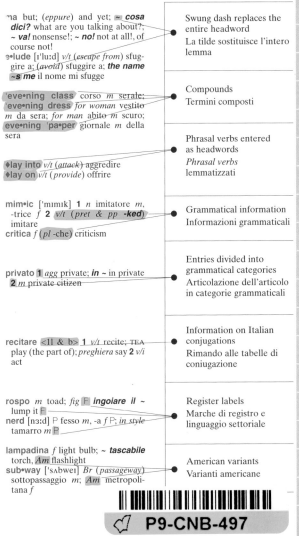

ma but; (*eppure*) and yet; **~ cosa dici?** what are you talking about?; **~ va!** nonsense!; **~ no!** not at all!, of course not!	Swung dash replaces the entire headword La tilde sostituisce l'intero lemma
e•lude [ɪ'luːd] *v/t* (*escape from*) sfuggire a; (*avoid*) sfuggire a; **the name ~s me** il nome mi sfugge	
'eve•ning class corso *m* serale; 'eve•ning dress *for woman* vestito *m* da sera; *for man* abito *m* scuro; eve•ning 'pa•per giornale *m* della sera	Compounds Termini composti
◆lay into *v/t* (*attack*) aggredire ◆lay on *v/t* (*provide*) offrire	Phrasal verbs entered as headwords *Phrasal verbs* lemmatizzati
mim•ic ['mɪmɪk] **1** *n* imitatore *m*, -trice *f* **2** *v/t* (*pret & pp* **-ked**) imitare critica *f* (*pl* -che) criticism	Grammatical information Informazioni grammaticali
privato **1** *agg* private; **in ~** in private **2** *m* private citizen	Entries divided into grammatical categories Articolazione dell'articolo in categorie grammaticali
recitare <ll & b> **1** *v/t* recite; TEA play (the part of); *preghiera* say **2** *v/i* act	Information on Italian conjugations Rimando alle tabelle di coniugazione
rospo *m* toad; *fig* F **ingoiare il ~** lump it F nerd [nɜːd] P fesso *m*, -a f P; *in style* tamarro *m* P	Register labels Marche di registro e linguaggio settoriale
lampadina *f* light bulb; **~ tascabile** torch, *Am* flashlight sub•way ['sʌbweɪ] *Br* (*passageway*) sottopassaggio *m*; *Am* metropolitana *f*	American variants Varianti americane

P9-CNB-497

Langenscheidt

Pocket Italian Dictionary

Italian – English
English – Italian

edited by the
Langenscheidt editorial staff

in cooperation with Paravia

Langenscheidt

New York · Berlin · Munich · Vienna · Zurich

Compiled by Lexus Ltd., Glasgow,
with contributions by
Jane Goldie
Loredana Riu
Debora Mazza
Pat Bulhosen
Carla Zipoli
Peter Terrell
Francesca Logi

10 09 08 07 06
5. 4. 3. 2.

© 2006 Langenscheidt KG, Berlin and Munich
Printed in Germany

Preface

Here is a new dictionary of English and Italian, a tool with some 45,000 references for those who work with the English and Italian languages at beginner's or intermediate level.

Focusing on modern usage, the dictionary offers coverage of everyday language – and this means including vocabulary from areas such as computer use and business.

Having made the selection of vocabulary items to include, the editors of this book have set out to provide the means to enable you, the user of the dictionary, to get straight to the translation that fits a particular context of use. Is the *mouse* you need for your computer, for example, the same in Italian as the *mouse* you don't want in the house? Is *flimsy* referring to furniture the same in Italian as *flimsy* referring to an excuse? This dictionary is rich in sense distinctions like this – and in translation options tied to specific, identified senses.

Vocabulary needs grammar to back it up. So in this dictionary you'll find irregular verb forms, in both English and Italian, irregular English plural forms as well as detailed guidance on Italian plural and feminine endings.

And vocabulary items are often only clearly understood in a context. So a large number of idiomatic phrases are given to show how the two languages correspond in context.

All in all, this is a book full of information, which will, we hope, become a valuable part of your language toolkit.

Contents

How to use the dictionary

To get the most out of your dictionary you should understand how and where to find the information you need. Whether you are yourself writing text in a foreign language or wanting to understand text that has been written in a foreign language, the following pages should help.

1. How and where do I find a word?

1.1 The word list for each language is arranged in alphabetical order and also gives irregular forms of verbs and nouns in their correct alphabetical order.

Sometimes you might want to look up terms made up of two separate words, for example **falling star,** or hyphenated words, for example **absent-minded.** These words are treated as though they were a single word and their alphabetical ordering reflects this.

The only exception to this strict alphabetical ordering is made for English *phrasal verbs* – words like **go off, go out, go up.** These are positioned in an alphabetical block directly after their main verb (in this case **go**).

1.2 Italian feminine headwords of the form **-trice** are shown as follows:

> **albergatore** *m,* **-trice** *f* hotel keeper

Here **-trice** means **albergatrice**.

1.3 Pronunciation for English headwords is given in square brackets. You can look up the spelling of a word in your dictionary in the same way as you would in a spelling dictionary. American spelling variants are marked *Am.* If just a single letter is omitted in the American spelling, this is put between round brackets:

> **colo(u)r — hono(u)r — travel(l)er**

2. How do I split a word?

Italians find English hyphenation very difficult. All you have to do with this dictionary is look for the bold dots between syllables. These dots show you where you can split a word at the end of a line but you should avoid having just one letter before or after the hyphen as in **a•mend** or **thirst•y.** In such cases it is better to take the entire word over to the next line.

3. Swung dashes and long dashes

3.1 A swung dash (~) replaces the entire headword when the headword is repeated within an entry:

> **face** [feɪs] **1** *n* viso *m,* faccia *f;* **~ to ~** faccia a faccia

Here **~ to ~** means **face to face**.

> **incanto**[1] *m* (*incantesimo*) spell; **come per ~** as if by magic

Here **come per ~** means **come per incanto**.

3.2 When a headword changes form in an entry, for example if it is put in the past tense or in the plural, then the past tense or plural ending is added to the swung dash – but only if the rest of the word doesn't change:

> **flame** [fleɪm] *n* fiamma *f*; *go up in* ~*s* incendiarsi
> **top** [tɒp] ... **3** *v/t* (*pret & pp* **-ped**): *~ped with cream* ricoperto
> di crema

But:

> ◆**make up 1** *v/i* ... *be made up of* essere composto da
> **sup•ply** [səˈplaɪ] ... **2** *v/t* ... *be supplied with* fitted with etc
> essere dotato di

3.3 Double headwords are replaced by a single swung dash:

> '**one-track mind** *hum*: *have a* ~ essere fissato col sesso
> **sliced 'bread** [slaɪst] pane *m* a cassetta; *the greatest thing
> since* ~ F il non plus ultra

3.4 In the Italian-English part of the dictionary, when a headword is repeated in a phrase or compound with an altered form, a long dash is used:

> **impronta** *f* impression, mark; *-e pl digitali* fingerprints

Here **-e digitali** means **impronte digitali**.

4. What do the different typefaces mean?

4.1 All Italian and English headwords and the Arabic numerals differentiating between parts of speech appear in **bold**:

> **incisivo 1** *agg* incisive **2** *m* dente incisor
> **itch** [ɪtʃ] **1** *n* prurito *m* **2** *v/i* prudere

4.2 *Italics* are used for :

a) abbreviated grammatical labels: *adj, adv, v/i, v/t* etc

b) gender labels: *m, f, mpl* etc

c) all the indicating words which are the signposts pointing to the correct translation for your needs, eg:

> **mix•ture** [ˈmɪkstʃə(r)] miscuglio *m*; *medicine* sciroppo *m*
> **pro•fuse•ly** [prəˈfjuːslɪ] *adv thank* con grande effusione; *bleed*
> copiosamente
> **rugoso** rough; *pelle* wrinkled; *albero* gnarled
> **terra** *f* earth; (*regione, proprietà, terreno agricolo*) land; (*superficie del suolo*) ground; (*pavimento*) floor

4.3 All phrases (examples and idioms) are given in ***secondary bold italics***:

> **sym•pa•thet•ic** [sɪmpəˈθetɪk] *adj* ... *be ~ towards an idea* simpatizzare per un'idea
> **premio** *m* (*pl* -mi) ... *~ Nobel per la pace* Nobel peace prize

4.4 The normal typeface is used for the translations. It is also used for Italian plural forms.

4.5 If a translation is given in italics, and not in the normal typeface, this means that the translation is more of an *explanation* in the other language and that an explanation has to be given because there just is no real equivalent:

>'Mid•lands *npl regione f nell'Inghilterra centrale*
>ragioneria *f* book-keeping; EDU *high school specializing in business studies*

5. Stress

To indicate where to put the **stress** in English words, the stress marker ' appears before the syllable on which the main stress falls:

>on•ion ['ʌnjən] cipolla *f*
>rec•ord[1] ['rekɔːd] *n* MUS disco *m* ...
>record[2] [rɪ'kɔːd] *v/t electronically* registrare ...

Stress is shown either in the pronunciation or, if there is no pronunciation given, in the actual headword or compound itself.

>'rec•ord hold•er primatista *m/f*

6. What do the various symbols and abbreviations tell you?

6.1 A solid blue diamond is used to indicate a phrasal verb:

>♦auction off *v/t* vendere all'asta

6.2 A white diamond is used to divide up longer entries into more easily digested chunks of related bits of text:

>a *prp* ◊ *stato in luogo*: *a Roma* in Rome; *a casa* at home
>◊ *moto a luogo*: *andare a Roma* go to Rome; *andare a casa* go home ◊ *tempo* ...

6.3 The abbreviation F tells you that the word or phrase is used colloquially rather than in formal contexts. The abbreviation V warns you that a word or phrase is vulgar or taboo. Be careful how you use these words. Words or phrases labelled P are slang.

These abbreviations, F, V and P are used both for headwords/phrases and for the translations of headwords/phrases. They come after the headword and before any phrase or indicated sense to be translated. They are given after the translation, but only if the translation has the same register as the headword/example. If there is no such label given, then the word or phrase is neutral.

6.4 A colon before an English or Italian phrase means that usage is restricted to this specific example (at least as far as this dictionary's translation is concerned):

>tru•ant ['truːənt]: *play* ~ marinare la scuola
>tuck [tʌk] ... 2 *v/t*: ~ *sth into sth* infilare qc in qc
>'shoe•string *n*: *do sth on a* ~ fare qc con pochi soldi

7. Does the dictionary deal with grammar too?

7.1 All English headwords are given a part of speech label:

> **tooth•less** ['tu:θlɪs] *adj* sdentato
> **top•ple** ['tɒpl] **1** *v/i* crollare **2** *v/t government* far cadere

But if a headword can only be used as a noun (in ordinary English) then no part of speech is given:

> **tooth•paste** dentifricio *m*

7.2 Italian headwords are not given parts of speech in cases where the grammar of the translation matches the grammar of the Italian:

> **esclusivo** exclusive
> **piuttosto** rather

But:

> **planetario** (*pl* -ri) **1** *agg* planetary **2** *m* planetarium

And Italian gender markers are given, as well as Italian plural forms:

> **pinacoteca** *f* (*pl* -che) art gallery
> **farmacista** *m/f* (*mpl* -i) chemist, *Am* pharmacist

7.3 If an English translation of an Italian adjective can only be used in front of a noun, and not after it, this is marked with *attr*:

> **fiabesco** (*pl* -chi) fairytale *attr*

7.4 If the Italian, unlike the English, doesn't change form if used in the plural, this is marked with *inv*:

> **fine settimana** *m inv* weekend

7.5 If the English, in spite of appearances, is not a plural form, this is marked with *nsg*:

> **mea•sles** ['mi:zlz] *nsg* morbillo *m*

7.6 Irregular English plurals are identified:

> **the•sis** ['θi:sɪs] (*pl* **theses** ['θi:si:z]) tesi *f inv*
> **thief** [θi:f] (*pl* **thieves** [θi:vz]) ladro *m*, -a *f*
> **trout** [traʊt] (*pl* **trout**) trota *f*

7.7 Words like **physics** or **media studies** have not been given a label to say if they are singular or plural for the simple reason that they can be either, depending on how they are used.

7.8 Irregular and semi-irregular verb forms are identified:

> **sim•pli•fy** ['sɪmplɪfaɪ] *v/t* (*pret & pp* **-ied**) semplificare
> **sing** [sɪŋ] *v/t & v/i* (*pret* **sang**, *pp* **sung**) cantare

7.9 Cross-references are given to tables of Italian conjugations:

> **finire** <4d> **fischiare** <1k>

7.10 Grammatical information is provided on the prepositions you'll need in order to create complete sentences:

> **ear•mark** ['ɪəmɑːk] *v/t* riservare; ~ *sth for sth* riservare qc a qc
> **tremare** <1b> tremble, shake (*di, per* with)

Abbreviations

see	→	vedi	feminine plural	fpl	femminile plurale
registered trademark	®	marchio registrato	railway	FERR	ferrovia
abbreviation	abbr	abbreviazione	figurative	fig	figurato
adjective	adj	aggettivo	philosophy	FIL	filosofia
adverb	adv	avverbio	financial	FIN	finanze
adjective	agg	aggettivo	physics	FIS	fisica
agriculture	AGR	agricoltura	physiology	FISIOL	fisiologia
mountaineering	ALP	alpinismo	formal usage	fml	uso formale
American	Am	inglese	photography	FOT	fotografia
English		americano	future	fut	futuro
anatomy	ANAT	anatomia	cooking	GASTR	gastronomia
architecture	ARCHI	architettura	generally	gen	generalmente
article	art	articolo	geography	GEOG	geografia
astronomy	AST	astronomia	geology	GEOL	geology
astrology	ASTR	astrologia	gerund	ger	gerundio
attributive usage	attr	uso attributivo	grammatical	GRAM	grammatica
motoring	AUTO	automobilismo	humorous	hum	uso spiritoso
civil aviation	AVIA	aviazione	imperative	imper	imperativo
adverb	avv	avverbio	imperfect	imperf	imperfetto
biology	BIO	biologia	indicative	ind	indicativo
botany	BOT	botanica	IT term	INFOR	informatica
British English	Br	inglese britannico	interjection	int	interiezione
chemistry	CHEM	chimica	invariable	inv	invariabile
chemistry	CHIM	chimica	ironic	iron	ironico
commerce,	COM	commercio	law	LAW	diritto
business			masculine	m	maschile
computers,	COMPUT	informatica	masculine noun	m/agg	sostantivo mas-
IT term			and adjective		chile e aggettivo
conditional	cond	condizionale	masculine and	m/f	maschile e
conjunction	cong	congiunzione	feminine		femminile
subjunctive	congiunt	congiuntivo	masculine plural	mpl	maschile plurale
conjunction	conj	congiunzione	nautical	MAR	marineria,
law	DIR	diritto			navigazione
et cetera	ecc	eccetera	mathematics	MAT	matematica
education	EDU	educazione	mathematics	MATH	matematica
for example	eg	per esempio	medicine	MED	medicina
electricity,	EL	elettricità,	metallurgy	METAL	metallurgia
electronics		elettronica	meteorology	METEO	meteorologia
electricity,	ELEC	elettricità,	military	MIL	militare
electronics		elettronica	mineralogy	MIN	mineralogia
especially	esp	specialmente	motoring	MOT	automobilismo
et cetera	etc	eccetera	music	MUS	musica
euphemistic	euph	eufemismo	noun	n	sostantivo
familiar, colloquial	F	familiare	nautical	NAUT	marineria,
feminine	f	femminile			navigazione
feminine noun	f/agg	sostantivo fem-	negative	neg	in senso negativo
and adjective		minile e aggettivo	plural noun	npl	sostantivo plurale

singular noun	*nsg*	sostantivo singolare	something	qc	qualcosa
optics	OPT	ottica	someone	qu	qualcuno
oneself	o.s.	sé, se stesso	radio	RAD	radio
optics	OTT	ottica	railway	RAIL	ferrovia
popular, slang	P	popolare	religion	REL	religione
painting	PAINT	pittura	skiing	SCI	sci
pejorative	*pej*	spregiativo	singular	sg	singolare
photography	PHOT	fotografia	someone	s.o.	qualcuno
physics	PHYS	fisica	sports	SP	sport
painting	PITT	pittura	humorous	*spir*	uso spiritoso
plural	*pl*	plurale	pejorative	*spreg*	spregiativo
politics	POL	politica	something	sth	qualcosa
past participle	*pp*	participio passato	theatre	TEA	teatro
present participle	*p pr*	participio presente	technology	TEC	tecnica
			technology	TECH	tecnica
present	*pr*	presente	telecommunications	TELEC	telecomunicazione
past historic	*p.r.*	passato remoto	theatre	THEA	teatro
present subjunctive	*pr congiunt*	presente congiuntivo	typography, typesetting	TIP	tipografia
preposition	*prep*	preposizione	television	TV	televisione
preterite	*pret*	preterito	vulgar	V	volgare
present indicative	*pr ind*	presente indicativo	auxiliary verb	*v/aus*	verbo ausiliario
pronoun	*pron*	pronome	auxiliary verb	*v/aux*	verbo ausiliario
preposition	*prp*	preposizione	intransitive verb	*v/i*	verbo intransitivo
psychology	PSI	psicologia	reflexive verb	*v/r*	verbo riflessivo
psychology	PSYCH	psicologia	transitive verb	*v/t*	verbo transitivo
			zoology	ZO	zoologia

Italian Spelling and Pronunciation

1. The Italian Alphabet

The twenty-one letters of the Italian alphabet are listed below with their names and with their sounds given as approximate English equivalents.

LETTER	NAME	APPROXIMATE SOUND
a	a	Like *a* in English *father*, eg **facile**, **padre**.
b	bi	Like *b* in English *boat*, eg **bello**, **abate**.
c	ci	When followed by **e** or **i**, like *ch* in English *cherry*, eg **cento**, **cinque**; if the **i** is unstressed and followed by another vowel, its sound is not heard, eg **ciaria**, **cieco**. When followed by **a**, **o**, **u**, or a consonant like *c* in English *cook*, eg **casa**, **come**, **cura**, **credere**. **Ch**, which is used before **e** and **i**, has likewise the sound of *c* in English *cook*, eg **chiesa**, **perché**.
d	di	Like *d* in English *dance*, eg **dare**, **madre**.
e	e	Has two sounds. One like *a* in English *make*, eg **ferro**; and one like *e* in English *met*, eg **festa**.
f	effe	Like *f* in English *fool*, eg **farina**, **efelide**.
g	gi	When followed by **e** or **i**, like *g* in English *general*, eg **gelato**, **ginnasta**; if the **i** is unstressed and followed by another vowel, its sound is not heard, eg **giallo**, **giorno**. When followed by **a**, **o**, **u**, or a consonant, like *g* in English *go*, eg **gamba**, **goccia**, **gusto**, **grado**. **Gh**, which is used before **e** and **i**, has likewise the sound of *g* in English *go*, eg **ghisa**. When the combination **gli** (a) is a form of the definite article or the personal pronoun, (b) is final in a word, or (c) comes between two vowels, it has the sound of Castilian *ll*, which is somewhat like *lli* in English *million*, eg (a) **gli uomini**, **gli ho parlato ieri**, (b) **battagli**, (c) figlio, migliore. When it is (a) initial (except in the word **gli**, above), (b) preceded by a consonant, or (c) followed by a consonant, it is pronounced like *gli* in English *negligence*, eg (a) **glioma**, (b) **ganglio**, (c) **negligenza**. The combination **gl** followed by **a**, **e**, **o**, or **u** is pronounced like *gl* in English *globe*, eg **glabro**, **gleba**, **globo**, **gluteo**, **inglese**. **Gn** has the sound of Castilian ñ, which is somewhat like *ni* in English *onion*, eg **signore**, **gnocco**.
h	acca	Always silent, eg **ah**, **hanno**. See **ch** under **c** above and **gh** under **g** above.
i	i	Like *i* in English *machine*, eg **piccolo**, **sigla**.

		When unstressed and followed by another vowel, like *y* in English *yes*, eg **piatto**, **piede**, **fiore**, **fiume**.
		For **i** in *ci*, see **c** above, in *gi*, see **g** above, and in *sci*, see **s** below.
l	elle	Like *l* in English *lamb*, eg **labbro**, **lacrima**.
m	emme	Like *m* in English *money*, eg **mano**, **come**.
n	enne	Like *n* in English *net*, eg **nome**, **cane**.
o	o	Has two sounds. One like *o* in English *note*, eg **sole**; and one like *o* in English hot, eg **donna**.
p	pi	Like *p* in English *pot*, eg **passo**, **carpa**.
q	cu	This letter is always followed by the letter **u** and the combination has the sound of *qu* in English *quart*, eg **quanto**, **questo**.
r	erre	Like *r* in English *rubber*, with a slight trill, eg **roba**, **carta**.
s	esse	Has two sounds.
		When initial and followed by a vowel, when preceded by a consonant and followed by a vowel, and when followed by **c** [k] **f**, **p**, **q**, or **t**, like *s* in English *see*, eg **sale**, **falso**, **scappare**, **spazio**, **stoffa**.
		When standing between two vowels and when followed by **b**, **d**, **g** [g], **l**, **m**, **n**, **r** or **v**, like *z* in English *zero*, eg **paese**, **sbaglio**, **svenire**.
		However, **s** standing between two vowels in some words and initial *s* followed by **b**, **d**, **g** [g], **l**, **m**, **n**, **r**, or **v** in some foreign borrowings are pronounced like *s* in *see*, eg **casa**, **tesa**, **smoking**, **slam**.
		When initial s stands between two vowels in a compound, its pronunciation remains that of initial s, eg **autoservizio**.
		Sc, when followed by **e** or **i** has the sound of *sh* in English *shall*, eg **scelta**, **scimmia**; if the **i** is unstressed and followed by another vowel, its sound is not heard, eg **sciame**, **sciopero**.
		Sch has the sound of *sc* in English *scope*, eg **scherzo**, **schiavo**.
		An **s** coming between two vowels is generally pronounced like *z* English *zero* in the north of Italy.
t	ti	Like *t* in English *table*, eg **terra**, **pasto**.
u	u	Like *u* in English *rule*, eg **luna**, **mulo**. When followed by a vowel, like *w* in English *was*, eg **quanto**, **guerra**, **nuovo**.
v	vu	Like *v* in English *vain*, eg **vita**, **uva**.
z	zeta	Has two sounds. One like *ts* in English *nuts*, eg **grazia**, **zuccero**; and one like *dz* in English *adze*, eg **zero**, **mezzo**.

The following five letters are found in borrowings from other languages.

LETTER	NAME	EXAMPLES
j	i lunga	**jazz**
k	cappa	**ko**
w	vu doppia	**whisky**
x	ics	**xenofobo**, *xilofono*
y	ìpsilon	**yacht**, **yoghurt**

Consonants written double are longer than consonants written single, that is, it takes a longer time to pronounce them, eg **camino** *chimney*, and **cammino** *road*, **capello** *hair* and **cappello** *hat*. Special attention is called to the following double consonants: **cc** followed by **e** or **i** has the sound of *ch ch* in English *beach chair*, that is a lengthened *ch*, eg **accento**; **cch** has the sound of *kk* in English *book-keeper*, eg **becchino**; **cq** has the sound of *kk* in English *book-keeper*, eg **acqua**; **gg** followed by **e** or **i** has the sound of *ge j* in English *carriage joiner*, eg **peggio**; **ggh** has the sound of *g g* in English *tag game*, eg **agghindare**.

2. Stress and Accent Marks

Whenever stress is shown as part of regular spelling, it is shown on **a**, **i**, and **u** by the grave accent mark, eg **libertà**, **giovedì**, **gioventù**, on close **e** and **o** by the acute accent mark, eg **perché**, and on open **e** and **o** by the grave accent mark, eg **caffè**, **parlò**.

Guidelines on Stress

(a)   In words of two syllables, the stress falls on the syllable next to the last, eg **casa**, **muro**, **terra**. If the syllable next to the last contains a diphthong, that is, a combination of a strong vowel (**a**, **e**, or **o**) and a weak vowel (**i** or **u**), the strong vowel is stressed, regardless of which vowel comes first, eg **daino**, **eroico**, **neutro**, **fiato**, **duale**, **siepe**, **fiore**, **buono**.

(b)   In words of more than two syllables, the stress may fall on the syllable next to the last, eg **andata**, **canzone**, **pastore** or on a preceding syllable, eg **missile**, **gondola**, **mandorla**. In these positions also the stressed syllable may contain a diphthong, eg **incauto**, **idraulico**, **fiocina**.

(c)   If a weak vowel in juxtaposition with a strong vowel is stressed, the two vowels constitute two separate syllables, eg **abba•ino**, **ero•ina**, **pa•ura**, **miriade**, **via**.

(d)   Two strong vowels in juxtaposition constitute two separate syllables, eg **pa•ese**, **aureola**, **idea**, **oceano**.

(e)   Two weak vowels in juxtaposition generally consitute a diphthong in which the first vowel is stressed in some words, eg **fluido** and the second vowel in others, eg **piuma**.

(f)   If a word ends in a diphthong, the diphthong is stressed, eg **marinai**, **parlai**, **eroi**.

English Pronunciation

Vowels

[ɑ:]	*father*	['fɑːðə(r)]
[æ]	*man*	[mæn]
[e]	*get*	[get]
[ə]	*about*	[ə'baʊt]
[ɜ:]	*absurd*	[əb'sɜːd]
[ɪ]	*stick*	[stɪk]
[iː]	*need*	[niːd]
[ɒ]	*hot*	[hɒt]
[ɔ:]	*law*	[lɔː]
[ʌ]	*mother*	['mʌðə(r)]
[ʊ]	*book*	[bʊk]
[uː]	*fruit*	[fruːt]

Diphthongs

[aɪ]	*time*	[taɪm]
[aʊ]	*cloud*	[klaʊd]
[eɪ]	*name*	[neɪm]
[eə]	*hair*	[heə(r)]
[ɪə]	*here*	[hɪə(r)]
[ɔɪ]	*point*	[pɔɪnt]
[əʊ]	*oath*	[əʊθ]
[ʊə]	*tour*	[tʊə(r)]

Consonants

[b]	*bag*	[bæg]
[d]	*dear*	[dɪə(r)]
[f]	*fall*	[fɔːl]
[g]	*give*	[gɪv]
[h]	*hole*	[həʊl]
[j]	*yes*	[jes]
[k]	*come*	[kʌm]
[l]	*land*	[lænd]
[m]	*mean*	[miːn]
[n]	*night*	[naɪt]
[p]	*pot*	[pɒt]
[r]	*right*	[raɪt]
[(r)]	pronounced only at the end of a word followed by a word starting with a vowel: *where* [weə(r)]	
[s]	*sun*	[sʌn]
[t]	*take*	[teɪk]
[v]	*vain*	[veɪn]
[w]	*wait*	[weɪt]
[z]	*rose*	[rəʊz]
[ŋ]	*bring*	[brɪŋ]
[ʃ]	*she*	[ʃiː]
[ʧ]	*chair*	[ʧeə(r)]
[dʒ]	*join*	[dʒɔɪn]
[ʒ]	*leisure*	['leʒə(r)]
[θ]	*think*	[θɪŋk]
[ð]	*the*	[ðə]
[']	means that the following syllable is stressed: *ability* [ə'bɪlətɪ]	

A *abbr* (= *autostrada*) M (= motorway)

a *prp* ◊ *stato in luogo*: **a Roma** in Rome; **a casa** at home ◊ *moto a luogo*: **andare a Roma** go to Rome; **andare a casa** go home ◊ *tempo*: **alle quattro** at four o'clock; **a Natale** at Christmas; **a maggio** in May; **a vent'anni** at the age of twenty; **a giorni** any day now; **a domani!** see you tomorrow! ◊ *modo*: **a piedi** on foot; **alla moda** in fashion; **al burro** GASTR in butter ◊ *mezzo*: **ricamato a mano** embroidered by hand, hand-embroidered; **fatto a macchina** machine-made ◊ *con valore distributivo*: **a due a due** two at a time; **a poco a poco** little by little ◊ *prezzo, misura*: **a che prezzo** at what price; **al metro** by the metre; **100 km all'ora** 100 km an hour

AAS *abbr* (= *Azienda Autonoma di Soggiorno*) tourist board

ab. *abbr* (= *abitanti*) inhabitants

abate *m* abbot

abbacchiato downhearted

abbacchio *m* (*pl* -cchi) GASTR young lamb

abbagliante 1 *agg* dazzling **2** *m gen pl* -**i** AUTO full beam

abbagliare <1g> dazzle

abbaglio *m* (*pl* -gli): **prendere un ~** make a blunder

abbaiare <1i> bark

abbandonare <1a> abandon

abbandono *m* abandon; (*rinuncia*) abandonment; **stato di ~** state of disrepair

abbassamento *m* lowering

abbassare <1a> *prezzo* lower; *radio* turn down; **~ la voce** lower one's voice

abbassarsi (*chinarsi*) bend down; *prezzo* come down; *fig* **~ a** stoop to

abbasso *int*: **~ la scuola!** down with school!

abbastanza enough; (*alquanto*) quite; **ho mangiato ~** I've had enough to eat; **sono ~ soddisfatto** I'm quite satisfied

abbattere <3a> knock down; *casa* demolish; *albero* cut down; *aereo* shoot down; *fig* dishearten

abbattersi fall; *fig* become disheartened

abbattimento *m* knocking down; *casa* demolition; *albero* cutting down; *aereo* shooting down; *fig* despondency

abbattuto disheartened

abbazia *f* abbey

abbellire <4d> embellish

abbeverare <1m> water

abbi, abbia → **avere**

abbicci *m inv* abc; *fig* basics *pl*

abbigliamento *m* clothing; **~ sportivo** sportswear; **industria** *f* **dell'~** clothing industry

abbinare <1a> match; (*combinare*) combine

abboccare <1d> *di pesce* bite; TEC join; *fig* swallow the bait

abboccato *vino* medium sweet

abbonamento *m a giornale*, TEA subscription; *a treno, bus* season-ticket; **~ annuale** yearly subscription; yearly ticket; **~ mensile** monthly subscription; monthly ticket

abbonare <1c & o> take out a subscription for; (*condonare*) deduct

abbonarsi subscribe

abbonato *m* subscriber; TELEC **elenco** *m* **degli -i** telephone directory

abbondante abundant; *porzione* generous; *vestito* loose; *nevicata* heavy

abbondanza *f* abundance

abbordabile *persona* approachable;

prezzo reasonable

abbordare <1a> **1** *v/t persona* approach; F *persona dell'altro sesso* chat up F; *argomento* tackle **2** *v/t* MAR board

abbottonare <1a> button up

abbozzare <1c> sketch; **~ un sorriso** smile faintly

abbozzo *m* sketch

abbracciare <1f> embrace, hug; *fig* take up

abbracciarsi embrace, hug

abbraccio *m* (*pl* -cci) embrace, hug; **un ~** *a fine lettera* love

abbreviare <1k & b> abbreviate

abbreviazione *f* abbreviation

abbronzante *m* sun-tan lotion; **lettino** *m* **~** sunbed

abbronzare <1a> *pelle* tan

abbronzarsi get a tan

abbronzato tanned

abbronzatura *f* tan

abbrustolire <4d> roast

abbuffarsi <1a> stuff o.s. (**di** with)

abbuono *m* FIN discount

abdicare <1l & d> abdicate

abdicazione *f* abdication

abete *m* fir

abile good (**in** at); fit (**a** for)

abilità *f inv* ability

abilitazione *f* qualification

abisso *m* abyss

abitabile habitable; **cucina** *f* **~** dining kitchen

abitacolo *m* AUTO passenger compartment

abitante *m/f* inhabitant

abitare <1l> **1** *v/t* live in **2** *v/i* live

abitato 1 *agg* inhabited **2** *m* built-up area

abitazione *f* house

abiti *mpl* clothes

abito *m* dress; *da uomo* suit; **~ da sera** evening dress

abituale usual

abituare <1l> accustom (**a** to)

abituarsi: **~ a** get used to

abitudinario (*pl* -ri) **1** *agg* of fixed habits **2** *m* creature of habit

abitudine *f* habit

abolire <4d> abolish

abolizione *f* abolition

abominevole abominable

aborigeno 1 *agg* aboriginal **2** *m* aboriginal

abortire <4d> MED miscarry; *volontariamente* have an abortion; *fig* fail

abortista *m/f* pro-choice campaigner

aborto *m* MED miscarriage; *provocato* abortion

abrogare <1e & c or 1l> repeal

abrogazione *f* repeal

abusare <1a>: **~ di** abuse; (*approfittare*) take advantage of; **~ nel bere** drink to excess

abusivo illegal

abuso *m* abuse; **~ sessuale** sexual abuse

a.C. *abbr* (= **avanti Cristo**) BC (= before Christ)

acacia *f* (*pl* -cie) acacia

acca *f*: **non capire un'~** not understand a thing

accademia *f* academy; **~ di belle arti** art college

accademico (*pl* -ci) academic

accadere <2c> happen

accaduto *m*: **raccontami l'~** tell me what happened

accaldarsi <1a> get overheated

accaldato overheated

accalorarsi <1a> *fig* get excited

accampamento *m* camp

accampare <1a> **1** *v/t*: **~ scuse** come up with excuses **2** *v/i e* **accamparsi** camp

accanimento *m* (*tenacia*) tenacity; (*furia*) rage

accanirsi <4d> (*ostinarsi*) persist; **~ contro qu** rage against s.o.

accanito *odio* fierce; *tifoso* dedicated; *fumatore* inveterate; **lavoratore** *m* **~** hard worker

accanto 1 *prp* **~ a** next to **2** *avv* near, nearby; *abitare* next door

accantonare <1a> put aside

accappatoio *m* (*pl* -oi) bathrobe; *da mare* beachrobe

accarezzare <1a> caress; *speranza* cherish; *animale* stroke accasciarsi <1f> flop down

accatastare <1a> pile up

accattonaggio *m* begging

accattone *m* beggar

accavallare <1a> cross

accavallarsi *fig* overlap

accecare <1b & d> **1** *v/t* blind **2** *v/i* be blinding

accedere <3a>: ~ *a* enter

accelerare <1b & m> speed up; AUTO accelerate

accelerato **1** *agg* fast; *treno* slow **2** *m* slow train

acceleratore *m* AUTO accelerator

accelerazione *f* acceleration

accendere <3c> light; RAD, TV turn on

accendersi light up; *apparecchio* come on

accendino *m*, **accendisigari** *m inv* lighter

accennare <1a> indicate; *con parole* mention; ~ *a fare qc* show signs of doing sth

accenno *m* (*cenno*) gesture; (*indizio*) sign; (*allusione*) hint

accensione *f* ignition; AUTO ~ *elettronica* electronic ignition

accento *m* accent

accentuare <1b & m> accentuate

accertare <1b> check

accertarsi: ~ *di qc* check sth

acceso *colore* bright; *motore* running; *TV, luce* on

accessibile accessible; *prezzo* reasonable

accesso *m* access; *fig e* MED fit; *divieto d' ~* no entry

accessori *mpl* accessories

accessoriato AUTO complete with accessories

accessorio secondary

accetta *f* ax(e)

accettabile acceptable

accettare <1b> accept

accettazione *f* acceptance; (*di albergo*) reception; ~ *bagagli* check-in

accetto: *bene/male ~* welcome/not welcome

acchiappare <1a> catch

acciaio *m* (*pl* -ai) steel; ~ *inossi-*

dabile stainless steel

accidentale accidental

accidentato *terreno* rough

accidenti *int* F damn! F; *di sorpresa* wow!

accigliato frowning

accingersi <3d>: ~ *a fare qc* be about to do sth

acciottolato *m* cobbles *pl*

acciuffare <1a> grab

acciuga *f* (*pl* -ghe) anchovy

acclamare <1a>applaud

acclimatarsi <1m> get acclimatized

accludere <3q> enclose

accluso enclosed; *qui ~* enclosed

accogliente welcoming

accogliere <3ss> welcome; *richiesta* grant

accollare <1c> shoulder

accollarsi take on

accollato *abito* high-necked

accoltellare <1b> knife

accolto *pp* → *accogliere*

accomodamento *m* arrangement; (*accordo*) agreement

accomodante accommodating

accomodare <1c & m> (*riparare*) mend; *lite* resolve; (*sistemare*) arrange

accomodarsi make o.s. at home; *si accomodi!* come in!; (*sedersi*) have a seat!

accompagnamento *m* accompaniment; *lettera f di ~* covering letter

accompagnare <1a> accompany

accompagnatore *m*, **-trice** *f* escort; MUS accompanist

acconciatura *f* hairdo

acconsentire <4b> consent (*a* to)

accontentare <1b> satisfy

accontentarsi be happy (*di* with)

acconto *m* deposit

accoppiare <1k & c> couple; *animali* mate

accoppiarsi pair off

accorciare <1f> shorten

accorciarsi get shorter

accordare <1c> grant; MUS tune; (*armonizzare*) harmonize

accordarsi agree; *di colori* match

accordo *m* agreement; (*armonia*)

harmony; MUS chord; **essere d'~** agree; **mettersi d'~** reach an agreement; **d'~!** OK!

accorgersi <3d>: **~ di** notice

accorrere <3o> hurry; **~ in aiuto di qu** rush to help s.o.

accortezza *f* forethought

accorto **1** *pp* → **accorgersi 2** *agg* shrewd

accostare <1c> approach; *porta* leave ajar

accostarsi get close

accreditare <1b & m> confirm; FIN credit

accredito *m* credit

accrescere <3n> increase

accrescersi grow bigger

accudire <4d> **1** *v/t* look after **2** *v/i:* **~ a qc** attend to sth

accumulare <1m> accumulate

accumulatore *m* battery

accumulazione *f* accumulation

accuratezza *f* care

accurato careful

accusa *f* accusation; DIR charge; **Pubblica Accusa** public prosecutor

accusare <1a> accuse; DIR charge; **~ ricevuta** acknowledge receipt

accusato *m*, **-a** *f* accused

accusatore *m* prosecutor

acerbo unripe

acero *m* maple

aceto *m* vinegar; **~ balsamico** balsamic vinegar; **mettere sott'~** pickle

acetone *m* nail varnish remover

ACI *abbr* (= **Automobile Club d'Italia**) Automobile Club of Italy

acidità *f* acidity; **~ di stomaco** heartburn

acido **1** *agg* acid; *fig* sour; **piogge fpl acide** acid rain *sg* **2** *m* acid

ACLI *abbr* (= **Associazione Cristiana dei Lavoratori Italiani**) Italian trade union association

acne *f* acne

acqua *f* water; **~ corrente** running water; **~ minerale** mineral water; **~ potabile** drinking water; **~ di rubinetto** tap water; **~ ossigenata** hydrogen peroxide; **una teoria che fa ~** a theory that doesn't hold water; **~ in bocca!** keep it under your hat!; **ha l'~ alla gola** (*non ha tempo*) he's pushed for time; **-e** *pl* waters; **-e** *pl* **territoriali** territorial waters; **in cattive -e** in deep water

acquaforte *f* etching

acquaio *m* (*pl* -ai) sink

acquaragia *f* turpentine

acquario *m* (*pl* -ri) aquarium; ASTR **Acquario** Aquarius

acquatico (*pl* -ci) aquatic; **sci m ~** water skiing; *oggetto* waterski; **uccello m ~** waterfowl

acquavite *f* brandy

acquazzone *m* downpour

acquedotto *m* aqueduct

acqueo: **vapore** *m* **~** water vapo(u)r

acquerello *m* water-colo(u)r

acquirente *m/f* purchaser

acquisizione *f* acquisition

acquistare <1a> **1** *v/t* buy; *fig* gain **2** *v/i* improve (**in** in)

acquisto *m* purchase; **potere m d'~** purchasing power; **~ a rate** hire purchase, *Am* installment plan

acquolina *f:* **mi viene l'~ in bocca** my mouth's watering

acre sour; *voce* harsh

acrilico (*pl* -ci) acrylic

acrobata *m/f* acrobat

acustica *f* acoustics

acustico (*pl* -ci) acoustic

acuto **1** *agg* intense; *nota, dolore* sharp; *suono, voce* shrill; MED acute **2** *m* MUS high note

ad *prp* → **a** (*before vowels*)

adagiare <1f> *persona* lay down

adagiarsi lie down

adagio **1** *avv* slowly; **con cautela** cautiously **2** *m* (*pl* -gi) MUS adagio

adattamento *m* adaptation; (*rielaborazione*) reworking

adattare <1a> adapt

adattarsi (*adeguarsi*) adapt (**a** to); (*addirsi*) be suitable (**a** for); **questo colore non ti si adatta** the colour doesn't suit you

adattatore *m* adaptor

adatto right (**a** for)

addebitare <1m>: FIN ~ *qc a qu* debit s.o. with sth; *fig* ascribe sth to s.o.

addebito *m* FIN debit; *nota f di* ~ debit note

addensarsi <1b> thicken

addestramento *m* training

addestrare <1b> train

addetto 1 *agg* assigned (*a* to) **2** *m*, -*a f* person responsible; ~ *alle pubbliche relazioni* public relations officer; *fig* ~ *ai lavori* expert; ~ *culturale* cultural attaché; *vietato l'ingresso ai non -i* authorized personnel only

addio 1 *int* goodbye **2** *m* goodbye, farewell

addirittura (*assolutamente*) absolutely; (*perfino*) even

additivo *m* additive

addizionare <1a> add

addizione *f* addition

addobbare <1c> decorate

addobbo *m* decoration

addolcire <4d> sweeten; *fig* soften

addolorare <1a> grieve

addome *m* abdomen

addomesticare <1b, d & n> tame

addominale abdominal

addormentare <1b> get (off) to sleep

addormentarsi fall asleep

addormentato asleep; (*assonnato*) sleepy

addossare <1c> (*appoggiare*) lean (*a* on); *fig colpa* put, lay (*a* on)

addossarsi lean (*a* on); *fig* shoulder

addosso 1 *prp* on; *vicino* next to **2** *avv*: *avere* ~ *vestiti* have on; *avere* ~ *qu* have s.o. breathing down one's neck

addurre <3e> produce

adeguare <1a> adjust

adeguarsi conform; ~ *alle circostanze* adjust to circumstances

adeguato adequate

adempiere <4d & g>: ~ *a dovere* carry out, do

aderente 1 *agg vestito* tight **2** *m/f* follower

aderire <4d>: ~ *a* adhere to; *partito* support; *richiesta* agree to

adesione *f* adhesion; (*consenso*) agreement

adesivo 1 *agg* adhesive **2** *m* sticker

adesso now; *da* ~ *in poi* from now on; *fino* ~ up to now; *per* ~ for the moment

adiacente adjacent; ~ *a* next to, adjacent to

adibire <4d> use

adirarsi <1a> get angry

adirato angry

adolescente *m/f* adolescent, teenager

adolescenza *f* adolescence, teens *pl* F

adoperare <1m & c> use

adorare <1a> adore

adorazione *f* adoration

adornare <1a> adorn

adottare <1c> adopt

adottivo *genitori* adoptive; *figlio* adopted

adozione *f* adoption

adrenalina *f* adrenalin

adriatico (*pl* -ci) **1** *agg* Adriatic; *mare m Adriatico* Adriatic Sea **2** *m*: *Adriatico* Adriatic

adulare <1a> flatter

adulazione *f* flattery

adulterare <1m> adulterate

adulterio *m* (*pl* -ri) adultery

adulto1 *agg* adult **2** *m*, -*a f* adult

adunare <1a> assemble

aerare <1l> air

aerazione *f* airing

aereo 1 *agg* air *attr*; *fotografia*, *radici* aerial; *base f* -*a* air base; *compagnia f* -*a* airline; *ponte m* ~ airlift; *posta f* -*a* airmail **2** *m* plane; ~ *di linea* airliner

aerobica *f* aerobics *sg*

aerobus *m inv* plane that makes short-haul flights

aerodinamico aerodynamic

aeronautica *f* aeronautics; ~ *militare* Air Force

aeroplano *m* plane, aeroplane, *Am* airplane

aeroporto *m* airport

aerosol *m inv contenitore* aerosol

aerospaziale aerospace *attr*

aerostato *m* aerostat, lighter-than-air aircraft

aerostazione *f* air terminal

afa *f* closeness, mugginess

affabile affable

affaccendarsi <1b> busy o.s. (*in* with)

affaccendato busy

affacciarsi <1f> appear

affamato starving

affannato breathless

affanno *m* breathlessness; *fig* anxiety

affare *m* matter, business; FIN transaction; *-i pl* business *sg*; **non sono -i tuoi** it's none of your business; **uomo** *m* **d'-i** businessman; **ministro** *m* **degli Affari Esteri** Foreign Secretary; **giro** *m* **d'-i** turnover

affarista *m/f* (*mpl* -i) wheeler-dealer

affascinante fascinating

affascinare <1m> fascinate

affaticare <1d> tire

affaticarsi tire o.s. out

affatto completely; **non è ~ vero!** there's not the slightest bit of truth in it!

affermare <1a> state

affermarsi become established

affermazione *f* assertion; (*successo*) achievement

afferrare <1b> seize, grab F; (*comprendere*) grasp

afferrarsi cling (*a* to), hold on (*a* to)

affettare[1] <1a> (*tagliare*) slice

affettare[2] <1b> *ammirazione ecc* affect

affettato[1] *m* sliced meat

affettato[2] *agg* affected

affettatrice *f* slicer

affetto *m* affection

affettuoso affectionate

affezionarsi <1a>: **~ a qu** become fond of s.o.

affezionato: **~ a qu** fond of s.o.

affiancare <1d> place side by side; *fig* support

affibbiare <1k>: **~ qc a qu** saddle s.o. with sth

affidabilità *f* dependability

affidamento *m* trust; **fare ~ su** rely on

affidare <1a> entrust

affidarsi: **~ a** rely on

affiggere <3mm> *avviso* put up

affilare <1a> sharpen; *fig* make thinner

affilato sharp; *naso* thin

affiliare <1g> *a una società* affiliate

affiliato 1 *m*, **-a** *f* member **2** *agg*: **società** *f* **-a** affiliate

affiliazione *f* affiliation

affinché so that

affine similar

affinità *f inv* affinity

affiorare <1a> *dall'acqua* emerge; *fig* (*mostrarsi*) appear

affissione *f* bill-posting

affisso 1 *pp* → **affiggere 2** *m* bill

affittacamere *m/f* landlord; *donna* landlady

affittare <1a> *locali, terre* let; (*prendere in affitto*) rent; **affittasi** to let

affitto *m* rent; **dare in ~** let; **prendere in ~** rent

affliggere <3cc> distress; *di malattia* trouble, plague

afflitto distressed

affluente *m* tributary

affluenza *f fig* influx

affluire <4d> flow; *di persone* pour in

afflusso *m* influx

affogare <1c & e> *v/t & v/i* drown

affollamento *m* crowd

affollare <1c>, **affollarsi** crowd

affollato crowded

affondare <1a> *v/t & v/i* sink

affrancare <1d> free; *posta* frank

affrancatura *f* franking; *tassa di spedizione* postage

affresco *m* (*pl* -chi) fresco

affrettare <1a> speed up

affrettarsi hurry

affrontare <1a> face, confront; *spese* meet

affronto *m* insult

affumicare <1d & m> *stanza* fill with smoke; *alimenti* smoke

affumicato smoked

affusolato tapering

afoso sultry

Africa f Africa

africano 1 agg African **2** m, **-a** f African

afrodisiaco m/agg aphrodisiac

agave f agave

agenda f diary

agente m/f agent; ~ **di cambio** stockbroker; ~ **immobiliare** estate agent, Am realtor; ~ **inquinante** pollutant; ~ **di pubblica sicurezza** police officer; ~ **di vendita** sales representative; ~ **di viaggio** travel agent

agenzia f agency; ~ **di cambio** bureau de change; ~ **immobiliare** estate agency, Am real estate office; ~ **pubblicitaria** advertising agency; ~ **di viaggi** travel agency

agevolare <1m> make easier

agevolato FIN on easy terms

agevolazione f FIN special term

agevole easy

agganciare <1f> hook; cintura, collana fasten

aggeggio m (pl -ggi) gadget

aggettivo m adjective

agghiacciante spine-chilling

aggiornamento m updating; (rinvio) postponement; **corso** m **d'** ~ refresher course

aggiornare <1a> (mettere al corrente) update; (rinviare) postpone

aggiornarsi keep up to date

aggirare <1a> surround; fig ostacolo get round

aggirarsi hang about; FIN be in the region of

aggiudicare <1d & m> award; all'asta knock down

aggiungere <3d> add

aggiunta f addition

aggiustare <1a> (riparare) repair; (sistemare) settle

agglomerato m: ~ **urbano** built-up area

aggrapparsi <1a> cling, hold on (a to)

aggravante 1 agg aggravating **2** f aggravation

aggravare <1a> punizione increase; (peggiorare) make worse

aggravarsi worsen, deteriorate

aggravio m (pl -vi): ~ **fiscale** tax increase

aggraziato graceful

aggredire <4d> attack

aggressione f aggression; (attacco) attack, POL **patto** m **di non** ~ non-aggression pact

aggressività f aggressiveness

aggressivo aggressive

aggressore m attacker; POL aggressor

agguato m ambush; **tendere un** ~ **a qu** ambush s.o., set an ambush for s.o.

agguerrito hardened

agiatezza f comfort

agiato comfortable, well-off; (comodo) comfortable

agibile fit for human habitation

agile agile

agilità f agility; fig liveliness

agio m (pl -gi) ease; **vivere negli agi** live in comfort; **sentirsi a proprio** ~ feel at ease

agire <4d> act; comportarsi behave; act; di medicina take effect; DIR take action (contro against)

agitare <1l> shake; fazzoletto wave; fig (turbare) upset, agitate; ~ **prima dell'uso** shake before use

agitato agitated; mare rough

agitazione f agitation

agli prp **a** and art **gli**

aglio m (pl -gli) garlic

agnello m lamb

agnolotti mpl type of ravioli

ago m (pl -ghi) needle

agonia f agony

agonismo m competitiveness

agonistico (pl -ci) competitive

agopuntura f acupuncture

agorafobia f agoraphobia

agosto m August; **in** ~ in August

agraria f agriculture

agrario (pl -ri) agricultural

agricolo agricultural

agricoltore m farmer

agricoltura f agriculture

agrifoglio m holly

agriturismo m farm holidays pl

agro sour

agrodolce bittersweet; GASTR sweet and sour

agronomo *m*, **-a** *f* agricultural economist

agrumi *mpl* citrus fruit *sg*

aguzzare <1a> sharpen; **~ la vista** keep one's eyes peeled

aguzzo pointed

ah! oh!

ahi! ouch!

ai *prp* **a** and *art* **i**

Aids *m o f* Aids

airbag *m inv* airbag

A.I.R.E. *abbr* (= **Anagrafe degli Italiani Residenti all'Estero**) register of Italian citizens resident overseas

airone *m* heron

aiuola *f* flower bed

aiutante *m/f* assistant

aiutare <1a> help

aiuto *m* help, assistance; *persona* assistant; **~ allo sviluppo** development aid *or* assistance; **chiedere ~ a qu** ask s.o. for help

aizzare <1a> incite

al *prp* **a** and *art* **il**

ala *f* (*pl* -i) wing

alabastro *m* alabaster

alano *m* Great Dane

alba *f* dawn; **all'~** at dawn

albanese *agg*, *m/f* Albanian

Albania *f* Albania

albeggiare <1f> dawn

alberato tree-lined

albergare <1b & e> put up

albergatore *m*, **-trice** *f* hotel keeper

alberghiero hotel *attr*

albergo *m* (*pl* -ghi) hotel; **guida** *f* **degli -ghi** hotel guide

albero *m* tree; MAR mast; AVIA, AUTO shaft; **~ genealogico** family tree; **~ motore** drive shaft; **~ di Natale** Christmas tree

albicocca *f* (*pl* -cche) apricot

albicocco *m* (*pl* -cchi) apricot (tree)

albo *m* notice board; (*registro*) register; **radiare dall'~** strike off

album *m inv* album

albume *m* albumen

alcalino alkaline

alcol *m* alcohol

alcolico (*pl* -ci) **1** *agg* alcoholic; **gradazione** *f* **-a** alcohol content **2** *m* alcoholic drink

alcolismo *m* alcoholism

alcolizzato *m*, **-a** *f* alcoholic

alcoltest *m inv* Breathalyzer®

alcuno 1 *agg* any; **non ~** no, not any **2** *pron* any; **-i** *pl* some, a few

aldilà *m*: **l'~** the next world

aletta *f* fin

alfabetico (*pl* -ci) alphabetical

alfabeto *m* alphabet

alfanumerico (*pl* -ci) INFOR alphanumeric

alfiere *m* scacchi bishop

alfine eventually

alga *f* (*pl* -ghe) seaweed

algebra *f* algebra

Algeria *f* Algeria

algerino 1 *agg* Algerian **2** *m*, **-a** *f* Algerian

aliante *m* glider

alice *f* anchovy

alienare <1b> DIR transfer; *persone* alienate

alienarsi become lienated

alienato 1 *agg* alienated **2** *m*, **-a** *f* madman; *donna* madwoman

alienazione *f* alienation; **~ mentale** madness

alimentare <1a> **1** *v/t* feed **2** *agg* food *attr*; **generi** *mpl* **-i** foodstuffs

alimentazione *f* feeding

alimento *m* food; **~ base** basic food(stuff); **-i** *pl* DIR alimony *sg*

aliquota *f* share; **~ d'imposta** rate of taxation

aliscafo *m* hydrofoil

alito *m* breath

all. *abbr* (= **allegato**) enc(l). (= enclosed)

all', **alla** *prp* **a** and *art* **l'**, **la**

allacciamento *m* TEC connection

allacciare <1f> fasten; TEC connect

allagamento *m* flooding

allagare <1e> flood

allargare <1e> widen; *vestito* let out; *braccia* open

allargarsi widen

allarmare <1a> alarm

allarmarsi become alarmed

allarme m alarm; **dare l'~** raise the alarm; **~ smog** smog alert

allattare <1a> *bambino* feed

alle *prp* **a** and *art* **le**

alleanza f alliance

allearsi <1b> ally o.s.

alleato 1 *agg* allied **2** m, **-a** f ally

allegare <1e> *documento* enclose

allegato m enclosure; INFOR attachment; **qui ~** enclosed

alleggerire <4d> lighten; *fig dolore* ease

allegria f cheerfulness

allegro 1 *agg* cheerful; *colore* bright **2** m MUS allegro

allenamento m training

allenare <1b>, **allenarsi** train (*per* for; **a** in)

allenatore m, **-trice** f trainer

allentare <1b> **1** *v/t* loosen; *fig disciplina* relax **2** *v/i e* **allentarsi** loosen

allergia f allergy

allergico (*pl* -ci) allergic (**a** to)

allestimento m preparation; MAR fitting out; TEA **~ scenico** sets *pl*, scenery

allestire <4d> prepare; MAR fit out; TEA stage

allevamento m BOT, ZO breeding

allevare <1b> BOT, ZO breed; *bambini* bring up, raise

allevatore m, **-trice** f breeder

alleviare <1b & k> alleviate

allievo m, **-a** f pupil, student

alligatore m alligator

allineamento m alignment

allineare <1m> line up; FIN adjust; TIP align

allinearsi line up; *fig* **~ con** *qu* align o.s. with s.o.

allo *prp* **a** and *art* **lo**

allodola f skylark

alloggiare <1f & c> **1** *v/t* put up; MIL billet **2** *v/i* stay, put up

alloggio m (*pl* -ggi) accommodation; **dare ~ a** *qu* put s.o. up; **vitto e ~** bed and board

allontanare <1a> take away; *fig pericolo, sospetto* avert

allontanarsi go away; *fig* grow apart

allora 1 *avv* then **2** *cong* then; **d'~ in poi** from then on; **fin d'~** since then

alloro m laurel; GASTR bay

alluce m big toe

allucinante F incredible, mind-blowing F

allucinazione f hallucination

alludere <3q> allude (**a** to)

alluminio m aluminium, *Am* aluminum

allungamento m lengthening

allungare <1e> lengthen; (*diluire*) dilute; *mano* stretch out, put out

allungarsi *di giorni* get longer; *di persona* stretch out, lie down

allusione f allusion

alluvione f flood

almeno at least

alogena f halogen

Alpi *fpl* Alps

alpinismo m mountaineering

alpinista m/f mountain climber

alpino Alpine

alquanto 1 *agg* some **2** *avv* a little, somewhat

alt *int* stop

altalena f swing

altare m altar

alterare <1l> alter

alterarsi (*guastarsi*) go bad *or* off; (*irritarsi*) get angry

alterazione f alteration

alterco m (*pl* -chi) altercation

alternare <1b>, **alternarsi** alternate

alternativa f alternative

alternativo alternative

alternato: corrente f **-a** alternating current

alterno: a giorni *pl* **-i** on alternate days

altezza f height; *titolo* Highness

alticcio (*pl* -cci) tipsy

altitudine f GEOG altitude

alto 1 *agg* high; *persona* tall; **a voce -a** in a loud voice; *leggere* aloud; **in ~** at the top; *moto* up; **a notte -a** in the middle of the night **2** m top

altoatesino 1 *agg* South Tyrolean **2** m, **-a** f person from South Tyrol

altoforno m blast furnace

altoparlante m loudspeaker

altopiano *m* (*pl* altipiani) plateau

altrettanto *agg, pron* as much; **-i** *pl* as many

altrimenti (*in modo diverso*) differently; (*in caso contrario*) otherwise

altro 1 *agg* other; **un ~** another; *l'altr'anno* last year; *l'~ giorno* the other day; *l'~ ieri* the day before yesterday 2 *pron* other; *l'un l'~* one another; *gli altri* other people; *tra l'~* what's more, moreover; *desidera ~?* anything else?; *tutt'~ che* anything but

altronde: *d'~* on the other hand

altrove elsewhere

altruismo *m* altruism

altura *f* hill

alunno *m*, **-a** *f* pupil, student

alzacristallo *m inv* AUTO window winder

alzare <1a> raise, lift; *prezzi* increase, raise; (*costruire*) build, erect; **~ le spalle** shrug (one's shoulders)

alzarsi stand up, rise; *da letto* get up; *di sole* come up, rise

amabile lovable; (*gentile*) pleasant, kind; *vino* sweet

amabilità *f* pleasantness

amaca *f* (*pl* -che) hammock

amalgamare <1m> amalgamate

amante *m/f* lover

amare <1a> love; *amico* be fond of

amareggiare <1f> embitter

amareggiato embittered

amarena *f* sour black cherry

amarezza *f* bitterness

amaro 1 *agg* bitter 2 *m liquore* bitters *pl*

ambasciata *f* embassy

ambasciatore *m*, **-trice** *f* ambassador

ambedue both

ambientale environmental

ambientalista 1 *agg* environmental 2 *m/f* environmentalist

ambientarsi <1b> become acclimatized

ambiente *m* BIO environment; **~ di lavoro** work environment; **protezione** *f* **dell'~** environmental protection

ambiguità *f inv* ambiguity

ambiguo ambiguous

ambito *m* sphere

ambizione *f* ambition

ambizioso ambitious

ambo 1 *agg* both; *in -i casi* in both cases 2 *m* (*lotteria*) double

ambulante 1 *agg* travel(l)ing 2 *m/f* pedlar

ambulanza *f* ambulance

ambulatorio *m* MED (*pl* -ri) outpatients

America *f* America

americano 1 *agg* American 2 *m*, **-a** *f* American 3 *m* American English

ametista *f* amethyst

amianto *m* asbestos

amichevole friendly

amicizia *f* friendship

amico (*pl* -ci) 1 *agg* friendly 2 *m*, **-a** *f* (*pl* -che) friend; **~ intimo** close friend

amido *m* starch

ammaccare <1d> dent; *frutta* bruise

ammaccatura *f* dent; *su frutta* bruise

ammaestrare <1b> teach; *animali* train

ammalarsi <1a> fall ill

ammalato 1 *agg* ill 2 *m*, **-a** *f* ill person

ammanco *m* (*pl* -chi) deficit

ammanettare <1a> handcuff, put handcuffs on

ammarare <1a> *di aereo* put down in the water; *di navetta spaziale* splash down

ammassare <1a>, **ammassarsi** mass

ammasso *m* pile; GEOL mass

ammazzare <1a> kill; *animali* slaughter

ammazzarsi (*suicidarsi*) kill o.s.

ammenda *f* (*multa*) fine; *fare ~ di* make amends for

ammesso *pp* → **ammettere**

ammettere <3ee> admit; (*supporre*) suppose; (*riconoscere*) acknowledge; **ammesso che …** supposing (that) …

amministrare <1a> administer; *azienda* manage, run

amministrativo administrative

amministratore *m*, **-trice** *f* administrator; *di azienda* manager; *~* **delegato** managing director

amministrazione *f* administration; *~* **comunale** local council; **pubblica** *~* public administration; **spese** *fpl* **d'~** administrative costs

ammiraglia *f* flagship

ammiraglio *m* (*pl* -gli) admiral

ammirare <1a> admire

ammiratore *m*, **-trice** *f* admirer

ammirazione *f* admiration

ammirevole admirable

ammissibile admissible

ammobiliare <1g> furnish

ammobiliato furnished

ammodo 1 *agg inv* respectable **2** *avv* properly

ammollo: in ~ soaking

ammonimento *m* reprimand, admonishment; (*consiglio*) warning

ammonire <4d> reprimand, admonish; (*avvertire*) warn; DIR caution

ammonizione *f* reprimand, admonishment; SP warning; DIR caution

ammontare 1 *v/i* <1a>: *~* **a** amount to **2** *m* amount; **per un ~ di ...** in the amount of ...

ammorbidire <4d> soften

ammortamento *m* FIN amortization

ammortizzare <1a> FIN amortize

ammortizzatore *m* AUTO shock absorber

ammucchiare <1g> pile up

ammucchiarsi pile up, accumulate

ammuffire <4d> go mo(u)ldy; *fig* mo(u)lder away

ammutolire <4d> be struck dumb

amnesia *f* amnesia

amnistia *f* amnesty

amo *m* hook; *fig* bait

amore *m* love; **per l'~ di qu** for love of s.o.; **per l'amor di Dio** for goodness' sake, for the love of God; **fare l'~ con qu** make love to s.o.

amoreggiare <1f> flirt

amorevole loving

amoroso loving, affectionate; *sguardo* amorous; *lettera, poesia* love *attr*

amperaggio *m* (*pl* -gi) amperage

ampiezza *f di stanza* spaciousness; *di* *gonna* fullness; *fig di cultura* breadth; *fig ~* **di vedute** broadmindedness

ampio (*pl* -pi) *stanza* spacious, large; *abito* roomy; *gonna* full

ampliamento *m* broadening, widening; *di edificio* extension

ampliare <1l> broaden, widen; *edificio* extend

amplificare <1m & d> TEC *suono* amplify

amplificatore *m* amplifier

ampolla *f* cruet

amputare <1l> amputate

amputazione *f* amputation

amuleto *m* amulet

anabbagliante dipped

anabolizzante *m* anabolic steroid

anacronistico (*pl* -ci) anachronistic

anagrafe *f ufficio* registry office

analcolico (*pl* -ci) **1** *agg* non-alcoholic **2** *m* non-alcoholic drink

anale anal

analfabeta *m/f* (*mpl* -i) illiterate person, person who cannot read or write

analfabetismo *m* illiteracy

analgesico (*pl* -ci) *m/agg* analgesic

analisi *f inv* analysis; *~* **del sangue** blood test

analista *m/f* (*mpl* -i) analyst; *~* **programmatore** systems analyst

analizzare <1a> analyse, *Am* analyze

analogia *f* analogy

analogo (*pl* -ghi) analogous

ananas *m inv* pineapple

anarchia *f* anarchy

anarchico (*pl* -ci) **1** *agg* anarchic **2** *m*, **-a** *f* anarchist

ANAS *abbr* (= **Azienda Nazionale Autonoma della Strada**) Italian Roads Department

anatomia *f* anatomy

anatomico (*pl* -ci) anatomical

anatra *f* duck

anca *f* (*pl* -che) hip

anche too, also, as well; (*perfino*) even; *~* **se** even if

ancora[1] *avv* still; *di nuovo* again; *di più* (some) more; **non ~** not yet; *~*

una volta once more, one more time; *dammene ~ un po'* give me a bit more

ancora² f anchor; *gettare l'~* drop anchor

ancoraggio m (pl -ggi) anchoring; *luogo* anchorage

ancorare <1l> anchor

ancorarsi anchor; *fig ~ a* cling to

andamento m *di vendite* performance

andare <1p> **1** v/i go; (*funzionare*) work; ~ *via* (*partire*) leave; *di macchia* come out; ~ *bene* suit; *taglia* fit; ~ *a cavallo* ride; ~ *a passeggio* walk; ~ *a male* go off; ~ *a finire* turn out; ~ *in bicicletta* cycle; *come va?* how are you?, how are things?; *non mi va di vestito* it doesn't fit me; *non mi va di venire* I don't feel like coming **2** m: *coll'~ del tempo* with the passage of time; *a lungo ~* in the long run

andarsene go away

andata f outward journey; *c'era più traffico all'~* there was more traffic on the way there; *biglietto m di ~* single (ticket), *Am* oneway ticket; *biglietto m di ~ e ritorno* return (ticket), *Am* roundtrip ticket

andatura f walk; SP pace

andirivieni m inv toing and froing

androne m hallway

aneddoto m anecdote

anello m ring; ~ *di fidanzamento* engagement ring

anemia f an(a)emia

anemico (pl -ci) an(a)emic

anemone m anemone

anestesia f an(a)esthesia; *sostanza* an(a)esthetic

anestesista m/f (mpl -i) an(a)esthetist

anestetico m (pl -ci) an(a)esthetic

anfetamina f amphetamine

anfibio (pl -bi) **1** agg amphibious **2** m ZO amphibian; MIL amphibious vehicle

anfiteatro m amphitheatre, *Am* -theater

anfora f amphora

angelo m angel; ~ *custode* guardian angel

anglicano **1** agg Anglican **2** m, -a f Anglican

anglista m/f student of English

anglosassone Anglo-Saxon

angolare angular

angolo m corner; MAT angle; ~ *cottura* kitchenette; MAT ~ *retto* right angle; SP *calcio m d'~* corner kick;

angoloso angular

angoscia f (pl -sce) anguish

angoscioso *pieno d'angoscia* anguished; *che da angoscia* distressing, heart-rending

anguilla f eel

anguria f water melon

angusto narrow

anice m GASTR aniseed

anidride f: ~ *carbonica* carbon dioxide

anima f soul; *non c'è ~ viva* there isn't a soul to be seen; F *rompere l'~ a qu* get on s.o.'s nerves F

animale **1** agg animal *attr* **2** m animal; ~ *domestico* pet

animare <1l> give life to; *conversazione* liven up; (*promuovere*) promote

animato *strada* busy; *conversazione*, *persona* animated

animatore m, -trice f *di gruppo* leader

animazione f animation; INFOR ~ *al computer* computer animation

animo m nature; (*coraggio*) heart; *farsi ~* be brave; *perdersi d'~* lose heart

anisetta f aniseed-flavoured liqueur

anitra f duck

annacquare <1a> water down

annaffiare <1k> water

annaffiatoio m (pl -oi) watering can

annali mpl annals

annata f vintage; (*anno*) year; *importo* annual amount

annegare <1e> **1** v/t drown **2** v/i e *annegarsi* drown

annerire <4d> **1** v/t blacken **2** v/i e *annerirsi* turn black, blacken annessione *f* POL annexation

annesso **1** *pp* → **annettere 2** *agg* annexed; (*allegato*) enclosed, attached **3** *m edificio* annex(e)

annettere <3m> POL annex; ARCHI add; (*allegare*) enclose, attach

annidarsi <1a> nest

anniversario *m* (*pl* -ri) anniversary

anno *m* year; **buon ~!** Happy New Year!; **~ finanziario** financial year; **~ scolastico** school year; **quanti -i hai?** how old are you?; **ho 33 -i** I'm 33 (years old)

annodare <1c> tie (together); *cravatta* tie, knot

annoiare <1i> bore; (*dare fastidio a*) annoy

annoiarsi get bored

annoiato bored

annotare <1c> make a note of; *testo* annotate

annotazione *f* note; *in testo* annotation

annuale annual, yearly; *di un anno* year-long

annuario *m* (*pl* -ri) yearbook

annuire <4d> (*assentire*) assent (**a** to)

annullamento *m* cancellation; *di matrimonio* annulment

annullare <1a> cancel; *matrimonio* annul; *gol* disallow; (*vanificare*) cancel out

annunciare <1f> announce

annunciatore *m*, **-trice** *f* RAD, TV announcer

Annunciazione *f* REL Annunciation

annuncio *m* (*pl* -ci) announcement; *in giornale* advertisement; **-i** *pl* **economici** classified ads, classifieds; **~ pubblicitario** ad(vert), advertisement

annunziare <1a> → **annunciare**

annuo annual, yearly

annusare <1a> sniff; *fig* smell

annuvolarsi <1a> cloud over

anomalo anomalous

anonimo anonymous; **società** *f* **-a** limited company

anoressia *f* anorexia

anoressico anorexic

anormale abnormal

ANSA *abbr* (= **Agenzia Nazionale Stampa Associata**) Italian Press Agency

ansa *f* handle; *di un fiume* bend

ansia *f* anxiety; **con ~** anxiously

ansimare <1l> wheeze

ansioso anxious

antagonismo *m* antagonism

antagonista *m/f* (*mpl* -i) antagonist

antartico (*pl* -ci) Antarctic *attr*

antecedente **1** *agg* preceding **2** *m* precedent

antefatto *m* prior event

anteguerra *m* pre-war years *pl*

antenato *m, f* ancestor

antenna *f* RAD, TV aerial; ZO antenna; **~ parabolica** satellite dish

anteporre <3ll> put before

anteposto *pp* → **anteporre**

anteprima *f* preview

anteriore front; *precedente* previous

anti ... anti ...

antiatomico (*pl* -ci) anti-nuclear; **rifugio** *m* **~** fallout shelter

antibiotico (*pl* -ci) *m/agg* antibiotic

anticamente in ancient times

anticamera *f* ante-room; **fare ~** be kept waiting

antichità *f inv* antiquity; **negozio** *m* **d'~** antique shop

anticiclone *m* anticyclone

anticipare <1m> anticipate; *denaro* pay in advance; *partenza, riunione ecc* bring forward

anticipo *m* advance; (*caparra*) deposit; **in ~** ahead of time, early

antico (*pl* -chi) **1** *agg* ancient; *mobile* antique **2 gli -chi** *pl* the ancients

anticoncezionale *m/agg* contraceptive

anticonformista *m/f* (*mpl* -i) nonconformist

anticongelante *m* anti-freeze

anticorpo *m* antibody

anticostituzionale unconstitutional

antidoto *m* antidote

antifurto **1** *adj* antitheft **2** *m* anti-theft device

antigas *inv* gas *attr*

antincendio *inv* fire *attr*

antinebbia *m inv* foglamp
antiorario: *in senso* ~ anticlockwise, *Am* counterclockwise
antipasto *m* starter
antipatia *f* antipathy
antipatico (*pl* -ci) disagreeable
antiquariato *m* antique business, antiques; *negozio m di* ~ antique shop
antiquario *m* (*pl* -ri), **-a** *f* antique dealer
antiquato antiquated
antiriflesso *inv* anti-glare
antiruggine *m* rust inhibitor
antirumore: *protezione f* ~ sound-proofing
antisemitismo *m* anti-Semitism
antisettico (*pl* -ci) *m/agg* antiseptic
antisismico (*pl* -ci) earthquake-proof
antitesi *f* FIL antithesis
antiurto shockproof
antologia *f* anthology
antracite *f* anthracite
antropologia *f* anthropology
anulare *m* ring finger
anzi in fact; (*o meglio*) (or) better still
anzianità *f* old age; ~ *di servizio* seniority
anziano **1** *agg* elderly; *per servizio* (most) senior **2** *m*, **-a** *f* old man; *donna* old woman; *gli -i* the elderly
anziché rather than
anzitutto first of all
aorta *f* aorta
apatia *f* apathy
apatico (*pl* -ci) apathetic
ape *f* bee
aperitivo *m* aperitif
aperto **1** *pp* → **aprire 2** *agg* open; *di mentalità aperta* broad-minded; *all'* ~ *piscina* open-air; *mangiare all'*~ eat outside *or* in the open air
apertura *f* opening; PHOT aperture; ~ *di credito* loan agreement; ~ *alare* wingspan
apice *m* apex; *fig* height
apicoltore *m*, **-trice** *f* bee-keeper
apicoltura *f* bee-keeping
apnea *f* SP free diving
apolide **1** *agg* stateless **2** *m* stateless person

apolitico (*pl* -ci) apolitical
apoplessia *f* apoplexy
apostolico (*pl* -ci) apostolic
apostolo *m* apostle
apostrofare <1m & c> reprimand; GRAM add an apostrophe to
apostrofo *m* apostrophe
appagare <1e> satisfy
appaiare <1i> match
appallottolare <1c & n> roll up into a ball
appalto *m* (*contratto*) contract; *dare in* ~ contract out; *prendere in* ~ win the contract for; *gara f di* ~ call for tenders
appannare <1a> mist up
appannarsi *di vetro* mist up; *di vista* grow dim
apparato *m* TEC, *fig* apparatus; ~ *digerente* digestive system
apparecchiare <1g> *tavola* set, lay; (*preparare*) prepare
apparecchiatura *f* equipment
apparecchio *m* (*pl* -cchi) TEC device; AVIA F plane; *per denti* brace; ~ *fotografico* camera; F *portare l'*~ wear a hearing aid
apparente apparent
apparenza *f* appearance; *salvare le -e* save face
apparire <4e> appear
appariscente striking, eyecatching
apparizione *f* apparition
appartamento *m* flat, *Am* apartment
appartarsi <1a> withdraw
appartenere <2q> belong
appassionare <1a> excite; (*commuovere*) move
appassionarsi become excited (*a* by)
appassionato passionate
appassire <4d> wither
appellarsi <1b> appeal (*a* to; *contro* against)
appello *m* appeal; *fare* ~ *a qu* appeal to s.o.; DIR *ricorrere in* ~ lodge an appeal
appena **1** *avv* just **2** *cong* as soon as
appendere <3c> hang
appendiabiti *m* hatstand

appendice *f* appendix
appendicite *f* appendicitis
Appennini *mpl* Apennines
appesantire <4d> make heavier
appesi, appeso *pp* → **appendere**
appetito *m* appetite; **buon ~!** enjoy your meal!
appetitoso appetizing
appianare <1a> level; *lite* smooth over
appiattire <4d> flatten
appicccicare <1m & d> stick
appicccicarsi stick
appiccicoso sticky; *fig* clingy
appigliarsi <1g> grab hold (**a** of)
appiglio *m* (*pl* -gli) fingerhold; *per piedi* toehold; *fig* excuse
applaudire <4a or d> *v/t & v/i* applaud
applauso *m* applause
applicare <1l & d> *etichetta* attach; *regolamento* apply
applicarsi: ~ **a qc** apply o.s. to sth
applicazione *f* application
appoggiare <1f & c> lean (**a** against); (*posare*) put; *fig* support back
appoggiarsi: ~ **a** lean on; *fig* rely on, lean on
appoggiatesta *m inv* headrest
appoggio *m* (*pl* -ggi) support
apporre <3ll> put; ~ **la firma su qc** put one's signature to sth
apportare <1c> bring; *fig* (*causare*) cause
apposito appropriate
apposta deliberately, on purpose; *specialmente* specifically
apprendere <3c> learn; *notizia* hear
apprendista *m/f* (*mpl* -i) apprentice
apprendistato *m* apprenticeship
apprensione *f* apprehension
apprensivo apprehensive
appreso *pp* → **apprendere**
appresso **1** *prp* close, near; (*dietro*) behind; ~ **a qu** near s.o., close to s.o. **2** *avv* near, close by; **portarsi qc ~** bring sth (with one)
apprezzare <1b> appreciate
approccio *m* (*pl* -cci) approach
approdare <1c> land; *di barca* moor,

tie up; *fig* **non ~ a nulla** come to nothing
approdo *m* landing; *luogo* landing stage
approfittare <1a>: ~ **di qc** take advantage of sth
approfondire <4d> deepen; *fig* study in depth
appropriarsi <1m & c>: ~ **di qc** appropriate sth
appropriato appropriate
approvare <1c> approve of; *legge* approve
approvazione *f* approval
approvvigionamento *m* supply
appuntamento *m* appointment
appuntare <1a> pin; *avviso* pin up
appuntito pointed; *matita* sharp
appunto **1** *m* note; **prendere -i** take notes **2** *avv*: (**per l'**)~ exactly
apribottiglie *m inv* bottle opener
aprile *m* April
aprire <4f> open; *rubinetto* turn on
aprirsi open; ~ **con qu** confide in s.o., open up to s.o.
apriscatole *m inv* can-opener, *Br* tin-opener
aquila *f* eagle
aquilone *m* kite
arabesco *m* (*pl* -chi) arabesque; *spir* scrawl, scribble
Arabia Saudita *f* Saudi (Arabia)
arabo 1 *agg* Arab **2** *m*, **-a** *f* Arab **3** *m* Arabic
arachide *f* peanut
aragosta *f* lobster
arancia *f* (*pl* -ce) orange
aranciata *f* orangeade
arancio 1 *agg inv* orange **2** *m* (*pl* -ci) *albero* orange tree; *colore* orange
arancione *m/agg* orange
arare <1a> plough, *Am* plow
aratro *m* plough, *Am* plow
arazzo *m* tapestry
arbitraggio *m* (*pl* -ggi) arbitration; SP refereeing
arbitrare <1l> arbitrate in; SP referee
arbitrario (*pl* -ri) arbitrary
arbitro *m* arbiter; SP referee
arbusto *m* shrub
arca *f* (*pl* -che) (*cassa*) chest; REL **l'~**

di Noè Noah's Ark

arcaico (*pl* -ci) archaic

arcangelo *m* archangel

arcata *f* ANAT, ARCHI arch

archeologia *f* arch(a)eology

archeologo *m* (*pl* -gi), **-a** *f* arch(a)eologist

archetto *m* MUS bow

architetto *m* architect

architettonico (*pl* -ci) architectural

archiviare <1k> file

archivio *m* (*pl* -vi) archives, records

arcipelago *m* (*pl* -ghi) archipelago

arcivescovo *m* archbishop

arco *m* (*pl* -chi) bow; ARCHI arch; ~ **di tempo** space of time; **orchestra** *f* **d'-chi** string orchestra

arcobaleno *m* rainbow

ardente *fig* ardent

ardere <3uu> *v/t & v/i* burn

area *f* surface; *zona* area; ~ **fabbricabile** site that may be built on; SP ~ **di rigore** penalty area; ~ **di servizio** service area

arena *f* arena

arenarsi <1a> run aground; *fig* come to a halt

areo ... → **aereo** ...

argano *m* winch

argentato silver-plated

argenteria *f* silver(ware)

Argentina *f* Argentina

argentino 1 *agg* Argentinian **2** *m*, **-a** *f* Argentinian

argento *m* silver; ~ **vivo** quicksilver; FERR **carta** *f* **d'~** *travel pass for people over a certain age;* **nozze** *fpl* **d'~** silver wedding *sg*

argilla *f* clay

argilloso clayey

arginare <1l> embank

argine *m* embankment

argomento *m* argument; (*contenuto*) subject; **cambiare** ~ change the subject

arguto witty; (*perspicace*) shrewd

arguzia *f* wit; *espressione* witticism, witty remark; (*perspicacia*) shrewdness

aria *f* **1** air; ~ **condizionata** air conditioning; **all'~ aperta** in the fresh air; **mandare all'~ qc** ruin sth **2** (*aspetto*) appearance; (*espressione*) air; **aver l'~ stanca** look tired; **ha l'~ di non capire** he looks as if he doesn't understand; **darsi delle -e** give o.s. airs **3** MUS tune; *di opera* aria

aridità *f* dryness

arido dry, arid

arieggiare <1f> *stanza* air

ariete *m* ZO ram; ASTR **Ariete** Aries

aringa *f* (*pl* -ghe) herring

arista *f* GASTR chine of pork

aristocratico (*pl* -ci) **1** *agg* aristocratic **2** *m*, **-a** *f* aristocrat

aristocrazia *f* aristocracy

aritmetica *f* arithmetic

arma *f* (*pl* -i) weapon; ~ **da fuoco** firearm; **-i** *pl* **convenzionali** conventional weapons; **-i** *pl* **nucleari** nuclear weapons; **-i** *pl* **atomiche, biologiche e chimiche** atomic, biological and chemical weapons; **chiamare alle -i** call up; *fig* **essere alle prime -i** be just starting out

armadio *m* (*pl* -di) cupboard; ~ **a muro** fitted cupboard

armamentario *m* (*pl* -ri) *gen spir* paraphernalia

armamento *m* armament; **industria** *f* **degli -i** armaments industry

armare <1a> arm; ARCHI reinforce

armarsi arm o.s. (**di** with)

armata *f* army; MAR fleet

armato armed

armatore *m* shipowner

armatura *f* armo(u)r; (*struttura*) framework

armistizio *m* (*pl* -zi) armistice

armonia *f* harmony

armonica *f* (*pl* -che) harmonica; ~ **a bocca** mouth organ

armonico (*pl* -ci) harmonic

armonioso harmonious

armonizzare <1a> *v/t & v/i* harmonize

arnese *m* tool

arnia *f* beehive

aroma *m* (*pl* -i) aroma

aromatico (*pl* -ci) aromatic

aromatizzare <1a> flavo(u)r

aromaterapia *f* aromatherapy
arpa *f* harp
arpione *m pesca* harpoon
arrabattarsi <1a> do everything one can
arrabbiarsi <1k> get angry
arrabbiato angry; *(idrofobo)* rabid
arrampicarsi <1m & d> climb
arrampicata *f* climb
arrampicatore *m*, **-trice** *f* climber; ~ **sociale** social climber
arrangiamento *m* arrangement
arrangiare <1f> arrange
arrangiarsi *(accordarsi)* agree (**su** on); *(destreggiarsi)* manage
arrecare <1b & d> bring; *fig* cause
arredamento *m* décor; *mobili* furniture; *arte* interior design
arredare <1b> furnish
arredatore *m*, **-trice** *f* interior designer
arrendersi <3c> surrender; *fig* give up
arrendevole soft, yielding
arrestare <1b> stop, halt; DIR arrest
arrestarsi stop
arresto *m* coming to a stop; DIR arrest
arretrato **1** *agg* in arrears; *paese* underdeveloped; **numero** *m* ~ **di giornale** back number **2 -i** *mpl* arrears
arricchire <4d> *fig* enrich
arricchirsi get rich
arricciare <1f> *capelli* curl; ~ **il naso** turn up one's nose
arringa *f* (*pl* -ghe) DIR closing speech for the defence
arrivare <1a> arrive; ~ **a** reach; ~ **primo** arrive first; ~ **puntuale** arrive on time; ~ **a fare qc** manage to do sth; F **non ci arriva** he doesn't get it F, he doesn't understand
arrivederci, **arrivederla** goodbye
arrivista *m/f* (*mpl* -i) social climber
arrivo *m* arrival; SP finishing line; **-i internazionali** international arrivals
arrogante arrogant
arroganza *f* arrogance
arrossire <4d> blush

arrostire <4d> *carne* roast; **ai ferri** grill
arrosto *m* roast; ~ **d'agnello** roast lamb
arrotolare <1m & c> roll up
arrotondare <1a> round off; *stipendio* supplement
arroventato red-hot
arruffare <1a> *capelli* ruffle
arruffato ruffled
arrugginire <4d> **1** *v/t* rust **2** *v/i* e **arrugginirsi** rust; *fig* become rusty
arruolamento *m* enlistment
arruolare <1o> enlist
arruolarsi enlist, join up
arsenale *m* arsenal; MAR dockyard
arso **1** *pp* → **ardere** **2** *agg* burnt; *(secco)* dried-up
arsura *f* blazing heat
arte *f* art; *(abilità)* gift; **le -i** *pl* **figurative** the figurative arts; **-i** *pl* **grafiche** graphic arts; **storia** *f* **dell'~** history of art; **un discorso fatto ad ~** a masterly speech
artefatto *voce* disguised
artefice *m/f fig* author, architect
arteria *f* artery; ~ **stradale** arterial road
arterioso arterial
artico (*pl* -ci) Arctic *attr*
articolare **1** *agg* articular **2** *v/t* <1m> articulate; *(suddividere)* divide
articolazione *f* ANAT articulation
articolo *m* item, article; GRAM ~ **determinativo** definite article; GRAM ~ **indeterminativo** indefinite article; **-i** *pl* **di consumo** consumer goods; ~ **di fondo** leading article; ~ **di prima necessità** basic
artificiale artificial
artificio *m* (*pl* -ci) artifice; **fuochi** *mpl* **d'~** fireworks
artificioso *maniere* artificial
artigianale handmade, handcrafted
artigianato *m* craftsmanship
artigiano *m*, **-a** *f* craftsman; *donna* craftswoman
artiglieria *f* artillery
artiglio *m* (*pl* -gli) claw
artista *m/f* (*mpl* -i) artist
artistico (*pl* -ci) artistic

arto *m* limb

artrite *f* arthritis

artrosi *f* rheumatism

ascella *f* armpit

ascendente **1** *agg* ascending; *strada* sloping upwards; *movimento* upwards **2** *m* ASTR ascendant; *fig* influence

ascensione *f di montagna* ascent; REL Ascension

ascensore *m* lift, *Am* elevator

ascesa *f* ascent

ascesso *m* abscess

asceta *m* (*pl* -i) ascetic

ascia *f* (*pl* -sce) ax(e)

asciugacapelli *m* hairdryer

asciugamano *m* towel; **~ da bagno** bath towel

asciugare <1e> dry

asciugarsi dry o.s.; **~ i capelli** dry one's hair

asciugatrice *f* tumble dryer

asciutto **1** *agg* dry **2** *m: fig trovarsi all'~** be stony broke

ascoltare <1a> listen to

ascoltatore *m*, **-trice** *f* listener

ascolto *m* listening; **dare / prestare ~** listen (*a* to); **indice m di ~** ratings *pl*

asettico (*pl* -ci) aseptic

asfaltare <1a> asphalt

asfalto *m* asphalt

asfissia *f* asphyxia

asfissiare <1k> asphyxiate

Asia *f* Asia

asiatico (*pl* -ci) **1** *agg* Asian **2** *m*, **-a** *f* Asian

asilo *m* shelter; **richiesta f di ~ politico** request for political asylum; **~ infantile** nursery school; **~ nido** day nursery

asimmetrico (*pl* -ci) asymmetrical

asino *m* ass (*anche fig*)

asma *f* asthma

asmatico (*pl* -ci) asthmatic

asociale antisocial

asola *f* buttonhole

asparago *m* (*pl* -gi) spear of asparagus; **-gi** asparagus *sg*

aspettare <1b> wait for; **~ un bambino** be expecting a baby; **farsi ~** keep people waiting

aspettarsi expect; **dovevo aspettarmelo** I should have expected it

aspettativa *f* expectation; **da lavoro** unpaid leave

aspetto[1] *m* look, appearance; *di problema* aspect; **sotto quest' ~** from that point of view

aspetto[2] *m: **sala f d'~** waiting room

aspirante **1** *agg* TEC suction *attr* **2** *m/f* applicant

aspirapolvere *m* vacuum cleaner

aspirare <1a> *v/t* inhale; TEC suck up **2** *v/i:* **~ a qc** aspire to sth

aspirina *f* aspirin

asportare <1c> take away

aspro sour; (*duro*) harsh; *litigio* bitter

assaggiare <1f> taste, sample

assaggio *m* (*pl* -ggi) taste, sample

assai **1** *agg* a lot of **2** *avv con verbo* a lot; *con aggettivo* very; (*abbastanza*) enough

assalire <4m> attack

assaltare <1a> → **assalire**

assalto *m* attack; *fig* **prendere d'~** storm

assassinare <1a> murder; POL assassinate

assassinio *m* murder; POL assassination

assassino **1** *agg* murderous **2** *m*, **-a** *f* murderer; POL assassin

asse[1] *f* board; **~ da stiro** ironing board

asse[2] *m* TEC axle; MAT axis

assecondare <1a> support; (*esaudire*) satisfy

assediare <1k> besiege

assedio *m* (*pl* -di) siege

assegnare <1a> *premio* award; (*destinare*) assign

assegno *m* cheque, *Am* check; **~ in bianco** blank cheque (*Am* check); **~ sbarrato** crossed cheque (*Am* check); **~ turistico** traveller's cheque, *Am* traveler's check; **contro ~** cash on delivery; **-i familiari** child benefit; **emettere un ~** issue *or* write a cheque (*Am* check)

assemblea *f* meeting; **~ generale** annual general meeting

assennato sensible

assentarsi <1b> go away, leave

assente absent, away; *fig* absent-minded

assenza *f* absence; *~ di qc* lack of sth

assessore *m* council(l)or; *~ comunale* local councillor

assetato thirsty

assetto *m* order; MAR trim

assicurare <1a> insure; (*legare*) secure; *lettera, pacco* register

assicurarsi make sure, ensure

assicurata *f* registered letter

assicurato 1 *agg* insured; *lettera, pacco* registered **2** *m*, **-a** *f* person with insurance

assicurazione *f* insurance; *~ dei bagagli* luggage insurance; *~ di responsabilità civile* liability insurance; *~ sulla vita* life insurance; *~ casco* comprehensive insurance

assideramento *m* exposure

assiduo (*diligente*) assiduous; (*regolare*) regular

assieme together

assillante nagging

assillare <1a> pester

assillo *m fig persona* pest, nuisance; (*preoccupazione*) nagging thought

assimilare <1m> assimilate

assimilazione *f* assimilation

assise *fpl*: *Corte f d'~* Crown Court

assistente *m/f* assistant; *~ sociale* social worker; *~ di volo* flight attendant

assistenza *f* assistance; *~ medica* medical care; *~ sociale* social work; *~ tecnica* after-sales service

assistere <3f> **1** *v/t* assist, help; (*curare*) nurse **2** *v/i* (*essere presente*) be present (*a* at), attend (*a* sth)

asso *m* ace; *fig piantare in ~* leave in the lurch

associare <1f> take into partnership; *fig ~ qu a qc* associate s.o. with sth

associarsi enter into partnership (*a* with); (*unirsi*) join forces; (*iscriversi*) subscribe (*a* to); (*prendere parte*) join (*a* sth)

associazione *f* association; *~ per la difesa dei consumatori* consumer association

assoggettare <1b> subject

assolato sunny

assolo *m inv* MUS solo

assolto *pp* → **assolvere**

assolutamente absolutely

assoluto absolute

assoluzione *f* DIR acquittal; REL absolution

assolvere <3g> DIR acquit; *da un obbligo* release; *compito* carry out, perform; REL absolve, give absolution to

assomigliare <1g>: *~ a qu* be like s.o., resemble s.o.

assomigliarsi be like *or* resemble each other

assonnato sleepy

assorbente 1 *agg* absorbent **2** *m*: *~ igienico* sanitary towel

assorbire <4c or 4d> absorb

assordante deafening

assordare <1a> **1** *v/t* deafen **2** *v/i* go deaf

assortimento *m* assortment

assortito assorted; *essere ben ~ con* go well with

assorto engrossed

assuefare <3aa> accustom (*a* to)

assuefarsi become accustomed (*a* to)

assuefatto *pp* → **assuefare**

assuefazione *f* resistance, tolerance; *agli alcolici, alla droga* addiction

assumere <3h> *impiegato* take on, hire; *incarico* take on

assunzione *f di impiegato* employment, hiring; REL **Assunzione** Assumption

assurdità *f* absurdity

assurdo absurd

asta *f* pole; FIN auction; *mettere all'~* sell at auction, put up for auction

astemio (*pl* -mi) **1** *agg* abstemious **2** *m*, **-a** *f* abstemious person

astenersi <2q>: *~ da* abstain from

astensione *f* abstention; *~ dal voto* abstention

asterisco *m* (*pl* -chi) asterisk

astigmatismo *m* astigmatism

astinenza *f* abstinence

astio *m* (*pl* -ti) ranco(u)r

astratto abstract

astringente *m/agg* MED astringent

astro *m* star

astrologia *f* astrology

astrologo *m* (*pl* -gi), **-a** *f* astrologer

astronauta *m/f* (*mpl* -i) astronaut

astronave *f* spaceship

astronomia *f* astronomy

astronomico (*pl* -ci) astronomical

astronomo *m*, **-a** *f* astronomer

astuccio *m* (*pl* -cci) case

astuto astute

ateismo *m* atheism

ateneo *m* university

ateo *m*, **-a** *f* atheist

atlante *m* atlas

atlantico (*pl* -ci) Atlantic; *Oceano m Atlantico* Atlantic Ocean

atleta *m/f* (*mpl* -i) athlete

atletica *f* athletics; **~ leggera** track and field (events)

atletico (*pl* -ci) athletic

atmosfera *f* atmosphere

atmosferico (*pl* -ci) atmospheric

atomico (*pl* -ci) atomic

atomo *m* atom

atrio *m* (*pl* -ri) foyer; **~ della stazione** station concourse

atroce appalling

atrocità *f* atrocity

attaccabrighe *m o f inv* F troublemaker

attaccamento *m* attachment

attaccante *m* SP forward

attaccapanni *m inv* clothes hook; *a stelo* clothes hanger

attaccare <1d> **1** *v/t* attach; (*incollare*) stick; (*appendere*) hang; (*assalire*) attack; (*iniziare*) begin, start **2** *v/i* stick; F **~ a fare qc** start doing sth

attaccarsi stick; (*aggrapparsi*) hold on (**a** to)

attacco *m* (*pl* -cchi) attack; (*punto di unione*) junction; EL socket; SCI binding; MED fit; (*inizio*) beginning

attardarsi <1a> linger

atteggiamento *m* attitude

atteggiarsi <1f>: **~ a** pose as

attendere <3c> **1** *v/t* wait for **2** *v/i*: **~ a** attend to

attendibile reliable

attenersi <2q> stick (**a** to)

attentare <1b>: **~ a** attack; **~ alla vita di qu** make an attempt on s.o.'s life

attentato *m* attempted assassination

attento **1** *agg* attentive; **stare ~ a** be careful of **2** *int* **~!** look out!, (be) careful!

attenuante *f* extenuating circumstance

attenuare <1m & b> reduce; *colpo* cushion

attenuarsi lessen, decrease

attenzione *f* attention; **~!** look out!, (be) careful!; **far ~ a qc** mind *or* watch sth

atterraggio *m* (*pl* -ggi) landing; **~ di fortuna** emergency landing

atterrare <1b> **1** *v/t avversario* knock down; *edificio* demolish, knock down **2** *v/i* land

attesa *f* waiting; (*tempo d'attesa*) wait; (*aspettativa*) expectation

atteso *pp* → **attendere**

attestare <1b> certify

attestato *m* certificate; **~ di frequenza** good attendance certificate

attico *m* (*pl* -ci) attic

attiguo adjacent (**a** to)

attimo *m* moment

attinente relevant (**a** to)

attirare <1a> attract

attitudine *f* attitude; **avere ~ per qc** have an aptitude for sth

attivare <1a> activate

attività *f* activity; *pl* FIN assets; **che ~ svolgi?** what do you do (for a living)?; **avere un'~ in proprio** have one's own business

attivo **1** *agg* active; FIN **bilancio** *m* **~** credit balance **2** *m* FIN assets *pl*; GRAM active voice

atto *m* act; (*gesto*) gesture; *documento* deed; **~ di fede** act of faith; **all'~ pratico** when it comes to the crunch; **mettere in ~** carry out; **prendere ~ di** note; DIR **mettere**

agli -i enter in the court records

attorcigliare <1g>, **attorcigliarsi** twist

attore *m*, **-trice** *f* actor; *donna* actress

attorno: ~ *a qc* round sth; *qui* ~ around here

attraccare <1d> MAR berth, dock

attracco *m* (*pl* -cchi) MAR berth

attraente attractive

attrarre <3xx> attract

attrattiva *f* attraction

attratto *pp* → **attrarre**

attraversare <1b> *strada, confine* cross; ~ *un momento difficile* be going through a bad time

attraverso across

attrazione *f* attraction

attrezzare <1a> equip

attrezzarsi get o.s. kitted out

attrezzato equipped

attrezzatura *f* equipment, gear

attrezzo *m* piece of equipment; **-i** *pl* **da ginnastica** apparatus

attribuire <4d> attribute

attributo *m* attribute

attrice *f* → **attore**

attrito *m* friction

attuale current

attualità *f* news; *d'*~ topical

attualizzare <1a> update

attuare <1l> put into effect

attuazione *f* putting into effect

audace bold

audacia *f* boldness

audioleso **1** *agg* hearing-impaired **2** *m*, **-a** *f* person with hearing difficulties, person who is hearing-impaired

audiovisivo audiovisual

audizione *f* audition

augurare <1l> wish; ~ *a qu buon viaggio* wish s.o. a good trip

augurio *m* (*pl* -ri) wish; *fare gli* **-ri** *di Buon Natale a qu* wish s.o. a Merry Christmas; *tanti* **-ri!** all the best!

aula *f* *di scuola* class room; *di università* lecture theatre *or* room

aumentare <1a> **1** *v/t* increase; *prezzi* increase, raise, put up **2** *v/i* increase; *di prezzi* increase, rise, go up

aumento *m* increase, rise; ~ *salariale* pay rise; ~ *dei prezzi* increase *or* rise in prices

aureo golden

aureola *f* halo

auricolare *m* earphone

aurora *f* dawn; ~ *boreale* northern lights *pl*

ausiliare **1** *agg* auxiliary **2** *m* GRAM auxiliary

ausiliario (*pl* -ri) auxiliary

austerità *f* austerity

australe southern

Australia *f* Australia

australiano **1** *agg* Australian **2** *m*, **-a** *f* Australian

Austria *f* Austria

austriaco (*mpl* -ci) **1** *agg* Austrian **2** *m*, **-a** *f* Austrian

autenticare <1m, d & b> authenticate

autenticità *f* authenticity

autentico (*pl* -ci) authentic

autista *m/f* (*mpl* -i) driver

auto *f inv* → **automobile**

autoadesivo **1** *agg* self-adhesive **2** *m* sticker

autoambulanza *f* ambulance

autobiografia *f* autobiography

autobomba *f* car bomb

autobus *m* bus; ~ *di linea* city bus

autocaravan *f* camper van

autocarro *m* truck, *Br* lorry

autocisterna *f* tanker

autocontrollo *m* self-control

autocritica *f* self-criticism

autodidatta *m/f* (*mpl* -i) self-taught person

autodifesa *f* self-defence, *Am* -defense

autodromo *m* motor racing circuit

autofinanziamento *m* self-financing

autogol *m inv* own goal

autografo *m* autograph

autogrill *m inv* motorway café

autolavaggio *m* (*pl* -ggi) car-wash

automa *m* (*pl* -i) robot

automatico (*pl* -ci) **1** *agg* automatic **2** *m bottone* press stud fastener

automezzo *m* motor vehicle

automobile *f* car; ~ *da corsa* racing

car; **~ da noleggio** hire car

automobilismo *m* driving; SP motor racing

automobilista *m/f* (*mpl* -i) driver

autonoleggio *m* (*pl* -ggi) car rental; (*azienda*) car-rental firm

autonomia *f* autonomy; TEC battery life

autonomo autonomous

autoradio *f inv* car radio

autore *m*, **-trice** *f* author; DIR perpetrator

autorevole authoritative

autorimessa *f* garage

autorità *f inv* authority; **~ portuale** port authorities *pl*

autoritario (*pl* -ri) authoritarian

autorizzare <1a> authorize

autorizzazione *f* authorization

autoscatto *m* automatic shutter release

autoscuola *f* driving school

autosilo *m inv* multistorey car park, *Am* parking garage

autosoccorso *m* self-help

autostop *m*: **fare l'~** hitchhike

autostoppista *m/f* (*mpl* -i) hitchhiker

autostrada *f* motorway, *Am* highway; **~ informatica** information highway

autotreno *m* articulated lorry, *Am* semi

autovettura *f* motor vehicle

autrice *f* → **autore**

autunno *m* autumn, *Am* fall

avambraccio *m* (*pl* -cci) forearm

avanguardia *f* avant-garde; **all'~** avant-garde *attr*; *azienda* leading-edge; **essere all'~ in** lead the way in

avanti 1 *avv* in front, ahead; **d'ora in ~** from now on; **andare ~** *di orologio* be fast; **mandare ~** be the head of; **essere ~ nel programma** be ahead of schedule **2** *int* **~!** come in! **3** *m* SP forward

avanzare <1a> **1** *v/i* advance; *fig* make progress; (*rimanere*) be left over **2** *v/t* put forward

avanzo *m* remainder; FIN surplus; **gli -i** *pl* the leftovers

avaria *f* failure

avariato damaged; *cibi* spoiled

avarizia *f* avarice

avaro 1 *agg* miserly **2** *m*, **-a** *f* miser

avena *f* oats *pl*

avere <2b> **1** *v/t* have; **~ 20 anni** be 20 (years old); **~ fame/sonno** be hungry/sleepy; **~ caldo/freddo** be hot/cold; **~ qualcosa da fare** have something to do; **avercela con qu** have it in for s.o.; **che hai?** what's up with you? **2** *v/aus* have; **hai visto Tony?** have you seen Tony?; **hai visto Tony ieri?** did you see Tony yesterday? **3** *m* FIN credit; **dare e ~** debits and credits; **-i** *mpl* wealth *sg*

avi *mpl* ancestors

aviatore *m* flyer

aviazione *f* aviation; MIL Air Force

avidità *f* avidness

avido avid

aviogetto *m* jet

AVIS *abbr* (= *Associazione Volontari Italiani del Sangue*) Italian blood donors' association

avocado *m* avocado

avorio *m* ivory

avvalersi <2r>: **~ di qc** avail o.s. of sth

avvallamento *m* depression

avvantaggiare <1f> favo(u)r

avvantaggiarsi: **~ di qc** take advantage of sth

avvedersi <2s>: **~ di qc** notice sth

avveduto astute

avvelenamento *m* poisoning

avvelenare <1a> poison

avvelenarsi poison o.s.

avvenimento *m* event

avvenire <4p> **1** *v/i* (*accadere*) happen **2** *m* future

Avvento *m* Advent

avventore *m* regular customer

avventura *f* adventure

avventurarsi <1a> venture

avventuriero *m*, **-a** *f* adventurer; *donna* adventuress

avventuroso adventurous

avvenuto *pp* → **avvenire**

avverarsi <1a> come true

bacinella

avverbio m (pl -bi) adverb

avversario (pl -ri) **1** agg opposing **2** m, **-a** f opponent

avversione f aversion (**per** to)

avvertenza f (ammonimento) warning; (premessa) foreword; **avere l'~ di** be careful to; **-e** pl (istruzioni per l'uso) instructions

avvertimento m warning

avvertire <4b> warn; (percepire) catch

avviamento m introduction; TEC, AUTO start-up

avviare <1h> start

avviarsi set out, head off

avviato established

avvicendare <1b> alternate

avvicendarsi alternate

avvicinamento m approach

avvicinare <1a> approach; **~ qc a qc** move sth closer to sth

avvicinarsi approach, near (**a** sth)

avvilire <4d> depress; mortificare humiliate

avvilirsi demean o.s.; scoraggiarsi become depressed

avvilito scoraggiato depressed

avvio m: **dare l'~ a qc** get sth under way

avvisare <1a> (informare) inform, advise; (mettere in guardia) warn

avviso m notice; **a mio ~** in my opinion; **mettere qu sull'~** warn s.o.

avvitare <1a> screw in; fissare screw

avvocato m lawyer

avvolgere <3d> wrap

avvolgibile m roller blind

avvolto pp → **avvolgere**

avvoltoio m (pl -oi) vulture

azienda f business; **~ a conduzione familiare** family business; **~ autonoma di soggiorno** tourist information office

aziendale company attr

azionare <1a> activate; allarme set off

azionario share; **capitale** m **~** share capital

azione f action; (effetto) influence; FIN share; FIN **~ ordinaria** ordinary share; **emettere -i** issue shares

azionista m/f (mpl -i) shareholder; **maggiore ~** majority shareholder

azoto m nitrogen

azzannare <1a> bite into

azzardarsi <1a> dare

azzardato foolhardy

azzardo m hazard; **gioco** m **d'~** game of chance

azzerare <1b> TEC reset

azzuffarsi <1a> come to blows

azzurro 1 agg blue **2** m colore blue; SP **gli -i** pl the Italians, the Italian national team

B

babbo m F dad F, Am pop F; **Babbo Natale** Father Christmas, Santa (Claus)

babbuino m baboon

babordo m MAR port (side)

baby-sitter m/f inv baby-sitter

bacato wormeaten

bacca f (pl -cche) berry

baccalà m inv dried salt cod

baccano m din

bacchetta f rod; MUS del direttore d'orchestra baton; per suonare il tamburo (drum) stick; **~ magica** magic wand

bacheca f (pl -che) notice board; di museo showcase

baciare <1f> kiss

baciarsi kiss (each other)

bacillo m bacillus

bacinella f basin; FOT tray

bacino m basin; ANAT pelvis; MAR port

bacio m (pl -ci) kiss

baco m (pl -chi) worm; **~ da seta** silkworm

bada f: **tenere a ~ qu** keep s.o. at bay

badare <1a> **: ~ a** look after; (fare attenzione a) look out for, mind; **~ ai fatti propri** mind one's own business; **non ~ a spese** spare no expense

baffo m: **-i** pl m(o)ustache; di animali whiskers

bagagliaio m (pl -ai) FERR luggage van, Am baggage car; AUTO boot, Am trunk

bagaglio m (pl -gli) luggage, Am baggage; **deposito** m **-i** left luggage (office), Am baggage checkroom; **fare i -i** pack; **spedire come ~ appresso** send as accompanied luggage

bagliore m glare; di speranza glimmer

bagnante m/f bather

bagnare <1a> wet; (immergere) dip; (inzuppare) soak; (annaffiare) water; di fiume flow through

bagnarsi get wet; in mare ecc swim, bathe

bagnato wet; **~ di sudore** dripping with sweat; **~ fradicio** soaked, wet through

bagnino m, **-a** f lifeguard

bagno m bath; stanza bathroom; gabinetto toilet; **~ di fango** mud bath; **fare il ~** have a bath; **mettere a ~** soak; nel mare ecc (have a) swim; **~ degli uomini** gents, Am men's room; **~ per donne** ladies' (room)

bagnomaria m inv double boiler, bain marie

baia f bay

baio m (pl bai): **cavallo** m **~** bay

baita f mountain chalet

balaustra f balustrade

balbettare <1a> stammer; bambino babble, prattle

balbettio m stammering; di bambino babble, prattle

balbuzie f stutter

balbuziente m/f stutterer

balcanico (pl -ci) Balkan; **paesi** mpl **-ci** Balkans

balconata f TEA dress circle, Am balcony

balcone m balcony

baldoria f revelry; **fare ~** have a riotous time

balena f whale

balenare <1a>: fig **gli è balenata un'idea** an idea flashed through his mind

baleno m lightning; **in un ~** in a flash

balestra f AUTO leaf spring

balia[1] f: **in ~ di** at the mercy of

balia[2] f: **~ asciutta** nanny

balla f bale; fig F (frottola) fib F

ballare <1a> v/t & v/i dance

ballata f MUS ballad

ballerina f dancer; di balletto ballet dancer; di rivista chorus girl; (scarpa) ballet shoe; ZO wagtail

ballerino m dancer; di balletto ballet dancer

balletto m ballet

ballo m dance; (il ballare) dancing; (festa) ball; **corpo** m **di ~** corps de ballet; **essere in ~** persona be involved; essere in gioco be at stake; **abbiamo in ~ un lavoro importante** we've got a big job on at the moment; **tirare in ~ qc** bring sth up

balneare località, centro seaside attr; **stagione** f **~** swimming season; **stabilimento** m **~** lido; **stazione** f **~** seaside resort

balocco m (pl -cchi) toy

balordo 1 agg ragionamento shaky; idea stupid; tempo, consiglio unreliable **2** m (teppista) lout

balsamico (pl -ci) aceto balsamic; aria balmy

balsamo m per i capelli hair conditioner; fig balm, solace

baltico (pl -ci) Baltic

balzare <1a> jump, leap; **~ in piedi** jump or leap to one's feet; fig **un errore che balza subito agli occhi** a mistake that suddenly jumps out at you

balzo m jump, leap; fig **cogliere la**

B

palla al ~ jump at the chance
bambagia *f* cotton wool, *Am* absorbent cotton
bambinaia *f* nanny
bambino *m*, **-a** *f* child; *in fasce* baby; ~ *in provetta* test-tube baby
bambola *f* doll
bambolotto *m* baby boy doll
bambù *m* bamboo; *canna f di* ~ bamboo cane
banale banal
banalità *f inv* banality
banana *f* banana
banano *m* banana tree
banca *f* (*pl* -che) bank; INFOR ~ *dati* data bank; ~ *degli organi* organ bank
bancarella *f* stall
bancario (*pl* -ri) **1** *agg istituto, segreto* banking *attr; deposito, estratto conto* bank *attr* **2** *m*, **-a** *f* bank employee
bancarotta *f* bankruptcy
banchetto *m* banquet
banchiere *m* banker
banchina *f* FERR platform; MAR quay; *di strada* verge; *di autostrada* hard shoulder; ~ *spartitraffico* central reservation, *Am* median strip
banchisa *f* ice floe
banco *m* (*pl* -chi) FIN bank; *di magistrati, di lavoro* bench; *di scuola* desk; *di bar* bar; *di chiesa* pew; *di negozio* counter; ~ *corallino* coral reef; ~ *di sabbia* sandbank; ~ *del lotto* place *that sells State lottery tickets;* **vendere qc sotto** ~ sell sth under the counter
bancogiro *m* giro
bancone *m* (work)bench
bancomat® *m inv* (*distributore*) cash-point, *Am* ATM; (*carta*) cash card
banconota *f* banknote, *Am* bill
banda *f* band; *di delinquenti* gang; INFOR ~ *perforata* punched tape
banderuola *f* weathercock (*anche fig*)
bandiera *f* flag
bandire <4d> proclaim; *concorso* announce; (*esiliare*) banish; *fig* (*abolire*) dispense with

bandito *m* bandit
banditore *m* *all'asta* auctioneer
bando *m* proclamation; (*esilio*) banishment
bar *m inv* bar
bara *f* coffin
baracca *f* (*pl* -cche) hut; *spreg* hovel; F *mandare avanti la* ~ keep one's head above water
baraccopoli *f inv* shanty town
barare <1a> cheat
baratro *m* abyss
barattare <1a> barter
baratto *m* barter
barattolo *m* tin, *Am* can; *di vetro* jar
barba *f* beard; *farsi la* ~ shave; *fig* *che* ~*!* what a nuisance!, what a pain! F
barbabietola *f* beetroot, *Am* red beet; ~ *da zucchero* sugar beet
barbarico (*pl* -ci) barbaric
barbarie *f* barbarity
barbaro 1 *agg* barbarous **2** *m* barbarian
barbecue *m inv* barbecue
barbiere *m* barber
barboncino *m* (miniature) poodle
barbone[1] *m* (*cane*) poodle
barbone[2] *m*, **-a** *f* (*vagabondo*) tramp
barca *f* (*pl* -che) boat; ~ *a remi* rowing boat, *Am* rowboat; ~ *a vela* sailing boat, *Am* sailboat
barcaiolo *m* boatman
barcollare <1c> stagger
barcone *m* barge
barella *f* stretcher
baricentro *m* centre of gravity
barile *m* barrel
barista *m/f* (*mpl* -i) barman, *Am* bartender; *donna* barmaid; *proprietario* bar owner
baritono *m* baritone
baro *m* cardsharp
barocco (*pl* -cchi) *m/agg* Baroque
barometro *m* barometer
barone *m*, **-essa** *f* baron; *donna* baroness; *fig* ~ *dell'industria* tycoon
barra *f* bar; MAR tiller; ~ *spaziatrice* space bar
barricare <1l & d> barricade
barricata *f* barricade

B

barriera *f* barrier (*anche fig*); ~ **doga-nale** tariff barrier

baruffa *f* (*litigio*) squabble; (*zuffa*) brawl; *far* ~ squabble; (*venirse alle mani*) brawl

barzelletta *f* joke

basare <1a> base

basarsi be based (**su** on)

basco (*pl* -chi) **1** *agg* Basque **2** *m*, -a *f* Basque **3** *m* (*berretto*) beret

base *f* base; *fig* basis; *in* ~ *a* on the basis of

basette *fpl* sideburns

basilare basic

basilica *f* (*pl* -che) basilica

basilico *m* basil

bassezza *f* lowness; *fig* (*viltà, azione meschina*) vileness

basso **1** *agg* low; *di statura* short; MUS bass; *fig* despicable; *a capo* ~ with bowed head; *a occhi -i* looking downwards, with lowered eyes; *fare man -a di qc* steal sth **2** *avv*: *in* ~ *stato* down below; *più in* ~ further down; *da* ~ *in una casa* downstairs **3** *m* MUS bass

bassopiano *m* (*pl* bassipiani) GEOG lowland

bassorilievo *m* (*pl* bassorilievi) bas-relief

bassotto *m* dachshund

basta → **bastare**

bastardo *m*, -a *f cane* mongrel; *fig* bastard

bastare <1a> be enough; (*durare*) last; *basta!* that's enough!; *adesso basta!* enough is enough!; *basta che* (*purché*) as long as

bastimento *m* ship

bastonare <1a> beat

bastone *m* stick; *di pane* baguette, French stick; *fig il* ~ *e la carota* the carrot and stick (approach); ~ *da passeggio* walking stick

battaglia *f* battle (*anche fig*)

battagliero combative

battello *m* boat

battente *m di porta* wing; *di finestra* shutter

battere <3a> **1** *v/i* (*bussare, dare colpi*) knock **2** *v/t* beat; *record* break;

senza ~ *ciglio* without batting an eyelid; ~ *le mani* clap (one's hands); ~ *i piedi* stamp one's feet; *batteva i denti dal freddo* his teeth were chattering with cold; ~ *a macchina* type; ~ *bandiera* fly a flag

battersela run off

battersi fight

batteria *f* battery; MUS drums *pl*

batteri *mpl* bacteria

batterista *m/f* (*pl* -i) drummer

battesimo *m* christening, baptism

battezzare <1a> christen, baptize

battibaleno *m*: *in un* ~ in a flash

battibecco *m* (*pl* -cchi) argument

batticuore *m* palpitations *pl*; *fig con un gran* ~ with great anxiety

battimano *m* applause

battipanni *m inv* carpet beater

battistero *m* baptistry

battistrada *m inv* AUTO tread

battito *m del polso* pulse; *delle ali* flap (of its wings); *della pioggia* beating; ~ *cardiaco* heartbeat

battuta *f* beat; *in dattilografia* keystroke; MUS bar; TEA cue; *nel tennis* service; *fare una* ~ *di caccia* go hunting; ~ *di spirito* wisecrack; *non perdere una* ~ not miss a word

baule *m* trunk; AUTO boot, *Am* trunk

bavaglino *m* bib

bavaglio *m* (*pl* -gli) gag

bavero *m* collar

bazar *m inv* bazaar

bazzecola *f* trifle

bazzicare <1l & d> **1** *v/t un posto* haunt; *persone* associate with **2** *v/i* hang about

Bce *abbr* (= **Banca centrale europea**) Central European Bank

beatificare <1n & d> beatify

beatitudine *f* bliss

beato happy; REL blessed; ~ *te!* lucky you!

beauty-case *m inv* toilet bag

bebè *m inv* baby

beccaccia *f* (*pl* -cce) woodcock

beccare <1d> peck; F *fig* (*cogliere sul fatto*) nab F; F *fig malattia* catch, pick up F

beccarsi *fig bisticciare* squabble; F

malattia catch, pick up F

beccheggiare <1f> MAR pitch

becchino *m* grave digger

becco *m* (*pl* -cchi) beak; *di teiera ecc* spout; CHIM ~ *Bunsen* Bunsen burner; F *chiudi il ~!* shut up! F, shut it! F; *non avere il ~ di un quattrino* be broke

befana *f* kind old witch who brings presents to children on Twelfth Night; REL Twelfth Night; *fig* old witch

beffa *f* hoax; *farsi -e di qu* make a fool of s.o.

beffardo scornful

beffare <1b> mock

beffarsi: ~ *di* mock

bega *f* (*pl* -ghe) (*litigio*) fight, argument; (*problema*) can of worms

begli → *bello*

begonia *f* begonia

Bei *abbr* (= *Banca europea per gli investimenti*) EIB (= European Investment Bank)

bei → *bello*

belare <1b> bleat

belga (*mpl* -gi) *agg*, *m/f* Belgian

Belgio *m* Belgium

belladonna *f* BOT deadly nightshade

bellezza *f* beauty; *istituto m di* ~ beauty salon; *prodotti mpl di* ~ cosmetics

bellico (*pl* -ci) (*di guerra*) war *attr*, (*del tempo di guerra*) wartime *attr*

bellicoso bellicose

bello 1 *agg* beautiful; *uomo* handsome; *tempo* fine, nice, beautiful; *questa è -a!* that's a good one!; *a-a posta* on purpose; *hai un bel dire* in spite of what you say; *nel bel mezzo* right in the middle; *farsi* ~ get dressed up; *scamparla* ~ have a narrow escape 2 *m* beauty; *sul più* ~ at the worst possible moment

belva *f* wild beast

belvedere *m inv* viewpoint

bemolle *m inv* MUS flat

benché though, although

benda *f* bandage; *per occhi* blindfold

bendare <1b> MED bandage

bene 1 *avv* well; ~! good!; *per* ~ properly; *stare* ~ *di salute* be well; *di*

vestito suit; *ben ti sta!* serves you right!; *va* ~! OK!; *andare* ~ *a qu di abito* fit s.o.; *di orario, appuntamento* suit s.o.; *di* ~ *in meglio* better and better; *sentirsi* ~ feel well 2 *m* good; *fare* ~ *alla salute* be good for you; *per il tuo* ~ for your own good; *voler* ~ *a qu* love s.o.; (*amare*) love s.o.; *-i pl* assets, property *sg*; *-i pl di consumo* consumer goods; *-i pl culturali* cultural heritage *sg*; *-i pl immobili* real estate *sg*; *-i pl pubblici* public property *sg*

benedetto 1 *pp* → *benedire* 2 *agg* blessed; REL *acqua f -a* holy water

benedire <3t> bless

benedizione *f* blessing

beneducato well-mannered

benefattore *m*, **-trice** *f* benefactor

beneficenza *f* charity; *spettacolo m di* ~ benefit (performance)

beneficio *m* (*pl* -ci) benefit; *a* ~ *di* for the benefit of

benefico (*pl* -ci) beneficial; *organizzazione, istituto* charitable; *spettacolo* charity *attr*

benemerito worthy

benessere *m* well-being; (*agiatezza*) affluence

benestante 1 *agg* well-off 2 *m/f* person with money

benestare *m* consent

benevolenza *f* benevolence

benevolo benevolent

benigno MED benign

beninteso of course; ~ *che* provided that

benone splendid

benpensante *m/f* moderate; *spreg* conformist

benservito *m*: *dare il* ~ *a qu* thank s.o. for their services

bensì but rather

bentornato welcome back

benvenuto 1 *agg* welcome 2 *m* welcome; *dare il* ~ *a qu* welcome s.o.

benvisto well thought of

benvolere: *farsi* ~ *da qu* win s.o. over

benvoluto well-liked

benzina *f* petrol, *Am* gas; *serbatoio*

B

m **della ~** petrol (*Am* gas) tank; **~ normale** 4-star, *Am* premium; **~ senza piombo** unleaded petrol (*Am* gas); **fare ~** get petrol (*Am* gas)

benzinaio *m* (*mpl* -ai), **-a** *f* petrol or *Am* gas station attendant

bere 1 *v/t* <3i> drink; *fig* swallow; *fig* **darla a ~ a qu** take s.o. in **2** *m* *bevanda* drink; *atto* drinking

berlina *f* AUTO saloon

berlinese 1 *agg* Berlin **2** *m/f* Berliner

Berlino *m* Berlin

bermuda *mpl* Bermuda shorts

bernoccolo *m* bump; *fig* flair; **aver il ~ di qc** have a flair for sth

berretto *m* cap

berrò → bere

bersaglio *m* (*pl* -gli) target; *fig* *di scherzi* butt

besciamella *f* béchamel

bestemmia *f* swear-word

bestemmiare <1k> **1** *v/i* swear (**contro** at) **2** *v/t* curse

bestia *f* animal; *persona brutale* beast; *persona sciocca* blockhead; *fig* **andare in ~** fly into a rage

bestiale bestial; F (*molto intenso*) terrible

bestiame *m* livestock

bettola *f spreg* dive

betulla *f* birch

bevanda *f* drink

beve → bere

bevibile drinkable

bevitore *m*, **-trice** *f* drinker

bevuta *f* drink; *azione* drinking

biada *f* fodder

biancheria *f* linen; **~ intima** underwear

bianco (*pl* -chi) **1** *agg* white; *foglio* blank; **dare carta -a a qu** give s.o. a free hand, give s.o. carte blanche; **notte f -a** sleepless night **2** *m* white; **~ d'uovo** egg white; **lasciare in ~** leave blank; **di punto in ~** point-blank; GASTR **riso m in ~** rice with butter and cheese; **mangiare in ~** avoid rich food; **in ~ e nero** film black and white; **in ~** assegno blank

biancospino *m* hawthorn

biasimare <1l> blame

biasimevole blameworthy

biasimo *m* blame

bibbia *f* bible

biberon *m inv* baby's bottle

bibita *f* soft drink

bibliografia *f* bibliography

bibliografico (*pl* -ci) bibliographical

biblioteca *f* (*pl* -che) library; *mobile* book-case

bibliotecario *m* (*pl* -ri), **-a** *f* librarian

bicamerale POL two-chamber

bicameralismo *m* two-chamber system

bicamere *m inv* two-room flat (*Am* apartment)

bicarbonato *m*: **~** (**di sodio**) bicarbonate of soda

bicchiere *m* glass; **un ~ di birra** a glass of beer; **~ da birra** beer-glass; **~ di carta** paper cup

bicentenario *m* bicentenary

bici *f inv* F bike F

bicicletta *f* bike, bicycle; **andare in ~** cycle, ride a bicycle; **~ pieghevole** folding bike; **~ da corsa** racing bike; **gita f in ~** bike ride

bidè *m inv* bidet

bidone *m* drum; *della spazzatura* (dust)bin, *Am* garbage can; F (*imbroglio*) swindle F

biella *f* TEC connecting rod

biennale 1 *agg che si fa ogni due anni* biennial; *che dura due anni* two-year **2** **Biennale** *f* (**di Venezia**) Venice Arts Festival

biennio *m* (*pl* -nni) period of two years

bietola *f* beet

bifase two-phase

bifora *f* ARCHI mullioned window

biforcarsi <1d> fork

biforcazione *f* fork

bigamia *f* bigamy

bigamo *m*, **-a** *f* bigamist

bigiotteria *f* costume jewellery, *Am* costume jewelry; (*negozio*) jewel-(l)er's

bigliettaio *m* (*pl* -ai), **-a** *f* booking office clerk; *sul treno, tram* conductor

biglietteria *f* ticket office, booking office; *di cinema, teatro* box office

biglietto *m* ticket; **~ aereo** airline *or* plane ticket; **~ d'andata e ritorno** return ticket, *Am* roundtrip ticket; **~ d'auguri** (greetings) card; **~ da visita** business card; **~ di banca** banknote, *Am* bill; **~ della lotteria** lottery ticket; **un ~ da 10 dollari** a ten-dollar bill; **fare il ~** buy the ticket

bigodino *m* roller

bigotto 1 *agg* bigoted **2** *m*, **-a** *f* bigot

bikini *m inv* bikini

bilancia *f* (*pl* -ce) scales; FIN balance; ASTR **Bilancia** Libra; **~ commerciale** balance of trade; **~ dei pagamenti** balance of payments

bilanciare <1f> balance; (*pareggiare*) equal, be equal to; *fig* weigh up; FIN **~ un conto** balance an account

bilanciarsi balance

bilancio *m* (*pl* -ci) balance; (*rendiconto*) balance sheet; **~ annuale** annual accounts; **~ consuntivo** closing balance; **~ dello Stato** national budget; **~ preventivo** budget; **fare il ~** draw up a balance sheet; *fig* take stock; **relazione** *f* **annuale di ~** annual report

bilaterale bilateral

bile *f* bile; *fig* rage

biliardo *m* billiards *sg*

bilico *m*: **essere in ~** be precariously balanced; *fig* be undecided

bilingue bilingual

bilione *m* (*mille miliardi*) million million, *Am* trillion; (*miliardo*) billion

bilocale *m* two-room flat (*Am* apartment)

bimbo *m*, **-a** *f* child

bimensile every two weeks, *Br* fortnightly

bimestrale *ogni due mesi* bimonthly; *che dura due mesi* two-month (long)

bimotore 1 *agg* twin-engine **2** *m* twin-engine plane

binario 1 *agg* binary **2** *m* (*pl* -ri) track; (*marciapiede*) platform

binocolo *m* binoculars *pl*

biochimica *f* biochemistry

biodegradabile biodegradable

biodinamica *f* biodynamics

biografia *f* biography

biografico (*pl* -ci) biographical

biografo *m*, **-a** *f* biographer

biologia *f* biology

biologico (*pl* -ci) biological; (*verde*) organic; **da culture -che** organic

biologo *m* (*pl* -gi), **-a** *f* biologist

biondo blonde

bioritmo *m* biorhythm

biossido *m* dioxide

biotopo *m* biotope

biplano *m* biplane

bipolare bipolar

biposto *m/agg* two-seater

birbante *m* rascal

birichino 1 *agg* naughty **2** *m*, **-a** *f* little devil

birillo *m* skittle

biro® *f inv* biro, ballpoint (pen)

birra *f* beer; **~ chiara** lager; **~ scura** brown ale; **~ in lattina** canned beer; **~ alla spina** draught (beer); **lievito** *m* **di ~** brewer's yeast; **a tutta ~** flat out

birreria *f* pub that sells only beer; *fabbrica* brewery

bis *m inv, int* encore

bisbetico (*pl* -ci) bad-tempered

bisbigliare <1g> whisper

bisbiglio *m* whisper

bisca *f* (*pl* -che) gambling den

biscia *f* (*pl* -sce) grass snake

biscotto *m* biscuit, *Am* cookie

bisessuale bisexual

bisestile: **anno** *m* **~** leap year

bisettimanale every two weeks, *Br* fortnightly

bisnonno *m*, **-a** *f* great-grandfather; *donna* great-grandmother

bisognare <1a>: **bisogna farlo** it must be done, it needs to be done; **non bisogna farlo** it doesn't have to be done, there's no need to do it

bisogno *m* need; (*mancanza*) lack; (*fabbisogno*) requirements; **in caso di ~** if necessary, if need be; **avere ~ di qc** need sth; **non ce n'è bisogno** there is no need

bisognoso needy

B

bisonte *m* ZO bison
bistecca *f* (*pl* -cche) steak; **~ ai ferri** grilled *or Am* broiled steak; **~ alla fiorentina** charcoal grilled steak
bisticciare <1f> quarrel
bisticcio *m* (*pl* -cci) quarrel
bisturi *m inv* MED scalpel
bit *m inv* INFOR bit
bitter *m inv* aperitif
bivaccare <1d> bivouac
bivacco *m* (*pl* -cchi) bivouac
bivio *m* (*pl* -vi) junction; *fig* crossroads
bizantino Byzantine
bizzarro bizarre
bizzeffe: a ~ galore
blando mild, gentle
blatta *f* cockroach
blindare <1a> armo(u)r-plate
blindato armo(u)red
blitz *m inv* blitz
bloccare <1c & d> block; MIL blockade; (*isolare*) cut off; *prezzi, conto* freeze
bloccarsi *di ascensore, persona* get stuck; *di freni, porta* jam
bloccaruota *m* AUTO wheel clamp, *Am* Denver boot; **mettere il ~ a** clamp
bloccasterzo *m* AUTO steering lock
blocchetto *m per appunti* notebook
blocco *m* (*pl* -cchi) block; *di carta* pad; MIL blockade; **~ stradale** road block; **~ dei fitti** rent control; **comprare in ~** buy in bulk; **~ dei prezzi** price-freeze; **~ delle esportazioni** export ban, embargo
bloc-notes *m inv* writing pad
blu blue
blusa *f* blouse
boa[1] *m inv* ZO boa constrictor
boa[2] *f* MAR buoy
boato *m* rumble
bob *m inv* SP bobsleigh, bobsled
bobbista *m/f* (*pl* -i) bobsledder
bobina *f* spool; *di film* reel; AUTO **~ d'accensione** ignition coil
bocca *f* (*pl* -cche) mouth; (*apertura*) opening; **igiene** *f* **della ~** oral hygiene; **in ~ al lupo!** good luck!; **vuoi essere sulla ~ di tutti?** do you want

to be the talk of the town?; **lasciare la ~ amara** leave a bad taste; **rimanere a ~ aperta** be dumbfounded; *fig* **rimanere a ~ asciutta** come away empty-handed
boccaccia *f* (*pl* -cce) (*smorfia*) grimace
boccaglio *m* (*pl* -gli) *di maschera per il nuoto* mouthpiece
boccale *m* jug; *da birra* tankard
boccetta *f* small bottle
boccheggiare <1f> gasp
bocchino *m per sigarette* cigarette holder; MUS, *di pipa* mouthpiece
boccia *f* (*pl* -cce) (*palla*) bowl; **gioco** *m* **delle -cce** bowls
bocciare <1c & f> (*respingere*) reject, vote down; EDU fail; *boccia* hit, strike
bocciatura *f* failure
bocciolo *m* bud
bocconcino *m* morsel
boccone *m* mouthful; **~ amaro** bitter pill
bocconi face down
body *m inv* body
boia *m inv* executioner; F **fa un freddo ~** it's bloody freezing F
boicottaggio *m* boycott
boicottare <1c> boycott
bolgia *f fig* bedlam
bolide *m* AST meteor; **come un ~** like greased lightning
bolla[1] *f* bubble; MED blister
bolla[2] *f documento* note, docket; **~ di consegna** delivery note
bollare <1a> stamp; *fig* brand
bollente boiling hot
bolletta *f* bill; **~ della luce** electricity bill; **~ di consegna** delivery note; F **essere in ~** be hard up F
bollettino *m*: **~ meteorologico** weather forecast
bollire <4c> *v/t & v/i* boil
bollito **1** *agg* boiled **2** *m* boiled meat
bollitore *m* kettle
bollo *m* stamp; **~ (di circolazione)** road tax (disk); **marca** *f* **da ~** revenue stamp
bomba *f* bomb; **a prova di ~** bombproof; **~ a mano** hand grenade; **~ a**

orologeria time bomb; ~ **atomica** atomic bomb

bombardamento *m* shelling, bombardment; (*attacco aereo*) air raid; *fig* bombardment

bombardare <1a> bomb; *fig* bombard

bombardiere *m* bomber

bombola *f* cylinder; ~ (**di gas**) gas bottle, gas cylinder

bomboniera *f* wedding keep-sake

bonaccia *f* MAR calm

bonaccione *m*, **-a** *f* kind-hearted person

bonario (*pl* -ri) kind-hearted

bonifica *f* (*pl* -che) reclamation

bonificare <1m & d> FIN (*scontare*) allow, discount; (*accreditare*) credit; AGR reclaim; (*prosciugare*) drain

bonifico *m* FIN (*sconto*) allowance, rebate; (*trasferimento*) (money) transfer

bontà *f inv* goodness; (*gentilezza*) kindness

bonus-malus *m inv assicurazione* no-claims bonus system

bora *f* bora (*a cold north wind*)

borbottare <1a> mumble

bordello *m* brothel; *fig* F bedlam F; (*disordine*) mess

bordo *m* (*orlo*) edge; MAR, AVIA, AUTO **a** ~ on board; **salire a** ~ board, go on board

boreale northern; **aurora** *f* ~ northern lights *pl*

borgata *f* village; (*rione popolare*) suburb

borghese 1 *agg* middle-class; **in** ~ in civilian clothes; **poliziotto** *m* **in** ~ plainclothes policeman **2** *m/f* middle-class person; **piccolo** ~ petty bourgeois, lower middle-class person

borghesia *f* middle classes *pl*

borgo *m* (*pl* -ghi) village

boria *f* conceit

borico (*pl* -ci): **acido** *m* ~ boric acid

borotalco *m* talcum powder, talc

borraccia *f* (*pl* -cce) flask

borsa *f* bag; (*borsetta*) handbag, *Am* purse; *per documenti* briefcase; FIN

Stock Exchange; ~ **della spesa** shopping bag; ~ **termica** cool bag; ~ **di studio** scholarship; ~ **merci** Commodities Exchange; ~ **nera** black market; ~ **valori** Stock Exchange; **bollettino** *m* (o **listino** *m*) **di** ~ share index; **metter mano alla** ~ put one's hand in one's pocket

borsaiolo *m*, **-a** *f* pickpocket

borseggio *m* (*pl* -ggi) pickpocketing

borsellino *m* purse, *Am* coin purse

borsetta *f* handbag, *Am* purse

borsista *m/f* (*mpl* -i) *speculatore* speculator; *studente* scholarship holder

boscaglia *f* brush, scrub

boscaiolo *m* woodcutter

bosco *m* (*pl* -schi) wood

boscoso wooded

bossolo *m* di proiettili (shell) case

BOT, bot *abbr* (= **Buono Ordinario del Tesoro**) treasury bond

botanica *f* botany

botanico (*pl* -ci) **1** *agg* botanical **2** *m*, **-a** *f* botanist

botola *f* trapdoor

botta *f* blow; (*rumore*) bang; **fare a -e** come to blows

botte *f* barrel; ARCHI **volta** *f* **a** ~ barrel vault

bottega *f* (*pl* -ghe) shop; (*laboratorio*) workshop

bottegaio *m* (*pl* -ai), **-a** *f* shopkeeper

botteghino *m* box office; (*del lotto*) *sales outlet for lottery tickets*

bottiglia *f* bottle

bottiglieria *f* wine merchant's

bottino *m* loot

botto *m* (*rumore*) bang; **di** ~ all of a sudden

bottone *m* button; ~ **automatico** press-stud, *Am* snap fastener; **attaccare un** ~ **a** s.o. sew a button on for s.o.; *fig* buttonhole s.o.

bovino 1 *agg* bovine **2** *m*: **-i** *pl* cattle

box *m inv* per auto lock-up garage; *per bambini* playpen; *per cavalli* loose box

boxe *f* boxing

bozza *f* draft; TIP proof

bozzetto *m* sketch

B

bozzolo m cocoon

braccetto m: **a ~** arm in arm

bracciale m bracelet; (fascia) armband; di orologio watch strap

braccialetto m bracelet

bracciante m/f day labo(u)rer

bracciata f nel nuoto stroke

braccio m (pl le braccia e i bracci) arm; **~ di mare** sound; **a -a aperte** with open arms; **portare in ~ qu** carry s.o.; fig **essere il ~ destro di qu** be s.o.'s right-hand man; **incrociare le -a** fold one's arms; fig go on strike

bracciolo m arm(rest)

bracco m (pl -cchi) hound

bracconiere m poacher

brace f embers pl; **alla ~** char-grilled, Am -broiled

braciola f GASTR chop

branca f (pl -che) branch (anche fig)

branchia f gill

branco m (pl -chi) ZO di cani, lupi pack; di pecore, uccelli flock; fig spreg gang

brancolare <1l> grope

branda f camp-bed

brandello m shred, scrap; **a -i** in shreds or tatters

brano m di testo, musica passage

brasato m GASTR di manzo braised beef

Brasile m Brazil

brasiliano 1 agg Brazilian **2** m, -a f Brazilian

bravata f boasting; azione bravado

bravo good; (abile) clever, good; **~!** well done!

bravura f skill

break m inv break

breccia f (pl -cce) breach

bretella f (raccordo) slip road, Am ramp; **-e** pl braces, Am suspenders

breve short; **in ~** briefly, in short

brevettare <1a> patent

brevetto m patent; di pilota licence, Am license; **ufficio** m **dei -i** patent office

brevità f shortness

brezza f breeze

bricco m (pl -cchi) jug, Am pitcher

briciola f crumb

briciolo m fig grain, scrap

bricolage m do-it-yourself

briga f (pl -ghe): **darsi la ~ di fare qc** take the trouble to do sth; **attaccar ~ con qu** pick a quarrel with s.o.

brigadiere m MIL sergeant

brigante m bandit

brigata f party, group; MIL brigade

briglia f rein; fig **a ~ sciolta** at breakneck speed

brillante 1 agg sparkling; colore bright; fig brilliant **2** m diamond

brillare <1a> **1** v/i shine **2** v/t mina blow up

brillo tipsy

brina f hoar-frost

brindare <1a> drink a toast (**a** to), toast (**a** sth); **~ alla salute di qu** drink to or toast s.o.

brindisi m inv toast

brio m liveliness; MUS brio

brioche f inv brioche

brioso lively

britannico (pl -ci) **1** agg British **2** m, -a f Briton

brivido m di freddo, spavento shiver; di emozione thrill

brizzolato capelli greying, Am graying

brocca f (pl -cche) jug, Am pitcher

broccato m brocade

broccoli mpl broccoli sg

brodo m (clear) soup; di pollo, di manzo, di verdura stock; **minestra** f **in ~** soup; **~ ristretto** consommé

brodoso watery, thin

bronchiale bronchial

bronchite f bronchitis

broncio m: **avere** (o **tenere**) **il ~** sulk; **mi ha tenuto il ~ per tre giorni** he sulked for three days

broncopolmonite f bronchopneumonia

brontolare <1l> grumble; di stomaco rumble

brontolio m grumble; di stomaco rumble

brontolone 1 agg grumbling **2** m, -a f grumbler

bronzo m bronze

bruciapelo: *a* ~ point-blank

bruciare <1f> **1** *v/t* burn; (*incendiare*) set fire to; ~ **le tappe** forge ahead **2** *v/i* burn; *fig di occhi* sting

bruciarsi burn o.s.

bruciato burnt; *dal sole* scorched, parched

bruciatura *f* burn

bruciore *m* burning sensation; ~ **di stomaco** heartburn

bruco *m* (*pl* -chi) grub; (*verme*) worm

brufolo *m* spot

brughiera *f* heath, moor

brulicare <1l & d> swarm

brulichio *m* swarming

brullo bare

bruno brown; *capelli* dark

brusco (*pl* -schi) sharp; *persona, modi* brusque, abrupt; (*improvviso*) sudden

brutale brutal

brutalità *f inv* brutality

bruto **1** *agg*: **forza** *f* -**a** brute force **2** *m* brute

brutta *f*: (*copia* *f*) ~ rough copy

bruttezza *f* ugliness

brutto ugly; (*cattivo*) bad; *tempo, tipo, situazione, affare* nasty

Bruxelles *f* Brussels

buca *f* (*pl* -che) hole; (*avvallamento*) hollow; *del biliardo* pocket; ~ **delle lettere** letter-box, *Am* mailbox

bucaneve *m inv* snowdrop

bucare <1d> make a hole in; (*pungere*) prick; *biglietto* punch; ~ **una gomma** have a puncture, *Am* have a flat (tire); *fig* **avere le mani bucate** be a spendthrift

bucarsi prick o.s.; *con droga* shoot up

bucato *m* washing, laundry; **fare il** ~ do the washing

buccia *f* (*pl* -cce) peel

bucherellare <1b> make holes in; **bucherellato dai tarli** riddled with woodworm

buco *m* (*pl* -chi) hole; ~ **dell' ozono** hole in the ozone layer; ~ **nero** black hole

budello *m* (*pl le* budella) gut; (*vicolo*) alley

budget *m inv* budget

budino *m* pudding

bue *m* (*pl* buoi) ox, *pl* oxen; *carne* beef

bufalo *m* buffalo

bufera *f* storm; ~ **di neve** snow-storm

buffet *m inv* buffet; *mobile* sideboard

buffo funny

buffone *m*, -**a** *f* buffoon, fool; *di corte* fool, jester

bugia[1] *f* candle holder

bugia[2] *f* (*menzogna*) lie; **dire** -**e** tell lies, lie

bugiardo **1** *agg* lying **2** *m*, -**a** *f* liar

bugigattolo *m* cubby-hole

buio **1** *agg* dark **2** *m* darkness; **al** ~ in the dark; ~ **pesto** pitch dark

bulbo *m* BOT bulb

Bulgaria *f* Bulgaria

bulgaro **1** *agg* Bulgarian **2** *m*, -**a** *f* Bulgarian

bulletta *f* tack

bullone *m* bolt

buoi → **bue**

buon → **buono**

buonafede *f*: **in** ~ in good faith

buonanotte *int, f* good night; **dare la** ~ say good night

buonasera *int, f* good evening; **dare la** ~ say good evening

buongiorno *int, m* good morning, hello; **dare il** ~ say good morning *or* hello

buongustaio *m* (*pl* -ai), -**a** *f* gourmet

buongusto *m* good taste; **di** ~ in good taste

buono **1** *agg* good; (*valido*) good, valid; *momento, occasione* right; **alla** -**a** informal, casual; **di buon'ora** early; **di buon grado** willingly; **avere buon naso** have a good sense of smell; ~ **a nulla** good-for-nothing **2** *m* good; FIN bond; (*tagliando*) coupon, voucher; ~ **del tesoro** Treasury bond; ~ **pasto** *o* **mensa** luncheon voucher; ~ **regalo** gift voucher; ~ **sconto** money-off coupon

buonsenso *m* common sense

B

buonuscita f (*liquidazione*) golden handshake
burattino m puppet
burbero gruff, surly
burla f practical joke, trick
burlarsi <1a>: ~ *di qu* make fun of s.o.
burlone m, **-a** f joker
burocrate m bureaucrat
burocratico (*pl* -ci) bureaucratic
burocrazia f bureaucracy
burrasca f (*pl* -sche) storm
burrascoso stormy
burro m butter; GASTR **al** ~ in butter; **tenero come il** ~ soft as butter
burrone m ravine
bussare <1a> knock; ~ **alla porta** knock at the door
bussola f compass; ~ **magnetica** magnetic compass; **perdere la** ~ lose one's bearings

busta f per lettera envelope; per documenti folder; (*astuccio*) case; ~ **paga** pay packet
bustarella f bribe
bustina: ~ **di tè** tea bag
busto m ANAT torso; scultura bust; (*corsetto*) girdle
buttafuori m inv TEA call-boy; di locale notturno bouncer
buttare <1a> **1** v/i BOT shoot, sprout **2** v/t throw; ~ **via** throw away; fig waste; ~ **giù** knock down; lettera scribble down; boccone gulp down; F ~ **la pasta** put the pasta on
buttarsi throw o.s.; fig have a go (**in** at); ~ **giù** (*saltare*) jump; fig lose heart, get discouraged
by-pass m inv by-pass
byte m inv INFOR byte

C

ca. abbr (= **circa**) ca (= circa)
c.a. abbr (= **corrente alternata**) AC (= alternating current)
cabaret m inv cabaret
cabina f di nave, aereo cabin; di ascensore, funivia cage; ~ **balneare** beach hut; ~ **di guida** driver's cab; ~ **elettorale** polling booth; ~ **telefonica** phone box, Am pay phone
cabinato m cabin cruiser
cabriolè, **cabriolet** m inv convertible
cacao m cocoa
caccia (*pl* -cce) **1** f hunting; **andare a** ~ go hunting (**di** sth); **dare la** ~ **a qu** chase after s.o. **2** m MIL aereo fighter; nave destroyer
cacciagione f GASTR game
cacciare <1f> hunt; (*scacciare*) drive out; (*ficcare*) shove; ~ (**via**) chase away
cacciarsi: **dove ti eri cacciato?**

where did you get to?
cacciatora f: GASTR **alla** ~ stewed
cacciatore m, **-trice** f hunter; ~ **di frodo** poacher
cacciavite m inv screwdriver
cachemire m inv cashmere
cachet m inv MED capsule
cacio m cheese
cactus m inv cactus
cadavere m corpse
cadente: **stella** f ~ shooting star
cadere <2c> fall; di edificio fall down; di capelli, denti fall out; di aereo crash; ~ **dalle nuvole** be thunderstruck; lasciar ~ drop; lasciarsi ~ **su una poltrona** collapse into an armchair
caduta f fall; ~ **massi** falling rocks; ~ **di tensione** drop in voltage
caffè m inv coffee; locale café; ~ **corretto** espresso with a shot of alcohol; ~ **macchiato** espresso with a

splash of milk

caffeina f caffeine; **senza ~** caffeine free

caffellatte m inv hot milk with a small amount of coffee

caffettiera f (bricco) coffee pot; (macchinetta) coffee maker

cafone m boor

cagionevole delicate, sickly

cagliare <1g> curdle

cagna f bitch

calabrese agg, m/f Calabrian

calabrone m hornet

calamari mpl squid

calamita f magnet

calamità f inv calamity; **~ naturale** natural disaster

calante f luna f ~ waning moon

calare <1a> **1** v/t lower; prezzi reduce, lower **2** v/i di vento drop; di prezzi fall, come down; di siparo fall; di sole set, go down; di peso lose weight; **è calato del 20%** it's down 20%

calca f throng

calcagno m (pl i calcagni o le calcagna) heel

calcare¹ <1d> (pigiare) press down; con i piedi tread; parole emphasize; **~ la mano** exaggerate; **~ le scene** become an actor, take up acting

calcare² m limestone

calcareo chalky

calce¹ f lime

calce² m fig: **in ~** below

calcestruzzo m concrete

calciare <1f> kick

calciatore m footballer, soccer player

calcina f (malta) mortar

calcinaccio m (pl -cci) (intonaco) bit of plaster; di muro bit of rubble

calcio m (pl -ci) kick; attività football, soccer; MIL butt; CHIM calcium; **giocare al ~** play football or soccer; **campionato m di ~** football or soccer championship; **~ di rigore** penalty kick

calco m (pl -chi) mo(u)ld

calcolare <1l> calculate; (valutare) weigh up

calcolatore m calculator; fig calculating person; elettronico computer

calcolatrice f calculator; **~ tascabile** pocket calculator; **~ da tavolo** desktop calculator

calcolo m calculation; MED stone; **~ preventivo** estimate

caldaia f boiler

caldarrosta f roast chestnut

caldo 1 agg warm; (molto caldo) hot; **non mi fa né ~ né freddo** it's all the same to me **2** m warmth; molto caldo heat; **ho ~** I'm warm; I'm hot

calendario m (pl -ri) calendar; **~ delle manifestazioni** calendar of events

calibrare <1a> calibrate

calibro m calibre, Am caliber; TEC callipers

calice m goblet; REL chalice

calle f a Venezia lane

calligrafia f calligraphy

callo m corn; **fare il ~ a qc** become hardened to sth

calma f calm; **prendersela con ~** take it easy

calmante m sedative

calmare <1a> calm; dolore soothe

calmarsi di dolore ease (off)

calmo calm

calo m di peso loss; dei prezzi drop, fall

calore m warmth; intenso heat

caloria f calorie

caloroso fig warm

calpestare <1a> walk on; fig trample over

calunnia f slander

calunniare <1k> slander

calura f heat

calvario m REL Calvary; fig ordeal

calvizie f baldness

calvo bald

calza f da donna stocking; da uomo sock; **~ elastica** support stocking; **fare la ~** knit

calzamaglia f tights pl, Am pantyhose; da ginnastica leotard

calzare <1a> **1** v/t scarpe put on; (indossare) wear **2** v/i fig fit

calzascarpe m shoehorn

calzatoio *m* (*pl* -oi) shoehorn

calzature *fpl* footwear *sg*

calzaturificio *m* (*pl* -ci) shoe factory

calzettone *m* knee sock

calzino *m* sock

calzolaio *m* (*pl* -ai) shoemaker

calzoleria *f* shoe shop

calzoncini *mpl* shorts; **~ da bagno** (swimming) trunks

calzone *m* GASTR folded-over pizza

calzoni *mpl* trousers, *Am* pants

camaleonte *m* chameleon

cambiale *f* bill (of exchange); **~ in bianco** blank bill; **girare una ~** endorse a bill; **pagare una ~** hono(u)r a bill; **~ a vista** sight bill; **~ a scadenza fissa** fixed-term bill

cambiamento *m* change; **~ climatico** climate change

cambiare <1k> **1** *v/t* change; (*scambiare*) exchange; AUTO **~ la marcia** change gear; **~ casa** move (house); **~ idea** change one's mind **2** *v/i e* **cambiarsi** change

cambiavalute *m* o *f inv* currency dealer, money-broker

cambio *m* (*pl* -bi) change; FIN, (*scambio*) exchange; AUTO, TEC gear; **~ automatico** automatic gearshift; **~ dell'olio** oil change; **~ d'indirizzo** change of address; **in ~** in exchange (**di** for); **dare il ~ a qu** relieve s.o.; **fare ~ con qu** swap *or* exchange with s.o.

camelia *f* camellia

camera *f* room; **~ da letto** bedroom; **~ singola** single room; **~ matrimoniale** double room; **a due letti** twin room; **~ d'albergo** hotel room; **~ blindata** strong room; **Camera dei Deputati** House of Commons; FOT **~ oscura** darkroom; **~ d'aria** inner tube; **~ dell'industria e del commercio** *chamber of commerce*

cameraman *m inv* cameraman

camerata *f stanza* dormitory; *in ospedale* ward

cameriera *f* waitress; (*domestica*) maid

cameriere *m* waiter; (*domestico*) manservant

camerino *m* dressing room

camice *m di medico* white coat; *di chirurgo* gown

camicetta *f* blouse

camicia *f* (*pl* -cie) shirt; **~ sportiva** sports shirt; **~ da notte** nightdress

caminetto *m* fireplace

camino *m* chimney; (*focolare*) fireplace

camion *m inv* truck, *Br* lorry

camioncino *m* van

camionista *m* (*pl* -i) truck driver, *Br* lorry driver

cammello *m* camel; *stoffa* camel hair

camminare <1a> walk; (*funzionare*) work, go

camminata *f* walk

cammino *m*: **un'ora di ~** an hour's walk; **mettersi in ~** set out

camomilla *f* camomile; (*infuso*) camomile tea

camoscio *m* (*pl* -sci) chamois; **scarpe fpl di ~** suede shoes

campagna *f* country; *fig*, POL campaign; **vivere in ~** live in the country; **~ pubblicitaria** advertising campaign; **~ elettorale** election campaign

campana *f* bell

campanello *m* bell; *della porta* doorbell; **~ d'allarme** alarm bell

campanile *m* bell tower

campanula *f* campanula

campare <1a> live; **~ alla giornata** live for the moment

campeggiare <1f> camp

campeggiatore *m* camper

campeggio *m* camping; *posto* camp site

camper *m inv* camper van

campestre rural

camping *m* camp site

campionario *m* (*pl* -ri) samples

campionato *m* championship; **~ mondiale** world championship

campione *m* sample; (*esemplare*) specimen; *di stoffa* swatch; SP champion

campo *m* field; **~ giochi** playground; **~ di golf** golf course; **~ di calcio** football *or* soccer pitch; **~ di con-**

centramento concentration camp; **~ da tennis** tennis court; **~ di ricerche** area of research; **~ sportivo** sports ground; **~ profughi** refugee camp

camposanto m (pl camposanti) cemetery

camuffare <1a> disguise

Canada m Canada

canadese 1 agg Canadian **2** m/f Canadian **3** f half-litre (Am -liter) bottle of beer

canale m channel; artificiale canal

canalizzazione f channelling; (conduttura) pipe

canapa f hemp

canarino m canary

cancellare <1b> cross out; con gomma rub out, erase; INFOR delete; debito write off, cancel; appuntamento cancel

cancellata f railings pl

cancelleria f: **articoli** mpl **di ~** stationery

cancelliere m chancellor; DIR clerk of the court

cancello m gate

cancerogeno carcinogenic

cancrena f gangrene

cancro m MED cancer; ASTR, GEOG **Cancro** Cancer

candeggiante m stain remover

candeggina f bleach

candela f candle; **~ d'accensione** spark plug

candelabro m candelabra

candeliere m candlestick

candidarsi <1l> stand (for election)

candidato m, **-a** f candidate

candidatura f candidacy, candidature

candido pure white; (sincero) frank; (innocente) innocent, pure; (ingenuo) naive

canditi mpl candied fruit

cane m dog; di arma da fuoco hammer, cock; **~ da guardia** guard dog; **freddo ~** freezing cold; **non c'era un ~** there wasn't a soul about; F **fatto da -i** botched F

canestro m basket

canguro m kangaroo

canile m (casotto) kennel; luogo kennels

canino 1 agg dog attr **2** m (dente) canine (tooth)

canna f reed; (bastone) stick; P joint P; **~ fumaria** flue; **~ da pesca** fishing rod; **~ da zucchero** sugar cane

cannella f GASTR cinnamon

cannelloni mpl cannelloni sg

cannibale m cannibal

cannocchiale m telescope

cannonata f fig: **è una ~** it's terrific

cannone m MIL gun, cannon; (asso) ace

cannuccia f (pl -cce) straw

canoa f canoe

canone m FIN rental (fee); RAD, TV licence (fee); (norma) standard

canottaggio m a pagaie canoeing; a remi rowing; **circolo** m **di ~** rowing club

canottiera f vest

canotto m rowing boat, Am rowboat; **~ pneumatico** rubber dinghy; **~ di salvataggio** lifeboat

cantante m/f singer

cantare <1a> sing

cantautore m, **-trice** f singer-songwriter

cantiere m building or construction site; MAR shipyard

cantina f cellar; locale wineshop

canto¹ m (canzone) song; (il cantare) singing; **~ popolare** folk song; **~ del cigno** swan song

canto² m: **dal ~ mio** for my part; **d'altro ~** on the other hand

cantonata f (grosso sbaglio) blunder

cantone m POL canton; **Lago** m **dei Quattro Cantoni** Lake Lucerne

canzonare <1a> tease

canzone f song; **la solita ~** the same old story

canzoniere m songbook

caos m chaos

caotico (pl -ci) chaotic

C.A.P. abbr (= **Codice di Avviamento Postale**) postcode, Am zip code

capace capable; (ampio) large, capacious; **~ di fare qc**

capable of doing sth

capacità *f inv* ability; (*capienza*) capacity; FIN ~ **di acquisto** purchasing power; INFOR ~ **di memoria** memory

capanna *f* hut

capannone *m* shed; AVIA hangar

caparra *f* FIN deposit

capello *m* hair; **-i** *pl* hair *sg*; GASTR **-i d'angelo** very thin noodles; **ne ho fin sopra i -i!** I've had it up to here!; **per un** ~ by the skin of one's teeth

capezzolo *m* nipple

capiente large, capacious

capienza *f* capacity

capigliatura *f* hair

capillare MED capillary

capire <4d> understand; **capisco** I see; **si capisce!** naturally!, of course!; **far** ~ **qc a qu** make s.o. understand sth, get s.o. to see sth; **farsi** ~ make o.s. understood

capitale 1 *agg* capital; *fig* major **2** *f città* capital **3** *m* FIN capital; ~ **d'esercizio** working capital; ~ **disponibile** available capital; ~ **fisso** fixed capital; ~ **iniziale** start-up capital; **fuga** *f* **di -i** flight of capital; ~ **proprio** equity capital; ~ **sociale** share capital

capitalismo *m* capitalism

capitalista *agg*, *m/f* (*mpl* -i) capitalist

capitaneria *f*: ~ **di porto** port authorities *pl*

capitano *m* captain

capitare <1l> *di avvenimento* happen; *di persona* find o.s.; **se mi capita l'occasione di venire** if I get a chance to come; ~ **in cattive mani** fall into the wrong hands; **mangio dove capita** I don't always eat in the same place; ~ **a proposito** come along at the right time; **sono cose che capitano** these things happen

capitello *m* ARCHI capital

capitolo *m* chapter; **avere voce in** ~ have a say in the matter

capitombolo *m* tumble, fall

capo *m* ANAT head; *persona* head, chief, boss F; GEOG cape; ~ **del governo** head of government; ~ **dello**

Stato head of state; ~ **di vestiario** item of clothing; **da** ~ from the beginning; **ti seguirò in** ~ **al mondo** I'll follow you to the ends of the earth; **per sommi -i** briefly; **andare a** ~ start a new paragraph; **non venire a** ~ **di nulla** be unable to come to any kind of conclusion; **questa storia non ha né** ~ **né coda** this story just doesn't make sense

capobanda *m/f di delinquenti* ringleader

capodanno *m* New Year's Day

capofamiglia *m/f* head of the family

capofitto: **a** ~ headlong

capogiro *m* dizzy spell

capogruppo *m/f* group leader; POL leader

capolavoro *m* masterpiece

capolinea *m* terminus

capolista *f* SP leaders *pl*

capoluogo *m* (*pl* capoluoghi) principal town

capomastro *m* (*pl* capomastri) master builder

caporeparto *m/f* (*mpl* capireparto, *fpl* caporeparto) *di fabbrica* foreman; *donna* forewoman; *di ufficio* superintendent

caposala *m/f* (*mpl* capisala, *fpl* caposala) *in ospedale* ward sister; *uomo* charge nurse

caposaldo *m* (*pl* capisaldi) stronghold

caposezione *m/f* (*mpl* capisezione, *fpl* caposezione) section chief

capostazione *m/f* (*mpl* capistazione, *fpl* capostazione) station master

capostipite *m/f* founder

capotavola: **a** ~ at the head of the table

capote *f inv* AUTO hood, (soft) top

capotreno *m/f* (*mpl* capitreno, *fpl* capotreno) guard

capoufficio *m/f* (*mpl* capiufficio, *fpl* capoufficio) supervisor

capoverso *m* (*pl* capoversi) paragraph; TIP indent(ation)

capovolgere <3d> turn upside down; *piani* upset; *situazione* reverse

capovolgersi turn upside down; *di barca* capsize

capovolgimento *m* complete change

capovolto *pp* → **capovolgere**

cappa *f* (*mantello*) cloak; *di cucina* hood; **~ del camino** cowl

cappella *f* chapel

cappellano *m* chaplain

cappelletti *mpl* pasta, shaped like little hats, with meat, cheese and egg filling

cappello *m* hat; **~ di paglia** straw hat; **senza ~** hatless; **mettersi il ~** put one's hat on

cappero *m* caper

cappio *m* noose

cappone *m* capon; **far venire la pelle di ~ a qu** give s.o. the creeps

cappotto *m* coat

cappuccino *m bevanda* cappuccino

cappuccio *m* (*pl* -cci) hood; *di penna* top, cap

capra *f* (nanny)goat; (*cavalletto*) trestle

capretto *m* kid

capriccio *m* (*pl* -cci) whim; *di bambini* tantrum; **fare i ~i** have tantrums

capriccioso capricious; *bambino* naughty; *tempo* changeable

Capricorno ASTR, GEOG Capricorn

capriola *f* somersault

capriolo *m* roe deer; GASTR venison

capro *m* billy goat; **~ espiatorio** scapegoat

capsula *f* capsule; *di dente* crown; **~ spaziale** space capsule

captare <1a> RAD pick up

carabina *f* carbine

carabiniere *m* police officer

caraffa *f* carafe

caramella *f* sweet

caramello *m* caramel

carato *m* carat

carattere *m* character; (*caratteristica*) characteristic; (*lettera*) character, letter; **-i** *pl* TIP typeface; INFOR font

caratteristica *f* characteristic

caratteristico (*pl* -ci) characteristic

caratterizzare <1a> characterize

caravan *m inv* caravan

caravanning *m inv* caravanning

carboidrato *m* carbohydrate

carbone *m* coal

carbonella *f* charcoal

carburante *m* fuel

carburatore *m* carburet(t)or

carcassa *f di animale* carcass; TEC (*inteliatura*) frame; MAR, F wreck

carcerato *m*, **-a** *f* prisoner

carcerazione *f* imprisonment; **~ preventiva** preventive detention

carcere *m* (*pl* le -ri) jail, prison

carceriere *m*, **-a** *f* jailer, gaoler

carciofo *m* artichoke

cardellino *m* goldfinch

cardiaco (*pl* -ci) cardiac, heart

cardinale 1 *agg* cardinal; **punto** *m* **~** cardinal point **2** *m* REL cardinal

cardine *m* hinge

cardiologia *f* cardiology

cardiologo *m* (*pl* -gi), **-a** *f* (*pl* -ghe) heart specialist, cardiologist

cardo *m* thistle

carena *f* MAR keel

carenza *f* lack (**di** of)

carestia *f* shortage

carezza *f* caress

carezzare <1a> caress

cargo *m aereo* air freighter; *nave* cargo ship

cariato: **dente** *m* **~** decayed tooth

carica *f* (*pl* -che) (*incarico*) office; *fig* (*slancio*, *energia*) drive; TEC load; MIL (*attacco*) charge; SP tackle; **in ~** in office; **durata** *f* **della ~** term of office; **tornare alla ~** insist

caricare <1d & l> load; MIL charge; *orologio* wind up

caricarsi overload o.s. (**di** with); PSI psych o.s. up; **~ di debiti** get heavily into debt

caricatura *f* caricature

caricaturista *m/f* (*mpl* -i) caricaturist

carico (*pl* -chi) **1** *agg* loaded; EL charged; *caffè* strong; *colore* deep; *orologio* wound up **2** *m* load; FIN charge, expense; MAR cargo; DIR **a ~ di** (*contro*) against; **essere a ~ di qu**

be dependent on s.o.; ~ **utile** payload; **lettera** f (o **polizza** f) **di** ~ bill of lading; ~ **di lavoro** workload

carie f inv tooth decay

carino (grazioso) pretty; (gentile) nice

carisma m charisma

carità f charity; **per** ~! for goodness sake!, for pity's sake!

carnagione f complexion

carnale carnal; **fratello** m ~ blood brother

carne f flesh; GASTR meat; ~ **di maiale** / **manzo** pork / beef; ~ **tritata** mince

carneficina f slaughter

carnevale m carnival

carnivoro m carnivore

carnoso fleshy

caro 1 agg dear; (costoso) dear, expensive; **mi è molto** ~ I am very fond of him/it; **a** ~ **prezzo** dearly 2 avv a lot; **costare** ~ be very expensive; fig have a high price 3 m dear; -**i** pl loved ones, family

carogna f carrion; F swine

carosello m merry-go-round

carota f carrot

carotide f carotid artery

carovana f caravan

carovita m high cost of living; **indennità** f **di** ~ cost of living allowance

carpa f carp

carpentiere m carpenter

carpire <4d>: ~ **qc a qu** get sth out of s.o.

carponi on all fours

carrabile → **carraio**

carraio: **passo** m ~ driveway

carreggiata f roadway; **rimettersi in** ~ fig catch up

carrello m trolley; AVIA undercarriage; ~ **elevatore** fork-lift truck; ~ **portabagagli** baggage trolley, Am baggage cart

carretto m cart

carriera f career; **fare** ~ come a long way; **di gran** ~ at top speed

carriola f wheelbarrow

carro m cart; AST Bear; FERR ~ **bestiame** cattle truck; FERR ~ **merci** goods wagon, Am freight car; ~ **armato** tank; ~ **attrezzi** breakdown van, tow truck, Am wrecker; ~ **funebre** hearse

carrozza f FERR carriage; ~ **con cuccette** sleeper; ~ **ristorante** restaurant car

carrozzella f per bambini pram; per invalidi wheelchair

carrozzeria f bodywork, coachwork

carrozziere m AUTO (progettista) (car) esigner; (costruttore) coachbuilder; chi fa riparazioni panel beater

carrozzina f pram

carta f paper; GASTR (menù) menu; GEOG ~ **geografica** map; ~ **assegni** cheque (guarantee) card; ~ **da bollo** official stamped paper; ~ **da gioco** (playing) card; ~ **da lettere** note paper; ~ **da macero** waste paper (for pulping); ~ **da parati** wallpaper; ~ **d'argento** card that entitles people over a certain age to reduced fares; ~ **di credito** credit card; ~ **d'identità** identity card; AVIA ~ **d'imbarco** boarding pass; ~ **igienica** toilet paper; ~ **stagnola** silver paper; GASTR tinfoil; ~ **stradale** road map; ~ **telefonica** phone card; ~ **velina** tissue paper; AUTO ~ **verde** green card; ~ **vetrata** sandpaper

cartacarbone f carbon paper

cartamodello m (pl cartamodelli) pattern

cartamoneta f inv paper money

cartapecora f parchment, vellum

cartapesta f papier-mâché

cartastraccia f waste paper

carteggio m (pl -ggi) correspondence

cartella f (borsa) briefcase; di alunno schoolbag, satchel; copertina per documenti folder, file; foglio dattiloscritto page; ~ **clinica** medical record

cartellino m (etichetta) label; **con prezzo** price tag; (scheda) card; SP ~ **giallo** / **rosso** yellow/red card; ~ **orario** clocking-in card

cartello m sign; nelle dimostrazioni

placard; FIN cartel; **~ stradale** road sign

cartellone *m pubblicitario* hoarding, *Am* billboard; TEA bill

cartiera *f* paper mill

cartilagine *f* cartilage

cartina *f* GEOG map; *(bustina)* packet; *per sigarette* cigarette paper

cartoccio *m* (*pl* -cci) paper bag; *a cono* paper cone; GASTR **al ~** baked in tinfoil, en papillote

cartografia *f* cartography

cartoleria *f* stationer's

cartolina *f* postcard; **~ illustrata** picture postcard; **~ postale** postcard

cartoncino *m* (thin) cardboard; *(biglietto)* card

cartone *m* cardboard; **-i** *pl* **animati** cartoons

cartuccia *f* (*pl* -cce) cartridge

casa *f edificio* house; *(abitazione)* home; FIN company; **~ di cura** nursing home; **~ editrice** publishing house; **~ dello studente** hall of residence; **~ a schiera** terraced house; **~ unifamiliare** single-family dwelling; **~ per le vacanze** holiday home; **case popolari** council houses; **seconda ~** second home; **essere di ~** be like one of the family; **dove stai di ~?** where do you live?; **cambiare ~** move (house); **fatto in ~** home-made; **andare a ~** go home; **essere a ~** be at home; SP **giocare in/fuori** play at home/away

casalinga *f* (*pl* -ghe) housewife

casalingo (*pl* -ghi) domestic; *(fatto in casa)* home-made; *persona* home-loving; **cucina *f* -a** home cooking; **-ghi** *mpl* household goods

cascare <1d> fall (down); *fig* **cascarci** fall for it

cascata *f* waterfall

cascina *f* (*casa colonica*) farmhouse; *(caseificio)* dairy farm

casco *m* (*pl* -chi) helmet; *dal parrucchiere* hair dryer; **-chi** *pl* **blu** UN forces, blue berets F

caseggiato *m* (*edificio*) block of flats, *Am* apartment block

caseificio *m* (*pl* -ci) dairy

casella *f di schedario* pigeon hole; *(quadratino)* square; **~ postale** post office box

casellario *m* (*pl* -ri) pigeon holes; **~ giudiziario** criminal records (office)

casello *m autostradale* toll booth

casereccio (*pl* -cci) homemade

caserma *f* barracks

casino P *m* brothel; *(rumore)* din, racket; *(disordine)* mess; **~ di caccia** hunting lodge

casinò *m inv* casino

caso *m* case; *(destino)* chance; *(occasione)* opportunity; **~ d'emergenza** emergency; **per ~** by chance; **a ~** at random; **(in) ~ che** in case; **in ~ contrario** should that not be the case; **in ogni ~** in any case, anyway; **in nessun ~** under no circumstances; **nel peggiore dei -i** if the worst comes to the worst

casolare *m* farmhouse

caspita! goodness (gracious)!, good heavens!

cassa *f case*; *di legno* crate; *di negozio* till; *sportello* cash desk, cashpoint; *(banca)* bank; **~ acustica** speaker; **~ comune** kitty; **~ continua** night safe; **~ da morto** coffin; **~ di risparmio** savings bank; **~ integrazione** form of income support; **~ malattia** department administering health insurance scheme; **~ toracica** ribcage; **orario *m* di ~** opening hours

cassaforte *f* (*pl* casseforti) safe

cassapanca *f* (*pl* cassapanche) chest

casseruola *f* (sauce)pan

cassetta *f* box; *per frutta, verdura* crate; *(musicassetta)* cassette; **~ delle lettere** (*buca*) post box, *Am* mailbox; *(casella)* letterbox, *Am* mailbox; **~ del pronto soccorso** first-aid kit; **~ di sicurezza** strong box; **successo *m* di ~** box office hit; **pane *m* a ~** sliced loaf

cassetto *m* drawer; AUTO **~ portaoggetti** glove compartment

cassettone *m* chest of drawers; **soffitto *m* a -i** panelled ceiling cassiere *m*, **-a** *f* cashier; *di banca* teller; *di supermercato* checkout assistant

cassonetto *m* dustbin

casta *f* caste

castagna *f* chestnut

castagno *m* chestnut (tree)

castano *capelli* chestnut; *occhi* brown

castello *m* castle; TEC (*impalcatura*) scaffolding; **letti** *mpl* **a ~** bunk beds

castigare <1e> punish

castigo *m* (*pl* -ghi) punishment

castità *f* chastity

castoro *m* beaver

castrare <1a> castrate; *gatto* neuter; *femmina di animale* spay

casual **1** *agg* casual **2** *m* casual clothes, casual wear

casuale chance, casual

casualità *f* chance nature

cataclisma *m* (*pl* -i) disaster

catacomba *f* catacomb

catalizzatore *m* catalyst; AUTO catalytic converter; **~ a tre vie** three-way catalytic converter

catalogare <1m & e> catalog(ue)

catalogo *m* (*pl* -ghi) catalog(ue); **~ di vendita per corrispondenza** mail order catalog(ue)

catapecchia *f* shack

catapultare <1a> catapult

catarifrangente *m* reflector; *lungo la strada* reflector, Br cat's eye

catarro *m* catarrh

catasta *f* pile, heap

catasto *m* land register

catastrofe *f* catastrophe

catastrofico (*pl* -ci) catastrophic

categoria *f* category; *di albergo* class; **~ a rischio** at risk category

categorico (*pl* -ci) categoric(al)

catena *f* chain; **-e** *pl* **da neve** snow chains; **reazione** *f* **a ~** chain reaction; **~ di montaggio** assembly line; **~ montuosa** mountain range, chain of mountains

catenaccio *m* (*pl* -cci) bolt; SP defensive tactics

cateratta *f* (*chiusa*) sluice(gate); (*cascata*) falls; MED cataract

catino *m* basin

catrame *m* tar

cattedra *f scrivania* desk; *incarico di insegnamento* teaching post; **~ universitaria** university chair

cattedrale *f* cathedral

cattiveria *f* wickedness; *di bambini* naughtiness; *azione* nasty thing to do; *parole crudeli* nasty thing to say

cattività *f* captivity

cattivo bad; *bambino* naughty, bad; **con le buone o con le -e** by hook or by crook

cattolicesimo *m* (Roman) Catholicism

cattolico (*pl* -ci) **1** *agg* (Roman) Catholic **2** *m*, **-a** *f* (Roman) Catholic

cattura *f* capture; (*arresto*) arrest

catturare <1a> capture; (*arrestare*) arrest

caucciù *m* rubber

causa *f* cause; (*motivo*) reason; DIR lawsuit; **fare ~** sue (**a qu** s.o.); **a ~ di** because of; **per ~ tua** because of you

causale *f* cause, reason

causare <1a> cause

cautela *f* caution; (*precauzione*) precaution

cauto cautious

cauzione *f* (*deposito*) security; *per la libertà provvisoria* bail

Cav. *abbr* (= **Cavaliere**) *Italian title awarded for services to the country*

cava *f* quarry

cavalcare <1d> ride

cavalcata *f* ride

cavalcavia *m inv* flyover

cavalcioni: **a ~** astride

cavaliere *m* rider; *accompagnatore* escort; *al ballo* partner

cavalla *f* mare

cavallerizzo *m*, **-a** *f* horseman; *donna* horsewoman

cavalletta *f* grasshopper

cavalletto *m* trestle; FOT tripod; *da pittore* easel

cavallo *m* horse; *scacchi* knight; *dei pantaloni* crotch; **~ da corsa** race horse; AUTO **~ vapore** horsepower;

andare a ~ go riding; **vivere a ~ di due secoli** straddle two centuries

cavallone *m* breaker

cavalluccio *m* (*pl* -cci): **~ marino** sea horse

cavare <1a> take out; *dente* take out, extract; **cavarsela** manage, get by

cavarsi: ~ da un impiccio get out of trouble

cavatappi *m inv* corkscrew

caverna *f* cave

cavernoso: una voce -a a deep voice

cavia *f* guinea pig *(anche fig)*

caviale *m* caviar

caviglia *f* (*pl* -glie) ANAT ankle

cavillo *m* quibble

cavità *f inv* cavity

cavo 1 *agg* hollow **2** *m* cable; **~ d'accensione** plug lead; **~ di avviamento** jump leads; **~ di ormeggio** mooring rope; **~ da rimorchio** tow rope; **~ in fibra ottica** optic fibre cable; **televisione** *f* **via ~** cable TV

cavolfiore *m* cauliflower

cavolo *m* cabbage; **~ di Bruxelles** Brussels sprout; **~ rapa** kohlrabi; **~ verzotto** Savoy cabbage

cazzo *m* V prick V; **~!** fuck! V

CC *abbr* (= **Carabinieri**) Italian police force

cc *abbr* (= **centimetri cubici**) cc (= cubic centimetres)

c.c. *abbr* (= **corrente continua**) DC (= direct current)

c/c *abbr* (= **conto corrente**) current account, *Am* checking account

CD *m inv* CD; **lettore** *m* **~** CD player; **CD-Rom** *m inv* CD-Rom; **drive** *m* **per ~** CD-Rom drive

ce → **ci** (*before* **lo, la, li, le, ne**)

c'è there is

cecchino *m* sniper

cece *m* chickpea

cecità *f* blindness

ceco 1 *agg* Czech **2** *m*, **-a** *f* Czech

cecoslovacco (*pl* -cchi) **1** *agg* Czechoslovakian **2** *m*, **-a** *f* Czechoslovakian

cedere <3a> **1** *v/t* (*dare*) hand over, give up; (*vendere*) sell, dispose of; **~**

il posto give up one's seat **2** *v/i* give in, surrender (**a** to); *muro, terreno* collapse, give way; **non ~!** don't give in!

cedevole soft

cedibile transferable, assignable

cedola *f* coupon; **~ di consegna** delivery note

cedro *m del Libano* cedar

CEE, Cee *abbr* (= **Comunità Economica Europea**) EEC (= European Economic Community)

cefalo *m* ZO mullet

ceffone *m* slap

celebrare <1l & b> celebrate

celebrazione *f* celebration

celebre famous

celebrità *f inv* fame; (*persona*) celebrity

celere fast, speedy, swift; **posta** *f* **~** swiftair®, *Am* Fedex®

celeste sky blue; (*divino*) heavenly *(anche fig)*

celibato *m* celibacy

celibe 1 *agg* single, unmarried **2** *m* bachelor

cella *f* cell

cellula *f* cell; **~ fotoelettrica** photoelectric cell; **~ solare** solar cell

cellulare 1 *agg* cell *attr*; **telefono** *m* **~** mobile phone, *Am* cell(ular) phone **2** *m* prison van; (*telefono*) mobile

cellulite *f* cellulite

cellulosa *f* cellulose

celtico (*pl* -ci) Celtic

cemento *m* cement; **~ armato** reinforced concrete

cena *f* supper, evening meal; *importante, con ospiti* dinner; **~ in piedi** buffet

cenacolo *m* PITT Last Supper

cenare <1a> have supper; *formalmente* dine

cencio *m* (*pl* -ci) rag, piece of cloth; (*per spolverare*) duster; **bianco come un ~** white as a sheet

cenere *f* ash; **le Ceneri** *fpl* Ash Wednesday

cenno *m* sign; *della mano* wave; *del capo* nod; *con gli occhi* wink; (*breve notizia*) mention; (*allusione*) hint;

far ~ a qu *con la mano* wave to s.o.; *con il capo* nod to s.o.; *con gli occhi* wink at s.o.; **far ~ di voler andare** signal that one wants to leave; **far ~ di sì** nod (one's head); **far ~ di no** shake one's head

cenone *m* feast, banquet; **~ di San Silvestro** special celebratory meal on New Year's Eve

censimento *m* census

censura *f* censorship

censurare <1a> censor

centenario (*pl* -ri) **1** *agg* hundred-year-old **2** *m* (*persona*) centenarian; (*anniversario*) centenary

centesimo **1** *agg* hundredth **2** *m*: **~ di dollaro** cent; **badare al ~** count every penny

centigrado *m* centigrade

centimetro *m* centimetre, *Am* -meter; **~ cubo** cubic centimetre (*Am* -meter); **~ quadrato** square centimetre (*Am* -meter)

centinaio *m* (*pl* le centinaia) hundred; **un ~ di** about a hundred, a hundred or so

cento hundred; **per ~** per cent; **~ per ~** one hundred per cent; **~ di questi giorni** many happy returns

centrale **1** *agg* central **2** *f* station, plant; **~ atomica** o **nucleare** nuclear power station

centralinista *m/f* switchboard operator

centralino *m* switchboard

centralizzare <1a> centralize

centrare <1b> TEC centre, *Am* center; **~ il bersaglio** hit a bull's eye

centrifuga **1** *agg* centrifugal **2** *f* spin-dryer; TEC centrifuge

centrifugare <1e & m> spin-dry; TEC centrifuge

centro *m* centre, *Am* center; *di bersaglio* bull's eye; **~ commerciale** shopping centre; **~ della città** town or city centre, *Am* downtown; **~ residenziale** residential area; **~ storico** old (part of) town; **fare ~** hit the bull's eye; *fig* hit the nail on the head

ceppo *m*: **~ bloccaruota** wheel

clamp; **mettere il ~ a** clamp

cera[1] *f* wax; *per lucidare* polish; **~ da scarpe** shoe polish

cera[2] *f* look; **avere una brutta ~** look awful

ceralacca *f* sealing wax

ceramica *f* (*pl* -che) *arte* ceramics *sg*; *oggetto* piece of pottery

cerata *f* oilskins *pl*

cerca *f*: **in ~ di ...** in search of ...

cercare <1d> **1** *v/t* look for **2** *v/i*: **~ di fare** try to do

cerchia *f* circle

cerchio *m* (*pl* -chi) circle

cerchione *m* TEC rim

cereale **1** *agg* grain *attr* **2** **-i** *mpl* grain, cereals

cerealicoltura *f* grain farming

cerebrale: **commozione** *f* **~** concussion

cerimonia *f* ceremony; REL service; **-e** *pl* (*convenevoli*) pleasantries; **fare ~** stand on ceremony; **senza tante ~** (*bruscamente*) unceremoniously

cerimoniale *m/agg* ceremonial

cerimonioso ceremonious

cerino *m* (wax) match

cernia *f* grouper

cerniera *f* hinge; **~ lampo** zip (fastener), *Am* zipper

cernita *f* selection, choice

cero *m* (large) candle

cerotto *m* (sticking) plaster

certezza *f* certainty

certificare <1m & d> certify

certificato *m* certificate; **~ medico** medical certificate; **~ di garanzia** guarantee; **~ di nascita** birth certificate; **~ di sana e robusta costituzione** certificate of good health

certo **1** *agg* (*sicuro*) certain, sure (*di* of; *che* that); **un ~ signor Federici** a (certain) Mr Federici; **ci vuole un ~ coraggio** it takes (some) courage; **di una -a età** of a certain age; **-i** some; **-e cose non si dicono** there are some things you just don't say; **un ~ non so che** a certain something, a certain je ne sais quoi **2** *avv* (*certamente*) certainly; (*naturalmente*) of course; ~ *che ...* surely ... 3 *pron*: *-i*, *-e* some, some people

certosa *f* Carthusian monastery

cervello *m* (*pl* i cervelli, le cervella) brain; GASTR brains; *farsi saltare le -a* blow one's brains out; *lambiccarsi il* ~ rack one's brains

cervo *m* deer; *carne* venison; *~ volante* stag beetle

cesareo: *taglio m* ~ C(a)esarean (section), C section

cesellare <1b> chisel

cesello *m* chisel

cesoie *fpl* shears

cespuglio *m* (*pl* -gli) bush, shrub

cessare <1b> stop, cease

cessate il fuoco *m* ceasefire

cessazione *f di contratto* termination; *~ di esercizio* closure, going out of business

cessione *f* transfer, handover

cesso *m* P bog P

cesta *f* basket

cestinare <1a> throw away, bin F

cestino *m* little basket; *per la carta* wastepaper basket

cesto *m* basket

cetaceo *m* cetacean

ceto *m* (social) class; *~ medio* middle class

cetra *f* zither

cetriolino *m* gherkin

cetriolo *m* cucumber

cf., **cfr.** *abbr* (= *confronta*) cf (= compare)

cg *abbr* (= *centigrammo*) cg (= centigram)

CGIL *abbr* (= *Confederazione Generale Italiana del Lavoro*) Italian trade union organization

chalet *m inv* chalet

charter *m inv* charter

che 1 *agg* what; *a* ~ *cosa serve?* what is that for?; *~ brutta giornata!* what a filthy day! **2** *pron persona*: soggetto who; *persona*: oggetto who, that, *fml* whom; *cosa* that, which; *~?* what?; *ciò* ~ what; *non c'e di* ~ don't mention it, you're welcome **3** *cong dopo il comparativo* than;

sono tre anni ~ *non la vedo* I haven't seen her for three years

check-in *m inv* AVIA check-in; *fare il* ~ check in

chemioterapia *f* chemotherapy, chemo F

chetichella: *alla* ~ stealthily

chi who; *di* ~ *è il libro?* whose book is this? *a* ~ *ha venduto la casa?* who did he sell the house to?; *c'è* ~ *dice che* some people say that; *~ ... ~* some ... others

chiacchiera *f* chat; (*maldicenza*) gossip; (*notizia infondata*) rumo(u)r; *far due -e con qu* have a chat with s.o.

chiacchierare <1l> chat, chatter; *spreg* gossip

chiacchierata *f* chat

chiacchierone 1 *agg* talkative, chatty; (*pettegolo*) gossipy **2** *m*, *-a f* chatterbox; (*pettegolo*) gossip

chiamare <1a> call; TELEC (tele)phone, ring; *andare a* ~ *qu* go and get s.o., fetch s.o.; *mandare a* ~ *qu* send for s.o.; (*convocare*) call in; TELEC ~ *in teleselezione* call direct, dial direct

chiamarsi be called; *come ti chiami?* what's your name?; *mi chiamo ...* my name is ...

chiamata *f* call; TELEC (tele)phone call; *~ a carico del destinatario* reverse charge call, *Am* collect call; *~ interurbana* long-distance call

chiara *f* egg white

chiarezza *f* clarity

chiarimento *m* clarification

chiarire <4d> clarify

chiarirsi become clear

chiaro 1 *agg* clear; *colore* light, pale; (*luminoso*) bright; *~ e tondo* definite **2** *m* light; *~ di luna* moonlight; *mettere in* ~ (*appurare*) throw light on; (*spiegare*) clarify **3** *avv* plainly; (*con franchezza*) frankly

chiaroscuro *m* PITT chiaroscuro

chiaroveggente *m/f* clairvoyant

chiasso *m* din, racket; *fare* ~ make a din *or* racket; *fig* cause a sensation chiassoso noisy

chiatta *f* barge; **ponte *m di* -e** pontoon bridge

chiave **1** *agg inv* key **2** *f* key; MUS clef; ~ **d'accensione** ignition key; ~ **della macchina** car key; ~ **inglese** spanner, *Am* monkey wrench; **sotto ~** under lock and key

chiavistello *m* bolt

chiazza *f* (*macchia*) stain; *sulla pelle, di colore* patch

chic *inv* chic, stylish, elegant

chicco *m* (*pl* -chi) grain; (*di caffè*) bean; ~ **d'uva** grape

chiedere <3k> *per sapere* ask (**di** about); *per avere* ask for; (*esigere*) demand, require; ~ **qc a qu** ask s.o. sth; ~ **di qu** (*chiedere notizie di*) ask about s.o.; *per parlargli* ask for s.o.; ~ **un piacere a qu** ask s.o. a favo(u)r, ask a favo(u)r of s.o.; ~ **scusa a qu** apologize to s.o.

chiedersi wonder (**se** whether)

chiesa *f* church

chiesto *pp* → **chiedere**

chiglia *f* MAR keel

chilo *m* kilo; **mezzo ~** half a kilo

chilogrammo *m* kilogram

chilometraggio *m* AUTO *mileage*

chilometrico *indennità* per chilometre

chilometro *m* kilometre, *Am* -meter; **-i** *pl* **all'ora** kilometres (*Am* -meters) per hour

chilowatt *m inv* kilowatt

chimica *f* chemistry

chimico (*pl* -ci) **1** *agg* chemical; **sostanze** *fpl* **-che** chemicals **2** *m,* **-a** *f* chemist

chinare <1a> *testa* bend; *occhi* lower

chinarsi stoop, bend down

chincaglierie *fpl* knick-knacks, ornaments

chinino *m* quinine

chioccia *f fig* mother hen

chiocciola *f* snail; **scala** *f a* ~ spiral staircase

chiodato: SP **scarpe** *fpl* **-e** spikes

chiodo *m* nail; ~ **di garofano** clove; *fig* ~ **fisso** obsession, idée fixe; **roba da -i!** it's unbelievable!

chioma *f* mane; *di cometa* tail

chiosco *m* (*pl* -chi) kiosk

chiostro *m* cloister

chip *m inv* chip

chiromante *m/f* palmist

chiropratico *m,* **-a** *f* chiropractor

chirurgia *f* surgery

chirurgico (*pl* -ci) surgical

chirurgo *m* (*pl* -ghi) surgeon

chissà who knows; (*forse*) maybe

chitarra *f* guitar

chitarrista *m/f* (*mpl* -i) guitarist

chiudere <3b> close, shut; *a chiave* lock; *strada* close off; *gas, luce* turn off; *fabbrica, negozio per sempre* close down, shut down; *fig* ~ **un occhio** turn a blind eye; FIN ~ **in pareggio** break even; ~ **in perdita / in attivo** show a loss / a profit

chiudersi *di porta, ombrello* close, shut; *di ferita* heal up; ~ **in se stesso** withdraw into o.s.

chiunque anyone; *relativo* whoever

chiusa *f di fiume* lock; *di discorso* conclusion

chiuso **1** *pp* → **chiudere** **2** *agg* closed, shut; *a chiave* locked; (*nuvoloso*) cloudy, overcast; *persona* reserved

chiusura *f* closing, shutting; AUTO ~ **centralizzata** central locking; ~ **lampo** zip (fastener), *Am* zipper; **ora** *f di* ~ closing time

choc *m inv* shock

ci **1** *pron* us; **non ~ ha parlato** he didn't speak to us; ~ **siamo divertiti molto** we had a great time; ~ **vogliamo bene** we love each other; ~ **penso** I'm thinking about it **2** *avv* here; (*lì*) there; ~ **sei?** are you there?; **c'è ...** there is ...; ~ **sono ...** there are ...; ~ **vuole tempo** it takes time

C.ia *abbr* (= **compagnia**) Co. (= company)

ciabatta *f* slipper

cialda *f* wafer

ciambella *f* GASTR type of cake, baked in a ring-shaped mo(u)ld; (*salvagente*) lifebelt

cianfrusaglia *f* knick-knack

ciao! *nell'incontrarsi* hi!; *nel congedarsi* 'bye!, cheerio!

ciarlatano *m* charlatan

ciarpame *m* junk

ciascuno 1 *agg* each; *(ogni)* every **2** *pron* everyone

cibarsi <1a> feed on, eat *(di* sth)

cibernetica *f* cybernetics

cibo *m* food; *-i pl* foodstuffs, foods; **~ pronto** fast food

cicala *f (insetto)* cicada

cicalino *m* buzzer, bleeper

cicatrice *f* scar

cicatrizzare <1a>, **cicatrizzarsi** heal

cicca *f (pl* -che*) (mozzicone)* stub, butt; *(gomma da masticare)* (chewing) gum

ciccia *f (grasso)* flab

ciccione *m*, **-a** *f* fatty

cicciottello chubby

cicerone *m* guide

ciclamino *m* cyclamen

ciclico cyclical

ciclismo *m* cycling, bike riding

ciclista *m/f (mpl* -i*)* cyclist

ciclistico bike *attr*, cycle *attr*

ciclo *m* cycle

ciclomotore *m* moped

ciclone *m* cyclone

cicloturismo *m* cycling holidays

cicogna *f* stork

cicoria *f* chicory

cieco *(pl* -chi*)* **1** *agg* blind; *vicolo m ~* dead end, blind alley **2** *m*, **-a** *f* blind man; *donna* blind woman

cielo *m* sky; REL heaven; *grazie al ~* thank heaven(s)

cifra *f* figure; *(monogramma)* monogram; *(somma)* amount, sum; *(codice)* cipher, code; *~ d'affari* turnover; *numero m di sei -e* six digit number

cifrato *(messaggio)* in cipher, in code

ciglio *m (pl* le ciglia*)* ANAT eyelash; *(pl* i cigli*) (bordo)* edge

cigno *m* swan

cigolare <1l> squeak

cigolio *m* squeak

Cile *m* Chile

cilecca: far ~ di *arma da fuoco* mis-
fire

cileno 1 *agg* Chilean **2** *m*, **-a** *f* Chilean

ciliegia *f (pl* -ge*)* cherry

ciliegio *m (pl* -gi*)* cherry (tree)

cilindrata *f* TEC cubic capacity; *automobile f di media ~* middle of the range car

cilindrico *(pl* -ci*)* cylindrical

cilindro *m* cylinder; *cappello* top hat

cima *f* top; *in ~ all'armadio* on top of the wardrobe; *da ~ a fondo* from top to bottom; *fig* from beginning to end; *non è una ~* he's no Einstein

cimentarsi <1l>: *~ in* embark on

cimice *f* bug; *dei letti* bed bug; *(puntina da disegno)* drawing-pin

ciminiera *f* smokestack

cimitero *m* cemetery

Cina *f* China

cinciallegra *f* great tit

cincilla, **cincillà** *f* chinchilla

cin cin! F cheers!

cineamatore *m* video enthusiast

cineforum *m inv* film *followed by a discussion*; club film club

cinema *m inv* cinema, *Am luogo* movie theater; *~ d'essai* experimental cinema; *luogo* art cinema, art house

cinematografia *f* cinematography; *industria* film *or* movie industry

cinematografico *(pl* -ci*)* film *attr*, movie *attr*

cinepresa *f* cine camera

cinese *agg*, *m/f* Chinese

cineteca *f* film library

cinetico *(pl* -ci*)* kinetic

cingere <3d> *(circondare)* surround

cinghia *f* strap; *(cintura)* belt; *tirare la ~* tighten one's belt

cinghiale *m* wild boar; *pelle f di ~* pigskin

cinguettare <1a> twitter

cinguettio *m* twittering

cinico *(pl* -ci*)* **1** *agg* cynical **2** *m* **-a** *f* cynic

cinismo *m* cynicism

cinquanta fifty

cinquantenario *m* fiftieth anniversary

cinquantenne *m/f* 50-year-old
cinquantesimo *m/agg* fiftieth
cinquantina *f*: *una ~ di* about 50
cinque five
cinquecento **1** *agg* five hundred **2** *m*: *il Cinquecento* the sixteenth century
cinquemila five thousand
cintare <1a> enclose
cinto *pp* → *cingere*
cintura *f* belt; (*vita*) waist; *~ di salvataggio* lifebelt; *~ di sicurezza* seat-belt
cinturino *m* strap
ciò (*questo*) this; (*quello*) that; *~ che* what; *con tutto ~* even so, in spite of all that; *~ nonostante* nevertheless
ciocca *f* (*pl* -cche) *di capelli* lock
cioccolata *f* chocolate
cioccolatino *m* chocolate
cioccolato *m* chocolate
cioè that is, i.e.
ciondolare <1l> dangle; *fig* hang about
ciondolo *m* pendant
ciotola *f* bowl
ciottolo *m* pebble
cipolla *f* onion; *di pianta* bulb
cipollina *f* small onion; *erba f ~* chives *pl*
cipresso *m* cypress (tree)
cipria *f* (face) powder
circa **1** *avv* (round) about **2** *prp* about
circo *m* (*pl* -chi) circus
circolare **1** *v/i* <1l> circulate; *di persone* move along; *le auto non possono ~* it's impossible to drive **2** *agg* circular **3** *f lettera* circular
circolazione *f* traffic; MED circulation; DIR *libera ~* freedom of movement; *~ del sangue* circulation of the blood; *mettere in ~ voci* spread; *ritirare dalla ~* withdraw from circulation
circolo *m* circle; (*club*) club; *~ vizioso* vicious circle
circondare <1a> surround
circonferenza *f* circumference
circonvallazione *f* ring road
circoscrivere <3tt> circumscribe

circoscrizione *f* area, district; *~ elettorale* constituency
circostante surrounding
circostanza *f* circumstance; (*occasione*) occasion
circuito *m* SP (*percorso*) track; EL circuit; EL *corto ~* short circuit
CISL *abbr* (= *Confederazione Italiana Sindacati Lavoratori*) Italian trade union organization
cisterna *f* cistern; (*serbatoio*) tank; *nave f ~* tanker
cisti *f* ANAT cyst
cistifellea *f* gall bladder
cistite *f* cystitis
CIT *abbr* (= *Compagnia Italiana del Turismo*) Italian Tourist Board
citare <1a> quote; *come esempio* cite, quote; DIR *testimone* summons; *in giudizio* sue
citazione *f* quotation, quote; DIR summons
citofono *m* entry phone; *in uffici* intercom
città *f* town; *grande* city; *~ dormitorio* dormitory town; *~ giardino* garden city; *~ universitaria* university town (*in the provinces*); *la ~ vecchia* the old (part of) town; *Città del Vaticano* Vatican City; *la ~ eterna* the Eternal City
cittadina *f* (small) town
cittadinanza *f* citizenship; (*popolazione*) citizens; *~ onoraria* freedom of the city
cittadino **1** *agg* town *attr*, city *attr* **2** *m*, *-a f* citizen; (*abitante di città*) city dweller
ciuccio *m* F (*succhiotto*) dummy, *Am* pacifier
ciuffo *m* tuft
civetta *f* ZO (little) owl; *fig far la ~* flirt
civico (*pl* -ci) (*della città*) municipal, town *attr*; *delle persone* civic; *numero ~* (street) number
civile **1** *agg* civil; *civilizzato* civilized; (*non militare*) civilian; *guerra f ~* civil war; *matrimonio m ~* civil marriage; *stato m ~* marital status **2** *m* civilian

civiltà f inv civilization; (*cortesia*) civility

clacson m inv horn

clamoroso fig sensational

clandestino 1 agg clandestine; (*illegale*) illegal **2** m, **-a** f stowaway

clarinetto m clarinet

classe f class; (*aula*) classroom; ~ **operaia** working class; ~ **turistica** tourist class; **di ~** classy

classicismo m classicism

classico (*pl* -ci) **1** agg classical; (*tipico*) classic **2** m classic

classifica f classification; (*elenco*) list; *sportiva* league standings, league table; *musicale* charts

classificare <1m & d> classify

classificatore m (*cartella*) folder; *mobile* filing cabinet, *Am* file cabinet

classismo m class consciousness

clausola f clause; (*riserva*) proviso

claustrofobia f claustrophobia

clavicola f collar-bone, clavicle

clemente merciful; *tempo* mild

clemenza f clemency; *di tempo* mildness

cleptomane m/f kleptomaniac

clericale clerical

clero m clergy

clessidra f hourglass

clic m inv click; **mediante ~** by clicking

cliccare <1d> INFOR click (**su** on)

cliché m inv fig cliché

cliente m/f customer; *di professionista* client; *di albergo* guest; MED patient; ~ **abituale** regular

clientela f customers pl, clientele; *di professionista* clients pl; *di medico* patients pl; ~ **abituale** patrons pl, regular customers pl

clima m (*pl* -i) climate

climatico (*pl* -ci) climate attr, climatic; **stazione** f **climatica** health resort

clinica f (*pl* -che) (*ospedale*) clinic; (*casa di cura*) nursing home; ~ **medica** clinical medicine

clinico (*pl* -ci) **1** agg clinical **2** m clinician

clip m inv clip

clonare <1a> BIO clone

cloro m chlorine

clorofilla f chlorophyl(l)

cloroformio m chloroform

club m inv club

cm abbr (= **centimetro**) cm (= centimetre)

c.m. abbr (= **corrente mese**) of this month, inst.

CNR abbr (= **Consiglio Nazionale delle Ricerche**) Italian National Research Council

coabitare <1m> share a flat (*Am* an apartment), be flatmates (*Am* roommates)

coagularsi <1m> *di sangue* coagulate, clot; *di latte* curdle

coalizione f coalition; **governo** m **di ~** coalition government

coalizzarsi <1a> join forces; POL form a coalition

cobra m inv cobra

cocaina f cocaine

cocainomane 1 agg addicted to cocaine **2** m/f cocaine addict

coccinella f ladybird, *Am* ladybug

coccio m (*pl* -cci) earthenware; *frammento* fragment (of pottery), shard

cocciuto stubborn, obstinate

cocco 1 m (*pl* -cchi) (*albero*) coconut palm *or* tree; **noce** f **di ~** coconut **2** m, **-a** f (*persona prediletta*) darling

coccodrillo m crocodile

coccolare <1l & c> F cuddle; (*viziare*) spoil

cocente scorching; fig scathing

cocktail m inv bevanda cocktail; *festa* cocktail party

cocomero m water melon

coda f tail; (*fila*) queue, *Am* line; *di veicolo, treno* rear; MUS coda; ~ **di paglia** guilty conscience; ~ **dell'occhio** corner of the eye; *piano* m **a ~** grand piano; **fare la ~** queue (up), *Am* stand in line

codardo 1 agg cowardly **2** m, **-a** f coward

codazzo m swarm

codesto 1 *agg* that **2** *pron* that one

codice *m* code; **~ a barre** bar code; **~
civile** civil code; **~ di avviamento
postale** post code, *Am* zip code; **~
fiscale** tax code; **~ stradale** Highway Code

codificare <1m & d> *dati* encode;
DIR codify

codino *m* pigtail, plait

coefficiente *m* coefficient

coerente coherent; *fig* consistent

coerenza *f* coherence; *fig* consistency

coesione *f* cohesion

coesistenza *f* coexistence

coetaneo 1 *agg* the same age (**di** as)
2 *m*, **-a** *f* contemporary, person of
the same age

cofanetto *m* casket

cofano *m* AUTO bonnet, *Am* hood

cogestione *f* joint management; **~
aziendale** worker participation

cogliere <3ss> pick; (*raccogliere*)
gather; (*afferrare*) seize; *occasione*
take, seize, jump at; (*capire*) grasp; **~
di sorpresa** catch unawares, take
by surprise; **~ sul fatto** catch in the
act, catch red-handed

cognac *m inv* cognac

cognato *m*, **-a** *f* brother-in-law;
donna sister-in-law

cognizione *f* knowledge; FIL cognition; *parla con ~ di causa* he knows
what he's talking about

cognome *m* surname; *nome m e ~*
full name

coi *prp* **con** and *art* **i**

coincidenza *f* coincidence; FERR
connection; *perdere la ~* miss one's
connection

coincidere <3q> coincide

coinquilino *m*, **-a** *f in condominio* fellow tenant; *in appartamento*
flatmate; *Am* roommate

coinvolgere <3d> involve (**in** in)

coinvolto *pp* → *coinvolgere*

col *prp* **con** and *art* **il**

colabrodo *m inv* strainer

colapasta *m inv* colander

colare <1a> **1** *v/t* strain; *pasta* drain
2 *v/i* drip; (*perdere*) leak; *di naso*

run; *di cera* melt; **~ a fondo** *o* **a pico**
sink, go down

colata *f di metallo* casting; *di lava*
flow

colazione *f prima* breakfast; *di mezzogiorno* lunch; **~ al sacco** picnic;
far ~ have breakfast, breakfast

colei *pron f* the one; **~ che** the one
that

colera *m* cholera

colesterolo *m* cholesterol

colica *f* (*pl* -che) colic

colino *m* strainer

colla *f* glue; *di farina* paste

collaborare <1m> co-operate, collaborate; *con giornale* contribute

collaboratore *m*, **-trice** *f* collaborator; *di giornale* contributor; **~atore**
m esterno freelance(r); **-trice** *f*
domestica home help

collaborazione *f* co-operation, collaboration

collana *f* necklace; *di libri* series

collant *m inv* tights *pl*, *Am* pantyhose

collare *m* collar

collasso *m* collapse; **~ cardiaco**
heart failure

collaudare <1a> test; *fig* put to the
test

collaudo *m* test

colle *m* hill; (*valico*) pass

collega *m/f* (*mpl* -ghi) colleague,
co-worker

collegamento *m* connection; MIL liaison; RAD, TV link; **~ aereo** /
ferroviario connecting flight / train

collegare <1a> connect, link

collegarsi RAD, TV link up

collegiale 1 *agg* collective **2** *m/f*
boarder

collegio *m* (*pl* -gi) boarding school;
~ elettorale constituency

collera *f* anger; *andare in ~* get angry; *essere in ~ con qu* be angry
with s.o.

collerico (*pl* -ci) irascible

colletta *f* collection

collettività *f* community

collettivo *m/agg* collective

colletto *m* collar

collezionare <1a> collect

comandante

collezione f collection; **fare ~ di qc** collect sth, make a collection of sth

collezionista m/f collector; **~ di francobolli** stamp collector

collina f hill

collinoso hilly

collirio m eyewash

collisione f collision; **entrare in ~** collide

collo m neck; (bagaglio) piece or item of luggage; (pacco) package; **~ del piede** instep

collocamento m placing; (impiego) employment; **agenzia f di ~** employment agency; **ufficio m di ~** Jobcentre

collocare <1l & d> place, put; **~ a riposo** retire

collocazione f place, job

colloquiale colloquial

colloquio m (pl -qui) talk, conversation; ufficiale interview; (esame) oral (exam)

colluttazione f scuffle

colmare <1a> fill (di of); fig di gentilezze overwhelm (di with); **~ un vuoto** bridge a gap

colmo 1 agg full (di of) **2** m summit, top; fig (culmine) height; **è il ~!** that's the last straw!

colomba f ZO, fig dove

colombo m pigeon

colon m colon

Colonia f: **acqua f di ~** eau de Cologne

colonia f colony; per bambini holiday camp; **~ marina** seaside holiday camp

coloniale colonial

colonico (pl -ci): **casa f -a** farmhouse

colonizzare <1a> colonize

colonna f column; di veicoli line; fig mainstay; **~ sonora** sound track; **~ vertebrale** spinal column

colonnato m colonnade

colonnello m colonel

colonnina f della benzina petrol (Am gas) pump

colorante m dye; **senza -i** with no artificial colo(u)rings

colorare <1a> colo(u)r; disegno colo(u)r in

colorato colo(u)red

colorazione f colo(u)ring

colore m colo(u)r; carte suit; poker flush; **gente f di ~** colo(u)red people; **scatola f dei -i** paint box; **~ a olio** oil (paint); **a -i** film, televisione colo(u)r attr; **farne di tutti i -i** get up to all sorts of mischief

colorito 1 agg volto rosy-cheeked; fig (vivace) colo(u)rful **2** m complexion

coloro pron pl the ones; **~ che** those who

colossale colossal

colosso m colossus

colpa f fault; REL sin; **dare a qu la ~ di qc** blame s.o. for sth; **non è ~ sua** it's not her fault; **per ~ tua** because of you; **senso m di ~** sense of guilt; **sentirsi in ~** feel guilty

colpevole 1 agg guilty **2** m/f culprit, guilty party

colpire <4d> hit, strike; fig impress, leave an impression on; **~ nel segno** hit the nail on the head

colpo m blow; (fig) blow, shock; di pistola shot; MED stroke; **~ apoplettico** apoplectic fit; **~ di calore** heat stroke; **~ di sole** sunstroke; **~ di stato** coup d'état; **~ di telefono** phone call; **~ di testa** whim; **fare ~** make an impact; **sul ~, di ~** suddenly

coltellata f ferita stab wound

coltello m knife

coltivare <1a> AGR, fig cultivate

coltivatore m farmer

coltivazione f cultivation; di prodotti agricoli e piante growing; **campi coltivati** crops

colto¹ agg cultured, learned

colto² pp → **cogliere**

coltura f growing; piante crop

colui pron m the one; **~ che** the one that

coma m coma

comandamento m commandment

comandante m commander; AVIA, MAR captain

comandare <1a> **1** v/t (*ordinare*) order, command; *esercito* command; *nave* captain, be captain of; FIN *merci* order; TEC control; ~ **a distanza** operate by remote control **2** v/i be in charge

comando m order, command; TEC control; ~ **a distanza** remote control

combaciare <1f> fit together; *fig* correspond

combattente m soldier, serviceman

combattere <3a> v/t & v/i fight

combattimento m fight; SP match, fight

combinare <1a> combine; (*organizzare*) arrange; ~ **un guaio** make a mess; **oggi ho combinato poco** I got very little done today

combinarsi go well together

combinazione f combination; (*coincidenza*) coincidence; **per** ~ by chance

combustibile **1** agg combustible **2** m fuel

combustione f combustion

come **1** avv as; (*in modo simile o uguale*) like; *interrogativo, esclamativo* how; (*prego?*) pardon?; **fa' ~ ti ho detto** do as I told you; **lavora ~ insegnante** he works as a teacher; ~ **me** like me; **un cappello ~ il mio** a hat like mine; ~ **sta?** how are you?, how are things?; **com'è bello!** how nice it is!; ~ **mai?** how come?, why?; **oggi ~ oggi** nowadays; ~ **se** as if **2** cong (*come se*) as if, as though; (*appena, quando*) as (soon as); ~ **se niente fosse** as if nothing had happened

cometa f comet

comfort m inv comfort; **dotato di tutti i ~ moderni** with all mod cons

comicità f funniness

comico (*pl* -ci) **1** agg funny, comical; *genere* comic **2** m, **-a** f comedian; *donna* comedienne

comignolo m chimney pot

cominciare <1f> start, begin (**a** to); **a ~ da oggi** (starting) from today; **tanto per** ~ to begin or start with

comitato m committee; ~ **direttivo** steering committee

comitiva f group, party

comizio m meeting

Comm. abbr (= **Commendatore**) *Italian title awarded for services to the country*

commando m commando

commedia f comedy; *fig* play-acting

commediografo m, **-a** f playwright

commemorare <1m & b> commemorate

commemorazione f commemoration

commentare <1a> comment on

commentatore m, **-trice** f commentator

commento m comment

commerciale commercial; *relazioni, trattative* trade attr; *lettera* business attr

commercialista m/f accountant

commercializzare <1a> market

commerciante m/f merchant; (*negoziante*) shopkeeper

commerciare <1b & f> deal (**in** in)

commercio m (*pl* -ci) trade, business; *internazionale* trade; *di droga* traffic; ~ **all'ingrosso** wholesale trade; ~ **al minuto** retail trade; **camera** f **di** ~ chamber of commerce; **essere in** ~ be available; **mettere in** ~ **qc** put sth on the market

commessa f (*ordinazione*) order

commesso m, **-a** f shop assistant, Am sales clerk; (*impiegato*) clerk; ~ **viaggiatore** travel(l)ing salesman

commestibile **1** agg edible **2** -i mpl foodstuffs

commettere <3ee> commit; *errore* make

commiserare <1m> feel sorry for

commissariato m: ~ (**di pubblica sicurezza**) police station

commissario m (*pl* -ri) di polizia (police) superintendent; *membro di commissione* commissioner

commissionare <1a> FIN commission

commissione f commission; (*incarico*) errand; **Commissione europea** European Commission; **-i** pl shopping sg; **fatto su ~** made to order

commosso 1 pp → **commuovere 2** agg fig moved, touched

commovente moving, touching

commozione f emotion; **~ cerebrale** concussion

commuovere <3ff> move, touch

commuoversi be moved or touched

comò m inv chest of drawers

comodino m bedside table

comodità f inv comfort; (*vantaggio*) convenience

comodo 1 agg comfortable; *vestito* loose, comfortable; (*facilmente raggiungibile*) easy to get to; (*utile*) useful, handy; F *persona* laid back F; **stia ~!** don't get up! **2** m comfort; **con ~** at one's convenience; **far ~ di denaro** come in useful, be handy; **le fa ~ così** she finds it easier that way; **fare il propio ~** do as one pleases

compagnia f company; (*gruppo*) group; REL order; **~ aerea** airline; **~ di assicurazioni** insurance company; **far ~ a qu** keep s.o. company

compagno m, **-a** f companion; (*convivente*), FIN partner; POL comrade; **~ di scuola** schoolfriend, schoolmate; **~ di squadra** team mate; **~ di viaggio** travelling companion

comparativo m/agg comparative

comparire <4e> appear; (*essere pubblicato*) come out, appear; (*far figura*) stand out

comparizione f: DIR **mandato** m **di ~** summons

comparsa f appearance; TEA person with a walk-on part; *in film* extra

comparso pp → **comparire**

compartimento m compartment

compassione f compassion, pity; **provare ~ per qu** feel sorry for s.o.

compasso m (pair of) compasses

compatibile compatible

compatire <4d>: **~ qu** feel sorry for s.o.

compatriota m/f (mpl -i) compatriot

compatto compact; *folla* dense; fig united

compensare <1b> (*controbilanciare*) compensate for, make up for; (*ricompensare*) reward; (*risarcire*) pay compensation to

compenso m (*ricompensa, risarcimento*) compensation; (*retribuzione*) fee; **in ~** (*d'altra parte*) on the other hand; **dietro ~** for a fee

compera f purchase; **fare le -e** go shopping

competente competent; (*responsabile*) appropriate

competenza f (*esperienza*) competence; **essere di ~ di qu** be s.o.'s responsibility

competere <3a> (*gareggiare*) compete

competitività f competitiveness

competitivo competitive

competizione f competition

compiacente too eager to please

compiacenza f overeagerness to please

compiacere <2k> please

compiacersi (*provare piacere*) be pleased (**di** with); **mi compiaccio con te** congratulations

compiaciuto pp → **compiacere**

compiangere <3d> pity; *per lutto* mourn

compianto pp → **compiangere**

compiere <4g> (*finire*) complete, finish; (*eseguire*) carry out; **~ gli anni** have one's birthday

compiersi (*avverarsi*) happen

compilare <1a> compile; *modulo* complete, fill in

compilatore m INFOR compiler

compilazione f compilation

compimento m completion

compito[1] agg polite

compito[2] m task; EDU **i -i** pl homework sg

compiuto *lavoro, opera* completed, finished; **ha 10 anni -i** he's 10

compleanno m birthday; **buon ~!** happy birthday!

complementare complementary

complemento m complement;

GRAM object

complessato full of complexes

complessivo all-in

complesso 1 agg complex, complicated 2 m complex; MUS group; di circostanze set, combination; in o nel ~ on the whole

completamento m completion

completare <1b> complete

completo 1 agg complete; (pieno) full; TEA sold out 2 m set; (vestito) suit; al ~ (pieno) full (up); TEA sold out

complicare <1l & d> complicate

complicarsi get complicated

complicato complicated, complex

complicazione f complication

complice m/f DIR accomplice

complimentarsi: ~ con qu congratulate s.o. (per on)

complimento m compliment; fare un ~ a qu pay s.o. a compliment; -i! congratulations!; non fare -i! help yourself!

componente 1 m component 2 m/f (persona) member

componibile modular; cucina fitted

componimento m composition; DIR settlement

comporre <3ll> (mettere in ordine) arrange; MUS compose; TELEC ~ un numero dial a number

comporsi: ~ di consist of, be made up of

comportamento m behavio(u)r

comportare <1c> involve

comportarsi behave

compositore m, -trice f composer

composizione f composition; di fiori arrangement; DIR settlement

composta f stewed fruit; (terricciato) compost

composto 1 pp → comporre 2 agg compound; abiti, capelli tidy, neat; ~ da made up of; stai ~ keep still; seduto sit properly 3 m compound

comprare <1a> buy, purchase; (corrompere) bribe, buy off

compratore m, -trice f buyer, purchaser

compravendita f buying and selling

comprendere <3c> (includere) comprise, include; (capire) understand

comprensibile understandable

comprensione f understanding

comprensivo (tollerante) understanding; ~ di inclusive of

compreso 1 pp → comprendere 2 agg inclusive; (capito) understood; tutto ~ all in; ~ te including you

compressa f (pastiglia) tablet; di garza compress

compresso pp → comprimere

comprimere <3r> press; (reprimere) repress; FIS compress

compromesso 1 pp → compromettere 2 m compromise; DIR ~ di vendita agreement to sell

compromettere <3ee> compromise

compromettersi compromise o.s.

computer m inv computer; assistito dal ~ computer-assisted; ~ portatile portable (computer), laptop

computerizzare <1a> computerize

computisteria f book-keeping, accountancy

comunale del comune municipal, town attr; consiglio m ~ town council; palazzo m ~ town hall

comune 1 agg common; amico mutual; (ordinario) ordinary, common; in ~ in common; non ~ unusual, uncommon; fuori del ~ out of the ordinary 2 m municipality; palazzo m del ~ town hall

comunemente commonly

comunicare <1m & d> 1 v/t notizia pass on, communicate; contagio pass on; REL give Communion to 2 v/i (esprimersi) communicate; di persone keep in touch, communicate

comunicato m announcement, communiqué; ~ stampa press release

comunicazione f communication; (annuncio) announcement; TELEC (collegamento) connection; dare ~ di qc a qu tell s.o. about sth; TELEC la ~ si è interrotta I've been cut off; TELEC ~ internazionale international call

comunione *f* REL communion; *di idee* sharing

comunismo *m* Communism

comunista *m/f* (*mpl* -i) Communist

comunità *f* community; **Comunità europea** European Community

comunitario community *attr*; *dell'UE* Community *attr*

comunque 1 *cong* however, no matter how; **~ vadano le cose** whatever happens **2** *avv* (*in ogni modo*) in any case, anyhow; (*in qualche modo*) somehow; (*tuttavia*) however

con with; (*mezzo*) by; **~ questo tempo** in this weather; **~ tutto ciò** for all that; **avere ~ sé** have with *or* on one

conato *m*: **~ di vomito** retching

concedere <3l> grant; *premio* award; **ti concedo che** I admit that

concedersi: **~ qc** treat o.s. to sth

concentramento *m* concentration

concentrare <1b>, **concentrarsi** concentrate

concentrazione *f* concentration

concentrico (*pl* -ci) concentric

concepibile conceivable

concepimento *m* conception

concepire <4d> conceive; (*ideare*) devise, conceive

concernere <3a> concern; **per quanto mi concerne** as far as I'm concerned

concerto *m* concert; *composizione* concerto

concessionario *m* (*pl* -ri) agent; **~ esclusivo** sole agent

concessione *f* concession

concesso *pp* → **concedere**

concetto *m* concept; (*giudizio*) opinion

concezione *f* conception; *fig* idea (*di* for)

conchiglia *f* shell

conciare <1f> *pelle* tan; (*sistemare*) arrange; **come ti sei conciato!** what a state *or* mess you're in!; **~ qu per le feste** tan s.o.'s hide, give s.o. a good hiding

conciliare <1k> reconcile; *multa* pay, settle; **~ il sonno** be conducive to sleep

conciliazione *f* reconciliation; DIR settlement

concimare <1a> *pianta* feed

concime *m* manure; **~ chimico** chemical fertilizer

conciso concise

concitato excited

concittadino *m*, **-a** *f* fellow citizen

concludere <3q> conclude; (*portare a termine*) achieve, carry off; **~ un affare** clinch a deal; **non ho concluso nulla** I got nowhere

concludersi end, close

conclusione *f* conclusion; **in ~** in short

conclusivo conclusive

concluso *pp* → **concludere**

concordanza *f* agreement

concordare <1c> **1** *v/t* agree (on); GRAM make agree **2** *v/i* (*essere d'accordo*) agree; (*coincidere*) tally

concordato 1 *agg* agreed on **2** *m* agreement; REL concordat; DIR settlement

concorde *agg* in agreement; (*unanime*) unanimous; (*simultaneo*) simultaneous

concordia *f* harmony

concorrente 1 *agg* (*rivale*) competing, rival **2** *m/f in una gara, gioco* competitor, contestant; FIN competitor

concorrenza *f* competition

concorrenziale competitive

concorrere <3o> (*contribuire*) concur; (*competere*) compete (**a** for); *di strade* converge; **~ per un posto** compete for a position

concorso 1 *pp* → **concorrere 2** *m* (*competizione*) competition, contest; **bandire un ~** announce a competition

concreto concrete; (*pratico*) practical

condanna *f* DIR sentence

condannare <1a> condemn (**a** to); DIR sentence (**a** to)

condensare <1b>, **condensarsi** condense

condensazione *f* condensation

condimento *m* seasoning; *di*

insalata dressing
condire <4d> season; *insalata* dress; *fig* spice up
condito seasoned
condividere <3q> share
condiviso *pp* → **condividere**
condizionale **1** *m/agg* conditional **2** *f* suspended sentence
condizionamento *m* PSI conditioning; ~ *dell'aria* air conditioning
condizionare <1a> PSI condition
condizionato: *con aria -a* with air conditioning, air-conditioned
condizionatore *m* air conditioner
condizione *f* condition; *-i pl di lavoro* working conditions; *a ~ che* on condition that
condoglianze *fpl* condolences; *fare le ~ a qu* express one's condolences to s.o.
condominio *m* (*comproprietà*) joint ownership; *edificio* block of flats, *Am* condo
condomino *m* owner-occupier, *Am* condo owner
condonare <1a> remit
condono *m* remission; ~ *fiscale* conditional amnesty for tax evaders
condotta *f* (*comportamento*) behavio(u)r, conduct; (*canale*) piping
condotto **1** *pp* → **condurre 2** *m* pipe; ANAT duct
conducente *m/f* driver; ~ *di autobus* bus driver
condurre <3e> lead; (*accompagnare*) take; *veicolo* drive; *azienda* run; *acque, gas* carry, take
conduttore *m*, -trice *f* RAD, TV presenter; FERR (*controllore*) conductor
conduttura *f* (*condotto*) pipe
confederazione *f* confederation
conferenza *f* conference; ~ *al vertice* summit (conference); ~ *stampa* press conference
conferimento *m* conferring
conferire <4d> **1** *v/t* (*dare*) confer; *premio* award **2** *v/i*: ~ *con qu* confer with s.o.
conferma *f* confirmation
confermare <1a> confirm

confessare <1b>, **confessarsi** confess
confessione *f* confession
confessore *m* confessor
confetto *m* GASTR sugared almond; MED pill
confettura *f* jam
confezionare <1a> *merce* wrap, package; *abiti* make
confezione *f* wrapping, packaging; *di abiti* making; ~ *regalo* gift wrap; *-i pl* garments
conficcare <1d> hammer, drive
confidare <1a> **1** *v/t* confide **2** *v/i*: ~ *in* trust in, rely on
confidarsi: ~ *con* confide in
confidenza *f* (*familiarità*) familiarity; (*fiducia*) confidence, trust; *avere ~ con qu* be familiar with s.o.; *prendere ~ con qc* familiarize o.s. with sth
confidenziale (*riservato*) confidential; *strettamente ~* strictly confidential
configurare <1a> configure
configurazione *f* configuration
confinante neighbo(u)ring
confinare <1a> border (*con* sth); *fig* confine
confine *m* border; *fra terreni*, *fig* boundary
confisca *f* (*pl* -che) seizure
confiscare <1d> confiscate
conflitto *m* conflict
confluire <4d> merge
confondere <3bb> confuse, mix up; (*imbarazzare*) embarrass
confondersi get mixed up
conformare <1a> (*rendere adatto*) adapt
conformarsi: ~ *a* conform to; (*adattarsi*) adapt to
conforme (*simile*) similar; ~ *a* in accordance with; *copia f ~* (certified) true copy
conformismo *m* conformity
conformista *m/f* (*mpl* -i) conformist
conformità *f* conformity; *in ~ a* in accordance with
confortare <1c> comfort
confortevole comfortable

conforto *m* comfort

confrontare <1a> compare

confronto *m* confrontation; (*comparazione*) comparison; **a ~ di**, **in ~ a** compared with; **maleducato nei -i di qu** rude to s.o.

confusione *f* confusion; (*disordine*) muddle, mess; (*baccano*) noise, racket; (*imbarazzo*) embarrassment

confuso **1** *pp* → **confondere** **2** *agg* (*non chiaro*) confused, muddled; (*imbarazzato*) embarrassed

congedare <1b> dismiss; MIL discharge

congedarsi take leave (**da** of)

congedo *m* (*permesso*) leave; MIL *assoluto* discharge

congelare <1b> **1** *v/t* freeze **2** *v/i e* **congelarsi** freeze

congelato frozen

congelatore *m* freezer

congenito congenital

congestionare <1a> congest

congestionato congested; *volto* flushed

congestione *f* congestion

congettura *f* conjecture

congiungere <3d> join

congiungersi join (up)

congiuntivite *f* conjunctivitis

congiuntivo *m* GRAM subjunctive

congiunto **1** *pp* → **congiungere** **2** *m*, **-a** *f* relative, relation

congiuntura *f* ANAT joint; **~ economica** economic situation

congiunzione *f* GRAM conjunction

congiura *f* conspiracy, plot

congratularsi <1m>: **~ con qu** congratulate (**per** on)

congratulazioni *fpl*: **fare le propie ~ a qu** congratulate s.o.; **-i!** congratulations!

congressista *m/f* (*mpl* -i) convention participant

congresso *m* convention

conguaglio *m* (*pl* -gli) balance

CONI *abbr* (= **Comitato Olimpico Nazionale Italiano**) Italian Olympic Committee

coniare <1k & c> mint; *fig* coin

conifere *fpl* conifers

coniglio *m* (*pl* -gli) rabbit

coniugare <1l, c & e> conjugate

coniugato married

coniugazione *f* conjugation

coniuge *m/f* spouse; **-i** *pl* husband and wife; **i -i Rossi** Mr and Mrs Rossi

connazionale *m/f* compatriot

connessione *f* connection

connotati *mpl* features

cono *m* cone; **~ gelato** ice-cream cone

conoscente *m/f* acquaintance

conoscenza *f* knowledge; *persona* acquaintance; (*sensi*) consciousness; **per ~ cc**; **fare la ~ di qu** make s.o.'s acquaintance, meet s.o.; **perdere ~** lose consciousness, faint

conoscere <3n> know; (*fare la conoscenza di*) meet; **~ qu di vista** know s.o. by sight

conoscitore *m*, **-trice** *f* connoisseur

conosciuto well-known, famous

conquista *f* conquest

conquistare <1a> conquer; *fig* win

consacrare <1a> consecrate; *sacerdote* ordain; (*dedicare*) dedicate

consacrarsi devote o.s. (**a** to)

consacrazione *f* consecration; *di sacerdote* ordination

consanguineo *m*, **-a** *f* blood relative

consapevole: **~ di** conscious of, aware of

consapevolezza *f* consciousness, awareness

conscio conscious, aware

consecutivo (*di seguito*) consecutive; **tre giorni -i** three consecutive days, three days in a row

consegna *f di lavoro, documento* handing in; *di prigionero, ostaggio* handover; **~ a domicilio** home delivery; **~ bagagli** left luggage, *Am* baggage checkroom

consegnare <1a> *lavoro, documento* hand in; *prigionero, ostaggio* hand over; *merci, posta* deliver

conseguente consequent

conseguenza *f* consequence; **di ~** consequently; **in ~ di qc** as a result of sth

conseguire <4a> **1** v/t achieve; *laurea* obtain **2** v/i follow

consenso m (*permesso*) consent, permission

consentire <4b> **1** v/i (*accondiscendere*) consent **2** v/t allow

conserva f preserve; **~ di pomodoro** tomato purée; **~ di frutta** jam

conservante m preservative

conservare <1b> keep; GASTR preserve

conservarsi keep; *in salute* keep well

conservatore m, **-trice** f conservative

conservatorio m (*pl* -ri) music school, conservatoire

conservazione f preservation

considerare <1m> consider

considerazione f consideration; (*osservazione*) remark, comment; **prendere in ~** take into consideration

considerevole considerable

consigliare <1g> advise; (*raccomandare*) recommend

consigliarsi ask for advice

consigliere m adviser; **~ municipale** town council(l)or

consiglio m (*pl* -gli) piece of advice; (*organo amministrativo*) council; **~ d'amministrazione** board (of directors); **Consiglio d'Europa** Council of Europe; **~ dei ministri** Cabinet

consistente substantial; (*denso*) thick

consistenza f (*densità*) consistency, thickness; *di materiale* texture; *di argomento* basis

consistere <3f> consist (*in, di* of)

consocio m (*pl* -ci), **-a** f associate

consolare[1] <1c> console, comfort

consolare[2] agg consular

consolarsi console o.s.

consolato m consulate; **~ generale** consulate general

consolazione f consolation

console[1] m *diplomatico* consul; **~ generale** consul general

console[2] f *mobile* console

consolidare <1m & c> consolidate

consolidarsi stabilize

consonante f consonant

consorte m/f spouse; **principe** m **~** prince consort

consorzio m (*pl* -zi) *di imprese* consortium

constatare <1l> ascertain, determine; (*notare*) note

constatazione f statement

consueto usual

consuetudine f habit, custom; (*usanza*) custom, tradition

consulente m/f consultant; **~ legale** legal adviser; **~ tributario** tax consultant

consulenza f consultancy; **~ aziendale** management consultancy

consultare <1a> consult

consultarsi: **~ con qu** consult s.o.

consultazione f consultation; **opera** f **di ~** reference book

consultorio m family planning clinic

consumare <1a> *acqua, gas* use, consume; (*logorare*) wear out; (*mangiare*) eat, consume; (*bere*) drink

consumarsi wear out

consumatore m, **-trice** f consumer

consumazione f food; (*bevanda*) drink

consumismo m consumerism

consumo m consumption; (*usura*) wear; **beni** mpl **di ~** consumer goods

consuntivo m FIN closing balance

contabile m/f book keeper

contabilità f FIN *disciplina* accounting; *ufficio* accounts department; **tenere la ~** keep the books

contachilometri m inv mileometer, clock F

contadino 1 agg rural, country attr **2** m, **-a** f peasant

contagiare <1f> infect

contagio m (*pl* -gi) infection; *per contatto diretto* contagion; (*epidemia*) outbreak

contagioso infectious

contagiri m inv rev(olution) counter

contagocce m inv dropper

container m inv container

contaminare <1m> contaminate, pollute

contaminazione f contamination, pollution

contante m cash; *in -i* cash

contare <1a> **1** v/t count **2** v/i count; *~ di fare qc* plan on doing sth

contascatti m inv time meter on phone

contatore m meter

contatto m contact

conte m count

contegno m behavio(u)r; (*atteggiamento*) restraint

contemplare <1b> contemplate; DIR provide for

contemplazione f contemplation

contemporaneamente at the same time

contemporaneo 1 agg contemporary (*di* with); *movimenti* simultaneous **2** m, *-a* f contemporary

contendere <3c> **1** v/t: *~ qc a qu* compete with s.o. for sth **2** v/i (*competere*) contend

contendersi contend for, compete for

contenere <2q> contain, hold; (*reprimere*) repress; (*limitare*) limit

contenersi contain o.s.

contenitore m container

contentare <1b> please

contentarsi be content (*di* with)

contentezza f happiness

contento pleased (*di* with); (*lieto*) glad, happy

contenuto m contents pl

contesa f dispute

conteso pp → **contendere**

contessa f countess

contestare <1b> protest; DIR serve

contestatore m, *-trice* f protester

contestazione f protest

contesto m context

contiene → **contenere**

contiguo adjacent (*a* to)

continentale continental

continente m continent

continuare <1m> **1** v/t continue, carry on (*a fare* doing) **2** v/i continue

continuazione f continuation; *di film* sequel; *in ~* over and over again; (*ininterrottamente*) non stop

continuità f continuity

continuo (*ininterrotto*) continuous; (*molto frequente*) continual; *di ~* (*ininterrottamente*) continuously; (*molto spesso*) continually; EL *corrente f -a* direct current

conto m (*calcolo*) calculation; FIN account; *in ristorante* bill, Am check; *~ corrente* current account, Am checking account; *~ corrente postale* Post Office account; *~ profitti e perdite* profit and loss account; *~ vincolato* term deposit; *rendere di qc* account for sth; *rendersi ~ di qc* realize sth; *fare ~ su qu* count on s.o.; *tenere ~ di qc* take sth into account; *~ alla rovescia* countdown; *per ~ mio* (*secondo me*) in my opinion; (*da solo*) on my own; *sapere qc sul ~ di qu* know sth about s.o.; *in fin dei -i* when all's said and done, after all

contorcere <3d> twist

contorcersi: *~ dal dolore / dalle risate* roll about in pain / laughing

contorno m outline, contour; GASTR accompaniment

contorto twisted

contrabbandare <1a> smuggle

contrabbandiere m smuggler

contrabbando m contraband

contrabbasso m MUS double bass

contraccambiare <1k> return

contraccambio m (pl -bi) return

contraccettivo m contraceptive

contraccezione f contraception

contraccolpo m rebound; *di arma da fuoco* recoil

contraddire <3t> contradict

contraddizione f contradiction

contraffare <3aa> (*falsificare*) forge; (*imitare*) imitate

contraffatto forged; *voce* imitated

contraffazione f (*imitazione*) imitation; (*falsificazione*) forgery

contralto m MUS (contr)alto

contrappeso m counterbalance

contrapporre <3ll> set against

contrapporsi (*contrastare*) clash; *~ a* oppose

contrapposizione f opposition;

mettere in ~ contrast
contrapposto *pp* → **contrapporre**
contrariamente: ~ *a* contrary to
contrariare <1k> *piani* thwart, oppose; *persona* irritate, annoy
contrariato irritated, annoyed
contrarietà *fpl inv* difficulties, problems
contrario (*pl* -ri) **1** *agg* contrary; *direzione* opposite; *vento* adverse; *essere* ~ be against (*a* sth) **2** *m* contrary, opposite; *al* ~ on the contrary
contrarre <3xx> contract
contrarsi contract
contrassegnare <1a> mark
contrassegno *m* mark; FIN (*in*) ~ cash on delivery
contrastante contrasting
contrastare <1a> **1** *v/t* contrast; (*ostacolare*) hinder **2** *v/i* contrast (*con* with)
contrasto *m* contrast; (*litigio, discordia*) disagreement, dispute
contrattacco *m* (*pl* -cchi) counterattack
contrattare <1a> negotiate; *persona* hire
contrattempo *m* hitch
contratto[1] *pp* → **contrarre**
contratto[2] *m* contract; ~ *d'affitto* lease
contrattuale contractual
contravvenire <4p> contravene
contravvenzione *f* contravention; (*multa*) fine
contrazione *f* contraction; (*riduzione*) reduction
contribuente *m/f* taxpayer
contribuire <4d> contribute
contributo *m* contribution; *-i pl sociali* social security (*Am* welfare) contributions
contro against
controbattere <3a> (*replicare*) answer back; (*confutare*) rebut
controcorrente **1** *agg* non-conformist **2** *avv* against the current; *in fiume* upstream
controffensiva counter-offensive
controfigura *f in film* stand in
controfirmare <1a> countersign

controindicazione *f* MED contraindication
controllare <1c> control; (*verificare*) check
controllo *m* control; (*verifica*) check; MED check-up; ~ *alla frontiera* customs inspection; ~ *dei biglietti* ticket inspection; ~ (*dei*) *passaporti* passport control; ~ *della qualità* quality control
controllore *m* controller; *di bus, treno* ticket inspector; ~ *di volo* air-traffic controller
controluce *f*: *in* ~ against the light
contromano: *andare a* ~ be going the wrong way
contromarca *f* (*pl* -che) token
contromisura *f* countermeasure
controproducente counterproductive
controproposta *f* counter-proposal
contrordine *m* counterorder
controsenso *m* contradiction in terms; (*assurdità*) nonsense
controversia *f* controversy, dispute; DIR litigation
controverso controversial
controvoglia unwillingly
contusione *f* bruise
contuso bruised
convalescente **1** *agg* convalescent **2** *m/f* person who is convalescent
convalescenza *f* convalescence; *essere in* ~ be convalescing
convalidare <1m> validate
convegno *m* convention; *luogo* meeting place
convenevoli *mpl* pleasantries
conveniente (*vantaggioso*) good; (*opportuno*) appropriate
convenienza *f di prezzo, offerta* good value; *di gesto* appropriateness; *fare qc per* ~ do sth out of self-interest
convenire <4p> **1** *v/i* gather, meet; (*concordare*) agree; (*essere opportuno*) be advisable, be better **2** *v/t* (*stabilire*) stipulate
convento *m di monache* convent; *di monaci* monastery
convenuto *pp* → **convenire**

convenzionale conventional

convenzione f convention; (accordo) agreement, convention

convergere <3uu> converge

conversare <1b> talk, make conversation

conversazione f conversation

conversione f conversion; AUTO U-turn

convertibile convertible

convertibilità f convertibility

convertire <4b or d> convert

convertirsi be converted

convincere <3d> convince

convinto pp → **convincere**

convinzione f conviction

convivente m/f common-law husband; donna common-law wife

convivenza f living together, cohabitation

convivere <3zz> live together

convocare <1l, c & d> call, convene

convocazione f calling, convening

convoglio m (pl -gli) MIL, MAR convoy; FERR train

cooperare <1m & c> co-operate (a in); (contribuire) contribute (a to)

cooperativa f: (società f) ~ co-operative; ~ di consumo cooperative (store)

cooperativo cooperative

cooperazione f cooperation

coordinamento m co-ordination

coordinare <1m> co-ordinate

coordinata f MAT co-ordinate

coordinatore m, -trice f co-ordinator

coordinazione f co-ordination

coperchio m (pl -chi) lid, top

coperta f blanket; MAR deck; ~ **imbottita** quilt

copertina f cover

coperto 1 pp → **coprire** 2 agg covered (di with); cielo overcast, cloudy 3 m cover, shelter; piatti e posate place; prezzo cover charge; essere al ~ be under cover, be sheltered

copertone m AUTO tyre, Am tire

copertura f cover; ~ **delle spese** covering one's costs

copia f copy; FOT print, copy; in **duplice** ~ in duplicate

copiare <1k & c> copy

copione m per attore script

copioso copious, abundant

copisteria f copy centre (Am center)

coppa f cup; (calice) glass; ~ (**di**) **gelato** dish of ice-cream; AUTO ~ **dell'olio** oil sump

coppetta f di gelato tub

coppia f couple, pair; gara f a -e doubles

copricapo m inv head covering

copricostume m inv beachrobe

coprifuoco m curfew

copriletto m inv bedspread, coverlet

coprire <4f & c> cover; errore, suono cover up

coprirsi (vestirsi) put something on; (rannuvolarsi) become overcast

coproduzione f co-production, joint production

coraggio m courage; (sfacciataggine) nerve; farsi ~ be brave

coraggioso brave, courageous

corallo m coral

Corano m Koran

corazza f MIL armo(u)r; ZO shell

corazzata f battleship

corazzato MIL armo(u)red; fig hardened (contro to)

corda f cord; (fune) rope; (cordicella) string; MUS string; ~ **vocale** vocal cord; essere giù di ~ feel down or depressed; tenere qu sulla ~ keep s.o. in suspense or on tenterhooks; tagliare la ~ cut and run

cordame m MAR rigging

cordata f ALP rope, roped party

cordiale 1 agg cordial; -i saluti mpl kind regards 2 m cordial

cordialità f cordiality

cordoglio m (dolore) grief, sorrow; (condoglianze) condolences pl

cordone m cord; di marciapiedi kerb, Am curb; (sbarramento) cordon; ~ **ombelicale** umbilical cord

coreografia f choreography

coreografo m, -a f choreographer

coriandolo m BOT coriander; -i mpl confetti

coricare <1l, c & d> (adagiare) lay

down; (*mettere a letto*) put to bed

coricarsi lie down

cornacchia f crow

cornamusa f bagpipes *pl*

cornea f cornea

cornetta f MUS cornet

cornetto m (*brioche*) croissant; (*gelato*) cone, cornet

cornice f frame

cornicione m ARCHI cornice

corno m (*pl gen* le corna) horn; *ramificate* antlers; ~ **da scarpe** shoehorn; *fig* F **fare le -a a qu** cheat on s.o. F; **facciamo le -a!** touch wood!; **F non m'importa un ~** I don't give a damn F

cornuto F cheated, betrayed

coro m chorus; *cantori* choir; **in ~** (*insieme*) all together

corona f crown; (*rosario*) rosary; ~ **di fiori** wreath

coronaria f ANAT coronary artery

coronario: *vasi* mpl -**i** coronary arteries

corpetto m *da donna* bodice

corpo m body; MIL corps; ~ **celeste** heavenly body; ~ **diplomatico** diplomatic corps; ~ **di ballo** dancers *pl*; (**a**) ~ **a** ~ hand-to-hand

corporatura f build

corporazione f corporation

corpulento stout, corpulent

Corpus Domini m Corpus Christi

corredo m equipment; *da sposa* trousseau; *da neonato* layette

correggere <3cc> correct

correggersi correct o.s.

correlazione f correlation

corrente 1 agg current; *acqua* running; *lingua* fluent; **di uso** ~ in common use **2** m: **essere al** ~ know (*di* sth); **tenersi qu al** ~ keep s.o. up to date, keep s.o. informed **3** f current; *fig di opinione* trend; *fazione* faction; ~ **continua** direct current; ~ **d'aria** draught

correre <3o> **1** v/t run; ~ **il pericolo** run the risk **2** v/i run; (*affrettarsi*) hurry; *di veicolo* speed; *di tempo* fly; ~ **in aiuto di qu** rush to help s.o.; ~ **dietro a qu** run after s.o.; *lascia* ~!

let it go!, leave it!; **corre voce** it is rumo(u)red

correttezza f correctness; (*onestà*) honesty

corretto 1 pp → **correggere 2** agg correct

correzione f TIP correction

corrida f bullfight

corridoio m (*pl* -oi) corridor; *in aereo, teatro* aisle

corridore m *in auto* racing driver; *a piedi* runner

corriera f coach, bus

corriere m courier; ~ **della droga** drugs courier, mule P

corrispondente 1 agg corresponding **2** m/f correspondent; ~ **estero** foreign correspondent

corrispondenza f correspondence; (*posta*) post; **vendita** f **per** ~ mail order (shopping)

corrispondere <3hh> **1** v/t (*pagare*) pay; (*ricambiare*) reciprocate **2** v/i correspond; (*coincidere*) coincide; (*equivalere*) be equivalent

corrisposto 1 pp → **corrispondere 2** agg reciprocated

corrodere <3b>, **corrodersi** corrode, rust

corrompere <3rr> corrupt; *con denaro* bribe

corrosione f corrosion

corrosivo corrosive

corroso pp → **corrodere**

corrotto 1 pp → **corrompere 2** agg corrupt

corrugare <1e> wrinkle; ~ **la fronte** frown

corruzione f corruption; *con denaro* bribery

corsa f run; *attività* running; *di autobus* trip, journey; (*gara*) race; ~ **agli armamenti** arms race; ~ **a ostacoli** *ippica* steeplechase; *atletica* hurdles; **di** ~ at a run; *in fretta* in a rush; **vettura f da** ~ racing car; **fare una** ~ rush, dash; -**e** pl races

corsia f aisle; *di ospedale* ward; AUTO lane; ~ **di emergenza** emergency lane; ~ **di sorpasso** overtaking lane; **a tre -e** three-lane

77 costruttore

Corsica f Corsica

corsivo m italics pl

corso¹ 1 agg Corsican 2 m, -a f Corsican

corso² 1 pp → correre 2 m course; (strada) main street; FIN di moneta circulation; di titoli rate; ~ d'acqua watercourse; ~ di lingue language course; ~ dei cambi exchange rate, rate of exchange; ~ di chiusura closing rate; FIN fuori ~ out of circulation; TIP in ~ di stampa being printed; lavori mpl in ~ work in progress; si sposeranno nel ~ dell'anno they'll get married this year

corte f court; Corte di giustizia europea European Court of Justice

corteccia f (pl -cce) bark

corteggiare <1f> court

corteo m procession

cortese polite, courteous

cortesia f politeness, courtesy; per ~! please!

cortile m courtyard

cortina f curtain

corto short; tagliar ~ cut it short; essere a ~ di quattrini be short of money

cortocircuito m short (circuit)

cortometraggio m short

corvo m rook; ~ imperiale raven

cosa f thing; (che) ~ what; qualche ~ something; dimmi una ~ tell me something; una ~ da nulla a trifle; un'altra ~ another thing; -e pl da vedere sights; fra le altre -e among other things; tante belle -e! all the best!

coscia f (pl -sce) thigh; GASTR leg

cosciente conscious

coscienza f conscience; (consapevolezza) consciousness; agire secondo ~ listen to one's conscience; senza coscienza unscrupulous

coscienzioso conscientious

così so; (in questo modo) like this; ~ ~ so-so; e ~ via and so on; per ~ dire so to speak; proprio ~! exactly!; basta ~! that's enough!

cosicché and so

cosiddetto so called

cosiffatto such

cosmesi f cosmetics pl

cosmetico (pl -ci) 1 agg cosmetic 2 m cosmetic

cosmico (pl -ci) cosmic

cosmo m cosmos

cosmonauta m/f (pl -ti) cosmonaut

cosmopolita cosmopolitan

coso m F what-d'you-call-it F

cospargere <3uu> sprinkle; (coprire) cover (di with)

cosparso pp → cospargere

cospirare <1a> conspire

cospiratore m, -trice f conspirator

cospirazione f conspiracy

costa f coast, coastline; (pendio) hillside; ANAT rib; di libro spine

costante 1 agg constant, steady; MAT constant 2 f MAT constant

costanza f perseverance

costare <1c> cost; ~ caro be expensive, cost a lot; fig cost dearly; quanto costa? how much is it?

costata f rib steak; ~ di agnello lamb chop

costeggiare <1f> skirt, hug

costellazione f constellation

costiero coastal

costituire <4d> constitute; società form, create

costituirsi give o.s. up

costituzionale constitutional

costituzione f constitution

costo m cost; ~ della vita cost of living; prezzo m di ~ cost price; -i pl di produzione production costs; a ~ di perdere even if it means losing; ad ogni ~ at all costs

costola f rib; di libro spine

costoletta f GASTR cutlet

costoro pron pl they; complemento them

costoso expensive, costly

costretto pp → costringere

costringere <3d> force, compel

costrizione f constraint

costruire <4d> build, construct

costruttivo fig constructive

costruttore m, -trice f builder; (fab-

bricante) manufacturer

costruzione f building, construction; GRAM construction

costui *pron m* he; *complemento* him

costume *m* (*usanza*) custom; (*condotta*) morals *pl*; (*indumento*) costume; **~ da bagno** swimming costume, swimsuit; **da uomo** (swimming) trunks; **~ nazionale** national costume

cotechino *m* kind of pork sausage

cotenna f pigskin; *della pancetta* rind

cotoletta f cutlet; **~ alla milanese** breaded cutlet fried in butter

cotone *m* cotton; MED **~ idrofilo** cotton wool, *Am* absorbent cotton

cotta f F crush

cottimo *m*: **lavorare a ~** do piecework

cotto 1 *pp → cuocere* **2** *agg* done, cooked; F *fig* head over heels in love (**di** with)

cottura f cooking

coupon *m inv* coupon

covare <1a> **1** *v/t* sit on, hatch; *fig malattia* sicken for, come down with; *rancore* harbo(u)r **2** *v/i* sit on eggs

covo *m* den; (*nido*) nest; *fig* hideout

covone *m* sheaf

cozza f mussel

cozzare <1c>: **~ contro** crash into; *fig* clash with

C.P. *abbr* (= **Casella Postale**) PO Box (= Post Office Box)

crac *m inv fig* crash

crampo *m* cramp

cranio *m* (*pl* -ni) skull

crash *m* INFOR: **andare in ~** crash

cratere *m* crater

cravatta f tie; **~ a farfalla** bow-tie

crawl *m* SP crawl, freestyle

creare <1b> create; *fig* (*causare*) cause

creatività f creativity

creativo 1 *agg* creative **2** *m* copywriter

creato 1 *pp → creare* **2** *m* creation

creatore 1 *agg* creative **2** *m* Creator **3** *m*, **-trice** f creator

creatura f creature

creazione f creation

credente *m/f* believer

credenza[1] f belief

credenza[2] f mobile dresser

credenziali *fpl* credentials

credere <3a> **1** *v/t* believe; (*pensare*) believe, think; **lo credo bene!** I should think so too!; **credersi** believe *or* think o.s. to be **2** *v/i* believe; **~ a qu** believe s.o.; **~ in qu** believe in s.o.; **credo in Dio** I believe in God; **non ci credo** I don't believe it; **non credevo ai miei occhi** I couldn't believe my eyes

credibile credible

credibilità f credibility

credito *m* credit; *fig* trust; (*attendibilità*) reliability; **comprare a ~** buy on credit; **dare ~ a qc** believe sth; **fare ~ a qu** give s.o. credit

creditore *m*, **-trice** f creditor

credo *m inv* credo

crema f cream; *di latte e uova* custard; **~ da barba** shaving foam; **~ idratante** moisturizer, moisturizing cream; **~ solare** suntan lotion

cremare <1b> cremate

cremazione f cremation

cren *m* horseradish

crepa f crack

crepaccio *m* (*pl* -cci) cleft; *di ghiacciaio* crevasse

crepare <1b> (*spaccarsi*) crack; F (*morire*) kick the bucket; **~ dalle risa** split one's sides laughing

crêpe f inv pancake

crepitare <1l & b> crackle

crepuscolo *m* twilight

crescendo *m* MUS crescendo

crescente growing; *luna* waxing

crescere <3n> **1** *v/t* bring up, raise **2** *v/i* grow; (*aumentare*) grow, increase

crescione *m* watercress

crescita f growth; (*aumento*) growth, increase; **~ economica** economic growth

cresima f confirmation

cresimare <1l & b> confirm

crespo *capelli* frizzy

cresta f crest; *di montagna* peak

creta f clay

cretino F **1** *agg* stupid, idiotic **2** *m*, **-a** *f* idiot

CRI *abbr* (= *Croce Rossa Italiana*) Italian Red Cross

cric *m inv* AUTO jack

criminale 1 *agg* criminal **2** *m/f* criminal; **~ di guerra** war criminal

criminalità *f* crime

criminalizzare <1a> criminalize

crimine *m* crime

criniera *f* mane

cripta *f* crypt

crisantemo *m* chrysanthemum

crisi *f* crisis; MED fit; **~ energetica** energy crisis; **~ degli alloggi** housing shortage

cristallizzare, cristallizzarsi <1a> crystallize

cristallo *m* crystal; **bicchiere m di ~** crystal glass

cristianesimo *m* Christianity

cristianità *f* (*i cristiani*) Christendom

cristiano 1 *agg* Christian **2** *m*, **-a** *f* Christian

Cristo *m* Christ

criterio *m* (*pl* -ri) criterion; (*buon senso*) common sense

critica *f* (*pl* -che) criticism

criticare <1l & d> criticize

critico (*pl* -ci) **1** *agg* critical **2** *m*, **-a** *f* critic

croato 1 *agg* Croatian **2** *m*, **-a** *f* Croat, Croatian

Croazia *f* Croatia

croccante 1 *agg* crisp, crunchy **2** *m* GASTR nut brittle

crocchetta *f* GASTR potato croquette

croce *f* cross; **Croce Rossa** Red Cross; **farsi il segno della ~** cross o.s.; **a occhio e ~** at a rough guess

crocevia *m* crossroads *inv*

crociata *f* crusade

crociera *f* cruise; ARCHI crossing; **velocità f di ~** cruising speed

crocifiggere <3mm> crucify

crocifissione *f* crucifixion

crocifisso 1 *pp* → **crocifiggere 2** *m* crucifix

croco *m* BOT crocus

crollare <1c> collapse

crollo *m* collapse

cromare <1c> chromium-plate

cromatico (*pl* -ci) MUS chromatic

cromo *m* chrome

cronaca *f* (*pl* -che) chronicle; *di partita* commentary; **fatto di ~** news item; **~ nera** crime news; **essere al centro della ~** be front-page news

cronico (*pl* -ci) chronic

cronista *m/f* (*mpl* -i) reporter; *di partita* commentator

cronologia *f* chronology

cronologico (*pl* -ci) chronological

cronometrare <1a> time

cronometro *m* chronometer; SP stopwatch

crosta *f* crust; MED scab; *di formaggio* rind

crostacei *mpl* shellfish

crostata *f* GASTR tart

crostino *m* GASTR crouton

cruciale crucial

cruciverba *m* *inv* crossword (puzzle)

crudele cruel

crudeltà *f* cruelty

crudo raw

crumiro *m*, **-a** *f* scab

crusca *f* bran

cruscotto *m* dashboard; *scomparto* glove compartment

c.s. *abbr* (= *come sopra*) as above

CSI *abbr* (= *Comunità di Stati Indipendenti*) CIS (= Commonwealth of Independent States)

c.to *abbr* (= *conto*) acct (= account)

Cuba *f* Cuba

cubano 1 *agg* Cuban **2** *m*, **-a** *f* Cuban

cubetto *m* (small) cube; **~ di ghiaccio** ice cube

cubico (*pl* -ci) cubic

cubo 1 *agg* cubic **2** *m* cube

cuccagna *f*: (*paese m della*) **~** land of plenty

cuccetta *f* FERR couchette; MAR berth

cucchiaiata *f* spoonful

cucchiaino *m* teaspoon

cucchiaio *m* (*pl* -ai) spoon; **~ da**

tavola tablespoon

cuccia f (pl -cce) dog's basket; *esterna* kennel

cucciolo m cub; *di cane* puppy

cucina f kitchen; *cibi* food; ~ **casalinga** home cooking; ~ **gas** gas cooker or stove; **libro di** ~ cook book

cucinare <1a> cook

cucinino m kitchenette

cucire <4a> sew; **macchina** f **da** ~ sewing-machine

cucito 1 agg sewn **2** m sewing

cucitura f seam

cuculo m cuckoo

cuffia f da piscina swimming cap; RAD, TV headphones pl; ~ **da bagno** shower cap

cugino m, **-a** f cousin

cui persona who, whom fml; cose which; **la casa in** ~ **abitano** the house they live in, the house in which they live, the house where they live; **il** ~ **nome** whose name; **per** ~ so

culinario cookery attr, culinary; **arte** f **-a** culinary art, cookery

culla f cradle

cullare <1a> rock

culminante: **punto** m ~ climax

culminare <1l> culminate

culmine m peak

culo V m arse V, Am ass V

culto m cult; religione religion

cultura f culture; ~ **di massa** mass culture; ~ **generale** general knowledge

culturale cultural

culturismo m body-building

cumulativo cumulative; **biglietto** m ~ group ticket

cumulo m heap, pile

cuneo m wedge

cunetta f fondo stradale bump

cuocere <3p> cook; pane bake

cuoco m (pl -chi), **-a** f cook

cuoio m leather; ~ **capelluto** scalp; F

tirare le -a kick the bucket F

cuore m heart; carte **-i** pl hearts; **di** ~ wholeheartedly; **senza** ~ heartless; fig **nel** ~ **di** in the heart of; **nel** ~ **della notte** in the middle of the night; **stare a** ~ **a qu** be very important to s.o.

cupo gloomy; suono deep

cupola f dome

cura f care; MED treatment; ~ **dimagrante** diet; **avere** ~ **di qc** take care of sth; **casa** f **di** ~ nursing home

curabile curable

curare <1a> take care of; MED treat

curarsi look after o.s.; **non curarti di loro** don't care about them

curato m parish priest

curatore m, **-trice** f fiduciario trustee; di testo editor; ~ **fallimentare** official receiver

curia f curia

curiosare <1a> have a look around; spreg pry (**in** into)

curiosità f inv curiosity

curioso curious

cursore m INFOR cursor

curva f curve

curvare <1a> curve; schiena bend

curvarsi bend

curvatura f curve

curvo curved; persona bent

cuscinetto m TEC bearing; ~ **a sfere** ball bearing; POL **stato** m ~ buffer state

cuscino m cushion; (guanciale) pillow

custode m/f caretaker; **angelo** m ~ guardian angel

custodia f care; DIR custody; (astuccio) case

custodire <4d> (conservare) keep

CV abbr (= **Cavallo Vapore**) HP (= horsepower); (= **curriculum vitae**) CV (= curriculum vitae)

cyclette f exercise bike

D

da *prp stato in luogo* at; *moto da luogo* from; *moto a luogo* to; *tempo* since; *con verbo passivo* by; **viene ~ Roma** he comes from Rome; **sono ~ mio fratello** I'm at my brother's (place); **l'ho fatto ~ me** I did it myself; **ero ~ loro** I was at their place; **passo ~ Firenze** I'm going via Florence; **vado dal medico** I'm going to the doctor's; **~ ieri** since yesterday; **~ oggi in poi** from now on, starting from today; **~ bambino** as a child; **qualcosa ~ mangiare** something to eat; **francobollo ~ 1000 lire** 1000 lire stamp; **la donna –i capelli grigi** the woman with grey hair

dà → **dare**

daccapo → **capo**

dado *m* dice; GASTR stock cube; TEC nut

dagli *prp* **da** and *art* **gli**

dai[1] *prp* **da** and *art* **i**

dai[2] → **dare**

daino *m* deer; (*pelle*) buckskin

dal *prp* **da** and *art* **il**

dalia *f* dahlia

dall', dalla, dalle, dallo *prp* **da** and *art* **l', la, le, lo**

daltonico *agg* (*pl* -ci) colo(u)r-blind

dama *f* lady; *gioco* draughts, *Am* checkers

damasco *m* (*pl* -chi) damask

damigiana *f* demijohn

danaro *m* → **denaro**

danese 1 *m/agg* Danish **2** *m/f* Dane

Danimarca *f* Denmark

danneggiare <1f> (*rovinare*) damage; (*nuocere*) harm

danno *m* damage; (*a persona*) harm; **risarcire i –i a qu** compensate s.o. for the damage; **–i** *pl* **all'ambiente** environmental damage, damage to the environment

dannoso harmful

danza *f* dance; **~ classica** ballet

danzare <1a> *v/t & v/i* dance

dappertutto everywhere

dappoco *agg inv* (*inetto*) worthless; (*irrilevante*) minor, unimportant

dapprima at first

dare <1r> **1** *v/t* give; **~ qc a qu** give s.o. sth, give sth to s.o.; **~ uno sguardo a qc** have a look at sth; **dammi del tu** call me 'tu'; **mi dia del lei** address me as 'lei'; SP **~ il via** give the off; *fig* **~ il via a qc** get sth under way **2** *v/i di finestra* overlook (*su* sth); *di porta* lead into (*su* sth); *fig* **~ nell'occhio** attract attention, be noticed **3** *m* FIN debit; **~ e avere** debit and credit

darsi *v/r* give each other; (*dedicarsi*) devote o.s. (*a* to); **~ al commercio** go into business; **darsela a gambe** take to one's heels; **può ~** perhaps

darsena *f* dock

data *f* date; **~ di nascita** date of birth; **~ di scadenza** expiry date; **senza indicazione di ~** undated

datare <1a> **1** *v/t* date; *lettera* date, put the date on **2** *v/i:* **a ~ da oggi** from today

dato 1 *pp* → **dare 2** *agg* (*certo*) given, particular; (*dedito*) addicted (*a* to); **in -i casi** in certain cases; **~ che** given that **3** *m* piece of data; **-i** *pl* data; INFOR **elaborazione** *f* **dei data** data processing; **supporto** *m* **~** data medium

datore *m*, **-trice** *f*: **~ di lavoro** employer

dattero *m* date; (*albero*) date palm

dattilografare <1n> type

dattilografia *f* typing

dattilografo *m*, **-a** *f* typist

davanti 1 *prp:* **~ a** in front of **2** *avv* in front; (*dirimpetto*) opposite; **se mi stai ~** if you stand in front of me

3 *agg inv* front **4** *m* front
davanzale *m* window sill
davanzo more than enough
davvero really
dazio *m* (*pl* -zi) duty; (*posto*) customs; ~ *d'importazione* import duty; ~ *d'esportazione* export duty; *esente da* ~ duty-free
d.C. *abbr* (= *dopo Cristo*) AD (= *anno domini*)
dea *f* goddess
debito 1 *agg* due, proper **2** *m* debt; (*dovere*) duty; FIN ~ *pubblico* national debt; *avere un* ~ *con qu* be in debt to s.o.; *fig sentirsi in* ~ *verso qu* feel indebted to s.o.
debitore *m*, **-trice** *f* debtor; *essere* ~ *di qc a qu* owe s.o. sth, owe sth to s.o.
debole 1 *agg* weak; (*voce*) weak, faint; (*luce*) dim **2** *m* weakness; *avere un* ~ *per qu* have a soft spot for s.o.
debolezza *f* weakness
debuttante *m/f* beginner; *artista* performer at the start of his / her career
debuttare <1a> make one's début
debutto *m* début
decadente decadent
decadenza *f* decadence
decaffeinato decaffeinated, decaff F
decalcomania *f* transfer, *Am* decal
decano *m* dean
decappottabile *f/agg* AUTO convertible
decathlon *m* decathlon
decedere <3l>: *è deceduto ieri* he died yesterday
decelerare <1b & m> *v/t* & *v/i* slow down
decennio *m* (*pl* -ni) decade
decente *agg* decent
decentramento *m* decentralization
decentrare <1b> decentralize
decesso *m* death
decidere <3q> **1** *v/t questione* settle; *data* decide on, settle on; ~ *di fare qc* decide to do sth **2** *v/i* decide
decidersi decide (*a* to), make up one's mind (*a* to)
decifrare <1a> decipher
decimale *m/agg* decimal

decimetro *m* decimetre, *Am* -meter
decimo *m/agg* tenth
decina *f* MATH ten; *una* ~ about ten
decisione *f* decision; (*risolutezza*) decisiveness; *prendere una* ~ make a decision; ~ *della maggioranza* majority decision
decisivo decisive
deciso 1 *pp* → **decidere 2** *agg* (*definito*) definite; (*risoluto*) determined; (*netto*) clear; (*spiccato*) marked
declassare <1a> *oggetto* downgrade; *persona* demote
declinare <1a> **1** *v/t* decline; ~ *ogni responsabilità* disclaim all responsibility **2** *v/i* (*tramontare*) set; (*diminuire*) decline
declinazione *f* GRAM declension
declino *m fig* decline
decodificatore *m* decoder
decollare <1c> take off
decollo *m* take-off
decomporre <3ll> **1** *v/i* (*putrefarsi*) decompose **2** *v/t* CHIM break down
decomposizione *f* decomposition; CHIM breaking down
decompressione *f* decompression
decongestionare <1a> *strada*, MED relieve congestion in; ~ *il traffico* relieve traffic congestion
decorare <1b> decorate
decoratore *m*, **-trice** *f* decorator
decorazione *f* decoration
decoro *m* decorum
decoroso decorous
decorrenza *f*: *con immediata* ~ with immediate effect
decorrere <3o> *v/i* pass; *a* ~ *da oggi* with effect from today
decorso 1 *pp* → **decorrere 2** *m di malattia* course
decrepito decrepit
decrescere <3n> decrease, fall
decreto *m* decree; ~~*legge* *m* *decree passed in exceptional circumstances that has the force of law*
dedica *f* (*pl* -che) dedication
dedicare <1b & d> dedicate
dedicarsi dedicate o.s.
dedito dedicated (*a* to); *a un vizio* addicted (*a* to)

dedizione *f* dedication

dedurre <3e> deduce; FIN deduct; (*derivare*) derive

deduttivo deductive

deduzione *f* deduction

defalcare <1d> deduct

defalco *m* (*pl* -chi) deduction

defezione *f* defection

deficiente 1 *agg* (*mancante*) deficient, lacking (*di* in) 2 *m/f* backward person; *insulto* idiot, moron

deficienza *f* (*scarsezza*) deficiency, lack (*di* of)

deficit *m inv* deficit; ~ *del bilancio pubblico* budget deficit, public spending deficit

definire <4d> define; (*risolvere*) settle

definitivo definitive

definizione *f* definition; DIR settlement

deflettore *m* AUTO quarterlight

deflusso *m* ebb

deformare <1a> deform; *legno* warp; *metallo* buckle; *fig* distort

deformarsi *di legno* warp; *di metallo* buckle; *di scarpe* lose their shape

deformazione *f* deformation; *di legno* warping; *di metallo* buckling; *fisica* deformity; *fig*, OTT distortion

deforme deformed

defunto 1 *agg* dead; *fig* defunct 2 *m*, -a *f* DIR: *il* ~ the deceased

degenerare <1m & b> degenerate (*in* into)

degente *m/f* patient

degenza *f* stay (in bed / hospital)

degli *prp di* and *art* gli

degnare <1a> 1 *v/t*: ~ *qu di una parola* deign to speak to s.o. 2 *v/i e* degnarsi: ~ *di* deign to, condescend to

degno worthy; ~ *di nota* noteworthy; ~ *di un re* fit for a king

degradante degrading, demeaning

degradare <1a> degrade; *da un rango* demote

degradarsi demean o.s., lower o.s.; CHIM degrade; *di ambiente, edifici* deteriorate

degradazione *f* degradation

degrado *m* deterioration; ~ *ambientale* damage to the environment

degustazione *f* tasting; ~ *del vino* wine tasting

dei¹ *prp di* and *art i*

dei² (*pl di dio*): *gli* ~ *mpl* the Gods

del *prp di* and *art il*

delatore *m*, -trice *f* informer

delega *f* (*pl* -ghe) delegation; (*procura*) proxy

delegare <1b> delegate

delegato 1 *agg*: *amministratore m* ~ managing director 2 *m*, -a *f* delegate; ~ *sindacale* (trade) union delegate

delegazione *f* delegation

delfino *m* dolphin

deliberare <1m> 1 *v/t* decide 2 *v/i* DIR deliberate (*su* on)

delicatezza *f* delicacy; (*discrezione*) tact, delicacy; (*debolezza*) frailty, delicacy

delicato delicate; (*persona*) frail, delicate; (*colore*) soft

delimitare <1m> define

delineare <1m> outline

delinquente *m/f* criminal; *fig* scoundrel; ~ *minorile* juvenile delinquent

delinquenza *f* crime; ~ *minorile* juvenile delinquency; ~ *organizzata* organized crime

delirare <1a> be in raptures, rave; MED be delirious

delirio *m* (*pl* -ri) delirium; *fig* frenzy

delitto *m* crime; *corpo del* ~ corpus delicti

delizia *f* delight

delizioso delightful; *cibo* delicious

dell', della, delle, dello *prp di* and *art l'*, *la*, *le*, *lo*

delta *m* delta

deltaplanista *m/f* (*mpl* -ti) hang-glider

deltaplano *m* hang-glider; *attività* hang-gliding

deludere <3q> disappoint

delusione *f* disappointment

deluso disappointed

demagogo *m* (*pl* -ghi) demagog(ue)

demanio *m* State property

demente *m/f* MED person with dementia; F lunatic

demenza *f* MED dementia; F lunacy F, madness F

democratico (*pl* -ci) **1** *agg* democratic **2** *m*, **-a** *f* democrat

democrazia *f* democracy

democristiano *m/agg* Christian Democrat

demografia *f* demography

demografico demographic

demolire <4d> demolish (*anche fig*); *macchine* crush

demolizione *f* demolition; *di macchine* crushing

demone *m* spirit

demonio *m* (*pl* -ni) devil

demoralizzarsi <1a> become demoralized, lose heart

demotivato demotivated

denaro *m* money; ~ **contante** cash

denatalità *f* decline in the birth rate

denaturato CHIM: **alcol** *m* ~ methlyated spirits *pl*

denominare <1m & c> name, call

denominazione *f* name; ~ **di origine controllata** term signifying that a wine is of a certain origin and quality

denotare <1l & b or c> denote, be indicative of

densità *f* density; *della nebbia* thickness, density; ~ **della popolazione** population density

denso dense; *fumo, nebbia* thick, dense

dentario (*pl* -ri) dental

dentata *f* bite; *segno* toothmark

dente *m* tooth; ~ **del giudizio** wisdom tooth; ~ **di leone** dandelion; **mal** *m* **di -i** toothache; *fig* **stringere i -i** grit one's teeth; **parlare fra i -i** mumble; GASTR **al** ~ al dente, *still slightly firm*

dentice *m* fish native to the Mediterranean

dentiera *f* dentures

dentifricio *m* (*pl* -ci) toothpaste

dentista *m/f* (*mpl* -ti) dentist

dentro 1 *prp* in, inside; (*entro*) within; ~ **di sé** inwardly **2** *avv* in, inside; (*nell' intimo*) inwardly; **qui/lì** ~ in here / there; F **metter** ~ put inside *or* away

denuclearizzato nuclear-free, denuclearized

denuncia *f* (*pl* -ce) denunciation; *alla polizia, alla società di assicurazione* complaint, report; *di nascita, morte* registration; ~ **dei redditi** income tax return

denunciare <1f> denounce; *alla polizia, alla società di assicurazione* report; *nascita* register

denunzia → **denuncia**

denutrito undernourished

deodorante *m* deodorant

depilare <1a> *con pinzette* pluck; *con rasoio* shave; *con ceretta* wax

depilatorio (*pl* -ri) **1** *agg* depilatory **2** *m* hair-remover, depilatory

dépliant *m inv* leaflet; (*opuscolo*) brochure

deplorare <1c> deplore

deplorevole deplorable

deporre <3ll> **1** *v/t* put down; *uova* lay; *re, presidente* depose; ~ **il falso** commit perjury **2** *v/i* DIR testify, give evidence (**a favore di** for, **a carico di** against)

deportare <1c> deport

depositare <1m & c> deposit; (*posare*) put down, deposit; (*registrare*) register

depositato: marchio *m* ~ registered trademark

deposito *m* deposit; (*magazzino*) warehouse; MIL, *rimessa* depot; FERR ~ **bagagli** left-luggage office, *Am* baggage checkroom; ~ **di munizioni** ammunition dump; FIN ~ **vincolato** term deposit

deposizione *f* deposition; *da un'alta carica* removal; *di regnante*; overthrow

deposto *pp* → **deporre**

depravato *m*, **-a** *f* depraved person

depressione *f* depression; ~ **atmosferica** atmospheric depression; **zona** *f* **di** ~ **atmosferica** area of low pressure, low

depresso 1 pp → **deprimere 2** *agg* depressed

deprezzamento *m* depreciation

deprezzare <1b> lower the value of

deprezzarsi depreciate

deprimente depressing

deprimere <3r> depress

deprimersi get depressed

depurare <1a> purify

depuratore *m* purifier

depurazione *f* purification; **impianto** *m* **di ~** purification plant

deputato *m*, **-a** *f* Member of Parliament, *Am* Representative

deragliare <1g> FERR go off *or* leave the rails; **far ~** derail

deridere <3g> deride

derisione *f* derision

deriso pp → **deridere**

deriva *f* MAR drift; **andare alla ~** drift

derivare <1a> **1** *v/t* derive **2** *v/i*: **~ da** come from, derive from

derivazione *f* derivation; *(discendenza)* origin; EL shunt; TELEC extension

dermatologia *f* dermatology

dermatologo *m* (*pl* -gi), **-a** *f* dermatologist

derrate *fpl* food

derubare <1a> rob

descritto pp → **descrivere**

descrivere <3tt> describe

descrizione *f* description

deserto 1 *agg* deserted; **isola** *f* **-a** desert island **2** *m* desert

desiderare <1m> *(volere)* want, wish; *intensamente* long for, crave; *sessualmente* desire; **desidera?** can I help you?; **farsi ~** play hard to get; *(tardare)* keep people waiting; **lascia a ~** it leaves a lot to be desired

desiderio *m* (*pl* -ri) wish (**di** for); *intenso* longing (**di** for); *sessuale* desire (**di** for)

design *m inv* design

designare <1a> *(nominare)* appoint, name; *(fissare)* fix, set

designer *m/f inv* designer

desistere <3f>: **~ da** desist from

desolante distressing

desolato desolate; **sono ~!** I am so sorry

desolazione *f* desolation; *(dolore)* distress

dessert *m inv* dessert

destare <1a> *fig* (a)rouse, awaken

destarsi *fig* be aroused, be awakened

destinare <1a> destine; *(assegnare)* assign; **con il pensiero** mean, intend; *data* fix, set; *(indirizzare)* address (**a** to)

destinatario *m* (*pl* -ri), **-a** *f di lettera* addressee

destinazione *f*: *(luogo m di)* ~ destination

destino *m* destiny

destra *f* right; *(mano)* right hand; **a ~ stato** on the right, to the right; **moto** to the right

destreggiarsi <1f> manœuvre, *Am* maneuver

destrezza *f* skill, dexterity

destro right; *(abile)* skil(l)ful, dexterous

destrorso 1 *agg persona* right-handed; TEC clockwise **2** *m*, **-a** *f* right-hander, right-handed person

detenere <2q> hold; *in prigione* detain, hold

detenuto *m*, **-a** *f* prisoner

detenzione *f imprigionamento* detention; **~ abusiva di armi** possession of illegal weapons

detergente *m* detergent; *per cosmesi* cleanser

deteriorabile perishable

deteriorarsi <1a> deteriorate

determinare <1m & b> determine, establish; *(causare)* cause, lead to

determinato certain; *(specifico)* particular, specific; *(risoluto)* determined

determinazione *f* determination

detersivo *m* detergent; *per piatti* washing-up liquid, *Am* dishwashing liquid; *per biancheria* detergent, *Br* washing powder

detestare <1b> hate, detest

detonare <1c> detonate

detrarre <3xx> deduct (**da** from)

detratto $pp \rightarrow$ **detrarre**

detrazione f deduction

detrito m debris; GEOL detritus

detta f: **a ~ di** according to

dettaglio m (pl -gli) detail; FIN **commercio** m **al ~** retail trade

dettare <1a> dictate; **~ legge** lay down the law

dettato m dictation

dettatura f dictation; **scrivere sotto ~** take dictation

detto 1 pp $\rightarrow$ **dire**; **~ fatto** no sooner said than done; **come non ~** let's forget it **2** agg said; (soprannominato) known as **3** m saying

devastare <1a> devastate

devastazione f devastation

deve, devi $\rightarrow$ **dovere**

deviare <1h> **1** v/t traffico, sospetti divert **2** v/i deviate

deviazione f deviation; di traffico diversion

devo $\rightarrow$ **dovere**

devolvere <3g> POL devolve

devoluto pp $\rightarrow$ **devolvere**

devoluzione f POL devolution

devoto 1 agg devoted; REL devout **2** m, **-a** f devotee; REL **i -i** the devout

devozione f devotion; REL devoutness

di 1 prp of; con il comparativo than; **~ ferro** (made of) iron; **io sono ~ Roma** I'm from Rome; **l'auto ~ mio padre** my father's car; **una tazza ~ caffè** a cup of coffee; **~ giorno** by day; **parlare ~ politica** talk about politics; **d'estate** in the summer; **~ questo passo** at this rate; **~ chi è questo libro?** whose is this book?, who does this book belong to?; **più bello ~** prettier than **2** art some; interrogativo any, some; neg any; **del vino** some wine

di' $\rightarrow$ **dire**

dia $\rightarrow$ **dare**

diabete m diabetes

diabetico (pl -ci) **1** agg diabetic **2** m, **-a** f diabetic

diadema m diadem

diaframma m (pl -i) diaphragm

diagnosi f inv diagnosis

diagnosticare <1n, c & d> diagnose

diagonale 1 agg diagonal **2** f diagonal (line)

diagramma m (pl -i) diagram

dialetto m dialect

dialisi f inv dialysis

dialogo m (pl -ghi) dialog(ue)

diamante m diamond

diametro m diameter

diapason m inv tuning fork

diapositiva f FOT slide

diario m (pl -ri) diary

diarrea f diarrh(o)ea

diavolo m devil; **un buon ~** a good fellow; **mandare qu al ~** tell s.o. to get lost

dibattere <3a> debate, discuss

dibattersi struggle; fig struggle (**in** with)

dibattito m debate

dicembre m December

diceria f rumo(u)r

dichiarare <1a> state; ufficialmente declare; nei giochi di carte bid; **ha qualcosa da ~?** anything to declare?

dichiararsi declare o.s.

dichiarazione f declaration; **~ dei redditi** income tax statement; **~ doganale** customs declaration

diciannove nineteen

diciannovesimo m/agg nineteenth

diciassette seventeen

diciassettesimo m/agg seventeenth

diciottenne m/f eighteen-year-old

diciotto eighteen

diciottesimo m/agg eighteenth

didattica f didactics

dieci ten; **alle / verso le ~** at / about ten (o'clock)

diesel m diesel

dieta f diet; **essere a ~** be on a diet

dietetica f dietetics

dietetico (pl -ci) diet attr

dietista m/f dietitian, dietician

dietro 1 prp behind; **~ l'angolo** round the corner; **~ di me** behind me; **uno ~ l'altro** nello spazio one behind the other; nel tempo one after the other; **~ ricevuta** on receipt

2 *avv* behind; *in auto* in the back; ***di ~ stanza***, *porta* back; *zampe* hind; AUTO rear **3** *m inv* back

difatti *cong* in fact

difendere <3c> defend; (*proteggere*) protect

difensiva *f* defensive; ***stare sulla ~*** be on the defensive

difensivo defensive

difensore *m* defender; ***~ d'ufficio*** legal aid lawyer, *Am* public defender

difesa *f* defence, *Am* defense; ***~ dei consumatori*** consumer protection; ***legittima ~*** self-defence (*Am* -defense)

difeso *pp* → **difendere**

difetto *m* (*imperfezione*) defect; *morale* fault, flaw; (*mancanza*) lack; ***far ~*** be lacking

difettoso defective

diffamare <1a> slander; *scrivendo* libel

diffamazione *f* defamation of character

differente different (***da*** from, *Am* than)

differenza *f* difference; ***~ di prezzo*** difference in price; ***a ~ di*** unlike

differenziare <1f> differentiate

differenziarsi differ (***da*** from)

differire <4d> postpone

difficile difficult; (*improbabile*) unlikely

difficoltà *f inv* difficulty; ***senza ~*** easily, without any difficulty

diffida *f* DIR injunction

diffidare <1a> **1** *v/t* DIR issue an injunction against; ***~ qu dal fare qc*** warn s.o. not to do sth **2** *v/i*: ***~ di qu*** distrust s.o., mistrust s.o.

diffidente distrustful, mistrustful

diffidenza *f* distrust, mistrust

diffondere <3bb> diffuse; *fig* spread

diffondersi *fig* spread; (*dilungarsi*) enlarge

diffusione *f di luce, calore* diffusion; *di giornale* circulation

diffuso 1 *pp* → **diffondere 2** *agg* widespread; (*luce*) diffuse

difterite *f* diphtheria

diga *f* (*pl* -ghe) *fluviale* dam; *litoranea* dyke; *portuale* breakwater

digerire <4d> digest; F (*tollerare*) stomach F

digestione *f* digestion

digestivo 1 *agg* digestive **2** *m afterdinner drink*, digestif

digitale digital; ***impronta f ~*** fingerprint

digitare <1l> INFOR key

digiunare <1a> fast

digiuno 1 *agg* fasting; *fig privo* lacking (***di*** in); ***essere ~ di notizie*** have no news, not have any news **2** *m* fast; ***a ~*** on an empty stomach

dignità *f* dignity

dignitoso dignified

digrignare <1a> gnash

dilagare <1e> flood; *fig* spread rapidly

dilaniare <1k> tear apart

dilapidare <1m> squander

dilatare <1a> FIS expand; *occhi* open wide

dilatarsi *di materiali, metalli* expand; *di pupilla* dilate

dilatazione *f* expansion; *di pupilla* dilation

dilazionare <1a> defer, delay

dilazione *f* extension

dileguarsi <1a> vanish, disappear

dilemma *m* (*pl* -i) dilemma

dilettante *m/f* amateur; *spreg* dilettante

dilettare <1b> delight

dilettarsi: ***~ di qc*** dabble in sth, do sth as a hobby; ***~ a fare qc*** take delight in doing sth

diletto[1] **1** *agg* beloved **2** *m*, **-a** *f* beloved

diletto[2] *m* (*piacere*) delight; ***fare qc per ~*** do sth for pleasure

diligente diligent; (*accurato*) accurate

diligenza *f* diligence

diluire <4d> dilute

dilungarsi <1e> *fig* dwell (***su*** on)

diluviare <1k> pour down

diluvio *m* downpour; *fig* deluge; ***~ universale*** Flood

dimagrante: ***cura f ~*** diet

dimagrire <4d> lose weight

dimenare <1a> wave; *coda* wag

dimenarsi throw o.s. about

dimensione f dimension; (*grandezza*) size; (*misure*) dimensions

dimenticanza f forgetfulness, absent-mindedness; (*svista*) oversight

dimenticare <1m & d> forget

dimenticarsi forget (*di* sth; *di fare qc* to do sth)

dimestichezza f familiarity

dimettere <3ee> dismiss (*da* from); *da ospedali* discharge, release (*da* from); *da carceri* release (*da* from)

dimettersi resign (*da* from)

dimezzare <1b> halve; (*dividere*) halve, divide in two

diminuire <4d> **1** v/t reduce, diminish; *prezzi* reduce, lower **2** v/i decrease, diminish; *di prezzi, valore* fall, go down; *di vento, rumore* die down

diminuzione f decrease; *di prezzi, valore* fall, drop (*di* in)

dimissioni fpl resignation sg; *dare le ~* resign, hand in one's resignation

dimora f residence; *senza fissa ~* of no fixed abode

dimostrare <1a> demonstrate; (*interesse*) show; (*provare*) prove, show

dimostrarsi prove to be

dimostrazione f demonstration; (*prova*) proof

dinamica f dynamics

dinamico (*pl* -ci) dynamic

dinamismo m dynamism

dinamite f dynamite

dinamo f inv dynamo

dinanzi prp: *~ a al cospetto di* before

dinastia f dynasty

dingo m inv dingo

dinosauro m dinosaur

dintorno **1** avv around **2** m: *-i* pl neighbo(u)rhood

dio m (*pl* gli dei) *idolo* god; *Dio* God; *grazie a Dio!* thank God!, thank goodness!; *per l'amor di Dio* for God's or goodness sake

diocesi f inv diocese

diossina f dioxin

dipartimento m department

dipendente **1** agg dependent **2** m/f employee

dipendenza f dependence; (*edificio*) annex(e); *essere alle ~ di* work for

dipendere <3c>: *~ da* (*essere subordinato a*) depend on; (*essere mantenuto da*) be dependent on; (*essere causato da*) derive from, be due to; *dipende* it depends; *questo dipende da te* it's up to you

dipeso pp → **dipendere**

dipingere <3d> paint; *fig* describe, depict

dipinto **1** pp → **dipingere** **2** m painting, picture

diploma m (*pl* -i) diploma, certificate; *~ di laurea* degree (certificate)

diplomarsi <1c> obtain a diploma

diplomatico (*pl* -ci) **1** agg diplomatic **2** m diplomat

diplomato **1** agg qualified **2** m, -a f holder of a diploma

diplomazia f diplomacy

diporto m: *imbarcazione* f *da ~* pleasure boat

diradare <1a> thin out

diradarsi thin out; *di nebbia* clear, lift

dire <3t> **1** v/t say; (*raccontare*) tell; *~ qc a qu* tell s.o. sth; *vale a ~* that is, in other words; *a ~ il vero* to tell the truth; *come si dice ... in inglese?* what's the English for ... ?; *voler ~* mean **2** v/i *~ bene di qu* speak highly of s.o.; *dico sul serio* I'm serious **3** m: *per sentito ~* by hearsay; *hai un bel ~* say what you like

direttissima f ALP shortest or most direct route; DIR *processo* m *per ~* summary proceedings pl

direttiva f directive

direttivo **1** agg *di direzione di società* managerial; *comitato, consiglio*, POL executive attr **2** m *di società* board (of directors); POL leadership

diretto **1** pp → **dirigere** **2** agg (*immediato*) direct; *~ a* aimed at; *lettera* addressed to; *essere ~ a casa* be heading for home; RAD, TV *in* (*ripresa*) *-a* live **3** m direct train; SP straight

direttore *m*, **-trice** *f* manager; *più in alto nella gerarchia* director; MUS conductor; EDU headmaster, headmistress *f*, *Am* principal; *di giornale, rivista* editor (in chief); **~ generale** chief executive officer; **~ delle vendite** sales manager; **~ d'orchestra** conductor; **~ tecnico** technical manager; SP coach and team manager

direzione *f* direction; *di società* management; *di partito* leadership; *ufficio* office; *sede generale* head office; **in ~ di Roma** in the direction of Rome

dirigente 1 *agg classe, partito* ruling; *personale* managerial **2** *m/f* executive; POL leader

dirigere <3u> direct; *azienda* run, manage; *orchestra* conduct

dirigersi head (**a, verso** for, towards)

dirigibile *m* airship, dirigible

dirimpetto opposite, across the way; **~ a** facing, in front of

diritto 1 *agg* straight **2** *avv* straight **3** *m* right; DIR law; **-i** *pl* (*il compenso*) fees; **-i d'autore** copyright; **~ commerciale** commercial law; **~ costituzionale** constitutional law; **~ internazionale** international law; **~ di precedenza** right of way; **~ di voto** right to vote; **-i** *pl* **umani** human rights; **parità f di -i** equal rights; **aver ~ a** be entitled to; **di ~** by rights

dirittura *f* straight line; SP straight; *fig* rectitude; **in ~ d'arrivo** in the home straight

diroccato ramshackle

dirottamento *m* hijack(ing)

dirottare <1c> *traffico* divert; *aereo* reroute; *con intenzioni criminali* hijack

dirottatore *m*, **-trice** *f* hijacker

dirotto: **piove a ~** it's pouring

dirupo *m* precipice

disabile 1 *agg* disabled **2** *m/f* disabled person

disabitato uninhabited

disabituare <1n>: **~ qu a qc** get s.o. out of the habit of sth

disaccordo *m* disagreement

disadattato 1 *agg* maladjusted **2** *m/f* (social) misfit

disadatto unsuitable (**a** for); *persona* unsuited (**a un lavoro** to a job)

disadorno bare, unadorned

disagiato uncomfortable; *vita* hard

disagio *m* (*pl* -gi) (*difficoltà*) hardship; (*scomodità*) discomfort; (*imbarazzo*) embarrassment; **essere a ~** be ill at ease

disambientato out of place

disapprovare <1c> disapprove of

disapprovazione *f* disapproval

disappunto *m* disappointment

disarmare <1a> disarm

disarmato unarmed; *fig* defenceless

disarmo *m* POL disarmament

disastro *m* disaster

disastroso disastrous

disattento inattentive

disattenzione *f* inattention, lack of attention; *errore* careless mistake

disavanzo *m* deficit; **~ della bilancia commerciale** trade deficit; **~ commerciale con l'estero** foreign trade deficit

disavventura *f* misadventure

disboscamento *m* deforestation

disboscare <1d> deforest

disbrigo *m* (*pl* -ghi) dispatch

discapito *m*: **a ~ di qu** to the detriment *or* disadvantage of s.o.

discarica *f* (*pl* -che) dumping; (*luogo*) dump

discendente 1 *agg inv* descending **2** *m/f* descendant

discendenza *f* descent; (*discendenti*) descendants

discendere <3c> descend; (*trarre origine*) be a descendant (**da** of), be descended (**da** from); *da veicoli, da cavallo* alight (**da** from)

discepolo *m* disciple

discesa *f* descent; (*pendio*) slope; *di bus* exit; SCI **~ libera** downhill (race); **strada f in ~** street that slopes downwards

dischetto *m* INFOR diskette, floppy

disciogliere <3ss> dissolve; *neve* melt

disciolto pp → **disciogliere**

disciplina f discipline

disciplinare 1 agg disciplinary **2** v/t <1a> discipline

disciplinato disciplined

disco m (pl -chi) disc, Am disk; SP discus; MUS record; INFOR disk; INFOR ~ **rigido** hard disk; AUTO ~ **orario** parking disc; ~ **volante** flying saucer

discobolo m discus thrower

discografia f elenco recordings, discography; attività record industry

discolo 1 agg wild, unruly **2** m troublemaker

discolpare <1a> clear

discontinuo intermittent; (disuguale) erratic

discorde not in agreement, clashing

discordia f discord; (differenza di opinioni) disagreement; (litigio) argument

discorrere <3o> talk (di about)

discorso 1 pp → **discorrere 2** m pubblico, ufficiale speech; (conversazione) conversation, talk; **che ~i!** what rubbish!

discoteca f (pl -che) locale disco; raccolta record library

discrepanza f discrepancy

discreto (riservato) discreet; (abbastanza buono) fairly good; (moderato) moderate, fair

discrezione f discretion; **a ~ di** at the discretion of

discriminare <1m> **1** v/i discriminate **2** v/t stranieri, donne discriminate against

discriminazione f discrimination

discussione f discussion; (litigio) argument

discusso pp → **discutere**

discutere <3v> **1** v/t proposta, caso discuss, talk about; questione debate; (mettere in dubbio) question; (contestare) dispute **2** v/i talk; (litigare) argue; (negoziare) negotiate

discutibile debatable

disdegnare <1a> disdain

disdetta f DIR notice; fig bad luck

disdetto pp → **disdire**

disdire <3t> impegno cancel; contratto terminate

disegnare <1a> draw; (progettare) design

disegnatore m, **-trice** f draughtsman, Am draftsman; donna draughtswoman, Am draftswoman; (progettista) designer

disegno m drawing; (progetto) design; ~ **di legge** bill

diserbante m weed-killer, herbicide

diserbare <1a> weed

diseredare <1b> disinherit

diseredato underprivileged, disadvantaged

disertare <1b> **1** v/t desert; ~ **una riunione** not attend a meeting **2** v/i desert

disertore m deserter

diserzione f desertion

disfare <3aa> undo; letto strip; (distruggere) destroy; ~ **la valigia** unpack

disfarsi di neve, ghiaccio melt; ~ **di** get rid of

disfatta f defeat

disfatto pp → **disfare**

disfunzione f MED disorder

disgelo m thaw

disgrazia f misfortune; (incidente) accident; (sfavore) disgrace; **per ~** unfortunately

disgraziato 1 agg (sfortunato) unlucky, unfortunate **2** m, **-a** f poor soul; F (farabutto) bastard F

disgregare <1b> break up

disgregarsi break up, disintegrate

disguido m hiccup, hitch

disgustare <1a> disgust

disgustarsi be disgusted (di by)

disgusto m disgust

disgustoso disgusting

disidratato dehydrated

disilludere <3b> disillusion

disillusione f disillusionment

disilluso disillusioned

disimparare <1a> forget

disinfettante m disinfectant

disinfettare <1b> disinfect

disinfezione f disinfection

disingannare <1a> disillusion

disinibito uninhibited

disinnescare <1d> *bomba* defuse

disinnestare <1a> AUTO *marcia* disengage

disinquinare <1a> clean up

disinserire <4d> disconnect

disinteressarsi take no interest (*di* in)

disinteressato disinterested

disinteresse *m* lack of interest; (*generosità*) unselfishness

disintossicare <1m, c & d> detoxify

disintossicazione *f* treatment for drug / alcohol addiction, *Am* detox F

disinvolto confident

disinvoltura *f* confidence

dislessia *f* dyslexia

dislessico dyslexic

dislivello *m* difference in height; *fig* difference

disobbedire → *disubbidire*

disoccupato 1 *agg* unemployed, jobless **2** *m*, **-a** *f* person who is unemployed, person without a job; *i -i* the unemployed, the jobless

disoccupazione *f* unemployment; *~ giovanile* unemployment among the young, youth unemployment

disonestà *f* dishonesty

disonesto dishonest

disonorare <1a> bring dishono(u)r on

disonore *m* dishono(u)r

disopra 1 *avv* above; *al ~ di* above **2** *agg* upper **3** *m* top

disordinato untidy, messy

disordine *m* untidiness, mess; *in ~* untidy, in a mess; *-i pl* riots, public disorder *sg*

disorganizzazione *f* disorganization, lack of organization

disorientare <1b> disorient(ate)

disorientamento *m* disorientation

disorientato disorient(at)ed

disotto 1 *avv* below; *al ~ di* beneath **2** *agg* lower **3** *m* underside

dispari odd

disparità *f* disparity

disparte: *in ~* aside, to one side

dispendio *m* waste

dispendioso expensive

dispensa *f stanza* larder; *mobile* cupboard; *pubblicazione* instal(l)ment; DIR exemption; *~ universitaria* duplicated lecture notes

dispensare <1b> dispense; (*esonerare*) exonerate

disperare <1b> despair (*di* of); *far ~ qu* drive s.o. to despair

disperarsi despair

disperato desperate

disperazione *f* despair, desperation

disperdere <3uu> disperse; *energie, sostanze* squander; *non ~ nell'ambiente* please dispose of carefully

disperdersi disperse

dispersione *f* dispersal; CHIM, FIS dispersion; *fig di energie* waste

disperso 1 *agg* → *disperdere* **2** *agg* scattered; (*sperduto*) lost, missing

dispetto *m* spite; *per ~* out of spite; *a ~ di qc* in spite of sth; *fare -i a qu* annoy *or* tease s.o.

dispettoso mischievous

dispiacere 1 *v/i* <2k> (*causare dolore*) upset (*a* s.o.); (*non piacere*) displease (*a* s.o.); *mi dispiace* I'm sorry; *le dispiace se apro la finestra?* do you mind if I open the window? **2** *m* (*rammarico*) regret, sorrow; (*dolore*) grief, sadness; (*delusione*) disappointment; *-i* (*preoccupazioni*) worries, troubles

display *m* display

disponibile available; (*cortese*) helpful, obliging

disponibilità *f* availability; (*cortesia*) helpfulness

disporre <3ll> **1** *v/t* arrange; (*stabilire*) order **2** *v/i* (*decidere*) make arrangements; *abbiamo già disposto diversamente* we've made other arrangements; *~ di qc* have sth (at one's disposal)

dispositivo *m* TEC device

disposizione *f* arrangement; (*norma*) provision; (*attitudine*) aptitude (*a* for); *stare / mettere a ~ di qu* be / put at s.o.'s disposal

disposto 1 *pp* → *disporre* **2** *agg*: *~ a* ready to, willing to; *essere ben ~*

D

verso qu be well disposed to s.o.

dispotico (*pl* -ci) despotic

disprezzare <1b> despise

disprezzo *m* contempt

disputa *f* dispute, argument

disputare <1l> 1 *v/i* argue 2 *v/t* SP take part in; *disputarsi qc* compete for sth

dissanguare <1a> *fig* bleed dry, bleed white

disseminare <1m> scatter, disseminate; *fig* spread

dissenso *m* dissent; (*dissapore*) argument, disagreement

dissenteria *f* dysentery

dissentire <4b> disagree (*da* with)

disseppellire <4d> exhume

dissertazione *f* dissertation

disservizio *m* (*pl* -zi) poor service; (*inefficienza*) inefficiency; (*cattiva gestione*) mismanagement

dissestare <1b> FIN destabilize

dissestato *strada* uneven; *finanze* precarious

dissesto *m* ruin, failure; **~ ecologico** environmental meltdown

dissetante thirst-quenching

dissetare <1a>: **~ qu** quench s.o.'s thirst

dissetarsi quench one's thirst

dissidente *m/f* dissident

dissimulare <1m> conceal, hide

dissimulazione *f* concealment

dissipare <1l> dissolve; (*sperperare*) squander

dissociare <1f> dissociate

dissociarsi dissociate o.s. (*da* from)

dissodare <1c> till

dissoluto dissolute

dissolvere <3g> dissolve; *dubbi, nebbia* dispel

dissolversi dissolve; (*svanire*) vanish

dissonante dissonant; *fig* discordant

dissonanza *f* MUS dissonance; *fig* clash

dissuadere <2i>: **~ qu da fare qc** dissuade s.o. from doing sth

dissuaso *pp* → **dissuadere**

distaccare <1d> detach; SP leave behind

distaccarsi *da persone* detach o.s.

(*da* from)

distacco *m* (*pl* -cchi) detachment (*anche fig*); (*separazione*) separation; SP lead

distante distant, remote, far-off; **~ da** far from

distanza *f* distance (*anche fig*); **comando m a ~** remote control

distanziare <1g> 1 *v/t* space out; SP leave behind; (*superare*) overtake

distare <1a>: *l'albergo dista 100 metri dalla stazione* the hotel is 100 metres from the station; *quanto dista da qui?* how far is it from here?

distendere <3c> (*adagiare*) lay; *gambe, braccia* stretch out; *muscoli* relax; *bucato* hang out; *nervi* calm

distendersi lie down; (*rilassarsi*) relax

distensione *f* relaxation; POL détente

distensivo relaxing

distesa *f* expanse

disteso 1 *pp* → **distendere** 2 *agg* stretched out; (*rilassato*) relaxed

distillare <1a> distil, *Am* distill

distilleria *f* distillery

distinguere <3d> distinguish

distintivo 1 *agg* distinctive 2 *m* badge

distinto 1 *pp* → **distinguere** 2 *agg* (*diverso*) different, distinct; (*chiaro*) distinct; *fig* distinguished; *-i saluti* yours faithfully

distinzione *f* distinction

distorsione *f* distortion; MED sprain

distrarre <3xx> distract; (*divertire*) entertain

distrarsi (*non essere attento*) get distracted; (*svagarsi*) take one's mind off things

distratto 1 *pp* → **distrarre** 2 *agg* absent-minded

distrazione *f* absent-mindedness; (*errore*) inattention; (*svago*) amusement; *che distrae da un'attività* distraction

distretto *m* district

distribuire <4d> distribute; *premi* award, present

93

distributore *m* distributor; ~ (*di benzina*) (petrol, *Am* gas) pump; ~ *automatico* vending machine; ~ *automatico di biglietti* ticket machine

distribuzione *f* distribution; *posta* delivery

distruggere <3cc> destroy

distruttivo destructive

distrutto *pp* → *distruggere*

distruzione *f* destruction

disturbare <1a> disturb; (*dare fastidio a*) bother; (*sconvolgere*) upset

disturbarsi: *non si disturbi* please don't bother

disturbi *mpl* RAD interference *sg*

disturbo *m* trouble, bother; MED *-i pl di circolazione* circulation problems

disubbidiente disobedient

disubbidienza *f* disobedience

disubbidire <4d>: ~ *a* disobey

disuguaglianza *f* disparity, difference

disuguale different; *terreno* uneven; *fig* inconsistent, erratic

disumano inhuman

disuso *m*: *in* ~ in disuse, disused

ditale *m* thimble

dito *m* (*pl le dita*) finger; *del piede* toe; *un* ~ *di vino* a drop of wine

ditta *f* company, firm; ~ *fornitrice* supplier; ~ *di vendite per corrispondenza* mail-order company

dittafono® *m* dictaphone®

dittatore *m* dictator

dittatura *f* dictatorship

diurno daytime *attr*; *albergo m* ~ *place where travellers can have a shower/shave*

diva *f* diva

divagare <1e> digress

divampare <1a> *di rivolta, incendio* break out; *di passione* blaze

divano *m* sofa; ~ *letto* sofa bed

divaricare <1m & d> open (wide)

divario *m* (*pl -ri*) difference

divenire <4p> become

diventare <1b> become; *rosso, bianco* turn, go; ~ *grande* grow up

diverbio *m* (*pl -bi*) argument

divergente diverging, divergent

divergenza *f* divergence; *di opinioni* difference

divergere <3uu & 3a> diverge

diversamente differently; (*altrimenti*) otherwise

diversificare <1n & d> **1** *v/t* diversify **2** *v/i e* **diversificarsi** differ

diversità *f* difference; (*varietà*) diversity

diversivo *m* diversion, distraction

diverso 1 *agg* (*differente*) different (*da* from, *Am* than); *-i pl* several; *da -i giorni* for the past few days **2** *mpl -i* several people

divertente amusing

divertimento *m* amusement; *buon ~!* have a good time!, enjoy yourself/yourselves!

divertire <4b> amuse

divertirsi enjoy o.s., have a good time

dividendo *m* dividend

dividere <3q> divide; (*condividere*) share

dividersi *di coppia* separate; (*scindersi*) be split, be divided (*in* into)

divieto *m* ban; ~ *d'importazione* import ban; AUTO ~ *di segnalazioni acustiche* please do not use your horn; ~ *di sosta* no parking

divincolarsi <1m> twist, wriggle

divinità *f inv* divinity

divino divine

divisa *f* uniform; FIN currency

divisione *f* division; ~ *del lavoro* division of labo(u)r

divisorio (*pl -ri*) **1** *agg* dividing; *parete f -a* partition wall, stud wall **2** *m* partition

divo *m* star

divorare <1c> devour

divorziare <1c & g> get a divorce

divorziato divorced

divorzio *m* (*pl -zi*) divorce

divulgare <1e> divulge, reveal; (*rendere accessibile*) popularize

divulgazione *f* divulging; *scientifica ecc* popularization

dizionario *m* (*pl -ri*) dictionary

DNA *abbr* (= *acido deossiribonucleico*) DNA (= deoxyribonucleic acid)

do[1] → *dare*

do[2] *m inv* MUS C; *nel solfeggio della scala* doh

dobbiamo → *dovere*

D.O.C., doc *abbr* (= *Denominazione d'Origine Controllata*) *term signifying that a wine is of a certain origin and quality*

doccia *f* (*pl* -cce) shower; *fare la* ~ take a shower

docente 1 *agg* teaching; *personale m* ~ teaching staff **2** *m/f* teacher

docile docile

documentare <1a> document

documentarsi collect information

documentario *m* documentary

documentazione *f* documentation

documento *m* document; *-i pl* papers; *-i dell'autoveicolo* car documents

dodici twelve

dogana *f* customs; (*dazio*) (customs) duty

doganale customs *attr*; *controllo m* ~ customs check; *dichiarazione f* ~ customs declaration; *formalità fpl* -*i* customs formalities

doganiere *m* customs officer

doglie *fpl*: *avere le* -*e* be in labo(u)r

dogma *m* (*pl* -i) dogma

dolce 1 *agg* sweet; *carattere, voce, pendio* gentle; *acqua* fresh; *clima* mild; *ricordo* pleasant; *suono* soft **2** *m* (*portata*) dessert, sweet; *di sapore* sweetness; (*torta*) cake; *-i pl* sweet things

dolcezza *f* sweetness; *di carattere, voce* gentleness; *di clima* mildness; *di ricordo* pleasantness; *di suono* softness

dolciastro sweetish; *fig* syrupy, sugary

dolcificante *m* sweetener

dolciumi *mpl* sweets, *Am* candy *sg*

dolente painful, sore

dolere <2e> hurt, be painful; *mi duole la schiena* my back hurts, I have a sore back

dolersi be sorry (*di* for); (*lagnarsi*) complain (*di* about)

dollaro *m* dollar

dolo *m* malice

Dolomiti *fpl* Dolomites

dolorante sore, painful

dolore *m* pain

doloroso painful

doloso malicious

domanda *f* question; (*richiesta*) request; FIN demand; *fare una* ~ *a qu* ask s.o. a question; ~ *e offerta* supply and demand

domandare <1a> **1** *v/t per sapere*: *nome, ora, opinione ecc* ask; *per ottenere*: *informazioni, aiuto ecc* ask for; ~ *un favore a qu* ask s.o. a favour; ~ *scusa* apologize **2** *v/i*: ~ *a qu* ask s.o.; ~ *di qu per sapere come sta* ask after s.o.; *per parlargli* ask for s.o.

domandarsi wonder, ask o.s.

domani 1 *avv* tomorrow; ~ *mattina* tomorrow morning; ~ *sera* tomorrow evening; *a* ~*!* see you tomorrow! **2** *m* tomorrow

domare <1a> tame; *fig* control

domattina tomorrow morning

domenica *f* (*pl* -che) Sunday; *la* ~, *di* ~ on Sundays

domestico (*pl* -ci) **1** *agg* domestic; *animale m* ~ pet **2** *m*, *-a f* servant; *donna* maid

domiciliato: ~ *a* domiciled at

domicilio *m* domicile; (*casa*) home

dominante dominant; *idee* prevailing; *classe* ruling

dominare <1l & c> **1** *v/t* dominate; *materia* master; *passioni* master, overcome **2** *v/i* rule (*su* over), be master (*su* of); *fig di confusione* reign

dominazione *f* domination

dominio *m* (*pl* -ni) (*controllo*) control, power; *fig* (*campo*) domain, field

domino *m* mask, domino

donare <1a> donate, give; *sangue* give

donatore *m*, **-trice** *f* donor; ~ *di sangue* blood donor

donazione *f* donation

dondolare <1l> **1** *v/t culla* rock; *testa* nod **2** *v/i* sway; (*oscillare*) swing

dondolarsi *su altalena* swing; *su sedia* rock; *fig* hang around

dondolio *m* (gentle) rocking

dondolo *m*: **cavallo** *m* **a ~** rocking horse; **sedia** *f* **a ~** rocking chair

donna *f* woman; *carte da gioco* queen; **~ di servizio** home help; **scarpe** *fpl* **da ~** women's *or* ladies' shoes

donnola *f* weasel

dono *m* gift

dopo 1 *prp* after; **~ di te** after you; **~ mangiato** after eating, after meals; **subito ~ il bar** just past the bar **2** *avv* (*in seguito*) afterward(s), after; (*poi*) then; (*più tardi*) later; **il giorno ~** the day after, the next day **3** *conj*: **~ che** after

dopobarba *m inv* aftershave

dopodomani the day after tomorrow

dopoguerra *m inv* post-war period

dopopranzo *m* afternoon

doposci *m inv* après-ski; **~** *pl stivali* après-ski boots

dopotutto after all

doppiaggio *m di film* dubbing

doppiare <1k> *film* dub; SP lap; MAR round

doppiatore *m*, **-trice** *f* dubber

doppio (*pl* -pi) **1** *agg* double **2** *m* double; SP doubles

doppine *m* duplicate

doppipetto *m* double-breasted jacket

dorare <1c> gild; GASTR brown

dorato 1 *pp* → **dorare 2** *agg* gilded; *sabbia*, *riflessi* golden; GASTR browned

dorico (*pl* -ci) ARCHI Doric

dormicchiare <1k> doze

dormiglione *m*, **-a** *f* late riser

dormire <4c> sleep

dormita *f* (good) night's sleep

dormitorio *m* (*pl* -ri) dormitory

dormiveglia *m*: **essere nel ~** be only half awake

dorso *m* back; (*di libro*) spine; SP backstroke

dosaggio *m* (*pl* -gi) proportion; *di medicina* dosage

dosare <1c> measure out; *fig* be sparing with; *parole* weigh

dose *f* quantity, amount; MED dose; **una buona ~ di coraggio** a lot of courage

dosso *m di strada* hump; **togliersi gli abiti di ~** get undressed, take one's clothes off

dotare <1c> provide, supply (*di* with); *fig* provide, endow (*di* with)

dotato gifted; **~ di** equipped with

dotazione *f* equipment; *finanziaria* endowment; **dato in ~ a qu** issued to s.o.

dote *f* dowry; *fig* gift

dott. *abbr* (= **dottore**) Dr (= doctor)

dotto 1 *agg* learned **2** *m* scholar

dottorato *m* doctorate; **~ di ricerca** doctorate in scientific research

dottore *m* doctor (**in** of)

dottoressa *f* (woman) doctor

dottrina *f* doctrine

dott.ssa *abbr* (= **dottoressa**) Dr (= doctor)

dove where; **~ sei?** where are you?; **di ~ sei?** where are you from?; **fin ~?** how far?; **per ~ si passa?** which way do you go?; **mettilo ~ vuoi** put it wherever you like

dovere <2f> **1** *v/i* have to, must; **devo averlo** I must have it, I have to have it; **non devo dimenticare** I mustn't forget; **deve arrivare oggi** she is supposed to arrive today; **come si deve** (*bene*) properly; *persona* very decent; **doveva succedere** it was bound to happen; **dovresti avvertirlo** you ought to *or* should let him know **2** *v/t* owe **3** *m* duty; **per ~** out of duty

dovunque 1 *avv* (*dappertutto*) everywhere; (*in qualsiasi luogo*) anywhere **2** *conj* wherever

dovuto 1 *pp* → **dovere 2** *agg* due; **~ a** because of, due to

dozzina *f* dozen; **una ~ di uova** a dozen eggs; **se ne vendono a ~** they are sold by the dozen

dragare <1e> dredge

drago *m* (*pl* -ghi) dragon

dragoncello *m* tarragon

dramma *m* (*pl* -i) drama

drammatico (*pl* -ci) dramatic

drammatizzare <1a> dramatize

drammaturgia *f* theatre, *Am* theater

drammaturgo *m* (*pl* -ghi) play-wright

drastico (*pl* -ci) drastic

drenaggio *m* drainage

drenare <1a> drain

dribblare <1a> SP dribble

dritto **1** *agg* straight **2** *avv* straight (ahead) **3** *m di indumento, tessuto* right side **4** *m*, **-a** *f* F crafty devil F

drive *m inv* INFOR drive

drizzare <1a> (*raddrizzare*) straighten; (*erigere*) put up, erect; **~ le orecchie** prick up one's ears

drizzarsi: **~ in piedi** rise to one's feet

droga *f* (*pl* -ghe) drug; **-ghe pesanti/leggere** hard/soft drugs

drogare <1c & e> drug

drogarsi SP take drugs

drogato *m*, **-a** *f* drug addict

drogheria *f* grocer's

dubbio (*pl* -bbi) **1** *agg* doubtful; (*equivoco*) dubious **2** *m* doubt; **essere in ~ fra** hesitate between; **mettere qc in ~** doubt sth; **senza ~** undoubtedly, without a doubt

dubbioso doubtful

dubitare <1l> doubt (*di* sth); **dubito che venga** I doubt whether he'll come

duca *m* (*pl* -chi) duke

ducato *m* (*territorio*) duchy

duchessa *f* duchess

due two; **a ~ a ~** in twos, two by two; **tutt'e ~** both of them; **vorrei dire ~ parole** I'd like to say a word or two

duecento **1** *agg* two hundred **2** *m*: **il Duecento** the thirteenth century

duello *m* duel

duemila two thousand

duepezzi *m inv* bikini; (*vestito*) two-piece (suit)

duetto *m* duet; (*persone*) duo, couple

duna *f* (sand) dune

dunque **1** *conj* so; (*allora*) well (then) **2** *m*: **venire al ~** come to the crunch

duomo *m* cathedral

duplex *m inv* party line

duplicato *m* duplicate

duplice double; **in ~ copia** in duplicate

durante *prp* during; **vita natural ~** for ever and ever

durare <1a> last; (*conservarsi*) keep, last

durata *f* duration, length; *di prodotto* life; **per tutta la ~ di** throughout; **~ di volo** flight time

duraturo lasting

durevole lasting

durezza *f* hardness; *di carne* toughness; (*asprezza*) harshness

duro **1** *agg* hard; *carne, persona* tough; *inverno, voce* harsh; *congegno, meccanismo* stiff; *pane* stale; (*ostinato*) stubborn; F (*stupido*) thick F; **~ d'orecchi** hard of hearing; **tieni ~!** don't give up!, hang in there! **2** *m* tough guy

durone *m* callous

duttile ductile; *fig* malleable

E

E *abbr* (= *est*) E (= east)

e and

è → *essere*

ebanista *m/f* (*mpl* -i) cabinet maker

ebano *m* ebony

ebbe, ebbi → *avere*

ebbene well

ebbrezza *f* drunkenness; *fig* thrill

ebraico (*pl* -ci) **1** *agg* Hebrew; *religione* Jewish **2** *m* Hebrew

ebreo 1 *m*, **-a** *f* Jew; **gli -i** the Jews **2** *agg* Jewish

ecc. *abbr* (= *eccetera*) etc (= et cetera)

eccedente excess

eccedenza *f* excess; (*il di più*) surplus; **peso** *m* **in ~** excess weight

eccedere <3a> **1** *v/t* exceed, go beyond **2** *v/i* go too far; **~ nel bere** drink too much

eccellente excellent

eccentrico (*pl* -ci) eccentric

eccessivo excessive

eccesso *m* excess; **~ di personale** overmanning; **~ di velocità** speeding

eccetera et cetera

eccetto except

eccettuare <1m & b> except

eccezionale exceptional; **in via ~** as an exception

eccezionalmente exceptionally

eccezione *f* exception

ecchimosi *f inv* bruise

eccitante 1 *agg* exciting **2** *m* stimulant

eccitare <1l & b> excite

eccitarsi get excited

eccitazione *f* excitement

ecclesiastico (*pl* -ci) **1** *agg* ecclesiastical **2** *m* priest

ecco (*qui*) here; (*là*) there; **~ come** this is how; **~ fatto** that's that; **~ tutto** that's all; **~mi** here I am; **~li**

here they are; **~ti il libro** here is your book

eclissare <1a> eclipse

eclissarsi *fig* slip away

eclisse *f*, **eclissi** *f inv* eclipse; **~ solare** solar eclipse; **~ lunare** lunar eclipse

eco *m/f* (*pl* gli echi) echo

ecografia *f* scan

ecologia *f* ecology

ecologico (*pl* -ci) ecological

ecologista 1 *m/f* ecologist **2** *agg* ecological

ecologo *m* (*pl* -gi), **-a** *f* ecologist

economia *f* economy; *scienza* economics *sg*; **fare ~** economize (**di** on); **~ di mercato** market economy; **università Economia e Commercio** business school; **-e** *pl* savings

economico (*pl* -ci) economic; (*poco costoso*) economical; **classe** *f* **~** economy class

economista *m/f* (*mpl* -i) economist

economizzare <1a> **1** *v/t* save **2** *v/i* economize (**su** on)

economo 1 *agg* thrifty **2** *m*, **-a** *f* bursar

ecosistema *m* ecosystem

eczema *m* (*pl* -i) eczema

ed and

edera *f* ivy

edicola *f* newspaper kiosk

edificare <1m & d> build; *fig* edify

edificio *m* (*pl* -ci) building; *fig* structure

edile construction *attr*, building *attr*

edilizia *f* construction, building; (*urbanistica*) town planning

editare <1a> INFOR edit

editore 1 *agg* publishing **2** *m*, **-trice** *f* publisher; (*curatore*) editor

editoria *f* publishing

editoriale 1 *agg* publishing **2** *m* editorial

edizione *f* edition; **~ straordinaria** *di telegiornale* special news bulletin; *di giornale* extra (edition); **la quarta ~ del congresso XY** the fourth XY conference

educare<1l, b & d> educate; (*allevare*) bring up; *gusto, orecchio, mente* train

educativo education *attr*; (*istruttivo*) educational

educata (ben) ~ well brought-up, polite

educazione *f* education; *dei figli* upbringing; (*buone maniere*) (good) manners; **~ fisica** physical education

effervescente *bibita* fizzy, effervescent; *aspirina* soluble; *personalità* bubbly, effervescent

effettivamente (*in effetti*) in fact; *per rafforzare un'affermazione* really, actually

effettivo 1 *agg* (*reale*) real, actual; (*efficace*) effective; *personale* permanent; MIL regular **2** *m* FIN sum total

effetto *m* (*conseguenza*) effect; (*impressione*) impression; FIN (*cambiale*) bill (of exchange); **~ serra** greenhouse effect; **fare ~** (*funzionare*) work; (*impressionare*) make an impression; **fare l'~ di essere ...** give the impression of being ...; **-i** *pl* **collaterali** side effects; **-i** *pl* **personali** personal effects *or* belongings; **a tutti gli -i** to all intents and purposes; **in -i** in fact

effettuare<1m & b> carry out; *pagamento* make

effettuarsi take place; **il servizio non si effettua la domenica** there is no Sunday service

efficace effective

efficacia *f* effectiveness

efficiente efficient; (*funzionante*) in working order

efficienza *f* efficiency

Egitto *m* Egypt

egiziano 1 *agg* Egyptian **2** *m*, **-a** *f* Egyptian

egizio ancient Egyptian

egli *pron m* he

egocentrico egocentric

egoismo *m* selfishness, egoism

egoista 1 *agg* selfish **2** *m/f* (*mpl* -i) selfish person, egoist

egr. *abbr* (= **egregio**) *form of address used in correspondence*

egregio (*pl* -gi) distinguished; *nelle lettere* **~ signore** Dear Sir

eguale → **uguale**

eh? eh?, what?

ehi! oi!

E.I. *abbr* (= **Esercito Italiano**) Italian army

elaborare<1m> elaborate; *dati* process; *piano* draw up, work out

elaborato elaborate

elaboratore *m*: **~ elettronico** computer

elaborazione *f* elaboration; **~ elettronica dei dati** electronic data processing; **~ dei testi** word processing

elasticità *f* elasticity; (*agilità*) agility, suppleness; *fig* flexibility; *della mente* quickness

elastico (*pl* -ci) **1** *agg* elastic; *norme, orari* flexible **2** *m* rubber band

elefante *m* elephant

elegante elegant

eleganza *f* elegance

eleggere<3cc> elect

elementare elementary; **scuola ~** primary school, *Am* elementary school

elemento *m* element; (*componente*) component; **-i** *pl* (*rudimenti*) rudiments; (*fatti*) data

elemosina *f* charity; **chiedere l'~** beg

elemosinare<1n & c> *v/t & v/i* beg

elencare<1b & d> list

elenco *m* (*pl* -chi) list; **~ telefonico** phone book F, telephone directory

eletto 1 *pp* → **eleggere 2** *agg* chosen

elettorale electoral

elettorato *m* electorate

elettore *m*, **-trice** *f* voter

elettrauto *m inv* *auto* electrics garage; *persona* car electrician

elettricista *m/f* (*pl* -i) electrician

elettricità f electricity

elettrico (pl -ci) electric; **centrale** f **-a** power station

elettrocardiogramma m (pl -i) electrocardiogram

elettrodo m electrode

elettrodomestico m (pl -ci) household appliance

elettrolisi f electrolysis

elettromagnetico electromagnetic

elettromotore m electric motor

elettromotrice f FERR electric locomotive

elettrone m electron

elettronica f electronics

elettronico electronic

elettroshock electroshock

elettrotecnica f electrical engineering

elettrotecnico (pl -ci) **1** agg electrical **2** m electrical engineer

elevare <1b> raise; costruzioni erect; (promuovere) promote; fig migliorare better

elevato high; fig elevated, lofty

elevazione f elevation

elezione f election

eliambulanza f air ambulance

elica f (pl -che) MAR propeller, screw; AVIA propeller

elicottero m helicopter

eliminare <1m> eliminate

eliminatoria f SP heat

eliminazione f elimination

elio m helium

eliporto m heliport

élite f elite, élite

ella pron f she

ellenico (pl -ci) Hellenic

ellenismo m Hellenism

ellepì m inv LP

elmetto m helmet

elmo m helmet

elogiare <1f & c> praise

elogio m (pl -gi) praise

eloquente eloquent

eloquenza f eloquence

eludere <3q> elude; sorveglianza, domanda evade

elusivo elusive

elvetico (pl -ci) Swiss

emanare <1a> **1** v/t give off; legge pass **2** v/i emanate, come (da from)

emanazione f di calore, raggi emanation; di legge passing

emancipare <1m> emancipate

emanciparsi become emancipated

emancipazione f emancipation

emarginare <1m> marginalize

emarginato m, **-a** f person on the fringes of society

ematoma m (pl -i) h(a)ematoma

embargo m (pl -ghi) embargo

emblema m (pl -i) emblem

embolia f embolism

embrione m embryo

emergenza f emergency; **freno** m **d'~** emergency brake; **in caso di ~** in an emergency

emergere <3uu> emerge; (distinguersi) stand out

emersione f emersion

emerso pp → **emergere**

emesso pp → **emettere**

emettere <3ee> luce give out, emit; grido, verdetto give; calore give off; FIN issue; TEC emit

emicrania f migraine

emigrante m/f emigrant

emigrare <1a> emigrate

emigrato m, **-a** f person who has emigrated

emigrazione f emigration

emisfero m hemisphere

emissario m (pl -ri) GEOG outlet; (agente segreto) emissary

emissione f emission; di denaro, francobolli issue; RAD broadcast; **banca** f **di ~** bank of issue, issuing bank; **data** f **di ~** date of issue; **-i** pl **inquinanti** toxic emissions

emittente 1 agg issuing; (trasmittente) broadcasting **2** f RAD transmitter; TV channel; **~ privata** commercial channel

emoglobina f h(a)emoglobin

emorragia f h(a)emorrhage

emorroidi fpl h(a)emorrhoids

emostatico m h(a)emostat

emotivo emotional; (sensibile) sensitive

emozionante exciting, thrilling

E

emozionato excited; (*agitato*) nervous; (*commosso*) moved; (*turbato*) upset

emozionare <1a> (*appassionare*) excite; (*commuovere*) move; (*turbare*) upset

emozionarsi get excited; (*commuoversi*) be moved

emozione *f* emotion; (*agitazione*) excitement

empirico (*pl* -ci) empirical

emporio *m* (*pl* -ri) *negozio* department store

emulsione *f* emulsion

enciclopedia *f* encyclop(a)edia

enciclopedico (*pl* -ci) encyclop(a)edic

endovenoso intravenous

ENEL *abbr* (= *Ente Nazionale per l'Energia Elettrica*) Italian electricity board

energetico *fabbisogno, consumo ecc* energy *attr*; *alimento* energy-giving

energia *f* energy; ~ *eolica* wind power; ~ *nucleare* nuclear energy; ~ *solare* solar power

energico (*pl* -ci) strong, energetic

enfasi *f* emphasis

enfatizzare <1a> emphasize

ENI *abbr* (= *Ente Nazionale Idrocarburi*) state-owned oil company

enigma *m* (*pl* -i) enigma

enigmatico (*pl* -ci) enigmatic

ENIT *abbr* (= *Ente Nazionale Italiano per il Turismo*) Italian tourist board

ennesimo MAT nth; F *per l'-a volta* for the hundredth time F

enorme enormous

enoteca *f* (*pl* -che) (*negozio*) wine merchant's (*specializing in fine wines*)

ente *m* organization; FIL being; ~ *per il turismo* tourist board; *gli enti locali* the local authorities

entrambi both

entrare <1a> (*andare dentro*) go in, enter; (*venire dentro*) come in, enter; *la chiave non entra* the key won't go in, the key doesn't fit; *fig questo non c'entra* that has noth-

ing to do with it; ~ *in una stanza* enter a room, go into / come into a room; ~ *in carica* take up one's duties; *non entro più nei pantaloni* I can't get into my trousers any more

entrata *f* entrance; *in parcheggio* entrance, way in; *in un paese* entry; INFOR input; FIN -*e pl* (*reddito*) income; (*guadagno*) earnings; ~ *libera* admission free

entro within

entroterra *m inv* hinterland

entusiasmare <1a> arouse enthusiasm in

entusiasmo *m* enthusiasm

entusiasta enthusiastic

entusiastico (*pl* -ci) enthusiastic

enumerare <1m> enumerate

enumerazione *f* enumeration

enzima *m* (*pl* -i) enzyme

epatite *f* hepatitis; ~ *virale* viral hepatitis

epica *f* epic

epicentro *m* epicentre, *Am* -center; *fig* centre

epidemia *f* epidemic; ~ *di influenza* flu epidemic

epidermide *f* skin; MED epidermis

Epifania *f* Epiphany

epilessia *f* epilepsy

epilettico (*pl* -ci) **1** *agg* epileptic **2** *m, -a f* epileptic

episodio *m* (*pl* -di) episode

epistolare: *stile m* ~ style of letter-writing

epoca *f* (*pl* -che) age; (*periodo*) period, time; *auto f d'*~ vintage car; *mobili mpl d'*~ period furniture

epurare <1a> *fig* purge

eppure (and) yet

E.P.T. *abbr* (= *Ente Provinciale per il Turismo*) provincial tourist board

equatore *m* equator

equatoriale equatorial

equazione *f* equation

equilatero equilateral

equilibrare <1a> balance

equilibrato balanced; *fig* well-balanced

equilibrio *m* (*pl* -ri) balance; *fig* common sense

equino horse *attr*; *carne f -a* horse-meat

equinozio *m* (*pl* -zi) equinox

equipaggiamento *m* equipment

equipaggiare <1f> equip; MAR, AVIA *con personale* man, crew

equipaggio *m* (*pl* -ggi) crew

equiparare <1m> make equal

equipazione *f* equalization; *~ di diritti* equal rights

équipe *f inv* team; *lavoro m di ~* team work

equitazione *f* horse riding

equivalente *m/agg* equivalent

equivalenza *f* equivalence

equivoco (*pl* -ci) **1** *agg* ambiguous; (*sospetto*) suspicious; F (*losco*) shady F **2** *m* misunderstanding

era *f* (*epoca*) age, era; GEOL era; *~ atomica* atomic age; *~ glaciale* Ice Age

era, erano → *essere*

erba *f* grass; GASTR *-e pl* herbs; *-e aromatiche* herbs; *alle -e* with herbs; *fig in ~* budding

erbaccia *f* (*pl* -cce) weed

erborista *m/f* (*pl* -i) herbalist

erboristeria *f* herbalist's

erboso grassy

erede *m/f* heir; *donna* heiress

eredità *f* inheritance; BIO heredity

ereditare <1m & b> inherit

ereditarietà *f* heredity

ereditario (*pl* -ri) hereditary

ereditiera *f* heiress

eremita *m* (*pl* -i) hermit

eremo *m* (*pl* -i) hermitage

eresia *f* heresy

eretico 1 *agg* heretical **2** *m* (*pl* -ci), *-a f* heretic

eretto 1 *pp* → *erigere* **2** *agg* erect

erezione *f* building; FISIOL erection

ergastolano *m*, *-a f* person serving a life sentence, lifer F

ergastolo *m* life sentence

ergonomico (*pl* -ci) ergonomic

erica *f* heather

erigere <3u> erect; *fig* (*fondare*) establish, found

erigersi *fig* set o.s. up (*a* as)

eritema *m* (*pl* -i) *cutaneo* rash; *~ solare* sunburn

ermafrodito *m* hermaphrodite

ermellino *m* ermine

ermetico (*pl* -ci) (*a tenuta d'aria*) airtight; *fig* obscure

ernia *f* MED hernia; *~ del disco* slipped disc

ero → *essere*

eroe *m* hero

erogare <1l, b & e> *denaro* allocate; *gas, acqua* supply

erogazione *f di denaro* allocation; *di gas ecc* supply

eroico (*pl* -ci) heroic

eroina *f droga* heroin; *donna eroica* heroine

eroinomane *m/f* heroin addict

erosione *f* GEOL erosion

erotico (*pl* -ci) erotic

erotismo *m* eroticism

errare <1b> wander, roam; (*sbagliare*) be mistaken

errata corrige *m inv* correction

erroneamente mistakenly

errore *m* mistake, error; *~ di battitura* typographical error, typo F; *~ di calcolo* mistake in the addition; *~ di ortografia* spelling mistake; *~ di stampa* misprint; *~ giudiziario* miscarriage of justice; *per ~* by mistake

erta *f*: *stare all'~* be on the alert

erudito 1 *agg* erudite, learned **2** *m*, *-a f* erudite person

erudizione *f* erudition, learning

eruttare <1a> *di vulcano* erupt

eruzione *f* eruption; MED rash

es. *abbr* (= *esempio*) eg (= for example)

esagerare <1m> **1** *v/t* exaggerate **2** *v/i* exaggerate; (*eccedere*) go too far (*in* in)

esagerato 1 *agg* exaggerated; *zelo* excessive; *prezzo* exorbitant **2** *m*, *-a f*: *sei il solito ~!* you're exaggerating as usual!

esagerazione *f* exaggeration

esagonale hexagonal, six-sided

esagono *m* hexagon

esalare <1a> **1** *v/t odori* give off; *~ il respiro* exhale **2** *v/i* come, emanate (*da* from)

esaltare <1a> exalt; (*entusiasmare*) elate

esaltarsi become elated

esaltato 1 *agg* elated; (*fanatico*) fanatical **2** *m* fanatic

esaltazione *f* exaltation; (*eccitazione*) elation

esame *m* exam(ination); MED (*test*) test; (*visita*) examination; **~ d'idoneità** aptitude test; **~ di guida** driving test; **prendere in ~** examine

esaminare <1m> examine (*anche* MED)

esaminatore *m*, **-trice** *f* examiner

esasperante exasperating

esasperare <1m> (*inasprire*) exacerbate; (*irritare*) exasperate

esasperarsi become exasperated

esasperato exasperated

esasperazione *f* exasperation

esattezza *f* accuracy; **con ~** exactly; **per l'~** to be precise

esatto 1 *pp* → **esigere 2** *agg* exact; *risposta* correct, right; *in punto* exactly; **~!** that's right!

esattoria *f* tax office

esaudire <4d> grant; *speranze* fulfil

esauriente exhaustive

esaurimento *m* exhaustion; FIN **svendita** *f* **fino a ~ della merce** clearance sale; MED **~ nervoso** nervous breakdown

esaurire <4d> exhaust; *merci* run out of

esaurito (*esausto*) exhausted; FIN sold out; *pubblicazioni* out of print; TEA **fa il tutto ~** it is playing to a full house

esausto exhausted

esca *f* (*pl* -che) bait (*anche fig*)

esce → **uscire**

eschimese *agg*, *m/f* Inuit, Eskimo

esclamare <1a> exclaim

esclamazione *f* exclamation

escludere <3q> exclude; *possibilità*, *ipotesi* rule out

esclusione *f* exclusion

esclusiva *f* exclusive right, sole right; FIN **~ di vendita** sole agency

esclusivo exclusive

escluso 1 *pp* → **escludere 2** *agg* excluded; (*impossibile*) out of the question, impossible **3** *m*, **-a** *f* person on the fringes of society

esco → **uscire**

escogitare <1m & c> contrive

escoriazione *f* graze

escrementi *mpl* excrement *sg*

escursione *f* trip, excursion; *a piedi* hike; **~ di un giorno** day trip

escursionismo *m* touring; *a piedi* hiking, walking

escursionista *m/f* tourist; *a piedi* hiker, walker

esecutivo *m/agg* executive

esecutore *m*, **-trice** *f* DIR executor; MUS performer; **~ testamentario** executor

esecuzione *f* (*realizzazione*) carrying out; MUS performance; DIR execution; **~ capitale** execution

eseguire <4b or 4d> carry out; MUS perform

esempio *m* (*pl* -pi) example; **per ~, ad ~** for example; **prendere ~ da qu** follow s.o.'s example

esemplare 1 *agg* exemplary **2** *m* specimen; (*copia*) copy

esentare <1b> exempt (*da* from)

esente exempt; **~ da tasse** tax free

esequie *fpl* funeral (service) *sg*

esercente *m/f* shopkeeper

esercitare <1m & b> exercise; (*addestrare*) train; *professione* practise

esercitarsi practise

esercitazione *f* exercise

esercito *m* army

esercizio *m* (*pl* -zi) exercise; (*pratica*) practice; *di impianti* operation, use; (*anno finanziario*) financial year, *Am* fiscal year; FIN *azienda* business; *negozio* shop; **~ pubblico** commercial premises

esibire <4d> *documenti* produce; *mettere in mostra* display

esibirsi *in uno spettacolo* perform; *fig* show off

esibizione *f* exhibition; (*ostentazione*) showing off; (*spettacolo*) performance

esibizionista *m/f* show-off; PSI exhibitionist

esigente exacting, demanding

esigenza f demand; (bisogno) need

esigere <3w> demand; (riscuotere) exact

esile slender; (voce) faint

esiliare <1k> exile

esilio m (pl -li) exile

esistente existing

esistenza f existence

esistere <3f> exist

esitare <1l & b> hesitate

esitazione f hesitation

esito m result, outcome; FIN sales, turnover

eskimo m inv giacca parka

esodo m exodus; di capitali flight

esofago m (pl -ghi) œsophagus, Am esophagus

esonerare <1m & c> exempt (da from)

esonero m exemption

esorbitante exorbitant

esordiente m/f beginner

esordio m (pl -di) introduction, preamble; (inizio) beginning; TEA début

esordire <4d> begin; TEA make one's début

esortare <1c> (incitare) urge; (pregare) beg

esortazione f urging

esoterico (pl -ci) esoteric

esoterismo m esotericism

esotico (pl -ci) exotic

espandere <3uu> expand

espandersi expand; (diffondersi) spread

espansione f expansion

espansività f fig warmth, friendliness

espansivo FIS, TEC expansive; fig warm, friendly

espatriare <1m & k> leave one's country

espatrio m (pl -i) expatriation

espediente m expedient; vivere di -i live by one's wits

espellere <3y> expel

esperienza f experience; per ~ from experience

esperimento m experiment

esperto m/agg expert

espiare <1h> atone for

espirare <1a> breathe out, exhale

espirazione f exhalation

esplicito explicit

esplodere <3q> 1 v/t colpo fire 2 v/i explode

esplorare <1c> explore

esploratore m, -trice f explorer; giovane m ~ boy scout

esplorazione f exploration

esplosione f explosion; fig ~ demografica population explosion

esplosivo m/agg explosive

esploso pp → esplodere

esponente m/f exponent

esporre <3ll> expose (anche PHOT); avviso put up; in una mostra exhibit, show; (riferire) present; ragioni, caso state; teoria explain

esporsi expose o.s. (a to); (compromettersi) compromise o.s.

esportare <1c> export

esportatore 1 agg exporting; paese m ~ exporting country, exporter 2 m, -trice f exporter

esportazione f export

esposimetro m FOT exposure meter

espositore m, -trice f exhibitor

esposizione f (mostra) exhibition; (narrazione) presentation; FOT exposure

esposto 1 pp → esporre 2 agg in mostra on show; ~ a exposed to; critiche open to; ~ a sud south facing 3 m statement; (petizione) petition

espressione f expression

espressivo expressive

espresso 1 pp → esprimere 2 agg express 3 m posta express letter; FERR express; (caffè m) ~ espresso; macchina f ~ espresso machine; per ~ express

esprimere <3r> express

esprimersi express o.s.

espropriare <1m & c> expropriate

espropriazione f expropriation

esproprio m expropriation

espulsione f expulsion

espulso pp → **espellere**

essa pron f persona she; cosa, animale it

essenza f essence

essenziale 1 agg essential 2 m: l'~ è the main thing is

essere <3z> 1 v/i be; ~ **di** (provenire di) be or come from; ~ **di qu** (appartenere a) belong to s.o.; **lei è di Roma** she is or comes from Rome; **è di mio padre** it is my father's, it belongs to my father; **c'è** there is; **ci sono** there are; **sono io** it's me; **cosa c'è?** what's the matter?, what's wrong?; **non c'è di che!** don't mention it!; **chi è?** who is it?; **ci siamo!** here we are!; **sono le tre** it's three o'clock; **siamo in quattro** there are four of us; **se fossi in te** if I were you; **sarà!** if you say so! 2 v/aus: **siamo arrivati alle due** we arrived at two o'clock; **non siamo ancora arrivati** we haven't arrived yet; **è stato investito** he has been run over 3 m being; ~ **umano** human being

esso pron m persona he; cosa, animale it

est m east; **a** ~ **di** east of

estasi f ecstasy

estate f summer; ~ **di San Martino** Indian summer; **in** ~, **d'**~ in (the) summer

estendere <3c> extend

estendersi di territorio extend; (allungarsi) stretch; fig (diffondersi) spread

estensione f extension; (vastità) expanse; MUS range

estenuante exhausting

esteriore m/agg exterior, outside

esteriorità f appearance

esterno 1 agg external; **per uso** ~ for external use only 2 m outside; in film location shot; **all'**~ on the outside

estero 1 agg foreign; **ministro m degli Affari -i** Foreign Secretary, Am Secretary of State 2 m foreign countries; **all'**~ abroad

esteso 1 pp → **estendere** 2 agg extensive; (diffuso) widespread; **per** ~ in full

estetica f (a)esthetics

estetista f beautician

estinguere <3d> extinguish, put out; debito pay off; sete quench

estinguersi die out

estinto 1 pp → **estinguere** 2 agg extinct; debito paid off 3 m, -a f deceased

estintore m fire extinguisher

estinzione f extinction; FIN redemption, paying off

estirpare <1a> uproot; dente extract; fig eradicate

estivo summer attr

estorcere <3d> denaro extort

estorsione f extortion

estorto pp → **estorcere**

estradare <1a> extradite

estradizione f extradition

estraneo 1 adj outside (**a** sth); **corpo** m ~ foreign body 2 m, -a f stranger; persona non autorizzata unauthorized person

estrarre <3xx> extract; pistola draw out; ~ **a sorte** draw

estratto 1 pp → **estrarre** 2 m extract; documento abstract; FIN ~ **conto** statement (of account)

estrazione f extraction

estremista m/f (pl -i) extremist

estremità f inv extremity; di corda end; (punta) tip; (punto superiore) top

estremo 1 agg extreme; (più lontano) farthest; (ultimo nel tempo) last, final; l'-a sinistra the far or extreme left; l'Estremo Oriente the Far East 2 m (estremità) extreme; gli -i di un documento the main points

estro m (ispirazione artistica) inspiration

estromettere <3ee> expel, Am expell

estroverso extrovert(ed)

estuario m (pl -ri) estuary

esuberante (vivace) exuberant

esuberanza f exuberance

esule m/f exile

esultare <1a> rejoice

età *f inv* age; **all'~ di** at the age of; **~ della pietra** Stone Age; **raggiungere la maggiore ~** come of age; **limiti** *mpl* **d'~** age limit; **avere la stessa ~** be the same age; **di mezz' ~** middle-aged

etere *m* ether

eternità *f* eternity

eterno eternal; *(interminabile)* endless, never-ending; *questione, problema* age-old; **in ~** for ever and ever

eterogeneo heterogen(e)ous

eterosessuale heterosexual

etica *f* ethics

etichetta *f* label; *cerimoniale* etiquette

etico ethical

etimologia *f* etymology

etiope *agg, m/f* Ethiopian

Etiopia *f* Ethiopia

etiopico *m/agg* Ethiopian

etnico *(pl* -ci) ethnic

etrusco *(pl* -chi) **1** *agg* Etruscan **2** *m*, **-a** *f* Etruscan

ettaro *m* hectare

etto *m* hundred grams

ettogrammo *m* *(pl* -i) hundred grams *pl*, hectogram

ettolitro *m* hectolitre, *Am* -liter

eucalipto *m* eucalyptus

eucaristia *f* REL Eucharist

euforia *f* euphoria

euforico *(pl* -ci) euphoric

euro *m inv* euro

eurocheque *m inv* Eurocheque

eurodeputato *m*, **-a** *f* Euro MP

eurodollaro *m* Eurodollar

euromercato *m* euromarket

Europa *f* Europe

europeo **1** *agg* European **2** *m*, **-a** *f* European

eurovisione *f* Eurovision

evacuare <1m> evacuate

evacuazione *f* evacuation

evadere <3q> **1** *v/t* evade; *(sbrigare)* deal with; **~ le tasse** evade taxes **2** *v/i* escape **(da** from)

evaporare <1m> evaporate

evaporazione *f* evaporation

evasione *f* escape; *fig* escapism; **~ fiscale** *f* tax evasion

evasivo evasive

evaso 1 *pp* → **evadere 2** *m*, **-a** *f* fugitive

evasore *m:* **~ fiscale** tax evader

evenienza *f* eventuality

evento *m* event

eventuale possible

eventualità *f inv* eventuality; **nell'~ che** in the event that; **per ogni ~** for every eventuality

eventualmente if necessary

evidente evident

evidenza *f* evidence; **mettere in ~** emphasize, highlight

evidenziatore *m* highlighter

evitare <1l & b> avoid; **~ il fastidio a qu** spare s.o. the trouble

evoluto 1 *pp* → **evolvere 2** *agg* developed; *(progredito)* progressive, advanced; *senza pregiudizi* open minded, broad-minded

evoluzione *f* evolution

evolvere <3s> **1** *v/t* develop **2** *v/i e* **evolversi** evolve, develop

evviva hurray

ex ... *(nelle parole composte)* ex-, former

expertise *f inv* expertise

extra 1 *agg inv* extra; **di qualità ~** top quality **2** *m inv* extra

extracomunitario 1 *agg* non-EC, non-EU **2** *m*, **-a** *f* non-EC *or* non-EU citizen

extraconiugale extramarital

extraeuropeo non-European

extraterrestre *agg, m/f* extraterrestrial

F

fa 1 → **fare** 2 *avv*: **5 anni** ~ 5 years ago; **3 m** MUS F; *nel solfeggio della scala* fa(h)

fabbisogno *m* needs *pl*, requirements *pl*

fabbrica *f* (*pl* -che) factory, *Am* plant

fabbricante *m/f* manufacturer

fabbricare <1l & d> manufacture; ARCHI build; *fig* fabricate

fabbricato *m* building

fabbricazione *f* manufacturing; ARCHI building

fabbro *m*: ~ (**ferraio**) blacksmith

faccenda *f* matter

faccende *fpl* housework *sg*

facchino *m* porter

faccia *f* (*pl* -cce) face; (*risvolto, aspetto*) facet; (*lato*) side; ~ **tosta** cheek; ~ **a** ~ face to face; **è** ~ **a** opposite, in front of; **in** ~ in the face; **gliel'ha detto in** ~ he told him to his face

facciata *f* ARCHI front, façade; *di foglio* side; *fig* (*esteriorità*) appearance

faccio → **fare**

facile easy; *di carattere* easy-going; (*incline*) prone (**a** to); **è ~ a dirsi!** easier said than done!; **è ~ che venga** he is likely to come; **non è mica una cosa** ~ it isn't that easy

facilità *f* ease; (*attitudine*) aptitude, facility; **con** ~ easily; INFOR ~ **d'uso** user-friendliness

facilitare <1m> facilitate

facilitazione *f* facility; **-i** *pl* **di prezzo** easy terms

facilmente easily

facoltà *f inv* faculty; (*potere*) power; **avere la ~ di scelta** have a choice, be able to choose

facoltativo optional

facoltoso wealthy

facsimile *m* facsimile

faggio *m* (*pl* -ggi) beech (tree)

fagiano *m* pheasant

fagiolini *mpl* green beans

fagiolo *m* bean

fagotto *m* bundle; MUS bassoon; *fig* **far** ~ pack up and leave

fai → **fare**

fai da te *m inv* do-it-yourself, DIY

falce *f* scythe

falciare <1f> cut (with a scythe); *fig* mow down

falciatrice *f* lawn-mower

falco *m* (*pl* -chi) hawk

falda *f* layer; GEOL stratum; *di cappello* brim; (*pendio*) slope; (*piede di monte*) foot; ~ **acquifera** water table

falegname *m* carpenter

falegnameria *f* carpentry

falena *f* moth

falla *f* MAR leak; **tappare una** ~ stop *or* plug a leak (*anche fig*)

fallimento *m* failure; FIN bankruptcy

fallire <4d> 1 *v/t* miss 2 *v/i* fail; FIN go bankrupt

fallito 1 *agg* unsuccessful, failed; FIN bankrupt 2 *m* failure; FIN bankruptcy

fallo *m* fault; (*errore*) error, mistake; SP foul; **mettere il piede in** ~ lose one's footing; **cogliere in ~ qu** catch s.o. out; (*in flagrante*) catch s.o red-handed

falò *m inv* bonfire

falsare <1a> *verità, fatti* distort

falsario *m* (*pl* -ri) forger

falsificare <1m & d> forge

falsificazione *f* forgery

falsità *f* falsity, falseness; (*menzogna*) lie; (*ipocrisia*) insincerity

falso 1 *agg* false; (*sbagliato*) incorrect, wrong; *oro, gioielli* imitation, fake F; (*falsificato*) forged, fake F 2 *m* (*falsità*) falsehood; *oggetto falsificato* forgery, fake F; DIR forgery

fama *f* fame; (*reputazione*) reputation; *di ~ mondiale* world-famous

fame *f* hunger; *aver* ~ be hungry

famiglia *f* family; *~ numerosa* large family

familiare 1 *agg* family *attr*; (*conosciuto*) familiar; (*semplice*) informal **2** *m/f* relative, relation

familiarità *f* familiarity

familiarizzare <1a> familiarize

familiarizzarsi familiarize o.s.

famoso famous

fanale *m* AUTO, MAR, AVIA, FERR light; (*lampione*) street lamp

fanalino *m* AUTO: *~ di coda* tail-light; *fig essere il ~ di coda* bring up the rear

fanatico (*pl* -ci) **1** *agg* fanatical **2** *m*, *-a f* fanatic

fanciullo *m*, *-a f lit* (young) boy; *ragazza* (young) girl

fandonia *f* lie

fango *m* (*pl* -ghi) mud; MED *-ghi pl* mud-baths

fangoso muddy

fannullone *m*, *-a f* lazy good-for-nothing

fantascienza *f* science fiction

fantasia *f* fantasy; (*immaginazione*) imagination; (*capriccio*) fancy; MUS fantasia

fantasma *m* (*pl* -i) ghost

fantasticare <1m & d> day-dream (*di* about)

fantastico (*pl* -ci) fantastic

fante *m carte da gioco* jack

fanteria *f* MIL infantry

fantoccio *m* (*pl* -cci) puppet (*anche fig*)

farabutto *m* nasty piece of work

faraona *f*: (*gallina f*) ~ guinea fowl

farcire <4d> GASTR stuff; *torta* fill

farcito stuffed; *dolce* filled

fard *m inv* blusher

fardello *m* bundle; *fig* burden

fare <3aa> **1** *v/t* do; *vestito*, *dolce*, *errore* make; *biglietto*, *benzina* buy, get; ~ (*dello*) *sport* play sport; *~ il pieno* fill up; *~ un bagno* have a bath; *~ il conto al ristorante* prepare the bill; *~ il medico / l'insegnante* be a doctor / teacher; *non fa niente* it

doesn't matter; *~ vedere qc a qu* show sth to s.o.; *farcela* manage; *non ce la faccio più* I can't take any more; *2 più 2 fa 4* 2 and 2 make(s) 4; *quanto fa?* how much is it?; *far ~ qc a qu* get s.o. to do sth **2** *v/i*: *questo non fa per me* this isn't for me; *faccia pure!* go ahead!, carry on!; *qui fa bello / brutto* the weather here is nice / awful; *fa freddo / caldo* it's cold / warm

farsi (*diventare*) grow; F (*drogarsi*) shoot up F; *~ grande* grow tall; *si sta facendo tardi* it's getting late; *~ avanti* step forward; *~ la barba* shave; *~ male* hurt o.s.

farfalla *f* butterfly

farina *f* flour

farinaceo 1 *agg* starchy **2** *-cei mpl* starchy foodstuffs

faringe *f* pharynx

faringite *f* inflammation of the pharynx

farmaceutico (*pl* -ci) pharmaceutical

farmacia *f* pharmacy; *negozio* chemist's, *Am* drugstore

farmacista *m/f* (*mpl* -i) chemist, *Am* pharmacist

farmaco *m* (*pl* -ci) drug

faro *m* MAR lighthouse; AVIA beacon; AUTO headlight; *-i pl fendinebbia* fog lamps *or* lights

farsa *f* farce

fascia *f* (*pl* -sce) band; MED bandage; *~ elastica* crepe bandage; *~ oraria* (time) slot

fasciare <1f> MED bandage

fasciatura *f* (*fascia*) bandage; *azione* bandaging

fascicolo *m* (*opuscolo*) booklet, brochure; (*incartamento*) file, dossier

fascino *m* fascination, charm

fascio *m* (*pl* -sci) bundle; *di fiori* bunch; *di luce* beam

fascismo *m* Fascism

fascista *agg*, *m/f* (*mpl* -i) Fascist

fase *f* phase; AUTO stroke; *fig essere fuori ~* be out of sorts; *~ di lavorazione* production stage

fastidio *m* (*pl* -di) bother, trouble;

dare ~ a qu bother s.o.; **le dà ~ se ... ?** do you mind if ... ?; **un sacco di -i** a lot of bother

fastidioso (*irritante*) irritating, annoying; (*irritabile*) irritable

fasto *m* pomp

fastoso sumptuous

fata *f* fairy

fatale fatal; **era ~ che non si sarebbero mai più rivisti** they were fated never to meet again

fatalità *f inv* (*il fato*) fate; (*disavventura*) misfortune

fatato magic, enchanted

fatica *f* (*pl* -che) (*sforzo*) effort; (*stanchezza*) fatigue; **a ~ with a** great deal of effort; **faccio ~ a crederci** I find it hard to believe

faticare <1d> toil; **~ a** find it difficult to

faticoso tiring; (*difficile*) laborious

fatt. *abbr* (= **fattura**) inv (= invoice)

fattibile feasible

fatto 1 *pp* → **fare** 2 *agg* done; AGR ripe; **~ a mano** hand-made; **~ di legno** made of wood; **~ in casa** home-made; **~ per qu/qc** (tailor-)made for s.o./sth 3 *m* fact; (*avvenimento*) event; (*faccenda*) affair, business; **il ~ è che ...** the fact is that ...; **cogliere sul ~** catch redhanded; **di ~** *agg* real; *avv* in fact, actually; **passare a vie di ~** come to blows; **in ~ di** as regards

fattore *m* (*elemento*) factor; AGR farm manager; **~ di protezione antisolare** sun protection factor

fattoria *f* farm; (*casa*) farmhouse

fattorino *m* messenger; *per consegne* delivery man; *posta* postman, *Am* mailman

fattura *f* (*lavorazione*) workmanship; *di abiti* cut; FIN invoice; **rilasciare una ~ a qu** invoice s.o.

fatturare <1a> FIN invoice

fatturato *m* FIN (*giro d'affari*) turnover

fauna *f* fauna

fava *f* broad bean

favola *f* (*fiaba*) fairy tale; (*storia*) story; *morale* fable; (*meraviglia*)

dream; **una vacanza da ~** a dream holiday

favoloso fabulous

favore *m* favo(u)r; **prezzo** *m* **di ~** special deal; **a ~ di qu** in favo(u)r of s.o.; **per ~!** please!; **fare un ~ a qu** do s.o. a favo(u)r

favorevole favo(u)rable

favorire <4d> 1 *v/t* favo(u)r; (*promuovere*) promote 2 *v/i*: **vuol ~?** would you care to join me/us?; **favorisca i documenti!** your papers, please!; **favorisca nello studio** would you go into the study please

favorito *m/agg* favo(u)rite

fax *m inv* fax; **mandare un ~ a qc** send s.o. a fax, fax s.o.

faxare <1a> fax

fazione *f* faction

fazzolettino *m*: **~ di carta** tissue

fazzoletto *m* handkerchief; **per la** *testa* headscarf

f.co *abbr* (= **franco**) free

febbraio *m* February

febbre *f* fever; **ha la ~** he has a *or* is running a temperature; **~ da fieno** hay fever

febbrifugo *m* (*pl* -ghi) MED *drug that reduces the temperature*

febbrile feverish

fecondare <1a> fertilize

fecondazione *f* fertilization; **~ artificiale** artificial insemination

fecondità *f* fertility

fecondo fertile

fede *f* faith; (*fedeltà*) loyalty; *anello* wedding ring; **aver ~ in qc** have faith in s.o.; **tener ~ a una promessa** keep a promise

fedele 1 *agg* faithful; (*esatto, conforme all'originale*) true 2 *m* REL believer; **i -i** *pl* the faithful

fedeltà *f* faithfulness; MUS **alta ~** hi-fi, high fidelity

federa *f* pillowcase

federale federal

federazione *f* federation

fegato *m* liver; *fig* courage, guts *pl* F

felce *f* fern

felice happy; (*fortunato*) lucky

felicità *f* happiness

felicitarsi <1m>: ~ *con qu per qc* congratulate s.o. on sth

felicitazioni *fpl* congratulations

felino feline

felpa *f* sweatshirt

feltro *m* felt

femmina *f* (*figlia*) girl, daughter; ZO, TEC female

femminile 1 *agg* feminine; (*da donna*) women's **2** *m* GRAM feminine

femminilità *f* feminity

femminismo *m* feminism

femminista *m/f* (*mpl* -i) feminist

femore *m* femur

fendinebbia *m inv* fog lamp *or* light

fenicottero *m* flamingo

fenomeno *m* phenomenon

feriale: *giorno m* ~ weekday

ferie *fpl* holiday *sg*, *Am* vacation *sg*; *andare in* ~ go on holiday (*Am* vacation)

ferimento *m* wounding

ferire <4d> wound; *in incidente* injure; *fig* hurt

ferirsi injure o.s.

ferita *f* wound; *in incidente* injury

ferito 1 *agg* wounded; *in incidente* injured; *fig sentimenti* hurt; *orgoglio* injured **2** *m* casualty

fermacarte *m inv* paperweight

fermacravatta *m* tiepin

fermaglio *m* (*pl* -gli) clasp; *per capelli* hair slide; (*gioiello*) brooch

fermare <1a> stop; DIR detain

fermarsi stop; (*restare*) stay, remain

fermata *f* stop; ~ *dell' autobus* bus stop; ~ *facoltativa o* ~ *a richiesta* request stop

fermentare <1a> ferment

fermentazione *f* fermentation

fermento *m* yeast; *fig* ferment

fermezza *f* firmness

fermo 1 *agg* still, motionless; *veicolo* stationary; (*saldo*) firm; *mano* steady; *star* ~ (*non muoversi*) keep still; *l'orologio è* ~ the watch has stopped **2** *int* ~! (*alt!*) stop!; (*immobile!*) keep still! **3** *m* DIR detention

fermoposta *m* poste restante

feroce fierce, ferocious; *animale* wild; (*insopportabile*) dreadful

ferocia *f* ferocity

ferragosto *m* August 15 public holiday; *periodo* August holidays

ferramenta *f* hardware; *negozio* hardware store, ironmonger's *Br*

ferrato FERR: *strada f* -*a* railway line, *Am* railroad; *fig essere* ~ *in qc* be well up in sth

ferro *m* iron; (*arnese*) tool; *fig di* ~ *memoria*, *salute* excellent; *stomaco* cast-iron; ~ *da calza* knitting needle; ~ *da stiro a vapore* steam iron; ~ *di cavallo* horseshoe; ~ *battuto* wrought iron; GASTR *ai* -*i* grilled, *Am* broiled

ferrovia *f* railway, *Am* railroad; ~ *metropolitana o sotterranea* underground, *Am* subway

ferrovecchio *m* (*pl* -cchi) scrap merchant

ferroviario (*pl* -ri) rail(way) *attr*, *Am* railroad *attr*

ferroviere *m* rail (*Am* railroad) worker

fertile fertile

fertilità *f* fertility

fertilizzante *m* fertilizer

fesso *m* F idiot F; *far* ~ *qu* con s.o F

fessura *f* (*spaccatura*) crack; (*fenditura*) slit, slot

festa *f* feast; *di santo* feast day; (*ricevimento*) party; (*compleanno*) birthday; (*onomastico*) name day; ~ *della mamma / del papà* Mother's/ Father's Day; ~ *nazionale* national holiday; *buone* -*e! a Natale* Merry Christmas and a happy New Year!

festeggiamenti *mpl* celebrations

festeggiare <1f> celebrate; *persona* have a celebration for

festival *m inv* festival

festività *f inv* festival; ~ *pl* celebrations, festivities

festivo festive; *giorno m* ~ holiday

festoso happy, cheerful

feto *m* f(o)etus

fetta *f* slice; *a* -*e* sliced

feudale feudal

fiaba *f* fairy tale

fiabesco (*pl* -chi) fairytale *attr*

fiacca *f* weariness; (*svogliatezza*)

laziness; **battere la ~** slack, be a shirker

fiacco (*pl* -cchi) (*debole*) weak; (*svogliato*) lazy; FIN *mercato* sluggish

fiaccola *f* torch

fiala *f* phial

fiamma *f* flame; MAR pennant; GASTR **alla ~** flambé

fiammante: rosso m ~ fiery red; **nuovo ~** brand new

fiammifero *m* match

fiancheggiare <1f> border; *fig* support

fianco *m* (*pl* -chi) side; ANAT hip; **~ a ~** side by side; **di ~ a qu** beside s.o.; **al tuo ~** by your side

fiasco *m* (*pl* -chi) flask; *fig* fiasco

fiato *m* breath; **senza ~** breathless; MUS **strumento m a ~** wind instrument; **tutto d'un ~** in one go; **riprendere ~** catch one's breath

fibbia *f* buckle

fibra *f* fibre, *Am* fiber; **di forte ~** robust, sturdy; **~ morale** moral fibre (*Am* fiber); **~ sintetica** synthetic; **~ di vetro** fibreglass, *Am* fiberglass

fibroso fibrous

ficcanaso *m/f* F nosy parker F

ficcare <1d> thrust; F (*mettere*) shove F

ficcarsi get; **~ nei guai** get into hot water; **~ qc in testa** get sth into one's head; **dove s'è ficcato?** where can it / he have got to?

fico *m* (*pl* -chi) *frutto* fig; *albero* fig (tree); **~ d'India** prickly pear

fidanzamento *m* engagement

fidanzarsi <1a> get engaged

fidanzata *f* fiancée

fidanzato *m* fiancé; **i -i** *pl* the engaged couple

fidarsi: ~ di qu / qc trust s.o. / sth, rely on s.o. / sth; **non mi fido di chiederlo a mio padre** I don't dare ask my father

fidato trustworthy

fideiussione *f* DIR guarantee

fido 1 *agg* trusted, trusty **2** *m* FIN credit

fiducia *f* confidence; **avere ~ in qu** have faith in s.o.; **di ~ persona** reli-

able, trustworthy; *incarico* responsible

fiduciaria *f* ~ FIN trust company

fiduciario (*pl* -ri) **1** *agg* DIR *atto, società* trust *attr* **2** *m* trustee

fiducioso trusting

fienile *m* barn

fieno *m* hay

fiera[1] *f animale* wild beast

fiera[2] *f mostra* fair

fierezza *f* pride

fiero proud

fifa F *f* nerves, jitters F; **aver ~** have the jitters, be jittery

figlia *f* daughter

figliastra *f* stepdaughter

figliastro *m* stepson

figlio *m* (*pl* -gli) son; **avere -gli** *pl* have children; **essere ~ unico** be an only child

figlioccia *f* (*pl* -cce) goddaughter

figlioccio *m* (*pl* -cci) godson

figura *f* figure; (*illustrazione*) illustration; (*apparenza*) appearance; **far brutta ~** make a bad impression

figurare <1a> **1** *v/t fig* imagine; **figurati!** just imagine!, just think!; **si figuri!** not at all!, of course not! **2** *v/i* (*apparire*) appear; (*far figura*) make a good impression

figurato (*illustrato*) illustrated; *linguaggio, espressione* figurative

figurina *f da raccolta* collector card, trading card

figurino *m* fashion sketch

fila *f* line, row; (*coda*) queue, *Am* line; **di ~** in succession; **tre giorni di ~** three days running, three days in succession; **in ~ indiana** in single file; **fare la ~** queue, *Am* wait in line

filamento *m* filament

filare <1a> **1** *v/t* spin **2** *v/i di ragno* spin; *di ragionamento* make sense; *di formaggio* go stringy; *di veicolo* travel; F (*andarsene*) take off F; **fila!** go away!, shoo!; **~ diritto** (*comportarsi bene*) behave (o.s.) **3** *m di alberi* row

filarmonico (*pl* -ci) philharmonic

filastrocca *f* (*pl* -cche) *m* nursery rhyme

filatelia f philately

filato 1 agg (logico) logical; **andare di ~ a casa** go straight home; **per 10 ore filate** for ten hours straight **2** m yarn; **per cucire** thread

file m inv INFOR file

filetto m GASTR fillet; TEC thread

filiale f branch; (società affiliata) affiliate

filigrana f su carta watermark; in oreficeria filigree

film m inv film, movie; **~ giallo** thriller; **~ in bianco e nero** black and white film

filmare <1a> film

filmato m short (film)

filo m (pl anche le -a) thread; metallico wire; di lama edge; d'erba blade; fig **un ~ di vergogna/rispetto** an ounce of shame/respect; fig **~ conduttore** lead; **~ interdentale** (dental) floss; **~ spinato** barbed wire; **~ di voce** whisper; **per ~ e per segno** in detail; **dare del ~ da torcere a qu** make things difficult for s.o.

filobus m inv trolley(bus)

filodrammatica f amateur dramatic society

filologia f philology

filologo m (pl -gi) philologist

filone m MIN vein; pane French stick; fig tradition

filosofia f philosophy

filosofico (pl -ci) philosophic(al)

filosofo m philosopher

filovia f trolley(bus)

filtrare <1a> **1** v/t strain, filter **2** v/i fig filter out

filtro m filter; **~ dell'olio** oil filter; **~ di carta** filter paper

fin → **fine, fino**

finale 1 agg final **2** m end **3** f SP final

finalista m/f finalist

finalmente (alla fine) at last; (per ultimo) finally

finanza f finance; **-e** pl finances; **ministro m delle -e** Minister of Finance

finanziamento m funding

finanziare <1g> fund, finance

finanziario (pl -ri) financial

finanziere m financier; (guardia di finanza) Customs and Excise officer; lungo le coste coastguard

finché until; (per tutto il tempo che) as long as

fine 1 agg fine; (sottile) thin; udito, vista sharp, keen; (raffinato) refined **2** m aim; **al ~ di ...** in order to ...; **secondo ~** ulterior motive **3** f end; **alla ~** in the end; **alla fin ~, in fin dei conti** after all, when all's said and done; **senza ~** endless

fine settimana m inv weekend

finestra f window

finestrino m window; AUTO **~ posteriore** rear window

finezza f fineness; (sottigliezza) thinness; (raffinatezza) refinement

fingere <3d> **1** v/t **~ sorpresa/dolore** pretend to be surprised/to be in pain **2** v/i: **~ di** pretend to

fingersi pretend to be

finire <4d> **1** v/t finish, end; **finiscila!** stop it! **2** v/i end, finish (in in); **andrà a ~ male** cosa this will all end in tears; persona he/she will come to no good

finito finished; (venduto) sold out; **è finita** it's over; **farla finita con qc** put an end to sth

finlandese 1 m/agg Finnish **2** m/f Finn

Finlandia f Finland

fino¹ agg fine; (acuto) sharp; oro pure

fino² prp tempo till, until; luogo as far as; **~ a domani** until tomorrow; **~ a che** (per tutto il tempo che) as long as; (fino al momento in cui) until; **fin da ieri** since yesterday

fino³ avv even; **fin troppo** more than enough

finocchio m (pl -cchi) fennel

finora so far

finta f pretence, Am pretense, sham; SP feint; **far ~ di** pretend to

fintantoché until

finto 1 pp → **fingere 2** agg false; (artificiale) artificial; (simulato) feigned

finzione f pretence, Am pretense, sham

fiocco m (pl -cchi) bow; ~ **di neve** snowflake; -**cchi** pl **d'avena** oat flakes, rolled oats; fig **coi -cchi** first-rate

fioco (pl -chi) weak; luce dim

fionda f catapult

fioraio m (pl -ai), -**a** f florist

fiordaliso m cornflower

fiordo m fjord

fiore m flower; fig **il** (**fior**) ~ the cream; nelle carte -**i** pl clubs; **disegno** m **a -i** floral design; **a fior d'acqua** on the surface of the water; **essere in** ~ be in flower

fiorente flourishing

fiorentino 1 agg Florentine **2** m, -**a** f Florentine; GASTR **alla -a** with spinach; bistecca charcoal grilled **3** f GASTR T-bone steak

fioretto m SP foil

fiorire <4d> flower; fig flourish

fioritura f flowering (anche fig)

Firenze f Florence

firma f signature; (il firmare) signing; FIN **avere la** ~ be an authorized signatory

firmamento m firmament

firmare <1a> sign

firmatario m (pl -ri) signatory

firmato abito, borsa designer attr

fisarmonica f (pl -che) accordion

fiscale tax, fiscal; fig spreg rigid, unbending

fiscalità f taxation; (pignoleria) rigidity, lack of flexibility

fischiare <1k> **1** v/t whistle; ~ **qu** boo s.o. **2** v/i di vento whistle

fischio m (pl -chi) whistle; SP ~ **finale** final whistle

fisco m tax authorities pl, Inland Revenue, Am Internal Revenue; **il** ~ the taxman

fisica f physics; ~ **nucleare** nuclear physics

fisico (pl -ci) **1** agg physical **2** m physicist; ANAT physique

fisiologia f physiology

fisionomia f face; fig di popolo, città appearance; (carattere) character

fisioterapia f physiotherapy

fisioterapista m/f (mpl -i) physiotherapist

fissare <1a> (fermare) fix; (guardare intensamente) stare at; (stabilire) arrange; (prenotare) book

fissarsi (stabilirsi) settle; (ostinarsi) set one's mind (**di** on); (avere un'idea fissa) become obsessed (**di** with); ~ **in mente** memorize

fissatore m (per capelli) hair-spray; FOT fixer

fissazione f (mania) fixation (**di** about)

fisso 1 agg fixed; stipendio, cliente regular; lavoro permanent **2** avv fixedly

fitta f sharp pain

fitto¹ 1 agg (denso) thick; ~ **di** full of **2** avv nevicare, piovere hard

fitto² m rent

fiume m river; fig flood, torrent; **letto** m **del** ~ river bed

fiutare <1a> smell; cocaina snort; ~ **un imbroglio** smell a rat

fiuto m sense of smell; fig nose

flacone m bottle

flagrante flagrant; **cogliere qu in** ~ catch s.o. red-handed

flanella f flannel

flash m inv FOT flash; stampa newsflash

flatulenza f flatulence

flauto m flute

flemma f calm

flemmatico (pl -ci) phlegmatic

flessibile flexible

flessione f bending; GRAM inflection; (diminuzione) dip, (slight) drop

flipper m inv pinball machine; **giocare a** ~ play pinball

flirt m inv flirtation

flirtare <1a> flirt

F.lli abbr (= **fratelli**) Bros (= brothers)

floppy disk m inv floppy (disk)

flora f flora

floreale floral

floricultura f flower-growing industry

florido flourishing

floscio (*pl* -sci) limp; *muscoli* flabby

flotta *f* fleet

fluido *m/agg* fluid

fluorescente fluorescent

fluoro *m* fluorine

flusso *m* flow; **~ e riflusso** ebb and flow

fluttuare <1l> FIN, *fig* fluctuate

fluttuazione *f* fluctuation; **~ dei prezzi** price fluctuation

fluviale river *attr*

f.m. *abbr* (= **fine mese**) end of the month

FMI *abbr* (= **Fondo Monetario Internazionale**) IMF (= International Monetary Fund)

f.to *abbr* (= **firmato**) sgd (= signed)

foca *f* (*pl* -che) seal

focaccia *f* (*pl* -cce) focaccia; *dolce sweet type of bread*; **rendere pan per ~** give tit for tat

focalizzare <1a> focus on

foce *f* mouth

focolaio *m* (*pl* -ai) *fig* hotbed

focolare *m* hearth; TEC furnace

focoso fiery

fodera *f interna* lining; *esterna* cover

foderare <1l & c> *all'interno* line; *all'esterno* cover

fodero *m* sheath

foggia *f* (*pl* -gge) *f di abito, acconciatura* style

foglia *f* leaf

fogliame *m* foliage

foglio *m* (*pl* -gli) sheet; INFOR **~ elettronico** spreadsheet; **~ rosa** *provisional driving licence*; **~ di via obbligatorio** expulsion order

fogna *f* sewer

fognatura *f* sewers *pl*, sewage pipes *pl*

folata *f* gust

folclore *m* folklore

folcloristico (*pl* -ci) folk *attr*

folgorare <1l> *di fulmine, idea* strike; *di corrente elettrica* electrocute; **~ qu con lo sguardo** glare at s.o.

folgorato struck

folklore *m* → **folclore**

folla *f* crowd; *fig* host

folle[1] *agg* mad

folle[2] AUTO: **in ~** in neutral

follia *f* madness

folto thick

fondale *m* MAR sea bed; TEA backcloth, backdrop

fondamentale fundamental

fondamento *m* foundation; **le -a** *fpl* the foundations; **senza ~** unfounded

fondare <1a> found

fondarsi be based (**su** on)

fondato founded

fondatore *m*, **-trice** *f* founder

fondazione *f* foundation

fondere <3bb> **1** *v/t* (*liquefare*) melt; METAL smelt; *colori* blend **2** *v/i* melt

fondersi melt; FIN merge

fonderia *f* foundry

fondiario (*pl* -ri) land *attr*

fondo 1 *agg* deep **2** *m* bottom; (*sfondo*) background; *terreno* property; FIN fund; SP long-distance; SCI cross-country, langlauf; **-i** *pl di denaro* funds; **a ~** (*profondamente*) in depth; *fig* **in ~** basically; **in ~ alla strada / al corridoio** at the end *or* bottom of the road / of the corridor; **essere in ~ al treno** be at the rear of the train; FIN **~ d'ammortamento** depreciation fund; **andare a ~** (*affondare*) sink; (*approfondire*) get to the bottom (**di** of); **-i** *pl di magazzino* old *or* unsold stock *sg*

fondotinta *m inv* foundation

fonduta *f cheese fondue*

fonetica *f* phonetics

fontana *f* fountain

fonte *m/f* spring; *fig* source; **~ energetica** source of energy; **da ~ attendibile** from a reliable source

footing *m* jogging

foraggio *m* (*pl* -ggi) forage

forare <1a> *di proiettile* pierce; *con il trapano* drill; *biglietto* punch; *pneumatico* puncture

foratura *f di pneumatico* puncture

forbici *fpl* scissors; **un paio di ~** a pair of scissors

forca *f* (*forcone*) pitchfork

forcella *f* TEC fork

forchetta *f* fork; **essere una buona**

~ have a big appetite

forcina f hairpin

forcipe m forceps pl

forcone m pitchfork

foresta f forest

forestale forest attr

foresteria f guest accommodation

forestiero 1 agg foreign **2** m, **-a** f foreigner

forfait m inv lump sum; SP withdrawal; **a ~** on a lump-sum basis

forfettario flat-rate, all in; **prezzo** m **~** lump sum

forfora f dandruff

forma f form; (sagoma) shape; TEC (stampo) mo(u)ld; **essere in ~** be in good form

formaggiera f dish for grated cheese

formaggino m processed cheese

formaggio m (pl -ggi) cheese

formale formal

formalità f inv formality

formare <1a> shape; TELEC **~ il numero** dial the number

formarsi form; (svilupparsi) develop; di un'idea take shape

formato m size; di libro format

formattare <1a> INFOR format

formazione f formation; fig addestramento training; SP line-up; **~ professionale** vocational training

formica[1] f (pl -che) ZO ant

formica[2]® Formica®

formicaio m (pl -ai) anthill

formicolare <1m> di mano, gamba tingle; fig **~ di** teem with

formicolio m sensazione pins and needles pl

formidabile (straordinario) incredible; (poderoso) powerful

formula f formula

formulare <1l> teoria, ipotesi formulate; (esprimere) express

fornaio m (pl -ai) baker; negozio bakery

fornello m stove

fornire <4d> supply (**qc a qu** s.o. with sth)

fornirsi get (**di** sth), get hold (**di** of)

fornitore m supplier

fornitura f supply

forno m oven; (panetteria) bakery; **~ a microonde** microwave (oven); GASTR **al ~ carne, patate** roast; **mele, pasta** baked

foro[1] m (buco) hole

foro[2] m romano forum; DIR (tribunale) (law) court

forse perhaps, maybe; **mettere in ~** cast doubt on

forte 1 agg strong; suono loud; pioggia heavy; taglia large; somma considerable, substantial; dolore severe **2** avv (con forza) hard; (ad alta voce) loudly; (velocemente) fast **3** m (fortezza) fort; **questo è il suo ~** it's his strong point

fortezza f MIL fortress; **~ d'animo** strength of character

fortificare <1m & d> rendere più **forte** strengthen; MIL fortify

fortino m MIL blockhouse

fortuito chance

fortuna f fortune; **avere ~** be successful; (essere fortunato) be lucky; **buona ~!** good luck!; **fare ~** make a fortune; **per ~** luckily; **di ~** makeshift; **atterraggio** m **di ~** emergency landing

fortunatamente fortunately

fortunato lucky, fortunate

foruncolo m pimple

forza f strength; (potenza) power; muscolare force; **~ di gravità** force of gravity; **per cause di ~ maggiore** because of circumstances beyond my/our control; **a viva ~** by force; **a ~ di ...** by dint of ...; **per ~** against my/our will; **per ~!** (naturalmente) of course!; **~!** come on!; **-e** pl (armate) MIL armed forces

forzare <1c> force

foschia f haze

fosco (pl -schi) dark

fosfato m phosphate

fosforescente phosphorescent

fosforo m phosphorus

fossa f pit, hole; (tomba) grave; **~ comune** mass grave

fossato m ditch; di fortezza moat

fossetta f dimple

fossile 1 agg fossil attr **2** m fossil

fosso *m* ditch

foto *f inv* photo, snap

fotocellula *f* photocell

fotocopia *f* photocopy

fotocopiare <1k & c> photocopy

fotocopiatrice *f* photocopier

fotogenico (*pl* -ci) photogenic

fotografare <1m & c> photograph

fotografia *f arte* photography; (*foto*) photograph; ~ **formato tessera** passport-size photograph; ~ **aerea** aerial photograph; ~ **a colori** colo(u)r photograph

fotografico (*pl* -ci) photographic; **macchina** *f* -**a** camera; **articoli** *mpl* -**ci** photographic equipment

fotografo *m* photographer

fotomontaggio *m* (*pl* -gi) photomontage

fotoreporter *m/f inv* photo journalist

fotoromanzo *m* story told in pictures

fra *prp* ◊ between; ~ **Roma e Londra** between Rome and London ◊ among; ~ **questi ragazzi** out of all these boys; ~ **di noi** between you and me; ~ **l'altro** what's more ◊ in; ~ **breve** in a very short time, soon; ~ **tre giorni** in three days ◊ ~ **sé e sé** to himself/herself

frac *m inv* tails

fracassare <1a> smash

fracasso *m di persone* din; *di oggetti che cadono* crash

fradicio (*pl* -ci) rotten; (*bagnato*) soaked, soaking wet; **ubriaco** ~ blind drunk F, blotto F

fragile fragile; *persona* frail, delicate

fragola *f* strawberry

fragore *m* roar; *di tuono* rumble

fraintendere <3c> misunderstand

frammentario (*pl* -ri) fragmentary

frammento *m* fragment

frana *f* landslide

franare <1a> collapse

francamente frankly

francese **1** *m/agg* French **2** *m/f* Frenchman; *donna* Frenchwoman; *i* -*i pl* the French

franchezza *f* frankness

franchigia *f* FIN exemption; *posta* freepost; ~ **doganale** exemption from customs duties

Francia *f* France

franco (*pl* -chi) **1** *agg* frank; FIN free; **farla** -**a** get away with it; ~ **domicilio** free delivery, carriage paid **2** *m* FIN franc

francobollo *m* stamp; **due** -**i da ... lire** two ... lire stamps

frangente *m* (*onda*) breaker; (*situazione*) (difficult) situation

frangia *f* (*pl* -ge) fringe

frantumare <1a> shatter

frantumi *mpl* splinters; **in** ~ in smithereens; **mandare in** ~ smash to smithereens

frappé *m inv* milkshake

frase *f* phrase; ~ **fatta** cliché

frassino *m* ash (tree)

frastagliato: **costa** *f* -**a** jagged coastline

frastuono *m* racket

frate *m* REL friar, monk

fratellastro *m* step-brother; *con legami di consanguineità* half-brother

fratello *m* brother; -*i pl fratello e sorella* brother and sister

fraterno brotherly, fraternal

frattaglie *fpl* GASTR offal *sg*; *di pollo* giblets

frattanto meanwhile, in the meantime

frattempo *m:* **nel** ~ meanwhile, in the meantime

frattura *f* fracture

fratturare <1a> fracture

fratturarsi: ~ **una gamba** break one's leg

frazionare <1a> (*dividere in parti*) break up, split up

frazionarsi split (**in** into)

frazione *f* fraction; POL small group; (*borgata*) hamlet; ~ **decimale** decimal fraction; **una** ~ **di secondo** a split second

freccia *f* (*pl* -cce) arrow; AUTO ~ (**di direzione**) indicator

freddezza *f* coldness

freddo **1** *agg* cold; *fig* **a sangue** ~ in cold blood **2** *m* cold; **ho** ~ I'm cold;

fa ~ it's cold

freddoloso: essere ~ feel the cold

freddura f pun, play on words

freezer m inv freezer

fregare <1e> rub; F (*imbrogliare*) swindle F; F (*battere*) beat, wipe the floor with F; F *a un esame* fail; F (*rubare*) pinch F, lift F; P **me ne frego di quello che pensano** I don't give a damn what they think F

fregata f MAR frigate

fregatura f F (*imbroglio*) rip-off F; (*ostacolo, contrarietà*) pain F

fregio m ARCHI frieze

fremere <3a> (*tremare*) tremble, quiver

frenare <1a> AUTO brake; *folla, lacrime, risate* hold back; *entusiasmo, impulso* restrain

frenarsi (*dominarsi*) restrain o.s.

frenata f braking; **fare una ~** brake; *segni* mpl *di* ~ tyre marks

freno m AUTO brake; *del cavallo* bit; **~ d'allarme** emergency brake; **~ a mano** handbrake, Am parking brake; **~ a pedale** foot-brake; *porre* **~ a qc** curb sth; *fig senza* **~** without restraint; *tenere a* **~ la lingua** curb one's tongue

frequentare <1b> *luoghi* frequent; *scuola, corso* attend; *persona* associate with

frequentato popular; *strada* busy

frequente frequent; *di* **~** frequently

frequenza f frequency; *scolastica* attendance; *un'alta* **~ di spettatori** a large audience; *con* **~** frequently

freschezza f freshness; *di temperatura* coolness

fresco (*pl* -chi) **1** agg fresh; *temperatura* cool; *fig* **stai ~ !** you're for it! F, you've had it! F **2** m coolness; *prendere il* **~** take the air; *fa* **~** it's cool; *mettere in* **~** put in a cool place; *fig* F *al* **~** inside F

frescura f cool(ness)

fretta f hurry; *aver* **~** be in a hurry; *non c'è* **~** there's no hurry, there's no rush; *in tutta* **~**, *in* **~** *e furia* in great haste

frettoloso *saluto, sorriso* hurried;

lavoro rushed; *persona* in a hurry

fricassea f GASTR fricassee

friggere <3cc> **1** v/t fry **2** v/i sizzle

friggitoria f *shop that sells deep fried fish etc*

friggitrice f deep fryer

frigido MED frigid

frigo m fridge

frigorifero 1 agg cold *attr; camion, nave, vagone* refrigerated **2** m refrigerator

fringuello m chaffinch

frittata f GASTR omelette, Am omelet; *fig* **ormai la ~ è fatta** the damage is done

frittella f fritter; *fig* (*macchia*) grease stain

fritto 1 pp → **friggere 2** agg fried **3** m fried food; **~ misto** assortment of deep-fried food

frittura f *metodo* frying; **~ di pesce** fried fish

frivolo frivolous

frizionare <1a> rub

frizione f friction; AUTO clutch

frizzante *bevanda* fizzy, sparkling; *aria* crisp; *fig parola, motto* biting, sharp

frodare <1c> defraud (*di* of); **~ il fisco** evade *or* dodge F tax

frode f fraud

frontale frontal; **scontro** m **~** head-on collision

fronte 1 f forehead; *di* **~** *a* (*dirimpetto*) opposite, facing; *in presenza di* before; *a confronto di* compared to *or* with; *la casa, vista dal di* **~** the house, seen from the front **2** m front; **~ caldo** warm front; *far* **~ agli impegni** face up to one's responsibilities; *far* **~ alle spese** make ends meet

fronteggiare <1f> (*stare di fronte a*) face; (*far fronte a*) face, confront

frontespizio m (*pl* -zi) title page; ARCHI frontispiece

frontiera f border, frontier; *guardia* f *di* **~** border guard; *valico* m *di* **~** border crossing

frontone m ARCHI pediment

fronzolo m frill

frottola *f* F **fib** F

frugale frugal

frugare <1e> **1** *v/i* (*rovistare*) rummage **2** *v/t* (*cercare con cura*) search, rummage through

fruire <4d> ~ *di qc* benefit from sth

frullare <1a> GASTR blend, liquidize; *uova* whisk

frullato *m* milk-shake

frullatore *m* liquidizer, blender

frullino *m* whisk

frumento *m* wheat

frusciare <1f> rustle

fruscio *m* rustle

frusta *f* whip; GASTR whisk

frustare <1a> whip

frustino *m* riding crop

frustrare <1a> frustrate

frustrazione *f* frustration

frutta *f* fruit; ~ *candita* candied fruit; ~ *fresca* fresh fruit; ~ *secca* nuts

fruttare <1a> **1** *v/t* yield **2** *v/i* fruit

frutteto *m* orchard

fruttifero fruitful; FIN interest-bearing

fruttivendolo *m*, **-a** *f* greengrocer

frutto *m* fruit; **-i** *pl di mare* seafood *sg*

fruttuoso profitable

FS *abbr* (= *Ferrovie dello Stato*) Italian State railways

fu → *essere*

fucilare <1a> shoot

fucilata *f* shot

fucile *m* rifle

fucina *f* forge

fuga *f* (*pl* -ghe) escape; MUS fugue; ~ *di gas* gas leak; FIN ~ *di capitali* flight of capital

fuggevole fleeting

fuggiasco *m* (*pl* -schi) fugitive

fuggifuggi *m inv* stampede

fuggire <4a> flee

fuggitivo *m* fugitive

fulcro *m* fulcrum

fuliggine *f* soot

fuligginoso sooty

fulminante *sguardo* withering; *malattia* which strikes suddenly

fulminare <1l> *di sguardo* look daggers at, glare at; *rimanere fulminato da fulmine* be struck by lightning; *da elettricità* be electrocuted; *fig* be thunderstruck

fulminarsi *di lampadina* blow

fulmine *m* lightning

fulmineo fast, rapid

fumaiolo *m* MAR funnel; FERR chimney; *di casa* chimney pot

fumare <1a> smoke

fumatore *m*, **-trice** *f* smoker; FERR *scompartimento m per -i / non -i* smoking / non-smoking compartment

fumetto *m* comic strip; **-i** *pl per ragazzi* comics

fumo *m* smoke; (*vapore*) steam; *fig andare in* ~ (*fallire*) go up in smoke; (*svanire*) come to nothing; *mandare in* ~ shatter

fumoso smoky; *fig* (*oscuro*) muddled

fune *f* rope; (*cavo*) cable; *tiro m alla* ~ tug-of-war

funebre funeral *attr*; *fig* gloomy, funereal; *carro m* ~ hearse

funerale *m* funeral

fungere <3d> act (*da* as)

fungo *m* (*pl* -ghi) mushroom; MED fungus; ~ *velenoso* poisonous mushroom; ~ *prataiolo* field mushroom

funicolare *f* funicular railway

funivia *f* cableway

funzionamento *m* operation, functioning

funzionare <1a> operate, function; *non* ~ be out of order; *di orologio* have stopped

funzionario *m* (*pl* -ri) official, civil servant

funzione *f* function; (*carica*) office; REL service, ceremony; *mettere in* ~ put into operation; *in* ~ *di ...* depending on; *variare in* ~ *di ...* vary with ...

fuoco *m* (*pl* -chi) fire; FIS, FOT focus; *dar* ~ *a qc* set fire to sth; **-chi** *d'artificio* fireworks; MIL *far* ~ (open) fire; FOT *mettere a* ~ focus

fuorché except

fuori 1 *prp stato* outside, out of; *moto* out of, away from; ~ *di casa* outside the house; ~ *città* out of town; ~

luogo out of place; **~ mano** out of the way; **~ di sé** beside o.s.; **~ uso** out of use **2** *avv* outside; **all'aperto** out of doors; SP out; **di ~** outside; **~!** out!

fuoribordo *m inv* motorboat; *motore* outboard motor

fuoriclasse *agg*, *m/f inv* champion

fuorigioco *m inv* offside; **essere nel ~** be offside

fuoriserie 1 *agg* made to order, custom made **2** *f inv* AUTO custom-built model

fuoristrada *m inv* off-road vehicle

fuoriuscita *f di gas* leakage, escape

fuoriuscito *m* exile

fuorviare <1h> **1** *v/i* go astray **2** *v/t* lead astray

furbizia *f* cunning

furbo cunning, crafty

furfante *m* rascal, rogue

furgoncino *m* (small) van

furgone *m* van

furia *f* fury, rage; **a ~ di …** by dint of …

furibondo furious, livid

furioso furious; *vento*, *lotta* violent

furore *m* fury, rage; **far ~** be all the rage

furtivo furtive

furto *m* theft; **~ con scasso** burglary

fusa *fpl*: **fare le ~** purr

fuscello *m* twig

fuseaux *mpl* leggings

fusibile *m* EL fuse

fusione *f* fusion; FIN merger; **~ nucleare** nuclear fusion

fuso¹ *pp* → **fondere**; METAL molten; *burro* melted

fuso² *m* spindle; **~ orario** time zone

fusto *m* (*tronco*) trunk; (*stelo*) stem, stalk; *di metallo* drum; *di legno* barrel

futile futile

futilità *f* futility

futuristico futuristic

futuro *m/agg* future; **in ~** in future; **in un lontano / prossimo ~** in the distant / near future

G

g *abbr* (= **grammo**) g (= gram)

gabbia *f* cage; **~ di mattia** *fig* madhouse; **~ toracica** rib cage

gabbiano *m* (sea)gull

gabinetto *m* toilet; POL cabinet; **~ medico / dentistico** doctor's / dentist's surgery; POL **~ ombra** shadow cabinet

gaffe *f* blunder, gaffe

gaelico *m* Gaelic

gala *f* (*ricevimento*) gala; **serata *f* di ~** gala evening

galante gallant

galanteria *f* gallantry

galantuomo (*pl* -uomini) *m* gentleman

galassia *f* galaxy

galateo *m libro* book of etiquette; *comportamento* etiquette, (good) manners

galera *f* (*prigione*) jail, prison

galla *f* BOT gall; **a ~** afloat; **venire a ~** (come to the) surface; *fig* come to light; **tenersi a ~** stay *or* keep afloat

galleggiante 1 *agg* floating **2** *m* (*boa*) buoy

galleggiare <1f> float

galleria *f* gallery; *passaggio con negozi* (shopping) arcade; FERR, MIN tunnel; TEA circle

Galles *m* Wales

gallese 1 *m/agg* Welsh **2** *m/f* Welshman; *donna* Welshwoman

gallina *f* hen

gallo *m* cock; SP **peso** *m* **~** bantam weight

gallone m MIL stripe; *unità di misura* gallon

galoppare <1c> gallop

galoppo m gallop; *al ~* at a gallop

gamba f leg; *fig* **in ~** (*capace*) smart, bright; (*in buona salute*) healthy, (*fighting*) fit; *persona anziana* spry, sprightly; *darsela a -e* take to one's heels

gamberetto m shrimp

gambero m prawn

gambo m *di fiore, bicchiere* stem; *di pianta, fungo* stalk

gamma f range; MUS scale

gancio m (*pl* -ci) hook; *~ di traino* tow-hook

gara f competition; *di velocità* race; *~ automobilistica* car race; *~ eliminatoria* heat; *fare a ~* compete

garage m inv garage; *~ sotterraneo* underground car park (*Am* parking garage)

garagista m (*pl* -i) (*custode*) garage attendant; (*meccanico*) mechanic

garante m guarantor.

garantire <4d> 1 v/t guarantee; (*assicurare*) ensure 2 v/i (*farsi garante*) stand guarantor (*per* for)

garantito guaranteed

garanzia f guarantee; *essere in ~* be under guarantee

garbato courteous, polite

garbo m courtesy, politeness; (*modi gentili*) good manners *pl*; (*tatto*) tact

gardenia f gardenia

gareggiare <1f> compete

gargarismo m gargle; (*collutorio*) mouthwash; *fare i -i* gargle

garofano m carnation; GASTR *chiodi mpl di ~* cloves

garza f gauze

garzone m boy

gas m inv gas; *a ~* gas *attr*; AUTO *dare ~* accelerate; *~ asfissiante* poison gas; *~ lacrimogeno* tear gas; *~ naturale* natural gas; *~ di scarico* exhaust (fumes)

gasato 1 agg *bibita* fizzy; (*eccitato*) excited 2 m, *-a* f bighead

gasolio m *per riscaldamento* oil; AUTO diesel fuel

gastrico (*pl* -ci) gastric; *succhi mpl -ci* digestive juices

gastrite f gastritis

gastronomia f gastronomy

gastronomico (*pl* -ci) gastronomic

gatta f (*female*) cat

gattino m kitten

gatto m cat; *maschio* (tom) cat; *c'era-no quattro -i* there was hardly any-body there

gavetta f MIL mess tin; *fare la ~* come up through the ranks

gay m/agg gay

gazza f magpie

gazzella f gazelle

gazzetta f gazette; *~ ufficiale* offi-cial journal, gazette

gazzosa f fizzy drink

GB abbr (= **Gran Bretagna**) GB (= Great Britain)

G.d.F. abbr (= **Guardia di Finanza**) Customs and Excise

gel m inv gel

gelare <1b> 1 v/t freeze 2 v/i e **gelarsi** freeze; *mi si è gelato il san-gue* my blood ran cold

gelata f frost

gelateria f ice-cream parlo(u)r

gelatina f gelatine; *~ di frutta* fruit jelly

gelato 1 agg frozen 2 m ice cream; *~ alla vaniglia* vanilla ice cream; *~ di fragola* strawberry ice cream

gelido freezing

gelo m (*brina*) frost; *fig* chill

gelosia f jealousy

geloso jealous (*di* of)

gelso m mulberry (tree)

gelsomino m jasmine

gemellaggio m twinning

gemello 1 agg twin 2 m *di camicia* cuff link 3 m, *-a* f twin; ASTR *Ge-melli pl* Gemini

gemere <3a> groan

gemito m groan

gemma f (*pietra preziosa*) gem, jewel; BOT bud; *fig* gem

gene m BIO gene

genealogia f genealogy

genealogico (*pl* -ci) genealogical; *albero* m *~* family tree

G

generale 1 *agg* general; **in ~** in general 2 *m* MIL general

generalità *f inv* general nature; **le ~** *pl* personal details

generalizzare <1a> generalize

generalmente generally

generare <1l & b> (*dar vita a*) give birth to; (*causare*) generate, create; *sospetti* arouse; *elettricità, calore* generate

generatore *m* EL generator

generazione *f* generation

genere *m* (*tipo, specie*) kind; BIO genus; GRAM gender; **in ~** generally; **unico nel suo ~** unique; **-i** *pl* **alimentari** foodstuffs; **-i** *pl* **di consumo** consumer goods; **~ umano** mankind, humanity

generico (*pl* -ci) generic

genero *m* son-in-law

generosità *f* generosity

generoso generous (**con** to)

genesi *f* genesis

genetico (*pl* -ci) genetic; **ingegneria** *f* **-a** genetic engineering

gengiva *f* gum

geniale ingenious; *idea* brilliant

genialità *f* genius; (*ingegnosità*) ingeniousness

genio *m* (*pl* -ni) genius; (*inclinazione*) talent; **andare a ~** be to one's liking; **lampo** *m* **di ~** brainwave

genitali *mpl* genitals

genitori *mpl* parents

gennaio *m* January

genocidio *m* genocide

Genova Genoa

genovese *m/agg* Genoese

gentaglia *f* scum

gente *f* people *pl*; **quanta ~ !** what a crowd!; *iron* **~ bene** upper-crust

gentile kind; *nelle lettere* **~ signora** Dear Madam

gentilezza *f* kindness

gentiluomo (*pl* -uomini) *m* gentleman

genuino genuine; *prodotto alimentare* traditionally made; *risata* spontaneous

genziana *f* gentian

geografia *f* geography; **~ economica** economic geography

geografico (*pl* -ci) geographic

geologia *f* geology

geologico (*pl* -ci) geological

geologo *m* (*pl* -gi), **-a** *f* geologist

geometra *m/f* surveyor

geometria *f* geometry

geometrico (*pl* -ci) geometric(al)

geranio *m* (*pl* -ni) geranium

gerarchia *f* hierarchy

gerarchico (*pl* -ci) hierarchical; **per via -a** through the proper channels

gerente *m/f* manager

gergo *m* (*pl* -ghi) slang; *di una professione* jargon

geriatrico (*pl* -ci) geriatric; **istituto** *m* **~** old people's home

Germania *f* Germany

germe *m* germ; *fig* (*principio*) seeds *pl*; **in ~** in embryo

germinare <1l & b> germinate

germogliare <1g & c> sprout

germoglio *m* (*pl* -gli) shoot

geroglifico *m* (*pl* -ci) hieroglyph

gerundio *m* (*pl* -di) gerund

gesso *m* MIN gypsum; MED, *scultura* plaster cast; *per scrivere* chalk

gesticolare <1m> gesticulate

gestione *f* management

gestire <4d> manage

gesto *m con il braccio, la mano* gesture; *con la testa* nod

gestore *m* manager

Gesù *m* Jesus; **~ bambino** baby Jesus

gettare <1b> throw; *fondamenta* lay; *grido* give, let out; **~ fuori** throw out; **~ via** throw away

gettarsi throw o.s.; *di fiume* flow, empty (**in** into)

getto *m* jet; **di ~** in one go; **a ~ continuo** continuously

gettone *m* token; *per giochi* counter; *per giochi d'azzardo* chip; **~ (telefonico)** (telephone) token; **~ di presenza** (*indennità*) attendance fee; **telefono** *m* **a ~** phone taking tokens

ghetto *m* ghetto

ghiacciaio *m* (*pl* -ai) glacier

ghiacciare <1f> *v/t & v/i* freeze

ghiacciato *lago, stagno* frozen; *bibita*

ice-cold; **tè** *m* ~ iced tea

ghiaccio *m* (*pl* -cci) ice; *sulla strada* black ice

ghiacciolo *m* icicle; (*gelato*) ice lolly

ghiaia *f* gravel

ghianda *f* acorn

ghiandola *f* gland

ghigliottina *f* guillotine

ghignare <1a> sneer

ghigno *m* sneer

ghiotto *persona* greedy; *fig: di notizie ecc* avid (**di** for); (*appetitoso*) appetizing

ghiottoneria *f difetto* gluttony; *cibo* delicacy

ghirigoro *m* doodle

ghirlanda *f* garland

ghiro *m* dormouse; **dormire come un** ~ sleep like a log

ghisa *f* cast iron

già already; (*ex*) formerly; **~!** of course!

giacca *f* (*pl* -cche) jacket; *di abito maschile* jacket; **~ a vento** windproof jacket, windcheater; **~ di pelle** leather jacket

giacché since

giacenza *f* (*pl* -ze) (*merce per la vendita*) stock; (*merce invenduta*) unsold goods *pl*; *periodo* stock time; **~ di cassa** cash in *or* on hand; **-e** *pl* **di magazzino** stock in hand

giacere <2k> lie

giacimento *m* MIN deposit

giacinto *m* hyacinth

giada *f* jade

giaggiolo *m* iris

giaguaro *m* jaguar

giallo 1 *agg* yellow; **libro** *m* **~, film** *m* **~** thriller **2** *m* yellow; (*libro, film*) thriller

Giappone *m* Japan

giapponese *agg, m/f* Japanese

giardinaggio *m* gardening

giardiniera *f donna* gardener; *mobile* plant stand; GASTR (mixed) pickles

giardiniere *m* gardener

giardino *m* garden; **~ botanico** botanical gardens *pl*; **~ d'infanzia** kindergarten; **~ pubblico** park

giarrettiera *f* garter

giavellotto *m* javelin

gigante 1 *agg* gigantic, giant *attr* **2** *m* giant

gigantesco (*pl* -chi) gigantic

giglio *m* (*pl* -gli) lily

gilè *m inv* waistcoat, *Am* vest

gin *m inv* gin

ginecologo *m* (*pl* -gi), **-a** *f* gyn(a)ecologist

ginepro *m* juniper

ginestra *f* broom

gingillarsi <1a> fiddle; (*perder tempo*) fool around

gingillo *m* plaything; (*ninnolo*) knick-knack

ginnastica *f* exercises *pl*; *disciplina sportiva* gymnastics; *in palestra* P.E., physical education; **~ presciistica** warm-up exercises (for skiers); **una ~ mentale** a mental exercise

ginocchio *m* (*pl* -cchi *e le* -cchia) knee; **stare in** ~ be on one's knees, be kneeling

giocare <1o> **1** *v/i* play; *d'azzardo, in Borsa* gamble; (*scommettere*) bet; **~ a** tennis, flipper play; **~ d'astuzia** use cunning **2** *v/t* play; (*ingannare*) trick

giocarsi (*perdere al gioco*) gamble away; (*beffarsi*) make fun; *carriera* destroy, throw away

giocatore *m*, **-trice** *f* player; *d'azzardo* gambler

giocattolo *m* toy

gioco *m* (*pl* -chi) game; **il ~** gambling; **~ d'azzardo** game of chance; **~ da bambini** child's play; **~ di prestigio** conjuring trick; **~ elettronico** computer game; **Giochi Olimpici** Olympic Games; **l'ho detto per ~ !** I was joking!

giocoliere *m* juggler

gioia *f* joy; (*gioiello*) jewel; *fig* **darsi alla pazza** ~ go wild (with excitement)

gioielleria *f* jeweller's (shop), *Am* jewelry store

gioielliere *m*, **-a** *f* jeweller, *Am* jeweler

gioiello *m* jewel

gioire <4d> rejoice (**di** in)

giornalaio *m* (*pl* -ai), **-a** *f* newsagent

giornale *m* (news)paper; (*rivista*) magazine; (*registro*) journal; **~ radio** news (bulletin); **~ scandalistico** *testata* tabloid; *stampa in genere* gutter press

giornaliero 1 *agg* daily; **abbonamento** *m* **~** day pass; **spese** *fpl* **-e** day-to-day expenses **2** *m* day labo(u)rer

giornalino *m per ragazzi* comic; **~ aziendale** inhouse newspaper, staff magazine

giornalismo *m* journalism

giornalista *m/f* (*mpl* -sti) journalist, reporter

giornalistico (*pl* -ci) *attività, esperienza* journalistic; *agenzia, servizio* news *attr*

giornalmente daily

giornata *f* day; **~** (*lavorativa*) **di 8 ore** 8-hour day; **lo finiremo in ~** we'll finish it today *or* by the end of the day; **vivere alla ~** live from day to day

giorno *m* day; **~ di arrivo / partenza** arrival / departure date; **~ di paga** payday; (*mescolare*) mix; FIN endorse weekday, working day; **~ festivo** (public) holiday; **illuminato a ~** floodlit; **l'altro ~** the other day; **ogni ~** every day; **a ~** (*fra pochi giorni*) in a few days (time); **al ~** a day; **al ~ d'oggi** nowadays; **in pieno ~** in broad daylight; **di ~** by day

giostra *f* merry-go-round, *Am* carousel

giovane 1 *agg* young; (*giovanile*) youthful **2** *m/f* young man, youth; *ragazza* young woman, girl; **i -i** *pl* young people

giovanile youthful

giovanotto *m* young man, youth

giovare <1a> (*essere utile*) be useful (**a** to); (*far bene*) be good (**a** for)

giovarsi: ~ di make use of; *consigli* take

Giove *m* Jupiter

giovedì *m inv* Thursday; **di ~** on Thursdays

gioventù *f* youth; (*i giovani*) young people *pl*

gioviale jovial, jolly

giovinezza *f* youth

giradischi *m* record player

giraffa *f* giraffe

giramondo *m/f* rolling stone, wanderer

girandola *f* (*fuoco d'artificio*) Catherine wheel; (*giocattolo*) windmill; (*banderuola*) weather vane

girare <1a> **1** *v/t* turn; *ostacolo* get round; *posto, città, negozi* go round; *mondo, paese* travel round; *film* shoot; (*mescolare*) mix; FIN endorse **2** *v/i* turn; *rapidamente* spin; (*andare in giro*) wander *or* roam around; **con un veicolo** drive around; **mi gira la testa** I feel dizzy, my head is spinning

girarrosto *m* GASTR spit

girasole *m* sunflower

girata *f* turn; (*passeggiata a piedi*) walk, stroll; *in macchina* drive; FIN endorsement; **~ in bianco** blank endorsement

giravolta *f* turn; AUTO spin; *fig* U-turn

girevole revolving

girino *m* tadpole

giro *m* turn; (*circolo*) circle; (*percorso abituale*) round; (*deviazione*) detour; (*passeggiata a piedi*) walk, stroll; *in macchina* drive; *in bicicletta* ride; *di pista* lap; *di motore* rev(olution); (*viaggio*) tour; **~ d'affari** turnover; **~ di capitali** circulation of capital; **~ turistico della città** city sightseeing tour; **fare il ~ dei negozi** go round the shops; **nel ~ di una settimana** within a week; **senza tanti -i di parole** without beating about the bush so much; **~ di prova** test drive; **essere in ~** (*da qualche parte*) be around (somewhere); (*fuori*) be out; **mettere in ~** spread; *fig* **prendere in ~ qu** pull s.o.'s leg; **a ~ di posta** by return of post

girocollo *m inv*: **maglione** *m* **a ~** crewneck (sweater)

gironzolare <1m> hang around; **~ per negozi** wander about the shops girovagare <1m, c & e> wander about

girovago (pl -ghi) **1** agg gente nomadic **2** m wanderer; (ambulante) itinerant

gita f trip, excursion; **andare in ~** go on a trip or excursion; **~ domenicale** Sunday outing; **~ in bicicletta** bike ride

gitano m, **-a** f gypsy

gitante m/f (day) tripper

giù down; (sotto) below; (da basso) downstairs; **andar ~** go down; fig **non mi va ~** it sticks in my throat; fig **essere ~** be down or depressed; di salute be run down; **mandar ~** swallow (anche fig); **un po' più in ~** a bit lower down; **su e ~** up and down; **da Roma in ~** south of Rome

giubbotto m sports jacket; **~ di salvataggio** life jacket

giudicare <1m & d> **1** v/t judge; (considerare) consider, judge; **~ male qu** misjudge s.o.; **lo hanno giudicato colpevole** he has been found guilty. **2** v/i judge

giudice m judge; **~ istruttore** examining magistrate; **~ di gara** referee

giudiziario (pl -ri) judicial; **vendita f -a** sale by order of the court

giudizio m (pl -zi) judg(e)ment; (senno) wisdom; DIR (causa) trial; (sentenza) verdict; **a mio ~** in my opinion; **~ civile** civil action, lawsuit; **mettere ~** turn over a new leaf

giudizioso sensible

giugno m June

giunco m (pl -chi) reed

giungere <3d> **1** v/t: **~ le mani** clasp one's hands **2** v/i: arrive (**a** in, at), reach (**a** sth); **~ a Roma/alla stazione** arrive in Rome/at the station, reach Rome/the station; fig **~ in porto** reach one's goal; **questa mi giunge nuova** it's news to me

giungla f jungle

giunta f addition; POL junta; **~ comunale** town council; **per ~** in addition, moreover

giunto pp → **giungere**

giuntura f ANAT joint

giuramento m oath; **falso ~** perjury; **fare un ~** swear an oath; **prestare ~** take the oath

giurare <1a> swear

giurato **1** agg sworn **2** m member of the jury

giuria f jury

giuridico (pl -ci) legal

giurisdizione f jurisdiction

giurisprudenza f jurisprudence

giurista m/f (mpl -sti) jurist

giustezza f accuracy; di argomentazione soundness; TIP justification

giustificare <1m & d> justify

giustificazione f justification

giustizia f justice; **fare ~ sommaria** administer summary justice

giusto **1** agg just, fair; (adatto) right, appropriate; (esatto) correct, right, exact **2** avv correctly; mirare accurately; (proprio, per l'appunto) just; **~!** that's right! **3** m (uomo giusto) just man; **pretendo solo il ~** I just want what is rightfully mine

glaciale glacial, icy

gladiolo m gladiolus

glassa f GASTR icing

gli **1** art mpl the; **avere gli occhi azzurri** have blue eyes **2** pron (a lui) (to) him; (a esso) (to) it; (a loro) (to) them; **dagli i libri** give him/them the books, give the books to him/them

glicemia f glyc(a)emia

glicerina f glycerine

glicine m wisteria

glie: **~la, ~lo, ~li, ~le, ~ne** = pron gli or le with pron la, lo, li, le, ne

globale global

globo m globe; **~ oculare** eyeball; **~ terrestre** globe

globulo m globule; MED corpuscle; **~ rosso/bianco** red/white blood cell

gloria f glory

glorificare <1m & d> glorify

glorioso glorious

glossa f gloss

glossario m (pl -ri) glossary

glucosio m glucose

gnocchi mpl (di patate) gnocchi (small potato dumplings)

G

gnorri m F: **fare lo ~** act dumb F

goal m inv SP goal

gobba f hump

gobbo **1** agg hunchbacked **2** m hunchback

goccia f (pl -cce) drop; **a ~ a ~** little by little

gocciolare <1l> drip

gocciolio m (pl -ii) drip

godere <2a> **1** v/t enjoy; **godersela** enjoy o.s. **2** v/i (rallegrarsi) be delighted (**di** at)

godimento m enjoyment

goffo awkward, clumsy

gol m inv SP goal

gola f throat; (ingordigia) greed(iness), gluttony; GEOG gorge; **mal m di ~** sore throat; **far ~ a** tempt

golf m inv golf; (cardigan) cardigan; (maglione) sweater; **giocatore** m **di ~** golf player, golfer

golfista m/f golfer

golfo m gulf

golosità f (ghiottoneria) greed(iness), gluttony; (leccornia) delicacy

goloso greedy; **essere ~ di dolci** have a sweet tooth

golpe m inv coup

gomito m elbow; **curva** f **a ~** sharp bend; fig **alzare il ~** hit the bottle

gomitolo m ball (of wool)

gomma f rubber; per cancellare eraser; (pneumatico) tyre, Am tire; **~ da masticare** (chewing) gum; AUTO **~ di scorta** spare tyre (Am tire); **avere una ~ a terra** have a flat tyre (Am tire)

gommapiuma f foam rubber

gommato carta gummed; tessuto rubberized

gommista m (pl -i) tyre (Am tire) specialist

gommone m rubber dinghy

gondola f gondola

gondoliere m gondolier

gonfiare <1k> **1** v/t con aria inflate; le guance puff out; fig (esagerare) exaggerate, magnify **2** v/i e **gonfiarsi** swell up; fig puff up

gonfio (pl -fi) swollen; pneumatico inflated; stomaco bloated; fig puffed up (**di** with); fig **a -e vele** splendidly

gonfiore m swelling

gonna f skirt; **~ a pieghe** pleated skirt; **~ pantalone** culottes pl

gorgo m (pl -ghi) whirlpool

gorgogliare <1g> di stomaco rumble; dell'acqua gurgle

gorilla m inv gorilla; F (guardia del corpo) bodyguard, gorilla F

gotico (pl -ci) m/agg Gothic

gotta f MED gout

governante **1** f housekeeper **2** m ruler

governare <1b> POL govern, rule; MAR steer

governativo government attr; scuola state attr

governatore m governor

governo m government; MAR steering; **~ di coalizione** coalition government; **~ di minoranza** minority government

gozzo m MED goitre, Am goiter

gozzovigliare <1g> make merry

gracchiare <1k> di corvo caw; di rane croak; di persona squawk

gracidare <1l> croak

gracile (debole) delicate

gradasso m boaster

gradazione f gradation; (sfumatura) shade; **~ alcolica** alcohol(ic) content

gradevole pleasant, agreeable

gradimento m liking

gradinata f flight of steps; stadio stand; a teatro gallery, balcony

gradino m step

gradire <4d> like; (desiderare) wish; **gradirei sapere** I would like to know; **gradisce un po' di vino?** would you like some wine?

gradito pleasant; (bene accetto) welcome

grado[1] m degree; in una gerarchia, MIL rank; **30 -i all'ombra** 30 degrees in the shade; **in ~ di lavorare** capable of working, fit for work; **essere in ~ di** be in a position to; **per -i** by degrees

grado[2] m: **di buon ~** willingly

graduale gradual
graduare <1l> graduate
graduatoria f list
graduazione f graduation
graffa f TIP brace
graffiare <1k> scratch
graffio m (pl -ffi) scratch
graffiti mpl graffiti
grafia f (hand)writing
grafica f graphics pl
grafico (pl -ci) **1** agg graphic **2** m (diagramma) graph; (disegnatore) graphic artist
grafite f graphite
grafologia f handwriting analysis
grammatica f grammar
grammaticale grammatical
grammo m gram(me)
gran → **grande**
grana 1 f grain; F (seccatura) trouble; F soldi dough F, cash; F **piantare una** ~ stir up trouble; F **pieni di** ~ rolling in money F **2** m inv cheese similar to Parmesan
granaio m (pl -ai) barn
granata f MIL grenade; BOT pomegranate
Gran Bretagna f Great Britain
granchio m (pl -chi) crab; fig blunder; fig **prendere un** ~ make a blunder
grandangolare m FOT wide-angle lens
grande big, large; (alto) big, tall; (largo) wide; fig (intenso, notevole) great; (adulto) grown-up, big; (vecchio) old; FERR ~ **velocità** high speed; **non è un gran che** it's nothing special
grandezza f (dimensione) size; (larghezza) width; (ampiezza) breadth; (altezza) height; fig (eccellenza) greatness; (grandiosità) grandeur
grandinare <1l> hail
grandinata f hailstorm
grandine f hail
grandioso grand
granduca m (pl -chi) grand duke
granducato m grand duchy
granduchessa f grand duchess
granello m grain; ~ **di pepe** pepper-

corn; ~ **di polvere** speck of dust; ~ **di sabbia** grain of sand
granita f type of ice made of frozen crystals of coffee or fruit syrup
granito m granite
grano m (chicco) grain; (frumento) wheat; fig grain, ounce
granturco m maize, corn
grappa f grappa, brandy made from the remains of the grapes used in wine-making
grappolo m bunch
grassetto m TIP bold (type)
grasso 1 agg fat; (unto) greasy; cibo fatty **2** m fat; di bue, pecora suet; **macchia f di** ~ grease stain; ~ **lubrificante** grease; **privo di -i** fat-free
grassoccio (pl -cci) plump
grata f grating
gratella f, **graticola** f GASTR grill
gratifica f bonus
gratin m: **al** ~ au gratin
gratinato → **al gratin**
gratis free (of charge)
gratitudine f gratitude
grato grateful; (gradito) welcome; **vi sarei grato se ...** I would be grateful if ..., I would appreciate it if ...
grattacapo m problem, headache F
grattacielo m skyscraper
grattare <1a> scratch; (raschiare) scrape; (grattugiare) grate; F swipe F, pinch F
grattugia f (pl -ge) grater
grattugiare <1f> grate; **pane** m **grattugiato** breadcrumbs pl
gratuito free (of charge); (infondato) gratuitous
gravare <1a> **1** v/t burden **2** v/i weigh (su on)
grave (pesante) heavy; (serio) serious; (difficile) hard
gravidanza f pregnancy
gravità f seriousness, gravity; FIS (forza f di) ~ (force of) gravity
gravoso onerous
grazia f grace; (gentilezza) favo(u)r; REL grace; DIR pardon; **in** ~ **di** thanks to; **con** ~ gracefully; **colpo** m **di** ~ coup de grâce
graziare <1g> pardon

grazie *int* thank you, thanks; **tante ~** thank you so much; **~ a** thanks to; **~ a Dio!** thank goodness!

grazioso charming; (*carino*) pretty

Grecia *f* Greece

greco (*pl* -ci) **1** *agg* Greek **2** *m*, -a *f* Greek

gregge *m* (*pl* le -ggi) flock

greggio (*pl* -ggi) **1** *agg* (*non lavorato*) raw, crude (*petroleum*)

grembiule *m* apron

grembo *m* lap; (*materno*) womb; *fig* bosom

gremito crowded

gretto (*avaro*) mean; (*di mente ristretta*) narrow-minded

gridare <1a> **1** *v/t* shout, yell; **~ aiuto** shout for help **2** *v/i* shout, yell; (*strillare*) scream

grido *m* (*pl gen* le -da) shout, cry

grigio (*pl* -gi) grey, *Am* gray; *fig* (*triste*) sad; (*scialbo*) dull, dreary

grigiore *m* greyness, *Am* grayness; *fig* (*monotonia*) dullness, dreariness

griglia *f* (*grata*) grating; GASTR grill; **alla ~** grilled

grilletto *m* trigger

grillo *m* cricket; *fig* (*capriccio*) fancy, whim

grimaldello *m device for picking locks*

grinfie *fpl fig* clutches

grinta *f* grit; *fig* determination

grinza *f di stoffa* crease

grinzoso *viso* wrinkled; (*spiegazzato*) creased

grissino *m* bread stick

grondaia *f* gutter

grondare <1a> **1** *v/i* (*colare*) pour; (*gocciolare*) drip; **~ di sudore** be dripping with sweat **2** *v/t* drip with

groppa *f* back

groppo *m*: **avere un ~ alla gola** have a lump in one's throat

grossezza *f* (*dimensione*) size; (*spessore*) thickness; (*l'essere grosso*) largeness

grossista *m/f* (*mpl* -i) wholesaler

grosso 1 *agg* big, large; (*spesso*) thick; *mare* rough; *sale*, *ghiaia* coarse;

F pezzo m **~** big shot F; **questa è -a!** this is too much!; **sbagliarsi di ~** make a big mistake; **farla -a** make a fine mess **2** *m* bulk

grossolano coarse; *errore* serious

grossomodo roughly

grotta *f* cave; *artificiale* grotto

grottesco (*pl* -chi) grotesque

groviglio *m* (*pl* -gli) tangle; *fig* muddle

gru *f inv* crane

gruccia *f* (*pl* -cce) crutch; *per vestiti* hanger

grumo *m* clot; *di farina* lump

gruppo *m* group; **~ sanguigno** blood group; **~ di lavoro** working group; **a -i** in groups

guadagnare <1a> earn; (*ottenere*) gain

guadagno *m* gain; (*profitto*) profit; (*entrate*) earnings *pl*; **margine m di ~** profit margin

guaina *f* sheath; (*busto*) corset, girdle

guaio *m* (*pl* -ai) trouble; (*danno*) damage; **-ai a te se lo fai!** woe betide you if you do!; **essere nei -ai** be in trouble

guancia *f* (*pl* -ce) cheek

guanciale *m* pillow

guanto *m* glove

guantone *m*: **~ da boxe** boxing glove

guardaboschi *m inv* forest ranger

guardacaccia *m inv* gamekeeper

guardacoste *m inv* MAR coastguard

guardalinee *m inv* SP assistant referee, linesman

guardamacchine *m* car park (*Am* parking lot) attendant

guardare <1a> **1** *v/t* look at; (*osservare, stare a vedere*) watch; (*custodire*) watch, look after; (*esaminare*) check **2** *v/i* look; (*controllare*) check; *di finestra* overlook (**su** sth); *di porta* lead (**su** to); **~ a sud** face south

guardarsi look at o.s.; **~ da** beware of; (*astenersi*) refrain from

guardaroba *m inv* cloakroom, *Am* checkroom; *armadio* wardrobe

guardarobiere *m*, **-a** *f* cloakroom attendant

guardia *f* guard; ~ **forestale** forest ranger; ~ **di finanza** Customs and Excise officer; ~ **di pubblica sicurezza** policeman; ~ **del corpo** bodyguard; ~ **medica, medico** *m* **di** ~ doctor on duty; **fare la** ~ keep guard; **stare in** ~ be on one's guard

guardiano *m* **-a** *f* (*custode*) warden; (*portiere*) caretaker; (*guardia*) guard; *di parco* keeper; ~ **notturno** night watchman

guardone *m* voyeur

guardrail *m inv* guardrail

guarigione *f* recovery; **in via di** ~ on the mend

guarire <4d> **1** *v/t* cure **2** *v/i* recover; *di ferita* heal

guarnire <4d> decorate; *abiti* trim; GASTR garnish

guarnizione *f* (*abbellimento*) trimming; GASTR garnish; *di rubinetto* washer; AUTO ~ **del freno** brake lining

guastafeste *m/f inv* spoilsport

guastare <1a> spoil, ruin; *meccanismo* break

guastarsi break down; *di tempo* change for the worse; *di cibi* go bad, spoil

guasto 1 *agg* broken; *telefono, ascensore* out of order; AUTO broken down; *cibi* bad, off F; *dente* rotten, decayed **2** *m* fault, failure; AUTO breakdown

guerra *f* war; ~ **civile** civil war; ~ **lampo** blitz; ~ **fredda** Cold War

guerrafondaio *m* (*pl* -ai) warmonger

guerriglia *f* guerrilla warfare

guerrigliero *m*, **-a** *f* guerrilla

gufo *m* owl

guida *f* guidance; (*persona, libro*) guide; AUTO driving; ~ **alpina** mountain guide; ~ **telefonica** phone book; ~ **turistica** tourist guide; AUTO ~ **a destra/a sinistra** right-hand/left-hand drive

guidare <1a> guide; AUTO drive

guidatore *m*, **-trice** *f* driver

guinzaglio *m* (*pl* -gli) lead, leash

guizzare <1a> dart

guscio *m* (*pl* -sci) shell

gustare <1a> taste; *fig* enjoy

gusto *m* taste; (*sapore*) flavo(u)r; *fig* (*piacere*) pleasure; **buon/cattivo** ~ good/bad taste; **senza** ~ tasteless

gustoso tasty; *fig* delightful

H

h *abbr* (= **ora**) h (= hour)

ha *abbr* (= **ettaro**) ha (= hectare)

ha, hai, hanno → **avere**

habitat *m inv* BIO habitat

habitué *m/f inv* regular customer

hacker *m/f* INFOR *inv* hacker

hall *f inv* foyer

hamburger *m inv* hamburger

handicap *m inv* handicap

handicappato 1 *agg* disabled, handicapped **2** *m*, **-a** *f* disabled *or* handicapped person

hard disk *m inv* INFOR hard disk

hardware *m inv* INFOR hardware

harem *m inv* harem

hashish *m inv* hashish

henné *m inv* henna

herpes *m inv* herpes

hg *abbr* (= **ettogrammo**) hg (= hectogram)

hinterland *m inv* hinterland

hit parade *f inv* hit parade

hl *abbr* (= **ettolitro**) hl (= hectolitre)

hm *abbr* (= **ettometro**) hm (= hectometre)

ho → **avere**

hobby *m inv* hobby
hockey *m inv* hockey; **~ su ghiaccio** ice hockey
holding *f inv* holding

hostess *f inv* hostess; **~ di terra** (*guida*) member of ground staff
hotel *m inv* hotel
hot dog *m inv* hot dog

I

i *art mpl* the
iberico (*pl* -ci) Iberian
iceberg *m inv* iceberg
icona *f* icon
iconografia *f* iconography
Iddio *m* God
idea *f* idea; (*opinione*) opinion; **~ fissa** obsession, idée fixe; **cambiare ~** change one's mind; **non avere la minima ~ di qc** not have the slightest idea about sth; **scambio** *m* **di -e** exchange of views; **neanche per ~!** of course not!
ideale *m/agg* ideal
idealizzare <1a> idealize
ideare <1b> *scherzo, scusa* think up; *metodo, oggetto nuovo* invent; *piano, progetto* devise
ideatore *m*, **-trice** *f* originator; *di metodo, oggetto nuovo* inventor
idem ditto
identico (*pl* -ci) identical
identificare <1n & d> identify
identificazione *f* identification
identikit® *m inv* Identikit
identità *f inv* identity
ideologia *f* ideology
ideologico (*pl* -ci) ideological
idioma *m* (*pl* -i) idiom
idiomatico (*pl* -ci) idiomatic
idiota **1** *agg* idiotic, stupid **2** *m/f* (*mpl* -i) idiot, fool
idiozia *f* stupidity, idiocy; (*assurdità*) nonsense; **un'~** a stupid *or* idiotic thing to do/say
idolo *m* idol
idoneità *f* suitability; *qualifica* qualification

idoneo suitable (**a** for)
idrante *m* hydrant
idratante *della pelle* moisturizing
idratare <1a> *la pelle* moisturize
idrico water *attr*
idraulico **1** *agg* hydraulic; **impianto** *m* **~** plumbing **2** *m* (*pl* -ci) plumber
idromassaggio *m* Jacuzzi®, whirlpool bath
idroelettrico hydroelectric
idrofilo: cotone *m* **~** cotton wool, *Am* absorbent cotton
idrofobo ZO rabid; (*furioso*) foaming at the mouth
idrogeno *m* hydrogen
idroplano *m* hydroplane
iena *f* hyena
ieri yesterday; **~ l'altro, l'altro ~** the day before yesterday; **~ mattina** yesterday morning
igiene *f* hygiene; **~ del corpo** personal hygiene; **ufficio** *m* **d'~** public health office
igienico (*pl* -ci) hygienic; **carta** *f* **-a** toilet paper
ignaro unaware (**di** of)
ignorante (*non informato*) ignorant; (*incolto*) uneducated; (*maleducato*) rude
ignoranza *f* ignorance
ignorare <1a> (*non considerare*) ignore; (*non sapere*) not know; **lo ignoro** I don't know
ignoto unknown
il *art m sg* the; **~ signor Conte** Mr Conte; **~ martedì** on Tuesdays; **3000 lire ~ chilo** 3000 lire a kilo; **mi piace il caffè** I like coffee

illecito illicit

illegale illegal

illegalità *f* illegality

illeggibile illegible

illegittimo illegitimate

illeso unhurt

illimitato unlimited

ill.mo *abbr* (= *illustrissimo*) *formal style of address in correspondence*

illogico (*pl* -ci) illogical

illudere <3q> deceive

illudersi delude o.s.

illuminare <1m> light up; *fig* enlighten

illuminazione *f* lighting; *fig* flash of inspiration; **~ stradale** street lighting

illusione *f* illusion

illuso **1** *pp → illudere* **2** *m/f* (*sognatore*) dreamer

illusorio (*pl* -ri) illusory

illustrare <1a> illustrate

illustratore *m*, **-trice** *f* illustrator

illustrazione *f* illustration

illustre illustrious

imballaggio *m* (*pl* -ggi) *operazione* packing; (*involucro*) package

imballare <1a> pack; *AUTO* **~ il motore** race the engine

imballo *m → imballaggio*

imbalsamare <1a> embalm; *animale* stuff

imbambolato *occhi, sguardo* blank; *dal sonno* bleary-eyed; **non star lí fermo ~!** don't stand there gawping!

imbarazzante embarrassing

imbarazzare <1a> embarrass

imbarazzato embarrassed

imbarazzo *m* embarrassment; (*disturbo*) trouble; **non avere che l' ~ della scelta** be spoilt for choice; **~ di stomaco** upset stomach; **mettere in ~ qu** embarrass s.o.

imbarcadero *m* landing stage

imbarcare <1d> embark; *carico* load

imbarcarsi go on board, embark; **~ in un'impresa** embark on an undertaking

imbarcazione *f* boat; **~ da diporto** pleasure boat

imbarco *m* (*pl* -chi) *di passeggeri* boarding, embarkation; *di carico* loading; (*banchina*) landing stage

imbattersi <3a>: **~ in qu** bump into s.o.

imbattibile unbeatable

imbecille **1** *agg* idiotic, stupid **2** *m/f* imbecile, fool

imbiancare <1d> **1** *v/t* whiten; *con pitture* paint; *tessuti* bleach **2** *v/i e* **imbiancarsi** go white

imbianchino *m* (house) painter

imboccare <1d> *persona* feed; *fig* prompt; **~ una strada** turn into a road

imboccatura *f* (*apertura*) opening; (*ingresso*) entrance; *MUS* mouthpiece

imbocco *m* entrance

imboscata *f* ambush

imbottigliamento *m* bottling; *AUTO* traffic jam

imbottigliare <1g> bottle; *di veicoli* hold up; **sono rimasto imbottigliato nel traffico** I was stuck in a traffic jam

imbottire <4d> stuff; *giacca* pad; *fig* (*riempire*) cram, stuff

imbottito stuffed; *panino* filled

imbottitura *f* stuffing; *di giacca* padding

imbranato clumsy

imbrattare <1a> soil; (*macchiare*) stain

imbrattatele *m/f inv* dauber

imbrogliare <1g & c> **1** *v/t* (*raggirare*) take in; (*truffare*) cheat, swindle; *fig* confuse **2** *v/i* cheat

imbroglio *m* (*pl* -gli) (*truffa*) trick; *fig* (*pasticcio*) mess

imbroglione *m*, **-a** *f* cheat, swindler

imbronciato sulky

imbrunire <4d> get dark

imbruttire <4d> **1** *v/t* make ugly **2** *v/i* become ugly

imbucare <1d> *posta* post, *Am* mail

imburrare <1a> butter

imbuto *m* funnel

imitare <1a or 1l> imitate

imitazione *f* imitation

immagazzinare <1a> store

immaginare <1m> imagine; (*supporre*) suppose; **s'immagini!** not at all!

immaginario (*pl* -ri) imaginary

immaginazione *f* imagination

immagine *f* image

immancabile *cortesia, sorriso* unfailing; *persona* ever present; *macchina fotografica* inevitable

immangiabile inedible

immatricolare <1n> register

immatricolarsi enrol, *Am* enroll; *all'università* matriculate, enrol

immatricolazione *f* registration; *all'università* matriculation, enrol(l)ment

immaturità *f* immaturity

immaturo *persona* immature; (*precoce*) premature; *frutto* unripe

immedesimarsi <1n> identify (*in* with)

immediatamente immediately

immediato immediate; (*pronto*) prompt

immenso immense

immergere <3uu> immerse, dip; (*lasciare immerso*) soak

immergersi plunge; *di subacqueo, sottomarino* dive; *fig* immerse o.s. (*in* in)

immeritato undeserved

immersione *f* immersion; *di subacqueo, sottomarino* dive

immerso 1 *pp* → **immergere 2** *agg* immersed

immettere <3ee> introduce (*in* into); INFOR *dati* enter; (*portare*) lead (*in* into)

immettersi: ~ **in** get into

immigrante *m/f* immigrant

immigrare <1a> immigrate

immigrato *m*, **-a** *f* immigrant

immigrazione *f* immigration; (*immigrati*) immigrants *pl*; FIN inflow

imminente imminent; *pericolo* impending; *pubblicazione* forthcoming

imminenza *f* imminence

immischiare <1k> involve

immischiarsi meddle (*in* with), interfere (*in* in)

immissione *f* introduction; *di manodopera* intake; INFOR *di dati* entry

immobile 1 *agg* motionless, still **2** *mpl*: **-i** real estate *sg*

immobiliare: **agente** *m/f* ~ estate agent, *Am* realtor; **società** *f* ~ *di compravendita* property company; *di costruzione* construction company

immobilismo *m* inactivity; POL opposition to progress

immobilità *f* immobility; POL, FIN inactivity

immobilizzare <1a> immobilize; FIN *capitali* tie up

immondizia *f* (*gen pl*) rubbish, refuse, *Am* trash

immorale immoral

immoralità *f* immorality

immortale immortal

immortalità *f* immortality

immune MED immune (*a* to); (*esente*) free (*da* from)

immunità *f* immunity

immunitario: **sistema** *m* ~ immune system

immunizzare <1a> immunize

immunodeficienza *f* immunodeficiency

immutabile *decisione, legge* unchangeable; *principi, tradizioni* unchanging

immutato unchanged

impacchettare <1a> (*confezionare*) wrap (up); (*mettere in pacchetti*) package

impacciare <1f> *movimenti* hamper; *persona* hinder

impacciato (*imbarazzato*) embarrassed; (*goffo*) awkward, clumsy

impaccio *m* (*pl* -cci) (*ostacolo*) hindrance; (*situazione difficile*) awkward situation; (*imbarazzo*) awkwardness

impacco *m* (*pl* -chi) MED compress

impadronirsi <4d>: ~ **di qc** take possession of sth, seize sth; *fig* master sth

impagabile priceless

impaginare <1m> TIP paginate

impaginazione *f* pagination

impalcatura *f temporanea* scaffolding; *fig* framework, structure

impallidire <4d> *di persona* turn pale

impanare <1a> GASTR coat with breadcrumbs

impanato in breadcrumbs, breaded

impantanarsi <1a> get bogged down

impaperarsi <1m> falter

imparare <1a> learn (*a* to)

imparentarsi <1b>: ~ *con qu* become related to s.o.

impari unequal; MAT odd

impartire <4d> give

imparziale impartial

imparzialità *f* impartiality

impassibile impassive

impastare <1a> mix; *pane* knead

impasto *m* GASTR dough; (*mescolanza*) mixture

impatto *m* impact

impaurire <4d> frighten

impaurirsi become frightened

impaziente impatient

impazienza *f* impatience

impazzata: *all'~ correre* at breakneck speed; *colpire* wildly

impazzire <4d> go mad *or* crazy; *far ~ qu* drive s.o. mad *or* crazy

impeccabile impeccable

impedimento *m* hindrance; (*ostacolo*) obstacle; DIR impediment; *essere d'~* be a hindrance

impedire <4d> prevent; (*ostruire*) block, obstruct; (*impacciare*) hinder; *~ a qu di fare qc* prevent s.o. *or* keep s.o. from doing sth

impegnare <1a> (*dare come pegno*) pawn; (*riservare*) reserve, book; *spazio, corsia* occupy, take up; SP *avversario* keep under pressure; (*costringere*) oblige; *~ qu di lavoro* keep s.o. busy *or* occupied; *~ qu per contratto* bind s.o. by contract

impegnarsi (*prendersi l'impegno*) commit o.s., undertake (*a* to); (*concentrarsi*) apply o.s. (*in* to); *mi sono impegnata a farlo* I've committed myself to doing it, I've undertaken to do it

impegnativo (*che richiede impegno*) demanding; *pranzo, serata, abito* formal; (*vincolante*) binding

impegnato (*occupato*) busy; *fig* (politically) committed; *sono già ~* I've made other arrangements, I'm doing something else

impegno *m* commitment; (*appuntamento*) engagement; (*zelo*) zeal, care; COM *senza ~* with no commitment

impensabile unthinkable

impensato unexpected

imperante (*dominante*) prevailing

imperare <1b> rule (*su* over)

imperativo *m/agg* imperative

imperatore *m*, **-trice** *f* emperor; *donna* empress

impercettibile imperceptible

imperdonabile unforgivable

imperfetto *m/agg* imperfect

imperfezione *f* imperfection

impermeabile 1 *agg* waterproof **2** *m* raincoat

impermeabilità *f* impermeability

impermeabilizzare <1a> waterproof

impero *m* empire; (*potere*) rule

impersonale impersonal

impersonare <1a> personify; (*interpretare*) play (the part of)

impertinente impertinent

impertinenza *f* impertinence

imperturbabile imperturbable

imperturbabilità *f* imperturbability

imperversare <1b> rage; *fig di moda* be all the rage

impeto *m* impetus, force; (*accesso*) outburst; (*slancio*) passion, heat; *parlare con ~* speak forcefully

impetuoso impetuous

impiantare <1a> *azienda, ufficio* set up; *congegno, apparecchiatura* install; MED implant

impianto *m operazione* installation; (*apparecchiature*) plant; (*sistema*) system; MED implant; *~ elettrico* wiring; *~ di risalita* ski lift; *~ di riscaldamento* heating system; *~ stereo* stereo (system); *-i pl sanitari* bathroom fixtures and fittings

impiastro *m* poultice; *fig* pain in the neck

impiccare <1d> hang

impiccarsi hang o.s.

impicciare <1f> be in the way

impicciarsi: ~ *di o in qc* interfere *or* meddle in sth

impiccio *m* (*pl* -cci) (*ostacolo*) hindrance; (*seccatura*) bother; **essere d'~** be in the way; **essere in un ~** in trouble

impiegare <1b & e> (*usare*) use; *tempo, soldi* spend; (*metterci*) take; (*assumere*) employ; **ho impiegato un'ora** it took me an hour

impiegato *m*, **-a** *f* employee; **~ di banca** bank clerk; **~ di ruolo** permanent employee

impiego *m* (*pl* -ghi) (*uso*) use; (*occupazione*) employment; (*posto*) job; FIN investment; **domanda** *f* **d'~** job application; **offerta** *f* **d'~** job offer

impietosire <4d> move to pity

impietosirsi be moved to pity

impigliare <1g> entangle

impigliarsi get entangled

impigrire <4d> **1** *v/t* make lazy **2** *v/i e* **impigrirsi** get lazy

implacabile implacable

implicare <1l & d> (*coinvolgere*) implicate; (*comportare*) imply

implicito implicit

implorare <1c> implore

impolverato dusty, covered with *or* in dust

imponente imposing, impressive

imponibile 1 *agg* taxable **2** *m* taxable income

impopolare unpopular

impopolarità *f* unpopularity

imporre <3ll> impose; *prezzo* fix

imporsi (*farsi valere*) assert o.s.; (*avere successo*) be successful, become established; (*essere necessario*) be necessary

importante important

importanza *f* importance; **darsi ~** give o.s. airs; **senza ~** not important, unimportant

importare <1c> **1** *v/t* FIN, INFOR import **2** *v/i* matter, be important;

(*essere necessario*) be necessary; **e a te che te ne importa?** what's it to you?; **non importa** it doesn't matter; **non gliene importa niente** he couldn't care less

importatore *m*, **-trice** *f* importer

importazione *f* import; **~ clandestina** smuggling; **permesso** *m* **d'~** import permit

importo *m* amount

importunare <1a> (*assillare*) pester; (*disturbare*) bother

importuno troublesome; *domanda, osservazione* ill-timed

imposizione *f* imposition; (*tassazione*) taxation; (*tassa*) tax

impossessarsi <1b>: **~ di** seize

impossibile impossible

impossibilità *f* impossibility

imposta[1] *f* tax; **~ di consumo** excise duty; **~ diretta / indiretta** direct / indirect tax; **~ sul reddito** income tax; **~ sul valore aggiunto** value added tax; **~ sul fatturato** sales tax; **ufficio** *m* **delle -e** tax office

imposta[2] *f di finestra* shutter

impostare <1c> *lavoro* plan; *problema* set out; *lettera* post, *Am* mail

imposto *pp* → **imporre**

impostore *m* impostor

impotente powerless; (*inefficace*) ineffectual; MED impotent

impotenza *f* powerlessness; MED impotence

impraticabile *strada* impassable

impratichirsi <4d> get practice (**in** in)

imprecare <1d & b> curse, swear (**contro** at)

imprecazione *f* curse

imprecisato *numero, quantità* indeterminate; *motivi, circostanze* not clear

imprecisione *f* inaccuracy

impreciso inaccurate

impregnare <1a> impregnate; (*imbevere*) soak

impregnarsi become impregnated (**di** with)

imprenditore *m*, **-trice** *f* entrepreneur

imprenditoriale entrepreneurial

impreparato unprepared

impresa f (*iniziativa*) enterprise, undertaking; (*azienda*) business, firm; **~ familiare** family business; **piccola ~** small business; **~ di servizi pubblici** utility company

impresario m (pl -ri) contractor; TEA impresario

impressionabile impressionable; FOT sensitive

impressionante impressive; (*spaventoso*) frightening; (*sconvolgente*) upsetting, shocking

impressionare <1a> (*turbare*) upset, shock; (*spaventare*) frighten; (*colpire*) impress; FOT expose

impressionato FOT exposed; **~ favorevolmente** (favourably) impressed

impressione f impression; (*turbamento*) shock; (*paura*) fright; TIP printing

impresso pp → **imprimere**

imprevedibile unforeseeable; *persona* unpredictable

imprevisto 1 agg unexpected **2** m unforeseen event; **salvo imprevisti** all being well

imprigionare <1a> imprison

imprimere <3r> impress; fig *nella mente* fix firmly, imprint; *movimento* impart; TIP print

improbabile unlikely, improbable

improbabilità f unlikelihood, improbability

improduttivo unproductive

impronta f impression, mark; (*orma*) footprint; (*traccia*) track; fig mark; **-e** pl **digitali** fingerprints

improprio (pl -ri) improper

improvvisamente suddenly

improvvisare <1a> improvize

improvvisarsi take on the role of

improvvisata f surprise

improvvisato improvized, impromptu

improvviso sudden; (*inaspettato*) unexpected; **all'~** suddenly; (*inaspettatamente*) unexpectedly

imprudente careless; (*non saggio*) imprudent, rash

imprudenza f carelessness; (*mancanza di saggezza*) imprudence, rashness

impugnare <1a> grasp; DIR contest

impugnatura f grip; (*manico*) handle

impulsivo impulsive

impulso m impulse

impunità f impunity

impunito unpunished

impuntarsi (*ostinarsi*) dig one's heels in

imputato m, **-a** f accused

imputazione f charge

imputridire rot

in prp in; *moto a luogo* to; **~ casa** at home; **è ~ Scozia** he is in Scotland; **va ~ Inghilterra** he is going to England; **~ italiano** in Italian; **~ campagna** in the country; **essere ~ viaggio** be travelling; **viaggiare ~ macchina** travel by car; **nel 1999** in 1999; **una giacca ~ pelle** a leather jacket; **~ vacanza** on holiday; **se fossi ~ te** if I were you, if I were in your place

inabile unfit (**a** for); (*disabile*) disabled

inabitabile uninhabitable

inabitato uninhabited

inaccessibile inaccessible, out of reach; fig *persona* unapproachable; *prezzi* exorbitant

inaccettabile unacceptable

inacidire <4d>, **inacidirsi** turn sour

inadatto unsuitable (**a** for), unsuited (**a** to)

inadeguato inadequate

inafferrabile elusive; (*incomprensibile*) incomprehensible

inalare <1a> inhale

inalatore m inhaler, puffer F

inalazione f inhalation

inalterabile *sentimento* unchangeable; *colore* fast; *metallo* non-tarnish

inalterato unchanged

inamidare <1m> starch

inammissibile inadmissible

inanimato inanimate; (*senza vita*) lifeless

inappellabile final, irrevocable

inappetenza f lack of appetite

inarcare <1d> *schiena* arch; *sopracciglia* raise

inaridire <4d> **1** v/t parch **2** v/i dry up

inaspettato unexpected

inasprimento m (*intensificazione*) worsening; *di carattere* embitterment

inasprire <4d> exacerbate, make worse; *carattere* embitter

inasprirsi get worse; *di persona* become embittered

inattaccabile unassailable

inattendibile unreliable

inatteso unexpected

inattività f inactivity

inattivo *persona, capitale* idle; *vulcano* dormant

inattuabile (*non fattibile*) impracticable; (*non realistico*) unrealistic

inaugurare <1m> *mostra* (officially) open, inaugurate; *lapide, monumento* unveil; F *oggetto nuovo* christen F

inaugurazione f *di mostra* (official) opening, inauguration; *di lapide* unveiling; F *di oggetto nuovo* christening F

inavvertenza f inadvertence

inavvertito unnoticed

incagliarsi <1g> MAR run aground

incalcolabile incalculable

incalzante *pericolo* imminent; *richieste* pressing

incalzare <1a> pursue; *fig con richieste* ply

incamminarsi <1m> set out

incandescente incandescent; *fig* heated

incantare <1a> enchant

incantarsi (*restare affascinato*) be spellbound; (*sognare a occhi aperti*) be in a daze; TEC jam

incantato *per effetto di magia* enchanted; (*trasognato*) in a daze; (*affascinato*) spellbound

incantesimo m spell

incantevole delightful, charming

incanto[1] m (*incantesimo*) spell; **come per ~** as if by magic

incanto[2] m COM auction; **mettere**

all'~ sell at auction, put up for auction

incapace 1 agg incapable (**di** of); (*incompetente*) incompetent **2** m/f incompetent person

incapacità f (*inabilità*) inability; (*incompetenza*) incompetence

incappare <1a>: **~ in** nebbia, difficoltà run into

incapricciarsi <1f>: **~ di qu** take a liking to s.o.

incarcerare <1m> imprison

incaricare <1m & d> (*dare istruzioni a*) instruct; **~ qu di fare qc** tell or instruct s.o. to do sth

incaricarsi: **~ di qc** (*occuparsi di*) see to sth, deal with sth

incaricato m, **-a** f (*responsabile*) person in charge; (*funzionario*) official, representative

incarico m (*pl* -chi) (*compito*) task, assignment; (*nomina*) appointment; **per ~ di** on behalf of

incarnare <1a> embody

incarnazione f incarnation

incartamento m file, dossier

incartare <1a> wrap (up) (in paper)

incarto m wrapping; (*incartamento*) file, dossier

incassare <1a> COM (*riscuotere*) cash; *fig colpi, insulti ecc* take

incasso m (*riscossione*) collection; (*somma incassata*) takings *pl*

incastonare <1a> set

incastonatura f setting

incastrare <1a> fit in; F *fig* (*far apparire colpevole*) frame F; (*mettere in una posizione difficile*) corner F

incastro m joint

incatenare <1a> chain

incavato hollow; *occhi* deep-set

incendiare <1b & k> set fire to

incendiario m (*pl* m -ri), **-a** f arsonist, firebug F

incendio m (*pl* -di) fire; **~ doloso** arson

incenerimento m incineration

incenerire <4d> reduce to ashes

inceneritore m incinerator

incenso m incense

incensurato irreproachable; DIR **es-**

sere ~ have a clean record
incentivare <1a> (*incrementare*) boost
incentivo *m* incentive
incerata *f* oilcloth
incertezza *f* uncertainty
incerto 1 *agg* uncertain **2** *m* uncertainty
incessante incessant
incetta *f*: *fare* ~ *di qc* stockpile sth
inchiesta *f* investigation; FIN ~ *di mercato* market survey; **commissione** *f* **d'**~ committee *or* board of inquiry
inchinare <1a> bow
inchinarsi bow
inchino *m* bow; *di donna* curtsy
inchiodare <1c> **1** *v/t* nail; *coperchio* nail down; *fig* **essere inchiodato in un luogo** be stuck in a place **2** *v/i* AUTO jam on the brakes
inchiostro *m* ink; ~ *di china* Indian ink
inciampare <1a> trip (*in* over); ~ *in qu* run into s.o.
incidentale (*casuale*) accidental; (*secondario*) incidental
incidente *m* (*episodio*) incident; ~ *aereo* plane crash; ~ *stradale* road accident
incidere[1] <3q> *v/i* affect (*su* sth)
incidere[2] <3q> *v/t* engrave; (*tagliare*) cut; (*registrare*) record
incidersi *fig* (*restare impresso*) be engraved (*in* on)
incinta pregnant
incirca: *all'*~ more or less
incisione *f* engraving; (*acquaforte*) etching; (*taglio*) cut; MED incision; (*registrazione*) recording
incisivo 1 *agg* incisive **2** *m* (*dente*) incisor
incitare <1l> incite
incivile uncivilized; (*villano*) rude, impolite
inclinare <1a> **1** *v/t* tilt **2** *v/i*: ~ *a* (*tendere a*) be inclined to
inclinato tilted
inclinazione *f* inclination
incline inclined (*a* to)
includere <3q> include; (*allegare*)

enclose, inclose; *incluso il servizio* service included
inclusivo inclusive
incluso 1 *pp* → **includere 2** *agg* included; (*compreso*) inclusive; (*allegato*) enclosed
incoerente (*incongruente*) inconsistent
incoerenza *f* inconsistency
incognita *f* unknown quantity
incognito *m*: *in* ~ incognito
incollare <1c> stick; *con colla liquida* glue
incollarsi stick (*a* to)
incolonnare <1a> *numeri ecc* put in a column; *persone* line up
incolore colo(u)rless
incolpare <1a> blame
incolparsi ~ *a vicenda* blame each other
incolto uneducated; (*trascurato*) unkempt; AGR uncultivated
incolume unharmed
incolumità *f* safety
incombente *pericolo* impending
incombenza *f* task
incominciare <1f> start, begin (*a* to)
incomodare <1m & c> inconvenience
incomodarsi put o.s. out; *non si incomodi!* don't put yourself out!, please don't go to any trouble!
incomodo 1 *agg* (*inopportuno*) inconvenient; (*scomodo*) uncomfortable **2** *m* inconvenience
incompatibile incompatible; (*intollerabile*) unacceptable
incompatibilità *f* incompatibility
incompetente incompetent; *sono* ~ *in materia* I'm no expert
incompetenza *f* incompetence
incompiuto unfinished
incompleto incomplete
incomprensibile incomprehensible, impossible to understand
incomprensione *f* lack of understanding; (*malinteso*) misunderstanding
incompreso misunderstood
inconcepibile inconceivable

inconciliabile irreconcilable

inconcludente inconclusive; *persona* ineffectual

incondizionato unconditional

inconfondibile unmistakable

inconfutabile indisputable

inconsapevole (*ignaro*) unaware

inconsapevolezza *f* lack of awareness

inconscio *m/agg* unconscious

inconsistente insubstantial; *fig* (*infondato*) unfounded; (*vago*) vague

inconsistenza *f* flimsiness

inconsolabile inconsolable

inconsueto unusual

incontentabile hard to please, very demanding; (*perfezionista*) perfectionist

incontestato undisputed

incontrare <1a> 1 *v/t* meet; *difficoltà* come up against, encounter 2 *v/i e* **incontrarsi** meet (**con** s.o.)

incontrario: *all'~* the other way round; (*nel modo sbagliato*) the wrong way round

incontrastato undisputed

incontro 1 *m* meeting; **~ di calcio** football match; POL **~ al vertice** summit (meeting) 2 *prp:* **~ a** towards; *andare* **~ a qu** go and meet s.o.; *fig* meet s.o. halfway

inconveniente *m* (*svantaggio*) drawback; (*ostacolo*) hitch

incoraggiamento *m* encouragement

incoraggiante encouraging

incoraggiare <1f> encourage

incorniciare <1f> frame

incoronare <1a> crown

incoronazione *f* coronation

incorporare <1m & c> incorporate

incorreggibile incorrigible

incorrere <3o>: **~ in sanzioni** incur; *errore* make

incorruttibile incorruptible

incosciente unconscious; (*irresponsabile*) reckless

incoscienza *f* unconsciousness; (*insensatezza*) recklessness

incostante changeable; *negli affetti* fickle

incostanza *f* changeableness; *negli affetti* fickleness

incostituzionale unconstitutional

incostituzionalità *f* unconstitutionality

incredibile incredible

incredulo incredulous, disbelieving

incrementare <1a> increase

incremento *m* increase, growth; **~ demografico** population growth

increspare <1a> *acque* ripple; *capelli* frizz; *tessuto* gather

incriminare <1m> indict

incrociare <1f> 1 *v/t* cross 2 *v/i* MAR, AVIA cruise

incrocio *m* (*pl* -ci) (*intersezione*) crossing; (*crocevia*) crossroads; *di razze animali* cross(-breed)

incrollabile indestructible; *fig* unshakeable

incubatrice *f* incubator

incubazione *f* incubation

incubo *m* nightmare

incudine *f* anvil

incurabile incurable

incurante heedless (**di** of)

incuria *f* negligence

incuriosire <4d>: **~ qu** make s.o. curious, arouse s.o.'s curiosity

incuriosirsi become curious

incursione *f* raid; **~ aerea** air raid

incurvare <1a> bend

incustodito unattended, unguarded; *passaggio a livello* unmanned

indaco *m/agg* indigo

indaffarato busy

indagare <1e> 1 *v/t cause, fenomeni* investigate 2 *v/i* investigate (**su, intorno a** sth)

indagine *f* (*ricerca, studio*) research; *della polizia* investigation; **~ di mercato** market survey; **~ demoscopica** (public) opinion poll

indebitare <1m>, **indebitarsi** get into debt

indebitato in debt

indebolimento *m* weakening

indebolire <4d> *v/t & v/i* weaken

indecente indecent

indecenza *f* (*vergogna*) disgrace,

outrage; (*mancanza di pudore*) indecency

indecisione *f* indecision; *abituale* indecisiveness

indeciso undecided; *abitualmente* indecisive

indefinito indefinite

indegno unworthy

indelebile indelible; *colore* fast

indenne *persona* uninjured; *cosa* undamaged

indennità *f inv* (*gratifica*) allowance, benefit; (*risarcimento*) compensation; ~ *di trasferta* travel allowance; ~ *parlamentare* MP's allowance

indennizzare <1a> compensate (*per* for)

indennizzo *m* (*compenso*) compensation

indescrivibile indescribable

indesiderato unwanted

indeterminato *tempo* unspecified, indefinite; *quantità* indeterminate

India *f* India

indiano 1 *agg* Indian; *in fila -a* in single file **2** *m*, **-a** *f* Indian

indicare <1l & d> show, indicate; *col dito* point at *or* to; (*consigliare*) suggest, recommend; (*significare*) mean

indicativo *m* GRAM indicative

indicato (*consigliabile*) advisable; (*adatto*) suitable

indicatore 1 *agg* indicative; *cartello m* ~ road sign **2** *m* indicator; (*strumento*) gauge, indicator; ~ *del livello di carburante* fuel gauge; AUTO ~ *di direzione* indicator

indicazione *f* indication; (*direttiva*) direction; (*informazione*) piece of information; MED *-i pl* directions (for use); *-i pl stradali* road signs

indice *m* index; ANAT index finger, forefinger; TV ~ *di ascolto* ratings *pl*

indicibile indescribable

indietreggiare <1f> draw back; *camminando all'indietro* step back; MIL retreat

indietro behind; *tornare, girarsi* back; **essere** ~ *con il lavoro* be behind; *mentalmente* be backward; *nei pagamenti* be in arrears; *di orologio* be slow; *dare* ~ (*restituire*) give back; *tirarsi* ~ draw back; *fig* back out; *all'*~ backwards; AUTO *fare marcia* ~ reverse; *fig* back-pedal

indifeso undefended; (*inerme*) defenceless, helpless

indifferente indifferent; *lasciare qu* ~ leave s.o. cold, cut no ice with s.o.; *non* ~ appreciable, considerable; *per me è* ~ it's all the same to me

indifferenza *f* indifference

indigeno 1 *agg* native, indigenous **2** *m*, **-a** *f* native

indigestione *f* indigestion

indigesto indigestible

indignare <1a>: ~ *qu* make s.o. indignant, arouse s.o.'s indignation

indignarsi get indignant (*per* about)

indignazione *f* indignation

indimenticabile unforgettable

indipendente independent (*da* of); ~ *dalla mia volontà* outside my control

indipendentemente independently; ~ *dall'età* regardless of age, whatever the age

indipendenza *f* independence

indire <3t> *conferenza, elezioni, sciopero* call; *concorso* announce

indiretto indirect

indirizzare <1a> direct; *lettera* address; (*spedire*) send

indirizzario *m* address book; *per spedizione* mailing list

indirizzo *m* address; (*direzione*) direction

indisciplina *f* lack of discipline, indiscipline

indisciplinato undisciplined

indiscreto indiscreet

indiscrezione *f* indiscretion

indiscriminato indiscriminate

indiscusso unquestioned

indiscutibile unquestionable

indispensabile 1 *agg* indispensable, essential **2** *m* essentials *pl*

indispettire <4d> irritate

indispettirsi get irritated

indispettito irritated

indisporre <3ll> irritate
indisposizione f indisposition
indisposto (*ammalato*) indisposed
indistinto indistinct, faint
indistruttibile indestructible
indivia f endive
individuale individual
individualismo m individualism
individualista m/f (mpl -i) individualist
individualità f individuality
individuo m individual
indivisibile indivisible
indiviso undivided
indizio m (pl -zi) clue; (*segno*) sign; (*sintomo*) symptom; DIR **-i** pl circumstantial evidence sg
indole f nature
indolente indolent
indolenza f indolence
indolore painless
indomani m: **l'~** the next day
indossare <1c> (*mettersi*) put on; (*portare*) wear
indossatore m, **-trice** f model
indotto pp → **indurre**
indovinare <1a> guess; *futuro* predict
indovinato (*ben riuscito*) successful; (*ben scelto*) well chosen
indovinello m riddle
indovino m, **-a** f fortune-teller
indubbiamente undoubtedly
indugiare <1f> **1** v/t *partenza* delay **2** v/i (*tardare*) delay; (*esitare*) hesitate; (*attardarsi*) linger
indugiarsi linger
indugio m (pl -gi) delay; **senza ~** without delay
indulgente indulgent; *giudice, sentenza* lenient
indulgenza f indulgence; *di giudice, sentenza* leniency
indumento m garment, item of clothing; **gli -i** pl clothes
indurire <4d> **1** v/t harden; *fig cuore* harden; *corpo* toughen (up) **2** v/i e **indurirsi** go hard, harden
indurito hardened
indurre <3e> induce
industria f industry; (*operosità*) industriousness; **~ automobilistica** car industry; **~ dei servizi** service industry, services; **~ pesante** heavy industry
industriale 1 agg industrial **2** m industrialist
industrializzare <1a> industrialize
industrializzazione f industrialization
ineccepibile irreproachable; *ragionamento* faultless
inedito unpublished; *fig* novel
inefficace ineffective
inefficacia f ineffectiveness
inefficiente inefficient
inefficienza f inefficiency
ineguagliabile (*senza rivali*) unrivalled; (*senza confronto*) incomparable, beyond compare
ineguaglianza f inequality
ineguale (*non uguale*) unequal; (*discontinuo*) uneven
inequivocabile unequivocal
inerte (*inoperoso*) idle; (*immobile*) inert, motionless; (*senza vita*) lifeless; FIS inert
inerzia f inertia; (*inattività*) inactivity; **forza f d'~** force of inertia
inesattezza f inaccuracy
inesatto inaccurate
inesauribile inexhaustible
inesorabile inexorable
inesperienza f inexperience, lack of experience
inesperto inexperienced
inesplicabile inexplicable
inesplorato unexplored
inesploso unexploded
inesprimibile (*indicibile*) indescribable
inestimabile inestimable; *bene* invaluable
inetto inept
inevaso pending
inevitabile inevitable
inezia f trifle
infallibile infallible
infame 1 agg (*turpe*) infamous, foul; *spir* horrible, terrible **2** m/f P (*delatore*) grass P
infantile *letteratura, giochi* children's;

malattie childhood; (*immaturo*) childish, infantile

infanzia f childhood; (*primi mesi*) infancy (*anche fig*); (*bambini*) children

infarinare <1a> (dust with) flour

infarinatura f fig smattering

infarto m cardiaco heart attack

infastidire <4d> annoy, irritate

infaticabile tireless

infatti in fact

infatuarsi <1m>: ~ *di qu* become infatuated with s.o.

infedele 1 agg unfaithful; *traduzione* inaccurate **2** m/f REL infidel

infedeltà f inv unfaithfulness

infelice unhappy; (*inopportuno*) unfortunate; (*malriuscito*) bad

infelicità f unhappiness

inferiore 1 agg lower; fig inferior (a to); *di qualità* ~ of inferior quality; **essere ~ a qu** be inferior to s.o., be s.o.'s inferior; ~ *alla media* below average **2** m/f inferior; (*subalterno*) subordinate

inferiorità f inferiority; *complesso m d'~* inferiority complex

infermeria f infirmary

infermiere m, **-a** f nurse

infermità f inv illness

infermo 1 agg (*ammalato*) ill; (*invalido*) invalid **2** m, **-a** f invalid

infernale infernal

inferno m hell

inferriata f grating; (*cancellata*) railings pl

infertilità f infertility

infestare <1b> infest

infettare <1b> infect

infettarsi become infected

infettivo infectious

infetto infected

infezione f infection

infiammabile flammable

infiammare <1a> fig, MED inflame

infiammarsi become inflamed

infiammazione f inflammation; ~ *alla gola* inflammation of the throat

inferire <4d> *di maltempo, malattie* rage; ~ *su o contro* savagely attack

infilare <1a> *fili, corde, ago* thread;

(*inserire*) insert, put in; (*indossare*) put on; *strada* take; ~ *le mani in tasca* put one's hands in one's pockets; ~ *la porta uscendo / entrando* slip out / in

infilarsi *indumento* slip on; (*conficcarsi*) stick; (*introdursi*) slip (*in* into); (*stiparsi*) squeeze (*in* into)

infiltrare <1a> infiltrate

infiltrarsi seep; fig infiltrate

infiltrazione f infiltration; *di liquidi* seepage

infilzare <1a> pierce; *perle* thread; fig string together

infimo lowest

infine (*alla fine*) finally, eventually; (*insomma*) in short

infinità f infinity; *ho un'~ di cose da fare* I've got no end of things to do

infinito 1 agg infinite **2** m infinity; GRAM infinitive; *ripetere all'~* say over and over again

infischiarsi <1k> F: ~ *di* not give a hoot about F; *me ne infischio* I couldn't care less F

infittire v/t & v/i <4d> thicken

inflazione f inflation; *tasso m d'~* (rate of) inflation

inflessibile inflexible

inflessibilità f inflexibility

inflessione f inflection

infliggere <3cc> inflict

inflitto pp → **infliggere**

influente influential

influenza f influence; MED flu, influenza

influenzabile easily influenced, impressionable

influenzare <1b> influence

influire <4d>: ~ *su* influence, have an effect on

influsso m influence

infondato unfounded, without foundation

infondere <3bb> fig instil

inforcare <1d> *occhiali* put on; *bicicletta* get on, mount

informale informal

informare <1a> inform (*di* of)

informarsi find out (*di, su* about)

informatica f *scienza* information

technology, computer science

informatico (*pl* -ci) **1** *agg* computer attr **2** *m*, **-a** *f* computer scientist

informato informed

informatore *m*, **-trice** *f* informant; *della polizia* informer

informazione *f* piece of information; *ufficio* *m* **-i** information office

informe shapeless

informicolirsi <4d> have pins and needles

infortunio *m* (*pl* -ni) accident; **~ sul lavoro** accident at work, industrial accident; **assicurazione** *f* **contro gli -i** accident insurance

infossato *occhi* deep-set, sunken

infrangere <3d> break

infrangibile unbreakable; **vetro** *m* **~** shatterproof glass

infranto *pp* → **infrangere**

infrarosso infrared

infrasettimanale midweek

infrastruttura *f* infrastructure

infrazione *f* offence, *Am* offense; **~ al codice stradale** traffic offence (*Am* offense)

infreddatura *f* cold

infruttuoso fruitless

infuocare *fig* inflame

infuocato (*caldissimo*) scorching, blistering; *discorso, tramonto* fiery

infuori: **all'~** outwards; **all'~ di** except

infuriare <1k> **1** *v/t* infuriate, enrage **2** *v/i* rage

infuriarsi fly into a rage

infuriato furious

infusione *f*, **infuso** *m* infusion; (*tisana*) herbal tea

ingaggiare <1f> (*reclutare*) recruit; *attore, cantante lirico* engage; SP sign (up); (*iniziare*) start, begin

ingaggio *m* (*pl* -ggi) (*reclutamento*) recruitment; SP signing; (*somma*) fee

ingannare <1a> deceive; **~ il tempo** kill time

ingannarsi deceive o.s.

inganno *m* deception, deceit

ingarbugliare <1g> tangle; *fig* confuse, muddle

ingarbugliarsi get entangled; *fig* get confused

ingegnarsi <1a> do one's utmost (**a, per** to)

ingegnere *m* engineer

ingegneria *f* engineering; **~ genetica** genetic engineering; **~ meccanica** mechanical engineering

ingegno *m* (*mente*) mind; (*intelligenza*) brains *pl*; (*genio*) genius; (*inventiva*) ingenuity

ingegnoso ingenious

ingelosire <4d> **1** *v/t* make jealous **2** *v/i* be jealous

ingente enormous

ingenuità *f* ingenuousness

ingenuo ingenuous

ingerenza *f* interference

ingerire <4d> swallow

ingerirsi interfere

ingessare <1b> put in plaster

ingessatura *f* plaster

Inghilterra *f* England

inghiottire <4d> swallow

ingiallire <4d> *v/t* & *v/i* yellow, turn yellow

ingiallito yellowed

inginocchiarsi <1k> kneel (down)

ingiù: **all'~** down(wards)

ingiungere <3d>: **~ a qu di fare qc** order s.o. to do sth

ingiunzione *f* injunction; **~ di pagamento** final demand

ingiuria *f* insult

ingiuriare <1k> insult

ingiustificato unjustified

ingiustizia *f* injustice

ingiusto unjust, unfair

inglese 1 *m/agg* English **2** *m/f* Englishman; *donna* Englishwoman *f*

ingoiare <1i> swallow

ingolfare <1a>, **ingolfarsi** flood

ingombrante cumbersome, bulky

ingombrare <1a> *passaggio* block (up); *stanza, mente* clutter (up)

ingombro 1 *agg passaggio* blocked; *stanza, mente* cluttered (up) **2** *m* hindrance, obstacle; **essere d'~** be in the way

ingordo greedy

ingorgare <1e> block

ingorgarsi get blocked

ingorgo *m* (*pl* -ghi) blockage; **~ stradale** traffic jam

ingovernabile ungovernable

ingozzare <1a> *cibo* devour, gobble up; *persona* stuff (*di* with)

ingozzarsi stuff o.s (*di* with)

ingranaggio *m* (*pl* -ggi) gear; *fig* machine;

ingranare <1a> engage; *fig* F **le cose cominciano a ~** things are beginning to work out

ingrandimento *m* enlargement; *di azienda, città* expansion, growth

ingrandire <4d> enlarge; *azienda, città* expand, develop; (*esagerare*) exaggerate

ingrandirsi grow

ingrassare <1a> **1** *v/t animali* fatten (up); (*lubrificare*) grease **2** *v/i* get fat, put on weight; *di birra, burro ecc* be fattening

ingratitudine *f* ingratitude

ingrato ungrateful; *lavoro, compito* thankless

ingrediente *m* ingredient

ingresso *m* entrance; (*atrio*) hall; (*accesso*) admittance; INFOR input; **~ libero** admission free; **vietato l'~** no entry, no admittance

ingrossare <1c> **1** *v/t* make bigger; (*gonfiare, accrescere*) swell **2** *v/i e* **ingrossarsi** get bigger; (*gonfiarsi*) swell

ingrossato swollen

ingrosso: all'~ (*all'incirca*) roughly, about; COM wholesale; **commercio** *m* **all'~** wholesale (trade)

ingualcibile crease-resistant

inguaribile incurable

inguinale groin *attr*; **ernia** *f* **~** hernia

inguine *m* ANAT groin

ingurgitare <1m> gulp down

inibire <4d> prohibit, forbid; PSI inhibit

inibito inhibited

inibizione *f* PSI inhibition

iniettare <1b> inject; **~ qc a qu** inject s.o. with sth; **occhi** *mpl* **iniettati di sangue** bloodshot eyes

iniettarsi: ~ qc inject o.s with sth

iniezione *f* injection; **motore** *m* **a ~** fuel-injection engine

inimicarsi <1d> fall out (**con** with)

inimicizia *f* enmity

inimitabile inimitable

inimmaginabile unimaginable

ininterrotto continuous

iniziale 1 *agg* initial; **stipendio** *m* **~** starting salary **2** *f* initial

inizializzare <1a> INFOR initialize

iniziare <1g> **1** *v/t* begin, start; *ostilità, dibattito* open; *fig* initiate **2** *v/i* begin, start; *di ostilità, dibattito* open; **~ a fare qc** begin *or* start doing sth, begin *or* start to do sth

iniziativa *f* initiative; **~ privata** private enterprise; **di mia ~** on my own initiative; **spirito** *m* **d'~** initiative

inizio *m* (*pl* -zi) start, beginning; **avere ~** start, begin; **dare ~ a qc** start sth

in loco on the premises

innaffiare <1k> water

innaffiatoio *m* (*pl* -oi) watering can

innalzare <1a> raise; (*erigere*) erect

innalzarsi rise

innamorarsi <1a> fall in love (**di** with)

innamorato 1 *agg* in love (**di** with) **2** *m*, **-a** *f* boyfriend; *donna* girlfriend

innanzi 1 *prp* before; **~ a** in front of; **~ tutto** first of all; (*soprattutto*) above all **2** *avv stato in luogo* in front; (*avanti*) forward; (*prima*) before; **d'ora** **~** from now on

innato innate, inborn

innaturale unnatural

innervosire <4d>: **~ qu** make s.o. nervous; (*irritare*) get on s.o.'s nerves

innervosirsi get nervous; (*irritarsi*) get irritated

innestare <1b> BOT, MED graft; EL *spina* insert; AUTO *marcia* engage

innesto *m* BOT, MED graft; AUTO clutch; EL connection

inno *m* hymn; **~ nazionale** national anthem

innocente innocent

innocenza *f* innocence

innocuo innocuous, harmless

innovativo innovative

innovazione *f* innovation

innumerevole innumerable

inodore odo(u)rless

inoffensivo harmless, inoffensive

inoltrare <1a> forward

inoltrarsi advance, penetrate (*in* into)

inoltrato late

inoltre besides

inondare <1a> flood

inondazione *f* flood

inoperoso idle

inopportuno (*inadatto*) inappropriate; (*intempestivo*) untimely; *persona* tactless

inorridire <4d> **1** *v/t* horrify **2** *v/i* be horrified

inorridito horrified

inospitale inhospitable, unwelcoming

inosservato unobserved, unnoticed; (*non rispettato*) disregarded; **passare ~** go unnoticed

inossidabile stainless

inquadrare <1a> *dipinto, fotografia* frame; *fig* put into context

inquadrarsi be part of

inquadratura *f* frame

inqualificabile *fig* unspeakable

inquietante *che preoccupa* worrying; *che turba* disturbing

inquietare <1b> (*preoccupare*) worry; (*turbare*) disturb; **fare ~ qu** make s.o. cross

inquietarsi (*preoccuparsi*) get worried; (*impazientirsi*) get cross

inquieto restless; (*preoccupato*) worried, anxious; (*adirato*) angry

inquietudine *f* anxiety

inquilino *m*, -a *f* tenant

inquinamento *m* pollution; *da sostanze radioattive* contamination; **~ acustico** noise pollution; **~ atmosferico** air pollution; **~ dell'ambiente** pollution

inquinante **1** *agg* polluting; **non ~** environmentally friendly; **sostanza** *f* **~** pollutant **2** *m* pollutant

inquinare <1a> pollute; *fig* (*corrom-*

pere) corrupt; DIR *prove* tamper with

insabbiamento *m di porto* silting up; *fig* shelving

insabbiare <1k> *fig* shelve

insabbiarsi *di porto* get silted up; *fig* grind to a halt

insaccare <1d> put in bags

insaccati *mpl* sausages

insalata *f* salad; **~ mista** mixed salad; **~ verde** green salad

insalatiera *f* salad bowl

insanabile (*incurabile*) incurable; *fig* (*irrimediabile*) irreparable

insanguinato bloodstained

insaponare <1a> soap

insapore tasteless

insaporire <4d> flavo(u)r

insaputa **all'~ di qu** unknown to s.o.

insaziabile insatiable

inscatolare <1m> tin, can

inscenare <1a> stage

inscindibile inseparable

insegna *f* sign; (*bandiera*) flag; (*stemma*) symbol; (*decorazione*) decoration

insegnamento *m* teaching

insegnante **1** *agg* teaching; **corpo** *m* **~** staff **2** *m/f* teacher

insegnare <1a> teach; **~ qc a qu** teach s.o. sth

inseguimento *m* chase, pursuit

inseguire <4b> chase, pursue

inseminazione *f* insemination; **~ artificiale** artificial insemination

insenatura *f* inlet

insensato **1** *agg* senseless, idiotic **2** *m*, -a *f* fool, idiot

insensibile insensitive (*a* to); *parte del corpo* numb

insensibilità *f* insensitivity; *di parte del corpo* numbness

inseparabile inseparable

inserire <4d> insert; (*collegare: in elettrotecnica*) connect; *annuncio* put in, place

inserirsi fit in; *in una conversazione* join in

inserto *m* (*pubblicazione*) supplement; (*insieme di documenti*) file

inservibile unusable

inserviente *m/f* attendant

inserzione *f* insertion; *sul giornale* ad(vert), advertisement

insetticida *m* (*pl* -i) insecticide

insettifugo *m* (*pl* -ghi) insect repellant

insetto *m* insect

insicurezza *f* insecurity, lack of security

insicuro insecure

insidia *f* (*tranello*) snare; (*inganno*) trick

insidioso insidious

insieme 1 *avv* together; (*contemporaneamente*) at the same time **2** *prp*: ~ **a**, ~ **con** together with **3** *m* whole; *di abiti* outfit; **nell'**~ on the whole

insignificante insignificant

insinuare <1m> insert; *fig dubbio, sospetto* sow the seeds of; ~ **che** insinuate that

insinuarsi penetrate; *fig* ~ **in** creep into

insinuazione *f* insinuation

insipido insipid

insistente insistent

insistenza *f* insistence

insistere <3f> insist; (*perseverare*) persevere; ~ **a fare qc** insist on doing sth

insoddisfacente unsatisfactory

insoddisfatto unsatisfied; (*scontento*) dissatisfied

insoddisfazione *f* dissatisfaction

insofferente intolerant

insofferenza *f* intolerance

insolazione *f* sunstroke

insolente insolent

insolenza *f* insolence; *espressione* insolent remark

insolito unusual

insolubile insoluble

insoluto unsolved; *debito* unpaid, outstanding

insolvente insolvent

insolvenza *f* insolvency

insolvibile insolvent

insomma (*in breve*) briefly, in short; ~**!** well, really!

insonne sleepless

insonnia *f* insomnia

insonnolito sleepy

insonorizzazione *f* soundproofing

insopportabile unbearable, intolerable

insorgere <3d> rise (up) (**contro** against); *di difficoltà* come up, crop up

insormontabile insurmountable

insorto 1 *pp* → **insorgere 2** *m* rebel

insospettabile above suspicion; (*impensato*) unsuspected

insospettato unsuspected

insospettire <4d> **1** *v/t*: ~ **qu** make s.o. suspicious, arouse s.o.'s suspicion **2** *v/i e* **insospettirsi** become suspicious

insostenibile untenable; (*insopportabile*) unbearable

insostituibile irreplaceable

insperato unhoped for; (*inatteso*) unexpected

inspiegabile inexplicable

inspirare <1a> breathe in, inhale

instabile unstable; *tempo* changeable

instabilità *f* instability; *del tempo* changeability

installare <1a> install

installazione *f* installation

instancabile tireless, untiring

insù all'~ upwards

insubordinato insubordinate

insubordinazione *f* insubordination

insuccesso *m* failure

insufficiente insufficient; (*inadeguato*) inadequate

insufficienza *f* (*scarsità*) insufficiency; (*inadeguatezza*) inadequacy; ~ **cardiaca** cardiac insufficiency

insulare *popolazione, flora ecc* island *attr*

insulina *f* insulin

insulso *fig* (*privo di vivacità*) dull; (*vacuo*) inane; (*sciocco*) silly

insultare <1a> insult

insulto *m* insult

insuperabile insuperable; (*ineguagliabile*) incomparable

insuperato unsurpassed

insurrezione *f* insurrection

intaccare <1d> (*corrodere*) corrode;

fig (*danneggiare*) damage; *scorte, capitale* make inroads into

intagliare <1g> carve

intaglio *m* carving

intanto (*nel frattempo*) meanwhile; (*per ora*) for the time being; (*invece*) yet; ~ **che** while

intarsio *m* (*pl* -si) inlay

intasamento *m* blockage; ~ **del traffico** traffic jam

intasare <1a> block

intasarsi get blocked

intasato blocked

intascare <1d> pocket

intatto intact

integrale 1 *agg* whole; MAT integral; *edizione* unabridged; **pane** *m* ~ wholemeal bread **2** *m* MAT integral

integrare <1l> integrate; (*aumentare*) supplement

integrarsi integrate

integrazione *f* integration; **cassa** *f* ~ *form of income support*

integrità *f* integrity

intelaiatura *f* framework

intelletto *m* intellect

intellettuale *agg*, *m/f* intellectual

intelligente intelligent

intelligenza *f* intelligence; ~ **artificiale** artifical intelligence, AI

intendere <3c> (*comprendere*) understand; (*udire*) hear; (*voler dire*) mean; (*avere intenzione*) intend; (*pretendere*) want; **s'intende!** naturally!, of course!

intendersi (*capirsi*) understand each other; (*accordarsi*) agree; ~ **di qc** know a lot about sth; **intendersela** have an affair (**con** with)

intenditore *m*, **-trice** *f* connoisseur, expert

intensificare <1n & d> intensify

intensificarsi intensify

intensità *f* intensity; EL strength

intensivo intensive

intenso intense

intento 1 *agg* engrossed (**a** in), intent (**a** on) **2** *m* aim, purpose

intenzionale intentional, deliberate

intenzione *f* intention; **avere l'~ di fare qc** intend to do sth; **con** ~ in-

tentionally; **senza** ~ unintentionally

interamente entirely, wholly

interagire <4d> interact

interattivo interactive

interazione *f* interaction

intercalare 1 *v/t* insert **2** *m* stock phrase

intercambiabile interchangeable

intercapedine *f* cavity

intercedere <3a> intercede (**presso** with; **per** on behalf of)

intercettare <1b> intercept

intercettazione *f* interception; **-i** *pl* **telefoniche** phone tapping *sg*

intercontinentale intercontinental

intercorrere <3o> *di tempo* elapse; (*esserci*) exist, be

interdentale: filo *m* ~ (dental) floss

interdetto 1 *pp* → **interdire 2** *agg* (*sbalordito*) astonished; (*sconcertato*) puzzled **3** *m*, **-a** *f* idiot F

interdire <3t> forbid; ~ **a qu di fare qc** forbid s.o. to do sth; DIR ~ **qu** deprive s.o. of his / her civil rights

interdizione *f* ban

interessamento *m* interest; (*intervento*) intervention

interessante interesting; **in stato** ~ pregnant

interessare <1b> **1** *v/t* interest; (*riguardare*) concern **2** *v/i* matter

interessarsi be interested, take an interest (**a, di** in); (*occuparsi*) take care (**di** of)

interessato 1 *agg* interested (**a** in); (*implicato*) involved (**a** in); *spreg parere, opinione* biased; *persona* self-interested **2** *m*, **-a** *f* person concerned

interesse *m* interest; (*tornaconto*) benefit; **tasso** *m* **d'**~ interest rate; ~ **composto** compound interest; **per** ~ out of self-interest; **senza** ~ of no interest; FIN **senza -i** interest-free

interfaccia *f* (*pl* -cce) INFOR interface

interferenza *f* interference

interferire <4d> interfere

interfono *m* intercom

interiezione *f* interjection

interiora *fpl* entrails

interiore *m/agg* interior

interlocutore *m*, **-trice** *f*: **la sua -trice** the woman he was in conversation with

interludio *m* interlude

intermediario *m* (*pl* -ri), **-a** *f* intermediary

intermedio (*pl* -di) intermediate; *bilancio, relazione* interim

intermezzo *m* intermezzo

interminabile interminable

intermittente intermittent

internamento *m* internment; *in manicomio* committal

internare <1b> intern; *in manicomio* commit

internazionale international

internet *m* Internet; **navigare nell'~** surf the Net

internista *m/f* (*pl* -i) internist

interno 1 *agg* internal, inside *attr*; GEOG inland; POL, FIN domestic; *fig* inner; **alunno** *m* ~ boarder **2** *m* (*parte interna*) inside, interior; GEOG interior; TELEC extension; **via Dante n. 6 – 9** 6 via Dante, Flat 9; **ministero** *m* **dell'Interno** *o* **degli Interni** Home Office, *Am* Department of the Interior; **all'~** inside; SP ~ **destro / sinistro** inside right / left

intero whole, entire; (*completo*) complete; **latte** *m* ~ whole milk; MAT **numero** ~ integer; **l'-a somma** the full amount

interpellare <1b> consult

interporre <3ll> *autorità, influenza* bring to bear

interporsi intervene

interpretare <1m & b> interpret; *personnagio* play; MUS play, perform

interpretazione *f* interpretation; TEA, MUS, *film* performance

interprete *m/f* interpreter; *attore, musicista* performer; ~ **simultaneo** (*-a*) interpreter; **fare da** ~ interpret, act as interpreter

interpunzione *f* punctuation

interrogare <1m, b & e> question; EDU test

interrogativo 1 *agg* GRAM interrogative; *occhiata* questioning; **pun-**

to *m* ~ question mark **2** *m* (*domanda*) question; (*dubbio*) doubt

interrogatorio *m* (*pl* -ri) questioning

interrogazione *f* questioning; *domanda* question; EDU oral test

interrompere <3rr> interrupt; (*sospendere*) break off, stop; *comunicazioni, forniture* cut off

interrotto *pp* → **interrompere**

interruttore *m* EL switch

interruzione *f* interruption

intersecare <1m, b & d> intersect

intersezione *f* intersection

interurbana *f* long-distance (phone) call

interurbano intercity; **comunicazione** *f* **-a** long-distance (phone) call

intervallo *m* interval; *di scuola, lavoro* break

intervenire <4p> intervene; (*partecipare*) take part, participate (**a** in); MED operate

intervento *m* intervention; (*partecipazione*) participation; MED operation; **pronto** ~ emergency services

intervista *f* interview

intervistare <1a> interview

intervistatore *m*, **-trice** *f* interviewer

intesa *f* (*accordo*) understanding, (*patto*) agreement; SP team work

inteso 1 *pp* → **intendere 2** *agg* (*capito*) understood; (*destinato*) intended, meant (**a** to); **siamo -i?** agreed?; **ben** ~ needless to say, of course

intestare <1b> *assegno* make out (**a** to); *proprietà* register (**a** in the name of); **carta** *f* **intestata** letterhead, letterheaded notepaper

intestatario *m* (*pl* -ri), **-a** *f di assegno* payee; *di proprietà* registered owner

intestazione *f* heading; *su carta da lettere* letterhead

intestinale intestinal

intestino *m* intestine, gut

intimare <1l *or* 1a> order

intimazione *f* order

intimidazione *f* intimidation

intimidire <4d> intimidate

intimità *f* privacy; *di un rapporto* intimacy

intimo 1 *agg* intimate; (*segreto*) private; (*accogliente*) cosy, *Am* cozy; *amico* close, intimate **2** *m persona* close friend, intimate; (*abbigliamento*) underwear

intimorire <4d> frighten

intingere <3d> dip

intingolo *m* sauce

intitolare <1m> (*dare il titolo a*) call, entitle; (*dedicare*) dedicate (**a** to)

intitolarsi be called

intollerabile intolerable

intollerante intolerant

intolleranza *f* intolerance

intonacare <1m, c & d> plaster

intonaco *m* (*pl* -chi) plaster

intonare <1c> *strumento* tune; *colori* co-ordinate

intonarsi (*armonizzare*) go well (**a**, **con** with)

intonato MUS in tune; *colori pl* -i colours that go well together

intontire <4d> daze

intontito dazed

intoppo *m* (*ostacolo*) hindrance; (*contrattempo*) snag

intorno 1 *prp*: ~ **a** around; (*circa*) (round) about, around; (*riguardo a*) about **2** *avv* around; **tutt'**~ all around; **guardarsi** ~ look around

intossicare <1m, c & d> poison

intossicazione *f* poisoning; ~ **alimentare** food poisoning

intralciare <1f> hinder, hamper

intralcio *m* (*pl* -ci) hindrance

intramuscolare MED intramuscular

intransigente intransigent

intransitivo intransitive

intraprendente enterprising

intraprendenza *f* enterprise

intraprendere <3c> undertake

intrattabile intractable; *prezzo* fixed, non-negotiable

intrattenere <2q> entertain; ~ **buoni rapporti con qu** be on good terms with s.o.

intrattenersi dwell (**su** on)

intravedere <2s> glimpse, catch a

glimpse of; *fig* (*presagire*) anticipate, see

intravisto *pp* → **intravedere**

intrecciare <1f> plait, braid; (*intessere*) weave

intrecciarsi intertwine

intreccio *m* (*pl* -cci) *fig* (*trama*) plot

intricato tangled; *disegno* intricate; *fig* complicated

intrigante scheming; (*affascinante*) intriguing

intrigo *m* (*pl* -ghi) plot

intrinseco (*pl* -ci) intrinsic

introdurre <3e> introduce; (*inserire*) insert

introdursi get in

introduzione *f* introduction

introito *m* income; (*incasso*) takings *pl*

intromettersi <3ee> interfere; (*interporsi*) intervene

intromissione *f* interference; (*intervento*) intervention

introvabile impossible to find

introverso 1 *agg* introverted **2** *m*, **-a** *f* introvert

intrufolarsi <1m> sneak in

intruglio *m* (*pl* -gli) concoction

intrusione *f* intrusion

intruso *m*, **-a** *f* intruder

intuire <4d> know instinctively

intuito *m* intuition

intuizione *f* intuition

inumano inhuman

inumidire <4d> dampen, moisten

inumidirsi get damp

inutile useless; (*superfluo*) unnecessary, pointless

inutilità *f* uselessness

inutilizzabile unusable

inutilizzato unused

inutilmente pointlessly, needlessly

invadente 1 *agg* nosy **2** *m/f* busybody

invadenza *f* nosiness

invadere <3q> invade; (*occupare*) occupy; (*inondare*) flood

invaghirsi <4d>: ~ **di** take a fancy to

invalidare <1m> invalidate

invalidità *f* disability

invalido 1 *agg* disabled; DIR invalid

2 *m*, **-a** *f* disabled person

invano in vain

invariabile invariable

invariabilità *f* unchanging nature

invariato unchanged

invasione *f* invasion (*di* of)

invasore *m* invader

invecchiare <1k> **1** *v/t* age **2** *v/i* age, get older; *di vini, cibi* mature; *fig* (*cadere in disuso*) date

invece instead; (*ma*) but; ~ *di fare* instead of doing

inveire <4d>: ~ *contro* inveigh against

invenduto unsold

inventare <1b> invent

inventario *m* (*pl* -ri) inventory

inventore *m*, **-trice** *f* inventor

invenzione *f* invention

invernale winter *attr*; *sport mpl* **-i** winter sports

inverno *m* winter; *d'~* in winter

inverosimile improbable, unlikely

inversione *f* (*scambio*) reversal; AUTO ~ *di marcia* U-turn

inverso **1** *agg* reverse **2** *m* opposite

invertire <4b or 4d> reverse; (*capovolgere*) turn upside down; CHIM, EL invert; ~ *la marcia* turn round; ~ *le parti* exchange roles

investigare <1m, b & e> investigate

investigatore *m*, **-trice** *f* investigator

investigazione *f* investigation

investimento *m* investment; *di veicolo* crash; *di pedone* running over; ~ *di capitali* capital investment

investire <4d or 4b> *pedone* run over; *veicolo* smash into, collide with; FIN, *fig* invest

inviare <1h> send

inviato *m*, **-a** *f* envoy; *di giornale* correspondent

invidia *f* envy

invidiare <1k> envy

invidioso envious

invincibile invincible

invio *m* (*pl* -vii) dispatch; INFO **tasto** *m* **d'~** enter key

inviolabile inviolable

invisibile invisible

invitante *profumo* enticing; *offerta* tempting

invitare <1a> invite

invitato *m*, **-a** *f* guest

invito *m* invitation; ~ *a presentarsi* summons *sg*

invocare <1c & d> invoke; (*implorare*) plead for, beg for

invocazione *f* invocation; (*richiesta*) plea

invogliare <1g & c> induce

involontario (*pl* -ri) involuntary

involtini *mpl* GASTR rolled stuffed slices of meat

involto *m* bundle; (*pacco*) parcel

involucro *m* wrapping

inzaccherare <1m> spatter with mud

inzuppare <1a> soak; (*intingere*) dip

inzuppato soaked

io 1 *pron* I; ~ *stesso* myself; *sono* ~! it's me! **2** *m inv* ego

iodio *m* iodine

ionico (*pl* -ci) ARCHI Ionic

iosa: *a* ~ in abundance, aplenty

iperalimentazione *f* overfeeding

iperattivo hyperactive

iperbole *f figura retorica* hyperbole; MAT hyperbola

ipermercato *m* hypermarket

ipersensibile hypersensitive

ipertensione *f* high blood pressure

ipnosi *f* hypnosis

ipnotizzare <1a> hypnotize

ipocalorico (*pl* -ci) low in calories

ipocrisia *f* hypocrisy

ipocrita 1 *agg* hypocritical **2** *m/f* (*mpl* -i) hypocrite

ipoteca *f* (*pl* -che) mortgage; *accendere un'~* take out a mortgage

ipotecare <1b & d> mortgage

ipotesi *f* hypothesis

ipotetico (*pl* -ci) hypothetical

ipotizzare <1a> hypothesize

ippica *f* (horse) riding

ippocastano *m* horse chestnut

ippodromo *m* race-course

ippopotamo *m* hippo(potamus)

ira *f* anger; *avere uno scatto d'~* fly into a rage

iracheno 1 *agg* Iraqi **2** *m*, **-a** *f* Iraqi

Iran *m* Iran

iraniano **1** *agg* Iranian **2** *m*, **-a** *f* Iranian

Iraq *m* Iraq

irascibile irritable, irascible

iride *f* (*arcobaleno*) rainbow; ANAT, BOT iris

Irlanda *f* Ireland

irlandese **1** *agg* Irish **2** *m* Irish Gaelic **3** *m/f* Irishman; *donna* Irishwoman

ironia *f* irony

ironico (*pl* -ci) ironic(al)

ironizzare <1a> be ironic

IRPEF *abbr* (= *Imposta sul Reddito delle Persone Fisiche*) income tax

irradiare <1k> *v/t* & *v/i* radiate

irradiazione *f* radiation

irraggiungibile unattainable

irragionevole unreasonable

irrazionale irrational

irreale unreal

irrealizzabile unattainable

irrefrenabile uncontrollable

irregolare irregular

irregolarità *f inv* irregularity

irreparabile irreparable

irreperibile impossible to find

irreprensibile irreproachable

irreprimibile irrepressible

irrequietezza *f* restlessness

irrequieto restless

irresistibile irresistible

irresponsabile irresponsible

irresponsabilità *f* irresponsibility

irrestringibile non-shrink; *parzialmente* shrink-resistant

irrevocabile irrevocable

irriconoscibile unrecognizable

irrigare <1e> irrigate

irrigazione *f* irrigation

irrigidire <4d> stiffen; *fig disciplina* tighten

irrigidirsi stiffen

irrigidito stiff

irrilevante irrelevant

irrimediabile irremediable

irrinunciabile *diritto* inalienable

irripetibile unrepeatable

irrisorio (*pl* -ri) derisive; *quantità, somma di denaro* derisory; *prezzo*

ridiculously low

irritabile irritable

irritabilità *f* irritability

irritante irritating

irritare <1l or 1a> irritate

irritarsi become irritated

irrobustire <4d> strengthen, build up

irrompere <3rr> burst (*in* into)

irruzione *f*: *fare ~ in* burst into; *di polizia* raid

iscritto **1** *pp* → *iscrivere* **2** *m*, **-a** *f* member; *a gare, concorsi* entrant; EDU pupil, student **3** *m*: *per ~ in* writing

iscrivere <3tt> register; *a gare, concorsi* enter (**a** for, in); EDU enrol(l) (**a** at)

iscriversi *in un elenco* register; ~ **a** *partito, associazione* join; *gara* enter; EDU enrol(l) at

iscrizione *f* inscription

islamico (*pl* -ci) Islamic

Islanda *f* Iceland

islandese **1** *m/agg* Icelandic **2** *m/f* Icelander

isola *f* island; ~ **pedonale** pedestrian precinct; ~ **spartitraffico** traffic island

isolamento *m* isolation; TEC insulation; ~ **acustico** soundproofing

isolano *m*, **-a** *f* islander

isolante **1** *agg* insulating **2** *m* insulator

isolare <1l> isolate; TECH insulate

isolarsi isolate o.s., cut o.s. off

isolato **1** *agg* isolated; TECH insulated **2** *m* outsider; *di case* block

ispettore *m*, **-trice** *f* inspector

ispezionare <1a> inspect

ispezione *f* inspection

ispirare <1a> inspire

ispirarsi *di artista* get inspiration (**a** from)

ispirazione *f* inspiration; (*impulso*) impulse; (*idea*) idea

Israele *m* Israel

israeliano *m*, **-a** *f* Israeli

issare <1a> hoist

istallare <1a> → *installare*

istantanea *f* snap

istantaneo instantaneous
istante *m* instant; **all'~** instantly
istanza *f (esigenza)* need; *(domanda)*
application; DIR petition
ISTAT *abbr* (= *Istituto Centrale di
Statistica*) central statistics office
isterico (*pl* -ci) hysterical
istigare <ll & e> instigate
istintivo instinctive
istinto *m* instinct
istituire <4d> establish
istituto *m* institute; *assistenziale* institution, home; **~ di bellezza** beauty
salon; **~ di credito** bank
istituzione *f* institution
istmo *m* isthmus
istruire <4d> educate, teach; *(dare*

istruzioni a, addestrare) instruct
istruirsi educate o.s.
istruito educated
istruttivo instructive
istruttore *m*, **-trice** *f* instructor
istruzione *f* education; *(direttiva)* in-
struction; **-i** *pl* **per l'uso** instructions
(for use)
Italia *f* Italy
italiano **1** *m/agg* Italian; **parla ~?** do
you speak Italian? **2** *m*, **-a** *f* Italian
itinerario *m* (*pl* -ri) route, itinerary
ittico (*pl* -ci) fish
iugoslavo → **yugoslavo**
iuta *f* jute
IVA *abbr* (= *Imposta sul Valore Aggiunto*) VAT (= value-added tax)

J

jazz *m* jazz
jazzista *m/f (mpl* -i) jazz musician
jeans *mpl* jeans
jeep *f inv* jeep
jet *m inv* jet
jet-lag *m inv* jet lag
jet-set *m inv* jet set
jockey *m inv* jockey
jogging *m* jogging; **fare ~** jog, go for

a jog
joint-venture *f inv* joint venture
jolly *m inv* joker
joule *m inv* joule
joy-stick *m inv* joystick
judo *m* judo
juke-box *m inv* jukebox
jumbo *m* jumbo
junior *m/agg* (*pl* juniores) junior

K

karatè *m* karate
kg *abbr* (= *chilogrammo*) kg (= kilogram)
killer *m inv* killer
kit *m inv* kit
kitsch *agg inv*, *m* kitsch
kiwi *m inv* BOT kiwi (fruit)

km *abbr* (= *chilometro*) km (= kilometre)
km/h *abbr* (= *chilometri all'ora*)
km/h (= kilometres per hour)
kmq *abbr* (= *chilometri quadrati*)
km² (= square kilometres)
knock-out knock-out

k.o.: *mettere qu* ~ knock s.o. out; *fig* trounce s.o.
kolossal *m inv* epic
krapfen *m inv* GASTR doughnut
kümmel *m* kümmel

kV *abbr* (= *chilovolt*) kV (= kilovolt)
kW *abbr* (= *chilowatt*) kW (= kilowatt)
kWh *abbr* (= *chilowattora*) kWh (= kilowatt hour)

L

L *abbr* (= *lira*) L (= lire)
l *abbr* (= *litro*) l (= litre)
l' = *lo, la*
la¹ *art fsg* the; ~ *signora Rossi* Mrs Rossi; ~ *domenica* on Sundays; *mi piace la birra* I like beer
la² *pron* **1** *sg* (*persona*) her; (*cosa, animale*) it; ~ *prenderò* I'll take it **2** *anche* **La** *sg* you
la³ *m* MUS A; *nel solfeggio della scala* la(h)
là there; *di* ~that way; (*in quel luogo*) in there; *di* ~ *di* on the other side of; *più in* ~ further on; *nel tempo* later on
labbro *m* (*pl* le -a) lip
labile (*passeggero*) fleeting, short-lived
labirinto *m* labyrinth
laboratorio *m* (*pl* -ri) lab, laboratory; (*officina*) workshop
laboriosità *f* laboriousness; *di persona* industriousness
laborioso laborious; *persona* hard-working, industrious
laburista **1** *agg* Labo(u)r **2** *m/f* Labo(u)r Party member; *elettore* Labo(u)r supporter
lacca *f* (*pl* -cche) lacquer; *per capelli* hair spray, lacquer
laccare <1d> lacquer
laccio *m* (*pl* -cci) tie, (draw)string; *-cci pl delle scarpe* shoe laces
lacerante *dolore, grido* piercing
lacero tattered, in tatters
lacrima *f* tear
lacrimare <1l> water

lacrimevole heart-rending; *film m* ~ tear-jerker
lacrimogeno: *gas m* ~ tear gas
lacuna *f* gap
lacunoso incomplete
ladino 1 *agg* South Tyrolean **2** *m*, -a *f* South Tyrolean
ladro *m*, -a *f* thief
laggiù down there; *distante* over there
laghetto *m* pond
lagna *f* (*lamentela*) whining; *persona* whiner; (*cosa noiosa*) bore
lagnanza *f* complaint
lagnarsi <1a> complain (*di* about)
lago *m* (*pl* -ghi) lake; ~ *artificiale* reservoir; ~ *di Garda* Lake Garda
laguna *f* lagoon
laico (*pl* -ci) **1** *agg scuola, stato* secular **2** *m*, -a *f* member of the laity
lama *f* blade; ~ *di coltello* knife blade
lamentare <1a> lament, deplore
lamentarsi complain (*di* about)
lamentela *f* complaint
lamento *m* whimper
lamentoso whining
lametta *f*: ~ (*da barba*) razor blade
lamiera *f* metal sheet; ~ *ondulata* corrugated iron
lamina *f* foil; ~ *d'oro* gold leaf
lampada *f* lamp; ~ *alogena* halogen lamp; ~ *a stelo* floor lamp, *Br* standard lamp; ~ *al neon* neon light
lampadario *m* (*pl* -ri) chandelier
lampadina *f* light bulb; ~ *tascabile*

torch, *Am* flashlight

lampante blindingly obvious

lampeggiare <1f> flash

lampeggiatore *m* AUTO indicator; FOT flashlight

lampione *m* streetlight

lampo *m* lightning; *in un ~* in a flash

lampone *m* raspberry

lana *f* wool; *pura ~ vergine* pure new wool

lancetta *f* needle, indicator; *di orologio* hand

lancia *f* (*pl* -ce) spear; MAR launch; *~ di salvataggio* lifeboat

lanciare <1f> throw; *prodotto* launch; *~ un'occhiata* glance, take a quick look; *~ un urlo* give a shout, shout

lanciarsi rush; *~ contro* throw o.s at, attack; F *~ in un' impresa* embark on a venture; F *mi lancio* I'll go for it F, I'll take the plunge F

lancinante *dolore* piercing

lancio *m* (*pl* -ci) throwing; *di prodotto* launch; *~ del disco* discus; *~ del giavellotto* javelin; *~ del peso* putting the shot

languire <4a or 4d> languish

languore *m* lang(u)or; *ho un ~ allo stomaco* I'm feeling peckish

lanificio *m* (*pl* -ci) wool mill

lanterna *f* lantern; (*faro*) lighthouse

lapide *f* gravestone; *su monumento* plaque

lapis *m inv* pencil

lardo *m* lard

larghezza *f* width, breadth; *~ di vedute* broad-mindedness

largo (*pl* -ghi) **1** *agg* wide, broad; *indumento* loose, big; (*abbondante*) large, generous; *~ di manica* generous **2** *m* width; (*piazza*) square; *andare al ~* head for the open sea; *al ~ di* off the coast of; *farsi ~* elbow one's way through; *stare alla -a da* steer clear of, keep away from

larice *m* larch

laringe *f* larynx

laringite *f* laryngitis

larva *f* ZO larva

lasagne *fpl* lasagne *sg*

lasciapassare *m inv* pass

lasciare <1f> leave; (*abbandonare*) give up; (*concedere*) let; (*smettere di tenere*) let go; *lascia andare!, lascia perdere!* forget it!

lasciarsi separate, leave each other; *~ andare* let o.s. go

lascito *m* legacy

lascivo lascivious

laser *m inv, agg inv* laser

lassativo *m/agg* laxative

lasso *m*: *~ di tempo* period of time

lassù up there

lastra *f di pietra* slab; *di metallo, ghiaccio, vetro* sheet; MED x-ray

lastrico *m* (*pl* -chi *o* -ci): *fig ridursi sul ~* lose everything

latente latent

laterale lateral

laterizio *m* (*mpl* -zi) bricks and tiles *pl*

latino 1 *agg* Latin; *~-americano* Latin-American **2** *m* Latin; *~-americano, -a* Latin-American

latitante *m/f* fugitive

latitudine *f* latitude

lato *m* side; *a ~ di, di ~ a* beside; *d'altro ~* on the other hand

latrare <1a> bark

latrato *m* barking

latrina *f* latrine

latta *f* can, tin; *~ di benzina* petrol can, *Am* gas can

lattaio *m* (*pl* -ai), *-a f* milkman; *donna* milkwoman

lattante *m* infant, small baby

latte *m* milk; *~ a lunga conservazione* long-life milk; *~ intero* whole milk; *~ materno* mother's milk; *~ scremato* skim(med) milk

latteo milk *attr*; *Via f Lattea* Milky Way

latteria *f* dairy

lattice *m* latex

latticinio *m* (*pl* -ni) dairy product

lattina *f* can, tin

lattuga *f* (*pl* -ghe) lettuce

laurea *f* degree

laurearsi <1l> graduate

laureato *m*, *-a f* graduate

lava *f* lava

L

lavabile washable; **~ in lavatrice** machine-washable

lavabo *m* basin

lavacristallo *m* AUTO windscreen (*Am* windshield) washer

lavaggio *m* (*pl* -ggi) washing; **~ a secco** dry-cleaning; **~ del cervello** brainwashing

lavagna *f* blackboard; GEOL slate; **~ luminosa** overhead projector

lavanda *f* BOT lavender

lavanderia *f* laundry; **~ a gettone** laundrette

lavandino *m* basin; *nella cucina* sink

lavapiatti *m/f inv* dishwasher

lavare <1a> wash; **~ i panni** do the washing

lavarsi wash; **~ le mani** wash one's hands; **~ i denti** brush *or* clean one's teth

lavastoviglie *f inv* dishwasher

lavatoio *m* (*pl m* -oi) laundry; *di casa* laundry (room), utility room

lavatrice *f* washing machine

lavello *m* basin; *nella cucina* sink

lavina *f* avalanche

lavorare <1a> **1** *v/i* work **2** *v/t materia prima* process; *legno* carve; *terra* work

lavorativo: **giorno** *m* **~** working day

lavorato *legno* carved

lavoratore *m*, **-trice** *f* worker; **~ autonomo** self-employed person; **~ dipendente** employee

lavorazione *f di materia prima* processing; *di legno* carving

lavoro *m* work; (*impiego*) job; **~ di gruppo** teamwork; **~ nero** moonlighting; **-i** *pl* **occasionali** *o* **saltuari** odd jobs; **per ~** on business; **condizioni** *fpl* **di ~** working conditions; **permesso** *m* **di ~** work permit; **posto** *m* **di ~** place of work, workplace; **-i in corso** roadworks, work in progress; **senza ~** unemployed

le¹ *art fpl* the

le² *pron fsg* to her; *fpl* them; *anche* **Le** you

leader *m/f inv* leader

leale loyal

lealtà *f* loyalty

lebbra *f* leprosy

lebbroso *m*, **-a** *f* leper

lecca-lecca *m inv* lollipop

leccare <1d> lick; **F ~ qu** suck up to s.o. F, lick s.o.'s boots F

leccio *m* (*pl* -cci) holm oak

leccornia *f* appetizing dish, delicacy

lecito legal, permissible; **se mi è ~** if I may

lega *f* (*pl* -ghe) league; METAL alloy

legale 1 *agg* legal **2** *m/f* lawyer

legalità *f* legality

legalizzare <1a> legalize

legame *m* tie, relationship; (*nesso*) link, connection

legamento *m* ANAT ligament

legare <1e> tie; *persona* tie up; (*collegare*) link; *fig di lavoro* tie down

legarsi *fig* tie o.s. down

legazione *f* legation

legge *f* law; **studiare ~** study *or* read law; **a norma di ~** up to standard; **a norma di ~ ...** complies with ...; **fuori ~** illegal, unlawful

leggenda *f* legend; *di carta geografica ecc* key

leggendario (*pl* -ri) legendary

leggere <3cc> read; **~ le labbra** lipread; **~ nel pensiero a qu** read s.o.'s mind

leggerezza *f* lightness; *fig* casualness; **con ~** thoughtlessly, unthinkingly

leggero light; (*lieve, di poca importanza*) slight; (*superficiale*) thoughtless; *caffè* weak; **alla -a** lightly, lightheartedly

leggibile legible

leggio *m* (*pl* -ii) lectern; MUS music stand

legislativo legislative

legislatore *m* legislator

legislatura *f periodo* term of parliament

legislazione *f* legislation

legittimare <1m> approve

legittimazione *f* approval

legittimo legitimate

legna *f* (fire)wood; *far* ~ collect firewood

legname *m* timber; ~ *da costruzione* lumber

legno *m* (*pl* i -i) wood; *di* ~ wooden

legumi *mpl* peas and beans; *secchi* pulses

lei *pron fsg soggetto* she; *oggetto, con preposizione* her; ~ *stessa* herself; *anche* **Lei** you; *dare del* ~ *a qu* address s.o. as 'lei'

lembo *m di gonna* hem, bottom; *di terra* stip

lente *f* lens; *-i pl* glasses, spectacles, specs F; *-i pl* (*a contatto*) contact lenses, contacts F; ~ *d'ingrandimento* magnifying glass

lentezza *f* slowness

lenticchia *f* lentil

lentiggine *f* freckle

lento slow; (*allentato*) slack; *abito* loose

lenza *f* fishing rod

lenzuolo *m* (*pl* i -i -e *le* -a) sheet

leone *m* lion; ASTR **Leone** Leo

leonessa *f* lioness

leopardo *m* leopard

lepre *f* hare

lercio filthy

lesbica *f* lesbian

lesionare damage

lesione *f* MED injury

lessare <1a> boil

lessico *m* (*pl* -ci) vocabulary; (*dizionario*) glossary

lesso **1** *agg* boiled **2** *m* boiled beef

letale lethal

letame *m* manure, dung

letargo *m* (*pl* -ghi) lethargy

lettera *f* letter; *alla* ~ to the letter; ~ *assicurata* registered letter; ~ *commerciale* business letter; ~ *di accompagnamento* covering letter; FIN ~ *di cambio* bill of exchange; ~ *espresso* (letter sent) express delivery; ~ *raccomandata* recorded delivery letter

letterale literal

letterario (*pl* -ri) literary

letterato *m*, **-a** *f* man / woman of letters

letteratura *f* literature

lettino *m* cot; *dal medico* bed; *dallo psicologo* couch; ~ *solare* sunbed

letto[1] *m* bed; ~ *a una piazza* single bed; ~ *matrimoniale* double bed; *andare a* ~ go to bed; *essere a* ~ be in bed

letto[2] *pp* → **leggere**

lettore *m*, **-trice** *f* reader; *all' università* lecturer in a foreign language; INFOR disk drive; ~ *compact disc* CD player; ~ *ottico* optical character reader

lettura *f* reading

leucemia *f* leuk(a)emia

leva *f* lever; MIL call-up, *Am* draft; AUTO ~ *del cambio* gear lever

levante *m* east

levare <1b> (*alzare*) raise, lift; (*togliere*) take, (re)move; (*rimuovere*) take out, remove; *macchia* remove, get out; *dente* take out, extract; ~ *l'ancora* weigh anchor

levarsi get up, rise; *di sole* rise, come up; *indumento* take off; ~ *il vizio di fare qc* get out of the habit of doing sth; *levatelo dalla testa!* you can get that idea out of your head!

levata *f di posta* collection

levatrice *f* midwife

levigare <1l, b & e> smooth down

levigato smooth

lezione *f* lesson; *all'università* lecture; *fig* *dare una* ~ *a qu* teach s.o. a lesson

li *pron mpl* them

lì there; ~ *per* ~ there and then; *giù di* ~ thereabouts; *di* ~ *a pochi giorni* a few days later

libanese *agg*, *m/f* Lebanese

Libano *m* (the) Lebanon

libbra *f* pound

libellula *f* dragon-fly

liberale **1** *agg* generous; POL liberal **2** *m/f* liberal

liberalità *f* generosity

liberalizzare <1a> liberalize

liberalizzazione *f* liberalization

liberamente freely

liberare <1l> release, free;

(*sgomberare*) empty; *stanza* vacate

liberarsi: ~ *di* get rid of

liberazione *f* release; *di nazione* liberation

libero free; *camera d'albergo* vacant, free

libertà *f inv* freedom, liberty; **mettersi in** ~ change into more comfortable clothes; ~ *di stampa* freedom of the press; **prendersi la** ~ *di fare qc* take the liberty of doing sth; ~ **provvisoria** bail

Libia *f* Libya

libico (*pl* -ci) **1** *agg* Libyan **2** *m*, -a *f* Libyan

libraio *m* (*pl* -ai) bookseller

librario (*pl* -ri) book *attr*

libreria *f* bookstore, *Br* -shop; (*biblioteca*) book collection, library; *mobile* bookcase

libretto *m* booklet; MUS libretto; ~ *di assegni* cheque book, *Am* check book; AUTO ~ *di circolazione* registration document; ~ *di risparmio* bank book

libro *m* book; ~ *di testo* textbook; ~ *illustrato* picture book

licenza *f* FIN licence, *Am* license, permit; MIL leave; EDU school leaving certificate; ~ *di costruzione* building *or* construction permit; ~ *di esercizio* trading licence (*Am* license)

licenziamento *m* dismissal; *per motivi economici* dismissal, *Br* redundancy

licenziare <1g> dismiss; *per motivi economici* dismiss, lay off, *Br* make redundant; ~ *alle stampe* pass for press

licenziarsi resign

liceo *m* high school; ~ *classico* (*scientifico*) *high school that specializes in arts* (*science*) *subjects*

lido *m* beach

lieto happy; ~ *di conoscerla* nice *or* pleased to meet you

lieve light; (*di poca gravità*) slight, minor; *sorriso, rumore* faint

lievitare <1l & b> rise; *fig* rise, be on the increase

lievito *m* yeast; ~ *in polvere* baking powder

lilla *m/agg* lilac

lillà *m* lilac (tree)

lima *f* file

limare <1a> file

limetta *f* emery board; *di metallo* nail file

limitare <1l> limit, restrict (*a* to); (*contenere*) limit, contain

limitato limited; FIN **società** *f* **a responsabilità -a** limited company; **è** ~ *di persona* he's got his limitations

limitazione *f* limitation; ~ *delle nascite* birth control; *senza* -i without restriction

limite *m* limit; (*confine*) boundary; ~ *di età* age limit; ~ *di velocità* speed limit; *al* ~ at most, at the outside; *nei* -i *del possibile* to the best of one's ability

limitrofo bordering, neighbo(u)ring

limonata *f* lemonade

limone *m* lemon; (*albero*) lemon tree

limpidezza *f* cleanness

limpido clear; *acqua* crystal-clear, limpid

lince *f* lynx

linciare <1f> lynch

linea *f* line; ~ *dell'autobus* bus route; **mantenere la** ~ keep one's figure; TELEC **restare in** ~ stay on the line, not hang up

lineamenti *mpl* (*fisionomia*) features

lineare linear

lineetta *f* dash

linfonodo *m* lymph node

lingotto *m* ingot

lingua *f* tongue; (*linguaggio*) language; ~ *madre* mother tongue; ~ *parlata* colloquial language; ~ *straniera* foreign language; ~ *nazionale* official language

linguaggio *m* (*pl* -ggi) language; ~ *tecnico* technical language, jargon; INFOR ~ *di programmazione* programming language

linguistica *f* linguistics

lino *m* BOT flax; *tessuto* linen

liofilizzato freeze-dried

liquidare <1l> (*pagare*) pay; *merci* clear; *azienda* liquidate; *fig questione* settle; *problema* dispose of; *persona* F liquidate F, dispose of F

liquidazione *f* liquidation; **~ totale** clearance sale

liquidità *f* liquid assets *pl*, liquidity

liquido *m/agg* liquid

liquirizia *f* liquorice

liquore *m* liqueur

lira *f* lira

lirica *f* (*pl* -che) lyric poem; MUS **la ~** opera

lirico (*pl* -ci) lyric; *cantante* opera *attr*; **teatro m ~** opera house

lisca *f* (*pl* -che) fishbone

lisciare <1f> smooth (down); (*accarezzare*) stroke; *capelli* straighten

liscio (*pl* -sci) smooth; *bevanda* straight, neat; *fig* **passarla -a** get away with it

liso worn

lista *f* (*elenco*) list; (*striscia*) strip; **~ d'attesa** waiting list; **in ~ d'attesa** on the waiting list, wait-listed; AVIA on standby; **~ dei vini** wine list

listino *m*: **~ di borsa** share index; **~ prezzi** price list

Lit. *abbr* (= *lire italiane*) L (= lire)

lite *f* quarrel, argument; JUR lawsuit; **~ coniugale** marital dispute

litigare <1l & e> quarrel, argue

litigio *m* (*pl* -gi) quarrel, argument

litigioso argumentative, quarrelsome

litografia *f* lithography

litografo *m* lithograph

litorale **1** *agg* coastal **2** *m* coast

litoranea *f* coast road

litoraneo coast *attr*, coastal

litro *m* litre, *Am* liter

Lituania *f* Lithuania

lituano **1** *agg* Lithuanian **2** *m*, **-a** *f* Lithuanian

liturgia *f* liturgy

liturgico (*pl* -ci) liturgical

liutaio *m* (*pl* -ai) lute maker

liuto *m* lute

livella *f* level

livellamento *m* levelling

livellare <1b> level

livello *m* level; AUTO **~ dell'olio** oil level; *fig* **ad altissimo ~** first-class, first-rate; **sopra il ~ del mare** above sea level; **~ di vita** standard of living

livido **1** *agg* livid; *braccio, viso* black and blue; *occhio* black; *per il freddo* blue **2** *m* bruise

lo **1** *art m/sg* the **2** *pron m/sg* him; *cosa, animale* it; **non ~ so** I don't know

lobo *m* lobe

locale **1** *agg* local; MED **anestesia** *f* **~** local an(a)esthetic **2** *m* room; *luogo pubblico* place; FERR local train

località *f inv* town; **~ balneare** seaside resort; **~ turistica** tourist resort

localizzare <1a> locate; (*delimitare*) localize

locandina *f* TEA bill

locatario *m* (*pl* -ri), **-a** *f* tenant

locatore *m*, **-trice** *f* landlord; *donna* landlady

locazione *f* rental

locomotiva *f* locomotive

locomozione *f* locomotion; **mezzo m di ~** means of transport

locuzione *f* fixed expression

lodare <1c> praise

lode *f* praise

lodevole praiseworthy, laudable

loggia *f* (*pl* -gge) loggia

loggione *m* TEA gallery

logica *f* logic

logico (*pl* -ci) logical

logorare <1l> wear out

logorio *m* wear and tear

logoro *indumento* worn (out), threadbare

lombaggine *f* lumbago

Lombardia *f* Lombardy

lombardo **1** *agg* of Lombardy **2** *m*, **-a** *f* native of Lombardy

lombata *f* loin

lombo *m* loin

lombrico *m* (*pl* -chi) earthworm

Londra *f* London

longevo longlived

longitudine *f* GEOG longitude

lontananza *f* distance; *tra persone* separation

lontano **1** *agg* far; *nel tempo* far-off;

L

passato, futuro, parente distant; **alla -a** *concoscenze* vaguely, slightly; **siamo cugini alla -a** we're distant cousins **2** *avv* far (away); **da ~** from a distance; **abita molto ~?** do you live very far away?

lontra *f* otter

loquace talkative

lordo dirty; *peso, reddito ecc* gross

loro 1 *pron soggetto* they; *oggetto* them; *forma di cortesia, anche* **Loro** you **2** *possessivo* their; *forma di cortesia, anche* **Loro** your; **il ~ amico** their / your friend; **i ~ genitori** their / your parents **3** *pron:* **il ~** theirs; *forma di cortesia, anche* **Loro** yours

lotta *f* struggle; SP wrestling; *fig* fight

lottare <1c> wrestle, struggle (**con** with); *fig* fight (**contro** against; **per** for)

lottatore *m* wrestler

lotteria *f* lottery; **biglietto** *m* **della ~** lottery ticket

lotto *m* lottery; *di terreno* plot

lozione *f* lotion; **~ dopobarba** aftershave

L.st. *abbr* (= **lira sterlina**) £ (= pound)

lubrificante *m* lubricant; AUTO lubricating oil

lubrificare <1m & d> lubricate

lucchetto *m* padlock

luccicare <1l & d> sparkle

luccio *m* (*pl* -cci) pike

lucciola *f* glowworm

luce *f* light; **~ al neon** neon light; **dare alla ~ un figlio** give birth to a son; *fig* **far ~ su qc** shed light on sth; AUTO **-i pl di posizione** side lights; **-i** *pl* **posteriori** rear lights

lucente shining, gleaming

lucentezza *f* shininess

lucertola *f* lizard

lucidare <1l> polish; *disegno* trace

lucidatrice *f* floor polisher

lucido 1 *agg superficie, scarpe* shiny; FOT glossy; *persona* lucid **2** *m* polish; *disegno* transparency; **~ da scarpe** shoe polish

lucrativo lucrative

lucro *m:* **a scopo di ~** profit-making;

senza fini di ~ non-profit-making

luglio *m* July

lugubre sombre, *Am* somber, lugubrious

lui *pron msg soggetto* he; *oggetto* him; **a ~** to him; **~ stesso** himself

lumaca *f* (*pl* -che) slug

lume *m* (*lampada*) lamp; *luce* light; *fig* **perdere il ~ della ragione** lose one's mind

luminosità *f* luminosity; FOT speed

luminoso luminous; *stanza* bright, full of light; **sorgente** *f* **-a** light source

luna *f* moon; *fig* **avere la ~ storta** be in a mood; **~ crescente / calante** crescent / waning moon; **~ piena** full moon; **~ di miele** honeymoon

luna-park *m inv* amusement park, *Br* funfair

lunario *m:* **sbarcare il ~** make ends meet

lunatico (*pl* -ci) moody

lunedì *m inv* Monday; **il o di ~** on Mondays

lunetta *f* ARCHI lunette

lunghezza *f* length

lungo (*pl* -ghi) **1** *agg* long; *caffè* weak; **non essere ~!** don't be long!, don't take forever!; **a ~** at length, for a long time; *fig* **alla -a** in the long run; **andare per le -ghe** drag on; **di gran -a** by far **2** *prp* along; (*durante*) throughout

lungolago *m* (*pl* -ghi) lakeside, lakeshore

lungomare *m inv* sea front

lunotto *m* AUTO rear window

luogo *m* (*pl* -ghi) place; **~ di nascita** birthplace, place of birth; **avere ~** take place, be held; **fuori ~** out of place; **in primo ~** in the first place; **in qualche ~** somewhere, someplace; **in nessun ~** nowhere

lupo *m* wolf

lurido filthy

lusinga *f* (*pl* -ghe) flattery

lusingare <1e> flatter

lusinghiero flattering

lussazione *f* dislocation

lusso *m* luxury; **albergo** *m* **di ~**

luxury hotel
lussuoso luxurious
lustrare <1a> polish

lustro *m* shine, lustre, *Am* luster; *fig* prestige; (*periodo*) five-year period
lutto *m* mourning

M

m *abbr* (= **metro**) m (= metre)
ma but; (*eppure*) and yet; ~ **cosa dici?** what are you talking about?; ~ **va!** nonsense!; ~ **no!** not at all!, of course not!
maccheroni *mpl* macaroni *sg*
macchia *f* spot; *di sporco* stain; (*bosco*) scrub; **allargarsi a ~ d'olio** spread like wildfire
macchiare <1k> stain, mark
macchiato stained; **caffè** *m* ~ *espresso with a splash of milk*
macchina *f* machine; (*auto*) car; *fig* machinery; **fotografica** camera; ~ **da cucire** sewing machine; ~ **da presa** cine camera; ~ **da scrivere** typewriter; **sportiva** sports car; ~ **a noleggio** hire car, rental car; **fatto a ~** machine made
macchinario *m* (*pl* -ri) machinery
macchinista *m* (*pl* -i) FERR train driver
macedonia *f*: ~ (**di frutta**) fruit salad
macellaio *m* (*pl* -ai), **-a** *f* butcher
macellare <1b> butcher
macelleria *f* butcher's
macerie *fpl* rubble *sg*
macigno *m* boulder
macinacaffè *m inv* coffee mill, coffee grinder
macinapepe *m inv* pepper mill, pepper grinder
macinare <1l> grind
macinino *m* mill; *spir* old banger
macrobiotica *f* health food; **negozio** *m* **di ~** health food shop
macrobiotico (*mpl* -ci) macrobiotic
macroscopico (*pl* -ci) *fig* huge,

enormous; *errore* monumental, colossal
Madonna *f* Madonna, Our Lady; PITT ~ **con bambino** Madonna and Child
madonnaro *m* pavement artist specializing in sacred images
madre *f* mother
madrelingua **1** *f* mother tongue **2** *m/f* native speaker
madrepatria *f* native land, mother country
madreperla *f* mother-of-pearl
madrevite *f* nut
madrina *f* godmother
maestà *f* majesty
maestoso majestic
maestrale *m* north-west wind
maestranze *fpl* workers
maestria *f* mastery
maestro **1** *agg* (*principale*) main; MAR **albero** *m* ~ main mast; **muro** *m* ~ loadbearing wall **2** *m* master; MUS, PITT maestro, master; **colpo** *m* **da ~** masterstroke **3** *m*, **-a** *f* teacher; ~ **di nuoto** swimming teacher *or* instructor; ~ **di sci** ski instructor
mafia *f* Mafia
maga *f* witch
magari **1** *avv* maybe, perhaps **2** *int* ~! if only! **3** *cong* ~ **venisse** if only he would come
magazzinaggio *m* storage
magazzino *m* warehouse; *di negozio* stock room; (*emporio*) factory shop; **grandi -i** *pl* department stores
maggio *m* May
maggiolino *m* June bug, May beetle
maggiorana *f* marjoram

maggioranza f majority; **~ azionaria** majority shareholding

maggiorare <1a> increase

maggiore 1 agg bigger; (più vecchio) older; MUS major; **il ~** the biggest; figlio the oldest; artista the greatest; azionista the major, the largest; **la maggior parte del tempo/di noi** most of the time/of us, the majority of the time/of us; **andare per la ~** be a crowd pleaser **2** m MIL major

maggiorenne adult attr

maggioritario (pl -ri) majority; **sistema** m **~** first-past-the-post system

magia f magic

magico (pl -ci) magic(al)

magistrale (eccellente) masterful; **istituto** m **~** teacher training college

magistrato DIR m magistrate

maglia f top; (maglione) sweater; SP shirt, jersey; ai ferri stitch; **lavorare a ~** knit; SP **~ gialla** yellow jersey

maglieria f knitwear

maglietta f tee-shirt

maglione m sweater

magnanimo magnanimous

magnesia f magnesia

magnesio m magnesium

magnete m magnet

magnetico (pl -ci) magnetic

magnifico (pl -ci) magnificent

magnolia f magnolia

mago m **1** (pl -ghi) wizard **2** (pl -gi) **i re -gi** the Three Wise Men, the Magi

magro thin; cibo low in fat; fig consolazione small; guadagno meagre, Am meager

mai never; (qualche volta) ever; **~ più** never again; **più che ~** more than ever; **non accetterò ~ e poi ~** I will never agree, never; **chi ha ~ detto che ...** who said that ...; **come ~?** how come?; **se ~** if ever; **meglio tardi che ~** better late than never; **dove/perché ~?** where/why on earth?

maiale m pig; (carne f di) **~** pork

maiolica f (pl -che) majolica

maionese f mayonnaise

mais m maize

maiuscola f capital (letter)

maiuscolo capital

mal → male

malandato vestito, divano, macchina dilapidated; persona poorly, not very well

malanno m misfortune; (malattia) illness

malapena: a ~ hardly, barely

malaria f malaria

malaticcio (pl -cci) sickly

malato 1 agg ill; **essere ~ di cuore** have heart problems; **~ di mente** mentally ill **2** m, **-a** f ill person

malattia f illness; **essere/mettersi in ~** be/go on sick leave; **~ infettiva** infectious disease; **-e** pl **della pelle** skin diseases; **-e** pl **veneree** sexually transmitted diseases

malavita f underworld

malavoglia f unwillingness, reluctance; **di ~** unwillingly, grudgingly, reluctantly

malconcio (pl -ci) vestito, divano, macchina dilapidated, the worse for wear; persona poorly, not very well

malcontento 1 agg discontented, dissatisfied **2** m discontent

malcostume m immorality

maldestro awkward, clumsy

male 1 m evil; **che c'è di ~?** where's the harm in it?; **andare a ~** go off, go bad; **aversela** o **prendersela a ~** take it the wrong way; MED **mal di gola** sore throat; **mal di testa/di denti** headache/toothache; **mal di mare** seasickness; **far ~ a qu** hurt s.o.; **mi fa ~ il braccio** my arm hurts; **il cioccolato mi fa ~** chocolate doesn't agree with me; **fare ~ alla salute** be bad for you; **farsi ~** hurt o.s. **2** avv badly; **capire ~** misunderstand; **di ~ in peggio** from bad to worse; **meno ~!** thank goodness!; **stare ~** (essere malato) be ill; (essere giù) be depressed; **il giallo mi sta ~** yellow doesn't suit me, I don't suit yellow; **il divano sta ~ qui** the couch doesn't look right here; **sta ~ ...** it's not done to ...; **mi ha**

risposto ~ he gave me a rude answer

maledetto 1 *pp* → **maledire 2** *agg* dratted, damn(ed)

maledire <3t> curse

maledizione *f* curse; ~! damn!

maleducato bad-mannered, uncouth

malessere *m* indisposition; *fig* malaise

malfamato disreputable

malfatto *cosa* badly made

malfattore *m* criminal

malformazione *f* MED, BIO malformation

malgoverno *m* POL misgovernment

malgrado 1 *prp* in spite of, despite **2** *avv* **mio/tuo** ~ against my/your will **3** *cong* although

maligno malicious, spiteful; MED malignant

malinconia *f* melancholy

malinconico (*pl* -ci) melancholic

malincuore: a ~ reluctantly, unwilling

malintenzionato 1 *agg* shady, suspicious **2** *m*, **-a** *f* shady character

malinteso *m* misunderstanding

malizia *f* (*cattiveria*) malice, spite; (*astuzia*) trick; **con** ~ maliciously, spitefully

malizioso malicious, spiteful; *sorriso* mischievous

malloppo *m* (*refurtiva*) loot

malmenare <1a> mistreat

malmesso *vestito, divano, macchina* the worse for wear; **sono un po'** ~ I'm a bit hard up

malnutrito under-nourished

malnutrizione *f* malnutrition

malore *m*: **è stato colto da un** ~ he was suddenly taken ill

malsano unhealthy

malsicuro unsafe

malta *f* mortar

maltempo *m* bad weather

malto *m* malt

maltrattare <1a> mistreat, ill-treat

malumore *m* bad mood; **essere di** ~ be in a bad mood

malvagio (*pl* -gi) evil, wicked

malvisto unpopular

malvivente *m* lout

malvolentieri unwillingly, reluctantly

mamma *f* mother, mum; ~ **mia!** goodness!

mammella *f* breast

mammifero *m* mammal

mammografia *f* mammography

manager *m/f* manager

manageriale managerial, management *attr*

mancanza *f* lack (**di** of); (*errore*) oversight; ~ **di abitazioni** housing shortage; ~ **di corrente** power failure; ~ **di personale** lack of staff, staff shortage; **per** ~ **di tempo** for lack of time

mancare <1d> *v/i* be missing; (*venire meno*) fail; (*morire*) pass away; **a qu manca qc** s.o. lacks sth; **mi mancano le forze** I don't have the strength; **mi manca la casa** I miss home; **mi mancano 5000 lire** I'm 5000 lire short; **manca la benzina nella macchina** the car needs filling up; **mancano tre mesi a Natale** it's three months to Christmas; **sentirsi** ~ feel faint; **non mancherò** I'll do that, I'll be sure to do it; **c'è mancato poco che cadesse** he almost fell; **ci mancherebbe altro!** no way!, you must be joking!; ~ **di qc** (*non avere*) lack sth, be lacking in sth; ~ **di fare qc** fail *or* omit to do sth; ~ **di parola** break one's promise **2** *v/t* miss

mancato *occasione* missed, lost; *tentativo* unsuccessful; **è un poeta** ~ he should have been a poet; ~ **pagamento** non-payment

manchevole faulty, defective

mancia *f* (*pl* -ce) tip

manciata *f* handful

mancino 1 *agg* left-handed; *fig* **colpo** *m* ~ blow beneath the belt, dirty trick **2** *m*, **-a** *f* left-hander

mandante *m/f* DIR client; F *person who hires a contract killer*

mandare <1a> send; ~ **qu a prendere qc** send s.o. for sth; ~ **a monte**

M

ruin, send up in smoke F; *fig* **~ giù** digest, take in

mandarino *m* BOT mandarin (orange)

mandato *m* POL mandate; DIR warrant; **~ bancario** banker's order; **~ di pagamento** payment order; **~ d'arresto** arrest warrant

mandibola *f* jaw

mandolino *m* mandolin

mandorla *f* almond

mandorlo *m* almond tree

mandria *f* herd

maneggevole easy to handle, manageable

maneggiare <1f> handle (*anche fig*)

maneggio *m* (*pl* -ggi) handling; *per cavalli* riding school

manesco (*pl* -chi) a bit too ready with one's fists

manette *fpl* handcuffs

manganello *m* truncheon

mangereccio (*pl* -ci) edible

mangiabile edible

mangiacassette *m inv*, **mangianastri** *m inv* cassette player

mangiare 1 *v/t* <1f> eat; *fig* squander; *mangiarsi le parole* mumble; *mangiarsi un'occasione* throw away *or* waste an opportunity **2** *m* food

mangime *m* fodder

mangiucchiare <1g> snack, eat between meals

mango *m* (*pl* -ghi) mango

mania *f* mania

Manica *f*: *la ~* the (English) Channel

manica *f* (*pl* -che) sleeve; *senza -che* sleeveless; *è un altro paio di -che!* that's another kettle of fish

manicaretto *m* delicacy

manichino *m* dummy

manico *m* (*pl* -chi o -ci) handle; *di violino* neck

manicomio *m* (*pl* -mi) mental home

manicotto *m* TEC sleeve

manicure *f inv* manicure; (*persona*) manicurist

maniera *f* (*modo*) way, manner; (*stile*) manner; *-e* manners

manifattura *f* manufacture; (*stabili-*

---

mento) factory

manifestante *m/f* demonstrator

manifestare <1b> **1** *v/t* (*esprimere*) express; (*mostrare*) show, demonstrate **2** *v/i* demonstrate

manifestarsi appear, show up; *di malattia* manifest itself

manifestazione *f* expression; *il mostrare* show, demonstration; **~ di protesta** demonstration, demo F; **~ sportiva** sporting event

manifesto 1 *agg* obvious **2** *m* poster

maniglia *f* handle; *di autobus, metro* strap

manipolare <1m> manipulate; *vino* adulterate

manipolazione *f* manipulation; *di vino* adulteration

mano *f* (*pl* -i) hand; *fuori* ~ out of the way, not easy to get at; *fig* **alla ~** approachable; *di seconda* ~ secondhand; *dare una* ~ *a qu* give s.o. a hand; *mettere* ~ *a qc* start sth; *lavo le pentole che sporco a* ~ *a* ~ I wash the dirty pots as I go along; *tenersi per* ~ hold hands; *man* ~ *che* as (and when); *-i in alto!* hands up!

manodopera *f* labo(u)r

manomettere <3ee> tamper with

manopola *f* knob

manoscritto *m* manuscript

manovale *m* hod carrier

manovella *f* starting handle; TEC crank

manovra *f* manoeuvre, *Am* maneuver

manovrare <1c> **1** *v/t* TEC operate; FERR shunt; *fig* manipulate **2** *v/i* manoeuvre, *Am* maneuver

mansarda *f* (*locale*) attic

mansueto docile

mantello *m* (*cappa*) cloak; *di animale* coat; (*strato*) covering, layer

mantenere <2q> keep; *famiglia* keep, maintain; *in buono stato* maintain; *mantenersi in forma* keep in shape

mantenimento *m* maintenance; *di famiglia* keep

manto *m* cloak; *di animale* coat; *fig* ~

di neve mantle of snow

Mantova f Mantua

mantovano 1 agg Mantuan **2** m, **-a** f native of Mantua

manuale 1 agg manual **2** m manual, handbook

manubrio m (pl -ri) handlebars pl

manutenzione f maintenance

manzo m steer, bullock; *carne* beef

mappa f map

mappamondo m globe

maratona f marathon

maratoneta m/f (mpl -i) marathon runner

marca f (pl -che) brand, make; (etichetta) label; *~ da bollo* revenue stamp

marcare <1d> mark; *goal* score

marcato accento, lineamenti strong

marchiare <1k> brand (anche fig)

marchio m (pl -chi) FIN brand; *~ depositato* registered trademark

marcia f (pl -ce) march; SP walk; TEC AUTO gear; *~ indietro* reverse; *mettersi in ~* set off

marciapiede m pavement, Am sidewalk; FERR platform

marciare <1f> march

marcio (pl -ci) bad, rotten; (corrotto) corrupt, rotten to the core; *avere torto ~* be totally wrong

marcire <4d> go bad, rot; fig rot

marco m (pl -chi) mark

mare m sea; *in alto ~* on the high seas

marea f tide; fig *una ~ di* loads of; *alta ~* high tide; *bassa ~* low tide; *~ nera* oil slick

mareggiata f storm

maremoto m tidal wave

margarina f margarine

margherita f marguerite

margheritina f daisy

margine m margin; (orlo) edge, brink; *vivere ai -i della società* live on the fringes of society

marina f coast(line); MAR navy; PITT seascape

marinaio m (pl -ai) sailor

marinare <1a> GASTR marinate; F *~ la scuola* play truant, Br bunk off school F

marinato GASTR marinated

marino sea, marine

marionetta f puppet, marionette

marito m husband

marittimo maritime

marmellata f jam; *~ di arance* marmalade

marmitta f AUTO silencer, Am muffler; *~ catalitica* catalytic converter

marmo m marble

marmotta f marmot; *dormire come una ~* sleep like a log

marocchino 1 agg Moroccan **2** m, **-a** f Moroccan

Marocco m Morocco

marrone 1 agg (chestnut) brown **2** m colore (chestnut) brown; (castagno) chestnut

marsala m Marsala, dessert wine

marsina f tails

Marte m Mars

martedì m inv Tuesday; *~ grasso* Shrove Tuesday, Br Pancake Day F

martello m hammer; *~ pneumatico* pneumatic drill

martire m/f martyr

martirio m (pl -ri) martyrdom

martora f marten

marxismo m Marxism

marxista m/f (mpl -i) Marxist

marzapane m marzipan

marziano m Martian

marzo m March

mascalzone m rogue, rascal

mascara m inv mascara

mascarpone m mascarpone

mascella f jaw

maschera f mask; in cinema, teatro usher; donna usherette; *~ antigas* gas mask; *~ subacquea* face mask; *ballo m in ~* masked ball

mascherare <1l> mask; fig camouflage, conceal

mascherarsi put on a mask; (travestirsi) dress up (da as)

maschile spogliatoio, abito men's; caratteristica male; GRAM masculine

maschilista (pl -i) **1** m male chauvinist, sexist **2** agg chauvinistic, sexist

maschio (pl -chi) **1** agg male; *hanno*

tre **figli -i** they have three sons or boys **2** m (*ragazzo*) boy; (*uomo*) man; ZO male

mascolino masculine

mascotte f inv mascot

massa f mass; EL earth; F **una ~ di cosa da fare** masses of things to do F

massacrare <1a> massacre

massacro m massacre

massaggiare <1f> massage

massaggiatore m, **-trice** f masseur; *donna* masseuse

massaggio m (pl -ggi) massage

massaia f housewife

massiccio (pl -cci) **1** agg massive; *oro, noce ecc* solid **2** m massif

massima f saying, maxim; (*temperatura*) maximum; **di ~** *progetto* preliminary; **in linea di ~** generally speaking, on the whole

massimale m maximum

massimo 1 agg greatest, maximum **2** m maximum; **al ~** at most

mass media mpl ~ mass media

masso m rock

masterizzare <1a> INFOR burn

masterizzatore m INFOR writer

masticare <1l & d> chew

mastice m mastic; (*stucco*) putty

mastino m mastiff

mastodontico (pl -ci) gigantic, enormous

masturbare <1a>, gen **masturbarsi** masturbate

masturbazione f masturbation

matassa f skein

matematica f mathematics, maths F, *Am* math F

matematico (pl -ci) **1** agg mathematical **2** m, **-a** f mathematician

materassino m airbed, lilo®

materasso m mattress

materia f matter; (*materiale*) material; (*disciplina*) subject; **~ facoltativa** optional subject; **~ obbligatoria** compulsory subject; **~ prima** raw material; **~ sintetica** synthetic (material)

materiale 1 agg material; (*rozzo*) coarse, rough **2** m material; TEC equipment

materialista (mpl -i) **1** agg materialistic **2** m/f materialist

maternità f inv motherhood; *in ospedale* maternity

materno maternal; **scuola** f **-a** nursery school

matita f pencil; **~ colorata** colo(u)red pencil; **~ per gli occhi** eye pencil; **~ per sopracciglia** eyebrow pencil

matrice f matrix

matricola f register; *all'università* first-year student

matrigna f stepmother

matrimoniale matrimonial

matrimonio m (pl -ni) marriage; *rito* wedding

mattina f morning; **di ~** in the morning; **questa ~** this morning; **domani ~** tomorrow morning

mattinata f morning; TEA matinee

mattiniero: essere ~ be an early bird

mattino m morning; **di buon ~** early in the morning

matto 1 agg mad, crazy, insane (**per** about); **avere una voglia -a di qc** be dying for sth; **essere ~ da legare** be insane, be mad as a hatter **2** m, **-a** f madman, lunatic; *donna* madwoman, lunatic; **mi piace da -i andare al cinema** I'm mad about the cinema

mattone m brick; *fig* **che ~!** what a turgid piece of writing!

mattonella f tile

mattutino morning attr

maturare <1a> *interessi* accrue; **~ una decisione** reach a decision

maturità f maturity; (*diploma*) A level

maturo *frutto* ripe; *persona* mature; **i tempi sono -i** the time is ripe

mausoleo m mausoleum

mazza f club; (*martello*) sledgehammer; *da baseball* bat; **~ da golf** golf club

mazzo m bunch, bundle; **~ di fiori** bunch of flowers, bouquet; **~ di chiavi** bunch of keys; **~ di carte** pack or deck of cards

mc *abbr* (= **metro cubo**) m³ (= cubic metre)

me (= **mi** before **lo, la, li, le, ne**) me; **dammelo** give me it, give it to me; **come ~** like me; **fai come ~** do what I do; **per ~** for me; **secondo ~** in my opinion

meccanica *f* mechanics; *di orologio* mechanism; **la ~ di un incidente** how an accident happened; **~ di precisione** precision engineering

meccanicamente mechanically

meccanico (*pl* -ci) **1** *agg* mechanical **2** *m* mechanic

meccanismo *m* mechanism

mecenate *m/f* sponsor

mèche *f inv* streak

medaglia *f* medal

medesimo (very) same; **il ~** the (very) same; **la -a** the (very) same

media *f* average; **in ~** on average; **superiore** (**inferiore**) **alla ~** above (below) average; **~ oraria** average speed

mediano 1 *agg* central, middle **2** *m* SP half-back

mediante by (means of)

mediatore *m*, **-trice** *f* mediator

mediazione *f* mediation

medicamento *m* medicine

medicare <1l, b & d> *persona* treat; *ferita* clean, disinfect

medicazione *f* treatment; (*bende*) dressing

medicina *f* medicine; **~ interna** internal medicine; **~ legale** forensic medicine; **~ sportiva** sports medicine

medicinale 1 *agg* medicinal **2** *m* medicine

medico (*pl* -ci) **1** *agg* medical; **visita** *f* **-a** medical examination, physical F **2** *m* doctor; **~ generico** general practitioner, *Br* GP; **~ di famiglia** family doctor; **~ di guardia** duty doctor

medievale medi(a)eval

medio (*pl* -di) **1** *agg* *età, classe ecc* middle *attr; guadagno, statura, rendimento* average **2** *m* middle finger

mediocre mediocre

mediocrità *f* mediocrity

medioevo *m* Middle Ages

meditare <1l & b> **1** *v/t* think about; (*progettare*) plan **2** *v/i* meditate; (*riflettere*) think; **~ su qc** think about sth

meditazione *f* meditation; (*riflessione*) consideration, reflection

mediterraneo 1 *agg* Mediterranean **2** *m* **Mediterraneo** Mediterranean (Sea)

medium *m/f inv* medium

medusa *f* ZO jellyfish

megalomania *m* megalomania

meglio 1 *avv* better; **~!, tanto ~!** so much the better!, good!; **alla ~** to the best of one's ability; **di bene in ~** better and better **2** *agg* better; *superlativo* best **3** *m* best; **fare del proprio ~** do one's best **4** *f* **avere la ~ su** get the better of

mela *f* apple

melagrana *f* pomegranate

melanzana *f* aubergine, *Am* eggplant

melma *f* mud

melo *m* apple (tree)

melodia *f* melody

melodico (*pl* -ci) melodic

melodramma *m* (*pl* -i) melodrama

melodrammatico melodramatic

melograno *m* pomegranate tree

melone *m* melon

membrana *f* membrane; **~ del timpano** eardrum

membro *m* (*pl* le **membra**) ANAT limb; *persona* (*pl* i -i) member

memorabile memorable

memorandum *m inv* memo(random); (*promemoria*) memo

memoria *f* memory; INFOR storage capacity; **a ~** by heart; **in ~ di** in memory of; **~ centrale** main memory; **questo nome non ti richiama alla ~ niente** doesn't that name remind you of anything?; **-e** *pl* memoirs

memorizzare <1a> memorize; INFOR save

menare <1a> lead; F (*picchiare*) hit

mendicante *m/f* beggar

M

mendicare <1l, d or 1d> **1** *v/t* beg (for); *aiuto, lavoro ecc* beg for, plead for **2** *v/i* beg

menefreghismo *m* couldn't-care-less attitude

meninge *f*: F *spremersi le -i* rack one's brains F

meningite *f* meningitis

meno 1 *avv* less; *superlativo* least; MATH minus; *il ~ possibile* as little as possible; *di ~* at least; *a ~ che* unless; *per lo ~* at least; *sono le sei ~ un quarto* it's a quarter to six; *sempre ~* less and less; *fare a ~ di qc* do without sth; *venir ~ a qcno* forze desert s.o.; *venir ~ alla parola data* not keep one's word **2** *prp* except

menomato damaged; (*handicappato*) disabled

menomazioni *fpl* damage *sg*

mensa *f di fabbrica* canteen; MIL mess; *~ universitaria* refectory

mensile 1 *agg* monthly; *tessera f ~ per treno, autobus* monthly season ticket **2** *m* (*periodico*) monthly

mensilità *f inv* salary

mensola *f* bracket

menta *f* mint; *~ piperita* peppermint

mentale mental

mentalità *f inv* mentality

mentalmente mentally

mente *f* mind; *malato di ~* mentally ill; *avere in ~ di fare qc* be planning to do sth, be thinking about doing sth; *tenere a ~ qc* bear sth in mind; *non mi viene in ~ il nome di ...* I can't remember the name of ...; *mi è uscito di ~* it slipped my mind

mentire <4d or b> lie

mento *m* chin

mentre while

menù *m inv* menu *anche* INFOR

menzionare <1a> mention

menzogna *f* lie

meraviglia *f* wonder; *a ~* marvel(l)ously, wonderfully

meravigliare <1g> astonish

meravigliarsi *~ di* be astonished by;

mi meraviglio di te you astonish me

meravigliato astonished

meraviglioso marvel(l)ous, wonderful

mercante *m* merchant

mercanteggiare <1f> bargain, haggle

mercantile 1 *agg nave* cargo *attr*; *porto* commercial **2** *m* cargo ship

mercanzia *f* merchandise

mercato *m* market; *~ coperto* covered market, indoor market; *~ estero* foreign market; *~ mondiale* world market; *~ interno* domestic market; *~ unico europeo* single European market; *~ nero* black market; *~ delle pulci* flea market; *a buon ~* cheap, inexpensive

merce *f* goods; *~ di contrabbando* contraband

merceria *f (pl -ie)* haberdashery

mercoledì *m inv* Wednesday; *~ delle Ceneri* Ash Wednesday

mercurio *m* mercury; AST **Mercurio** Mercury

merda P shit P

merenda *f* snack

meridiana *f* sundial

meridiano 1 *agg* midday *attr* **2** *m* meridian

meridionale 1 *agg* southern; *Italia f ~* southern Italy **2** *m/f* southerner

meridione *m* south; *il Meridione* southern Italy

meringa *f (pl -ghe)* meringue

meritare <1l & b> **1** *v/t* deserve; *non merita un prezzo così alto* it's not worth that much **2** *v/i*: *un libro che merita* a worthwhile book; *non ti arrabbiare, non merita* don't get angry, it's / he's not worth it

meritevole worthy (*di* of)

merito *m* merit; *in ~ a* as regards; *per ~ suo* thanks to him

merletto *m* lace

merlo *m* ZO blackbird; ARCHI *-i pl* battlements

merluzzo *m* cod

meschino mean, petty; (*infelice*) wretched

mescolanza f mixture

mescolare <1l> mix; *insalata* toss; *caffè* stir

mescolarsi mix, blend

mese m month; *una volta al* ~ once a month; *ai primi del* ~ on the first of every month

messa[1]: ~ *in piega* set; ~ *in scena* production; AUTO ~ *in marcia* starting; ~ *in moto* start-up; FOT ~ *a fuoco* focussing; ~ *a punto di meccanismo* adjustment; *di motore* (fine-)tuning; *di testo* finalization

messa[2] f REL mass; ~ *solenne* high mass

messaggero m messenger

messaggio m (pl -ggi) message

messale m missal

messicano 1 agg Mexican **2** m, -a f Mexican

Messico m Mexico

messinscena f production; fig act

messo pp → **mettere**

mestiere m trade; (professione) profession; *essere del* ~ be a professional or an expert

mestolo m ladle

mestruazione f menstruation

meta f destination; SP try; fig goal, aim

metà f inv half; *punto centrale* middle, centre; *siamo a* ~ *del viaggio* we're half-way there; *a* ~ *prezzo* half price; *a* ~ *strada* halfway; *fare a* ~ go halves (*di* on)

metabolico metabolic

metabolismo m metabolism

metadone m methadone

metafora f metaphor

metaforico (pl -ci) metaphorical

metallico (pl -ci) metallic

metallizzato metallic

metallo m metal; ~ *prezioso* precious metal

metallurgia f metallurgy

metamorfosi f inv metamorphosis

metano m methane

metanodotto m gas pipeline

meteora f meteor

meteorite m o f meteorite

meteorologico (pl -ci) meteoro-

logical, weather attr; *bollettino* m ~ weather forecast; *servizio* m ~ weather service

meticoloso meticulous

metodico (pl -ci) methodical

metodo m method

metrica f metrics

metrico (pl -ci) metric

metro[1] m metre, Am meter; ~ *quadrato* square metre (Am meter); ~ *cubo* cubic metre (Am meter)

metrò[2] m inv (metropolitana) underground, Am subway

metronotte m inv night watchman

metropoli f inv metropolis

metropolitana f underground, Am subway

mettere <3ee> put; *vestito* put on; ~ *a punto meccanismo* adjust; *motore* (fine-)tune; ~ *in moto* start (up); ~ *in ordine* tidy up; ~ *al sicuro* put away safely; ~ *su casa* set up house; *mettiamo che* let's assume that

mettersi *abito, cappello ecc* put on; ~ *a letto* go to bed, take to one's bed; ~ *a sedere* sit down; AVIA, AUTO ~ *la cintura* fasten one's seat belt; ~ *a fare qc* start to do sth; ~ *in cammino* set out, get going

mezzaluna f (pl mezzelune) half moon, crescent; GASTR two-handled chopper

mezzanino m mezzanine

mezzanotte f midnight

mezzo 1 agg half; *uno e* ~ one and a half; *mezz'ora* half-hour; *le sei e* ~ half-past six; ~ *chilo* a half kilo; *a -a strada* halfway; *di -a età* middle-aged **2** avv half **3** m (parte centrale) middle; (metà) half; (strumento) means sg; (veicolo) means sg of transport; *prendere un* ~ *pubblico* use public transport; *-i pl di comunicazione di massa* mass media; *-i pl di pagamento* means of payment; *per* ~ *di* by means of; *a* ~ *posta* by post,; *in* ~ *a due persone, due libri* between; *in* ~ *a quei documenti* in the middle of or among those papers; *in* ~ *alla stanza* in the middle of the room;

M

nel ~ di in the middle of; **giusto ~** happy medium

mezzobusto *m* (*pl* mezzibusti) half-length photograph / portrait

mezzofondo *m* middle distance

mezzogiorno *m* midday; GEOG **Mezzogiorno** south (of Italy), southern Italy

mezzoservizio *m*: **lavorare a ~** work part-time

mg *abbr* (= **milligrammo**) mg (= milligram)

mi[1] *m* MUS E; *nel solfeggio della scala* me, mi

mi[2] *pron* me; *riflessivo* myself; **eccomi** here I am

miagolare <1l> miaow, mew

miagolio *m* miaowing, mewing

mica: non ho ~ finito I'm nowhere near finished; **non è - vero** there's not the slightest bit of truth in it; **~ male** not bad at all

miccia *f* fuse

micidiale *veleno*, *clima* deadly; *fatica*, *sforza* exhausting, killing

micio F *m* (*pl* -ci) (pussy) cat

micosi *f inv* mycosis

microbiologia *f* microbiology

microbo *m* microbe

microcamera *f* miniature camera

microchirurgia *f* microsurgery

microclima *m* microclimate

microcomputer *m inv* microcomputer

microcosmo *m* microcosm

microfilm *m inv* microfilm

microfono *m* microphone, mike F

microonda *f* microwave; **forno a a -e** microwave (oven)

microprocessore *m* microprocessor

microrganismo *m* microorganism

microscopico (*pl* -ci) microscopic

microscopio *m* (*pl* -pi) microscope

midollo *m* marrow; **~ osseo** bone marrow; **~ spinale** spinal cord

miei *mpl* di **mio** my

miele *m* honey

mietere <3a> harvest

migliaio *m* (*pl* -aia *f*) thousand; **un ~** a *or* one thousand; *fig* **un ~ di per-**

sone thousands of people; **a migliaia** in their thousands

miglio[1] *m* (*pl* -glia *f*) *misura* mile; **~ marino** nautical mile

miglio[2] *m grano* millet

miglioramento *m* improvement

migliorare <1a> **1** *v/t* improve **2** *v/i e* **migliorarsi** improve, get better

migliore better; **il ~** the best

mignolo *m* (*o* **dito ~**) little finger; *del piede* little toe

migrare <1a> migrate

migrazione *f* migration

-mila thousand; **due~** two thousand

milanese 1 *agg* of Milan **2** *m/f* inhabitant of Milan

Milano *f* Milan

miliardario *m* (*pl* -ri), **-a** *f* billionaire, multimillionaire

miliardo *m* billion

milionario *m* (*pl* -ri), **-a** *f* millionaire; *donna* millionairess

milione *m* million

militare <1l> fight, militate (**contro** against; **per** for); **~ in un partito** be a member of a party **2** *agg* military **3** *m* soldier; **fare il ~** do one's military service

militarismo *m* militarism

militarista *m/f* (*mpl* -i) militarist

militarizzare <1a> hand over to the military; *partito* structure like the army

milite *m* soldier; **il ~ ignoto** the Unknown Soldier

militesente exempt from military service

milizia *f* militia

mille (*pl* mila) a thousand

millefoglie *m inv* vanilla slice

millennio *m* (*pl* -nni) millennium

millepiedi *m inv* millipede

millesimo *m/agg* thousandth

milligrammo *m* milligram(me)

millimetro *m* millimetre, *Am* -meter

milza *f* spleen

mimetizzare <1a> MIL camouflage

mimetizzarsi camouflage o.s.; *fig* **~ tra la folla** get lost in the crowd

mimica *f* mime

mimo *m* mime

mimosa *f* mimosa

mina *f* mine; *di matita* lead

minaccia *f* (*pl* -cce) threat

minacciare <1f> threaten

minaccioso threatening

minare <1a> mine; *fig* undermine

minato: *campo m* ~ minefield

minareto *m* minaret

minatore *m* miner

minatorio (*pl* -ri) threatening

minerale *m*/*agg* mineral

minestra *f* soup; **~ di fagioli** bean soup; **~ di verdura** vegetable soup

minestrina *f* clear soup, broth

minestrone *m* minestrone

miniatura *f* miniature

miniera *f* mine (*anche fig*)

minigolf *m inv* miniature golf

minigonna *f* mini(skirt)

minimizzare <1a> minimize

minimo 1 *agg* least, slightest; *prezzo, offerta* lowest; *salario, temperatura* minimum 2 *m* minimum; **come ~, dovresti ...** you should at least ...

ministero *m* ministry; (*gabinetto*) government, ministry; **pubblico ~** state prosecutor

ministro *m* minister; **~ degli Esteri** Foreign Secretary, *Am* Secretary of State; **~ degli Interni** Home Secretary, *Am* Secretary of the Interior; **primo ~** Prime Minister; **consiglio m dei -i** Cabinet

minoranza *f* minority

minorato 1 *agg* severely handicapped 2 *m*, **-a** *f* severely handicapped person

minore *agg* minor; *di età* younger; *distanza* shorter; *più piccolo* smaller; 2 *m*/*f*: **vietato ai -i di 18 anni** no admittance to those under 18 years of age; *film* X-rated

minorenne 1 *agg* under-age 2 *m*/*f* minor

minuscola *f* small letter, lower case letter

minuscolo tiny, miniscule

minuto 1 *agg persona* tiny; *oggetto* minute; *descrizione, indagine* detailed; **commercio m al ~** retail trade 2 *m* minute; **60 pulsazioni al**

~ 60 beats a minute; **ho i -i contati** I don't have a minute to spare

minuzioso *descrizione* detailed; *ricerca* meticulous

mio (*pl* miei) 1 *agg* my; **un ~ amico** a friend of mine, one of my friends; **i miei amici** my friends 2 *pron*: **il ~** mine; **questo libro è ~** this book is mine, this is my book; **i miei** my parents

miope short-sighted

miopia *f* short-sightedness, myopia

mira *f* aim; (*obiettivo*) target; **prendere la ~** take aim; **prendere di ~** aim at; *fig* **prendere di ~ qu** have it in for s.o.

miracolo *m* miracle; **per ~** by a miracle, miraculously

miraggio *m* (*pl* -ggi) mirage

mirare <1a> aim (**a** at)

mirino *m* MIL sight; FOT viewfinder

mirtillo *m* bilberry

mirto *m* myrtle

miscela *f* mixture; *di caffè, tabacco* blend

miscelatore *m* GASTR mixer; *rubinetto* mixer tap

mischia *f* (*rissa*) scuffle; SP, (*folla*) scrum

mischiare <1k> mix; *carte* shuffle

mischiarsi mix

miscuglio *m* (*pl* -gli) mixture

miserabile wretched, miserable

miserevole pitiful

miseria *f* (*povertà*) poverty; (*infelicità*) misery; **costare una ~** cost next to nothing; F **porca ~!** damn and blast! F

misericordia *f* mercy; **avere ~ di qu** have pity on s.o.

misero wretched

misfatto *m* misdeed

missaggio *m* (*pl* -ggi) → **mixaggio**

missare → **mixare**

missile *m* missile; **~ a lunga gittata** long-range missile

missionario *m* (*pl* -ri), **-a** *f* missionary

missione *f* mission

misterioso mysterious

mistero *m* mystery

mistico (*pl* -ci) mystic(al)

misto 1 *agg* mixed **2** *m* mixture; ~ *lana* wool mix

misura *f* measurement; (*taglia*) size; (*provvedimento*), *fig* measure; MUS bar; **-e** *pl* **preventive** preventive measures; **unità** *f* **di** ~ unit of measurement; **con** ~ in moderation; **su** ~ made to measure

misurabile measurable, which can be measured

misurare <1a> measure; *vestito* try on; ~ **le spese** limit one's spending

misurarsi *in una gara* compete; ~ **con** compete with

misurato restrained

misurino *m* measuring spoon

mite *persona, inverno* mild; *condanna* light

mitigare <1l & e> lessen; *dolore* ease, lessen

mito *m* myth

mitologia *f* mythology

mitologico (*pl* -ci) mythological

mitra *m inv*, **mitragliatrice** *f* machine gun

mitt. *abbr* (= **mittente**) from

mittente *m/f* sender

mixaggio *m* mixing

mixare <1k> mix

ml *abbr* (= **millilitro**) ml (= millilitre)

M.M. *abbr* (= **Marina Militare**) Italian navy

mm *abbr* (= **millimetro**) mm (= millimetre)

mobile 1 *agg* mobile; *ripiano, pannello* removeable; **squadra** *f* ~ flying squad **2** *m* piece of furniture; **-i** *pl* furniture

mobilia *f* furnishings

mobilificio *m* furniture-making factory

mobilio *m* → **mobilia**

mobilità *f* mobility

mobilitare <1m> mobilize

moca *m* mocha

mocassino *m* moccasin

moda *f* fashion; **alla** ~ fashionable, in fashion; *vestirsi* fashionably; **di** ~ fashionable, in fashion; **fuori** ~ out of fashion, unfashionable

modalità *f inv* method

modella *f* model

modellare <1b> model

modello 1 *agg* model **2** *m* model; (*indossatore*) male model; *di vestito* style; (*formulario*) form

modem *m inv* INFOR modem

moderare <1l & c> moderate

moderato moderate

moderatore *m*, **-trice** *f* moderator

moderazione *f* moderation

modernizzare <1a> modernize

moderno modern

modestia *f* modesty

modesto modest; *prezzo* very reasonable

modico (*pl* -ci) reasonable

modifica *f* (*pl* -che) modification

modificare <1m & d> modify

modo *m* (*maniera*) way, manner; (*mezzo*) way; MUS mode; GRAM mood; ~ **di dire** expression; ~ **di vedere** way of looking at things; **per** ~ **di dire** so to speak; **se hai** ~ **di passare da me** if you could drop by; **a** ~ **mio** in my own way; **ad ogni** ~ anyway, anyhow; **di** ~ **che** so that; **in che** ~? how?; **in special** ~ especially

modulo *m* form; (*elemento*) module; ~ **di domanda** application form; ~ **d'iscrizione** registration form; ~ **di versamento** *banca* pay-in slip

mogano *m* mahogany

moglie *f* (*pl* -gli) wife

mola *f* grindstone; *di mulino* millstone

molare 1 *v/t* <1c> grind **2** *m* molar

mole *f* (*grandezza*) size

molecola *f* molecule

molestare <1b> bother, trouble; *sessualmente* sexually harass

molestia *f* bother, nuisance; ~ **sessuale** sexual harassment

molesto annoying

molla *f* spring; *fig* spur; **-e** *pl* tongs

mollare <1c> *corda* release, let go; F *schiaffo, ceffone* give; F *fidanzato* dump; ~ **la presa** let go

molle soft; (*bagnato*) wet

molleggiare <1f> be springy

molleggio *m* springs

molletta *f* hairgrip; *da bucato* clothes peg *or* pin

mollica *f* (*pl* -che) crumb

mollusco *m* (*pl* -chi) mollusc, *Am* mollusk

molo *m* pier

molotov *f inv* Molotov cocktail

molteplice multifaceted

moltiplicare <1m & d> **1** *v/t* multiply (*per* by) **2** *v/i e* **moltiplicarsi** multiply

moltitudine *f* multitude, host

molto **1** *agg* a lot of; *con nomi plurali* a lot of, many **2** *avv* a lot; *con aggettivi* very; **~ meglio** much better, a lot better; *da ~* for a long time; *fra non ~* before long

momentaneo momentary, temporary

momento *m* moment; *dal ~ che* from the moment that; *causale* since; *a -i* sometimes, at moments; *per il ~* for the moment; *del ~* short-lived; *sul ~* at the time

monaca *f* (*pl* -che) nun

monaco *m* (*pl* -ci) monk

monarca *m* (*pl* -chi) monarch

monarchia *f* monarchy

monarchico (*pl* -ci) **1** *agg* monarchical **2** *m*, **-a** *f* monarchist

monastero *m* monastery; *di monache* convent

mondano society; (*terreno*) worldly; *fare vita -a* go out

mondare <1a> *frutta* peel

mondiale **1** *agg* world *attr*, *economia* world *attr*, global; *fenomeno, scala* worldwide; *di fama ~* world-famous **2** *m*: *i -i di calcio* the World Cup

mondo *m* world; *giro m del ~* world tour, tour round the world; *l'altro ~* the next world; *il più bello del ~* the most beautiful in the world; *divertirsi un ~* enjoy o.s. enormously *or* a lot

monello *m*, **-a** *f* imp, little devil

moneta *f* coin; (*valuta*) currency; (*denaro*) money; (*spiccioli*) change; *~ d'oro* gold coin

monetario (*pl* -ri) monetary; *Fondo*

m ~ internazionale International Monetary Fund

mongolfiera *m* hot-air balloon

monito *m* reprimand

monografia *f* monograph

monogramma *m* (*pl* -i) monogram

monolocale *m* bedsit

monologo *m* (*pl* -ghi) monolog(ue)

monopattino *m* child's scooter

monopolio *m* (*pl* -li) monopoly

monopolizzare <1a> monopolize

monoposto *m* single-seater

monotonia *f* monotony

monotono monotonous

monouso disposable, throwaway

montacarichi *m inv* hoist

montaggio *m* (*pl* -ggi) TECH assembly; *di film* editing

montagna *f* mountain; *fig* **-e** *pl* **russe** rollercoaster *sg*

montagnoso mountainous

montanaro *m*, **-a** *f* person who lives in the mountains

montare <1a> **1** *v/t* go up, climb; *cavallo* get onto, mount; TEC assemble; *film* edit; GASTR whip; *~ la guardia* mount guard **2** *v/i* go up; *venire* come up; *~ in macchina* get into; *~ su scala* climb; *pullman* get on

montarsi: *~ la testa* get a swollen head, get bigheaded

montatura *f di occhiali* frame; *di gioiello* mount; *fig* set-up F, frame-up F

monte *m* mountain; *fig* mountain, pile; *a ~* upstream; *fig* *mandare a ~* ruin, mess up F

montone *m* ram; *pelle, giacca* sheepskin

montuoso mountainous

monumento *m* monument

moquette *f inv* fitted carpet

mora *f* BOT *del gelso* mulberry; *del rovo* blackberry

morale **1** *agg* moral **2** *f* morals *pl*; *di favola ecc* moral **3** *m* morale; *essere giù di ~* be feeling a bit down; *tirare su il ~ a qu* cheer s.o. up, lift s.o.'s spirits

moralista *m/f* (*mpl* -i) moralist

morbidezza f softness
morbido soft
morbillo m measles sg
morbo m disease
morboso fig unhealthy, unnatural; *curiosità* morbid
mordace fig biting, mordant
mordere <3uu> bite
morena f moraine
morfina f morphine
moribondo dying
morire <4k> die; fig ~ *di paura* be scared to death; F *muoio dalla voglia di una birra* I could murder a pint F, I'm dying for a beer F
mormorare <1l> murmur; (*bisbigliare, lamentarsi*) mutter
mormorio m murmuring; (*brontolio*) muttering
morsetto m TEC clamp; EL terminal
morsicare <1l, c & d> bite
morso 1 pp → *mordere* **2** m bite; *di cibo* bit, mouthful; *per cavallo* bit; *i -i pl della fame* the pangs of hunger
mortale *ferita, malattia* fatal; *offesa, nemico* deadly; *uomo* mortal
mortalità f mortality
morte f death
mortificare <1m & d> mortify
mortificazione f mortification
morto 1 pp → *morire* **2** agg dead; *stanco ~* dead tired **3** m, *-a* f dead man; *donna* dead woman; *i -i* pl the dead
mortorio m: F *essere un ~* be deadly dull *or* boring
mortuario (pl -ri) death; *camera* f *-a* chapel
mosaico m (pl -ci) mosaic
mosca f (pl -che) fly; *peso* m ~ flyweight; ~ *cieca* blindman's buff; *restare con un pugno di -e* come away empty-handed
moscatello m muscatel
moscato 1 agg muscat; *noce* f *-a* nutmeg **2** m muscatel
moscerino m gnat, midge
moschea f mosque
moscio (pl -sci) thin, flimsy; fig limp, washed out
moscone m ZO bluebottle; (*imbar-*

cazione) pedalo
mossa f movement; fig e di judo, karate move
mosso 1 pp → *muovere* **2** agg mare rough
mostarda f mustard
mosto m must, *unfermented grape juice*
mostra f show; (*esposizione*) exhibition; fig *mettere in ~* show off
mostrare <1a> show; (*indicare*) point out
mostrarsi appear
mostro m monster
mostruoso monstrous
motel m inv motel
motivare <1a> cause; *personale* motivate; (*spiegare*) explain, give reasons for
motivazione f (*spiegazione*) explanation; (*stimolo*) motivation
motivo m reason; MUS theme, motif; *su tessuto* pattern; *per quale ~?* for what reason?, why?
moto[1] m movement; *fare ~* get some exercise; *mettere in ~ motore* start (up); fig set in motion
moto[2] f (motor)bike
motocicletta f motorcycle
motociclista m/f (mpl -i) motorcyclist
motociclo m motorcycling
motore m engine; ~ *Diesel* diesel engine; ~ *a due tempi* two-stroke engine; ~ *a quattro tempi* four-stroke engine; ~ *a combustione* internal combustion engine; INFOR ~ *di ricerca* search engine; ~ *fuoribordo* outboard (motor *or* engine); *veicolo* m *a ~* motor vehicle; *accendere il ~* start (up) the engine, turn the key in the ignition; *fermare il ~* turn off the engine
motorino m moped; ~ *d'avviamento* starter
motorizzato motorized; F *sei ~* have you got wheels? F
motoscafo m motorboat
motoscooter m inv (motor) scooter
motrice f FERR railcar
motteggio m (pl -ggi) joke

motto *m* motto

mouse *m inv* INFOR mouse

movente *m* motive

movimento *m* movement; (*vita*) life, bustle

mozione *f* motion; ~ **di fiducia** vote of confidence

mozzarella *f* mozzarella, *buffalo-milk cheese*

mozzicone *m* cigarette end, (cigarette) stub

mozzo *m* TEC hub

mq *abbr* (= **metro quadrato**) sq m (= square metre)

mucca *f* (*pl* -cche) cow

mucchio *m* (*pl* -cchi) pile, heap

muco *m* (*pl* -chi) mucus

mucosa *f* mucous membrane

muffa *f* mo(u)ld; **sapere di ~** taste mo(u)ldy; **fare la ~** go mo(u)ldy

mughetto *m* lily-of-the-valley

mugolare <1l> *di cane* whine; (*gemere*) moan, whine

mugolio *m* whining

mugugnare <1a> grumble

mulattiera *f* mule track

mulatto *m*, **-a** *f* mulatto

mulinello *m su canna da pesca* reel; *vortice d'acqua* eddy

mulino *m* mill; ~ **a vento** windmill

mulo *m* mule

multa *f* fine

multare <1a> fine

multicolore multicolo(u)red

multiculturale multicultural

multimediale multimedia

multinazionale *f*agg multinational

multiplo multiple

multiuso multipurpose

mungere <3d> milk

municipale municipal; **consiglio** *m* ~ town council

municipio *m* (*pl* -pi) town council, municipality; *edificio* town hall

munire <4d>: ~ **di** supply with, provide with

munizioni *fpl* ammunition

muovere <3ff> **1** *v/t* move **2** *v/i partire* move off (**da** from); ~ **incontro a qu** move towards s.o.

muoversi move; F (*sbrigarsi*) get a

move on F

muraglia *f* wall

murale **1** *agg* wall *attr* **2** *m* PITT mural

murare <1a> (*chiudere*) wall up

muratore *m* bricklayer

muratura *f* brickwork

murena *f* moray (eel)

muro *m* (*pl anche* le mura) wall; ~ **del suono** sound barrier; *fig* **mi ha messo con le spalle al** ~ he'd got my back against the wall; **le -a** *fpl* (city) walls

muschio *m* (*pl* -chi) BOT moss

muscolare muscular; **strappo** *m* ~ strained muscle

muscolatura *f* muscles *pl*

muscolo *m* muscle

muscoloso muscular

museo *m* museum; ~ **etnologico** folk museum; ~ **d'arte** museum

museruola *f* muzzle

musica *f* music; ~ **da camera** chamber music; ~ **leggera** light music, easy-listening music

musicale musical; **strumento** *m* ~ musical instrument

musicassetta *f* (music) tape

musicista *m/f* (*mpl* -i) musician

muso *m di animale* muzzle; **tenere il ~ a qu** be in a huff with s.o.

musone *m* sulker

musulmano **1** *agg* Muslim, Moslem **2** *m*, **-a** *f* Muslim, Moslem

muta *f di cani* pack; SP wetsuit

mutabile changeable

mutamento *m* change

mutande *fpl di donna* knickers; *di uomo* (under)pants

mutandine *fpl* knickers; ~ (**da bagno**) (swimming) trunks

mutare <1a> *v/t & v/i* change

mutevole → **mutabile**

mutilare <1l> mutilate

mutilato *m* disabled ex-serviceman

mutilazione *f* mutilation

muto **1** *agg* dumb; (*silenzioso*) silent, dumb; **essere ~ dallo stupore** be struck dumb with astonishment; **film** *m* ~ silent movie **2** *m*, **-a** *f* mute

mutua *f* fund that pays out sickness benefit; **medico** *m* **della ~a** doctor recognized by the mutua

mutuato *m*, **-a** *f* person entitled to

sickness benefit

mutuo 1 *agg* mutual **2** *m* mortgage

N

N *abbr* (= **nord**) N (= north)

n. *abbr* (= **numero**) No. (= number)

nacchere *fpl* castanets

nafta *f* naphtha

nano 1 *agg* dwarf **2** *m*, **-a** *f* dwarf

napoletano 1 *agg* Neapolitan **2** *m*, **-a** *f* Neapolitan

Napoli *f* Naples

nappa *f* tassel; (*pelle*) nappa (*type of soft leather*)

narciso *m* BOT narcissus

narcosi *f inv* narcosis

narcotico *m* (*pl* -ci) narcotic

narcotizzare <1a> drug

narice *f* nostril

narrare <1a> tell, narrate

narratore, **-trice** *f* narrator

nascere <3gg> be born; BOT come up; *fig* develop, grow up; *di sole* rise, come up; *sono nato a Roma* I was born in Rome; *le è nata una figlia* she's had a little girl

nascita *f* birth; *fin dalla ~* from birth

nascondere <3hh> hide, conceal

nascondersi hide

nascondiglio *m* (*pl* -gli) hiding place

nascosto 1 *pp* → **nascondere 2** *avv*: *di ~* in secret; *di ~ a qu* unbeknownst to s.o.

nasello *m* (*pesce*) hake

naso *m* nose

nastro *m* tape; *per capelli*, *di decorazione* ribbon; *~ adesivo* adhesive tape, Sellotape®, *Am* Scotch tape®; *~ isolante* insulating tape, *Am* friction tape; *~ magnetico* magnetic tape

Natale *m* Christmas; *vigilia f di ~*

Christmas Eve; *buon ~!* Merry Christmas!

natale *agg* of one's birth

natalità *f* birth rate, number of births

natalizio (*pl* -zi) Christmas

natante 1 *agg* floating **2** *m* boat

nativo 1 *agg* native **2** *m*, **-a** *f* native

NATO *abbr* (= **Organizzazione del Trattato nord-atlantico**) NATO (= North Atlantic Treaty Organization

nato → **nascere**

natura *f* nature; PITT ~ *morta* still life; *contro ~* unnatural; *essere paziente per ~* be patient by nature, be naturally patient; *secondo ~* in harmony with nature

naturale natural; *scienze fpl -i* natural sciences

naturalezza *f* naturalness; *con ~* naturally

naturalizzare <1a>: *è naturalizzato americano* he's a naturalized American

naturalmente naturally, of course; *comportarsi* naturally

naufragare <1l & e> *di nave* be wrecked; *di persona* be shipwrecked; *fig* be ruined, come to grief

naufragio *m* (*pl* -gi) shipwreck; *fig* ruin; *fare ~ di nave* be wrecked; *di persona* be shipwrecked

naufrago *m* (*pl* -ghi), **-a** *f* survivor of a shipwreck

nausea *f* nausea; *avere la ~* feel sick, *Am* feel nauseous; *dare la ~ a qu* make s.o. feel sick, nauseate s.o. (*anche fig*)

nauseare <1l> nauseate (*anche fig*)

nautica *f* seamanship

nautico (*pl* -ci) nautical

navale; *cantiere m* ~ shipyard

navata *f* ARCHI: ~ *centrale* nave; ~ *laterale* aisle

nave *f* ship; ~ *da carico* cargo ship *or* vessel; ~ *passeggeri* passenger ship; ~ *traghetto* ferry

navetta 1 *agg inv: bus m* ~ shuttle bus 2 *f* shuttle; ~ *spaziale* space shuttle

navicella *f di astronave* nose cone

navigabile navigable

navigare <11 & e> sail; INFOR navigate

navigatore *m* navigator

navigazione *f* navigation

nazionale 1 *agg* national 2 *f* national team; *la ~ italiana* the Italian team

nazionalismo *m* nationalism

nazionalista *m/f* (*mpl* -i) nationalist

nazionalistico (*pl* -ci) nationalistic

nazionalità *f inv* nationality

nazionalizzare <1a> nationalize

nazione *f* nation

N.B. *abbr* (= *nota bene*) NB (= nota bene)

N.d.A. *abbr* (= *nota dell'autore*) author's note

N.d.E. *abbr* (= *nota dell'editore*) publisher's note

N.d.T. *abbr* (= *nota del traduttore*) translator's note

NE *abbr* (= *nord-est*) NE (= northeast)

ne 1 *pron* (*di lui*) about him; (*di lei*) about her; (*di loro*) about them; (*di ciò*) about it; ~ *sono contento* I'm happy about it; ~ *ho abbastanza* I have enough 2 *avv* from there; ~ *vengo adesso* I've just come back from there

né: ~ ... ~ neither ... nor; *non l'ho trovato ~ a casa ~ in ufficio* I couldn't find him either at home or in the office

neanche neither; *io non vado – neanch'io* I'm not going – neither am I *or* me neither F; *non l'ho visto* I didn't even see him; ~ *per sogno!* in your dreams!

nebbia *f* fog

nebbioso foggy

nebulosa *f* AST nebula

nebuloso *fig* vague, hazy

necessaire *m inv*: ~ (*da viaggio*) beauty case

necessario (*pl* -ri) 1 *agg* necessary 2 *m*: *il ~ per vivere* the basic necessities *pl*

necessità *f inv* need; *ho ~ di parlarti* I need to talk to you; *articolo m di prima ~* essential; *in caso di ~* if necessary, if need be; *fare qc senza* ~ do sth needlessly; *per* ~ out of necessity

nefrite *f* MED nephritis

negare <1e> deny; (*rifiutare*) refuse

negativa *f* negative

negativo *m/agg* negative

negato: *essere ~ per qc* be hopeless at sth

negazione *f* denial; GRAM negative

negli *prp* **in** and *art* **gli**

negligente careless, negligent

negligenza *f* carelessness, negligence

negoziante *m/f* shopkeeper

negoziare <1g & c> 1 *v/t* negotiate 2 *v/i* negotiate, bargain; FIN ~ *in* trade in, deal in

negoziato *m* negotiation; *-i pl di pace* peace negotiations

negoziazione *f* negotiation

negozio *m* (*pl* -zi) shop; (*affare*) deal; ~ *di generi alimentari* food shop; ~ *specializzato* specialist shop

negro 1 *agg* black 2 *m*, *-a f* black (man/woman)

nei, nel, nell', nella, nelle, nello *prp* **in** and *art* **i, il, l', la, le, lo**

nemico (*pl* -ci) 1 *agg* enemy *attr* 2 *m*, *-a f* enemy

nemmeno neither; ~ *io* me neither; ~ *per idea!* don't even think about it!

neo *m* mole; *fig* flaw

neonato *m*, *-a f* infant, newborn baby

neppure not even; *non ci vado – – io* I'm not going – neither am I *or* me neither F

N

nero 1 *agg* black; *fig giornata, periodo* black; *umore* awful, filthy F **2** *m* black; *di seppia* ink **3** *m*, **-a** *f* black (man / woman)

nerofumo *m* lampblack

nervo *m* nerve; **dare sui** (*o ai*) **-i a qu** get on s.o.'s nerves

nervosismo *m* nervousness

nervoso 1 *agg* nervous; (*irritabile*) edgy; (*asciutto*) sinewy; **esaurimento** *m* ~ nervous breakdown **2** *m* F: **il ~** irritation; **mi viene il ~** I'm beginning to get really irritated, this is getting on my nerves

nespola *f* medlar

nespolo *m* medlar (tree)

nessuno 1 *agg* no; **non chiamare in nessun caso** don't call in any circumstances; **c'è -a notizia?** is there any news? **2** *pron* nobody, no one; **hai visto ~?** did you see anyone *or* anybody?

nettezza *f* cleanliness; **~ urbana** cleansing department

netto clean; (*chiaro*) clear; *reddito, peso* net; **interrompere qu di ~** break in on s.o.

netturbino *m*, **-a** *f* dustman

neurologia *f* neurology

neurologico neurological

neurologo *m* (*pl* -gi), **-a** *f* neurologist

neutrale neutral

neutralità *f* neutrality

neutralizzare <1a> neutralize

neutro neutral; GRAM neuter

neve *f* snow

nevicare <1l & d> snow

nevicata *f* snowfall

nevoso snowy

nevralgia *f* neuralgia

nevralgico (*pl* -ci) neuralgic; **punto** *m* ~ specially painful point; *fig* weak point

nevrosi *f* neurosis

nevrotico (*pl* -ci) **1** *agg* neurotic; F short-tempered, quick to fly off the handle F **2** *m*, **-a** *f* neurotic

nicchia *f* niche

nichel *m* nickel

nicotina *f* nicotine

nido *m* nest

niente 1 *pron m* nothing **2** *avv* nothing; **non ho ~** I don't have anything, I have nothing; **lo fai tu? – ~ affatto!** are you going to do it? – no, I am not!; **tu hai detto che … – ~ affatto!** you said that … – no, I did not!; **non ho per ~ fame** I'm not at all hungry; **non ho capito per ~** I didn't understand a thing

niente(di)meno no less; **~!** that's incredible! you don't say!

ninfea *f* water-lily

nipote *m/f di zio* nephew; *donna, ragazza* niece *f*; *di nonno* grandson; *donna, ragazza* granddaughter *f*

nitidezza *f* clarity, clearness; FOT sharpness

nitido clear; FOT sharp

nitrire <4d> neigh

NO *abbr* (= *nord-ovest*) NW (= northwest)

no no; **~ e poi ~** absolutely not!, no and that's final!; **come ~!** of course!, naturally!; **se ~** otherwise; **dire di ~** say no; **credo di ~** I don't think so

nobile 1 *agg* noble **2** *m/f* aristocrat

nobiltà *f* nobility

nocca *f* (*pl* -cche) knuckle

nocciola *f* hazelnut; **color** *m* ~ hazel

nocciolina *f*: **~ (americana)** peanut, ground-nut, monkey-nut

nocciolo¹ *m* (*albero*) hazel (tree)

nocciolo² *m di frutto* stone; *di questione* heart, kernel

noce 1 *m* walnut (tree); (*legno*) walnut **2** *f* walnut; **~ di cocco** coconut; **~ moscata** nutmeg

nocepesca *f* nectarine

nocivo harmful

nodo *m* knot; *fig* crux; FERR junction; **avere un ~ in gola** have a lump in one's throat

noi *pron soggetto* we; *con prp* us; **a ~** to us; *con* **~** with us; **senza di ~** without us

noia *f* boredom; **-e** *pl* trouble *sg*; **dar ~ a qu** annoy s.o.; **venire a ~ a qu** start to bore s.o.

noioso boring; (*molesto*) annoying

noleggiare <1f> hire; MAR, AVIA charter

noleggio *m* hire; MAR, AVIA charter; ~ (*di*) *bicicletta* bike hire

nolo *m* hire; *prendere a ~* hire; *dare a ~* hire out

nome *m* name; GRAM noun; ~ *di battesimo* Christian name; ~ *e cognome* full name; *conoscere qu di ~* know s.o. by name; *in ~ di* in the name of

nomignolo *m* nickname

nomina *f* appointment

nominare <1l & c> (*menzionare*) mention; *a un incarico* appoint (*a* to)

non not; ~ *ho fratelli* I don't have any brothers, I have no brothers; ~ *ancora* not yet; ~ *che io non voglia* not that I don't want to; ~ *cedibile* not transferable, non-transferable

nonché let alone; (*e anche*) as well as

noncurante nonchalant, casual; ~ *di* mindless of, heedless of

noncuranza *f* nonchalance, casualness

nondimeno nevertheless

nonno *m*, -**a** *f* grandfather; *donna* grandmother; -*i pl* grandparents

nonnulla *m inv* trifle

nono *m/agg* ninth

nonostante despite; *ciò ~* however

nonsenso *m* nonsense

non stop *agg inv* nonstop

nontiscordardimé *m inv* forget-me-not

non vedente *m/f* blind person

nord *m* north; *mare m del ~* North Sea; *a(l) ~ di* (to the) north of

nordest *m* north-east

nordico (*pl* -ci) northern; *lingue* Nordic

nordovest *m* north-west

norma *f* (*precetto*) rule, precept; TEC standard; -*e per l'uso* instructions (for use); *a ~ di legge* up to standard; *a ~ di legge ...* complies with ...

normale normal

normalità *f* normality

normalizzare <1a> normalize;

(*uniformare*) standardize

norvegese *agg*, *m/f* Norwegian

Norvegia *f* Norway

nostalgia *f* nostalgia; *avere ~ di casa* feel homesick; *avere ~ di qu* miss s.o.

nostrale local, home *attr*

nostrano local, home *attr*

nostro 1 *agg* our; *i -i genitori pl* our parents; *un ~ amico* a friend of ours 2 *pron*: *il ~* ours

nota *f* note; FIN bill; *degno di ~* noteworthy; ~ *spese* expense account; *prendere ~ di qc* make a note of sth; *situazione, comportamento* take note of sth

notaio *m* (*pl* -ai) notary (public)

notare <1c> (*osservare*) notice; (*annotare*) make a note of, note down; *con segni* mark; *è da ~ che* please note that; *ti faccio ~ che* I'll have you know that

notariato *m* notaryship

notarile notarial

notevole *degno di nota* notable, noteworthy; *grande* considerable, substantial

notificare <1m & d> serve (*a* on)

notizia *f* piece *or* bit *or* item of news; *avere -e di qu* have news of s.o., hear from s.o.; -*e pl sportive* sports news; *le ultime -e pl* the latest news

notiziario *m* (*pl* -ri) RAD, TV news

noto well-known; *rendere ~* announce

notorietà *f* fame; *spreg* notoriety

notorio (*pl* -ri) well-known; *spreg* notorious

nottambulo *m*, -**a** *f* night owl

nottata *f* night; *fare la ~* stay up all night

notte *f* night; *di ~* at night; *buona ~!* good night!; *nel cuore della ~* in the middle of the night

notturno night(-time) *attr*; *animale* nocturnal; *ore fpl -e* hours of darkness

novanta ninety

novantesimo *m/agg* ninetieth

nove nine

novecento 1 *agg* nine hundred 2 *m*:

il Novecento the twentieth century

novella *f* short story

novembre *m* November

novità *f inv* novelty; *(notizia)* piece *or* item of news; *essere una ~ sul mercato* be new on the market

novizio (*pl* -zi) **1** *agg* novice **2** *m*, *-a f* beginner, novice; REL novice

nozione *f* notion, idea; *-i pl di base* rudiments

nozionistico (*pl* -ci) superficial

nozze *fpl* wedding *sg*; *~ d'argento* silver wedding (anniversary); *sposarsi in seconde ~* get married for the second time, remarry

ns. *abbr* (= *nostro*) our(s), *used in correspondence*

NU *abbr* (= *Nazioni Unite*) UN (= United Nations); (= *nettezza urbana*) cleansing department

nube *f* cloud

nubifragio *m* (*pl* -gi) cloudburst

nubile *donna* single, unmarried

nuca *f* (*pl* -che) nape of the neck

nucleare nuclear

nucleo *m* FIS nucleus (*anche fig*); *~ urbano* urban centre

nudismo *m* naturism, nudism

nudista *m/f* (*mpl* -i) naturist, nudist

nudità *f* nudity, nakedness

nudo 1 *agg* nude, naked; *(spoglio)* bare; *a occhio ~* to the naked eye **2** *m* PITT nude

nulla 1 *avv* nothing; *è solo una cosa da ~* it's nothing; *per ~* for nothing; *non per ~* not for nothing **2** *m* nothing; *non ti ho portato un bel ~* I haven't brought you anything at all

nullaosta *m: fig ottenere il ~* get the green light *or* go-ahead

nullo invalid; *gol* disallowed; *voto* spoiled; *dichiarare ~* declare null and void

numerale *m* numeral

numerare <1l> number

numerato numbered

numerico (*pl* -ci) numerical

numero *m* number; *arabo, romano* numeral; *di scarpa* size; *~ di casa* home (tele)phone number; *~ di targa* registration number, *Am* license number; *~ di telefono* phone number; *~ di volo* flight number; TELEC *sbagliare ~* dial the wrong number; *~ verde* 0800 number, *Am* toll-free number; *~ legale* quorum; EDU *~ chiuso* restricted enrol(l)ment; *sono venuti in gran ~* lots of them came; F *dare i -i* talk nonsense

numeroso numerous; *famiglia*, *classe* large

nuocere <3ii>: *~ a* harm; *il fumo nuoce alla salute* smoking is bad for you

nuora *f* daughter-in-law

nuotare <1c> swim

nuotata *f* swim

nuotatore *m*, *-trice f* swimmer

nuoto *m* swimming; *attraversare la Manica a ~* swim across the Channel

nuovamente again

nuovo 1 *agg* new; *di ~* again; *essere ~ in una città* be new to a town; *~ fiammante* brand new **2** *m: che c'è di ~?* what's new?

nutriente nourishing

nutrimento *m* food

nutrire <4d or 4a> feed

nutrirsi: *~ di* live on

nutritivo nutritious

nutrizione *f* nutrition

nuvola *f* cloud; *fig cadere dalle -e* be taken aback

nuvoloso cloudy

nylon *m* nylon

N

O

O *abbr* (= **ovest**) W (= west)

o *cong* or; **~ ... ~** either ... or

oasi *f inv* oasis

obbedire → **ubbidire**

obbligare <1l, c & e>: **~ qu a fare qc** oblige *or* compel s.o. to do sth

obbligarsi commit o.s. (*a fare* to doing), undertake (*a fare* to do)

obbligatorio (*pl* -ri) obligatory, compulsory

obbligazione *f* obligation; FIN bond

obbligo *m* (*pl* -ghi) obligation; **d'~** obligatory

obesità *f* obesity

obeso obese

obiettare <1b> object, say (*a* to)

obiettivo **1** *agg* objective **2** *m* aim, objective; FOT lens

obiettore *m*: **~ di coscienza** conscientious objector

obiezione *f* objection; **fare ~ di coscienza** be a conscientious objector

obliquo oblique

obliterare <1m> *biglietto* punch

oblò *m inv* MAR porthole

oca *f* (*pl* -che) *f* goose; *fig* silly woman

occasionale casual; **i rapporti** *mpl* **-i** casual sex

occasionalmente occasionally

occasione *f* (*opportunità*) opportunity, chance; (*evento*) occasion; (*affare*) bargain; **automobile** *f* **d'~** second-hand *or* used car; **cogliere l'~** seize the opportunity, jump at the chance F; **all'~** if necessary; **in ~ di** on the occasion of

occhiaie *fpl* bags under the eyes

occhiali *mpl* glasses, specs *Br* F; **~ da sole** sunglasses

occhiata *f* look, glance; **dare un'~ a** have a look at, glance at; (*sorvegliare*) keep an eye on

occhiello *m* buttonhole

occhio *m* (*pl* -chi) eye; **a ~ nudo** to the naked eye; **a ~ e croce** roughly; **dare nell'~** attract attention, be noticed; **a quattr' -i** in private

occidentale western; **Europa** *f* **~** Western Europe

occidente *m* west; **a ~ di** (to the) west of

occorrente **1** *agg* necessary **2** *m* necessary materials *pl*

occorrenza *f*: **all'~** if necessary, if need be

occorrere <3o> be necessary; (*accadere*) occur; **mi occorre** I need; **Le occorre altro?** (do you need) anything else?; **occorre programmare le cose** we / you need to plan things; **non occorre!** there's no need!

occupare <1l & c> *spazio* take up, occupy; *tempo* occupy, fill; *posto* have, hold; *persona* keep busy; *di esercizio* occupy

occuparsi take care (*di* of), deal (*di* with); **occupati degli affari tuoi!** mind your own business!; **~ di qu** look after s.o., take care of s.o.

occupato TELEC engaged, *Am* busy; *posto, appartamento* taken; *gabinetto* engaged; *persona* busy; *città, nazione* occupied

occupazione *f* *di città, paese* occupation; (*attività*) pastime; (*impiego*) job

oceano *m* ocean; **Oceano Atlantico** Atlantic Ocean; **Oceano Pacifico** Pacific Ocean

OCSE *abbr* (= **Organizzazione per la Cooperazione e lo Sviluppo Economico**) OECD (= Organization for Economic Co-operation and Development)

oculista *m/f* (*pl* -i) ophthalmologist

od = o (*before a vowel*)

O

odiare <1k> hate, detest

odierno modern-day *attr* of today, today's

odio *m* hatred

odioso hateful, odious

odontotecnico *m*, **-a** *f* dental technician

odorare <1a> **1** *v/t* smell **2** *v/i* smell (**di** of)

odorato *m* sense of smell

odore *m* smell, odo(u)r; **-i** *pl* GASTR herbs

odoroso fragrant, sweet-smelling

offendere <3c> offend

offendersi take offence, *Am* offense

offensiva *f* offensive

offensivo offensive

offerente *m* bidder; **maggior ~** highest bidder

offerta *f* offer; FIN supply; REL offering; (*dono*) donation; *in asta* bid; **~ d'impiego** job offer; **~ pubblica di acquisto** takeover bid; **~ speciale** special offer

offesa *f* offence, *Am* offense

offeso *pp* → **offendere**

officina *f* workshop; *per macchine* garage

offrire <4f & c> offer; **ti offro da bere** I'll buy *or* stand F you a drink; **posso offrirti qualcosa?** can I get you anything?

oggettivo objective

oggetto *m* object; **-i** *pl* **di valore** valuables

oggi today; **d'~** of today, today's; **da ~ a domani** overnight; **da ~ in poi** from now on; **~ stesso** today, this very day; **~ come ~** at the moment; **~ pomeriggio** this afternoon

oggigiorno nowadays

ogni every; **~ tanto** every so often; **~ sei giorni** every six days

Ognissanti *m inv* All Saints Day

ognuno everyone, everybody

Olanda *f* Holland

olandese **1** *agg m* Dutch **2** *m/f* Dutchman; *donna* Dutchwoman

oleandro *m* oleander

oleoso oily

olfatto *m* sense of smell

oliare <1k> oil

oliera *f* type of cruet for oil and vinegar bottles

Olimpiadi *fpl* Olympic Games, Olympics; **~ invernali** Winter Olympics

olimpionico (*pl* -ci) **1** *agg* Olympic *attr* **2** *m*, **-a** *f* Olympic contestant

olio *m* (*pl* -li) oil; **~ dei freni** brake fluid; **~ lubrificante** lubricating oil, lube; **~ per il cambio** gearbox oil; **~ extra-vergine d'oliva** extra-virgin olive oil; **~ solare** suntan oil

oliva *f* olive

olivo *m* olive (tree)

olmo *m* elm (tree)

OLP *abbr* (= **Organizzazione per la Liberazione della Palestina**) PLO (= Palestine Liberation Organization)

oltraggiare <1f> offend, outrage

oltraggio *m* (*pl* -ggi) offence, *Am* offense, outrage

oltre **1** *prp in spazio, tempo* after, past; (*più di*) over; **vai ~ il semaforo** go past the traffic lights; **aspetto da ~ un'ora** I've been waiting for more than *or* over an hour; **~ a** apart from **2** *avv nello spazio* further; *nel tempo* longer

oltremare overseas

omaggio *m* (*pl* -ggi) homage; (*dono*) gift; **copia (in) ~** free *or* complimentary copy; **~ pubblicitario** (free) gift; **essere in ~ con** come free with

ombelico *m* (*pl* -chi) navel

ombra *f* shadow; *zona non illuminata* shade; *fig* **un'~ di tristezza** a touch of sadness; **all'~** in the shade

ombrello *m* umbrella

ombrellone *m* parasol; *sulla spiaggia* beach umbrella

ombretto *m* eye shadow

ombroso shady; *fig persona* touchy

omelette *f inv* omelette, *Am* omelet

omeopatia *f* homeopathy

omeopatico (*pl* -ci) **1** *agg* homeopathic **2** *m*, **-a** *f* homeopath

omero *m* humerus

omesso *pp* → **omettere**

omettere <3ee> omit, leave out

omicida (*mpl* -di) **1** *agg* murderous **2** *m/f* murderer

omicidio *m* (*pl* -di) murder; ~ *colposo* manslaughter; **tentato ~** attempted murder

omogeneizzato homogenized

omogeneo homogenous

omologare <1m, c & e> approve

omonimo **1** *agg* of the same name **2** *m* homonym **3** *m*, **-a** *f* namesake

omosessuale *agg, m/f* homosexual

omosessualità *f* homosexuality

OMS *abbr* (= *Organizzazione Mondiale della Sanità*) WHO (= World Health Organization)

on. *abbr* (= *onorevole*) Hon (= honourable)

oncologia *f* oncology

oncologo *m*, **-a** *f* oncologist

onda *f* wave; **-e** *pl* **corte** short wave; **-e** *pl* **lunghe** long wave; **-e** *pl* **medie** medium wave; RAD **andare in ~** go on the air

ondata *f* wave; ~ *di caldo* heat wave; ~ *di freddo* cold spell

ondeggiare <1f> *di barca* rock; *di bandiera* flutter

ondulato *capelli* wavy; *superficie* uneven; *cartone, lamiera* corrugated

onestà *f* honesty

onesto honest; *prezzo, critica* fair

onice *m* onyx

onnipotente omnipotent

onnipotenza *f* omnipotence

onnipresente ubiquitous

onnisciente omniscient

onniscienza *f* omniscience

onnivoro **1** *agg* omnivorous **2** *m*, **-a** *f* omnivore

onomastico *m* (*pl* -ci) name day

onorare <1a> be a credit to; ~ *qu di qc* hono(u)r s.o. with sth

onorario (*pl* -ri) **1** *agg* honorary **2** *m* fee

onorato respected, hono(u)red

onore *m* hono(u)r; *in* ~ *di* in hono(u)r of

onorevole **1** *agg* hono(u)rable **2** Onorevole *m/f* Member of Parliament

onorificenza *f* hono(u)r

ONU *abbr* (= *Organizzazione delle Nazioni Unite*) UN (= United Nations)

OPA *abbr* (= *Offerta Pubblica di Acquisto* (*di azioni di società*)) takeover bid

opacità *f di vetro* opaqueness; *di colore, foto* darkness

opaco (*pl* -chi) *vetro* opaque; *calze, rossetto* dark

opera *f* work; MUS opera; ~ *d'arte* work of art; ~ *buona* good deed; *mettersi all'~* set to work

operaio (*pl* -ai) **1** *agg* working **2** *m*, **-a** *f* worker; ~ *specializzato* skilled worker

operare <1l & c> **1** *v/t cambiamento* make; *miracoli* work; MED operate on **2** *v/i* act

operativo operational; *ricerca* applied; *ordine* operative; **piano** *m* ~ plan of operations

operatore *m*, **-trice** *f* operator; *televisivo, cinematografico* cameraman; ~ *di Borsa* market trader; ~ *sociale* social worker; ~ *turistico* tour operator

operazione *f* operation; ~ *finanziaria* transaction

operetta *f* operetta

operoso hard-working, industrious

opinione *f* opinion; *secondo la tua* ~ in your opinion

oppio *m* opium

opporre <3ll> put forward, offer; *scuse, resistenza* offer

opporsi be opposed

opportunista *m/f* opportunist

opportunità *f inv* opportunity; *di decisione* timeliness; *pari* ~ *pl* equal opportunities

opportuno suitable, appropriate; *al momento* ~ at a suitable time, at the opportune moment

opposizione *f* opposition; POL *all'*~ in opposition

opposto **1** *pp* → **opporre 2** *agg* opposite **3** *m* POL opposition

oppressione *f* oppression

oppressore *m* oppressor

opprimente oppressive

O

opprimere <3r> oppress
oppure or (else)
optare <1c>: ~ **per** choose, opt for
opuscolo *m* brochure
opzione *f* option
ora [1] *f* time; *unità di misura* hour; *che ~ è?, che -e sono?* what time is it?, what's the time?; ~ **legale** daylight saving time; ~ **locale** local time; **-e** *pl* **straordinarie** overtime *sg*; ~ **di punta** rush hour; TELEC peak time; **di buon'~** early
ora [2] *avv* now; *sono rientrato or* ~ I've only just got back; **per** ~ for the moment, for the time being; ~ **come** ~ at the moment; **d'~ in poi** from now on **2** *cong* now
orafo *m*, **-a** *f* goldsmith
orale 1 *agg* oral **2** *m* oral (exam)
orario (*pl* -ri) **1** *agg* *tariffa*, hourly; *velocità* per hour; RAD **segnale ~** time signal; **in senso ~** clockwise **2** *m di treno, bus, aeroplano* timetable, *Am* schedule; *di negozio* hours of business; *al lavoro* hours of work; ~ **di apertura/chiusura** opening/closing time; ~ **di sportello** banking hours; ~ **flessibile** flexitime; **in ~** on time
orata *f* gilthead bream
oratore *m*, **-trice** *f* speaker
oratorio 1 *agg* (*pl* -ri) as an orator **2** *m* oratory
orbita *f*; AST orbit; ANAT eye-socket; **in ~** in orbit
orchestra *f* orchestra; (*luogo*) (orchestra) pit
orchestrale 1 *agg* orchestral **2** *m/f* member of an orchestra
orchestrare <1b> orchestrate (*anche fig*)
orchestrazione *f* orchestration
orchidea *f* orchid
ordigno *m* device; ~ **esplosivo** explosive device
ordinale *m/agg* ordinal
ordinamento *m* rules and regulations; ~ **sociale** rules governing society
ordinare <1l> order; *stanza* tidy up; MED prescribe; REL ordain

ordinario (*pl* -ri) ordinary; *mediocre* pretty average
ordinato tidy
ordinazione *f* order; REL ordination
ordine *m* order; **mettere in ~** tidy up; ~ **alfabetico** alphabetical order; ~ **di pagamento** payment order; **di prim'~** first-rate, first-class; ~ **del giorno** agenda; **l'~ dei medici** the medical association; ~ **permanente** FIN standing order
orecchino *m* earring
orecchio *m* (*pl* -cchi) ear; MUS **a ~** by ear
orecchioni *mpl* mumps *sg*
orefice *m/f* goldsmith
oreficeria *f* goldsmithing; (*gioielleria*) jewel(l)er's
orfano 1 *agg* orphan **2** *m*, **-a** *f* orphan
orfanotrofio *m* orphanage
organico (*pl* -ci) organic
organismo *m* organism; *fig* body
organista *m/f* (*mpl* -i) organist
organizzare <1a> organize
organizzazione *f* organization
organo *m* organ
orgasmo *m* orgasm
orgoglio *m* pride
orgoglioso proud
orientabile adjustable, swivelling
orientale 1 *agg* eastern; (*dell'Oriente*) Oriental; *Europa f ~* Eastern Europe **2** *m/f* Oriental
orientamento *m*: **senso** *m* **d'~** sense of direction; ~ **professionale** professional advice
orientare <1b> *antenna, schermo* turn; ~ **qu verso una carriera** guide *or* steer s.o. towards a career
orientarsi get one's bearings
oriente *m* east; **l'Oriente** the Orient; **Medio Oriente** Middle East; **Estremo Oriente** Far East; **ad ~ di** (to the) east of
origano *m* oregano
originale *m/agg* original
originalità *f* originality
originalmente originally
originario (*pl* -ri) original; **essere ~ di** come from, be a native of;

popolo originate in

origine *f* origin; *in* ~ originally

origliare <1g> eavesdrop

orizzontale horizontal

orizzonte *m* horizon

orlare <1a> hem

orlo *m* edge; *di vestito* hem

orma *f* footprint; *fig* **seguire le -e di qu** follow in s.o.'s footsteps

ormai by now

ormonale hormonal

ormone *m* hormone

ornamentale ornamental

ornamento *m* ornament

ornare <1a> decorate

ornitologia *f* ornithology

ornitologico ornithological

ornitologo *m*, **-a** *f* ornithologist

oro *m* gold; **d'~** (made of) gold

orologeria *f* clock- and watch-making; *negozio* watchmaker's

orologiaio *m* (*pl* -ai) (clock- and) watch-maker

orologio *m* (*pl* -gi) clock; *portatile* watch; ~ **a cucù** cuckoo clock; ~ **da polso** wristwatch; ~ **da tasca** pocket watch; ~ **subacqueo** waterproof watch

oroscopo *m* horoscope

orrendo horrendous

orribile horrible

orrore *m* horror (**di** of); *avere qc in* ~ hate sth

Orsa *f*: ~ **maggiore** / **minore** Ursa Major / Minor, the Great / Little Bear

orsacchiotto *m* bear cub; (*giocattolo*) teddy (bear)

orso *m* bear; *fig* hermit; ~ **bianco** polar bear

ortaggio *m* (*pl* -ggi) vegetable

ortica *f* (*pl* -che) nettle

orticaria *f* nettle rash

orticoltura *f* horticulture

orto *m* vegetable garden, kitchen garden; ~ **botanico** botanical gardens

ortodossia *f* orthodoxy

ortodosso orthodox

ortografia *f* spelling

ortolano *m*, **-a** *f* market gardener

ortopedia *f* orthop(a)edics

ortopedico (*pl* -ci) **1** *agg* orthop(a)edic **2** *m*, **-a** *f* orthop(a)edist

orzaiolo *m* stye

orzata *f* drink made from crushed almonds, sugar and water

orzo *m* barley; ~ **perlato** pearl barley

osare <1c> dare

oscenità *f inv* obscenity

osceno obscene

oscillare <1a> *di corda* sway, swing; *di barca* oscillate; FIS oscillate; *fig di persona* waver, hesitate; *di prezzi* fluctuate

oscillazione *f di barca* rocking; ~ **dei prezzi** price fluctuations *pl*

oscurare <1a> obscure; *luce* block out

oscurità *f* darkness; *fig* obscurity; **nell'~** in the dark

oscuro **1** *agg* dark; (*sconosciuto*) obscure **2** *m* dark; *essere all'~ di qc* be in the dark about sth

ospedale *m* hospital

ospitale hospitable

ospitalità *f* hospitality

ospitare <ll & c> put up; SP be at home to

ospite *m/f* guest; *chi ospita* host; *donna* hostess

ospizio *m* (*pl* -zi) old folk's home

ossatura *f* bone structure; *fig*, ARCHI structure

osseo bone *attr*

osservare <1b> (*guardare*) look at, observe; (*notare*) see, notice, observe; (*far notare*) point out, remark; (*seguire*) abide by, obey; ~ **una dieta** keep to a diet, follow a diet; *le faccio* ~ *che* I'll have you know that

osservatore *m*, **-trice** *f* observer, watcher

osservatorio *m* (*pl* -ri) AST observatory; ~ **meteorologico** *f* weather station

osservazione *f* observation; (*affermazione*) remark, observation

ossessione *f* obsession (**di** with); *avere l'~ di* be obsessed with

ossessivo obsessive

O

ossia or rather
ossidabile liable to tarnish
ossidare <1l & c> tarnish
ossidazione f tarnish
ossigeno m oxygen; **tenda** f ~ oxygen tent
osso m (ANAT pl le ossa) bone; **di** ~ bone attr, made of bone; ~ **sacro** sacrum; **in carne e -a** in the flesh
ossobuco m (pl ossibuchi) marrowbone; GASTR ossobuco, stew made with knuckle of veal
ostacolare <1m> hinder
ostacolo m obstacle; nell'atletica hurdle; nell'equitazione fence, jump; fig stumbling block, obstacle
ostaggio m (pl -ggi) hostage; **prendere qu in** ~ take s.o. hostage
ostello m: ~ **della gioventù** youth hostel
osteoporosi f osteoporosis
osteria f inn
ostetrica f obstetrician; (levatrice) midwife
ostetricia f obstetrics
ostetrico (pl -ci) **1** agg obstetric(al) **2** m obstetrician
ostia f Host
ostile hostile
ostilità f inv hostility
ostinarsi <1a> dig one's heels in; ~ **a fare qc** persist in doing sth
ostinato obstinate
ostinazione f obstinacy
ostrica f (pl -che) oyster
ostruire <4d> block, obstruct
ostruito blocked
ostruzione f (ostacolo) obstruction, blockage
otite f ear infection
otorinolaringoiatra m/f (pl -i) ear, nose and throat specialist, ENT specialist
ottagonale octagonal
ottagono octagon
ottano m octane; **numero m di -i** octane rating or number

ottanta eighty
ottantesimo m/agg eightieth
ottava f MUS octave
ottavo m/agg eighth
ottenere <2q> get, obtain
ottengo → **ottenere**
ottenibile obtainable
ottica f optics; fig viewpoint, point of view
ottico (pl -ci) **1** agg optical **2** m optician
ottimale optimum
ottimismo m optimism
ottimista m/f (mpl -i) optimist
ottimistico (pl -ci) optimistic
ottimizzare <1a> optimize
ottimo excellent, extremely good
otto **1** agg eight; **oggi a** ~ a week today **2** m eight; ~ **volante** big dipper
ottobre m October
ottocento **1** agg eight hundred **2** m: **il Ottocento** the nineteenth century
ottone m brass; MUS **-i** pl brass (instruments)
otturare <1a> block; dente fill
otturatore m FOT shutter
otturazione f blocking; di dente filling
ottuso obtuse
ovaia f ANAT ovary
ovale m/agg oval
ovazione f ovation
overdose f inv overdose
ovest m west
ovile m sheep pen; fig fold
ovini mpl sheep
ovunque everywhere
ovvero or rather; (cioè) that is
ovvio (pl -vvi) obvious
oziare <1g> laze around, be idle
ozio m (pl -zi) laziness, idleness
ozioso lazy, idle
ozono m ozone; **buco m nell'**~ hole in the ozone layer; **strato m d'** ~ ozone layer

P

p. *abbr* (= *pagina*) p (= page)

pacato calm, unhurried

pacchetto *m* package, small parcel; *di sigarette, biscotti* packet; **~ azionario** block of shares; **~ turistico** package holiday

pacchiano vulgar, in bad taste

pacco *m* (*pl* -cchi) parcel, package; **~ bomba** parcel bomb; **~ postale** parcel

pace *f* peace; *lasciare in* **~ qu** leave s.o. alone *or* in peace

pacifico (*pl* -ci) **1** *agg* peaceful **2** *m*: *il Pacifico* the Pacific

pacifismo *m* pacifism

pacifista *m/f* (*mpl* -i) pacifist

padano *agg* of the Po; *pianura f* **-a** Po Valley

padella *f di cucina* frying pan

padiglione *m* pavilion; **~ auricolare** auricle

Padova *f* Padua

padovano 1 *agg* Paduan **2** *m*, **-a** native of Padua

padre *m* father

padrino *m* godfather

padronanza *f* (*controllo*) control; (*conoscenza*) mastery; **~ di sé** self-control

padrone *m*, **-a** *f* boss; (*proprietario*) owner; *di cane* master; *donna* mistress; **~ di casa** man / lady of the house; *per inquilino* landlord; *donna* landlady

paesaggio *m* (*pl* -ggi) scenery; PITT, GEOG landscape

paesaggista *m/f* PITT landscape painter *or* artist

paesano 1 *agg* country *attr* **2** *m*, **-a** *f* person from the country; *spreg* country bumpkin

paese *m* country; (*villaggio*) village; (*territorio*) region, area; *i Paesi Bassi pl* the Netherlands; **~ d'origi-ne** country of origin; **-i** *pl in via di sviluppo* developing countries; **~ membro** member state

paga *f* (*pl* -ghe) pay

pagabile payable; **~ a vista** payable at sight

pagamento *m* payment; **~ anticipa-to** payment in advance; **~ alla consegna** cash on delivery; **~ in contanti** payment in cash, cash payment; **~ a rate** payment in insta(l)lments; *altre sono a* **~** others you have to pay for

pagare <1e> **1** *v/t acquisto* pay for; *conto, fattura, debito* pay; *ti pago qualcosa da bere* I'll buy you *or* stand you a drink; *gliela faccio* **~** he'll pay for this **2** *v/i* pay; **~** *anticipatamente* pay in advance; **~** *in contanti* pay (in) cash; **~** *a rate* pay in instal(l)ments

pagella *f* report, *Am* report card

paghetta *f* pocket money

pagina *f* page; *a* **~ 10** on page 10; **-e gialle** Yellow Pages; **~ elettronica** screen page; **~ Web** Web site

paglia *f* straw

paio *m* (*pl* le paia): *un* **~ di scarpe,** *guanti ecc* a pair of; *un* **~ di volte** a couple of times

pala *f* shovel; *di elica, turbina, remo* blade; **~ d'altare** altarpiece

palasport *m inv* indoor sports arena

palato *m* palate

palazzina *f* luxury home

palazzo *m* palace; (*edificio*) building; *con appartamenti* block of flats, *Am* apartment block; **~ comunale** town hall; **~ di giustizia** courthouse; **~ dello sport** indoor sports arena

palco *m* (*pl* -chi) dais; TEA stage

palcoscenico *m* (*pl* -ci) stage

palese obvious

Palestina *f* Palestine

palestinese *agg, m/f* Palestinian

palestra *f* gym

paletta *f* shovel; *per la spiaggia* spade; FERR signal(l)ing paddle

paletto *m* tent peg

palla *f* ball; **~ di neve** snowball; *fig* **cogliere la ~ al balzo** jump at the chance

pallacanestro *f* basketball

pallanuoto *f* water polo

pallavolo *f* volley ball

palliativo *m* palliative

pallido pale

pallina *f* **di vetro** marble; **~ da golf** golf ball; **~ da tennis** tennis ball

pallino *m* nel biliardo cue ball; *nelle bocce* jack; *munizione* pellet; *fig* **avere il ~ della pesca** be mad about fishing, be fishing mad; **a -i** *pl* with spots, spotted

palloncino *m* balloon

pallone *m* ball; *calcio* football, soccer; AVIA balloon; **~ sonda** weather balloon

pallore *m* paleness, pallor

pallottola *f* pellet; *di pistola* bullet

palma *f* palm

palmo *m* hand's breadth; ANAT palm; **a ~ a ~** gradually, bit by bit, inch by inch

palo *m* pole; *nel calcio* (goal)post

palombaro *m* diver

palpabile *fig* palpable

palpare <1a> feel; MED palpate

palpebra *f* eyelid

palpitare <1l> *del cuore* pound

palpitazione *f* palpitation

palpito *m* del cuore beat

paltò *m inv* overcoat, heavy coat

palude *f* marsh

paludoso marshy

palustre marshy; *pianta* marsh

panacea *f* panacea

panca *f* (*pl* -che) bench; *in chiesa* pew

pancarré *m* sliced loaf

pancetta *f* pancetta, *cured belly of pork*

panchetto *m* footstool

panchina *f* bench

pancia *f* (*pl* -ce) *m* stomach, belly F; *di animale* belly; **mal** *m* **di ~** stomach-ache, belly-ache F; **mettere su ~** develop a paunch

panciotto *m* waistcoat, *Am* vest

panciuto big-bellied

pancreas *m inv* pancreas

pane *m* bread; **~ bianco** white bread; **~ nero** (*o* **di segala**) black *or* rye bread; **~ integrale** wholewheat bread

panetteria *f* bakery

panettiere *m/f* baker

panettone *m* panettone, *cake made with candied fruit*

panfilo *m* yacht; **~ a motore** motor yacht

pangrattato *m* breadcrumbs *pl*

panico (*pl* -ci) *m* panic

paniere *m* basket

panificio *m* (*pl* -ci) bakery

panino *m* roll; **~ imbottito** filled roll

paninoteca *f* sandwich shop

panna *f* cream; **~ montata** whipped cream

panne *f*: **essere in ~** have broken down, have had a breakdown

pannello *m* panel; **~ solare** solar panel

panno *m* pezzo di stoffa cloth; **-i** *pl* clothes; **se fossi nei tuoi -i** if I were in your shoes

pannocchia *f* cob

pannolino *m* nappy; *per donne* sanitary towel

panorama *m* (*pl* -i) panorama; *fig* overview

panoramica *f* FOT panorama, panoramic view; *fig* overview

pantaloncini *mpl* shorts

pantaloni *mpl* trousers, *Am* pants

pantera *f* ZO panther

pantofola *f* slipper

pantomima *f* pantomime

paonazzo purple

papà *m inv* daddy, dad

papa *m* Pope

papale papal

paparazzo *m*: **i ~i** *pl* the paparazzi

papavero *m* poppy

papera *f* *fig* (*errore*) slip of the tongue

papero *m*, **-a** *f* gosling
papillon *m inv* bow tie
papiro *m* papyrus
pappa *f* food
pappagallo *m* parrot
paprica *f* paprika
par. *abbr* (= **paragrafo**) para (= paragraph)
parabrezza *m inv* windscreen, *Am* windshield
paracadutare <1a> parachute in
paracadute *m inv* parachute
paracadutista *m/f* (*mpl* -i) parachutist
paracarro *m* post
paradiso *m* heaven, paradise; **~ terrestre** heaven on earth, Eden
paradossale paradoxical
paradosso *m* paradox
parafango *m* (*pl* -ghi) mudguard, *Am* fender
parafulmine *m* lightning rod
paraggi *mpl* neighbo(u)rhood *sg*; **nei ~ di** (somewhere) near
paragonabile comparable
paragonare <1a> compare
paragone *m* comparison; **a ~ di** compared with, in *or* by comparison with; **senza ~** incomparable
paragrafo *m* paragraph
paralisi *f* paralysis
paralitico *m*, **-a** *f* (*mpl* -ci) paralyzed person
paralizzare <1a> paralyze
parallela *f* parallel line; **-e** *pl* parallel bars
parallelo *m/agg* parallel
paraluce *m inv* FOT lens hood
paralume *m* lampshade
parametro *m* parameter
paranoia *f* paranoia
paranoico (*pl* -ci) **1** *agg* paranoid **2** *m*, **-a** *f* person with paranoia
paranormale *m/agg* paranormal
paraocchi *mpl* blinkers (*anche fig*)
parapendio *m* SP paragliding
parapetto *m* parapet; MAR rail
paraplegico 1 *agg* paraplegic **2** *m*, **-a** *f* paraplegic
parare <1a> **1** *v/t ornare* decorate; *proteggere* shelter; *occhi* shield; *scan-*

sare parry **2** *v/i* save
parasole *m* parasol; FOT lens hood
parassita *m/f* (*mpl* -i) parasite
parata *f* parade
paraurti *m inv* bumper
parcheggiare <1f> *v/t & v/i* park
parcheggio *m* parking; *luogo* car park, *Am* parking lot; **~ sotterraneo** underground car park; **divieto di ~** no parking
parchimetro *m* parking meter
parco¹ (*pl* -chi) *agg*: **essere ~ nel mangiare** eat sparingly
parco² *m* (*pl* -chi) park; **~ dei divertimenti** amusement park; **~ naturale** nature reserve; **~ nazionale** national park; **~ macchine** fleet (of vehicles)
parecchio 1 *agg* a lot of **2** *pron* **parecchi** *mpl*, **parecchie** *fpl* quite a few **3** *avv* quite a lot
pareggiare <1f> **1** *v/t* even up; (*uguagliare*) match, equal; *conto* balance **2** *v/i* SP draw
pareggio *m* (*pl* -ggi) SP draw
parente *m/f* relative
parentela *f* relationship; *parenti* relatives, relations
parentesi *f* bracket; (*detto*) **fra ~** by the by; *fig* **aprire una ~** digress slightly
parere 1 *v/i* <2h> seem, appear; **pare che** it seems that, it would appear that; **che te ne pare?** what do you think (of it)?; **non ti pare?** don't you think?; **a quanto pare** by all accounts; **non mi pare vero!** I can't believe it! **2** *m* opinion; **a mio ~** in my opinion, to my way of thinking
parete *f* wall; **~ divisoria** partition wall
pari 1 *agg* equal; *numero* even; **essere di ~ altezza** be the same height; **al ~ di** like; **alla ~** the same; SP **finire alla ~** end in a draw; **senza ~** unrivalled, unequalled **2** *m* (social) equal, peer; **da ~ a ~** as an equal
Parigi Paris
parigino (of) Paris, Parisian
parità *f* equality, parity; **~ di diritti** equal rights; **a ~ di condizioni** all

things being equal

parka *m inv* parka

parlamentare 1 *agg* Parliamentary **2** *v/i* <1a> negotiate **3** *m/f* (*pl* -ri) Member of Parliament, MP

parlamento *m* Parliament; *Parlamento europeo* European Parliament

parlare <1a> talk, speak (*a qu* to s.o.; *di qc* about sth); ~ *del più e del meno* make small talk; *parla inglese?* do you speak English?

parmigiano *m* (*formaggio*) Parmesan

parodia *f* parody

parola *f* word; (*facoltà*) speech; ~ *d'ordine* password; *-e pl crociate* crossword (puzzle) *sg*; *essere di* ~ keep one's word; *chiedere la* ~ ask for the floor; ~ *per* ~ word for word

parolaccia *f* swear word

parquet *m* parquet floor

parrocchia *f* parish

parrochiale parish *attr*

parroco *m* (*pl* -ci) parish priest

parrucca *f* (*pl* -cche) wig

parrucchiere *m*, *-a f* hairdresser; ~ *per signora* ladies' hairdresser

parte *f* part; (*porzione*) portion; (*lato*) side; DIR party; ~ *civile* plaintiff; *far* ~ *di una società* belong to a society, be a member of a society; *prendere* ~ take part in; *a* ~ separate; *scherzi a* ~ joking apart; *mettere da* ~ *qc* put sth aside; *dall'altra* ~ *della strada* on the other side of the street; *da nessuna* ~ nowhere; *da tutte le -i* everywhere; *da* ~ *mia* for my part, as far as I'm concerned; *regalo ecc from* me; *in* ~ in part, partly; *in gran* ~ largely

partecipante *m/f* participant

partecipare <1m> **1** *v/t* announce **2** *v/i*: ~ *a gara* take part in; *dolore, gioia* share

partecipazione *f* (*intervento*) participation; (*annunzio*) announcement; FIN holding; ~ *agli utili* profit-sharing

parteggiare <1f>: ~ *per* support

partenza *f* departure; SP start; INFOR ~ *a freddo* cold start; *essere di* ~ be just about to leave, be on the point of leaving; *fig punto m di* ~ starting point, point of departure

participio *m* (*pl* -pi) participle

particolare 1 *agg* particular; *segretario* private; *in* ~ in particular **2** *m* particular, detail

particolareggiato detailed

particolarità *f inv* special nature

partigiano *m*, *-a f* partisan

partire <4a> leave; AUTO, SP start; ~ *per* leave for; ~ *per l'estero* go abroad

partita *f* SP match; *di carte* game; *di merce* shipment; ~ *IVA* VAT registration number; ~ *amichevole* friendly (match); ~ *di calcio* football match

partito *m* POL party; ~ *d'opposizione* opposition (party); *prendere* ~ make up one's mind; *essere ridotto a mal* ~ be in a bad way

partitura *f* score

partner *m/f inv* partner

parto *m* birth; ~ *cesareo* C(a)esarean (section)

partorire <4d> give birth to

part time 1 *agg* part-time **2** *avv* part time

parziale partial; *fig* biased

pascolo *m* pasture

Pasqua *f* Easter

pasquale Easter *attr*

Pasquetta *f* Easter Monday

passaggio *m* (*pl* -ggi) passage; *in macchina* lift, *Am* ride; *atto* passing; SP pass; *essere di* ~ be passing through; ~ *pedonale* pedestrian crossing, *Br* zebra crossing; ~ *a livello* level crossing, *Am* grade crossing; *dare un* ~ *a qu* give s.o. a lift (*Am* ride)

passante *m/f* passer-by

passaporto *m* passport; *controllo m dei -i* passport control

passare <1a> **1** *v/i* (*trasferirsi*) go (*in* into); SP pass; *di legge* be passed, pass; *di tempo* go by *or* past, pass; ~ *attraverso delle difficoltà* have a difficult time; ~ **da** / **per Milano** go through Milan; ~ **dal panettiere** drop by the baker's; *mi è passato di mente* it slipped my mind; ~ **di moda** go out of fashion; ~ **inosservato** go unnoticed; ~ **per imbecille** be taken for a fool **2** *v/t* *confine* cross; (*sorpassare*) overstep; (*porgere*) pass; (*trascorrere*) spend; TELEC *ti passo Claudio* here's Claudio

passata *f* quick wipe; GASTR ~ (**di pomodoro**) passata, *sieved tomato pulp*

passatempo *m* pastime, hobby

passato 1 *pp* → **passare 2** *agg* past; *alimento* pureed; *l'anno* ~ last year **3** *m* past; GASTR puree

passatoia *f* runner

passaverdura *m inv* food mill

passeggero 1 *agg* passing, short-lived **2** *m*, *-a f* passenger

passeggiare <1f> stroll, walk

passeggiata *f* stroll, walk; (*percorso*) walk

passeggino *m* pushchair

passeggio *m* (*pl* -ggi): *andare a* ~ go for a walk

passe-partout *m inv* (*chiave*) master key

passerella *f* (foot)bridge; MAR gangway; AVIA ramp; *per sfilate* catwalk

passero *m* sparrow

passionale passionate; *delitto* of passion

passione *f* passion; REL Passion

passivo 1 *agg* passive; *fumo m* ~ second-hand smoke **2** *m* GRAM passive; FIN liabilities *pl*

passo *m* step; (*impronta*) footprint; *di libro* passage; GEOG pass; *a* ~ *di lumaca* at a snail's pace; ~ *falso* false move; AUTO *avanzare a* ~ *d'uomo* crawl; ~ *carrabile* driveway; *fare due* -*i* go for a walk *or* a stroll; *fig fare il primo* ~ take the first step

pasta *f* paste; (*pastasciutta*) pasta; (*impasto*) dough; (*dolce*) pastry; ~ *dentifricia* toothpaste; ~ *frolla* shortcrust pastry; ~ *sfoglia* puff pastry

pastasciutta *f* pasta

pastella *f* batter

pastello *m* pastel

pasticca *f* (*pl* -cche) pastille

pasticceria *f* pastries *pl*, cakes *pl*; *negozio* cake shop

pasticciere *m*, *-a f* confectioner

pasticcino *m* pastry

pasticcio *m* (*pl* -cci) GASTR pie; *fig* mess; ~ *di fegato d'oca* pâté de foie gras; *essere nei* -*i* be in a mess

pastiglia *f* MED tablet, pill

pastina *f* small pasta shapes for soup

pasto *m* meal

pastorale 1 *m* bishop's staff, crozier **2** *f* REL pastoral letter

pastore 1 *m*, *-a f* shepherd **2** *m* REL: ~ (**evangelico**) pastor

pastorizzato pasteurized

patata *f* potato; -*e pl fritte* (French) fries, *Br* chips; -*e pl lesse* boiled potatoes; -*e pl arrosto* roast potatoes

patatine *fpl* crisps, *Am* chips; (*fritte*) French fries, *Br* chips

patente *f*: ~ (**di guida**) driving licence, *Am* driver's license

paternalismo *m* paternalism

paternità *f* paternity

paterno paternal, fatherly

patetico (*pl* -ci) pathetic

patire <4d> **1** *v/i* suffer (*di* from) **2** *v/t* suffer (from)

patito 1 *agg* of suffering **2** *m*, *-a f* fan; ~ *del jazz* jazz fan

patologia *f* pathology

patologico pathological

patria *f* homeland

patrigno *m* stepfather

patrimonio *m* (*pl* -ni) estate; ~ *artistico* artistic heritage; ~ *ereditario* genetic inheritance; *fig un* ~ a fortune

patriota *m/f* (*mpl* -i) patriot

patriottico patriotic

patriottismo *m* patriotism

patrocinio *m* support, patronage

patrono *m*, *-a f* REL patron saint

patteggiare <1f> negotiate

P

pattinaggio *m* (*pl* -ggi) skating; ~ *artistico* figure skating; ~ *su ghiaccio* ice skating; ~ *a rotelle* roller skating

pattinare <1l> skate; AUTO skid

pattinatore *m*, **-trice** *f* skater

pattino *m* SP skate; ~ *a rotelle* roller skate; ~ *in linea* roller blade

patto *m* pact; *a ~ che* on condition that; *venire a -i* come to terms

pattuglia *f* patrol

pattumiera *f* dustbin

paura *f* fear; *avere ~ di* be frightened of; *mettere* (*o fare*) *~ a qu* frighten s.o.

pauroso fearful; *che fa paura* frightening

pausa *f* pause; *durante il lavoro* break

pavimento *m* floor

pavone *m* peacock

pazientare <1b> be patient

paziente *agg, m/f* patient

pazienza *f* patience

pazzesco (*pl* -chi) crazy

pazzia *f* madness

pazzo 1 *agg* mad, crazy; *è ~ da legare* he's off his head; *andare ~ per* be mad *or* crazy about 2 *m*, **-a** *f* madman; *donna* madwoman

p.c. *abbr* (= *per conoscenza*) cc (= carbon copy)

p.e. *abbr* (= *per esempio*) eg (= for example)

pecca *f* (*pl* -cche) fault

peccare <1b & d> sin; ~ *di* be guilty of

peccato *m* sin; (*che*) *~ !* what a pity!

pecora *f* sheep

pecorino *m/agg*: (*formaggio m*) ~ pecorino (*ewe's milk cheese*)

peculiarità *f inv* special feature, peculiarity

pedaggio *m* (*pl* -ggi) toll

pedalare <1a> pedal

pedale *m* pedal; ~ *dell'acceleratore* accelerator

pedalò *m inv* pedalo

pedana *f* footrest; SP springboard

pedante pedantic

pedata *f* kick; (*impronta*) footprint

pediatra *m/f* (*mpl* -i) p(a)ediatrician

pediatria *f* p(a)ediatrics

pedicure 1 *m/f* chiropodist, *Am* podiatrist 2 *m inv* pedicure

pedina *f* draughtsman; *fig* cog in the wheel

pedinare <1a> shadow, follow

pedofilia *f* p(a)edophilia

pedofilo *m*, **-a** *f* p(a)edophile

pedonale pedestrian; *zona f ~* pedestrian precinct; *strisce fpl -i* pedestrian crossing *sg*

pedone *m* pedestrian

peggio 1 *avv* worse 2 *m*: *il ~ è che* the worst of it is that; *avere la ~* get the worst of it; *di male in ~* from bad to worse

peggioramento *m* deterioration, worsening

peggiorare <1a> 1 *v/t* make worse, worsen 2 *v/i* get worse, worsen

peggiore worse; *superlativo* worst; *il ~* the worst; *nel ~ dei casi* if the worst comes to the worst

pegno *m d'amore, respetto ecc* token; *dare qc in ~* pawn sth

pelare <1a> peel; *pollo* pluck; *fig* F fleece F

pellame *m* skin, pelt

pelle *f* skin; ~ *scamosciata* suede; *avere la ~ d'oca* have gooseflesh; *fig essere ~ e ossa* be nothing but skin and bones

pellegrinaggio *m* (*pl* -ggi) pilgrimage

pellegrino *m*, **-a** *f* pilgrim

pelletteria *f* leatherwork; **-e** *pl* leather goods

pellicano *m* pelican

pelliccieria *f* furrier's

pelliccia *f* (*pl* -cce) fur; *cappotto* fur coat

pellicola *f* film; ~ *a colori* colo(u)r film; ~ *trasparente* cling film

pelo *m* hair, coat; (*pelliccia*) coat; *a ~ dell'acqua* on the surface of the water; *fig per un ~* by the skin of one's teeth

peluria *f* down

pena *f* (*sofferenza*) pain, suffering; (*punizione*) punishment; ~ *di morte* death penalty; *stare in ~ per qu* worry about s.o.; *vale la ~ soffrire tanto?* is it worth suffering so much?; *non ne vale la ~* it's not worth it; *mi fa ~* I feel sorry for him / her; *a mala ~* hardly

penale 1 *agg* criminal; *codice* penal **2** *f* penalty

penalista *m/f* (*mpl* -i) criminal lawyer

penalità *f inv* penalty

penalizzare <1a> penalize

pendenza *f* slope

pendere <3a> hang; (*essere inclinato*) slope; *fig* ~ *dalle labbra di qu* hang on s.o.'s every word

pendio *m* slope

pendolare *m/f* commuter

pendolo *m* pendulum

pene *m* penis

penetrante *dolore, freddo* piercing; *fig sguardo* piercing, penetrating; *analisi* penetrating

penetrare <1l & b> **1** *v/t* penetrate **2** *v/i*: ~ *in* enter

penicillina *f* penicillin

peninsulare peninsular

penisola *f* peninsula; ~ *iberica* Iberian peninsula

penitenza *f* REL penance; *in gioco* forfeit

penitenziario *m* (*pl* -ri) prison

penna *f* pen; *di uccello* feather; ~ *biro®* ballpoint (pen), biro; ~ *stilografica* fountain pen; ~ *a feltro* felt-tip (pen)

pennarello *m* felt-tip (pen)

pennello *m* brush

penombra *f* half-light

penoso painful

pensare <1b> think; ~ *a* think about or of; ~ *a fare qc* (*ricordarsi di*) remember to do sth; ~ *di fare qc* think of doing sth; *che ne pensa?* what do you think?; *cosa stai pensando?* what are you thinking about?; *ci penso io* I'll take care of it; *senza* ~ without thinking

pensiero *m* thought; (*preoccupazione*) worry; *stare in* ~ be worried or anxious (*per* about); *un piccolo* ~ (*regalo*) a little something

pensieroso pensive

pensile hanging

pensilina *f* shelter

pensionamento *m* retirement

pensionato *m*, -*a* *f* pensioner, retired person; (*alloggio*) boarding house

pensione *f* pension; (*albergo*) boarding house; ~ *completa* full board; *mezza* ~ half board; *andare in* ~ retire

pensoso pensive, thoughtful

pentagono *m* pentagon

Pentecoste *f* Whitsun

pentimento *m* remorse

pentirsi <4b or 4d> *di peccato* repent; ~ *di aver fatto qc* be sorry for doing sth

pentola *f* pot, pan; ~ *a pressione* pressure cooker

penultimo last but one, penultimate

penuria *f* shortage (*di* of); ~ *di alloggi* housing shortage

penzolare <1l> dangle

penzoloni dangling

peonia *f* peony

pepare <1a> pepper

pepato peppered

pepe *m* pepper

peperone *m* pepper

per 1 *prp* for; *mezzo* by; ~ *qualche giorno* for a few days; ~ *questa ragione* for that reason; ~ *tutta la notte* throughout the night; ~ *iscritto* in writing; ~ *esempio* for example; *dieci* ~ *cento* ten per cent; *uno* ~ *uno* one by one **2** *cong*: ~ *fare qc* (in order) to do sth; *stare* ~ be about to

pera *f* pear

peraltro however

perbene 1 *agg* respectable **2** *avv* properly

percento 1 *m* percentage **2** *avv* per cent

percentuale *f/agg* percentage

percepire <4d> perceive; (*riscuotere*) cash

percezione *f* perception

perché because; (*affinché*) so that; ~*?* why?

perciò so, therefore

percorrere <3o> *distanza* cover; *strada, fiume* travel along

percorso 1 *pp* → **percorrere 2** *m* (*tragitto*) route

percossa *f* blow

percosso → **percuotere**

percuotere <3ff> strike

percussione *f* percussion; MUS *-i pl* percussion

perdere <3b & 3uu> **1** *v/t* lose; *treno, occasione* miss; *~ tempo* waste time; *~ di vista* lose sight of; *fig* lose touch with **2** *v/i* lose; *di rubinetto, tubo* leak; *a ~* disposable

perdersi get lost; *~ d'animo* lose heart

perdita *f* loss; *di gas, di acqua* leak; *essere in ~* be making a loss; *~ di tempo* waste of time; *si estendeva a ~ d'occhio* it stretched as far as the eye could see

perditempo 1 *m/f inv* idler **2** *m inv* waste of time

perdonare <1a> forgive

perdono *m* forgiveness; *ti chiedo ~* please forgive me

perenne eternal, never-ending; BOT perennial

perfettamente perfectly

perfetto 1 *agg* perfect **2** *m* GRAM perfect (tense)

perfezionamento *m* adjustment, further improvement; *corso m di ~* further training

perfezionare <1a> perfect, further improve

perfezione *f* perfection; *a ~* to perfection, perfectly

perfezionista *m/f* perfectionist

perfido treacherous

perfino even

perforare <1c> drill through

perforazione *f* perforation

pergola *f* pergola

pergolato *m* pergola

pericolante on the verge of collapse

pericolo *m* danger; (*rischio*) risk; *fuori ~* out of danger; *mettere in ~* endanger, put at risk

pericoloso dangerous

periferia *f* periphery; *di città* outskirts

periferico (*pl* -ci) peripheral; *quartiere* outlying; INFOR *unità f -a* peripheral

perifrasi *f inv* circumlocution

periodico (*pl* -ci) **1** *agg* periodic **2** *m* periodical; *~ mensile* monthly

periodo *m* period; *~ di transizione* transition period

peripezia *f* misadventure

perito 1 *agg* expert **2** *m*, *-a f* expert

peritonite *f* peritonitis

perizia *f* skill, expertise; *esame* examination (by an expert)

perla *f* pearl; *~ coltivata* cultured pearl; *collana f di -e* pearl necklace

perlina *f* bead

perlomeno at least

perlopiù usually

perlustrare <1a> patrol

permaloso easily offended, touchy

permanente 1 *agg* permanent **2** *f* perm

permanenza *f* permanence; *in un luogo* stay

permesso 1 *pp* → **permettere 2** *m* permission; (*breve licenza*) permit; MIL leave; *~ d'atterraggio* permission to land; *~ di lavoro* work permit; *~ di soggiorno* residence permit; *(è) ~?* may I?; *con ~* excuse me

permettere <3ee> allow, permit

permettersi afford

pernacchia *f* F raspberry F

pernice *f* partridge

perno *m* pivot

pernottamento *m* night, overnight stay

pernottare <1c> spend the night, stay overnight

pero *m* pear (tree)

però but

perpendicolare *f/agg* perpendicular

perpetuo perpetual

perplesso perplexed

perquisire <4d> search

perquisizione *f* search; *~ personale* body search; *mandato m di ~* search warrant

persecuzione *f* persecution; *mania*

f di ~ persecution complex

perseguitare <1m> persecute

perseguitato *m*: ~ *politico* person being persecuted for their political views

perseverante persevering

perseveranza *f* perseverance

perseverare <1m & b> persevere

persiana *f* shutter

persiano Persian

persino → **perfino**

persistente persistent

persistenza *f* persistence

persistere <3f> persist

perso *pp* → **perdere**

persona *f* person; *a (o per)* ~ a head, each; *in* ~, *di* ~ in person, personally

personaggio *m* (*pl* -ggi) character; (*celebrità*) personality

personale 1 *agg* personal **2** *m* staff, personnel; AVIA ~ *di terra* ground staff *or* crew; *riduzione f del* ~ cuts in staff, personnel cutbacks

personalità *f inv* personality

personalmente personally

personificare <1n & d> personify

perspicace shrewd

perspicacia *f* shrewdness

persuadere <2i> convince; ~ *qu a fare qc* persuade s.o. to do sth

persuasione *f* persuasion

persuasivo persuasive

persuaso *pp* → **persuadere**

pertanto and so, therefore

pertinente relevant, pertinent

pertinenza *f* relevance, pertinence

perturbazione *f* disturbance; ~ *atmosferica* atmospheric disturbance

peruviano 1 *agg* Peruvian **2** *m*, *-a f* Peruvian

pervenire <4p> arrive; *far* ~ send

perverso perverse

pervertito *m*, *-a f* pervert

p.es. *abbr* (= *per esempio*) eg (= for example)

pesante heavy; *fig libro, film* boring

pesantezza *f* heaviness; ~ *di stomaco* indigestion

pesapersone *f inv* scales; *in negozio ecc* weighing machine

pesare <1a> **1** *v/t* weigh; *ingredienti* weigh out **2** *v/i* weigh

pesca[1] *f* (*pl* -che) (*frutto*) peach

pesca[2] *f* fishing; ~ *con la lenza* angling

pescare <1d> fish for; (*prendere*) catch; *fig* dig up; *ladro, svaligiatore ecc* catch (red-handed)

pescatore *m* fisherman

pesce *m* fish; ~ *spada* swordfish; ~ *d'aprile* April Fool; ASTR *Pesci pl* Pisces

pescecane *m* (*pl* pescicani) shark

peschereccio *m* (*pl* -cci) fishing boat

pescheria *f* fishmonger's

pescivendolo *m*, *-a f* fishmonger

pesco *m* (*pl* -chi) peach (tree)

pescoso with abundant supplies of fish

peso *m* weight; ~ *netto* net weight; *di nessun* ~ of no importance, unimportant; *a* ~ by weight; *fig non voglio essere un* ~ *per te* I don't want to be a burden to you

pessimismo *m* pessimism

pessimista 1 *agg* pessimistic **2** *m/f* (*mpl* -i) pessimist

pessimistico (*pl* -ci) pessimistic

pessimo very bad, terrible

pestaggio *m* (*pl* -ggi) F going-over F

pestare <1a> *carne, prezzemolo* pound; *con piede* step on; (*picchiare*) beat up

peste *f* plague; *persona* pest

pesticida *m* (*pl* -i) pesticide

pesto *m* pesto, *paste of basil, olive oil and pine nuts*

petalo *m* petal

petardo *m* banger

petizione *f* petition

peto *m* F fart F

petroliera *f* (oil) tanker

petrolifero oil *attr*

petrolio *m* oil, petroleum, ~ *greggio* crude

pettegolare <1m> gossip

pettegolezzo *m* piece *or* item of gossip

pettegolo 1 *agg* gossipy **2** *m*, *-a f* gossip

P

pettinare <1l & b> comb

pettinarsi comb one's hair

pettinatura *f* hairstyle, hairdo

pettine *m* comb

pettirosso *m* robin

petto *m* chest; (*seno*) breast; **~ di pollo** chicken breast; **a doppio ~** double-breasted

pezza *f* cloth; (*toppa*) patch

pezzo *m* piece; *di motore* part; **da / per un ~** for a long time; **due -i** bikini; **~ di ricambio** spare (part); *fig* **~ grosso** big shot; **andare in -i** break into pieces; **in -i da cento mila lire** in denominations of one hundred thousand lira

ph *m* pH

piacente attractive

piacere 1 *v/i* <2k>: **le piace il vino?** do you like wine?; **non mi piace il cioccolato** I don't like chocolate; **non mi piacciono i tuoi amici** I don't like your friends; **mi piacerebbe saperlo** I'd really like to know; **faccio come mi pare e piace** I do as I please **2** *m* pleasure; (*favore*) favo(u)r; **~!** pleased to meet you!; **viaggio** *m* **di ~** pleasure trip; **aver ~ di** be delighted to; **mi fa ~** I'm happy to; **con ~** with pleasure; **per ~** please; **serviti a ~** take as much as you like

piacevole pleasant

piacimento *m*: **a ~** as much as you like

piaga *f* (*pl* -ghe) (*ferita*) wound; *fig* scourge; **agitare il coltello nella ~** rub salt into the wound

pialla *f* plane

piallare <1a> plane

piana *f* plain

pianerottolo *m* landing

pianeta *m* planet

piangere <3d> **1** *v/i* cry, weep **2** *v/t* mourn

pianificare <1m & d> plan

pianificazione *f* planning

pianista *m/f* (*mpl* -i) pianist

piano 1 *agg* flat **2** *avv* (*adagio*) slowly; (*a voce bassa*) quietly, in a low voice **3** *m* plan; (*pianura*) plane; *di edificio* floor; MUS piano; **~ rialzato** mezzanine (floor); *primo* **~** foreground; PHOT close-up

pianoforte *m* piano; **~ a coda** grand piano

pianta *f* plant; *di città* map; *del piede* sole; **~ di appartamento** house plant; **~ medicinale** medicinal plant; *di sana* **~** from start to finish

piantare <1a> plant; *chiodo* hammer in; F **piantala!** cut that out! F; F **~ qu** dump s.o. F; **~ grane** make difficulties

piantarsi F: **si sono piantati** they've split up F

pianterreno *m* ground floor, *Am* first floor

pianto 1 *pp* → **piangere 2** *m* crying, weeping; (*lacrime*) tears

pianura *f* plain

piastra *f* plate

piastrella *f* tile

piattaforma *f* platform; **~ di lancio** launch pad

piattino *m* saucer

piatto 1 *agg* flat **2** *m* plate; GASTR dish; MUS **~i** *pl* cymbals; **~ forte** main course; **~ fondo** soup plate; **~ nazionale** national dish; **~ piano** flat plate; *primo* **~** first course; **~ del giorno** day's special

piazza *f* square; COM market (place); *fig* **fare ~ pulita** make a clean sweep

piazzale *m* large square; *in autostrada* toll-booth area

piazzare <1a> place, put; (*vendere*) sell

piazzista *m/f* salesman; *donna* saleswoman

piazzola *f* small square; **~ di sosta** layby

piccante spicy, hot

picchiare <1a> beat

picchiata *f* AVIA nosedive

picchio *m* (*pl* -cchi) ZO woodpecker

picciionaia *f* TEA gods

piccione *m* pigeon; **~ viaggiatore** carrier pigeon; **prendere due -i con una fava** kill two birds with one stone

picco *m* (*pl* -cchi) peak; MAR **colare**

a ~ sink

piccolezza *f* smallness; (*inezia*) trifle; *fig* pettiness, small-mindedness

piccolo 1 *agg* small, little; *di statura* short; *meschino* petty **2** *m*, *-a f* child; *la gatta con i suoi -i* the cat and her young; *da* ~ as a child; *fin da* ~ since I/he was a child

piccozza *f* ice ax(e)

picnic *m inv* picnic; *fare un* ~ have a picnic, picnic

pidocchio *m* (*pl* -cchi) louse

piede *m* foot; *-i pl piatti* flat feet; P cops P, flatfoots P; *a -i* on foot; *su due -i* suddenly; *stare in -i* stand; *a ~ libero* at large; *a -i nudi* barefoot, with bare feet

piedistallo *m* pedestal

piega *f* (*pl* -ghe) wrinkle; *di pantaloni* crease; *di gonna* pleat; *a -ghe* pleated

piegare <1b & e> **1** *v/t* bend; (*ripiegare*) fold **2** *v/i* bend

piegarsi bend; *fig* ~ *a* comply with

pieghevole *sedia* folding

Piemonte *m* Piedmont

piemontese *agg*, *m/f* Piedmontese

piena *f* flood; *a teatro* full house

pienezza *f* fullness

pieno 1 *agg* full (*di* of); (*non cavo*) solid; *in* ~ *giorno* in broad daylight; *in -a notte* in the middle of the night **2** *m*: *nel* ~ *dell'inverno* in the depths of winter; AUTO *fare il* ~ fill up

pietà *f* pity (*di* for); PITT pietà; *avere* ~ *di qu* take pity on s.o.; *senza* ~ pitiless, merciless

pietanza *f* dish

pietoso pitiful; (*compassionevole*) merciful

pietra *f* stone; ~ *focaia* flint; ~ *preziosa* precious stone; ~ *miliare* milestone (*anche fig*)

pietrina *f* flint

pietroso stony

pigiama *m* pyjamas *pl*, PJs F

pigiare <1f> crush

pigione *f* rent

pigliare <1g> catch; ~ *fiato* catch

one's breath

pigmeo *m*, *-a f* pygmy

pigna *f* pinecone

pignolo pedantic, nit-picking F

pignoramento *m* distraint

pignorare <1a> distrain

pigrizia *f* laziness

pigro lazy

PIL *abbr* (= *prodotto interno lordo*) GDP (= gross domestic product)

pila *f* EL battery; (*catasta*) pile, heap

pilastro *m* pillar

pillola *f* pill; ~ (*anticoncezionale*) pill; *prendere la* ~ be on the pill

pilone *m* pier; EL pylon

pilota (*pl* -i) **1** *m/f* AVIA, MAR pilot; AUTO driver; ~ *automatico* automatic pilot **2** *agg* pilot *attr*

pilotare <1c> pilot; AUTO drive

pinacoteca *f* (*pl* -che) art gallery

pineta *f* pine forest

ping-pong *m* table tennis, ping-pong

pinna *f* di *pesce* fin; SP flipper

pino *m* pine

pinolo *m* pine nut

pinza *f* pliers *pl*; MED forceps *pl*

pinzare <1a> staple

pinzatrice *f* stapler

pinzette *fpl* tweezers

pio pious

pioggerella *f* drizzle

pioggia *f* (*pl* -gge) rain; ~ *acida* acid rain

piombare <1a> **1** *v/t dente* fill **2** *v/i* fall; *precipitarsi* rush (*su* at); *mi è piombato in casa* he dropped in unexpectedly

piombatura *f* di *dente* filling

piombino *m* sinker

piombo *m* lead; *a* ~ plumb; *con/ senza* ~ *benzina* leaded/unleaded; *fig andare con i piedi di* ~ tread carefully

pioniere *m*, *-a f* pioneer

pioppo *m* poplar

piovere <3kk> rain; *piove a dirotto* it's raining cats and dogs

piovigginare <1m> drizzle

piovigginoso drizzly

piovoso rainy

piovra *f* octopus

pipa f pipe; **fumare la ~** smoke a pipe

pipì f F pee F; F **fare la ~** go for a pee F

pipistrello m bat

piramide f pyramid

pirata m (pl -i) pirate; **~ dell'aria** hijacker; **~ della strada** hit-and-run driver; (guidatore spericolato) roadhog

pirofila f oven-proof dish

piroscafo m steamer, steamship

pirotecnica f fireworks pl

pirotecnico (pl -ci) fireworks attr

pisciare <1f> P piss P

piscina f (swimming) pool; **~ coperta** indoor pool

pisello m pea

pisolino m nap

pista f di atletica track; di circo ring; (traccia) trail; di autostrada toll-lane; **~ d'atterraggio** runway; **~ da ballo** dance floor; **~ da sci** ski slope; **~ da sci da fondo** cross country ski trail; **~ ciclabile** bike path

pistacchio m (pl -cchi) pistachio

pistola f pistol; **~ ad acqua** water pistol; **~ automatica** automatic (pistol); **~ a spruzzo** spray gun

pistone m piston

pittore m, -trice f painter

pittoresco (pl -chi) picturesque

pittura f painting

pitturare <1a> paint

più 1 avv more (**di, che** than); superlativo most; MAT plus; **~ grande** bigger; **il ~ grande** the biggest; **di ~** more; **non ~** no more; tempo **non ~** no longer; **~ o meno** more or less; **per di ~** what's more; **mai ~** never again; **al ~ presto** as soon as possible; **al ~ tardi** at the latest 2 agg more; superlativo most; **~ volte** several times 3 m more; MAT plus sign; **per lo ~** mainly; **i ~, le ~** the majority

piuma f feather

piumaggio m plumage

piumino m down; giacca down jacket

piumone m Continental quilt, duvet

piuttosto rather

pizza f pizza

pizzaiolo m pizza maker

pizzeria f pizzeria, pizza parlo(u)r

pizzicare <ll & d> 1 v/t braccio, persona pinch; F ladro catch (redhanded), nick F 2 v/i pinch

pizzico m (pl -chi) pinch

pizzicotto m pinch

pizzo m (merletto) lace

placare <1d> placate; dolore ease

placca f (pl -cche) plate; (targhetta) plaque; **~ dentaria** plaque

placcare <1d> plate; nel rugby tackle; **placcato d'oro** gold-plated

placido placid

planare <1a> glide

planata f: **fare una ~** glide

plancia f bridge; (passerella) gangway, gangplank

planetario (pl -ri) 1 agg planetary 2 m planetarium

plasma m plasma; **~ sanguigno** blood plasma

plasmabile malleable

plasmare <1a> mo(u)ld

plastica f plastic; MED plastic surgery; **posate fpl di ~** plastic cutlery

plastico (pl -ci) 1 agg plastic 2 m ARCHI scale model; **esplosivo m al ~** plastic bomb

plastilina® f Plasticine®

platano m plane (tree)

platea f TEA stalls

platino m platinum

plausibile plausible

plenilunio m (pl -ni) full moon

pletora f fig plethora

plettro m plectrum

pleurite f pleurisy

plico m (pl -chi) envelope; **in ~ separato** under separate cover

plurale m/agg plural

pluripartitico (pl -ci) multiparty

plusvalore m capital gains; **tassa f sul ~** capital gains tax

plutonio m plutonium

pneumatico (pl -ci) 1 agg pneumatic 2 m tyre, Am tire; **-i da neve** pl snow tyres (Am tires)

PNL abbr (= **prodotto nazionale lordo**) GNP (= gross national product)

po¹: *un* ~ a little (*di* sth), a little bit (*di* of); *un bel* ~ quite a lot

poco (*pl* -chi) **1** *agg* little; *con nomi plurali* few **2** *avv* not much; *con aggettivi* not very, not greatly; *senti un po'!* just listen!; *a* ~ *a* ~ little by little, gradually; ~ *fa* a little while ago; *fra* ~ in a little while, soon; ~ *dopo* a little while later, soon after; *per* ~ cheap; *(quasi)* almost, nearly

podere *m* farm

podio *m* (*pl* -di) podium, dais; MUS podium

podismo *m* walking

poesia *f* poetry; *componimento* poem

poeta *m* (*pl* -i), **-essa** *f* poet

poetico (*pl* -ci) poetic

poggiare <1f & c> lean; *(posare)* put, place

poggiarsi: ~ *a* lean on

poggiatesta *m inv* head rest

poggio *m* (*pl* -ggi) mound

poi *avv* then; *d'ora in* ~ from now on; *questa* ~! well I'm blowed!; *dalle 6 in* ~ from 6 o'clock on(wards); *prima o* ~ sooner or later

poiché since

poker *m* poker

polacco (*pl* -cchi) **1** *m/agg* Polish **2** *m*, **-a** *f* Pole

polare Polar; *circolo m* ~ *artico / antartico* Arctic / Antarctic circle

polarizzare <1a> polarize

polemica *f* (*pl* -che) argument; *fare -che* argue

polemico (*pl* -ci) argumentative

polemizzare <1a> argue

polenta *f* polenta, *kind of porridge made from cornmeal*

policlinico *m* (*pl* -ci) general hospital

poliglotta **1** *agg* multilingual **2** *m/f* polyglot

poligono *m* MAT polygon; MIL ~ *di tiro* firing range

polio *f* F polio F

poliomielite *f* poliomyelitis

polipo *m* polyp

politica *f* politics; *(strategia)* policy; ~ *estera* foreign policy; ~ *interna* domestic policy; ~ *sanitaria* health policy

politico (*pl* -ci) **1** *agg* political **2** *m*, **-a** *f* politician

polizia *f* police; ~ *ferroviaria* transport police; ~ *stradale* (o *della strada*) traffic police, *Am* highway patrol; *agente m di* ~ police officer

poliziesco (*pl* -chi) police *attr*; *romanzo m* ~ detective story

poliziotto **1** *m* policeman **2** *agg*: *donna f* **-a** policewoman; *cane m* ~ police dog

polizza *f* policy; ~ *di assicurazione* insurance policy

pollame *m* poultry

pollice *m* thumb; *unità di misura* inch

polline *m* pollen

pollo *m* chicken; ~ *arrosto* roast chicken

polmonare pulmonary

polmone *m* lung

polmonite *f* pneumonia

polo¹ *m* GEOG pole; ~ *nord* North Pole; ~ *sud* South Pole

polo² **1** *m* SP polo **2** *f inv* polo shirt

Polonia *f* Poland

polpa *f* flesh; *di manzo, vitello* meat

polpaccio *m* (*pl* -cci) calf

polpastrello *m* fingertip

polpetta *f* di carne meatball

polpettone *m* meat loaf

polpo *m* octopus

polposo fleshy

polsino *m* cuff

polso *m* ANAT wrist; *di camicia* cuff; *pulsazione* pulse; *tastare il* ~ *a qu* take s.o.'s pulse

poltiglia *f* mush

poltrire <4d> laze around

poltrona *f* armchair; TEA stall (seat)

poltrone *m*, **-a** *f* lazybones

polvere *f* dust; *(sostanza polverizzata)* powder; *caffè m in* ~ instant coffee; *latte m in* ~ powdered milk

polverina *f* powder

polverizzare <1a> crush, pulverize; *fig* pulverize

polveroso dusty

pomata *f* cream

pomello *m* cheek; *di porta* knob

P

pomeridiano afternoon *attr*; *alle tre -e* at three in the afternoon, at three pm

pomeriggio *m* (*pl* -ggi) afternoon; *di ~, nel ~* in the afternoon; *domani ~* tomorrow afternoon

pomice *f* agg: (*pietra f*) ~ pumice (stone)

pomo *m* knob; ~ *d'Adamo* Adam's apple

pomodoro *m* tomato

pompa[1] *f* pomp; *impresa f di -e funebri* undertaker's, *Am* mortician

pompa[2] *f* TEC pump

pompelmo *m* grapefruit

pompiere *m* firefighter, *Br* fireman; *-i pl* firefighters, *Br* fire brigade

pomposo pompous

ponderare <1l & c> ponder

ponderato *decisione*, *scelta* carefully considered; *persona* reflective

pone → *porre*

ponente *m* west

pongo → *porre*

ponte *m* bridge; ARCHI scaffolding; MAR deck; ~ *girevole* swing bridge; ~ *sospeso* suspension bridge; ~ *radio* radio link; ~ *aereo* airlift; *fare il ~* have a four-day weekend

pontefice *m* pontiff

ponteggio *m* scaffolding

ponticello *m* MUS bridge

pontificio (*pl* -ci) papal; *Stato m ~* Papal States *pl*

pontile *m* jetty

pop: *musica f ~* pop (music)

popolamento *m di città*, *Stato* population

popolare **1** *agg* popular; *quartiere* working-class; *ballo m ~* folk dance **2** *v/t* <1l>populate

popolarità *f* popularity

popolato populated; (*abitato*) inhabited; (*pieno*) crowded

popolazione *f* population

popolo *m* people

poppa *f* MAR stern

porcellana *f* porcelain, china

porcellino *m* piglet; ~ *d'India* guinea-pig

porcheria *f* disgusting thing; *fig una*

~ filth; *mangiare -e* eat junk food

porchetta *f suckling pig roasted whole in the oven*

porcile *m* pigsty, *Am* pigpen

porcino *m* cep

porco *m* (*pl* -chi) pig

porcospino *m* porcupine

porgere <3d> *mano*, *oggetto* hold out; *aiuto*, *saluto ecc* proffer

porno F **1** *agg* porn(o) F **2** *m* porn F

pornografia *f* pornography

pornografico (*pl* -ci) pornographic

poro *m* pore

poroso porous

porre <3ll> place, put; ~ *una domanda* ask a question; *poniamo che ...* let's suppose (that) ...

porro *m* leek; MED wart

porta *f* door; ~ *scorrevole* sliding door; *a -e chiuse* behind closed doors

portabagagli *m inv* luggage rack; AUTO roof rack

portacenere *m inv* ashtray

portachiavi *m inv* keyring

portacipria *m inv* powder compact

portafinestra *f* (*pl* portefinestre) French window

portafoglio *m* (*pl* -gli) wallet

portafortuna *m inv* good luck charm, talisman

portale *m* door

portalettere *m/f inv* → *postino*

portamento *m* bearing

portamonete *m inv* purse

portaombrelli *m inv* umbrella stand

portapacchi *m inv di macchina* roof rack; *di bicicletta* carrier

portapenne *m inv* pencil case

portare <1c> (*trasportare*) carry; (*accompagnare*) take; (*avere addosso*) wear; (*condurre*) lead; ~ *via* take away; *mi ha portato un regalo* he brought me a present; *portale un regalo* take her a present; ~ *in tavola* serve; *essere portato per qc* / *per fare qc* have a gift for sth / for doing sth; ~ *fortuna* be lucky; *porta bene i propri anni* he doesn't look his age

portasci *m inv* AUTO ski rack

portasigarette *m inv* cigarette case

portata *f* GASTR course; *di danni* extent; TEC *di camion* load capacity; *di cannocchiale* range; **alla ~ di** *film, libro ecc* suitable for; **a ~ di mano** within reach

portatile portable; **computer** *m* ~ portable (computer); **radio** *f* ~ portable (radio); **telefono** *m* ~ mobile (phone), *Am* cell(ular) phone; **farmacia** *f* ~ first-aid kit

portatore *m*, **-trice** *f* bearer; *di malattia* carrier

portauovo *m inv* eggcup

portavoce *m/f inv* spokesperson

portico *m* (*pl* -ci) porch; **-i** *pl* arcades

portiera *f* door

portiere *m* doorman; (*portinaio*) caretaker; SP goalkeeper, goalie F

portinaio *m* (*pl* -ai), **-a** *f* caretaker

portineria *f* caretaker's flat (*Am* apartment)

porto¹ *pp* → **porgere**

porto² *m posta* postage; **~ d'armi** gun licence (*Am* license)

porto³ *m* MAR port; **~ d'imbarco** port of embarkation

Portogallo *m* Portugal

portoghese *agg*, *m/f* Portuguese

portone *m* main entrance

porzione *f* share; GASTR portion

posa *f di cavi, tubi* laying; FOT exposure; FOT **mettersi in ~** pose

posacenere *m inv* ashtray

posare <1c> **1** *v/t* put, place **2** *v/i* (*stare in posa*) pose; **~ su** rest on; *fig* **~ da intellettuale** pose as an intellectual

posarsi alight

posate *fpl* cutlery *sg*

posato composed

positivo positive

posizione *f* position; **~ chiave** key position

possedere <2o> own, possess

possedimento *m* possession

possessivo possessive

possesso *m* possession

possessore *m* owner, possessor

possiamo → **potere**

possibile **1** *agg* possible; **il più**

presto ~ as soon as possible **2** *m*: **fare il ~** do everything one can, do one's best

possibilità *f inv* possibility; (*occasione*) opportunity, chance; **~ di guadagno** earning potential

possibilmente if possible, if I / you *etc* can

posso → **potere**

posta *f* mail, *Br* post; (*ufficio postale*) post office; **~ aerea** airmail; **per ~** by post; **a giro di ~** by return of post; INFOR **~ elettronica** e-mail; **fermo ~** poste restante

postale postal; **servizio** *m* ~ postal service; **cartolina** *f* ~ postcard

postdatare <1a> postdate

posteggiare <1f> park

posteggio *m* (*pl* -ggi) carpark; **~ dei taxi** taxi rank

posteriore back *attr*, rear *attr*; (*successivo*) later; **sedile** *m* ~ back seat

posticipare <1m> postpone

posticipato: **pagamento** *m* ~ payment in arrears

postino *m*, **-a** *f* postman, *Am* mailman; *donna* postwoman, *Am* mailwoman

posto¹ *pp* → **porre**; **~ che** supposing that

posto² *m* place; (*lavoro*) job, position; **mettere a ~ stanza** tidy (up); **la tua camera è a ~?** is your room tidy?; **~ macchina** parking space; **~ finestrino / corridoio** window / aisle seat; **ho trovato solo un ~ in piedi** I had to stand; **~ a sedere** seat; **~ di guardia** guard post; INFOR **~ di lavoro** workstation; **~ di polizia** police station; **~ di pronto soccorso** first aid post; **~ di villeggiatura** holiday resort; **vado io al ~ tuo** I'll go in your place, I'll go instead of you; **fuori ~** out of place

postoperatorio (*pl* -ri) postoperative

postumo posthumous

potabile fit to drink; **acqua** *f* ~ drinking water

potare <1a> prune

potassio *m* potassium

potente powerful; (*efficace*) potent

potenza *f* power; ~ *mondiale* world power; ~ *del motore* engine power

potenziare <1a> strengthen

potere 1 *v/i* <2l> can, be able to; *non posso andare* I can't go; *non ho potuto farlo* I couldn't do it, I was unable to do it; *posso fumare?* do you mind if I smoke?; *formale* may I smoke?; *può essere* perhaps, maybe; ~*può darsi* perhaps, maybe **2** *m* power; ~ *d'acquisto* purchasing power; *essere al* ~ be in power

poveraccio *m* (*pl* -cci), **-a** *f* poor thing, poor creature

poveretto *m*, **poverino** *m* poor man

povero 1 *agg* poor **2** *m*, **-a** *f* poor man; *donna* poor woman; *i -i pl* the poor

povertà *f* poverty

pozzanghera *f* puddle

pozzo *m* well; ~ *petrolifero* oil well

pp. *abbr* (= *pagine*) pp (= pages)

p.p. *abbr* (= *per procura*) pp (= for, on behalf of); (= *pacco postale*) small parcel

PP.TT. *abbr* (= *Poste e Telecomunicazioni*) Italian Post Office

pranzare <1a> *a mezzogiorno* have lunch; *la sera* have dinner

pranzo *m a mezzogiorno* lunch; *la sera* dinner

prassi *f inv* standard procedure

prataiolo *m* field mushroom

pratica *f* (*pl* -che) practice; (*esperienza*) experience; (*atto*) file; *mettere in* ~ put into practice; *fare* ~ gain experience, become more experienced; *-che pl* papers, documents; *fare le -che necessarie per qc* take the necessary steps for sth; *fare le -che per passaporto* gather together the necessary documentation for; *in* ~ in practice; *avere* ~ *di qc* have experience of sth

praticabile *sport* which can be practised; *strada* passable

praticantato *m* apprenticeship

praticare <1l & d> *virtù*, *pazienza* show; *professione*, *sport* practise;

locale frequent; ~ *molto sport* do a lot of sport

pratico (*pl* -ci) practical; *essere* ~ *di conoscere bene* know a lot about

prato *m* meadow

preavviso *m* notice

precario (*pl* -ri) precarious

precauzione *f* caution; *-i pl* precautions

precedente 1 *agg* preceding **2** *m* precedent; *avere dei -i penali* have a record

precedenza *f* precedence; AUTO *diritto m di* ~ right of way; *avere la* ~ have precedence; AUTO have right of way; *dare la* ~ give priority; AUTO give way

precedere <3a> precede

precipitare <1m> **1** *v/t* throw; *fig* rush **2** *v/i* fall, plunge

precipitarsi (*affrettarsi*) rush

precipitazione *f* (*fretta*) haste, hurry; *-i pl atmosferiche* atmospheric precipitation *sg*

precipitoso hasty

precipizio *m* (*pl* -zi) precipice

precisamente precisely

precisare <1a> specify

precisione *f* precision, accuracy; *con* ~ precisely

preciso accurate; *persona* precise; *alle tre -e* at three o'clock exactly *o* precisely, at three o'clock sharp

precoce precocious; *pianta* early

precotto *m* ready-made, pre-cooked

preda *f* prey; *in* ~ *alla disperazione* in despair

predecessore *m*, **-a** *f* predecessor

predestinare <1a> predestine

predica *f* (*pl* -che) sermon

predicare <1l, b & d> preach

prediletto 1 *pp* → *prediligere* **2** *agg* favo(u)rite

predilezione *f* predilection

prediligere <3u> prefer

predire <3t> predict

predisporre <3ll> draw up in advance; ~ *a* encourage, promote

predisposto *pp* → *predisporre*

predominare <1m & c> predominate

predominio *m* (*pl* -ni) predominance

prefabbricato 1 *agg* prefabricated **2** *m* prefabricated building

prefazione *f* preface

preferenza *f* preference

preferenziale preferential

preferire <4d> prefer

preferito favo(u)rite

prefetto *m* prefect

prefettura *f* prefecture

prefiggersi <3mm> set o.s.

prefisso 1 *pp* → **prefiggersi 2** *m* TELEC code

pregare <1b & e> beg (**di fare** to do); *divinità* pray to; **ti prego di ascoltarmi** please listen to me; **farsi ~** be coaxed; **prego** please; **prego?** I'm sorry (what did you say)?; **grazie! – prego!** thank you! – you're welcome! *or* not at all!

preghiera *f* request; REL prayer

pregiato *metallo, pietra* precious

pregio *m* (*qualità*) good point

pregiudicato *m*, **-a** *f* previous offender

pregiudizio *m* (*pl* -zi) prejudice

preg.mo *abbr* (= **pregiatissimo**) formal style of address used in correspondence

pregustare <1a> look forward to

preistoria *f* prehistory

preistorico (*pl* -ci) prehistoric

prelato *m* REL prelate

prelavaggio *m* pre-wash

prelevamento *m di sangue, campione* taking; FIN withdrawal; **~ in contanti** cash withdrawal

prelevare <1b> *sangue, campione* take; *denaro* withdraw

prelibato exquisite

prelievo *m* (*prelevamento*) taking; FIN withdrawal; **~ del sangue** blood sample

pre-maman 1 *agg* maternity *attr* **2** *m inv* maternity dress

prematrimoniale premarital

prematuro premature

premeditato premeditated

premere <3a> **1** *v/t* press **2** *v/i* press (**su** on); **mi preme che** it is

important to me that

premessa *f* introduction

premesso *pp* → **premettere**

premettere <3ee> say first

premiare <1k & b> give an award *or* prize to; *onestà, coraggio* reward

premiato prize-winning, award-winning

premiazione *f* award ceremony

premio *m* (*pl* -mi) prize, award; FIN premium; **~ Nobel per la pace** Nobel peace prize; **assegnare un ~** award a prize

premura *f* (*fretta*) hurry, rush; **essere pieno di -e nei confronti di qu** be very attentive to s.o.; **mettere ~ a qu** hurry s.o. along; **non c'è ~** there's no hurry *o* rush

premuroso attentive

prenatale prenatal

prendere <3c> **1** *v/t* take; *malattia, treno* catch; **cosa prendi?** what will you have?; **~ qu per un italiano** take *or* mistake s.o. for an Italian; **andare / venire a ~ qu** fetch s.o.; **~ fuoco** catch fire; **~ il sole** sunbathe; **~ paura** take fright, get frightened; AVIA **~ quota** gain height; **~ in giro qu** pull s.o.'s leg; **prendersela** get upset (**per** about; **con** with); **che ti prende?** what's got into you? **2** *v/i* **~ a destra** turn right

prendisole *m inv* sundress

prenotare <1c> book, reserve

prenotato booked, reserved

prenotazione *f* booking, reservation

preoccupare <1m & c> worry, preoccupy

preoccuparsi worry

preoccupato worried, preoccupied

preoccupazione *f* worry

preparare <1a> prepare

prepararsi get ready (*a* to), prepare (*a* to)

preparativi *mpl* preparations

preparato 1 *agg* ready, prepared **2** *m* preparation

preparazione *f* preparation

preposizione *f* preposition

prepotente domineering; *bisogno* pressing

P

prepotenza *f di persona* domineering nature; *di bisogno* pressing nature

presa *f* grip, hold; **abbandonare la ~** let go; **fare una ~** *presso corriere* call a courier; EL **~ di corrente** socket; *fig* **~ di possesso** conquest, capture; **essere alle -e con qc** be grappling with sth

presagio *m* (*pl* -gi) omen, sign

presalario *m* scholarship

presbite far-sighted, long-sighted

prescindere <3v>: **~ da** have nothing to do with, not be connected with

prescritto *pp* → **prescrivere**

prescrivere <3tt> prescribe

prescrizione *f* prescription

presentare <1b> *documenti, biglietto* show, present; *domanda* submit; *scuse* make; TEA present; (*contenere*) contain; (*far conoscere*) introduce (*a* to)

presentarsi look; (*esporre*) show itself; *occasione* present itself, occur

presentatore *m*, **-trice** *f* presenter

presentazione *f* presentation; *di richiesta* submission; **fare le -i** make the introductions

presente 1 *agg* present; **hai ~ il negozio ... ?** do you know the shop ... ? **2** *m* present; GRAM present (tense); **i -i** *pl* those present, those in attendance

presentimento *m* premonition

presenza *f* presence; **alla** (*o* **in**) **~ di** in the presence of; **di bella ~** fine-looking

presepe *m*

presepio *m* (*pl* -pi) crèche

preservare <1b> protect, keep (*da* from)

preservativo *m* condom

presidente *m/f* chairman; POL **Presidente dello Stato** President; **~ del Consiglio** (**dei ministri**) Prime Minister

presidenza *f* chairmanship; POL presidency

preso *pp* → **prendere**

pressappoco more or less

pressare <1b> crush; TEC press

pressione *f* pressure; **~ atmosferica** atmospheric pressure; **~ delle gomme** tyre pressure; **~ sanguigna** blood pressure; *fig* **far ~ su** put pressure on, press

presso 1 *prp* (*vicino a*) near; **nella sede di** on the premises of; *posta* care of; **vive ~ i genitori** he lives with his parents; **lavoro ~ la FIAT** I work for Fiat **2** *m*: **nei -i di** in the vicinity of, in the neighbo(u)rhood of

pressoché almost

prestare <1b> lend; **~ ascolto / aiuto a qu** listen to / help s.o.; **~ un servizio** provide a service

prestarsi offer one's services; (*essere adatto*) lend itself (*a* to)

prestatore *m di servizio* provider

prestazione *f* service

prestigio *m* prestige

prestito *m* loan; **in ~** on loan; **dare in ~** lend; **prendere in ~** borrow

presto (*fra poco*) soon; (*in fretta*) quickly; (*di buon'ora*) early; **a ~!** see you soon!; **far ~** be quick

presumere <3h> presume

presuntuoso presumptuous

presunzione *f* presumption

prete *m* priest

pretendente *m/f* claimant

pretendere <3c> claim

pretensioso pretentious

pretesa *f* pretension; **avanzare -e** put forward claims; **senza -e** unpretentious

pretesto *m* pretext

pretore *m* magistrate

pretura *f* magistrates' court

prevalenza *f* prevalence; **in ~** prevalently

prevalere <2r> prevail

prevedere <2s> foresee, predict; *tempo* forecast; *di legge* provide for

prevedibile predictable

prevendita *f* advance sale

prevenire <4p> *domanda, desiderio* anticipate; (*evitare*) prevent

preventivo 1 *agg* preventive **2** *m* estimate

prevenzione *f* prevention

previdente foresighted

previdenza f foresight; **~ sociale** social security, Am welfare

previsione f forecast; **-i pl del tempo** weather forecast sg

previsto pp → **prevedere**

prezioso precious

prezzemolo m parsley

prezzo m price; **~ di listino** recommended retail price; **~ promozionale** special introductory price; **aumento m del ~** price increase; **a buon ~** cheap; fig **a caro ~** dearly; **a metà ~** half-price; **a qualunque ~** at any cost; **~ netto** net price

prigione f prison

prigionia f imprisonment

prigioniero m, **-a** f prisoner; **fare ~** take prisoner

prima¹ avv before; (in primo luogo) first; **~ di** before; **~ di fare qc** before doing sth; **~ o poi** sooner or later; **~ che** before; **quanto ~** as soon as possible

prima² f FERR first class; AUTO first gear; TEA first night

primario (pl -ri) prime

primavera f spring

primaverile spring attr

primitivo primitive; (iniziale) original

primizia f early crop

primo 1 agg first; **~ piano** m first floor; **in -a visione** film just out 2 m, **-a** f first; **ai -i del mese** at the beginning of the month; **sulle -e** at the beginning, at first 3 m GASTR first course, starter

primogenito 1 agg first-born 2 m, **-a** f first-born

principale 1 agg main 2 m boss

principato m principality

principe m prince

principessa f princess

principiante m/f beginner

principio m (pl -pi) (inizio) start, beginning; (norma) principle; **al ~** at the start, in the beginning; **da ~** from the start or beginning or outset; **per ~** as a matter of principle; **in**

linea di ~ in theory

privare <1a> deprive (**di** of)

privarsi deprive o.s. (**di** of)

privatizzare <1a> privatize

privato 1 agg private; **in ~** in private 2 m private citizen

privazione f deprivation; (sacrificio) privation

privilegiare <1f> favo(u)r, prefer

privilegiato privileged

privilegio m (pl -gi) privilege

privo: **~ di** lacking in, devoid of; **~ di sensi** unconscious

pro 1 m inv: **i ~ e i contro** the pros and cons; **a che ~?** what's the point or use? 2 prp for; **~ capite** per capita, each

probabile probable

probabilità f inv probability

problema m (pl -i) problem

problematico (pl -ci) problematic

proboscide f trunk

procedere <3a> carry on; fig (agire) proceed; DIR **~ contro qu** take legal proceedings against s.o.

procedimento m process

procedura f procedure; DIR proceedings pl

processare <1b> try

processione f procession

processo m process; DIR trial; **~ civile** civil proceedings; **~ di fabbricazione** manufacturing process; **~ verbale** minutes pl; **essere sotto ~** be on trial

processuale DIR trial attr

procinto m: **essere in ~ di** be about to, be on the point of

proclamare <1a> proclaim

proclamazione f proclamation

procura f power of attorney; **Procura di Stato** public prosecutor's office; **per ~** by proxy

procurare <1a> (causare) cause; **~ qc a qu** cause s.o. sth

procurarsi get hold of, obtain

procuratore m, **-trice** f person with power of attorney; DIR lawyer for the prosecution; **~ generale** Attorney General

prodigio m (pl -gi) prodigy

P

prodigioso tremendous, prodigious
prodotto 1 *pp* → **produrre 2** *m*
product; **-i** *pl* **alimentari** foodstuffs;
-i *pl* **farmaceutici** pharmaceuticals;
~ finito finished product; **~ interno/**
nazionale lordo gross domestic/
national product; **-i** *pl* **di bellezza**
cosmetics
produco → **produrre**
produrre <3e> produce; *danni* cause
produttività *f* productivity
produttivo productive
produttore *m*, **-trice** *f* producer
produzione *f* production; **~ giorna-**
liera daily production *or* output; **~**
in serie mass production
prof. *abbr* (= **professore**) Prof. (=
Professor)
profanare <1a> desecrate
profano 1 *agg* profane **2** *m fig*: **sono**
un ~ di I know nothing about
professionale *esperienza, impegno*
professional; *scuola, corso* vocational
professione *f* profession; **~ di fede**
profession of faith; **calciatore** *m* **di**
~ professional footballer
professionista *m/f* (*mpl* -i) professional, pro F; **libero ~** self-employed
person
professore *m*, **-essa** *f* teacher; *d'uni-*
versità professor
profeta *m* (*pl* -i) prophet
profezia *f* prophecy
proficuo profitable
profilassi *f inv* prophylaxis
profilattico (*pl* -ci) prophylactic
profilo *m* profile
profitto *m* (*vantaggio*) advantage;
FIN **conto -i e perdite** profit and
loss account
profondità *f inv* depth; FOT **~ di cam-**
po depth of field
profondo deep
prof. ssa *abbr* (= **professoressa**)
Prof. (= Professor)
profugo *m* (*pl* -ghi), **-a** *f* refugee
profumare <1a> perfume, scent
profumatamente: **pagare ~** pay
through the nose, pay a fortune
profumeria *f* perfume shop

profumo *m* perfume
progettare <1b> plan
progettazione *f* design
progetto *m* design; *di costruzione*
project; **~ pilota** pilot project; **~ di**
legge bill
prognosi *f inv* prognosis
programma *m* (*pl* -i) programme,
Am program; INFOR program; **~**
applicativo application; **~ di scrit-**
tura word processor; **~ televisivo**
TV program(me); **fuori ~** unsched-
uled; **avere in ~ qualcosa** have
something planned
programmare <1a> plan; INFOR
program
programmatore *m*, **-trice** *f* pro-
grammer
programmazione *f* programming;
FIN **~ economica** economic planning; INFOR **linguaggio** *m* **di ~** programming language
progredire <4d> progress
progredito advanced
progressione *f* progression
progressivo progressive
progresso *m* progress; **fare -i** make
progress
proibire <4d> ban, prohibit; **~ a qu di**
fare qc forbid s.o. to do sth
proibizione *f* ban
proiettare <1b> throw; *film* screen,
show; *fig* project
proiettile *m* projectile
proiettore *m* projector; **~ per dia-**
positive slide projector
proiezione *f* projection; *di film*
screening, showing
prole *f* children, offspring
proletario (*pl* -ri) **1** *agg* proletariat
2 *m* proletarian
pro loco *f inv* local tourist board
prologo *m* (*pl* -ghi) prolog(ue)
prolunga *f* EL extension cord
prolungamento *m* extension
prolungare <1e> *nel spazio* extend;
nel tempo prolong, extend
prolungarsi *di strada* extend; *di riu-*
nione go on, continue
promemoria *m inv* memo
promessa *f* promise

promesso pp → **promettere**

promettente promising

promettere <3ee> promise; ~ **bene** look promising

promontorio m (pl -ri) promontory, headland

promosso pp → **promuovere**

promozione f promotion; EDU year; ~ **delle vendite** sales promotion

promuovere <3ff> promote; EDU move up

pronipote m/f di nonni great-grandson; donna, ragazza great-granddaughter; di zii great-nephew; donna, ragazza great-niece

pronome m pronoun

prontezza f readiness, promptness; (rapidità) speediness, promptness; ~ **di spirito** quick thinking

pronto (preparato) ready (**a fare qc** to do sth; **per qc** for sth); (rapido) speedy, prompt; TELEC ~! hello!; **pagamento** m **-a cassa** payment in cash, cash payment; ~ **soccorso** first aid; in ospedale accident and emergency, A&E; ~ **per l'uso** ready to use

pronuncia f pronunciation

pronunciare <1f> pronounce; **non ha pronunciato una parola** he didn't say a word

pronunciarsi give an opinion (**su** on)

pronunciato fig definite, pronounced

propaganda f propaganda; POL ~ **elettorale** electioneering

propagare <1e> propagate; fig spread

propagarsi spread (anche fig)

propano m propane

propenso inclined (**a fare qc** to do sth)

propizio (pl -zi) suitable

propongo → **proporre**

proponimento m resolution; **fare ~ di fare qc** decide or make up one's mind to do sth

proporre <3ll> propose

proporsi stand (**come** as); ~ **di fare qc** intend to do sth

proporzionale proportional

proporzionato in proportion (**a** to)

proporzione f proportion; **in ~** in proportion (**a, con** to)

proposito m intention; **a che ~?** what about?; **a ~** by the way; **a ~ di** about, with reference to; **di ~** deliberately, on purpose; **capitare a ~** turn up at just the right moment

proposizione f GRAM sentence

proposta f proposal

proposto pp → **proporre**

propriamente really

proprietà f inv property; diritto ownership; ~ **privata** private property; **essere di ~ di qu** belong to s.o., be s.o.'s property

proprietario m (pl -ri), **-a** f owner

proprio (pl -ri) **1** agg own; (caratteristico) typical; (adatto) proper; **nome** m ~ proper noun; **amor** m ~ pride; **a -e spese** at one's own expense **2** avv (davvero) really; **è ~ lui che me l'ha chiesto** he's the one who asked me!; **è ~ impossibile** that is quite impossible **3** m (beni) personal property; **lavorare in ~** be self-employed

propulsione f propulsion

propulsore m propeller

prora f prow

proroga f (pl -ghe) postponement; (prolungamento) extension

prorogare <1l, e & c> (rinviare) postpone; (prolungare) extend

prosa f prose

prosciogliere <3ss> release; DIR acquit

prosciugare <1e> drain; di sole dry up

prosciutto m ham, prosciutto; ~ **cotto** cooked ham; ~ **crudo** salted air-dried ham

proseguimento m continuation

proseguire <4a> **1** v/t continue **2** v/i continue, carry on, go on

prosperare <1l & c> prosper

prosperità f prosperity

prospero prosperous

prospettiva f perspective; (panorama) view; fig point of view;

senza -e without prospects

prospetto *m disegno* elevation; (*facciata*) facade; (*tabella*) table; ~ **pubblicitario** brochure

prossimamente shortly, soon

prossimità *f inv* proximity; *in ~ di* near, close to

prossimo 1 *agg* close; *la -a volta* the next time; *il lavoro è ~ alla fine* the work is nearly finished **2** *m* fellow human being, neighbo(u)r

prostituta *f* prostitute

prostituzione *f* prostitution

protagonista *m/f* (*mpl* -i) protagonist

proteggere <3cc> protect (*da* from)

proteico protein *attr*

proteina *f* protein

protesi *f inv* prosthesis; ~ *dentaria* false teeth, dentures

protesta *f* protest

protestante *agg, m/f* Protestant

protestare <1b> *v/t & v/i* protest

protettivo protective

protetto *pp* → *proteggere*

protezione *f* protection; ~ *degli animali* prevention of cruelty to animals; ~ *dell'ambiente* environmental protection, protection of the environment; ~ *del paesaggio* nature conservation; ~ *delle acque* prevention of water pollution; INFOR ~ *dati* data protection

protocollare 1 *agg* official **2** *v/t* <1c> register

protocollo *m* protocol; (*registro*) register; TEC standard; *foglio m* ~ foolscap; *mettere a* ~ register

prototipo *m* prototype

prova *f* (*esame*) test; (*tentativo*) attempt; (*testimonianza*) proof; *di abito* fitting; SP heat; TEA *-e pl* rehearsal *sg*; TEA *-e pl generali* dress rehearsal *sg*; ~ *di laboratorio* lab test; *banco m di* ~ test bench; *a* ~ *di bomba* bombproof; *salvo* ~ *contraria* unless otherwise stated; *per insufficienza di -e* for lack of evidence; *mettere alla* ~ put to the test

provare <1c> test, try out; *vestito* try (on); (*dimostrare*) prove; TEA re-

hearse; ~ *a fare qc* try to do sth

provato proven; *fig* marked (*da* by)

provengo → *provenire*

provenienza *f* origin

provenire <4p> come (*da* from)

proventi *mpl* income *sg*

proverbio *m* (*pl* -i) proverb

provetta *f* test-tube; *bambino m in ~* test-tube baby

provincia *f* (*pl* -ce) province

provinciale 1 *agg* provincial; *strada f ~ B* road **2** *m/f* provincial **3** *f B* road

provino *m* screen-test; (*campione*) sample

provocante provocative

provocare <1l, c & d> (*causare*) cause; (*sfidare*) provoke; *invidia* arouse

provvedere <2s> **1** *v/t* provide (*di* with) **2** *v/i*: ~ *a* take care of

provvedimento *m* measure; ~ *d'urgenza* emergency measure

provvidenza *f* providence

provvigione *f* commission

provvisorio (*pl* -ri) provisional

provvista *f: fare ~* go (food) shopping; *far ~ di qc* stock up on sth

provvisto 1 *pp* → *provvedere* **2** *agg: essere ~ di* be provided with, have; *essere ben ~ di qc* have lots of sth

prozio *m*, *-a* *f* great-uncle; *donna* great-aunt

prua *f* prow

prudente careful, cautious

prudenza *f* care, caution

prudere <3a>: *mi prude la mano* my hand itches

prugna *f* plum; ~ *secca* prune

prurito *m* itch

P.S. *abbr* (= *Pubblica Sicurezza*) police; (= *post scriptum*) PS (= post scriptum)

pseudo ... pseudo ...

pseudonimo *m* pseudonym

psicanalisi *f* psychoanalysis

psicanalista *m/f* (*mpl* -i) psychoanalyst

psiche *f* psyche

psichiatra *m/f* (*mpl* -i) psychiatrist

psichiatria *f* psychiatry

psichiatrico (*pl* -ci) psychiatric

psicologia *f* psychology

psicologico (*pl* -ci) psychological

psicologo *m* (*pl* -gi), **-a** *f* psychologist

psicosi *f inv* psychosis

psicoterapia *f* psychotherapy

P.T.P. *abbr* (= *Posto Telefonico Pubblico*) public telephone

pubblicare <1l & d> publish

pubblicazione *f* publication; *-i pl* **matrimoniali** banns

pubblicità *f inv* publicity, advertising; *annuncio* ad(vert); ~ *televisiva* TV ad, *Br* commercial; *fare ~ a evento* publicize; *prodotto* advertise

pubblicitario 1 *agg* advertising **2** *m*, **-a** *f* publicist

pubblico (*pl* -ci) **1** *agg* public; *Pubblico Ministero* public prosecutor **2** *m* public; (*spettatori*) audience; *in ~* in public

pube *m* pubis

pubertà *f* puberty

pudore *m* modesty; *senza ~* shameless, immodest

pugilato *m* boxing; *incontro m di ~* boxing match

pugile *m* boxer

pugnalare <1a> stab

pugnale *m* dagger

pugno *m* fist; (*colpo*) punch; *quantità* handful; *di proprio ~* in one's own handwriting; *avere in ~ qc* have sth in one's grasp; *ti ho in ~* I've got you now; *rimanere con un ~ di mosche* come away empty-handed; *fare a -i* fight, come to blows

pulce *f* flea

pulcino *m* chick

puledro *m*, **-a** *f* colt; (*femmina*) filly

pulire <4d> clean

pulito clean; *fig* cleaned-out

pulitura *f* cleaning; ~ *a secco* dry cleaning

pulizia *f* cleanliness; *fig* ~ *etnica* ethnic cleansing; *donna f delle* **-e** cleaner; *fare le* **-e** do the cleaning, clean

pullman *m inv* coach, bus

pullover *m inv* pullover

pullulare <1l>: ~ *di* be teeming or swarming with

pulpito *m* pulpit

pulsante *m* button

pulsare <1a> pulsate

pulsazione *f* pulsation

pulviscolo *m* dust

pungente *foglia* prickly; *freddo, parola* sharp, biting; *desiderio* sharp

pungere <3d> prick; *di ape, vespa* sting; ~ *qu sul vivo* cut s.o. to the quick

pungiglione *m* sting

punibile punishable (*con* by)

punire <4d> punish

punizione *f* punishment; SP *calcio m di ~* free kick

punta *f di spillo, coltello* point; *di dita, lingua* tip; GEOG peak; *fig* touch, trace; *ora f di ~* peak hour; *ce l'ho sulla ~ della lingua* it's on the tip of my tongue; *fig* *prendere qc di ~* face sth head-on

puntare <1a> **1** *v/t* pin (*su* to); (*dirigere*) point (*verso* at); (*scommettere*) bet (*su* on); *fig ~ i piedi* dig one's heels in **2** *v/i* (*dirigersi*) head (*verso* for); ~ *a successo, matrimonio* aspire to, set one's sights on; ~ *su contare su* rely on

puntata *f* instal(l)ment; (*scommessa*) bet

punteggiatura *f* punctuation

punteggio *m* score

puntiglio *m* obstinacy

puntiglioso punctilious

puntina *f*; *di giradischi* stylus; ~ (*da disegno*) drawing pin, *Am* thumbtack

puntino *m* dot; *a ~* perfectly, to perfection

punto 1 *pp* → *pungere* **2** *m* point; MED, (*maglia*) stitch; ~ *di vista* point of view, viewpoint; ~ *cardinale* point of the compass; ~ *culminante* height; ~ *di partenza* starting point; ~ *di fusione* melting point; *fino a che ~ sei arrivato?* how far have you got?; *alle dieci in ~* at ten o'clock exactly *or* on the dot; ~ *fermo* full stop, *Am* period; *due -i* colon; ~ *e virgola* semi-colon;

P

~ esclamativo exclamation mark; **~ interrogativo** question mark; **di ~ in bianco** suddenly, without warning; **essere sul ~ di fare qc** be on the point of doing sth, be about to do sth

puntuale punctual

puntualità f punctuality

puntualizzare <1a> make clear

puntura f *di ape, vespa* sting; *di ago* prick; MED injection; **~ d'insetto** insect bite

punzecchiare <1k> prick; fig (*provocare*) tease

può, **puoi** → **potere**

pupazzo m puppet; **~ di neve** snowman

pupilla f pupil

purché provided, on condition that

pure 1 cong even if; (*tuttavia*) (and) yet **2** avv too, as well; **pur di** in order to; **venga ~ avanti !** do come in!

purè m puree

purezza f purity

purga f (pl -ghe) purge

purgante m laxative

puro pure

purtroppo unfortunately

pus m pus

pustola f pimple

putrefare <3aa> rot, putrefy

puttana f P whore P

puzza f stink

puzzare <1a> stink (**di** of)

puzzo m stink

puzzola f ZO polecat

puzzolente stinking, evil-smelling

p.v. abbr (= **prossimo venturo**) next

Q

q abbr (= **quintale**) 100 kilograms

qua here; **passa di ~** come this way; **al di ~ di** on this side of

quaderno m exercise book

quadrangolare four-sided

quadrangolo m quadrangle

quadrante m quadrant; *di orologio* dial

quadrare <1a> **1** v/t MAT square; *conti* balance **2** v/i *di conti* balance, square F; *fig* **i conti non quadrano** there's something fishy going on

quadrato 1 agg square; *fig persona* rational **2** m square; *tabella ecc* list

quadrifoglio m (pl -gli) four-leaf clover

quadro 1 agg square **2** m painting, picture; MAT square; *fig* **nel ~ di** as part of; **~ (sinottico)** table; **-i** pl *direttivi* senior executives, senior management sg; **~ di comando** control panel; **~ a olio** oil painting; **a -i** check attr

quadruplo m/agg quadruple

quaggiù down here

quaglia f quail

qualche a few; (*un certo*) some; *interrogativo* any; **rimango ~ giorno** I'm staying for a few days; **~ giorno usciamo insieme** we'll go out some day; **~ cosa** something; **~ volta** sometime; *alcune volte* a few times; *a volte* sometimes; **in ~ luogo** somewhere; **~ mese fa** a few months ago; **in ~ modo** somehow

qualcheduno someone, somebody

qualcosa something; *interrogativo* anything, something; **qualcos'altro** something else; **~ da mangiare** something to eat; **~ di bello** something beautiful

qualcuno someone, somebody; *in interrogazioni anche* anyone, anybody; **qualcun'altro** someone *or* somebody else; **c'è ~?** (is) anybody *or* anyone home?

quale 1 *agg* what; **~ *libro vuoi?*** which book do you want?; *città* **~ *Roma*** cities like Rome **2** *pron*: **prendi un libro – ~?** take a book – which one?; *il/la ~ persona* who, that; *cosa* which, that; *la persona della ~ stai parlando* the person you're talking about **3** *avv* as

qualifica *f* (*pl* -che) qualification; *~ professionale* profession

qualificare <1m & d> qualify; (*definire*) describe

qualificarsi give one's name (*come* as); *a esame, gara* qualify

qualificato qualified

qualificazione *f* qualification

qualità *f inv* quality; *merce f di prima ~* top quality goods; *~ della vita* quality of life

qualora in the event that

qualsiasi any; *non importa quale* whatever; *~ persona* anyone; *~ cosa faccia* whatever I do

qualunque any; *uno ~* any one; *~ cosa* anything; *~ cosa faccia* whatever I do; *in ~ stagione* whatever the season; *l'uomo ~* the man in the street

qualvolta: *ogni ~* every time that

quando when; *per ~?* when?; *da ~?* how long?; *~ vengo* when I come; *ogni volta che* whenever I come; *di ~ in ~* now and then, from time to time

quantità *f inv* quantity, amount

quantitativo *m* quantity, amount

quanto 1 *agg* how much; *con nomi plurali* how many; *tutto ~ il libro* the whole book; *tutti -i pl* every single one *sg*; *-i ne abbiamo oggi?* what is the date today?, what is today's date? **2** *avv*: *~ dura ancora?* how long will it go on for?; *~ a me* for me; *~ costa?* how much is it?; *~ prima* as soon as possible; *in ~* since, because; *per ~ ne sappia* as far as I know **3** *m*: *teoria f dei -i* quantum theory

quaranta forty

quarantena *f* quarantine

quarantenne 1 *agg* forty or so **2** *m/f*

person in his/her forties

quarantesimo *m/agg* fortieth

quaresima *f* Lent

quarta *f* AUTO fourth (gear)

quartiere *m* district; MIL quarters *pl*; *~ generale* headquarters

quarto 1 *agg* fourth **2** *m* fourth; (*quarta parte*) quarter; *~ d'ora* quarter of an hour; *sono le due e un ~* it's (a) quarter past two; *un ~ di rosso* a quarter-litre (*Am* liter) of red; *-i di finale* quarter-finals

quarzo *m* quartz; *orologio m al ~* quartz watch

quasi almost; *~ mai* hardly ever

quassù up here

quattordicesimo *m/agg* fourteenth

quattordici fourteen

quattrini *mpl* money *sg*, cash *sg*

quattro four; *al ~ per cento* at four per cent; *fare ~ passi* go for a stroll; *farsi in ~ per fare qc* go to a lot of trouble to do sth

quattrocchi *m inv*: *a ~* in private

quattrocento 1 *agg* four hundred **2** *m*: *il Quattrocento* the fifteenth century

quattromila four thousand

quegli, quei → **quello**

quello 1 *agg* that, *pl* those **2** *pron* that (one), *pl* those (ones); *~ che* the one that; *tutto ~ che* all (that), everything (that)

quercia *f* (*pl* -ce) oak

querela *f* legal action; *sporgere ~ contro qc* take legal action against s.o., sue s.o.; *~ per diffamazione* action for slander

quesito *m* question

questi → **questo**

questionario *m* (*pl* -ri) questionnaire

questione *f* question; *~ di fiducia* question *or* matter of trust; *qui non è ~ di* it is not a question *or* matter of; *è ~ di fortuna* it's a matter of luck; *è fuori ~* it is out of the question; *mettere qc in ~* cast doubt on sth

questo 1 *agg* this, *pl* these; *quest'oggi* today **2** *pron* this (one), *pl* these (ones); **~ qui** this one here; **con ~** with that; **per ~** for that reason; **quest'oggi** today; **-a poi!** well I'm blowed!; **ci mancherebbe anche -a!** that's all we'd need!; **-a non me l'aspettavo** I wasn't expecting this

questore *m* chief of police

questura *f* offices of the chief of police

qui here; **~ vicino** near here; **fin ~** up to here; **passa di ~!** come this way!; **voglio uscire di ~** I want to get out of here; **di ~ a un mese** a month from now, in a month's time

quietanza *f* receipt

quiete *f* peace and quiet

quieto quiet

quindecismo *m/agg* fifteenth

quindi 1 *avv* then **2** *cong* therefore

quindici fifteen; **tra ~ giorni** in two weeks (time), *Br* in a fortnight('s time)

quindicina *f*: **una ~** about fifteen;

una ~ di giorni about two weeks, *Br* about a fortnight

quinta *f* AUTO fifth (gear); TEA **le -e** the wings; *fig* **dietro le -e** behind the scenes

quintale *m* hundred kilos; **mezzo ~** fifty kilos

quinto *m/agg* fifth

quota *f* (*parte*) share, quota; (*altitudine*) altitude; **perdere ~** lose altitude; **prendere ~** gain altitude

quotare <1c> (*valutare*) value; FIN **azioni** *pl* **quotate in borsa** shares listed *or* quoted on the Stock Exchange

quotato respected

quotazione *f di azioni* value, price; **~ d'acquisto** bid price; **~ di vendita** offer price

quotidianamente daily

quotidiano 1 *agg* daily **2** *m* daily (newspaper)

quoziente *m*: **~ d'intelligenza** IQ

R

R. *abbr* (= **raccomandata**) recorded delivery, *Am* certified mail

rabarbaro *m* rhubarb

rabbia *f* rage; (*stizza*) anger; MED rabies; **accesso** *m* **di ~** fit of rage; **fare ~ a qu** make s.o. cross

rabbino *m* rabbi

rabbioso *gesto, sguardo* of rage; *cane* rabid

rabbrividire <4d> shudder; *per paura* shiver

rabbuiarsi <1i> get dark, darken; *fig* darken

racc. *abbr* (= **raccomandata**) recorded delivery, *Am* certified mail

raccapricciante appalling, sickening

raccattare <1a> (*tirar su*) pick up

racchetta *f* racquet; **~ da sci** ski pole

racchiudere <3b> contain

raccogliere <3ss> (*tirar su*) pick up; (*radunare*) gather, collect; AGR harvest; **~ i frutti di qc** reap the benefits of sth

raccoglitore *m* ring binder; **~ del vetro** bottle bank

raccolgo → **raccogliere**

raccolta *f* collection; AGR harvest; **fare ~ di francobolli** collect stamps

raccolto 1 *pp* → **raccogliere 2** *m* harvest

raccomandabile: **un tipo poco ~** a shady character

raccomandare <1a> **1** *v/t* recommend **2** *v/i*: **~ a qu di fare qc** tell s.o. to do sth

raccomandata *f* recorded delivery (letter), *Am* certified mail

raccomandazione f recommendation

raccontare <1a> tell; **~ per filo e per segno** tell in great detail

racconto m story

raccordo m TEC connection; *strada* slip road; **~ anulare** ring road; **~ autostradale** junction

rada f roads pl, roadstead

radar m inv radar; **impianto** m **~** radar installation; **uomini** pl **~** air traffic controllers

raddolcire <4d> sweeten; *fig* soften

raddolcirsi *di aria* grow milder; *di carattere* mellow

raddoppiare <1k> double; *sforzi* redouble

raddrizzare <1a> straighten

raddrizzarsi straighten up

radere <3b> shave; *sfiorare* skim; **~ al suolo** raze (to the ground)

radersi shave

radiare <1k> strike off

radiatore m radiator

radiazione f radiation

radicale radical

radice f root; **~ quadrata** square root; **mettere -i** put down roots

radio f inv radio; (*stazione*) radio station; **giornale** m **~** (radio) news; **via ~** by radio; **ascoltare la ~** listen to the radio

radioascoltatore m, **-trice** f (radio) listener

radioattività f radioactivity

radioattivo radioactive

radiocronaca f (radio) commentary

radiocronista m/f (pl -i) (radio) commentator

radiodramma m (pl -i) (radio) play

radiofonico radio attr

radiografia f x-ray

radiografico (pl -ci): **esame** m **~** x-ray

radioregistratore m radio cassette recorder

radioso radiant

radiosveglia f clock radio

radiotaxi m inv taxi, cab

radiotelefono m radio

radioterapia f radiation treatment

radiotrasmittente f *apparecchio* radio transmitter; *stazione* radio station

rado *pettine* wide-toothed; *alberi, capelli* sparse; **di ~** seldom

radunare <1a> collect, gather

radunarsi collect, gather

raduno m rally

rafano m horseradish

raffermo *pane* stale

raffica f (pl -che) gust; *di mitragliatrice* burst

raffigurare <1a> represent

raffinare <1a> refine

raffinatezza f refinement; **gli piacciono le -e** he likes the finer things in life

raffinato *fig* refined

raffineria f refinery

rafforzare <1c> strengthen

raffreddamento m cooling; **~ ad acqua** water cooling

raffreddare <1a> cool

raffreddarsi cool down; MED catch cold

raffreddato *fig*: **essere molto ~** have a very bad cold

raffreddore m cold; **~ da fieno** hay fever

rag. *abbr* (= **ragioniere**) accountant

ragazza f girl; **la mia ~** my girlfriend; **~ alla pari** au pair; **nome** m **da ~** maiden name

ragazzo m boy; **il mio ~** my boyfriend

raggio m (pl -ggi) ray; MAT radius; **~ d'azione** range; *fig* duties, responsibilities; **~ di sole** ray of sunshine; **-i** pl **X** x-rays; **-i** pl **infrarossi** / **ultravioletti** infrared / ultraviolet rays

raggirare <1a> fool, take in

raggiro m trick

raggiungere <3d> *luogo* reach, get to; *persona* join; *scopo* achieve

raggomitolare <1n> wind or roll into a ball

raggomitolarsi curl up

raggrinzito wrinkled

ragionamento m reasoning

ragionare <1a> reason; **~ di** talk about, discuss

R

ragione f reason; (*diritto*) right; ~ *sociale* company name; *per -i di salute* for health reasons; *aver ~* be right; *dare ~ a qu* admit that s.o. is right; *a ~, con ~* rightly; *senza ~* for no reason

ragioneria f book-keeping; EDU *high school specializing in business studies*

ragionevole reasonable

ragioniere m, **-a** f accountant

ragnatela f spider's web

ragno m spider

ragù m inv *meat sauce for pasta*

RAI-TV abbr (= *Radio Televisione Italiana*) *Italian state radio and television*

rallegramenti mpl congratulations

rallegrare <1a> cheer up, brighten up

rallegrarsi cheer up, brighten up; ~ *con qu di qc* congratulate s.o. on sth

rallentare <1b> slow down; *fig* ~ *il lavoro* ease off in one's work

rallentatore m: *al* ~ in slow motion

ramanzina f lecture

rame m copper

ramificarsi <1m & d> *di fiume* branch

ramificazione f ramification

ramino m (*gioco*) rummy

rammaricare <1m & d> disappoint

rammaricarsi be disappointed (*di* at)

rammarico m (*pl* -chi) regret

rammendare <1a> darn

rammendo m darn

rammollire <4d> v/t & v/i soften

ramo m branch

ramoscello m twig

rampa f flight; ~ *di carico* loading ramp; ~ *d'accesso* slip road; ~ *di lancio* launch(ing) pad

rampicante 1 agg climbing; *pianta* f ~ climber **2** m climber

rampone m crampon

rana f frog; *uomo* m ~ frogman

rancido rancid

rancore m ranco(u)r

randagio (*pl* -gi) stray

randello m club

rango m (*pl* -ghi) rank

rannicchiarsi <1k> huddle up

rannuvolamento m clouding over

rannuvolarsi <1m> cloud over

ranocchio m (*pl* -cchi) frog

rapa f turnip

rapace 1 m bird of prey **2** agg fig predatory; *uccello* m ~ bird of prey

rapida f rapids pl

rapidità f speed, rapidity

rapido 1 agg quick, fast; *crescita, aumento* rapid **2** m (*treno* m) ~ intercity train

rapimento m abduction, kidnap-(p)ing

rapina f robbery

rapinare <1a> rob

rapinatore m, **-trice** f robber

rapire <4d> abduct, kidnap

rapitore m, **-trice** f abductor, kidnap(p)er

rappacificare <1n & d> reconcile

rappacificazione f reconciliation

rappezzare <1b> patch; *fig discorso, articolo* cobble together

rappezzo m patch

rapporto m *resoconto* report; *relazione* relationship; *nesso* connection, link; *-i pl interpersonali* personal relationships; *avere -i pl di lavoro con qu* be a colleague of s.o., work with s.o.; *in ~ a* in connection with; *le due cose sono in ~* the two things are related *or* connected

rappresentante m/f representative

rappresentanza f agency; ~ *esclusiva* sole agency

rappresentare <1b> represent; TEA perform

rappresentazione f representation; TEA performance

rarità f inv rarity

raro rare

rasare <1a> shave

rasatura f shaving

raschiare <1k> scrape; *ruggine, sporco* scrape off

raschiarsi ~ *la gola* clear one's throat

rasentare <1b> (*sfiorare*) scrape; *fig* (*avvicinarsi*) verge on; ~ *il muro* hug the wall

rasente: ~ *a* very close to

rasoio *m* (*pl* -oi) razor; ~ *di sicurezza* safety razor; ~ *elettrico* electric razor

raspo *m* cluster

rassegna *f* festival; *di pittura ecc* exhibition; *passare in* ~ review

rassegnare <1a> resign o.s (*a* to)

rassegnato resigned

rassegnazione *f* resignation

rasserenare <1a> calm down

rasserenarsi *di cielo, tempo* clear up

rassicurare <1a> reassure

rassicurarsi feel reassured

rassomigliante similar

rassomiglianza *f* resemblance

rassomigliare <1g>: ~ *a* look like, resemble

rassomigliarsi look like *or* resemble each other

rastrellare <1b> rake; *fig* comb

rastrelliera *f* rack; ~ *per biciclette* bike rack

rastrello *m* rake

rata *f* instal(l)ment; *a -e* in instalments; ~ *qc a rate* buy sth on hire purchase *or Am* the installment plan

rateale: *pagamento m* ~ payment in insta(l)lments; *vendita f* ~ hire purchase, *Am* installment plan

ratificare <1m & d> ratify

ratto *m* ZO rat

rattoppare <1c> patch

rattoppo *m* patch

rattrappire <4d>, **rattrappirsi** go stiff

rattrappito stiff

rattristare <1a> sadden, make sad

rattristarsi become sad

raucedine *f* hoarseness

rauco (*pl* -chi) hoarse

ravanello *m* radish

ravioli *mpl* ravioli *sg*

ravvicinamento *m* approach; *fig* reconciliation

ravvicinare <1a> move closer; *fig* (*confrontare*) compare; (*riappacificare*) reconcile

ravvivare <1a> revive

razionale rational

razionalizzare <1a> rationalize

razionare <1a> ration

razione *f* ration

razza *f* race; *fig* sort, kind; ZO breed

razzia *f* raid

razziale racial

razzismo *m* racism

razzista *agg*, *m/f* (*mpl* -i) racist

razzo *m* rocket; *come un* ~ like greased lightning, like a bat out of hell

re *m inv* king; MUS D

reagire <4d> react (*a* to)

reale *vero* real; *regale* royal

realismo *m* realism

realista *m/f* (*mpl* -i) realist

realistico (*pl* -ci) realistic

realizzabile feasible

realizzare <1a> realize; *piano, progetto* carry out

realizzarsi *di sogno* come true; *di persona* find o.s., find fulfilment

realizzazione *f* fulfilment; (*cosa realizzata*) achievement

realmente really

realtà *f* reality; *in* ~ in fact, actually; ~ *virtuale* virtual reality

reato *m* (criminal) offence (*Am* offense); *-i pl minori* minor offences

reattore *m* AVIA jet engine; *aereo* jet; ~ *nucleare* nuclear reactor

reazionario (*pl* -ri) **1** *agg* reactionary **2** *m*, **-a** *f* reactionary

reazione *f* reaction

recapitare <1m> deliver

recapito *m* delivery; (*indirizzo*) address; ~ *telefonico* phone number

recare <1d> *portare* bring; *arrecare* cause

recarsi go

recensione *f* review

recensire <4d> review

recensore *m* reviewer, critic

recente recent

recentemente recently

recintare <1a> enclose

recinto *m* enclosure; *per animali* pen, enclosure; *steccato* fence

recipiente *m* container, recipient

reciproco (*pl* -ci) mutual, reciprocal

recita f performance

recitare <1l & b> **1** v/t recite; TEA play (the part of); *preghiera* say **2** v/i act

reclamare <1a> **1** v/i complain **2** v/t claim

réclame f inv advert

reclamizzare <1a> advertise

reclamo m complaint

reclusione f seclusion

recluso m prisoner

recluta f recruit

record m inv record; *stabilire il* ~ set the record; *a tempo di* ~ in record time

recuperare → **ricuperare**

recupero → **ricupero**

redatto pp → **redigere**

redattore m, **-trice** f editor; *di articolo* writer; ~ **capo** editor-in-chief

redazione f editorial staff; *di articolo* writing

redditizio (pl -zi) profitable

reddito m income; ~ **annuo** annual income

Redentore m REL Redeemer

redigere <3oo> *testo, articolo* write; *lista* draw up

redini fpl reins

reduce m/f ex-serviceman

referendum m inv referendum

referenza f reference

referto m (official) report

refettorio m (pl -ri) refectory

refill m inv refill

refrigerante cooling

refrigerare <1m> refrigerate

refrigerio m (pl -ri) coolness

refurtiva f stolen property

regalare <1a> give; *regalarsi qc* treat o.s. to sth

regale regal

regalino m gift, present, little something F

regalo m gift, present; *articolo* m *da* ~ gift

regata f (boat) race

reggere <3cc> **1** v/t (*sostenere*) support; (*tenere in mano*) hold; (*sopportare*) bear; GRAM take **2** v/i *di tempo* last; *di ragionamento* stand up; fig

non reggo più I can't take any more

reggersi stand

reggia f (pl -gge) palace

reggicalze m inv suspender belt

reggipetto m, **reggiseno** m bra, Am brassiere

regia f production; *di film* direction

regime m régime; MED diet; MED *essere a* ~ be on a diet

regina f queen

regionale regional

regione f region

regista m/f director; TEA producer

registrare <1a> *in un registro* enter, record, register; *rilevare* show, register; *canzone, messaggio* record

registratore m: ~ (*a cassetta*) cassette recorder; ~ **a nastro** tape recorder; ~ **di cassa** cash register

registrazione f recording

registro m register

regnare <1a> reign

regno m kingdom; *periodo* reign

regola f rule; *in* ~ in order; *di* ~ as a rule

regolabile adjustable

regolamento m regulation; ~ **dei conti** settling of accounts

regolare **1** v/t <1l & b> regulate; *spese, consumo* cut down on; TEC adjust; *questione* sort out, settle; *conto, debito* settle **2** agg regular

regolarità f regularity

regolarizzare <1a> *situazione* sort out, put in order

regredire <4d> regress

regressione f regression

regressivo regressive

regresso m regression

reimpiego m (pl -ghi) *di capitali* reinvestment; *di personale* re-employment

relatività f relativity; *teoria* f *della* ~ theory of relativity

relativo relative (*a* to); (*corrispondente*) relevant

relatore m, **-trice** f speaker

relazione f *legame* relationship; *esposizione* report; *avere una* ~ *con qu* have an affair or a relationship

with s.o.; **in ~ a** with reference to; **-i pubbliche** public relations, PR
religione f religion
religiosa f nun
religiosità f religion
religioso 1 agg religious **2** m monk
relitto m wreck
remare <1b> row
rematore m rower
remo m oar
remoto remote
remunerare <1m> pay
remunerativo remunerative, well-paid; **non ~** unpaid
remunerazione f payment, remuneration
rendere <3c> restituire give back, return; fruttare yield; senso, idea render; **~ un servizio a qu** do s.o. a favo(u)r; **~ conto a qu di qc** account to s.o. for sth; **~ felice** make happy
rendimento m di macchina, impiegato performance; **~ giornaliero** daily output or production
rendita f income; **~ vitalizia** annuity; **vivere di ~** have private means
rene m kidney
reparto m department
repentaglio m: **mettere a ~** risk, endanger
reperibile available; **difficilmente ~** difficult to find
reperire <4d> find
reperto m find; DIR exhibit
repertorio m (pl -ri) TEA, MUS repertory
replica f (pl -che) (copia) replica; TV repeat; TEA repeat performance; (risposta) answer, response; **il suo tono non ammette -e** his tone of voice leaves no room for discussion
replicare <1l, b & d> ripetere repeat; ribattere reply, answer
reportage m inv report
reporter m/f inv reporter, journalist
repressione f repression
repressivo repressive
represso pp → **reprimere**
reprimere <3r> repress
repubblica f (pl -che) republic

repubblicano republican
repulsione f repulsion
reputare <1l & b> consider, deem
reputarsi consider o.s.
reputazione f reputation
requisire <4d> requisition
requisito m requirement
resa f surrender; restituzione return; **~ dei conti** settling of accounts
residence m inv block of service flats (Am apartments)
residente resident
residenza f (official) address; sede seat; soggiorno stay
residenziale residential; **zona** f **~** residential area
residuo m remainder
resina f resin
resistente sturdy, strong; **~ al fuoco** fire-resistant
resistenza f resistance; instancabilità stamina
resistere <3f> al freddo ecc stand up to; opporsi resist; **non resisto più** I can't take any more
reso pp → **rendere**
resoconto m report
respingere <3d> richiesta, pretendente reject, turn down; nemico, attacco repel
respinto pp → **respingere**
respirare <1a> **1** v/t breathe (in) **2** v/i breathe; fig draw breath
respiratore m respirator; per apnea snorkel
respirazione f breathing; **~ artificiale** artificial respiration
respiro m breathing; **trattenere il ~** hold one's breath; fig **un attimo di ~** a moment's rest
responsabile responsible (**di** for); DIR liable (**di** for)
responsabilità f inv responsibility; DIR liability; **~ civile** civil liability; **~ limitata** limited liability
ressa f crowd
restare <1b> stay, remain; avanzare be left; **~ indietro** stay behind; **~ perplesso / vedovo** be puzzled / widowed; **restarci male** be hurt
restaurare <1a> restore

R

restauratore *m*, **-trice** *f* restorer

restauro *m* restoration; **chiuso per -i** closed for restoration

restituire <4d> return; *saluto* restore

restituzione *f* return

resto *m* rest, remainder; *(soldi)* change; **-i** *pl* remains; **del ~** anyway, besides

restringere <3d> narrow; *vestito, giacca* take in

restringersi *di strada* narrow; *di stoffa* shrink

restrizione *f* restriction

rete *f per pescare ecc* net; SP goal; INFOR, TELEC, FERR network; **~ autostradale** road network

retina *f* ANAT retina

retribuire <4d> pay

retribuzione *f* payment

retroattivo retroactive

retrobottega *m inv* back shop

retrocedere <3l> retreat; *fig* lose ground

retrodatare <1a> backdate

retrogrado reactionary

retromarcia *f* (*pl* -ce) AUTO reverse (gear)

retroscena *mpl fig* background *sg*

retrospettivo *mostra* retrospective

retroterra *m inv* hinterland

retrovisivo: **specchietto** *m* **~** rear-view mirror

retta[1] *f somma* fee

retta[2] *f* MAT straight line

retta[3] *f*: **dare ~ a qu** listen to s.o.

rettangolare rectangular

rettangolo *m* rectangle

rettifica *f* (*pl* -che) correction

rettificare <1m & d> correct

rettile *m* reptile

rettilineo straight

rettorato *m* rectorship

rettore *m* rector

reumatico (*pl* -ci) rheumatic

reumatismo *m* rheumatism

revisionare <1a> *conti* audit; AUTO MOT, put through the MOT test; *testo* revise

revisione *f di conti* audit; AUTO MOT; *di testo* revision

revoca *f* (*pl* -che) repeal

revocare <1l, b & d> repeal, revoke

R.I. *abbr* (= **Repubblica Italiana**) Italian Republic

ri- *prefisso* re-.

riabilitare <1n> rehabilitate

riabilitazione *f* rehabilitation

riacquistare <1a> get back, regain; *casa* buy back

riagganciare <1f> TELEC hang up

riallacciare <1f> refasten; TELEC reconnect

rialzare <1a> *alzare di nuovo* pick up; *aumentare* raise, increase

rialzo *m* rise, increase

rianimare <1m> *speranze, entusiasmo* revive; *(rallegrare)* cheer up; MED resuscitate

rianimarsi revive

rianimazione *f* resuscitation; **centro** *m* **di ~** intensive care unit, ICU

riapertura *f* reopening

riaprire <4f> reopen

riarmare <1a> rearm

riarmo *m* rearmament

riassettare <1b> tidy up

riassetto *m* tidy-up

riassumere <3h> re-employ; *(riepilogare)* summarize

riassunto **1** *pp* → **riassumere 2** *m* summary

riavere <2b> get back, regain; **ho riavuto il raffreddore** I've got another cold

riaversi recover (**da** from), get over (**da** sth)

riavviare <1h> INFOR reboot

ribaltabile folding

ribaltare <1a> **1** *v/t* overturn **2** *v/i di macchina, barca* turn over

ribassare <1a> **1** *v/t* lower **2** *v/i* fall, drop

ribasso *m* fall, drop; *sconto* discount; **essere in ~** be falling *or* dropping

ribattere <3a> **1** *v/t argomento* refute **2** *v/i (replicare)* answer back; *(insistere)* insist; **~ a un'accusa** deny an accusation

ribellarsi <1b> rebel (**a** against)

ribelle **1** *agg* rebellious **2** *m/f* rebel

ribellione *f* rebellion

ribes *m inv* currant; **~ nero**

blackcurrant; **~ rosso** redcurrant

ribrezzo *m* horror; **fare ~ a** disgust

ricadere <2c> fall; *cadere di nuovo* fall back; *fig* relapse

ricaduta *f* relapse

ricamare <1a> embroider

ricambiare <1k> change; *contraccambiare* return, reciprocate

ricambio *m* change; *(sostituzione)* replacement; *pezzo* (spare) part; **pezzo m di ~** spare part

ricamo *m* embroidery

ricapitolare <1n> sum up, recapitulate

ricaricare <1m & d> *batteria* recharge

ricattare <1a> blackmail

ricattatore *m*, **-trice** *f* blackmailer

ricatto *m* blackmail

ricavare <1a> derive; *denaro* get

ricavato *m di vendita* proceeds

ricchezza *f* wealth

riccio[1] *m (pl* -cci*)* ZO hedgehog; BOT *spiny outer casing of the chestnut;* **~ di mare** sea urchin

riccio[2] *(pl* -cci*)* **1** *agg* curly **2** *m* curl

ricciolo *m* curl

ricco *(pl* -cchi*)* **1** *agg* rich, wealthy; **~ di** rich in **2** *m*, **-a** *f* rich *or* wealthy man/woman; **i - i** *pl* the rich

ricerca *f (pl* -che*)* research; *di persona scomparsa, informazione ecc* search *(di* for*)*; EDU project; **alla ~ di** in search of

ricercare <1d> *(cercare di nuovo)* look again for; *(cercare con cura)* search *or* look for

ricercato 1 *agg oggetto, artista* sought-after **2** *m* man wanted by the police

ricercatore *m*, **-trice** *f* researcher

ricetta *f* prescription; GASTR recipe

ricevere <3a> receive; *di medico* see patients; **~ gente** have guests

ricevimento *m* receipt; *festa* reception

ricevitore *m* receiver

ricevuta *f* receipt; **accusare ~** acknowledge receipt

richiamare <1a> *(chiamare di nuovo)* call again; *(chiamare indietro)* call back; *attirare* draw; *fig rimproverare* rebuke, reprimand; **~ l'attenzione di qu** draw s.o.'s attention *(su* to*)*; **~ qu all'ordine** call s.o. to order

richiamarsi: **~ a** refer to

richiedente *m/f* applicant

richiedere <3k> ask for again; *(necessitare di)* take, require; *documento* apply for

richiesta *f* request *(di qc* for sth*)*; FIN demand; **a (o su) ~ di** at the request of; **più informazioni saranno disponibili su ~** further information on request

richiesto 1 *pp* → **richiedere 2** *agg:* **molto ~** much in demand, much sought after

riciclaggio *m (pl* -ggi*)* recycling

riciclare <1a> recycle

ricompensa *f* reward

ricompensare <1b> reward *(qu di qc* s.o. for sth*)*

riconciliare <1g> reconcile

riconciliazione *f* reconciliation

ricondurre <3e> *(riportare)* take back *(a* to*)*; *(imputare)* attribute *(a* to*)*

riconoscente grateful; **mostrarsi ~** show one's gratitude

riconoscenza *f* gratitude; **per ~** out of gratitude

riconoscere <3n> recognise; *ammettere* acknowledge; **riconosco che** I admit that; **non si riconosce più** he's unrecognisable

riconoscibile recognizable

riconoscimento *m* recognition

riconquistare <1a> reconquer

ricordare <1c> remember; *(menzionare)* mention; **~ qc a qu** remind s.o. of sth

ricordarsi remember *(di qc* sth; *di fare qc* to do sth*)*

ricordo *m* memory; *oggetto* memento; **~ di viaggio** souvenir

ricorrente recurrent, recurring

ricorrenza *f* recurrence; *di evento* anniversary

ricorrere <3o> *di date, di festa* take place, happen; **~ a qu** turn to s.o.; **~ a qc** have recourse to sth; **oggi**

ricorre l'aniversario del nostro matrimonio today is our wedding anniversary

ricorso 1 pp → **ricorrere 2** m DIR appeal; **avere ~ a** *avvocato, medico* see; **avere ~ all'aiuto di qu** ask for s.o.'s help; **presentare ~** appeal

ricostruire <4d> rebuild; *fig* reconstruct

ricostruzione f rebuilding; *fig* reconstruction

ricotta f ricotta, *soft cheese made from ewe's milk*

ricoverare <1m & c> admit

ricoverato 1 *agg* admitted **2** m, **-a** f *in ospedale* patient

ricovero m *in ospedale* admission; (*refugio*) shelter

ricreazione f recreation; *nelle scuole* break, recreation, *Am* recess

ricredersi <3a> change one's mind

ricuperare <1m> **1** v/t get back, recover; *libertà, fiducia* regain; *spazio* gain; *tempo* make up; **~ il tempo perso** make up for lost time **2** v/i catch up

ricupero m recovery; **~ del centro storico** development of the old part of town; **~ di debiti** debt collection; EDU **corso** m **di ~** remedial course; **materiale** m **di ~** scrap; SP **partita** f **di ~** rescheduled match

ricurvo bent, crooked

ridare <1r> *restituire* give back, return; *fiducia, forze* restore

ridere <3b> laugh (*di* at); **far ~ di sé** make a fool of o.s.; **se la ride del parere degli altri** he couldn't care less what people think

ridicolizzare <1a> ridicule

ridicolo 1 *agg* ridiculous **2** m ridicule; **mettere qu in ~, gettare il ~ su qu** ridicule s.o.

ridimensionare <1a> downsize; *fig* get into perspective

ridotto 1 pp → **ridurre 2** *agg*: **a prezzi -i** at reduced prices

riduco → **ridurre**

ridurre <3e> reduce (**a** to); *prezzi, sprechi* reduce, cut; *personale* reduce, cut back; **~ al silenzio** reduce to silence

ridursi decrease, diminish; **~ a fare qc** be reduced to doing sth; **~ male** be in a bad way; **~ in miseria** ruin o.s.

riduzione f reduction, cut; **~ del personale** staff cutbacks

riempire <4g> fill (up); *formulario* fill in

rientrare <1a> come back; *a casa* come home; **questo non rientrava nei miei piani** that was not part of the plan

rientro m return; **al tuo ~** when you get back

rifare <3aa> do again; (*rinnovare*) do up; *stanza* tidy (up); *letto* make

rifarsi *vita* rebuild; *casa* renovate; *guardaroba* replace; **~ di qc** make up for sth

riferimento m reference; **punto** m **di ~** point of reference; **con ~ a** with reference to

riferire <4d> report

riferirsi: **~ a** refer to

rifiutare <1a> e **rifiutarsi** refuse

rifiuto m refusal; **-i** pl waste sg, refuse sg; (*spazzatura*) rubbish sg; **-i tossici** toxic waste

riflessione f thought, reflection; FIS reflection

riflessivo thoughtful; GRAM reflexive

riflesso 1 pp → **riflettere 2** m reflection; (*gesto istintivo*) reflex (movement); **ho agito di ~** it was a reflex action, I did it automatically

riflettere <3qq> **1** v/t reflect **2** v/i think; **~ su qc** think about sth, reflect on sth

riflettersi be reflected

riflettore m floodlight

riflusso m ebb

riforma f reform; REL Reformation; **~ monetaria** monetary reform

riformare <1a> (*rifare*) re-shape, reform; (*cambiare*) reform; MIL declare unfit

riformato REL Reformed; MIL declared unfit

rifornimento *m* AVIA refuelling; *-i pl* supplies, provisions; *fare ~ di cibo* stock up on food; *fare ~ di benzina* fill up

rifornire <4d> *macchina* fill (up); *frigo* restock, fill (*di* with); *~ il magazzino* restock

rifornirsi stock up (*di* on)

rifugiarsi <1f> take refuge

rifugiato *m*, *-a f* refugee; *~ politico* political refugee

rifugio *m* (*pl* -gi) shelter; *~ alpino* mountain hut; *~ antiaereo* air-raid shelter

riga *f* (*pl* -ghe) *f* line; (*fila*) row; (*regola*) rule; *in stoffa* stripe; *nei capelli* parting, *Am* part; *stoffa f a -ghe* striped fabric

rigatoni *mpl* rigatoni *sg*

rigenerare <1m & b> regenerate

rigenerazione *f* regeneration

rigetto *m* MED rejection; *fig* mental block

rigido (*duro*) rigid; *muscolo, articolazione* stiff; *clima* harsh; *fig: severo* strict

rigirare <1a> **1** *v/i* walk around **2** *v/t* turn over and over; *denaro* launder; *~ il discorso* change the subject

rigirarsi turn round; *nel letto* toss and turn

rigo *m* (*pl* -ghi) line; *~ musicale* staff, stave

rigoglioso lush, luxuriant

rigore *m di clima* harshness; (*severità*) strictness; SP (*anche calcio m di ~*) penalty (kick); *area f di ~* penalty area; *di ~* compulsory

rigoroso rigorous

riguardante about, regarding

riguardare <1a> look at again; (*rivedere*) review, look at; (*riferirsi*) be about, concern; *per quanto riguarda ...* as far as ... is concerned; *non ti riguarda* it's none of your business, it doesn't concern you

riguardarsi take care of o.s.

riguardo *m* (*attenzione*) care; (*rispetto*) respect; *mancanza f di ~* lack of respect; *di ~* important; *~ a*

as regards, about; *senza ~* carelessly

rilasciare <1f> release; *documento* issue

rilascio *m* release; *di passaporto* issue

rilassamento *m* relaxation

rilassare <1a> e **rilassarsi** relax

rilassato relaxed

rilegare <1e> *libro* bind

rilegatore *m* bookbinder

rilegatura *f* binding

rilevare <1b> (*ricavare*) find; (*osservare*) note, notice; *ditta* acquire, buy up; *da quanto è successo si rileva che ...* from what has happened, we can gather that ...

rilievo *m* relief; *fig dare ~ a qc, mettere qc in ~* emphasize or highlight sth; *di ~* important; *di nessun ~* of no importance

rima *f* rhyme; *far ~* rhyme

rimandare <1a> send again; (*restituire*) send back, return; *palla* return; (*rinviare*) postpone

rimanente 1 *agg* remaining **2** *m* rest, balance

rimanenza *f* remainder

rimanere <2m> stay, remain; (*avanzare*) be left (over); *rimanerci male* be hurt; *come siete rimasti per stasera?* what arrangements did you make for this evening?

rimango → **rimanere**

rimarginare <1m> e **rimarginarsi** heal

rimasto *pp* → **rimanere**

rimbalzare <1a> bounce

rimbalzo *m* bounce

rimboccare <1d> *coperte* tuck in; *rimboccarsi le maniche* roll up one's sleeves

rimborsare <1a> reimburse, refund, pay back

rimborso *m* reimbursement, repayment; *~ spese* reimbursement of expenses; *contro ~* COD, cash on delivery

rimboschimento *m* reforestation

rimboschire <4d> reforest

rimediare <1k & b> **1** *v/i* ~ *a* make

up for, remedy; **come posso ~?** how can I put things right? **2** v/t find, scrape together

rimedio m (pl -di) remedy; MED medicine; **senza ~** hopeless

rimescolare <1m> mix again; più volte mix thoroughly; caffè stir again

rimessa f di auto garage; degli autobus depot; FIN remittance; SP **~ laterale** throw-in

rimettere <3ee> put back, return; (affidare) refer; vomitare bring up; **~ a posto** put back; **~ in ordine** tidy up; **ci ho rimesso molti soldi** I lost a lot of money

rimettersi di tempo improve; **~ da qc** get over sth; **~ a qu** put o.s. in s.o.'s hands

rimmel® m inv mascara

rimodernare <1b> modernize

rimorchiare <1k & c> AUTO tow (away)

rimorchiatore m tug

rimorchio m AUTO tow; veicolo trailer

rimorso m remorse

rimozione f removal

rimpatriare <1k & m> **1** v/t repatriate **2** v/i return or go home

rimpatrio m (pl -ri) repatriation

rimpiangere <3d> regret (**di avere fatto qc** doing sth); tempi passati, giovinezza miss

rimpianto 1 pp → **rimpiangere 2** m regret

rimpiazzare <1a> replace

rimpicciolire <4d> **1** v/t make smaller **2** v/i become smaller, shrink

rimproverare <1m & c> scold; impiegato reprimand; **~ qc a qu** reproach s.o. for sth

rimprovero m scolding; dal capo reprimand; **-i** pl reproaches

rimuovere <3ff> remove; muovere di nuovo move again

rinascere <3gg> be born again; di passione, speranza be revived; fig **sentirsi ~** feel rejuvenated

Rinascimento m Renaissance

rincarare <1a> **1** v/i increase, put up; **~ la dose** make matters worse **2** v/i

increase in price

rincaro m increase in price

rincasare <1a> venire come home; andare go home

rinchiudere <3b> shut up

rinchiudersi shut o.s. up

rincorrere <3o> run or chase after

rincorsa f run-up

rincorso pp → **rincorrere**

rincrescere <3n>: **mi rincresce** I'm sorry; **se non ti rincresce** if you don't mind

rincrescimento m regret

rinfacciare <1f>: **~ qc a qu** cast sth up to s.o.

rinforzare <1c> strengthen

rinforzarsi get stronger

rinforzo m reinforcement; MIL **-i** pl reinforcements

rinfrescare <1d> **1** v/t cool down, make cooler; (ristorare) refresh; (rinnovare) freshen up; **~ la memoria a qu** refresh s.o.'s memory **2** v/i cool down

rinfrescarsi freshen up

rinfresco m (pl -chi) buffet (party)

rinfusa: **alla ~** any which way, all higgledy-piggledy

ringhiare <1k> growl

ringhiera f railing

ringiovanire <4d> **1** v/t make feel younger; di aspetto make look younger **2** v/i feel younger; di aspetto look younger

ringraziamento: **un ~** a word of thanks; **lettera f di ~** thank you letter, letter of thanks; **i miei -i** pl my thanks

ringraziare <1g> thank (**di** for)

rinnovamento m change; di contratto, tessera renewal

rinnovare <1c> renovate; guardaroba replace; abbonamento renew; (ripetere) renew, repeat

rinnovarsi renew itself; (ripetersi) be repeated, happen again

rinnovo m renovation; di guardaroba replacement; di abbonamento renewal; di richiesta repetition

rinsavire <4d> **1** v/t: **~ qu** bring s.o. back to his / her senses **2** v/i come to one's senses

rintanarsi <1a> hide, go to earth

rintracciare <1f> track down

rinuncia f (pl -ce) renunciation (a of)

rinunciare <1f> give up (a sth)

rinunzia → *rinuncia*

rinvenimento m recovery; di resti discovery

rinvenire <4p> 1 v/t recover; resti discover 2 v/i regain consciousness, come round

rinviare <1h> (mandare indietro) return; (posticipare) postpone, put off; a letteratura refer

rinvio m (pl -vii) return; di riunione postponement; in un testo cross-reference

rione m district

riordinare <1m> tidy up; ~ le idee set one's ideas in order

riorganizzare <1a> reorganize

riorganizzazione f reorganization

riparare <1a> 1 v/t (proteggere) protect (da from); (aggiustare) repair; un torto make up for 2 v/i escape

ripararsi dalla pioggia shelter, take shelter (da from)

riparato sheltered

riparazione f repair; fig di torta, ingiustizia putting right, reparation; officina f -i garage

riparo m shelter; mettersi al ~ take shelter

ripartire¹ v/i <4a> leave again

ripartire² v/t <4d> divide (up)

ripartizione f division

ripassare <1a> 1 v/i → *passare* 2 v/t col ferro iron; lezione revise, Am review

ripensamento m: avere un ~ have second thoughts

ripensare <1b> riflettere think; ~ a qc think about sth again; ci ho ripensato I've changed my mind

ripetere <3a> repeat; ti ho ripetuto mille volte la stessa cosa I've told you the same thing a thousand times

ripetizione f repetition; dare -i a qu tutor s.o.

ripetuto repeated

ripido steep

ripiegare <1b & e> 1 v/t fold (up) again 2 v/i fall back

ripiego m (pl -ghi) makeshift (solution)

ripieno 1 agg full; GASTR stuffed 2 m stuffing

riporre <3ll> put away; speranze place

riportare <1c> take back; (riferire) report; vittoria, successo achieve; MAT carry over; tasche sew on; danni, ferite sustain

riporto m amount carried over

riposare <1c> v/t & v/i rest

riposarsi rest

riposato: a mente -a once I've / you've had some rest

riposo m rest; giorno m di ~ day off; collocare a ~ retire; senza ~ nonstop

ripostiglio m (pl -gli) boxroom, storeroom

riprendere <3c> take again; (prendere indietro) take back; lavoro go back to; FOT record; ~ coscienza regain consciousness; ~ a fare qc start doing sth again

riprendersi: ~ da qc get over sth

ripresa f resumption; di vestito alteration; film shot; AUTO acceleration; RAD, TV in ~ diretta (broadcast) live; a più -e several times, on several occasions

riproduco → *riprodurre*

riprodurre <3e> reproduce

riprodursi di animali breed, reproduce; di situazione happen again

riproduzione f reproduction; ~ vietata copyright

riprovare <1c> 1 v/t feel again; vestito try on again 2 v/i try again

ripugnante disgusting, repugnant

ripugnanza f disgust, repugnance

ripugnare <1a>: ~ a qu disgust s.o.

ripulire <4d> clean again; (rimettere in ordine) tidy (up); spir empty, clean out

risa fpl laughter sg

risaia f rice field

R

risalire <4m> **1** v/t scale go back up **2** v/i (rincarare) go up again; **~ alle origini** go back to source

risalita f ascent; **impianti** mpl **di ~** ski lifts

risaltare <1a> stand out

risalto m: **fare ~** stand out; **mettere in ~, dare ~ a** highlight

risanamento m redevelopment; FIN improvement; **~ del deficit pubblico** reduction in the public deficit

risanare <1a> redevelop; FIN improve

risarcimento m compensation

risarcire <4d> persona compensate (**di** for); danno compensate for

risata f laugh

riscaldamento m heating; **~ centrale** central heating system (for a block of flats)

riscaldare <1a> heat or warm up

riscaldarsi warm o.s.

rischiararsi clear (up); cielo clear (up); **~ in volto** cheer up

rischiare <1k> **1** v/t risk **2** v/i: **~ di sbagliare** risk making a mistake

rischio m (pl -chi) risk; **a ~ della propria vita** risking one's own life; **mettere a ~** put at risk

rischioso risky

riscontrare <1a> (confrontare) compare; (controllare) check; (incontrare) come up against; errori come across

riscontro m comparison; check; **in ~ alla Vostra** in response to yours

riscuotere <3ff> FIN soldi draw; assegno cash; fig earn

risentimento m resentment

risentire <4b> **1** v/t hear again **2** v/i feel the effects (**di** of)

risentirsi TELEC talk again; (offendersi) take offence (Am offense)

riserbo m reserve; **senza ~** openly

riserva f reserve; (scorta) stock, reserve; fig reservation; AUTO **essere in ~** be running out of fuel; **fondo m di ~** reserve stock; **avere delle -e pl su qc** have reservations about sth; **senza -e** without reservation, wholeheartedly; **~ naturale** nature

reserve; **fare ~ di** stock up on

riservare <1b> keep; (prenotare) book, reserve

riservarsi reserve; **mi riservo di non accettare** I reserve the right not to accept

riservatezza f reserve

riservato reserved; (confidenziale) confidential

risiedere <3a> be resident, reside

riso[1] **1** pp → ridere **2** m laughing

riso[2] m rice

risolto pp → risolvere

risolutezza f determination, resolution; **con ~** with determination

risoluto determined

risoluzione f resolution; (soluzione) solution; **~ d'un contratto** cancellation of a contract; **prendere una ~** make a decision

risolvere <3g> solve; (decidere) resolve

risolversi be solved; (decidersi) decide, resolve; **~ in nulla** come to nothing

risonanza f MUS resonance; fig: di scandolo reverberations pl

risorgere <3d> rise; fig: di industria ecc experience a rebirth

Risorgimento m Risorgimento, the reunification of Italy

risorsa f resource

risotto m risotto

risparmiare <1k> save; fig spare

risparmiarsi conserve one's energy

risparmiatore m saver

risparmio m (pl -mi) saving; **-i** pl savings; **cassa f di ~** savings bank

rispecchiare <1k> reflect

rispettare <1b> respect; legge, contratto abide by

rispettivo respective

rispetto **1** m respect **2** prp: **~ a** (confronto a) compared with; (in relazione a) as regards

risplendere <3a> shine, glitter

rispondere <3hh> answer (**a** sth), reply (**a** to); (reagire) respond; saluto acknowledge; **~ alle speranze** come up to expectations; **~ di qc** be accountable for sth (**a** to); **~ male**

answer back; TELEC **non risponde** there's no answer

risposta *f* answer, reply; *(reazione)* response; **~ pagata** reply paid

rissa *f* brawl

ristabilimento *m di ordine* restoration; *di regolamento* re-introduction; *(guarigione)* recovery

ristabilire <4d> *ordine* restore; *regolamento* re-introduce; **~ la verità** set the record straight

ristabilirsi recover

ristampa *f* reprint

ristampare <1a> reprint

ristorante *m* restaurant

ristrettezza *f di idee* narrowness; **vivere nelle -e** live in straitened circumstances

ristretto: **caffè** *m inv* **~** very strong coffee

ristrutturare <1a> *azienda* restructure

ristrutturazione *f* restructuring

risultare <1a> *(derivare)* result; *(rivelarsi)* turn out; **mi risulta che …** as far as I know ...

risultato *m* result; **senza ~** unsuccessfully

risurrezione *f* REL Resurrection

risvegliare <1g>, **risvegliarsi** *fig* awaken

risveglio *m (pl -gli)* awakening; *fig* reawakening; **al mio ~** when I woke

ritardare <1a> **1** *v/t* delay **2** *v/i* be late; *orologio* be slow

ritardatario *m (pl -ri)*, **-a** *f* latecomer

ritardo *m* delay; **senza ~** without delay; **essere in ~** be late

ritenere <2q> *(credere)* believe

ritenersi: **si ritiene molto intelligente** he thinks he is very intelligent

ritenuta *f* deduction *(su* from); **~ alla fonte** deduction at source

ritirare <1a> withdraw, pull back; *(tirare di nuovo)* throw again; *proposta* withdraw; *(prelevare)* collect, pick up

ritirarsi *(restringersi)* shrink; **~ a vita privata** retire into private life; **~ da**

gara, esame ecc withdraw from

ritiro *m* withdrawal

ritmo *m* rhythm

rito *m* ceremony; **essere di ~** be customary

ritoccare <1d> touch up

ritornare <1a> **1** *v/i venire* get back, come back, return; *andare* go back, return; *su argomento* go back *(su* over); **~ verde** turn green again; **~ in sé** come to one's senses **2** *v/t* return

ritornello *m* refrain

ritorno *m* return; **far ~** come back, return; **essere di ~** be back; **viaggio** *m di* **~** return trip

ritrarre <3xx> pull away; PITT paint; *(rappresentare)* depict

ritrattare <1a> retract

ritrattazione *f* retraction

ritratto *m* portrait; *fig* **il ~ di qu** the spitting image of s.o.

ritrovare <1c> find; *(riacquistare)* regain

ritrovarsi meet again; *(capitare)* find o.s.; *(orientarsi)* get one's bearings

ritrovo *m* meeting; *luogo* meeting place; **~ notturno** nightclub

ritto straight

riunificazione *f* reunification

riunione *f* meeting; *di amici, famiglia* reunion

riunire <4d> gather

riunirsi meet

riuscire <4o> succeed; *(essere capace)* manage; **non riesco a capire** I can't understand; **~ bene / male** be a success / a failure; *di foto* come out well / badly; **~ in qc** be successful in sth

riuscita *f* success

riuscito successful

riutilizzare <1a> re-use

riutilizzazione *f* re-use

riva *f* shore

rivale 1 *agg* rival *attr* **2** *m/f* rival

rivaleggiare <1f> compete

rivalità *f* rivalry

rivalutare <1a> revalue; *persona* change one's mind about

rivalutazione *f* revaluation

R

rivedere <2s> see again; (*ripassare*) review, look at again; (*verificare*) check

rivelare <1a> reveal

rivelazione *f* revelation

rivendere <3a> resell

rivendicare <1m & d> demand

rivendicazione *f* demand; **-i** *pl* **salariali** wage demands

rivendita *f negozio* retail outlet

rivenditore *m*, **-trice** *f* retailer; ~ **specializzato** dealer

rivestimento *m* covering

rivestire <4b> (*foderare*) cover; *ruolo* play; *carica* fill

rivestirsi get dressed again

rivincita *f* return match; **prendersi la ~** get one's revenge

rivista *f* magazine; TEA revue; MIL review; ~ **di moda** fashion magazine

rivolgere <3d> turn; *domanda* address (*a qu* to s.o.); **non mi rivolge mai il saluto** he never acknowledges me; ~ **la parola a qu** speak to s.o., address s.o.; ~ **l'attenzione a qc** turn one's attention to sth

rivolgersi: ~ **a qu** apply to s.o. (**per** for)

rivolgimento *m fig* upheaval

rivolta *f* revolt

rivoltare <1c> turn; (*mettere sottosopra*) turn upside down; (*disgustare*) revolt

rivoltella *f* revolver

rivoluzionario (*pl* -ri) revolutionary

rivoluzione *f* revolution

rizzare <1a> put up; *bandiera* raise; *orecchie* prick up

rizzarsi straighten up; **mi si sono rizzati i capelli in testa** my hair stood on end

roba *f* things *pl*, stuff; ~ **da mangiare** food, things *or* stuff to eat; ~ **da matti!** would you believe it!

robot *m inv* robot; **da cucina** food processor

robustezza *f* sturdiness

robusto sturdy

rocca *f* (*pl* -cche) fortress

roccia *f* (*pl* -cce) rock

rocciatore *m* rock climber

roccioso rocky

rock *m inv* MUS rock; **concerto** *m* ~ rock concert

rockettaro *m*, **-a** *f* rocker

roco (*pl* -chi) hoarse

rodaggio *m* running in; *fig* **sono ancora in** ~ I'm still finding my feet; **in** ~ running in

rodere <3b> gnaw at

rodersi: ~ **dalla gelosia** be eaten up with jealousy

roditore *m* rodent

rogna *f* F *di cane* mange; *problema* hassle

rognone *m di animale* kidney

Roma *f* Rome

romanico (*pl* -ci) Romanesque

romano 1 *agg* Roman; **fare alla -a** go Dutch 2 *m*, **-a** *f* Roman

romanticismo *m* Romanticism

romantico (*pl* -ci) 1 *agg* romantic 2 *m*, **-a** *f* romantic

romanziere *m* novelist

romanzo 1 *agg* Romance 2 *m* novel; ~ **giallo** thriller

rombare <1a> rumble

rombo[1] *m* rumble

rombo[2] *m* ZO turbot

rombo[3] *m* MAT rhombus

romeno 1 *agg* Romanian 2 *m*, **-a** *f* Romanian

rompere <3rr> 1 *v/t* break; F ~ **le scatole a qu** get on s.o.'s nerves F 2 *v/i* F be a pain F; *fig* ~ **con qu** break it off with s.o.

rompersi break; ~ **un braccio** break one's arm

rompicapo *m inv* puzzle; (*problema*) headache

rompighiaccio *m inv* ice-breaker; ALP ice-pick

rondine *f* swallow

ronzare <1a> buzz

ronzio *m* buzzing

rosa 1 *f* rose; ~ **dei venti** wind rose 2 *m/agg inv* pink

rosaio *m* (*pl* -ai) *pianta* rosebush

rosario *m* (*pl* -ri) REL rosary

rosato *m* rosé

rosbif *m inv* roast beef

roseo pink; *avvenire* rosy

roseto *m* rose garden

rosmarino *m* rosemary

rosolare <1l & c> brown

rosolia *f* German measles *sg*

rosone *m* ARCHI rose window

rospo *m* toad; *fig* F **ingoiare il ~** lump it F

rossastro reddish

rossetto *m* lipstick

rossiccio (*pl* -cci) reddish

rosso 1 *agg* red **2** *m* red; **~ d'uovo** egg yolk; **fermarsi al ~** stop at a red light; **passare col ~** go through a red light

rossore *m* red patch

rosticceria *f* rotisserie (*shop selling roast meat*)

rotaia *f* rail

rotare <1o> rotate

rotatoria *f* roundabout, *Am* traffic circle

rotazione *f* rotation

rotella *f* castor

rotocalco *m* (*pl* -chi) magazine

rotolare <1l & c> *v/t & v/i* roll

rotolarsi roll (around)

rotolino *m* FOTO film

rotolo *m* roll; FOTO film; **andare a -i** go to rack and ruin; **mandare a -i** ruin

rotondo round

rotta *f* MAR, AVIA course; *fig* (*giusta direzione*) straight and narrow; **cambiare ~** change course; **a ~ di collo** at breakneck speed

rottame *m* wreck

rotto 1 *pp* → **rompere 2** *agg* broken

rottura *f* breaking; F *tra innamorati* break-up; F **che ~!** what a pain! F

rotula *f* kneecap

roulotte *f inv* caravan

routine *f* routine

rovesciare <1f & b> *liquidi* spill; *oggetto* knock over; (*capovolgere*) overturn, upset; *fig* turn upside down

rovesciarsi overturn, capsize

rovesciata *f calcio* bicycle kick

rovescio (*pl* -sci) reverse; *in tennis* backhand; *fig* **~ d'acqua** downpour, cloudburst; **~ di fortuna** reversal of

fortune; **il ~ della medaglia** the other side of the coin; **mettersi una maglia al ~** put a sweater on inside out

rovina *f* ruin; **andare in -e** go to rack and ruin; **mandare in -e** ruin; **-e** *pl* ruins

rovinare <1a> ruin

rovinarsi ruin o.s.

rovo *m* bramble

rozzo rough and ready

RSM *abbr* (= **Repubblica di San Marino**) Republic of San Marino

R.U. *abbr* (= **Regno Unito**) UK (= United Kingdom)

ruba *f*: **andare a ~** sell like hot cakes, walk out the door

rubare <1a> steal

rubinetto *m* tap; **~ dell'acqua calda** hot water tap

rubino *m* ruby

rubrica *f* (*pl* -che) *di libro* table of contents; *quaderno* address book; *di giornale* column; TV report

rude rough and ready

rudere *m* ruin; **-i** *pl* ruins

rudimentale rudimentary, basic

rudimenti *mpl* basics, rudiments

ruga *f* (*pl* -ghe) wrinkle, line

ruggine *f* rust

ruggire <4d> roar

ruggito *m* roar

rugiada *f* dew

rugoso rough; *pelle* wrinkled; *albero* gnarled

rullare <1a> MAR roll; AVIA taxi

rullino *m* FOTO film

rullio *m* roll

rullo *m* roll; **~ compressore** steam roller

rum *m* rum

ruminare <1a> chew the cud; *fig* ruminate

rumore *m* noise; **far ~** make a noise, be noisy

rumoreggiare <1f> be noisy; *di tuono* growl, rumble; *di folla* mutter

rumoroso noisy

ruolo *m* role; **personale** *m* **di ~** (permanent) members of staff

ruota *f* wheel; **~ anteriore** front

R

wheel; ~ **dentata** cog; ~ **posteriore** back wheel; ~ **motrice** drive wheel; ~ **di scorta** spare wheel; *fig* **mettere i bastoni tra le -e a qu** put a spoke in s.o.'s wheel

rupe *f* cliff

rupestre *inv* rock *attr*; **arte** *f* ~ wall painting

ruscello *m* stream

russare <1a> snore

Russia *f* Russia

russo 1 *agg* Russian **2** *m*, **-a** *f* Russian

rustico (*pl* -ci) rural, rustic; *fig* unsophisticated

ruttare <1a> belch; *di bambino* burp

ruttino *m* burp

rutto *m* belch

ruvidezza *f* roughness

ruvido rough

ruzzolare <1l> fall

ruzzolone *m* fall; **fare un** ~ fall

S

S *abbr* (= **sud**) S (= south)

S. *abbr* (= **santo**) St (= Saint)

s *abbr* (= **secondo**) s, sec (= second)

S.A. *abbr* (= **Società Anonima**) Ltd (= Limited)

sa → **sapere**

sabato *m* Saturday; **di** ~ on Saturdays; **è meglio uscire di** ~ it's better to go out on a Saturday

sabbia *f* sand

sabbioso sandy

sabotaggio *m* sabotage

sabotare <1a> sabotage

sabotatore *m*, **-trice** *f* saboteur

sacca *f* (*pl* -cche) bag; ANAT, BIO sac

saccarina *f* saccharin

saccheggiare <1f> sack; *spir* raid

saccheggio *m* (*pl* -ggi) sack, sacking

sacchetto *m* bag

sacco *m* (*pl* -chi) sack; *fig* F **un ~ di** piles of F; **costa un** ~ it costs a fortune; ~ **a pelo** sleeping bag; ~ **da montagna** backpack, rucksack; *fig* **vuotare il** ~ spill the beans; *confidarsi* pour one's heart out

saccopelista *m/f* backpacker, hiker

sacerdote *m* priest

sacramento *m* sacrament

sacrificare <1m & d> sacrifice

sacrificarsi sacrifice o.s.

sacrificio *m* (*pl* -ci) sacrifice

sacrilegio *m* sacrilege

sacro sacred; **osso** *m* ~ sacrum

sadico (*pl* -ci) **1** *agg* sadistic **2** *m*, **-a** *f* sadist

sadismo *m* sadism

safari *m inv* safari; ~ **fotografico** photo safari

saggezza *f* wisdom

saggiare <1f> test

saggio[1] (*pl* -ggi) **1** *agg* wise **2** *m* wise man, sage

saggio[2] *m* (*pl* -ggi) test; (*campione*) sample; *scritto* essay; *di danza, musica* end of term show; ~ **d'interesse** interest rate, rate of interest; ~ **di sconto** discount rate

saggista *m/f* essayist

saggistica *f* essay-writing

Sagittario *m* ASTR Sagittarius

sahariana *f* safari jacket

sala *f* room; (*soggiorno*) living room; ~ **da pranzo** dining room; ~ **di lettura** reading room; ~ **giochi** amusement arcade; ~ **operatoria** (operating) theatre, *Am* operating room

salamandra *f* salamander

salame *m* salami

salamoia *f*: **in** ~ in brine

salare <1a> salt

salariale pay *attr*

salariato *m* employee

salario *m* (*pl* -ri) salary, wages; **~ base** basic salary *or* wage

salatino *m* savo(u)ry

salato savo(u)ry; *acqua* salt; *cibo* salted; F (*caro*) steep F; **troppo ~** salty

saldare <1a> weld; *ossa* set; *fattura* pay (off)

saldatura *f* welding; **una ~** a weld

saldo 1 *agg* steady, secure; *fig* **essere ~ nelle proprie convinzioni** be unshakeable in one's beliefs; **tenersi ~** hold on tight **2** *m* payment; *in svendita* sale item; (*resto*) balance; **-i** *pl* **di fine stagione** end-of-season sales; **articolo in ~** sale item; **~ attivo** net assets; **~ passivo** net liabilities

sale *m* salt; **ha poco ~ in zucca** he's not very bright

salgo → **salire**

salice *m* willow; **~ piangente** weeping willow

saliera *f* salt cellar

salina *f* salt works

salire <4m> **1** *v/i* climb; *di livello, prezzi, temperatura,* rise; **~ in macchina** get in; **~ su** *scala* climb; *treno, autobus* get on **2** *v/t:* **~ le scale** andare go up, climb; *venire* come up, climb

saliscendi *m inv:* **finestra f a ~** sash window

salita *f* climb; *strada* slope; **strada f in ~** steep street

saliva *f* saliva

salma *f* corpse, body

salmastro 1 *agg* briny **2** *m* salt

salmone *m* salmon; **~ affumicato** smoked salmon

salmonella *f* salmonella (poisoning)

salone *m* living room; (*esposizione*) show; **~ dell'automobile** motor show; **~ di bellezza** beauty salon

salotto *m* lounge

salpare <1a> sail

salsa *f* sauce; **~ di pomodoro** tomato sauce

salsiccia *f* (*pl* -cce) sausage

saltare <1a> **1** *v/t* jump; (*omettere*) skip; **~ (in padella)** sauté **2** *v/i* jump; *di bottone* come off; *di fusibile* blow;

F *di impegno* be cancelled; **~ (giù) dal letto** jump out of bed; **~ dalla gioia** jump for joy; **è saltata la corrente** there's been a power cut; **~/ far ~ in aria** blow up; **~ fuori** turn up

saltellare <1b> hop

saltimbocca *m inv* fried veal topped with prosciutto and a sage leaf

salto *m* jump; (*dislivello*) change in level; **~ mortale** somersault; **~ in alto** high jump; **~ in lungo** long jump; *fig* **~ nel buio** leap in the dark; **faccio un ~ da te** I'll drop by *or* in

saltuariamente occasionally

saltuario (*pl* -ri) occasional; **lavoro** *m* **~** casual work

salubre healthy

salumeria *f* shop that sells salumi

salumi *mpl* cold meat *sg*

salutare 1 *agg* healthy; *fig discussione* helpful **2** *v/t* <1a> say hello to, greet; **salutami la tua famiglia** say hello to the family for me

salute *f* health; **~!** cheers!; **alla tua ~!** cheers!, here's to you!

salutista *m/f* (*mpl* -i) health fanatic

saluto *m* wave; **tanti -i** greetings

salvagente *m inv* lifebelt; *giubbotto* life jacket; *per bambini* ring; (*isola spartitraffico*) traffic island

salvaguardare <1a> protect, safeguard

salvaguardia *f* protection

salvare <1a> save, rescue

salvataggio *m* (*pl* -ggi) salvage; **barca** *f* **di ~** lifeboat

salve! hello!

salvezza *f* salvation

salvia *f* sage

salvietta *f* napkin, *Br* serviette

salvo 1 *agg* safe **2** *prp* except; **~ che** unless; **~ imprevisti** barring accidents, all being well **3** *m:* **mettersi in ~** take shelter

sambuco *m* (*pl* -chi) elder

San = **Santo**

sanare <1a> heal; FIN, ARCHI restore

sanatorio *m* (*pl* -ri) sanatorium, *Am* sanitarium

sandalo *m* sandal; BOT sandalwood

sangue *m* blood; **a ~ freddo** in cold

blood; **donare il ~** give blood; GASTR **al ~** rare

sanguigno: **gruppo** m **~** blood group; **vaso** m **~** blood vessel

sanguinare <11> bleed; **mi sanguina il naso** my nose is bleeding

sanguinoso bloody

sanguisuga f (pl -ghe) leech

sanità f health; **amministrazione** health care

sanitario (pl -ri) health attr; **assistenza** f **-a** health care

sanno → **sapere**

sano healthy; **~ e salvo** safe and sound

santo **1** agg holy; **acqua** f **-a** holy water; **tutto il ~ giorno** the whole blessed day **2** m, **-a** f saint; davanti al nome St

santuario m (pl -ri) sanctuary

sanzione f sanction

sapere <2n> **1** v/t know; (essere capace di) be able to; (venire a) ~ hear; **sai nuotare?** can you swim?; **lo so** I know **2** v/i: **far ~ qc a qu** let s.o. know sth; **saperla lunga** know all about it; **non si sa mai** you never know; **per quel che ne so** as far as I know; **~ di** (avere sapore di) taste of; **non sa di nulla** it doesn't taste of anything **3** m knowledge

sapiente **1** agg wise **2** m/f (scienzato) scientist

sapienza f wisdom

sapone m soap

saponetta f toilet soap

sapore m taste (di of); **-i** pl aromatic herbs; **avere ~ di qc** taste of sth; **senza ~** tasteless

saporito tasty

saracinesca f (pl -sche) roller shutter

sarcasmo m sarcasm; **non fare ~!** don't be sarcastic!

sarcastico (pl -ci) sarcastic

sarcofago m (pl -gi e -ghi) sarcophagus

Sardegna f Sardinia

sardina f sardine

sardo **1** agg Sardinian **2** m, **-a** f Sardinian

sarò → **essere**

sarto m, **-a** f tailor; **per donne** dressmaker

sartoria f tailor's; **per donne** dressmaker's

sasso m stone; **restare di ~** be thunderstruck

sassofonista m/f (mpl -i) saxophone player, saxophonist

sassofono m saxophone

satellite **1** m satellite **2** agg satellite attr; **città** f **~** satellite town

satira f satire

satirico (pl -ci) satirical

saturare <1l> saturate (**di** with)

saturazione f saturation

saturo saturated

sauna f sauna

saziare <1g> satiate

saziarsi eat one's fill; **non ~ mai di fare qc** never get tired of doing sth

sazietà f: **mangiare a ~** eat one's fill

sazio (pl -zi) full (up)

sbadato absent-minded

sbadigliare <1g> yawn

sbadiglio m (pl -gli) yawn

sbagliare <1g> **1** v/i e **sbagliarsi** make a mistake; **hai sbagliato a dirle la verità** you were wrong to tell her the truth **2** v/t make a mistake; **~ persona** have the wrong person; **~ strada** go the wrong way

sbagliato wrong

sbaglio m (pl -gli) mistake; **per ~** by mistake; **senza -i** flawless

sbalordimento m amazement, stupefaction

sbalordire <4d> stun, amaze

sbalorditivo amazing, incredible

sbalzare <1a> throw; **temperatura** change

sbalzo m jump; **~ di temperatura** change in temperature

sbandare <1a> AUTO skid; FERR, fig go off the rails

sbandata f AUTO skid; F **prendersi una ~ per qu** develop a crush on s.o.

sbarazzare <1a> clear

sbarazzarsi: **~ di** get rid of

sbarcare <1d> **1** v/t merci unload; persone disembark; fig **~ il lunario** make ends meet **2** v/i disembark

sbarco m (pl -chi) di merce unloading; di persone disembarkation

sbarra f bar; **essere alla ~** be on trial

sbarramento m fence; (ostacolo) barrier

sbarrare <1a> bar; assegno cross; occhi open wide

sbarrato assegno crossed; occhi wide open

sbattere <3a> **1** v/t porta slam, bang; (urtare) bang; GASTR beat; **~ la porta in faccia a qu** close the door in s.o.'s face **2** v/i bang

sbattitore m hand mixer

sbendare <1b> take the bandage(s) off

sberla f F slap

sbiadire <4d> fade

sbiadito faded; stile colo(u)rless

sbiancare <1d> **1** v/t bleach **2** v/i turn pale

sbilanciare <1f> unbalance, throw off balance

sbilanciarsi lose one's balance; fig commit o.s.

sbizzarrirsi <4d> indulge o.s.

sbloccare <1c & d> clear; macchina unblock; prezzi deregulate

sblocco m (pl -cchi) f clearing; di macchina unblocking; di prezzi deregulation

sboccare <1d>: **~ in** di fiume flow into; di strada lead to

sbocciare <1f & c> open (out)

sbocco m (pl -cchi) FIN outlet; di situazione way out; **strada f senza ~** dead end, cul-de-sac

sbornia f F hangover; **prendersi una ~** get drunk

sborsare <1a> F cough up F

sbottonare <1a> unbutton

sbottonarsi fig open up (con to); **~ la giacca** unbutton one's jacket

sbozzare <1c> draft, rough out

sbraitare <1a> shout, yell

sbranare <1a> tear apart

sbriciolare <1l> spread crumbs

sbrigare <1e> attend to

sbrigarsi hurry up

sbrigativo (rapido) hurried, rushed;

(brusco) brusque

sbrinare <1a> frigorifero defrost

sbrinatore m defrost control

sbrogliare <1g & c> untangle, disentangle; **sbrogliarsela** sort things out

sbronza f F hangover

sbronzarsi <1a> F get drunk

sbronzo F tight F, sloshed F

sbucare <1d> emerge; **da dove sei sbucato?** where did you spring from?

sbucciare <1f> frutta, patate peel; **sbucciarsi le ginocchia** skin one's knees

sbucciato peeled; ginocchio skinned

sbucciatura f graze

s.c. abbr (= **sopra citato**) above-mentioned

scabroso rough, uneven; fig offensive

scacchiera f chessboard

scacciare <1f> chase away

scacco m (pl -cchi) (chess) piece; fig setback; **~ matto** checkmate; **-cchi** pl chess sg; **giocare a -cchi** play chess; **a -cchi** checked

scadente 1 → **scadere** 2 agg second-rate

scadenza f deadline; su alimento best before date; **~ del termine** deadline, last date; **a breve ~** short-term; **a lunga ~** long-term

scadere <2c> di passaporto expire; di cambiale fall due; (perdere valore) decline (in quality)

scaduto expired; alimento past its sell-by date

scaffale m shelves pl

scaglia f flake; di legno chip; di pesce scale

scagliare <1g> hurl

scagliarsi: ~ contro attack

scala f staircase; GEOG scale; **~ (a pioli)** ladder; **~ mobile** escalator; FIN sliding scale; **~ musicale** (musical) scale; **disegno m in ~** scale drawing; **su larga ~** on a large scale; **su ~ nazionale** country-wide; **fare le -e** climb the stairs

scalare <1a> climb

scalata f climb; **~ al successo** rise to fame

scalatore m, **-trice** f climber

scaldabagno m water heater

scaldare <1a> heat (up); fig **~ la testa a qu** get s.o. worked up

scaldarsi warm up; fig get worked up, get excited

scaldavivande m inv food warmer

scalinata f steps pl

scalino m step

scalo m AVIA stop; MAR port of call; **volo** m **senza ~** nonstop flight; **fare ~ a** call at

scalogna f bad luck; **portare ~** be unlucky

scalognato unlucky

scaloppina f escalope

scalpello m chisel

scaltro shrewd

scalzo barefoot

scambiare <1k> (confondere) mistake (per for); (barattare) exchange, swap F (con for)

scambio m (pl -bi) exchange; di persona mistake; FERR points pl; **-i pl commerciali** trade sg; **~ di lettere** exchange of letters; **~ d'opinioni** exchange of views; **-i pl culturali** cultural exchange sg; **libero ~** free trade

scampagnata f day out in the country

scampanellare <1b> ring

scampanellata f ring

scampi mpl ZO scampi

scampo m escape, way out

scampolo m remnant

scandagliare <1g> sound; fig sound out

scandalistico (pl -ci) scandal-mongering

scandalizzare <1a> scandalize, shock

scandalizzarsi be scandalized or shocked (di by)

scandalizzato scandalized

scandalo m scandal

scandaloso scandalous

scandinavo 1 agg Scandinavian **2** m, **-a** f Scandinavian

scanner m inv INFOR scanner

scannerizzare <1a> INFOR scan

scansafatiche m/f inv lazybones

scansare <1a> (allontanare) move; (evitare) avoid

scansarsi move out of the way

scansia f bookcase

scantinato m cellar

scapito m: **a ~ di** to the detriment of

scapola f shoulder blade, ANAT scapula

scapolo 1 agg single, unmarried **2** m bachelor

scappamento m TEC exhaust

scappare <1a> (fuggire) run away; (affrettarsi) rush, run; **lasciarsi ~ l'occasione** let the opportunity slip; **mi è scappata la pazienza** I lost patience

scappatella f di bambino escapade; **fare delle -lle** get into mischief

scappatoia f way out

scarabocchiare <1k & c> scribble

scarabocchio m (pl -cchi) scribble

scarafaggio m (pl -ggi) cockroach

scaraventare <1b> throw, hurl

scaraventarsi throw or hurl o.s. (contro at)

scarcerare <1l> release

scarcerazione f release

scardinare <1l> take off the hinges

scarica f (pl -che) discharge

scaricare <1l & d> unload; batteria run down; rifiuti, sostanze nocive dump; responsabilità offload, get rid of; **~arsi la coscienza** ease one's conscience; F **~ qu** get rid of s.o.; INFOR **~ dalla rete** download; INFOR **~ su dischetto** download to disk

scaricarsi relax, unwind F; di batteria run down

scarico (pl -chi) **1** agg camion empty; batteria run-down **2** m di merce unloading; luogo dump; di responsabilità offloading; **gas** m **di ~** exhaust (fumes); **tubo** m **di ~** exhaust (pipe); **divieto di ~** no dumping; **-chi pl industriali** industrial waste sg

scarlattina f scarlet fever

scarpa f shoe; **-e pl da uomo / da**

donna men's/women's shoes

scarpata f (*burrone*) escarpment

scarpetta f shoe; **-e** pl **da ginnastica** trainers

scarpinare <1a> trek

scarpinata f trek

scarpone m (heavy) boot; **~ da sci** ski boot

scarseggiare <1f> become scarce; **~ di qc** not have much of sth, be short of sth

scarsezza f, **scarsità** f shortage, scarcity; **~ di viveri** food shortage

scarso scarce, in short supply; **esse-re ~ di qc** be lacking in sth; **quattro chilometri -si** barely four kilometres

scartare <1a> (*svolgere*) unwrap; (*eliminare*) reject

scarto m rejection; (*cosa scartata*) re-ject; **merce f di ~** imperfect goods

scassare <1a> F ruin, wreck

scassarsi F give up the ghost F

scassato F done for F

scassinare <1a> force open

scassinatore m, **-trice** f burglar

scasso m forced entry; **furto m con ~** breaking and entering, burglary

scatenare <1a> fig unleash

scatenarsi fig: *di tempesta* break; *di collera* break out; *di persona* let one's hair down

scatenato unrestrained

scatola f box; *di tonno*, *piselli* tin, can; **in ~** *cibo* tinned, canned; AVIA **~ nera** black box

scattare <1a> **1** v/t FOT take **2** v/i go off; *di serratura* catch; (*arrabbiarsi*) lose one's temper; *di atleta* put on a spurt; **~ in piedi** jump up; **far ~** acti-vate

scatto m click; SP spurt; FOTO expo-sure; *di foto* taking; TELEC unit; FOTO **~ automatico** automatic timer; **uno ~ di rabbia** an angry ges-ture; **~ di stipendio** automatic raise

scavalcare <1d> *muro* climb (over)

scavare <1a> *con pala* dig; *con trivella* excavate

scavi mpl archeologici dig sg

scegliere <3ss> choose, pick, select

scelgo → **scegliere**

scelta f choice, selection; **di prima ~** first-rate; **prendine uno a ~** take your pick

scelto 1 pp → **scegliere 2** agg hand-picked; *merce*, *pubblico* (specially) selected

scemo 1 agg stupid, idiotic **2** m, **-a** f idiot

scena theatre, Am theater; (*scenata*) scene; fig **colpo** m **di ~** coup de théâtre; **mettere in ~** produce; fig **fare ~ muta** be struck dumb

scenario m (pl -ri) screenplay; fig scenery

scenata f scene; **fare una ~** (**a qu**) make a scene

scendere <3c> **1** v/i andare go down, descend; *venire* come down, de-scend; *da cavallo* get down, dis-mount; *dal treno, dall' autobus* get off; *dalla macchina* get out; *di temperatura, prezzi* go down, drop; **~ a terra** come (back) down to earth **2** v/t: **~ le scale** andare go down the stairs; *venire* come down the stairs

scendiletto m bedside rug

sceneggiatura f screenplay

scenografia f sets pl

scenografo m, **-a** f set designer

scetticismo m scepticism, Am skep-ticism

scettico 1 agg sceptical, Am skepti-cal **2** m, **-a** f sceptic, Am skeptic

scheda f card; (*formulario*) form; **~ elettorale** ballot (paper); INFOR **~ grafica** graphics card; **~ telefonica** phonecard

schedario m (pl -ri) file

schedina f pools coupon

scheggia f (pl -gge) sliver

scheletro m skeleton

schema m (pl -i) diagram; (*abboz-zo*) outline

schematico (pl -ci) general; *disegno* schematic

schematizzare <1a> outline

scherma f fencing; **tirare di ~** fence

schermo m screen; (*riparo*) shield

scherzare <1a> play; (*burlare*) joke

scherzo m joke; MUS scherzo;

S

essere uno ~ (*facile*) be child's play; **-i a parte** joking aside; **per ~ fare**, **dire qc** as a joke

scherzoso playful

schiaccianoci *m inv* pair of nutcrackers, nutcrackers *pl*

schiacciare <1f> **1** *v/t* crush; *noce* crack; **~ un piede a qu** step on s.o.'s toes; F **~ un sonnellino** have a snooze F, have forty winks F **2** *v/i* SP smash

schiacciato crushed, squashed

schiaffeggiare <1f> slap

schiaffo *m* slap

schiamazzare <1a> make a din

schiamazzo *m* yell, scream

schiantare <1a> **1** *v/t* crash, smash **2** *v/i e* **schiantarsi** crash

schianto *m* crash

schiarire <4d> lighten

schiarirsi brighten up

schiarita *f* bright spell

schiavitù *f* slavery

schiavo 1 *agg*: **essere ~ di** be a slave to **2** *m*, **-a** *f* slave

schiena *f* back; **mal di ~** back ache

schienale *m di sedile* back

schiera *f* group; **a ~** in ranks

schierare <1b> line up

schierarsi: **~ in favore di qu** come out in favo(u)r of s.o.

schietto pure; *fig* frank

schifezza *f*: **che ~!** how disgusting!

schifo *m* disgust; **fare ~ a qu** disgust s.o.

schifoso disgusting; (*pessimo*) dreadful

schioppo *m* shotgun

schiuma *f* foam; **~ da bagno** bubble bath; **~ da barba** shaving foam

schiumoso foamy

schivare <1a> avoid, dodge F

schivo shy

schizzare <1a> **1** *v/t* (*spruzzare*) squirt; (*abbozzare*) sketch **2** *v/i* squirt; (*saltare*) jump

schizzinoso fussy

schizzo *m* squirt; (*abbozzo*) (*lightning*) sketch

sci *m inv* ski; *attività* skiing; **~ acquatico** water ski/skiing; **~ di**

fondo cross-country ski/skiing

sciacquare <1a> rinse

sciacquatura *f* rinse

sciagura *f* disaster

sciagurato *giorno*, *evento* unfortunate

scialle *m* shawl

scialuppa *f* dinghy; **~ di salvataggio** lifeboat

sciame *m* swarm

sciare <1h> ski

sciarpa *f* scarf

sciatica *f* sciatica

sciatore *m*, **-trice** *f* skier

sciatteria *f* untidiness, sloppiness F

sciatto untidy, sloppy F

scientifico (*pl* -ci) scientific

scienza *f* science; **-e** *pl* **naturali** natural science

scienziato *m*, **-a** *f* scientist

scimmia *f* monkey

scimmiottare <1c> ape

scimpanzè *m inv* chimpanzee, chimp F

scintilla *f* spark

scintillante sparkling

scintillare <1a> sparkle

scintillio *m* sparkle

sciocchezza *f* (*idiozia*) stupidity; **è solo una ~** it's nothing

sciocco (*pl* -cchi) **1** *agg* silly **2** *m*, **-a** *f* silly thing

sciogliere <3ss> untie; *capelli* undo, let down; *matrimonio* dissolve; *neve* melt; *dubbio*, *problema* clear up

sciogliersi *di corda*, *nodo* come undone; *di burro*, *neve* melt; *di questione*, *problema* resolve itself

scioglilingua *m inv* tongue-twister

scioltezza *f* nimbleness; *fisica* agility

sciolto 1 *pp* → **sciogliere 2** *agg neve*, *ghiaccio* melted; *matrimonio* dissolved; **a briglia -a** at breakneck speed

scioperante *m/f* striker

scioperare <1l & c> strike

sciopero *m* strike; **fare ~** go on strike; **~ bianco** work-to-rule; **~ generale** general strike; **~ della fame** hunger strike

sciovia *f* ski-lift

sciovinismo *m* chauvinism

sciovinista *m/f* (*mpl* -i) chauvinist

scipito bland

scippatore *m*, **-trice** *f* bag-snatcher

scippo *m* bag-snatching

scirocco *m* sirocco

sciroppo *m* syrup

scissione *f* splitting

scisto *m* GEOL schist

sciupare <1a> (*logorare*) wear out; *salute* ruin; *tempo, denaro* waste, fritter away

sciupato *persona* drawn; *cosa* worn out

scivolare <1l> slide; (*cadere*) slip

scivolo *m* slide; (*caduta*) slip; *gioco* chute; **~ d'emergenza** escape chute

scivoloso slippery

sclerosi *f inv* MED sclerosis; **~ multipla** multiple sclerosis, MS

scocciare F <1f> bother, annoy, hassle F

scocciatore F *m*, **-trice** *f* pest F, nuisance F

scocciatura F *f* nuisance F

scodella *f* bowl

scogliera *f* cliff

scoglio *m* (*pl* -gli) rock; *fig* stumbling block

scoiattolo *m* squirrel

scolapasta *m inv* colander

scolare <1a> drain

scolaro *m*, **-a** *f* schoolboy; *ragazza* schoolgirl

scolastico (*pl* -ci) school *attr*

scoliosi *f inv* curvature of the spine

scollato low-necked; *donna* wearing a low neck

scollatura *f* neck(line)

scollo *m* neck

scolo *m* drainage

scolorire <4d> **1** *v/t* fade **2** *v/i e* **scolorirsi** fade

scolorito faded

scolpire <4d> *marmo, statua* sculpt; *legno* carve; *fig* engrave

scommessa *f* bet

scommesso *pp* → **scommettere**

scommettere <3ee> bet

scomodare <1l & c> disturb

scomodarsi put o.s. out; **non si scomodi** please don't go to any bother

scomodo uncomfortable; (*non pratico*) inconvenient

scomparire <4e> disappear

scomparsa *f* disappearance

scomparso *pp* → **scomparire**

scompartimento *m* compartment; FERR **~ per (non) fumatori** (non-)smoking compartment

scompenso *m* imbalance; **~ cardiaco** cardiac insufficiency

scompigliare <1g> *persona* ruffle the hair of; *capelli* ruffle

scompiglio *m* (*pl* -gli) confusion

scomponibile flat pack *attr*, modular

scomporre <3ll> break down

scomporsi: senza ~ without showing any emotion

sconcertante disconcerting

sconcio (*pl* -ci) indecent; *parola* disgusting, filthy

sconclusionato incoherent

sconfiggere <3cc> defeat

sconfinare <1a> trespass; MIL cross the border

sconfinato vast, boundless

sconfitta *f* defeat

sconfitto *pp* → **sconfiggere**

sconfortante discouraging, disheartening

sconfortare <1c> discourage, dishearten

sconforto *m* discouragement

scongelare <1b> thaw

scongiurare <1a> beg; *pericolo* avert

sconosciuto 1 *agg* unknown **2** *m*, **-a** *f* stranger

sconsolato disconsolate

scontare <1a> FIN deduct, discount; *pena* serve

scontato discounted; (*previsto*) expected; **~ del 30%** 30% discount *or* deduction

scontento 1 *agg* unhappy, not satisfied (*di* with) **2** *m* unhappiness, dissatisfaction

sconto *m* discount; **praticare uno ~**

give a discount

scontrarsi <1a> collide (**con** with); *fig* clash (**con** with)

scontrino m receipt; **fare lo ~ alla cassa** please pay at the cash desk before ordering

scontro m AUTO collision; *fig* clash

scontroso unpleasant, disagreeable

sconveniente inappropriate, unacceptable

sconvolgente upsetting, distressing; **di un'intelligenza ~** incredibly intelligent

sconvolgere <3d> upset

sconvolto **1** pp → **sconvolgere** **2** agg paese in upheaval

scopa f broom

scopare <1a> sweep; P shag P

scoperchiare <1k> pentola take the lid off

scoperta f discovery

scoperto **1** pp → **scoprire** **2** agg pentola uncovered; **a capo** bareheaded; **assegno** m **~** bad cheque, rubber cheque F **3** m FIN overdraft; **allo ~** in the open

scopo m aim, purpose; **allo ~ di fare qc** in order to do sth; **senza ~** aimlessly

scoppiare <1k & c> di bomba, petardo explode; di palloncino, pneumatico burst; **~ in lacrime** burst into tears; **~ a ridere** burst out laughing; **~ di caldo** be boiling hot

scoppio m (pl -ppi) explosion; di palloncino bursting; fig outbreak

scoprire <4f> contenitore take the lid off; (denudare) uncover; piani, verità discover, find out

scoraggiare <1f> discourage, dishearten

scoraggiarsi become discouraged, lose heart

scoraggiato discouraged, disheartened

scorciatoia f short cut

scordare <1c>, **scordarsi di** forget

scordato MUS out of tune

scoreggia f (pl -gge) F fart F

scoreggiare <1f> F fart F

scorgere <3d> see, make out; **non**

farsi ~ not let o.s. be seen

scoria f waste

scorpione m scorpion; ASTR **Scorpione** Scorpio

scorrere <3o> **1** v/i flow, run; di tempo go past, pass **2** v/t giornale skim

scorretto (errato) incorrect; (non onesto) unfair

scorrevole porta sliding; stile flowing

scorso **1** pp → **scorrere** **2** agg: **l'anno ~** last year

scorta f escort; (provvista) supply, stock

scortare <1c> escort

scortese rude, discourteous

scortesia f rudeness, lack of courtesy

scorto pp → **scorgere**

scorza f peel; fig exterior

scossa f shake; **~ di terremoto** (earth) tremor; **~ elettrica** electric shock

scosso pp → **scuotere**

scostare <1c> move away (**da** from)

scostarsi move (aside); fig **~ della retta via** leave the straight and narrow

scottante delicate

scottare <1c> **1** v/t burn; GASTR verdure blanch; **mi sono scottato le dita** I burned my fingers **2** v/i burn; **scotta!** it's hot!

scottato verdure blanched

scottatura f burn; **ho già avuto troppe -e** I've had my fingers burned once too often

Scozia f Scotland

scozzese **1** agg Scottish **2** m/f Scot

screditare <1l> discredit

scremato skimmed; **parzialmente ~** semi-skimmed

screpolare <1l & b> e **screpolarsi** crack

screpolatura f crack

scricchiolare <1l> creak

scricchiolio m (pl -ii) creak

scricciolo m ZO wren

scritta f inscription

scritto **1** pp → **scrivere** **2** m writing; **per ~** in writing

scrittore m, **-trice** f writer

scrittura f writing; REL scripture

scritturare <1a> engage, sign F

scrivania f desk

scrivere <3tt> write; (annotare) write down; **come si scrive ... ?** how do you spell ... ?

scroccare <1c & d> F scrounge F

scrollare <1c> shake; **~ le spalle** shrug (one's shoulders)

scrosciare <1f & c> di pioggia fall in torrents

scrupolo m scruple; **senza -i** unscrupulous

scrupolosità f scrupulousness

scrupoloso scrupulous

scrutare <1a> look at intently; orizzonte scan

scrutatore m, **-trice** f POL person counting votes

scrutinio m (pl -ni) POL counting; EDU teachers' meeting to discuss pupils' performance

scucire <4a> unpick; F **scuci i soldi!** cough up! F

scucirsi come apart at the seams

scuderia f stable

scudetto m SP championship

scudo m shield

sculacciare <1f> spank

scultore m, **-trice** f sculptor

scultura f sculpture

scuola f school; **~ di lingue** language school; **~ elementare** primary school; **~ media** secondary school; **~ parificata** private school officially recognized by the state; **~ serale** evening classes pl; **~ superiore** high school; **~ guida** driving school; **andare a ~** go to school

scuotere <3ff> shake

scuotersi shake off

scure f ax(e)

scurire <4d> v/t & v/i darken

scuro 1 agg dark **2** m darkness; **essere allo ~ di qc** be in the dark about sth

scusa f excuse; **chiedere ~** apologize

scusare <1a> forgive; (giustificare) excuse; **mi scusi** I'm sorry; **scusi, scusa** excuse me

scusarsi apologize

S.C.V. abbr (= **Stato della Città del Vaticano**) Vatican City

s.d. abbr (= **senza data**) undated

sdebitarsi <1l> pay one's debts

sdegnare <1a> (disprezzare) despise; (fare arrabbiare) incense

sdegnarsi get angry (**con** with)

sdegno m moral indignation

sdentato toothless

sdoganamento m customs clearance

sdoganare <1a> clear through customs

sdolcinato sloppy

sdraiare <1i> lay

sdraiarsi lie down

sdraiato lying down

sdraio m: **(sedia f a) ~** deck chair

se¹ cong if; **~ mai** if need be; **~ mai arrivasse ...** should he arrive ...; **come** as if; **~ no** if not

se² pron = **si** in front of **lo, la, li, le, ne**

sé oneself; lui himself; lei herself; loro themselves; esso, essa itself; **da ~** (by) himself / herself / themselves

sebbene even though, although; **~ abbia detto la verità** even though he told the truth

secca f (pl -cche) shallows

seccante fig annoying

seccare <1d> **1** v/t dry; fig annoy **2** v/i e **seccarsi** primary dry; fig get annoyed

seccatore m, **-trice** f nuisance, pest

seccatura f nuisance

secchio m (pl -cchi) bucket, pail

secco (pl -cchi) **1** agg dry; fiori, pomodori dried; risposta, tono curt; **frutta f -a** dried fruit; (noci) nuts pl **2** m: **rimanere a ~** run out of petrol; fig run out of money; **pulire a ~** dryclean

secolare albero, tradizione hundred-year old

secolo m century; **ti ho aspettato un ~!** I waited hours for you!

seconda f AUTO second (gear); FERR second class; EDU second year

secondario (pl -ri) secondary

secondo 1 agg second; **di -a mano** second-hand; **~ fine** ulterior motive, hidden agenda **2** *prp* according to; ~ **me** in my opinion; ~ **le istruzioni** as per instructions **3** *m* second; GASTR main course

secrétaire *m inv* mobile writing desk

sedano *m* celery

sedare <1b> calm (down)

sedativo *m* sedative

sede *f* headquarters; **la Santa Sede** the Holy See

sedentario (*pl* -ri) sedentary

sedere **1** *m* F rear end F **2** *v/i* <2o> e **sedersi** sit down

sedia *f* chair; ~ **a sdraio** deck chair; ~ **a dondolo** rocking chair; ~ **a rotelle** wheelchair

sedicesimo *m/agg* sixteenth

sedicente so-called, self-styled

sedici sixteen

sedile *m* seat; AUTO ~ **posteriore** back seat

seducente attractive

sedurre <3e> seduce; (*attrarre*) attract

seduta *f* session; (*posa*) sitting; ~ **plenaria** plenary session

seduto seated

seduttore *m*, -**trice** *f* seducer; *donna* seductress

seduzione *f* seduction

S.E. e O. *abbr* (= **salvo errori e omissioni**) E & OE (= errors and omissions excepted)

seg. *abbr* (= **seguente**) foll. (= following)

sega *f* (*pl* -ghe) saw

segale *f* rye; **pane m di ~** rye bread

segare <1e> saw

segatura *f* sawdust

seggio *m* (*pl* -ggi) seat; ~ (**elettorale**) polling station

seggiola *f* chair

seggiolino *m di macchina, bicicletta* child's seat

seggiolone *m* high chair

seggiovia *f* chair lift

seggo → **sedere**

segnalare <1a> signal; (*annunciare*) report

segnale *m* signal; (*segno*) sign; ~ **d'allarme** alarm; ~ **orario** (**alla ra-**

dio) time signal; ~ **stradale** road sign

segnaletica *f* signs *pl*; ~ **stradale** road signs *pl*

segnalibro *m* bookmark

segnare <1a> (*marcare*) mark; (*annotare*) note down; SP score; ~ **a dito qu** point s.o. out, point to s.o.; **sentirsi segnato a dito** feel the finger pointed at you; **ha segnato due gol** he scored two goals

segno *m* sign; (*traccia*) mark, trace; (*cenno*) gesture, sign; -**i caratteristici** distinguishing marks; *fig* **non dar -i di vita** not get in touch; **cogliere nel ~** hit the nail on the head; ~ **zodiacale** sign of the zodiac; **farsi il ~ della croce** cross o.s.; **lasciare il ~** leave a mark

segretaria *f* secretary; ~ **di direzione** executive secretary

segretariato *m* secretariat

segretario *m* (*pl* -ri) secretary; POL ~ **di partito** party leader

segreteria *f carica* secretaryship; *ufficio* administrative office; *attività* secretarial duties *pl*; ~ **telefonica** answering machine, answerphone

segreto **1** *agg* secret **2** *m* secret; ~ **professionale** confidentiality

seguace *m/f* disciple, follower

seguente next, following

seguire <4a> **1** *v/t* follow; *corso* take **2** *v/i* follow (**a qc** sth); **come segue** as follows

seguitare <1l>: ~ **a fare qc** carry on doing sth

seguito *m persone* retinue; (*sostenitori*) followers; *di film* sequel; **di ~** one after the other, in succession; **in ~** after that; **in ~ a** following, in the wake of

sei[1] → **essere**

sei[2] six

seicento **1** *agg* six hundred **2** *m*: **il Seicento** the seventeenth century

selciato *m* paving

selezione *f* selection

self-service *m inv* self-service

sella *f* saddle

sellino *m* saddle

seltz m: **acqua f di** ~ soda (water)

selva f forest

selvaggina f game

selvaggio (pl -ggi) **1** agg animale, fiori wild; tribù, omicidio savage **2** m, **-a** f savage

selvatico (pl -ci) wild

semaforo m traffic lights

sembrare <1a> seem; (assomigliare a) resemble, look like

seme m seed

semestre m six months; EDU term

semicerchio m (pl -chi) semi-circle, half-moon

semicircolare semi-circular

semiconduttore m EL semi-conductor

semifinale f semi-final

semifreddo m soft icecream

semilavorato m semi-finished

semina f sowing

seminare <1l> sow

seminario m (pl -ri) seminar

seminudo half-naked

seminuovo practically new

semisfera f hemisphere

semolino m semolina

semplice simple; (non doppio) single; (spontaneo) natural

semplicità f simplicity

semplificare <1m & d> simplify

semplificazione f simplification

sempre always; **ci conosciamo da ~** we've known each other practically for ever; **è quello di ~** he's the same as always; **per** ~ for ever; ~ **più** more and more; ~ **più vecchio** older and older; **piove ~ di più** the rain's getting heavier and heavier; ~ **che** as long as, on condition that

sen. abbr (= **senatore**) Sen (= senator)

senape f mustard

senato m senate

senatore m, **-trice** f senator

senile senile

senno m common sense; **uscire di** ~ lose one's mind; (arrabbiarsi) lose control

seno m breast; GEOG inlet; MAT sine; **in ~ a** in

sensato sensible

sensazionale sensational

sensazione f sensation, feeling; (impressione) feeling; **fare** ~ cause a sensation; **ho la ~ che** I have a feeling that

sensibile sensitive; (evidente) significant, substantial

sensibilità f sensitivity

sensibilizzare <1a> make more aware (**a** of)

senso m sense; (significato) meaning; (direzione) direction; **buon** ~ common sense; ~ **unico** one way; ~ **vietato** no entry; **in ~ orario** clockwise; **privo di -i** unconscious; **perdere i -i** faint

sensore m TEC sensor

sensuale sensual

sensualità f sensuality

sentenza f DIR verdict; ~ **di morte** death sentence

sentenziare <1g> fig pass judgment

sentiero m path

sentimentale sentimental

sentimento m feeling, sentiment

sentinella f sentry

sentire <4b> feel; (udire) hear; (ascoltare) listen to; odore smell; cibo taste

sentirsi feel; **sentirsela di fare qc** feel up to doing sth

senza without; **senz'altro** definitely; ~ **dubbio** more than likely, probably; ~ **impegno** (with) no obligation or commitment; ~ **di me** without me

senzatetto m/f inv homeless person; **i -i** pl the homeless

separare <1a or 1l & b> separate

separarsi separate, split up

separazione f separation; ~ **dei beni** division of property

sepolto pp → **seppellire**

sepoltura f burial

seppellire <4d> bury

seppia f cuttle fish

seppure even if

sequestrare <1b> confiscate; DIR impound, seize; (rapire) kidnap

sequestro m kidnap(ping); DIR

impounding, seizure

sera f evening; **di ~** in the evenings; **questa ~** this evening; **verso ~** towards evening

serale evening *attr*

serata f evening; (*festa*) party; **~ danzante** dance; **~ di gala** gala (evening)

serbatoio m (*pl* -oi) tank; **~ di riserva** reserve tank

serbo¹ **1** *agg* Serbian **2** m, **-a** f Serb

serbo² m: **tenere in ~** keep; **avere qc in ~** have sth in store

serenata f serenade

serenità f serenity

sereno serene; *fig* relaxed, calm

serial m *inv* serial

seriale INFOR serial; **porta** f **~** serial port

sericoltura f silk-worm farming

serie f *inv* series; **articolo** m **di ~** mass produced item; **produzione** f **in ~** mass production

serietà f seriousness

serigrafia f silk-screen printing

serio (*pl* -ri) **1** *agg* serious; (*affidabile*) reliable **2** m: **sul ~** seriously

sermone m sermon

serpe f grass snake

serpeggiare <1f> wind

serpente m snake

serpentina f *linea* wavy line; *strada* winding street

serra f greenhouse

serramanico m: **coltello** m **a ~** flick knife

serranda f shutter

serrare <1b> close; *denti, pugni* clench; **~ il ritmo** step up the pace

serrata f lock-out

serratura f lock; **~ a combinazione** combination lock

servire <4b> **1** v/i: *non mi serve* I don't need it; **a che serve questo?** what's this for?; **~ da bere a qu** pour s.o. a drink **2** v/t serve; *mi serve aiuto* I need help

servirsi (*usare*) use (**di** sth); **prego, si serva!** *a tavola* please help yourself!

servitù f slavery, servitude; (*persona-le*) servants *pl*

servizio m (*pl* -zi) service; (*favore*) favo(u)r; (*dipartimento*) department; *in giornale* feature (story); **lavorare a mezzo ~** work part-time; **~ assistenza tecnica** after-sales service; **~ civile** community service in lieu of military service; **~ militare** military service; **~ d'emergenza** emergency service; **~ da tavola** dinner service; **di ~** on duty; **fuori ~** out of order; **in ~** on duty; **-zi** *pl* services

servofreno m servo brake

servosterzo m power steering

sesamo m sesame

sessanta sixty

sessantenne sixty-year-old

sessantesimo m/agg sixtieth

sessantina f: **una ~** about sixty (**di** sth); **sulla ~** about sixty

sesso m sex

sessuale sexual

sessualità f sexuality

sesto m/agg sixth

seta f silk; **~ artificiale** artificial silk

sete f thirst; **aver ~** be thirsty

setola f bristle

setta f sect

settanta seventy

settantenne seventy-year-old

settantesimo m/agg seventieth

settantina f: **una ~** about seventy (**di** sth); **sulla ~** about seventy

settare <1a> *macchina, computer* set up

sette seven

settecento **1** *agg* seven hundred **2** m: **il Settecento** the eighteenth century

settembre m September

settentrionale **1** *agg* northern **2** m/f northerner

settentrione m north

setticemia f septic(a)emia

settimana f week; **~ corta** five-day week; **~ santa** Easter week

settimanale m/agg weekly

settimo m/agg seventh

settore m sector

severità f severity

severo severe

sezione f section

sfaccendato idle

sfacchinata f backbreaking job

sfacciato cheeky

sfacelo m ruin

sfamare <1a> feed

sfarfallio m flicker

sfarzo m splendo(u)r

sfarzoso magnificent

sfasciare <1f> smash; MED unbandage

sfasciarsi smash

sfaticato m, **-a** f idler

sfavillare <1a> di occhi sparkle; di fuoco flicker

sfavillio m di occhi sparkle

sfavore m disadvantage

sfavorevole unfavourable

sfera f sphere; ~ **d'azione** responsibilities, duties; ~ **di competenza** area of expertise

sferico (pl -ci) spherical

sfida f challenge

sfidare <1a> challenge

sfiducia f distrust, mistrust; **voto di** ~ vote of no confidence

sfiduciato discouraged, disheartened

sfigurare <1a> **1** v/t disfigure **2** v/i look out of place

sfigurato disfigured

sfilare <1a> **1** v/t unthread; (togliere) take off **2** v/i parade

sfilata f: ~ **di moda** fashion show

sfinimento m exhaustion

sfinito exhausted

sfiorare <1a> brush; argomento touch on

sfiorire <4d> fade, wither

sfitto empty, not let

sfocato foto blurred

sfociare <1f> flow

sfogare <1e> rabbia, frustrazione vent, get rid of (**con**, **su** on)

sfogarsi vent one's feelings; **non ti sfogare su di me** don't take it out on me; ~ **con qu** confide in s.o., pour one's heart out to s.o.

sfoglia: **pasta** f ~ puff pastry

sfogliare <1g & c> libro leaf through

sfogo m (pl -ghi) outlet; MED rash

sfoltire <4d> thin

sfondare <1a> break; porta break down; muro knock down; pavimento break through

sfondo m background

sformare <1a> stretch out of shape

sformato m GASTR soufflé

sfornito: **essere** ~ **di qc** be out of sth

sfortuna f bad luck, misfortune

sfortunatamente unfortunately

sfortunato unlucky, unfortunate

sforzare <1c> strain

sforzarsi try very hard, make every effort

sforzo m effort; fisico strain; **fare uno** ~ make an effort; fisicamente strain o.s.; **senza** ~ effortlessly

sfracellarsi <1b> break into pieces, shatter

sfrattare <1a> evict

sfratto m eviction; avviso notice to quit

sfregare <1e> rub

sfrenato unrestrained

sfrontato insolent

sfruttamento m exploitation

sfruttare <1a> exploit

sfuggevole fleeting

sfuggire <4a> (scampare) escape (**a** from); **mi è sfuggito di mente** it slipped my mind

sfuggita f: **di** ~ in passing

sfumatura f nuance; di colore shade

sfuriata f (angry) tirade

sfuso loose; burro melted; vino in bulk

sgabello m stool

sgabuzzino m cupboard

sgambetto m: **fare lo** ~ **a qu** trip s.o. up

sganciare <1f> unhook; FERR uncouple; F soldi fork out F

sganciarsi become unhooked; di persona release o.s.; fig free o.s.

sgarbato rude

sgarbo m discourtesy

sgelare <1b> thaw

sgelo m thaw

sghembo crooked; **di** ~ crookedly, not in a straight line

S

sgobbare <1c> slave

sgobbone *m*, **-a** *f* F swot F

sgocciolare <1l> *v/t & v/i* drip

sgomberare <1l> → **sgombrare**

sgombero *m di strada* clearing; *(trasloco)* removal

sgombrare <1a> *strada*, *stanza* clear; *ostacolo* remove; *appartamento* clear out, empty

sgombro[1] *agg strada*, *stanza* empty

sgombro[2] *m* mackerel

sgomentare <1a> frighten

sgomentarsi be frightened

sgomento *m* fear

sgonfiare <1k> **1** *v/t* let the air out of **2** *v/i e* **sgonfiarsi** become deflated; *il braccio si è sgonfiato* the swelling in the arm has gone down

sgonfio *(pl* -fi) flat; MED not swollen

sgradevole unpleasant

sgradito unwelcome

sgranchire <4d>, **sgranchirsi**: **~ le gambe** stretch one's legs

sgraziato awkward

sgridare <1a> scold, tell off F

sgridata *f* scolding, telling off F

sguaiato raucous

sgualdrina *f* tart

sguardo *m* look; *(occhiata)* glance; *al primo ~* at first glance

sguazzare <1a> splash about; *fig* F **~ nei soldi** be rolling (in it) F

sgusciare <1f> **1** *v/t* shell **2** *v/i* slip away; *mi è sgusciato di mano* it slipped out of my hand

shampoo *m inv* shampoo

shock *m inv* shock; **~ culturale** culture shock

si[1] *pron* oneself; *lui* himself; *lei* herself; *esso*, *essa* itself; *loro* themselves; *reciproco* each other; **spazzolarsi i capelli** brush one's hair; **~ è spazzolato i capelli** he brushed his hair; **~ dice** they say; **cosa ~ può dire?** what can one say?, what can I say?; **~ capisce da sé** it's self-evident

si[2] *m* MUS B

sì *avv* yes; **dire di ~** say yes; **~ e no** yes and no; **penso di ~** I think so

sia: **~ ... ~ ...** both ... and ...; *(o l'uno o l'altro)* either ... or ...; **~ che ... ~ che ...** whether ... or whether ...

siamo → **essere**

sibilare <1l> hiss; *di vento* whistle

sibilo *m* hiss; *di vento* whistle

sicario *m* hired killer, hit man F

sicché (and) so

siccità *f* drought

siccome since

Sicilia *f* Sicily

siciliano 1 *agg* Sicilian **2** *m*, **-a** *f* Sicilian

sicura *f* safety catch

sicurezza *f* security; *(protezione)* safety; *(certezza)* certainty; **pubblica ~** police; **cintura** *f* **di ~** safety belt; **misure** *fpl* **di ~** safety measures

sicuro 1 *agg luogo* safe; *investimento* sound, safe; *(certo)* sure; **~ di sé** self-confident, sure of o.s.; **di ~** definitely **2** *m*: **essere al ~ da qc** be safe from sth; **mettere al ~** put in a safe place

siderurgia *f* iron and steel industry

sidro *m* cider

siedo → **sedere**

siepe *f* hedge

siero *m* MED serum

sieropositivo HIV positive

siesta *f* siesta

siete → **essere**

sifilide *f* MED syphilis

sig. *abbr* (= **signore**) Mr (= mister)

sigaretta *f* cigarette; **~ col filtro** filter tip

sigaro *m* cigar

sigg. *abbr* (= **signori**) Messrs

sigillare <1a> seal

sigillo *m* seal

sigla *f* initials *pl*; *musicale* theme (tune)

sig.na *abbr* (= **signorina**) Miss, Ms

significare <1m & d> mean

significativo significant

significato *m* meaning

signora *f* lady; **mi scusi, ~!** excuse me!; **la ~ Rossi** Mrs Rossi; **-e e signori** ladies and gentlemen

signore *m* gentleman; **mi scusi, ~!** excuse me!; **il signor Rossi** Mr Rossi; **i -i Rossi** Mr and Mrs Rossi

signorile *appartamento* luxury; *modi* gentlemanly

signorina *f* young lady; *è ancora ~* she's not married; *la ~ Rossi* Miss Rossi

sig.ra *abbr* (= *signora*) Mrs

silenziatore *m* silencer, *Am* muffler

silenzio *m* silence; *fare ~* be quiet; *~!* silence!, quiet!

silenzioso silent

sillaba *f* syllable

sillabare <1l> split into syllables

silo *m* silo

siluro *m* MAR torpedo

simboleggiare <1f> symbolize

simbolico (*pl* -ci) symbolic

simbolismo *m* symbolism

simbolo *m* symbol

simile similar

simmetria *f* symmetry

simmetrico (*pl* -ci) symmetric(al)

simpatia *f* liking; (*affinità*) sympathy; *avere ~ per qu* like s.o.

simpatico (*pl* -ci) likeable

simpatizzare <1a> become friends

simposio *m* (*pl* -si) symposium

simulare <1l> feign; TEC simulate

simulazione *f* pretence, *Am* pretense; TECH simulation; *~ elettronica* electronic simulation

sinagoga *f* (*pl* -ghe) synagogue

sinceramente sincerely; (*in verità*) honestly

sincerarsi <1b> make sure

sincerità *f* sincerity

sincero sincere

sincronizzare <1a> synchronize

sindacalista *m/f* (*mpl* -i) trade unionist

sindacato *m* trade union

sindaco *m* (*pl* -ci) mayor

sinfonia *f* symphony

sinfonico (*pl* -ci) symphonic

singhiozzare <1a> sob

singhiozzo *m*: *avere il ~* have hiccups; *-zi pl* sobs

single *m/f inv* single

singolare **1** *agg* singular; (*insolito*) unusual; (*strano*) strange **2** *m* singular; SP singles

singolo **1** *agg* individual; *camera,* *letto* single **2** *m* individual; SP singles

sinistra *f* left; *a ~* on the left; *andare a ~* to the left

sinistro **1** *agg* left, left-hand; *fig* sinister **2** *m* accident

sino → *fino*

sinonimo **1** *agg* synonymous **2** *m* synonym

sintesi *f inv* synthesis; (*riassunto*) summary

sintetico (*pl* -ci) synthetic; (*riassunto*) brief; *materiale m ~* synthetic (material)

sintetizzare <1a> synthesize; (*riassumere*) summarize, sum up

sintomo *m* symptom

sintonia *f* RAD tuning; *fig essere in ~* be on the same wavelength (*con* as)

sintonizzare <1a> RAD tune

sintonizzarsi <1a> tune in (*su* to)

sinusite *f* sinusitis

sipario *m* (*pl* -ri) curtain

sirena *f* siren; *mitologica* mermaid; *~ d'allarme* alarm

siringa *f* (*pl* -ghe) MED syringe; *~ monouso* disposable syringe

sismico (*pl* -ci) seismic

sistema *m* (*pl* -i) system; *~ antibloccaggio* anti-lock braking system; *~ elettorale proporzionale* proportional representation; *~ immunitario* immune system; *~ monetario* monetary system; INFOR *~ operativo* operating system

sistemare <1b> put; (*mettere in ordine*) arrange; *casa* do up

sistemarsi tidy o.s. up; (*trovare casa, sposarsi*) settle down

sistematico (*pl* -ci) systematic

sistemazione *f* place; (*lavoro*) job; *in albergo* accommodation

sito site; *in ~* on the premises

situare <1l> locate, find

situato: *essere ~* be situated

situazione *f* situation

slacciare <1f> undo

slalom *m* slalom

slanciato slender

slancio *m* (*pl* -ci) impulse

slavo **1** *agg* Slav, Slavonic **2** *m*, *-a f* Slav

sleale disloyal
slealtà f disloyalty
slegare <1e> untie
slegarsi free o.s.
slegato fig incoherent, disjointed
slip m inv underpants; da donna knickers; ~ da bagno bathing trunks
slitta f sledge
slittino m sled; SP bobsleigh
s.l.m. abbr (= sul livello del mare) above sea level
slogan m inv slogan
slogare <1e> dislocate
slogarsi: ~ una caviglia sprain one's ankle
slogatura f sprain
sloggiare <1f> move out
smacchiare <1k> take the stains out of
smacchiatore m stain remover
smagliatura f ladder, Am run; MED stretch mark
smaltare <1a> enamel
smaltimento m FIN disposal of stock; di rifiuti tossici disposal
smaltire <4d> dispose of
smalto m enamel; per ceramiche glaze; ~ per unghie nail varnish or polish
smantellamento m dismantling
smantellare <1b> dismantle
smarrimento m loss
smarrire <4d> lose
smarrirsi get lost
smarrito 1 pp → **smarrire** 2 agg lost
smascherare <1l> unmask
Sme abbr (= Sistema monetario europeo) EMS (= European Monetary System)
smemorato forgetful
smentire <4d> prove to be wrong; non si smentisce mai! he doesn't change!
smentita f denial
smeraldo 1 m emerald 2 agg emerald (green)
smercio m (pl -ci) sale
smesso pp → **smettere**
smettere <3ee> 1 v/t stop; abiti stop

wearing 2 v/i stop (di fare qc doing sth)
smilitarizzare <1a> demilitarize
smilitarizzazione f demilitarization
sminuire <4d> problema downplay; persona belittle
smistamento m FERR shunting
smistare <1a> FERR shunt
smisurato boundless
smodato excessive
smog m smog
smontabile which can be taken apart, Am knockdown
smontaggio m dismantling
smontare <1a> 1 v/i (da cavallo) dismount 2 v/t dismantle; persona deflate
smorfia f grimace
smorfioso affected, simpering
smorto persona deathly pale; colore dull
smorzare <1c> colore tone down; luce dim; entusiasmo dampen
smuovere <3ff> shift, move
snellezza f slenderness
snellire <4d> slim down; fig pare down
snello slim, slender
snervante irritating, wearing on the nerves
snob 1 agg snobbish 2 m/f inv snob
SO abbr (= sud-ovest) SW (= southwest)
so → **sapere**
sobborgo m (pl -ghi) suburb
sobrietà f sobriety
sobrio (pl -ri) sober
Soc. abbr (= società) Co (= company); soc. (= society)
socchiudere <3b> half-close
socchiuso 1 pp → **socchiudere** 2 agg half-closed; porta ajar
soccombere <3a> succumb
soccorrere <3o> help
soccorritore m rescue worker
soccorso 1 pp → **soccorrere** 2 m rescue; venire in ~ a qu come to s.o.'s rescue; pronto ~ first aid; ~ stradale breakdown service, Am wrecking service; segnale m di ~ distress signal

sociale social

socialismo *m* socialism

socialista (*mpl* -i) *agg, m/f* socialist

socializzare <1a> socialize

società *f inv* company; (*associazione*) society; ~ *a responsabilità limitata* limited liability company; ~ *in nome collettivo* general partnership; ~ *per azioni* joint stock company; ~ *del benessere* welfare society; ~ *dei consumi* consumer society

socievole sociable

socio *m* (*pl* -ci), -a *f* member; FIN partner

sociologia *f* sociology

sociologo *m* (*pl* -gi), -a *f* sociologist

soddisfacente satisfying

soddisfare <3aa> satisfy

soddisfatto 1 *pp* → soddisfare 2 *agg* satisfied; *essere ~ di qu* be satisfied with s.o.

soddisfazione *f* satisfaction

sodio *m* sodium

sodo *uovo* hard-boiled; *fig venire al* ~ get down to brass tacks

sofà *m inv* sofa

sofferente suffering

sofferenza *f* suffering

soffermare <1a> *attenzione* turn

soffermarsi dwell (*su* on)

sofferto *pp* → soffrire

soffiare <1k> blow; F swipe F; *~arsi il naso* blow one's nose

soffice soft

soffio *m* puff

soffitta *f* attic

soffitto *m* ceiling

soffocante suffocating

soffocare <1l, c & d> suffocate

soffriggere <3cc> fry gently

soffrire <4f> 1 *v/t* suffer; *persone* bear, stand 2 *v/i* suffer (*di* from)

sofisticato sophisticated

software *m inv* software

softwarista *m/f* software engineer

soggettivo subjective

soggetto 1 *agg* subject; ~ *a tassa* subject to tax; *andare ~ a qc* suffer from sth 2 *m* GRAM subject

soggezione *f* subjection

soggiornare <1a> stay

soggiorno *m* stay; *permesso m di ~* residence permit

soglia *f* threshold

sogliola *f* sole

sognare <1a> *e* sognarsi dream (*di* about, of)

sognatore *m*, -trice *f* dreamer

sogno *m* dream; *neppure per ~!* in your dreams!

soia *f* soya

sol *m inv* MUS G

solaio *m* (*pl* -ai) attic, loft

solamente only; ~ *ieri* just yesterday

solare solar

solarium *m inv* solarium

solco *m* (*pl* -chi) furrow

soldato *m* soldier

soldi *mpl* money *sg*

sole *m* sun; *c'è il ~* it's sunny; *colpo m di ~* sunstroke; *prendere il ~* sunbathe

soleggiare <1f> dry in the sun

soleggiato sun-dried

solenne solemn

solennità *f inv* solemnity

solere <2p>: ~ *fare* be in the habit of doing

soletta *f* insole

solforico (*pl* -ci) sulphur, Am sulfur *attr*; *acido m ~* sulphuric, Am sulfuric acid

solidale *fig* in agreement

solidarietà *f* solidarity

solidarizzare <1a> agree, be in agreement

solidità *f* solidity

solido solid; (*robusto*) sturdy

solista *m/f* (*mpl* -i) soloist

solitario (*pl* -ri) 1 *agg* solitary; *luogo* lonely; *navigatore solo* 2 *m* solitaire; *gioco* patience

solito usual, same; *al o di ~* usually; *come al ~* as usual; *più del ~* more than usual

solitudine *f* solitude, being alone

sollecitare <1m> (*stimolare*) urge; *risposta* ask (again) for

sollecito 1 *agg persona* diligent; *risposta, reazione* prompt; *lettera f di ~* reminder 2 *m* reminder

sollecitudine *f di persona* diligence; *di risposta* promptness

solleticare <1m & d> tickle; *appetito* whet

solletico *m* tickling; **fare il ~ a qu** tickle s.o.; **soffrire il ~** be ticklish

sollevamento *m* lifting; *(insurrezione)* rising; **~ pesi** weightlifting

sollevare <1b> lift; *problema, obiezione* bring up

sollevarsi *di popolo* rise up; AVIA climb, rise

sollievo *m* relief

solo 1 *agg* lonely; *(non accompagnato)* alone; *(unico)* only; MUS solo; **da ~** by myself / yourself etc, on my / your etc own **2** *avv* only **3** *m* MUS solo

solstizio *m* (*pl* -zi) solstice

soltanto only; **~ ieri** only yesterday

solubile soluble

soluzione *f* solution; **~ provvisoria** stopgap

solvente 1 *agg* FIN solvent **2** *m* CHIM solvent

somigliante similar

somiglianza *f* resemblance

somigliare <1g> **~ a qu** resemble s.o.

somma *f (addizione)* addition; *risultato* sum; *(importo)* amount (of money), sum; **fare la ~ di** add (up); *fig* **tirare le -e** sum up

sommare <1a> add; **~ a** total, come to

sommario (*pl* -ri) **1** *agg* summary **2** *m* summary; *di libro* table of contents

sommato: tutto ~ all things considered, on the whole

sommergere <3uu> submerge; *fig* overwhelm (**di** with)

sommergersi submerge, dive

sommergibile *m* submarine

sommerso *città* submerged; *strade* inches deep in water

sommesso *voce* quiet

somministrare <1a> MED administer

sommo 1 *agg* supreme **2** *m* summit; *fig* height

sommossa *f* uprising

sondaggio *m* (*pl* -ggi): **~ (d'opinione)** (opinion) poll

sondare <1a> sound; *fig* test

sonnambulo *m*, **-a** *f* sleepwalker

sonnecchiare <1k> doze

sonnifero *m* sleeping tablet

sonno *m* sleep; **aver ~** be sleepy; **prendere ~** fall asleep

sonnolento drowsy

sonnolenza *f* drowsiness

sono → **essere**

sonorità *f inv* sonority

sonoro sound *attr; risa, applausi* loud; **colonna f -a** sound-track

sontuosità *f* magnificence

sontuoso sumptuous, magnificent

soppesare <1a> weigh; *fig* weigh up

sopportabile bearable, tolerable

sopportare <1c> *peso* bear; *fig* bear, stand F

soppressione *f* deletion; *di regola* abolition

soppresso *pp* → **sopprimere**

sopprimere <3r> delete; *regola* abolish

sopra 1 *prp* on; (*più in alto di*) above; (*riguardo a*) about, on; **~ il tavolo** on the table; **l'uno ~ l'altro** one on top of the other; **i bambini ~ cinque anni** children over five; **5 gradi ~ zero** 5 degrees above zero; **al di ~ di qc** over sth **2** *avv* on top; *(al piano superiore)* upstairs; **dormirci ~** sleep on it; **vedi ~** see above; **la parte di ~** the top *or* upper part

soprabito *m* (over)coat

sopracciglio *m (fpl* -a) eyebrow

sopraccoperta *f di letto* bedspread; *di libro* dustjacket

sopraffare <3aa> overwhelm

sopraggiungere <3d> *di persona* turn up, arrive on the scene; *di difficoltà* arise, come up F

sopralluogo *m* (*pl* -ghi) inspection (of the site)

soprammobile *m* ornament

soprannaturale supernatural

soprannome *m* nickname

soprannumero *m*: **in ~** overcrowded

soprano *m* soprano; **mezzo ~**

mezzo(-soprano)

soprappensiero → *sovrappensiero*

soprassalto: di ~ with a start

soprattassa *f* surcharge

soprattutto particularly, (e)specially, above all

sopravvalutare <1a> overvalue; *fig* overestimate

sopravvenire <4p> turn up, appear

sopravvento *m*: **avere o prendere il ~** have the upper hand

sopravvissuto 1 *agg* surviving **2** *m*, **-a** *f* survivor

sopravvivenza *f* survival

sopravvivere <3zz> survive, outlive (**a qu**)

soprintendente *m/f* supervisor

sopruso *m* abuse of power

soqquadro *m*: **mettere a ~** turn upside down

sorbetto *m* sorbet

sorbire <4d> sip

sorbirsi put up with

sorcio *m* (*pl* -ci) mouse

sordina *f* mute; **in ~** in secret, on the quiet F

sordità *f* deafness

sordo deaf

sordomuto deaf and dumb

sorella *f* sister

sorellastra *f* stepsister

sorgente *f* spring; *fig* source

sorgere <3d> *di sole* rise, come up; *fig* arise, come up

sormontare <1a> *difficoltà* overcome, surmount

sorpassare <1a> go past; AUTO pass, overtake; *fig* exceed

sorpassato out of date

sorpasso *m*: **divieto di ~** no passing, no overtaking; **fare un ~** pass, overtake

sorprendente surprising

sorprendere <3c> surprise; (*cogliere sul fatto*) catch

sorpresa *f* surprise

sorpreso *pp* → *sorprendere*

sorridere <3b> smile

sorriso 1 *pp* → *sorridere* **2** *m* smile

sorseggiare <1f> sip

sorso *m* mouthful

sorta *f* sort, kind

sorte *f* fate; **tirare a ~** draw lots

sorteggiare <1f> draw

sorteggio *m* (*pl* -ggi) draw

sorto *pp* → *sorgere*

sorveglianza *f* supervision; *di edificio* security

sorvegliare <1g> supervise; *edificio* provide security for; *bagagli ecc* look after, take care of

sorvolare <1a> **1** *v/t* AVIA fly over **2** *v/i fig*: **~ su** skim over, skip

sosia *m inv* double

sospendere <3c> suspend; (*appendere*) hang

sospensione *f* suspension

sospeso 1 *pp* → *sospendere* **2** *agg* hanging; *fig questione* pending; **tenere in ~** *persona* keep in suspense

sospettare <1b> suspect; **~ qu o di qu** suspect s.o.

sospetto 1 *agg* suspicious **2** *m*, **-a** *f* suspect

sospettoso suspicious

sospirare <1a> **1** *v/i* sigh **2** *v/t* long for

sospiro *m* sigh

sosta *f* stop; (*pausa*) break, pause; **senza ~** nonstop; **divieto di ~** no parking

sostantivo *m* noun

sostanza *f* substance; **in ~** in short, to sum up

sostare <1c> stop

sostegno *m* support; **a ~ di** in support of

sostenere <2q> support; (*affermare*) maintain

sostengo → *sostenere*

sostenitore *m*, **-trice** *f* supporter

sostentamento *m* support

sostenuto *stile* formal; *velocità* high

sostituibile which can be replaced, replaceable

sostituire <4d>: **~ X con Y** replace X with Y, substitute Y for X

sostituto *m*, **-a** *f* substitute, replacement

sostituzione *f* substitution, replacement

S

sottaceti *mpl* pickles

sottana *f* slip, underskirt; (*gonna*) skirt; REL cassock

sotterranea *f* underground

sotterraneo 1 *agg* underground *attr* **2** *m* cellar

sotterrare <1b> bury

sottile fine; *fig* subtle; *udito* keen

sottintendere <3c> imply

sottinteso 1 *pp* → **sottintendere** **2** *m* allusion

sotto 1 *prp* under; **i bambini ~ cinque anni** children under five; **5 gradi ~ zero** 5 degrees below (zero); **~ la pioggia** in the rain; **al di ~ di qc** under sth **2** *avv* below; (*più in basso*) lower down; (*al di sotto*) underneath; (*al piano di ~*) downstairs

sottobanco under the counter

sottobraccio: camminare ~ walk arm-in-arm; **prendere qu ~** take s.o.'s arm

sottocchio: tenere ~ qc keep an eye on sth

sottochiave under lock and key

sottocosto at less than cost price

sottoesposto FOT underexposed

sottofondo *m* background

sottolineare <1n> *anche fig* underline

sottomarino 1 *agg* underwater *attr* **2** *m* submarine

sottomesso 1 *pp* → **sottomettere** **2** *agg* submissive; *popolo* subject *attr*

sottomettere <3ee> submit; *popolo* subdue

sottomissione *f* submission

sottopassaggio *m* (*pl* -ggi) underpass

sottoporre <3ll> submit

sottoporsi: ~ a undergo

sottoscritto 1 *pp* → **sottoscrivere** **2** *m* undersigned

sottoscrivere <3tt> *documento* sign; *teoria* subscribe to; *abbonamento* take out

sottoscrizione *f* signing; (*abbonamento*) subscription

sottosopra *fig* upside-down

sottosuolo *m* subsoil; **ricchezze** *fpl*

del ~ mineral wealth; **nel ~** underground

sottosviluppato underdeveloped

sottovalutare <1a> undervalue; *persona* underestimate

sottoveste *f* slip, underskirt

sottovoce quietly, sotto voce

sottrarre <3xx> MAT subtract; *denaro* embezzle

sottrarsi: ~ a qc avoid sth

sottratto *pp* → **sottrarre**

sottrazione *f* MAT subtraction; *di denaro* embezzlement

sottufficiale *m* non-commissioned officer, NCO

souvenir *m inv* souvenir

sovietico (*pl* -ci) Soviet

sovrabbondante overabundant

sovrabbondanza *f* overabundance

sovrabbondare <1a> be overabundant; **~ di** have an overabundance of

sovraccarico 1 *agg* overloaded (**di** with) **2** *m* overload

sovrano 1 *agg* sovereign **2** *m*, **-a** *f* sovereign

sovrappensiero: essere ~ be lost in thought

sovrappeso 1 *agg* overweight **2** *m* excess weight

sovrappopolato overpopulated

sovrapporre <3ll> overlap

sovrapposizione *f* overlapping

sovrapproduzione *f* overproduction

sovrastare <1a> overlook, dominate

sovrintendente *m/f* → **soprintendente**

sovrumano superhuman

sovvenzionare <1a> give a grant to

sovvenzione *f* grant

sovversivo subversive

S.P. *abbr* (= **Strada Provinciale**) B road

S.p.A. *abbr* (= **Società per Azioni**) joint stock company

spaccare <1d> break in two; *legna* split, chop

spaccarsi break in two

spaccatura *f* crevice

spacciare <1f> *droga* deal in, push F; **siamo spacciati!** we've had it!

spacciarsi: ~ **per** pass o.s. off as

spacciatore *m*, **-trice** *f* di droga dealer

spaccio *m* (*pl* -cci) *di droga* dealing; *negozio* general store

spacco *m* (*pl* -cchi) *m in gonna* slit; *in giacca* vent

spaccone *m*, **-a** *f* braggart

spada *f* sword

spadroneggiare <1f> throw one's weight around

spaesato disorient(at)ed, confused

spaghetti *mpl* spaghetti *sg*

Spagna *f* Spain

spagnolo 1 *m/agg* Spanish 2 *m*, **-a** *f* Spaniard

spago *m* (*pl* -ghi) string

spalancare <1d> open wide

spalla *f* shoulder; **girare le -e a qu** turn one's back on s.o.; **era di -e** he had his back to me; **stringersi nelle -e** shrug; **vivere alle -e di qu** live off s.o.

spalleggiare <1f> support, back up

spalliera *f* wallbars

spallina *f* shoulder pad

spalmare <1a> spread

spalti *mpl* terraces

spandere <3a> spread

spandersi spread

spanto *pp* → **spandere**

sparare <1a> 1 *v/i* shoot (*a* at) 2 *v/t*: ~ **un colpo** fire a shot

sparatoria *f* gunfire, series of shots

sparecchiare <1k> clear

spareggio *m* SP play-off

spargere <3uu> spread; *lagrime*, *sangue* shed

sparire <4d or 4e> disappear

sparizione *f* disappearance

sparo *m* (gun)shot

sparpagliare <1g> scatter

sparso 1 *pp* → **spargere** 2 *agg* scattered

spartiacque *m inv* watershed

spartire <4d> divide (up), split F

spartito *m* score

spartitraffico *m* (*pl* -ci) traffic island

spartizione *f* division

spasimante *m/f* admirer

spasimo *m* agony

spasmo *m* MED spasm

spasso *m* fun; **andare a** ~ go for a walk; *fig* **essere a** ~ be out of work, be unemployed; **è uno** ~ he/it's a good laugh; **per** ~ as a joke, for fun

spassoso very funny

spastico (*pl* -ci) spastic

spaurito frightened

spavaldo cocky, over-confident

spaventapasseri *m inv* scarecrow

spaventare <1b> frighten, scare

spaventarsi be frightened, be scared

spavento *m* fright; **mi sono preso uno** ~ I got a fright

spaventoso frightening

spaziale space *attr*

spazientirsi <4d> get impatient, lose one's patience

spazio *m* (*pl* -zi) space; ~ **aereo** airspace

spazioso spacious

spazzacamino *m* chimney sweep

spazzaneve *m inv* snowplough, *Am* -plow

spazzare <1a> sweep

spazzatura *f* rubbish, garbage

spazzino *m*, **-a** *f* street sweeper

spazzola *f* brush

spazzolare <1l> brush

spazzolino *m* brush; ~ **da denti** toothbrush

specchiarsi <1k> look at o.s.; (*riflettersi*) be mirrored, be reflected

specchietto *m* mirror; (*prospetto*) table; AUTO ~ **retrovisore** rear-view mirror

specchio *m* (*pl* -cchi) mirror

speciale special

specialista *m/f* (*mpl* -i) specialist

specialità *f inv* special(i)ty

specializzarsi <1a> specialize

specialmente especially

specie 1 *f inv* species; **una** ~ **di** a sort or kind of 2 *avv* especially

specificare <1m & d> specify

specifico (*pl* -ci) specific

speculare <1l & b> speculate (**in** in, **su** on)

speculativo speculative
speculatore *m*, **-trice** *f* speculator
speculazione *f* speculation
spedire <4d> send
spedito fast
spedizione *f* dispatch, sending; *di merce* shipping; (*viaggio*) expedition; *agenzia f di* ~ shipping agency; *spese pl di* ~ shipping costs
spedizioniere *m* courier
spegnere <3vv> put out; *luce, motore, radio* turn off, switch off
spegnersi *di fuoco* go out; *di motore* stop, die F
spellare <1a> skin
spellarsi peel
spelonca *f* (*pl* -che) cave
spendere <3c> spend; *fig* invest
spennare <1a> *pollo* pluck
spensierato carefree
spento *pp* → **spegnere**
speranza *f* hope; *senza* ~ hopeless
sperare <1b> **1** *v/t* hope for **2** *v/i* trust (*in* in)
sperduto lost; *luogo* remote, isolated
spergiuro 1 *m* perjury **2** *m*, **-a** *f* perjurer
sperimentale experimental
sperimentare <1a> try; *in laboratorio* test; *fig: fatica, dolore* feel; *droga* experiment with
sperma *m* sperm
sperperare <1l & b> fritter away, squander
sperpero *m* frittering away, squandering
spesa *f* expense; *fare la* ~ do the shopping; *fare -e* go shopping; *-e pl di produzione* production costs; *-e pl di pubblicità* advertising costs; *-e pl vive* incidental expenses; *a proprie -e* at one's own expense
spesso 1 *agg* thick; *-e volte* many times, often **2** *avv* often, frequently
spessore *m* thickness
spett. *abbr* (= **spettabile**) Messrs; *in lettera* **Spett. Ditta** Dear Sirs
spettacolare spectacular
spettacolo *m* show; (*panorama*) spectacle, sight; ~ *teatrale* show
spettare <1b>: *questo spetta a te*

this is yours; *non spetta a te giudicare* it's not up to you to judge
spettatore *m*, **-trice** *f* spectator; TEA member of the audience
spettinare <1l & b>: ~ *qu* ruffle s.o.'s hair
spettro *m* ghost; FIS spectrum
spezie *fpl* spices
spezzare <1b> break in two
spezzarsi break
spezzatino *m* stew
spezzato 1 *agg* broken (in two) **2** *m* co-ordinated two-piece suit
spezzettare <1a> break up
spia *f* spy; TEC pilot light; *fare la* ~ tell, sneak
spiacente: *essere* ~ be sorry; *sono molto* ~ I am very sorry
spiacere <2k>: *mi spiace* I am sorry
spiacevole unpleasant
spiaggia *f* (*pl* -gge) beach
spianare <1a> roll
spiare <1h> spy on
spiazzo *m* empty space; *in bosco* clearing
spiccato strong
spicchio *m* (*pl* -cchi) *di frutto* section; ~ *d'aglio* clove of garlic
spicciarsi <1f> hurry up
spiccioli *mpl* (small) change *sg*
spiedo *m* spit; *allo* ~ spit-roasted
spiegabile possible to explain
spiegare <1b & e> (*stendere*) spread; (*chiarire*) explain
spiegarsi explain what one means; *mi spiego?* have I made myself clear?; *non so se mi spiego* I don't know if I make myself clear
spiegazione *f* explanation
spiegazzare <1a> crease
spietato merciless, pitiless
spiga *f* (*pl* -ghe) *di grano* ear
spigato herring-bone *attr*
spigliato confident
spigola *f* sea bass
spigolo *m* corner
spilla *f gioiello* brooch; ~ *da balia* safety pin
spillo *m* pin; ~ *di sicurezza* safety pin
spina *f* BOT thorn; ZO spine; *di pesce*

bone; EL plug; ANAT ~ *dorsale* spine; *parcheggio m a ~ di pesce* angle parking; *birra f alla ~* draught beer, beer on tap; *fig* **stare sulle -e** be on tenterhooks

spinaci *mpl* spinach *sg*

spinale spinal

spinello F *m* joint F

spingere <3d> push; *fig* drive

spino *m* thorn

spinoso thorny

spinta *f* push

spinterogeno *m* AUTO distributor

spinto *pp* → **spingere**

spionaggio *m* (*pl* -ggi) espionage

spiraglio *m* (*pl* -gli) crack; *di luce, speranza* gleam, glimmer

spirale *f* spiral; *contraccettivo* coil

spirare <1a> blow; *fig* die

spirito *m* spirit; (*disposizione*) mind; (*umorismo*) wit; *avere ~ d'osserva-zione* be observant; *fare dello ~* be witty

spiritoso witty

spirituale spiritual

splendere <3a> shine

splendente bright

splendido wonderful, splendid

splendore *m* splendo(u)r

spogliare <1g> undress; (*rubare*) rob

spogliarsi undress, strip; *~ di qc* give sth up

spogliarello *m* striptease

spogliatoio *m* (*pl* -oi) dressing room, locker room

spoglio (*pl* -gli) bare

spola *f*: *fare la ~ da un posto all'altro* shuttle backwards and for-wards between two places

spolverare <1l> dust

spolverizzare <1a> dust (*di* with)

sponda *f di letto* edge, side; *di fiume* bank; *nel biliardo* cushion

sponsor *m inv* sponsor

sponsorizzare <1a> sponsor

spontaneità *f* spontaneity

spontaneo spontaneous

sporadico (*pl* -ci) sporadic

sporcare <1c & d> dirty

sporcarsi get dirty

sporcizia *f* dirt

sporco (*pl* -chi) **1** *agg* dirty **2** *m* dirt

sporgere <3d> **1** *v/t* hold out; *denun-cia* make **2** *v/i* jut out

sporgersi lean out

sport *m inv* sport; *~pl invernali* win-ter sports; *fare dello ~* do sport; *per ~* for fun

sporta *f* shopping bag; *di vimini* shopping basket

sportello *m* door; *~ automatico* au-tomatic teller machine, cash dis-penser

sportivo 1 *agg* sports *attr*; *persona* sporty; *campo m ~* playing field **2** *m*, *-a f* sportsman; *donna* sports-woman

sporto *pp* → **sporgere**

sposa *f* bride; *abito m da ~* wedding dress

sposare <1c> marry

sposarsi get married

sposato married

sposo *m* bridegroom; *-i pl* newly-weds

spostare <1a> (*trasferire*) move, shift; (*rimandare*) postpone

spostarsi move

S.P.Q.R. *abbr* (= *Senatus Popu-lusque Romanus*) the Senate and People of Rome

spranga *f* (*pl* -ghe) bar

sprangare <1e> bar

sprecare <1b & d> waste, squander

spreco *m* (*pl* -chi) waste

spregevole contemptible, despi-cable

spregiudicato unprejudiced, unbi-ased; *spreg* unscrupulous

spremere <3a> squeeze

spremilimoni *m inv* lemon squeezer

spremuta *f* juice; *~ di limone* lemon juice; *~ d'arancia* orange juice

sprizzare <1a> spurt; *fig* exude

sprofondare <1a> sink; *fig ~ dalla vergogna* be overcome with em-barrassment

spronare <1a> spur on

sprone *m* spur

sproporzionato disproportionate (*a* to), out of proportion (*a* to)

sproposito *m* blunder; *fare uno ~*

S

do something silly; **costare uno ~** cost a fortune; **a ~** out of turn

sprovveduto inexperienced

sprovvisto: ~ di lacking; **sono ~ di ...** I don't have any ...; **alla -a** unexpectedly

spruzzare <1a> spray

spruzzatore m spray

spruzzo m spray; *fango* splatter

spudorato shameless

spugna f sponge

spuma f foam

spumante: (vino m**) ~** sparkling wine

spumeggiante frothy; *persona* bubbly

spuntare <1a> stick out; BOT come up; *di sole* appear; *di giorno* break; **gli è spuntato un dente** he has cut a tooth

spuntino m snack

spunto m suggestion; **prendere ~ da** be inspired by

sputare <1a> **1** v/i spit **2** v/t spit out

sputo m spittle

squadra f *strumento* set square; *(gruppo)* squad; SP team; **~ volante** flying squad

squalifica f (*pl* -che) disqualification

squalificare <1m & d> disqualify

squallido squallid

squallore m squalor

squalo m shark

squama f flake; *di pesce* scale

squarcio m (*pl* -ci) *in stoffa* rip, tear; *in nuvole* break

squilibrato 1 *agg* insane **2** m, -a f lunatic

squilibrio m (*pl* -ri) imbalance

squillare <1a> ring

squillo m ring; **ragazza** f **~** callgirl

squisito *cibo* delicious

sradicare <1l & d> uproot; *fig (eliminare)* eradicate, uproot

S.r.l. *abbr* (= **Società a responsabilità limitata**) Ltd (= limited)

SS. *abbr* (= **santi**) Saints

S.S. *abbr* (= **Sua Santità**) His Holiness (the Pope); (= **Strada Statale**) A road

stabile 1 *agg* steady; *(duraturo)* stable; *tempo* settled **2** m building

stabilimento m (*fabbrica*) plant, Br factory; **~ balneare** lido

stabilire <4d> *data, obiettivi, record* set; *(decidere)* decide, settle

stabilirsi settle

stabilità f steadiness; *di relazione, moneta* stability

stabilizzare <1a> stabilize

staccare <1d> remove, detach; EL unplug; TELEC **~ il ricevitore** lift the receiver

stadio m (*pl* -di) stage; SP stadium

staffa f stirrup; **perdere le -e** blow one's top

staffetta f SP relay; **corsa** f **a ~** relay race

stage m inv training period

stagionale seasonal

stagionare <1a> age, mature; *legno* season

stagionato aged, mature; *legno* seasoned

stagione f season; **alta ~** high season; **bassa ~** low season; **~ morta** off-season; **frutta** f **di ~** fruit in season, seasonal fruit

stagnare <1a> *dell'acqua* grow stagnant; FIN stagnate

stagnante stagnant

stagno 1 m pond; TEC tin **2** *agg* watertight

stalla f *per bovini* cowshed; *per cavalli* stable

stamani, stamattina this morning

stambecco m (*pl* -cchi) ibex

stampa f press; *tecnica* printing; FOT print; *posta* **-e** *pl* printed matter; **libro** m **in corso di ~** book that has gone to press; **~ locale** local press; **~ scandalistica** tabloids, gutter press; **libertà** f **di ~** freedom of the press

stampante f INFOR printer; **~ a getto di inchiostro** ink-jet printer; **~ laser** laser printer

stampare <1a> print

stampatello m block letters *pl*

stampato m INFOR printout, hard copy

stampella f crutch
stampo m mo(u)ld
stancare <1d> tire (out)
stancarsi get tired, tire
stanchezza f tiredness, fatigue
stanco (pl -chi) tired; ~ **morto** dead beat
stand m inv stand
standard m/agg inv standard
standardizzare <1a> standardize
standardizzazione f standardization
stanga f (pl -ghe) bar
stanghetta f leg
stanotte tonight; (la notte scorsa) last night
stantuffo m piston
stanza f room
stanziare <1g> somma di denaro allocate, earmark
stanzino m boxroom
stappare <1a> take the top off
star f inv star
stare <1q> be; (restare) stay; (abitare) live; ~ **in piedi** stand; ~ **bene** be well; di vestiti suit; ~ **per fare qc** be about to do sth; **stammi a sentire** listen to me; **lascialo** ~ leave him alone, let him be; ~ **telefonando** be on the phone, be making a phonecall; **come sta?** how are you?, how are things?; **ben ti sta!** serves you right!; **ci sto!** here I am!; **sta bene** all right, ok
starnutire <4d> sneeze
starnuto m sneeze
start m inv off
starter m inv SP starter; AUTO choke
stasera this evening, tonight
statale 1 agg state attr **2** m/f (gen pl -i) civil servant **3** f main road
statistica f (pl -che) statistics
Stati Uniti d'America mpl United States of America, USA
statizzare <1a> nationalize
stato 1 pp → **essere** e **stare 2** m anche POL state; ~ **assistenziale** Welfare State; ~ **civile** marital status; ~ **maggiore** general staff; ~ **di salute** state of health, condition; **essere in ~ di fare** be in a position

to do; **essere in ~ interessante** be pregnant
statua f statue
statunitense 1 agg US attr, American **2** m/f US citizen, citizen of the United States
statura f height; fig stature
statuto m statute
stavolta this time
stazionamento m parking
stazionare <1a> be parked
stazionario (pl -ri) stationary
stazione f station; ~ **di servizio** service station; ~ **balneare** seaside resort; ~ **centrale** main station; ~ **climatica** health resort; ~ **termale** spa; ~ **trasmittente** radio station
stecca f (pl -cche) di biliardo cue; di sigarette carton; MED splint; MUS wrong note
stecchino m toothpick
stella f star; ~ **alpina** edelweiss; ~ **polare** North Star, Pole Star; ~ **cadente** shooting star; ~ **di mare** starfish; fig **vedere le -e** see stars
stelo m stem, stalk
stemma m (pl -i) coat of arms
stendere <3c> spread; braccio stretch out; biancheria hang out, hang up; verbale draw up
stendersi stretch out
stendibiancheria m inv clothes dryer
stenodattilografa f shorthand typist
stenodattilografia f shorthand typing
stenografare <1m & c> take down in shorthand
stenografia f shorthand
stentare <1b>: ~ **a fare qc** find it hard to do sth, have difficulty doing sth
stento m: **a** ~ with difficulty; **-i** pl hardship
stereo m inv stereo
stereotipo 1 agg stereotypical **2** m stereotype
sterile sterile
sterilità f sterility
sterilizzare <1a> sterilize

S

sterilizzazione *f* sterilization
sterlina *f* sterling
sterminare <1l & b> exterminate
sterminato vast
sterminio *m* (*pl* -ni) extermination
sterno *m* breastbone, ANAT sternum
sterzare <1b> steer; **~ a sinistra** turn left
sterzata *f* swerve
sterzo *m* AUTO steering
steso *pp* → **stendere**
stesso same; **lo ~, la stessa** the same one; **è lo ~** it's all the same; **oggi ~** this very day; **io ~** myself; **se ~** himself; **l'ho visto coi miei stessi occhi** I saw it with my very own eyes
stile *m* style; SP **~ libero** freestyle
stilografica *f* fountain pen
stima *f* (*ammirazione*) esteem; (*valutazione*) estimate
stimare <1a> *persona* esteem; *oggetto* value, estimate (the value of); (*ritenere*) think, consider
stimarsi think *or* consider o.s.
stimato respected
stimolante 1 *agg* stimulating **2** *m* stimulant
stimolare <1l> stimulate
stimolo *m* stimulus
stinco *m* (*pl* -chi) shin
stingere <3d> **1** *v/t* fade **2** *v/i e* **stingersi** fade
stinto *pp* → **stingere**
stipare <1a> cram
stipato crammed (*di* with)
stipendiato *m*, **-a** *f* person on a salary
stipendio *m* (*pl* -di) salary
stipulare <1l> stipulate
stipulazione *f* stipulation
stiramento *m* MED pulled muscle
stirare <1a> iron; **non si stira** it's non-iron
stirarsi pull
stiratura *f* ironing
stiro *m*: **ferro m da ~** iron; **non ~** non-iron
stirpe *f* (*origine*) birth
stitichezza *f* constipation
stivale *m* boots; **-i** *pl* **di gomma** rubber boots, *Br* wellingtons

sto → **stare**
stoccafisso *m* stockfish (*air-dried cod*)
stoccaggio *m* (*pl* -ggi) stocking
stoffa *f* material; *fig* **avere ~** be talented
stomaco *m* (*pl* -chi) stomach; **dolori mpl di ~** stomach pains; **mi sono tolto un peso dallo ~** I got it off my chest
stonare <1c> *di cantante* sing out of tune; *fig* be out of place; *di colori* clash
stonato *persona* tone deaf; *nota* false; *strumento* out of tune
stop *m inv* AUTO brake light; *cartello* stop sign
stoppare <1c> stop
storcere <3d> twist; **~ il naso** make a face
storcersi bend; **~ un piede** twist one's ankle
stordimento *m* dizziness
stordire <4d> stun
stordito stunned
storia *f* history; (*narrazione*) story; **~ dell'arte** history of art; **non far -e!** don't make a fuss *or* scene!
storico (*pl* -ci) *agg* historical; (*memorabile*) historic **2** *m*, **-a** *f* historian
storiografia *f* historiography
storiografo *m*, **-a** *f* historirapher
storione *m* sturgeon
stormo *m* *di uccelli* flock
stornare <1a> *pericolo* avert
storno *m* *uccello* starling
storpio (*pl* -pi) **1** *agg* crippled **2** *m* **-a** *f* cripple
storta *f*: **prendere una ~ al piede** twist one's ankle
storto crooked
stoviglie *fpl* dishes
strabico (*pl* -ci) cross-eyed
strabismo *m* strabismus
stracarico (*pl* -chi) overloaded
stracaro exceedingly expensive
stracciare <1f> tear up
stracciatella *f* *type of soup*; *gelato* chocolate chip
stracciato in shreds

straccio (*pl* -cci) **1** *m per pulire* cloth; *per spolverare* duster **2** *agg*: **carta** *f* **-a** waste paper

strada *f* road; **per ~** down the road; **sono (già) per ~** I'm coming, I'm on my way; **~ provinciale** B road; **~ a senso unico** one-way street; **~ statale** A road; **farsi ~** push one's way through; *nella vita* get on in life; **a mezza ~** half-way

stradale road *attr*; **incidente** *m* **~** road accident; **polizia** *f* **~** traffic police; **regolamento** *m* **~** rule of the road; **rete** *f* **~** road network

stradario *m* street-finder, street map

strafare <3aa> exaggerate

strage *f* slaughter; **fare ~ di cuori** be a heartbreaker

stragrande: **la ~ maggioranza** the vast majority

stranezza *f* strangeness

strangolare <1l> strangle

straniero **1** *agg* foreign **2** *m*, **-a** *f* foreigner

strano strange

straordinario (*pl* -ri) **1** *agg* special; *eccezionale* extraordinary **2** *m* overtime

strapazzare <1a> treat badly; **uova** *fpl* **strapazzate** scrambled eggs

strapazzarsi overdo it

strapazzo *m* strain; **essere uno ~** be exhausting; **da ~** third-rate

strapieno crowded

strapiombo *m*: **a ~** overhanging

strappare <1a> tear, rip; (*staccare*) tear down; (*togliere*) grab, snatch (**a qu** out of s.o.'s hands)

strappo *m* tear, rip; MED torn ligament; *fig* **uno ~ alla regola** an exception to the rule

straricco (*pl* -cchi) extremely rich

straripare <1a> flood, overflow its banks

strascico *m* (*pl* -chi) train; *fig* aftereffects

stratagemma *m* (*pl* -i) stratagem

strategia *f* strategy

strategico (*pl* -ci) strategic

strato *m* layer; **~ d'ozono** ozone layer; **~ protettivo** protective coating; **~ sociale** social stratum

stravagante extravagant

stravaganza *f* extravaganza

stravecchio (*pl* -cchi) ancient

stravedere <2s>: **~ per qu** worship s.o.

stravincere <3d> win by a mile

stravolgere <3d> change radically; (*travisare*) twist; (*stancare*) exhaust

stravolto **1** *pp* → **stravolgere 2** *agg* (*stanco*) exhausted

strazio *m* (*pl* -zi): **era uno ~** it was painful

strega *f* (*pl* -ghe) witch

stregare <1e> bewitch

stregone *m* wizard

stremare <1b> exhaust

stremato exhausted

stress *m inv* stress

stressante stressful

stressare <1b> stress

stretta *f* hold; **~ di mano** handshake; **mettere qu alle -e** put s.o. in a tight corner

strettamente closely; **tenere qc ~ (in mano)** clutch sth (in one's hand)

strettezza *f* narrowness

stretto **1** *pp* → **stringere 2** *agg* narrow; *vestito, scarpe* too tight; **lo ~ necessario** the bare minimum **3** *m* GEOG strait

strettoia *f* bottleneck

stridere <3a> *di porta* squeak; *di colori* clash

stridulo shrill

strillare <1a> scream

strillo *m* scream

striminzito skimpy

strimpellare <1b> strum

stringa *f* (*pl* -ghe) lace

stringere <3d> **1** *v/t* make narrower; *abito* take in; *vite* tighten; **~ amicizia** become friends **2** *v/i di tempo* press

stringersi *intorno a tavolo* squeeze up

striscia *f* (*pl* -sce) strip; *dipinta* stripe; **-sce** *pl* **pedonali** pedestrian crossing *sg*, *Br* zebra crossing *sg*; **a -sce** striped

strisciare <1f> **1** *v/t piedi* scrape; (*sfiorare*) brush, smear (**contro** against) **2** *v/i* crawl

striscio *m* MED smear

striscione *m* banner

strizzare <1a> wring; **~ l'occhio a qu** wink at s.o.

strofa *f* verse

strofinaccio *m* (*pl* -cci) dish towel

strofinare <1a> rub

stroncare <1d> *albero* knock down; *vita* snuff out; F *idea* shoot down

stropicciare <1f> crush, wrinkle

strozzare <1c> strangle

strozzatura *f* narrowing

strozzino *m*, **-a** *f* loan shark F

struggente all-consuming

struggere <3cc> consume

strumentalizzare make use of

strumento *m* instrument; **~ musicale** musical instrument; **~ ad arco / a fiato** string / wind instrument

strutto *m* lard

struttura *f* structure

strutturale structural

strutturare <1a> structure

struzzo *m* ZO ostrich

stuccare <1d> plaster

stucco *m* (*pl* -cchi) plaster; **rimanere di ~** be thunderstruck, Br be gobsmacked F

studente *m*, **-essa** *f* student; **casa f dello ~** hall of residence

studiare <1k> study

studio *m* (*pl* -di) study; *di artista*, RAD, TV studio; *di professionista* office; *di medico* surgery; **borsa f di ~** bursary

studioso 1 *agg* studious **2** *m*, **-a** *f* scholar

stufa *f* stove; **~ elettrica / a gas** electric / gas fire

stufare <1a> GASTR stew; *fig* bore

stufarsi get bored (**di** with)

stufato *m* stew

stufo: essere ~ di qc be bored with sth

stuolo *m* host

stupefacente 1 *agg* amazing, stupefying **2** *m* narcotic

stupefatto amazed, stupefied

stupendo stupendous

stupidaggine *f* stupidity; **è una ~**

(*cosa senza importanza*) it's nothing

stupidità *f* stupidity

stupido 1 *agg* stupid **2** *m*, **-a** *f* idiot

stupire <4d> **1** *v/t* amaze **2** *v/i* e **stupirsi** be amazed

stupore *m* amazement

stuprare <1a> rape

stupratore *m* rapist

stupro *m* rape

sturare <1a> clear, unblock

stuzzicadenti *m inv* toothpick

stuzzicare <1l & d> tease; **~ l'appetito** whet the appetite

su 1 *prp* on; *argomento* about; (*circa*) (round) about; **sul tavolo** on the table; **sul mare** by the sea; **sulle tremila lire** round about three thousand lire; **~ misura** made to measure; **nove volte ~ dieci** nine times out of ten **2** *avv* up; (*al piano di sopra*) upstairs; **~!** come on!; **avere ~** *vestito* have on; **guardare in ~** look up

sub *m/f inv* skin diver

subacqueo 1 *agg* underwater **2** *m*, **-a** *f* skin diver

subaffittare <1a> sublet

subaffitto *m* sublet

subdolo underhand

subentrare <1a>: **~ a qu** replace s.o., take s.o.'s place

subire <4d> *danni*, *perdita* suffer

subito immediately

subordinare <1m> subordinate

suburbano suburban

succedere <3a or 3l> (*accadere*) happen; **~ a una persona** succeed; **che succede?** what's going on?

successione *f* succession

successivo successive

successo 1 *pp* → **succedere 2** *m* success; **di ~** successful

successore *m* successor

succhiare <1k> suck

succo *m* (*pl* -cchi) juice; **~ d'arancia** orange juice

succoso juicy

succursale *f* branch

sud *m* south; **~ ovest** south-west; **~ est** south-east; **al ~ di** (to the) south of

sudare <1a> perspire, sweat
sudata *f* perspiration, sweat
sudato sweaty
suddividere <3q> subdivide
suddivisione *f* subdivision
sudicio (*pl* -ci) **1** *agg* dirty **2** *m* dirt
sudiciume *m* dirt
sudore *m* perspiration, sweat
sufficiente sufficient
sufficienza *f* sufficiency; *a ~* enough
suffragio *m* (*pl* -gi) suffrage; *~ universale* universal suffrage
suggerimento *m* suggestion
suggerire <4d> suggest; TEA prompt
suggeritore *m* TEA prompter
suggestionare <1a> influence
suggestione *f* influence
suggestivo picturesque
sughero *m* cork
sugli *prp su* and *art* **gli**
sugo *m* (*pl* -ghi) sauce; *di arrosto* juice; *al ~* with sauce
sui *prp su* and *art* **i**
suicida *m/f* suicide (victim)
suicidarsi <1a> commit suicide, kill o.s.
suicidio *m* (*pl* -di) suicide
suino pork *attr*
sul *prp su* and *art* **il**
sull', **sulla, sulle, sullo** *prp su* and *art* **l', la, le, lo**
suo **1** *agg* his; *di cosa* its; *-a f* her; *di cosa* its; *il ~ maestro* his teacher; *i suoi amici* his friends; *questo libro è ~* this is his book; *Suo* your **2** *pron*: *il ~* his; *di cosa* its; *la -a f* hers; *di cosa* its
suocera *f* mother-in-law
suocero *m* father-in-law; *-i pl* mother- and father-in-law, in-laws F
suola *f* sole
suolo *m* ground; (*terreno*) soil
suonare <1o> **1** *v/t* play; *campanello* ring **2** *v/i* play; *alla porta* ring
suono *m* sound
suora *f* REL nun
super *f inv* F 4-star
superare <1l> go past; *fig* overcome; *esame* pass
superato out of date
superbia *f* haughtiness

superbo haughty
superficiale superficial
superficie *f* surface; *in ~* on the surface
superfluo superfluous
superiora *f* Mother Superior
superiore **1** *agg* top; *qualità* superior; *~ alla media* better than average **2** *m* superior
superiorità *f* superiority
superlativo *m/agg* superlative
supermarket *m inv*, **supermercato** *m* supermarket
superstite **1** *agg* surviving **2** *m/f* survivor
superstizione *f* superstition
superstizioso superstitious
superstrada *f* motorway, *Am* highway (*with no tolls*)
superuomo *m* (*pl* -uomini) superman
suppergiù about
supplementare additional, supplementary
supplemento *m* supplement; *~ intercity* intercity supplement; FERR *fare il ~* pay a supplement
supplente *m/f* replacement; EDU supply teacher
supplenza *f* supply teaching
supplicare <1l & d> beg
supplizio *m* (*pl* -zi) torture
suppongo → **supporre**
supporre <3ll> suppose
supporto *m* TEC support; INFOR *~ dati* data support
supposizione *f* supposition
supposta *f* MED suppository
supposto *pp* → **supporre**
suppurare <1a> MED suppurate
suppurazione *f* suppuration
supremazia *f* supremacy
supremo supreme
surf *m inv* surfboard; *fare ~* surf, go surfing
surfista *m/f* (*mpl* -i) surfer
surgelare <1b> freeze
surgelato **1** *agg* frozen **2** *m*: *-i pl* frozen food *sg*
surriscaldare <1a> overheat
surrogato *m* substitute

suscettibile touchy; **è ~ di miglioramento** it's likely to improve
suscettibilità f touchiness
suscitare <1l> arouse
susina f plum
susino m plum (tree)
sussidio m (pl -di) grant, allowance; **~ di disoccupazione** unemployment benefit
sussultare <1a> start, jump
sussulto m start, jump
sussurrare <1a> v/t & v/i whisper
sussurro m whisper
sutura f MED stitches pl
svagarsi <1e> take one's mind off things
svago m (pl -ghi) distraction; **per ~** to take one's mind off things
svaligiare <1f> burgle, Am burglarize
svalutare <1a> devalue
svalutazione f devaluation
svanire <4d> vanish
svantaggio m (pl -ggi) disadvantage
svantaggioso disadvantageous
svariato varied
svedese **1** m/agg Swedish **2** m/f Swede
sveglia f alarm clock
svegliare <1g> waken (up)
svegliarsi waken up
sveglio awake; fig alert
svelare <1a> segreto reveal
svelto quick; **alla -a** quickly
svendere <3a> sell at a reduced price
svendita f clearance

svenimento m fainting fit
svenire <4p> faint
sventolare <1l & b> v/t & v/i wave
sventura f misfortune
sventurato unfortunate
svenuto pp → **svenire**
svergognato shameless
svernare <1b> spend the winter in
svestire <4b> undress
svestirsi get undressed, undress
Svezia f Sweden
sviare <1h> deflect; fig divert
svignarsela <1a> slip away
sviluppare <1a> develop
svilupparsi develop
sviluppato developed
sviluppo m development
svincolo m di strada junction
svista f oversight; **per ~** by some oversight
svitare <1a> unscrew
svitato unscrewed; fig **essere ~** have a screw loose
Svizzera f Switzerland
svizzero 1 agg Swiss **2** m, **-a** f Swiss
svogliatezza f laziness
svogliato lazy
svolazzare <1a> flutter
svolgere <3d> rotolo unwrap; tema develop; attività carry out
svolgersi happen; di film be set
svolgimento m course; di tema development
svolta f turning; fig turning point
svoltare <1c>: **~ a destra** turn right
svolto pp → **svolgere**
svuotare <1c> empty

T

t abbr (= **tonnellata**) t (= tonne)
tabaccaio m (pl -ai), **-a** f tobacconist
tabaccheria f tobacconist's
tabacco m (pl -cchi) tobacco

tabagismo m smoking
tabella f table; **~ dei prezzi** price list; fig **~ di marcia** schedule
tabellina f multiplication table

tabellone *m* board; *per avvisi* notice board; ~ **pubblicitario** billboard

tabernacolo *m* tabernacle

tabù *m/agg inv* taboo

tabulato *m* printout

TAC *abbr* (= *Tomografia Assiale Computerizzata*) CAT (= computerized axial tomography)

taccagno mean, stingy F

taccheggio *m* shoplifting

tacchino *m* turkey

tacco *m* (*pl* -cchi) heel

taccuino *m* notebook

tacere <2k> **1** *v/t* keep quiet about, say nothing about **2** *v/i* not say anything, be silent

tachicardia *f* tachycardia

tachimetro *m* speedometer

tacitare <1l> *scandalo* hush up

tacito tacit

taciturno taciturn

tafano *m* ZO horsefly

tafferuglio *m* (*pl* -gli) scuffle

taglia *f* (*misura*) size; **di ~ media** medium; ~ **forte** outsize; ~ **unica** one size

tagliacarte *m inv* paper-knife

tagliando *m* coupon; AUTO service; **fare il** ~ have the vehicle serviced

tagliare <1g> cut; *albero* cut down; *legna* chop; ~ **i capelli** have one's hair cut; *fig* ~ **la strada a qu** cut in front of s.o.

tagliarsi cut o.s.; **mi sono tagliata un dito** I've cut my finger

tagliatelle *fpl* tagliatelle *sg*

tagliente sharp

tagliere *m* chopping board

taglierini *mpl* type of noodles

taglio *m* (*pl* -gli) cut; ~ **cesareo** C(a)esarean (section)

tailleur *m inv* suit

talco *m* (*pl* -chi) talc, talcum powder

tale such a; *-i pl* such; ~ **e quale** just like; **un** ~ someone; **il signor tal dei -i** Mr So-and-so

talento *m* talent

tallonare <1a> *persona* follow close behind; *nel rugby* heel

talloncino *m* coupon

tallone *m* heel

talmente so

talora sometimes

talpa *f* mole

talvolta sometimes

tamburo *m* drum

tamponamento *m* AUTO collision; ~ **a catena** multi-vehicle pile-up

tamponare <1a> *falla* plug; AUTO collide with, crash into

tampone *m* MED swab; *per donne* tampon; *per timbri* (ink) pad; INFOR buffer

tana *f* den

tandem *m inv* tandem

tangente *f* MAT tangent; F (*percentuale illecita*) kickback F; F (*bustarella*) bribe; F (*pizzo*) protection money

tangenziale *f* ring road

tanica *f* container; MAR *per fuoribordo* tank

tanto 1 *agg* so much; *-i pl* so many; *-i saluti* best wishes; ~ **e grazie** thank you so much, many thanks **2** *pron* much; *-i pl* many **3** *avv* (*così*) so; *con verbi* so much; **di ~ in ~** from time to time; ~ **quanto** as much as; **è da** ~ (*tempo*) **che non lo vedo** I haven't seen him for a long time; ~ **per cambiare** for a change

tappa *f* stop; *di viaggio* stage

tappare <1a> plug; *bottiglia* put the cork in

tapparella *f* rolling shutter

tappeto *m* carpet

tappezzare <1a> (wall)paper

tappezzeria *f di pareti* wallpaper; *di sedili* upholstery

tappo *m* cap, top; *di sughero* cork; *di lavandini, vasche* plug

tarare <1a> TEC calibrate

tarchiato stocky

tardare <1a> **1** *v/t* delay **2** *v/i* be late

tardi late; **più** ~ later (on); **al più** ~ at the latest; **a più** ~! see you!; **far** ~ (*arrivare in ritardo*) be late; (*stare alzato*) stay up late; **in ufficio** work late

tardivo late; *fig* retarded, slow

tardo late

targa *f* (*pl* -ghe) nameplate; AUTO numberplate

targhetta *f* tag; *su porta* nameplate

tariffa *f* rate; *nei trasporti* fare; *doganale* tariff

tarlato worm-eaten

tarlo *m* woodworm

tarma *f* (clothes) moth

tartaro *m* tartar

tartaruga *f* (*pl* -ghe) *terrestre* tortoise; *aquatica* turtle

tartina *f* canapé

tartufo *m* truffle

tasca *f* (*pl* -che) pocket; **ne ho piene le -che** I'm fed up with this

tascabile 1 *agg* pocket *attr* **2** *m* paperback

tassa *f* tax; ~ **di circolazione** road tax; ~ **di soggiorno** visitor tax; **esente da** ~ tax free; **soggetto a** ~ subject to tax

tassametro *m* meter, clock F

tassare <1a> tax

tassello *m nel muro* plug

tassista *m/f* (*mpl* -i) taxi driver

tasso[1] *m* FIN rate; ~ **d'inflazione** inflation rate, rate of inflation; ~ **d'interesse** interest rate; ~ **di sconto** discount rate

tasso[2] *m* ZO badger

tasso[3] *m* BOT yew

tastare <1a> feel; *fig* ~ **il terreno** test the water, see how the land lies

tastiera *f* keyboard

tastierista *m/f* (*mpl* -i) keyboarder

tasto *m* key; INFOR ~ **operativo** function key

tattica *f* (*pl* -che) tactics *pl*

tattico (*pl* -ci) tactical

tatto *m* (*senso*) touch; *fig* tact; **mancanza di** ~ tactlessness, lack of tact

tatuaggio *m* (*pl* -ggi) tattoo

tatuare <1l> tattoo

taverna *f country-style restaurant*

tavola *f* table; (*asse*) plank, board; *in libro* plate; ~ **calda** snackbar; ~ **rotonda** round table; SP ~ **a vela** sailboard; **mettersi a** ~ sit down to eat; **a** ~! lunch / dinner is ready!, come and get it! F

tavoletta *f*: ~ **di cioccolata** bar of chocolate

tavolo *m* table

taxi *m inv* taxi

tazza *f* cup

tazzina *f* espresso cup

tbc, TBC *abbr* (= **tubercolosi**) TB (= tuberculosis)

TCI *abbr* (= **Touring Club Italiano**) Italian motoring organization

te you; ~ **l'ho venduto** I sold it to you

tè *m* tea; ~ **freddo** iced tea; **sala** *f* **da** ~ tearoom; **tazza** *f* **da** ~ teacup

teatrale theatre, *Am* theater; *fig* theatrical; **rappresentazione** *f* ~ play

teatro *m* theatre, *Am* theater; *fig* (*luogo*) scene; ~ **all'aperto** open air theatre (*Am* theater); ~ **lirico** opera (house)

tecnica *f* (*pl* -che) technique; (*tecnologia*) technology

tecnico (*pl* -ci) **1** *agg* technical **2** *m* technician

tecnologia *f* technology; **alta** ~ high technology, high tech F

tecnologico (*pl* -ci) technological

tedesco (*pl* -chi) **1** *m/agg* German **2** *m*, **-a** *f* German

tegame *m* (sauce)pan

teglia *f* baking tin

tegola *f* tile

teiera *f* teapot

tel. *abbr* (= **telefono**) tel (= telephone)

tela *f* cloth; PITT canvas; ~ **cerata** oilcloth

telaio *m* (*pl* -ai) loom; *di automobile* chassis; *di bicicletta, finestra* frame

telecamera *f* television camera

telecomando *m* remote control

telecomunicazioni *fpl* telecommunications, telecomms

telefax *m inv* fax

teleferica *f* (*pl* -che) cableway

telefilm *m inv* film made for television

telefonare <1m & b> (tele)phone, ring (**a qu** s.o.)

telefonata *f* (tele)phone call; ~ **interurbana** long-distance (phone) call; ~ **urbana** local call; **fare una** ~ **a qu** ring *or* phone s.o.

telefonico (*pl* -ci) (tele)phone *attr*

telefonista *m/f* (*mpl* -i) (switchboard) operator

telefonino *m* mobile (phone), *Am* cell(ular) phone

telefono *m* (tele)phone; ~ *a gettoni* telephone that takes tokens; ~ *a scheda* (*magnetica*) cardphone; ~ *a tastiera* push-button (tele)phone; ~ *cellulare* cellphone, cellular (tele)phone; *dare un colpo di ~ a qu* give s.o. a ring

telegiornale *m* news *sg*

telegrafare <1m & b> telegraph

telegrafico (*pl* -ci) *stile* telegraphic; *risposta* very brief

telegrafo *m* telegraph

telegramma *m* (*pl* -i) telegram

teleguidato remote controlled

telelavoro *m* teleworking

teleobiettivo *m* telephoto lens

telepatia *f* telepathy

teleschermo *m* TV screen

telescopio *m* (*pl* -pi) telescope

teleselezione *f* STD

telespettatore *m*, **-trice** *f* TV viewer

televisione *f* television, TV; ~ *via cavo* cable television *or* TV; ~ *via satellite* satellite television *or* TV

televisivo television *attr*, TV *attr*

televisore *m* television (set), TV (set); ~ *a colori* colo(u)r TV

telex *m inv* telex

telone *m* tarpaulin; TEA curtain

tema *m* theme, subject

temerario (*pl* -ri) reckless

temere <2a> be afraid *or* frightened of

temperamatite *m inv* pencil sharpener

temperamento *m* temperament

temperare <1l & b> *acciaio* temper; *matita* sharpen

temperato *acciaio* tempered; *matita* sharp; *clima* temperate

temperatura *f* temperature; ~ *ambiente* room temperature

tempesta *f* storm

tempestoso stormy

tempia *f* temple

tempio *m* (*pl* -pli) temple

tempo *m* time; METEO weather; ~ *libero* free time; *a ~ parziale* part-

time; *a ~ perso* in one's spare time; *a ~ pieno* full-time; SP **-i** *pl* **supplementari** extra time *sg*, *Am* overtime *sg*; *a ~, in ~* in time; *col ~* in time, eventually; *un ~* once, long ago; *per ~* (*presto*) in good time; (*di buon'ora*) early; *non ho ~* I don't have (the) time; *lavora da molto ~* he has been working for a long time; *fa bel / brutto ~* the weather is lovely / nasty

temporale *m* thunderstorm

temporaneo temporary

tenace *materiali, sostanze* strong; *fig* tenacious

tenacia *f fig* tenacity

tenaglie *fpl* pincers *pl*

tenda *f* curtain; *da campeggio* tent

tendenza *f* tendency

tendere <3c> **1** *v/t molla, elastico, muscoli* stretch; *corde del violino* tighten; *mano* hold out, stretch out; *fig trappola* lay; ~ *un braccio per fare qc* reach out to do sth; ~ *le braccia a qu* hold one's arms out to s.o. **2** *v/i*: ~ *a* (*aspirare a*) aim at; (*essere portati a*) tend to; (*avvicinarsi a*) verge on

tendina *f* net curtain

tendine *m* tendon

tenebre *fpl* darkness *sg*

tenente *m* lieutenant

tenere <2q> **1** *v/t* hold; (*conservare, mantenere*) keep; (*gestire*) run; *spazio* take up; *conferenza* give; ~ *d'occhio* keep an eye on, watch **2** *v/i* hold (on); ~ *a* (*dare importanza a*) care about; SP support

tenerezza *f* tenderness

tenero tender; *pietra, legno* soft

tenersi (*reggersi*) hold on (*a* to); (*mantenersi*) keep o.s.; ~ *in piedi* stand (up)

tengo → **tenere**

tennis *m* tennis; ~ *da tavolo* table tennis

tennista *m/f* (*mpl* -i) tennis player

tenore *m* MUS tenor; ~ *di vita* standard of living

tensione *f* voltage; *fig* tension

tentare <1b> try, attempt; (*allettare*)

tempt; **~ tutto il possibile** do everything possible

tentativo *m* attempt

tentazione *f* temptation

tenue *colore* pale; *luce, speranza* faint

tenuta *f (capacità)* capacity; *(resistenza)* stamina; *(divisa)* uniform; *(abbigliamento)* outfit; AGR estate; **a ~ d'aria** airtight; AUTO **~ di strada** roadholding ability

teologia *f* theology

teologico (*pl* -ci) theological

teologo *m* (*pl* -gi), **-a** *f* theologian

teorema *m* (*pl* -i) theorem

teoria *f* theory

teorico (*pl* -ci) theoretical

tepore *m* warmth

teppista *m/f* (*pl* -i) hooligan

terapia *f* therapy

tergicristallo *m* AUTO windscreen (*Am* windshield) wiper

termale thermal; **stazione** *f* **~** spa; **stabilimento** *m* **~** baths *pl*

terme *fpl* baths

terminal *m inv* AVIA air terminal, terminal building

terminale 1 *agg* terminal; **stazione** *f* **~** terminus **2** *m* INFOR, EL terminal

terminare <1l & b> *v/t* & *v/i* end, finish, terminate

termine *m* end; *(confine)* limit; FIN *(scadenza)* deadline; *(parola)* term; **-i di consegna** terms of delivery; **~ tecnico** technical term; **a breve / lungo ~** in the short / long term; **in altri -i** in other words; **volgere al ~** come to an end

termocoperta *f* electric blanket

termometro *m* thermometer

termos *m inv* thermos®

termosifone *m* radiator

termostato *m* thermostat

terra *f* earth; *(regione, proprietà, terreno agricolo)* land; *(superficie del suolo)* ground; *(pavimento)* floor; **a ~** on the ground; AVIA, MAR **scendere a ~** get off; TEC **mettere a ~** earth; **cadere a** *o* **per ~** fall (down)

terracotta *f* (*pl* terrecotte) terracotta

terraferma *f* dry land, terra firma

terrapieno *m* embankment

terrazza *f*, **terrazzo** *m* balcony, terrace

terremoto *m* earthquake

terreno 1 *agg* earthly; *piano* ground, *Am* first **2** *m (superficie)* ground; *(suolo, materiale)* soil; *(appezzamento)* plot of land; *fig (settore, tema)* field, area; **perdere / guadagnare ~** lose / gain ground; **~ fabbricabile** land that may be built on

terrestre land *attr*, terrestrial; *della Terra* of the Earth; **globo** *m* **~** globe

terribile terrible

terrina *f* bowl

territoriale territorial

territorio *m* (*pl* -ri) territory

terrore *m* terror

terrorismo *m* terrorism

terrorista *m/f* (*pl* -i) terrorist

terrorizzare <1a> terrorize

terza *f* AUTO third (gear)

terziario *m* (*pl* -ri) tertiary sector, services *pl*

terzino *m* SP back

terzo 1 *agg* third; **il ~ mondo** the Third World; **-a pagina** arts page **2** *m* third

teschio *m* (*pl* -chi) skull

tesi *f inv* **~ (di laurea)** thesis

teso 1 *pp* → **tendere 2** *agg* taut; *fig* tense

tesoro *m* treasure; *(tesoreria)* treasury

tessera *f* card; **~ d'abbonamento** season ticket

tessile 1 *agg* textile **2** **-i** *mpl* textiles

tessuto *m* fabric, material; **~ di lana** wool; **-i** *pl* fabrics, material *sg*

test *m inv* test

testa *f* head; **a ~** each, a head; **alla ~ di** at the head of; **essere in ~** lead

testamento *m* will

testardaggine *f* stubbornness

testardo stubborn

testata *f (giornale)* newspaper; *di letto* headboard; AUTO cylinder head; **~ nucleare** nuclear warhead

teste *m/f* witness

testicolo *m* testicle

testimone *m/f* witness; **~ oculare**

eyewitness; **Testimoni** pl **di Geova** Jehovah's Witnesses

testimonianza f testimony; (prova) proof

testimoniare <1k & c> **1** v/i testify, give evidence **2** v/t fig testify to; DIR **~ il falso** commit perjury

testo m text

tetano m tetanus

tetro gloomy

tetto m roof

tettoia f roof

Tevere m Tiber

TG abbr (= **Telegiornale**) TV news

thermos → **termos**

ti you; riflessivo yourself

tibia f shinbone, tibia

tic m inv di orologio tick; MED tic

ticchettio m di orologio ticking; di pioggia patter

ticket m inv MED charge

tiene → **tenere**

tiepido lukewarm, tepid; fig half-hearted, lukewarm

tifo m MED typhus; fig **fare il ~ per una squadra** be a fan or supporter of a team

tifoso m, **-a** f fan, supporter

tiglio m (pl -gli) lime tree

tigre f tiger

timbrare <1a> stamp

timbro m stamp; MUS timbre; **~ postale** postage stamp

timidezza f shyness, timidity

timido shy, timid

timo m BOT thyme

timone m MAR, AVIA rudder; fig helm

timoniere m helmsman

timore m fear

timoroso timorous

timpano m MUS kettledrum; ANAT eardrum

tingere <3d> dye

tinta f (colorante) dye; (colore) colo(u)r

tintarella f (sun)tan

tinto pp → **tingere**

tintoria f dry-cleaner's

tintura f dyeing; (colorante) dye; **~ di iodio** iodine

tipico (pl -ci) typical

tipo m sort, kind, type; F fig guy

tipografia f printing; stabilimento printer's

tipografo m printer

tipografico typographical

tir m heavy goods vehicle, HGV

tiranneggiare <1f> tyrannize

tirannia f tyranny

tiranno 1 agg tyrannical **2** m tyrant

tirare <1a> **1** v/t pull; (tendere) stretch; (lanciare) throw; (sparare) fire; (tracciare) draw; **~ fuori** take out; **~ su** da terra pick up; bambino bring up; **~ giù** take down **2** v/i pull; di abito be too tight; di vento blow; (sparare) shoot; **~ avanti** (arrangiarsi) get by, manage; (continuare) keep going; **~ dritto** go straight on; **~ a sorte** draw lots

tirarsi: **~ indietro** back off; fig back out

tiratore m, **-trice** f shot

tiratura f di libro print run; di giornale circulation

tirchio (pl -chi) **1** agg mean, stingy F **2** m, **-a** f miser, skinflint F

tiro m (lancio) throw; (sparo) shot; **~ con l'arco** archery; fig **un brutto ~** a nasty trick; **essere a ~** be within range

tirocinante m/f trainee

tirocinio m (pl -ni) training

tiroide f thyroid

tirolese agg, m/f Tyrolean, Tyrolese

Tirolo m Tyrol

tisana f herbal tea, tisane

titolare m/f owner

titolo m title; dei giornali headline; FIN security; **~ a reddito fisso** fixed income security; **a ~ di** as; **~ di studio** qualification

titubare <1l> hesitate

tizio m, **-a** f: **un ~** somebody, some man; **una -a** somebody, some woman

toccare <1d> **1** v/t touch; (riguardare) concern, be about **2** v/i happen (a to); **gli tocca metà dell'eredità** half the estate is going to him; **tocca a me** it's my turn; **mi tocca partire** I must go, I have to go

tocco *m* (*pl* -cchi) touch

togliere <3ss> take (away), remove; (*eliminare*) take off; (*tirare fuori*) take out, remove; (*revocare*) lift, raise; *dente* take out, extract; **~ di mezzo** get rid of; **ciò non toglie che** the fact remains that

togliersi *giacca* take off, remove; (*spostarsi*) take o.s. off; **~ dai piedi** get out of the way

tolgo → **togliere**

tollerante tolerant

tolleranza *f* tolerance

tollerare <1l & c> tolerate

tolto *pp* → **togliere**

tomba *f* grave

tombola *f* bingo

tomografia *f* MED tomography; **~ assiale computerizzata** computerized axial tomography

tonaca *f* (*pl* -che) habit

tonalità *f inv* tonality

tondeggiante roundish

tondo round; (*grassoccio*) plump; **chiaro e ~** quite clearly

tonfo *m* **in acqua** splash

tonico *m* (*pl* -ci) tonic

tonificare <1m & d> tone up

tonnellata *f* tonne

tonno *m* tuna

tono *m* tone; **rispondere a ~** (*a proposito*) answer to the point; **per le rime** answer back

tonsille *fpl* ANAT tonsils

tonsillite *f* tonsillitis

topazio *m* (*pl* -zi) topaz

topo *m* mouse

topografia *f* topography

Topolino *m* Mickey Mouse

toppa *f* (*serratura*) keyhole; (*rattoppo*) patch

torace *m* chest

torbido *liquid* cloudy

torcere <3d> twist; *biancheria* wring

torchio *m* (*pl* -chi) press

torcia *f* (*pl* -ce) *f* torch

torcicollo *m* stiff neck

tordo *m* thrush

torinese of Turin

Torino *f* Turin

tormenta *f* snowstorm

tormentare <1a> torment

tormentarsi torment o.s.

tormento *m* torment

tornaconto *m* benefit

tornante *m* hairpin bend

tornare <1a> *venire* come back, return; *andare* go back, return; (*quadrare*) balance; **~ utile** prove useful; **~ a fare / dire qc** do / say sth again; **ben tornato!** welcome back!; **~ in sé** come to one's senses

torneo *m* tournament; **Torneo delle Sei Nazioni** Six Nations Cup

tornio *m* (*pl* -ni) lathe

toro *m* bull; ASTR **Toro** Taurus

torpedine *f* ZO electric ray

torpore *m* torpor

torre *f* tower

torrefare <3aa> roast

torrefazione *f* roasting

torreggiare <1f> tower (**su** over)

torrente *m* stream

torrido torrid

torrone *m* nougat

torsione *f* twisting; TEC torsion

torso *m* torso

torsolo *m* core

torta *f* cake

tortellini *mpl* tortellini *sg*

torto *m* wrong; **aver ~** be wrong; **a ~** wrongly

tortora *f* turtledove

tortuoso (*sinuoso*) winding; (*ambiguo*) devious

tortura *f* torture

torturare <1a> torture

torvo *sguardo* dark, black

tosaerba *f e m* lawnmower

tosare <1a> *pecore* shear

Toscana *f* Tuscany

toscano Tuscan

tosse *f* cough; **~ canina** whooping cough; **aver la ~** have a cough

tossico (*pl* -ci) **1** *agg* toxic **2** *m*, **-a** *f* F druggie F

tossicodipendente *m/f* drug addict

tossicodipendenza *f* drug addiction

tossicomane *m/f* drug addict

tossire <4a & d> cough

tostapane *m* toaster

tostare <1c> *pane* toast; *caffè* roast
tot 1 *agg* so many **2** *pron* so much
totale *m/agg* total
totalità *f (interezza)* entirety, totality; **nella ~ dei casi** in all cases
totip *m competition similar to football pools, based on horse racing*
totocalcio *m competition similar to football pools*
tovaglia *f* tablecloth
tovagliolo *m* napkin, serviette
tozzo 1 *agg* stocky **2** *m di pane* crust
tra → **fra**
traballare <1a> stagger; *mobile* wobble
traboccare <1d> overflow (*anche fig*)
traccia *f (pl -cce) (orma)* footprint; *di veicolo* track; *(indizio)* clue; *(segno)* trace; *(abbozzo)* sketch
tracciare <1f> *linea* draw; *(delineare)* outline; *(abbozzare)* sketch
trachea *f* windpipe
tracolla *f* (shoulder) strap; **a ~** slung over one's shoulder; **borsa f a ~** shoulder bag
tracollo *m* collapse
tradimento *m* betrayal; POL treason; **a ~** treacherously
tradire <4d> betray; *coniuge* be unfaithful to
tradirsi give o.s. away
traditore 1 *agg (infedele)* unfaithful **2** *m*, **-trice** *f* traitor
tradizionale traditional
tradizione *f* tradition
tradotto *pp* → **tradurre**
tradurre <3e> translate; **~ in inglese** translate into English
traduttore *m*, **-trice** *f* translator
traduzione *f* translation
trafficante *m/f spreg* dealer; **~ di droga** drug dealer
trafficare <1l & d> deal, trade (**in** in); *spreg* traffic (**in** in); *(armeggiare)* tinker; *(affaccendarsi)* bustle about
traffico *m (pl -chi e -ci)* traffic; **~ aereo** air traffic; **~ stradale** road traffic; **densità f del ~** volume of traffic
traforo *m* tunnel

tragedia *f* tragedy
traghettare <1a> ferry
traghetto *m* ferry
tragico (*pl* -ci) tragic
tragitto *m* journey
traguardo *m* finishing line
traiettoria *f* trajectory
trainare <1l> *(rimorchiare)* tow; *di animali* pull, draw
traino *m* towing; *veicolo* vehicle on tow; **a ~** on tow
tralasciare <1f> *(omettere)* omit, leave out; *(interrompere)* interrupt
traliccio *m (pl* -cci) EL pylon; TEC trellis
tram *m inv* tram
trama *f fig* plot
tramandare <1a> hand down
tramare <1a> *fig* plot
trambusto *m (confusione)* bustle; *(tumulto)* uproar, commotion
tramezzino *m* sandwich
tramezzo *m* partition
tramite 1 *m (collegamento)* link; *(intermediario)* go-between **2** *prep* through
tramontana *f* north wind
tramontare <1a> set
tramonto *m* sunset; *fig* decline
trampolino *m* diving board; SCI ski jump
tranello *m* trap
tranne except
tranquillante *m* tranquil(l)izer
tranquillità *f* peacefulness, tranquillity
tranquillizzare <1a>: **~ qu** set s.o.'s mind at rest
tranquillo calm, peaceful
transatlantico (*pl* -ci) **1** *agg* transatlantic **2** *m* liner
transazione *f* DIR settlement; FIN transaction
transenna *f* barrier
transistor *m inv* transistor
transitabile *strada* passable
transitare <1l> pass
transitivo GRAM transitive
transito *m* transit; **divieto di ~** no thoroughfare
transitorio (*pl* -ri) transitory

transizione f transition

transoceanico (pl -ci) ocean attr

trantran m F routine

tranviere m (manovratore) tram driver; (controllore) tram conductor

trapanare <1l> drill

trapano m drill; **~ a percussione** percussion drill

trapezio m (pl -zi) trapeze; MAT trapezium

trapezista m/f (mpl -i) trapeze artist

trapiantare <1a> transplant

trapianto m transplant

trappola f trap

trapunta f quilt

trarre <3xx> conclusioni draw; vantaggio derive; **tratto da un libro di** taken from a book by

trasalire <4m> jump

trasandato scruffy; lavoro slipshod

trasbordare <1a> transfer

trasbordo m transfer

trascinare <1a> drag; (travolgere) sweep away; fig (entusiasmare) carry away

trascorrere <3o> **1** v/t spend **2** v/i pass, go by

trascorso pp → **trascorrere**

trascrivere <3tt> transcribe

trascrizione f transcription

trascurabile unimportant

trascurare <1a> neglect; (tralasciare) ignore; **~ di fare qc** fail to do sth

trascuratezza f negligence

trascurato careless, negligent; (trasandato) slovenly; (ignorato) neglected

trasferibile transferable

trasferimento m transfer

trasferire <4d> transfer

trasferirsi move

trasferta f transfer; SP away game

trasformare <1a> transform; TEC process; nel rugby convert

trasformarsi change, turn (in into)

trasformatore m transformer

trasformazione f transformation

trasfusione f transfusion

trasgredire <4d> disobey

trasgressione f disobedience

trasgressore m transgressor

traslocare <1c & d> v/t & v/i move

trasloco m (pl -chi) move

trasmettere <3ee> pass on; RAD, TV broadcast, transmit; DIR diritti transfer

trasmissibile transmissible

trasmissione f transmission; RAD, TV broadcast, transmission; (programma) programme, Am program; RAD, TV **~ in diretta** live broadcast; INFOR **~ dati** data transmission

trasognato dreamy

trasparente 1 agg transparent **2** m transparency

trasparenza f transparency

trasportare <1c> transport

trasporto m transport; **~ combinato rotaia-strada** piggyback transport; **-i** pl **pubblici** public transport sg

trasversale 1 agg transverse **2** f MAT transversal

tratta f trade; FIN draft

trattamento m treatment

trattare <1a> **1** v/t treat; TEC treat, process; FIN deal in; (negoziare) negotiate **2** v/i deal; **~ di** be about; FIN **~ in** deal in

trattarsi: **di che si tratta?** what's it about?

trattative fpl negotiations, talks

trattato m treatise; DIR, POL treaty; **~ di pace** peace treaty

trattenere <2q> (far restare) keep, hold; (far perder tempo) hold up; (frenare) restrain; fiato, respiro hold; lacrime hold back; somma withhold

trattenersi (rimanere) stay; (frenarsi) restrain o.s.; **~ dal fare qc** refrain from doing sth

trattenuta f deduction

trattino m dash; in parole composte hyphen

tratto 1 pp → **trarre 2** m di spazio, tempo stretch; di penna stroke; (linea) line; **a un ~** all of a sudden; **-i** pl (lineamenti) features; **a -i** at intervals

trattore m tractor

trattoria f restaurant

trauma m (pl -i) trauma

traumatico (*pl* -ci) traumatic

travaglio *m*: MED ~ **di parto** labo(u)r

travasare <1a> decant

trave *f* beam

traversa *f* crossbeam

traversare <1b> cross

traversata *f* crossing

traverso: *flauto m* ~ flute; *andare di* ~ *di cibi* go down the wrong way; *per vie* -*e* by devious means

travestimento *m* disguise

travestire <4b> disguise

travestirsi disguise o.s., dress up (*da* as)

travestito *m* transvestite

travolgere <3d> carry away (*anche fig*); *con un veicolo* run over

travolto *pp* → **travolgere**

trazione *f* TEC traction; AUTO ~ *anteriore* / *posteriore* front- / rearwheel drive

tre three

trebbiare <1k> AGR thresh

treccia *f* (*pl* -cce) plait

trecento **1** *agg* three hundred **2** *m*: *il Trecento* the fourteenth century

tredicesimo *m*/*agg* thirteenth

tredici thirteen

tregua *f* truce; *fig* break, let-up

trekking *m* hiking

tremante trembling, shaking

tremare <1b> tremble, shake (*di, per* with)

tremendo terrible, tremendous

tremila three thousand

treno *m* train; ~ *intercity* intercity train; ~ *merci* goods train; *in* ~ by train

trenta thirty

trentenne *agg*, *m*/*f* thirty-year-old

trentesimo *m*/*agg* thirtieth

trentina: *una* ~ about thirty; *essere sulla* ~ be about thirty, be in one's thirties

treppiedi *m inv* tripod

treruote *m inv* three-wheeler

triangolare triangular

triangolo *m* triangle; AUTO warning triangle

tribù *f inv* tribe

tribuna *f* platform

tribunale *m* court; ~ *per i minorenni* juvenile court

tributario (*pl* -ri) tax

tributo *m* tax; *fig* tribute

tricheco *m* (*pl* -chi) walrus

triciclo *m* tricycle

tricolore **1** *agg* tricolo(u)r(ed) **2** *m* tricolo(u)r

triennale *contratto*, *progetto* threeyear; *mostra*, *festival* three-yearly

triennio *m* (*pl* -nni) three-year period

triestino of Trieste

trifoglio *m* (*pl* -gli) clover

triglia *f* red mullet

trilaterale trilateral

trillare <1a> trill

trillo *m* trill

trim. *abbr* (= **trimestre**) term

trimestrale quarterly

trimestre *m* quarter; EDU term

trincea *f* trench

trincerare <1b> entrench

trincerarsi entrench o.s.

trinchetto *m* foremast

trinciare <1f> cut up, chop

Trinità *f* Trinity

trio *m* trio

trionfare <1a> triumph (*su* over)

trionfo *m* triumph

triplicare <1l & d> triple

triplice triple

triplo **1** *agg* triple **2** *m*: *il* ~ three times as much (*di* as)

trippa *f* tripe

triste sad

tristezza *f* sadness

tritacarne *m inv* mincer

tritare <1a> mince

tritatutto *m inv* mincer

trito minced; *fig* ~ *e ritrito* rehashed

trittico *m* (*pl* -ci) triptych

triturare <1a> grind

trivellare <1b> drill

trivella *f* drill

triviale trivial

trofeo *m* trophy

tromba *f* MUS trumpet; AUTO horn; ~ *d'aria* whirlwind; ~ *delle scale* stairwell

trombone *m* trombone

T

trombosi *f* thrombosis

troncare <1d> cut off; *fig* break off

tronchese *m* wire cutters *pl*

tronco *m* (*pl* -chi) ANAT, BOT trunk; FERR section; *licenziare in ~* fire on the spot *or* there and then

trono *m* throne

tropicale tropical

tropici *mpl* tropics

troppo 1 *agg* too much; *-i pl* too many **2** *avv* too much; *non ~* not too much; *è ~ tardi* it's too late

trota *f* trout

trottare <1c> trot

trotto *m* trot

trottola *f* (spinning) top

trovare <1c> find; (*inventare*) find, come up with; *andare a ~ qu* (go and) see s.o.

trovarsi be; *~ bene* be happy

trovata *f* good idea

truccare <1d> make up; *motore* soup up; *partita, elezioni* fix

truccarsi put on one's make-up

truccatore *m*, **-trice** *f* make-up artist

trucco *m* (*pl* -cchi) make-up; (*inganno, astuzia*) trick

truce fierce; (*crudele*) cruel

truffa *f* fraud

truffare <1a> defraud (*di* of)

truffatore *m*, **-trice** *f* trickster, con artist F

truppa *f* troops *pl*; *fig* horde

tu you; *dammi del tu* call me 'tu'; *sei ~?* is that you?

tuba *f* tuba

tubatura *f*, **tubazione** *f* pipes *pl*, piping

tubercolosi *f* tuberculosis

tubero *m* tuber

tubetto *m* tube

tubo *m* pipe; *flessibile* hose; AUTO *~ di scappamento* exhaust (pipe); *~ fluorescente* fluorescent light

tuffare <1a> dip

tuffarsi (*immergersi*) dive; (*buttarsi dentro*) throw o.s. (*anche fig*)

tuffo *m* dip; SP dive

tugurio *m* (*pl* -ri) hovel

tulipano *m* tulip

tumore *m* tumo(u)r

tumulto *m* riot

tumultuoso tumultuous

tunica *f* (*pl* -che) tunic

Tunisia *f* Tunisia

tunisino 1 *agg* Tunisian **2** *m*, **-a** *f* Tunisian

tunnel *m inv* tunnel; *~ dell'orrore* ghost train

tuo (*pl* tuoi) **1** *agg* your; *il ~ amico* your friend; *un ~ amico* a friend of yours **2** *pron*: *il ~* yours

tuonare <1c> thunder

tuono *m* thunder

tuorlo *m* yolk

turare <1a> stop; *bottiglia* put the top on

turbamento *m* perturbation

turbante *m* turban

turbare <1a> upset, disturb

turbina *f* turbine

turbine *m* whirlwind

turbolenza *f* turbulence

turboreattore *m* turbojet

turchese *m/agg* turquoise

Turchia *f* Turkey

turco (*pl* -chi) **1** *m/agg* Turkish **2** *m*, **-a** *f* Turk

turismo *m* tourism; *~ di massa* mass tourism

turista *m/f* (*mpl* -i) tourist

turistico (*pl* -ci) tourist; *assegno m ~* traveller's cheque, *Am* traveler's check

turno *m* turn; *di lavoro* shift; *a ~* in turn; *di ~* on duty; *è il mio ~* it's my turn; *~ di riposo* rest day; *darsi il ~* take turns

tuta *f da lavoro* boiler suit, overalls; *~ da ginnastica* track suit; *~ da sci* salopettes

tutela *f* protection; DIR guardianship

tutelare <1b> protect

tutore *m*, **-trice** *f* guardian

tuttavia still

tutto 1 *agg* whole; *-i, -e pl* all; *~ il libro* the whole book; *-i i giorni* every day; *-i e tre* all three; *noi -i* all of us **2** *avv* all; *era ~ solo* he was all alone; *del ~* quite; *in ~* altogether, in all **3** *pron* all; *gente* everybody, everyone; *cose* everything; *lo ha*

mangiato ~ he ate it all
tuttora still

TV *abbr* (= *televisione*) TV (= television)

U

ubbidiente obedient
ubbidienza *f* obedience
ubbidire <4d> obey; ~ *ai genitori* obey one's parents
ubriacare <1d>: ~ **qu** get s.o. drunk
ubriacarsi get drunk
ubriachezza *f* drunkenness
ubriaco (*pl* -chi) **1** *agg* drunk **2** *m*, -**a** *f* drunk
uccello *m* bird; ~ *rapace* bird of prey
uccidere <3q> kill
uccidersi kill o.s.
ucciso *pp* → *uccidere*
uccisione *f* killing
udienza *f* (audience) audience; DIR hearing
udire <4n> hear
udito *m* hearing
uditorio *m* (*pl* -ri) audience
Ue *abbr* (= *Unione europea*) EU (= European Union)
Uem *abbr* (= *Unione economica e monetaria europea*) EMU (= Economic and Monetary Union)
ufficiale 1 *agg* official; *non* ~ unofficial **2** *m* official; MIL officer
ufficio *m* (*pl* -ci) office; ~ *cambi* bureau de change; ~ *oggetti smarriti* lost property; ~ *postale* post office; ~ *stampa* press office; ~ *di collocamento* Jobcentre; ~ *turistico* tourist information office
ufficioso unofficial
ufo¹ *m*: **a** ~ at other people's expense, free (of charge)
ufo² *m* UFO
uguaglianza *f* equality
uguagliare <1g> make equal; (*livellare*) level; (*essere pari a*) equal
uguale equal; *lo stesso* the same;

terreno level
UIL *abbr* (= *Unione Italiana del Lavoro*) Italian trade union organization
ulcera *f* ulcer; ~ *gastrica* gastric ulcer
ulteriore further
ultimamente recently
ultimare <1l> complete
ultimatum *m inv* ultimatum
ultimo 1 *agg* last; *più recente* latest; ~ *piano* top floor **2** *m*, -**a** *f* last; *fino all'*~ till the end
ultracorto: *onde fpl* -**e** ultrashort waves
ultrasuono *m* ultrasound
ultravioletto ultraviolet
ululare <1l> howl
ululato *m* howl
umanità *f* humanity
umanitario (*pl* -ri) humanitarian
umano human; *trattamento ecc* humane
Ume *abbr* (= *unione monetaria* (*europea*)) EMU (= European Monetary Union)
umidificatore *m* humidifier
umidità *f* dampness
umido 1 *agg* damp **2** *m* dampness; GASTR *in* ~ stewed
umile (*modesto*) humble; *mestiere* menial
umiliante humiliating
umiliare <1g> humiliate
umiliazione *f* humiliation
umiltà *f* humility
umore *m* mood; *di buon* ~ in a good mood; *di cattivo* ~ in a bad mood
umorismo *m* humo(u)r
umorista *m/f* (*mpl* -i) humorist

U

un, una → uno
unanime unanimous
unanimità f unanimity; all'~ unanimously
uncinetto m crochet hook; lavorare all'~ crochet
uncino m hook
undicesimo m/agg eleventh
undici eleven
ungere <3d> grease
ungherese agg, m/f Hungarian
Ungheria f Hungary
unghia f nail
unguento m ointment, cream
unico (pl -ci) only; (senza uguali) unique; moneta f -a single currency
unifamiliare: casa f ~ detached house
unificare <1m & d> unify
unificazione f unification
uniformare <1a> standardize
uniformarsi: ~ a conform to; regole, direttive comply with
uniforme f agg uniform
uniformità f uniformity
unione f union; fig unity; Unione economica e monetaria Economic and Monetary Union; Unione europea European Union; Unione monetaria (europea) (European) Monetary Union
unire <4d> unite; congiungere join
unirsi unite; ~ in matrimonio marry
unità f inv unit; ~ monetaria monetary unit; ~ di misura unit of measurement; INFOR ~ a dischi flessibili disk drive; ~ pl periferiche peripherals
unito united
universale f universal
università f inv university
universitario (pl -ri) 1 agg university attr 2 m, -a f university student; (professore) university lecturer
universo m universe
uno 1 art a; before a vowel or silent h an; un' uovo an egg 2 agg a, one 3 m one; ~ e mezzo one and a half 4 pron one; a ~ a ~ one by one; l'~ dopo l'altro one after the other; l'un l'altro each other, one another

unto 1 pp → ungere 2 agg greasy 3 m grease
unzione f: estrema ~ last rites
uomo m (pl uomini) man; ~ d'affari businessman; ~ di fiducia right-hand man; ~ qualunque man in the street; da ~ abbigliamento ecc for men, men's
uovo m (pl le -a) egg; ~ alla coque soft-boiled egg; ~ di Pasqua Easter egg; ~ al tegame fried egg; -a pl strapazzate scrambled eggs
uragano m hurricane
uranio m uranium
urbanistica f town planning
urbano urban; fig urbane
uretra f urethra
urgente urgent
urgenza f urgency; in caso d'~ in an emergency
urina f urine
urlare <1a> scream
urlo m (pl anche le -a) scream
urna f urn; elettorale ballot box
urologo m (pl -gi), -a f urologist
urrà! hooray!
urtare <1a> bump into, collide with; con un veicolo hit; fig offend; ~ i nervi a qu get on s.o.'s nerves
urto m bump; (scontro) collision
u.s. abbr (= ultimo scorso) last, ult.
USA abbr (= Stati uniti d'America) USA (= United States of America)
usa: ~ e getta disposable
usanza f custom, tradition
usare <1a> 1 v/t use 2 v/i use; (essere di moda) be in fashion
usato used; (di seconda mano) second-hand
uscire <4o> come out; (andare fuori) go out
uscita f exit, way out; INFOR output; ~ di sicurezza emergency exit; via d'~ way out
usignolo m nightingale
uso m use; (abitudine) custom; pronto per l'~ ready to use; fuori ~ out of use; ~ indebito misuse; per ~ interno for internal use; per ~ esterno not to be taken internally
US(S)L, Us(s)l abbr (= Unità

(**Socio-**)**sanitaria Locale**) local health authority

ustionarsi <1a> burn o.s.

ustione f burn

usuale usual

usufruire <4d>: **~ di qc** have the use of sth

usura f di denaro illegal money lending; (logorio) wear and tear

usuraio m (pl -i) loan shark

utensile 1 agg: **macchina** f **~** machine tool **2** m utensil

utente m/f user; **~ della strada** road user

utero m womb

utile 1 agg useful; **in tempo ~** within the time limit **2** m FIN profit; **unire l'~ al dilettevole** combine business with pleasure; **~ netto** net profit; **~ d'esercizio** operating profit

utilità f usefulness

utilitaria f economy car

utilizzare <1a> use

utilizzazione f use

utopia f utopia

utopista m/f (mpl -i) dreamer

uva f grapes pl; **~ passa** raisins pl; **~ spina** gooseberry

V

V abbr (= **volt**) V (= volt)

V. abbr (= **via**) St (= street)

v. abbr (= **vedi**) see

va → andare

vacante vacant

vacanza f holiday; **-e** pl **estive** summer holiday(s); **andare in ~** go on holiday

vacca f (pl -cche) cow

vaccinare <1a> vaccinate

vaccinazione f vaccination; **~ antitetanica** tetanus injection or shot

vaccino m vaccine

vado → andare

vagabondare <1a> wander

vagabondo 1 agg (girovago) wandering; (fannullone) idle **2** m, **-a** f (giramondo) wanderer; (fannullone) idler, layabout F; (barbone) tramp

vagare <1e> wander (aimlessly)

vagina f ANAT vagina

vaglia m inv: **~** (**postale**) postal order; **~ bancario** bill of exchange, draft

vago (pl -ghi) vague

vagone m carriage; **~ letto** sleeper; **~ merci** goods wagon; **~ ristorante**

dining car

vai → andare

vaiolo m smallpox

valanga f (pl -ghe) avalanche

valere <2r> be worth; (essere valido) be valid; **non vale nulla** it's worthless, it isn't worth anything; **far ~ diritti, autorità** assert; **non vale!** that's not fair!

valersi: **~ di qc** avail o.s. of sth

valeriana f valerian

valevole valid

valgo → valere

valico m (pl -chi) pass

validità f validity

valido valid; persona fit; **non ~** invalid

valigia f (pl -gie) suitcase; **fare le -e** pack

valle f valley

valore m value; (coraggio) bravery, valo(u)r; **~ aggiunto** added value; **~ commerciale** market value; **~ corrente** current value; **~ energetico** energy value; **-i** pl securities; **di ~** valuable; **senza ~** worthless

valorizzare <1a> increase the value of; (far risaltare) show off

valoroso courageous

valuta f currency; *stabilità f della ~* monetary stability

valutare <1a> value

valutario monetary

valutazione f valuation

valvola f valve; EL fuse; *~ dell'aria* air valve

valzer m inv waltz

vandalismo m vandalism

vandalo m vandal

vanga f (pl -ghe) spade

vangelo m gospel

vaniglia f vanilla

vanità f vanity

vanitoso vain

vanno → **andare**

vano 1 agg minacce, promesse empty; (inutile) vain **2** m (spazio vuoto) hollow; (stanza) room; AUTO *~ porta-oggetti* glove compartment

vantaggio m (pl -ggi) advantage; *in gara* lead

vantaggioso advantageous

vantare <1a> speak highly of; possedere boast

vantarsi boast (**di** of)

vanto m boast

vapore m vapo(u)r; MAR steamer; *~ (d'acqua)* steam

vaporetto m water bus

vaporizzare <1a> (nebulizzare) spray

vaporoso floaty; (vago) woolly

variabile 1 agg changeable **2** f MAT variable

variare <1k> v/t & v/i vary

variazione f variation

varice f varicose vein

varicella f chickenpox

varietà 1 f inv variety **2** m inv variety, Am vaudeville; (spettacolo m di) *~* variety (Am vaudeville) show

vario (pl -ri) varied; **-ri** pl various

variopinto multicolo(u)red

vasca f (pl -che) (serbatoio, cisterna) tank; (lunghezza di piscina) length; di fontana basin; *~ (da bagno)* bath, (bath)tub

vaselina f vaseline

vasellame m dishes

vaso m pot; ANAT vessel

vassoio m (pl -oi) tray

vasto vast

V.d.F. abbr (= **vigili del fuoco**) fire brigade, Am fire department

ve = **vi** (before **lo, la, li, le, ne**)

vecchiaia f old age

vecchio (pl -cchi) **1** agg old **2** m, **-a** f old man; donna old woman

vece f: *in ~ di* instead of; *fare le -i di qu* take s.o.'s place

vedere <2s> see; *far ~* show; *stare a ~* watch

vedovo 1 agg widowed **2** m, **-a** f widower; donna widow

veduta f view (**su** of); *~ aerea* aerial view; fig *larghezza f di -e* broadmindedness

vegetale 1 agg vegetable attr; regno, vita plant attr **2** m plant

vegetare <1l & b> vegetate

vegetariano 1 agg vegetarian attr **2** m, **-a** f vegetarian

vegetazione f vegetation

vegeto vecchio spry; *vivo e ~* hale and hearty

veggente m/f (chiaroveggente) clairvoyant

veglia f (l'essere svegli) wakefulness; (il vegliare) vigil; *essere tra la ~ e il sonno* be half asleep

vegliare <1g> **1** v/i keep watch **2** v/t: *~ qu* watch over s.o.

veicolo m vehicle; *~ spaziale* spaceship

vela f sail; attività sailing; *fare ~* set sail; *tutto è andato a gonfie -e* everything went swimmingly

veleggiare <1f> sail

veleno m poison; di animali venom (anche fig)

velenoso poisonous; fig venomous

veliero m sailing ship

velina: *carta f ~ per imballaggio* tissue paper

velismo m sailing

velista m/f sailor

velivolo m aircraft

velluto m velvet; *~ a coste* corduroy

velo m veil

veloce fast, quick

velocemente quickly

velocità *f inv* speed; *limite m di ~* speed limit; *eccesso m di ~* speeding; *~ della luce* speed of light; *~ di crociera* cruising speed

velodromo *m* velodrome

vena *f* vein; *essere in ~* be in the mood

vendemmia *f* (grape) harvest

vendemmiare <1k> *v/t v/i* harvest

vendere <3a> sell; *~ all'ingrosso* sell wholesale; *~ al minuto* retail

vendetta *f* revenge

vendicare <1f & d> avenge

vendicarsi get one's revenge (*di qu* on s.o.; *di qc* for sth)

vendita *f* sale; *~ di fine stagione* end-of-season sale; *~ diretta* direct selling

venditore *m*, -trice *f* salesman; *donna* saleswoman

venerare <1l & b> revere

venerazione *f* veneration

venerdì *m inv* Friday; *Venerdì Santo* Good Friday

Venere *f* Venus

Venezia *f* Venice

veneziano 1 *agg* of Venice, Venetian 2 *m*, -a *f* Venetian

vengo → venire

venire <4p> come; (*riuscire*) turn out; *come ausiliare* be; *i suoi disegni vengono ammirati da tutti* his drawings are admired by all; *~ a costare* total, work out at; *~ a sapere qc* learn sth, find sth out; *~ al dunque* get to the point; *mi sta venendo fame* I'm getting hungry

ventaglio *m* (*pl* -gli) fan

ventenne *agg*, *m/f* twenty-year-old

ventesimo *m/agg* twentieth

venti twenty

ventilatore *m* fan

ventilazione *f* ventilation

ventina *f*: *una ~* about twenty

ventiquattrore *f inv* (*valigetta*) overnight bag

vento *m* wind; *c'è ~* it's windy

ventoso windy

ventre *m* stomach; *basso ~* lower abdomen

venturo next

venuta *f* arrival

venuto 1 *pp* → *venire* 2 *m*, -a *f*: *il primo ~* just anyone; *non è certo il primo ~* he's not just anyone

veramente really

veranda *f* veranda

verbale 1 *agg* verbal 2 *m* record; *di riunione* minutes *pl*

verbalizzare <1a> record (in writing), take down; *riunione* take the minutes of; (*esprimere a parole*) verbalize

verbalmente verbally

verbo *m* GRAM verb

verde 1 *agg* green; *benzina* unleaded; *numero ~* freephone number; *essere al ~* be broke 2 *m* green; POL *i -i pl* the Greens

verdetto *m* verdict

verdura *f* vegetables *pl*

vergine 1 *agg* virgin *attr* 2 *f* virgin; ASTR *Vergine* Virgo

verginità *f* virginity

vergogna *f* shame; (*timidezza*) shyness

vergognarsi <1a> be ashamed; (*essere timido*) be shy

vergognoso ashamed; (*timido*) shy; *azione* shameful

verifica *f* (*pl* -che) check

verificare <1m & d> check

verificarsi (*accadere*) occur, take place; (*avverarsi*) come true

verità *f* truth

verme *m* worm; *~ solitario* tapeworm

vermut *m* vermouth

vernice *f* paint; *trasparente* varnish; *pelle* patent leather; *fig* veneer; *~ antiruggine* rust-proofing paint; *~ fresca* wet paint; *~ protettiva* protective coating

verniciare <1f> paint; *con vernice trasparente* varnish; *verniciato di fresco* wet paint

verniciatura *f* painting; *con vernice trasparente* varnishing; *fig* veneer

vero 1 *agg* (*rispondente a verità*) true; (*autentico*) real; *sei contento, ~?* you're happy, aren't you?; *ti piace il*

V

gelato, **~?** you like icecream, don't you?; **fosse ~!** if only (it were true)! **2** *m* truth; PITT **dal ~** from life

veronese 1 *agg* of Verona **2** *m/f* inhabitant of Verona

verosimile likely

verruca *f* (*pl* -che) wart

versamento *m* payment; **ricevuta** *f* **di ~** receipt for payment

versante *m* slope

versare <1b> **1** *v/t vino* pour; *denaro* pay; (*rovesciare*) spill **2** *v/i* (*trovarsi*, *essere*) be

versione *f* version; (*traduzione*) translation; **in ~ originale** original language version

verso 1 *prp* towards; **andare ~ casa** head for home; **~ le otto** about eight o'clock **2** *m di poesie* verse; (*modo*) manner; **non c'è ~** there is no way

vertebra *f* vertebra

vertebrale: **colonna** *f* **~** spinal column

verticale 1 *agg* vertical **2** *f* vertical (line); *in ginnastica* handstand

vertice *m* summit; **incontro** *m* **al ~** summit (meeting)

vertigine *f* vertigo, dizziness; **ho le -i** I feel dizzy

vertiginoso *altezza* dizzy; *prezzi* staggering, sky-high; *velocità* breakneck

verza *f* savoy (cabbage)

vescica *f* (*pl* -che) ANAT bladder

vescovo *m* bishop

vespa *f* ZO wasp

vespaio *m* (*pl* -ai) wasps' nest; *fig* hornets' nest

vestaglia *f* dressing gown, *Am* robe

veste *f fig* (*capacità*, *funzione*) capacity; **in ~ ufficiale** in an offical capacity

vestiario *m* wardrobe

vestire <4b> dress; (*portare*) wear

vestirsi get dressed; *in un certo modo* dress; **~irsi da** (*travestirsi*) dress up as

vestito *m da uomo* suit; *da donna* dress; (*capo di vestiario*) item of clothing, garment; **-i** *pl* clothes; **-i** *pl* **da uomo** men's wear

veterinario *m* (*pl* -ri), **-a** *f* veterinary surgeon, vet F

veto *m* veto; **porre il ~ a** veto

vetraio *m* (*pl* -i), (*installatore*) glazier

vetrata *f finestra* large window; *porta* glass door; *di chiesa* stained-glass window

vetreria *f* (*fabbrica*) glass works; (*negozio*) glazier's

vetrina *f* (shop) window; *mobile* display cabinet; *di museo*, *fig* showcase

vetrinista *m/f* (*mpl* -i) window dresser

vetro *m* glass; *di finestra*, *porta* pane; **di ~** glass *attr*; **~ armato** reinforced glass; **~ smerigliato** frosted glass

vetta *f* top; *di montagna* peak

vettura *f* AUTO car; FERR carriage; **~ da corsa** racing car; **in ~!** all aboard!

vi 1 *pron* you; *riflessivo* yourselves; *reciproco* each other **2** *avv* → **ci**

via 1 *f* street, road; *fig* way; **~ Marconi** Marconi St; **lettera** *f* (**per**) **~ aerea** airmail letter; **Via lattea** Milky Way; **ricorrere alle -e legali** take legal action; **in ~ eccezionale** as an exception; **per ~ di** by; (*a causa di*) because of **2** *m* off, starting signal; SP **dare il ~** give the off; **dare il ~ a qc** get sth under way **3** *avv* away; **andar ~** go away, leave; **~ ~** (*gradualmente*) little by little, gradually; (*man mano*) as (and when); **e così ~** and so on; **~! per scacciare** go away!, scram! F; (*suvvia*) come on! **4** *prp* via, by way of

viabilità *f* road conditions *pl*; (*rete stradale*) road network; (*traffico stradale*) road traffic

viadotto *m* viaduct

viaggiare <1f> travel; **~ per affari** travel on business

viaggiatore *m*, **-trice** *f* travel(l)er

viaggio *m* (*pl* -ggi) journey; **~ aereo** flight; **~ per mare** voyage; **~ di nozze** honeymoon; **~ in comitiva** group travel; **~ in treno** train journey; **~ d'affari** business trip; **~ di studio** study trip; **cestino** *m* **da ~** packed meal; **mettersi in ~** set out;

essere in ~ be away, be travelling

viale *m* avenue

viavai *m inv* coming and going

vibrare <1a> vibrate

vibrazione *f* vibration

vice- *prefisso* vice-

vice *m/f inv* deputy

vicedirettore *m* assistant manager

vicenda *f* (*episodio*) event; (*storia*) story; *alterne ~e* changing fortunes; *a ~* (*a turno*) in turn; (*scambievolmente*) each other, one another

viceversa vice versa

vicinanza *f* nearness, proximity; *-e pl* neighbo(u)rhood *sg*, vicinity *sg*

vicinato *m* neighbo(u)rhood; (*persone*) neighbo(u)rs *pl*

vicino 1 *agg* near, close; *~ a* near, close to; (*accanto a*) next to; (*da ~ esaminare*) closely; *visto* close up **2** *avv* nearby, close by **3** *m*, *-a f* neighbo(u)r

vicolo *m* lane; *~ cieco* dead end

videata *f* INFOR display

video *m* video; F (*schermo*) screen

videocamera *f* videocamera

videocassetta *f* video (cassette)

videocontrollo *m* video surveillance

videogioco *m* video game

videoregistratore *m* video (recorder)

videoteca *f* video library; (*negozio*) video shop

videotel *m inv Italian Videotex®*

videotelefono *m* videophone, viewphone

vietare <1b> forbid; *~ a qu di fare qc* forbid s.o. to do sth

vietato: *~ fumare* no smoking

vigente in force

vigilante *m* security guard

vigilanza *f* vigilance; *sotto ~* under surveillance

vigilare <1l> *persone* watch (over); (*pattugliare*) patrol

vigile 1 *agg* watchful **2** *m/f:* ~ (*urbano*) local police officer; *~ del fuoco* firefighter

vigilia *f* night before, eve; *~ di Natale* Christmas Eve

vigliacco (*pl* -cchi) **1** *agg* cowardly

2 *m*, *-a f* coward

vigna *f* (small) vineyard

vigneto *m* vineyard

vignetta *f* cartoon

vigore *m* vigo(u)r

vigoroso vigorous

vile 1 *agg* vile; (*codardo*) cowardly **2** *m* coward

villa *f* villa

villaggio *m* (*pl* -ggi) village; *~ turistico* holiday village

villeggiatura *f* holiday

villino *m* house

vincere <3d> **1** *v/t* win; *avversario, nemico* defeat, beat; *difficoltà* overcome **2** *v/i* win

vincersi (*dominarsi*) control o.s.

vincita *f* win

vincitore *m*, **-trice** *f* winner

vincolare <1l> bind; *capitale* tie up

vincolo *m* bond

vino *m* wine; *~ bianco* white wine; *~ rosso* red wine; *~ da pasto* table wine

vinto *pp* → **vincere**

viola *f* MUS viola; BOT violet; *~ del pensiero* pansy

violare <1l> violate; *legge* break

violazione *f* violation; *di leggi, patti, accordi* breach; *~ di domicilio* unlawful entry

violentare <1b> rape

violentatore *m* rapist

violento violent

violenza *f* violence

violinista *m/f* (*mpl* -i) violinist

violino *m* violin

violoncello *m* cello

vipera *f* viper

virgola *f* comma; MAT decimal point

virile manly, virile

virtù *f inv* virtue

virtuoso 1 *agg* virtuous **2** *m* virtuoso

virus *m inv* virus

viscere *fpl* insides; *fig: della terra* bowels

vischio *m* (*pl* -chi) mistletoe

viscido slimy

viscosa *f* viscose

viscoso viscous

visibile visible

V

visibilità f visibility

visiera f di berretto peak; di casco visor

visione f sight, vision; **prendere ~ di qc** have a look at sth; **in ~** for examination

visita f visit; **~ medica** medical (examination); **far ~ a qu** visit s.o.

visitare <1l> visit; MED examine

visitatore m, **-trice** f visitor

visivo visual

viso m face

visone m mink

vissuto pp → **vivere**

vista f (senso) sight; (capacità visiva) eyesight; (veduta) view; **a prima ~** at first sight; MUS at sight; **in ~ di** in sight of; fig in view of; **conoscere qu di ~** know s.o. by sight; fig **perdere qu di ~** lose touch with s.o.

visto 1 pp → **vedere**; **~ che** seeing that **2** m visa; **~ d'entrata** entry visa; **~ di transito** transit visa; **~ d'uscita** exit visa

vistoso eye-catching

visuale 1 agg visual **2** f (veduta) view

vita f life; (durata della vita) lifetime; ANAT waist; **a ~** for life; **costo m della ~** cost of living; **senza ~** lifeless

vitale vital; persona lively, full of life

vitalità f inv vitality

vitamina f vitamin

vite[1] f TEC screw

vite[2] f AGR vine

vitello m calf; GASTR veal

viticoltore m vinegrower

viticoltura f vinegrowing

vitreo fig: sguardo, occhio glazed, glassy

vittima f victim

vitto m diet food; **~ e alloggio** bed and board

vittoria f victory

vittorioso victorious

vivace lively; colore bright

vivacità f liveliness; di colori brightness

vivaio m di pesci tank; di piante nursery; fig breeding ground

vivanda f food

viva voce m inv speakerphone

vivente living

vivere <3zz> **1** v/i live (**di** on) **2** v/t (passare, provare) experience; **~ una vita tranquilla** live quietly, lead a quiet life

viveri mpl food (supplies)

vivisezione f vivisection

vivo 1 agg (in vita) alive; (vivente) living; colore bright; **farsi ~** get in touch; (arrivare) turn up; **~ e vegeto** hale and hearty **2** m: **dal ~** trasmissione, concerto live; **entrare nel ~ della questione** get to the heart of the matter; **i -i** pl the living

viziare <1g> persona spoil

viziato persona spoiled; aria f **-a** stale air

vizio m (pl -zi) vice; (cattiva abitudine) (bad) habit; (dipendenza) addiction; **~ cardiaco** heart defect

vizioso persona dissolute; **circolo m ~** vicious circle

v.le abbr (= **viale**) St (= street)

vocabolario m (pl -ri) (lessico) vocabulary; (dizionario) dictionary

vocabolo m word

vocale 1 agg vocal **2** f vowel

vocazione f vocation

voce f voice; fig rumo(u)r; in dizionario, elenco entry; **ad alta ~** in a loud voice, loudly; **a bassa ~** in a low voice, quietly; **spargere la ~** spread rumo(u)rs

voglia f (desiderio) wish, desire; (volontà) will; sulla pelle birthmark; **avere ~ di fare qc** feel like doing sth; **morire dalla ~ di fare qc** be dying to do sth; **contro ~, di mala ~** unwillingly, reluctantly

voglio → **volere**

voi you; riflessivo yourselves; reciproco each other; **a ~** to you; **senza di ~** without you

vol. abbr (= **volume**) vol (= volume)

volano m shuttlecock

volante 1 agg flying **2** m AUTO (steering) wheel **3** f flying squad

volantino m leaflet

volare <1a> fly

volata f SP final sprint; **di ~** in a rush

volenteroso willing

volentieri willingly; **~!** with pleasure!

volere **1** <2t> *v/t* & *v/i* want; *vorrei ...* I would *or* I'd like ...; *vorrei partire* I'd like to leave; **~ dire** mean; **~ bene a qu** (*amare*) love s.o.; *ci vogliono dieci mesi* it takes ten months; *senza ~* without meaning to **2** *m* will

volgare vulgar

volgarità *f* vulgarity

volgere <3d> **1** *v/t*: **~ le spalle** turn one's back **2** *v/i*: **~ al termine** draw to a close; *il tempo volge al brutto* the weather is getting worse; **~ al peggio** take a turn for the worse

volo *m* flight; (*caduta*) fall; *prendere il ~ di uccello* fly away; *di persona* run away; **~ a vela** gliding; **~ diretto** direct flight; **~ di linea** scheduled flight; **~ internazionale** international flight; **~ nazionale** domestic flight; **~ senza scalo** nonstop flight; *fig afferrare qc al ~ be* quick to grasp sth

volontà *f* will; *a ~* as much as you like; *buona ~* goodwill

volontariato *m* voluntary work

volontario (*pl* -ri) **1** *agg* voluntary **2** *m*, *-a f* volunteer

volpe *f* fox; *femmina* vixen

volt *m inv* volt

volta *f* time; (*turno*) turn; ARCHI vault; *una ~* once; *due -e* twice; *qualche ~* sometimes; *questa ~* this time; *ogni ~* every time; *una ~ per sempre* once and for all; *poco per ~* little by little; *un'altra ~ ancora una volta* one more time; *lo faremo un'altra ~* we'll do it some other time; *molte -e* many times, often

voltaggio *m* (*pl* -ggi) voltage

voltare <1c> **1** *v/t* turn; *pagina* turn (over); **~ le spalle a qu** *azione* turn one's back on s.o.; *posizione* have one's back to s.o. **2** *v/i* turn; **~ a destra** turn right

voltarsi turn (round)

volto[1] *m* face

volto[2] *pp* → **volgere**

volume *m* volume

voluminoso bulky

voluttà *f* voluptuousness

vomitare <1l & c> vomit, throw up F; *fig mi fa ~* it makes me sick

vomito *m* vomit

vongola *f* ZO, GASTR clam

voragine *f* chasm, abyss

vortice *m* whirl; *in acqua* whirlpool; *di vento* whirlwind

vostro **1** *agg* your; *i -i amici* your friends **2** *pron*: *il ~* yours; *questi libri sono -i* these books are yours

votare <1a> vote

votazione *f* vote

voto *m* POL vote; EDU mark; REL, *fig* vow; *mettere qc ai -i* put sth to the vote, take a vote on sth

v.r. *abbr* (= *vedi retro*) see over

Vs. *abbr* (= *vostro*) your

v.s. *abbr* (= *vedi sopra*) see above

V.U. *abbr* (= *Vigili Urbani*) police

vulcanico (*pl* -ci) volcanic

vulcano *m* volcano

vulnerabile vulnerable

vuole → **volere**

vuotare <1c> empty

vuotarsi empty

vuoto **1** *agg* empty; (*non occupato*) vacant; (*privo*) devoid (*di* of) **2** *m* (*spazio*) empty space; (*recipiente*) empty; FIS vacuum; *fig* void; **~ d'aria** air pocket; **~ a perdere** non-return-able container; **~ a rendere** return-able container; *andare a ~* fall through; (*confezionato*) *sotto ~* vacuum-packed

V

W

W *abbr* (= **watt**) W (= watt); (= **viva**) long live
walkman *m inv* Walkman®
watt *m inv* watt
WC *abbr* (= **gabinetto**) WC (= water closet)
week-end *m inv* weekend

western *m inv* Western; **~ all'italiana** spaghetti Western
whisky *m inv* whisky
windsurf *m inv* (*tavola*) sailboard; *attività* windsurfing; **fare ~** go windsurfing
W.L. *abbr* (= **vagone letto**) sleeper

XY

X, x *f* x; **raggi** *mpl* **~** X-rays
xenofobia *f* xenophobia
xenofobo 1 *agg* xenophobic **2** *m*, **-a** *f* xenophobe
xilofono *m* xylophone

yacht *m inv* yacht
yoga *m* yoga
yogurt *m inv* yoghurt
yugoslavo 1 *agg* Yugoslav(ian) **2** *m*, **-a** *f* Yugoslav(ian)

Z

zabaione *m* zabaglione
zafferano *m* saffron
zaffiro *m* sapphire
zagara *f* orange blossom
zaino *m* rucksack
zampa *f* ZO (*piede*) paw; *di uccello* claw; (*zoccolo*) hoof; (*arto*) leg; GASTR *di maiale* trotter; *fig* **giù le -e!** hands off!; **a ~ di elefante** flared
zampillare <1a> gush
zampillo *m* spurt
zampone *m* GASTR stuffed pig's trotter
zanzara *f* mosquito

zanzariera *f* mosquito net; *su finestre* insect screen
zappa *f* hoe
zappare <1a> hoe
zapping *m inv* **fare lo ~** zap
zattera *f* raft
zavorra *f* ballast
zebra *f* zebra
zecca[1] *f* (*pl* -cche) ZO tick
zecca[2] *f* (*pl* -cche) Mint; **nuovo di ~** brand-new
zelante zealous
zelo *m* zeal
zenit *m* zenith

W

zenzero *m* ginger

zeppo: pieno ~ crammed (**di** with)

zerbino *m* doormat

zero *m* zero; *nel tennis* love; *nel calcio* nil; *fig* **partire da ~** start from scratch; **2 gradi sotto ~** 2 degrees below zero

zigomo *m* cheekbone

zigzag *m inv* zigzag

zimbello *m* decoy; *fig* laughing stock

zinco *m* zinc

zingaro m, **-a** *f* gipsy

zio *m*, **-a** *f* uncle; *donna* aunt

zitto quiet; **sta ~!** be quiet!; *in tono minaccioso* keep your mouth shut! F

zoccolo *m* clog; ZO hoof; ARCHI base

zodiacale: segni *mpl* **-i** signs of the Zodiac

zodiaco *m* Zodiac

zolfo *m* sulphur, *Am* sulfur

zona *f* zone, area; **~ di libero scambio** free trade area; **~ disco** short-stay parking area; **~ industriale** industrial area; **~ pedonale** pedestrian precinct; **~ residenziale** residential area; **~ verde** green belt

zonzo: andare a ~ wander around

zoo *m inv* zoo

zoppicare <1l, c & d> limp; *di mobile* wobble

zoppo lame; (*zoppicante*) limping; *mobile* wobbly

zucca *f* (*pl* -cche) marrow; *fig* F (*testa*) bonce F, nut F

zuccherare <1l> sugar

zuccheriera *f* sugar bowl

zucchero *m* sugar; **~ greggio** brown sugar; **~ vanigliato** vanilla sugar; **~ in zollette** sugar cubes

zucchini *mpl* courgettes, *Am* zucchini(s)

zuffa *f* scuffle

zuppa *f* soup; **~ di verdura** vegetable soup; **~ di pesce** fish soup; **~ inglese** trifle

zuppiera *f* tureen

zuppo soaked, wet through

Z

A

a [ə] *stressed* [eɪ] *art* un *m*, una *f*; *masculine before s + consonant, gn, ps, z* uno; *feminine before vowel* un'; **~ cat** un gatto; **~ joke** uno scherzo; **~ girl** una ragazza; **an island** un'isola; **£5 ~ ride** una corsa 5 sterline; **£2 ~ litre** 2 sterline al litro; **five flights ~ day** cinque voli al giorno

a·back [ə'bæk] *adv*: **taken ~** preso alla sprovvista

a·ban·don [ə'bændən] *v/t* abbandonare; *hope, scheme* rinunciare a

a·bashed [ə'bæʃt] *adj* imbarazzato

a·bate [ə'beɪt] *v/i of storm, flood waters* calmarsi

ab·at·toir ['æbətwɑː(r)] *m* mattatoio *m*

ab·bey ['æbɪ] abbazia *f*

ab·bre·vi·ate [ə'briːvɪeɪt] *v/t* abbreviare

ab·bre·vi·a·tion [əbriːvɪ'eɪʃn] abbreviazione *f*

ab·di·cate ['æbdɪkeɪt] *v/i* abdicare

ab·di·ca·tion [æbdɪ'keɪʃn] abdicazione *f*

ab·do·men ['æbdəmən] addome *m*

ab·dom·i·nal [æb'dɒmɪnl] *adj* addominale

ab·duct [əb'dʌkt] *v/t* sequestrare, rapire

ab·duc·tion [əb'dʌkʃn] sequestro *m*, rapimento *m*

ab·hor·rence [əb'hɒrəns] *fml* orrore *m*

ab·hor·rent [əb'hɒrənt] *adj fml* ripugnante

♦ **abide by** [ə'baɪd] *v/t* attenersi a

a·bil·i·ty [ə'bɪlətɪ] abilità *f inv*

a·blaze [ə'bleɪz] *adj* in fiamme

a·ble ['eɪbl] *adj* (*skilful*) capace; **be ~ to** essere capace a; **I wasn't ~ to see / hear** non ero in grado di vedere / sentire

a·ble-bod·ied [eɪbl'bɒdɪːd] *adj* robusto; *MIL* abile

ab·nor·mal [æb'nɔːml] *adj* anormale

ab·nor·mal·ly [æb'nɔːməlɪ] *adv* in modo anomalo

a·board [ə'bɔːd] **1** *prep* a bordo di **2** *adv*: **be ~** essere a bordo; **go ~** salire a bordo

a·bol·ish [ə'bɒlɪʃ] *v/t* abolire

ab·o·li·tion [æbə'lɪʃn] abolizione *f*

a·bort [ə'bɔːt] *v/t mission, rocket launch* annullare; *COMPUT: program* interrompere

a·bor·tion [ə'bɔːʃn] aborto *m*; **have an ~** abortire

a·bor·tive [ə'bɔːtɪv] *adj* fallito; **the plan proved ~** il piano si è rivelato un fallimento

a·bout [ə'baʊt] **1** *prep* (*concerning*) su; *I'll tell you all ~ it* ti dirò tutto al riguardo; **talk ~ sth** parlare di qc; **be angry ~ sth** essere arrabbiato per qc; **there's nothing you can do ~ it** non ci puoi fare niente; **what's it ~?** *of book, film* di cosa parla?; *of complaint, problem* di cosa si tratta? **2** *adv* (*roughly*) intorno a, verso; (*nearly*) quasi; **it's ~ ready** è quasi pronto; **be ~ to ...** (*be going to*) essere sul punto di ...; **be ~** (*somewhere near*) essere nei paraggi; **there are a lot of people** c'è un sacco di gente qui

a·bove [ə'bʌv] **1** *prep* (*higher than*) sopra; (*more than*) sopra, oltre; **~ all** soprattutto **2** *adv* sopra; **on the floor ~** al piano di sopra

a·bove-men·tioned [əbʌv'menʃnd] *adj* suddetto

ab·ra·sion [ə'breɪʒn] abrasione *f*

ab·ra·sive [ə'breɪsɪv] *adj personality* ruvido

a·breast [ə'brest] *adv* fianco a fianco; **keep ~ of** tenere al corrente di

a·bridge [ə'brɪdʒ] *v/t* ridurre

a·broad [ə'brɔːd] *adv* all'estero

a·brupt [əˈbrʌpt] *adj departure* improvviso; *manner* brusco

a·brupt·ly [əˈbrʌptlɪ] *adv leave* improvvisamente; *say* bruscamente

ab·scess [ˈæbsɪs] ascesso *m*

ab·sence [ˈæbsəns] assenza *f*

ab·sent [ˈæbsənt] *adj* assente

ab·sen·tee [æbsənˈtiː] *n* assente *m/f*

ab·sen·tee·ism [æbsənˈtiːɪzm] assenteismo *m*

ab·sent-mind·ed [æbsəntˈmaɪndɪd] *adj* distratto

ab·sent-mind·ed·ly [æbsəntˈmaɪndɪdlɪ] *adv* distrattamente

ab·so·lute [ˈæbsəluːt] *adj power* assoluto; *idiot* totale

ab·so·lute·ly [ˈæbsəluːtlɪ] *adv* (*completely*) assolutamente; **~ not!** assolutamente no!; *do you agree?* – ~ sei d'accordo? – assolutamente sì

ab·so·lu·tion [æbsəˈluːʃn] REL assoluzione *f*

ab·solve [əbˈzɒlv] *v/t* assolvere

ab·sorb [əbˈsɔːb] *v/t* assorbire; **~ed in ...** assorto in ...

ab·sorb·en·cy [əbˈsɔːbənsɪ] assorbenza *f*

ab·sorb·ent [əbˈsɔːbənt] *adj* assorbente

ab·sorb·ing [əbˈsɔːbɪŋ] *adj* avvincente

ab·stain [əbˈsteɪn] *v/i from voting* astenersi

ab·sten·tion [əbˈstenʃn] *in voting* astensione *f*

ab·sti·nence [ˈæbstɪnəns] astinenza *f*

ab·stract [ˈæbstrækt] *adj* astratto

ab·struse [əbˈstruːs] *adj* astruso

ab·surd [əbˈsɜːd] *adj* assurdo

ab·surd·i·ty [əbˈsɜːdətɪ] assurdità *f*

ab·surd·ly [əbˈsɜːdlɪ] *adv* in modo assurdo

a·bun·dance [əˈbʌndəns] abbondanza *f*

a·bun·dant [əˈbʌndənt] *adj* abbondante

a·buse¹ [əˈbjuːs] *n* abuso *m*; (*ill treatment*) maltrattamento *m*; (*insults*) insulti *mpl*

a·buse² [əˈbjuːz] *v/t* abusare di; (*treat badly*) maltrattare; (*insult*) insultare

a·bu·sive [əˈbjuːsɪv] *adj language* offensivo; **become ~** diventare aggressivo

a·bys·mal [əˈbɪzml] *adj* F (*very bad*) pessimo

a·byss [əˈbɪs] abisso *m*

AC [ˈeɪsiː] *abbr* (= **alternating current**) c.a. (corrente *f* alternata)

ac·a·dem·ic [ækəˈdemɪk] **1** *n* docente *m/f* universitario, -a **2** *adj* accademico; *person* portato per lo studio

a·cad·e·my [əˈkædəmɪ] accademia *f*

ac·cede [əkˈsiːd] *v/i:* **~ to throne** salire a

ac·cel·e·rate [əkˈseləreɪt] *v/t & v/i* accelerare

ac·cel·e·ra·tion [əkseləˈreɪʃn] *of car* accelerazione *f*

ac·cel·e·ra·tor [əkˈseləreɪtə(r)] *of car* acceleratore *m*

ac·cent [ˈæksənt] accento *m*

ac·cen·tu·ate [əkˈsentjueɪt] *v/t* accentuare

ac·cept [əkˈsept] *v/t* accettare

ac·cep·ta·ble [əkˈseptəbl] *adj* accettabile

ac·cept·ance [əkˈseptəns] accettazione *f*

ac·cess [ˈækses] **1** *n* accesso *m*; **have ~ to** *computer* avere accesso a; *child* avere il permesso di vedere **2** *v/t* accedere a

'ac·cess code COMPUT codice *m* di accesso

ac·ces·si·ble [əkˈsesəbl] *adj* accessibile

ac·ces·sion [əkˈseʃn] ascesa *f*

ac·ces·so·ry [əkˈsesərɪ] *for wearing* accessorio *m*; LAW complice *m/f*

'ac·cess road svincolo *m*

'ac·cess time COMPUT tempo *m* di accesso

ac·ci·dent [ˈæksɪdənt] incidente *m*; **by ~** per caso

ac·ci·den·tal [æksɪˈdentl] *adj* accidentale

ac·ci·den·tal·ly [æksɪˈdentlɪ] *adv* accidentalmente

ac·claim [əˈkleɪm] **1** *n* consenso *m* **2** *v/t* acclamare ac·cla·ma·tion [ækləˈmeɪʃn] acclamazioni *fpl*

ac·cli·mate, **ac·cli·ma·tize** [əˈklaɪmət, əˈklaɪmətaɪz] **1** *v/t* acclimatare **2** *v/i* acclimatarsi

ac·com·mo·date [əˈkɒmədeɪt] *v/t* ospitare; *special requirements* tenere conto di

ac·com·mo·da·tion [əkɒməˈdeɪʃn] sistemazione *f*

ac·com·pa·ni·ment [əˈkʌmpənɪmənt] MUS accompagnamento *m*

ac·com·pa·nist [əˈkʌmpənɪst] MUS: **with Gerald Moore as his ~** con l'accompagnamento di Gerald Moore

ac·com·pa·ny [əˈkʌmpənɪ] *v/t* (*pret & pp* **-ied**) accompagnare

ac·com·plice [əˈkʌmplɪs] complice *m/f*

ac·com·plish [əˈkʌmplɪʃ] *v/t task* compiere; *goal* conseguire

ac·com·plished [əˈkʌmplɪʃt] *adj* dotato

ac·com·plish·ment [əˈkʌmplɪʃmənt] *of a task* realizzazione *f*; (*talent*) talento *m*; (*achievement*) risultato *m*

accord [əˈkɔːd] accordo *m*; **of his / my own ~** di sua / mia spontanea volontà

ac·cord·ance [əˈkɔːdəns]: **in ~ with** conformemente a

ac·cord·ing [əˈkɔːdɪŋ] *adv*: **~ to** secondo

ac·cord·ing·ly [əˈkɔːdɪŋlɪ] *adv* di conseguenza

ac·cor·di·on [əˈkɔːdɪən] fisarmonica *f*

ac·cor·di·on·ist [əˈkɔːdɪənɪst] fisarmonicista *m/f*

ac·count [əˈkaʊnt] *financial* conto *m*; (*report, description*) resoconto *m*; **give an ~** fare un resoconto di; **on no ~** per nessuna ragione; **on ~ of** a causa di; **take ... into ~, take ~ of ...** tenere conto di ...

♦ **account for** *v/t* (*explain*) giustificare; (*make up, constitute*) ammontare a

ac·count·abil·i·ty [əkaʊntəˈbɪlətɪ]

responsabilità *f*

ac·coun·ta·ble [əˈkaʊntəbl] *adj* responsabile; **be held ~** essere considerato responsabile

ac·coun·tant [əˈkaʊntənt] contabile *m/f*; *running own business* commercialista *m/f*

ac'count hol·der titolare *m/f* di conto; *of current account* correntista *m/f*

ac'count num·ber numero *m* di conto

ac·counts [əˈkaʊnts] *npl* contabilità *f*

ac·cu·mu·late [əˈkjuːmjʊleɪt] **1** *v/t* accumulare **2** *v/i* accumularsi

ac·cu·mu·la·tion [əkjuːmjʊˈleɪʃn] accumulazione *f*

ac·cu·ra·cy [ˈækjʊrəsɪ] precisione *f*

ac·cu·rate [ˈækjʊrət] *adj* preciso

ac·cu·rate·ly [ˈækjʊrətlɪ] *adv* con precisione

ac·cu·sa·tion [ækjuːˈzeɪʃn] accusa *f*

ac·cuse [əˈkjuːz] *v/t* accusare; **he ~d me of lying** mi ha accusato di mentire; **be ~d of ...** LAW essere accusato di ...

ac·cused [əˈkjuːzd] *n* LAW accusato *m*, -a *f*

ac'cus·ing [əˈkjuːzɪŋ] *adj* accusatorio

ac'cus·ing·ly [əˈkjuːzɪŋlɪ] *adv look, point* con aria accusatoria; *say* con tono accusatorio

ac·cus·tom [əˈkʌstəm] *v/t*: **get ~ed to** abituarsi a; **be ~ed to** essere abituato a

ace [eɪs] *in cards* asso *m*; (*in tennis: shot*) ace *m inv*

ache [eɪk] **1** *n* dolore *m* **2** *v/i* fare male; **my head ~s** mi fa male la testa

a·chieve [əˈtʃiːv] *v/t* realizzare; *success, fame* ottenere

a·chieve·ment [əˈtʃiːvmənt] *of ambition* realizzazione *f*; (*thing achieved*) successo *m*

ac·id [ˈæsɪd] *n* acido *m*

a·cid·i·ty [əˈsɪdətɪ] *also fig* acidità *f*

ac·id 'rain pioggia *f* acida

'ac·id test *fig* prova *f* della verità

ac·knowl·edge [ək'nɒlɪdʒ] *v/t* riconoscere; *by smile, nod* far capire di aver notato; *he ~d the applause with a smile* ha risposto all'applauso con un sorriso; *~ (receipt of) a letter* accusare ricezione di una lettera

ac·knowl·edg(e)·ment [ək'nɒlɪdʒmənt] riconoscimento *m*; *(smile, nod)* cenno *m*; *(letter)* lettera *f* di accusata ricezione; *in ~ of thanking* come pegno di riconoscenza di; *~s (in book)* ringraziamenti *mpl*

ac·ne ['æknɪ] MED acne *m*

a·corn ['eɪkɔːn] BOT ghianda *f*

a·cous·tics [ə'kuːstɪks] acustica *f*

ac·quaint [ə'kweɪnt] *v/t*: *be ~ed with fml* conoscere

ac·quain·tance [ə'kweɪntəns] *person* conoscenza *f*

ac·qui·esce [ækwɪ'es] *v/i fml* acconsentire

ac·qui·es·cence [ækwɪ'esns] *fml* consentimento *m*

ac·quire [ə'kwaɪə(r)] *v/t* acquisire

ac·qui·si·tion [ækwɪ'zɪʃn] acquisizione *f*

ac·quis·i·tive [ə'kwɪzətɪv] *adj* avido

ac·quit [ə'kwɪt] *v/t* LAW assolvere

ac·quit·tal [ə'kwɪtl] LAW assoluzione *f*

a·cre ['eɪkə(r)] acro *m*

a·cre·age ['eɪkrɪdʒ] estensione *f* in acri

ac·rid ['ækrɪd] *adj smell* acre

ac·ri·mo·ni·ous [ækrɪ'məʊnɪəs] *adj* aspro

ac·ro·bat ['ækrəbæt] acrobata *m/f*

ac·ro·bat·ic [ækrə'bætɪk] *adj* acrobatico

ac·ro·bat·ics [ækrə'bætɪks] *npl* acrobazie *fpl*

ac·ro·nym ['ækrənɪm] acronimo *m*

a·cross [ə'krɒs] **1** *prep on other side of* dall'altro lato di; *sail ~ the Atlantic* attraversare l'Atlantico in barca a vela; *walk ~ the street* attraversare la strada; *a bridge ~ the river* un ponte sul fiume; *~ Europe all over in* tutta Europa **2** *adv to other side* dall'altro lato; *10 m ~* largo 10 m; *they*

came to the river and swam ~ sono arrivati al fiume e l'hanno attraversato a nuoto

a·cryl·ic [ə'krɪlɪk] *adj* acrilico

act [ækt] **1** *v/i* agire; THEA recitare; *(pretend)* fare finta; *~ as* fare le funzioni di **2** *n (deed)* atto *m*; *of play* atto *m*; *in variety show* numero *m*; *(pretence)* finta *f*; *(law)* atto *m*; *~ of God* causa *f* di forza maggiore

act·ing ['æktɪŋ] **1** *n* recitazione *f*; *she went into ~* si è data alla recitazione **2** *adj (temporary)* facente funzione; *the ~ president* il facente funzione di presidente

ac·tion ['ækʃn] azione *f*; *out of ~ (not functioning)* fuori uso; *take ~* agire; *bring an ~ against* LAW fare causa a

ac·tion 're·play TV replay *m inv*

ac·tive ['æktɪv] *adj* attivo; GRAM attivo

ac·tiv·ist ['æktɪvɪst] POL attivista *m/f*

ac·tiv·i·ty [æk'tɪvəti] attività *f*

ac·tor ['æktə(r)] attore *m*

ac·tress ['æktrɪs] attrice *f*

ac·tu·al ['æktʃʊəl] *adj* reale; *cost* effettivo; *the ~ ceremony starts at 10* la cerimonia vera e propria comincia alle 10

ac·tu·al·ly ['æktʃʊəli] *adv (in fact, to tell the truth)* in realtà; *expressing surprise* veramente; *~ I do know him* stressing the converse a dire il vero, lo conosco

ac·u·punc·ture ['ækjʊpʌŋktʃə(r)] agopuntura *f*

a·cute [ə'kjuːt] *adj pain, sense* acuto; *shortage* estremo

a·cute·ly [ə'kjuːtli] *adv (extremely)* estremamente

AD [eɪ'diː] *abbr (= anno domini)* d.C. (= dopo Cristo)

ad [æd] → *advertisement*

ad·a·mant ['ædəmənt] *adj* categorico

ad·a·mant·ly ['ædəməntli] *adv* categoricamente

Ad·am's ap·ple [ædəmz'æpəl] pomo *m* di Adamo

a·dapt [ə'dæpt] **1** *v/t* adattare **2** *v/i of*

person adattarsi

a·dapt·a·bil·i·ty [ədæptə'bɪlətɪ] adattabilità *f*

a·dap·ta·ble [ə'dæptəbl] *adj* adattabile

a·dap·ta·tion [ædæp'teɪʃn] *of play etc* adattamento *m*

a·dapt·or [ə'dæptə(r)] *electrical* adattatore *m*

add [æd] **1** *v/t* aggiungere; MATH addizionare **2** *v/i of person* fare le somme

♦ **add on** *v/t 15% etc* aggiungere

♦ **add up 1** *v/t* sommare **2** *v/i fig* quadrare

ad·der ['ædə(r)] vipera *f* rossa

ad·dict ['ædɪkt] *to football, chess* maniaco *m*, -a *f*; ***drug* ~** tossicomane *m/f*, tossicodipendente *m/f*; **heroin ~** eroinomane *m/f*; **TV ~** teledipendente *m/f*

ad·dic·ted [ə'dɪktɪd] *adj* dipendente; **be ~ to** *drugs, alcohol* essere dedito a; *football, computer games etc* essere un maniaco di

ad·dic·tion [ə'dɪkʃn] *to drugs* dipendenza *f*, assuefazione *f*; *to TV, chocolate etc* dipendenza *f*

ad·dic·tive [ə'dɪktɪv] *adj*: **be ~ of** *drugs* provocare dipendenza o assuefazione; *of TV, chocolate etc* provocare dipendenza

ad·di·tion [ə'dɪʃn] MATH addizione *f*; *to list, company etc* aggiunta *f*; **in ~ to** in aggiunta a

ad·di·tion·al [ə'dɪʃnl] *adj* aggiuntivo

ad·di·tive ['ædɪtɪv] additivo *m*

add-on ['ædɒn] complemento *m*

ad·dress [ə'dres] **1** *n* indirizzo *m*; **form of ~** appellativo *m* **2** *v/t letter* indirizzare; *audience* tenere un discorso a; *person* rivolgersi a

ad·dress book indirizzario *m*

ad·dress·ee [ædre'siː] destinatario *m*, -a *f*

ad·ept [ə'dept] *adj* esperto; **be ~ at** essere esperto in

ad·e·quate ['ædɪkwət] *adj* adeguato

ad·e·quate·ly ['ædɪkwətlɪ] *adv* adeguatamente

ad·here [əd'hɪə(r)] *v/i* aderire

♦ **adhere to** *v/t surface* aderire a; *rules* attenersi a

ad·he·sive [əd'hiːsɪv] *n* adesivo *m*

ad·he·sive 'plas·ter cerotto *m*

ad·he·sive 'tape nastro *m* adesivo

ad·ja·cent [ə'dʒeɪsnt] *adj* adiacente

ad·jec·tive ['ædʒɪktɪv] aggettivo *m*

ad·join [ə'dʒɔɪn] *v/t* essere adiacente a

ad·join·ing [ə'dʒɔɪnɪŋ] *adj* adiacente

ad·journ [ə'dʒɜːn] *v/i* aggiornare

ad·journ·ment [ə'dʒɜːnmənt] aggiornamento *m*

ad·just [ə'dʒʌst] *v/t* regolare; **~ o.s. to** adattarsi a

ad·just·a·ble [ə'dʒʌstəbl] *adj* regolabile

ad·just·ment [ə'dʒʌstmənt] regolazione *f*; *psychological* adattamento *m*

ad lib [æd'lɪb] **1** *adj & adv* a braccio F **2** *v/i* (*pret & pp* **-bed**) improvvisare

ad·min·is·ter [əd'mɪnɪstə(r)] *v/t medicine* somministrare; *company* amministrare; *country* governare

ad·min·is·tra·tion [ədmɪnɪ'streɪʃn] amministrazione *f*; (*government*) governo *m*

ad·min·is·tra·tive [ədmɪnɪ'strətɪv] *adj* amministrativo

ad·min·is·tra·tor [əd'mɪnɪstreɪtə(r)] amministratore *m*, -trice *f*

ad·mi·ra·ble ['ædmərəbl] *adj* ammirevole

ad·mi·ra·bly ['ædmərəblɪ] *adv* ammirevolmente

ad·mi·ral ['ædmərəl] ammiraglio *m*

ad·mi·ra·tion [ædmə'reɪʃn] ammirazione *f*

ad·mire [əd'maɪə(r)] *v/t* ammirare

ad·mir·er [əd'maɪərə(r)] ammiratore *m*, -trice *f*

ad·mir·ing [əd'maɪərɪŋ] *adj* ammirativo

ad·mir·ing·ly [əd'maɪərɪŋlɪ] *adv* con ammirazione

ad·mis·si·ble [əd'mɪsəbl] *adj* ammissibile

ad·mis·sion [əd'mɪʃn] (*confession*) ammissione *f*; **~ free** entrata *f* libera

ad·mit [əd'mɪt] *v/t* (*pret & pp* **-ted**)

ammettere; *to a place* lasciare entrare; *to school, club etc* ammettere; *to hospital* ricoverare

ad·mit·tance [əd'mɪtəns]: *no ~* vietato l'accesso

ad·mit·ted·ly [əd'mɪtedlɪ] *adv* effettivamente

ad·mon·ish [əd'mɒnɪʃ] *v/t fml* ammonire

a·do [ə'duː]: *without further ~* senza ulteriori indugi

ad·o·les·cence [ædə'lesns] adolescenza *f*

ad·o·les·cent [ædə'lesnt] **1** *n* adolescente *m/f* **2** *adj* adolescenziale

a·dopt [ə'dɒpt] *v/t* adottare

a·dop·tion [ə'dɒpʃn] adozione *f*

adop·tive par·ents [ədɒptɪv 'peərənts] *npl* genitori *mpl* adottivi

a·dor·a·ble [ə'dɔːrəbl] *adj* adorabile

ad·o·ra·tion [ædə'reɪʃn] adorazione *f*

a·dore [ə'dɔː(r)] *v/t* adorare

a·dor·ing [ə'dɔːrɪŋ] *adj* in adorazione

ad·ren·al·in [ə'drenəlɪn] adrenalina *f*

a·drift [ə'drɪft] *adj* alla deriva; *fig* sbandato

ad·u·la·tion [ædjʊ'leɪʃn] adulazione *f*

ad·ult ['ædʌlt] **1** *n* adulto *m*, -a *f* **2** *adj* adulto

ad·ult ed·u·ca·tion corsi *mpl* per adulti

a·dul·ter·ous [ə'dʌltərəs] *adj relationship* extraconiugale

a·dul·ter·y [ə'dʌltərɪ] adulterio *m*

'adult film *euph* film *m inv* per adulti

ad·vance [əd'vɑːns] **1** *n* (*money*) anticipo *m*; *in science etc* progresso *m*; MIL avanzata *f*; *in ~* in anticipo; *make ~s* (*progress*) fare progressi; *sexually* fare le avances **2** *v/i* MIL avanzare; (*make progress*) fare progressi **3** *v/t theory* avanzare; *sum of money* anticipare; *human knowledge, a cause* fare progredire

ad·vance 'book·ing prenotazione *f*

ad·vanced [əd'vɑːnst] *adj country, level* avanzato; *learner* di livello avanzato

ad·vance 'no·tice preavviso *m*

ad·vance 'pay·ment pagamento *m* anticipato

ad·van·tage [əd'vɑːntɪdʒ] vantaggio *m*; *it's to your ~* è a tuo vantaggio; *take ~ of opportunity* approfittare di

ad·van·ta·geous [ædvən'teɪdʒəs] *adj* vantaggioso

ad·vent ['ædvent] *fig* avvento *m*

'ad·vent cal·en·dar *calendario m dell'Avvento con finestrelle numerate che i bambini aprono giorno per giorno*

ad·ven·ture [əd'ventʃə(r)] avventura *f*

ad·ven·tur·ous [əd'ventʃərəs] *adj* avventuroso

ad·verb ['ædvɜːb] avverbio *m*

ad·ver·sa·ry ['ædvəsərɪ] avversario *m*, -a *f*

ad·verse ['ædvɜːs] *adj* avverso

ad·vert ['ædvɜːt] → *advertisement*

ad·ver·tise ['ædvətaɪz] **1** *v/t job* mettere un annuncio per; *product* reclamizzare **2** *v/i for job* mettere un annuncio; *for product* fare pubblicità

ad·ver·tise·ment [əd'vɜːtɪsmənt] annuncio *m*, inserzione *f*; *for product* pubblicità *f inv*

ad·ver·tis·er ['ædvətaɪzə(r)] acquirente *m/f* di uno spazio pubblicitario; *in magazine, newspaper* inserzionista *m/f*

ad·ver·tis·ing ['ædvətaɪzɪŋ] pubblicità *f inv*

'ad·ver·tis·ing a·gen·cy agenzia *f* pubblicitaria; **'ad·ver·tis·ing budg·et** budget *m inv* per la pubblicità; **'ad·ver·tis·ing cam·paign** campagna *f* pubblicitaria; **'ad·ver·tis·ing rev·e·nue** proventi *mpl* della pubblicità

ad·vice [əd'vaɪs] consigli *mpl*; *legal, financial* consulenza *f*; *a bit of ~* un consiglio; *take s.o.'s ~* seguire il consiglio di qu

ad·vis·a·ble [əd'vaɪzəbl] *adj* consigliabile

ad·vise [əd'vaɪz] *v/t person* consigliare a; *caution etc* consigliare; **~ s.o. to ...** consigliare a qu di ...

ad·vis·er [əd'vaɪzə(r)] consulente *m/f*

ad·vo·cate ['ædvəkeɪt] *v/t* propugnare

aer·i·al ['eərɪəl] *n* antenna *f*

aer·i·al 'pho·to·graph fotografia *f* aerea

aer·o·bics [eə'rəʊbɪks] *nsg* aerobica *f*

aer·o·dy·nam·ic [eərəʊdaɪ'næmɪk] *adj* aerodinamico

aer·o·nau·ti·cal [eərəʊ'nɔːtɪkl] *adj* aeronautico

aer·o·plane ['eərəpleɪn] aeroplano *m*

aer·o·sol ['eərəsɒl] spray *m inv*

aer·o·space in·dus·try ['eərəʊspeɪs ɪndʌstrɪ] industria *f* aerospaziale

aes·thet·ic [iːs'θetɪk] *adj* estetico

af·fa·ble ['æfəbl] *adj* affabile

af·fair [ə'feə(r)] (*matter*) affare *m*; (*event*) caso *m*; (*business*) affare *m*; (*love*) relazione *f*; **foreign ~s** affari *mpl* esteri; **have an ~ with** avere una relazione con

affect [ə'fekt] *v/t* MED colpire; (*influence*) influire su; (*concern*) riguardare; (*cause feelings to*) colpire

af·fec·tion [ə'fekʃn] affetto *m*

af·fec·tion·ate [ə'fekʃnət] *adj* affettuoso

af·fec·tion·ate·ly [ə'fekʃnətlɪ] *adv* affettuosamente

af·fin·i·ty [ə'fɪnətɪ] affinità *f inv*

af·fir·ma·tive [ə'fɜːmətɪv] *adj* affermativo; **answer in the ~** rispondere affermativamente

af·flict [ə'flɪkt] *v/t* tormentare; **be ~ed with** soffrire di

af·flu·ence ['æfluəns] benessere *m*

af·flu·ent ['æfluənt] *adj* benestante; **~ society** società *f inv* del benessere

af·ford [ə'fɔːd] *v/t*: **be able to ~ sth** *financially* potersi permettere qc; **I can't ~ the time** non ne ho il tempo; **it's a risk we can't ~ to take** è un rischio che non possiamo permetterci di correre

af·ford·a·ble [ə'fɔːdəbl] *adj* abbordabile

af·front [ə'frʌnt] *n* affronto *m*

a·float [ə'fləʊt] *adj* boat a galla; **keep the company ~** tenere a galla l'azienda

a·fraid [ə'freɪd] *adj*: **be ~** avere paura; **be ~ of** avere paura di; **I'm ~** *expressing regret* sono spiacente; **I'm ~ so** temo che sia così; **I'm ~ not** purtroppo no

a·fresh [ə'freʃ] *adv* da capo

Af·ri·ca ['æfrɪkə] Africa *f*

Af·ri·can ['æfrɪkən] **1** *n* africano *m*, -a *f* **2** *adj* africano

af·ter ['ɑːftə(r)] **1** *prep* dopo; **~ her/me/you** dopo di lei/me/te; **~ all** dopo tutto; **~ that** dopo; **the day ~ tomorrow** dopodomani **2** *adv* dopo; **the day ~** il giorno dopo

af·ter·math ['ɑːftəmɑːθ]: **the ~ of war** il dopoguerra; **in the ~ of** nel periodo immediatamente successivo a

afternoon [ɑːftə'nuːn] pomeriggio *m*; **in the ~** nel pomeriggio; **this ~** oggi pomeriggio; **good ~** buon giorno

'af·ter sales serv·ice servizio *m* dopovendita; **'af·ter·shave** dopobarba *m inv*; **'af·ter·taste** retrogusto *m*

af·ter·wards ['ɑːftəwədz] *adv* dopo

a·gain [ə'geɪn] *adv* di nuovo; **I never saw him ~** non l'ho mai più visto

a·gainst [ə'geɪnst] *prep lean* contro; **America ~ Brazil** SP America contro Brasile; **I'm ~ the idea** sono contrario all'idea; **what do you have ~ her?** cos'hai contro di lei?; **~ the law** contro la legge

age [eɪdʒ] **1** *n* (*also era*) età *f inv*; **at the ~** all'età di; **under ~** minorenne; **she's five years of ~** ha cinque anni; **I've been waiting for ~s** F ho aspettato un secolo F **2** *v/i* invecchiare

aged¹ [eɪdʒd] *adj*: **a boy ~ 16** un ragazzo di 16 anni; **he was ~ 16** aveva 16 anni

aged² ['eɪdʒɪd] **1** *adj*: **her ~ parents** i

suoi anziani genitori **2** *n*: *the ~* gli
anziani

'age group fascia *f* d'età

'age lim·it limite *m* d'età

a·gen·cy ['eɪdʒənsɪ] agenzia *f*

a·gen·da [ə'dʒendə] ordine *m* del
giorno; *on the ~* all'ordine del giorno

a·gent ['eɪdʒənt] agente *m/f*

ag·gra·vate ['ægrəveɪt] *v/t* aggravare; (*annoy*) seccare

ag·gre·gate ['ægrɪgət] *n* insieme *m*;
in (*the*) *~* nel complesso; *win on ~*
SP vincere ai punti

ag·gres·sion [ə'greʃn] aggressione *f*

ag·gres·sive [ə'gresɪv] *adj* (*also dynamic*) aggressivo

ag·gres·sive·ly [ə'gresɪvlɪ] *adv* con
aggressività

ag·gro ['ægrəʊ] P grane *fpl*

a·ghast [ə'ɡɑːst] *adj* inorridito

ag·ile ['ædʒaɪl] *adj* agile

a·gil·i·ty [ə'dʒɪlətɪ] agilità *f*

ag·i·tate ['ædʒɪteɪt] *v/i*: *~ for /
against* mobilitarsi per / contro

ag·i·tat·ed ['ædʒɪteɪtɪd] *adj* agitato

ag·i·ta·tion [ædʒɪ'teɪʃn] agitazione *f*

ag·i·ta·tor [ædʒɪ'teɪtə(r)] agitatore
m, -trice *f*

AGM [eɪdʒiː'em] *abbr* (= *annual
general meeting*) assemblea *f* annuale

ag·nos·tic [æg'nɒstɪk] *n* agnostico
m, -a *f*

a·go [ə'ɡəʊ] *adv*: *2 days ~* due giorni
fa; *long ~* molto tempo fa; *how long
~?* quanto tempo fa?

ag·o·nize ['ægənaɪz] *v/i* angosciarsi;
~ over angosciarsi per

ag·o·niz·ing ['ægənaɪzɪŋ] *adj* ango-
sciante

ag·o·ny ['ægənɪ] agonia *f*; *mental* angoscia *f*

a·gree [ə'ɡriː] **1** *v/i* essere d'accordo;
of figures, accounts quadrare; (*reach
agreement*) mettersi d'accordo; *I ~*
sono d'accordo; *it doesn't ~ with
me of food* mi fa male **2** *v/t price*
concordare; *~ that sth should be
done* concordare che si dovrebbe
fare qc

a·gree·a·ble [ə'ɡriːəbl] *adj* (*pleasant*) piacevole; *be ~* (*in agreement*)
essere d'accordo

a·gree·ment [ə'ɡriːmənt] (*consent,
contract*) accordo *m*; *reach ~ on* trovare un accordo su

ag·ri·cul·tur·al [ægrɪ'kʌltʃərəl] *adj*
agricolo

ag·ri·cul·ture ['ægrɪkʌltʃə(r)] agricoltura *f*

ahead [ə'hed] *adv* davanti; (*in advance*) avanti; *200 m ~* 200 m più
avanti; *be ~ of* essere davanti a;
plan / think ~ programmare per
tempo; *arrive ~ of the others* arrivare prima degli altri

aid [eɪd] **1** *n* aiuto *m* **2** *v/t* aiutare

aide [eɪd] assistente *m/f*

Aids [eɪdz] Aids *inv*

ail·ing ['eɪlɪŋ] *adj economy* malato

ail·ment ['eɪlmənt] disturbo *m*

aim [eɪm] **1** *n in shooting* mira *f*; (*objective*) obiettivo *m*; *take ~* prendere la mira; **2** *v/i in shooting* mirare; *~
at doing sth, ~ to do sth* aspirare a
fare qc **3** *v/t*: *be ~ed at of remark etc*
essere rivolto a; *of guns* essere
puntato contro

aim·less ['eɪmlɪs] *adj* senza obiettivi;
wandering senza meta

air [eə(r)] **1** *n* aria *f*; *by ~ travel* in aereo; *send mail* per via aerea; *in the
open ~* all'aperto; *on the ~* RAD, TV
in onda **2** *v/t room* arieggiare; *fig:
views* rendere noto

'air·bag airbag *m inv*; 'air·base base
f aerea; 'air-con·di·tioned *adj* con
aria condizionata; 'air-con·di·tion-
ing aria *f* condizionata; 'air·craft
aereo *m*; 'air·craft car·ri·er portae-
rei *f inv*; 'air fare tariffa *f* aerea;
'air·field campo *m* d'aviazione; 'air
force aeronautica *f* militare; 'air
host·ess hostess *f inv*; 'air let·ter
aerogramma *m*; 'air·lift **1** *n* ponte *m*
aereo **2** *v/t* trasportare per via aerea; 'air·line compagnia *f* aerea;
'air·lin·er aereo *m* di linea; 'air·
mail: *by ~* per via aerea; 'air·plane
aeroplano *m*; 'air·pock·et vuoto *m*
d'aria; 'air pol·lu·tion inquinamen-

to *m* atmosferico; '**air·port** aeroporto *m*; '**air·sick**: **get** ~ soffrire il mal d'aereo *o* l'aereo; '**air·space** spazio *m* aereo; '**air ter·mi·nal** terminale *m*; '**air·tight** *adj* container ermetico; '**air traf·fic** traffico *m* aereo; '**air-traf·fic con·trol** controllo *m* del traffico aereo; **air-traf·fic con'trol·ler** controllore *m* di volo

air·y ['eərɪ] *adj* room arieggiato; *attitude* noncurante

aisle [aɪl] corridoio *m*; *in supermarket* corsia *f*; *in church* navata *f* laterale

aisle seat posto *m* corridoio

a·jar [ə'dʒɑː(r)] *adj*: **be** ~ essere socchiuso

a·lac·ri·ty [ə'lækrətɪ] alacrità *f*

a·larm [ə'lɑːm] **1** *n* allarme *m*; *raise* ***the*** ~ dare l'allarme **2** *v/t* allarmare

a'larm clock sveglia *f*

a·larm·ing [ə'lɑːmɪŋ] *adj* allarmante

a·larm·ing·ly [ə'lɑːmɪŋlɪ] *adv* in modo allarmante

al·bum ['ælbəm] *for photographs*, (*record*) album *m inv*

al·co·hol ['ælkəhɒl] alcol *m*; ~**-free** analcolico

al·co·hol·ic [ælkə'hɒlɪk] **1** *n* alcolizzato *m*, -a *f* **2** *adj* alcolico

a·lert [ə'lɜːt] **1** *n* (*signal*) allarme *m*; *be on the* ~ stare all'erta; *of troops*, *police* essere in stato di allerta **2** *v/t* mettere in guardia **3** *adj* all'erta *inv*

A-lev·el ['eɪlevl] diploma *f* di scuola media superiore in Gran Bretagna che permette di accedere all'università

al·ge·bra ['ældʒɪbrə] algebra *f*

al·i·bi ['ælɪbaɪ] alibi *m inv*

a·li·en ['eɪlɪən] **1** *n* (*foreigner*) straniero *m*, -a *f*; *from space* alieno *m*, -a *f* **2** *adj* estraneo; *be* ~ *to s.o.* essere estraneo a qu

a·li·en·ate ['eɪlɪəneɪt] *v/t* alienarsi

a·light [ə'laɪt] *adj*: *be* ~ essere in fiamme; *set sth* ~ dare fuoco a qc

a·lign [ə'laɪn] *v/t* allineare

a·like [ə'laɪk] **1** *adj* simile; *be* ~ assomigliarsi **2** *adv*: *it appeals to old and young* ~ attira vecchi e giovani allo stesso tempo

al·i·mo·ny ['ælɪmənɪ] alimenti *mpl*

a·live [ə'laɪv] *adj*: *be* ~ essere vivo; ~ *and kicking* vivo e vegeto

all [ɔːl] **1** *adj* tutto; (*any whatever*) qualsiasi; ~ *day* / *month* tutto il giorno / mese; *beyond* ~ *doubt* al di là di qualsiasi dubbio **2** *pron* tutto; ~ *of us* / *them* tutti noi / loro; *he ate* ~ *of it* lo ha mangiato tutto; *that's* ~, *thanks* è tutto, grazie; *for* ~ *I care* per quello che me ne importa; *for* ~ *I know* per quel che ne so; ~ *at once* tutto in una volta; (*suddenly*) tutt'a un tratto; ~ *but* (*nearly*) quasi; ~ *but John agreed* (*except*) erano tutti d'accordo tranne John; ~ *the better* molto meglio; ~ *the time* tutto il tempo; *they're not at* ~ *alike* non si assomigliano affatto; *not at* ~! niente affatto!; *two* ~ SP due pari; ~ *right* → **alright**

al·lay [ə'leɪ] *v/t* attenuare

al·le·ga·tion [ælɪ'geɪʃn] accusa *f*

al·lege [ə'ledʒ] *v/t* dichiarare

al·leged [ə'ledʒd] *adj* presunto

al·leg·ed·ly [ə'ledʒɪdlɪ] *adv* a quanto si suppone

al·le·giance [ə'liːdʒəns] fedeltà *f*

al·ler·gic [ə'lɜːdʒɪk] *adj* allergico; *be* ~ *to* essere allergico a

al·ler·gy ['ælədʒɪ] allergia *f*

al·le·vi·ate [ə'liːvɪeɪt] *v/t* alleviare

al·ley ['ælɪ] vicolo *m*

al·li·ance [ə'laɪəns] alleanza *f*

al·lied ['ælaɪd] MIL alleato

al·lo·cate ['æləkeɪt] *v/t* assegnare

al·lo·ca·tion [ælə'keɪʃn] assegnazione *f*; (*amount*) parte *f*

al·lot [ə'lɒt] *v/t* (*pret* & *pp* **-ted**) assegnare

al·lot·ment [ə'lɒtmənt] *Br* lotto *m* da coltivare

al·low [ə'laʊ] *v/t* (*permit*) permettere; (*calculate for*) calcolare; *be* ~**ed** essere autorizzato; *it's not* ~**ed** è vietato; *passengers are not* ~**ed to smoke** è vietato ai passeggeri fumare; *dogs not* ~**ed to** vietato l'ingresso ai cani; ~ *s.o. to ...* permettere a qu di ...

♦ **allow for** *v/t* tenere conto di

al·low·ance [əˈlauəns] (*money*) sussidio *m*; (*pocket money*) paghetta *f*; **make ~s for sth** tenere conto di qc; **make ~s for s.o.** essere indulgente con qu

al·loy [ˈælɔɪ] lega *m*

'all-pur·pose *adj* multiuso *inv*; **'all-round** *adj improvement* generale; *person* eclettico; **'all-time: be at an ~ low** *of inflation, unemployment* aver raggiunto il minimo storico

♦ **allude to** [əˈluːd] *v/t* alludere a

al·lur·ing [əˈluːrɪŋ] *adj* attraente

al·lu·sion [əˈluːʒn] allusione *f*

al·ly [ˈælaɪ] *n* alleato *m*, -a *f*

Al·might·y [ɔːlˈmaɪtɪ]: **the ~** l'Onnipotente

al·mond [ˈɑːmənd] mandorla *f*

al·most [ˈɔːlməust] *adv* quasi

a·lone [əˈləʊn] *adj* solo

a·long [əˈlɒŋ] **1** *prep* lungo; **walk ~ the street** camminare lungo la strada **2** *adv*: **~ with** insieme con; **all ~** (*all the time*) per tutto il tempo; **we're going, would you like to come ~?** noi andiamo, vuoi venire con noi?

a·long·side [əlɒŋˈsaɪd] *prep* di fianco a; *person* al fianco di; **draw up ~** accostare; **draw up ~ s.o.** accostare vicino a qu; **~ him** al suo fianco

a·loof [əˈluːf] *adj* in disparte

a·loud [əˈlaʊd] *adv* ad alta voce; *laugh, call* forte

al·pha·bet [ˈælfəbet] alfabeto *m*

al·pha·bet·i·cal [ælfəˈbetɪkl] *adj* alfabetico

al·pine [ˈælpaɪn] *adj* alpino

Alps [ælps] *npl* Alpi *fpl*

al·read·y [ɔːlˈredɪ] *adv* già

al·right [ɔːlˈraɪt] *adj*: **it's ~** va bene; **are you ~?** (*not hurt*) stai bene?; **I'm ~** (*not hurt*) sto bene; (*have got enough*) va bene così; **is the monitor ~?** (*in working order*) funziona il monitor?; **is it ~ with you if I ...?** ti va bene se ...?; **~, you can have one!** va bene, puoi averne uno!; **~, I heard you!** sì, ti ho sentito!; **everything is ~ now between them** adesso va tutto bene tra di loro;

that's ~ (*don't mention it*) non c'è di che; (*I don't mind*) non fa niente; **~, that's enough!** basta così!

Al·sa·tian [ælˈseɪʃn] *Br* pastore *m* tedesco

al·so [ˈɔːlsəʊ] *adv* anche

al·tar [ˈɒltə(r)] REL altare *m*

al·ter [ˈɒltə(r)] *v/t* modificare; *clothes* aggiustare

al·ter·a·tion [ɒltəˈreɪʃn] modifica *f*

al·ter·nate [ˈɒltəneɪt] **1** *v/i* alternare **2** *adj* [ˈɒltənət] alternato; **on ~ days** a giorni alterni; **on ~ Mondays** un lunedì su due

al·ter·nat·ing 'cur·rent [ˈɒltəneɪtɪŋ] corrente *f* alternata

al·ter·na·tive [ɒlˈtɜːnətɪv] **1** *n* alternativa *f* **2** *adj* alternativo

al·ter·na·tive·ly [ɒlˈtɜːnətɪvlɪ] *adv* alternativamente

al·though [ɔːlˈðəʊ] *conj* benché, sebbene

al·ti·tude [ˈæltɪtjuːd] altitudine *f*

al·to·geth·er [ɔːltəˈgeðə(r)] *adv* (*completely*) completamente; (*in all*) complessivamente

al·tru·ism [ˈæltruːɪzm] altruismo *m*

al·tru·is·tic [æltruːˈɪstɪk] *adj* altruistico

a·lu·min·i·um [æljuˈmɪnɪəm], *Am* **a·lu·mi·num** [əˈluːmɪnəm] alluminio *m*

al·ways [ˈɔːlweɪz] *adv* sempre

a.m. [eɪˈem] *abbr* (= *ante meridiem*) di mattina

a·mal·gam·ate [əˈmælgəmeɪt] *v/i of companies* fondersi

a·mass [əˈmæs] *v/t* accumulare

am·a·teur [ˈæmətə(r)] *n* (*unskilled*) dilettante *m/f*; SP non professionista *m/f*

am·a·teur·ish [ˈæmətərɪʃ] *adj pej* dilettantesco

a·maze [əˈmeɪz] *v/t* stupire

a·mazed [əˈmeɪzd] *adj* stupito

a·maze·ment [əˈmeɪzmənt] stupore *m*

a·maz·ing [əˈmeɪzɪŋ] *adj* (*surprising*) sorprendente; F (*good*) incredibile

a·maz·ing·ly [əˈmeɪzɪŋlɪ] *adv* incredibilmente

am·bas·sa·dor [æm'bæsədə(r)] ambasciatore *m*, -trice *f*

am·ber ['æmbə(r)] *n* ambra *f*; **at ~** giallo

am·bi·dex·trous [æmbɪ'dekstrəs] *adj* ambidestro

am·bi·ence ['æmbɪəns] atmosfera *f*

am·bi·gu·i·ty [æmbɪ'gjuːətɪ] ambiguità *f*

am·big·u·ous [æm'bɪgjʊəs] *adj* ambiguo

am·bi·tion [æm'bɪʃn] ambizione *f*

am·bi·tious [æm'bɪʃəs] *adj* ambizioso

am·biv·a·lent [æm'bɪvələnt] *adj* ambiguo

am·ble ['æmbl] *v/i* camminare con calma; **we were ambling along the riverbank** stavamo passeggiando lungo il fiume

am·bu·lance ['æmbjʊləns] ambulanza *f*

am·bush ['æmbʊʃ] **1** *n* agguato *m* **2** *v/t* tendere un agguato a; **be ~ed by** subire un agguato da parte di

a·mend [ə'mend] *v/t* emendare

a·mend·ment [ə'mendmənt] emendamento *m*

a·mends [ə'mendz]: **make ~** fare ammenda

a·men·i·ties [ə'miːnətɪz] *npl* comodità *fpl*

A·mer·i·ca [ə'merɪkə] America *f*

A·mer·i·can [ə'merɪkən] **1** *n* americano *m*, -a *f* **2** *adj* americano

a·mi·a·ble ['eɪmɪəbl] *adj* amichevole

a·mi·ca·ble ['æmɪkəbl] *adj* amichevole

a·mi·ca·bly ['æmɪkəblɪ] *adv* amichevolmente

am·mu·ni·tion [æmjʊ'nɪʃn] munizioni *fpl*; *fig* arma *f*

am·ne·sia [æm'niːzɪə] amnesia *f*

am·nes·ty ['æmnəstɪ] amnistia *f*

a·mong(st) [ə'mʌŋ(st)] *prep* tra

a·mor·al [eɪ'mɒrəl] *adj* amorale

a·mount [ə'maʊnt] quantità *f inv*; (*sum of money*) importo *m*

♦ **amount to** *v/t of income, sum* ammontare a; (*be equal to*) equivalere a

am·phib·i·an [æm'fɪbɪən] anfibio *m*

am·phib·i·ous [æm'fɪbɪəs] *adj* animal anfibio; *vehicle* anfibio

am·phi·the·a·ter *Am*, **am·phi·the·a·tre** ['æmfɪθɪətə(r)] anfiteatro *m*

am·ple ['æmpl] *adj* abbondante; (*more than enough*) in abbondanza

am·pli·fi·er ['æmplɪfaɪə(r)] amplificatore *m*

am·pli·fy ['æmplɪfaɪ] *v/t* (*pret & pp* **-ied**) *sound* amplificare

am·pu·tate ['æmpjʊteɪt] *v/t* amputare

am·pu·ta·tion [æmpjʊ'teɪʃn] amputazione *f*

a·muse [ə'mjuːz] *v/t* (*make laugh etc*) divertire; (*entertain*) intrattenere

a·muse·ment [ə'mjuːzmənt] (*merriment*) divertimento *m*; (*entertainment*) intrattenimento *m*; **~s** (*games*) divertimenti *mpl*; **to our great ~** con nostro grande divertimento

a'muse·ment ar·cade sala *f* giochi

a'muse·ment park parco *m* giochi

a·mus·ing [ə'mjuːzɪŋ] *adj* divertente

an [æn] → **a**

an·a·bol·ic 'ster·oid [ænə'bɒlɪk] anabolizzante *m*

an·ae·mi·a [ə'niːmɪə] anemia *f*

an·aem·ic [ə'niːmɪk] *adj* anemico

an·aes·thet·ic [ænəs'θetɪk] *n* anestetico *m*

an·aes·the·tist [ə'niːsθətɪst] anestesista *m/f*

an·a·log ['ænəlɒg] *adj* COMPUT analogico

a·nal·o·gy [ə'nælədʒɪ] analogia *f*

an·a·lyse ['ænəlaɪz] *v/t* analizzare; (*psychoanalyse*) psicanalizzare

a·nal·y·sis [ə'næləsɪs] (*pl* **analyses** [ə'næləsiːz]) analisi *f inv*

an·a·lyst ['ænəlɪst] *also* PSYCH analista *m/f*

an·a·lyt·i·cal [ænə'lɪtɪkl] *adj* analitico

an·a·lyze *Am* → **analyse**

an·arch·y ['ænəkɪ] anarchia *f*

a·nat·o·my [ə'nætəmɪ] anatomia *f*

an·ces·tor ['ænsestə(r)] antenato *m*, -a *f*

an·chor ['æŋkə(r)] **1** n NAUT ancora f **2** v/i NAUT gettare l'ancora

'an·chor·man TV presentatore m, anchorman m inv

an·cient ['eɪnʃənt] adj antico

an·cil·lar·y [æn'sɪlərɪ] adj staff ausiliario

and [ənd] stressed [ænd] conj e; **5 ~ 5 makes 10** 5 più 5 fa 10; **three hundred ~ sixty** trecentosessanta; **worse ~ worse** sempre peggio; **I'll come ~ pick you up** vengo a prenderti

an·ec·dote ['ænɪkdəʊt] aneddoto m

a·ne·mi·a etc Am → **anaemia** etc

an·es·thet·ic etc Am → **anaesthetic** etc

an·gel ['eɪndʒl] REL, fig angelo m

an·ger ['æŋgə(r)] **1** n rabbia f **2** v/t fare arrabbiare

an·gi·na [æn'dʒaɪnə] angina f (pectoris)

an·gle ['æŋgl] n angolo m; (position, fig) angolazione f

an·gler ['æŋglə(r)] pescatore m, -trice f (con amo e lenza)

An·gli·can ['æŋglɪkən] REL **1** adj anglicano **2** n anglicano m, -a f

An·glo-Sax·on [æŋgləʊ'sæksn] **1** adj anglosassone **2** n person anglosassone m/f

an·gry ['æŋgrɪ] adj arrabbiato; **be ~ with s.o.** essere arrabbiato con qu

an·guish ['æŋgwɪʃ] angoscia f

an·gu·lar ['æŋgjʊlə(r)] adj face, shape spigoloso

an·i·mal ['ænɪml] animale m

an·i·mat·ed ['ænɪmeɪtɪd] adj animato

an·i·ma·ted car'toon cartone m animato

an·i·ma·tion [ænɪ'meɪʃn] animazione f

an·i·mos·i·ty [ænɪ'mɒsətɪ] animosità f

an·kle ['æŋkl] caviglia f

an·nex [ə'neks] v/t state annettere

an·nexe ['æneks] n (building) edificio m annesso; to document annesso m

an·ni·hi·late [ə'naɪəleɪt] v/t annientare

an·ni·hi·la·tion [ənaɪə'leɪʃn] annientamento m

an·ni·ver·sa·ry [ænɪ'vɜːsərɪ] (wedding ~) anniversario m

an·no·tate ['ænəteɪt] v/t report annotare

an·nounce [ə'naʊns] v/t annunciare

an·nounce·ment [ə'naʊnsmənt] annuncio m

an·nounc·er [ə'naʊnsə(r)] TV, Radio annunciatore m, -trice f

an·noy [ə'nɔɪ] v/t infastidire; **be ~ed** essere infastidito

an·noy·ance [ə'nɔɪəns] (anger) irritazione f; (nuisance) fastidio m

an·noy·ing [ə'nɔɪɪŋ] adj irritante

an·nu·al ['ænjʊəl] adj annuale

an·nu·al gen·er·al 'meet·ing assemblea f annuale

an·nu·i·ty [ə'njuːətɪ] rendita f annuale

an·nul [ə'nʌl] v/t (pret & pp **-led**) marriage annullare

an·nul·ment [ə'nʌlmənt] annullamento m

a·non·y·mous [ə'nɒnɪməs] adj anonimo

an·o·rak ['ænəræk] Br giacca f a vento

an·o·rex·i·a [ænə'reksɪə] anoressia f

an·o·rex·ic [ænə'reksɪk] adj anoressico

an·oth·er [ə'nʌðə(r)] **1** adj un altro m, un'altra f **2** pron un altro m, un'altra f; **one ~** l'un l'altro; **do they know one ~?** si conoscono?

ans·wer ['ɑːnsə(r)] **1** n to letter, person, problem risposta f **2** v/t letter, person rispondere a; **~ the door** aprire la porta; **~ the telephone** rispondere al telefono

◆ **answer back 1** v/t person ribattere a **2** v/i ribattere

◆ **answer for** v/t rispondere di

an·swer·ing ma·chine ['ɑːnsərɪŋ] TELEC segreteria f telefonica

ans·wer·phone ['ɑːnsəfəʊn] segreteria f telefonica

ant [ænt] formica f

an·tag·o·nis·m [æn'tægənɪzm] antagonismo m

an·tag·o·nis·tic [æntægə'nɪstɪk] *adj* ostile

an·tag·o·nize [æn'tægənaɪz] *v/t* contrariare

Ant·arc·tic [ænt'ɑːktɪk] *n* Antartico *m*

an·te·lope ['æntɪləup] antilope *f*

an·te·na·tal [æntɪ'neɪtl] *adj* durante la gravidanza; ~ *classes* corso *m* di preparazione al parto; ~ *clinic* clinica *f* per gestanti

an·ten·na [æn'tenə] antenna *f*

an·thol·o·gy [æn'θɒlədʒɪ] antologia *f*

an·thro·pol·o·gy [ænθrə'pɒlədʒɪ] antropologia *f*

an·ti·bi·ot·ic [æntɪbaɪ'ɒtɪk] *n* antibiotico *m*

an·ti·bod·y ['æntɪbɒdɪ] anticorpo *m*

an·tic·i·pate [æn'tɪsɪpeɪt] *v/t* prevedere

an·tic·i·pa·tion [æntɪsɪ'peɪʃn] previsione *f*

an·ti·clock·wise ['æntɪklɒkwaɪz] *Br* **1** *adj* antiorario **2** *adv* in senso antiorario

an·tics ['æntɪks] *npl* buffonate *fpl*

an·ti·dote ['æntɪdəut] antidoto *m*

an·ti·freeze ['æntɪfriːz] antigelo *m inv*

an·tip·a·thy [æn'tɪpəθɪ] antipatia *f*

an·ti·quat·ed ['æntɪkweɪtɪd] *adj* antiquato

an·tique [æn'tiːk] *n* pezzo *m* d'antiquariato

an'tique dealer antiquario *m*, -a *f*

an·tiq·ui·ty [æn'tɪkwətɪ] antichità *f inv*

an·ti·sep·tic [æntɪ'septɪk] **1** *adj* antisettico **2** *n* antisettico *m*

an·ti·so·cial [æntɪ'səuʃl] *adj* asociale

an·ti·vi·rus pro·gram [æntɪ'vaɪrəs] COMPUT programma *m* antivirus

anx·i·e·ty [æŋ'zaɪətɪ] ansia *f*

anx·ious ['æŋkʃəs] *adj* ansioso; *be ~ for ...* *for news etc* essere ansioso di avere ...

an·y ['enɪ] **1** *adj* qualche; *are there ~ diskettes / glasses?* ci sono dei dischetti / bicchieri?; *is there ~ bread?* c'è del pane?; *is there ~*

improvement? c'è qualche miglioramento?; *there aren't ~ diskettes / glasses* non ci sono dischetti / bicchieri; *there isn't ~ bread* non c'è pane; *there isn't ~ improvement* non c'è nessun miglioramento; *have you ~ idea at all?* hai qualche idea?; *take ~ one you like* prendi quello che vuoi **2** *pron*: *do you have ~?* ne hai?; *there aren't ~ left* non ce ne sono più; *there isn't ~ left* non ce n'è più; *~ of them could be guilty* chiunque di loro potrebbe essere colpevole **3** *adv* un po'; *is that ~ better / easier?* è un po' meglio / più facile?; *I don't like it ~ more* non mi piace più

an·y·bod·y ['enɪbɒdɪ] *pron* qualcuno; *with negative* nessuno; (*whoever*) chiunque; *is there ~ there?* c'è qualcuno?; *there wasn't ~ there* non c'era nessuno; *~ could do it* lo potrebbe fare chiunque

an·y·how ['enɪhau] comunque; *if I can help you ~, let me know* se ti posso aiutare in qualsiasi modo, fammi sapere

an·y·one ['enɪwʌn] → *anybody*

an·y·thing ['enɪθɪŋ] *pron* qualcosa; *with negatives* niente, nulla; *I didn't hear ~* non ho sentito niente *o* nulla; *~ but* per niente; *she was ~ but helpful* non è stata per niente d'aiuto; *~ else?* qualcos'altro?

an·y·way ['enɪweɪ] → *anyhow*

an·y·where ['enɪweə(r)] *adv* da qualche parte; *with negative* da nessuna parte; (*wherever*) dovunque; *I can't find it ~* non riesco a trovarlo da nessuna parte

a·part [ə'pɑːt] *adv in distance* distante; *the two cities are 250 miles ~* le due città distano 250 miglia l'una dall'altra; *live ~ of people* vivere separati; *~ from* (*excepting*) a parte, tranne; (*in addition to*) oltre a

a·part·ment [ə'pɑːtmənt] appartamento *m*

a'part·ment block *Am* palazzo *m* (d'appartamenti)

ap·a·thet·ic [æpə'θetɪk] *adj* apatico

ap·a·thy ['æpəθɪ] apatia *f*

ape [eɪp] scimmia *f*

a·pe·ri·tif [ə'perɪti:f] aperitivo *m*

ap·er·ture ['æpətʃə(r)] PHOT apertura *f*

a·piece [ə'pi:s] *adv* l'uno *m*, l'una *f*;
you can have one ~ potete averne uno a testa

a·pol·o·get·ic [əpɒlə'dʒetɪk] *adj letter, smile* di scuse; **he was very ~ for being late** si è scusato molto di essere in ritardo

a·pol·o·gize [ə'pɒlədʒaɪz] *v/i* scusarsi; **~ to s.o.** scusarsi con qu

a·pol·o·gy [ə'pɒlədʒɪ] scusa *f*; **make an ~ to s.o.** fare le proprie scuse a qu

a·pos·tle [ə'pɒsl] REL apostolo *m*

a·pos·tro·phe [ə'pɒstrəfɪ] GRAM apostrofo *m*

ap·pal [ə'pɔ:l] *v/t* sconvolgere

ap·pal·ling [ə'pɔ:lɪŋ] *adj* sconvolgente; *language* scioccante

ap·pa·ra·tus [æpə'reɪtəs] apparecchio *m*

ap·par·ent [ə'pærənt] *adj* evidente; *(seeming real)* apparente; **become ~ that ...** diventare evidente che ...

ap·par·ent·ly [ə'pærəntlɪ] *adv* apparentemente

ap·pa·ri·tion [æpə'rɪʃn] *(ghost)* apparizione

ap·peal [ə'pi:l] **1** *n (charm)* attrattiva *f; for funds etc,* LAW appello *m* **2** *v/i* LAW fare appello

◆ **appeal to** *(be attractive to)* attirare

◆ **appeal for** *v/t blood, help* fare un appello per ottenere; **the President appealed for calm** il Presidente ha fatto appello alla calma

ap·peal·ing [ə'pi:lɪŋ] *adj idea, offer* allettante; *glance* supplichevole

ap·pear [ə'pɪə(r)] *v/i* apparire, comparire; *in film etc* apparire; *of new product* comparire; *in court* comparire; *(look, seem)* apparire; **it ~s that ...** sembra che ...

ap·pear·ance [ə'pɪərəns] *(arrival)* apparizione *f*, comparsa *f; in film etc*

apparizione *f; in court* comparizione *f, (look)* aspetto *m;* **put in an ~** fare un salto; **judge by ~s** giudicare dalle apparenze

ap·pease [ə'pi:z] *v/t gods, anger* placare; *tyrant* compiacere

ap·pen·di·ci·tis [əpendɪ'saɪtɪs] appendicite *f*

ap·pen·dix [ə'pendɪks] MED, *of book etc* appendice *f*

ap·pe·tite ['æpɪtaɪt] appetito *m;* **~ for sth** *fig* sete *f* di qc

ap·pe·tiz·er ['æpɪtaɪzə(r)] *food* stuzzichino *m; drink* aperitivo *m*

ap·pe·tiz·ing ['æpɪtaɪzɪŋ] *adj* appetitoso

ap·plaud [ə'plɔ:d] **1** *v/i* applaudire **2** *v/t also fig* applaudire

ap·plause [ə'plɔ:z] applauso *m; (praise)* approvazione *f*

ap·ple ['æpl] mela *f*

ap·ple 'pie torta *f* di mele

ap·ple 'sauce composta *f* di mele

ap·pli·ance [ə'plaɪəns] apparecchio *m; household* elettrodomestico *m*

ap·plic·a·ble [ə'plɪkəbl] *adj* applicabile

ap·pli·cant ['æplɪkənt] candidato *m,* -a *f*

ap·pli·ca·tion [æplɪ'keɪʃn] *for job etc* candidatura *f; for passport, visa* domanda *f,* richiesta *f; for university* domanda *f* di iscrizione

ap·pli·ca·tion form modulo *m* di richiesta; *for passport, visa* modulo *f* di richiesta; *for university* modulo *f* di richiesta di iscrizione

ap·ply [ə'plaɪ] *(pret & pp -ied)* **1** *v/t* applicare **2** *v/i of rule, law* applicarsi

◆ **apply for** *v/t job, passport* fare domanda per; *university* fare domanda di iscrizione a

◆ **apply to** *v/t (contact)* rivolgersi a; *(affect)* applicarsi a

ap·point [ə'pɔɪnt] *v/t to position* nominare

ap·point·ment [ə'pɔɪntmənt] *to position* nomina *f; (meeting)* appuntamento *m*

ap'point·ments di·a·ry agenda *f* degli appuntamenti

A

ap·prais·al [əˈpreɪz(ə)l] valutazione f

ap·pre·cia·ble [əˈpriːʃəbl] adj notevole

ap·pre·ci·ate [əˈpriːʃieɪt] **1** v/t apprezzare; (*acknowledge*) rendersi conto di; *thanks, I ~ it* grazie, te ne sono grato; *I ~ that …* mi rendo conto che … **2** v/i FIN rivalutarsi

ap·pre·ci·a·tion [əpriːʃiˈeɪʃn] *of kindness etc* riconoscenza f; *of music etc* apprezzamento m

ap·pre·ci·a·tive [əˈpriːʃətɪv] adj (*showing gratitude*) riconoscente; (*showing pleasure*) soddisfatto

ap·pre·hen·sion [æprɪˈhenʃn] apprensione f

ap·pre·hen·sive [æprɪˈhensɪv] adj apprensivo

ap·pren·tice [əˈprentɪs] apprendista m/f

ap·pren·tice·ship [əˈprentɪsʃɪp] apprendistato m

ap·proach [əˈprəʊtʃ] **1** n avvicinamento m; (*proposal*) contatto m; *to problem* approccio m **2** v/t (*get near to*) avvicinarsi a; (*contact*) contattare; *problem* abbordare

ap·proach·a·ble [əˈprəʊtʃəbl] adj *person* abbordabile

ap·pro·pri·ate¹ [əˈprəʊprɪət] adj appropriato

ap·pro·pri·ate² [əˈprəʊprɪeɪt] v/t also euph appropriarsi di

ap·prov·al [əˈpruːvl] approvazione f

ap·prove [əˈpruːv] v/t & v/i approvare

♦ **approve of** v/t approvare

ap·prox·i·mate [əˈprɒksɪmət] adj approssimativo

ap·prox·i·mate·ly [əˈprɒksɪmətlɪ] adv approssimativamente

ap·prox·i·ma·tion [əprɒksɪˈmeɪʃn] approssimazione f

APR [eɪpiːˈɑː] abbr (= *annual percentage rate*) tasso m di interesse annuale

a·pri·cot [ˈeɪprɪkɒt] albicocca f

A·pril [ˈeɪprəl] aprile m

a·pron [ˈeɪprən] grembiule m

apt [æpt] adj *pupil* portato; *remark*

appropriato; *be ~ to …* avere tendenza a …

ap·ti·tude [ˈæptɪtjuːd] attitudine f

'ap·ti·tude test test m inv attitudinale

aq·ua·lung [ˈækwəlʌŋ] autorespiratore m

a·quar·i·um [əˈkweərɪəm] acquario m

A·quar·i·us [əˈkweərɪəs] ASTR Acquario m

a·quat·ic [əˈkwætɪk] adj acquatico

Ar·ab [ˈærəb] **1** n arabo m, -a f **2** adj arabo

Ar·a·bic [ˈærəbɪk] **1** n arabo m **2** adj arabo

ar·a·ble [ˈærəbl] adj coltivabile

ar·bi·tra·ry [ˈɑːbɪtrərɪ] adj arbitrario

ar·bi·trate [ˈɑːbɪtreɪt] v/i arbitrare

ar·bi·tra·tion [ɑːbɪˈtreɪʃn] arbitrato m

ar·bi·tra·tor [ˈɑːbɪtreɪtə(r)] arbitro m

ar·cade [ɑːˈkeɪd] (*games ~*) sala f giochi

arch [ɑːtʃ] n arco m

ar·chae·o·log·i·cal [ɑːkɪəˈlɒdʒɪkl] adj archeologico

ar·chae·ol·o·gist [ɑːkɪˈɒlədʒɪst] archeologo m, -a f

ar·chae·ol·o·gy [ɑːkɪˈɒlədʒɪ] archeologia f

ar·cha·ic [ɑːˈkeɪɪk] adj arcaico

arch·bish·op [ɑːtʃˈbɪʃəp] arcivescovo m

ar·che·ol·o·gy etc Am → **archaeology** etc

ar·cher [ˈɑːtʃə(r)] arciere m, -a f

ar·chi·tect [ˈɑːkɪtekt] architetto m

ar·chi·tec·tur·al [ɑːkɪˈtektʃərəl] adj architettonico

ar·chi·tec·ture [ˈɑːkɪtektʃə(r)] architettura f

ar·chives [ˈɑːkaɪvz] npl archivi mpl

arch·way [ˈɑːtʃweɪ] arco m

Arc·tic [ˈɑːktɪk] n Artico m

ar·dent [ˈɑːdənt] adj ardente

ar·du·ous [ˈɑːdjʊəs] adj arduo

ar·e·a [ˈeərɪə] area f; (*region*) zona f

'ar·e·a code Am TELEC prefisso m

telefonico; *official name* indicativo *m* distrettuale

a·re·na [ə'ri:nə] SP arena *f*

Ar·gen·ti·na [ɑːdʒən'ti:nə] Argentina *f*

Ar·gen·tin·i·an [ɑːdʒən'tɪnɪən] **1** *adj* argentino **2** *n* argentino *m*, -a *f*

ar·gu·a·bly ['ɑːgjʊəblɪ] *adv* probabilmente; *he's ~ the best* si può dire che è il migliore

ar·gue ['ɑːgju:] **1** *v/i* (*quarrel*) litigare; (*reason*) sostenere **2** *v/t*: *~ that ...* sostenere che ...

ar·gu·ment ['ɑːgjʊmənt] (*quarrel*) litigio *m*; (*reasoning*) argomento *m*

ar·gu·men·ta·tive [ɑːgjʊ'mentətɪv] *adj* polemico

a·ri·a ['ɑːrɪə] MUS aria *f*

ar·id ['ærɪd] *adj* land arido

Ar·i·es ['eərɪːz] ASTR Ariete *m*

a·rise [ə'raɪz] *v/i* (*pret arose*, *pp arisen*) *of situation*, *problem* emergere

a·ris·en [ə'rɪzn] *pp* → *arise*

a·ris·toc·ra·cy [ærɪ'stɒkrəsɪ] aristocrazia *f*

a·ris·to·crat ['ærɪstəkræt] aristocratico *m*, -a *f*

a·ris·to·crat·ic [ærɪstə'krætɪk] *adj* aristocratico

a·rith·me·tic [ə'rɪθmətɪk] aritmetica *f*

arm[1] [ɑːm] *n of person* braccio *m*; *of chair* bracciolo *m*

arm[2] [ɑːm] *v/t* armare; *~ s.o. / sth with sth* armare qu / qc di qc

ar·ma·ments [ɑː'mɑːməmənts] *npl* armamenti *mpl*

arm·chair ['ɑːmtʃeə(r)] poltrona *f*

armed [ɑːmd] *adj* armato

armed 'forc·es *npl* forze *fpl* armate

armed 'rob·ber·y rapina *f* a mano armata

ar·mor *Am*, **ar·mour** ['ɑːmə(r)] armatura *f*; (*metal plates*) blindatura *f*

ar·mored ve·hi·cle *Am*, **ar·moured ve·hi·cle** [ɑːməd'viːɪkl] veicolo *m* blindato

arm·pit ['ɑːmpɪt] ascella *f*

arms [ɑːmz] *npl* (*weapons*) armi *fpl*

ar·my ['ɑːmɪ] esercito *m*

a·ro·ma [ə'rəʊmə] aroma *m*

a·rose [ə'rəʊz] *pret* → *arise*

a·round [ə'raʊnd] **1** *prep* (*in circle*, *roughly*) intorno a; *room*, *world* attraverso; *it's ~ the corner* è dietro l'angolo **2** *adv* (*in the area*) qui intorno; (*encircling*) intorno; *he lives ~ here* abita da queste parti; *walk ~* andare in giro; *she has been ~* (*has travelled*, *is experienced*) ha girato; *he's still ~* F (*alive*) è ancora in circolazione

a·rouse [ə'raʊz] *v/t* suscitare; (*sexually*) eccitare

ar·range [ə'reɪndʒ] *v/t* (*put in order*) sistemare; *music* arrangiare; *meeting*, *party etc* organizzare; *time and place* combinare; *I've ~d to meet her* ho combinato di incontrarla

♦ **arrange for** *v/t* provvedere a; *I've arranged for him to meet us* ho provveduto affinché ci incontrasse

ar·range·ment [ə'reɪndʒmənt] (*agreement*) accordo *m*; *of party*, *meeting* organizzazione *f*; (*layout: of furniture etc*) disposizione *f*; *of music* arrangiamento *m*; *~s for party*, *meeting* preparativi *mpl*; *make ~s* prendere disposizioni

ar·rears [ə'rɪəz] *npl* arretrati *mpl*; *be in ~ of person* essere in arretrato; *be paid in ~ for job* essere pagato a lavoro effettuato

ar·rest [ə'rest] **1** *n* arresto *m*; *be under ~* essere in arresto **2** *v/t* arrestare

ar·riv·al [ə'raɪvl] arrivo *m*; *~s at airport* arrivi *mpl*

ar·rive [ə'raɪv] *v/i* arrivare

♦ **arrive at** *v/t place*, *decision* arrivare a

ar·ro·gance ['ærəgəns] arroganza *f*

ar·ro·gant ['ærəgənt] *adj* arrogante

ar·ro·gant·ly ['ærəgəntlɪ] *adv* con arroganza

ar·row ['ærəʊ] freccia *f*

arse [ɑːs] V culo *m* V

ar·se·nic ['ɑːsənɪk] arsenico *m*

ar·son ['ɑːsn] incendio *m* doloso

ar·son·ist ['ɑːsənɪst] piromane *m/f*

art [ɑːt] arte *f*; *the ~s* l'arte

ar·te·ry ['ɑːtərɪ] MED arteria *f*

'art gal·ler·y galleria *f* d'arte

ar·thri·tis [ɑː'θraɪtɪs] artrite *f*

ar·ti·choke ['ɑːtɪʃəʊk] carciofo *m*

ar·ti·cle ['ɑːtɪkl] articolo *m*

ar·tic·u·late [ɑː'tɪkjʊlət] *adj speech* chiaro; *be ~ of person* esprimersi bene

ar·tic·u·lat·ed 'lor·ry [ɑːtɪkjʊleɪtɪd] *Br* autoarticolato *m*

ar·ti·fi·cial [ɑːtɪ'fɪʃl] *adj* artificiale; (*not sincere*) finto

ar·ti·fi·cial in'tel·li·gence intelligenza *f* artificiale

ar·til·le·ry [ɑː'tɪlərɪ] artiglieria *f*

ar·ti·san ['ɑːtɪzæn] artigiano *m*, -a *f*

ar·tist ['ɑːtɪst] artista *m/f*

ar·tis·tic [ɑː'tɪstɪk] *adj* artistico

'arts de·gree laurea *f* in discipline umanistiche

as [æz] **1** *conj* (*while, when*) mentre; (*because*) dato che; (*like*) come; *~ he grew older, ...* diventando più vecchio, ...; *~ if* come se; *~ usual* come al solito; *~ necessary* in base alla necessità; **2** *adv*: *~ high / pretty / ...* alto / carino come ...; *~ much ~ that?* così tanto?; *run ~ fast ~ you can* corri più veloce che puoi **3** *prep* come; *~ a child* da bambino; *~ a schoolgirl* quando andava a scuola; *I'm talking to you ~ a friend* ti parlo come amico; *dressed ~ a policeman* vestito da poliziotto; *work ~ a teacher / translator* essere insegnante / traduttore; *~ for* quanto a; *~ Hamlet* nel ruolo di Amleto

asap ['eɪzæp] *abbr* (= *as soon as possible*) quanto prima

as·bes·tos [æz'bestɒs] amianto *m*

As·cen·sion [ə'senʃn] REL Ascensione *f*

as·cent [ə'sent] *path* salita *f*; *of mountain* ascensione *f*; *fig* ascesa *f*

ash [æʃ] cenere *f*; *~es* ceneri *fpl*

a·shamed [ə'ʃeɪmd] *adj*: *be ~* vergognarsi di; *you should be ~ of yourself* dovresti vergognarti

a·shore [ə'ʃɔː(r)] *adv* a terra; *go ~* sbarcare

ash·tray ['æʃtreɪ] posacenere *m*, portacenere *m*

Ash 'Wednes·day mercoledì *m inv* delle Ceneri

A·sia ['eɪʃə] Asia *f*

A·sian ['eɪʃən] **1** *n* asiatico *m*, -a *f*; (*Indian, Pakistani*) indiano *m*, -a *f* **2** *adj* asiatico; (*Indian, Pakistani*) indiano

a·side [ə'saɪd] *adv* da parte; *take s.o. ~* prendere a parte qu; *joking ~* scherzi a parte; *~ from* a parte

ask [ɑːsk] **1** *v/t person* chiedere a; (*invite*) invitare; *question* fare; *favour* chiedere; *can I ~ you something?* posso chiederti una cosa?; *~ s.o. about sth* chiedere a qu di qc; *~ s.o. for ...* chiedere a qu ...; *~ s.o. to ...* chiedere a qu di ... **2** *v/i* chiedere

♦ **ask after** *v/t person* chiedere di

♦ **ask for** *v/t* chiedere; *person* chiedere di

♦ **ask out** *v/t for a drink, night out* chiedere di uscire a

ask·ing price ['ɑːskɪŋpraɪs] prezzo *m* di domanda

a·sleep [ə'sliːp] *adj*: *he's (fast) ~* sta dormendo (profondamente); *fall ~* addormentarsi

as·par·a·gus [ə'spærəgəs] asparagi *mpl*

as·pect ['æspekt] aspetto *m*

as·phalt ['æsfælt] *n* asfalto *m*

as·phyx·i·ate [æ'sfɪksɪeɪt] *v/t* asfissiare

as·phyx·i·a·tion [əsfɪksɪ'eɪʃn] asfissia *f*

as·pi·ra·tion [æspə'reɪʃn] aspirazione *f*

as·pi·rin ['æsprɪn] aspirina *f*

ass [æs] F (*idiot*) cretino *m*, -a; *Am* P (*backside*) culo *m* P

as·sai·lant [ə'seɪlənt] assalitore *m*, -trice *f*

as·sas·sin [ə'sæsɪn] assassino *m*, -a *f*

as·sas·sin·ate [ə'sæsɪneɪt] *v/t* assassinare

as·sas·sin·a·tion [əsæsɪ'neɪʃn] assassinio *m*

as·sault [ə'sɒlt] **1** *n* assalto *m*; LAW aggressione *f* **2** *v/t* aggredire

as·sem·ble [ə'sembl] **1** v/t parts assemblare, montare **2** v/i of people radunarsi

as·sem·bly [ə'semblɪ] assemblea f; of parts assemblaggio m

as·sem·bly line catena f di montaggio

as·sem·bly plant officina f di montaggio

as·sent [ə'sent] v/i acconsentire

as·sert [ə'sɜːt]: v/t: **~ o.s.** farsi valere

as·ser·tive [ə'sɜːtɪv] adj person sicuro di sé

as·sess [ə'ses] v/t valutare

as·sess·ment [ə'sesmənt] valutazione f

as·set ['æset] FIN attivo m; fig: thing vantaggio m; person elemento m prezioso

as·sign [ə'saɪn] v/t: person destinare; thing assegnare

as·sign·ment [ə'saɪnmənt] (task, study) compito m

as·sim·i·late [ə'sɪmɪleɪt] v/t information assimilare; person into group integrare

as·sist [ə'sɪst] v/t assistere

as·sist·ance [ə'sɪstəns] assistenza f

as·sis·tant [ə'sɪstənt] assistente m/f; in shop commesso m, -a f

as·sis·tant di·rec·tor vice-direttore m; of film aiuto-regista m/f

as·sis·tant 'man·ag·er vice-responsabile m/f; of hotel, restaurant vice-direttore m

as·so·ci·ate [ə'səʊʃɪeɪt] **1** v/t associare **2** v/i: **~ with** frequentare **3** n [ə'səʊʃɪət] socio m, -a f

as·so·ci·ate pro'fes·sor professore m associato, professoressa f associata

as·so·ci·a·tion [əsəʊsɪ'eɪʃn] associazione f; **in ~ with** in associazione con

as·sort·ed [ə'sɔːtɪd] adj assortito

as·sort·ment [ə'sɔːtmənt] assortimento m; **there was a whole ~ of people** c'era gente di tutti i tipi

as·sume [ə'sjuːm] v/t (suppose) supporre

as·sump·tion [ə'sʌmpʃn] supposizione f; **The Assumption** REL l'Assunzione f

as·sur·ance [ə'ʃʊərəns] assicurazione f, garanzia f; (confidence) sicurezza f; **he gave me his personal ~ that ...** mi ha assicurato personalmente che ...

as·sure [ə'ʃʊə(r)] v/t (reassure): **~ s.o. of sth** assicurare qc a qu

as·sured [ə'ʃʊəd] adj (confident) sicuro

as·ter·isk ['æstərɪsk] asterisco m

asth·ma ['æsmə] asma f

asth·mat·ic [æs'mætɪk] adj asmatico

as·ton·ish [ə'stɒnɪʃ] v/t sbalordire; **be ~ed** essere sbalordito

as·ton·ish·ing [ə'stɒnɪʃɪŋ] adj sbalorditivo

as·ton·ish·ing·ly [ə'stɒnɪʃɪŋlɪ] adv in modo sbalorditivo

as·ton·ish·ment [ə'stɒnɪʃmənt] stupore m

as·tound [ə'staʊnd] v/t stupefare

as·tound·ing [ə'staʊndɪŋ] adj stupefacente

a·stray [ə'streɪ] adv: **go ~** smarrirsi; morally uscire dalla retta via

a·stride [ə'straɪd] **1** adv a cavalcioni **2** prep a cavalcioni di

as·trol·o·ger [ə'strɒlədʒə(r)] astrologo m, -a f

as·trol·o·gy [ə'strɒlədʒɪ] astrologia f

as·tro·naut ['æstrənɔːt] astronauta m/f

as·tron·o·mer [ə'strɒnəmə(r)] astronomo m, -a f

as·tro·nom·i·cal [æstrə'nɒmɪkl] adj price etc astronomico

as·tron·o·my [ə'strɒnəmɪ] astronomia f

as·tute [ə'stjuːt] adj astuto

a·sy·lum [ə'saɪləm] mental manicomio m; political asilo m

at [ət] stressed [æt] prep (with places) a; **he works ~ the hospital** lavora in ospedale; **~ the baker's** dal panettiere o in panetteria; **~ Joe's** da Joe; **~ the door** alla porta; **~ 10 pounds** a 10 sterline; **~ the age of 18** all'età di 18 anni; **~ 5 o'clock** alle cinque; **~ war** in guerra; **~ night** di notte; **~**

the moment you called nel momento in cui hai chiamato; **~ 150 km/h** a 150 km/h; **be good / bad ~ sth** essere / non essere bravo in qc

ate [eɪt] *pret of* **eat**

a·the·is·m ['eɪθɪɪzm] ateismo *m*

a·the·ist ['eɪθɪɪst] ateo *m*, -a *f*

ath·lete ['æθliːt] atleta *m/f*

ath·let·ic [æθ'letɪk] *adj* atletico

ath·let·ics [æθ'letɪks] *nsg* atletica *f*

At·lan·tic [ət'læntɪk] *n* Atlantico *m*

at·las ['ætləs] atlante *m*

at·mos·phere ['ætməsfɪə(r)] *of earth, mood* atmosfera *f*

at·mos·pher·ic pol·lu·tion [ætməs'ferɪk] inquinamento *m* atmosferico

at·om ['ætəm] atomo *m*

'at·om bomb bomba *f* atomica

a·tom·ic [ə'tomɪk] *adj* atomico

a·tom·ic 'en·er·gy energia *f* nucleare

a·tom·ic 'waste scorie *fpl* nucleari

a·tom·iz·er ['ætəmaɪzə(r)] vaporizzatore *m*

a·tone [ə'təun] *v/i:* **~ for** scontare

a·tro·cious [ə'trəuʃəs] *adj* atroce

a·troc·i·ty [ə'trosətɪ] atrocità *f inv*

at·tach [ə'tætʃ] *v/t* attaccare; *importance* attribuire; *document, file* allegare; **be ~ed to** (*fond of*) essere attaccato a

at·tach·ment [ə'tætʃmənt] (*fondness*) attaccamento *m*; *to email* allegato *m*

at·tack [ə'tæk] **1** *n* aggressione *f*; MIL attacco *m* **2** *v/t* aggredire; MIL attaccare

at·tempt [ə'tempt] **1** *n* tentativo *m* **2** *v/t* tentare; **~ to do sth**

at·tend [ə'tend] *v/t* wedding, funeral partecipare a; *school, classes* frequentare

♦ **attend to** *v/t* (*deal with*) sbrigare; *customer* servire; *patient* assistere

at·tend·ance [ə'tendəns] partecipazione *f*; *at school* frequenza *f*

at·tend·ant [ə'tendənt] *in museum etc* sorvegliante *m/f*

at·ten·tion [ə'tenʃn] attenzione *f*; **bring sth to s.o.'s ~** informare qu di qc; **your ~ please** attenzione; **pay ~**

fare attenzione; **for the ~ of** *in faxes etc* alla cortese attenzione di

at·ten·tive [ə'tentɪv] *adj listener* attento

at·tic ['ætɪk] soffitta *f*

at·ti·tude ['ætɪtjuːd] atteggiamento *m*

attn *abbr* (= **attention**) c.a. (= alla cortese attenzione di)

at·tor·ney [ə'tɜːnɪ] avvocato *m*; **power of ~** delega *f*

at·tract [ə'trækt] *v/t* attirare; **be ~ed to s.o.** essere attirato da qu

at·trac·tion [ə'trækʃn] attrazione *f*

at·trac·tive [ə'træktɪv] *adj* attrattivo; *person* attraente

at·trib·ute¹ [ə'trɪbjuːt] *v/t* attribuire; **~ sth to ...** attribuire qc a ...

at·trib·ute² ['ætrɪbjuːt] *n* attributo *m*

au·ber·gine ['əubəʒiːn] melanzana *f*

auc·tion ['ɔːkʃn] **1** *n* asta *f* **2** *v/t* mettere all'asta

♦ **auction off** *v/t* vendere all'asta

auc·tio·neer [ɔːkʃə'nɪə(r)] banditore *m*, -trice *f*

au·da·cious [ɔː'deɪʃəs] *adj* audace

au·dac·i·ty [ɔː'dæsətɪ] audacia *f*

au·di·ble ['ɔːdəbl] *adj* udibile

au·di·ence ['ɔːdɪəns] pubblico *m*; TV telespettatori *mpl*; *with the Pope etc* udienza *f*

au·di·o ['ɔːdɪəu] *adj* audio *inv*

au·di·o·vi·su·al [ɔːdɪəu'vɪʒuəl] *adj* audiovisivo

au·dit ['ɔːdɪt] **1** *n of accounts* revisione *f o* verifica *f* contabile; *software* **~** inventario *m* dei software **2** *v/t* verificare

au·di·tion [ɔː'dɪʃn] **1** *n* audizione *f* **2** *v/i* fare un'audizione

au·di·tor ['ɔːdɪtə(r)] revisore *m* contabile

au·di·to·ri·um [ɔːdɪ'tɔːrɪəm] *of theatre etc* sala *f*

Au·gust ['ɔːgəst] agosto *m*

aunt [ɑːnt] zia *f*

au pair (girl) [əu'peə(r)] ragazza *f* alla pari

au·ra ['ɔːrə]: **she has an ~ of confidence** emana sicurezza

aus·pic·es ['ɔːspɪsɪz]: **under the ~**

of sotto l'egida di
aus·pi·cious [ɔːˈspɪʃəs] *adj* propizio
aus·tere [ɔːˈstɪə(r)] *adj* austero
aus·ter·i·ty [ɒsˈterətɪ] *economic* austerità *f*
Aus·tra·li·a [ɒˈstreɪlɪə] Australia *f*
Aus·tra·li·an [ɒˈstreɪlɪən] **1** *adj* australiano **2** *n* australiano *m*, -a *f*
Aus·tri·a [ˈɒstrɪə] Austria *f*
Aus·tri·an [ˈɒstrɪən] **1** *adj* austriaco **2** *n* austriaco *m*, -a *f*
au·then·tic [ɔːˈθentɪk] *adj* autentico
au·then·tic·i·ty [ɔːθenˈtɪsətɪ] autenticità *f*
au·thor [ˈɔːθə(r)] autore *m*, autrice *f*
au·thor·i·tar·i·an [ɔːθɒrɪˈteərɪən] *adj* autoritario
au·thor·i·ta·tive [ɔːˈθɒrɪtətɪv] *adj* autoritario; *information* autorevole
au·thor·i·ty [ɔːˈθɒrətɪ] autorità *f inv*; (*permission*) autorizzazione *f*; **be in ~** avere l'autorità; **be an ~ on** essere un'autorità in materia di; **the authorities** le autorità
au·thor·i·za·tion [ɔːθəraɪˈzeɪʃn] autorizzazione *f*
au·thor·ize [ˈɔːθəraɪz] *v/t* autorizzare; **be ~d to ...** essere autorizzato a ...
au·tis·tic [ɔːˈtɪstɪk] *adj* autistico
au·to·bi·og·ra·phy [ɔːtəbaɪˈɒgrəfɪ] autobiografia *f*
au·to·crat·ic [ɔːtəˈkrætɪk] *adj* autocratico
au·to·graph [ˈɔːtəgrɑːf] autografo *m*
au·to·mate [ˈɔːtəmeɪt] *v/t* automatizzare
au·to·mat·ic [ɔːtəˈmætɪk] **1** *adj* automatico **2** *n car* macchina *f* con il cambio automatico; *gun* pistola *f* automatica; *washing machine* lavatrice *f* automatica
au·to·mat·i·cal·ly [ɔːtəˈmætɪklɪ] *adv* automaticamente
au·to·ma·tion [ɔːtəˈmeɪʃn] automazione *f*
au·to·mo·bile [ˈɔːtəməbiːl] automobile *f*
au·ton·o·mous [ɔːˈtɒnəməs] *adj* autonomo

au·ton·o·my [ɔːˈtɒnəmɪ] autonomia *f*
au·to·pi·lot [ˈɔːtəʊpaɪlət] pilota *m* automatico
au·top·sy [ˈɔːtɒpsɪ] autopsia *f*
au·tumn [ˈɔːtəm] autunno *m*
aux·il·ia·ry [ɔːgˈzɪlɪərɪ] *adj* ausiliario
a·vail [əˈveɪl] **1** *n*: **to no ~** invano **2** *v/t*: **~ o.s. of** avvalersi di
a·vai·la·ble [əˈveɪləbl] *adj* disponibile
av·a·lanche [ˈævəlɑːnʃ] valanga *f*
av·a·rice [ˈævərɪs] avarizia *f*
a·venge [əˈvendʒ] *v/t* vendicare
av·e·nue [ˈævənjuː] corso *m*; *fig* strada *f*
av·e·rage [ˈævərɪdʒ] **1** *adj* medio; (*of mediocre quality*) mediocre **2** *n* media *f*; *above / below* ~ sopra/sotto la media; *on* ~ in media, mediamente **3** *v/t* raggiungere in media
♦ **average out** *v/t* fare la media di
♦ **average out at** *v/t* risultare in media a
a·verse [əˈvɜːs] *adj*: *not be ~ to* non avere niente contro
a·ver·sion [əˈvɜːʃn] avversione *f*; *have an ~ to* avere un'avversione per
a·vert [əˈvɜːt] *v/t one's eyes* distogliere; *crisis* evitare
a·vi·a·ry [ˈeɪvɪərɪ] voliera *f*
a·vi·a·tion [eɪvɪˈeɪʃn] aviazione *f*; ~ *industry* industria *f* aeronautica
av·id [ˈævɪd] *adj* avido
av·o·ca·do [ævəˈkɑːdəʊ] avocado *m inv*
a·void [əˈvɔɪd] *v/t* evitare
a·void·a·ble [əˈvɔɪdəbl] *adj* evitabile
a·wait [əˈweɪt] *v/t* attendere
a·wake [əˈweɪk] *adj* sveglio; *it's keeping me ~* mi impedisce di dormire
a·ward [əˈwɔːd] **1** *n* (*prize*) premio *m* **2** *v/t* assegnare; *damages* riconoscere; *she was ~ed the Nobel Prize for ...* le hanno assegnato il premio Nobel per ...
a·ware [əˈweə(r)] *adj* conscio, consapevole; *be ~ of sth* essere conscio *o* consapevole di qc; *become ~ of sth*

rendersi conto di qc

a·ware·ness [əˈweənɪs] consapevolezza *f*

a·way [əˈweɪ] *adv* via; SP fuori casa; **be ~** *travelling, sick etc* essere via; **go/run ~** andare/correre via; **look ~** guardare da un'altra parte; **it's 2 miles ~** dista 2 miglia; **Christmas is still six weeks ~** mancano ancora sei settimane a Natale; **take sth ~ from s.o.** togliere qc a qu; **put sth ~** mettere via qc

a·way match SP partita *f* fuori casa

awe [ɔː] soggezione *f*

awe·some ['ɔːsm] *adj* F (*terrific*) fantastico

aw·ful ['ɔːfl] *adj* tremendo, terribile; **I feel ~** F sto da cani F

aw·ful·ly ['ɔːflɪ] *adv* F (*very*) da matti F

awk·ward ['ɔːkwəd] *adj* (*clumsy*) goffo; (*difficult*) difficile; (*embarrassing*) scomodo; **feel ~** sentirsi a disagio

awn·ing ['ɔːnɪŋ] tenda *f*

ax *Am*, **axe** [æks] **1** *n* scure *f*, accetta *f* **2** *v/t* *project, job* sopprimere

ax·le ['æksl] asse *f*

B

BA [biːˈeɪ] *abbr* (= **Bachelor of Arts**) (*degree*) laurea *f* in lettere; (*person*) laureato *m*, -a *f* in lettere

ba·by ['beɪbɪ] *n* bambino *m*, -a *f*

'baby boom baby boom *m inv*

ba·by·ish ['beɪbɪʃ] *adj* infantile

'baby-sit *v/i* (*pret & pp -sat*) fare il/la baby-sitter

'bab·y-sit·ter baby-sitter *m/f inv*

bach·e·lor ['bætʃələ(r)] scapolo *m*

back [bæk] **1** *n of person* schiena *f*; *of animal, hand* dorso *m*; *of car, bus* parte *f* posteriore; *of book, house* retro *m*; *of clothes* rovescio *m*; *of drawer* fondo *m*; *of chair* schienale *m*; SP terzino *m*; **in the ~** (*of the car*) (nei sedili) di dietro; **at the ~ of the bus** in fondo all'autobus; **~ to front** al contrario; **at the ~ of beyond** in capo al mondo **2** *adj door, steps* di dietro; *wheels, legs* posteriore; *garden, room* sul retro; *payment, issue* arretrato; **~ road** strada secondaria **3** *adv*: **please move/stand ~** indietro, per favore; **2 metres ~ from the edge** a 2 metri dal bordo; **~ in 1935** nel 1935; **give sth ~ to s.o.** restituire qc a qu; **she'll be ~**

tomorrow sarà di ritorno domani; **when are you coming ~?** quando torni?; **take sth ~ to the store** *because unsatisfactory* riportare qc indietro al negozio; **they wrote/phoned ~** hanno risposto alla lettera/telefonata; **he hit me ~** mi ha restituito il colpo **4** *v/t* (*support*) appoggiare; *car* guidare in retromarcia; *horse* puntare su; **~ the car into the garage** mettere la macchina in garage in retromarcia **5** *v/i of driver* fare retromarcia

♦ **back away** *v/i* indietreggiare

♦ **back down** *v/i fig* fare marcia indietro

♦ **back off** *v/i* spostarsi indietro; *from danger* tirarsi indietro

♦ **back onto** *v/t* dare su

♦ **back out** *v/i fig* tirarsi indietro

♦ **back up 1** *v/t* (*support*) confermare; *claim, argument* supportare; *file* fare un backup di; **back s.o. up** spalleggiare qu; **be backed up** *of traffic* essere congestionato **2** *v/i in car* fare retromarcia

'back·ache mal *m inv* di schiena;

back·bench·er [bæk'bentʃə(r)]

parlamentare *m/f* ordinario, -a;
'**back·bit·ing** maldicenze *fpl*;
'**back·bone** *also fig* spina *f* dorsale;
'**back·door** porta *f* di dietro
'**back-break·ing** *adj* massacrante;
back 'burn·er: *put sth on the ~*
accantonare qc; '**back·date** *v/t* retrodatare; '**back·door** porta *f* di dietro

back·er ['bækə(r)] FIN finanziatore *m*, -trice *f*

back'fire *v/i fig* avere effetto contrario; *~ on s.o.* ritorcersi contro qu; '**back·ground** *n* sfondo *m*; *fig: of person* background *m inv*; *of story, event* retroscena *mpl*; '**back·hand** *n in tennis* rovescio *m*; **back·hand·er** ['bækhændə(r)] F bustarella *f* F

'**back·ing** ['bækɪŋ] *n moral* appoggio *m*; *financial* finanziamento *m*; MUS accompagnamento *m*

'**back·ing group** MUS gruppo *m* d'accompagnamento

'**back·lash** reazione *f* violenta; '**back·log**: *~ of work* lavoro *m* arretrato; *~ of unanswered letters* corrispondenza *f* arretrata; '**backpack** *n* zaino *m*; '**back·pack·er** saccopelista *m/f*; '**back·pack·ing** *il viaggiare con zaino e sacco a pelo*; '**back·ped·al** *v/i fig* fare marcia indietro; '**back seat** *of car* sedile *m* posteriore; **back-seat 'driv·er**: *you're a terrible ~!* smettila di dire come si deve guidare!; '**back·side** F sedere *m*; '**back·space (key)** (tasto di) ritorno *m*; '**back·stairs** *npl* scala *f* di servizio; '**back streets** *npl* vicoli *mpl*; '**back·stroke** SP dorso *m*; '**back·track** *v/i* tornare indietro; '**back·up** (*support*) rinforzi *mpl*, COMPUT backup *m inv*; '**back·up disk** COMPUT disco *m* di backup

back·ward ['bækwəd] *adj child* tardivo; *society* arretrato; *glance* all'indietro

backwards ['bækwədz] *adv* indietro
back'yard cortile *m*; *not in my ~ fig* non in casa mia
ba·con ['beɪkn] pancetta *f*
bac·te·ri·a [bæk'tɪərɪə] *npl* batteri *mpl*

bad [bæd] *adj news, manners* cattivo; *weather, cold, headache* brutto; *mistake, accident* grave; *egg, food* guasto; *smoking is ~ for you* il fumo fa male; *it's not ~* non è male; *that's too ~ shame* peccato!; *feel ~ about sth (guilty)* sentirsi in colpa per qc; *be ~ at* essere negato per; *Friday's ~, how about Thursday?* venerdì non posso, che ne dici di giovedì?

bad 'debt debito *m* insoluto
badge [bædʒ] distintivo *m*
bad·ger ['bædʒə(r)] *v/t* tasso *m*
bad 'lan·guage parolacce *fpl*
bad·ly ['bædlɪ] *adv* male; *injured, damaged* gravemente; *he ~ needs a haircut / rest* ha urgente bisogno di tagliarsi i capelli / riposare; *he is ~ off (poor)* è povero
bad-man·nered [bæd'mænəd] *adj* maleducato
bad·min·ton ['bædmɪntən] badminton *m inv*
bad-tem·pered [bæd'tempəd] *adj* irascibile
baf·fle ['bæfl] *v/t*: *be ~d* essere perplesso
baf·fling ['bæflɪŋ] *adj* sconcertante
bag [bæg] borsa *f*; *plastic, paper* busta *f*
bag·gage ['bægɪdʒ] bagagli *mpl*
bag·gage re·claim ['riːkleɪm] ritiro *m* bagagli
bag·gage trol·ley carrello *m*
bag·gy ['bægɪ] *adj* senza forma
bag·pipes *npl* cornamusa *fsg*
bail [beɪl] *n* LAW cauzione *f*; *on ~* su cauzione
♦**bail out 1** *v/t* LAW scarcerare su cauzione; *fig* tirare fuori dai guai **2** *v/i of aeroplane* lanciarsi col paracadute
bai·liff ['beɪlɪf] *ufficiale m* giudiziario
bait [beɪt] *n* esca *f*
bake [beɪk] *v/t* cuocere al forno
baked 'beans [beɪkt] *npl* fagioli *mpl in salsa rossa*
baked po'ta·toes *npl* patate *fpl* cotte al forno con la buccia
bak·er ['beɪkə(r)] fornaio *m*, -a *f*

bak·er's ['beɪkəz] panetteria f
bak·er·y ['beɪkərɪ] panetteria f
bak·ing pow·der ['beɪkɪŋ] lievito m
bal·ance ['bæləns] **1** n equilibrio m; (remainder) resto m; of bank account saldo m **2** v/t tenere in equilibrio; ~ **the books** fare il bilancio **3** v/i stare in equilibrio; of accounts quadrare
bal·anced ['bælənst] adj (fair) obiettivo; diet, personality equilibrato
bal·ance of 'pay·ments bilancia f dei pagamenti
bal·ance of 'trade bilancia f commerciale
'bal·ance sheet bilancio m (di esercizio)
bal·co·ny ['bælkənɪ] of house balcone m; in theatre prima galleria f
bald [bɔːld] adj man calvo; **he's going** ~ sta perdendo i capelli
bald·ing ['bɔːldɪŋ] adj stempiato
Bal·kan ['bɔːlkən] adj balcanico
Bal·kans ['bɔːlkənz] npl: **the** ~ i Balcani mpl
ball¹ [bɔːl] palla f; football pallone m; **be on the** ~ essere sveglio; **play** ~ fig collaborare; **the** ~'s **in his court** la prossima mossa è sua
ball² [bɔːl] (dance) ballo m
bal·lad ['bæləd] ballata f
ball 'bear·ing cuscinetto m a sfere
bal·le·ri·na [bælə'riːnə] ballerina f
bal·let ['bæleɪ] art danza f classica; dance balletto m
'bal·let danc·er ballerino m classico, ballerina f classica
'ball game F: **that's a different** ~ è un altro paio di maniche
bal·lis·tic mis·sile [bə'lɪstɪk] missile m balistico
bal·loon [bə'luːn] child's palloncino m; for flight mongolfiera f
bal·loon·ist [bə'luːnɪst] aeronauta m/f
bal·lot ['bælət] **1** n votazione f **2** v/t members consultare tramite votazione
'bal·lot box urna f elettorale
'bal·lot pa·per scheda f elettorale
'ballpark F: **be in the right** ~ essere nell'ordine corretto di cifre; **'ball-**

park fig·ure F cifra f approssimativa
'ball·point (pen) penna f a sfera
balls [bɔːlz] npl V (also courage) palle fpl V
bam·boo [bæm'buː] n bambù m inv
ban [bæn] **1** n divieto m (**on** di) **2** v/t (pret & pp **-ned**) proibire
ba·nal [bə'nɑːl] adj banale
ba·na·na [bə'nɑːnə] banana f
band [bænd] banda f; pop gruppo m; of material nastro m
ban·dage ['bændɪdʒ] **1** n benda f **2** v/t bendare
B&B [biːn'biː] abbr (= **bed and breakfast**) pensione f familiare, bed and breakfast m inv
ban·dit ['bændɪt] brigante m
'band·wagon n: **jump on the** ~ seguire la corrente
ban·dy ['bændɪ] adj legs storto
bang [bæŋ] **1** n colpo m **2** v/t door chiudere violentemente; (hit) sbattere; **I –ed my knee on the table** ho battuto il ginocchio contro il tavolo **3** v/i sbattere; **the door ~ed shut** la porta si è chiusa con un colpo
bang·er ['bæŋə(r)] F (sausage) salamino m; **an old** ~ (car) una vecchia carretta
ban·gle ['bæŋgl] braccialetto m
ban·is·ters ['bænɪstəz] npl ringhiera fsg
ban·jo ['bændʒəʊ] banjo m inv
bank¹ [bæŋk] of river riva f
bank² [bæŋk] **1** n FIN banca f **2** v/i: ~ **with** avere un conto presso la banca **3** v/t money mettere in banca
♦ **bank on** v/t contare su; **don't bank on it** non ci contare; **bank on s.o. doing sth** dare per scontato che qu faccia qc
'bank ac·count conto m bancario
'bank bal·ance saldo m
bank·er ['bæŋkə(r)] banchiere m
'bank·er's card carta f assegni
'bank·er's 'or·der ordine m di pagamento
bank 'hol·i·day giorno m festivo
bank·ing ['bæŋkɪŋ] professione f bancaria

B

'bank loan prestito *m* bancario; 'bank man·ag·er direttore *m* di banca; 'bank note banconota *f*; 'bank rate tasso *m* ufficiale di sconto; 'bank·roll *v/t* finanziare

bank·rupt ['bæŋkrʌpt] **1** *adj* fallito; **go ~** fallire **2** *v/t* portare al fallimento

bank·rupt·cy ['bæŋkrʌpsɪ] bancarotta *f*

'bank state·ment estratto *m* conto

ban·ner ['bænə(r)] striscione *m*

banns [bænz] *npl* pubblicazioni *mpl* (matrimoniali)

ban·quet ['bæŋkwɪt] *n* banchetto *m*

ban·ter ['bæntə(r)] *n* scambio *m* di battute

bap·tis·m ['bæptɪzm] battesimo *m*

bap·tize [bæp'taɪz] *v/t* battezzare

bar¹ [bɑː(r)] *n of iron* spranga *f*; *of chocolate* tavoletta *f*; *for drinks* bar *m inv*; *(counter)* bancone *m*; **a ~ of soap** una saponetta; **be behind ~s** *(in prison)* essere dietro le sbarre

bar² [bɑː(r)] *v/t (pret & pp* **-red**) vietare l'ingresso a; **he's been ~red from the club** gli hanno vietato l'ingresso al club

bar³ [bɑː(r)] *prep (except)* tranne

bar·bar·i·an [bɑː'beərɪən] barbaro *m*, -a *f*

bar·bar·ic [bɑː'bærɪk] *adj* barbaro

bar·be·cue ['bɑːbɪkjuː] **1** *n* barbecue *m inv* **2** *v/t* cuocere al barbecue

barbed 'wire [bɑːbd] filo *m* spinato

bar·ber ['bɑːbə(r)] barbiere *m*

bar·bi·tu·rate [bɑː'bɪtjʊrət] barbiturico *m*

'bar code codice *m* a barre

bare [beə(r)] *adj (naked)* nudo; *(empty: room)* spoglio; *mountainside* brullo

'bare·foot *adj:* **be ~** essere scalzo

'bare·head·ed [beə'hedɪd] *adj* senza cappello

'bare·ly ['beəlɪ] *adv* appena

bar·gain ['bɑːgɪn] **1** *n (deal)* patto *m*; *(good buy)* affare *m*; **it's a ~!** *(deal)* è un affarone!; **into the ~** per giunta **2** *v/i* tirare sul prezzo

♦ bargain for *v/t (expect)* aspettarsi;

he got more than he bargained for non se l'aspettava

barge [bɑːdʒ] *n* NAUT chiatta *f*

♦ barge into *v/t* piombare su

bar·i·tone ['bærɪtəʊn] *n* baritono *m*

bark¹ [bɑːk] **1** *n of dog* abbaiare *m* **2** *v/i* abbaiare

bark² [bɑːk] *of tree* corteccia *f*

bar·ley ['bɑːlɪ] orzo *m*

'bar·maid barista *f*

'bar·man barista *m*

barm·y ['bɑːmɪ] *adj* F pazzoide F

barn [bɑːn] granaio *m*

ba·rom·e·ter [bə'rɒmɪtə(r)] *also fig* barometro *m*

Ba·roque [bə'rɒk] *adj* barocco

bar·racks ['bærəks] *npl* MIL caserma *fsg*

bar·rage ['bærɑːdʒ] MIL sbarramento *m*; *fig* raffica *f*

bar·rel ['bærəl] *(container)* barile *m*

bar·ren ['bærən] *adj land* arido

bar·ri·cade [bærɪ'keɪd] *n* barricata *f*

bar·ri·er ['bærɪə(r)] barriera *f*; *language ~* l'ostacolo *m* della lingua

bar·ring ['bɑːrɪŋ] *prep:* **~ accidents** salvo imprevisti

bar·ris·ter ['bærɪstə(r)] avvocato *m*

bar·row ['bærəʊ] carriola *f*

'bar ten·der barista *m/f*

bar·ter ['bɑːtə(r)] **1** *n* baratto *m* **2** *v/i* barattare

base [beɪs] **1** *n* base *f* **2** *v/t* basare; **~ sth on sth** basare qc su qc; **be ~d in** *in city, country* essere di base a; **be ~d on** essere basato su

'base·ball baseball *m inv*

'base·ball bat mazza *f* da baseball

'base·ball cap berretto *m* da baseball

base·less ['beɪslɪs] *adj* infondato

base·ment ['beɪsmənt] seminterrato *m*

'base rate FIN tasso *m* base

bash [bæʃ] **1** *n* F colpo *m* **2** *v/t* F sbattere

ba·sic ['beɪsɪk] *adj knowledge, equipment* rudimentale; *salary* di base; *beliefs* fondamentale

ba·sic·al·ly ['beɪsɪklɪ] *adv* essenzialmente

ba·sics ['beɪsɪks] *npl*: **the ~** i rudimenti *mpl*; **get down to ~** venire al sodo

bas·il ['bæzɪl] basilico *m*

ba·sil·i·ca [bə'zɪlɪkə] basilica *f*

ba·sin ['beɪsn] *for washing* lavandino *m*

ba·sis ['beɪsɪs] (*pl* **bases** ['beɪsiːz]) base *f*

bask [baːsk] *v/i* crogiolarsi

bas·ket ['baːskɪt] cestino *m*; *in basketball* cesto *m*

'bas·ket·ball basket *m inv*, pallacanestro *f*

bass [beɪs] **1** *n* (*part*) voce *f* di basso; (*singer*) basso *m*; (*double bass*) contrabbasso *m*; (*guitar*) basso *m* **2** *adj* di basso

bas·tard ['baːstəd] F bastardo *m*, -a *f* F

bat¹ [bæt] **1** *n* mazza *f*; *for table tennis* racchetta *f* **2** *v/i* (*pret & pp* **-ted**) SP battere

bat² [bæt] *v/t* (*pret & pp* **-ted**): **he didn't ~ an eyelid** non ha battuto ciglio

bat³ [bæt] (*animal*) pipistrello *m*

batch [bætʃ] *n of students* gruppo *m*; *of goods* lotto *m*; *of bread* infornata *f*

ba·ted ['beɪtɪd] *adj*: **with ~ breath** col fiato sospeso

bath [baːθ] bagno *m*; **have a ~, take a ~** fare il bagno

'bath·ing cos·tume, **'bath·ing suit** costume *m* da bagno

'bath mat tappetino *m* da bagno; **'bath·robe** accappatoio *m*; **'bath·room** (*stanza f da*) bagno *m*

baths [baːðz] *npl* Br bagni *mpl* pubblici

'bath tow·el asciugamano *m* da bagno

'bath·tub vasca *f* da bagno

bat·on ['bætən] *of conductor* bacchetta *f*

bat·tal·i·on [bə'tælɪən] MIL battaglione *m*

bat·ter ['bætə(r)] *n* pastella *f*

bat·tered ['bætəd] *adj* maltrattato;

old hat, suitcase etc malridotto

bat·ter·y ['bætrɪ] pila *f*; MOT batteria *f*

'bat·ter·y charg·er caricabatterie *m inv*

bat·ter·y-op·e·rat·ed [bætrɪ'ɒpəreɪtɪd] *adj* a pile

bat·tle ['bætl] **1** *n also fig* battaglia *f* **2** *v/i against illness etc* lottare

'bat·tle·field, **'bat·tle·ground** campo *m* di battaglia

'bat·tle·ship corazzata *f*

bawd·y ['bɔːdɪ] *adj* spinto

bawl [bɔːl] *v/i* (*shout*) urlare; (*weep*) strillare

♦ **bawl out** *v/t* F fare una lavata di capo a

bay [beɪ] (*inlet*) baia *f*

bay·o·net ['beɪənet] *n* baionetta *f*

bay 'win·dow bovindo *m*

BBC [biːbiː'siː] *abbr* (= **British Broadcasting Corporation**) BBC *f inv*

BC [biː'siː] *abbr* (= **before Christ**) a. C. (= avanti Cristo)

be [biː] *v/i* (*pret was / were, pp been*) essere; *it's me* sono io; *was she there?* era lì?; *how much is / are ...?* quant'è / quanto sono ...?; *there is, there are* c'è, ci sono; *~ careful* sta' attento; *don't ~ sad* non essere triste; *how are you?* come stai?; *he's very well* sta bene; *I'm hot / cold* ho freddo / caldo; *it's hot / cold* fa freddo / caldo; *he's seven* ha sette anni ◊ *has the postman been?* è passato il postino?; *I've never been to Japan* non sono mai stato in Giappone; *I've been here for hours* sono qui da tanto ◊ *tags*: *that's right, isn't it?* giusto, no?; *she's American, isn't she?* è americana, vero? ◊ *v aux*: *I am thinking* sto pensando; *he was running* stava correndo; *you're ~ing silly* stai facendo lo sciocco; *he's working in London* lavora a Londra; *I'll be waiting for an answer* aspetterò una risposta ◊ *obligation*: *you are to do what I tell you* devi fare quello che ti dico; *I*

B

was to tell you this dovevo dirtelo; **you were not to tell anyone** non dovevi dirlo a nessuno ◊ *passive* essere, venire (*not with past tenses*); **he was killed** è stato ucciso; **they have been sold** sono stati venduti; **it will ~ sold for £100** sarà *o* verrà venduto a 100 sterline

beach [biːtʃ] *n* spiaggia *f*
'beach ball pallone *m* da spiaggia
'beach·wear abbigliamento *m* da spiaggia

beads [biːdz] *npl* perline *fpl*
beak [biːk] becco *m*
bea·ker ['biːkə(r)] bicchiere *m*
'be-all: the ~ and end-all la cosa più importante
beam [biːm] **1** *n in ceiling etc* trave *f* **2** *v/i* (*smile*) fare un sorriso radioso **3** *v/t* (*transmit*) trasmettere
bean [biːn] (*vegetable*) fagiolo *m*; *of coffee* chicco *m*; **be full of ~s** F essere particolarmente vivace
'bean·bag *seat* poltrona *f* sacco
bear¹ [beə(r)] *animal* orso *m*
bear² [beə(r)] (*pret* **bore**, *pp* **borne**) **1** *v/t weight* portare; *costs* sostenere; (*tolerate*) sopportare; *child* dare alla luce **2** *v/i*: **bring pressure to ~ on** fare pressione su
◆ **bear out** *v/t* (*confirm*) confermare; **bear s.o. out** appoggiare qu
bear·a·ble ['beərəbl] *adj* sopportabile
beard [bɪəd] barba *f*
beard·ed ['bɪədɪd] *adj* con la barba
bear·ing ['beərɪŋ] *in machine* cuscinetto *m*; **that has no ~ on the case** ciò non ha alcuna attinenza col caso
'bear mar·ket FIN mercato *m* cedente
beast [biːst] bestia *f*
beat [biːt] **1** *n of heart* battito *m*; *of music* ritmo *m* **2** *v/i* (*pret* **beat**, *pp* **beaten**) *of heart* battere; *of rain* picchiettare; **~ about the bush** menar il can per l'aia **3** *v/t* (*pret* **beat**, *pp* **beaten**) *in competition* battere; (*hit*)

picchiare; *drum* suonare; **~ it!** F fila!; **it ~s me** non capisco
◆ **beat up** *v/t* picchiare
beat·en ['biːtən] **1** *adj*: **off the ~ track** fuori mano **2** *pp* → **beat**
beat·ing ['biːtɪŋ] (*physical*) botte *fpl*
beat-up *adj* F malconcio
beau·ti·cian [bjuːˈtɪʃn] estetista *m/f*
beau·ti·ful ['bjuːtɪful] *adj* bello; **thanks, that's just ~!** grazie, così va bene
beau·ti·ful·ly ['bjuːtɪflɪ] *adv* stupendamente
beau·ty ['bjuːtɪ] *of woman, sunset* bellezza *f*
'beau·ty sal·on istituto *m* di bellezza
◆ **beaver away** *v/i* F sgobbare F
be·came [bɪˈkeɪm] *pret* → **become**
be·cause [bɪˈkɒz] *conj* perché; **~ of** a causa di
beck·on ['bekn] *v/i* fare cenno
be·come [bɪˈkʌm] *v/i* (*pret* **became**, *pp* **become**) diventare; **what's ~ of her?** che ne è stato di lei?
be·com·ing [bɪˈkʌmɪŋ] *adj* grazioso
bed [bed] *n* letto *m*; **~ of flowers** aiuola *f*; **go to ~** andare a letto; **he's still in ~** è ancora a letto; **go to ~ with** andare a letto con
bed and 'breakfast pensione *f* familiare, bed and breakfast *m inv*
'bed·clothes *npl* coperte e lenzuola *fpl*
bed·ding ['bedɪŋ] materasso *m* e lenzuola *fpl*
bed·lam ['bedləm] F manicomio *m*
bed·rid·den ['bedrɪdən] *adj* costretto a letto; **'bed·room** camera *f* da letto; **'bed·side: be at the ~ of** essere al capezzale di; **bed·side 'lamp** lampada *f* da comodino; **bed·side 'ta·ble** comodino *m*; **'bed-sit, bed-'sit·ter** monolocale *m*; **'bed·spread** copriletto *m*; **'bed·time** ora *f* di andare a letto
bee [biː] ape *f*
beech [biːtʃ] faggio *m*
beef [biːf] **1** *n* manzo *m*; F (*complaint*) problema *m* **2** *v/i* F (*complain*) lagnarsi
◆ **beef up** *v/t* rinforzare

'beef·bur·ger hamburger *m inv*

'bee·hive alveare *m*

'bee·line: *make a ~ for* andare diritto a

been [biːn] *pp* → *be*

beep [biːp] **1** *n* bip *m inv* **2** *v/i* suonare **3** *v/t* (*call on pager*) chiamare sul cercapersone

beep·er ['biːpə(r)] (*pager*) cercapersone *m inv*

beer [bɪə(r)] birra *f*

bee·tle ['biːtl] coleottero *m*

beet·root ['biːtruːt] barbabietola *f*; *as red as a* ~ rosso come un peperone

be·fore [bɪ'fɔː(r)] **1** *prep* prima di; *~ eight o'clock* prima delle otto **2** *adv* prima; *have you been to England ~?* sei già stato in Inghilterra?; *I've seen this film ~* questo film l'ho già visto **3** *conj* prima che; *I saw him ~ he left* l'ho visto prima che partisse; *I saw him ~ I left* l'ho visto prima di partire

be·fore·hand *adv* prima

be·friend [bɪ'frend] *v/t* fare amicizia con

beg [beg] (*pret & pp -ged*) **1** *v/i* mendicare **2** *v/t:* ~ *s.o. to ...* pregare qu di ...

be·gan [bɪ'gæn] *pret* → *begin*

beg·gar ['begə(r)] *n* mendicante *m/f*

be·gin [bɪ'gɪn] *v/t & v/i* (*pret began*, *pp begun*) cominciare; *to ~ with* per cominciare

be·gin·ner [bɪ'gɪnə(r)] principiante *m/f*

be·gin·ning [bɪ'gɪnɪŋ] inizio *m*; (*origin*) origine *f*

be·grudge [bɪ'grʌdʒ] *v/t* (*envy*) invidiare; (*give reluctantly*) dare malvolentieri

be·gun [bɪ'gʌn] *pp* → *begin*

be·half: *on ~ of* a nome di; *on my / his ~* a nome mio / suo

be·have [bɪ'heɪv] *v/i* comportarsi; ~ (*o.s.*) comportarsi bene; ~ (*yourself*)! comportati bene!

be·hav·iour [bɪ'heɪvjə(r)] comportamento *m*

be·hind [bɪ'haɪnd] **1** *prep in position* dietro; *in progress* indietro rispetto a; *in order* dietro a; *be ~* (*responsible for*) essere dietro a; (*support*) appoggiare **2** *adv* (*at the back*) dietro; *she had to stay ~* è dovuta rimanere; *be ~ in match* essere in svantaggio; *be ~ with sth* essere indietro con qc

beige [beɪʒ] *adj* beige *inv*

be·ing ['biːɪŋ] (*existence*) esistenza *f*; (*creature*) essere *m*

be·lat·ed [bɪ'leɪtɪd] *adj* in ritardo

belch [beltʃ] **1** *n* rutto *m* **2** *v/i* ruttare

Bel·gian ['beldʒən] **1** *adj* belga **2** *n* belga *m/f*

Bel·gium ['beldʒəm] Belgio *m*

be·lief [bɪ'liːf] convinzione *f*; *in God* fede *f*; *your ~ in me* il fatto che tu creda in me

be·lieve [bɪ'liːv] *v/t* credere

◆ believe in *v/t God, person* credere in; *ghost, person* credere a

be·liev·er [bɪ'liːvə(r)] REL credente *m/f*; *I'm a great ~ in ...* credo fermamente in ...

be·lit·tle [bɪ'lɪtl] *v/t* sminuire

bell [bel] *in church, school* campana *f*; *on door* campanello *m*

bel·lig·er·ent [bɪ'lɪdʒərənt] *adj* bellicoso

bel·low ['beləʊ] **1** *n* urlo *m*; *of bull* muggito *m* **2** *v/i* urlare; *of bull* muggire

bel·ly ['belɪ] pancia *f*

'bel·ly·ache *v/i* F brontolare F

be·long [bɪ'lɒŋ] *v/i*: *where does this ~?* dove va questo?; *I don't ~ here* mi sento un estraneo; *at last he found a place where he ~ed* finalmente ha trovato un posto adatto a lui

◆ belong to *v/t* appartenere a

be·long·ings [bɪ'lɒŋɪŋz] *npl* cose *fpl*

be·lov·ed [bɪ'lʌvɪd] *adj* adorato

be·low [bɪ'ləʊ] **1** *prep* sotto **2** *adv* di sotto; *in text* sotto; *see* ~ vedi sotto; *10 degrees* ~ 10 gradi sotto zero

belt [belt] *n* cintura *f*; *tighten one's* ~ *fig* stringere la cinghia

◆ belt up *v/i* (*fasten seat belt*) allaccia-

B

re la cintura (di sicurezza); **belt up!**
F sta' zitto!

be·moan [bɪ'məʊn] *v/t* lamentarsi di

bench [bentʃ] *n (seat)* panchina *f*;
(work~) banco *m*

'**bench·mark** punto *m* di riferimento

bend [bend] **1** *n* curva *f* **2** *v/t (pret &
pp* **bent**) piegare **3** *v/i (pret & pp*
bent) curvarsi; *of person* inchinarsi
♦ **bend down** *v/i* chinarsi

bend·er ['bendə(r)] F sbronza *f* F

be·neath [bɪ'ni:θ] **1** *prep* sotto **2** *adv*
di sotto; *they think he's ~ her* lo
considerano inferiore a lei

ben·e·dic·tion [benɪ'dɪkʃn] benedizione *f*

ben·e·fac·tor ['benɪfæktə(r)] benefattore *m*, -trice *f*

ben·e·fi·cial [benɪ'fɪʃl] *adj* vantaggioso

ben·e·fit ['benɪfɪt] **1** *n (advantage)*
vantaggio *m*; *payment* indennità *f
inv* **2** *v/t* andare a vantaggio di **3** *v/i*
trarre vantaggio *(**from** da)*

be·nev·o·lence [bɪ'nevələns] benevolenza *f*

be·nev·o·lent [bɪ'nevələnt] *adj* benevolo

be·nign [bɪ'naɪn] *adj* benevolo; MED
benigno

bent [bent] **1** *adj* F corrotto **2** *pret &
pp* → **bend**

be·queath [bɪ'kwi:ð] *v/t also fig* lasciare in eredità

be·quest [bɪ'kwest] lascito *m*

be·reaved [bɪ'ri:vd] **1** *adj* addolorato **2** *n*: *the ~* i familiari *mpl* del defunto

be·ret ['bereɪ] berretto *m*

ber·ry ['berɪ] bacca *f*

ber·serk [bə'zɜːk] *adv*: *go ~* dare in escandescenze

berth [bɜːθ] *on ship, train* cuccetta *f*;
give s.o. a wide ~ stare alla larga da
qu

be·seech [bɪ'si:tʃ] *v/t*: *~ s.o. to do sth*
implorare qu di fare qc

be·side [bɪ'saɪd] *prep* accanto a; *be ~
o.s.* essere fuori di sé; *that's ~ the
point* questo non c'entra

be·sides [bɪ'saɪdz] **1** *adv* inoltre
2 *prep (apart from)* oltre a

be·siege [bɪ'si:dʒ] *v/t also fig* assediare

best [best] **1** *adj* migliore **2** *adv* meglio; *it would be ~ if ...* sarebbe
meglio se ...; *I like her ~* lei è quella
che mi piace di più **3** *n*: *do one's ~*
fare del proprio meglio; *the ~* il
meglio; *(outstanding thing or person)* il / la migliore; *they've done
the ~ they can* hanno fatto tutto il
possibile; *make the ~ of* cogliere il
lato buono di; *all the ~!* tanti auguri!

best be'fore date scadenza *f*; **best
'man** *at wedding* testimone *m* dello
sposo; '**best-sell·er** bestseller *m
inv*

bet [bet] **1** *n* scommessa *f* **2** *v/i* scommettere; *you ~!* ci puoi scommettere!

be·tray [bɪ'treɪ] *v/t* tradire

be·tray·al [bɪ'treɪəl] tradimento *m*

bet·ter ['betə(r)] **1** *adj* migliore; *get
~* migliorare **2** *adv* meglio; *you'd ~
ask permission* faresti meglio a
chiedere il permesso; *I'd really ~
not* sarebbe meglio di no; *all the ~
for us* tanto meglio per noi; *I like
her ~* lei mi piace di più

bet·ter 'off *adj*: *be ~* stare meglio
finanziariamente; *the ~* la classe
abbiente

be·tween [bɪ'twi:n] *prep* tra; *~ you
and me* tra me e te

bev·er·age ['bevərɪdʒ] *fml* bevanda *f*

be·ware [bɪ'weə(r)] *v/t*: *~ of ...!* (stai)
attento a ...!

be·wil·der [bɪ'wɪldə(r)] *v/t* sconcertare

be·wil·der·ment   [bɪ'wɪldəmənt]
perplessità *f inv*

be·yond [bɪ'jɒnd] **1** *prep* oltre, al di
là di; *it's ~ me (don't understand)*
non capisco; *(can't do it)* va oltre le
mie capacità **2** *adv* più in là

bi·as ['baɪəs] *n against* pregiudizio *m*;
in favour of preferenza *f*

bi·as(s)ed ['baɪəst] *adj* parziale

bib [bɪb] *for baby* bavaglino *m*

Bible ['baɪbl] bibbia f

bib·li·cal ['bɪblɪkl] adj biblico

bib·li·og·ra·phy [bɪblɪ'ɒɡrəfɪ] bibliografia f

bi·car·bon·ate of so·da [baɪ'kɑːbənət] bicarbonato m di sodio

bi·cen·te·na·ry [baɪsen'tiːnərɪ] bicentenario m

bi·ceps ['baɪseps] npl bicipiti mpl

bick·er ['bɪkə(r)] v/i bisticciare

bi·cy·cle ['baɪsɪkl] n bicicletta f

bid [bɪd] **1** n at auction offerta f; (attempt) tentativo m **2** v/t & v/i (pret & pp **bid**) at auction offrire

bid·der ['bɪdə(r)] offerente m/f

bi·en·ni·al [baɪ'enɪəl] adj biennale

bi·fo·cals [baɪ'fəʊkəlz] npl occhiali mpl bifocali

big [bɪg] **1** adj grande; **my ~ brother / sister** mio fratello / mia sorella maggiore; **~ name** nome importante **2** adv: **talk ~** sparararle grosse

big·a·mist ['bɪɡəmɪst] bigamo m, -a f

big·a·mous ['bɪɡəməs] adj bigamo

big·a·my ['bɪɡəmɪ] bigamia f

'big·head F pallone m gonfiato F

big·head·ed [bɪg'hedɪd] adj F presuntuoso

big·ot ['bɪgət] fanatico m, -a f

bike [baɪk] **1** n F bici f inv F **2** v/i andare in bici; **I ~d here** sono venuto in bici

bik·er ['baɪkə(r)] motociclista m/f; (courier) corriere m

bi·ki·ni [bɪ'kiːnɪ] bikini m inv

bi·lat·er·al [baɪ'lætərəl] adj bilaterale

bi·lin·gual [baɪ'lɪŋgwəl] adj bilingue

bill [bɪl] **1** n in hotel, restaurant conto m; (gas / electricity ~) bolletta f; (invoice) fattura f; Am: money banconota f; POL disegno m di legge; (poster) avviso m **2** v/t (invoice) mandare la fattura a

'bill·fold Am portafoglio m

bil·li·ards ['bɪljədz] nsg biliardo m

bil·li·on ['bɪljən] (1,000,000,000) miliardo m

bill of ex·change FIN cambiale f

bill of 'sale atto m di vendita

bin [bɪn] n bidone m

bi·na·ry ['baɪnərɪ] adj binario

bind [baɪnd] v/t (pret & pp **bound**) also fig legare; (LAW: oblige) obbligare

bind·ing ['baɪndɪŋ] **1** adj agreement, promise vincolante **2** n of book rilegatura f; of ski attacco m

bin·go ['bɪŋgəʊ] tombola f

bi·noc·u·lars [bɪ'nɒkjʊləz] npl binocolo msg

bi·o·chem·ist [baɪəʊ'kemɪst] biochimico m, -a f

bi·o·chem·is·try [baɪəʊ'kemɪstrɪ] biochimica f

bi·o·de·grad·a·bil·i·ty [baɪəʊdɪgreɪdə'bɪlɪtɪ] biodegradabilità f inv

bi·o·de·gra·da·ble [baɪəʊdɪ'greɪdəbl] adj biodegradabile

bi·og·ra·pher [baɪ'ɒgrəfə(r)] biografo m, -a f

bi·og·ra·phy [baɪ'ɒgrəfɪ] biografia f

bi·o·log·i·cal [baɪə'lɒdʒɪkl] adj biologico

bi·ol·o·gist [baɪ'ɒlədʒɪst] biologo m, -a f

bi·ol·o·gy [baɪ'ɒlədʒɪ] biologia f

bi·o·tech·nol·o·gy [baɪəʊtek'nɒlədʒɪ] biotecnologia f

bird [bɜːd] uccello m

'bird·cage gabbia f per uccelli; **bird of 'prey** (uccello m) rapace m; **'bird sanc·tu·a·ry** rifugio m per uccelli; **bird's eye 'view** vista f a volo d'uccello

bi·ro® ['baɪrəʊ] biro f

birth [bɜːθ] also fig nascita f; (labour) parto m; **give ~ to** child partorire; **date of ~** data di nascita

'birth cer·tif·i·cate certificato m di nascita; **'birth con·trol** controllo m delle nascite; **'birth·day** compleanno m; **happy ~!** buon compleanno!; **'birth·mark** voglia f; **'birth·place** luogo m di nascita; **'birth·rate** tasso m di nascita

bis·cuit ['bɪskɪt] biscotto m

bi·sex·u·al ['baɪseksjʊəl] **1** adj bisessuale **2** n bisessuale m/f

bish·op ['bɪʃəp] vescovo m

bit¹ [bɪt] n (piece) pezzo m; (part) parte f; COMPUT bit m inv; **a ~** (a

B

little) un po'; **a ~ of** (*a little*) un po' di; **a ~ of news / advice** una notizia / un consiglio; **~ by ~** poco a poco; **I'll be there in a ~** (*in a little while*) sarò lì tra poco

bit² [bɪt] *for a horse* morso m

bit³ [bɪt] *pret* → **bite**

bitch [bɪtʃ] **1** *n dog* cagna *f*; F *woman* bastarda *f* F, stronza *f* V **2** *v/i* F (*complain*) lamentarsi

bitch·y ['bɪtʃɪ] *adj* F *person, remark* velenoso

bite [baɪt] **1** *n* morso *m*; **let's have a ~** (*to eat*) mangiamo un boccone; **he didn't get a ~ of** *angler* non ha abboccato neanche un pesce **2** *v/t* (*pret* **bit**, *pp* **bitten**) mordere; *one's nails* mangiarsi **3** *v/i* (*pret* **bit**, *pp* **bitten**) mordere; *of fish* abboccare

bit·ten ['bɪtn] *pp* → **bite**

bit·ter ['bɪtə(r)] **1** *adj taste* amaro; *person* amareggiato; *weather* gelido; *argument* aspro **2** *n beer* birra *f* amara

bit·ter·ly ['bɪtəlɪ] *adv resent* profondamente; **~ cold** gelido

bi·zarre [bɪ'zɑː(r)] *adj* bizzarro

blab [blæb] *v/i* (*pret & pp* **-bed**) F spifferare F

blab·ber·mouth ['blæbəmaʊθ] F spione *m*, -a *f*

black [blæk] **1** *adj also fig* nero; *person* negro, nero; *tea* senza latte **2** *n* (*colour*) nero *m*; (*person*) nero *m*, -a *f*; **in the ~** FIN in attivo; **in ~ and white** *fig* nero su bianco

♦ **black out** *v/i* svenire

'**black·ber·ry** mora *f* di rovo; '**black·bird** merlo *m*; '**black·board** lavagna *f*; **black 'box** scatola *f* nera; **black e'con·o·my** economia *f* sommersa

black·en ['blækn] *v/t fig: person's name* infangare

black 'eye occhio *m* nero; '**black·head** punto *m* nero, comedone *m*; **black 'ice** ghiaccio *m* (sulla strada); '**black·list 1** *n* lista *f* nera **2** *v/t* mettere sulla lista nera; '**black·mail 1** *n also fig* ricatto *m* **2** *v/t* ricattare; '**black·mail·er** ricattatore *m*, -trice

f; **black 'mar·ket** mercato *m* nero

black·ness ['blæknɪs] *of night* oscurità *f inv*

'**black·out** ELEC black-out *m inv*; MED svenimento *m*

black 'pud·ding sanguinaccio *m*

'**black·smith** fabbro *m* ferraio

blad·der ['blædə(r)] vescica *f*

blade [bleɪd] *of knife, sword* lama *f*; *of helicopter* pala *f*; *of grass* filo *m*

blame [bleɪm] **1** *n* colpa *f*; (*responsibility*) responsabilità *f inv* **2** *v/t* biasimare; **~ s.o. for sth** ritenere qu responsabile di qc

bland [blænd] *adj smile, answer* insulso; *food* insipido

blank [blæŋk] **1** *adj* (*not written on*) bianco; *tape* vergine; *look* vuoto **2** *n* (*empty space*) spazio *m*; **my mind's a ~** ho la testa vuota

blank 'check *Am*, **blank 'cheque** assegno *m* in bianco

blan·ket ['blæŋkɪt] *n also fig* coperta *f*

blare [bleə(r)] *v/i* suonare a tutto volume

♦ **blare out 1** *v/i* strepitare **2** *v/t* fare rimbombare

blas·pheme [blæs'fiːm] *v/i* bestemmiare

blas·phe·my ['blæsfəmɪ] bestemmia *f*

blast [blɑːst] **1** *n* (*explosion*) esplosione *f*; (*gust*) raffica *f* **2** *v/t* far esplodere; **~!** accidenti!

♦ **blast off** *v/i of rocket* essere lanciato

blast fur·nace altoforno *m*

'**blast-off** lancio *m*

bla·tant ['bleɪtənt] *adj* palese

blaze [bleɪz] **1** *n* (*fire*) incendio *m*; **a ~ of colour** un'esplosione di colore **2** *v/i of fire* ardere

♦ **blaze away** *v/i with gun* sparare a raffica

blaz·er ['bleɪzə(r)] *blazer m inv*

bleach [bliːtʃ] **1** *n for clothes* varechina *f*; *for hair* acqua *f* ossigenata **2** *v/t hair* ossigenarsi

bleak [bliːk] *adj countryside* desolato; *weather* cupo; *future* deprimente

blear·y-eyed ['blɪəɹɪaɪd] *adj:* **be ~** avere lo sguardo appannato
bleat [bliːt] *v/i of sheep* belare
bled [bled] *pret & pp →* **bleed**
bleed [bliːd] (*pret & pp* **bled**) **1** *v/i* sanguinare **2** *v/t fig* dissanguare
bleed·ing ['bliːdɪŋ] *n* emorragia *f*
bleep [bliːp] **1** *n* blip *m inv* **2** *v/i* suonare **3** *v/t* (*call on pager*) chiamare sul cercapersone
bleep·er ['bliːpə(r)] (*pager*) cercapersone *m inv*
blem·ish ['blemɪʃ] **1** *n on skin* imperfezione *f*; *on fruit* ammaccatura *f* **2** *v/t reputation* infangare
blend [blend] **1** *n* miscela *f* **2** *v/t* miscelare
♦ **blend in 1** *v/i* inserirsi; (*look good*) armonizzare **2** *v/t in cooking* incorporare
blend·er ['blendə(r)] *machine* frullatore *m*
bless [bles] *v/t* benedire; (**God**) **~ you!** Dio ti benedica!; **~ you!** (*in response to sneeze*) salute!; **~ me!, ~ my soul!** santo cielo!; **be ~ed with** godere di
bless·ing ['blesɪŋ] *also fig* benedizione *f*
blew [bluː] *pret →* **blow**
blind [blaɪnd] **1** *adj* cieco; **be ~ to** *fig* non vedere **2** *n:* **the ~** i ciechi **3** *v/t* accecare
blind 'al·ley vicolo *m* cieco; **blind 'date** appuntamento *m* al buio; **'blind·fold 1** *n* benda *f* **2** *v/t* bendare (gli occhi a) **3** *adv* con gli occhi bendati
blind·ing ['blaɪndɪŋ] *adj* atroce; *light* accecante, abbagliante
blind·ly ['blaɪndlɪ] *adv feel, grope* a tastoni; *fig* ciecamente
'blind spot *in road* punto *m* cieco; (*ability that is lacking*) punto *m* debole
blink [blɪŋk] *v/i of person* sbattere le palpebre; *of light* tremolare
blink·ered ['blɪŋkəd] *adj fig* ottuso
blip [blɪp] *on radar screen* segnale *m*; *fig* battuta *f* d'arresto
bliss [blɪs] felicità *f inv*

blis·ter ['blɪstə(r)] **1** *n* vescichetta *f* **2** *v/i* formare una vescichetta; *of paint* formare delle bolle
blis·ter pack blister *m inv*
bliz·zard ['blɪzəd] bufera *f* di neve
bloat·ed ['bləʊtɪd] *adj* gonfio
blob [blɒb] *of liquid* goccia *f*
bloc [blɒk] POL blocco *m*
block [blɒk] **1** *n* blocco *m*; *in town* isolato *m*; *of shares* pacchetto *m*; (*blockage*) blocco *m*; **~ of flats** palazzo *m* (d'appartamenti) **2** *v/t* bloccare
♦ **block in** *v/t with vehicle* bloccare la macchina di; **somebody's car was blocking me in** qualcuno ha bloccato la mia macchina parcheggiando la sua
♦ **block out** *v/t light* impedire
♦ **block up** *v/t sink etc* otturare
block·ade [blɒ'keɪd] **1** *n* blocco *m* **2** *v/t* bloccare
block·age ['blɒkɪdʒ] ingorgo *m*
block·bust·er ['blɒkbʌstə(r)] successone *m*
block 'let·ters *npl* maiuscole *fpl*
bloke [bləʊk] F tipo *m* F
blond [blɒnd] *adj* biondo
blonde [blɒnd] *n* (*woman*) bionda *f*
blood [blʌd] sangue *m*; **in cold ~** a sangue freddo
'blood al·co·hol lev·el concentrazione *f* di alcol etilico nel sangue; **'blood bank** banca *f* del sangue; **'blood bath** bagno *m* di sangue; **'blood do·nor** donatore *m*, -trice *f* di sangue; **'blood group** gruppo *m* sanguigno
blood·less ['blʌdlɪs] *adj coup* senza spargimento di sangue
'blood poi·son·ing setticemia *f*; **'blood pres·sure** pressione *f* del sangue; **'blood re·la·tion, 'blood rel·a·tive** consanguineo *m*, -a *f*; **'blood sam·ple** prelievo *m* di sangue; **'blood·shed** spargimento *m* di sangue; **'blood·shot** *adj* iniettato di sangue; **'blood·stain** macchia *f* di sangue; **'blood·stain·ed** *adj* macchiato di sangue; **'blood·stream** circolazione *f* (del sangue); **'blood**

B

test analisi *f inv* del sangue; **'blood-thirst·y** *adj* assetato di sangue; **'blood trans·fu·sion** trasfusione *f* di sangue; **'blood ves·sel** vaso *m* sanguigno

blood·y ['blʌdɪ] **1** *adj hands etc* insanguinato; *battle* sanguinoso; F maledetto; **~ hell!** porca miseria! F; **it's a ~ nuisance** è una gran rottura F; **you're a ~ genius!** sei un geniaccio! F **2** *adv*: **that's ~ difficult / easy!** è facile / difficile da morire!; **I'm ~ tired** sono stanco morto; **you'll ~ well do it!** eccome se lo farai!

blood·y-mind·ed [blʌdɪ'maɪndɪd] *adj* F ostinato

bloom [bluːm] **1** *n* fiore *m*; **in full ~** in piena fioritura **2** *v/i also fig* fiorire

blos·som ['blɒsəm] **1** *n* fiori *mpl* **2** *v/i also fig* fiorire

blot [blɒt] **1** *n* macchia *f* **2** *v/t* (*pret & pp* **-ted**) (*dry*) asciugare

♦ **blot out** *v/t memory* cancellare; *view* nascondere

blotch [blɒtʃ] chiazza *f*

blotch·y ['blɒtʃɪ] *adj* coperto di chiazze

blouse [blaʊz] camicetta *f*

blow [bləʊ] **1** *n* colpo *m* **2** *v/t* (*pret* **blew**, *pp* **blown**) *of wind* spingere; *smoke* soffiare; F (*spend*) sperperare; F *opportunity* mandare all'aria; **~ a whistle** fischiare; **~ one's nose** soffiarsi il naso **3** *v/i* (*pret* **blew**, *pp* **blown**) *of wind, person* soffiare; *of fuse* saltare; *of tyre* scoppiare; **the whistle blew for half-time** è stato fischiato l'intervallo

♦ **blow off 1** *v/t* portar via **2** *v/i* volar via

♦ **blow out 1** *v/t candle* spegnere **2** *v/i of candle* spegnersi

♦ **blow over 1** *v/t* abbattere **2** *v/i of storm, upset* calmarsi

♦ **blow up 1** *v/t with explosives* far saltare; *balloon* gonfiare; *photograph* ingrandire **2** *v/i also fig* esplodere

'blow-dry *v/t* (*pret & pp* **-ied**) asciugare col phon

'blow job ∨ pompino *m* ∨

blown [bləʊn] *pp* → **blow**

'blow-out *of tyre* scoppio *m*; F (*big meal*) abbuffata *f*

'blow-up *of photo* ingrandimento *m*

blue [bluː] **1** *adj* blu; F *film* porno **2** *n* blu *m inv*

blue 'chip *adj* sicuro; *company* di alto livello; **blue-'col·lar work·er** operaio *m*, -a *f*; **'blue·print** cianografia *f*; (*fig: plan*) programma *m*

blues [bluːz] *npl* MUS blues *m inv*; **have the ~** essere giù

'blues sing·er cantante *m/f* blues

bluff [blʌf] **1** *n* (*deception*) bluff *m inv* **2** *v/i* bluffare

blun·der ['blʌndə(r)] **1** *n* errore *m* **2** *v/i* fare un errore

blunt [blʌnt] *adj* spuntato; *person* diretto

blunt·ly ['blʌntlɪ] *adv speak* senza mezzi termini

blur [blɜː(r)] **1** *n* massa *f* indistinta **2** *v/t* (*pret & pp* **-red**) offuscare

blurb [blɜːb] *on book* note *fpl* di copertina

♦ **blurt out** *v/t* spiattellare

blush [blʌʃ] **1** *n* rossore *m* **2** *v/i* arrossire

blush·er ['blʌʃə(r)] *cosmetic* fard *m inv*

blus·ter ['blʌstə(r)] *v/i* protestare

blus·ter·y ['blʌstərɪ] *adj* ventoso

BO [biː'əʊ] *abbr* (= **body odour**) odori *mpl* corporei

board [bɔːd] **1** *n* asse *f*; *for game* scacchiera *f*; *for notices* tabellone *m*; **~ (of directors)** consiglio *m* (d'amministrazione); **on ~** (*plane, train, boat*) a bordo; **take on ~** *comments etc* prendere in esame; (*fully realize truth of*) accettare; **across the ~** a tutti i livelli **2** *v/t aeroplane etc* salire a bordo di **3** *v/i of passengers* salire a bordo

♦ **board up** *v/t* chiudere con assi

♦ **board with** *v/t* essere a pensione da

board and 'lodg·ing vitto e alloggio *m*

board·er ['bɔːdə(r)] pensionante *m/f*; EDU convittore *m*, -trice *f*

'board game gioco *m* da tavolo

'board·ing card carta *f* d'imbarco;

'**board·ing house** pensione f;
'**board·ing pass** carta f d'imbarco;
'**board·ing school** collegio m
'**board meet·ing** riunione f di consiglio
'**board room** sala f del consiglio
boast [bəʊst] **1** n vanteria f **2** v/i vantarsi
boat [bəʊt] (*small, for leisure*) barca f; (*ship*) nave f; **go by ~** andare in nave
bob¹ [bɒb] (*haircut*) caschetto m
bob² [bɒb] v/i (*pret & pp -bed*) of *boat etc* andare su e giù
♦ **bob up** v/i spuntare
'**bob·sleigh**, '**bob·sled** bob m inv
bod·ice ['bɒdɪs] corpetto m
bod·i·ly ['bɒdɪlɪ] **1** adj corporale **2** adv eject di peso
bod·y ['bɒdɪ] corpo m; *dead* cadavere m; **~ of water** massa f d'acqua; **~** (*suit*) (*undergarment*) body m inv
'**bod·y ar·mour** giubbotto m antiproiettile; '**body·guard** guardia f del corpo; '**body lan·guage** linguaggio m del corpo; '**body o·dour** odori mpl corporei; '**body pierc·ing** piercing m inv; '**body shop** MOT carrozzeria f; '**body stock·ing** body m inv; '**body·work** MOT carrozzeria f
bog palude f
bog·gle ['bɒgl] v/i: **the mind ~s!** è incredibile!
bo·gus ['bəʊgəs] adj fasullo
boil¹ [bɔɪl] n (*swelling*) foruncolo m
boil² [bɔɪl] **1** v/t far bollire **2** v/i bollire
♦ **boil down to** v/t ridursi a
♦ **boil over** v/i of milk etc traboccare bollendo
boil·er ['bɔɪlə(r)] caldaia f
boil·ing point ['bɔɪlɪŋ] of liquid punto m d'ebollizione; **reach ~** fig perdere le staffe
bois·ter·ous ['bɔɪstərəs] adj turbolento
bold [bəʊld] **1** adj (*brave*) audace **2** print neretto m; **in ~** in neretto
bol·ster ['bəʊlstə(r)] v/t confidence rafforzare

bolt [bəʊlt] **1** n on door catenaccio m; (*metal pin*) bullone m; of lightning fulmine m; **like a ~ from the blue** come un fulmine a ciel sereno **2** adv: **~ upright** diritto come un fuso **3** v/t (*fix with bolts*) fissare con bulloni; (*close*) chiudere col catenaccio **4** v/i (*run off*) scappare via
bomb [bɒm] **1** n bomba f **2** v/t bombardare; (*blow up*) fare esplodere una bomba in, far saltare
bom·bard [bɒm'bɑːd] v/t (*attack*) bombardare; **~ with questions** bombardare di domande
'**bomb attack** attacco m dinamitardo
bomb·er ['bɒmə(r)] (*aeroplane*) bombardiere m; (*terrorist*) dinamitardo m, -a f
'**bomb·er jack·et** bomber m inv
'**bomb·proof** adj a prova di bomba; '**bomb scare** allarme-bomba m; '**bomb·shell** fig: news bomba f
bond [bɒnd] **1** n (*tie*) legame m; FIN obbligazione f; **government ~s** titoli mpl di Stato **2** v/i aderire
bone [bəʊn] **1** n osso m **2** v/t meat disossare; fish togliere la lisca a
bon·fire ['bɒnfaɪə(r)] falò m inv
bonk [bɒŋk] v/t & v/i P scopare P
bon·net ['bɒnɪt] of car cofano m
bo·nus ['bəʊnəs] (*money*) gratifica f; (*something extra*) vantaggio m in più
boo [buː] **1** n fischio m **2** v/t & v/i actor, speaker fischiare
boob¹ [buːb] **1** n F (*mistake*) errore m **2** v/i F (*make a mistake*) fare un errore
boob² [buːb] n P (*breast*) tetta f P
boo-boo ['buːbuː] n F → **boob¹**
book [bʊk] **1** n libro m; **~ of matches** bustina f di fiammiferi **2** v/t (*reserve*) prenotare; of policeman multare; sp ammonire **3** v/i (*reserve*) prenotare
♦ **book in 1** v/i prenotare una camera; (*check in*) registrarsi **2** v/t prenotare una camera per
'**book·case** scaffale m
booked up [bʊkt'ʌp] adj tutto esaurito; person occupatissimo
book·ie ['bʊkɪ] F allibratore m

B

book·ing ['bʊkɪŋ] (*reservation*) prenotazione *f*

'**book·ing clerk** impiegato *m* della biglietteria

'**book·ing of·fice** biglietteria *f*

'**book·keep·er** contabile *m/f*

'**book·keep·ing** contabilità *f inv*

book·let ['bʊklɪt] libretto *m*

'**book·mak·er** allibratore *m*

books [bʊks] *npl* (*accounts*) libri *mpl* contabili; **do the ~** tenere la contabilità; **cook the ~s** falsificare i libri contabili

'**book·sell·er** libraio *m*, -a *f*; '**book·shelf** mensola *f*; '**book·shop** libreria *f*; '**book·stall** edicola *f*; '**book to·ken** buono *m* libro

boom¹ [buːm] **1** *n* boom *m inv* **2** *v/i* of *business* andare a gonfie vele

boom² [buːm] **1** *n* (*bang*) rimbombo *m* **2** *v/i* rimbombare

boor [bɔː(r)] zotico *m*

boor·ish ['bɔːrɪʃ] *adj* da zotico

boost [buːst] **1** *n* spinta *f* **2** *v/t production, sales* incrementare; *confidence* aumentare

boot¹ [buːt] *n* stivale *m*; (*climbing ~*) scarpone *m*; *for football* scarpetta *m*

boot² [buːt] *of car* bagagliaio *m*

♦ **boot out** *v/t* F sbattere fuori F

♦ **boot up** *v/t & v/i* COMPUT inizializzare

booth [buːð] *at market, fair* bancarella *f*; (*telephone ~*) cabina *f*

booze [buːz] *n* F alcolici *mpl*

booz·er ['buːzə(r)] F (*pub*) pub *m inv*; (*person*) beone *m*, -a *f* F

'**booze-up** F bevuta *f*

bor·der ['bɔːdə(r)] **1** *n between countries* confine *m*; (*edge*) bordo *m* **2** *v/t country* confinare con

♦ **border on** *country* confinare con; (*be almost*) rasentare

'**bor·der·line** *adj* al limite; **a ~ case** un caso limite

bore¹ [bɔː(r)] *v/t hole* praticare

bore² [bɔː(r)] **1** *n* (*person*) persona *f* noiosa; **it's such a ~** è una seccatura **2** *v/t* annoiare

bore³ [bɔː(r)] *pret* → **bear²**

bored [bɔːd] *adj* annoiato; **I'm ~** mi sto annoiando

bore·dom ['bɔːdəm] noia *f*

bor·ing ['bɔːrɪŋ] *adj* noioso

born [bɔːn] *adj*: **be ~** essere nato; **where were you ~?** dove sei nato?; **be a ~ ...** essere un ... nato

borne [bɔːn] *pp* → **bear²**

bor·row ['bɒrəʊ] *v/t* prendere in prestito

bos·om ['bʊzm] *of woman* seno *m*

boss [bɒs] boss *m inv*

♦ **boss about** *v/t* dare ordini a

boss·y ['bɒsɪ] *adj* prepotente

bo·tan·i·cal [bə'tænɪkl] *adj* botanico

bo·tan·ic(·al) gar·dens *npl* orto *m* botanico

bot·a·nist ['bɒtənɪst] botanico *m*, -a *f*

bot·a·ny ['bɒtənɪ] botanica *f*

botch [bɒtʃ] *v/t* fare un pasticcio con

both [bəʊθ] **1** *adj pron* entrambi, tutti *mpl* e due, tutte *fpl* e due, tutt'e due; **I know ~ (of the) brothers** conosco tutt'e due i fratelli; **~ (of the) brothers were there** tutt'e due i fratelli erano lì; **~ of them** entrambi **2** *adv*: **~ my mother and I** sia mia madre che io; **is it business or pleasure? – ~** per piacere o per affari? – tutt'e due

both·er ['bɒðə(r)] **1** *n* disturbo *m*; **it's no ~** non c'è problema **2** *v/t* (*disturb*) disturbare; (*worry*) preoccupare **3** *v/i*: **don't ~** (*you needn't do it*) non preoccuparti; **you needn't have ~ed!** non dovevi!

bot·tle ['bɒtl] **1** *n* bottiglia *f*; *for baby* biberon *m* **2** *v/t* imbottigliare

♦ **bot·tle out** *v/i* P tirarsi indietro

♦ **bottle up** *v/t feelings* reprimere

'**bot·tle bank** contenitore *m* per la raccolta del vetro

bot·tled wa·ter ['bɒtld] acqua *f* in bottiglia

'**bot·tle·neck** *n* ingorgo *m*

'**bot·tle-o·pen·er** apribottiglie *m inv*

bot·tom ['bɒtəm] **1** *adj* più basso **2** *n* fondo *m*; (*buttocks*) sedere *m*; **at the ~ of the screen** in basso sullo schermo; **at the ~ of the page / street** in fondo alla pagina / strada; **she**

started at the ~ and she's a manager now ha cominciato dal basso e ora è dirigente

♦ **bottom out** *v/i* toccare il fondo

bot·tom '**line** (*fig: financial outcome*) risultato *m* finanziario; **the ~** (*the real issue*) l'essenziale *m*

bought [bɔːt] *pret & pp* → **buy**

boul·der ['bəʊldə(r)] macigno *m*

bounce [baʊns] **1** *v/t ball* far rimbalzare **2** *v/i of ball* rimbalzare; *on sofa etc* saltare; *of cheque* essere protestato

bounc·er ['baʊnsə(r)] buttafuori *m inv*

bouncy ['baʊnsɪ] *adj ball* che rimbalza bene; *chair* molleggiato

bound¹ [baʊnd] *adj*: **be ~ to do sth** (*sure to*) dover fare per forza qc; (*obliged to*) essere obbligato a fare qc; **the train is ~ to be late** il treno sarà senz'altro in ritardo

bound² [baʊnd] *adj*: **be ~ for** *of ship* essere diretto a

bound³ [baʊnd] **1** *n* (*jump*) balzo *m* **2** *v/i* saltellare

bound⁴ [baʊnd] *pret & pp* → **bind**

bound·a·ry ['baʊndərɪ] confine *m*

bound·less ['baʊndlɪs] *adj* illimitato

bou·quet [bʊ'keɪ] bouquet *m inv*

bour·bon ['bɜːbən] bourbon *m inv*

bout [baʊt] MED attacco *m*; *in boxing* incontro *m*

bou·tique [buː'tiːk] boutique *f inv*

bo·vine spon·gi·form en·ceph·a·lo·pa·thy [bəʊvaɪnspʌndʒɪfɔːmensefə'lɒpəθɪ] encefalite *f* spongiforme bovina

bow¹ [baʊ] **1** *n as greeting* inchino *m* **2** *v/i* inchinarsi **3** *v/t head* chinare

bow² [bəʊ] (*knot*) fiocco *m*; MUS archetto *m*

bow³ [baʊ] *of ship* prua *f*

bow·els ['baʊəlz] *npl* intestino *msg*

bowl¹ [bəʊl] (*container*) bacinella *f*; *for soup, cereal* ciotola *f*; *for cooking, salad* terrina *f*; *plastic* contenitore *m* di plastica

bowl² [bəʊl] **1** *n ball* boccia *f* **2** *v/i in bowling* lanciare

♦ **bowl over** *v/t* (*fig: astonish*) strabiliare

bowl·er ['bəʊlə(r)] (*hat*) bombetta *f*; *in cricket* lanciatore *m*

bowl·ing ['bəʊlɪŋ] bowling *m inv*

'**bowl·ing al·ley** pista *f* da bowling

bowls [bəʊlz] *nsg* (*game*) bocce *fpl*

bow 'tie (cravatta *f* a) farfalla *f*

box¹ [bɒks] *n container* scatola *f*; *on form* casella *f*

box² [bɒks] *v/i do boxing* fare pugilato; *he ~ed well* ha combattuto bene

box·er ['bɒksə(r)] pugile *m*

'**box·er shorts** *npl* boxer *mpl*

'**box·ing** ['bɒksɪŋ] pugilato *m*, boxe *f inv*

'**Box·ing Day** *Br* Santo Stefano; '**box·ing glove** guantone *m* da pugile; '**box·ing match** incontro *m* di pugilato; '**box·ing ring** quadrato *m*, ring *m inv*

'**box num·ber** *at post office* casella *f*

'**box of·fice** botteghino *m*

boy [bɔɪ] *child* bambino *m*; *youth* ragazzo *m*; *son* figlio *m*

boy·cott ['bɔɪkɒt] **1** *n* boicottaggio *m* **2** *v/t* boicottare

'**boy·friend** ragazzo *m*

boy·ish ['bɔɪɪʃ] *adj* da ragazzo

boy'scout boy-scout *m inv*

bra [brɑː] reggiseno *m*

brace [breɪs] *on teeth* apparecchio *m* (ai denti)

brace·let ['breɪslɪt] braccialetto *m*

brac·es ['breɪsɪs] *npl* bretelle *fpl*

brack·et ['brækɪt] *for shelf* staffa *f*; *in text* parentesi *f inv*

brag [bræg] *v/i* (*pret & pp* **-ged**) vantarsi

braid [breɪd] (*trimming*) passamaneria *f*

braille [breɪl] braille *m*

brain [breɪn] cervello *m*; *use your ~* usa il cervello

'**brain dead** *adj* MED cerebralmente morto

brain·less ['breɪnlɪs] *adj* F deficiente

brains [breɪnz] *npl* (*intelligence*) cervello *msg*

'**brain·storm** *Br* attacco *m* di follia; **brain·storm·ing** ['breɪnstɔːmɪŋ] brain-storming *m inv*; '**brain sur·geon** neurochirurgo *m*; '**brain sur·ger·y** neurochirurgia *f*; '**brain tu·mour** tumore *m* al cervello; '**brain·wash** *v/t* fare il lavaggio del cervello a; *we've been ~ed into believing that …* ci hanno fatto il lavaggio del cervello per convincerci che …; '**brain·wave** (*brilliant idea*) lampo *m* di genio

brain·y ['breɪnɪ] *adj* F geniale

brake [breɪk] **1** *n* freno *m* **2** *v/i* frenare

'**brake flu·id** MOT liquido *m* dei freni; '**brake light** MOT fanalino *m* d'arresto; '**brake ped·al** MOT pedale *m* del freno

branch [brɑːntʃ] *n of tree* ramo *m*; *of bank, company* filiale *f*

♦ **branch off** *v/i of road* diramarsi

♦ **branch out** *v/i* diversificarsi

brand [brænd] **1** *n* marca *f*; **2** *v/t*: *be ~ed a traitor* essere tacciato di tradimento

brand 'im·age brand image *f inv*

bran·dish ['brændɪʃ] *v/t* brandire

brand 'lead·er marca *f* leader di mercato; **brand 'loy·al·ty** fedeltà *f inv* alla marca; '**brand name** marca *f*

brand-'new *adj* nuovo di zecca

bran·dy ['brændɪ] brandy *m inv*

brass [brɑːs] (*alloy*) ottone *m*; *the ~* MUS gli ottoni

brass 'band fanfara *f*

bras·sière [brə'zɪə(r)] *Am* reggiseno *m*

brat [bræt] *pej* marmocchio *m*

bra·va·do [brə'vɑːdəʊ] spavalderia *f*

brave [breɪv] *adj* coraggioso

brave·ly ['breɪvlɪ] *adv* coraggiosamente

brav·er·y ['breɪvərɪ] coraggio *m*

brawl [brɔːl] **1** *n* rissa *f* **2** *v/i* azzuffarsi

brawn·y ['brɔːnɪ] *adj* muscoloso

Bra·zil [brə'zɪl] Brasile *m*

Bra·zil·ian [brə'zɪlɪən] **1** *adj* brasiliano **2** *n* brasiliano *m*, -a *f*

breach [briːtʃ] *n* (*violation*) violazione *f*; *in party* rottura *f*

breach of 'con·tract LAW inadempienza *f* di contratto

bread [bred] *n* pane *m*

'**bread·crumbs** *npl for cooking* pane *msg* grattato; *for bird* briciole *fpl*

'**bread knife** coltello *m* per il pane

breadth [bredθ] larghezza *f*

'**bread·win·ner**: *be the ~* mantenere la famiglia

break [breɪk] **1** *n also fig* rottura *f*; (*rest*) pausa *f*; *give s.o. a ~* F (*opportunity*) dare un'opportunità a qu; *take a ~* fare una pausa; *without a ~ work, travel* senza sosta; *lucky ~* colpo di fortuna **2** *v/t* (*pret* **broke**, *pp* **broken**) *china, egg, bone* rompere; *rules, law* violare; *promise* non mantenere; *news* comunicare; *record* battere **3** *v/i* (*pret* **broke**, *pp* **broken**) *of china, egg, toy* rompersi; *of news* diffondersi; *of storm* scoppiare; *of boy's voice* cambiare

♦ **break away** *v/i* scappare; *from organization, tradition* staccarsi

♦ **break down 1** *v/i of vehicle, machine* avere un guasto; *of talks* arenarsi; *in tears* scoppiare in lacrime; (*mentally*) avere un esaurimento **2** *v/t door* buttare giù; *figures* analizzare

♦ **break even** *v/i* COM coprire le spese

♦ **break in** *v/i* (*interrupt*) interrompere; *of burglar* entrare con la forza

♦ **break off 1** *v/t* staccare; *engagement* rompere; *they've broken it off* si sono lasciati **2** *v/i* (*stop talking*) interrompersi

♦ **break out** *v/i* (*start up*) scoppiare; *of prisoners* evadere; *he broke out in a rash* gli è venuta l'orticaria

♦ **break up 1** *v/t* (*into component parts*) scomporre; *fight* far cessare **2** *v/i of ice* spaccarsi; *of couple* separarsi; *of band, meeting* sciogliersi

break·a·ble ['breɪkəbl] *adj* fragile

break·age ['breɪkɪdʒ] danni *mpl*

'**break·down** *of vehicle, machine* guasto *m*; *of talks* rottura *f*; (*nervous ~*) esaurimento *m* (nervoso); *of figures* analisi *f inv*

'**break·down ser·vice** servizio *m* di soccorso stradale

'**break·down truck** carro *m* attrezzi

break-'e·ven point punto *m* di rottura di pareggio

break·fast ['brekfəst] *n* colazione *f*; **have ~** fare colazione

'**break·fast tel·e·vi·sion** programmi *mpl* televisivi del mattino

'**break-in** furto *m* (con scasso);

'**break·through** *in plan, negotiations* passo *m* avanti; *of science, technology* scoperta *f*; '**break·up** *of marriage, partnership* rottura *f*

breast [brest] *of woman* seno *m*

'**breast·feed** *v/t* (*pret & pp* **breastfed**) allattare

'**breast·stroke** nuoto *m* a rana

breath [breθ] respiro *m*; **there wasn't a ~ of air** non c'era un filo d'aria; **be out of ~** essere senza fiato; **take a deep ~** fai un respiro profondo

breath·a·lyse ['breθəlaɪz] *v/t* sottoporre ad alcoltest

breath·a·lys·er® ['breθəlaɪzə(r)] alcoltest *m inv*

breathe [briːð] *v/t & v/i* respirare

♦**breathe in** 1 *v/i* inspirare 2 *v/t* respirare

♦**breathe out** *v/i* espirare

breath·ing ['briːðɪŋ] *n* respiro *m*

breath·less ['breθlɪs] *adj* senza fiato

breath·less·ness ['breθlɪsnɪs] fiato *m* corto

breath·tak·ing ['breθteɪkɪŋ] *adj* mozzafiato

bred [bred] *pret & pp* → **breed**

breed [briːd] 1 *n* razza *f* 2 *v/t* (*pret & pp* **bred**) allevare; *fig* generare 3 *v/i* (*pret & pp* **bred**) *of animals* riprodursi

breed·er ['briːdə(r)] allevatore *m*, -trice *f*

breed·ing ['briːdɪŋ] allevamento *m*; *of person* educazione *f*

breed·ing ground *fig* terreno *m* fertile

breeze [briːz] brezza *f*

breez·i·ly ['briːzɪlɪ] *adv fig* con disinvoltura

breez·y ['briːzɪ] *adj* ventoso; *fig* brioso

brew [bruː] 1 *v/t beer* produrre; *tea* fare 2 *v/i of storm* prepararsi; **there's trouble ~ing** ci sono guai in vista

brew·er ['bruːə(r)] produttore *m* di birra

brew·er·y ['bruːərɪ] fabbrica *f* di birra

bribe [braɪb] 1 *n* bustarella *f* 2 *v/t* corrompere

brib·er·y ['braɪbərɪ] corruzione *f*

brick [brɪk] mattone *m*

'**brick·lay·er** muratore *m*

brid·al suite ['braɪdl] suite *f inv* nuziale

bride [braɪd] sposa *f*

'**bride·groom** sposo *m*

'**brides·maid** damigella *f* d'onore

bridge¹ [brɪdʒ] 1 *n* ponte *m*; *of ship* ponte *m* di comando; **~ of the nose** setto *m* nasale; 2 *v/t gap* colmare

bridge² [brɪdʒ] (*card game*) bridge *m inv*

bri·dle ['braɪdl] briglia *f*

brief¹ [briːf] *adj* breve

brief² [briːf] 1 *n* (*mission*) missione *f*; (P: *lawyer*) avvocato *m* 2 *v/t*: **~ s.o. on sth** *instruct* dare istruzioni a qu su qc; *inform* mettere qu al corrente di qc

'**brief·case** valigetta *f*

brief·ing ['briːfɪŋ] briefing *m inv*

brief·ly ['briːflɪ] *adv* (*for a short period of time*) brevemente; (*in a few words, to sum up*) in breve

briefs [briːfs] *npl* slip *m inv*

bright [braɪt] *adj colour* vivace; *smile, future* radioso; (*sunny*) luminoso; (*intelligent*) intelligente; **~ red** rosso vivo

♦**brighten up** ['braɪtn] 1 *v/t* ravvivare; 2 *v/i of weather* schiarirsi; *of face, person* rallegrarsi

bright·ly ['braɪtlɪ] *adv smile* in modo radioso; *shine, lit* intensamente; *coloured* in modo sgargiante

bright·ness ['braɪtnɪs] luminosità *f inv*

bril·liance ['brɪljəns] *of person*

B

genialità *f inv*; *of colour* vivacità *f inv*

bril·liant ['briljǝnt] *adj sunshine etc* sfolgorante; (*very good*) eccezionale; (*very intelligent*) brillante

brim [brim] *of container* orlo *m*; *of hat* falda *f*

brim·ful ['brimful] *adj* colmo

bring [briŋ] *v/t* (*pret & pp* **brought**) portare; *~ it here, will you* portalo qui, per favore; *can I ~ a friend?* posso portare un amico?

♦ **bring about** *v/t* causare

♦ **bring around** *v/t from a faint* far rinvenire; (*persuade*) convincere

♦ **bring back** *v/t* (*return*) restituire; (*re-introduce*) reintrodurre; *memories* risvegliare

♦ **bring down** *v/t tree, government, aeroplane* abbattere; *rates, inflation, price* far scendere

♦ **bring in** *v/t interest, income* rendere; *legislation* introdurre; *verdict* emettere; (*involve*) coinvolgere

♦ **bring on** *v/t illness* provocare

♦ **bring out** *v/t* (*produce: book*) pubblicare; *new product* lanciare

♦ **bring to** *v/t from a faint* far rinvenire

♦ **bring up** *v/t child* allevare; *subject* sollevare; (*vomit*) vomitare

brink [briŋk] *also fig* orlo *m*

brisk [brisk] *adj person, tone* spiccio; *walk* svelto; *trade* vivace

brist·les ['brislz] *npl* peli *mpl*

brist·ling ['brisliŋ] *adj*: *be ~ with* brulicare di

Brit [brit] F britannico *m*, -a *f*

Brit·ain ['britn] Gran Bretagna *f*

Brit·ish ['britiʃ] **1** *adj* britannico **2** *n*: *the ~* i britannici

Brit·on ['britn] britannico *m*, -a *f*

brit·tle ['britl] *adj* fragile

broach [brǝutʃ] *v/t subject* affrontare

broad [brɔːd] *adj* largo; (*general*) generale; *in ~ daylight* in pieno giorno

'broad·cast 1 *n* trasmissione *f* **2** *v/t* trasmettere

'broad·cast·er giornalista *m/f* radiotelevisivo, -a

'broad·cast·ing diffusione *f* radiotelevisiva

broad·en ['brɔːdn] **1** *v/i* allargarsi **2** *v/t* allargare

broad·ly ['brɔːdlɪ] *adv*: *~ speaking* parlando in senso lato

broad·mind·ed [brɔːd'maɪndɪd] *adj* di larghe vedute

broad·mind·ed·ness [brɔːd'maɪndɪdnɪs] larghezza *f* di vedute

broc·co·li ['brɒkǝlɪ] broccoli *mpl*

bro·chure ['brǝuʃǝ(r)] dépliant *m inv*, opuscolo *m*

broke [brǝuk] **1** *adj* al verde; *go ~* (*go bankrupt*) andare sul lastrico **2** *pret* → **break**

bro·ken ['brǝukn] **1** *adj* rotto; *English* stentato; *marriage* fallito; *she's from a ~ home* i suoi sono separati **2** *pp* → **break**

bro·ken-heart·ed [brǝukn'hɑːtɪd] *adj* col cuore spezzato

bro·ker ['brǝukǝ(r)] mediatore *m*, -trice *f*

brol·ly ['brɒlɪ] F ombrello *m*

bron·chi·tis [brɒŋ'kaɪtɪs] bronchite *f*

bronze [brɒnz] *n* bronzo *m*

brooch [brǝutʃ] spilla *f*

brood [bruːd] *v/i of person* rimuginare

broom [bruːm] scopa *f*

broth [brɒθ] (*soup*) minestra *f*; (*stock*) brodo *m*

broth·el ['brɒθl] bordello *m*

broth·er ['brʌðǝ(r)] fratello *m*; *they're ~s* sono fratelli; *~s and sisters* fratelli e sorelle

'broth·er-in-law (*pl* **brothers-in-law**) cognato *m*

broth·er·ly ['brʌðǝlɪ] *adj* fraterno

brought [brɔːt] *pret & pp* → **bring**

brow [brau] (*forehead*) fronte *f*; *of hill* cima *f*

brown [braun] **1** *n* marrone *m*; *eyes, hair* castano **2** *adj* marrone; (*tanned*) abbronzato **3** *v/t in cooking* rosolare **4** *v/i in cooking* rosolarsi

Brown·ie ['braunɪ] giovane esploratrice *f*

brown 'pa·per carta *f* da pacchi;

brown pa·per 'bag sacchetto *m* di carta; **'brown sug·ar** zucchero *m* non raffinato

browse [brauz] *v/i in shop* curiosare; **~ *through a book*** sfogliare un libro

brows·er ['brauzə(r)] COMPUT browser *m inv*

bruise [bru:z] **1** *n* livido *m*; *on fruit* ammaccatura *f* **2** *v/t person* fare un livido a; *fruit* ammaccare **3** *v/i of person* coprirsi di lividi; *of fruit* ammaccarsi

bruis·ing ['bru:zɪŋ] *adj fig* doloroso

brunch [brʌntʃ] brunch *m inv*

bru·nette [bru:'net] *n* brunetta *f*

brunt [brʌnt] *n*: **bear the ~ of ...** subire il peggio di ...

brush [brʌʃ] **1** *n* spazzola *f*; (*paint~*) pennello *m*; (*tooth~*) spazzolino *m* da denti; (*conflict*) scontro *m* **2** *v/t* spazzolare; (*touch lightly*) sfiorare; (*move away*) spostare; **~ *your teeth*** lavati i denti

♦ **brush against** *v/t* sfiorare

♦ **brush aside** *v/t* ignorare

♦ **brush off** *v/t* spazzolare via; *criticism* ignorare

♦ **brush up** *v/t* ripassare

'brush-off: **give s.o. the ~** F rispondere picche a qu F

'brush·work PAINT pennellata *f*

brusque [brusk] *adj* brusco

Brus·sels ['brʌslz] Bruxelles *f inv*

Brus·sels 'sprout cavolino *m* di Bruxelles

bru·tal ['bru:tl] *adj* brutale

bru·tal·i·ty [bru:'tælətɪ] brutalità *f inv*

bru·tal·ly ['bru:təlɪ] *adv* brutalmente

brute [bru:t] *n* bruto *m*

'brute force forza *f* bruta

BSE [bi:es'i:] *abbr* (= ***bovine spongiform encephalopathy***)

bub·ble ['bʌbl] *n* bolla *f*

'bub·ble bath bagnoschiuma *m inv*; **'bub·ble gum** gomma *f* da masticare; **'bub·ble wrap** *n* involucro *m* a bolle

bub·bly ['bʌblɪ] *n* F (*champagne*) champagne *m inv*

buck[1] [bʌk] *n Am* F (*dollar*) dollaro *m*

buck[2] [bʌk] *v/i of horse* sgroppare

buck[3] [bʌk] *n*: **pass the ~** scaricare la responsabilità

buck·et ['bʌkɪt] *n* secchio *m*

'buck·et shop agenzia *f* di viaggi che pratica forti sconti

buck·le[1] ['bʌkl] **1** *n* fibbia *f* **2** *v/t belt* allacciare

buck·le[2] ['bʌkl] *v/i of wood, metal* piegarsi

♦ **buck·le down** *v/i* mettersi a lavorare

bud [bʌd] *n* BOT bocciolo *m*

bud·dy ['bʌdɪ] F amico *m*, -a *f*

budge [bʌdʒ] **1** *v/t* smuovere; (*make reconsider*) far cambiare idea a **2** *v/i* muoversi; (*change one's mind*) cambiare idea

bud·ger·i·gar ['bʌdʒərɪgɑː(r)] pappagallino *m*

bud·get ['bʌdʒɪt] **1** *n* budget *m inv*; *of company* bilancio *m* preventivo; *of state* bilancio *m* dello Stato; **I'm on a ~** devo stare attento ai soldi **2** *v/i* prevedere le spese

♦ **budget for** *v/t* preventivare

bud·gie ['bʌdʒɪ] F pappagallino *m*

buff[1] [bʌf] *adj* (*colour*) beige *inv*

buff[2] [bʌf] *n* appassionato *m*, -a *f*

buf·fa·lo ['bʌfələu] bufalo *m*

buf·fer ['bʌfə(r)] RAIL respingente *m*; COMPUT buffer *m inv*; *fig* cuscinetto *m*

buf·fet[1] ['bufeɪ] *n* (*meal*) buffet *m inv*

buf·fet[2] ['bʌfɪt] *v/t of wind* sballottare

bug [bʌg] **1** *n* (*insect*) insetto *m*; (*virus*) virus *m inv*; (*spying device*) microspia *f*; COMPUT bug *m inv* **2** *v/t* (*pret & pp -ged*) *room* installare microspie in; *telephone* mettere sotto controllo; F (*annoy*) seccare

bug·gy ['bʌgɪ] *for baby* passeggino *m*

build [bɪld] **1** *n of person* corporatura *f* **2** *v/t* (*pret & pp* **built**) costruire

♦ **build up 1** *v/t relationship* consolidare; *collection* mettere insieme **2** *v/i of tension, traffic* aumentare; **build up one's strength** rimettersi in forze

'build·er ['bɪldə(r)] *person* muratore

m; company impresario *m* edile

build·ing ['bɪldɪŋ] edificio *m*, palazzo *m*; *(activity)* costruzione *f*

build·ing blocks *npl for child* mattoncini *mpl*; **'build·ing site** cantiere *m* edile; **'build·ing so·ci·e·ty** *Br* istituto *m* di credito immobiliare; **'build·ing trade** edilizia *f*

'build-up *of traffic, pressure* aumento *m*; *of arms, forces* ammassamento *m*; *(publicity)* pubblicità *f inv*

built [bɪlt] *pret & pp* → **build**

built-in ['bɪltɪn] *adj wardrobe* a muro; *flash* incorporato

built-up 'ar·e·a abitato *m*

bulb [bʌlb] BOT bulbo *m*; *(light ~)* lampadina *f*

bulge [bʌldʒ] **1** *n* rigonfiamento *m* **2** *v/i* sporgere

bu·lim·i·a [buˈlɪmɪə] bulimia *f*

bulk [bʌlk] grosso *m*; *in ~* in grande quantità; *wholesale* all'ingrosso

'bulk·y ['bʌlkɪ] *adj* voluminoso

bull [bʊl] toro *m*

bull·doze ['bʊldəʊz] *v/t (demolish)* abbattere con il bulldozer; ~ *s.o. into sth fig* costringere qu a fare qc

bull·doz·er ['bʊldəʊzə(r)] bulldozer *m inv*

bul·let ['bʊlɪt] proiettile *m*, pallottola *f*

bul·le·tin ['bʊlɪtɪn] bollettino *m*

'bul·le·tin board COMPUT bulletin board *m inv*; *Am: on wall* bacheca *f*

'bull mar·ket FIN mercato *m* in ascesa

'bull's-eye centro *m* del bersaglio; *hit the ~* fare centro

'bull·shit 1 *n* V stronzate *fpl* V **2** *v/i (pret & pp -ted)* V dire stronzate V

bul·ly ['bʊlɪ] **1** *n* prepotente *m/f* **2** *v/t (pret & pp -ied)* tiranneggiare

bul·ly·ing ['bʊlɪŋ] *n* prepotenze *fpl*

bum [bʌm] **1** *n* F *worthless person* mezza calzetta *f* F; *(Br: bottom)* sedere *m*; *(Am: tramp)* barbone *m* **2** *adj* F *(useless)* del piffero **3** *v/t (pret & pp -med)* F *cigarette etc* scroccare

♦ **bum around**, **bum about** *v/i* F *(travel)* vagabondare; *(be lazy)* oziare

'bum·bag F marsupio *m*

bum·ble·bee ['bʌmblbiː] bombo *m*

bump [bʌmp] **1** *n (swelling)* gonfiore *m*; *(lump)* bernoccolo *m*; *on road* cunetta *f*; *get a ~ on the head* prendere un colpo in testa **2** *v/t* battere

♦ **bump into** *v/t table* battere contro; *(meet)* incontrare

♦ **bump off** *v/t* F *(murder)* far fuori F

♦ **bump up** *v/t* F *(prices)* aumentare

bump·er ['bʌmpə(r)] **1** *n* MOT paraurti *m inv*; **the traffic was ~ to ~** c'era una coda di macchine **2** *adj (extremely good)* eccezionale

bumph [bʌmf] *Br* F scartoffie *fpl*

'bump-start *v/t car* mettere in moto a spinte; *(fig: economy)* dare una spinta a

bump·y ['bʌmpɪ] *adj road* accidentato; *flight* movimentato

bun [bʌn] *hairstyle* chignon *m inv*; *for eating* panino *m* dolce

bunch [bʌntʃ] *of people* gruppo *m*; *of keys, flowers* mazzo *m*; *a ~ of grapes* un grappolo d'uva

bun·dle ['bʌndl] *of clothes* fagotto *m*; *of wood* fascina *f*

♦ **bundle up** *v/t* fare un fagotto di; *(dress warmly)* coprire bene

bung [bʌŋ] *v/t* F buttare

bun·ga·low ['bʌŋgələʊ] bungalow *m inv*

bun·gee jump·ing ['bʌndʒɪdʒʌmpɪŋ] salto *m* con l'elastico

bun·gle ['bʌŋgl] *v/t* pasticciare

bunk [bʌŋk] cuccetta *f*

bunk beds *npl* letti *mpl* a castello

buoy [bɔɪ] *n* NAUT boa *f*

buoy·ant ['bɔɪənt] *adj (cheerful)* allegro; *fig: economy* sostenuto

bur·den ['bɜːdn] **1** *n* also *fig* peso *m* **2** *v/t*: ~ *s.o. with sth fig* opprimere qu con qc

bur·eau ['bjʊərəʊ] *(office)* ufficio *m*

bu·reauc·ra·cy [bjʊəˈrɒkrəsɪ] burocrazia *f*

bu·reau·crat ['bjʊərəkræt] burocrate *m/f*

bu·reau·crat·ic [bjʊərə'krætɪk] *adj* burocratico

burg·er ['bɜːgə(r)] hamburger *m inv*

bur·glar ['bɜːglə(r)] ladro *m*

'**bur·glar a·larm** antifurto *m*

bur·glar·ize ['bɜːgləraɪz] *v/t Am* svaligiare

bur·glar·y ['bɜːglərɪ] furto *m* (con scasso)

bur·gle ['bɜːgl] *v/t* svaligiare

bur·i·al ['berɪəl] sepoltura *f*

bur·ly ['bɜːlɪ] *adj* robusto

burn [bɜːn] **1** *n* bruciatura *f*; *superficial* scottatura *f*; *very serious* ustione *f* **2** *v/t* (*pret & pp* **burnt**) bruciare; *of sun* scottare **3** *v/i* (*pret & pp* **burnt**) ardere; *of house* bruciare; *of toast* bruciarsi; (*get sunburnt*) scottarsi, bruciarsi; *~ to death* morire carbonizzato

♦ **burn down 1** *v/t* dare alle fiamme **2** *v/i* essere distrutto dal fuoco

♦ **burn out** *v/t*: *burn o.s. out* esaurirsi; *a burned-out car* un'auto bruciata

burnt [bɜːnt] *pret & pp* → **burn**

burp [bɜːp] **1** *n* rutto *m* **2** *v/i* ruttare **3** *v/t baby* far fare il ruttino a

burst [bɜːst] **1** *n in water pipe* rottura *f*; *of gunfire* raffica *f*; *a ~ of energy* un'esplosione d'energia **2** *adj tyre* bucato **3** *v/t* (*pret & pp* **burst**) *balloon* far scoppiare **4** *v/i* (*pret & pp* **burst**) *of balloon, tyre* scoppiare; *~ into a room* irrompere in una stanza; *~ into tears* scoppiare in lacrime; *~ out laughing* scoppiare a ridere

bur·y ['berɪ] *v/t* (*pret & pp* **-ied**) seppellire; *hide* nascondere; *~ o.s. in work* immergersi nel lavoro

bus [bʌs] **1** *n* autobus *m inv*; (*long distance*) pullman *m inv* **2** *v/t* (*pret & pp* **-sed**) trasportare in autobus

'**bus driv·er** autista *m/f* di autobus

bush [bʊʃ] (*plant*) cespuglio *m*; (*land*) boscaglia *f*

bushed [bʊʃt] *adj* F (*tired*) distrutto

bush·y ['bʊʃɪ] *adj eyebrows* irsuto

busi·ness ['bɪznɪs] (*trade*) affari *mpl*; (*company*) impresa *f*; (*work*) lavoro

m; (*affair, matter*) faccenda *f*; (*as subject of study*) economia *f* aziendale; *in the insurance ~* (*sector*) nel campo delle assicurazioni; *on ~* per affari; *that's none of your ~!, mind your own ~!* fatti gli affari tuoi!

'**busi·ness card** biglietto *m* da visita (della ditta); '**busi·ness class** business class *f inv*; '**busi·ness hours** *npl* orario *msg* di apertura; **busi·ness·like** ['bɪznɪslaɪk] *adj* efficiente; '**busi·ness lunch** pranzo *m* d'affari; '**busi·ness·man** uomo *m* d'affari; '**busi·ness meet·ing** riunione *f* d'affari; '**busi·ness school** istituto *m* commerciale; '**busi·ness stud·ies** *nsg* (*course*) economia *f* aziendale; '**busi·ness trip** viaggio *m* d'affari; '**busi·ness·wom·an** donna *f* d'affari

busk·er ['bʌskə(r)] musicista *m/f* ambulante

'**bus lane** corsia *f* riservata (ai mezzi pubblici); '**bus shel·ter** pensilina *f* (dell'autobus); '**bus sta·tion** autostazione *f*; '**bus stop** fermata *f* dell'autobus

bust[1] [bʌst] *n of woman* petto *m*

bust[2] [bʌst] **1** *adj* F (*broken*) scassato; *go ~* fallire **2** *v/t* scassare

'**bus tick·et** biglietto *m* dell'autobus

♦ **bus·tle about** ['bʌsl] *v/i* affaccendarsi

'**bust-up** F rottura *f*

bust·y ['bʌstɪ] *adj* prosperoso

bus·y ['bɪzɪ] **1** *adj* occupato; *day* intenso; *street* animato; *shop, restaurant* affollato; TELEC occupato; *be ~ doing sth* essere occupato a fare qc; *I'm ~ talking to Gran* sto parlando con la nonna **2** *v/t* (*pret & pp* **-ied**): *~ o.s. with* tenersi occupato con

'**bus·y·bod·y** impiccione *m*, -a *f*

but [bʌt] *unstressed* [bət] **1** *conj* ma; *~ then* (*again*) d'altra parte **2** *prep*: *all ~ him* tutti tranne lui; *the last one* il penultimo; *the next ~ one* il secondo; *~ for you* se non fosse per te; *nothing ~ the best* solo il meglio

butch·er ['bʊtʃə(r)] macellaio *m*, -a *f*

butch·er's ['bʊtʃəz] macelleria *f*

butt [bʌt] **1** *n of cigarette* mozzicone *m; of joke* bersaglio *m; Am* P *(backside)* culo *m* P **2** *v/t* dare una testata a; *of goat, bull* dare una cornata a
♦ **butt in** *v/i* interrompere
but·ter ['bʌtə(r)] **1** *n* burro *m* **2** *v/t* imburrare
♦ **butter up** *v/t* F arruffianarsi F
'**but·ter·cup** ranuncolo *m*
'**but·ter·fly** *also swimming* farfalla *f*
but·tocks ['bʌtəks] *npl* natiche *fpl*
but·ton ['bʌtn] **1** *n* bottone *m; on machine* pulsante *m* **2** *v/t* abbottonare
♦ **button up** → **button**
'**but·ton·hole 1** *n suit* occhiello *m* **2** *v/t* attaccare un bottone a
but·tress ['bʌtrəs] contrafforte *m*
bux·om ['bʌksəm] *adj* formoso
buy [baɪ] **1** *n* acquisto *m* **2** *v/t (pret & pp* **bought**) comprare; *can I ~ you a drink?* posso offrirti da bere?; *£5 doesn't ~ much* con 5 sterline non si compra granché
♦ **buy off** *v/t (bribe)* comprare
♦ **buy out** *v/t* COM rilevare
♦ **buy up** *v/t* accaparrarsi
buy·er ['baɪə(r)] acquirente *m/f; for department store, supermarket* buyer *m inv*
buzz [bʌz] **1** *n* ronzio *m;* F *(thrill)* emozione *f* **2** *v/i of insect* ronzare; *with buzzer* suonare **3** *v/t with*

buzzer chiamare
♦ **buzz off** *v/i* F levarsi di torno F
buzz·er ['bʌzə(r)] cicalino *m*
by [baɪ] **1** *prep agency* da; *(near, next to)* vicino a, accanto a; *(no later than)* entro, per; *(past)* davanti a; *(mode of transport)* in; *side ~ side* fianco a fianco; *~ day/night* di giorno/notte; *~ bus/train* in autobus/treno; *~ the hour/ton* a ore/tonnellate; *~ my watch* secondo il mio orologio; *a book ~ ...* un libro di ...; *murdered ~ her husband* assassinata dal marito; *~ o.s.* da solo; *pay ~ cheque* pagare con un assegno; *~ a couple of minutes* per pochi minuti; *2 ÷ 4 (measurement)* 2 per 4; *~ this time tomorrow* domani a questo'ora **2** *adv: ~ and ~ (soon)* tra breve
bye(-bye) [baɪ] ciao
'**by-e·lec·tion** elezione *f straordinaria di un parlamentare;* **by·gone** ['baɪgɒn] **1** *n: let ~s be ~s* metterci una pietra sopra **2** *adj: in ~ days* nei giorni andati; '**by·pass 1** *n (road)* circonvallazione *f;* MED by-pass *m inv* **2** *v/t* aggirare; '**by-prod·uct** sottoprodotto *m;* **by·stand·er** ['baɪstændə(r)] astante *m/f*
byte [baɪt] byte *m inv*
'**by·word** *n: be a ~ for* essere sinonimo di

C

cab [kæb] *(taxi)* taxi *m inv; of truck* cabina *f; ~ driver* tassista *m/f*
cab·a·ret ['kæbəreɪ] spettacolo *m* di cabaret
cab·bage ['kæbɪdʒ] cavolo *m*
cab·in ['kæbɪn] *of plane, ship* cabina *f*
'**cab·in at·tend·ant** assistente *m/f* di volo
'**cab·in crew** equipaggio *m* di volo

cab·i·net ['kæbɪnɪt] armadietto *m;* POL Consiglio *m* dei ministri; *display ~* vetrina *f; drinks ~* mobile *m* bar
'**cab·i·net mak·er** ebanista *m/f;* '**cab·i·net meet·ing** riunione *f* del Consiglio dei ministri; '**cab·i·net min·is·ter** membro *m* del Consiglio dei ministri; '**cab·i·net re·shuf·fle**

calorie

rimpasto *m* del governo

ca·ble ['keɪbl] ELEC, *for securing* cavo *m*; ~ *(TV)* tv *f* via cavo

'**ca·ble car** cabina *f* (di funivia)

'**ca·ble tel·e·vi·sion** televisione *f* via cavo

cac·tus ['kæktəs] cactus *m inv*

CAD-CAM ['kædkæm] *abbr* (= ***computer assisted design-computer assisted manufacture***) CAD-CAM *m*

cad·die ['kædɪ] **1** *n in golf* portamazze *m inv* **2** *v/i* portare le mazze

ca·det [kə'det] cadetto *m*

cadge [kædʒ] *v/t:* ~ *sth from s.o.* scroccare qc a qu

Cae·sar·e·an [sɪ'zeərɪən] *n* parto *m* cesareo

caf·é ['kæfeɪ] caffè *m inv*, bar *m*

caf·e·te·ri·a [kæfə'tɪərɪə] tavola *f* calda

caf·feine ['kæfiːn] caffeina *f*

cage [keɪdʒ] gabbia *f*

ca·gey ['keɪdʒɪ] *adj* evasivo

ca·hoots [kə'huːts] F: *be in* ~ *with* essere in combutta con

ca·jole [kə'dʒəʊl] *v/t* convincere con le lusinghe

cake [keɪk] **1** *n* dolce *m*, torta *f*; *be a piece of* ~ F essere un gioco da ragazzi **2** *v/i* of mud, blood indurirsi

ca·lam·i·ty [kə'læmətɪ] calamità *f inv*

cal·ci·um ['kælsɪəm] calcio *m*

cal·cu·late ['kælkjʊleɪt] *v/t* calcolare

cal·cu·lat·ing ['kælkjʊleɪtɪŋ] *adj* calcolatore

cal·cu·la·tion [kælkjʊ'leɪʃn] calcolo *m*

cal·cu·la·tor ['kælkjʊleɪtə(r)] calcolatrice *f*

cal·en·dar ['kælɪndə(r)] calendario *m*

calf[1] [kɑːf] (*pl* ***calves*** [kɑːvz]) *young cow* vitello *m*

calf[2] [kɑːf] (*pl* ***calves*** [kɑːvz]) *of leg* polpaccio *m*

'**calf·skin** *n* vitello *m*

cal·i·ber *Am*, **cal·i·bre** ['kælɪbə(r)] *of gun* calibro *m*; *a man of his* ~ un uomo del suo calibro

call [kɔːl] **1** *n* (*phone* ~) telefonata *f*; (*shout*) grido *m*; (*demand*) richiesta *f*; (*visit*) visita *f*; *be on* ~ *of doctor* essere di guardia; *pay s.o. a* ~ far visita a qu **2** *v/t on phone* chiamare; (*summon*) chiamare; (*shout*) gridare; (*describe as*) definire; *meeting, election* indire, convocare; *what have they* ~*ed the baby?* come hanno chiamato il bambino?; ~ *s.o. as a witness* citare qu a testimoniare; ~ *a flight* annunciare un volo; ~ *s.o. names* dare dei titoli a qu **3** *v/i on phone* chiamare; (*shout*) gridare; (*visit*) passare

♦ **call at** (*stop at*) passare da

♦ **call back 1** *v/t also* TELEC richiamare **2** *v/i on phone* richiamare; (*make another visit*) ripassare

♦ **call for** *v/t* (*collect*) passare a prendere; (*demand*) reclamare; (*require*) richiedere

♦ **call in 1** *v/t* (*summon*) far venire **2** *v/i on phone* chiamare; *call in sick* chiamare per dire di essere ammalato

♦ **call off** *v/t strike* revocare; *wedding, appointment* disdire

♦ **call on** *v/t* (*urge*) sollecitare; (*visit*) visitare

♦ **call out** *v/t* (*shout*) chiamare ad alta voce; (*summon*) chiamare

♦ **call up** *v/t on phone* chiamare; COMPUT aprire

'**call box** cabina *f* telefonica

'**call cen·tre** centro *m* chiamate

call·er ['kɔːlə(r)] *on phone* persona *f* che ha chiamato; (*visitor*) visitatore *m*, -trice *f*

'**call girl** squillo *f inv*

cal·lous ['kæləs] *adj* freddo, insensibile

cal·lous·ly ['kæləslɪ] *adv* freddamente, insensibilmente

cal·lous·ness ['kæləsnɪs] freddezza *f*, insensibilità *f*

calm [kɑːm] **1** *adj* calmo **2** *n* calma *f*

♦ **calm down 1** *v/t* calmare **2** *v/i* calmarsi

calm·ly ['kɑːmlɪ] *adv* con calma

cal·o·rie ['kælərɪ] caloria *f*

cam·cor·der ['kæmkɔːdə(r)] video-camera *f*

came [keɪm] *pret* → **come**

cam·e·ra ['kæmərə] macchina *f* fotografica; (*video* ~) videocamera *f*; (*television* ~) telecamera *f*

'**cam·e·ra·man** cameraman *m inv*

cam·ou·flage ['kæməflɑːʒ] **1** *n* mimetizzazione *f*; *of soldiers* tuta *f* mimetica **2** *v/t* mimetizzare; *fig* mascherare

camp [kæmp] **1** *n* campo *m*; **make ~** accamparsi **2** *v/i* accamparsi

cam·paign [kæm'peɪn] **1** *n* campagna *f* **2** *v/i* militare

cam·paign·er [kæm'peɪnə(r)] militante *m/f*

camp·er ['kæmpə(r)] *person* campeggiatore *m*, -trice *f*; *vehicle* camper *m inv*

camp·ing ['kæmpɪŋ] campeggio *m*; **go ~** andare in campeggio

'**camp·site** camping *m inv*, campeggio *m*

cam·pus ['kæmpəs] campus *m inv*

can[1] [kæn] *unstressed* [kən] *v/aux* (*pret* **could**) ◊ (*ability*) potere; ~ **you hear me?** mi senti?; **I can't see** non vedo; ~ **you speak French?** sai parlare il francese?; ~ **he call me back?** mi può richiamare?; **as fast as you** ~ più veloce che puoi; **as well as you** ~ meglio che puoi ◊ (*permission*) potere; ~ **I help you?** posso aiutarla?; ~ **you help me?** mi può aiutare?; ~ **I have a beer / coffee?** posso avere una birra / un caffè?; **that can't be right** non può essere giusto

can[2] [kæn] **1** *n for drinks* lattina *f*; *for food* scatola *f* **2** *v/t* (*pret & pp* **-ned**) inscatolare

Can·a·da ['kænədə] Canada *m*

Ca·na·di·an [kə'neɪdɪən] **1** *adj* canadese **2** *n* canadese *m/f*

ca·nal [kə'næl] (*waterway*) canale *m*

ca·nar·y [kə'neərɪ] canarino *m*

can·cel ['kænsl] *v/t* annullare

can·cel·la·tion [kænsə'leɪʃn] annullamento *m*

can·cel·la·tion fee penalità *f* (*per annullamento*)

can·cer ['kænsə(r)] cancro *m*

Can·cer ['kænsə(r)] ASTR Cancro *m*

can·cer·ous ['kænsərəs] *adj* canceroso

c&f *abbr* (= **cost and freight**) c&f

can·did ['kændɪd] *adj* franco

can·di·da·cy ['kændɪdəsɪ] candidatura *f*

can·di·date ['kændɪdət] candidato *m*, -a *f*

can·did·ly ['kændɪdlɪ] *adv* francamente

can·died ['kændiːd] *adj* candito

can·dle ['kændl] candela *f*

'**can·dle·stick** portacandele *m inv*

can·dor *Am*, **can·dour** ['kændə(r)] franchezza *f*

can·dy ['kændɪ] *Am* (*sweet*) caramella *f*; (*sweets*) dolciumi *mpl*

can·dy-floss ['kændɪflɒs] zucchero *m* filato

cane [keɪn] canna *f*; *for walking* bastone *m*

can·is·ter ['kænɪstə(r)] barattolo *m*; *spray* bombola *f*

can·na·bis ['kænəbɪs] hashish *m*

canned [kænd] *adj fruit, tomatoes* in scatola; (*recorded*) registrato

can·ni·bal·ize ['kænɪbəlaɪz] *v/t* riciclare parti di

can·not ['kænɒt] → **can**[1]

can·ny ['kænɪ] *adj* (*astute*) arguto

ca·noe [kə'nuː] canoa *f*

'**can o·pen·er** apriscatole *m inv*

can't [kɑːnt] → **can**[1]

can·tan·ker·ous [kæn'tæŋkərəs] *adj* irascibile

can·teen [kæn'tiːn] *in factory* mensa *f*

can·vas ['kænvəs] tela *f*

can·vass ['kænvəs] **1** *v/t* (*seek opinion of*) fare un sondaggio tra **2** *v/i* POL fare propaganda elettorale

can·yon ['kænjən] canyon *m inv*

cap [kæp] (*hat*) berretto *m*; *of bottle, jar* tappo *m*; *of pen* cappuccio *m*; *for lens* coperchio *m*

ca·pa·bil·i·ty [keɪpə'bɪlətɪ] *of person* capacità *f inv*; MIL potenziale *m*

ca·pa·ble ['keɪpəbl] *adj* (*efficient*) capace; *be* **~** *of* essere capace di

ca·pac·i·ty [kə'pæsətɪ] capacità *f inv*; *of car engine* potenza *f*; *of factory* capacità *f inv* produttiva; *in my* **~** *as ...* in qualità di ...

cap·i·tal ['kæpɪtl] *n of country* capitale *f*; (*capital letter*) maiuscola *f*; *money* capitale *m*

cap·i·tal ex'pend·i·ture spese *fpl* in conto capitale

cap·i·tal 'gains tax imposta *f* sui redditi di capitale

cap·i·tal 'growth aumento *m* del capitale

cap·i·tal·is·m ['kæpɪtəlɪzm] capitalismo *m*

'cap·i·tal·ist ['kæpɪtəlɪst] **1** *adj* capitalista **2** *n* capitalista *m/f*

♦ **cap·i·tal·ize on** ['kæpɪtəlaɪz] *v/t* trarre vantaggio da

cap·i·tal 'let·ter lettera *f* maiuscola

cap·i·tal 'pun·ish·ment pena *f* capitale

ca·pit·u·late [kə'pɪtjʊleɪt] *v/i* capitolare

ca·pit·u·la·tion [kæpɪtjʊ'leɪʃn] capitolazione *f*

Cap·ri·corn ['kæprɪkɔːn] ASTR Capricorno *m*

cap·size [kæp'saɪz] **1** *v/i* ribaltarsi **2** *v/t* far ribaltare

cap·sule ['kæpsjuːl] *of medicine* cachet *m inv*; (*space ~*) capsula *f*

cap·tain ['kæptɪn] *n* capitano *m*

cap·tion ['kæpʃn] *n* didascalia *f*

cap·ti·vate ['kæptɪveɪt] *v/t* affascinare

cap·tive ['kæptɪv] *adj* prigioniero

cap·tiv·i·ty [kæp'tɪvətɪ] cattività *f*

cap·ture ['kæptʃə(r)] **1** *n of building, city* occupazione *f*; *of city* presa *f*; *of criminal, animal* cattura *f* **2** *v/t person, animal* catturare; *city, building* occupare; *city* prendere; *market share* conquistare; (*portray*) cogliere

car [kɑː(r)] macchina *f*, auto *f inv*; *of train* vagone *m*; *by* **~** in macchina

ca·rafe [kə'ræf] caraffa *f*

car·a·mel ['kærəmel] *sweet* caramella *f* morbida

car·at ['kærət] carato *m*

car·a·van ['kærəvæn] roulotte *f inv*

'car·a·van site campeggio *m* per roulotte

car·bo·hy·drate [kɑːbə'haɪdreɪt] carboidrato *m*

'car bomb autobomba *f*

car·bon mon·ox·ide [kɑːbənmɒn-'ɒksaɪd] monossido *m* di carbonio

car·bu·ret·or [kɑːbju'retə(r)] carburatore *m*

car·cass ['kɑːkəs] carcassa *f*

car·cin·o·gen ['kɑːsɪnədʒen] cancerogeno *m*

car·cin·o·gen·ic [kɑːsɪnə'dʒenɪk] *adj* cancerogeno

card [kɑːd] *to mark special occasion* biglietto *m*; (*post~*) cartolina *f*; (*business ~*) biglietto *m* (da visita); (*playing ~*) carta *f*; COMPUT scheda *f*; *material* cartoncino *m*

'card·board cartone *m*

card·board 'box scatola *f* di cartone

car·di·ac ['kɑːdɪæk] *adj* cardiaco

car·di·ac ar'rest arresto *m* cardiaco

car·di·gan ['kɑːdɪgən] cardigan *m inv*

car·di·nal ['kɑːdɪnl] *n* REL cardinale *m*

'card in·dex schedario *m*; **'card key** tessera *f* magnetica; **'card phone** telefono *m* a scheda

care [keə(r)] **1** *n of baby, pet* cure *fpl*; *of the elderly* assistenza *f*; *of the sick* cura *f*; (*worry*) preoccupazione *f*; *take* **~** (*be cautious*) fare attenzione; *take* **~** (*of yourself*)! (*goodbye*) stammi bene; *take* **~** *of* (*look after: baby, dog*) prendersi cura di; *tool, house, garden* tenere bene; (*deal with*) occuparsi di; (*handle*) *with* **~!** *on label* maneggiare con cura **2** *v/t* interessarsi; *I don't* **~!** non mi importa; *I couldn't* **~** *less* non potrebbe importarmene di meno

care of → *c/o*

♦ **care about** *v/t* interessarsi a

♦ **care for** *v/t* (*look after*) prendersi cura di; *I don't care for your tone* non mi piace il tuo tono; *would you* *care for a tea?* *fml* gradirebbe un tè?

ca·reer [kəˈrɪə(r)] (*profession*) carriera *f*; (*path through life*) vita *f*

ca·reers of·fi·cer consulente *m/f* professionale

'**care·free** *adj* spensierato

care·ful ['keəful] *adj* (*cautious*) attento; (*thorough*) attento; (*be*) *~!* (stai) attento!

care·ful·ly ['keəfulɪ] *adv* con cautela

care·less ['keəlɪs] *adj* incurante; *driver, worker* sbadato; *work* fatto senza attenzione; *error* di disattenzione; *you are so ~!* sei così sbadato!

care·less·ly ['keəlɪslɪ] *adv* senza cura

carer ['keərə(r)] accompagnatore *m*, -trice *f*

ca·ress [kəˈres] **1** *n* carezza *f* **2** *v/t* accarezzare

care·tak·er ['keəteɪkə(r)] custode *m/f*

'**care·worn** *adj* provato

'**car fer·ry** traghetto *m* (per le macchine)

car·go ['kɑːɡəʊ] carico *m*

'**car hire** autonoleggio *m*

'**car hire com·pa·ny** compagnia *f* di autonoleggio

car·i·ca·ture ['kærɪkətʊə(r)] *n* caricatura *f*

car·ing ['keərɪŋ] *adj* premuroso

'**car me·chan·ic** meccanico *m* per auto

car·nage ['kɑːnɪdʒ] carneficina *f*

car·na·tion [kɑːˈneɪʃn] garofano *m*

car·ni·val ['kɑːnɪvl] carnevale *m*

car·ol ['kærəl] *n* canzone *f* di Natale

car·ou·sel [kærəˈsel] *at airport* nastro *m* trasportatore; *for slide projector* carrello *m*

'**car park** parcheggio *m*

'**car park at·tend·ant** parcheggiatore *m*, -trice *f*

car·pen·ter ['kɑːpɪntə(r)] falegname *m*

car·pet ['kɑːpɪt] tappeto *m*; (*fitted ~*) moquette *f inv*

'**car phone** telefono *m* da automobi-

le; '**car·pool** *n uso m* condiviso della macchina dell'uno o dell'altro tra un gruppo di persone; '**car port** posto *m* auto coperto; **car 'ra·di·o** autoradio *f inv*

car·riage ['kærɪdʒ] carrozza *f*; COM trasporto *m*

car·ri·er ['kærɪə(r)] (*company*) compagnia *f* di trasporto; *of disease* portatore *m* sano, portatrice *f* sana

'**car·ri·er bag** sacchetto *m*

car·rot ['kærət] carota *f*

car·ry ['kærɪ] (*pret & pp -ied*) **1** *v/t* portare; *of pregnant woman* portare in grembo; *of ship, plane, bus etc* trasportare; *proposal* approvare; *get carried away* farsi prendere dall'entusiasmo **2** *v/i* of sound sentirsi

♦ **carry on 1** *v/i* (*continue*) andare avanti, continuare; (*make a fuss*) fare storie; (*have an affair*) avere una storia **2** *v/t* (*conduct*) portare avanti

♦ **carry out** *v/t survey etc* effettuare; *orders etc* eseguire

'**car·ry·cot** porte-enfant *m inv*

'**car seat** *for child* seggiolino *m* per auto

cart [kɑːt] carretto *m*

car·tel [kɑːˈtel] cartello *m*

car·ton ['kɑːtn] *for storage, transport* cartone *m*; *of cigarettes* stecca *f*

car·toon [kɑːˈtuːn] *in newspaper, magazine* fumetto *m*; *on TV, film* cartone *m* animato

car·toon·ist [kɑːˈtuːnɪst] *for newspaper etc* vignettista *m/f*

car·tridge ['kɑːtrɪdʒ] *for gun, printer* cartuccia *f*

carve [kɑːv] *v/t meat* tagliare; *wood* intagliare

carv·ing ['kɑːvɪŋ] *figure* scultura *f*

'**car wash** lavaggio *m* per auto

case[1] [keɪs] *for glasses, pen* astuccio *m*; *of whisky, wine* cassa *f*; (*suitcase*) valigia *f*; *glass ~* teca *f*

case[2] [keɪs] *n* (*instance, for police*), MED caso *m*; (*argument*) argomentazione *f*; LAW causa *f*; *in ~ ...* in caso ...; *take an umbrella in ~ it rains* prendi un ombrello in caso piovesse; **in any ~** in ogni caso; **in that ~** in questo caso

'**case his·to·ry** MED cartella *f* clinica

'**case·load** numero *m* di assistiti; *my doctor's ~* il numero dei pazienti del mio dottore

cash [kæʃ] **1** *n* contanti *mpl*; F (*money*) soldi *mpl*; *~ down* in contanti; *pay (in) ~* pagare in contanti; *~ in advance* pagamento *m* anticipato; *~ on delivery* → **COD 2** *v/t cheque* incassare

♦ **cash in on** *v/t* guadagnare su

'**cash card** carta *f* per prelievi; '**cash cow** vacca *f* da mungere; '**cash desk** cassa *f*; **cash 'dis·count** sconto *m* su pagamento in contanti; '**cash di·spens·er** (sportello *m*) Bancomat® *m*; '**cash flow** flusso *m* di cassa

cash·ier [kæ'ʃɪə(r)] *n* in shop etc cassiere *m*, -a *f*

'**cash ma·chine** (sportello *m*) Bancomat® *m*

cash·mere ['kæʃmɪər] *adj* cashmere *m inv*

'**cash·point** (sportello *m*) Bancomat® *m*

'**cash re·gis·ter** cassa *f*

ca·si·no [kə'siːnəʊ] casinò *m inv*

cas·ket ['kæskɪt] *Am* (*coffin*) bara *f*

cas·se·role ['kæsərəʊl] *n meal* stufato *m*; *container* casseruola *f*

cas·sette [kə'set] cassetta *f*

cas'sette play·er mangiacassette *m inv*

cas'sette re·cord·er registratore *m* (a cassette)

cast [kɑːst] **1** *n of play* cast *m inv*; (*mould*) stampo *m* **2** *v/t* (*pret & pp cast*) *doubt, suspicion* far sorgere (*on* su); *shadow* proiettare; *metal* colare (in uno stampo); *play* assegnare le parti per; *~ s.o. as ... for play* far fare a qu il ruolo di ...; *he was ~ as Romeo* gli è stata assegnata la parte di Romeo; *~ a glance at s.o. / sth* gettare uno sguardo su qu / qc

♦ **cast off** *v/i of ship* sciogliere gli ormeggi

caste [kɑːst] casta *f*

cast·er ['kɑːstə(r)] *on chair etc* rotella *f*

'**cast·er sug·ar** zucchero *m* raffinato

cast 'iron ghisa *f*

cast-'iron *adj* di ghisa

cas·tle ['kɑːsl] castello *m*

'**cast·or** ['kɑːstə(r)] → **caster**

cas·trate [kæ'streɪt] *v/t* castrare

cas·tra·tion [kæ'streɪʃn] castrazione *f*

cas·u·al ['kæʒʊəl] *adj* (*chance*) casuale; (*offhand*) disinvolto; (*irresponsible*) noncurante; *remark* poco importante; *clothes* casual *inv*; (*not permanent*) occasionale; *~ sex* rapporti *mpl* occasionali

cas·u·al·ly ['kæʒʊəli] *adv dressed* (in modo) casual; *say* con disinvoltura

cas·u·al·ty ['kæʒʊəltɪ] *dead person* vittima *f*; *injured* ferito *m*

'**cas·u·al wear** abbigliamento *m* casual

cat [kæt] gatto *m*; *wild* felino *m*

cat·a·log *Am*, **cat·a·logue** ['kætəlɒg] *n* catalogo *m*

cat·a·lyst ['kætəlɪst] catalizzatore *m*

cat·a·lyt·ic con·vert·er [kætə'lɪtɪk] marmitta *f* catalitica

cat·a·pult ['kætəpʌlt] **1** *v/t fig: to fame, stardom* catapultare **2** *n* catapulta *f*; *toy* fionda *f*

cat·a·ract ['kætərækt] MED cateratta *f*

ca·tas·tro·phe [kə'tæstrəfɪ] catastrofe *f*

cat·a·stroph·ic [kætə'strɒfɪk] *adj* catastrofico

catch [kætʃ] **1** *n* presa *f*; *of fish* pesca *f*; *on handbag, box* chiusura *f*; *on door, window* fermo *m*; *on brooch* fermaglio *m*; (*problem*) inghippo *m* **2** *v/t* (*pret & pp caught*) *ball, escaped prisoner* prendere; *bus, train* prendere; *fish* prendere; (*in order to speak to*) trovare; (*hear*) afferrare; *illness* prendere; *~ (a) cold* prendere un raffreddore; *~ s.o.'s eye of person, object* attirare l'attenzione di qu; *~ sight of, ~ a glimpse of* intravedere; *~ s.o. doing sth* sorprendere qu a fare qc

♦ **catch on** v/i (become popular) fare presa; (understand) afferrare

♦ **catch up** v/i recuperare; **catch up with s.o.** raggiungere qu; **catch up with sth** work, studies mettersi in pari con qc

♦ **catch up on** v/t recuperare

catch-22 [kætʃtwentɪ'tuː]: **it's a ~ situation** è una situazione senza via d'uscita

catch·ing ['kætʃɪŋ] adj also fig contagioso

catch·y ['kætʃɪ] adj tune orecchiabile

cat·e·gor·ic [kætə'gɒrɪk] adj categorico

cat·e·gor·i·cal·ly [kætə'gɒrɪklɪ] adv categoricamente

cat·e·go·ry ['kætɪgərɪ] categoria f

♦ **cater for** ['keɪtə(r)] v/t (meet the needs of) rispondere alle esigenze di; (provide food for) organizzare rinfreschi per

ca·ter·er ['keɪtərə(r)] ristoratore m, -trice f

ca·ter·pil·lar ['kætəpɪlə(r)] bruco m

ca·the·dral [kə'θiːdrl] cattedrale f, duomo m

Cath·o·lic ['kæθəlɪk] **1** adj cattolico **2** n cattolico m, -a f

Ca·thol·i·cism [kə'θɒlɪsɪzm] cattolicesimo m

'cat·nap 1 n pisolino m **2** v/i (pret & pp **-ped**) schiacciare un pisolino

'cat's eye on road catarifrangente m

cat·tle ['kætl] npl bestiame m

cat·ty ['kætɪ] adj maligno

'cat·walk passerella f

caught [kɔːt] pret & pp → **catch**

cau·li·flow·er ['kɒlɪflaʊə(r)] cavolfiore m

cause [kɔːz] **1** n causa f; (grounds) motivo m; (objective) causa f **2** v/t causare; **what ~d you to leave so early?** perché sei andato via così presto?

caus·tic ['kɔːstɪk] adj fig caustico

cau·tion ['kɔːʃn] **1** n (carefulness) cautela f, prudenza f; **~ is advised** si raccomanda la prudenza **2** v/t (warn) mettere in guardia

cau·tious ['kɔːʃəs] adj cauto, prudente

cau·tious·ly ['kɔːʃəslɪ] adv con cautela

cave [keɪv] caverna f, grotta f

♦ **cave in** v/i of roof crollare

cav·i·ar ['kævɪɑː(r)] caviale m

cav·i·ty ['kævətɪ] cavità f inv; in tooth carie f inv

cc [siː'siː] **1** abbr (= **carbon copy**) cc (= copia f carbone); (= **cubic centimetres**) cm m inv (= centimetri cubici); MOT cilindrata f **2** v/t memo fare una copia di; person mandare una copia per conoscenza a

CD [siː'diː] abbr (= **compact disc**) CD m inv

CD play·er lettore m CD; **CD-ROM** [siːdiː'rɒm] CD-ROM m inv; **CD-ROM drive** drive m inv per CD-ROM

cease [siːs] v/t & v/i cessare

'cease-fire cessate il fuoco m inv

cei·ling ['siːlɪŋ] of room soffitto m; (limit) tetto m, plafond m inv

cel·e·brate ['selɪbreɪt] **1** v/i festeggiare **2** v/t celebrare, festeggiare; (observe) festeggiare

cel·e·brat·ed ['selɪbreɪtɪd] adj acclamato; **be ~ for** essere famoso per

cel·e·bra·tion [selɪ'breɪʃn] celebrazione f, festeggiamento m

ce·leb·ri·ty [sɪ'lebrətɪ] celebrità f inv

cel·e·ry ['selərɪ] sedano m

cel·i·ba·cy ['selɪbəsɪ] celibato m

cel·i·bate ['selɪbət] adj man celibe; woman nubile

cell [sel] for prisoner cella f; BIO cellula f; in spreadsheet casella f, cella f

cel·lar ['selə(r)] of house cantina f; of wine collezione f di vini

cel·list ['tʃelɪst] violoncellista m/f

cel·lo ['tʃeləʊ] violoncello m

cel·lo·phane ['seləfeɪn] cellofan m inv

cel·lu·lar phone [selju:lər'fəʊn] telefono m cellulare, cellulare m

cel·lu·lite ['selju:laɪt] cellulite f

ce·ment [sɪ'ment] **1** n cemento m; (adhesive) mastice m **2** v/t cementare; friendship consolidare cem·e·tery ['semətrɪ] cimitero *m*

cen·sor ['sensə(r)] *v/t* censurare

cen·sor·ship ['sensəʃɪp] censura *f*

cen·sus ['sensəs] censimento *m*

cent [sent] centesimo *m*

cen·te·na·ry [sen'ti:nərɪ] centenario *m*

cen·ter *Am* → **centre**

cen·ti·grade ['sentɪgreɪd] *adj* centigrado; *10 degrees ~* 10 gradi centigradi

cen·ti·me·ter *Am*, **cen·ti·me·tre** ['sentɪmi:tə(r)] centimetro *m*

cen·tral ['sentrəl] *adj location, flat* centrale; *(main)* principale, centrale; *~ London / France* il centro di Londra / della Francia; *be ~ to sth* essere fondamentale per qc

cen·tral 'heat·ing riscaldamento *m* autonomo

cen·tral·ize ['sentrəlaɪz] *v/t decision making* accentrare

cen·tral 'lock·ing MOT chiusura *f* centralizzata

cen·tral 'pro·ces·sing u·nit unità *f inv* centrale

cen·tral res·er·va·tion MOT banchina *f* spartitraffico

cen·tre ['sentə(r)] **1** *n* centro *m*; *in the ~ of* al centro di **2** *v/t* centrare

♦ centre on *v/t* essere incentrato su

cen·tre of 'grav·i·ty centro *m* di gravità

cen·tu·ry ['sentʃərɪ] secolo *m*

CEO [si:i:'əʊ] *abbr* (= **Chief Executive Officer**) direttore *m* generale

ce·ram·ic [sɪ'ræmɪk] *adj* ceramico

ce·ram·ics [sɪ'ræmɪks] *(pl: objects)* ceramiche *fpl*; *(sg: art)* ceramica *f*

ce·re·al ['sɪərɪəl] *(grain)* cereale *m*; *(breakfast ~)* cereali *mpl*

cer·e·mo·ni·al [serɪ'məʊnɪəl] **1** *adj* da cerimonia **2** *n* cerimoniale *m*

cer·e·mo·ny ['serɪmənɪ] *(event)* cerimonia *f*; *(ritual)* cerimonie *fpl*

cer·tain ['sɜːtn] *adj (sure, particular)* certo; *it's ~ that ...* è certo che ...; *a ~ Mr S.* un certo Sig S.; *make ~* accertarsi; *know / say for ~* sapere / dire con certezza

cer·tain·ly ['sɜːtnlɪ] *adv* certamente; *~ not!* certo che no!

cer·tain·ty ['sɜːtntɪ] *(certezza f; it's a ~* è una cosa certa; *he's a ~ to win* vincerà di certo

cer·tif·i·cate [sə'tɪfɪkət] *qualification* certificazione *f*; *official paper* certificato *m*

cer·ti·fy ['sɜːtɪfaɪ] *v/t (pret & pp -ied)* dichiarare ufficialmente

Ce·sar·e·an *Am* → **Caesarean**

ces·sa·tion [se'seɪʃn] cessazione *f*

c/f *abbr* (= **cost and freight**) c/f

CFC [si:ef'si:] *abbr* (= **chlorofluorocarbon**) CFC *m inv* (= clorofluorocarburi *mpl*)

chain [tʃeɪn] **1** *n* catena *f* **2** *v/t*: *~ sth / s.o. to sth* incatenare qc/qu a qc

chain re'ac·tion reazione *f* a catena; 'chain smoke *v/i* fumare una sigaretta dopo l'altra; 'chain smok·er fumatore *m*, -trice *f* incallito; 'chain store *store* negozio *m* di una catena; *company* catena *f* di negozi

chair [tʃeə(r)] **1** *n* sedia *f*; *(arm ~)* poltrona *f*; *at university* cattedra *f*; *the ~ (electric ~)* la sedia elettrica; *at meeting* presidente *m/f*; *take the ~* presiedere **2** *v/t meeting* presiedere

'chair lift seggiovia *f*

'chair·man presidente *m*

chair·man·ship ['tʃeəmənʃɪp] presidenza *f*

'chair·per·son presidente *m/f*

'chair·wom·an presidente *f*

cha·let ['ʃæleɪ] chalet *m inv*

chal·ice ['tʃælɪs] REL calice *m*

chalk [tʃɔːk] gesso *m*

chal·lenge ['tʃælɪndʒ] **1** *n* sfida *f* **2** *v/t* sfidare; *(call into question)* mettere alla prova

chal·len·ger ['tʃælɪndʒə(r)] sfidante *m/f*

chal·len·ging ['tʃælɪndʒɪŋ] *adj job, undertaking* stimolante

'cham·ber·maid ['tʃeɪmbəmeɪd] cameriera *f*; 'cham·ber mu·sic musica *f* da camera; **Cham·ber of 'Com·merce** Camera *f* di Commercio

cham·ois (leather) ['ʃæmɪ] camoscio *m*

cham·pagne [ʃæm'peɪn] champagne *m inv*

cham·pi·on ['ʧæmpɪən] **1** *n* SP campione *m*, -essa *f*; *of cause* difensore *m*, -a *f* **2** *v/t* (*cause*) difendere

cham·pi·on·ship ['ʧæmpɪənʃɪp] *event* campionato *m*; *title* titolo *m* di campione; *of cause* difesa *f*

chance [ʧɑːns] (*possibility*) probabilità *f inv*; (*opportunity*) opportunità *f inv*, occasione *f*; (*risk*) rischio *m*; (*luck*) caso *m*; **by ~** per caso; **take a ~** correre un rischio; **I'm not taking any ~s** non voglio correre nessun rischio; **you don't stand a ~** non hai nessuna possibilità

Chan·cel·lor ['ʧɑːnsələ(r)] *in Germany* cancelliere *m*; **~ (of the Exchequer)** *in Britain* ministro *m* del tesoro

chan·de·lier [ʃændə'lɪə(r)] lampadario *m*

change [ʧeɪndʒ] **1** *n* cambiamento *m*; *small coins* moneta *f*; *from purchase* resto *m*; **for a ~** per cambiare; **a ~ of clothes** un ricambio di vestiti **2** *v/t* (*alter*) cambiare; *one's clothes* cambiarsi **3** *v/i* cambiare; (*put on different clothes*) cambiarsi; **you ~ at Crewe** devi cambiare a Crewe

change·a·ble ['ʧeɪndʒəbl] *adj* incostante; *weather* variabile

'change·o·ver passaggio *m*; *period* fase *f* di transizione; *in relay race* passaggio *m* del testimone

chang·ing room ['ʧeɪndʒɪŋ] SP spogliatoio *m*; *in shop* camerino *m*

chan·nel ['ʧænl] *on TV, in water* canale *m*

Chan·nel 'Tun·nel tunnel *m* della Manica

chant [ʧɑːnt] **1** *n* slogan *m inv*; REL canto *m* **2** *v/i* gridare; *of demonstrators* gridare slogan; REL cantare

cha·os ['keɪɒs] caos *m inv*

cha·ot·ic [keɪ'ɒtɪk] *adj* caotico

chap [ʧæp] *n* F tipo *m* F

chap·el ['ʧæpl] cappella *f*

chapped [ʧæpt] *adj* screpolato

chap·ter ['ʧæptə(r)] *of book* capitolo *m*; *of organization* filiale *f*

char·ac·ter ['kærɪktə(r)] (*nature*) carattere *m*; (*person*) tipo *m*; *in book, play* personaggio *m*; *in writing* carattere *m*; **he's a real ~** è un tipo speciale

char·ac·ter·is·tic [kærɪktə'rɪstɪk] **1** *n* caratteristica *f* **2** *adj* caratteristico

char·ac·ter·is·ti·cal·ly [kærɪktə'rɪstɪklɪ] *adv* in modo caratteristico; **he was ~ rude** era maleducato, come al solito

char·ac·ter·ize ['kærɪktəraɪz] *v/t* caratterizzare

cha·rade [ʃə'rɑːd] *fig* farsa *f*

char·coal ['ʧɑːkəʊl] *for barbecue* carbonella *f*; *for drawing* carboncino *m*

charge [ʧɑːdʒ] **1** *n* (*fee*) costo *m*; LAW accusa *f*; **free of ~** gratis; **be in ~** essere responsabile; **take ~** assumersi l'incombenza; **take ~ of sth** farsi carico di qc **2** *v/t sum of money* far pagare; *person* far pagare a; (*put on account*) addebitare; LAW accusare; *battery* caricare; **how much do you ~ for ...?** quanto prende per ...? **3** *v/i* (*attack*) attaccare

'charge ac·count conto *m* (spese)

'charge card carta *f* di addebito

cha·ris·ma [kə'rɪzmə] carisma *m*

char·is·mat·ic [kærɪz'mætɪk] *adj* carismatico

char·i·ta·ble ['ʧærɪtəbl] *adj institution* di beneficenza; *donation* in beneficenza; *person* caritatevole

char·i·ty ['ʧærətɪ] *assistance* carità *f*; *organization* associazione *f* di beneficenza

char·la·tan ['ʃɑːlətən] ciarlatano *m*, -a *f*

charm [ʧɑːm] **1** *n appealing quality* fascino *m*; *on bracelet etc* ciondolo *m* **2** *v/t* (*delight*) conquistare

charm·ing ['ʧɑːmɪŋ] *adj* affascinante; *house, village* incantevole

charred [ʧɑːd] *adj* carbonizzato

chart [ʧɑːt] *diagram* diagramma *m*; *for ship* carta *f* nautica; *for aeroplane* carta *f* aeronautica; **the ~s** MUS l'hit parade *f inv*

char·ter ['ʧɑ:tə(r)] *v/t plane, boat* noleggiare

'**char·ter flight** volo *m* charter *inv*

chase [ʧeɪs] **1** *n* inseguimento *m* **2** *v/t* inseguire

♦ **chase away** *v/t* cacciare (via)

chas·er ['ʧeɪsə(r)] alcolico bevuto dopo un altro di diverso tipo

chas·sis ['ʃæsɪ] *of car* telaio *m*

chat [ʧæt] **1** *n* chiacchierata *f; useless talk* chiacchiere *fpl* **2** *v/i* (*pret & pp* **-ted**) chiacchierare

♦ **chat up** *v/t* F abbordare F

'**chat room** stanza *f* di chat; '**chat show** talk show *m inv*; '**chat show host** conduttore *m*, -trice *f* di un talk show

chat·ter ['ʧætə(r)] **1** *n* parlantina *f* **2** *v/i* *talk* fare chiacchiere; *of teeth* battere

'**chat·ter·box** chiacchierone *m*, -a *f*

chat·ty ['ʧætɪ] *adj person* chiacchierone; *letter* familiare

chauf·feur ['ʃəʊfə(r)] *n* autista *m/f*

'**chauf·feur-driv·en** *adj* con autista

chau·vin·ist ['ʃəʊvɪnɪst] *n* sciovinista *m/f; (male ~)* maschilista *m*

chau·vin·ist·ic [ʃəʊvɪ'nɪstɪk] *adj* sciovinista

cheap [ʧi:p] *adj (inexpensive)* economico; *(nasty)* cattivo; *(mean)* tirchio

cheat [ʧi:t] **1** *n person* imbroglione *m*, -a *f; in cards* baro *m; (deception)* truffa *f* **2** *v/t* imbrogliare; **~ s.o. out of sth** estorcere qc a qn con l'inganno **3** *v/i* imbrogliare; *in cards* barare; **~ on one's wife** tradire la propria moglie

check[^1] [ʧek] **1** *adj shirt* a quadri **2** *n* quadro *m*

check[^2] [ʧek] **1** *n to verify sth* verifica *f*, **keep in ~, hold in ~** tenere sotto controllo; **keep a ~ on** tenere sotto controllo **2** *v/t (verify)* verificare; *(restrain)* controllare; *(stop)* bloccare; *with a tick* marcare **3** *v/i* verificare; **did you ~ check for signs of forced entry?** hai guardato se c'erano segni di infrazione?

♦ **check in** *v/i* registrarsi

♦ **check off** *v/t* segnare

♦ **check on** *v/t* controllare

♦ **check out 1** *v/i of hotel* saldare il conto **2** *v/t (look into)* verificare; *club, restaurant etc* provare

♦ **check up on** *v/t* fare dei controlli su

♦ **check with** *v/i of person* verificare con; *(tally)* combaciare con

check[^3] [ʧek] *Am* → **cheque**

checked [ʧekt] *adj material* a quadri

checkers ['ʧekəz] *nsg Am: game* dama *f*

'**check-in** (**coun·ter**) banco *m* dell'accettazione

'**check·ing ac·count** *Am* conto *m* corrente

'**check-in time** check in *m inv*; '**check·list** lista *f* di verifica; '**check·mark** *Am* segno *m*; '**check·mate** *n* scacco *m* matto; '**check·out** cassa *f*; '**check·out time** *from hotel* ora *f* di check-out; '**check·point** *military, police* posto *m* di blocco; '**check·room** *Am for coats* guardaroba *m inv*; '**check·up** *medical* check up *m inv*; *dental* visita *f* di controllo

cheek [ʧi:k] guancia *f; (impudence)* sfacciataggine *f*

'**cheek·bone** zigomo *m*

cheek·i·ly ['ʧi:kɪlɪ] *adv* sfacciatamente

cheek·y ['ʧi:kɪ] *adj* sfacciato

cheer [ʧɪə(r)] **1** *n* acclamazione *f; three ~s for ...* hip, hip, hurrà per ...; **~!** *(toast)* salute!; **~!** F *(thanks)* grazie! **2** *v/t* acclamare **3** *v/i* fare acclamazioni

♦ **cheer on** *v/t* incitare

♦ **cheer up 1** *v/i* consolarsi; **cheer up!** su con la vita! **2** *v/t* tirare su

cheer·ful ['ʧɪəfʊl] *adj* allegro

cheer·ing ['ʧɪərɪŋ] *n* acclamazioni *fpl*

cheer·i·o [ʧɪərɪ'əʊ] F ciao F

cheer·y ['ʧɪərɪ] *adj* → **cheerful**

cheese [ʧi:z] formaggio *m*

'**cheese·burg·er** cheeseburger *m inv*

'cheese·cake dolce m al formaggio

chef [ʃef] chef m/f inv

chem·i·cal ['kemɪkl] 1 adj chimico 2 n sostanza f chimica

chem·i·cal 'war·fare guerra f chimica

chemist ['kemɪst] in laboratory chimico m, -a f; who dispenses medicine farmacista m/f

chem·is·try ['kemɪstrɪ] chimica f; fig alchimia f

'chem·ist's (shop) farmacia f

chem·o·ther·a·py [kiːməʊˈθerəpɪ] chemioterapia f

cheque [tʃek] assegno m

'cheque·book libretto m degli assegni

cheque (guar·an·tee) card carta f assegni

cher·ish ['tʃerɪʃ] v/t avere a cuore

cher·ry ['tʃerɪ] fruit ciliegia f; tree ciliegio m

cher·ub ['tʃerəb] cherubino m

chess [tʃes] scacchi mpl

'chess·board scacchiera f

'chess·man, chess·piece pezzo m degli scacchi

chest [tʃest] of person petto m; (box) cassa f; I'm glad I've got that off my ~ sono contento di essermi tolto questo peso dallo stomaco

chest·nut ['tʃesnʌt] castagna f; tree castagno m

chest of 'drawers comò m inv, cassettone m

chew [tʃuː] v/t masticare; of dog, rats rosicchiare

chew·ing gum ['tʃuːɪŋ] gomma f da masticare

chic [ʃiːk] adj chic inv

chick [tʃɪk] pulcino m; F (girl) ragazza f

chick·en ['tʃɪkɪn] 1 n pollo m; F fifone m, -a f F 2 adj F (cowardly) fifone

♦ chicken out v/i F tirarsi indietro per la fifa F

'chick·en·feed F una bazzecola

'chick·en·pox varicella f

chief [tʃiːf] 1 n (head) principale m/f; of tribe capo m 2 adj principale

chief·ly ['tʃiːflɪ] adv principalmente

chil·blain ['tʃɪlbleɪn] gelone m

child [tʃaɪld] (pl children ['tʃɪldrən]) also pej bambino m, -a f; they have two children hanno due figli

'child a·buse violenza f sui minori;

'child·birth parto m; child·hood ['tʃaɪldhʊd] infanzia f

child·ish ['tʃaɪldɪʃ] adj pej infantile, puerile

child·ish·ly ['tʃaɪldɪʃlɪ] adv pej puerilmente

child·ish·ness ['tʃaɪldɪʃnɪs] pej puerilità f inv

child·less ['tʃaɪldlɪs] adj senza figli

child·like ['tʃaɪldlaɪk] adj innocente

'child·mind·er baby-sitter m/f inv

'chil·dren ['tʃɪldrən] pl → child

Chil·e ['tʃɪlɪ] Cile m

Chil·e·an ['tʃɪlɪən] 1 adj cileno 2 n cileno m, -a f

chill [tʃɪl] 1 n in air freddo m; illness colpo m di freddo; there's a ~ in the air l'aria è fredda 2 v/t wine mettere in fresco

♦ chill out v/i P rilassarsi

chil·li (pep·per) ['tʃɪlɪ] peperoncino m

chil·ly ['tʃɪlɪ] adj weather, welcome freddo; I'm feeling a bit ~ ho un po' freddo; it's a bit ~ this morning sta freddino stamattina

chime [tʃaɪm] v/i suonare

chim·ney ['tʃɪmnɪ] camino m

chim·pan·zee [tʃɪmpænˈziː] scimpanzé m inv

chin [tʃɪn] mento m

Chi·na ['tʃaɪnə] Cina f

chi·na ['tʃaɪnə] porcellana f

Chi·nese [tʃaɪˈniːz] 1 adj cinese 2 n language cinese m; person cinese m/f

chink [tʃɪŋk] gap fessura f; sound tintinnio m

chip [tʃɪp] 1 n fragment scheggia f; damage scheggiatura f; in gambling fiche f inv; COMPUT chip m inv; ~s patate fpl fritte; Am patatine fpl 2 v/t (pret & pp -ped) damage scheggiare

♦ chip in v/i (interrupt) intervenire; with money contribuire

chi·rop·o·dist [kɪˈrɒpədɪst] pedicure m/f inv

chi·ro·prac·tor [ˈkaɪrəʊpræktə(r)] chiroterapeuta m/f

chirp [tʃɜːp] v/i cinguettare

chis·el [ˈtʃɪzl] n scalpello m

chit-chat [ˈtʃɪtʃæt] chiacchiere fpl

chiv·al·rous [ˈʃɪvlrəs] adj cavalleresco

chive [tʃaɪv] erba f cipollina

chlo·rine [ˈklɔːriːn] cloro m

chlor·o·form [ˈklɒrəfɔːm] n cloroformio m

choc·a·hol·ic [tʃɒkəˈhɒlɪk] n F fanatico m, -a f del cioccolato

chock-a-block [tʃɒkəˈblɒk] adj F pieno zeppo

chock-full [tʃɒkˈfʊl] adj F strapieno

choc·o·late [ˈtʃɒkələt] cioccolato m; in box cioccolatino m; hot ~ cioccolata f calda

'choc·o·late cake dolce m al cioccolato

choice [tʃɔɪs] 1 n scelta f; I had no ~ non avevo scelta 2 adj (top quality) di prima scelta

choir [ˈkwaɪə(r)] coro m

'choir·boy corista m

choke [tʃəʊk] 1 n MOT starter m inv 2 v/i soffocare; he ~d on a bone si è strozzato con un osso 3 v/t soffocare

cho·les·te·rol [kəˈlestərɒl] colesterolo m

choose [tʃuːz] v/t & v/i (pret chose, pp chosen) scegliere

choos·ey [ˈtʃuːzɪ] adj F selettivo

chop [tʃɒp] 1 n action colpo m; meat braciola f 2 v/t (pret & pp -ped) wood spaccare; meat, vegetables tagliare a pezzi

♦ **chop down** v/t tree abbattere

chop·per [ˈtʃɒpə(r)] tool accetta f; F (helicopter) elicottero m

chop·ping board [ˈtʃɒpɪŋ] tagliere m

'chop·sticks npl bastoncini mpl (cinesi)

cho·ral [ˈkɔːrəl] adj corale

chord [kɔːd] MUS accordo m

chore [tʃɔː(r)] household faccenda f domestica

chor·e·o·graph [ˈkɒrɪəgrɑːf] v/t coreografare

chor·e·og·ra·pher [kɒrɪˈɒgrəfə(r)] coreografo m, -a f

chor·e·og·ra·phy [kɒrɪˈɒgrəfɪ] coreografia f

cho·rus [ˈkɔːrəs] singers, of song coro m

chose [tʃəʊz] pret → **choose**

cho·sen [ˈtʃəʊzn] pp → **choose**

Christ [kraɪst] Cristo m; ~! Cristo!

chris·ten [ˈkrɪsn] v/t battezzare

chris·ten·ing [ˈkrɪsnɪŋ] battesimo m

Chris·tian [ˈkrɪstʃən] 1 n cristiano m, -a f 2 adj cristiano; attitude da cristiano

Chris·ti·an·i·ty [krɪstɪˈænətɪ] cristianesimo m

'Chris·tian name nome m di battesimo

Christ·mas [ˈkrɪsməs] Natale m; at ~ a Natale; Merry ~! Buon Natale!

'Christ·mas card biglietto m di auguri natalizi; **Christ·mas 'Day** giorno m di Natale; **Christ·mas 'Eve** vigilia f di Natale; **'Christ·mas present** regalo m di Natale; **'Christ·mas tree** albero m di Natale

chrome, chro·mi·um [krəʊm, ˈkrəʊmɪəm] cromo m

chro·mo·some [ˈkrəʊməsəʊm] cromosomo m

chron·ic [ˈkrɒnɪk] adj cronico

chron·o·log·i·cal [krɒnəˈlɒdʒɪkl] adj cronologico; in ~ order in ordine cronologico

chrys·an·the·mum [krɪˈsænθəməm] crisantemo m

chub·by [ˈtʃʌbɪ] adj paffuto

chuck [tʃʌk] v/t F buttare

♦ **chuck out** v/t F object buttare via; person buttare fuori

chuck·ing-out time [ˈtʃʌkɪŋˈaʊt] F ora f di chiusura

chuck·le [ˈtʃʌkl] 1 n risatina f 2 v/i ridacchiare

chum [tʃʌm] amico m, -a f

chum·my [ˈtʃʌmɪ] adj F pappa e ciccia F; be ~ with essere pappa e ciccia con

chunk [tʃʌŋk] pezzo *m*

chunk·y ['tʃʌŋkɪ] *adj sweater* spesso; *tumbler* tozzo; *person, build* tarchiato

church [tʃɜːtʃ] chiesa *f*

church 'hall sala *f* parrocchiale; **church 'serv·ice** funzione *f* religiosa; **'church·yard** cimitero *m* (di una chiesa)

churl·ish ['tʃɜːlɪʃ] *adj* sgarbato

chute [ʃuːt] scivolo *m; for waste disposal* canale *m* di scarico

CIA [siːaɪ'eɪ] *abbr* (= **Central Intelligence Agency**) CIA *f*

ci·der ['saɪdə(r)] sidro *m*

CIF [siːaɪ'ef] *abbr* (= **cost insurance freight**) CIF

ci·gar [sɪ'gɑː(r)] sigaro *m*

cig·a·rette [sɪgə'ret] sigaretta *f*

cig·a·rette end mozzicone *m* di sigaretta; **cig·a·rette light·er** accendino *m;* **cig·a·rette pa·per** carta *f* per sigarette

cin·e·ma ['sɪnɪmə] cinema *m*

cin·na·mon ['sɪnəmən] canella *f*

cir·cle ['sɜːkl] **1** *n* cerchio *m;* (group) cerchia *f* **2** *v/t* (draw circle around) cerchiare **3** *v/i of plane* girare in tondo; *of bird* volteggiare

cir·cuit ['sɜːkɪt] ELEC circuito *m;* (lap) giro *m*

'cir·cuit board COMPUT circuito *m* stampato; **'cir·cuit break·er** ELEC interruttore *m* automatico; **'cir·cuit train·ing** SP percorso *m* ginnico

cir·cu·lar ['sɜːkjʊlə(r)] **1** *n giving information* circolare *f* **2** *adj* circolare

cir·cu·late ['sɜːkjʊleɪt] **1** *v/i* circolare **2** *v/t memo* far circolare

cir·cu·la·tion [sɜːkjʊ'leɪʃn] BIO circolazione *f; of newspaper, magazine* tiratura *f*

cir·cum·fer·ence [sə'kʌmfərəns] circonferenza *f*

cir·cum·stanc·es ['sɜːkəmstənsɪs] *npl* circostanze *fpl;* (financial) situazione *fsg* (economica); **under no ~** in nessuna circostanza; **under the ~** date le circostanze

cir·cus ['sɜːkəs] circo *m*

cir·rho·sis (of the liv·er) [sɪ'rəʊsɪs] cirrosi *f* (epatica)

cis·tern ['sɪstən] cisterna *f; of WC* serbatoio *m*

cite [saɪt] *v/t* citare

cit·i·zen ['sɪtɪzən] cittadino *m*, -a *f*

cit·i·zen·ship ['sɪtɪznʃɪp] cittadinanza *f*

cit·rus fruit ['sɪtrəs] agrume *m*

cit·y ['sɪtɪ] città *f inv*

city 'cen·tre centro *m* (della città)

city 'hall sala *f* municipale

civ·ic ['sɪvɪk] *adj* civico

civ·il ['sɪvl] *adj* civile

civ·il en·gi'neer ingegnere *m* civile

ci·vil·i·an [sɪ'vɪljən] **1** *n* civile *m/f* **2** *adj clothes* civile

ci·vil·i·ty [sɪ'vɪlɪtɪ] civiltà *f*

civ·i·li·za·tion [sɪvəlaɪ'zeɪʃn] civilizzazione *f*

civ·i·lize ['sɪvəlaɪz] *v/t person* civilizzare

civ·il 'rights *npl* diritti *mpl* civili; **civ·il 'ser·vant** impiegato *m*, -a *f* statale; **civ·il 'ser·vice** pubblica amministrazione *f;* **civ·il 'war** guerra *f* civile

claim [kleɪm] **1** *n* (request) richiesta *f;* (right) diritto *m;* (assertion) affermazione *f* **2** *v/t* (ask for as a right) rivendicare; *damages* richiedere; (assert) affermare; *lost property* reclamare; *they have ~ed responsibility for the attack* hanno rivendicato l'attentato

claim·ant ['kleɪmənt] richiedente *m/f*

clair·voy·ant [kleə'vɔɪənt] *n* chiaroveggente *m/f*

clam [klæm] vongola *f*

♦ **clam up** *v/i* (pret & pp **-med**) F chiudersi come un riccio

clam·ber ['klæmbə(r)] *v/i* arrampicarsi

clam·my ['klæmɪ] *adj hands* appiccicaticcio; *weather* afoso

clam·or *or Am*, **clam·our** ['klæmə(r)] *noise* clamore *m;* (outcry) protesta *f*

♦ **clamour for** *v/t* chiedere a gran voce

clamp [klæmp] **1** *n fastener* morsa *f;*

for wheel ceppo *m* (bloccaruote)
2 *v/t fasten* bloccare (con una morsa); *fig: hand etc* stringere; *car* mettere i ceppi a

♦ **clamp down** *v/i* usare il pugno di ferro

♦ **clamp down on** *v/t* mettere un freno a

clan [klæn] clan *m inv*

clan·des·tine [klæn'destɪn] *adj* clandestino

clang [klæŋ] **1** *n* suono *m* metallico **2** *v/i*: **~ shut** chiudersi con un suono metallico

clang·er ['klæŋə(r)] F gaffe *f inv*; **drop a ~** fare una gaffe

clap [klæp] *v/t & v/i* (*pret & pp* **-ped**) (*applaud*) applaudire

clar·et ['klærɪt] *wine* claret *m inv*

clar·i·fi·ca·tion [klærɪfɪ'keɪʃn] chiarimento *m*

clar·i·fy ['klærɪfaɪ] *v/t* (*pret & pp* **-ied**) chiarire

clar·i·net [klærɪ'net] clarinetto *m*

clar·i·ty ['klærətɪ] chiarezza *f*

clash [klæʃ] **1** *n* scontro *m* **2** *v/i* scontrarsi; *of opinions* essere in contrasto; *of colours* stonare; *of events* coincidere

clasp [klɑːsp] **1** *n fastener* chiusura *f* **2** *v/t in hand* stringere

class [klɑːs] **1** *n* (*lesson*) lezione *f*; (*group of people, category*) classe *f*; **social ~** classe *f* sociale **2** *v/t* classificare

clas·sic ['klæsɪk] **1** *adj* (*typical*) classico; (*definitive*) eccellente; **she wrote the ~ biography of ...** la sua biografia di ... è un classico **2** *n* classico *m*

clas·si·cal ['klæsɪkl] *adj* classico

clas·si·fi·ca·tion [klæsɪfɪ'keɪʃn] classificazione *f*

clas·si·fied ['klæsɪfaɪd] *adj information* riservato

'clas·si·fied ad·(·ver·tise·ment) inserzione *f*, annuncio *m*

clas·si·fy ['klæsɪfaɪ] *v/t* (*pret & pp* **-ied**) (*categorize*) classificare

'class·mate compagno *m*, -a *f* di classe; **'class·room** aula *f*; **class**

war·fare lotta *f* di classe

classy ['klɑːsɪ] *adj* F d'alta classe

clat·ter ['klætə(r)] **1** *n* frastuono *m* **2** *v/i* fare baccano; **~ down the stairs** scendere rumorosamente le scale

clause [klɔːz] *in agreement* articolo *m*; GRAM proposizione *f*

claus·tro·pho·bi·a [klɔːstrə'fəʊbɪə] claustrofobia *f*

claw [klɔː] **1** *n* artiglio *m*; *of lobster* chela *m* **2** *v/t* (*scratch*) graffiare

clay [kleɪ] argilla *f*

clean [kliːn] **1** *adj* pulito **2** *adv* F (*completely*) completamente **3** *v/t* pulire; *teeth* lavarsi; *car, hands, face* lavare; *clothes* lavare o pulire a secco

♦ **clean out** *v/t room, cupboard* pulire a fondo; *fig* ripulire

♦ **clean up 1** *v/t also fig* ripulire **2** *v/i* pulire; (*wash*) ripulirsi; *on stock market etc* fare fortuna

clean·er ['kliːnə(r)] *male* uomo *m* delle pulizie; *female* donna *f* delle pulizie; (*dry ~*) lavanderia *f*, tintoria *f*

'clean·ing wom·an donna *f* delle pulizie

cleanse [klenz] *v/t skin* detergere

cleans·er ['klenzə(r)] *for skin* detergente *m*

'cleans·ing cream ['klenzɪŋ] latte *f* detergente

clear [klɪə(r)] **1** *adj* chiaro; *weather, sky* sereno; *water, eyes* limpido; *skin* uniforme; *conscience* pulito; **I'm not ~ about it** non l'ho capito bene; **I didn't make myself ~** non mi sono spiegato bene; **I made it ~ to him** gliel'ho fatto capire **2** *adv*: **loud and ~** forte e chiaro; **stand ~ of** stare lontano da; **steer ~ of** stare alla larga da **3** *v/t roads etc* sgomb(e)rare; (*acquit*) scagionare; (*authorize*) autorizzare; (*earn*) guadagnare al netto; *fence* scavalcare con un salto; *debt* saldare; **~ one's throat** schiarirsi la gola; **~ the table** sparecchiare (la tavola) **4** *v/i of sky* schiarirsi; *of mist* diradarsi

♦ **clear away** v/t mettere via

♦ **clear off** v/i F filarsela F

♦ **clear out** 1 v/t *cupboard* sgomb(e)rare 2 v/i sparire

♦ **clear up** 1 v/i (*tidy up*) mettere in ordine; *of weather* schiarirsi; *of illness, rash* sparire 2 v/t (*tidy*) mettere in ordine; *mystery, problem* risolvere

clear·ance ['klıərəns] *space* spazio *m* libero; (*authorization*) autorizzazione *f*

clear·ance sale liquidazione *f*

clear·ing ['klıərıŋ] *in woods* radura *f*

clear·ly ['klıəlı] *adv* chiaramente

cleav·age ['kli:vıdʒ] décolleté *m inv*

cleav·er ['kli:və(r)] mannaia *f*

clem·en·cy ['klemənsı] clemenza *f*

clench [klentʃ] v/t serrare

cler·gy ['klɜ:dʒı] clero *m*

cler·gy·man ['klɜ:dʒımæn] ecclesiastico *m*

clerk [klɑ:k, *Am* klɜ:rk] impiegato *m*, -a *f*; *Am: in shop* commesso *m*, -a *f*

clev·er ['klevə(r)] *adj* intelligente; *gadget, device* ingegnoso; **don't get ~ with me** non fare il furbo con me

clev·er·ly ['klevəlı] *adv* intelligentemente

cli·ché ['kli:ʃeɪ] frase *f* stereotipata

cli·chéd ['kli:ʃeɪd] *adj* stereotipato

click [klık] 1 *n* COMPUT click *m inv* 2 v/i *of camera etc* scattare

♦ **click on** v/t COMPUT cliccare su

cli·ent ['klaɪənt] cliente *m/f*

cli·en·tele [kli:ən'tel] clientela *f*

cliff [klıf] scogliera *f*

cli·mate ['klaɪmət] clima *m*

'**cli·mate change** mutazione *f* climatica

cli·mat·ic [klaɪ'mætık] *adj* climatico

cli·max ['klaɪmæks] *n* punto *m* culminante

climb [klaɪm] 1 *n up mountain* scalata *f*, arrampicata *f* 2 v/t salire su; *clamber up* arrampicarsi su; *mountaineering* scalare 3 v/i *of plane, road, inflation* salire; *clamber* arrampicarsi

♦ **climb down** v/i scendere; *fig* fare marcia indietro

climb·er ['klaɪmə(r)] *person* alpinista *m/f*

climb·ing ['klaɪmıŋ] alpinismo *m*

climb·ing wall *parete f artificiale per esercitarsi nella scalata*

clinch [klıntʃ] v/t *deal* concludere; **that ~es it** questo risolve la questione

cling [klıŋ] v/i (*pret & pp* **clung**) *of clothes* essere attillato

♦ **cling to** v/t *of child* avvinghiarsi a; *ideas, tradition* aggrapparsi a

'**cling·film** pellicola *f* trasparente

cling·y ['klıŋı] *adj child, boyfriend* appiccicoso

clin·ic ['klınık] clinica *f*

clin·i·cal ['klınıkl] *adj* clinico

clink [klıŋk] 1 *n noise* tintinnio *m* 2 v/i tintinnare

clip[1] [klıp] 1 *n fastener* fermaglio *m*; *for hair* molletta *f*; *for paper* graffetta *f* 2 v/t (*pret & pp* **-ped**): **~ sth to sth** attaccare qc a qc

clip[2] [klıp] 1 *n from film* spezzone *f* 2 v/t (*pret & pp* **-ped**) *hair, hedge, grass* tagliare

'**clip·board** fermablocco *m inv*

clip·pers ['klıpəz] *npl for hair* rasoio *m*; *for nails* tronchesina *f*; *for gardening* tosasiepi *fpl*

clip·ping ['klıpıŋ] *from newspaper* ritaglio *m*

clique [kli:k] combriccola *f*

cloak *n* cappa *f*

'**cloak·room** guardaroba *m inv*; (*euph: toilet*) servizi *mpl*

clock [klɒk] orologio *m*; F (*speedometer*) contachilometri *m inv*

'**clock ra·di·o** radiosveglia *f*; '**clock·wise** *adv* in senso orario; '**clock·work** meccanismo *m* di orologio; **it went like ~** è andato liscio come l'olio

♦ **clog up** [klɒg] (*pret & pp* **-ged**) 1 v/i intasarsi 2 v/t intasare

clone [kləʊn] 1 *n* clone *m* 2 v/t clonare

close[1] [kləʊs] 1 *adj family, friend* intimo; *resemblance* stretto; **we are very ~** siamo molto uniti; **be ~ to s.o.** *emotionally* essere vicino a qu

2 *adv* vicino; **~ at hand** a portata di mano; **~ by** nella vicinanze

close² [kləʊz] **1** *v/t* chiudere **2** *v/i of door, eyes* chiudersi; *of shop* chiudere

♦ **close down** *v/t & v/i* chiudere

♦ **close in** *v/i* circondare; *of fog, night* calare

♦ **close up 1** *v/t building* chiudere **2** *v/i (move closer)* avvicinarsi

closed [kləʊzd] *adj* chiuso

closed-cir·cuit 'tel·e·vi·sion televisione *f* a circuito chiuso

'close-knit *adj* affiatato

close·ly ['kləʊslɪ] *adv listen, watch* attentamente; *cooperate* fianco a fianco

clos·et ['klɒzɪt] *Am* armadio *m*

close-up ['kləʊsʌp] primo piano *m*

clos·ing date ['kləʊzɪŋ] termine *m*

clos·ing time ['kləʊzɪŋ] ora *f* di chiusura

clo·sure ['kləʊʒə(r)] chiusura *f*

clot [klɒt] **1** *n of blood* grumo *m* **2** *v/i (pret & pp -ted) of blood* coagularsi

cloth [klɒθ] *(fabric)* tessuto *m*; *for cleaning* straccio *m*

clothes [kləʊðz] *npl* vestiti *mpl*

'clothes brush spazzola *f* per vestiti; **'clothes hang·er** attaccapanni *m inv*; **'clothes·horse** stendibiancheria *m inv*; **'clothes·line** filo *m* stendibiancheria *inv*; **'clothes peg** molletta *f* per i panni

cloth·ing ['kləʊðɪŋ] abbigliamento *m*

cloud [klaʊd] *n* nuvola *f*; **a ~ of smoke/dust** una nuvola di fumo/polvere

♦ **cloud over** *v/i of sky* rannuvolarsi

'cloud·burst temporale *m*

cloud·less ['klaʊdlɪs] *adj sky* sereno

cloud·y ['klaʊdɪ] *adj* nuvoloso

clout [klaʊt] F *(blow)* botta *f*; *(fig: influence)* impatto *m*

clove of 'gar·lic [kləʊv] spicchio *m* d'aglio

clown [klaʊn] *in circus* pagliaccio *m*; *(joker, also pej)* pagliaccio *m*

club [klʌb] *n weapon* clava *f*; *in golf* mazza *f*; *organization* club *m inv*

clue [kluː] indizio *m*; **I haven't a ~** F non ne ho la minima idea; **he hasn't a ~** *(is useless)* non ci capisce niente

clued-up [kluːd'ʌp] *adj* F beninformato

clump [klʌmp] *n of earth* zolla *f*; *group* gruppo *m*

clum·si·ness ['klʌmzɪnɪs] goffaggine *f*

clum·sy ['klʌmzɪ] *adj person* goffo, maldestro

clung [klʌŋ] *pret & pp* → **cling**

clus·ter ['klʌstə(r)] **1** *n* gruppo *m* **2** *v/i of people* raggrupparsi; *of houses* essere raggruppato

clutch [klʌtʃ] **1** *n* MOT frizione *f* **2** *v/t* stringere

♦ **clutch at** *v/t* cercare di afferrare

clut·ter ['klʌtə(r)] **1** *n* oggetti *mpl* alla rinfusa **2** *v/t (also: ~ up)* ingombrare

Co. *abbr* (= **Company**) C.ia (= compagnia)

c/o *abbr* (= **care of**) presso

coach [kəʊtʃ] **1** *n (trainer)* allenatore *m*, -trice *f*; *of singer etc* maestro *m*, -a *f*; *on train* vagone *m*; *(Br: bus)* pullman *m inv* **2** *v/t* allenare; *singer, actor* dare lezioni a

coach·ing ['kəʊtʃɪŋ] allenamento *m*; *of singer, actor* lezioni *fpl*

'coach par·ty gruppo *m* di turisti; **'coach sta·tion** stazione *f* dei pullman; **'coach tour** viaggio *m* turistico in pullman

co·ag·u·late [kəʊ'ægjʊleɪt] *v/i of blood* coagularsi

coal [kəʊl] carbone *m*

co·a·li·tion [kəʊə'lɪʃn] coalizione *f*

'coal·mine miniera *f* di carbone

coarse [kɔːs] *adj skin, fabric* ruvido; *hair* spesso; *(vulgar)* grossolano

coarse·ly ['kɔːslɪ] *adv (vulgarly)* grossolanamente; *ground* a grani grossi

coast [kəʊst] *n* costa *f*; **at the ~** sulla costa

coast·al ['kəʊstl] *adj* costiero

coast·er ['kəʊstə(r)] *for glass* sottobicchiere *m*; *for bottle* sottobottiglia *m* '**coast·guard** *organization, person* guardia *f* costiera

'**coast·line** costa *f*, litorale *m*

coat [kəʊt] **1** *n* (*over~*) cappotto *m*; *of animal* pelliccia *f*; *of paint etc* mano *f* **2** *v/t* (*cover*) ricoprire

'**coat·hang·er** attaccapanni *m inv*, gruccia *f*

coat·ing ['kəʊtɪŋ] strato *m*

co·au·thor ['kəʊɔːθə(r)] **1** *n* co-autore *m*, -trice *f* **2** *v/t* scrivere insieme

coax [kəʊks] *v/t* convincere con le moine; ~ **sth out of s.o.** ottenere qc da qu con le moine

cob·bled ['kɒbld] *adj* lastricato (a ciottoli)

cob·ble·stone ['kɒblstəʊn] ciottolo *m*

cob·web ['kɒbweb] ragnatela *f*

co·caine [kə'keɪn] cocaina *f*

cock [kɒk] *n chicken* gallo *m*; *any male bird* maschio *m* (di uccelli); V (*penis*) cazzo *m* V

cock·eyed [kɒk'aɪd] *adj* F *idea etc* strampalato

'**cock·pit** *of plane* cabina *f* (di pilotaggio)

cock·roach ['kɒkrəʊtʃ] scarafaggio *m*

'**cock·tail** cocktail *m inv*

'**cock·tail par·ty** cocktail party *m inv*

'**cock·tail shak·er** shaker *m inv*

cock·y ['kɒkɪ] *adj* F arrogante

co·coa ['kəʊkəʊ] *drink* cioccolata *f* calda

co·co·nut ['kəʊkənʌt] cocco *m*

co·co·nut palm palma *f* di cocco

COD [siːəʊ'diː] *abbr* (= *cash on delivery*) pagamento *m* contrassegno

cod·dle ['kɒdl] *v/t sick person* coccolare; *pej: child* viziare

code [kəʊd] *n* codice *m*

co·ed·u·ca·tion·al [kəʊedjʊ'keɪʃnl] *adj* misto

co·erce [kəʊ'ɜːs] *v/t* costringere

co·ex·ist [kəʊɪg'zɪst] *v/i* coesistere

co·ex·ist·ence [kəʊɪg'zɪstəns] coesistenza *f*

cof·fee ['kɒfɪ] caffè *m inv*

'**cof·fee bar** caffè *m inv*; '**cof·fee bean** chicco *m* di caffè; '**cof·fee break** pausa *f* per il caffè; '**cof·fee cup** tazza *f* da caffè; '**cof·fee grind·er** ['graɪndə(r)] macinacaffè *m inv*; '**cof·fee mak·er** caffettiera *f*; '**cof·fee pot** caffettiera *f*; '**cof·fee shop** caffetteria *f*; '**cof·fee ta·ble** tavolino *m*

cof·fin ['kɒfɪn] bara *f*

cog [kɒg] dente *m*

co·gnac ['kɒnjæk] cognac *m inv*

'**cog·wheel** ruota *f* dentata

co·hab·it [kəʊ'hæbɪt] *v/i* convivere

co·her·ent [kəʊ'hɪərənt] *adj* coerente

coil [kɔɪl] **1** *n of rope* rotolo *m* **2** *v/t*: ~ (*up*) avvolgere

coin [kɔɪn] *n* moneta *f*

co·in·cide [kəʊɪn'saɪd] *v/i* coincidere

co·in·ci·dence [kəʊ'ɪnsɪdəns] coincidenza *f*

coke [kəʊk] P (*cocaine*) coca P *f*

Coke® [kəʊk] Coca® *f*

cold [kəʊld] **1** *adj* freddo; *I'm* (*feeling*) ~ ho freddo; *it's* ~ *of weather* fa freddo; *in* ~ *blood* a sangue freddo; *get* ~ *feet* F farsi prendere dalla fifa F **2** *n* freddo *m*; MED raffreddore *m*; *I have a* ~ ho il raffreddore

cold-blood·ed [kəʊld'blʌdɪd] *adj also murder* a sangue freddo; *person* spietato

cold 'call·ing porta-a-porta *m*; *by phone* televendite *fpl*

'**cold cuts** *npl* affettati *mpl*

cold·ly ['kəʊldlɪ] *adv* freddamente

cold 'meat affettati *mpl*

cold·ness ['kəʊldnɪs] *fig* freddezza *f*

'**cold sore** febbre *f* del labbro

cole·slaw ['kəʊlslɔː] *insalata f di cavolo, carote, cipolle tritati e maionese*

col·ic ['kɒlɪk] colica *f*

col·lab·o·rate [kə'læbəreɪt] *v/i* collaborare

col·lab·o·ra·tion [kəlæbə'reɪʃn] collaborazione *f*; *with enemy* collaborazionismo *m*

col·lab·o·ra·tor [kə'læbəreɪtə(r)] collaboratore *m*, -trice *f*; *with enemy* collaborazionista *m/f*

col·lapse [kə'læps] *v/i* crollare; *of*

person accasciarsi

col·lap·si·ble [kəˈlæpsəbl] *adj* pieghevole

col·lar [ˈkɒlə(r)] collo *m*, colletto *m*; *of dog, cat* collare *m*

'col·lar-bone clavicola *f*

col·league [ˈkɒliːg] collega *m/f*

col·lect [kəˈlekt] **1** *v/t person*: go andare a prendere; *person*: come venire a prendere; *tickets, cleaning etc* ritirare; *as hobby* collezionare; *(gather)* raccogliere **2** *v/i (gather together)* radunarsi **3** *adv Am*: *call ~* telefonare a carico del destinatario

col·lect·ed [kəˈlektɪd] *adj person* controllato; *the ~ works of ...* l'opera omnia di ...

col·lec·tion [kəˈlekʃn] collezione *f*; *in church* colletta *f*; *of poems, stories* raccolta *f*

col·lec·tive [kəˈlektɪv] *adj* collettivo

col·lec·tive 'bar·gain·ing trattative *fpl* sindacali

col·lec·tor [kəˈlektə(r)] collezionista *m/f*

col·lege [ˈkɒlɪdʒ] istituto *m* parauniversitario; *at Oxford and Cambridge* college *m inv*

col·lide [kəˈlaɪd] *v/i* scontrarsi

col·li·sion [kəˈlɪʒn] collisione *f*, scontro *m*

col·lo·qui·al [kəˈləʊkwɪəl] *adj* colloquiale

co·lon [ˈkəʊlən] *punctuation* due punti *mpl*; ANAT colon *m inv*

colo·nel [ˈkɜːnl] colonnello *m*

co·lo·ni·al [kəˈləʊnɪəl] *adj* coloniale

co·lo·nize [ˈkɒlənaɪz] *v/t country* colonizzare

co·lo·ny [ˈkɒlənɪ] colonia *f*

col·or *etc Am* → **colour** *etc*

co·los·sal [kəˈlɒsl] *adj* colossale

col·our [ˈkʌlə(r)] **1** *n* colore *m*; *in cheeks* colorito *m*; *in ~ film etc* a colori; *~s* MIL bandiera *f* **2** *v/t* colorare; *one's hair* tingere **3** *v/i (blush)* diventare rosso

'col·our-blind *adj* daltonico

col·oured [ˈkʌləd] *adj person* di colore

'col·our fast *adj* con colori resistenti

col·our·ful [ˈkʌləful] *adj* pieno di colori; *account* pittoresco

col·our·ing [ˈkʌlərɪŋ] colorito *m*

'col·our pho·to·graph fotografia *f* a colori

'col·our scheme abbinamento *m* dei colori

'col·our TV tv *f inv* a colori

colt [kəʊlt] puledro *m*

col·umn [ˈkɒləm] colonna *f*; *(newspaper feature)* rubrica *f*

col·umn·ist [ˈkɒləm(n)ɪst] giornalista *m/f* che cura una rubrica

co·ma [ˈkəʊmə] coma *m inv*

comb [kəʊm] **1** *n* pettine *m* **2** *v/t* pettinare; *area* rastrellare

com·bat [ˈkɒmbæt] **1** *n* combattimento *m* **2** *v/t* combattere

com·bi·na·tion [kɒmbɪˈneɪʃn] combinazione *f*

com·bine [kəmˈbaɪn] **1** *v/t* unire; *ingredients* mescolare **2** *v/i of chemical elements* combinarsi

com·bine har·vest·er [kɒmbaɪnˈhɑːvɪstə(r)] mietitrebbia *f*

com·bus·ti·ble [kəmˈbʌstɪbl] *adj* combustibile

com·bus·tion [kəmˈbʌstʃn] combustione *f*

come [kʌm] *v/i (pret came, pp come)* venire; *of train, bus* arrivare; *you'll ~ to like it* finirà per piacerti; *how ~?* F come mai? F

♦ **come about** *v/i (happen)* succedere

♦ **come across 1** *v/t (find)* trovare **2** *v/i of idea, humour* essere capito; *she comes across as ...* dà l'impressione di essere ...

♦ **come along** *v/i (come too)* venire; *(turn up)* presentarsi; *(progress)* fare progressi; *how is it coming along?* come sta andando?; *your Italian has come along a lot* il tuo italiano è migliorato molto

♦ **come apart** *v/i* smontarsi; *(break)* andare in pezzi

♦ **come away** *v/i of person, button* venire via

♦ **come back** *v/i* ritornare; *it came back to me* mi è tornato in mente

♦ come by 1 v/i passare 2 v/t (*acquire*) ottenere

♦ come down v/i venire giù; *in price, amount etc* scendere; *of rain, snow* cadere; **he came down the stairs** è sceso dalle scale

♦ come for v/t (*attack*) assalire; (*collect*) venire a prendere

♦ come forward v/i (*present o.s.*) farsi avanti

♦ come from v/t venire da; **where do you come from?** di dove sei?

♦ come in v/i entrare; *of train, in race* arrivare; *of tide* salire; **come in!** entra!

♦ come in for v/t attirare; **come in for criticism** attirare delle critiche

♦ come in on v/t partecipare a; **come in on a deal** stare a un accordo

♦ come off v/i *of handle etc* staccarsi

♦ come on v/i (*progress*) fare progressi; **how's the work coming on?** come sta venendo il lavoro?; **come on!** dai!; *in disbelief* ma dai!

♦ come out v/i *of person, book, sun* uscire; *of results, product* venir fuori; *of stain* venire via; *of gay* rendere nota la propria omosessualità

♦ come round v/i *to s.o.'s home* passare; (*regain consciousness*) rinvenire

♦ come to 1 v/t *place, position* arrivare a; **that comes to £70** fanno 70 sterline 2 v/i (*regain consciousness*) rinvenire

♦ come up v/i salire; *of sun* sorgere; **something has come up** si è presentato qualcosa

♦ come up with v/t *new idea etc* venir fuori con

'come·back ritorno m; **make a ~** tornare alla ribalta

co·me·di·an [kə'miːdiən] comico m, -a f; *pej* buffone m

'come·down passo m indietro

com·e·dy ['kɒmədi] commedia f

com·et ['kɒmɪt] cometa f

come·up·pance [kʌm'ʌpəns] n F: **he'll get his ~** avrà quello che si merita

com·fort ['kʌmfət] 1 n comodità f inv; (*consolation*) conforto m 2 v/t confortare

'com·for·ta·ble ['kʌmfətəbl] adj chair, room comodo; **be ~ in chair** stare comodo; *in situation* essere a proprio agio; (*financially*) essere agiato

com·fy ['kʌmfɪ] adj F → **comfortable**

com·ic ['kɒmɪk] 1 n *to read* fumetto m; (*comedian*) comico m, -a f 2 adj comico

com·i·cal ['kɒmɪkl] adj comico

com·ic book fumetto m

com·ic strip striscia f (di fumetti)

com·ma ['kɒmə] virgola f

com·mand [kə'mɑːnd] 1 n comando m 2 v/t person comandare a

com·man·deer [kɒmən'dɪə(r)] v/t appropriarsi di

com·mand·er [kə'mɑːndə(r)] comandante m

com·mand·er-in-'chief comandante m in capo

com·mand·ing of·fi·cer [kə'mɑːndɪŋ] ufficiale m comandante

com·mand·ment [kə'mɑːndmənt]: **the Ten Commandments** REL i Dieci Comandamenti

com·mem·o·rate [kə'meməreɪt] v/t commemorare

com·mem·o·ra·tion [kəmemə'reɪʃn]: **in ~ of** in commemorazione di

com·mence [kə'mens] v/t & v/i cominciare

com·mend [kə'mend] v/t (*praise*) lodare; (*recommend*) raccomandare

com·mend·a·ble [kə'mendəbl] adj lodevole

com·men·da·tion [kɒmen'deɪʃn] *for bravery* riconoscimento m

com·men·su·rate [kə'menʃərət] adj: **~ with** commisurato a

com·ment ['kɒment] 1 n commento m; **no ~!** no comment! 2 v/i fare commenti

com·men·ta·ry ['kɒməntrɪ] cronaca f

com·men·tate ['kɒmenteɪt] v/i commentare

com·men·ta·tor [ˈkɒmənteɪtə(r)] *on TV* telecronista *m/f*; *on radio* radiocronista *m/f*

com·merce [ˈkɒmɜːs] commercio *m*

com·mer·cial [kəˈmɜːʃl] **1** *adj* commerciale **2** *n* (*advert*) pubblicità *f inv*

com·mer·cial ˈbreak interruzione *f* pubblicitaria

com·mer·cial·ize [kəˈmɜːʃlaɪz] *v/t Christmas etc* commercializzare

com·mer·cial ˈtel·e·vi·sion televisione *f* privata

com·mer·cial ˈtrav·el·ler rappresentante *m/f*

com·mis·e·rate [kəˈmɪzəreɪt] *v/i* esprimere rincrescimento (**with** a)

com·mis·sion [kəˈmɪʃn] **1** *n* (*payment*, *committee*) commissione *f*; (*job*) incarico *m* **2** *v/t for a job* incaricare

com·mis·sion·aire [kəmɪʃəˈneə(r)] portiere *m*

Com·mis·sion·er [kəˈmɪʃənə(r)] *in European Union* Commissario *m*, -a *f*

com·mit [kəˈmɪt] *v/t* (*pret & pp* **-ted**) *crime* commettere; *money* assegnare; **~ o.s.** impegnarsi

com·mit·ment [kəˈmɪtmənt] impegno *m*

com·mit·tee [kəˈmɪtɪ] comitato *m*

com·mod·i·ty [kəˈmɒdətɪ] prodotto *m*

com·mon [ˈkɒmən] *adj* comune; **in ~** in comune; **have sth in ~ with s.o.** avere qc in comune con qu

com·mon·er [ˈkɒmənə(r)] persona *f* non nobile

com·mon ˈlaw husband/ wife *convivente al quale spettano legalmente i diritti di una moglie/ un marito*

com·mon·ly [ˈkɒmənlɪ] *adv* comunemente

Com·mon ˈMar·ket Mercato *m* Comune

ˈcom·mon·place *adj* luogo *m* comune

Com·mons [ˈkɒmənz] *npl*: **the ~** la Camera dei Comuni

com·mon ˈsense buon senso *m*

com·mo·tion [kəˈməʊʃn] confusione *f*

com·mu·nal [ˈkɒmjʊnl] *adj* comune

com·mu·nal·ly [ˈkɒmjʊnəlɪ] *adv* in comune

com·mu·ni·cate [kəˈmjuːnɪkeɪt] *v/t & v/i* comunicare

com·mu·ni·ca·tion [kəmjuːnɪˈkeɪʃn] comunicazione *f*

com·mu·ni·ca·tions *npl* comunicazioni *fpl*

com·mu·ni·ca·tions sat·el·lite satellite *m* per telecomunicazioni

com·mu·ni·ca·tive [kəˈmjuːnɪkətɪv] *adj person* comunicativo

Com·mu·nion [kəˈmjuːnɪən] REL comunione *f*

com·mu·ni·qué [kəˈmjuːnɪkeɪ] comunicato *m* ufficiale

Com·mu·nis·m [ˈkɒmjʊnɪzm] comunismo *m*

Com·mu·nist [ˈkɒmjʊnɪst] **1** *adj* comunista **2** *n* comunista *m/f*

com·mu·ni·ty [kəˈmjuːnətɪ] comunità *f inv*

com·mu·ni·ty ˈcen·tre centro *m* comunitario

com·mu·ni·ty ˈserv·ice servizio *m* civile (come pena per reati minori)

com·mute [kəˈmjuːt] **1** *v/i* fare il/la pendolare **2** *v/t* LAW commutare

com·mut·er [kəˈmjuːtə(r)] pendolare *m/f*

com·mut·er ˈtraf·fic traffico *m* dei pendolari

com·mut·er ˈtrain treno *m* dei pendolari

com·pact [kəmˈpækt] **1** *adj* compatto **2** *n* [ˈkɒmpækt] *for powder* portacipria *m inv*

com·pact ˈdisc → *CD*

com·pan·ion [kəmˈpænjən] compagno *m*, -a *f*

com·pan·ion·ship [kəmˈpænjənʃɪp] compagnia *f*

com·pa·ny [ˈkʌmpənɪ] COM società *f inv*; (*ballet ~, theatre ~*) compagnia *f*; (*companionship*, *guests*) compagnia *f*

com·pa·ny: **keep s.o. ~** fare compagnia a qu

com·pa·ny 'car auto *f inv* della ditta

com·pa·ny 'law diritto *m* societario

com·pa·ra·ble ['kɒmpərəbl] *adj* paragonabile; (*similar*) simile

com·par·a·tive [kəm'pærətɪv] **1** *adj* (*relative*) relativo; *study, method* comparato; GRAM comparativo **2** *n* GRAM comparativo *m*

com·par·a·tive·ly [kəm'pærətɪvlɪ] *adv* relativamente

com·pare [kəm'peə(r)] **1** *v/t* paragonare; **~ sth with sth / s.o. with s.o.** paragonare qc a qc / qu a qu; **~d with ...** rispetto a ... **2** *v/i* reggere il confronto; *how did he ~?* com'era rispetto agli altri?

com·pa·ri·son [kəm'pærɪsn] paragone *m*, confronto *m*; *in ~ with* in confronto a; *there's no ~* non c'è paragone

com·part·ment [kəm'pɑːtmənt] scomparto *m*; RAIL scompartimento *m*

com·pass ['kʌmpəs] bussola *f*; (*pair of*) ~*es* for geometry compasso *m*

com·pas·sion [kəm'pæʃn] compassione *f*

com·pas·sion·ate [kəm'pæʃənət] *adj* compassionevole

com·pas·sion·ate leave congedo *m* per motivi familiari

com·pat·i·bil·i·ty [kəmpætə'bɪlɪtɪ] compatibilità *f inv*

com·pat·i·ble [kəm'pætəbl] *adj also* COMPUT compatibile; *we're not ~* siamo incompatibili

com·pel [kəm'pel] *v/t* (*pret & pp -led*) costringere

com·pel·ling [kəm'pelɪŋ] *adj* argument convincente; *film, book* avvincente

com·pen·sate ['kɒmpənseɪt] **1** *v/t with money* risarcire **2** *v/i:* **~ for** compensare

com·pen·sa·tion [kɒmpən'seɪʃn] *money* risarcimento *m*; *reward* vantaggio *m*; *comfort* consolazione *f*

com·père ['kɒmpeə(r)] presentatore *m*, -trice *f*

com·pete [kəm'piːt] *v/i* competere;

(*take part*) gareggiare; **~ for** contendersi

com·pe·tence ['kɒmpɪtəns] competenza *f*

com·pe·tent ['kɒmpɪtənt] *adj* competente

com·pe·tent·ly ['kɒmpɪtəntlɪ] *adv* con competenza

com·pe·ti·tion [kɒmpə'tɪʃn] (*contest*) concorso *m*; SP gara *f*; (*competing, competitors*) concorrenza *f*

com·pet·i·tive [kəm'petɪtɪv] *adj* competitivo; *sport* agonistico; *price, offer* concorrenziale

com·pet·i·tive·ly [kəm'petɪtɪvlɪ] *adv:* **~ priced** a prezzi concorrenziali

com·pet·i·tive·ness competitività *f inv*

com·pet·i·tor [kəm'petɪtə(r)] *in contest* concorrente *m/f*; *our ~s* COM la concorrenza

com·pile [kəm'paɪl] *v/t* compilare

com·pla·cen·cy [kəm'pleɪsənsɪ] autocompiacimento *m*

com·pla·cent [kəm'pleɪsənt] *adj* compiaciuto; *be ~ about sth* compiacersi di qc

com·plain [kəm'pleɪn] *v/i* lamentarsi; *to shop, manager* reclamare; **~ of** MED accusare

com·plaint [kəm'pleɪnt] lamentela *f*; *to shop* reclamo *m*; MED disturbo *m*

com·ple·ment ['kɒmplɪmənt] *v/t* completare; *they ~ each other* si completano bene

com·ple·men·ta·ry [kɒmplɪ'mentərɪ] *adj* complementare

com·plete [kəm'pliːt] **1** *adj* (*total*) completo; (*finished*) terminato; *I made a ~ fool of myself* mi sono comportato da perfetto idiota **2** *v/t task, building etc* completare; *form* compilare

com·plete·ly [kəm'pliːtlɪ] *adv* completamente

com·ple·tion [kəm'pliːʃn] completamento *m*; *payment on ~* pagamento a conclusione lavori

com·plex ['kɒmpleks] **1** *adj* complesso **2** *n also* PSYCH complesso *m*

com·plex·ion [kəm'plekʃn] *facial carnagione f*

com·plex·i·ty [kəm'pleksɪtɪ] complessità *f inv*

com·pli·ance [kəm'plaɪəns] conformità *f inv*

com·pli·cate ['kɒmplɪkeɪt] *v/t* complicare

com·pli·cat·ed ['kɒmplɪkeɪtɪd] *adj* complicato

com·pli·ca·tion [kɒmplɪ'keɪʃn] complicazione *f;* **~s** MED complicazioni

com·pli·ment ['kɒmplɪmənt] **1** *n* complimento *m* **2** *v/t* fare i complimenti a

com·pli·men·ta·ry [kɒmplɪ'mentərɪ] *adj* lusinghiero; (*free*) in omaggio

'com·pli·ments slip ['kɒmplɪmənts] biglietto *m* intestato della ditta

com·ply [kəm'plaɪ] *v/i (pret & pp -ied)* ubbidire; **~ with** osservare; *of products, equipment* essere conforme a

com·po·nent [kəm'pəʊnənt] componente *m*

com·pose [kəm'pəʊz] *v/t also* MUS comporre; **be ~d of** essere composto da; **~ o.s.** ricomporsi

com·posed [kəm'pəʊzd] *adj (calm)* calmo

com·pos·er [kəm'pəʊzə(r)] MUS compositore *m*, -trice *f*

com·po·si·tion [kɒmpə'zɪʃn] *also* MUS composizione *f;* (*essay*) tema *m*

com·po·sure [kəm'pəʊʒə(r)] calma *f*

com·pound ['kɒmpaʊnd] *n* CHEM composto *m*

com·pound 'in·ter·est interesse *m* composto

com·pre·hend [kɒmprɪ'hend] *v/t* (*understand*) capire

com·pre·hen·sion [kɒmprɪ'henʃn] comprensione *f*

com·pre·hen·sive [kɒmprɪ'hensɪv] *adj* esauriente

com·pre·hen·sive in'sur·ance polizza *f* casco

com·pre·hen·sive·ly [kɒmprɪ'hensɪvlɪ] *adv* in modo esauriente

com·pre·hen·sive school scuola *f* secondaria

com·press ['kɒmpres] **1** *n* MED impacco *m* **2** *v/t* [kəm'pres] *air, gas* comprimere; *information* condensare

com·prise [kəm'praɪz] *v/t* comprendere; (*make-up*) costituire; **be ~d of** essere composto da

com·pro·mise ['kɒmprəmaɪz] **1** *n* compromesso *m* **2** *v/i* arrivare a un compromesso **3** *v/t* (*jeopardize*) compromettere; **~ o.s.** compromettersi

com·pul·sion [kəm'pʌlʃn] PSYCH coazione *f*

com·pul·sive [kəm'pʌlsɪv] *adj behaviour* patologico; *reading, viewing* avvincente

com·pul·so·ry [kəm'pʌlsərɪ] *adj* obbligatorio; **~ education** scuola *f* dell'obbligo

com·put·er [kəm'pjuːtə(r)] computer *m inv;* **have sth on ~** avere qc sul computer

com·put·er-aid·ed de'sign progettazione *f* assistita dall'elaboratore; **com·put·er-aid·ed man·u'fac·ture** produzione *f* computerizzata; **com·put·er-con'trolled** *adj* controllato dal computer; **com'puter game** computer game *m inv*

com·put·er·ize [kəm'pjuːtəraɪz] *v/t* computerizzare

com·put·er 'lit·er·ate *adj* che ha dimestichezza con il computer; **com·put·er 'sci·ence** informatica *f;* **com·put·er 'sci·en·tist** informatico *m*, -a *f*

com·put·ing [kəm'pjuːtɪŋ] *n* informatica *f*

com·rade ['kɒmreɪd] *also* POL compagno *m*, -a *f*

com·rade·ship ['kɒmreɪdʃɪp] cameratismo *m*

con [kɒn] **1** *n* F truffa *f* **2** *v/t* (*pret & pp -ned*) F truffare; **~ s.o. into doing sth** far fare qc a qu con l'inganno

con·ceal [kən'siːl] *v/t* nascondere

con·ceal·ment [kən'siːlmənt] occultazione *f*

con·cede [kən'siːd] *v/t* (*admit*) am-

mettere; *goal* concedere
con·ceit [kən'siːt] presunzione *f*
con·ceit·ed [kən'siːtɪd] *adj* presuntuoso
con·cei·va·ble [kən'siːvəbl] *adj* concepibile
con·ceive [kən'siːv] *v/i of woman* concepire; ~ *of* (*imagine*) immaginare
con·cen·trate ['kɒnsəntreɪt] **1** *v/i* concentrarsi **2** *v/t one's attention, energies* concentrare
con·cen·trat·ed ['kɒnsəntreɪtɪd] *adj juice etc* concentrato
con·cen·tra·tion [kɒnsən'treɪʃn] concentrazione *f*
con·cept ['kɒnsept] concetto *m*
con·cep·tion [kən'sepʃn] *of child* concepimento *m*
con·cern [kən'sɜːn] **1** *n* (*anxiety*) preoccupazione *f*; (*care*) interesse *m*; (*business*) affare *m*; (*company*) impresa *f*; *there's no cause for* ~ non c'è motivo di preoccuparsi; *it's none of your* ~ non sono affari tuoi **2** *v/t* (*involve*) riguardare; (*worry*) preoccupare; ~ *o.s. with* preoccuparsi di
con·cerned [kən'sɜːnd] *adj* (*anxious*) preoccupato; (*caring*) interessato; (*involved*) in questione; *as far as I'm* ~ per quanto mi riguarda
con·cern·ing [kən'sɜːnɪŋ] *prep* riguardo a
con·cert ['kɒnsət] concerto *m*
con·cert·ed [kən'sɜːtɪd] *adj* (*joint*) congiunto
con·cer·to [kən'tʃeətəʊ] concerto *m*
con·ces·sion [kən'seʃn] (*compromise*) concessione *f*
con·cil·i·a·to·ry [kənsɪlɪ'eɪtərɪ] *adj* conciliatorio
con·cise [kən'saɪs] *adj* conciso
con·clude [kən'kluːd] **1** *v/t* concludere; ~ *sth from sth* concludere qc da qc **2** *v/i* concludere
con·clu·sion [kən'kluːʒn] conclusione *f*; *in* ~ in conclusione
con·clu·sive [kən'kluːsɪv] *adj* conclusivo

con·coct [kən'kɒkt] *v/t meal, drink* mettere insieme; *excuse, story* inventare
con·coc·tion [kən'kɒkʃn] *food, drink* intruglio *m*
con·crete¹ ['kɒŋkriːt] *adj* concreto
con·crete² ['kɒŋkriːt] *n* calcestruzzo *m*; ~ *jungle* giungla *f* di cemento
con·cur [kən'kɜː(r)] *v/i* (*pret & pp -red*) essere d'accordo
con·cus·sion [kən'kʌʃn] commozione *f* cerebrale
con·demn [kən'dem] *v/t action* condannare; *building* dichiarare inagibile; (*doom*) condannare
con·dem·na·tion [kɒndəm'neɪʃn] *of action* condanna *f*
con·den·sa·tion [kɒnden'seɪʃn] *on walls, windows* condensa *f*
con·dense [kən'dens] **1** *v/t* (*make shorter*) condensare **2** *v/i of steam* condensarsi
con·densed 'milk [kən'densd] latte *m* condensato
con·de·scend [kɒndɪ'send] *v/i: he ~ed to speak to me* si è degnato di rivolgermi la parola
con·de·scend·ing [kɒndɪ'sendɪŋ] *adj* (*patronizing*) borioso
con·di·tion [kən'dɪʃn] **1** *n* condizione *f*; MED malattia *f*; ~*s* (*circumstances*) condizioni; *on* ~ *that* a condizione che; *in / out of* ~ in / fuori forma **2** *v/t* PSYCH condizionare
con·di·tion·al [kən'dɪʃnl] **1** *adj* acceptance condizionale **2** *n* GRAM condizionale *m*
con·di·tion·er [kən'dɪʃnə(r)] *for hair* balsamo *m*; *for fabric* ammorbidente *m*
con·di·tion·ing [kən'dɪʃnɪŋ] PSYCH condizionamento *m*
con·do·lenc·es [kən'dəʊlənsɪz] *npl* condoglianze *fpl*
con·dom ['kɒndəm] preservativo *m*
con·done [kən'dəʊn] *v/t actions* scusare
con·du·cive [kən'djuːsɪv] *adj: be* ~ *to* favorire
con·duct ['kɒndʌkt] **1** *n* (*behaviour*)

con·dot·ta *f* **2** *v/t* [kənˈdʌkt] (*carry out*) condurre; ELEC condurre; MUS dirigere; **~ o.s.** comportarsi

con·duct·ed tour [kənˈdʌktɪd] visita *f* guidata

con·duc·tor [kənˈdʌktə(r)] MUS direttore *m* d'orchestra; *on bus* bigliettaio *m*; PHYS conduttore *m*

con·duc·tress [kənˈdʌktrɪs] bigliettaia *f*

cone [kəʊn] cono *m*; *of pine tree* pigna *f*; *on motorway* birillo *m*

♦ **cone off** *v/t* chiudere al traffico

con·fec·tion·er [kənˈfekʃənə(r)] pasticciere *m*, **-a** *f*

con·fec·tion·e·ry [kənˈfekʃənərɪ] dolciumi *mpl*

con·fed·e·ra·tion [kənfedəˈreɪʃn] confederazione *f*

con·fer [kənˈfɜː(r)] (*pret & pp* **-red**) **1** *v/t* (*bestow*) conferire **2** *v/i* (*discuss*) confabulare

con·fe·rence [ˈkɒnfərəns] congresso *m*; **family ~** consiglio *m* di famiglia

'con·fe·rence cen·tre centro *m* congressi

'con·fe·rence room sala *f* riunioni

con·fess [kənˈfes] **1** *v/t* *sin, crime* confessare **2** *v/i* confessare; REL confessarsi; **~ to sth** confessare qc; **~ to a weakness for sth** confessare di avere un debole per qc

con·fes·sion [kənˈfeʃn] confessione *f*

con·fes·sion·al [kənˈfeʃnl] REL confessionale *m*

con·fes·sor [kənˈfesə(r)] REL confessore *m*

con·fide [kənˈfaɪd] **1** *v/t* confidare **2** *v/i*: **~ in s.o.** confidarsi con qu

con·fi·dence [ˈkɒnfɪdəns] (*assurance*) sicurezza *f* (di sé); (*trust*) fiducia *f*; **in ~** in confidenza

con·fi·dent [ˈkɒnfɪdənt] *adj* sicuro; *person* sicuro di sé

con·fi·den·tial [kɒnfɪˈdenʃl] *adj* riservato, confidenziale; *adviser* di fiducia

con·fi·den·tial·ly [kɒnfɪˈdenʃlɪ] *adv* in confidenza

con·fi·dent·ly [ˈkɒnfɪdəntlɪ] *adv* con sicurezza

con·fine [kənˈfaɪn] *v/t* (*imprison*) richiudere; (*restrict*) limitare; **be ~d to one's bed** essere costretto a letto

con·fined [kənˈfaɪnd] *adj* *space* ristretto

con·fine·ment [kənˈfaɪnmənt] (*imprisonment*) reclusione *f*; MED parto *m*

con·firm [kənˈfɜːm] *v/t* confermare

con·fir·ma·tion [kɒnfəˈmeɪʃn] conferma *f*

con·firmed [kɒnˈfɜːmd] *adj* *bachelor* incallito

con·fis·cate [ˈkɒnfɪskeɪt] *v/t* sequestrare

con·flict [ˈkɒnflɪkt] **1** *n* conflitto *m* **2** *v/i* [kənˈflɪkt] *of statements, accounts* essere in conflitto; *of dates* coincidere

con·form [kənˈfɔːm] *v/i* conformarsi; **~ to** *of products, acts etc* essere conforme a

con·form·ist [kənˈfɔːmɪst] *n* conformista *m/f*

con·front [kənˈfrʌnt] *v/t* (*face*) affrontare; **~ s.o. with sth** mettere qu di fronte a; **the problems ~ing us** i problemi che dobbiamo affrontare

con·fron·ta·tion [kɒnfrənˈteɪʃn] scontro *m*

con·fuse [kənˈfjuːz] *v/t*) confondere; **~ s.o. with s.o.** confondere qu con qu

con·fused [kənˈfjuːzd] *adj* confuso

con·fus·ing [kənˈfjuːzɪŋ] *adj* che confonde

con·fu·sion [kənˈfjuːʒn] confusione *f*

con·geal [kənˈdʒiːl] *v/i* *of blood, fat* rapprendersi

con·gen·ial [kənˈdʒiːnɪəl] *adj* (*pleasant*) simpatico

con·gen·i·tal [kənˈdʒenɪtl] *adj* MED congenito

con·gest·ed [kənˈdʒestɪd] *adj* congestionato

con·ges·tion [kənˈdʒestʃn] congestione f; **traffic** ~ la congestione del traffico

con·grat·u·late [kən'grætjʊleɪt] v/t congratularsi con

con·grat·u·la·tions [kəngrætjʊ'leɪʃnz] npl congratulazioni fpl; **~ on ...** congratulaizioni per ...

con·grat·u·la·to·ry [kəngrætjʊ'leɪtərɪ] adj di congratulazioni

con·gre·gate ['kɒŋgrɪgeɪt] v/i (gather) riunirsi

con·gre·ga·tion [kɒŋgrɪ'geɪʃn] REL fedeli mpl

con·gress ['kɒŋgres] (conference) congresso m; **Congress** in US il Congresso

Con·gres·sion·al [kən'greʃnl] adj del Congresso

Con·gress·man ['kɒŋgresmən] membro m del Congresso

co·ni·fer ['kɒnɪfə(r)] conifera f

con·jec·ture [kən'dʒektʃə(r)] n (speculation) congettura f

con·ju·gate ['kɒndʒʊgeɪt] v/t GRAM coniugare

con·junc·tion [kən'dʒʌŋkʃn] GRAM congiunzione f; **in ~ with** insieme a

con·junc·ti·vi·tis [kəndʒʌŋktɪ'vaɪtɪs] congiuntivite f

♦ con·jure up ['kʌndʒə(r)] v/t (produce) far apparire (come) per magia; (evoke) evocare

con·jur·er, con·jur·or ['kʌndʒərə(r)] (magician) prestigiatore m, -trice f

'con·jur·ing tricks ['kʌndʒərɪŋ] npl giochi mpl di prestigio

con man ['kɒnmæn] F truffatore m

con·nect [kə'nekt] v/t (join, link) collegare; to power supply allacciare; ~ **s.o. with s.o.** TELEC mettere in comunicazione qu con qu

con·nect·ed [kə'nektɪd] adj: **be well-~** avere conoscenze influenti; **be ~ with ...** essere collegato con; **by marriage** essere imparentato con

con·nect·ing flight [kə'nektɪŋ] coincidenza f (volo)

con·nec·tion [kə'nekʃn] (link) collegamento m; when travelling coinci-

denza f; (personal contact) conoscenza f; **in ~ with** a proposito di

con·nois·seur [kɒnə'sɜː(r)] intenditore m, -trice f

con·quer ['kɒŋkə(r)] v/t conquistare; fig: fear etc vincere

con·quer·or ['kɒŋkərə(r)] conquistatore m, -trice f

con·quest ['kɒŋkwest] conquista f

con·science ['kɒnʃəns] coscienza f; **have a guilty / clear ~** avere la coscienza sporca / a posto; **on one's ~** sulla coscienza

con·sci·en·tious [kɒnʃɪ'enʃəs] adj coscienzioso

con·sci·en·tious·ness [kɒnʃɪ'enʃənəs] coscienziosità f inv

con·sci·en·tious ob'ject·or obiettore m di coscienza

con·scious ['kɒnʃəs] adj (aware) consapevole; (deliberate) conscio; MED cosciente; **be / become ~ of** rendersi conto di

con·scious·ly ['kɒnʃəslɪ] adv consapevolmente

con·scious·ness ['kɒnʃəsnɪs] (awareness) consapevolezza f; MED conoscenza f; **lose / regain ~** perdere / riprendere conoscenza

con·sec·u·tive [kən'sekjʊtɪv] adj consecutivo

con·sen·sus [kən'sensəs] consenso m

con·sent [kən'sent] **1** n consenso m **2** v/i acconsentire

con·se·quence ['kɒnsɪkwəns] (result) conseguenza f

con·se·quent·ly ['kɒnsɪkwəntlɪ] adv (therefore) di conseguenza

con·ser·va·tion [kɒnsə'veɪʃn] (preservation) tutela f

con·ser'va·tion area area f soggetta a vincoli urbanistici e ambientali

con·ser·va·tion·ist [kɒnsə'veɪʃnɪst] ambientalista m/f

con·ser·va·tive [kən'sɜːvətɪv] **1** adj (conventional) conservatore; clothes tradizionale; estimate cauto; **Conservative** Br POL conservatore **2** n Br POL **Conservative** conservatore m, -trice f

con·ser·va·to·ry [kən'sɜːvətrɪ] veranda f; MUS conservatorio m

con·serve ['kɒnsɜːv] **1** n (jam) marmellata f **2** v/t [kən'sɜːv] energy, strength risparmiare

con·sid·er [kən'sɪdə(r)] v/t (regard) considerare; (show regard for) tener conto di; (think about) pensare a; ~ **doing sth** prendere in considerazione la possibilità di fare qc; **it is ~ed to be his best work** è considerata la sua opera migliore

con·sid·er·a·ble [kən'sɪdrəbl] adj considerevole

con·sid·er·a·bly [kən'sɪdrəblɪ] adv considerevolmente

con·sid·er·ate [kən'sɪdərət] adj person, attitude premuroso; **be ~ of** avere riguardo per

con·sid·er·ate·ly [kən'sɪdərətlɪ] adv premurosamente

con·sid·er·a·tion [kənsɪdə'reɪʃn] (thought) considerazione f; (thoughtfulness, concern) riguardo m; (factor) fattore m; **take sth into ~** prendere in considerazione qc; **under ~** in esame

con·sign·ment [kən'saɪnmənt] COM consegna f

♦ **con·sist of** [kən'sɪst] v/t consistere in

con·sis·ten·cy [kən'sɪstənsɪ] (texture) consistenza f; (unchangingness) coerenza f

con·sis·tent [kən'sɪstənt] adj (unchanging) coerente

con·sis·tent·ly [kən'sɪstəntlɪ] adv in modo coerente; always costantemente

con·so·la·tion [kɒnsə'leɪʃn] consolazione f

con·sole [kən'səʊl] v/t consolare

con·sol·i·date [kən'sɒlɪdeɪt] v/t consolidare

con·so·nant ['kɒnsənənt] n GRAM consonante f

con·sor·ti·um [kən'sɔːtɪəm] consorzio m

con·spic·u·ous [kən'spɪkjʊəs] adj: **be / look ~** spiccare; **feel ~** sentirsi fuori posto

con·spi·ra·cy [kən'spɪrəsɪ] cospirazione f

con·spi·ra·tor [kən'spɪrətə(r)] cospiratore m, -trice f

con·spire [kən'spaɪə(r)] v/i cospirare

con·stant ['kɒnstənt] adj (continuous) costante

con·stant·ly ['kɒnstəntlɪ] adv costantemente

con·sti·pat·ed ['kɒnstɪpeɪtɪd] adj stitico

con·sti·pa·tion [kɒnstɪ'peɪʃn] stitichezza f

con·sti·tu·en·cy [kən'stɪtjʊənsɪ] Br POL circoscrizione f elettorale

con·sti·tu·ent [kən'stɪtjʊənt] n (component) componente m; Br POL elettore m, -trice f

con·sti·tute ['kɒnstɪtjuːt] v/t costituire

con·sti·tu·tion [kɒnstɪ'tjuːʃn] also POL costituzione f

con·sti·tu·tion·al [kɒnstɪ'tjuːʃənl] adj POL costituzionale

con·straint [kən'streɪnt] (restriction) restrizione f

con·struct [kən'strʌkt] v/t building etc costruire

con·struc·tion [kən'strʌkʃn] costruzione f; **under ~** in costruzione

con·struc·tion in·dus·try edilizia f; **con·struc·tion site** cantiere m edile; **con·struc·tion work·er** operaio m edile

con·struc·tive [kən'strʌktɪv] adj costruttivo

con·sul ['kɒnsl] console m

con·su·late ['kɒnsjʊlət] consolato m

con·sult [kən'sʌlt] v/t (seek the advice of) consultare

con·sul·tan·cy [kən'sʌltənsɪ] (company) società f inv di consulenza; (advice) consulenza f

con·sul·tant [kən'sʌltənt] n (adviser) consulente m/f

con·sul·ta·tion [kɒnsəl'teɪʃn] consultazione f

con·sult·ing hours orario m di visita

con·sult·ing room ambulatorio *m*

con·sume [kən'sjuːm] *v/t* consumare

con·sum·er [kən'sjuːmə(r)] (*purchaser*) consumatore *m*, -trice *f*

con·su·mer 'con·fi·dence fiducia *f* dei consumatori; **con'sum·er goods** *npl* beni *mpl* di consumo; **con'sum·er so·ci·e·ty** società *f inv* dei consumi

con·sump·tion [kən'sʌmpʃn] consumo *m*

con·tact ['kɒntækt] **1** *n* contatto *m*; (*person*) conoscenza *f*; **keep in ~ with s.o.** mantenere i contatti con qu **2** *v/t* mettersi in contatto con

'con·tact lens lente *f* a contatto

'con·tact num·ber numero *m* presso cui si è reperibili

con·ta·gious [kən'teɪdʒəs] *adj also fig* contagioso

con·tain [kən'teɪn] *v/t* (*hold*) contenere; *flood, disease, revolt* contenere; **~ o.s.** contenersi

con·tain·er [kən'teɪnə(r)] (*recipient*) contenitore *m*; COM container *m inv*

con'tain·er ship nave *f* portacontainer

con·tam·i·nate [kən'tæmɪneɪt] *v/t* contaminare

con·tam·i·na·tion [kəntæmɪ'neɪʃn] contaminazione *f*

con·tem·plate ['kɒntəmpleɪt] *v/t* (*look at*) contemplare; (*think about*) considerare; **~ doing sth** considerare la possibilità di fare qc

con·tem·po·ra·ry [kən'tempərərɪ] **1** *adj* contemporaneo **2** *n* coetaneo *m*, -a *f*

con·tempt [kən'tempt] disprezzo *m*; **be beneath ~** essere spregevole

con·temp·ti·ble [kən'temptəbl] *adj* spregevole

con·temp·tu·ous [kən'temptjʊəs] *adj* sprezzante

con·tend [kən'tend] *v/i*: **~ for sth** contendersi qc; **~ with s.o. / sth** confrontarsi con qc / qu

con·tend·er [kən'tendə(r)] *in sport, competition* concorrente *m/f*; *against*

champion sfidante *m/f*; POL candidato *m*, -a *f*

con·tent[1] ['kɒntent] *n* contenuto *m*

con·tent[2] [kən'tent] **1** *adj* contento **2** *v/t*: **~ o.s. with** accontentarsi di

con·tent·ed [kən'tentɪd] *adj* contento

con·ten·tion [kən'tenʃn] (*assertion*) opinione *f*; **be in ~ for** essere in lizza per

con·ten·tious [kən'tenʃəs] *adj* polemico

con·tent·ment [kən'tentmənt] soddisfazione *f*

con·tents ['kɒntents] *npl of house, letter, bag etc* contenuto *m*

con·test[1] ['kɒntest] *n* (*competition*) concorso *m*; (*struggle, for power*) lotta *f*

con·test[2] [kən'test] *v/t leadership etc* essere in lizza per; *will* impugnare

con·tes·tant [kən'testənt] concorrente *m/f*

con·text ['kɒntekst] contesto *m*; **look at sth in ~ / out of ~** considerare qc in / fuori contesto

con·ti·nent ['kɒntɪnənt] *n* continente *m*; **the ~** l'Europa continentale

con·ti·nen·tal [kɒntɪ'nentl] *adj* continentale

con·ti·nen·tal 'break·fast colazione *f* a base di caffè, pane, burro e marmellata

con·tin·gen·cy [kən'tɪndʒənsɪ] eventualità *f inv*

con·tin·u·al [kən'tɪnjʊəl] *adj* continuo

con·tin·u·al·ly [kən'tɪnjʊəlɪ] *adv* continuamente

con·tin·u·a·tion [kəntɪnjʊ'eɪʃn] seguito *m*

con·tin·ue [kən'tɪnjuː] **1** *v/t* continuare; **~ doing sth** continuare a fare qc; **to be ~d** continua ... **2** *v/i* continuare

con·ti·nu·i·ty [kɒntɪ'njuːətɪ] continuità *f inv*; *in films* ordine *m* della sceneggiatura

con·tin·u·ous [kən'tɪnjʊəs] *adj* ininterrotto

con·tin·u·ous·ly [kən'tɪnjʊəslɪ] *adv* ininterrottamente

con·tort [kən'tɔːt] *v/t* contorcere

con·tour ['kɒntʊə(r)] profilo *m*; *on map* curva *f* di livello

con·tra·cep·tion [kɒntrə'sepʃn] contraccezione *f*

con·tra·cep·tive [kɒntrə'septɪv] *n* anticoncezionale *m*, contraccettivo *m*

con·tract¹ ['kɒntrækt] *n* contratto *m*

con·tract² [kən'trækt] **1** *v/i* (*shrink*) contrarsi **2** *v/t illness* contrarre

con·trac·tor [kən'træktə(r)] appaltatore *m*, -trice *f*; *building* ~ ditta *f* di appalti (edili)

con·trac·tu·al [kən'træktjʊəl] *adj* contrattuale

con·tra·dict [kɒntrə'dɪkt] *v/t* contraddire

con·tra·dic·tion [kɒntrə'dɪkʃn] contraddizione *f*

con·tra·dic·to·ry [kɒntrə'dɪktrɪ] *adj account* contraddittorio

con·trap·tion [kən'træpʃn] F aggeggio *m*

con·trar·y¹ ['kɒntrərɪ] **1** *adj* contrario; ~ *to* contrariamente a **2** *n*: *on the* ~ al contrario

con·tra·ry² [kən'treərɪ] *adj*: *be* ~ (*perverse*) essere un bastian contrario

con·trast ['kɒntrɑːst] **1** *n* contrasto *m*; *by* ~ invece **2** *v/t* [kən'trɑːst] confrontare **3** *v/i* contrastare

con·trast·ing [kən'trɑːstɪŋ] *adj* contrastante

con·tra·vene [kɒntrə'viːn] *v/t* contravvenire a

con·trib·ute [kən'trɪbjuːt] **1** *v/i with money, material, time* contribuire; *to magazine, paper* collaborare (*to* con); *to discussion* intervenire (*to* in); (*help to cause*) contribuire a creare **2** *v/t money* contribuire con

con·tri·bu·tion [kɒntrɪ'bjuːʃn] *money* offerta *f*; *to political party, church* donazione *f*; *of time, effort* contributo *m*; *to debate* intervento *m*; *to magazine* collaborazione *f*

con·trib·u·tor [kən'trɪbjʊtə(r)] *of money* finanziatore *m*, -trice *f*; *to magazine* collaboratore *m*, -trice *f*

con·trol [kən'trəʊl] **1** *n* controllo *m*; *take* ~ *of* assumere il controllo di; *lose* ~ *of* perdere il controllo di; *lose* ~ *of o.s.* perdere il controllo; *circumstances beyond our* ~ cause indipendenti dalla nostra volontà; *be in* ~ *of sth* tenere qc sotto controllo; *get out of* ~ diventare incontrollabile; *the situation is under* ~ la situazione è sotto controllo; *bring a blaze under* ~ circoscrivere un incendio; ~*s* (*of aircraft, vehicle*) comandi; ~*s* (*restrictions*) restrizioni **2** *v/t* (*pret & pp* -*led*) (*govern*) controllare; *traffic* dirigere; (*restrict*) contenere; (*regulate*) regolare; ~ *o.s.* controllarsi

con·trol cen·ter *Am*, **con·trol cen·tre** centro *m* di controllo

con·trol freak F *persona f che vuole avere tutto e tutti sotto controllo*

con·trolled 'sub·stance [kən'trəʊld] sostanza *f* stupefacente

con·trol·ling 'in·ter·est [kən'trəʊlɪŋ] FIN maggioranza *f* delle azioni

con·trol pan·el quadro *m* dei comandi

con·trol tow·er torre *f* di controllo

con·tro·ver·sial [kɒntrə'vɜːʃl] *adj* controverso

con·tro·ver·sy ['kɒntrəvɜːsɪ] polemica *f*

con·va·lesce [kɒnvə'les] *v/i* rimettersi (in salute)

con·va·les·cence [kɒnvə'lesns] convalescenza *f*

con·vene [kən'viːn] *v/t* indire

con·ve·ni·ence [kən'viːnɪəns] *of having sth, location* comodità *f inv*; *at my / your* ~ a mio / tuo comodo; *all* (*modern*) ~*s* tutti i comfort

con·ve·ni·ence food scatolame *m*, cibi precotti ecc

con·ve·ni·ence store negozio *m* alimentari

con·ve·ni·ent [kən'viːnɪənt] *adj location, device* comodo; *whenever* *it's ~* quando ti va bene

con·ve·ni·ent·ly [kən'vi:nɪəntlɪ] *adv* comodamente

con·vent ['kɒnvənt] convento *m*

con·ven·tion [kən'venʃn] *(tradition)* convenzione *f*; *(conference)* congresso *m*

con·ven·tion·al [kən'venʃnl] *adj person, ideas* convenzionale; *method* tradizionale

◆ **con·verge on** [kən'vɜ:dʒ] *v/t* convergere su

con·ver·sant [kən'vɜ:sənt] *adj*: *be ~ with* essere pratico di

con·ver·sa·tion [kɒnvə'seɪʃn] conversazione *f*

con·ver·sa·tion·al [kɒnvə'seɪʃnl] *adj* colloquiale

con·verse ['kɒnvɜ:s] *n (opposite)* contrario *m*

con·verse·ly [kən'vɜ:slɪ] *adv* per contro

con·ver·sion [kən'vɜ:ʃn] conversione *f*; *of house* trasformazione *f*

con·ver·sion ta·ble tabella *f* di conversione

con·vert ['kɒnvɜ:t] **1** *n* convertito *m*, -a *f* **2** *v/t* [kən'vɜ:t] convertire **3** *v/i* trasformarsi (*into* in); *house, room* trasformare

con·ver·ti·ble [kən'vɜ:təbl] *n car* cabriolet *f inv*, decappottabile *f*

con·vey [kən'veɪ] *v/t (transmit)* comunicare; *(carry)* trasportare

con·vey·or belt [kən'veɪə(r)] nastro *m* trasportatore

con·vict ['kɒnvɪkt] **1** *n* carcerato *m*, -a *f* **2** *v/t* [kən'vɪkt] LAW condannare; *~ s.o. of sth* condannare qu per qc

con·vic·tion [kən'vɪkʃn] LAW condanna *f*; *(belief)* convinzione *f*

con·vince [kən'vɪns] *v/t* convincere

con·vinc·ing [kən'vɪnsɪŋ] *adj* convincente

con·viv·i·al [kən'vɪvɪəl] *adj (friendly)* gioviale

con·voy ['kɒnvɔɪ] convoglio *m*

con·vul·sion [kən'vʌlʃn] MED convulsione *f*

cook [kʊk] **1** *n* cuoco *m*, -a *f*; *I'm a*

good ~ cucino bene **2** *v/t vegetables, meat* cucinare; *meal, dinner* preparare; *a ~ed meal* un pasto caldo; *~ the books* F falsificare i registri **3** *v/i of person* cucinare; *of vegetables, meat* cuocere

'cook·book ricettario *m*

cook·er ['kʊkə(r)] cucina *f*

cook·e·ry ['kʊkərɪ] cucina *f*

'cook·e·ry book ricettario *m*

cook·ie ['kʊkɪ] *Am* biscotto *m*

cook·ing ['kʊkɪŋ] *food* cucina *f*; *he does all the ~* è lui che cucina

cool [ku:l] **1** *n* F: *keep / lose one's ~* conservare / perdere la calma **2** *adj weather, breeze, drink* fresco; *(calm)* calmo; *(unfriendly)* freddo **3** *v/i of food* raffreddarsi; *of tempers* calmarsi; *of interest* raffreddarsi **4** *v/t* F: *~ it!* calma!

◆ **cool down 1** *v/i* raffreddarsi; *of weather* rinfrescare; *fig: of tempers* calmarsi **2** *v/t food* raffreddare; *fig* calmare

cool·ing-'off pe·ri·od periodo *m* di riflessione

co·op·e·rate [kəʊ'ɒpəreɪt] *v/i* cooperare

co·op·e·ra·tion [kəʊɒpə'reɪʃn] cooperazione *f*

co·op·e·ra·tive [kəʊ'ɒpərətɪv] **1** *n* COM cooperativa *f* **2** *adj* COM cooperativo; *(helpful)* disponibile (a collaborare)

co·or·di·nate [kəʊ'ɔ:dɪneɪt] *v/t* coordinare

co·or·di·na·tion [kəʊɒ:dɪ'neɪʃn] *of activities* coordinamento *m*; *of body* coordinazione *f*

cop [kɒp] *n* F poliziotto *m*

cope [kəʊp] *v/i* farcela; *~ with* farcela con

cop·i·er ['kɒpɪə(r)] *machine* fotocopiatrice *f*

co·pi·lot ['kəʊpaɪlət] secondo pilota *m*

co·pi·ous ['kəʊpɪəs] *adj* abbondante

cop·per ['kɒpə(r)] *n metal* rame *m*

cop·y ['kɒpɪ] **1** *n* copia *f*; *written material* materiale *m*; *fair ~* bella copia *f*; *rough ~* brutta copia *f*;

make a ~ of a file fare una copia di un file **2** *v/t* (*pret & pp -ied*) copiare

'**cop·y cat** F copione *m*, -a f F;
'**cop·y·cat** '**crime** reato *m* a imitazione di un altro; '**cop·y·right** n diritti *mpl* d'autore, copyright *m inv*; '**cop·y-writ·er** in advertising copywriter *m*

cor·al ['kɒrəl] corallo *m*

cord [kɔːd] (*string*) corda f; (*cable*) filo *m*

cor·di·al ['kɔːdɪəl] adj cordiale

cord·less '**phone** ['kɔːdlɪs] cordless *m inv*

cor·don ['kɔːdn] cordone *m*

♦ **cor·don off** v/t transennare; *put cordon around* recintare

cords [kɔːdz] npl trousers pantaloni *mpl* di velluto a coste

cor·du·roy ['kɔːdərɔɪ] velluto *m* a coste

core [kɔː(r)] **1** n of fruit torsolo *m*; of problem nocciolo *m*; of organization, party cuore *m* **2** v/t fruit togliere il torsolo a **3** adj issue, meaning essenziale

cork [kɔːk] in bottle tappo *m* di sughero; (*material*) sughero *m*

'**cork·screw** n cavatappi *m inv*

corn [kɔːn] grain frumento *m*; Am (*maize*) granturco *m*

cor·ner ['kɔːnə(r)] **1** n of page, room, street angolo *m*; of table spigolo *m*; in football calcio *m* d'angolo, corner *m inv*; *in the ~* nell'angolo; *on the ~ of street* all'angolo; *around the ~* dietro l'angolo **2** v/t person bloccare; ~ *a market* prendersi il monopolio di un mercato **3** v/i of driver, car affrontare una curva

'**cor·ner kick** in football calcio *m* d'angolo

'**cor·ner shop** piccola drogheria f

'**corn·flakes** npl fiocchi *mpl* di granturco, cornflakes *mpl*

'**corn·flour** farina f di granturco

corn·y ['kɔːnɪ] adj F scontato; sentimental sdolcinato

cor·o·na·ry ['kɒrənərɪ] **1** adj coronario **2** n infarto *m*

cor·o·ner ['kɒrənə(r)] ufficiale *m*

pubblico che indaga sui casi di morte sospetta

cor·po·ral ['kɔːpərəl] n caporale *m* maggiore

cor·po·ral '**pun·ish·ment** punizione f corporale

cor·po·rate ['kɔːpərət] adj COM aziendale; ~ *image* corporate image f inv; *sense of ~ loyalty* corporativismo *m*

cor·po·ra·tion [kɔːpə'reɪʃn] (*business*) corporation f inv

corps [kɔː(r)] nsg corpo *m*

corpse [kɔːps] cadavere *m*

cor·pu·lent ['kɔːpjʊlənt] adj corpulento

cor·pus·cle ['kɔːpʌsl] globulo *m*

cor·rect [kə'rekt] **1** adj giusto; behaviour corretto; *she's ~* ha ragione **2** v/t correggere

cor·rec·tion [kə'rekʃn] correzione f

cor·rect·ly [kə'rektlɪ] adv giustamente; behave correttamente

cor·re·spond [kɒrɪ'spɒnd] v/i (*match, write*) corrispondere; ~ *to* corrispondere a; ~ *with* corrispondere con

cor·re·spon·dence [kɒrɪ'spɒndəns] (*agreement, letters*) corrispondenza f

cor·re·spon·dent [kɒrɪ'spɒndənt] corrispondente m/f

cor·re·spon·ding [kɒrɪ'spɒndɪŋ] adj (*equivalent*) corrispondente

cor·ri·dor ['kɒrɪdɔː(r)] in building corridoio *m*

cor·rob·o·rate [kə'rɒbəreɪt] v/t corroborare

cor·rode [kə'rəʊd] v/t & v/i corrodere

cor·ro·sion [kə'rəʊʒn] corrosione f

cor·ru·gated '**card·board** ['kɒrəgeɪtɪd] cartone *m* ondulato

cor·ru·gated '**i·ron** lamiera f (di ferro) ondulata

cor·rupt [kə'rʌpt] **1** adj also COMPUT corrotto **2** v/t morals, youth traviare; (*bribe*) corrompere

cor·rup·tion [kə'rʌpʃn] corruzione f

Cor·si·ca ['kɔːsɪkə] Corsica f

Cor·si·can ['kɔːsɪkən] **1** adj corso **2** n corso *m*, -a f

cos·met·ic [kɒz'metɪk] *adj* cosmetico; *surgery* estetico; *fig* di facciata
cos·met·ics [kɒz'metɪks] *npl* cosmetici *mpl*
cos·met·ic 'sur·geon chirurgo *m* estetico
cos·met·ic 'sur·ger·y chirurgia *f* estetica
cos·mo·naut ['kɒzmənɔːt] cosmonauta *m/f*
cos·mo·pol·i·tan [kɒzmə'pɒlɪtən] *adj city* cosmopolita
cost[1] [kɒst] **1** *n also fig* costo *m*; *at all ~s* a ogni costo; *I've learnt to my ~* l'ho imparato a mie spese; *~s* LAW spese **2** *v/t* (*pret & pp* **cost**) costare; FIN: *proposal, project* fare il preventivo di; *how much does it ~?* quanto costa?; *it ~ me my health* ci ho rimesso la salute
cost[2] [kɒst] *v/t* (*pret & pp* **costed**) FIN: *proposal, project* fare il preventivo di
cost and 'freight COM costo e nolo;
'cost-con·scious *adj*: *be ~* fare attenzione ai consumi; **'cost-ef·fec·tive** *adj* conveniente; **'cost, insurance and freight** COM costo, assicurazione e nolo
cost·ly ['kɒstlɪ] *adj mistake* costoso; *it would be a ~ mistake* potresti pagarla cara
cost of 'liv·ing costo *m* della vita
cost 'price prezzo *m* di costo
cos·tume ['kɒstjuːm] *for actor* costume *m*
cos·tume 'jew·el·lery, *Am* **cos·tume 'jew·el·ry** bigiotteria *f*
co·sy *adj* (*comfortable*) gradevole; (*intimate and friendly*) intimo; *be nice and ~ in bed* starsene al calduccio a letto; *a nice ~ little job* un lavoretto tranquillo
cot [kɒt] *for child* lettino *m*
cott·age ['kɒtɪdʒ] cottage *m inv*
cot·tage 'cheese fiocchi *mpl* di latte
cot·ton ['kɒtn] **1** *n* cotone *m* **2** *adj* di cotone
♦ **cotton on** *v/i* F afferrare F
♦ **cotton on to** *v/t* F afferrare F
cot·ton 'wool ovatta *f*

couch [kautʃ] *n* divano *m*
'couch po·ta·to F teledipendente *m/f*
cou·chette [kuː'ʃet] cuccetta *f*
cough [kɒf] **1** *n* tosse *f*; *to get attention* colpetto *m* di tosse **2** *v/i* tossire; *to get attention* tossicchiare
♦ **cough up 1** *v/t blood etc* sputare; F *money* cacciar fuori F **2** *v/i* F (*pay*) cacciare i soldi F
'cough medicine, 'cough syrup sciroppo *m* per la tosse
could[1] [kʊd] *v/aux*: *~ I have my key?* mi dà la chiave?; *~ you help me?* mi puoi dare una mano?; *this ~ be our bus* questo potrebbe essere il nostro autobus; *you ~ be right* magari hai ragione; *I ~n't say for sure* non potrei giurarci; *he ~ have got lost* può darsi che si sia smarrito; *you ~ have warned me!* in indignation avresti potuto avvisarmi!
could[2] [kʊd] *pret* → **can**
coun·cil ['kaunsl] *n* (*assembly*) consiglio *m*; (*city ~*) comune *m*
'coun·cil house casa *f* popolare
coun·cil·lor ['kaunsələ(r)] consigliere *m*, -a *f* (comunale)
'coun·cil tax imposta *f* comunale sugli immobili
coun·sel ['kaunsl] **1** *n* (*advice*) consiglio *m*; (*lawyer*) avvocato *m* **2** *v/t course of action* consigliare; *person* offrire consulenza a
coun·sel·ing *Am*, **coun·sel·ling** ['kaunslɪŋ] terapia *f*
coun·sel·lor, *Am* **coun·sel·or** ['kaunslə(r)] (*adviser*) consulente *m/f*
count[1] [kaunt] *aristocrat* conte *m*
count[2] [kaunt] **1** *n* conteggio *m*; *keep / lose ~ of* tenere / perdere il conto di; *what's your ~?* quanti ne hai contati? **2** *v/i* contare; *that doesn't ~* questo non conta **3** *v/t* contare; *~ yourself lucky* considerati fortunato
♦ **count on** *v/t* contare su
'count·down conto *m* alla rovescia
coun·te·nance ['kauntənəns] *v/t* approvare

coun·ter¹ ['kaʊntə(r)] *in shop, café* banco *m*; *in game* segnalino *m*

coun·ter² ['kaʊntə(r)] **1** *v/t* neutralizzare **2** *v/i* (*retaliate*) rispondere

coun·ter 3 ['kaʊntə(r)] *adv*: **run ~ to** andare contro

'**coun·ter·act** *v/t* neutralizzare

coun·ter-at·tack 1 *n* contrattacco *m* **2** *v/i* contrattaccare

'**coun·terbal·ance 1** *n* contrappeso *m* **2** *v/t* fare da contrappeso a

coun·ter·es·pi·o·nage controspionaggio *m*

coun·ter·feit ['kaʊntəfɪt] **1** *v/t* falsificare **2** *adj* falso

coun·ter·foil ['kaʊntəfɔɪl] matrice *f*

'**coun·ter·part** *person* omologo *m*, -a *f*

coun·ter·pro·duc·tive *adj* controproducente

'**coun·ter·sign** *v/t* controfirmare

coun·tess ['kaʊntes] contessa *f*

count·less ['kaʊntlɪs] *adj* innumerevole

coun·try ['kʌntrɪ] **1** *n* (*nation*) paese *m*; *as opposed to town* campagna *f*; *in the ~* in campagna **2** *adj roads, life* di campagna

coun·try and '**west·ern** MUS country and western *m inv*; '**country·man** (*fellow ~*) connazionale *m*; '**coun·try·side** campagna *f*

coun·ty ['kaʊntɪ] contea *f*

coup [kuː] POL colpo *m* di stato, golpe *m inv*; *fig* colpo *m*

cou·ple ['kʌpl] *n* coppia *f*; **just a ~** solo un paio; **a ~ of** un paio di

cou·pon ['kuːpɒn] buono *m*

cour·age ['kʌrɪdʒ] coraggio *m*

cou·ra·geous [kə'reɪdʒəs] *adj* coraggioso

cou·ri·er ['kʊrɪə(r)] (*messenger*) corriere *m*; *with tourist party* accompagnatore *m* turistico, accompagnatrice *f* turistica

course [kɔːs] *n series of lessons* corso *m*; *part of meal* portata *f*; *of ship, plane* rotta *f*; *for golf* campo *m*; *for race, skiing* pista *f*; **of ~** (*certainly*) certo; (*naturally*) ovviamente; **of ~ not** certo che no; **first ~** primo *m*;

second ~ secondo *m*; **~ of action** linea *f* di condotta; **~ of treatment** cura *f*; **in the ~ of** nel corso di

court [kɔːt] *n* LAW corte *f*; (*courthouse*) tribunale *m*; SP campo *m*; **take s.o. to ~** fare causa a qu; **out of ~** in via amichevole

'**court case** caso *m* (giudiziario)

cour·te·ous ['kɜːtɪəs] *adj* cortese

cour·te·sy ['kɜːtəsɪ] cortesia *f*

'**court·house** tribunale *m*, palazzo *m* di giustizia; **court 'mar·tial 1** *n* corte *f* marziale **2** *v/t* processare in corte marziale; '**court or·der** ingiunzione *f* del tribunale; '**court·room** aula *f* del tribunale; '**court·yard** cortile *m*

cous·in ['kʌzn] cugino *m*, -a *f*

cove [kəʊv] *small bay* cala *f*

cov·er ['kʌvə(r)] **1** *n protective* fodera *f*; *of book, magazine* copertina *f*; (*shelter*) riparo *m*; *insurance* copertura *f*; **~s for bed** coperte *fpl*; **take ~** ripararsi **2** *v/t* coprire; *distance* percorrere; *of journalist* fare un servizio su; **we're not ~ed for theft** non siamo coperti contro i furti

♦ **cover up 1** *v/t* coprire; *fig* insabbiare **2** *v/i*: **cover up for s.o.** *fig* coprire qu

cov·er·age ['kʌvərɪdʒ] *by media* copertura *f*; **the trial got a lot of ~** il processo ha avuto molta risonanza

cov·er·ing let·ter ['kʌvrɪŋ] lettera *f* d'accompagnamento

cov·ert [kəʊ'vɔːt] *adj* segreto

'**cov·er-up** insabbiamento *m*; **it looks like a ~** sembra che qualcuno stia cercando di insabbiare le prove

cow [kaʊ] mucca *f*

cow·ard ['kaʊəd] vigliacco *m*, -a *f*

cow·ard·ice ['kaʊədɪs] vigliaccheria *f*

cow·ard·ly ['kaʊədlɪ] *adj* vile

'**cow·boy** (*western*) cow-boy *m inv*

cow·er ['kaʊə(r)] *v/i* rannicchiarsi

coy [kɔɪ] *adj* (*evasive*) evasivo; (*flirtatious*) civettuolo

'**coz·y** *Am* → **cosy**

CPU [siːpiː'juː] *abbr* (= **central**

processing unit unità *f* centrale di elaborazione

crab [kræb] *n* granchio *m*

crack [kræk] **1** *n* crepa *f*; (*joke*) battuta *f* **2** *v/t cup, glass* incrinare; *nut* schiacciare; *code* decifrare; F (*solve*) risolvere; **~ a joke** fare una battuta **3** *v/i* incrinarsi; **get ~ing** F darsi una mossa F

♦ **crack down on** *v/t* prendere serie misure contro

♦ **crack up** *v/i* (*have breakdown*) avere un esaurimento; F (*laugh*) scoppiare a ridere

'**crack·brained** *adj* F pazzoide *f*

'**crack·down** intensificazione *f* dei controlli (**on** su)

cracked [krækt] *adj cup, glass* incrinato; F (*crazy*) tocco F

crack·er ['krækə(r)] *to eat* cracker *m inv*

crack·le ['krækl] *v/i of fire* schioppettare

cra·dle ['kreɪdl] *n for baby* culla *f*

craft[1] [krɑːft] NAUT imbarcazione *f*

craft[2] [krɑːft] (*skill*) attività *f inv* artigiana; (*trade*) mestiere *m*

crafts·man ['krɑːftsmən] artigiano *m*

craft·y ['krɑːftɪ] *adj* astuto

crag [kræg] *rock* rupe *f*

cram [kræm] *v/t papers, food* infilare; *people* stipare

cramp [kræmp] *n* crampo *m*

cramped [kræmpt] *adj room, flat* esiguo

cran·ber·ry ['krænbərɪ] mirtillo *m*

crane [kreɪn] **1** *n machine* gru *f inv* **2** *v/t*: **~ one's neck** allungare il collo

crank [kræŋk] *n strange person* tipo *m* strambo

'**crank·shaft** albero *m* a gomiti

crash [kræʃ] **1** *n noise* fragore *m*; *accident* incidente *m*; COM crollo *m*; COMPUT crash *m inv* **2** *v/i fall noisily* fracassarsi; *of thunder* rombare; *of car* schiantarsi; *of two cars* scontrarsi, schiantarsi; *of plane* precipitare; COM: *of market* crollare; COMPUT fare un crash; F (*sleep*) dormire **3** *v/t car* avere un incidente con

♦ **crash out** *v/i* F (*fall asleep*) addormentarsi; *without meaning to* crollare F

'**crash bar·ri·er** barriera *f* protettiva; '**crash course** corso *m* intensivo; '**crash di·et** dieta *f* lampo; '**crash hel·met** casco *m* (di protezione); '**crash-land** *v/i* fare un atterraggio di fortuna; '**crash land·ing** atterraggio *m* di fortuna

crate [kreɪt] (*packing case*) cassetta *f*

cra·ter ['kreɪtə(r)] *of volcano* cratere *m*

crave [kreɪv] *v/t* smaniare dalla voglia di

crav·ing ['kreɪvɪŋ] voglia *f*; *pej* smania *f*

crawl [krɔːl] **1** *n in swimming* crawl *m*, stile *m* libero; **at a ~** (*very slowly*) a passo d'uomo **2** *v/i on floor* andare (a) carponi; (*move slowly*) avanzare lentamente

♦ **crawl with** *v/t* brulicare di

cray·on ['kreɪən] *n* matita *f* colorata; *wax* pastello *m* a cera

craze [kreɪz] moda *f*

cra·zy ['kreɪzɪ] *adj* pazzo; **be ~ about s.o.** essere pazzo di qu; **be ~ about sth** andare matto per qc

creak [kriːk] **1** *n* scricchiolio *m* **2** *v/i* scricchiolare

creak·y ['kriːkɪ] *adj* che scricchiola

cream [kriːm] **1** *n for skin* crema *f*; *for coffee, cake* panna *f*; *colour* color *m* panna **2** *adj* color panna

cream 'cheese formaggio *m* fresco da spalmare

creamer ['kriːmə(r)] *for coffee* panna *f* liofilizzata

cream·y ['kriːmɪ] *adj* (*with lots of cream*) cremoso

crease [kriːs] **1** *n accidental* grinza *f*; *deliberate* piega *f* **2** *v/t accidentally* sgualcire

cre·ate [kriː'eɪt] *v/t* creare

cre·a·tion [kriː'eɪʃn] creazione *f*

cre·a·tive [kriː'eɪtɪv] *adj* creativo

cre·a·tor [kriː'eɪtə(r)] creatore *m*, -trice *f*; **the Creator** REL il Creatore

crea·ture ['kriːtʃə(r)] creatura *f*

crèche [kreʃ] *for children* asilo *m* nido; REL presepe *m*

cred·i·bil·i·ty [kredə'bɪlətɪ] credibilità *f inv*

cred·i·ble ['kredəbl] *adj* credibile

cred·it ['kredɪt] **1** *n* FIN credito *m*; (*honour*) merito *m*; **be in ~** avere un saldo attivo; **get the ~ for sth** prendersi il merito di qc **2** *v/t* (*believe*) credere; **~ an amount to an account** accreditare una cifra su un conto

cred·i·ta·ble ['kredɪtəbl] *adj* lodevole

'**cred·it card** carta *f* di credito

'**cred·it lim·it** limite *m* di credito

cred·i·tor ['kredɪtə(r)] creditore *m*, -trice *f*

'**cred·it·wor·thy** *adj* solvibile

cred·u·lous ['kredjʊləs] *adj* credulo

creed [kri:d] credo *m inv*

creep [kri:p] **1** *n pej* tipo *m* odioso **2** *v/i* (*pret & pp* **crept**) *quietly* avanzare quatto quatto; *slowly* avanzare lentamente

creep·er ['kri:pə(r)] BOT rampicante *m*

creeps [kri:ps] *npl* F: **the house / he gives me the ~** la casa / lui mi fa venire la pelle d'oca

creep·y ['kri:pɪ] *adj* F che dà i brividi; **be ~** F far paura

cre·mate [krɪ'meɪt] *v/t* cremare

cre·ma·tion [krɪ'meɪʃn] cremazione *f*

cre·ma·to·ri·um [kremə'tɔːrɪəm] crematorio *m*

crept [krept] *pret & pp* → **creep**

cres·cent ['kresənt] *n shape* mezzaluna *f*

crest [krest] *of hill, bird* cresta *f*

crest·fal·len *adj* abbattuto

cre·vasse [krə'væs] voragine *f*

crev·ice ['krevɪs] crepa *f*

crew [kru:] *n of ship, plane* equipaggio *m*; *of workers etc* squadra *f*; (*film ~*) troupe *f inv*; (*crowd, group*) ghenga *f*

'**crew cut** taglio *m* a spazzola

'**crew neck** girocollo *m*

crick [krɪk] *n*: **~ in the neck** torcicollo *m*

crick·et ['krɪkɪt] *insect* grillo *m*; *game* cricket *m inv*

crime [kraɪm] (*offence*) reato *m*; (*criminality*) criminalità *f inv*; (*shameful act*) crimine *m*

crim·i·nal ['krɪmɪnl] **1** *n* delinquente *m/f* **2** *adj* LAW penale; (*shameful*) vergognoso; **a ~ offence** un reato

crim·son ['krɪmzn] *adj* cremisi *inv*

cringe [krɪndʒ] *v/i* morire di vergogna

crip·ple ['krɪpl] **1** *n* (*disabled person*) invalido *m*, -a *f* **2** *v/t person* rendere invalido; *fig* paralizzare

cri·sis ['kraɪsɪs] (*pl* **crises** ['kraɪsi:z]) crisi *f inv*

crisp [krɪsp] *adj weather, air, lettuce, new shirt* fresco; *bacon, toast* croccante; *bank notes* nuovo di zecca

crisps [krɪsps] *npl Br* patatine *fpl*

cri·te·ri·on [kraɪ'tɪərɪən] criterio *m*

crit·ic ['krɪtɪk] critico *m*, -a *f*

crit·i·cal ['krɪtɪkl] *adj* critico

crit·i·cal·ly ['krɪtɪklɪ] *adv speak etc* criticamente; **~ ill** gravemente malato

crit·i·cis·m ['krɪtɪsɪzm] critica *f*

crit·i·cize ['krɪtɪsaɪz] *v/t* criticare

croak [krəʊk] **1** *n of frog* gracidio *m*; *of person* rantolo *m* **2** *v/i of frog* gracidare; *of person* parlare con voce rauca

cro·chet ['krəʊʃeɪ] **1** *n* lavoro *m* all'uncinetto **2** *v/t* lavorare all'uncinetto

crock·e·ry ['krɒkərɪ] stoviglie *fpl*

croc·o·dile ['krɒkədaɪl] coccodrillo *m*

cro·cus ['krəʊkəs] croco *m*

cro·ny ['krəʊnɪ] F amico *m*, -a *f*

crook [krʊk] *n* truffatore *m*, -trice *f*

crook·ed ['krʊkɪd] *adj streets* tortuoso; *picture* storto; (*dishonest*) disonesto

crop [krɒp] **1** *n* raccolto *m*; *type of grain etc* coltura *f*; *fig* scaglione *m* **2** *v/t* (*pret & pp* **-ped**) *hair, photo* tagliare

♦**crop up** *v/i* venir fuori

cross [krɒs] **1** *adj* (*angry*) arrabbiato **2** *n* croce *f* **3** *v/t* (*go across*) attraversare; **~ one's legs** accavallare le gambe; **keep one's fingers ~ed** fare gli scongiuri; **it never ~ed my mind** non mi è passato per la testa **4** *v/i* (*go across*) attraversare; *of lines* intersecarsi

♦ **cross off, cross out** *v/t* depennare

'**cross·bar** *of goal* traversa *f*; *of bicycle* canna *f*; *in high jump* asticella *f*

'**cross·check 1** *n* controllo *m* incrociato **2** *v/t* fare un controllo incrociato su

cross-'coun·try corsa *f* campestre

cross-coun·try ('ski·ing) sci *m inv* di fondo

crossed 'check *Am*, **crossed 'cheque** [krɒst] assegno *m* sbarrato

cross-ex·am·i'na·tion LAW interrogatorio *m* in contraddittorio

cross-ex'am·ine *v/t* LAW interrogare in contraddittorio

cross-eyed ['krɒsaɪd] *adj* strabico

cross·ing ['krɒsɪŋ] NAUT traversata *f*; *for pedestrians* attraversamento *m* pedonale

'**cross·roads** *nsg* incrocio *m*; *fig* bivio *m*; '**cross·sec·tion** *of people* campione *m* rappresentativo; '**cross·walk** *Am* passaggio *m* pedonale; '**cross·word (puz·zle)** cruciverba *m inv*

crotch [krɒtʃ] *of person* inguine *m*; *of trousers* cavallo *m*

crouch [krautʃ] *v/i* accovacciarsi

crow [krəʊ] *n bird* corvo *m*; **as the ~ flies** in linea d'aria

'**crow·bar** piede *m* di porco

crowd [kraud] *n* folla *f*

crowd·ed ['kraudɪd] *adj* affollato

crown [kraun] **1** *n* corona *f*; *on tooth* capsula *f* **2** *v/t king* incoronare; *tooth* incapsulare

cru·cial ['kruːʃl] *adj* essenziale

cru·ci·fix ['kruːsɪfɪks] crocifisso *m*

cru·ci·fix·ion [kruːsɪ'fɪkʃn] crocifissione *f*

cru·ci·fy ['kruːsɪfaɪ] *v/t* (*pret & pp* **-ied**) REL crocifiggere; *fig* fare a pezzi

crude [kruːd] **1** *adj* (*vulgar*) volgare; (*unsophisticated*) rudimentale **2** *n*: **~ (oil)** (petrolio *m*) greggio *m*

crude·ly ['kruːdlɪ] *adv speak* volgarmente; *made* rozzamente

cru·el ['kruːəl] *adj* crudele

cru·el·ty ['kruːəltɪ] crudeltà *f inv*

cruise [kruːz] **1** *n* crociera *f* **2** *v/i of people* fare una crociera; *of car, plane* viaggiare a velocità di crociera

'**cruise lin·er** nave *f* da crociera

'**cruis·ing speed** ['kruːzɪŋ] *also fig* velocità *f inv* di crociera

crumb [krʌm] briciola *f*

crum·ble ['krʌmbl] **1** *v/t* sbriciolare **2** *v/i of bread* sbriciolarsi; *of stonework* sgretolarsi; *fig: of opposition etc* crollare

crum·bly ['krʌmblɪ] *adj* friabile

crum·ple ['krʌmpl] **1** *v/t* (*crease*) sgualcire **2** *v/i* (*collapse*) accasciarsi

crunch [krʌntʃ] **1** *n* F: **when it comes to the ~** al momento cruciale **2** *v/i of snow, gravel* scricchiolare

cru·sade [kruː'seɪd] *n also fig* crociata *f*

crush [krʌʃ] **1** *n crowd* ressa *f*; **have a ~ on** avere una cotta per **2** *v/t* schiacciare; (*crease*) sgualcire; **they were ~ed to death** sono morti schiacciati **3** *v/i* (*crease*) sgualcire

crust [krʌst] *on bread* crosta *f*

crust·y ['krʌstɪ] *adj bread* croccante

crutch [krʌtʃ] *for injured person* stampella *f*

cry [kraɪ] **1** *n* (*call*) grido *m*; **have a ~** piangere **2** *v/t* (*pret & pp* **-ied**) (*call*) gridare **3** *v/i* (*pret & pp* **-ied**) (*weep*) piangere

♦ **cry out** *v/t* & *v/i* gridare

♦ **cry out for** *v/t* (*need*) aver fortemente bisogno di

cryp·tic ['krɪptɪk] *adj* sibillino

crys·tal ['krɪstl] **1** *n mineral* cristallo *m*; *glass* cristalli *mpl* **2** *adj* di cristallo

crys·tal·lize ['krɪstlaɪz] **1** *v/t* concretizzare **2** v/i of thoughts etc concretizzarsi

cub [kʌb] cucciolo m

Cu·ba ['kjuːbə] Cuba f

Cu·ban ['kjuːbən] **1** adj cubano **2** n cubano m, -a f

cube [kjuːb] shape cubo m

cu·bic ['kjuːbɪk] adj cubico

cu·bic ca·pac·i·ty TECH cilindrata f

cu·bi·cle ['kjuːbɪkl] (changing room) cabina f

cu·cum·ber ['kjuːkʌmbə(r)] cetriolo m

cud·dle ['kʌdl] **1** n coccole fpl **2** v/t coccolare

cud·dly ['kʌdlɪ] adj kitten etc tenero; liking cuddles coccolone

cue [kjuː] n for actor etc imbeccata f; for billiards stecca f

cuff [kʌf] **1** n of shirt polsino m; (blow) schiaffo m; Am (of trousers) risvolto m; **off the ~** improvvisando **2** v/t hit dare uno schiaffo a

'**cuff link** gemello m

'**cul-de-sac** ['kʌldəsæk] vicolo m cieco

cu·li·nar·y ['kʌlɪnərɪ] adj culinario

cul·mi·nate ['kʌlmɪneɪt] v/i culminare; **~ in** culminare in

cul·mi·na·tion [kʌlmɪ'neɪʃn] culmine m

cu·lottes ['kjuːlɒt] npl gonna f pantalone

cul·prit ['kʌlprɪt] colpevole m/f

cult [kʌlt] culto m

cul·ti·vate ['kʌltɪveɪt] v/t land coltivare; person coltivarsi

cul·ti·vat·ed ['kʌltɪveɪtɪd] adj person colto

cul·ti·va·tion [kʌltɪ'veɪʃn] of land coltivazione f

cul·tur·al ['kʌltʃərəl] adj culturale

cul·ture ['kʌltʃə(r)] n cultura f

cul·tured ['kʌltʃəd] adj (cultivated) colto

'**cul·ture shock** shock m inv culturale

cum·ber·some ['kʌmbəsəm] adj ingombrante; procedure macchinoso

cu·mu·la·tive ['kjuːmjʊlətɪv] adj cumulativo

cun·ning ['kʌnɪŋ] **1** n astuzia f **2** adj astuto

cup [kʌp] n tazza f; (trophy) coppa f; **a ~ of tea** una tazza di tè

cup·board ['kʌbəd] armadio m

'**cup fi·nal** finale f di coppa

cu·po·la ['kjuːpələ] cupola f

'**cup tie** partita f di coppa

cur·a·ble ['kjʊərəbl] adj curabile

cu·ra·tor [kjʊə'reɪtə(r)] direttore m, -trice di museo

curb [kɜːb] **1** n on powers etc freno m **2** v/t tenere a freno

cur·dle ['kɜːdl] v/i of milk cagliare

cure [kjʊə(r)] **1** n MED cura f **2** v/t MED guarire; by drying essiccare; by salting salare; by smoking affumicare

cur·few ['kɜːfjuː] coprifuoco m

cu·ri·os·i·ty [kjʊərɪ'ɒsətɪ] curiosità f inv

cu·ri·ous ['kjʊərɪəs] adj (inquisitive) curioso; (strange) strano

cu·ri·ous·ly ['kjʊərɪəslɪ] adv (inquisitively) con curiosità; (strangely) stranamente; **~ enough ...** sembrerà strano ma ...

curl [kɜːl] **1** n in hair ricciolo m; of smoke spirale f **2** v/t arricciare **3** v/i of hair arricciarsi; of leaf, paper etc accartocciarsi

♦ **curl up** v/i acciambellarsi

curl·y ['kɜːlɪ] adj hair riccio; tail a ricciolo

cur·rant ['kʌrənt] (dried fruit) uva f passa

cur·ren·cy ['kʌrənsɪ] money valuta f; **foreign ~** valuta estera

cur·rent ['kʌrənt] **1** n corrente f **2** adj (present) attuale

'**cur·rent ac·count** conto m corrente

cur·rent af·fairs, cur·rent e'vents npl attualità f inv

cur·rent af·fairs pro·gramme programma m di attualità

cur·rent·ly ['kʌrəntlɪ] adv attualmente

cur·ric·u·lum [kə'rɪkjʊləm] programma m (scolastico)

cur·ric·u·lum vi·tae ['viːtaɪ]

curriculum *m inv* vitae

cur·ry ['kʌrɪ] *dish* piatto *m* al curry; *spice* curry *m inv*

curse [kɜːs] **1** *n spell* maledizione *f*; (*swearword*) imprecazione *f* **2** *v/t* maledire; (*swear at*) imprecare contro **3** *v/i* (*swear*) imprecare

cur·sor ['kɜːsə(r)] COMPUT cursore *m*

cur·so·ry ['kɜːsərɪ] *adj* di sfuggita

curt [kɜːt] *adj* brusco

cur·tail [kɜː'teɪl] *v/t trip etc* accorciare

cur·tain ['kɜːtn] tenda *f*; THEA sipario *m*

curve [kɜːv] **1** *n* curva *f* **2** *v/i* (*bend*) fare una curva

cush·ion ['kʊʃn] **1** *n for couch etc* cuscino *m* **2** *v/t blow, fall* attutire

cus·tard ['kʌstəd] crema *f* (pasticcicra)

cus·to·dy ['kʌstədɪ] *of children* custodia *f*; **in ~** LAW in detenzione preventiva

cus·tom ['kʌstəm] (*tradition*) usanza *f*; COM clientela *f*; **as was his ~** com'era suo solito

cus·tom·a·ry ['kʌstəmərɪ] *adj* consueto; **it is ~ to ...** è consuetudine ...

cus·tom·er ['kʌstəmə(r)] cliente *m/f*

cus·tom·er re'la·tions *npl* relazione *f* clienti

cus·tom·er 'serv·ice servizio *m* assistenza al cliente

cus·toms ['kʌstəmz] *npl* dogana *f*

Cus·toms and 'Ex·cise Ufficio *m* Dazi e Dogana; **'cus·toms clear·ance** sdoganamento *m*; **'cus·toms in·spec·tion** controllo *m* doganale; **'cus·toms of·fi·cer** doganiere *m*, -a *f*

cut [kʌt] **1** *n with knife, of hair, clothes* taglio *m*; (*reduction*) riduzione *f*; **in public spending** taglio *m*; **my hair needs a ~** devo tagliarmi i capelli **2** *v/t* (*pret & pp* **cut**) tagliare; (*reduce*) ridurre; **get one's hair ~** tagliarsi i capelli; **I ~ my finger** mi sono tagliato un dito

♦ **cut back 1** *v/i in costs* limitare le spese **2** *v/t employees* ridurre

♦ **cut down 1** *v/t tree* abbattere **2** *v/i in smoking etc* limitarsi

♦ **cut down on** *v/t cigarettes, chocolate* ridurre la quantità di; **cut down on smoking** fumare di meno

♦ **cut off** *v/t with knife, scissors etc* tagliare; (*isolate*) isolare; **I've been cut off** TELEC è caduta la linea

♦ **cut out** *v/t with scissors* ritagliare; (*eliminate*) eliminare; **cut that out!** Ⓕ smettila!; **be cut out for sth** essere tagliato per qc

♦ **cut up** *v/t meat etc* sminuzzare

cut·back *in production* riduzione *f*; *in public spending* taglio *m*

cute [kjuːt] *adj* (*pretty*) carino; (*smart, clever*) furbo

cu·ti·cle ['kjuːtɪkl] pellicina *f*

cut·ler·y ['kʌtlərɪ] posate *fpl*

'cut-off date scadenza *f*

cut-'price *adj goods* a prezzo ridotto; *store* di articoli scontati

cut-'throat *adj competition* spietato

cut·ting ['kʌtɪŋ] **1** *n from newspaper etc* ritaglio *m* **2** *adj remark* tagliente

CV [siː'viː] *abbr* (= **curriculum vitae**) CV *m inv* (= curriculum *m inv* vitae)

'cy·ber·space ['saɪbəspeɪs] ciberspazio *m*

cy·cle ['saɪkl] **1** *n* (*bicycle*) bicicletta *f*; *of events* ciclo *m* **2** *v/i to work* andare in bicicletta

'cy·cle path pista *f* ciclabile

cy·cling ['saɪklɪŋ] ciclismo *m*; **he's taken up ~** ha cominciato ad andare in bicicletta

cy·clist ['saɪklɪst] ciclista *m/f*

cyl·in·der ['sɪlɪndə(r)] cilindro *m*

cy·lin·dri·cal [sɪ'lɪndrɪkl] *adj* cilindrico

cyn·ic ['sɪnɪk] cinico *m*, -a *f*

cyn·i·cal ['sɪnɪkl] *adj* cinico

cyn·i·cal·ly ['sɪnɪklɪ] *adv* cinicamente

cyn·i·cism ['sɪnɪsɪzm] cinismo *m*

cy·press ['saɪprəs] cipresso *m*

cyst [sɪst] cisti *f inv*

Czech [tʃek] **1** *adj* ceco; **the ~ Republic** la Repubblica Ceca **2** *n person* ceco *m*, -a *f*; *language* ceco *m*

D

dab [dæb] **1** n (small amount) tocco m, pochino m **2** v/t (remove) (pret & pp **-bed**) tamponare; (apply) applicare; una pomata sul taglio; **~ a cut with ointment** applicare una pomata sul taglio
♦ **dabble in** v/t dilettarsi di
dad [dæd] papà m inv
dad·dy ['dædɪ] papà m inv
dad·dy long·legs zanzarone m
daf·fo·dil ['dæfədɪl] trombone m
daft [dɑːft] adj stupido
dag·ger ['dægə(r)] pugnale m
dai·ly ['deɪlɪ] **1** n (paper) quotidiano m; (cleaning woman) domestica f **2** adj quotidiano
dain·ty ['deɪntɪ] adj aggraziato
dair·y cat·tle ['deərɪ] vacche fpl da latte; **'dair·y farm·ing** produzione f di latticini; **'dair·y prod·ucts** npl latticini mpl
dais ['deɪɪs] palco m
dai·sy ['deɪzɪ] margherita f
dam [dæm] **1** n for water diga f **2** v/t (pret & pp **-med**) river costruire una diga su
dam·age ['dæmɪdʒ] **1** n also fig danno m **2** v/t danneggiare; fig: reputation etc compromettere
dam·ages ['dæmɪdʒɪz] npl LAW risarcimento msg
dam·ag·ing ['dæmɪdʒɪŋ] adj nocivo
dame [deɪm] Am F (woman) tizia f F; **she's quite a ~!** che donna!
damn [dæm] **1** int F accidenti **2** F **I don't give a ~!** non me ne frega niente! F **3** adj F maledetto **4** adv F incredibilmente **5** v/t (condemn) maledire; **~ it!** F accidenti!; **I'm ~ed if I will** F non me lo sogno nemmeno
damned [dæmd] → **damn** adj & adv
damn·ing ['dæmɪŋ] adj evidence schiacciante; report incriminante
damp [dæmp] adj umido
damp·en ['dæmpən] v/t inumidire

dance [dɑːns] **1** n ballo m **2** v/i ballare; of ballerina danzare; **would you like to ~?** ti va di ballare?; fml posso invitarla a ballare?
danc·er ['dɑːnsə(r)] (performer) ballerino m, -a f; **be a good ~** ballare bene
danc·ing ['dɑːnsɪŋ] ballo m, danza f
dan·de·lion ['dændɪlaɪən] dente m di leone
dan·druff ['dændrʌf] forfora f
dan·druff sham'poo shampoo m inv antiforfora inv
Dane [deɪn] danese m/f
dan·ger ['deɪndʒə(r)] pericolo m; **be in ~** essere in pericolo; **out of ~** of patient fuori pericolo
dan·ger·ous ['deɪndʒərəs] adj pericoloso
dan·ger·ous 'driv·ing guida f pericolosa
dan·ger·ous·ly ['deɪndʒərəslɪ] adv drive spericolatamente; **~ ill** gravemente malato
dan·gle ['dæŋgl] **1** v/t dondolare **2** v/i pendere
Da·nish ['deɪnɪʃ] **1** adj danese **2** n (language) danese m
Da·nish ('pastry) dolcetto m ripieno
dare [deə(r)] **1** v/i osare; **~ to do sth** osare fare qc; **how ~ you!** come osi! **2** v/t: **~ s.o. to do sth** sfidare qu a fare qc
dare·dev·il ['deədevɪl] scavezzacollo m
dar·ing ['deərɪŋ] adj audace
dark [dɑːk] **1** n buio m, oscurità f; **after ~** dopo il calare della notte; **keep s.o. in the ~** fig tenere qu all'oscuro **2** adj room, night buio; hair, eyes, colour scuro; **~ green/blue** verde/blu scuro
dark·en ['dɑːkn] v/i of sky oscurarsi
dark 'glass·es npl occhiali mpl scuri

dark·ness ['dɑːknɪs] oscurità *f*

'dark·room PHOT camera *f* oscura

dar·ling ['dɑːlɪŋ] **1** *n* tesoro *m*; **be a ~ and ...** sii carino e ... **2** *adj* caro

darn [dɑːn] **1** *n* (*mend*) rammendo *m* **2** *v/t* (*mend*) rammendare

dart [dɑːt] **1** *n for throwing* freccetta *f* **2** *v/i* scagliarsi

darts [dɑːts] *nsg* (*game*) freccette *fpl*

'dart(s)·board tabellone *m* delle freccette

dash [dæʃ] **1** *n in punctuation* trattino *m*, lineetta *f*; *of whisky, milk* goccio *m*; *of salt* pizzico *m*; (MOT: *dashboard*) cruscotto *m*; **make a ~ for** precipitarsi su **2** *v/i* precipitarsi; **I must ~** devo scappare **3** *v/t hopes* stroncare

♦ **dash off 1** *v/i* scappare **2** *v/t* (*write quickly*) buttare giù

'dash·board cruscotto *m*

data ['deɪtə] *mpl*

'data·base base *f* dati; **da·ta 'cap·ture** inserimento *f* dati; **da·ta 'pro·cess·ing** elaborazione *f* dati; **da·ta pro'tec·tion** protezione *f* dati; **da·ta 'stor·age** memorizzazione *f* dati, archiviazione *f* dati

date¹ [deɪt] (*fruit*) dattero *m*

date² [deɪt] **1** *n* data *f*; (*meeting*) appuntamento *m*; **your ~ is here** è arrivato il tuo ragazzo, è arrivata la tua ragazza; **what's the ~ today?** quanti ne abbiamo oggi?; **out of ~** *clothes* fuori moda; *passport* scaduto; **up to ~** aggiornato; (*fashionable*) attuale **2** *v/t letter, cheque* datare; (*go out with*) uscire con; **that ~s you** (*shows your age*) quanto sei vecchio

dat·ed ['deɪtɪd] *adj* superato

daub [dɔːb] *v/t*: **~ paint on a wall** imbrattare il muro di vernice

daugh·ter ['dɔːtə(r)] figlia *f*

'daugh·ter-in-law (*pl* **daughters-in-law**) nuora *f*

daunt [dɔːnt] *v/t* scoraggiare

daw·dle ['dɔːdl] *v/i* ciondolare

dawn [dɔːn] **1** *n* alba *f*; *fig: of new age* albori *mpl* **2** *v/i*: **it ~ed on me that ...** mi sono reso conto che ...

day [deɪ] giorno *m*; **what ~ is it today?** che giorno è oggi?; **~ off** giorno *m* di ferie; **by ~** di giorno; **~ by ~** giorno per giorno; **the ~ after** il giorno dopo; **the ~ after tomorrow** dopodomani; **the ~ before** il giorno prima; **the ~ before yesterday** l'altro ieri; **~ in ~ out** senza tregua; **in those ~s** a quei tempi; **one ~** un giorno; **the other ~** (*recently*) l'altro giorno; **let's call it a ~!** lasciamo perdere!

'day boy alunno *m* esterno; **'day·break: at ~** allo spuntare del giorno; **'day care** asilo *m*; **'day·dream 1** *n* sogno *m* ad occhi aperti **2** *v/i* essere sovrappensiero; **'day dream·er** sognatore *m*, -trice *f*; **day girl** alunna *f* esterna; **day re'turn** biglietto *m* di andata e ritorno in giornata; **'day·time: in the ~** durante il giorno; **day·light 'sav·ing time** ora *f* legale; **'day-trip** gita *f* di un giorno

daze [deɪz] *n*: **in a ~** sbalordito

dazed [deɪzd] *adj by good / bad news* sbalordito; *by a blow* stordito

daz·zle ['dæzl] *v/t of light, fig* abbagliare

DC [diː'siː] *abbr* (= **direct current**) c.c.; (= corrente *f* continua); *District of Columbia*) DC

dead [ded] **1** *adj person, plant* morto; *battery* scarica; *phone* muto; *light bulb* bruciato; **be ~** *of place* essere un mortorio F **2** *adv* F (*very*) da matti F; **~ beat, ~ tired** stanco morto; **that's ~ right** è assolutamente vero; **it's ~ interesting** è interessante da matti F **3** *n*: **the ~** (*dead people*) i morti; **in the ~ of night** nel cuore della notte

dead·en ['dedn] *v/t pain* attenuare; *sound* attutire

dead 'end (*street*) vicolo *m* cieco; **dead-'end job** lavoro *m* senza prospettive; **dead 'heat** pareggio *m*; **'dead·line** scadenza *f*; *for newspaper, magazine* termine *m* per l'invio in stampa; **'dead·lock** *n in talks* punto *m* morto

dead·ly ['dedlɪ] *adj* (*fatal*) mortale; F

(*boring*) di una noia mortale F

deaf [def] *adj* sordo

deaf-and-'dumb *adj* sordomuto

deaf·en ['defn] *v/t* assordare

deaf·en·ing ['defnɪŋ] *adj* assordante

deaf·ness ['defnɪs] sordità *f inf*

deal [diːl] **1** *n* accordo *m*; *it's a ~!* affare fatto!; *a good ~ (bargain)* un affare; *(a lot)* molto; *a great ~ of (lots)* un bel po' di; *it's your ~ in games* tocca a te **2** *v/t* (*pret & pp* **dealt**) *cards* distribuire; *~ a blow to* inferire un duro colpo a

♦ **deal in** *v/t* (*trade in*) trattare; *drugs* trafficare

♦ **deal out** *v/t cards* distribuire

♦ **deal with** *v/t* (*handle*) occuparsi di; *situation* gestire; (*do business with*) trattare con

deal·er ['diːlə(r)] (*merchant*) commerciante *m/f*; (*drug ~*) spacciatore *m*, -trice *f*

deal·ing ['diːlɪŋ] (*drug ~*) spaccio *m*

deal·ings ['diːlɪŋz] *npl* (*business*) rapporti *mpl*

dealt [delt] *pret & pp* → **deal**

dean [diːn] *of college* preside *m*

dear [dɪə(r)] *adj* caro; *Dear Sir* Egregio Signore; *Dear Richard / Dear Margaret* caro Richard / cara Margareth; (*oh*) *~!, ~ me!* povero / a me!

dear·ly ['dɪəlɪ] *adv love* teneramente

death [deθ] morte *f*

'death cer·tif·i·cate certificato *m* di decesso; **'death pen·al·ty** pena *f* di morte; **'death toll** numero *m* delle vittime

de·ba·ta·ble [dɪ'beɪtəbl] *adj* discutibile

de·bate [dɪ'beɪt] **1** *n* dibattimento *m*; POL dibattito *m*; *after much ~* dopo molto dibattere **2** *v/i* dibattere; *~ with o.s. whether ...* considerare se ... **3** *v/t* dibattere su

de·bauch·er·y [dɪ'bɔːtʃərɪ] depravazione *f*

deb·it ['debɪt] **1** *n* addebito *m* **2** *v/t*: *~ £150 to s.o.'s account* addebitare £ 150 a qu; *~ an account with £ 150*

addebitare £ 150 su un conto

'deb·it card carta *f* di debito

deb·ris ['debriː] *of plane* rottami *mpl*; *of building* macerie *fpl*

debt [det] debito *m*; *be in ~ (financially)* avere dei debiti

debt·or ['detə(r)] debitore *m*, -trice *f*

de·bug [diː'bʌg] *v/t* (*pret & pp* **-ged**) *room* togliere le microspie da; COMPUT togliere gli errori di

dé·but ['deɪbjuː] *n* debutto *m*

dec·ade ['dekeɪd] decennio *m*, decade *f*

dec·a·dence ['dekədəns] decadenza *f*

dec·a·dent ['dekədənt] *adj* decadente

de·caf·fein·at·ed [dɪ'kæfɪneɪtɪd] *adj* decaffeinato

de·cant·er [dɪ'kæntə(r)] caraffa *f*

de·cap·i·tate [dɪ'kæpɪteɪt] *v/t* decapitare

de·cay [dɪ'keɪ] **1** *n of organic matter* decomposizione *f*; *of civilization* declino *m*; (*decayed matter*) marciume *m*; *in teeth* carie *f inv* **2** *v/i of organic matter* decomporsi; *of civilization* declinare; *of teeth* cariarsi

de·ceased [dɪ'siːst]: *the ~* il defunto *m*, la defunta *f*

de·ceit [dɪ'siːt] falsità *f*, disonestà *f*

de·ceit·ful [dɪ'siːtfʊl] *adj* falso, disonesto

de·ceive [dɪ'siːv] *v/t* ingannare

De·cem·ber [dɪ'sembə(r)] dicembre *m*

de·cen·cy ['diːsənsɪ] decenza *f*; *he had the ~ to ...* ha avuto la decenza di ...

de·cent ['diːsənt] *adj price, proposition* corretto; *meal, sleep* decente; (*adequately dressed*) presentabile; *a ~ guy* un uomo per bene; *that's very ~ of you* è molto gentile da parte tua

de·cen·tral·ize [diː'sentrəlaɪz] *v/t* decentralizzare

de·cep·tion [dɪ'sepʃn] inganno *m*

de·cep·tive [dɪ'septɪv] *adj* ingannevole

de·cep·tive·ly [dɪ'septɪvlɪ] *adv*: *it*

looks ~ simple sembra semplice solo all'apparenza

dec·i·bel ['desɪbel] decibel *m inv*

de·cide [dɪ'saɪd] **1** *v/t* (*make up one's mind*) decidere; (*conclude, settle*) risolvere **2** *v/i* decidere; *you ~* decidi tu

de·cid·ed [dɪ'saɪdɪd] *adj* (*definite*) deciso

de·cid·er [dɪ'saɪdə(r)]: *be the ~ of match etc* essere decisivo

de·cid·u·ous [dɪ'sɪdjʊəs] *adj* che perde le foglie in inverno

dec·i·mal ['desɪml] *n* decimale

dec·i·mal 'point punto *m* che separa i decimali; in Italy virgola *f*

dec·i·mate ['desɪmeɪt] *v/t* decimare

de·ci·pher [dɪ'saɪfə(r)] *v/t* decifrare

de·ci·sion [dɪ'sɪʒn] decisione *f*; (*conclusion*) risoluzione *f*; *come to a ~* prendere una decisione

de·ci·sion-mak·er responsabile *m/f*; *be a ~* (*be able to make decisions*) saper prendere delle decisioni

de·ci·sive [dɪ'saɪsɪv] *adj* risoluto; (*crucial*) decisivo

deck [dek] *of ship* ponte *m*; *of bus* piano *m*; *of cards* mazzo *m*

'deck·chair sedia *f* a sdraio, sdraio *f inv*

dec·la·ra·tion [deklə'reɪʃn] dichiarazione *f*

de·clare [dɪ'kleə(r)] *v/t* dichiarare

de·cline [dɪ'klaɪn] **1** *n in number, standards* calo *m*; *in health* peggioramento *m* **2** *v/t invitation* declinare; *~ to comment / accept* esimersi dal commentare / accettare **3** *v/i* (*refuse*) declinare; (*decrease*) diminuire; *of health* peggiorare

de·clutch [diː'klʌtʃ] *v/i* lasciare andare la frizione

de·code [diː'kəʊd] *v/t* decodificare

de·com·pose [diːkəm'pəʊz] *v/i* decomporsi

dé·cor ['deɪkɔː(r)] arredamento *m*

dec·o·rate ['dekəreɪt] *v/t with paint* imbiancare; *with paper* tappezzare; (*adorn*), MIL decorare

dec·o·ra·tion [dekə'reɪʃn] *paint* vernice *f*; *paper* tappezzeria *f*;

(*ornament*) addobbi *mpl*; MIL decorazione *f*

dec·o·ra·tive ['dekərətɪv] *adj* decorativo

dec·o·ra·tor ['dekəreɪtə(r)] (*interior ~*) imbianchino *m*

de·co·rum [dɪ'kɔːrəm] decoro *m*

de·coy ['diːkɔɪ] *n* esca *f*

de·crease ['diːkriːs] **1** *n* diminuzione *f* **2** *v/t* ridurre **3** *v/i* ridursi

de·crep·it [dɪ'krepɪt] *adj* decrepito

ded·i·cate ['dedɪkeɪt] *v/t book etc* dedicare; *~ o.s. to ...* consacrarsi a ...

ded·i·ca·ted ['dedɪkeɪtɪd] *adj* dedito

ded·i·ca·tion [dedɪ'keɪʃn] *in book* dedica *f*; *to cause, work* dedizione *f*

de·duce [dɪ'djuːs] *v/t* dedurre

de·duct [dɪ'dʌkt] *v/t* detrarre; *~ sth from sth* detrarre qc da qc

de·duc·tion [dɪ'dʌkʃn] *from salary* trattenuta *f*; (*conclusion*) deduzione *f*; *~ at source* ritenuta *f* alla fonte

dee·jay ['diːdʒeɪ] F dj *m/f inv*

deed [diːd] *n* (*act*) azione *f*; LAW atto *m*

deem [diːm] *v/t* ritenere

deep [diːp] *adj hole, water, voice, thinker* profondo; *colour* intenso; *you're in ~ trouble* sei davvero nei guai

deep·en ['diːpn] **1** *v/t* rendere più profondo **2** *v/i* diventare più profondo; *of crisis* aggravarsi; *of mystery* infittirsi

'deep freeze *n* congelatore *m*; **'deep-froz·en food** surgelati *mpl*; **'deep-fry** *v/t* (*pret & pp -ied*) friggere (immergendo nell'olio); **deep 'fry·er** padella *f* (per friggere); *electric* friggitrice *f*

deer [dɪə(r)] (*pl deer*) cervo *m*

de·face [dɪ'feɪs] *v/t* vandalizzare

def·a·ma·tion [defə'meɪʃn] diffamazione *f*

de·fam·a·to·ry [dɪ'fæmətərɪ] *adj* diffamatorio

de·fault ['dɪfɒlt] *adj* COMPUT di default

de·feat [dɪ'fiːt] **1** *n* sconfitta *f* **2** *v/t* sconfiggere; *this problem ~s me* questo problema è troppo grande per me

de·feat·ist [dɪˈfiːtɪst] *adj attitude* disfattista

de·fect [ˈdiːfekt] *n* difetto *m*

de·fec·tive [dɪˈfektɪv] *adj* difettoso

de·fend [dɪˈfend] *v/t* difendere

de·fend·ant [dɪˈfendənt] accusato *m*, -a *f*; *in criminal case* imputato *m*, -a *f*

de·fence [dɪˈfens] difesa *f*; **come to s.o.'s ~** venire in aiuto a qu

de·fence budg·et POL budget *m inv* della difesa

de·fence law·yer avvocato *m* difensore

de·fence·less [dɪˈfenslɪs] *adj* indifeso

de·fence play·er SP difensore *m*

de·fence wit·ness LAW testimone *m/f* della difesa

de·fense *etc Am* → **defence** *etc*

de·fen·sive [dɪˈfensɪv] **1** *n*: **on the ~** sulla difensiva; **go on the ~** mettersi sulla difensiva **2** *adj weaponry* difensivo; *person* sulla difensiva

de·fen·sive·ly [dɪˈfensɪvlɪ] *adv* sulla difensiva; *play ~* SP ritirarsi in difesa

de·fer [dɪˈfɜː(r)] *v/t* (*pret & pp* **-red**) (*postpone*) rinviare

def·er·ence [ˈdefərəns] deferenza *f*

def·er·en·tial [defəˈrenʃl] *adj* deferente

de·fi·ance [dɪˈfaɪəns] sfida *f*; *in ~ of* a dispetto di

de·fi·ant [dɪˈfaɪənt] *adj* provocatorio

de·fi·cien·cy [dɪˈfɪʃənsɪ] (*lack*) carenza *f*

de·fi·cient [dɪˈfɪʃənt] *adj* carente; *be ~ in …* essere carente di …

def·i·cit [ˈdefɪsɪt] deficit *m inv*

de·fine [dɪˈfaɪn] *v/t* definire

def·i·nite [ˈdefɪnɪt] *adj date, time, answer* preciso; *improvement* netto; (*certain*) certo; *are you ~ about that?* ne sei sicuro?; *nothing ~ has been arranged* non è stato previsto niente di preciso

def·i·nite 'ar·ti·cle GRAM articolo *m* determinativo

def·i·nite·ly [ˈdefɪnɪtlɪ] *adv* senza dubbio; *smell, hear* distintamente

def·i·ni·tion [defɪˈnɪʃn] definizione *f*

de·fin·i·tive [dɪˈfɪnətɪv] *adj biography* più completo; *performance* migliore

de·flect [dɪˈflekt] *v/t ball, blow* deviare; sviare; *be ~ed from* essere sviato da

de·for·est·a·tion [dɪfɒrɪsˈteɪʃn] disboscamento *m*

de·form [dɪˈfɔːm] *v/t* deformare

de·for·mi·ty [dɪˈfɔːmɪtɪ] deformità *f inv*

de·fraud [dɪˈfrɔːd] *v/t* defraudare; *Inland Revenue* frodare

de·frost [diːˈfrɒst] *v/t food* scongelare; *fridge* sbrinare

deft [deft] *adj* agile

de·fuse [diːˈfjuːz] *v/t bomb* disinnescare; *situation* placare

de·fy [dɪˈfaɪ] *v/t* (*pret & pp* **-ied**) (*disobey*) disobbedire a

de·gen·e·rate [dɪˈdʒenəreɪt] *v/i* degenerare; *~ into* degenerare in

de·grade [dɪˈɡreɪd] *v/t* degradare

de·grad·ing [dɪˈɡreɪdɪŋ] *adj position, work* degradante

de·gree [dɪˈɡriː] *from university* laurea *f*; *of temperature, angle, latitude* grado *m*; *a ~ of* (*amount*) un po' di; *by ~s* per gradi; *to a certain ~* fino a un certo punto; *there is a ~ of truth in that* c'è del vero in questo; *get one's ~* prendere la laurea

de·hy·drat·ed [diːhaɪˈdreɪtɪd] *adj* disidratato

de-ice [diːˈaɪs] *v/t* togliere il ghiaccio da

de-ic·er [diːˈaɪsə(r)] (*spray*) antigelo *m inv*

deign [deɪn] *v/i*: *~ to …* degnarsi di …

de·i·ty [ˈdiːɪtɪ] divinità *f inv*

de·ject·ed [dɪˈdʒektɪd] *adj* sconfortato

de·lay [dɪˈleɪ] **1** *n* ritardo **2** *v/t* ritardare; *be ~ed* (*be late*) essere in ritardo; *~ doing sth* tardare a fare qc; *sorry, I've been ~ed* scusa, sono stato trattenuto **3** *v/i* tardare

del·e·gate [ˈdelɪɡət] **1** *n* delegato *m*,

-a *f* **2** *v/t* ['deligeit] *task*, *person* delegare

del·e·ga·tion [deli'geiʃn] *of task* delega *f*; (*people*) delegazione *f*

de·lete [dɪ'liːt] *v/t* cancellare

de·lete key COMPUT tasto *m* 'cancella'

de·le·tion [dɪ'liːʃn] *act* cancellazione *f*; *that deleted* cancellatura *f*

del·i ['deli] → *delicatessen*

de·lib·e·rate [dɪ'lɪbərət] **1** *adj* deliberato **2** *v/i* [dɪ'lɪbəreit] riflettere

de·lib·e·rate·ly [dɪ'lɪbərətlɪ] *adv* deliberatamente

del·i·ca·cy ['delikəsɪ] delicatezza *f*; (*food*) prelibatezza *f*

del·i·cate ['delikət] *adj* delicato

del·i·ca·tes·sen [delikə'tesn] gastronomia *f*

del·i·cious [dɪ'lɪʃəs] *adj* delizioso, ottimo

de·light [dɪ'laɪt] *n* gioia *f*; **to my great ~** con mio grande piacere

de·light·ed [dɪ'laɪtɪd] *adj* lieto

de·light·ful [dɪ'laɪtful] *adj* molto piacevole

de·lim·it [diː'lɪmɪt] *v/t* delimitare

de·lin·quen·cy [dɪ'lɪŋkwənsɪ] delinquenza *f* (minorile)

de·lin·quent [dɪ'lɪŋkwənt] *n* delinquente *m/f*

de·lir·i·ous [dɪ'lɪrɪəs] *adj* MED delirante; (*ecstatic*) in delirio

de·liv·er [dɪ'lɪvə(r)] *v/t* consegnare; *message* trasmettere; *baby* far nascere; **~ a speech** tenere un discorso

de·liv·er·y [dɪ'lɪvərɪ] *of goods*, *mail* consegna *f*; *of baby* parto *m*

de·liv·er·y charge: **there is no ~** la consegna è gratuita; **de·liv·er·y date** termine *m* di consegna; **de·liv·er·y man** fattorino *m*; **de·liv·er·y note** bolla *f*, documento *m* di trasporto; **de·liv·er·y serv·ice** consegna *f* a domicilio; **de·liv·er·y van** furgone *m* delle consegne

de·lude [dɪ'luːd] *v/t* ingannare; **~ s.o. into believing sth** far credere qc a qu; **you're deluding yourself** ti sbagli

de·luge ['deljuːdʒ] **1** *n* temporale *m*; *fig* valanga *f* **2** *v/t fig* sommergere

de·lu·sion [dɪ'luːʒn] illusione *f*; *of others* inganno *m*

de luxe [də'lʌks] *adj* di lusso

♦ **delve into** [delv] *v/t* addentrarsi in; *s.o.'s past* scavare in

de·mand [dɪ'mɑːnd] **1** *n* rivendicazione *f*; COM domanda *f*; *in ~* richiesto **2** *v/t* esigere; (*require*) richiedere

de·mand·ing [dɪ'mɑːndɪŋ] *adj job* impegnativo; *person* esigente

de·mean·ing [dɪ'miːnɪŋ] *adj* avvilente

de·men·ted [dɪ'mentɪd] *adj* demente

de·mise [dɪ'maɪz] scomparsa *f*

dem·o ['deməʊ] (*protest*) manifestazione *f*; *of video etc* dimostrazione *f*

de·moc·ra·cy [dɪ'mɒkrəsɪ] democrazia *f*

dem·o·crat ['deməkræt] democratico *m*, -a *f*; **Democrat** POL democratico *m*, -a *f*

dem·o·crat·ic [demə'krætɪk] *adj* democratico

dem·o·crat·ic·al·ly [demə'krætɪklɪ] *adv* democraticamente

'**dem·o disk** disco *m* dimostrativo

de·mo·graph·ic [deməʊ'græfɪk] *adj* demografico

de·mol·ish [dɪ'mɒlɪʃ] *v/t* demolire

dem·o·li·tion [demə'lɪʃn] demolizione *f*

de·mon ['diːmən] demone *m*

dem·on·strate ['demənstreit] **1** *v/t* (*prove*) dimostrare; *machine* fare una dimostrazione di **2** *v/i politically* manifestare

dem·on·stra·tion [demən'streiʃn] dimostrazione *f*; (*protest*) manifestazione *f*

de·mon·stra·tive [dɪ'mɒnstrətɪv] *adj* espansivo

de·mon·stra·tor ['demənstreitə(r)] (*protester*) manifestante *m/f*

de·mor·al·ized [dɪ'mɒrəlaɪzd] *adj* demoralizzato

de·mor·al·iz·ing [dɪ'mɒrəlaɪzɪŋ] *adj* demoralizzante

de·mote [diː'məʊt] *v/t* retrocedere;

MIL degradare

de·mure [dɪ'mjʊə(r)] *adj* contegnoso

den [den] (*study*) studio *m*

de·ni·al [dɪ'naɪəl] *of rumour, accusation* negazione *f*, *of request, right* negazione *f*, rifiuto *m*

den·im ['denɪm] denim *m inv*

den·ims ['denɪmz] *npl* (*jeans*) jeans *m inv*

Den·mark ['denmɑːk] Danimarca *f*

de·nom·i·na·tion [dɪnɒmɪ'neɪʃn] *of money* banconota *f*; REL confessione *f*; *money in small ~s* denaro *m* in banconote di piccolo taglio

de·nounce [dɪ'naʊns] *v/t* denunciare

dense [dens] *adj* fitto; (*stupid*) ottuso

dense·ly ['densli] *adv*: *~ populated* densamente popolato

den·si·ty ['densɪti] *of population* densità *f inv*

dent [dent] **1** *n* ammaccatura *f* **2** *v/t* ammaccare

den·tal ['dentl] *adj treatment* dentario, dentale; *hospital* dentistico

dent·ed ['dentɪd] *adj* ammaccato

den·tist ['dentɪst] dentista *m/f*

den·tist·ry ['dentɪstrɪ] odontoiatria *f*

den·tures ['dentʃəz] *npl* dentiera *f*

de·ny [dɪ'naɪ] *v/t* (*pret & pp -ied*) negare; *rumour* smentire; *I was denied the right to ...* mi è stato negato il diritto di …

de·o·do·rant [diː'əʊdərənt] deodorante *m*

de·part [dɪ'pɑːt] *v/i* partire; *~ from* (*deviate from*) allontanarsi da

de·part·ment [dɪ'pɑːtmənt] *of university* dipartimento *m*; *of government* ministero *m*; *of store, company* reparto *m*

de·part·ment store grande magazzino *m*

de·par·ture [dɪ'pɑːtʃə(r)] partenza *f*; (*deviation*) allontanamento *m*; *a new ~ for government, organization* una svolta

de·par·ture lounge sala *f* partenze

de·par·ture time ora *f* di partenza

de·pend [dɪ'pend] *v/i*: *that ~s* dipen-

de; *it ~s on the weather* dipende dal tempo; *I am ~ing on you* conto su di te

de·pen·da·ble [dɪ'pendəbl] *adj* affidabile

de·pen·dant [dɪ'pendənt] → ***dependent***

de·pen·dence, de·pen·den·cy [dɪ'pendəns, dɪ'pendənsɪ] dipendenza *f*

de·pen·dent [dɪ'pendənt] **1** *n* persona *f* a carico; *a married man with ~s* un uomo sposato con famiglia a carico **2** *adj* dipendente; *~ children* figli *mpl* a carico

de·pict [dɪ'pɪkt] *v/t in painting, writing* raffigurare

de·plete [dɪ'pliːt] *v/t* intaccare

de·plor·a·ble [dɪ'plɔːrəbl] *adj* deplorevole

de·plore [dɪ'plɔː(r)] *v/t* deplorare, lamentarsi di

de·ploy [dɪ'plɔɪ] *v/t* (*use*) spiegare; (*position*) schierare

de·pop·u·la·tion [diːpɒpjʊ'leɪʃn] spopolamento *m*

de·port [dɪ'pɔːt] *v/t* deportare

de·por·ta·tion [diːpɔː'teɪʃn] deportazione *f*

de·por'ta·tion or·der ordine *m* di deportazione

de·pose [dɪ'pəʊz] *v/t* deporre

de·pos·it [dɪ'pɒzɪt] **1** *n in bank* versamento *m*, deposito *m*; *of mineral* deposito *m*; *on purchase* acconto *m*; (*against loss, damage*) cauzione *f* **2** *v/t money* versare, depositare; (*put down*) lasciare; *silt, mud* depositare

de'pos·it ac·count libretto *m* di risparmio

dep·ot ['depəʊ] (*train station*) stazione *f* ferroviaria; (*bus station*) rimessa *f* degli autobus; *for storage* magazzino *m*

de·praved [dɪ'preɪvd] *adj* depravato

de·pre·ci·ate [dɪ'priːʃɪeɪt] *v/i* FIN svalutarsi

de·pre·ci·a·tion [dɪpriːʃɪ'eɪʃn] FIN svalutazione *f*

de·press [dɪˈpres] *v/t person* deprimere

de·pressed [dɪˈprest] *adj person* depresso

de·press·ing [dɪˈpresɪŋ] *adj* deprimente

de·pres·sion [dɪˈpreʃn] depressione *f*

dep·ri·va·tion [deprɪˈveɪʃn] privazione *f*; (*lack: of sleep, food*) carenza *f*

de·prive [dɪˈpraɪv] *v/t*: ~ *s.o. of sth* privare qu di qc

de·prived [dɪˈpraɪvd] *adj* socialmente svantaggiato

depth [depθ] profondità *f inv*; *in* ~ (*thoroughly*) a fondo; *in the ~s of winter* in pieno inverno; *be out of one's* ~ *in water* non toccare (il fondo); *when they talk about politics I'm out of my* ~ la politica va al di là della mia comprensione

dep·u·ta·tion [depjʊˈteɪʃn] deputazione *f*

♦ **deputize for** [ˈdepjʊtaɪz] *v/t* fare le veci di

dep·u·ty [ˈdepjʊtɪ] vice *m/f inv*

ˈdep·u·ty lead·er *of party* vice segretario *m*

de·rail [dɪˈreɪl] *v/t*: *be ~ed of train* essere deragliato

de·ranged [dɪˈreɪndʒd] *adj* squilibrato

de·reg·u·late [diːˈregjʊleɪt] *v/t* deregolamentare

de·reg·u·la·tion [diːregjʊˈleɪʃn] deregolamentazione *f*

der·e·lict [ˈderəlɪkt] *adj* desolato

de·ride [dɪˈraɪd] *v/t* deridere

de·ri·sion [dɪˈrɪʒn] derisione *f*

de·ri·sive [dɪˈraɪsɪv] *adj remarks, laughter* derisorio

de·ri·sive·ly [dɪˈraɪsɪvlɪ] *adv* con aria derisoria

de·ri·so·ry [dɪˈraɪsərɪ] *adj amount, salary* irrisorio

de·riv·a·tive [dɪˈrɪvətɪv] *adj (not original)* derivato

de·rive [dɪˈraɪv] *v/t* trarre; *be ~d from of word* derivare da

der·ma·tol·o·gist [dɜːməˈtɒlədʒɪst]

dermatologo *m*, -a *f*

de·rog·a·to·ry [dɪˈrɒgətrɪ] *adj* peggiorativo

de·scend [dɪˈsend] **1** *v/t* scendere; *be ~ed from* discendere da **2** *v/i* scendere; *of mood, darkness* calare

de·scen·dant [dɪˈsendənt] discendente *m/f*

de·scent [dɪˈsent] discesa *f*; (*ancestry*) discendenza *f*; *of Chinese* ~ di origini cinesi

de·scribe [dɪˈskraɪb] *v/t* descrivere; ~ *sth as sth* descrivere qc come qc

de·scrip·tion [dɪˈskrɪpʃn] descrizione *f*

des·e·crate [ˈdesɪkreɪt] *v/t* profanare

des·e·cra·tion [desɪˈkreɪʃn] profanazione *f*

de·seg·re·gate [diːˈsegrəgeɪt] eliminare la segregazione in

des·ert[1] [ˈdezət] *n also fig* deserto *m*

des·ert[2] [dɪˈzɜːt] **1** *v/t (abandon)* abbandonare **2** *v/i of soldier* disertare

des·ert·ed [dɪˈzɜːtɪd] *adj* deserto

de·sert·er [dɪˈzɜːtə(r)] MIL disertore *m*

de·ser·ti·fi·ca·tion [dɪzɜːtɪfɪˈkeɪʃn] desertificazione *f*

de·ser·tion [dɪˈzɜːʃn] (*abandoning*) abbandono *m*; MIL diserzione *f*

des·ert 'is·land isola *f* deserta

de·serve [dɪˈzɜːv] *v/t* meritare

de·sign [dɪˈzaɪn] **1** *n* design *m*; *technical* progettazione *f*; (*drawing*) progetto *m*, disegno *m*; (*pattern*) motivo *m*; *the machine's unique* ~ la concezione unica della macchina **2** *v/t house, car* progettare; *clothes* disegnare; *this machine is not ~ed for …* questa macchina non è stata concepita per …

des·ig·nate [ˈdezɪgneɪt] *v/t person* designare; *it has been ~d a no smoking area* quest'area è riservata ai non fumatori

de·sign·er [dɪˈzaɪnə(r)] designer *m/f inv*; *of building, car, ship* progettista *m/f*; *costume* ~ costumista *m/f*; *fashion* ~ stilista *m/f*; *interior* ~ arredatore *m*, -trice *f* de·sign·er clothes *npl* abiti *mpl* firmati

de·sign fault difetto *m* di concezione

de·sign school scuola *f* di design

de·sir·a·ble [dɪ'zaɪrəbl] *adj* desiderabile; (*advisable*) preferibile

de·sire [dɪ'zaɪə(r)] *n* desiderio *m*

desk [desk] scrivania *f*; *in hotel* reception *f inv*

'desk clerk *Am* receptionist *m/f inv*; 'desk di·a·ry agenda *f* da tavolo; 'desk·top scrivania *f*; (*computer*) computer *m inv* da tavolo; (*screen*) desktop *m inv*; desk·top 'pub·lish·ing editoria *f* elettronica

des·o·late ['desələt] *adj* place desolato

de·spair [dɪ'speə(r)] **1** *n* disperazione *f*; *in ~* disperato **2** *v/i* disperare; *~ of sth / s.o.* aver perso la fiducia in qc / qu; *~ of doing sth* disperare di fare qc

des·per·ate ['despərət] *adj* disperato; *be ~ for a cigarette / drink* morire dalla voglia di una sigaretta / bere qualcosa

des·per·a·tion [despə'reɪʃn] disperazione *f*

des·pic·a·ble [dɪs'pɪkəbl] *adj* deplorevole

de·spise [dɪ'spaɪz] *v/t* disprezzare

de·spite [dɪ'spaɪt] *prep* malgrado, nonostante

de·spon·dent [dɪ'spɒndənt] *adj* abbattuto

des·pot ['despɒt] despota *m*

des·sert [dɪ'zɜːt] dolce *m*, dessert *m inv*

des·ti·na·tion [destɪ'neɪʃn] destinazione *f*

des·tined ['destɪnd] *adj*: *be ~ for fig* essere destinato a

des·ti·ny ['destɪnɪ] destino *m*

des·ti·tute ['destɪtjuːt] *adj* indigente

de·stroy [dɪ'strɔɪ] *v/t* distruggere

de·stroy·er [dɪ'strɔɪə(r)] NAUT cacciatorpediniere *m*

de·struc·tion [dɪ'strʌkʃn] distruzione *f*

de·struc·tive [dɪ'strʌktɪv] *adj* distruttivo; *child* scalmanato

de·tach [dɪ'tætʃ] *v/t* staccare

de·tach·a·ble [dɪ'tætʃəbl] *adj* staccabile

de·tached [dɪ'tætʃt] *adj* (*objective*) distaccato

de·tached house villetta *f*

de·tach·ment [dɪ'tætʃmənt] (*objectivity*) distacco *m*

de·tail ['diːteɪl] *n* dettaglio *m*; *in ~* dettagliatamente

de·tailed ['diːteɪld] *adj* dettagliato

de·tain [dɪ'teɪn] *v/t* (*hold back*) trattenere; *as prisoner* trattenere

de·tain·ee [diːteɪn'iː] detenuto *m*, -a *f*

de·tect [dɪ'tekt] *v/t* rilevare; *anxiety, irony* cogliere

de·tec·tion [dɪ'tekʃn] *of criminal, crime* investigazione *f*; *of smoke etc* rilevamento *m*

de·tec·tive [dɪ'tektɪv] (*policeman*) agente *m/f* investigativo

de·tec·tive nov·el romanzo *m* giallo, giallo *m*

de·tec·tor [dɪ'tektə(r)] rilevatore *m*

dé·tente ['deɪtɒnt] POL distensione *f*

de·ten·tion [dɪ'tenʃn] (*imprisonment*) detenzione *f*

de·ter [dɪ'tɜː(r)] *v/t* (*pret & pp* -red) dissuadere; *~ s.o. from doing sth* dissuadere qu dal fare qc

de·ter·gent [dɪ'tɜːdʒənt] detergente *m*

de·te·ri·o·rate [dɪ'tɪərɪəreɪt] *v/i* deteriorarsi

de·te·ri·o·ra·tion [dɪtɪərɪə'reɪʃn] deterioramento *m*

de·ter·mi·na·tion [dɪtɜːmɪ'neɪʃn] (*resolution*) determinazione *f*

de·ter·mine [dɪ'tɜːmɪn] *v/t* (*establish*) determinare

de·ter·mined [dɪ'tɜːmɪnd] *adj* determinato, deciso

de·ter·rent [dɪ'terənt] *n* deterrente *m*

de·test [dɪ'test] *v/t* detestare

de·test·a·ble [dɪ'testəbl] *adj* detestabile

de·to·nate ['detəneɪt] **1** *v/t* fare detonare **2** *v/i* detonare

de·to·na·tion [detə'neɪʃn] detonazione *f*

de·tour ['diːtʊə(r)] *n* deviazione *f*

♦ **de·tract from** [dɪ'trækt] *v/t merit, value* sminuire; *enjoyment* rovinare; *room, décor* rovinare l'effetto di

de·tri·ment ['detrɪmənt]: **to the ~ of** a scapito di

de·tri·men·tal [detrɪ'mentl] *adj* nocivo

deuce [djuːs] *in tennis* 40 pari *m inv*

de·val·u·a·tion [diːvæljʊ'eɪʃn] *of currency* svalutazione *f*

de·val·ue [diː'væljuː] *v/t currency* svalutare

dev·a·state ['devəsteɪt] *v/t also fig* devastare

dev·a·stat·ing ['devəsteɪtɪŋ] *adj* devastante

de·vel·op [dɪ'veləp] **1** *v/t film, business* sviluppare; *land, site* valorizzare; *(originate)* scoprire; *illness, cold* contrarre **2** *v/i (grow)* svilupparsi; **~ into** diventare

de·vel·op·er [dɪ'veləpə(r)] *of property* impresario *m*, a *f* edile

de·vel·op·ing coun·try paese *m* in via di sviluppo

de·vel·op·ment [dɪ'veləpmənt] sviluppo *m*; *of land, site* valorizzazione *f*; *(origination)* scoperta *f*

de·vice [dɪ'vaɪs] *(tool)* dispositivo *m*

dev·il ['devl] diavolo *m*

de·vi·ous ['diːvɪəs] *(sly)* subdolo

de·vise [dɪ'vaɪz] *v/t* escogitare

de·void [dɪ'vɔɪd] *adj*: **be ~ of** essere privo di

dev·o·lu·tion [diːvə'luːʃn] POL decentramento *m*

de·vote [dɪ'vəʊt] *v/t time, effort, money* dedicare

de·vot·ed [dɪ'vəʊtɪd] *adj son etc* devoto; **be ~ to a person** essere molto attaccato a una persona

dev·o·tee [devəʊ'tiː] appassionato *m*, -a *f*

de·vo·tion [dɪ'vəʊʃn] *to a person* attaccamento *m*; *to one's job* dedizione *f*

de·vour [dɪ'vaʊə(r)] *v/t food, book* divorare

de·vout [dɪ'vaʊt] *adj* devoto; **a ~ Catholic** un cattolico fervente

dew [djuː] rugiada *f*

dex·ter·i·ty [dek'sterətɪ] destrezza *f*

di·a·be·tes [daɪə'biːtiːz] *nsg* diabete *m*

di·a·bet·ic [daɪə'betɪk] **1** *n* diabetico *m*, -a *f* **2** *adj* diabetico; *foods* per diabetici

di·a·bol·i·cal [daɪə'bɒlɪkl] *adj* P *(very bad)* penoso

di·ag·nose ['daɪəgnəʊz] *v/t* diagnosticare

di·ag·no·sis [daɪəg'nəʊsɪs] *(pl diagnoses* [daɪəg'nəʊsiːz]*)* diagnosi *f inv*

di·ag·o·nal [daɪ'ægənl] *adj* diagonale

di·ag·o·nal·ly [daɪ'ægənlɪ] *adv* diagonalmente

di·a·gram ['daɪəgræm] diagramma *m*

di·al ['daɪəl] **1** *n of clock, meter* quadrante *m*; TELEC disco *m* combinatore **2** *v/i (pret & pp -led, Am -ed)* TELEC comporre il numero **3** *v/t (pret & pp -led, Am -ed)* TELEC *number* comporre

di·a·lect ['daɪəlekt] dialetto *m*

di·al·ling code ['daɪlɪŋ] prefisso *m*

'di·al·ling tone, *Am* **'dial tone** segnale *m* di linea libera

di·a·log *Am*, **di·a·logue** ['daɪəlɒg] dialogo *m*

di·a·logue box COMPUT riquadro *m* di dialogo

di·am·e·ter [daɪ'æmɪtə(r)] diametro *m*

di·a·met·ri·cal·ly [daɪə'metrɪkəlɪ] *adv*: **~ opposed** diametricalmente opposto

di·a·mond ['daɪəmənd] *(jewel)* diamante *m*; *(shape)* losanga *f*; **~s** *in cards* quadri *mpl*

di·a·per ['daɪəpər] *Am* pannolino *m*

di·a·phragm ['daɪəfræm] diaframma *m*

di·ar·rhe·a *Am*, **di·ar·rhoe·a** [daɪə'riːə] diarrea *f*

di·a·ry ['daɪərɪ] *for thoughts* diario *m*; *for appointments* agenda *f*

dice [daɪs] **1** *n* dado *m* **2** *v/t* (*cut*) tagliare a dadini

di·chot·o·my [daɪˈkɒtəmɪ] dicotomia *f*

dic·tate [dɪkˈteɪt] *v/t letter, novel* dettare; *course of action* imporre

dic·ta·tion [dɪkˈteɪʃn] dettatura *f*

dic·ta·tor [dɪkˈteɪtə(r)] POL dittatore *m*

dic·ta·to·ri·al [dɪktəˈtɔːrɪəl] *adj* dittatoriale

dic·ta·tor·ship [dɪkˈteɪtəʃɪp] dittatura *f*

dic·tion·a·ry [ˈdɪkʃnrɪ] dizionario *m*

did [dɪd] *pret* → **do**

die [daɪ] *v/i* morire; **~ of cancer/ Aids** morire di cancro/AIDS; **I'm dying to know/leave** muoio dalla voglia di sapere/andare via

♦ **die away** *v/i of noise* estinguersi

♦ **die down** *v/i of noise, fire* estinguersi; *of storm, excitement* placarsi

♦ **die out** *v/i of custom* scomparire; *of species* estinguersi

die·sel [ˈdiːzl] (*fuel*) diesel *m*

di·et [ˈdaɪət] **1** *n* dieta *f* **2** *v/i to lose weight* essere a dieta

di·e·ti·tian [daɪəˈtɪʃn] dietologo *m*, -a *f*

dif·fer [ˈdɪfə(r)] *v/i* (*be different*) differire, essere differente; (*disagree*) non essere d'accordo

dif·fe·rence [ˈdɪfrəns] differenza *f*; (*disagreement*) divergenza *f*; **it doesn't make any ~** non fa nessuna differenza

dif·fe·rent [ˈdɪfrənt] *adj* diverso, differente

dif·fe·ren·ti·ate [dɪfəˈrenʃɪeɪt]: *v/i* distinguere; **~ between** *things* distinguere tra; *people* fare distinzioni tra

dif·fe·rent·ly [ˈdɪfrəntlɪ] *adv* diversamente, differentemente

dif·fi·cult [ˈdɪfɪkəlt] *adj* difficile

dif·fi·cul·ty [ˈdɪfɪkəltɪ] difficoltà *f inv*; **with ~** a fatica

dif·fi·dence [ˈdɪfɪdəns] diffidenza *f*

dif·fi·dent [ˈdɪfɪdənt] *adj* diffidente

dig [dɪg] (*pret & pp* **dug**) **1** *v/t* scava-

re **2** *v/i*: **it was ~ging into me** mi si stava conficcando dentro

♦ **dig out** *v/t* tirar fuori

♦ **dig up** *v/t garden* scavare; *buried object* dissotterrare; *tree* sradicare; *information* scovare

di·gest [daɪˈdʒest] *v/t also fig* digerire

di·ges·ti·ble [daɪˈdʒestəbl] *adj food* digeribile

di·ges·tion [daɪˈdʒestʃn] digestione *f*

di·ges·tive [daɪˈdʒestɪv] *adj* digestivo; **~ juices** succhi *mpl* gastrici; **~ system** apparato *m* digerente

dig·ger [ˈdɪgə(r)] (*machine*) scavatrice *f*

di·git [ˈdɪdʒɪt] (*number*) cifra *f*; **a 4 ~ number** un numero di 4 cifre

di·gi·tal [ˈdɪdʒɪtl] *adj* digitale

dig·ni·fied [ˈdɪgnɪfaɪd] *adj* dignitoso

dig·ni·ta·ry [ˈdɪgnɪtərɪ] dignitario *m*

dig·ni·ty [ˈdɪgnɪtɪ] dignità *f*

di·gress [daɪˈgres] *v/i* fare una digressione

di·gres·sion [daɪˈgreʃn] digressione *f*

digs [dɪgz] *npl* camera *f* in affitto

dike [daɪk] *along a river* argine *m*; *across a river* diga *f*

di·lap·i·dat·ed [dɪˈlæpɪdeɪtɪd] *adj* rovinato; *house* cadente

di·late [daɪˈleɪt] *v/i of pupils* dilatarsi

di·lem·ma [dɪˈlemə] dilemma *m*; **be in a ~** trovarsi in un dilemma

dil·et·tante [dɪleˈtæntɪ] dilettante *m/f*

dil·i·gent [ˈdɪlɪdʒənt] *adj* diligente

di·lute [daɪˈluːt] *v/t* diluire

dim [dɪm] **1** *adj room* buio; *light* fioco; *outline* indistinto; (*stupid*) idiota; *prospects* vago **2** *v/t* (*pret & pp* **-med**): **~ the headlights** abbassare le luci **3** *v/i* (*pret & pp* **-med**) *of lights* abbassarsi

di·men·sion [daɪˈmenʃn] (*measurement*) dimensione *f*

di·min·ish [dɪˈmɪnɪʃ] *v/t & v/i* diminuire

di·min·u·tive [dɪˈmɪnjutɪv] **1** *n* diminutivo *m* **2** *adj* minuscolo

dim·ple [ˈdɪmpl] fossetta *f*

din [dɪn] *n* baccano *m*

dine [daɪn] *v/i fml* cenare

din·er ['daɪnə(r)] *in a restaurant* cliente *m/f*; **fellow ~** commensale *m/f*

din·ghy ['dɪŋgɪ] *small yacht* dinghy *m*; *rubber boat* gommone *m*

din·gy ['dɪndʒɪ] *adj atmosphere* offuscato; (*dirty*) sporco

din·ing car ['daɪnɪŋ] RAIL vagone *m* ristorante; **'din·ing room** *in house* sala *f* da pranzo; *in hotel* sala *f* ristorante; **'din·ing ta·ble** tavolo *m* da pranzo

din·ner ['dɪnə(r)] *in the evening* cena *f*; *at midday* pranzo *m*; *formal gathering* ricevimento *m*

'din·ner guest invitato *m*, -a *f*; **'din·ner jack·et** smoking *m inv*; **'dinner par·ty** cena *f*; **'din·ner serv·ice** servizio *m* (di piatti)

di·no·saur ['daɪnəsɔː(r)] dinosauro *m*

dip [dɪp] **1** *n* (*swim*) tuffo *m*; *for food* salsa *f*; *in road* pendenza *f* **2** *v/t* (*pret & pp* **-ped**) immergere; **~ the headlights** abbassare le luci **3** *v/i* (*pret & pp* **-ped**) *of road* scendere

di·plo·ma [dɪ'pləʊmə] diploma *m*

di·plo·ma·cy [dɪ'pləʊməsɪ] diplomazia *f*

di·plo·mat ['dɪpləmæt] diplomatico *m*, -a *f*

di·plo·mat·ic [dɪplə'mætɪk] *adj* diplomatico

dip·lo·mat·i·cal·ly [dɪplə'mætɪklɪ] *adv* con diplomazia

dip·lo·mat·ic im·mu·ni·ty immunità *f* diplomatica

dire ['daɪə(r)] *adj* tremendo

di·rect [daɪ'rekt] **1** *adj* diretto **2** *v/t play* mettere in scena; *film* curare la regia di; *attention* dirigere; **could you please ~ me to ...?** mi può per favore indicare la strada per ...?

di·rect 'cur·rent ELEC corrente *f* continua

di·rect 'deb·it FIN ordine *m* di addebito automatico

di·rec·tion [dɪ'rekʃn] direzione *f*; *of film, play* regia *f*; **~s** (*instructions*), *to a place* indicazioni *fpl*; *for use*

istruzioni *fpl*

di·rec·tion in·di·ca·tor MOT freccia *f*

di·rec·tive [dɪ'rektɪv] *of EU etc* direttiva *f*

di·rect·ly [dɪ'rektlɪ] **1** *adv* (*straight*) direttamente; (*soon, immediately*) immediatamente **2** *conj* (non) appena; **I'll do it ~ I've finished this** lo faccio (non) appena ho finito questo

di·rec·tor [dɪ'rektə(r)] *of company* direttore *m*, -trice *f*; *of play, film* regista *m/f*

di·rec·to·ry [dɪ'rektərɪ] elenco *m*; TELEC guida *f* telefonica

dirt [dɜːt] sporco *m*, sporcizia *f*

'dirt cheap *adj* F a un prezzo stracciato

dirt·y ['dɜːtɪ] **1** *adj* sporco; (*pornographic*) sconcio **2** *v/t* (*pret & pp* **-ied**) sporcare

dirt·y 'trick tiro *m* mancino

dis·a·bil·i·ty [dɪsə'bɪlətɪ] handicap *m inv*, invalidità *f inv*

dis·a·bled [dɪs'eɪbld] **1** *n* handicappato *m*, -a *f*; **the ~** i disabili **2** *adj* handicappato

dis·ad·van·tage [dɪsəd'vɑːntɪdʒ] (*drawback*) svantaggio *m*; **be at a ~** essere svantaggiato

dis·ad·van·taged [dɪsəd'vɑːntɪdʒd] *adj* penalizzato

dis·ad·van·ta·geous [dɪsædvɑːn'teɪdʒəs] *adj* svantaggioso

dis·a·gree [dɪsə'griː] *v/i with person* non essere d'accordo

♦ **disagree with** *v/t of person* non essere d'accordo con; *of food* fare male a

dis·a·gree·a·ble [dɪsə'griːəbl] *adj* sgradevole

dis·a·gree·ment [dɪsə'griːmənt] disaccordo *m*; (*argument*) discussione *f*

dis·al·low [dɪsə'laʊ] *v/t goal* annullare

dis·ap·pear [dɪsə'pɪə(r)] *v/i* sparire, scomparire

dis·ap·pear·ance [dɪsə'pɪərəns] sparizione *f*, scomparsa *f*

dis·ap·point [dɪsə'pɔɪnt] *v/t* delude-re

dis·ap·point·ed [dɪsə'pɔɪntɪd] *adj* deluso

dis·ap·point·ing [dɪsə'pɔɪntɪŋ] *adj* deludente

dis·ap·point·ment [dɪsə'pɔɪntmənt] delusione *f*

dis·ap·prov·al [dɪsə'pruːvl] disapprovazione *f*

dis·ap·prove [dɪsə'pruːv] *v/i* disapprovare; ~ *of* disapprovare

dis·ap·prov·ing [dɪsə'pruːvɪŋ] *adj look* di disapprovazione

dis·ap·prov·ing·ly [dɪsə'pruːvɪŋlɪ] *adv* con disapprovazione

dis·arm [dɪs'ɑːm] **1** *v/t* disarmare **2** *v/i* disarmarsi

dis·ar·ma·ment [dɪs'ɑːməmənt] disarmo *m*

dis·arm·ing [dɪs'ɑːmɪŋ] *adj* disarmante

dis·as·ter [dɪ'zɑːstə(r)] disastro *m*

di·sas·ter ar·e·a area *f* disastrata; (*fig: person*) disastro *m*

di·sas·trous [dɪ'zɑːstrəs] *adj* disastroso

dis·band [dɪs'bænd] **1** *v/t* sciogliere **2** *v/i* sciogliersi

dis·be·lief [dɪsbə'liːf] incredulità *f*; *in* ~ con incredulità

disc [dɪsk] disco *m*

dis·card [dɪ'skɑːd] *v/t* sbarazzarsi di

dis·cern [dɪ'sɜːn] *v/t improvement, intentions* percepire; *outline* distinguere

dis·cern·i·ble [dɪ'sɜːnəbl] *adj improvement* percepibile; *outline* distinguibile

dis·cern·ing [dɪ'sɜːnɪŋ] *adj person* perspicace; *the car for the ~ driver* la macchina per i guidatori che sanno fare la differenza

dis·charge ['dɪstʃɑːdʒ] **1** *n from hospital* dimissione *f*; *from army* congedo *m* **2** *v/t* [dɪs'tʃɑːdʒ] *from hospital* dimettere; *from army* congedare; *from job* licenziare; LAW prosciogliere

di·sci·ple [dɪ'saɪpl] discepolo *m*, -a *f*

dis·ci·pli·nar·y [dɪsɪ'plɪnərɪ] *adj* disciplinare

dis·ci·pline ['dɪsɪplɪn] **1** *n* disciplina *f* **2** *v/t child, dog* imporre disciplina a; *employee* applicare provvedimenti disciplinari a

'disc jock·ey disc jockey *m/f inv*

dis·claim [dɪs'kleɪm] *v/t* negare; *responsibility* declinare

dis·close [dɪs'kləʊs] *v/t* svelare, rivelare

dis·clo·sure [dɪs'kləʊʒə(r)] rivelazione *f*

dis·co ['dɪskəʊ] discoteca *f*

dis·col·or *Am*, **dis·col·our** [dɪs-'kʌlə(r)] *v/i* scolorire

dis·com·fort [dɪs'kʌmfət] *n* disagio *m*; (*pain*) fastidio *m*

dis·con·cert [dɪskən'sɜːt] *v/t* sconcertare

dis·con·cert·ed [dɪskən'sɜːtɪd] *adj* sconcertato

dis·con·nect [dɪskə'nekt] *v/t* (*detach*) sconnettere; *supply, telephones* staccare; **they'll ~ you if you don't pay your phone bill** ti staccheranno il telefono se non paghi la bolletta; **I was ~ed** TELEC è caduta la linea

dis·con·so·late [dɪs'kɒnsələt] *adj* sconsolato

dis·con·tent [dɪskən'tent] malcontento *m*

dis·con·tent·ed [dɪskən'tentɪd] *adj* scontento

dis·con·tin·ue [dɪskən'tɪnjuː] *v/t* interrompere; **be a ~d line** essere fuori produzione

dis·cord ['dɪskɔːd] MUS dissonanza *f*; *in relations* contrasto *m*

dis·co·theque ['dɪskətek] discoteca *f*

dis·count ['dɪskaʊnt] **1** *n* sconto *m*; **a 10% ~** uno sconto del 10% **2** *v/t* [dɪs'kaʊnt] *goods* scontare; *theory* trascurare

dis·cour·age [dɪs'kʌrɪdʒ] *v/t* (*dissuade*) scoraggiare

dis·cour·age·ment [dɪs'kʌrɪdʒmənt] *being disheartened* scoraggiamento *m*; **meet with ~** non avere incoraggiamento

dis·cov·er [dɪ'skʌvə(r)] v/t scoprire

dis·cov·er·er [dɪ'skʌvərə(r)] scopritore m, -trice f

dis·cov·e·ry [dɪ'skʌvərɪ] scoperta f

dis·cred·it [dɪs'kredɪt] v/t screditare

di·screet [dɪ'skriːt] adj discreto

di·screet·ly [dɪ'skriːtlɪ] adv discretamente

dis·crep·an·cy [dɪ'skrepənsɪ] incongruenza f

dis·cre·tion [dɪ'skreʃn] discrezione f; **at your ~** a tua discrezione

di·scrim·i·nate [dɪ'skrɪmɪneɪt] v/i: **~ against** discriminare; **~ between** (distinguish between) distinguere tra

di·scrim·i·nat·ing [dɪ'skrɪmɪneɪtɪŋ] adj esigente

di·scrim·i·na·tion [dɪ'skrɪmɪneɪʃn] sexual, racial etc discriminazione f

dis·cus ['dɪskəs] SP: object disco m; SP: event lancio m del disco

di·scuss [dɪ'skʌs] v/t discutere; of article trattare di; **the article ~es whether ...** l'articolo esamina se ...

di·scus·sion [dɪ'skʌʃn] discussione f

'dis·cus throw·er lanciatore m, -trice f di disco

dis·dain [dɪs'deɪn] n sdegno m

dis·ease [dɪ'ziːz] malattia f

dis·em·bark [dɪsəm'bɑːk] v/i sbarcare

dis·en·chant·ed [dɪsən'tʃɑːntɪd] adj disincantato; **~ with** disilluso di

dis·en·gage [dɪsən'geɪdʒ] v/t svincolare

dis·en·tan·gle [dɪsən'tæŋgl] v/t districare

dis·fig·ure [dɪs'fɪgə(r)] v/t sfigurare; fig deturpare

dis·grace [dɪs'greɪs] **1** n vergogna f; **it's a ~** è una vergogna; **in ~** in disgrazia **2** v/t disonorare

dis·grace·ful [dɪs'greɪsful] adj behaviour, situation vergognoso

dis·grun·tled [dɪs'grʌntld] adj scontento

dis·guise [dɪs'gaɪz] **1** n travestimento m; **be in ~** essere travestito **2** v/t one's voice, handwriting camuffare; fear, anxiety dissimulare; **~ o.s. as**

travestirsi da; **he was ~d as a woman** era travestito da donna

dis·gust [dɪs'gʌst] **1** n disgusto m; **in ~** disgustato **2** v/t disgustare

dis·gust·ing [dɪs'gʌstɪŋ] adj disgustoso

dish [dɪʃ] part of meal piatto m; for serving piatto m; for cooking recipiente m

'dish·cloth strofinaccio m

dis·heart·en·ed [dɪs'hɑːtnd] adj demoralizzato

dis·heart·en·ing [dɪs'hɑːtnɪŋ] adj demoralizzante

di·shev·eled [dɪ'ʃevld] adj person, appearance arruffato; after effort scompigliato

dis·hon·est [dɪs'ɒnɪst] adj disonesto

dis·hon·est·y [dɪs'ɒnɪstɪ] disonestà f

dis·hon·or etc Am → **dishonour** etc

dis·hon·our [dɪs'ɒnə(r)] n disonore m; **bring ~ on** coprire di disonore

dis·hon·our·a·ble [dɪs'ɒnərəbl] adj disdicevole

'dish·wash·er machine lavastoviglie f inv; person lavapiatti m/f inv

'dish·wash·ing liq·uid Am detersivo m per i piatti

'dish·wa·ter acqua f dei piatti

dis·il·lu·sion [dɪsɪ'luːʒn] v/t disilludere

dis·il·lu·sion·ment [dɪsɪ'luːʒnmənt] disillusione f

dis·in·clined [dɪsɪn'klaɪnd] adj restio (to a)

dis·in·fect [dɪsɪn'fekt] v/t disinfettare

dis·in·fec·tant [dɪsɪn'fektənt] disinfettante m

dis·in·her·it [dɪsɪn'herɪt] v/t diseredare

dis·in·te·grate [dɪs'ɪntəgreɪt] v/i disintegrarsi; of marriage, building andare in pezzi

dis·in·ter·est·ed [dɪs'ɪntərestɪd] adj (unbiased) disinteressato

dis·joint·ed [dɪs'dʒɔɪntɪd] adj sconnesso

disk [dɪsk] disco m; (diskette) dischetto m; **on ~** su dischetto m '**disk drive** COMPUT lettore *m o* drive *m inv* di dischetti

disk·ette [dɪs'ket] dischetto *m*

dis·like [dɪs'laɪk] **1** *n* antipatia *f*; **take a ~ to s.o.** prendere qu in antipatia **2** *v/t*: **I ~ cats** non mi piacciono i gatti; **I ~ watching TV** non mi piace guardare la TV

dis·lo·cate ['dɪsləkeɪt] *v/t shoulder* lussare

dis·lodge [dɪs'lɒdʒ] *v/t* rimuovere

dis·loy·al [dɪs'lɔɪəl] *adj* sleale

dis·loy·al·ty [dɪs'lɔɪəltɪ] slealtà *f*

dis·mal ['dɪzməl] *adj weather*, *news* deprimente; *person* (*sad*), *failure* triste; *person* (*negative*) ombroso

dis·man·tle [dɪs'mæntl] *v/t* smontare; *organization* demolire

dis·may [dɪs'meɪ] **1** *n* costernazione *f* **2** *v/t* costernare

dis·miss [dɪs'mɪs] *v/t employee* licenziare; *suggestion*, *possibility* scartare; *idea*, *thought* accantonare

dis·miss·al [dɪs'mɪsl] *of employee* licenziamento *m*

dis·mount [dɪs'maʊnt] *v/i* smontare

dis·o·be·di·ence [dɪsə'biːdɪəns] disobbidienza *f*

dis·o·be·di·ent [dɪsə'biːdɪənt] *adj* disobbidiente

dis·o·bey [dɪsə'beɪ] *v/t* disobbedire a

dis·or·der [dɪs'ɔːdə(r)] (*untidiness*) disordine *m*; (*unrest*) disordini *mpl*; MED disturbo *m*

dis·or·der·ly [dɪs'ɔːdəlɪ] *adj room*, *desk* in disordine; *mob* turbolento

dis·or·gan·ized [dɪs'ɔːɡənaɪzd] *adj* disorganizzato

dis·o·ri·ent·ed [dɪs'ɔːrɪəntɪd], **dis·o·ri·en·tat·ed** [dɪs'ɔːrɪənteɪtɪd] *adj* disorientato

dis·own [dɪs'əʊn] *v/t* disconoscere

dis·par·ag·ing [dɪ'spærɪdʒɪŋ] *adj* dispregiativo

dis·par·i·ty [dɪ'spærətɪ] disparità *f inv*

dis·pas·sion·ate [dɪ'spæʃənət] *adj* (*objective*) spassionato

dis·patch [dɪ'spætʃ] *v/t* (*send*) spedire

dis·pen·sa·ry [dɪ'spensərɪ] *in phar-* macy dispensario *m*

♦ **di·spense with** [dɪ'spens] *v/t* fare a meno di

di·sperse [dɪ'spɜːs] **1** *v/t* dissipare **2** *v/i of crowd* disperdersi; *of mist* dissiparsi

di·spir·it·ed [dɪs'pɪrɪtɪd] *adj* abbattuto

dis·place [dɪs'pleɪs] *v/t* (*supplant*) rimpiazzare

di·splay [dɪ'spleɪ] **1** *n* esposizione *f*, mostra *f*; *in shop window* articoli *mpl* in esposizione; COMPUT visualizzazione *f*; **be on ~** *at exhibition* essere in esposizione *o* mostra; (*be for sale*) essere esposto in vendita **2** *v/t emotion* manifestare; *at exhibition* esporre; (*for sale*) esporre in vendita; COMPUT visualizzare

di·splay cab·i·net *in museum* teca *f*; *in shop* vetrinetta *f*

dis·please [dɪs'pliːz] *v/t* contrariare; **they were ~d with her** erano contrariati con lei

dis·plea·sure [dɪs'pleʒə(r)] disappunto *m*

dis·po·sa·ble [dɪ'spəʊzəbl] *adj* usa e getta *inv*

dis·po·sa·ble 'in·come reddito *m* disponibile

dis·pos·al [dɪ'spəʊzl] (*getting rid of*) eliminazione *f*; *of pollutants*, *nuclear waste* smaltimento *m*; **I am at your ~** sono a tua disposizione; **put sth at s.o.'s ~** mettere qc a disposizione di qu

♦ **di·spose of** [dɪ'spəʊz] *v/t* (*get rid of*) sbarazzarsi di

di·sposed [dɪ'spəʊzd] *adj*: **be ~ to do sth** (*willing*) essere disposto a fare qc; **be well ~ towards** essere ben disposto verso

dis·po·si·tion [dɪspə'zɪʃn] (*nature*) indole *f*

dis·pro·por·tion·ate [dɪsprə'pɔːʃənət] *adj* sproporzionato

dis·prove [dɪs'pruːv] *v/t* smentire

di·spute [dɪ'spjuːt] **1** *n* controversia *f*; (*industrial*) contestazione *f*; **be in ~** essere controverso **2** *v/t* contestare; (*fight over*) contendersi

dis·qual·i·fi·ca·tion [dɪskwɒlɪfɪˈkeɪ
ʃn] squalifica *f*; *it's a* ~ è penalizzan-
te

dis·qual·i·fy [dɪsˈkwɒlɪfaɪ] *v/t* (*pret
& pp -ied*) squalificare

dis·re·gard [dɪsrəˈgɑːd] **1** *n* mancanza *f* di considerazione **2** *v/t* ignorare

dis·re·pair [dɪsrəˈpeə(r)]: *in a state
of* ~ in cattivo stato

dis·rep·u·ta·ble [dɪsˈrepjʊtəbl] *adj*
depravato; *area* malfamato

dis·re·spect [dɪsrəˈspekt] mancanza
f di rispetto

dis·re·spect·ful [dɪsrəˈspektfʊl] *adj*
irriverente

dis·rupt [dɪsˈrʌpt] *v/t train service*
creare disagi a; *meeting, class* disturbare; (*intentionally*) creare scompiglio in

dis·rup·tion [dɪsˈrʌpʃn] *of train service* disagio *m*; *of meeting, class* disturbo *m*; (*intentional*) scompiglio
m

dis·rup·tive [dɪsˈrʌptɪv] *adj influence*
deleterio; *he's very ~ in class* è un
elemento di disturbo nella classe

dis·sat·is·fac·tion [dɪssætɪsˈfækʃn]
insoddisfazione *f*

dis·sat·is·fied [dɪsˈsætɪsfaɪd] *adj* insoddisfatto

dis·sen·sion [dɪˈsenʃn] dissenso *m*

dis·sent [dɪˈsent] **1** *n* dissenso *m*
2 *v/i* ~ *from* dissentire da

dis·si·dent [ˈdɪsɪdənt] *n* dissidente
m/f

dis·sim·i·lar [dɪsˈsɪmɪlə(r)] *adj* dissi-
mile

dis·so·ci·ate [dɪˈsəʊʃɪeɪt] *v/t*: ~ *o.s.
from* dissociarsi da

dis·so·lute [ˈdɪsəluːt] *adj* dissoluto

dis·so·lu·tion [ˈdɪsəluːʃn] POL scio-
glimento *m*

dis·solve [dɪˈsɒlv] **1** *v/t substance*
sciogliere **2** *v/i of substance* sciogliersi

dis·suade [dɪˈsweɪd] *v/t* dissuadere;
~ *s.o. from doing sth* dissuadere qu
dal fare qc

dis·tance [ˈdɪstəns] **1** *n* distanza *f*; *in
the* ~ in lontananza **2** *v/t*: ~ *o.s.
from* prendere le distanze da

dis·tant [ˈdɪstənt] *adj* lontano

dis·taste [dɪsˈteɪst] avversione *f*

dis·taste·ful [dɪsˈteɪstfʊl] *adj* spiacevole

dis·till·er·y [dɪsˈtɪlərɪ] distilleria *f*

dis·tinct [dɪsˈtɪŋkt] *adj* (*clear*) netto;
(*different*) distinto; *as ~ from* contrariamente a

dis·tinc·tion [dɪsˈtɪŋkʃn] (*differentia-
tion*) distinzione *f*; *hotel* / *product
of* ~ hotel / prodotto d'eccezione

dis·tinc·tive [dɪsˈtɪŋktɪv] *adj* caratteristico

dis·tinct·ly [dɪsˈtɪŋktlɪ] *adv* distintamente; (*decidedly*) decisamente

dis·tin·guish [dɪsˈtɪŋgwɪʃ] *v/t* (*see*)
distinguere; ~ *between X and Y* distinguere tra X e Y

dis·tin·guished [dɪsˈtɪŋgwɪʃt] *adj*
(*famous*) insigne; (*dignified*) distinto

dis·tort [dɪsˈtɔːt] *v/t* distorcere

dis·tract [dɪsˈtrækt] *v/t person* distrarre; *attention* distogliere

dis·tract·ed [dɪsˈtræktɪd] *adj* assente

dis·trac·tion [dɪsˈtrækʃn] *of attention*
distrazione *f*; *drive s.o. to* ~ fare
impazzire qu

dis·traught [dɪsˈtrɔːt] *adj* affranto

dis·tress [dɪsˈtres] **1** *n* sofferenza *f*;
in ~ *of ship, aircraft* in difficoltà **2** *v/t*
(*upset*) angosciare

dis·tress·ing [dɪsˈtresɪŋ] *adj* sconvolgente

dis·tress sig·nal segnale *m* di pericolo

dis·trib·ute [dɪsˈtrɪbjuːt] *v/t* distribuire

dis·tri·bu·tion [dɪstrɪˈbjuːʃn] distribuzione *f*

dis·trib·u·tor [dɪsˈtrɪbjutə(r)] COM
distributore *m*

dis·trict [ˈdɪstrɪkt] quartiere *m*

dis·trust [dɪsˈtrʌst] **1** *n* diffidenza *f*
2 *v/t* non fidarsi di

dis·turb [dɪsˈtɜːb] *v/t* disturbare; *do
not* ~ non disturbare

dis·turb·ance [dɪsˈtɜːbəns] (*interruption*) fastidio *m*; ~*s* (*civil unrest*)
disordini *mpl*

dis·turbed [dɪ'stɜːbd] *adj* (*concerned, worried*) turbato; *psychologically* malato di mente

dis·turb·ing [dɪ'stɜːbɪŋ] *adj* inquietante

dis·used [dɪs'juːzd] *adj* inutilizzato

ditch [dɪtʃ] **1** *n* fosso *m* **2** *v/t* F *boyfriend* scaricare F; F *car* sbarazzarsi di

dith·er ['dɪðə(r)] *v/i* titubare

di·van [dɪ'væn] (*bed*) divano *m*

dive [daɪv] **1** *n* tuffo *m*; (*underwater*) immersione *f*; *of plane* picchiata *f*; F (*bar etc*) bettola *f* F; **take a ~** F *of sterling etc* crollare **2** *v/i* tuffarsi; (*underwater*) fare immersione; *of submarine* immergersi; *of plane* scendere in picchiata; *the goalie ~d for the ball* il portiere si è tuffato per prendere la palla

div·er ['daɪvə(r)] *off board* tuffatore *m*, -trice *f*; (*underwater*) sub *m/f inv*, sommozzatore *m*, -trice *f*

di·verge [daɪ'vɜːdʒ] *v/i* divergere

di·verse [daɪ'vɜːs] *adj* svariato

di·ver·si·fi·ca·tion [daɪvɜːsɪfɪ'keɪʃn] COM diversificazione *f*

di·ver·si·fy [daɪ'vɜːsɪfaɪ] *v/i* (*pret & pp -ied*) COM diversificare

di·ver·sion [daɪ'vɜːʃn] *for traffic* deviazione *f*; *to distract attention* diversivo *m*

di·ver·si·ty [daɪ'vɜːsətɪ] varietà *f inv*

di·vert [daɪ'vɜːt] *v/t traffic* deviare; *attention* sviare, distogliere

di·vest [daɪ'vest] *v/t*: **~ s.o. of sth** privare qu di qc

di·vide [dɪ'vaɪd] *v/t* dividere

div·i·dend ['dɪvɪdend] FIN dividendo *m*; **pay ~s** *fig* dare i suoi frutti

di·vine [dɪ'vaɪn] *adj* REL, F divino

div·ing ['daɪvɪŋ] *from board* tuffi *mpl*; (*scuba ~*) immersione *f*

'**div·ing board** trampolino *m*

di·vis·i·ble [dɪ'vɪzəbl] *adj* divisibile

di·vi·sion [dɪ'vɪʒn] divisione *f*; *of company* sezione *f*

di·vorce [dɪ'vɔːs] **1** *n* divorzio *m*; **get a ~** divorziare **2** *v/t* divorziare da; **get ~d** divorziare **3** *v/i* divorziare

di·vorced [dɪ'vɔːst] *adj* divorziato

di·vor·cee [dɪvɔː'siː] divorziato *m*, -a *f*

di·vulge [daɪ'vʌldʒ] *v/t* divulgare

DIY [diːaɪ'waɪ] *abbr* (= **do it yourself**) fai da te *m inv*, bricolage *m*

DI'Y store negozio *m* di bricolage; *smaller shop* ferramenta *f*

diz·zi·ness ['dɪzɪnɪs] giramento *m* di testa, vertigini *fpl*

diz·zy ['dɪzɪ] *adj* stordito; *I feel ~* mi gira la testa

DJ [diː'dʒeɪ] *abbr* (= **disc jockey**) dj *m/f inv*; (= **dinner jacket**) smoking *m inv*

DNA [diːen'eɪ] *abbr* (= **deoxyribonucleic acid**) DNA *m inv* (= acido *m* deossiribonucleico)

do [duː] (*pret* **did**, *pp* **done**) **1** *v/t* fare; *one's hair* farsi; *100mph etc* andare a; **~ the ironing / cooking** stirare / cucinare; *what are you ~ing tonight?* cosa fai stasera?; *I don't know what to ~* non so cosa fare; *no, I'll ~ it* no, lo faccio; *stress on I* no, lo faccio io; *~ it right now!* fallo subito!; *have you done this before?* lo hai già fatto?; *have one's hair done* farsi fare i capelli **2** *v/i* (*be suitable, enough*) andare bene; *that will ~!* basta così!; *~ well* (*do a good job*) essere bravo; (*be in good health*) stare bene; *of business* andare bene; *well done!* (*congratulations!*) bravo!; *how ~ you ~?* molto piacere **3** *v/aux*: *~ you know him?* lo conosci?; *I ~n't know* non (lo) so; *~ be quick* sii veloce; *~ you like London? – yes I ~* ti piace Londra? – sì (mi piace); *he works hard, doesn't he?* lavora sodo, no?; *~n't you believe me?* non mi credi?; *you ~ believe me, ~n't you?* mi credi, non è vero?; *you ~n't know the answer, ~ you? – no I ~n't* non sai la risposta, vero? – no, non la so

♦ **do away with** *v/t* (*abolish*) abolire

♦ **do in** *v/t* F (*exhaust*) stravolgere F; *I'm done in* sono stravolto

♦ **do out of** *v/t*: *do s.o. out of sth* F fregare qc a qu F

♦ **do up** *v/t* (*renovate*) restaurare;

(*fasten*) allacciare; **do up your buttons** abbottonati; **do up your shoe-laces** allacciati le scarpe

♦ **do with** v/t: **I could do with ...** mi ci vorrebbe ...; **he won't have anything to do with it** (*won't get involved*) non vuole averci niente a che fare

♦ **do without 1** v/i farne a meno **2** v/t fare a meno di

do•cile ['dəʊsaɪl] *adj* docile

dock[1] [dɒk] **1** *n* NAUT bacino *m* **2** v/i *of ship* entrare in porto; *of spaceship* agganciarsi

dock[2] [dɒk] LAW banco *m* degli imputati

dock•er ['dɒkə(r)] portuale *m*

'**dock•yard** cantiere *m* navale

doc•tor ['dɒktə(r)] *n* MED dottore *m*, -essa *f*

doc•tor•ate ['dɒktərət] dottorato *m*

doc•trine ['dɒktrɪn] dottrina *f*

doc•u•dra•ma ['dɒkjʊdrɑːmə] ricostruzione *f* filmata

doc•u•ment ['dɒkjʊmənt] *n* documento *m*

doc•u•men•ta•ry [dɒkjʊ'mentərɪ] *n programme* documentario *m*

doc•u•men•ta•tion [dɒkjʊmen'teɪʃn] documentazione *f*

dodge [dɒdʒ] v/t *blow* schivare; *person, issue* evitare; *question* aggirare

dodg•ems ['dɒdʒəms] *npl* autoscontro *m*

dog [dɒg] **1** *n* cane *m* **2** v/t (*pret & pp* **-ged**) *of bad luck* perseguitare

'**dog catch•er** accalappiacani *m inv*

dog-eared ['dɒgɪəd] *adj book* con le orecchie

dogged ['dɒgɪd] *adj* accanito

dog•gie ['dɒgɪ] *in children's language* cagnolino *m*

dog•gy bag ['dɒgɪbæg] *pacchetto m con gli avanzi di una cena al ristorante per l'asporto*

'**dog•house:** **be in the ~** F essere nei casini F

dog•ma ['dɒgmə] dogma *m*

dog•mat•ic [dɒg'mætɪk] *adj* dogmatico

do-good•er [duː'gʊdə(r)] *pej* impiccione *m*, -a *f*

dogs•bod•y ['dɒgzbɒdɪ] F bestia *m* da soma

dog-tired *adj* F stravolto

do-it-your•self [duːɪtjə'self] fai da te *m inv*

dol•drums ['dɒldrəmz]: **be in the ~** *of economy* essere in stallo; *of person* essere giù di corda

dole [dəʊl] *Br* F assegno *m* di disoccupazione; **be on the ~** ricevere l'assegno di disoccupazione

'**dole money** *Br* F assegni *mpl* di disoccupazione

♦ **dole out** v/t distribuire

doll [dɒl] *toy*, F *woman* bambola *f*

♦ **doll up** v/t: **get dolled up** mettersi in ghingheri

dol•lar ['dɒlə(r)] dollaro *m*

dol•lop ['dɒləp] *n* F cucchiaiata *f*

dol•phin ['dɒlfɪn] delfino *m*

dome [dəʊm] *of building* cupola *f*

do•mes•tic [də'mestɪk] *adj* domestico; *news, policy* interno

do•mes•tic 'an•i•mal animale *m* domestico

do•mes•ti•cate [də'mestɪkeɪt] v/t *animal* addomesticare; **be ~d** *of person* essere incline a fare i lavori di casa

do'mes•tic flight volo *m* nazionale

dom•i•nant ['dɒmɪnənt] *adj* dominante; *member* principale

dom•i•nate ['dɒmɪneɪt] v/t dominare

dom•i•na•tion [dɒmɪ'neɪʃn] dominio *m*

dom•i•neer•ing [dɒmɪ'nɪərɪŋ] *adj* autoritario

dom•i•no ['dɒmɪnəʊ] domino *m*; **play ~s** giocare a domino

do•nate [dəʊ'neɪt] v/t donare

do•na•tion [dəʊ'neɪʃn] donazione *f*

done [dʌn] *pp* → **do**

don•key ['dɒŋkɪ] asino *m*

do•nor ['dəʊnə(r)] donatore *m*, -trice *f*

do•nut ['dəʊnʌt] *Am* → **doughnut**

doo•dle ['duːdl] v/i scarabocchiare

doom [duːm] *n* (*fate*) destino *f*; (*ruin*) rovina *f*

doomed [du:md] *adj project* condannato al fallimento; **we are** ~ siamo condannati; **the ~ ship** la nave destinata ad affondare; **the ~ plane** l'aereo destinato a cadere

door [dɔ:(r)] porta *f*; *of car* portiera *f*; **there's someone at the ~** stanno suonando alla porta

'**door·bell** campanello *m*; '**door·knob** pomello *m* della porta; '**door·man** usciere *m*; '**door·mat** zerbino *m*; '**door·step** gradino *m* della porta; '**door·way** vano *m* della porta

dope [dəʊp] **1** *n* (*drugs*) droga *f* leggera; *in sport* doping *m inv*; F (*idiot*) cretino *m*, -a *f*; F (*information*) soffiata *f* **2** *v/t* dopare

dor·mant ['dɔ:mənt] *adj*: ~ **volcano** vulcano *m* inattivo; **lie** ~ *of plant* rimanere latente

dor·mi·to·ry ['dɔ:mɪtrɪ] dormitorio *m*

dos·age ['dəʊsɪdʒ] dosaggio *m*

dose [dəʊs] *n* dose *f*

dot [dɒt] *n* puntino *m*; *in email address* punto *m*; **on the ~** (*exactly*) in punto

♦ **dote on** [dəʊt] *v/t* stravedere per

dot·ing ['dəʊtɪŋ] *adj* adorante

dot·ted line ['dɒtɪd] linea *f* tratteggiata

dot·ty ['dɒtɪ] *adj* F svitato

dou·ble ['dʌbl] **1** *n* (*amount*) doppio; (*person*) sosia *m inv*; *of film star* controfigura *f*; (*room with two beds*) doppio; (*room with double bed*) matrimoniale **2** *adj* doppio; **in ~ fig·ures** a due cifre **3** *adv*: ~ **the amount** il doppio della quantità **4** *v/t* raddoppiare **5** *v/i* raddoppiare

♦ **double back** *v/i* (*go back*) fare dietrofront

♦ **double up** *v/i in pain* piegarsi in due; (*share a room*) dividere la stanza

dou·ble·'bass contrabbasso *m*; **dou·ble·'bed** letto *m* matrimoniale; **dou·ble·'breast·ed** *adj* a doppio petto; **dou·ble·'check** *v/t* & *v/i* ricontrollare; **dou·ble·'chin** doppio mento *m*; **dou·ble·'cross** *v/t* fare il

doppio gioco con; **dou·ble·'deck·er** '**bus** autobus *m inv* a due piani; **dou·ble·'glaz·ing** doppi vetri *mpl*; **dou·ble·'park** *v/i* parcheggiare in doppia fila; '**dou·ble·'quick** *adj*: *in* ~ *time* in un batter d'occhio; '**dou·ble room** *with two beds* camera *f* doppia; *with double bed* camera *f* matrimoniale

dou·bles ['dʌblz] *npl in tennis* doppio *msg*

doubt [daʊt] **1** *n* dubbio *m*; **be in** ~ essere in dubbio; **no** ~ (*probably*) senz'altro **2** *v/t*: ~ *s.o. / sth* dubitare di qu / qc; ~ *that ...* dubitare che ...

doubt·ful [daʊtfʊl] *adj remark, look* dubbio; **be** ~ *of person* essere dubbioso; *it is* ~ *whether ...* è in dubbio se ...

doubt·ful·ly [daʊtflɪ] *adv* con aria dubbiosa

doubt·less [daʊtlɪs] *adj* senza dubbio

dough [dəʊ] impasto *m*; F (*money*) quattrini *mpl*

dough·nut [dəʊnʌt] bombolone *m*, krapfen *m inv*

dove [dʌv] colomba *f*; *fig* pacifista *m/f*

dow·dy ['daʊdɪ] *adj* scialbo

down[1] [daʊn] *n* (*feathers*) piuma *f*, piumino *m*

down[2] [daʊn] **1** *adv* (*downwards*) giù; ~ *there* laggiù; *fall* ~ cadere giù; *die* ~ calmarsi; *£200* ~ (*as deposit*) un acconto di £200; ~ *south* a sud; *be* ~ *of price, rate* essere diminuito; (*not working*) non funzionare; F (*depressed*) essere giù **2** *prep* giù da; (*along*) lungo; *I looked* ~ *the list* ho scorso la lista; *the third door* ~ *this corridor* la terza porta lungo questo corridoio; *walk* ~ *a street* percorrere una strada **3** *v/t* (*swallow*) buttare giù; (*destroy*) abbattere

'**down-and-out** *n* senza tetto *m/f inv*; '**down·cast** *adj* (*dejected*) abbattuto; '**down·fall** rovina *f*; *of politician, government* caduta *f*; '**down·grade** *v/t* ridimensionare; *employee* retrocedere di livello; **down·heart·ed** [daʊnˈhɑːtɪd] *adj* abbattuto; **down·'hill** *adv* in discesa; **go ~** *fig* peggiorare; **'down·hill ski·ing** discesa *f* libera; **'down·load** *v/t* COMPUT scaricare; **'down·mark·et** *adj* di fascia medio-bassa; **'down pay·ment** deposito *m*, acconto *m*; **'down·play** *v/t* minimizzare; **'down·pour** acquazzone *m*; **'down·right 1** *adj*: **it's a ~ lie** è una bugia bella e buona; **he's a ~ idiot** è un perfetto idiota **2** *adv dangerous, stupid etc* assolutamente; **'downside** (*disadvantage*) contropartita *f*; **'down·size 1** *v/t: company* ridimensionare; **the ~ed version of car** la versione ridotta **2** *v/i of company* ridimensionarsi; **'down·stairs** *adj & adv* al piano di sotto; **down-to-'earth** *adj approach* pratico; **she's very ~ about it** ha i piedi molto per terra al riguardo; **'down·town** *adj & adv* in centro; **'down·turn** *in economy* flessione *f* **'down·wards** *adj & adv* verso il basso

doze [dəʊz] **1** *n* sonnellino *m* **2** *v/i* fare un sonnellino

♦ **doze off** *v/i* assopirsi

doz·en [ˈdʌzn] dozzina *f*; **~s of ...** F un sacco di ... F

drab [dræb] *adj* scialbo

draft [drɑːft] *of document* bozza *f*; *Am* MIL leva *f*; *Am →* **draught 2** *v/t document* fare una bozza di; *Am* MIL arruolare

'draft dodg·er *Am* MIL renitente *m* alla leva

drag [dræg] **1** *n*: **it's a ~ having to ...** F è una rottura dover ... F; **he's a ~** F è una pizza F; **the main ~** P il corso principale; **in ~** vestito da donna; *of show, film* **a man in ~** un travestito **2** *v/t* (*pret & pp* **-ged**) (*pull*) trascinare; (*search*) dragare **3** *v/i* (*pret & pp* **-ged**) *of time* non passare mai; *of show, film* trascinarsi; **~ s.o. into sth** (*involve*) tirare in ballo qu in qc; **~ sth out of s.o.** (*get information from*) tirare fuori qc da qu

♦ **drag away**: *v/t*: **drag o.s. away**

from the TV staccarsi dalla TV

♦ **drag in** *v/t into conversation* tirare fuori

♦ **drag on** *v/i* (*last long time*) trascinarsi

♦ **drag out** *v/t* (*prolong*) tirare per le lunghe

♦ **drag up** *v/t* F (*mention*) rivangare

drag·on [ˈdrægn] drago *m*; *fig* strega *f*

drain [dreɪn] **1** *n* (*pipe*) tubo *m* di scarico; *under street* tombino *m*; **a ~ on resources** un salasso per le risorse **2** *v/t water* fare colare; *oil* fare uscire; *vegetables* scolare; *land* drenare; *glass, tank* svuotare; (*exhaust: person*) svuotare **3** *v/i of dishes* scolare

♦ **drain away** *v/i of liquid* defluire

♦ **drain off** *v/t water* fare defluire

drain·age [ˈdreɪnɪdʒ] (*drains*) fognatura *f*; *of water from soil* drenaggio *m*

'drain·pipe tubo *m* di scarico

dra·ma [ˈdrɑːmə] (*art form*) arte *f* drammatica; (*acting*) recitazione *f*; (*excitement*) dramma *m*; (*play: on TV*) sceneggiato *m*; **~ classes** corso *m* di recitazione

dra·mat·ic [drəˈmætɪk] *adj* drammatico; (*exciting*) sorprendente; *gesture* teatrale

dra·mat·i·cal·ly [drəˈmætɪklɪ] *adv say* drammaticamente; *decline, rise, change etc* drasticamente

dram·a·tist [ˈdræmətɪst] drammaturgo *m*, -a *f*

dram·a·ti·za·tion [dræmətaɪˈzeɪʃn] (*play*) adattamento *m* teatrale

dram·a·tize [ˈdræmətaɪz] *v/t story* adattare; *fig* drammatizzare

drank [dræŋk] *pret →* **drink**

drape [dreɪp] *v/t cloth, coat* appoggiare; **~d in** (*covered with*) avvolto in

drap·er·y [ˈdreɪpərɪ] drappeggio *m*

drapes [dreɪps] *npl Am* tende *fpl*

dras·tic [ˈdræstɪk] *adj* drastico

draught [drɑːft] **1** *n of air* corrente *f* (d'aria); **~ (beer), beer on ~** birra *f* alla spina

draughts [drɑːfts] *nsg game* dama *f*

draughts·man [ˈdrɑːftsmən] disegnatore *m* industriale; *of plan* disegnatore *m*, -trice *f*

draught·y ['drɑːftɪ] *adj* pieno di correnti d'aria

draw [drɔː] **1** *n* in match, competition pareggio *m*; in lottery estrazione *f*, sorteggio *m*; (attraction) attrazione *f* **2** *v/t* (pret **drew**, pp **drawn**) picture, map disegnare; cart, curtain, tirare; in lottery, gun, knife estrarre; (attract) attirare; (lead) tirare; from bank account ritirare **3** *v/i* (pret **drew**, pp **drawn**) disegnare; in match, competition pareggiare; **~ near** avvicinarsi

♦**draw back 1** *v/i* (recoil) tirarsi indietro **2** *v/t* hand ritirare; curtains aprire

♦**draw on 1** *v/i* (approach) avvicinarsi **2** *v/t* (make use of) attingere a

♦**draw out** *v/t* wallet etc estrarre; money from bank ritirare

♦**draw up 1** *v/t* document redigere; chair accostare **2** *v/i* of vehicle fermarsi; **draw up alongside s.o.** accostarsi a qu

'**draw·back** inconveniente *m*

draw·er[1] [drɔː(r)] of desk etc cassetto *m*

draw·er[2] [drɔː(r)] (person) disegnatore *m*, -trice *f*; **she's a good ~** disegna bene

draw·ing ['drɔːɪŋ] disegno *m*

'**draw·ing board** tecnigrafo *m*; **go back to the ~** fig ricominciare da capo

'**draw·ing pin** puntina *f*

drawl [drɔːl] *n* pronuncia *f* strascicata

drawn [drɔːn] *pp* → **draw**

dread [dred] *v/t* aver il terrore di; **I ~ him finding it out** ho il terrore che lo scopra

dread·ful ['dredfʊl] *adj* terribile

dread·ful·ly ['dredflɪ] *adv* F (extremely) terribilmente; behave malissimo

dream [driːm] **1** *n* sogno *m* **2** *adj* F house etc dei sogni **3** *v/t* sognare **4** *v/i* sognare; **I ~t about you** ti ho sognato

♦**dream up** *v/t* sognare

dream·er ['driːmə(r)] (daydreamer)

sognatore *m*, -trice *f*

dream·y ['driːmɪ] *adj* voice, look sognante

drear·y ['drɪərɪ] *adj* deprimente; (boring) noioso

dredge [dredʒ] *v/t* harbour, canal dragare

♦**dredge up** *v/t* fig scovare

dregs [dregz] *npl* of coffee fondi *mpl*; **the ~ of society** la feccia della società

drench [drentʃ] *v/t* inzuppare; **get ~ed** inzupparsi; **I'm ~ed** sono fradicio

dress [dres] **1** *n* for woman vestito *m*; (clothing) abbigliamento *m* **2** *v/t* person vestire; wound medicare; salad condire; **get ~ed** vestirsi **3** *v/i* vestirsi; **~ in red** vestirsi di rosso

♦**dress up** *v/i* vestirsi elegante; (wear a disguise) travestirsi; **dress up as a ghost** travestirsi da fantasma

'**dress cir·cle** prima galleria *f*

dress·er ['dresə(r)] in kitchen credenza *f*

dress·ing ['dresɪŋ] for salad condimento *m*; for wound medicazione *f*

'**dress·ing down** sgridata *f*; '**dress·ing gown** vestaglia *f*; '**dress·ing room** in theatre spogliatoio *m*; '**dress·ing ta·ble** toilette *f inv*

'**dress·mak·er** sarto *m*, -a *f*

'**dress re·hears·al** prova *f* generale

dress·y ['dresɪ] *adj* F sull'elegante F

drew [druː] *pret* → **draw**

drib·ble ['drɪbl] *v/i* of person sbavare; of water gocciolare; SP dribblare

dried [draɪd] *adj* fruit etc essicato

dri·er ['draɪə(r)] → **dryer**

drift [drɪft] **1** *n* of snow cumulo *m* **2** *v/i* of snow accumularsi; of ship andare alla deriva; (go off course) uscire dalla rotta; of person vagabondare

♦**drift apart** *v/i* of couple allontanarsi (l'uno dall'altro)

drift·er ['drɪftə(r)] vagabondo *m*, -a *f*

drill [drɪl] **1** *n* (tool) trapano *m*; (exercise), MIL esercitazione *f* **2** *v/t* tunnel scavare; **~ a hole** fare un foro col trapano **3** *v/i for oil* trivellare; MIL addestrarsi

dril·ling rig ['drɪlɪŋrɪg] (*platform*) sonda *f*

dri·ly ['draɪlɪ] *adv remark* ironicamente

drink [drɪŋk] **1** *n* bevanda *f*; **non-alcoholic ~** bibita *f* (analcolica); **a ~ of ...** un bicchiere di ...; **go for a ~** andare a bere qualcosa **2** *v/t & v/i* (*pret* **drank**, *pp* **drunk**) bere; **I don't ~** non bevo

◆ **drink up 1** *v/i* (*finish drink*) finire il bicchiere **2** *v/t* (*drink completely*) finire di bere

drink·a·ble ['drɪŋkǝbl] *adj* potabile

drink 'driv·ing guida *f* in stato di ebbrezza

drink·er ['drɪŋkǝ(r)] bevitore *m*, -trice *f*

drink·ing ['drɪŋkɪŋ] *of alcohol* consumo *m* di alcolici; **he has a ~ problem** beve troppi alcolici

'drink·ing wa·ter acqua *f* potabile

'drinks ma·chine distributore *m* di bevande

drip [drɪp] **1** *n action* gocciolamento *m*; *amount* goccia *f*; MED flebo *f inv* **2** *v/i* (*pret & pp* **-ped**) gocciolare

'drip-dry *adj* non-stiro

drip·ping ['drɪpɪŋ] *adv*: **~ wet** fradicio

drive [draɪv] **1** *n* percorso *m* in macchina; (*outing*) giro *m* in macchina; (*driveway*) viale *m*; (*energy*) grinta *f*; COMPUT lettore *m*; (*campaign*) campagna *f*; **left-/right-hand ~** MOT guida *f* a sinistra/destra **2** *v/t* (*pret* **drove**, *pp* **driven**) *vehicle* guidare; (*take in car*) portare (in macchina); TECH azionare; **that noise/this man is driving me mad** questo rumore/quest'uomo mi fa diventare matto **3** *v/i* (*pret* **drove**, *pp* **driven**) guidare; **I ~ to work** vado al lavoro in macchina

◆ **drive at** *v/t*: **what are you driving at?** dove vuoi andare a parare?

◆ **drive away 1** *v/t* portare via (in macchina); (*chase off*) cacciare **2** *v/i* andare via (in macchina)

◆ **drive in** *v/t nail* piantare

◆ **drive off** → **drive away**

driv·el ['drɪvl] *n* sciocchezze *fpl*

driv·en ['drɪvn] *pp* → **drive**

driv·er ['draɪvǝ(r)] guidatore *m*, -trice *f*, conducente *m/f*; *of train* macchinista *m/f*; COMPUT driver *m inv*

'driv·er's li·cense *Am* patente *f* (di guida)

'drive·way viale *m*

driv·ing ['draɪvɪŋ] **1** *n* guida *f* **2** *adj rain* violento

driv·ing 'force elemento *m* motore; **'driving in·struct·or** istruttore *m*, -trice *f* di guida; **'driv·ing les·son** lezione *f* di guida; **'driv·ing li·cence** patente *f* (di guida); **'driv·ing school** scuola *f* guida; **'driv·ing test** esame *m* di guida

driz·zle ['drɪzl] **1** *n* pioggerella *f* **2** *v/i* piovvigginare

drone [drǝʊn] *n* (*noise*) ronzio *m*

droop [druːp] *v/i* abbassarsi; *of plant* afflosciarsi

drop [drɒp] **1** *n of rain* goccia *f*; (*small amount*) goccio *m*; *in price, temperature* calo *m*; *in number* calo *m* **2** *v/t* (*pret & pp* **-ped**) far cadere; *from plane* sganciare; *person from car* lasciare; *person from team* scartare; (*stop seeing*) smettere di frequentare; *charges, demand etc* abbandonare; (*give up*) lasciare perdere; **~ a line to** scrivere due righe a **3** *v/i* (*pret & pp* **-ped**) cadere; (*decline*) calare

◆ **drop in** *v/i* (*visit*) passare

◆ **drop off 1** *v/t person, goods* lasciare **2** *v/i* (*fall asleep*) addormentarsi; (*decline*) calare

◆ **drop out** *v/i from competition, school* ritirarsi

'drop-out (*from school*) persona *f* che ha abbandonato gli studi; (*from society*) emarginato *m*, -a *f*

drops [drɒps] *npl for eyes* collirio *m*

drought [draʊt] siccità *f*

drove [drǝʊv] *pret* → **drive**

drown [draʊn] **1** *v/i* annegare **2** *v/t person* annegare; *sound* coprire; **be ~ed** annegare

drow·sy ['draʊzɪ] *adj* sonnolento

drudg·e·ry ['drʌdʒərɪ] lavoro *m* ingrato

drug [drʌg] **1** *n* droga *f*; *be on ~s* drogarsi **2** *v/t* (*pret & pp* ***-ged***) drogare

'**drug addict** tossicodipendente *m/f*

'**drug deal·er** spacciatore *m*, -trice *f* (di droga)

'**drug·store** *esp Am* negozio-bar *m* che vende articoli vari, inclusi medicinali

'**drug traf·fick·ing** traffico *m* di droga

drum [drʌm] *n* MUS tamburo *m*; (*container*) bidone *m*; *~s in pop music* batteria *f*

♦ **drum into** *v/t* (*pret & pp* ***-med***): *drum sth into s.o.* inculcare qc in qu

♦ **drum up** *v/t*: *drum up support* cercare supporto

drum·mer ['drʌmə(r)] batterista *m/f*; *in brass band* percussionista *m/f*

'**drum·stick** MUS bacchetta *f*; *of poultry* coscia *f*

drunk [drʌŋk] **1** *n* ubriacone *m*, -a *f* **2** *adj* ubriaco; *get ~* ubriacarsi **3** *pp* → **drink**

drunk·en [drʌŋkn] *voices, laughter* da ubriaco; *~ party* festa *f* in cui si beve molto

drunk 'driv·ing guida *f* in stato di ebbrezza

dry [draɪ] **1** *adj* secco; (*ironic*) ironico; *clothes* asciutto; (*where alcohol is banned*) dove la vendita e il consumo di alcolici sono illegali **2** *v/t & v/i* (*pret & pp* ***-ied***) asciugare

♦ **dry out** *v/i* asciugare; *of alcoholic* disintossicarsi

♦ **dry up** *v/i* of river prosciugarsi; F (*be quiet*) stare zitto

'**dry-clean** *v/t* pulire *o* lavare a secco; '**dry clean·er** tintoria *f*; '**dry-clean·ing** (*clothes*) abiti *mpl* portati in tintoria

dry·er ['draɪə(r)] (*machine*) asciugatrice *f*

DTP [diːtiːˈpiː] *abbr* (= **desktop publishing**) desk-top publishing *m*, impaginazione *f* elettronica

du·al ['djuːəl] *adj* doppio

du·al 'car·riage·way *Br* carreggiata *f* a due corsie

dub [dʌb] *v/t* (*pret & pp* ***-bed***) film doppiare

du·bi·ous ['djuːbɪəs] *adj* equivoco; (*having doubts*) dubbioso

duch·ess duchessa *f*

duck [dʌk] **1** *n* anatra *f* **2** *v/i* piegarsi **3** *v/t one's head* piegare; *question* aggirare

dud [dʌd] *n* F (*false note*) falso *m*

due [djuː] *adj* (*owed, proper*) dovuto; *be ~ of train, baby etc* essere previsto; *I'm ~ to meet him* dovrei incontrarlo; *~ to* (*because of*) a causa di; *be ~ to* (*be caused by*) essere dovuto a; *in ~ course* a tempo debito

dues [djuːz] *npl* quota *fsg*

du·et [djuːˈet] MUS duetto *m*

dug [dʌg] *pret & pp* → **dig**

duke [djuːk] duca *m*

dull [dʌl] *adj weather* grigio; *sound, pain* sordo; (*boring*) noioso

du·ly ['djuːlɪ] *adv* (*as expected*) come previsto; (*properly*) debitamente

dumb [dʌm] *adj* (*mute*) muto; F (*stupid*) stupido

dumb·found·ed [dʌmˈfaʊndɪd] *adj* ammutolito

dum·my ['dʌmɪ] *for clothes* manichino *m*; *for baby* succhiotto *m*

dump [dʌmp] **1** *n for rubbish* discarica *f*; (*unpleasant place*) postaccio *m* **2** *v/t* (*deposit*) lasciare; (*dispose of*) scaricare; *toxic waste etc* sbarazzarsi di

dump·ling ['dʌmplɪŋ] *fagotto m di pasta ripieno, sia dolce che salato*

dune [djuːn] duna *f*

dung [dʌŋ] sterco *m*

dun·ga·rees [dʌŋgəˈriːz] *npl* salopette *f inv*

dunk [dʌŋk] *v/t in coffee etc* inzuppare

du·o ['djuːəʊ] MUS duo *m inv*

du·pli·cate ['djuːplɪkət] **1** *n* duplicato *m*; *in ~* in duplicato **2** *v/t* ['djuːplɪkeɪt] (*copy*) duplicare; (*repeat*) rifare

du·pli·cate 'key chiave *f* di scorta

du·ra·ble ['djʊərəbl] *adj material* resistente; *relationship* durevole
du·ra·tion [djʊə'reɪʃn] durata *f*
du·ress [djʊə'res]: *under* ~ sotto costrizione
dur·ing ['djʊərɪŋ] *prep* durante
dusk [dʌsk] crepuscolo *m*
dust [dʌst] **1** *n* polvere *f* **2** *v/t* spolverare; ~ *sth with sth* (*sprinkle*) spolverare qc con qc
'**dust·bin** bidone *m* della spazzatura
'**dust cov·er** *for book* sopraccoperta *f*
duster ['dʌstə(r)] (*cloth*) straccio *m* (per spolverare)
'**dust jack·et** *of book* sopraccoperta *f*; '**dust·man** spazzino *m*; '**dust·pan** paletta *f*
dust·y ['dʌsti] *adj table* impolverato; *road* polveroso
Dutch [dʌtʃ] **1** *adj* olandese; *go* ~ F fare alla romana F **2** *n language* olandese *m*; *the* ~ gli Olandesi
du·ty ['djuːti] dovere *m*; *on goods* tassa *f* doganale, dazio *m*; *be on* ~ essere di servizio; *be off* ~ essere fuori servizio

du·ty 'free 1 *adj* duty free *inv* **2** *n* acquisto *m* fatto in un duty free
du·ty free al'low·ance limite *m* di acquisto in un duty free
du·ty'free shop duty free *m inv*
dwarf [dwɔːf] **1** *n* nano *m*, -a *f* **2** *v/t* fare scomparire
♦ **dwell on** [dwel] *v/t* rimuginare
dwin·dle ['dwɪndl] *v/i* diminuire
dye [daɪ] **1** *n* tintura *f*; *for food* colorante *m* **2** *v/t* colorare, tingere
dy·ing ['daɪɪŋ] *adj person* morente; *industry*, *tradition* in via di disparizione; *his* ~ *day* il giorno della sua morte
dy·nam·ic [daɪ'næmɪk] *adj person* dinamico
dy·na·mism ['daɪnəmɪzm] dinamismo *m*
dy·na·mite ['daɪnəmaɪt] *n* dinamite *f*
dy·na·mo ['daɪnəməʊ] TECH dinamo *f inv*
dy·nas·ty ['dɪnəsti] dinastia *f*
dys·lex·i·a [dɪs'leksɪə] dislessia *f*
dys·lex·ic [dɪs'leksɪk] **1** *adj* dislessico **2** *n* dislessico *m*, -a *f*

E

each [iːtʃ] **1** *adj* ogni **2** *adv* ciascuno; *they're £1.50* ~ costano £1,50 ciascuno **3** *pron* ciascuno *m*, -a *f*, ognuno *m*, -a *f*; ~ *other* l'un l'altro *m*, l'una l'altra *f*; *we know* ~ *other* ci conosciamo; *we drive* ~ *other's car* guidiamo l'uno la macchina dell'altro
ea·ger ['iːgə(r)] *adj* entusiasta; *be* ~ *to do sth* essere ansioso di fare qc; *be* ~ *for* essere desideroso di
ea·ger 'bea·ver F fanatico *m*, -a *f* F
ea·ger·ly ['iːgəli] *adv* ansiosamente
ea·ger·ness ['iːgənɪs] smania *f*
ea·gle ['iːgl] aquila *f*

ea·gle-eyed [iːgl'aɪd] *adj*: *be* ~ *eyed* avere l'occhio di falco
ear¹ [ɪə(r)] *of person*, *animal* orecchio *m*
ear² [ɪə(r)] *of corn* spiga *f*
'**ear·ache** mal *m* d'orecchi
'**ear·drum** timpano *m*
earl [ɜːl] conte *m*
'**ear·lobe** lobo *m* dell'orecchio
ear·ly ['ɜːli] **1** *adj* (*not late*) primo; *arrival* anticipato; (*farther back in time*) antico; *in the* ~ *hours* nelle prime ore; *in the* ~ *stages* nelle fasi iniziali; *in* ~ *spring* all'inizio della primavera; ~ *October* inizio

ottobre; *at an ~ age* in giovane età; *I'm an ~ riser* mi alzo sempre presto; *let's have an ~ supper* ceniamo presto; *an ~ Picasso* un Picasso primo periodo; *the ~ Romans* gli antichi Romani; *~ music* musica *f* primitiva; *I look forward to an ~ reply* resto in attesa di una sollecita risposta **2** *adv* (*not late*) presto; (*ahead of time*) in anticipo; *it's too ~* è troppo presto; *you're a bit ~* sei un po' in anticipo

'ear•ly bird persona *f* mattiniera; *planning ahead* persona *f* previdente

ear•mark ['ɪəmɑːk] *v/t* riservare; *~ sth for sth* riservare qc a qc

earn [ɜːn] *v/t* guadagnare; *of interest* fruttare; *holiday, drink etc* guadagnarsi; *~ one's living* guadagnarsi da vivere; *his honesty ~ed him everybody's respect* la sua onestà gli è valsa il rispetto di tutti

ear•nest ['ɜːnɪst] serio; *in ~* sul serio

earn•ings ['ɜːnɪŋz] *npl* guadagno *m*

'ear•phones *npl* cuffie *fpl* (d'ascolto); 'ear-pierc•ing *adj* perforante; 'ear•ring orecchino *m*; 'ear•shot: *within ~* a portata d'orecchio; *out of ~* fuori dalla portata d'orecchio

earth [ɜːθ] (*soil, planet*) terra *f*; *where on ~ have you been?* F dove cavolo sei stato? F

earth•en•ware ['ɜːθnweə(r)] *n* terracotta *f*

earth•ly ['ɜːθlɪ] *adj* terreno; *it's no ~ use ...* F è perfettamente inutile ...

'earth•quake ['ɜːθkweɪk] terremoto *m*

earth-shat•ter•ing ['ɜːθʃætərɪŋ] *adj* sconvolgente

ease [iːz] **1** *n* facilità *f*; *be at (one's) ~, feel at ~* essere *o* sentirsi a proprio agio; *be or feel ill at ~* essere *o* sentirsi a disagio **2** *v/t* (*relieve*) alleviare; *it will ~ my mind* mi darà sollievo **3** *v/i of pain* alleviarsi

♦ ease off *v/t* (*remove*) togliere con cautela *v/i of pain, rain* diminuire

ea•sel ['iːzl] cavalletto *m*

eas•i•ly ['iːzəlɪ] *adv* (*with ease*) facilmente; (*by far*) di gran lunga

east [iːst] **1** *n* est *m* **2** *adj* orientale **3** *adv travel* a est

Eas•ter ['iːstə(r)] Pasqua *f*

Eas•ter 'Day il giorno *o* la domenica di Pasqua

'Eas•ter egg uovo *m* di Pasqua

eas•ter•ly ['iːstəlɪ] *adj*: *~ wind* vento *m* dell'est; *in an ~ direction* verso est

Eas•ter 'Mon•day lunedì *m inv* di Pasqua, Pasquetta *f*

east•ern ['iːstən] *adj* orientale

east•ward(s) ['iːstwəd(z)] *adv* verso est

eas•y ['iːzɪ] *adj* facile; (*relaxed*) tranquillo; *take things ~* (*slow down*) prendersela con calma; *take it ~!* (*calm down*) calma!; *I've had it ~* ho avuto una vita facile

'eas•y chair poltrona *f*

eas•y-go•ing ['iːzɪgəʊɪŋ] *adj*: *he's very ~* gli va bene quasi tutto

eat [iːt] *v/t & v/i* (*pret ate, pp eaten*) mangiare

♦ eat out *v/i* mangiare fuori

♦ eat up *v/t finish* finire di mangiare; *fig* mangiare; *with jealousy* consumare; *eat up your beans* eat them all mangia tutti i fagioli

eat•a•ble ['iːtəbl] *adj* commestibile; *lunch, dish* mangiabile

eat•en ['iːtn] *pp* → eat

eau de Co•logne [əʊdəkə'ləʊn] acqua *f* di Colonia

eaves [iːvz] *npl* cornicione *m*

eaves•drop ['iːvzdrɒp] *v/i* (*pret & pp -ped*) origliare; *~ on s.o. / sth* origliare qu / qc

ebb [eb] *v/i of tide* rifluire

♦ ebb away *v/i fig: of courage, strength* venire meno

ec•cen•tric [ɪk'sentrɪk] **1** *adj* eccentrico **2** *n* eccentrico *m*, -a *f*

ec•cen•tric•i•ty [ɪksen'trɪsɪtɪ] eccentricità *f inv*

echo ['ekəʊ] **1** *n* eco *f* **2** *v/i* risuonare **3** *v/t words* ripetere; *views* condividere

e•clipse [ɪ'klɪps] **1** *n* eclissi *f inv* **2** *v/t*

fig eclissare

e·co·lo·gi·cal [iːkəˈlɒdʒɪkl] *adj* ecologico; **~ balance** equilibrio *m* ecologico

e·co·lo·gi·cal·ly [iːkəˈlɒdʒɪklɪ] *adv* ecologicamente

e·co·lo·gi·cal·ly 'friend·ly *adj* ecologico

e·col·o·gist [ɪˈkɒlədʒɪst] ecologista *m/f*

e·col·o·gy [ɪˈkɒlədʒɪ] ecologia *f*

ec·o·nom·ic [iːkəˈnɒmɪk] *adj* economico

ec·o·nom·i·cal [iːkəˈnɒmɪkl] *adj* (*cheap*) economico; (*thrifty*) parsimonioso

ec·o·nom·i·cal·ly [iːkəˈnɒmɪklɪ] *adv* (*in terms of economics*) economicamente; (*thriftily*) con parsimonia

ec·o·nom·ics [iːkəˈnɒmɪks] *science* economia *f*; *financial aspects* aspetti *mpl* economici

e·con·o·mist [ɪˈkɒnəmɪst] economista *m/f*

e·con·o·mize [ɪˈkɒnəmaɪz] *v/i* risparmiare, fare economia

♦**economize on** *v/t* risparmiare su

e·con·o·my [ɪˈkɒnəmɪ] *of a country* economia *f*; (*saving*) risparmio *m*, economia *f*

e·con·o·my class classe *f* economica; **e'con·o·my drive** regime *m* di risparmio; **e'con·o·my size** confezione *f* famiglia

e·co·sys·tem [ˈiːkəʊsɪstm] ecosistema *m*

e·co·tour·ism [ˈiːkəʊtʊərɪzm] agriturismo *m*

ec·sta·sy [ˈekstəsɪ] estasi *f*

ec·sta·tic [ɪkˈstætɪk] *adj* in estasi

ec·ze·ma [ˈeksmə] eczema *m*

edge [edʒ] **1** *n of knife* filo *m*; *of table, seat, lawn* bordo *m*; *of road* ciglio *m*; *of cliff* orlo *m*; *in voice* sfumatura *f* tagliente; **there's an ~ of cynicism in his voice** c'è una punta di cinismo nella sua voce; **on ~** → **edgy 2** *v/t* profilare **3** *v/i* (*move slowly*) muoversi con cautela

edge·ways [ˈedʒweɪz] *adv*: **I couldn't get a word in ~** non sono

riuscito a piazzare una parola

edg·y [ˈedʒɪ] *adj* teso

ed·i·ble [ˈedɪbl] *adj* commestibile

ed·it [ˈedɪt] *v/t text* rivedere; *prepare for publication* curare; *newspaper* dirigere; *TV program, film* montare; COMPUT editare

e·di·tion [ɪˈdɪʃn] edizione *f*

ed·i·tor [ˈedɪtə(r)] *of text* revisore *m*; *of publication* curatore *m*, -trice *f*; *of newspaper* direttore *m*, -trice; *of TV program* responsabile *m/f* del montaggio; *of film* tecnico *m* del montaggio; **sports ~** redattore *m*, -trice sportivo, -a; *in charge* caporedattore *m*, -trice *f* sportivo, -a

ed·i·to·ri·al [edɪˈtɔːrɪəl] **1** *adj* editoriale; **the ~ staff** la redazione **2** *n* editoriale *m*, articolo *m* di fondo

EDP [iːdiːˈpiː] *abbr* (= **electronic data processing**) EDP (= elaborazione *f* elettronica dei dati)

ed·u·cate [ˈedjukeɪt] *v/t child* istruire; *consumers* educare; **he was ~d at Cambridge** ha studiato a Cambridge

ed·u·cat·ed [ˈedjukeɪtɪd] *adj person* istruito

ed·u·ca·tion [edjuˈkeɪʃn] istruzione *f*; **the ~ system** la pubblica istruzione

ed·u·ca·tion·al [edjuˈkeɪʃnl] *adj* didattico; (*informative*) istruttivo

eel [iːl] anguilla *f*

ee·rie [ˈɪərɪ] *adj* inquietante

ef·fect [ɪˈfekt] effetto *m*; **take ~** *of medicine, drug* fare effetto; **come into ~** *of law* entrare in vigore

ef·fec·tive [ɪˈfektɪv] *adj* (*efficient*) efficace; (*striking*) d'effetto; **~ May 1** con decorrenza dal 1 maggio; **a very ~ combination** un abbinamento di grande effetto

ef·fem·i·nate [ɪˈfemɪnət] *adj* effeminato

ef·fer·ves·cent [efəˈvesnt] *adj also fig* effervescente

ef·fi·cien·cy [ɪˈfɪʃənsɪ] efficienza *f*; *of machine* rendimento *m*

ef·fi·cient [ɪˈfɪʃənt] *adj* efficiente; *machine* ad alto rendimento

ef·fi·cient·ly [ɪ'fɪʃəntlɪ] *adv* con efficienza

ef·flu·ent ['efluənt] scarichi *mpl*

ef·fort ['efət] sforzo *m*; ***make an* ~ *to do sth*** fare uno sforzo per fare qc

ef·fort·less ['efətlɪs] *adj* facile

ef·fron·te·ry [ɪ'frʌntərɪ] sfrontatezza *f*, sfacciataggine *f*

ef·fu·sive [ɪ'fjuːsɪv] *adj thanks, welcome* caloroso

e.g. [iː'dʒiː] ad *o* per esempio

e·gal·i·tar·i·an [ɪgælɪ'teərɪən] *adj* egualitario

egg [eg] uovo *m*; *of woman* ovulo *m*

♦ **egg on** *v/t* istigare

'**egg·cup** portauovo *m inv*; '**egghead** F intellettualoide *m/f*; '**eggplant** F melanzana *f*; '**egg·shell** guscio *m* d'uovo; '**egg tim·er** timer *m* per misurare il tempo di cottura delle uova

e·go ['iːgəu] ego *m*

e·go·cen·tric [iːgəu'sentrɪk] *adj* egocentrico

e·go·ism ['iːgəuɪzm] egoismo *m*

e·go·ist ['iːgəuɪst] egoista *m/f*

E·gypt ['iːdʒɪpt] Egitto *m*

E·gyp·tian [ɪ'dʒɪpʃn] **1** *adj* egiziano **2** *n* egiziano *m*, -a *f*

ei·der·down ['aɪdədaun] *(quilt)* piumino *m*

eight [eɪt] otto

eigh·teen [eɪ'tiːn] diciotto

eigh·teenth [eɪ'tiːnθ] *n & adj* diciottesimo, -a

eighth [eɪtθ] *n & adj* ottavo, -a

eigh·ti·eth ['eɪtɪθ] *n & adj* ottantesimo, -a

eigh·ty ['eɪtɪ] ottanta

ei·ther ['aɪðə(r)] **1** *adj* l'uno o l'altro; *(both)* entrambi *pl*; *at ~ side of the street* da entrambi i lati della strada **2** *pron* l'uno o l'altro *m*, l'una o l'altra *f* **3** *adv* nemmeno, neppure; *I won't go* ~ non vado nemmeno *o* neppure io **4** *conj*: ~ *my mother or my sister* mia madre o mia sorella; *he doesn't like* ~ *wine or beer* non gli piacciono né il vino, né la birra; ~ *you write or phone* o scrivi, o telefoni

e·ject [ɪ'dʒekt] **1** *v/t* espellere **2** *v/i from plane* eiettarsi

♦ **eke out** [iːk] *v/t* usare con parsimonia; *grant etc* arrotondare

e·lab·o·rate [ɪ'læbərət] **1** *adj* elaborato **2** *v/i* [ɪ'læbəreɪt] fornire particolari

e·lab·o·rate·ly [ɪ'læbərətlɪ] *adv* in modo elaborato

e·lapse [ɪ'læps] *v/i* trascorrere

e·las·tic [ɪ'læstɪk] **1** *adj* elastico **2** *n* elastico *m*

e·las·ti·ca·ted [ɪ'læstɪkeɪtɪd] *adj* elasticizzato

e·las·tic 'band elastico *m*

e·las·ti·ci·ty [ɪlæs'tɪsətɪ] elasticità *f*

E·las·to·plast® [ɪ'læstəplɑːst] cerotto *m*

e·lat·ed [ɪ'leɪtɪd] *adj* esultante

el·at·ion [ɪ'leɪʃn] esultanza *f*

el·bow ['elbəu] **1** *n* gomito *m* **2** *v/t*: ~ *out of the way* allontanare a spintoni

el·der ['eldə(r)] **1** *adj* maggiore **2** *n* maggiore *m/f*; *she's two years my* ~ è più vecchia di me di due anni

el·der·ly ['eldəlɪ] *adj* anziano

el·dest ['eldəst] **1** *adj* maggiore **2** *n* maggiore *m/f*; *the* ~ il/la maggiore

e·lect [ɪ'lekt] **1** *v/t* eleggere; ~ *to ...* decidere di ... **2** *adj*: *the president* ~ il futuro presidente

e·lec·tion [ɪ'lekʃn] elezione *f*

e·lec·tion cam·paign campagna *f* elettorale

e·lec·tion day giorno *m* delle elezioni

e·lec·tive [ɪ'lektɪv] *adj* facoltativo

e·lec·tor [ɪ'lektə(r)] elettore *m*, -trice *f*

e·lec·to·ral sys·tem [ɪ'lektərəlsɪstm] sistema *m* elettorale

e·lec·to·rate [ɪ'lektərət] elettorato *m*

e·lec·tric [ɪ'lektrɪk] *adj also fig* elettrico

e·lec·tri·cal [ɪ'lektrɪkl] *adj* elettrico

e·lec·tri·cal en·gi·neer ingegnere *m* elettrico

e·lec·tri·cal en·gi·neer·ing ingegneria *f* elettrica

E

e·lec·tric 'blan·ket coperta *f* elettrica

e·lec·tric 'chair sedia *f* elettrica

e·lec·tri·cian [ɪlek'trɪʃn] elettricista *m/f*

e·lec·tri·ci·ty [ɪlek'trɪsətɪ] elettricità *f*

e·lec·tric 'ra·zor rasoio *m* elettrico

e·lec·tri·fy [ɪ'lektrɪfaɪ] *v/t* (*pret & pp -ied*) elettrificare; *fig* elettrizzare

e·lec·tro·cute [ɪ'lektrəkjuːt] *v/t* fulminare

e·lec·trode [ɪ'lektrəud] elettrodo *m*

e·lec·tron [ɪ'lektrɒn] elettrone *m*

e·lec·tron·ic [ɪlek'trɒnɪk] *adj* elettronico

e·lec·tron·ic da·ta 'pro·ces·sing elaborazione *f* elettronica dei dati

e·lec·tron·ic 'mail posta *f* elettronica

e·lec·tron·ics [ɪlek'trɒnɪks] elettronica *f*

el·e·gance ['elɪgəns] eleganza *f*

el·e·gant ['elɪgənt] *adj* elegante

el·e·gant·ly ['elɪgəntlɪ] *adv* elegantemente

el·e·ment ['elɪmənt] elemento *m*

el·e·men·ta·ry [elɪ'mentərɪ] *adj* (*rudimentary*) elementare

el·e·men·ta·ry school *Am* scuola *f* elementare

el·e·men·ta·ry teacher maestro *m*, -a *f* elementare

el·e·phant ['elɪfənt] elefante *m*

el·e·vate ['elɪveɪt] *v/t* elevare

el·e·va·tion [elɪ'veɪʃn] (*altitude*) altitudine *f*

el·e·va·tor ['elɪveɪtə(r)] *Am* ascensore *m*

el·e·ven [ɪ'levn] undici

el·e·venth [ɪ'levnθ] *n & adj* undicesimo, -a; *at the ~ hour* all'ultima ora, all'ultimo momento

el·i·gi·ble ['elɪdʒəbl] *adj*: *be ~ to do sth* avere il diritto di fare qc; *be ~ for sth* avere diritto a qc

el·i·gi·ble 'bach·e·lor buon partito *m*

e·lim·i·nate [ɪ'lɪmɪneɪt] *v/t* eliminare; *be ~d from competition* essere eliminato

e·lim·i·na·tion [ɪ'lɪmɪneɪʃn] eliminazione *f*

e·lite [eɪ'liːt] **1** *n* elite *f inv* **2** *adj* elitario

el·lipse [ɪ'lɪps] ellisse *f*

elm [elm] olmo *m*

e·lope [ɪ'ləup] *v/i* scappare (per sposarsi)

el·o·quence ['eləkwəns] eloquenza *f*

el·o·quent ['eləkwənt] *adj* eloquente

el·o·quent·ly ['eləkwəntlɪ] *adv* con eloquenza

else [els] *adv*: *anything ~* qualcos'altro; *anything ~? in shop* (desidera) altro?; *nothing ~* nient'altro; *if you've got nothing ~ to do* se non hai altro da fare; *nobody ~* nessun altro; *everyone ~ is going* tutti gli altri vanno; *who ~ was there?* chi altro c'era?; *someone ~* qualcun altro; *something ~* qualcos'altro; *let's go somewhere ~* andiamo da qualche altra parte; *or ~* altrimenti

else·where ['elsweə(r)] *adv* altrove

e·lude [ɪ'luːd] *v/t* (*escape from*) sfuggire a; (*avoid*) sfuggire a; *the name ~s me* il nome mi sfugge

e·lu·sive [ɪ'luːsɪv] *adj person* difficile da trovare; *quality* raro; *criminal* inafferrabile

e·ma·ci·ated [ɪ'meɪsɪeɪtɪd] *adj* emaciato

e-mail ['iːmeɪl] **1** *n* e-mail *m inv* **2** *v/t person* mandare un e-mail; *text* mandare per e-mail

'e-mail ad·dress indirizzo *m* e-mail

e·man·ci·pat·ed [ɪ'mænsɪpeɪtɪd] *adj woman* emancipato

e·man·ci·pa·tion [ɪmænsɪ'peɪʃn] emancipazione *f*

em·balm [ɪm'bɑːm] *v/t* imbalsamare

em·bank·ment [ɪm'bæŋkmənt] *of river* argine *m*; RAIL massicciata *f*

em·bar·go [em'bɑːgəu] embargo *m inv*

em·bark [ɪm'bɑːk] *v/i* imbarcarsi

♦ embark on *v/t* imbarcarsi in

em·bar·rass [ɪm'bærəs] *v/t* imbarazzare

em·bar·rassed [ɪmˈbærəst] *adj* imbarazzato

em·bar·rass·ing [ɪmˈbærəsɪŋ] *adj* imbarazzante

em·bar·rass·ment [ɪmˈbærəsmənt] imbarazzo *m*

em·bas·sy [ˈembəsɪ] ambasciata *f*

em·bel·lish [ɪmˈbelɪʃ] *v/t* ornare; *story* ricamare su

em·bers [ˈembəz] *npl* brace *fsg*

em·bez·zle [ɪmˈbezl] *v/t* appropriarsi indebitamente di

em·bez·zle·ment [ɪmˈbezlmənt] appropriazione *f* indebita

em·bez·zler [ɪmˈbezlə(r)] malversatore *m*, -trice *f*

em·bit·ter [ɪmˈbɪtə(r)] *v/t* amareggiare

em·blem [ˈembləm] emblema *f*

em·bod·i·ment [ɪmˈbɒdɪmənt] incarnazione *f*

em·bod·y [ɪmˈbɒdɪ] *v/t* (*pret & pp* **-ied**) incarnare

em·bo·lis·m [ˈembəlɪzm] embolia *f*

em·boss [ɪmˈbɒs] *v/t metal* lavorare a sbalzo; *paper, fabric* stampare in rilievo

em·brace [ɪmˈbreɪs] **1** *n* abbraccio *m* **2** *v/t* (*hug, include*) abbracciare **3** *v/i of two people* abbracciarsi

em·broi·der [ɪmˈbrɔɪdə(r)] *v/t* ricamare; *fig* ricamare su

em·broi·der·y [ɪmˈbrɔɪdərɪ] ricamo *m*

em·bry·o [ˈembrɪəʊ] embrione *m*

em·bry·on·ic [embrɪˈɒnɪk] *adj fig* embrionale

em·e·rald [ˈemərəld] *precious stone* smeraldo *m*; *colour* verde *m* smeraldo

e·merge [ɪˈmɜːdʒ] *v/i* (*appear*) emergere; *it has ~d that ...* è emerso che ...

e·mer·gen·cy [ɪˈmɜːdʒənsɪ] emergenza *f*, *in an ~* in caso di emergenza; **emer·gen·cy 'ex·it** uscita *f* di sicurezza; **e'mer·gen·cy land·ing** atterraggio *m* di fortuna; **e'mergen·cy serv·ices** *npl* servizi *mpl* di soccorso

em·er·y board [ˈemərɪbɔːd] limetta *f* (da unghie)

em·i·grant [ˈemɪgrənt] emigrante *m/f*

em·i·grate [ˈemɪgreɪt] *v/i* emigrare

em·i·gra·tion [emɪˈɡreɪʃn] emigrazione *f*

Em·i·nence [ˈemɪnəns]: REL *His ~* Sua Eminenza

em·i·nent [ˈemɪnənt] *adj* eminente

em·i·nent·ly [ˈemɪnəntlɪ] *adv* decisamente

e·mis·sion [ɪˈmɪʃn] *of gases* emanazione *f*

e·mit [ɪˈmɪt] *v/t (pret & pp* **-ted**) *heat, gases* emanare; *light, smoke* emettere; *smell* esalare

e·mo·tion [ɪˈməʊʃn] emozione *f*

e·mo·tion·al [ɪˈməʊʃnl] *adj problems, development* emozionale; (*causing emotion*) commovente; (*showing emotion*) commosso

em·pa·thize [ˈempəθaɪz] *v/i* immedesimarsi; *~ with s.o.* immedesimarsi con qu; *~ with sth* capire qc

em·pe·ror [ˈempərə(r)] imperatore *m*

em·pha·sis [ˈemfəsɪs] enfasi *f*; *on word* rilievo *m*

em·pha·size [ˈemfəsaɪz] *v/t* enfatizzare; *word* dare rilievo a

em·phat·ic [ɪmˈfætɪk] *adj* enfatico

em·pire [ˈempaɪə(r)] impero *m*

em·ploy [ɪmˈplɔɪ] *v/t* dare lavoro a; (*take on*) assumere; (*use*) impiegare; *she's ~ed as a secretary* lavora come segretaria; *he hasn't been ~ed for six months* non lavora da sei mesi

em·ploy·ee [emplɔɪˈiː] dipendente *m/f*

em·ploy·er [em plɔɪˈə(r)] datore *m*, -trice *f* di lavoro

em·ploy·ment [em plɔɪmənt] occupazione *f*; (*work*) impiego *m*; *be seeking ~* essere in cerca di occupazione

em·ploy·ment a·gen·cy agenzia *f* di collocamento

em·press [ˈempris] imperatrice *f*

emp·ti·ness [ˈemptɪnɪs] vuoto *m*

emp·ty [ˈemptɪ] **1** *adj* vuoto **2** *v/t*

(*pret* & *pp* **-ied**) vuotare 3 *v/i* (*pret* & *pp* **-ied**) *of room, street* svuotarsi

em·u·late ['emjʊleɪt] *v/t* emulare

e·mul·sion [ɪ'mʌlʃn] *n paint* emulsione *f*

en·a·ble [ɪ'neɪbl] *v/t person* permettere a; *thing* permettere; **~ s.o. to do sth** permettere a qu di fare qc

en·act [ɪ'nækt] *v/t law* emanare; THEA rappresentare

e·nam·el [ɪ'næml] smalto *m*

enc *abbr* (= **enclosure(s)**) all. (= allegato *m*)

en·chant [ɪn'tʃɑːnt] *v/t (delight)* incantare

en·chant·ing [ɪn'tʃɑːntɪŋ] *adj smile, village, person* incantevole

en·cir·cle [ɪn'sɜːkl] *v/t* circondare

encl *abbr* (= **enclosure(s)**) all. (= allegato *m*)

en·close [ɪn'kləʊz] *v/t in letter* allegare; **please find ~d ...** in allegato, ...; *area* recintare

en·clo·sure [ɪn'kləʊʒə(r)] *with letter* allegato *m*

en·core ['ɒŋkɔː(r)] bis *m inv*

en·coun·ter [ɪn'kaʊntə(r)] **1** *n* incontro *m* **2** *v/t* incontrare

en·cour·age [ɪn'kʌrɪdʒ] *v/t* incoraggiare

en·cour·age·ment [ɪn'kʌrɪdʒmənt] incoraggiamento *m*

en·cour·ag·ing [ɪn'kʌrɪdʒɪŋ] *adj* incoraggiante

♦ **encroach on** [ɪn'krəʊtʃ] *v/t land, time* invadere; *rights* violare

en·cy·clo·pe·di·a [ɪnsaɪklə'piːdɪə] enciclopedia *f*

end [end] **1** *n (extremity)* estremità *f inv*; *(conclusion)* fine *f*; *(purpose)* fine *m*; **in the ~** alla fine; **for hours on ~** senza sosta; **stand sth on ~** mettere qc verticale; **at the ~ of July** alla fine di luglio; **put an ~ to** mettere fine a **2** *v/t* terminare **3** *v/i* finire

♦ **end up** *v/i* finire; **I'll end up doing it myself** finirò per farlo io stesso

en·dan·ger [ɪn'deɪndʒə(r)] *v/t* mettere in pericolo

en·dan·gered spe·cies specie *f* in via d'estinzione

en·dear·ing [ɪn'dɪərɪŋ] *adj* accattivante

en·deav·our [ɪn'devə(r)] **1** *n* tentativo *m* **2** *v/t* tentare

en·dem·ic [ɪn'demɪk] *adj* endemico

end·ing ['endɪŋ] finale *m*; GRAM desinenza *f*

end·less ['endlɪs] *adj* interminabile

en·dorse [en'dɔːs] *v/t cheque* girare; *candidacy* appoggiare; *product* fare pubblicità a

en·dorse·ment [en'dɔːsmənt] *of cheque* girata *f*; *of candidacy* appoggio *m*; *of product* pubblicità *f*

end prod·uct prodotto *m* finale

end re·sult risultato *m* finale

en·dur·ance [ɪn'djʊrəns] resistenza *f*

en·dure [ɪn'djʊə(r)] **1** *v/t* sopportare **2** *v/i (last)* resistere

en·dur·ing [ɪn'djʊərɪŋ] *adj* durevole

end-us·er [end'juːzə(r)] utilizzatore *m* finale

en·e·my ['enəmɪ] nemico *m*, -a *f*

en·er·get·ic [enə'dʒetɪk] *adj* energico

en·er·get·ic·al·ly [enə'dʒetɪklɪ] *adv* con energia

en·er·gy ['enədʒɪ] energia *f*

en·er·gy-sav·ing ['enədʒɪseɪvɪŋ] *adj device* per risparmiare energia

'en·er·gy sup·ply rifornimento *m* di energia elettrica

en·force [ɪn'fɔːs] *v/t* far rispettare

en·gage [ɪn'geɪdʒ] **1** *v/t (hire)* ingaggiare **2** *v/i* TECH ingranare

♦ **engage in** *v/t* occuparsi di; *conversation* coinvolgere in

en·gaged [ɪn'geɪdʒd] *adj to be married* fidanzato; **get ~** fidanzarsi

en'gaged tone *Br* TELEC segnale *m* d'occupato

en·gage·ment [ɪn'geɪdʒmənt] *(appointment)* impegno *m*; *to be married* fidanzamento *m*; MIL scontro *m*

en'gage·ment ring anello *m* di fidanzamento

en·gag·ing [ɪn'geɪdʒɪŋ] *adj smile, person* accattivante

en·gine ['endʒɪn] motore *m*

en·gi·neer [endʒɪ'nɪə(r)] **1** *n* ingegnere *m*; *for sound, software* tecnico *m*; NAUT macchinista *m* **2** *v/t fig: meeting etc* macchinare, architettare

en·gi·neer·ing [endʒɪ'nɪərɪŋ] ingegneria *f*

Eng·land ['ɪŋglənd] Inghilterra *f*

Eng·lish ['ɪŋglɪʃ] **1** *adj* inglese **2** *n* (*language*) inglese *m*; **the ~** gli inglesi

Eng·lish 'Chan·nel Manica *f*

'En·glish·man inglese *m*

'En·glish·wom·an inglese *f*

en·grave [ɪn'greɪv] *v/t* incidere

en·grav·ing [ɪn'greɪvɪŋ] (*drawing*) stampa *f*; (*design*) incisione *f*

en·grossed [ɪn'grəʊst] *adj*: **~ in** assorto in

en·gulf [ɪn'gʌlf] *v/t* avvolgere

en·hance [ɪn'hɑːns] *v/t* accrescere; *performance, reputation* migliorare

e·nig·ma [ɪ'nɪgmə] enigma *m*

e·nig·mat·ic [enɪg'mætɪk] *adj* enigmatico

en·joy [ɪn'dʒɔɪ] *v/t*: **did you ~ the film?** ti è piaciuto il film?; **I ~ reading** mi piace leggere; **~ your meal!** buon appetito!; **~ o.s.** divertirsi

en·joy·a·ble [ɪn'dʒɔɪəbl] *adj* piacevole

en·joy·ment [ɪn'dʒɔɪmənt] piacere *m*, divertimento *m*

en·large [ɪn'lɑːdʒ] *v/t* ingrandire

en·large·ment [ɪn'lɑːdʒmənt] ingrandimento *m*

en·light·en [ɪn'laɪtn] *v/t* illuminare

en·list [ɪn'lɪst] **1** *v/i* MIL arruolarsi **2** *v/t*: **~ the help of ...** ottenere l'appoggio di ...

en·liv·en [ɪn'laɪvn] *v/t* animare

en·mi·ty ['enmətɪ] inimicizia *f*

e·nor·mi·ty [ɪ'nɔːmətɪ] enormità *f inv*

e·nor·mous [ɪ'nɔːməs] *adj* enorme

e·nor·mous·ly [ɪ'nɔːməslɪ] *adv* enormemente

e·nough [ɪ'nʌf] **1** *adj* sufficiente, abbastanza *inv* **2** *pron* abbastanza; **will £50 be ~?** saranno sufficienti £50?;

I've had ~! ne ho abbastanza!; *thanks, I've had ~* grazie, basta così; *that's ~, calm down!* adesso basta, calmati! **3** *adv* abbastanza; *strangely ~* per quanto strano

en·quire [ɪn'kwaɪə(r)] *v/i* chiedere informazioni, informarsi; **~ about sth** chiedere informazioni su qc; **~ into sth** fare delle ricerche su qc

en·quir·ing [ɪn'kwaɪərɪŋ] *adj*: **have an ~ mind** avere una mente curiosa

en·quir·y [ɪn'kwaɪərɪ] richiesta *f* di informazioni; (*public ~*) indagine *f*

en·raged [ɪn'reɪdʒd] *adj* arrabbiato

en·rich [ɪn'rɪtʃ] *v/t* arricchire

en·roll [ɪn'rəʊl] *v/i* iscriversi

en·rol·ment [ɪn'rəʊlmənt] iscrizione *f*

en·sue [ɪn'sjuː] *v/i* seguire

en suite (bath·room) ['ɒnswiːt] bagno *m* in camera

en·sure [ɪn'ʃʊə(r)] *v/t* assicurare

en·tail [ɪn'teɪl] *v/t* comportare

en·tan·gle [ɪn'tæŋgl] *v/t in rope* impigliare; **become ~d in** impigliarsi in; *in love affair* invischiarsi in

en·ter ['entə(r)] **1** *v/t room, house* entrare in; *competition* iscriversi a; *person, horse in race* iscrivere; (*write down*) registrare; COMPUT inserire **2** *v/i* entrare; THEA entrare in scena; *in competition* iscriversi **3** *n* COMPUT invio *m*

en·ter·prise ['entəpraɪz] (*initiative*) intraprendenza *f*; (*venture*) impresa *f*

en·ter·pris·ing ['entəpraɪzɪŋ] *adj* intraprendente

en·ter·tain [entə'teɪn] **1** *v/t* (*amuse*) intrattenere; (*consider: idea*) considerare **2** *v/i* (*have guests*) ricevere

en·ter·tain·er [entə'teɪnə(r)] artista *m/f*

en·ter·tain·ing [entə'teɪnɪŋ] *adj* divertente

en·ter·tain·ment [entə'teɪnmənt] *adj* divertimento *m*

en·thrall [ɪn'θrɔːl] *v/t* affascinare

en·thu·si·as·m [ɪn'θjuːzɪæzm] entusiasmo *m*

en·thu·si·ast [ɪn'θjuːzɪ'æst] appassionato *m*, -a *f*

en·thu·si·as·tic [ɪnθjuːzɪ'æstɪk] *adj* entusiasta

en·thu·si·as·tic·al·ly [ɪnθjuːzɪ'æs-tɪklɪ] *adv* con entusiasmo

en·tice [ɪn'taɪs] *v/t* attirare

en·tire [ɪn'taɪə(r)] *adj* intero

en·tire·ly [ɪn'taɪəlɪ] *adv* interamente

en·ti·tle [ɪn'taɪtl] *v/t* dare il diritto a; **be ~d to do sth** avere il diritto di fare qc

en·ti·tled [ɪn'taɪtld] *adj book* intitolato

en·trance ['entrəns] entrata *f*, ingresso *m*; THEA entrata *f* in scena; *(admission)* ammissione *f*

en·tranced [ɪn'trɑːnst] *adj* incantato

'en·trance ex·am·(i·na·tion esame *m* di ammissione

'en·trance fee quota *f* di ingresso

en·trant ['entrənt] concorrente *m/f*

en·treat [ɪn'triːt] *v/t* supplicare; **~ s.o. to do sth** supplicare qu di fare qc

en·trenched [ɪn'trentʃt] *adj attitudes* radicato

en·tre·pre·neur [ɒntrəprə'nɜː] imprenditore *m*, -trice *f*

en·tre·pre·neur·i·al [ɒntrəprə'nɜːrɪəl] *adj* imprenditoriale

en·trust [ɪn'trʌst] *v/t* affidare; **~ s.o. with sth, ~ sth to s.o.** affidare qc a qu

en·try ['entrɪ] entrata *f*; *(admission)* ingresso *m*; *in diary* annotazione *f*, *in accounts, dictionary* voce *f*

'en·try form modulo *m* d'iscrizione

'en·try·phone citofono *m*; **'en·try vi·sa** visto *m* d'ingresso

e·nu·me·rate [ɪ'njuːməreɪt] *v/t* enumerare

en·vel·op [ɪn'veləp] *v/t* avviluppare

en·ve·lope ['envələʊp] busta *f*

en·vi·a·ble ['envɪəbl] *adj* invidiabile

en·vi·ous ['envɪəs] *adj* invidioso; **be ~ of s.o.** essere invidioso di qu

en·vi·ron·ment [ɪn'vaɪərənmənt] ambiente *m*

en·vi·ron·men·tal [ɪnvaɪərən'mentl]

adj ambientale

en·vi·ron·men·tal·ist [ɪnvaɪərən-'mentəlɪst] ambientalista *m/f*

en·vi·ron·men·tal·ly friend·ly [ɪn-vaɪərən'mentəlɪ] *adj* ecologico

en·vi·ron·men·tal pol·lu·tion inquinamento *m* ambientale

en·vi·ron·men·tal pro·tec·tion tutela *f* dell'ambiente

en·vi·rons [ɪn'vaɪərənz] *npl* dintorni *mpl*

en·vis·age [ɪn'vɪzɪdʒ] *v/t* prevedere

en·voy ['envɔɪ] inviato *m*, -a *f*

en·vy ['envɪ] **1** *n* invidia *f*; **be the ~ of** essere invidiato da **2** *v/t (pret & pp -ied)*: **~ s.o. sth** invidiare qc a qu

e·phem·er·al *adj* effimero

ep·ic ['epɪk] **1** *n* epopea *f* **2** *adj journey* mitico; **a task of ~ proportions** un'impresa titanica

ep·i·cen·tre ['epɪsentr] epicentro *m*

ep·i·dem·ic [epɪ'demɪk] epidemia *f*

ep·i·lep·sy ['epɪlepsɪ] epilessia *f*

ep·i·lep·tic [epɪ'leptɪk] epilettico *m*, -a *f*

ep·i·lep·tic 'fit attacco *m* epilettico

ep·i·log *Am*, **ep·i·logue** ['epɪlɒg] epilogo *m*

ep·i·sode ['epɪsəʊd] episodio *m*

ep·i·taph ['epɪtɑːf] epitaffio *m*

e·poch ['iːpɒk] epoca *f*

e·poch-mak·ing ['iːpɒkmeɪkɪŋ] *adj* che fa epoca

e·qual ['iːkwl] **1** *adj* uguale, pari *inv*; **be ~ to task** essere all'altezza di **2** *n*: **be the ~ of** essere equivalente a; **treat s.o. as his ~** trattare qualcuno alla pari **3** *v/t (pret & pp -led, Am -ed)* *(be as good as)* uguagliare; **4 times 12 ~s 48** 4 per 12 fa 48

e·qual·i·ty [ɪ'kwɒlətɪ] uguaglianza *f*, parità *f*

e·qual·ize ['iːkwəlaɪz] **1** *v/t* uniformare **2** *v/i Br* SP pareggiare

e·qual·iz·er ['iːkwəlaɪzə(r)] *Br* SP gol *m inv* del pareggio

e·qual·ly ['iːkwəlɪ] *adv* ugualmente; **~, ...** allo stesso modo, ...

e·qual 'rights *npl* parità *f* di diritti

e·quate [ɪ'kweɪt] *v/t* equiparare; **~ sth with sth** equiparare qc e qc e·qua·tion [ɪ'kweɪʒn] MATH equazione f

e·qua·tor [ɪ'kweɪtə(r)] equatore m

e·qui·lib·ri·um [iːkwɪ'lɪbrɪəm] equilibrio m

e·qui·nox ['iːkwɪnɒks] equinozio m

e·quip [ɪ'kwɪp] v/t (pret & pp -ped) equipaggiare; ~ s.o. / sth with sth equipaggiare qu/qc di qc; he's not ~ped to handle it fig non ha la capacità di gestirlo

e·quip·ment equipaggiamento m; electrical, electronic apparecchiature fpl

equ·i·ty ['ekwətɪ] FIN capitale m azionario

e·quiv·a·lent [ɪ'kwɪvələnt] 1 adj equivalente; be ~ to essere equivalente a 2 n equivalente m

e·ra ['ɪərə] era f

e·rad·i·cate [ɪ'rædɪkeɪt] v/t sradicare

e·rase [ɪ'reɪz] v/t cancellare

e·ras·er [ɪ'reɪzə(r)] gomma f (da cancellare)

e·rect [ɪ'rekt] 1 adj eretto 2 v/t erigere

e·rec·tion [ɪ'rekʃn] erezione f

er·go·nom·ic [ɜːgəʊ'nɒmɪk] adj furniture ergonomico

e·rode [ɪ'rəʊd] v/t erodere; of acid corrodere; fig: rights, power eliminare

e·ro·sion [ɪ'rəʊʒn] erosione f; of acid corrosione f, fig eliminazione f

e·rot·ic [ɪ'rɒtɪk] adj erotico

e·rot·i·cism [ɪ'rɒtɪsɪzm] erotismo m

er·rand ['erənd] commissione f, run ~s fare commissioni

er·rat·ic [ɪ'rætɪk] adj irregolare

er·ror ['erə(r)] errore m

'er·ror mes·sage COMPUT messaggio m di errore

e·rupt [ɪ'rʌpt] v/i of volcano eruttare; of violence esplodere; of person dare in escandescenze

e·rup·tion [ɪ'rʌpʃn] of volcano eruzione f; of violence esplosione f

es·ca·late ['eskəleɪt] v/i of costs aumentare; of war intensificarsi

es·ca·la·tion [eskə'leɪʃn] escalation f inv

es·ca·la·tor ['eskəleɪtə(r)] scala f mobile

es·cape [ɪ'skeɪp] 1 n of prisoner, animal, gas fuga f; have a narrow ~ scamparla per un pelo 2 v/i of prisoner, animal scappare, fuggire; of gas fuoriuscire 3 v/t: the word ~s me la parola mi sfugge

es'cape chute AVIA scivolo m

es·cort ['eskɔːt] 1 n accompagnatore m, -trice f; (guard) scorta f 2 v/t [ɪ'skɔːt] socially accompagnare; act as guard to scortare

es·pe·cial [ɪ'speʃl] → special

es·pe·cial·ly [ɪ'speʃlɪ] adv specialmente

es·pi·o·nage ['espɪənɑːʒ] spionaggio m

es·pres·so (cof·fee) [es'presəʊ] espresso m

es·say ['eseɪ] n saggio m; in school tema m

es·sen·tial [ɪ'senʃl] adj essenziale

es·sen·tial·ly [ɪ'senʃlɪ] adv essenzialmente

es·tab·lish [ɪ'stæblɪʃ] v/t company fondare; (create, determine) stabilire; ~ o.s. as imporsi come

es·tab·lish·ment [ɪ'stæblɪʃmənt] firm azienda f; hotel, restaurant struttura f; the Establishment la classe dirigente

es·tate [ɪ'steɪt] (area of land) tenuta f; (possessions of dead person) patrimonio m

es'tate a·gen·cy agenzia f immobiliare; es'tate a·gent agente m/f immobiliare; es'tate car giardiniera f

es·thet·ic etc Am → aesthetic etc

es·ti·mate ['estɪmət] 1 n stima f, valutazione f; COM preventivo m 2 v/t stimare

es·ti·ma·tion [estɪ'meɪʃn] stima f; he has gone up / down in my ~ è salito / sceso nella mia stima; in my ~ (opinion) a mio giudizio

es·tranged [ɪs'treɪndʒd] adj wife, husband separato

es·tu·a·ry ['estjʊərɪ] estuario m

ETA [iːtiː'eɪ] abbr (= estimated time of arrival) ora f d'arrivo prevista

etc [et'setrə] *abbr* (= *et cetera*) ecc. (= eccetera)

etch·ing ['etʃɪŋ] acquaforte *f*

e·ter·nal [ɪ'tɜːnl] *adj* eterno

e·ter·ni·ty [ɪ'tɜːnətɪ] eternità *f*

eth·i·cal ['eθɪkl] *adj* etico

eth·ics ['eθɪks] etica *f*

eth·nic ['eθnɪk] *adj* etnico

eth·nic 'group gruppo *m* etnico, etnia *f*

eth·nic mi'nor·i·ty minoranza *f* etnica

EU [iː'juː] *abbr* (= *European Union*) UE *f* (= Unione *f* europea)

eu·phe·mism ['juːfəmɪzm] eufemismo *m*

eu·pho·ri·a [juː'fɔːrɪə] euforia *f*

eu·ro ['jʊərəʊ] euro *m inv*; 'Eu·ro·cheque Eurocheque *m inv*; Eu·ro·crat ['jʊərəʊkræt] funzionario *m*, -a *f* della Commissione europea; 'Eu·ro MP eurodeputato *m*, -a *f*

Eu·rope ['jʊərəp] Europa *f*

Eu·ro·pe·an [jʊərə'pɪən] 1 *adj* europeo 2 *n* europeo *m*, -a *f*; Eu·rope·an Com'mis·sion Commissione *f* europea; Eu·ro·pe·an Com'mis·sion·er Commissario *m* europeo; Eu·ro·pe·an 'Par·lia·ment Parlamento *m* europeo; Eu·ro·pe·an 'Un·ion Unione *f* europea

eu·tha·na·si·a [juːθə'neɪzɪə] eutanasia *f*

e·vac·u·ate [ɪ'vækjʊeɪt] *v/t* evacuare

e·vade [ɪ'veɪd] *v/t* eludere; *taxes* evadere

e·val·u·ate [ɪ'væljʊeɪt] *v/t* valutare

e·val·u·a·tion [ɪvæljʊ'eɪʃn] valutazione *f*

e·van·gel·ist [ɪ'vændʒəlɪst] evangelizzatore *m*, -trice *f*

e·vap·o·rate [ɪ'væpəreɪt] *v/i of water* evaporare; *of confidence* svanire

e·vap·o·ra·tion [ɪvæpə'reɪʃn] *of water* evaporazione *f*

e·va·sion [ɪ'veɪʒn] elusione *f*; *of taxes* evasione *f*

e·va·sive [ɪ'veɪsɪv] *adj* evasivo

eve [iːv] vigilia *f*

e·ven ['iːvn] 1 *adj* (*regular*) omogeneo; *breathing* regolare; *surface* piano; *hem* diritto; *(number)* pari *inv*; *players, game* alla pari; get ~ with ... farla pagare a ... 2 *adv* persino; *the car ~ has a CD player* la macchina ha persino un lettore CD; ~ *bigger* ancora più grande; ~ *better/worse* ancora meglio/peggio; *not* ~ nemmeno, neppure; ~ *so* nonostante questo; ~ *if* anche se 3 *v/t*: ~ *the score* pareggiare

eve·ning ['iːvnɪŋ] sera *f*; *in the* ~ di sera; *this* ~ stasera; *good* ~ buona sera

'eve·ning class corso *m* serale; 'eve·ning dress *for woman* vestito *m* da sera; *for man* abito *m* scuro; eve·ning 'pa·per giornale *m* della sera

e·ven·ly ['iːvnlɪ] *adv* (*regularly*) in modo omogeneo; *breathe* regolarmente

e·vent [ɪ'vent] evento *m*, avvenimento *m*; *social* manifestazione *f*; SP prova *f*; *at all* ~s ad ogni modo

e·vent·ful [ɪ'ventfʊl] *adj* movimentato

e·ven·tu·al [ɪ'ventjʊəl] *adj* finale

e·ven·tu·al·ly [ɪ'ventjʊəlɪ] *adv* finalmente, alla fine

ev·er ['evə(r)] *adv* mai; *have you ~ been to ...?* sei mai stato in ...?; *for* ~ per sempre; *as* ~ come sempre; ~ *more* sempre di più; ~ *since he left I have been worried* da quando è partito sono preoccupato; ~ *since his sister's death* dalla morte di sua sorella; *he's been depressed ~ since* è depresso da allora

ev·er·green ['evəgriːn] *n* sempreverde *m*

ev·er·last·ing [evə'lɑːstɪŋ] *adj* eterno

ev·ery ['evrɪ] *adj* ogni; *one in ~ ten houses* una casa su dieci; ~ *other day* un giorno sì, uno no; ~ *now and then* ogni tanto

ev·ery·bod·y ['evrɪbɒdɪ] → *everyone*

ev·ery·day ['evrɪdeɪ] *adj* di tutti i giorni

ev·e·ry·one ['evrɪwʌn] *pron* tutti *pl*

ev·e·ry·thing ['evrɪθɪŋ] *pron* tutto

ev·e·ry·where ['evrɪweə(r)] *adv* dovunque, dappertutto; (*wherever*) dovunque

e·vict [ɪ'vɪkt] *v/t* sfrattare

ev·i·dence ['evɪdəns] prova *f*; **give ~** testimoniare

ev·i·dent ['evɪdənt] *adj* evidente

ev·i·dent·ly ['evɪdəntlɪ] *adv* evidentemente

e·vil ['iːvl] **1** *adj* cattivo **2** *n* male *m*

e·voke [ɪ'vəʊk] *v/t image* evocare

ev·o·lu·tion [iːvə'luːʃn] evoluzione *f*

e·volve [ɪ'vɒlv] *v/i* evolvere

ewe [juː] pecora *f* femmina

ex- [eks] *pref* ex-

ex [eks] F (*former wife*) ex *f inv* F; (*former husband*) ex *m inv* F

ex·act [ɪg'zækt] *adj* esatto

ex·act·ing [ɪg'zæktɪŋ] *adj task* impegnativo; *employer* esigente; *standards* rigido

ex·act·ly [ɪg'zæktlɪ] *adv* esattamente; **~!** esatto!, esattamente!; **not ~** non esattamente

ex·ag·ge·rate [ɪg'zædʒəreɪt] *v/t & v/i* esagerare

ex·ag·ge·ra·tion [ɪgzædʒə'reɪʃn] esagerazione *f*

ex·am [ɪg'zæm] esame *m*; **sit an ~** dare *o* sostenere un esame; **pass an ~** passare *o* superare un esame; **fail an ~** essere bocciato a un esame

ex·am·i·na·tion [ɪgzæmɪ'neɪʃn] esame *m*; *of patient* visita *f*

ex·am·ine [ɪg'zæmɪn] *v/t* esaminare; *patient* visitare

ex·am·in·er [ɪg'zæmɪnə(r)] EDU esaminatore *m*, -trice *f*

ex·am·ple [ɪg'zɑːmpl] esempio *m*; **for ~** ad *o* per esempio; **set a good / bad ~** dare il buon / cattivo esempio

ex·as·pe·rat·ed [ɪg'zæspəreɪt] *adj* esasperato

ex·as·pe·rat·ing [ɪg'zæspəreɪtɪŋ] *adj* esasperante

ex·ca·vate ['ekskəveɪt] *v/t* (*dig*) scavare; *of archaeologist* riportare alla luce

ex·ca·va·tion [ekskə'veɪʃn] scavo *m*

ex·ca·va·tor ['ekskəveɪtə(r)] escavatrice *f*

ex·ceed [ɪk'siːd] *v/t* (*be more than*) eccedere, superare; (*go beyond*) oltrepassare, superare

ex·ceed·ing·ly [ɪk'siːdɪŋlɪ] *adj* estremamente

ex·cel [ɪk'sel] (*pret & pp -led*) **1** *v/i* eccellere; **~ at** eccellere in **2** *v/t*: **~ o.s.** superare se stesso

ex·cel·lence ['eksələns] eccellenza *f*

ex·cel·lent ['eksələnt] *adj* eccellente

ex·cept [ɪk'sept] *prep* eccetto; **~ for** fatta eccezione per; **~ that ...** eccetto che ...

ex·cep·tion [ɪk'sepʃn] eccezione *f*; **with the ~ of** con l'eccezione di; **take ~ to** avere da ridire su; (*be offended by*) risentirsi per

ex·cep·tion·al [ɪk'sepʃnl] *adj* eccezionale

ex·cep·tion·al·ly [ɪk'sepʃnlɪ] *adv* (*extremely*) eccezionalmente

ex·cerpt ['eksɜːpt] estratto *m*

ex·cess [ɪk'ses] **1** *n* eccesso *m*; **eat / drink to ~** mangiare / bere all'eccesso; **be in ~ of** eccedere **2** *adj* in eccesso

ex·cess 'bag·gage eccedenza *f* di bagaglio

ex·cess 'fare supplemento *m* tariffa

ex·ces·sive [ɪk'sesɪv] *adj* eccessivo

ex·change [ɪks'tʃeɪndʒ] **1** *n of views, information* scambio *m*; *between schools* scambio *m* culturale; **in ~ (for)** in cambio (di) **2** *v/t* cambiare; **~ sth for sth** cambiare qc con qc

ex'change rate FIN tasso *m* di cambio

ex·ci·ta·ble [ɪk'saɪtəbl] *adj* eccitabile

ex·cite [ɪk'saɪt] *v/t* (*make enthusiastic*) eccitare

ex·cit·ed [ɪk'saɪtɪd] *adj* eccitato; **get ~** eccitarsi; **get ~ about sth** eccitarsi per qc

ex·cite·ment [ɪk'saɪtmənt] eccitazione *f*

ex·cit·ing [ɪk'saɪtɪŋ] *adj* eccitante, emozionante

E

ex·claim [ɪkˈskleɪm] v/t esclamare

ex·cla·ma·tion [ekskləˈmeɪʃn] esclamazione f

ex·cla'ma·tion mark punto m esclamativo

ex·clude [ɪkˈskluːd] v/t escludere

ex·clud·ing [ɪkˈskluːdɪŋ] prep ad esclusione di

ex·clu·sive [ɪkˈskluːsɪv] adj esclusivo

ex·com·mu·ni·cate [ekskəˈmjuːnɪkeɪt] v/t REL scomunicare

ex·cru·ci·a·ting [ɪkˈskruːʃieɪtɪŋ] adj pain lancinante

ex·cur·sion [ɪkˈskɜːʃn] escursione f, gita f

ex·cuse [ɪkˈskjuːs] 1 n scusa f 2 v/t [ɪkˈskjuːz] scusare; ~ *s.o. from sth* dispensare qu da qc; ~ *me to get attention, interrupting* scusami, mi scusi fml; *to get past* permesso

ex·di'rec·to·ry: Br be ~ non comparire sull'elenco telefonico

ex·e·cute [ˈeksɪkjuːt] v/t criminal giustiziare; plan attuare

ex·e·cu·tion [eksɪˈkjuːʃn] of criminal esecuzione f; of plan attuazione f

ex·e·cu·tion·er [eksɪˈkjuːʃnə(r)] carnefice m

ex·ec·u·tive [ɪgˈzekjʊtɪv] dirigente m/f

ex·ec·u·tive 'brief·case ventiquattrore f inv

ex·ec·u·tive 'wash·room bagno m della direzione

ex·em·pla·ry [ɪgˈzemplərɪ] adj esemplare

ex·empt [ɪgˈzempt] adj: be ~ from essere esente da

ex·er·cise [ˈeksəsaɪz] 1 n (physical), EDU esercizio m; MIL esercitazione f; *take* ~ fare esercizio 2 v/t muscle fare esercizio con; dog far fare esercizio a; caution, restraint adoperare 3 v/i fare esercizio

'ex·er·cise bike cyclette f inv; **'ex·er·cise book** EDU quaderno m di esercizi; **'ex·er·cise class** esercitazione f

ex·ert [ɪgˈzɜːt] v/t authority esercitare; ~ *o.s.* sforzarsi

ex·er·tion [ɪgˈzɜːʃn] sforzo m

ex·hale [eksˈheɪl] v/t esalare

ex·haust [ɪgˈzɔːst] 1 n fumes gas mpl di scarico; pipe tubo m di scappamento 2 v/t (tire) estenuare; (use up) esaurire

ex·haust·ed [ɪgˈzɔːstɪd] adj (tired) esausto

ex'haust fumes npl gas mpl di scarico

ex·haust·ing [ɪgˈzɔːstɪŋ] adj estenuante

ex·haus·tion [ɪgˈzɔːstʃn] spossatezza f

ex·haus·tive [ɪgˈzɔːstɪv] adj esauriente

ex'haust pipe tubo m di scappamento

ex·hib·it [ɪgˈzɪbɪt] 1 n in exhibition oggetto m esposto; LAW prova f 2 v/t of gallery, artist esporre; (give evidence of) manifestare

exhibition [eksɪˈbɪʃn] esposizione f; of bad behaviour manifestazione f; of skill dimostrazione f

ex·hi·bi·tion·ist [eksɪˈbɪʃnɪst] esibizionista m/f

ex·hil·a·rat·ing [ɪgˈzɪləreɪtɪŋ] adj emozionante

ex·ile [ˈeksaɪl] 1 n esilio m; person esiliato m, -a f 2 v/t esiliare

ex·ist [ɪgˈzɪst] v/i esistere; ~ *on* vivere di

ex·ist·ence [ɪgˈzɪstəns] esistenza f; *in* ~ esistente; *come into* ~ nascere

ex·ist·ing [ɪgˈzɪstɪŋ] adj attuale

ex·it [ˈeksɪt] 1 n uscita f 2 v/i COMPUT uscire

ex·on·e·rate [ɪgˈzɒnəreɪt] v/t scagionare

ex·or·bi·tant [ɪgˈzɔːbɪtənt] adj esorbitante

ex·ot·ic [ɪgˈzɒtɪk] adj esotico

ex·pand [ɪkˈspænd] 1 v/t espandere 2 v/i espandersi; of metal dilatarsi

♦**expand on** v/t dilungarsi su

ex·panse [ɪkˈspæns] distesa f

ex·pan·sion [ɪkˈspænʃn] espansione f; of metal dilatazione f

ex·pa·tri·ate [eksˈpætrɪət] 1 adj

residente all'estero **2** *n* residente *m/f* all'estero

ex·pect [ɪk'spekt] **1** *v/t* aspettare; (*suppose, demand*) aspettarsi **2** *v/i*: **be ~ing** aspettare un bambino; **I ~ so** immagino di sì

ex·pec·tant [ɪk'spektənt] *adj* pieno di aspettativa

ex·pec·tant 'moth·er donna *f* in stato interessante

ex·pec·ta·tion [ekspek'teɪʃn] aspettativa *f*; **~s** (*demands*) aspettative *fpl*

ex·pe·di·ent [ɪk'spiːdiənt] *n* espediente *m*

ex·pe·di·tion [ekspɪ'dɪʃn] spedizione *f*; **go on a shopping/sight-seeing ~** andare a fare spese/in giro a visitare

ex·pel [ɪk'spel] *v/t* (*pret & pp -led*) espellere

ex·pend [ɪk'spend] *v/t energy* spendere

ex·pend·a·ble [ɪk'spendəbl] *adj person* sacrificabile

ex·pen·di·ture [ɪk'spendɪtʃə(r)] spesa *f*

ex·pense [ɪk'spens] spesa *f*; **at the company's ~** a spese della società; **a joke at my ~** uno scherzo a mie spese; **at the ~ of his health** a spese della sua salute

ex'pense ac·count nota *f* spese

ex·pen·ses [ɪk'spensɪz] *npl* spese *fpl*

ex·pen·sive [ɪk'spensɪv] *adj* caro

ex·pe·ri·ence [ɪk'spɪəriəns] **1** *n* esperienza *f* **2** *v/t pain, pleasure* provare; *problem, difficulty* incontrare

ex·pe·ri·enced [ɪk'spɪəriənst] *adj* con esperienza; **he's ~ in teaching** ha esperienza nell'insegnamento

ex·per·i·ment [ɪk'sperɪmənt] **1** *n* esperimento *m* **2** *v/i* fare esperimenti; **~ on** *animals* sperimentare su; **~ with** (*try out*) sperimentare

ex·per·i·men·tal [ɪksperɪ'mentl] *adj* sperimentale

ex·pert ['ekspɜːt] **1** *adj* esperto **2** *n* esperto *m*, -a *f*

ex·pert ad'vice parere *m* di un esperto

ex·pert·ise [ekspɜː'tiːz] competenza *f*

ex·pire [ɪk'spaɪə(r)] *v/i* scadere

ex·pi·ry [ɪk'spaɪərɪ] scadenza *f*

ex'pi·ry date data *f* di scadenza

ex·plain [ɪk'spleɪn] **1** *v/t* spiegare **2** *v/i* spiegarsi

ex·pla·na·tion [eksplə'neɪʃn] spiegazione *f*

ex·plic·it [ɪk'splɪsɪt] *adj instructions* esplicito

ex·plic·it·ly [ɪk'splɪsɪtlɪ] *adv state, forbid* esplicitamente

ex·plode [ɪk'spləʊd] **1** *v/i of bomb* esplodere **2** *v/t bomb* fare esplodere

ex·ploit[1] ['eksplɔɪt] *n* exploit *m inv*

ex·ploit[2] [ɪk'splɔɪt] *v/t person, resources* sfruttare

ex·ploi·ta·tion [eksplɔɪ'teɪʃn] sfruttamento *m*

ex·plo·ra·tion [eksplə'reɪʃn] esplorazione *f*

ex·plor·a·to·ry [ɪk'splɒrətərɪ] *adj surgery* esplorativo

ex·plore [ɪk'splɔː(r)] *v/t country, possibility etc* esplorare

ex·plor·er [ɪk'splɔːrə(r)] esploratore *m*, -trice *f*

ex·plo·sion [ɪk'spləʊʒn] esplosione *f*; **a population ~** un'esplosione demografica

ex·plo·sive [ɪk'spləʊsɪv] *n* esplosivo *m*

ex·port ['ekspɔːt] **1** *n action* esportazione *f*; *item* prodotto *m* di esportazione **2** *v/t goods*, COMPUT esportare

'ex·port cam·paign campagna *f* per l'esportazione

ex·port·er ['ekspɔːtə(r)] esportatore *m*, -trice *f*

ex·pose [ɪk'spəʊz] *v/t* (*uncover*) scoprire; *scandal, person* denunciare; **~ sth to sth** esporre qc a qc

ex·po·sure [ɪk'spəʊʒə(r)] esposizione *f*; *to cold weather* esposizione *f* prolungata al freddo; *of dishonest behaviour* denuncia *f*; PHOT posa *f*

ex·press [ɪk'spres] **1** *adj* (*fast, explicit*) espresso **2** *n* (*train*) espresso *m*

3 v/t (speak of, voice) esprimere; **~ o.s. well/clearly** esprimersi bene/chiaramente; **~ o.s.** (emotionally) esprimersi

ex·pres·sion [ɪk'spreʃn] espressione f; (expressiveness) espressività f

ex·pres·sive [ɪk'spresɪv] adj espressivo

ex·press·ly [ɪk'spreslɪ] adv espressamente

ex·press·way [ɪk'spreswei] autostrada f

ex·pul·sion [ɪk'spʌlʃn] espulsione f

ex·qui·site [ek'skwɪzɪt] adj (beautiful) squisito

ex·tend [ɪk'stend] **1** v/t estendere; house, repertoire ampliare; runway, path prolungare; contract, visa prorogare; thanks, congratulations porgere **2** v/i of garden etc estendersi

ex·ten·sion [ɪk'stenʃn] to house annesso m; of contract, visa proroga f; TELEC interno m

ex·ten·sion ca·ble prolunga f

ex·ten·sive [ɪk'stensɪv] adj ampio

ex·tent [ɪk'stent] ampiezza f, portata f; **to such an ~ that** a un punto tale che; **to a certain ~** fino a un certo punto

ex·ten·u·at·ing cir·cum·stanc·es [ɪk'stenjʊeitɪŋ] npl circostanze fpl attenuanti

ex·te·ri·or [ɪk'stɪərɪə(r)] **1** adj esterno **2** n of building esterno m; of person aspetto m esteriore

ex·ter·mi·nate [ɪk'stɜːmɪneit] v/t sterminare

ex·ter·nal [ɪk'stɜːnl] adj (outside) esterno

ex·tinct [ɪk'stɪŋkt] adj species estinto

ex·tinc·tion [ɪk'stɪŋkʃn] of species estinzione f

ex·tin·guish [ɪk'stɪŋgwɪʃ] v/t spegnere

ex·tin·guish·er [ɪk'stɪŋgwɪʃə(r)] estintore m

ex·tort [ɪk'stɔːt] v/t estorcere; **money from ...** estorcere denaro da ...

ex·tor·tion [ɪk'stɔːʃn] estorsione f

ex·tor·tion·ate [ɪk'stɔːʃənət] adj prices esorbitante; **that's ~!** è un furto!

ex·tra ['ekstrə] **1** n extra m inv **2** adj in più; **be ~** (cost more) essere a parte **3** adv particolarmente; **an ~ special day** un giorno particolarmente speciale

ex·tra 'charge costo m aggiuntivo

ex·tract¹ ['ekstrækt] n estratto m

ex·tract² [ɪk'strækt] v/t estrarre; information estorcere

ex·trac·tion [ɪk'strækʃn] estrazione f

ex·tra·dite ['ekstrədait] v/t estradare

ex·tra·di·tion [ekstrə'dɪʃn] estradizione f

ex·tra·di·tion trea·ty accordo m di estradizione

ex·tra·mar·i·tal [ekstrə'mærɪtl] adj extraconiugale

ex·tra·or·di·nar·i·ly [ekstrɔːdɪn'eərɪlɪ] adv eccezionalmente

ex·tra·or·di·na·ry [ɪk'strɔːdɪnərɪ] adj straordinario

ex·tra 'time SP tempi mpl supplementari

ex·trav·a·gance [ɪk'strævəgəns] stravaganza f

ex·trav·a·gant [ɪk'strævəgənt] adj with money stravagante

ex·treme [ɪk'striːm] **1** n estremo m **2** adj estremo

ex·treme·ly [ɪk'striːmlɪ] adv estremamente

ex·trem·ist [ɪk'striːmɪst] estremista m/f

ex·tri·cate ['ekstrɪkeit] v/t districare

ex·tro·vert ['ekstrəvɜːt] n/adj estroverso m, -a f

ex·u·be·rant [ɪg'zjuːbərənt] adj esuberante

ex·ult [ɪg'zʌlt] v/i esultare

eye [ai] **1** n occhio m; of needle cruna f; **keep an ~ on** tenere d'occhio **2** v/t scrutare

'eye·ball bulbo m oculare; **'eye·brow** sopracciglio m; **'eye·catch·ing** adj appariscente; **'eye·lash** ciglio m; **'eye·lid** palpebra f; **'eye·lin·er** eyeliner m inv; **'eye·sha·dow** ombretto m; **'eye·sight**

vista *f*; **'eye·sore** pugno *m* in un occhio; **'eye strain** affaticamento *m*

della vista; **'eye·wit·ness** testimone *m/f* oculare

F

F *abbr* (= **Fahrenheit**) F (= Fahrenheit)
fab·ric ['fæbrɪk] (*material*) tessuto *m*
fab·u·lous ['fæbjʊləs] *adj* fantastico
fab·u·lous·ly ['fæbjʊləslɪ] *adv* incredibilmente
fa·çade [fə'sɑːd] *of building, person* facciata *f*
face [feɪs] **1** *n* viso *m*, faccia *f*; **~ to ~** faccia a faccia; *lose* **~** perdere la faccia **2** *v/t person, the sea etc* essere di fronte a; *facts, truth* affrontare
♦ **face up to** *v/t* affrontare
'face·cloth guanto *m* di spugna; **'face·lift** lifting *m inv* del viso; **'face pack** maschera *f* di bellezza; **face 'val·ue** valore *m* nominale; *take sth at* **~** giudicare qc dalle apparenze
fa·cial ['feɪʃl] *n* pulizia *f* del viso
fa·cil·i·tate [fə'sɪlɪteɪt] *v/t* facilitare
fa·cil·i·ties [fə'sɪlətɪz] *npl* strutture *fpl*
fact [fækt] fatto *m*; *in* **~**, *as a matter of* **~** in realtà
faction ['fækʃn] fazione *f*
fac·tor ['fæktə(r)] fattore *m*
fac·to·ry ['fæktərɪ] fabbrica *f*
fac·ul·ty ['fækəltɪ] facoltà *f inv*
fad [fæd] mania *f* passeggera
fade [feɪd] *v/i of colours* sbiadire; *of light* smorzarsi; *of memories* svanire
fad·ed ['feɪdɪd] *adj colour, jeans* sbiadito
fag [fæg] F (*cigarette*) sigaretta *f*
'fag end F (*cigarette end*) mozzicone *m* di sigaretta
Fahr·en·heit ['færənhaɪt] *adj* Fahrenheit
fail [feɪl] **1** *v/i* fallire **2** *v/t test, exam*

essere bocciato a; *he ~ed to arrive in time* non è riuscito ad arrivare in tempo; *he never ~s to write* non manca mai di scrivere **2** *n*: *without* **~** con certezza
fail·ing ['feɪlɪŋ] *n* difetto *m*
fail·ure ['feɪljə(r)] fallimento *m*
faint [feɪnt] **1** *adj* vago **2** *v/i* svenire
faint·ly ['feɪntlɪ] *adv* vagamente
fair¹ [feə(r)] *n* (*fun* **~**) luna park *m inv*; COM fiera *f*
fair² [feə(r)] *adj hair* biondo; *complexion* chiaro; (*just*) giusto; *it's not* **~** non è giusto *adv*: **~** *enough* e va bene
fair·ly ['feəlɪ] *adv treat* giustamente; (*quite*) piuttosto
fair·ness ['feənɪs] *of treatment* giustizia *f*
fai·ry ['feərɪ] fata *f*
'fai·ry tale fiaba *f*, favola *f*
faith [feɪθ] fede *f*
faith·ful ['feɪθfl] *adj* fedele; *be* **~** *to one's partner* essere fedeli al proprio compagno
faith·ful·ly ['feɪθflɪ] *adv* fedelmente; *Yours* **~** distinti saluti
fake [feɪk] **1** *n* falso *m* **2** *adj* falso **3** *v/t* (*forge*) falsificare; (*feign*) simulare
fall¹ [fɔːl] *n Am* autunno *m*
fall² [fɔːl] **1** *v/i* (*pret* **fell**, *pp* **fallen**) *of person, government, night* cadere; *of prices, temperature* calare; *it ~s on a Tuesday* cade di martedì; **~** *ill* ammalarsi **2** *n of person, government* caduta *f*; *in price, temperature* calo *m*
♦ **fall back on** *v/t* ricorrere a
♦ **fall behind** *v/i with work, studies* rimanere indietro

♦ **fall down** v/i cadere
♦ **fall for** v/t (*fall in love with*) innamorarsi di; (*be deceived by*) abboccare a
♦ **fall out** v/i of hair cadere; (*argue*) litigare
♦ **fall over** v/i cadere
♦ **fall through** v/i of plans andare a monte

fal·len ['fɔːlən] pp → **fall**
fal·li·ble ['fæləbl] adj fallibile
'fallout precipitazione f
false [fɔːls] adj falso
false a'larm falso allarme m
false·ly ['fɔːlslɪ] adv: **be ~ accused of sth** essere ingiustamente accusato di qc
false 'start in race falsa partenza f
false 'teeth npl dentiera f
fal·si·fy ['fɔːlsɪfaɪ] v/t (*pret & pp -ied*) falsificare
fame [feɪm] fama f
fa·mil·i·ar [fə'mɪljə(r)] adj (*intimate*) intimo; *form of address*, (*well-known*) familiare; **be ~ with sth** conoscere bene qc; *that looks / sounds ~* ha un'aria familiare
fa·mil·i·ar·i·ty [fəmɪlɪ'jærɪtɪ] *with subject etc* buona conoscenza f
fa·mil·i·ar·ize [fəm'ɪljəraɪz] v/t familiarizzare; **~ o.s. with ...** familiarizzarsi con ...
fam·i·ly ['fæməlɪ] famiglia f
fam·i·ly 'doc·tor medico m di famiglia; **fam·i·ly 'name** cognome m; **fam·i·ly 'plan·ning** pianificazione f familiare; **fam·i·ly 'plan·ning clin·ic** consultorio m per la pianificazione familiare; **fam·i·ly 'tree** albero m genealogico
fam·ine ['fæmɪn] fame f
fam·ished ['fæmɪʃt] adj F affamato
fa·mous ['feɪməs] adj famoso; **be ~ for ...** essere noto per ...
fan¹ [fæn] n (*supporter*) fan m/f
fan² [fæn] n for cooling: *electric* ventilatore m; *handheld* ventaglio m **2** v/t (*pret & pp -ned*): **~ o.s.** farsi aria
fa·nat·ic [fə'nætɪk] n fanatico m, -a f
fa·nat·i·cal [fə'nætɪkl] adj fanatico

fa·nat·i·cism [fə'nætɪsɪzm] fanatismo m
'fan belt MOT cinghia f della ventola
'fan club fan club m inv
fan·cy ['fænsɪ] **1** adj design stravagante **2** n: as the ~ takes you quanto ti va; **take a ~ to s.o.** prendere a benvolere qu **3** v/t (*pret & pp -ied*) F avere voglia di; *I'm sure he fancies you* sono sicuro che gli piaci
fan·cy 'dress costume m
fan·cy-'dress par·ty festa f in maschera
fang [fæŋ] dente m aguzzo
'fan mail lettere fpl dei fans
fan·ta·size ['fæntəsaɪz] v/i fantasticare
fan·tas·tic [fæn'tæstɪk] adj (*very good*) fantastico; (*very big*) enorme
fan·tas·tic·al·ly [fæn'tæstɪklɪ] adv (*extremely*) incredibilmente
fan·ta·sy ['fæntəsɪ] fantasia f
far [fɑː(r)] adv lontano; (*much*) molto; **~ away** lontano; **how ~ is it to ...?** quanto dista ...?; **as ~ as the corner / hotel** fino all'angolo / hotel; **as ~ as I can see** per quanto posso vedere; **as ~ as I know** per quanto ne so; *you've gone too ~* in behaviour sei andato troppo oltre; **so ~ so good** fin qui tutto bene
farce [fɑːs] farsa f
fare [feə(r)] n for travel tariffa f
Far 'East Estremo Oriente m
fare·well [feə'wel] n addio m
fare'well par·ty festa f d'addio
far-'fetched [fɑː'fetʃt] adj inverosimile
farm [fɑːm] n fattoria f
farm·er ['fɑːmə(r)] agricoltore m, -trice f
'farm·house cascina f
farm·ing ['fɑːmɪŋ] n agricoltura f
'farm·work·er bracciante m/f
'farm·yard cortile m di una cascina
far-'off adj lontano
far-'sight·ed [fɑː'saɪtɪd] adj previdente; Am OPT presbite
fart [fɑːt] **1** n F scoreggia f F, peto m

2 *v/i* F scoreggiare F, petare

far·ther ['fɑːðə(r)] *adv* più lontano

far·thest ['fɑːðəst] *adv* travel etc più lontano

fas·ci·nate ['fæsɪneɪt] *v/t* affascinare; *I always was ~d by the idea of ...* mi ha sempre affascinato l'idea di ...

fas·ci·nat·ing ['fæsɪneɪtɪŋ] *adj* affascinante

fas·ci·na·tion [fæsɪ'neɪʃn] *with subject* fascino *m*

fas·cis·m ['fæʃɪzm] fascismo *m*

fas·cist ['fæʃɪst] **1** *n* fascista *m/f* **2** *adj* fascista

fash·ion ['fæʃn] *n* moda *f*; (manner) maniera *f*, modo *m*; *in ~* alla moda; *out of ~* fuori moda

fash·ion·a·ble ['fæʃnəbl] *adj* alla moda

fash·ion·a·bly ['fæʃnəblɪ] *adv* dressed alla moda

'**fash·ion-con·scious** *adj* fanatico della moda; '**fash·ion de·sign·er** stilista *m/f*; '**fash·ion mag·a·zine** rivista *f* di moda; '**fash·ion show** sfilata *f* di moda

fast[1] [fɑːst] **1** *adj* veloce, rapido; *be ~ of clock* essere avanti **2** *adv* velocemente; *stuck* fissato saldamente; *~ asleep* profondamente addormentato

fast[2] [fɑːst] *n not eating* digiuno *m*

fas·ten ['fɑːsn] **1** *v/t* chiudere; dress, seat-belt allacciare; *~ sth onto sth* attaccare qc a qc; brooch appuntare qc su qc **2** *v/i of dress etc* allacciarsi

fas·ten·er ['fɑːsnə(r)] chiusura *f*

fast food fast food *m*; **fast·food 'res·tau·rant** fast food *m inv*; **fast 'for·ward 1** *n on video etc* riavvolgimento *m* rapido **2** *v/i* riavvolgere rapidamente; '**fast lane** on road corsia *f* di sorpasso; *in the ~ fig*: of life a cento all'ora; '**fast train** rapido *m*

fat [fæt] **1** *adj* grasso **2** *n* grasso *m*

fa·tal ['feɪtl] *adj* fatale

fa·tal·i·ty [fə'tælətɪ] fatalità *f inv*

fa·tal·ly ['feɪtəlɪ] *adv*: *~ injured* ferito a morte

fate [feɪt] fato *m*

fat·ed ['feɪtɪd] *adj*: *be ~ to do sth* essere destinato a fare qc

fa·ther ['fɑːðə(r)] *n* padre *m*; *Father Martin* REL padre Martin

Fa·ther 'Christ·mas Babbo *m* Natale

fa·ther·hood ['fɑːðəhʊd] paternità *f*

'**fa·ther-in-law** (*pl* **fathers-in-law**) suocero *m*

fa·ther·ly ['fɑːðəlɪ] *adj* paterno

fath·om ['fæðəm] *n* NAUT fathom *m inv*

♦**fathom out** *v/t fig* spiegarsi; *I just can't fathom you out* proprio non ti capisco

fa·tigue [fə'tiːg] *n* stanchezza *f*

fat·so ['fætsəʊ] *n* F ciccione *m*, -a F

fat·ten ['fætn] *v/t animal* ingrassare

fat·ty ['fætɪ] **1** *adj* grasso **2** *n* F person ciccione *m*, -a F

fau·cet ['fɔːsɪt] *Am* rubinetto *m*

fault [fɔːlt] *n* (defect) difetto *m*; *it's your / my ~* è colpa tua / mia; *find ~ with* criticare

fault·less ['fɔːltlɪs] *adj person, performance* impeccabile

fault·y ['fɔːltɪ] *adj goods* difettoso

fa·vor *etc Am* → **favour** *etc*

fa·vour ['feɪvə(r)] **1** *n* favore *m*; *do s.o. a ~* fare un favore a qu; *do me a ~!* (don't be stupid) fammi il piacere!; *in ~ of ...* a favore di ...; *be in ~ of ...* essere a favore di ... **2** *v/t* (prefer) preferire, prediligere

fa·vou·ra·ble ['feɪvərəbl] *adj reply etc* favorevole

fa·vou·rite ['feɪvərɪt] **1** *n* prediletto *m*, -a *f*; (food) piatto *m* preferito; *in race, competition* favorito *m*, -a *f* **2** *adj* preferito

fa·vou·rit·ism ['feɪvrɪtɪzm] favoritismo *m*

fax [fæks] **1** *n* fax *m inv*; *send sth by ~* inviare qc per fax **2** *v/t* inviare per fax; *~ sth to s.o.* inviare qc per fax a qc

FBI *abbr* (= *Federal Bureau of Investigation*) FBI *f*

fear [fɪə(r)] **1** *n* paura *f* **2** *v/t* avere paura di

fear·less ['fɪəlɪs] *adj* intrepido

fear·less·ly ['fɪəlɪslɪ] *adv* intrepidamente

fea·si·bil·i·ty stud·y [fiːzə'bɪlətɪ] studio *m* di fattibilità

fea·si·ble ['fiːzəbl] *adj* fattibile

feast [fiːst] *n* banchetto *m*

feat [fiːt] prodezza *f*

feath·er ['feðə(r)] piuma *f*

fea·ture ['fiːtʃə(r)] **1** *n* on face tratto *m*; of city, building, plan, style caratteristica *f*; in paper servizio *m*; (film) lungometraggio *m*; **make a ~ of ...** mettere l'accento su ... **2** *v/t* of film avere come protagonista

'fea·ture film lungometraggio *m*

Feb·ru·a·ry ['februərɪ] febbraio *m*

fed [fed] *pret & pp* → **feed**

fed·e·ral ['fedərəl] *adj* federale

fed·e·ra·tion [fedə'reɪʃn] federazione *f*

fed 'up *adj* F stufo F; **be ~ with ...** essere stufo di ...

fee [fiː] tariffa *f*, of lawyer, doctor etc onorario *m*

fee·ble ['fiːbl] *adj* debole

feed [fiːd] *v/t* (pret & pp fed) nutrire; family mantenere; baby dare da mangiare a

'feed·back *n* riscontro *m*, feedback *m inv*

feel [fiːl] (pret & pp felt) **1** *v/t* (touch) toccare; (sense) sentire; pain, pleasure, sensation sentire; (think) pensare **2** *v/i* sentirsi; **it ~s like silk / cotton** sembra seta / cotone al tatto; **your hand ~s hot / cold** la tua mano è calda / fredda; **I ~ hungry** ho fame; **I ~ tired** sono stanco; **how are you ~ing today?** come ti senti oggi?; **how does it ~ to be rich?** che sensazione fa essere ricchi?; **do you ~ like a drink / meal?** hai voglia di bere / mangiare qualcosa?; **I ~ like going / staying** ho voglia di andare / rimanere; **I don't ~ like it** non ne ho voglia

♦ **feel up to** *v/t* sentirsi in grado di

feel·er ['fiːlə(r)] of insect antenna *f*

'feel·good fac·tor fattore *m* tranquillizzante

feel·ing ['fiːlɪŋ] sentimento *m*; (emotion) sensazione *f*; (sensation) sensibilità *f*; **what are your ~s about it?** quali sono le tue impressioni in proposito?; **I have mixed ~s about him** ho sensazioni contrastanti nei suoi riguardi; **I have this ~ that ...** ho la sensazione che ...

feet [fiːt] *pl* → **foot**

fe·line ['fiːlaɪn] *adj* felino

fell [fel] *pret* → **fall**

fel·low ['feləʊ] *n* (man) tipo *m*

fel·low 'cit·i·zen concittadino *m*, -a *f*; **fel·low 'coun·try·man** compatriota *m/f*; **fel·low 'man** prossimo *m*

fel·o·ny ['felənɪ] *Am* delitto *m*

felt¹ [felt] *n* feltro *m*

felt² [felt] *pret & pp* → **feel**

felt 'tip, felt-tip(·ped) 'pen pennarello *m*

fe·male ['fiːmeɪl] **1** *adj* femmina; typical of women femminile **2** *n* femmina *f*; F (woman) donna *f*

fem·i·nine ['femɪnɪn] **1** *adj* femminile **2** *n* GRAM femminile *m*

fem·i·nis·m ['femɪnɪzm] femminismo *m*

fem·i·nist ['femɪnɪst] **1** *n* femminista *f* **2** *adj* femminista

fence [fens] *n* round garden etc recinto *m*; F criminal ricettatore *m*, -trice *f*; **sit on the ~** non prendere partito

♦ **fence in** *v/t* land recintare

fenc·ing ['fensɪŋ] SP scherma *f*

fend [fend] *v/i*: **~ for o.s.** badare a se stesso

fer·ment¹ [fə'ment] *v/i* of liquid fermentare

fer·ment² ['fɜːment] *n* (unrest) fermento *m*

fer·men·ta·tion [fɜːmen'teɪʃn] fermentazione *f*

fern [fɜːn] felce *f*

fe·ro·cious [fə'rəʊʃəs] *adj* feroce

fer·ry ['ferɪ] *n* traghetto *m*

fer·tile ['fɜːtaɪl] *adj* fertile

fer·til·i·ty [fɜː'tɪlətɪ] fertilità *f*

fer·til·i·ty drug cura *f* per sviluppare la fertilità

fer·ti·lize ['fɜːtəlaɪz] *v/t* ovum fecondare

fer·ti·liz·er ['fɜːtəlaɪzə(r)] *for soil* fertilizzante *m*

fer·vent ['fɜːvənt] *adj* admirer fervente

fer·vent·ly ['fɜːvəntlɪ] *adv* ardentemente

fes·ter ['festə(r)] *v/i of wound* fare infezione

fes·ti·val ['festɪvl] festival *m inv*

fes·tive ['festɪv] *adj* festivo; **the ~ season** le festività

fes·tiv·i·ties [fe'stɪvətɪz] *npl* festeggiamenti *mpl*

fe·tal ['fiːtl] *adj* fetale

fetch [fetʃ] *v/t* (go and ~) andare a prendere; (come and ~) venire a prendere; *thing* prendere; *price* rendere

fe·tus ['fiːtəs] feto *m*

feud [fjuːd] **1** *n* faida *f* **2** *v/i* litigare

fe·ver ['fiːvə(r)] febbre *f*

fe·ver·ish ['fiːvərɪʃ] *adj also fig* febbrile; *I'm feeling ~* mi sento la febbre

few [fjuː] **1** *adj* (not many) pochi; *a ~ ...* alcuni ...; *a ~ people* alcune persone, qualche persona; *a ~ books* alcuni libri, qualche libro; *quite a ~, a good ~* (a lot) parecchi **2** *pron* (not many) pochi; *a ~* (some) alcuni; *quite a ~, a good ~* (a lot) parecchi

few·er ['fjuːə(r)] *adj* meno; *~ than ...* meno di ...

fi·an·cé [fɪ'ɒnseɪ] fidanzato *m*

fi·an·cée [fɪ'ɒnseɪ] fidanzata *f*

fi·as·co [fɪ'æskəʊ] fiasco *m*

fib [fɪb] *n* frottola *f*

fi·ber *Am* → **fibre**

fi·bre ['faɪbə(r)] *n* fibra *f*

'fi·bre·glass *n* fibra *f* di vetro; **fi·bre 'op·tic** *adj* fibra *f* ottica; **fi·bre 'op·tics** tecnologia *f* delle fibre ottiche

fick·le ['fɪkl] *adj* incostante

fic·tion ['fɪkʃn] *n* (novels) narrativa *f*; (made-up story) storia *f*

fic·tion·al ['fɪkʃnl] *adj* immaginario

fic·ti·tious [fɪk'tɪʃəs] *adj* fittizio

fid·dle ['fɪdl] **1** *n* F (violin) violino *m*; *it's a ~* F (cheat) è una fregatura F **2** *v/i*: *~ with ...* giocherellare con ...;

~ around with ... trafficare con ... **3** *v/t* accounts, results truccare

fi·del·i·ty [fɪ'delətɪ] fedeltà *f*

fid·get ['fɪdʒɪt] *v/i* agitarsi

fid·get·y ['fɪdʒɪtɪ] *adj* in agitazione; *get ~* mettersi in agitazione

field [fiːld] campo *m*; (competitors in race) formazione *f*; *that's not my ~* non è il mio campo

field·er ['fiːldə(r)] *in cricket* esterno *m*

'field e·vents *npl* atletica *f* leggera (escluse le specialità su pista)

fierce [fɪəs] *adj* animal feroce; wind, storm violento

fierce·ly ['fɪəslɪ] *adv* ferocemente; *say sth ~* dire qc in tono aggressivo

fi·er·y ['faɪərɪ] *adj* personality, temper focoso

fif·teen [fɪf'tiːn] quindici

fif·teenth [fɪf'tiːnθ] *n & adj* quindicesimo, -a

fifth [fɪfθ] *n & adj* quinto, -a

fifth·ly ['fɪfθlɪ] *adv* al quinto posto

fif·ti·eth ['fɪftɪɪθ] *n & adj* cinquantesimo, -a

fif·ty ['fɪftɪ] cinquanta

fif·ty-'fif·ty *adv* metà e metà; *go ~ with s.o.* fare a metà con qu

fig [fɪg] fico *m*

fight [faɪt] **1** *n* lotta *f*; in war combattimento *m*; (argument) litigio *m*; in boxing incontro *m* **2** *v/t* (pret & pp **fought**) (brawl) azzuffare; in war combattere; disease, injustice combattere; in boxing battersi contro; (argue) litigare

♦ **fight for** *v/t* one's rights, a cause lottare per

fight·er ['faɪtə(r)] combattente *m/f*; aeroplane caccia *m inv*; (boxer) pugile *m*; *she's a ~* è combattiva

fight·ing ['faɪtɪŋ] *n* risse *fpl*; *he's always in trouble for ~* è sempre nei guai perché scatena risse

fig·u·ra·tive ['fɪgjərətɪv] *adj* use of word figurato; art figurativo

fig·ure ['fɪgə(r)] *n* (digit) cifra *f*; of person linea *f*; (form, shape) figura *f*

◆ **figure out** v/t (*understand*) capire; *calculation* calcolare

'**fig·ure skat·er** pattinatore m, -trice f artistico, -a

'**fig·ure skat·ing** pattinaggio m artistico

file[1] [faɪl] **1** n *for papers* raccoglitore m; *contents* dossier m inv, pratica f; COMPUT file m inv; **on ~** in archivio **2** v/t *documents* schedare

◆ **file away** v/t *documents* archiviare

file[2] [faɪl] n *for wood, fingernails* lima f

'**file man·ag·er** COMPUT file manager m inv

fi·li·al ['fɪlɪəl] *adj* filiale

fil·ing cab·i·net ['faɪlɪŋkæbɪnət] schedario m

fill [fɪl] **1** v/t riempire; *tooth* otturare **2** n: *eat one's ~* mangiare a sazietà

◆ **fill in** v/t *form* compilare; *hole* riempire; **fill s.o. in** mettere al corrente qu

◆ **fill in for** v/t sostituire temporaneamente

◆ **fill out 1** v/t *form* compilare **2** v/i (*get fatter*) arrotondarsi

◆ **fill up 1** v/t riempire **2** v/i of *stadium, theatre* riempirsi

fil·let ['fɪlɪt] n filetto m

fil·let '**steak** filetto m

fill·ing ['fɪlɪŋ] **1** n in *sandwich* ripieno m; in *tooth* otturazione f **2** *adj food* pesante

'**fill·ing sta·tion** stazione f di rifornimento

film [fɪlm] **1** n *for camera* pellicola f; *at cinema* film m inv **2** v/t *person, event* riprendere, filmare; *scene* girare

'**film-mak·er** regista m/f

'**film star** stella f del cinema

fil·ter ['fɪltə(r)] **1** n filtro m **2** v/t *coffee, liquid* filtrare

◆ **filter through** v/i of *news, reports* diffondersi

'**fil·ter pa·per** carta f filtrante

'**fil·ter tip** (*cigarette*) filtro m

filth [fɪlθ] n sporcizia f; (*obscenities*) sconcezze fpl

filth·y [fɪlθɪ] *adj* sporco; *language etc* volgare

fin [fɪn] of *fish* pinna f

fi·nal ['faɪnl] **1** *adj* finale **2** n SP finale f

fi·na·le [fɪ'nɑːlɪ] finale m

fi·nal·ist ['faɪnəlɪst] finalista m/f

fi·nal·ize ['faɪnəlaɪz] v/t *plans, design* mettere a punto

fi·nal·ly ['faɪnəlɪ] *adv* infine; (*at last*) finalmente

fi·nals ['faɪnəlz] *npl* EDU esami mpl finali

fi·nance ['faɪnæns] **1** n finanza f **2** v/t finanziare

fi·nan·ces ['faɪnænsɪz] *npl* finanze fpl

fi·nan·cial [faɪ'nænʃl] *adj* finanziario

fi·nan·cial·ly [faɪ'nænʃəlɪ] *adv* finanziariamente

fi·nan·cial '**year** esercizio m (finanziario)

fi·nan·cier [faɪ'nænsɪə(r)] n finanziatore m, -trice f

find [faɪnd] v/t (*pret & pp found*) trovare; *if you ~ it too hot / cold* se lo trovi troppo caldo / freddo; **~ a person innocent / guilty** LAW giudicare una persona innocente / colpevole

◆ **find out** v/t & v/i scoprire

find·ings ['faɪndɪŋz] *npl of report* conclusioni fpl

fine[1] [faɪn] *adj day, weather, city* bello; *wine, performance* buono; *distinction, line* sottile; *how's that? – that's ~* com'è? – va benissimo; *that's ~ by me* a me sta bene; *how are you? – ~* come stai? – bene

fine[2] [faɪn] **1** n *penalty* multa f **2** v/t multare

fine-'tooth comb: *go through sth with a ~* passare qc al setaccio

fine-'tune v/t *also fig* mettere a punto

fin·ger ['fɪŋgə(r)] **1** n dito m **2** v/t passare le dita su

'**fin·ger·nail** unghia f; '**fin·ger·print 1** n impronta f digitale **2** v/t prendere le impronte digitali di; '**fin·ger·tip** punta f del dito; *have sth at one's ~s knowledge* sapere qc a menadito

fin·i·cky ['fɪnɪkɪ] *adj person* pignolo; *design, pattern* complicato

fin·ish ['fɪnɪʃ] **1** v/t finire; **~ doing sth** finire di fare qc **2** v/i finire **3** n of product finitura f; finishing line traguardo m

♦ **finish off** v/t finire

♦ **finish up** v/t food finire; **he finished up liking London** Londra ha finito per piacergli

♦ **finish with** v/t boyfriend etc lasciare

fin·ish·ing line ['fɪnɪʃɪŋ] traguardo m

Fin·land ['fɪnlənd] Finlandia f

Finn [fɪn] finlandese m/f

Finn·ish ['fɪnɪʃ] **1** adj finlandese, finnico **2** n language finlandese m

fir [fɜ:(r)] abete m

fire ['faɪə(r)] **1** n fuoco m; (blaze) incendio m; (bonfire, campfire etc) falò m inv; **be on ~** essere in fiamme; **catch ~** prendere fuoco; **set sth on ~, set ~ to sth** dare fuoco a qc **2** v/i (shoot) sparare **3** v/t F (dismiss) licenziare

'fire a·larm allarme m antincendio; **'fire·arm** arma f da fuoco; **'fire bri·gade** vigili mpl del fuoco; **'fire·crack·er** petardo m; **'fire door** porta f taglia-fuoco; **'fire drill** esercitazione f antincendio; **'fire en·gine** autopompa f; **'fire es·cape** scala f antincendio; **fire ex·tin·guish·er** ['faɪərɪkstɪŋgwɪʃə(r)] estintore m; **'fire fight·er** pompiere m; **'fire·guard** parafuoco m inv; **'fire·man** pompiere m; **'fire·place** camino m; **'fire sta·tion** caserma f dei pompieri; **'fire truck** Am autopompa f; **'fire·wood** legna f da ardere; **'fire·works** npl fuochi mpl d'artificio

firm¹ [fɜ:m] adj grip, handshake energico; flesh, muscles sodo; voice, parents deciso; decision risoluto; date, offer definitivo; control rigido; foundations solido; believer convinto; **a ~ deal** un accordo definito

firm² [fɜ:m] n COM azienda f

first [fɜ:st] **1** adj primo; **who's ~ please?** chi è il primo, per favore? **2** n primo m, -a f **3** adv arrive, finish per primo; (beforehand) prima; **~ of**

all (for one reason) innanzitutto; **at ~** in un primo tempo, al principio

first 'aid pronto soccorso m; **first-'aid box, first-'aid kit** cassetta f del pronto soccorso; **'first-born** adj primogenito; **'first class 1** adj di prima classe **2** adv travel in prima classe; **first 'floor** primo piano m; Am piano m terra; **first'hand** adj diretto; **First 'La·dy** of US First Lady f inv

first·ly ['fɜːstlɪ] adv in primo luogo

first 'name nome m di battesimo; **first 'night** prima serata f; **first of'fend·er** delinquente m/f non pregiudicato, -a; **first-'rate** adj di prima qualità

fis·cal ['fɪskl] adj fiscale

fish [fɪʃ] **1** n (pl fish) pesce m; **drink like a ~** F bere come una spugna F; **feel like a ~ out of water** sentirsi come un pesce fuor d'acqua **2** v/i pescare

fish and 'chips npl pesce e patate fritte

'fish·bone lisca f

fish·er·man ['fɪʃəmən] pescatore m

fish 'fin·ger bastoncino m di pesce

fish·ing ['fɪʃɪŋ] pesca f

'fish·ing boat peschereccio m; **'fishing line** lenza f; **'fish·ing rod** canna f da pesca

fish·mon·ger ['fɪʃmʌŋgə(r)] pescivendolo m

fish·y ['fɪʃɪ] adj F (suspicious) sospetto

fist [fɪst] pugno m

fit¹ [fɪt] n MED attacco m; **a ~ of rage / jealousy** un accesso di rabbia / gelosia

fit² [fɪt] adj physically in forma; morally adatto; **keep ~** tenersi in forma

fit³ [fɪt] **1** v/t (pret & pp -ted) of clothes andare bene a; (attach) installare **2** v/i (pret & pp -ted) of clothes andare bene; of piece of furniture etc starci **3** n: **it is a good ~** of piece of furniture etc ci sta perfettamente; of clothes calza a pennello; **it's a tight ~** of piece of furniture etc

fit in 400

ci sta appena; *of clothes* va giusto giusto

♦ **fit in 1** *v/i of person in group* integrarsi; *it fits in with our plans* si concilia con i nostri programmi **2** *v/t*: **fit s.o. in** *into schedule* fissare un appuntamento a qu

fit·ful ['fɪtfʊl] *adj sleep* a tratti

fit·ness ['fɪtnɪs] *physical* forma *f*

'fit·ness cen·ter *Am*, **'fit·ness cen·tre** palestra *f*

fit·ted 'car·pet ['fɪtɪd] moquette *f inv*; **fit·ted 'kitch·en** cucina *f* componibile; **fit·ted 'sheet** lenzuolo *m* con gli angoli

fit·ter ['fɪtə(r)] *n* assemblatore *m*, -trice *f*

fit·ting ['fɪtɪŋ] *adj* appropriato

fit·tings ['fɪtɪŋz] *npl* equipaggiamento *msg*

five [faɪv] cinque

fiv·er ['faɪvə(r)] F banconota *f* da cinque sterline

fix [fɪks] **1** *n (solution)* soluzione *f*; **be in a ~** F essere nei casini F **2** *v/t (attach)* fissare; *(repair)* aggiustare; *(arrange: meeting etc)* fissare; *lunch* preparare; *dishonestly: match etc* manipolare; **~ sth onto sth** attaccare qc a qc; **I'll ~ you a drink** ti preparo da bere

♦ **fix up** *v/t meeting* fissare; *it's all fixed up* è tutto stabilito

fixed [fɪkst] *adj in one position* fisso; *timescale, exchange rate* stabilito

fix·tures ['fɪkstʃəz] *npl in room* installazioni *fpl* fisse; SP incontro *m*

♦ **fiz·zle out** ['fɪzl] *v/i* F sfumare F

fiz·zy ['fɪzɪ] *adj drink* gassato

flab [flæb] *on body* ciccia *f*

flab·ber·gast ['flæbəɡɑːst] *v/t*: **be ~ed** cadere dalle nuvole

flab·by ['flæbɪ] *adj muscles, stomach* flaccido

flag¹ [flæɡ] *n* bandiera *f*

flag² [flæɡ] *v/i (pret & pp -ged) (tire)* soccombere

'flag·pole asta *f*

fla·grant ['fleɪɡrənt] *adj* flagrante

'flag·ship *fig* cavallo *m* di battaglia

'flag·staff asta *f*

'flag·stone lastra *f* di pietra

flair [fleə(r)] *n (talent)* talento *m*; *(style)* stile *m*

flake [fleɪk] *n of snow* fiocco *m*; *of paint, plaster* scaglia *f*

♦ **flake off** *v/i* squamarsi

flak·y ['fleɪkɪ] *adj* squamato

flak·y 'pas·try pasta *f* sfoglia

flam·boy·ant [flæm'bɔɪənt] *adj personality* esuberante

flam·boy·ant·ly [flæm'bɔɪəntlɪ] *adv dressed* in modo vistoso

flame [fleɪm] *n* fiamma *f*; **go up in ~s** incendiarsi

flam·ma·ble ['flæməbl] *adj* infiammabile

flan [flæn] sformato *m*

flank [flæŋk] **1** *n* fianco *m* **2** *v/t*: **be ~ed by** essere affiancato da

flan·nel ['flænl] *n for washing* guanto *m* di spugna

flap [flæp] **1** *n of envelope, pocket* falda *f*; *of table* ribalta *f*; **be in a ~** F essere in fibrillazione F **2** *v/t (pret & pp -ped) wings* sbattere **3** *v/i (pret & pp -ped) of flag etc* sventolare; F *(panic)* andare in fibrillazione F

flare [fleə(r)] **1** *n (distress signal)* razzo *m*; *in dress* svasatura *f*; **~s trousers** pantaloni *mpl* a zampa di elefante **2** *v/t nostrils* allargare

♦ **flare up** *v/i of violence, illness, temper* esplodere; *of fire* divampare

flash [flæʃ] **1** *n of light* lampo *m*; PHOT flash *m inv*; **in a ~** F in un istante; **have a ~ of inspiration** avere un lampo di genio; **~ of lightning** lampo *m* **2** *v/i of light* lampeggiare **3** *v/t*: **~ one's headlights** lampeggiare

'flash·back *in film* flashback *m inv*

flash·er ['flæʃə(r)] MOT freccia *f*; F *person* esibizionista *m*

'flash·light *esp Am* pila *f*; PHOT flash *m inv*

flash·y ['flæʃɪ] *adj pej* appariscente

flask [flɑːsk] *(vacuum ~)* termos *m inv*

flat¹ [flæt] **1** *adj surface, land, tone* piatto; *beer* sgassato; *battery, tyre* a terra; *shoes* basso; *A/B* – MUS la/si bemolle; **and that's ~** F punto e

basta F **2** adv MUS sotto tonalità; ~
out work, run, drive a tutto gas **3** n
gomma f a terra

flat² [flæt] n Br (apartment) appartamento m

flat-chest-ed [flæˈtʃestɪd] adj piatto

flat-ly [ˈflætlɪ] adv refuse, deny risoluta-
mente

'flat-mate persona f con cui si divide
la casa

'flat rate tariffa f forfettaria

flat-ten [ˈflætn] v/t land, road livellare; by bombing, demolition radere al
suolo

flat-ter [ˈflætə(r)] v/t adulare

flat-ter-er [ˈflætərə(r)] adulatore m,
-trice f

flat-ter-ing [ˈflætərɪŋ] adj
lusinghiero; **Jane's dress is very ~**
il vestito di Jane le dona molto

flat-ter-y [ˈflætərɪ] adulazione f

flat-u-lence [ˈflætjʊləns] flatulenza f

flat-ware [ˈflætweər] Am stoviglie fpl

flau-tist [ˈflɔːtɪst] flautista m/f

fla-vor etc Am → **flavour** etc

fla-vour [ˈfleɪvə(r)] **1** n gusto m **2** v/t
food insaporire

fla-vour-ing [ˈfleɪvərɪŋ] n aroma m

flaw [flɔː] n difetto m

flaw-less [ˈflɔːlɪs] adj perfetto

flea [fliː] n pulce f

fleck [flek] puntino m

fled [fled] pret & pp → **flee**

flee [fliː] v/i (pret & pp **fled**) scappare

fleece [fliːs] v/t F fregare F

fleet [fliːt] n NAUT flotta f; of taxis,
trucks parco m macchine

fleet-ing [ˈfliːtɪŋ] adj visit etc di sfuggita; **catch a ~ glimpse of** vedere di
sfuggita

flesh [fleʃ] carne f; of fruit polpa f;
meet / see a person in the ~ incontrare / vedere una persona in carne
e ossa

flex [fleks] **1** v/t muscles flettere **2** n
ELEC cavo m

flex-i-bil-i-ty [fleksəˈbɪlətɪ] flessibili-
tà f

flex-i-ble [ˈfleksəbl] adj flessibile; **I'm
quite ~ about arrangements, timing**

sono abbastanza flessibile

flex-(i)-time [ˈfleks(ɪ)taɪm] orario m
flessibile

flew [fluː] pret → **fly**

flick [flɪk] v/t tail agitare; **he ~ed a fly
off his hand** ha cacciato via una
mosca dalla mano; **she ~ed her hair
out of her eyes** si è tolta i capelli
dagli occhi con un gesto
♦ **flick through** v/t book, magazine
sfogliare

flick-er [ˈflɪkə(r)] v/i of light tremolare

'flick-knife coltello m a scatto

fli-er [ˈflaɪə(r)] (circular) volantino m

flies [flaɪz] npl on trousers patta f

flight [flaɪt] volo m; (fleeing) fuga f; ~
(of stairs) rampa f (di scale)

'flight at-tend-ant assistente m/f di
volo; **'flight crew** equipaggio m di
volo; **'flight deck** in aeroplane cabina f di pilotaggio; of aircraft carrier
ponte m di decollo; **'flight num-ber**
numero m di volo; **'flight path** rotta
f (di volo); **'flight re-cord-er** registratore m di volo; **'flight time**
departure orario m di volo; duration
durata f di volo

flight-y [ˈflaɪtɪ] adj volubile

flim-sy [ˈflɪmzɪ] adj structure, furniture leggero; dress, material sottile;
excuse debole

flinch [flɪntʃ] v/i sobbalzare

fling [flɪŋ] **1** v/t (pret & pp **flung**) scagliare; ~ **o.s. into a chair** buttarsi su
una sedia **2** n F (affair) avventura f
♦ **flip through** [flɪp] v/t (pret & pp
-ped) book, magazine sfogliare

flip-per [ˈflɪpə(r)] for swimming pinna f

flirt [flɜːt] **1** v/i flirtare **2** n flirt m inv

flir-ta-tious [flɜːˈteɪʃəs] adj civettuolo

float [fləʊt] v/i galleggiare; FIN fluttuare

float-ing vot-er [ˈfləʊtɪŋ] elettore che
cambia spesso opinione

flock [flɒk] **1** n of sheep gregge m
2 v/i accorrere in massa

flog [flɒg] v/t (pret & pp **-ged**)
(whip) fustigare; F (sell) vendere

F

flood [flʌd] **1** n inondazione f **2** v/t of river inondare; **~ its banks** of river straripare

♦ **flood in** v/i affluire

flood·ing ['flʌdɪŋ] n inondazione f

'**flood·light** n riflettore m

'**flood·lit** ['flʌdlɪt] adj match illuminato da riflettori

flood wa·ters ['flʌdwɔːtəz] npl acque fpl di inondazione

floor [flɔː(r)] n pavimento m; (storey) piano m

'**floor·board** asse f del pavimento; '**floor cloth** straccio m per lavare per terra; '**floor·lamp** Am lampada f a stelo

flop [flɒp] **1** v/i (pret & pp **-ped**) crollare; F (fail) fare fiasco **2** n F (failure) fiasco m

flop·py ['flɒpɪ] adj not stiff floscio; (weak) moscio

flop·py ('disk) floppy m inv, floppy disk m inv

Flor·ence ['flɒrəns] Firenze

Flor·en·tine ['flɒrəntaɪn] **1** adj fiorentino **2** n fiorentino m, -a f

flor·ist ['flɒrɪst] fiorista m/f

floss [flɒs] **1** n for teeth filo m interdentale **2** v/t: **~ one's teeth** passare il filo interdentale

flour ['flaʊə(r)] farina f

flour·ish ['flʌrɪʃ] v/i fiorire; of business, civilization prosperare

flour·ish·ing ['flʌrɪʃɪŋ] adj business, trade prospero

flow [fləʊ] **1** v/i of river, traffic, current scorrere; of work procedere **2** n of river, ideas flusso m

'**flow-chart** diagramma m (di flusso)

flow·er ['flaʊə(r)] **1** n fiore m **2** v/i fiorire

'**flow·er·bed** aiuola f; '**flow·er·pot** vaso m per fiori; '**flow·er show** esposizione f floreale

flow·er·y ['flaʊərɪ] adj pattern a fiori; style of writing fiorito

flown [fləʊn] pp → fly

flu [fluː] influenza f

fluc·tu·ate ['flʌktjʊeɪt] v/i oscillare

fluc·tu·a·tion [flʌktjʊ'eɪʃn] oscillazione f

flu·en·cy ['fluːənsɪ] in a language scioltezza f

flu·ent ['fluːənt] adj fluente; **he speaks ~ Spanish** parla correntemente lo spagnolo

flu·ent·ly ['fluːəntlɪ] adv speak, write correntemente

fluff [flʌf] material lanugine f; **a bit of ~** un po' di lanugine

fluff·y ['flʌfɪ] adj material, hair lanuginoso; clouds soffice; **~ toy** peluche m inv

fluid ['fluːɪd] n fluido m

flung [flʌŋ] pret & pp → **fling**

flunk [flʌŋk] v/t Am F essere bocciato a

flu·o·res·cent [fluə'resnt] adj light fluorescente

flur·ry ['flʌrɪ] of snow raffica f

flush [flʌʃ] **1** v/t toilet tirare l'acqua di; **~ sth down the toilet** buttare qc giù dal water **2** v/i (go red in the face) diventare rosso; **the toilet won't ~** lo sciacquone del bagno non funziona **3** adj (level) a filo; **be ~ with ...** essere a filo con ...

♦ **flush away** v/t down toilet buttare giù dal water

♦ **flush out** v/t rebels etc scovare

flus·ter ['flʌstə(r)] v/t mettere in agitazione; **get ~ed** mettersi in agitazione

flute [fluːt] MUS flauto m traverso; glass flute m inv

flut·ter ['flʌtə(r)] **1** v/i of bird sbattere le ali; of wings sbattere; of flag sventolare; of heart battere forte **2** n F (bet) piccola scommessa f

fly[1] [flaɪ] n insect mosca f

fly[2] [flaɪ] on trousers patta f

fly[3] [flaɪ] (pret **flew**, pp **flown**) **1** v/i volare; of flag sventolare; (rush) precipitarsi; **~ into a rage** perdere le staffe **2** v/t aeroplane pilotare; airline volare con; (transport by air) spedire per via aerea

♦ **fly away** v/i of bird, plane volare via

♦ **fly back** v/i (travel back) ritornare (in aereo)

♦ **fly in 1** v/i of plane, passengers arrivare **2** v/t supplies etc mandare per

via aerea
♦ **fly off** *v/i of hat etc* volare via
♦ **fly out** *v/i* partire in aereo
♦ **fly past** *v/i in formation* volare in formazione; *of time* volare
fly·ing ['flaɪɪŋ] *n* volare *m*
fly·ing 'sau·cer disco *m* volante
'fly·o·ver MOT cavalcavia *m inv*
foam [fəʊm] *n on liquid* schiuma *f*
foam 'rub·ber gommapiuma® *f*
FOB [efəʊ'biː] *abbr* (= *free on board*) FOB
fo·cus ['fəʊkəs] **1** *n of attention* centro *m*; PHOT fuoco *m*; **be in ~** / **be out of ~** PHOT essere a fuoco / non essere a fuoco **2** *v/t:* **~ one's attention on** focalizzare l'attenzione su **3** *v/i* mettere a fuoco
♦ **focus on** *v/t problem, issue* focalizzare l'attenzione su; PHOT mettere a fuoco
fod·der ['fɒdə(r)] foraggio *m*
foe·tal ['fiːtl] *adj* → **fetal**
foe·tus ['fiːtəs] → **fetus**
fog [fɒg] nebbia *f*
♦ **fog up** *v/i* (*pret & pp* **-ged**) appannarsi
'fog·bound *adj* bloccato dalla nebbia
fog·gy ['fɒgɪ] *adj* nebbioso; *I haven't the foggiest (idea)* non ne ho la più pallida idea
foi·ble ['fɔɪbl] fisima *f*
foil¹ [fɔɪl] *n* carta *f* stagnola
foil² [fɔɪl] *v/t (thwart)* sventare
fold¹ [fəʊld] **1** *v/t paper etc* piegare; **~ one's arms** incrociare le braccia **2** *v/i of business* chiudere i battenti **3** *n in cloth etc* piega *f*
♦ **fold up 1** *v/t chairs etc* chiudere; *clothes* piegare **2** *v/i of chair, table* chiudere
fold² [fəʊld] *n for sheep etc* ovile *m*
fold·er ['fəʊldə(r)] *for documents* cartellina *f*; COMPUT directory *f inv*
fold·ing ['fəʊldɪŋ] *adj* pieghevole; **~ chair** sedia *f* pieghevole
fo·li·age ['fəʊlɪɪdʒ] fogliame *m*
folk [fəʊk] (*people*) gente *f*; *my ~* (*family*) i miei parenti; *come in, ~s* F entrate, gente F

'folk dance danza *f* popolare; **'folk mu·sic** musica *f* folk; **'folk sing·er** cantante *m/f* folk; **'folk song** canzone *f* popolare
fol·low ['fɒləʊ] **1** *v/t* (*also understand*) seguire **2** *v/i* seguire; *logically* quadrare; *it ~s from this that ...* ne consegue che ...; *as ~s* quanto segue
♦ **follow up** *v/t letter, inquiry* dare seguito a
fol·low·er ['fɒləʊə(r)] *of politician etc* seguace *m/f*; *of football team* tifoso *m*, -a *f*; *are you a ~ of ...?* *of TV programme* segui ...?
fol·low·ing ['fɒləʊɪŋ] **1** *adj* seguente **2** *n people* seguito *m*; *the ~* quanto segue
'fol·low-up meet·ing riunione *f* ulteriore
'fol·low-up vis·it *to doctor etc* visita *f* successiva
fol·ly ['fɒlɪ] (*madness*) follia *f*
fond [fɒnd] *adj* (*loving*) affezionato; *memory* caro; *he is ~ of travel* gli piace viaggiare
fon·dle ['fɒndl] *v/t* accarezzare
fond·ness ['fɒndnɪs] *for person* affetto *m*; *for wine, food* gusto *m*
font [fɒnt] *for printing* carattere *m*; *in church* fonte *f* battesimale
food [fuːd] cibo *m*; *I like Italian ~* mi piace la cucina italiana; *there's no ~ in the house* non c'è niente da mangiare in casa
'food chain catena *f* alimentare
food·ie ['fuːdɪ] F buongustaio *m*, -a *f*
'food mix·er mixer *m inv*
food poi·son·ing ['fuːdpɔɪznɪŋ] intossicazione *f* alimentare
fool [fuːl] **1** *n* pazzo *m*, -a *f*; *make a ~ of o.s.* rendersi ridicolo **2** *v/t* ingannare; *~ s.o. into believing that ...* far credere a qu che ...
♦ **fool about, fool around** *v/i* fare lo sciocco; *sexually* avere l'amante
♦ **fool around with** *v/t knife, drill etc* trastullarsi con; *s.o.'s wife* avere una relazione con
'fool·har·dy *adj* temerario
fool·ish ['fuːlɪʃ] *adj* sciocco

fool·ish·ly ['fuːlɪʃlɪ] *adv* scioccamente

'**fool·proof** *adj* a prova di idiota

foot [fut] (*pl* **feet** [fiːt]) *also measurement* piede *m*; **on** ~ a piedi; *I've been on my feet all day* sono stato in piedi tutto il giorno; *be back on one's feet* essere di nuovo in piedi; *at the* ~ *of the page* a piè di pagina; *at the* ~ *of the hill* ai piedi della collina; *put one's* ~ *in it* F fare una gaffe

foot·age ['futɪdʒ] pellicola *f* cinematografica

'**foot·ball** (*soccer*) calcio *m*; *American style* football *m* americano; (*ball*) pallone *m* da calcio; *for American football* pallone *m* da football americano

foot·bal·ler ['futbɔːlə(r)] calciatore *m*, -trice *f*

'**foot·ball hoo·li·gan** teppista *m* del calcio; '**foot·ball pitch** campo *m* da calcio; '**foot·ball play·er** *soccer* calciatore *m*, -trice *f*; *American style* giocatore *m* di football americano; '**foot·bridge** passerella *f*

foot·er ['futə(r)] COMPUT piè *m* di pagina

foot·hills ['futhɪlz] *npl* colline *fpl* pedemontane

'**foot·hold** *in climbing* punto *m* d'appoggio; *gain a* ~ *fig* conquistarsi uno spazio

foot·ing ['futɪŋ] (*basis*) presupposti *mpl*; *lose one's* ~ perdere il punto d'appoggio; *be on the same* ~ / *a different* ~ essere sullo stesso piano / su un piano diverso; *be on a friendly* ~ *with ...* avere rapporti amichevoli con ...

foot·lights ['futlaɪts] *npl* luci *fpl* della ribalta; '**foot·mark** impronta *f* di piede; '**foot·note** nota *f* a piè di pagina; '**foot·path** sentiero *m*; '**foot·print** impronta *f* di piede; '**foot·step** passo *m*; *follow in s.o.'s* ~*s* seguire i passi di qu; '**foot·stool** sgabello *m* per i piedi; '**foot·wear** calzatura *f*

for [fə(r)], [fɔː(r)] *prep* ◊ *purpose,*

destination etc per; *a train* ~ *...* un treno per ...; *clothes* ~ *children* abbigliamento *m* per bambini; *it's too big / small* ~ *you* è troppo grande / piccolo per te; *here's a letter* ~ *you* c'è una lettera per te; *this is* ~ *you* questo è per te; *what is there* ~ *lunch?* cosa c'è per pranzo?; *the steak is* ~ *me* la bistecca è per me; *what is this* ~? a cosa serve?; *what* ~? a che scopo?, perché?; ◊ *time* per; ~ *three days / two hours* per tre giorni / due ore; *I have been waiting* ~ *an hour* ho aspettato (per) un'ora; *please get it done* ~ *Monday* per favore, fallo per lunedì; ◊ *distance* per; *I walked* ~ *a mile* ho camminato per un miglio; *it stretches* ~ *100 miles* si estende per 100 miglia; ◊ (*in favour of*) per; *campaign* ~ fare una campagna per; *I am* ~ *the idea* sono a favore dell'idea; ◊ (*instead of, on behalf of*) per; *let me do that* ~ *you* lascia che te lo faccia io, lascia che faccia questo per te; *we are agents* ~ *...* siamo rappresentanti di ...; ◊ (*in exchange for*) per; *I bought it* ~ *£25* l'ho comprato per 25 sterline; *how much did you sell it* ~? a quanto l'hai venduto?

for·bade [fə'bæd] *pret* → **forbid**

for·bid [fə'bɪd] *v/t* (*pret* **forbade**, *pp* **forbidden**) vietare, proibire; ~ *s.o. to sth* vietare *o* proibire a qu di fare qc

for·bid·den [fə'bɪdn] **1** *adj* vietato, proibito; *smok•ing* ~ vietato fumare; *park•ing* ~ divieto di sosta **2** *pp* → **forbid**

for·bid·ding [fə'bɪdɪŋ] *adj* ostile

force [fɔːs] **1** *n* (*violence*) forza *f*; *come into* ~ *of law etc* entrare in vigore; *the* ~*s* MIL le forze armate **2** *v/t door, lock* forzare; ~ *s.o. to do sth* forzare *o* costringere qu a fare qc; ~ *sth open* aprire qc con la forza

♦ **force back** *v/t tears etc* trattenere

forced [fɔːst] *adj laugh, smile* forzato

forced 'land·ing atterraggio *m* d'emergenza

force·ful ['fɔːsfʊl] *adj argument, speaker* convincente; *character* energico

force·ful·ly ['fɔːsflɪ] *adv* in modo energico

for·ceps ['fɔːseps] *npl* MED forcipe *f*

for·ci·ble ['fɔːsəbl] *adj entry* forzato; *argument* convincente

for·ci·bly ['fɔːsəblɪ] *adv restrain* con la forza

ford [fɔːd] *n* guado *m*

fore [fɔː(r)] *n*: **come to the ~** salire alla ribalta

'**fore·arm** avambraccio *m*; **fore·bears** ['fɔːbeəz] *npl* antenati *mpl*; **fore·bod·ing** [fəˈbəʊdɪŋ] presentimento *m*; '**fore·cast 1** *n* previsione *f* **2** *v/t* (*pret & pp* **forecast**) prevedere; '**fore·court** *of garage* area *f* di rifornimento; **fore·fa·thers** ['fɔːfɑːðəz] *npl* antenati *mpl*; '**fore·fin·ger** indice *m*; '**fore·front: be in the ~ of** essere all'avanguardia in; '**fore·gone** *adj*: **that's a ~ conclusion** è una conclusione scontata; '**fore·ground** primo piano *m*; '**fore·hand** *in tennis* diritto *m*; '**fore·head** fronte *f*

for·eign ['fɒrən] *adj* straniero; *trade, policy* estero

for·eign af·fairs *npl* affari *mpl* esteri; **for·eign 'aid** aiuti *mpl* ad altri paesi; **for·eign 'bod·y** corpo *m* estraneo; **for·eign 'cur·ren·cy** valuta *f* estera

for·eign·er ['fɒrənə(r)] straniero *m*, -a *f*

for·eign ex'change cambio *m* valutario; **for·eign 'lan·guage** lingua *f* straniera; '**For·eign Of·fice** *in UK* Ministero *m* degli esteri; **for·eign 'pol·i·cy** politica *f* estera; **For·eign 'Sec·re·ta·ry** *in UK* ministro *m* degli esteri

'**fore·man** caposquadra *m*

'**fore·most 1** *adv* (*uppermost*) soprattutto **2** *adj* (*leading*) principale

fo·ren·sic 'med·i·cine [fəˈrenzɪk] medicina *f* legale

fo·ren·sic 'scien·tist medico *m* legale

'**fore·run·ner** precursore *m*; **fore·'saw** *pret* → **foresee**; **fore·'see** *v/t* (*pret* **foresaw**, *pp* **foreseen**) prevedere; **fore·'see·a·ble** [fəˈsiːəbl] *adj* prevedibile; *in the ~ future* per quanto si possa prevedere in futuro; **fore·'seen** *pp* → **foresee**; '**fore·sight** lungimiranza *f*

for·est ['fɒrɪst] foresta *f*

for·est·er ['fɒrɪstə(r)] guardaboschi *m/f*

for·est·ry ['fɒrɪstrɪ] scienze *fpl* forestali

'**fore·taste** anteprima *m*, assaggio *m*

fore·'tell *v/t* (*pret & pp* **foretold**) predire

fore·'told *pret & pp* → **foretell**

for·ev·er [fəˈrevə(r)] *adv* per sempre; *it is ~ raining here* piova continuamente qui

for·gave [fəˈgeɪv] *pret* → **forgive**

fore·word ['fɔːwɜːd] prefazione *f*

for·feit ['fɔːfɪt] *v/t right, privilege etc* perdere

forge [fɔːdʒ] *v/t* (*counterfeit*) contraffare; *signature* falsificare

♦ **forge ahead** *v/i* prendere il sopravvento

forg·er ['fɔːdʒə(r)] falsario *m*, -a *f*

forg·er·y ['fɔːdʒərɪ] (*banknote*) falsificazione *f*; (*document*) falso *m*

for·get [fəˈget] *v/t* (*pret* **forgot**, *pp* **forgotten**) dimenticare; *~ it!* lasciolo perdere; *he's a waste of time* lasciolo perdere, ti fa solo perdere tempo

for·get·ful [fəˈgetfʊl] *adj* smemorato

for·get-me-not non-ti-scordar-di-me *m inv*

for·give [fəˈgɪv] *v/t & v/i* (*pret* **forgave**, *pp* **forgiven**) perdonare

for·giv·en [fəˈgɪvn] *pp* → **forgive**

for·give·ness [fəˈgɪvnɪs] perdono *m*

for·got [fəˈgɒt] *pret* → **forget**

for·got·ten [fəˈgɒtn] *pp* → **forget**

fork [fɔːk] *n for eating* forchetta *f*; *for gardening* forca *f*; *in road* biforcazione *f*

♦ **fork out** *v/t & v/i* F (*pay*) sborsare F

fork·lift 'truck muletto *m*

form [fɔːm] **1** *n* (*shape*) forma *f*; (*document*) modulo *m*; *in school* classe f; **be on / off ~** essere in / fuori forma; **in the ~ of** sotto forma di 2 v/t in clay etc modellare; friendship creare; opinion formarsi; past tense etc formare; (constitute) costituire 3 v/i (take shape, develop) formarsi

form·al ['fɔ:ml] adj formale

for·mal·i·ty [fɔ'mælətɪ] formalità f inv; **it's just a ~** è solo una formalità; **the formalities** le formalità

for·mal·ly ['fɔ:məlɪ] adv formalmente

for·mat ['fɔ:mæt] **1** v/t (pret & pp **-ted**) diskette formattare; document impaginare **2** n (size: of magazine etc) formato m; (makeup: of programme) formula f

for·ma·tion [fɔ'meɪʃn] formazione f

for·ma·tive ['fɔ:mətɪv] adj formativo; **in his ~ years** nei suoi anni formativi

for·mer ['fɔ:mə(r)] adj wife, president ex inv; statement, arrangement precedente; **the ~** quest'ultimo

for·mer·ly ['fɔ:məlɪ] adv precedentemente

for·mi·da·ble ['fɔ:mɪdəbl] adj imponente

for·mu·la ['fɔ:mjulə] formula f

for·mu·late ['fɔ:mjuleɪt] v/t (express) formulare

for·ni·cate ['fɔ:nɪkeɪt] v/i fml fornicare

for·ni·ca·tion [fɔ:nɪ'keɪʃn] fml fornicazione f

fort [fɔ:t] MIL forte m

forth [fɔ:θ] adv: **back and ~** avanti e indietro; **and so ~** eccetera; **from that day ~** da quel giorno in poi

forth·com·ing ['fɔ:θkʌmɪŋ] adj (future) prossimo; personality comunicativo

'forth·right adj schietto

for·ti·eth ['fɔ:tɪɪθ] n & adj quarantesimo, -a

fort·night ['fɔ:tnaɪt] due settimane

for·tress ['fɔ:trɪs] MIL fortezza f

for·tu·nate ['fɔ:tʃʊnət] adj fortunato

for·tu·nate·ly ['fɔ:tʃʊnətlɪ] adv fortunatamente

for·tune ['fɔ:tʃu:n] sorte f; (lot of money) fortuna f; **tell s.o.'s ~** predire il futuro a qu

'for·tune-tell·er chiromante m/f

for·ty ['fɔ:tɪ] quaranta; **have ~ winks** F fare un pisolino F

Fo·rum ['fɔ:rəm] Roman foro m

fo·rum ['fɔ:rəm] fig foro m

for·ward ['fɔ:wəd] **1** adv avanti **2** adj pej: person diretto **3** n SP attaccante m **4** v/t letter inoltrare

'for·ward·ing ad·dress ['fɔ:wədɪŋ] recapito m

'for·ward·ing a·gent COM spedizioniere m

'for·ward-look·ing adj progressista

fos·sil ['fɒsəl] fossile m

fos·sil·ized ['fɒsəlaɪzd] adj fossilizzato

fos·ter ['fɒstə(r)] v/t child avere in affidamento; attitude, belief incoraggiare

'fos·ter child figlio m, -a f in affidamento

'fos·ter home famiglia f di accoglienza

'fos·ter par·ents npl genitori mpl con affidamento

fought [fɔ:t] pret & pp → **fight**

foul [faul] **1** n SP fallo m **2** adj smell, taste pessimo; weather orribile **3** v/t SP fare un fallo contro

found[1] [faund] v/t school etc fondare

found[2] [faund] pret & pp → **find**

foun·da·tion [faun'deɪʃn] of theory etc fondamenta fpl; (organization) fondazione f; make-up fondotinta m

foun·da·tions [faun'deɪʃnz] npl of building fondamenta fpl

found·er ['faundə(r)] n fondatore m, -trice f

found·ing ['faundɪŋ] n fondazione f

foun·dry ['faundrɪ] fonderia f

foun·tain ['fauntɪn] fontana f

'foun·tain pen penna f stilografica

four [fɔ:(r)] **1** adj quattro **2** n: **on all ~s** a quattro zampe

four-let·ter 'word parolaccia f; **four-post·er** ('bed) letto m a baldacchino; 'four-star adj hotel etc a quattro stelle; **four-star** ('pet·rol) super f

four-teen [fɔːˈtiːn] quattordici

four-teenth [fɔːˈtiːnθ] n & adj quattordicesimo, -a

fourth [fɔːθ] n & adj quarto, -a

four-wheel '**drive** MOT quattro per quattro m inv

fowl [faʊl] pollame m

fox [fɒks] **1** n volpe f **2** v/t (puzzle) mettere in difficoltà

foy·er ['fɔɪeɪ] atrio m

frac·tion ['frækʃn] frazione f

frac·tion·al·ly ['frækʃnəlɪ] adv lievemente

frac·ture ['fræktʃə(r)] **1** n frattura f **2** v/t fratturare

frag·ile ['frædʒaɪl] adj fragile

frag·ment ['frægmənt] n frammento m

frag·men·tar·y [fræg'mentərɪ] adj frammentario

fra·grance ['freɪgrəns] fragranza f

fra·grant ['freɪgrənt] adj profumato

frail [freɪl] adj gracile

frame [freɪm] **1** n of picture, window cornice f; of glasses montatura f; of bicycle telaio m; ~ of mind stato m d'animo **2** v/t picture incorniciare; F person incastrare F

'**frame-up** F montatura f

'**frame·work** struttura f

France [frɑːns] Francia f

fran·chise ['fræntʃaɪz] n for business concessione f

frank [fræŋk] adj franco

frank·furt·er ['fræŋkfɜːtə(r)] wurstel m inv

frank·ly ['fræŋklɪ] adv francamente

frank·ness ['fræŋknɪs] franchezza f

fran·tic ['fræntɪk] adj search, attempt frenetico; (worried) agitatissimo

fran·ti·cal·ly ['fræntɪklɪ] adv freneticamente

fra·ter·nal [frə'tɜːnl] adj fraterno

fraud [frɔːd] frode f; person impostore m, -trice f

fraud·u·lent ['frɔːdjʊlənt] adj fraudolento

fraud·u·lent·ly ['frɔːdjʊləntlɪ] adv in modo fraudolento

frayed [freɪd] adj cuffs liso

---

freak [friːk] **1** n unusual event fenomeno m anomalo; two-headed person, animal etc scherzo m di natura; F strange person tipo m, -a f strambo, -a; **movie / jazz ~** F (fanatic) fanatico m, -a f del cinema / del jazz **2** adj wind, storm etc violento

freck·le ['frekl] lentiggine f

free [friː] **1** adj (at liberty, not occupied) libero; (no cost) gratuito; **are you ~ this afternoon?** sei libero oggi pomeriggio?; **~ and easy** spensierato; **for ~** travel, get sth gratis **2** v/t prisoners liberare

free·bie ['friːbɪ] F omaggio m

free·dom ['friːdəm] libertà f

free·dom of '**speech** libertà f di parola

free·dom of the '**press** libertà f di stampa

free 'en·ter·prise liberalismo m economico; **free 'kick** in soccer calcio m di punizione; **free·lance** ['friːlɑːns] **1** adj free lance inv **2** adv work free lance inv; **free·lanc·er** ['friːlɑːnsə(r)] free lance m/f inv

free·ly ['friːlɪ] adv admit apertamente

free mar·ket e'con·o·my economia f del libero mercato; **free-range** '**chick·en** pollo m ruspante; **free-range 'eggs** npl uova fpl di galline ruspanti; **free 'sam·ple** campione m gratuito; **free 'speech** libertà f di espressione; '**free·way** Am autostrada f; **free'wheel** v/i on bicycle andare a ruota libera

freeze [friːz] (pret froze, pp frozen) **1** v/t food, river gelare; wages, account congelare; video bloccare **2** v/i of water gelare

♦ **freeze over** v/i of river gelare

'**freeze-dried** adj liofilizzato

freez·er ['friːzə(r)] freezer m inv, congelatore m

freez·ing ['friːzɪŋ] **1** adj gelato; **it's ~ out here** si gela qui fuori; **it's ~** (cold) of weather si gela; of water è gelata; **I'm ~** (cold) sono congelato **2** n: **10 below ~** 10 gradi sotto zero '**freez·ing com·part·ment** freezer *m inv*

'**freez·ing point** punto *m* di congelamento

freight [freɪt] *n* carico *m*; *costs* trasporto *m*

freight·er ['freɪtə(r)] *ship* nave *f* da carico; *aeroplane* aereo *f* da carico

French [frenʃ] **1** *adj* francese **2** *n* (*language*) francese *m*; **the ~** i francesi

French 'bread baguette *fpl*; '**French fries** *npl* patate *fpl* fritte; '**French·man** francese *m*; **French 'stick** baguette *f inv*; **French 'win·dows** *npl* vetrata *f*; '**French·wom·an** francese *f*

fren·zied ['frenzɪd] *adj attack, activity* frenetico; *mob* impazzito

fren·zy ['frenzɪ] frenesia *f*

fre·quen·cy ['fri:kwənsɪ] frequenza *f*

fre·quent¹ ['fri:kwənt] *adj* frequente

fre·quent² [frɪ'kwent] *v/t bar etc* frequentare

fre·quent·ly ['fri:kwentlɪ] *adv* frequentemente

fres·co ['freskəʊ] affresco *m*

fresh [freʃ] *adj fruit, meat etc*, (*cold*) fresco; (*new: start*) nuovo

fresh 'air aria *f* fresca

fresh·en ['freʃn] *v/i of wind* rinfrescare

♦ **freshen up 1** *v/i* rinfrescarsi **2** *v/t room, paintwork* rinfrescare

'**fresh·er** ['freʃə(r)] matricola *f*

fresh·ly ['freʃlɪ] *adv* appena

fresh·ness ['freʃnɪs] *of fruit, meat, climate* freschezza *f*; *of style, approach* novità *f*

fresh 'or·ange spremuta *f* d'arancia

'**fresh·wa·ter** *adj* d'acqua dolce

fret [fret] *v/i* (*pret & pp -ted*) agitarsi

Freud·i·an ['frɔɪdɪən] *adj* freudiano

fric·tion ['frɪkʃn] PHYS frizione *f*; *between people* attrito *m*

Fri·day ['fraɪdeɪ] venerdì *m inv*

fridge [frɪdʒ] frigo *m*

fried 'egg [fraɪd] uovo *m* fritto

fried po'ta·toes *npl* patate *fpl* saltate

friend [frend] amico *m*, -a *f*; **make ~s** fare amicizia; **make ~s with s.o.** fare amicizia con qu

friend·li·ness ['frendlɪnɪs] amichevolezza *f*

friend·ly ['frendlɪ] **1** *adj* amichevole; (*easy to use*) facile da usare; **be ~ with s.o.** (*be friends*) essere in rapporti d'amicizia con qu; **they're very ~** *with each other* sono molto in confidenza; **he started getting too ~** ha cominciato a prendersi troppa confidenza **2** SP amichevole *f*

'**friend·ship** ['frendʃɪp] amicizia *f*

fries [fraɪz] *npl* patate *fpl* fritte

fright [fraɪt] paura *f*; **give s.o. a ~** far paura a qu

fright·en ['fraɪtn] *v/t* spaventare; **be ~ed** (*of*) aver paura (di); **don't be ~ed** non aver paura

♦ **frighten away** *v/t* far scappare

fright·en·ing ['fraɪtnɪŋ] *adj* spaventoso

fri·gid ['frɪdʒɪd] *adj sexually* frigido

frill [frɪl] *on dress etc* volant *m inv*; **~s** (*fancy extras*) fronzoli *mpl*

frill·y ['frɪlɪ] *adj* pieno di volant

fringe [frɪndʒ] frangia *f*; (*edge*) margini *mpl*

fringe ben·e·fits *npl* benefici *mpl* accessori

frisk [frɪsk] *v/t* F frugare F

frisk·y ['frɪskɪ] *adj puppy etc* vivace

♦ **fritter away** ['frɪtə(r)] *v/t time, fortune* sprecare

fri·vol·i·ty [frɪ'vɒlətɪ] frivolezza *f*

friv·o·lous ['frɪvələs] *adj person, pleasures* frivolo

frizz·y ['frɪzɪ] *adj hair* crespo

frog [frɒg] rana *f*

'**frog·man** sommozzatore *m*, -trice *f*

from [frɒm] *prep* ◊ *in time* da; **~ 9 to 5** (*o'clock*) dalle 9 alle 5; **~ the 18th century** dal XVIII secolo; **~ today on** da oggi in poi; **~ next Tuesday** da martedì della prossima settimana ◊ *in space* da; **~ here to there** da qui a lì; **we drove here ~ Paris** siamo venuti qui in macchina da Parigi ◊ *origin* di; **a letter ~ Jo** una lettera di Jo; **a gift ~ the management** un regalo della direzione; *it doesn't say who it's* ~ non c'è scritto di chi è; *I am* ~ *Liverpool* sono di Liverpool; *made* ~ *bananas* fatto di banane ◊ (*because of*) di; *tired* ~ *the journey* stanco del viaggio; *it's* ~ *overeating* è a causa del troppo mangiare

front [frʌnt] **1** *n of building* lato *m* principale; *of car, statue* davanti *m inv*; *of book* copertina *f*; (*cover organization*) facciata *f*; MIL, *of weather* fronte *m*; *in* ~ davanti; *in* ~ *of* davanti a; *at the* ~ davanti; *at the* ~ *of* of bus etc nella parte anteriore di **2** *adj* wheel, seat anteriore **3** *v/t* TV *programme* presentare

front 'bench POL principali esponenti *mpl del governo e dell'opposizione nel Parlamento*; **front 'cov·er** copertina *f*; **front 'door** porta *f* principale; **front 'en·trance** entrata *f* principale

fron·tier ['frʌntɪə(r)] *also fig* frontiera *f*

'front line MIL fronte *m*; **front 'page** *of newspaper* prima pagina *f*; **front page 'news** *nsg* notizia *f* di prima pagina; **front 'row** prima fila *f*; **front seat** 'pas·sen·ger *in car* passeggero *m* davanti; **front-wheel 'drive** trazione *f* anteriore

frost [frɒst] *n* brina *f*
'frost·bite congelamento *m*
'frost·bit·ten *adj* congelato
frosted glass ['frɒstɪd] vetro *m* smerigliato
frost·y ['frɒstɪ] *adj also fig* gelido
froth [frɒθ] *n* spuma *f*
froth·y ['frɒθɪ] *adj cream etc* spumoso
frown [fraʊn] **1** *n* cipiglio *m* **2** *v/i* aggrottare le sopracciglia
froze [frəʊz] *pret* → **freeze**
fro·zen ['frəʊzn] **1** *adj* gelato; *wastes* gelido; *food* surgelato; *I'm* ~ F sono congelato F **2** *pp* → **freeze**
fro·zen 'food cibi *mpl* surgelati
fruit [fruːt] *n* frutto *m*; *collective* frutta *f*
'fruit cake dolce *f* con frutta candita
fruit·ful ['fruːtfʊl] *adj discussions etc* fruttuoso

'fruit juice succo *m* di frutta; **'fruit ma·chine** slot machine *f inv*; **fruit 'sal·ad** macedonia *f*
frus·trate [frʌ'streɪt] *v/t person* frustrare; *plans* scombussolare
frus·trat·ed [frʌ'streɪtɪd] *adj look, sigh* frustrato
frus·trat·ing [frʌ'streɪtɪŋ] *adj* frustrante
frus·trat·ing·ly [frʌ'streɪtɪŋlɪ] *adv slow, hard* in modo frustrante
frus·tra·tion [frʌ'streɪʃn] frustrazione *f*; *sexual* ~ insoddisfazione *f* sessuale; *the* ~*s of modern life* le frustrazioni della vita moderna
fry [fraɪ] *v/t* (*pret & pp* **-ied**) friggere
fry·ing pan ['fraɪɪŋ] padella *f*
fuck [fʌk] *v/t* V scopare V; ~*!* cazzo!
♦ **fuck off** *v/i* V andare affanculo V; **fuck off!** vaffanculo!
fuck·ing ['fʌkɪŋ] **1** *adj* V del cazzo V **2** *adv* V; *I'm* ~ *late!* V sono in ritardo, cazzo!; *I'm* ~ *tired* cazzo, come sono stanco
fu·el ['fjuːəl] **1** *n* carburante *m* **2** *v/t fig* alimentare
fu·gi·tive ['fjuːdʒətɪv] *n* fuggiasco *m*, -a *f*
ful·fil, *Am* **ful·fill** [fʊl'fɪl] *v/t* (*pret & pp* **-led**) *dreams* realizzare; *needs, expectations* soddisfare; *contract* eseguire; *requirements* corrispondere a; *feel* ~*led in job, life* sentirsi soddisfatto
ful·fil·ment, *Am* **ful·fill·ment** [fʊl'fɪlmənt] *of contract* esecuzione *f*; *of dreams* realizzazione *f*; *moral, spiritual* soddisfazione *f*
full [fʊl] *adj* pieno (*of* di); *account, report* esauriente; *life* intenso; ~ *up hotel, with food* pieno; *in* ~ *write* per intero; *pay in* ~ saldare il conto
full 'board pensione *f* completa; **'full-grown** *adj* adulto; ~ **adult** *person* adulto in età matura; *animal* adulto completamente sviluppato; **'full-length** *adj dress* lungo; ~ *film* lungometraggio *m*; **full 'moon** luna *f* piena; **full 'stop** punto *m* fermo; **full-'time** *adj & adv worker, job* a tempo pieno

ful·ly ['fʊlɪ] *adv* booked, recovered completamente; *understand, explain* perfettamente; *describe* ampiamente

fum·ble ['fʌmbl] *v/t catch* farsi sfuggire
♦ **fumble about** *v/i in bags, pockets* frugare; *move in the dark* andare a tastoni; *search in the dark* cercare a tastoni

fume [fjuːm] *v/i:* **be fuming** F (*be very angry*) essere nero F

fumes [fjuːmz] *npl* esalazioni *fpl*

fun [fʌn] divertimento *m;* **it was great** ~ era molto divertente; **bye, have** ~! ciao, divertiti!; *for* ~ per divertirsi; (*joking*) per scherzo; **make** ~ **of** prendere in giro

func·tion ['fʌŋkʃn] **1** *n* (*purpose*) funzione *f;* (*reception etc*) cerimonia *f* **2** *v/i* funzionare; ~ *as* servire da

func·tion·al ['fʌŋkʃnl] *adj* funzionale

fund [fʌnd] **1** *n* fondo *m* **2** *v/t project etc* finanziare

fun·da·men·tal [fʌndə'mentl] *adj* fondamentale

fun·da·men·tal·ist [fʌndə'mentlɪst] *n* fondamentalista *m/f*

fun·da·men·tal·ly [fʌndə'mentlɪ] *adv* fondamentalmente

fund·ing ['fʌndɪŋ] *money* fondi *mpl*

fu·ne·ral ['fjuːnərəl] funerale *m*

'fu·ne·ral di·rec·tor impresario *m* delle pompe funebri

'fu·ne·ral home *Am,* **'fu·ne·ral par·lour** obitorio *m*

'fun·fair luna park *m inv*

fun·gus ['fʌŋgəs] fungo *m*

fu·nic·u·lar ('rail·way) [fjuː'nɪkjʊlə(r)] funicolare *f*

fun·nel ['fʌnl] *n of ship* imbuto *m*

fun·ni·ly ['fʌnɪlɪ] *adv* (*oddly*) stranamente; (*comically*) in modo divertente; ~ **enough** per quanto strano

fun·ny ['fʌnɪ] *adj* (*comical*) divertente; (*odd*) strano

'fun·ny bone osso *m* del gomito

fur [fɜː(r)] pelliccia *f; on animal* pelo *m*

fu·ri·ous ['fjʊərɪəs] *adj* (*angry*) furioso; (*intense*) spaventoso; *at a* ~ *pace* a tutta velocità

fur·nace ['fɜːnɪs] forno *m*

fur·nish ['fɜːnɪʃ] *v/t room* arredare; (*supply*) fornire

fur·ni·ture ['fɜːnɪtʃə(r)] mobili *mpl; a piece of* ~ un mobile

fur·ry ['fɜːrɪ] *adj animal* coperto di pelliccia

fur·ther ['fɜːðə(r)] **1** *adj* (*additional*) ulteriore; (*more distant*) più lontano; *until* ~ *notice* fino a nuovo avviso; *have you anything* ~ *to say?* ha qualcosa da aggiungere? **2** *adv* walk, drive oltre; ~, *I want to say ...* inoltre, volevo dire ...; *two miles* ~ (*on*) due miglia più avanti **3** *v/t* cause etc favorire

fur·ther ed·u·ca·tion istruzione *f* universitaria o para-universitaria

fur·ther·more *adv* inoltre

fur·thest ['fɜːðɪst] **1** *adj* più lontano **2** *adv:* *this is the* ~ *north* è il punto più a nord; *the* ~ *man has travelled in space* il punto più lontano che si è raggiunto nello spazio

fur·tive ['fɜːtɪv] *adj glance* furtivo

fur·tive·ly ['fɜːtɪvlɪ] *adv* furtivamente

fu·ry ['fjʊərɪ] (*anger*) furore *m*

fuse [fjuːz] **1** *n* ELEC fusibile *m* **2** *v/i* ELEC bruciarsi **3** *v/t* ELEC bruciare

'fuse·box scatola *f* dei fusibili

fu·se·lage ['fjuːzəlɑːʒ] fusoliera *f*

'fuse wire filo *m* per fusibili

fu·sion ['fjuːʒn] fusione *f*

fuss [fʌs] *n* agitazione *f; about film, event* scalpore *m;* **make a** ~ *complain* fare storie; *behave in exaggerated way* agitarsi; **make a** ~ **of** *be very attentive to* colmare qu di attenzioni

fuss·y ['fʌsɪ] *adj person* difficile; *design etc* complicato; *be a* ~ *eater* essere schizzinoso nel mangiare

fu·tile ['fjuːtaɪl] *adj* futile

fu·til·i·ty [fjuː'tɪlətɪ] futilità *f inv*

fu·ture ['fjuːtʃə(r)] **1** *n* futuro *m; in* ~ in futuro **2** *adj* futuro

fu·tures ['fju:tʃəz] *npl* FIN titoli *mpl* a termine

'**fu·tures mar·ket** FIN mercato *m* dei titoli a termine

fu·tur·is·tic [fju:tʃə'rıstık] *adj design* futuristico

fuzz·y ['fʌzı] *adj hair* crespo; (*out of focus*) sfuocato

G

gab [gæb] *n*: **have the gift of the ~** F avere la parlantina F

gab·ble ['gæbl] *v/i* parlare troppo in fretta

♦**gad about** [gæd] *v/i* (*pret & pp -ded*) andarsene in giro

gad·get ['gædʒıt] congegno *m*

Gael·ic ['geılık] *n language* gaelico *m*

gaffe [gæf] gaffe *f inv*

gag [gæg] **1** *n* bavaglio *m*; (*joke*) battuta *f* **2** *v/t* (*pret & pp -ged*) *person* imbavagliare; *the press* azzittire

gai·ly ['geılı] *adv* (*blythely*) allegramente

gain [geın] *v/t* (*acquire*) acquisire, acquistare; **~ speed** acquistare velocità; **~ 10 pounds** aumentare di 10 libbre

ga·la ['gɑ:lə] *concert etc* serata *f* di gala

gal·ax·y ['gæləksı] AST galassia *f*

gale [geıl] bufera *f*

gal·lant ['gælənt] *adj* galante

gall blad·der ['gɔ:lblædə(r)] cistifellea *f*

gal·le·ry ['gælərı] galleria *f*

gal·ley ['gælı] *on ship* cambusa *f*

♦**gal·li·vant around** ['gælıvænt] *v/i* andarsene a spasso

gal·lon ['gælən] gallone *m*; **~s of tea** F litri *mpl* di tè

gal·lop ['gæləp] *v/i* galoppare

gal·lows ['gæləuz] *npl* forca *fsg*

gall·stone ['gɔ:lstəun] calcolo *m* biliare

ga·lore [gə'lɔ:(r)] *adj*: *apples / novels* **~** mele / romanzi a iosa

gal·va·nize ['gælvənaız] *v/t* TECH galvanizzare; *fig* stimolare

gam·ble ['gæmbl] *v/i* giocare (d'azzardo)

gam·bler ['gæmblə(r)] giocatore *m*, -trice *f* (d'azzardo)

gam·bling ['gæmblıŋ] *n* gioco *m* (d'azzardo)

game [geım] *n* gioco *m*; (*match, in tennis*) partita *f*

'**game·keep·er** guardacaccia *m/f inv*

'**game re·serve** riserva *f* di caccia

gam·mon ['gæmən] coscia *f* di maiale affumicata

gang [gæŋ] banda *f*

♦**gang up on** *v/t* mettersi contro

'**gang rape 1** *n* stupro *m* collettivo **2** *v/t* stuprare in massa

gan·grene ['gæŋgri:n] MED cancrena *f*

gang·ster ['gæŋstə(r)] malvivente *m*, gangster *m inv*

'**gang war·fare** guerra *f* tra bande

'**gang·way** passaggio *m*; *for ship* passerella *f*

gaol [dʒeıl] → *jail*

gap [gæp] *in wall, for parking* buco *m*; *in conversation, life* vuoto *m*; *in time* intervallo *m*; *in story, education* lacuna *f*; *between two people's characters* scarto *m*

gape [geıp] *v/i of person* rimanere a bocca aperta; *of hole* spalancarsi

♦**gape at** *v/t* guardare a bocca aperta

gap·ing ['geıpıŋ] *adj hole* spalancato

'**gap year** *anno m* tra la fine del liceo e l'inizio dell'università dedicato ad altre attività

gar·age ['gærɪdʒ] *n for parking* garage *m inv*; *for petrol* stazione *f* di servizio; *for repairs* officina *f*

gar·bage ['gɑːbɪdʒ] rifiuti *mpl*; (*fig: nonsense*) idiozie *fpl*

gar·bled ['gɑːbld] *adj message* ingarbugliato

gar·den ['gɑːdn] giardino *m*; *for vegetables* orto *m*

'gar·den cen·ter *Am*, **'gar·den cen·tre** centro *m* per il giardinaggio

gar·den·er ['gɑːdnə(r)] giardiniere *m*, -a *f*

gar·den·ing ['gɑːdnɪŋ] giardinaggio *m*

gar·gle ['gɑːgl] *v/i* fare i gargarismi

gar·goyle ['gɑːgɔɪl] ARCHI gargouille *f inv*

gar·ish ['geərɪʃ] *adj* sgargiante

gar·land ['gɑːlənd] *n* ghirlanda *f*

gar·lic ['gɑːlɪk] aglio *m*

gar·lic 'bread pane *m* all'aglio

gar·ment ['gɑːmənt] capo *m* d'abbigliamento

gar·nish ['gɑːnɪʃ] *v/t* guarnire

gar·ret ['gærɪt] soffitta *f*

gar·ri·son ['gærɪsn] *n* guarnigione *f*

gar·ter ['gɑːtə(r)] giarrettiera *f*

gas [gæs] *n* gas *m inv*; (*esp Am: gasoline*) benzina *f*

'gas bill bolletta *f* del gas

gash [gæʃ] *n* taglio *m*

gas·ket ['gæskɪt] guarnizione *f*

'gas man impiegato *m* del gas

'gas me·ter contatore *m* del gas

gas·o·line ['gæsəliːn] *Am* benzina *f*

gasp [gɑːsp] **1** *n* sussulto *m* **2** *v/i* rimanere senza fiato; **~ for breath** essere senza fiato; *he collapsed ~ing for breath* si è accasciato senza fiato

'gas ped·al *Am* acceleratore *m*; **'gas pipe·line** gasdotto *m*; **'gas sta·tion** *Am* stazione *f* di rifornimento; **'gas stove** cucina *f* a gas

gas·tric ['gæstrɪk] *adj* MED gastrico

gas·tric 'flu MED influenza *f* intestinale; **gas·tric 'juices** *npl* succhi *mpl* gastrici; **gas·tric 'ul·cer** MED ulcera *f* gastrica

gate [geɪt] cancello *m*; *of city, castle, at airport* porta *f*

ga·teau ['gætəu] torta *f*

'gate·crash *v/t* intrufolarsi in

'gate·way ingresso *m*; *fig* via *f* d'accesso

gath·er ['gæðə(r)] **1** *v/t facts, information* raccogliere; **~ speed** acquistare velocità; *am I to ~ that …?* devo dedurre che …? **2** *v/i* (*understand*) dedurre

♦ **gather up** *v/t possessions* radunare

gath·er·ing ['gæðərɪŋ] *n* (*group of people*) raduno *m*

gau·dy ['gɔːdɪ] *adj* pacchiano

gauge [geɪdʒ] **1** *n* indicatore *m* **2** *v/t pressure* misurare; *opinion* valutare

gaunt [gɔːnt] *adj* smunto

gauze [gɔːz] *adj* garza *f*

gave [geɪv] *pret* → **give**

gaw·ky ['gɔːkɪ] *adj* impacciato

gawp [gɔːp] *v/i* F fissare come un ebete F; **~ at sth** fissare qc con aria inebetita

gay [geɪ] **1** *n* (*homosexual*) omosessuale *m/f* **2** *adj* omosessuale; *club* gay *inv*

gaze [geɪz] **1** *n* sguardo *m* **2** *v/i* fissare

♦ **gaze at** *v/t* fissare

GB [dʒiː'biː] *abbr* (= **Great Britain**) GB (= Gran Bretagna *f*)

GDP [dʒiːdiː'piː] *abbr* (= **gross domestic product**) PIL *m* (= prodotto *m* interno lordo)

gear [gɪə(r)] *n* (*equipment*) equipaggiamento *m*; *in vehicles* marcia *f*

'gear·box MOT scatola *f* del cambio

'gear le·ver, **'gear shift** MOT leva *f* del cambio

geese [giːs] *pl* → **goose**

gel [dʒel] *for hair, shower* gel *m inv*

gel·a·tine ['dʒelətiːn] gelatina *f*

gel·ig·nite ['dʒelɪgnaɪt] gelignite *f*

gem [dʒem] gemma *f*; *fig: book etc* capolavoro *m*; *person* perla *f* rara

Gem·i·ni ['dʒemɪnaɪ] ASTR Gemelli *mpl*

gen·der ['dʒendə(r)] genere *m*

gene [dʒiːn] gene *m*; *it's in his ~s* è una sua caratteristica innata

gen·er·al ['dʒenrəl] **1** *n* MIL generale *m*; **in ~** in generale **2** *adj* generale

gen·er·al e'lec·tion elezioni *fpl* politiche

gen·er·al·i·za·tion [dʒenrəlaɪ'zeɪʃn] generalizzazione *f*

gen·er·al·ize ['dʒenrəlaɪz] *v/i* generalizzare

gen·er·al·ly ['dʒenrəlɪ] *adv* generalmente; **~ speaking** in generale

gen·er·al prac'ti·tion·er medico *m* generico

gen·er·ate ['dʒenəreɪt] *v/t* generare; *in linguistics* formare

gen·er·a·tion [dʒenə'reɪʃn] generazione *f*

gen·er·a·tion gap scarto *m* generazionale

gen·er·a·tor ['dʒenəreɪtə(r)] ELEC generatore *m*

ge·ner·ic drug [dʒə'nerɪk] MED *medicina f senza una marca specifica*

gen·e·ros·i·ty [dʒenə'rosɪtɪ] generosità *f*

gen·e·rous ['dʒenərəs] *adj* generoso

ge·net·ic [dʒɪ'netɪk] *adj* genetico

ge·net·i·cal·ly [dʒɪ'netɪklɪ] *adv* geneticamente; **~ modified** transgenico

ge·net·ic 'code codice *m* genetico; **ge·net·ic en·gi·neer·ing** ingegneria *f* genetica; **ge·net·ic 'fin·ger·print** esame *m* del DNA

ge·net·i·cist [dʒɪ'netɪsɪst] genetista *m/f*

ge·net·ics [dʒɪ'netɪks] genetica *f*

ge·ni·al ['dʒiːnɪəl] *adj person, company* gioviale

gen·i·tals ['dʒenɪtlz] *npl* genitali *mpl*

ge·ni·us ['dʒiːnɪəs] genio *m*

Gen·o·a ['dʒenəuə] Genova *f*

gen·o·cide ['dʒenəsaɪd] genocidio *m*

gen·tle ['dʒentl] *adj* delicato; *breeze, slope* dolce

gen·tle·man ['dʒentlmən] signore *m*; **he's a real ~** è un vero gentleman

gen·tle·ness ['dʒentlnɪs] delicatezza *f*; *of breeze, slope* dolcezza *f*

gen·tly ['dʒentlɪ] *adv* delicatamente; *blow, slope* dolcemente

gents [dʒents] *toilet* bagno *m* degli uomini

gen·u·ine ['dʒenjuɪn] *adj* autentico; *(sincere)* sincero

gen·u·ine·ly ['dʒenjuɪnlɪ] *adv* sinceramente

ge·o·graph·i·cal [dʒɪə'græfɪkl] *adj* geografico

ge·og·ra·phy [dʒɪ'ɒgrəfɪ] geografia *f*

ge·o·log·i·cal [dʒɪə'lɒdʒɪkl] *adj* geologico

ge·ol·o·gist [dʒɪ'ɒlədʒɪst] geologo *m*, -a *f*

ge·ol·o·gy [dʒɪ'ɒlədʒɪ] geologia *f*

ge·o·met·ric, ge·o·met·ri·cal [dʒɪə-'metrɪk(l)] *adj* geometrico

ge·om·e·try [dʒɪ'ɒmətrɪ] geometria *f*

ge·ra·ni·um [dʒə'reɪnɪəm] geranio *m*

ger·i·at·ric [dʒerɪ'ætrɪk] **1** *adj* geriatrico **2** *n* anziano *m*, -a *f*

germ [dʒɜːm] *also fig* germe *m*

Ger·man ['dʒɜːmən] **1** *adj* tedesco **2** *n person* tedesco *m*, -a *f*; *language* tedesco *m*

Ger·man 'mea·sles *nsg* rosolia *f*

Ger·man 'shep·herd pastore *m* tedesco

Germany ['dʒɜːmənɪ] Germania *f*

ger·mi·nate ['dʒɜːmɪneɪt] *v/i of seed* germogliare

germ 'war·fare guerra *f* batteriologica

ges·tic·u·late [dʒe'stɪkjuleɪt] *v/i* gesticolare

ges·ture ['dʒestʃə(r)] *n also fig* gesto *m*

get [get] *v/t* (*pret & pp* **got**) *(obtain)* prendere; *(fetch)* andare a prendere; *(receive: letter)* ricevere; *(receive: knowledge, respect etc)* ottenere; *(catch: bus, train, flu)* prendere; *(become)* diventare; *(arrive)* arrivare; *(understand)* afferrare; **~ sth done** *causative* farsi fare qc; **~ s.o. to do sth** far fare qc a qu; **I'll ~ him to do it** glielo faccio fare; **~ to do sth** *have opportunity* avere occasione di fare qc; **~ one's hair cut** tagliarsi i capelli; **~ sth ready** preparare qc; **~**

G

going (*leave*) andare via; **have got** avere; **I have got to study / see him** devo studiare / vederlo; **I don't want to, but I've got to** non voglio, ma devo; **~ to know** venire a sapere

♦**get about** *v/i* (*travel*) andare in giro; (*be mobile*) muoversi

♦**get along** *v/i* (*progress*) procedere; **how is he getting along at school?** come se la cava a scuola?; *come to party etc* venire; *with s.o.* andare d'accordo

♦**get at** *v/t* (*criticize*) prendersela con; (*imply, mean*) volere arrivare a; **I don't understand what you're getting at** non capisco dove vuoi arrivare

♦**get away 1** *v/i* (*leave*) andare via **2** *v/t*: **get sth away from s.o.** togliere qc a qu

♦**get away with** *v/t* cavarsela per

♦**get back 1** *v/i* (*return*) ritornare; **I'll get back to you on that** ti faccio sapere **2** *v/t* (*obtain again*) recuperare

♦**get by** *v/i* (*pass*) passare; *financially* tirare avanti

♦**get down 1** *v/i from ladder etc* scendere; (*duck etc*) abbassarsi **2** *v/t* (*depress*) buttare giù

♦**get down to** *v/t* (*start: work*) mettersi a; (*reach: real facts*) arrivare a; **let's get down to business** parliamo d'affari

♦**get in 1** *v/i* (*arrive: of train, plane*) arrivare; (*come home*) arrivare a casa; *to car* salire; **how did they get in?** *of thieves, mice etc* come sono entrati? **2** *v/t to suitcase etc* far entrare

♦**get off 1** *v/i from bus etc* scendere; (*finish work*) finire; (*not be punished*) cavarsela **2** *v/t* (*remove*) togliere; *clothes, hat, footgear* togliersi; **get off the grass!** togliti dal prato!

♦**get off with** *v/t* F *sexually* rimorchiare F; **get off with a small fine** cavarsela con una piccola multa

♦**get on 1** *v/i to bike, bus, train* salire; (*be friendly*) andare d'accordo; (*advance: of time*) farsi tardi; (*become*

old*) invecchiare; (*make progress*) procedere; **he's getting on well at school** se la sta cavando bene a scuola; **it's getting on** *getting late* si sta facendo tardi; **he's getting on** *getting old* sta invecchiando; **he's getting on for 50** va per i 50 anni **2** *v/t*: **get on the bus / one's bike** salire sull'autobus / sulla bici; **get one's hat on** mettersi il cappello; **I can't get these trousers on** non riesco a mettermi questi pantaloni

♦**get out 1** *v/i of car etc* scendere; *of prison* uscire; **get out!** fuori!; **let's get out of here** usciamo da qui; **I don't get out much these days** non esco molto in questi giorni **2** *v/t* (*extract: nail, something jammed*) tirare fuori; (*remove: stain*) mandare via; (*pull out: gun, pen*) tirare fuori

♦**get over** *v/t fence, disappointment etc* superare; *lover etc* dimenticare

♦**get over with** *v/t* togliersi; **let's get it over with** togliamocelo

♦**get through** *v/i on telephone* prendere la linea; (*make self understood*) farsi capire; **get through to s.o.** (*make self understood*) farsi capire da qu; **I called you all day but I didn't manage to get through** ti ho chiamato tutto il giorno, ma era sempre occupato

♦**get up 1** *v/i of person, wind* alzarsi **2** *v/t* (*climb: hill*) salire su

'**get·a·way** *from robbery* fuga *f*

'**get·a·way car** macchina *f* per la fuga

'**get-to·geth·er** ritrovo *m*

ghast·ly ['gɑːstlɪ] *adj colour, experience, person etc* orrendo; **you look ~** hai un aspetto orribile

gher·kin ['gɜːkɪn] cetriolino *m* sotto aceto

ghet·to ['getəʊ] ghetto *m*

ghost [gəʊst] fantasma *m*, spettro *m*

ghost·ly ['gəʊstlɪ] *adj* spettrale

'**ghost town** città *f inv* fantasma

ghoul [guːl] persona *f* morbosa

ghoul·ish ['guːlɪʃ] *adj* macabro

gi·ant ['dʒaɪənt] **1** *n* gigante *m* **2** *adj* gigante

gib·ber·ish ['dʒɪbərɪʃ] F bestialità *fpl* F

gibe [dʒaɪb] *n* frecciatina *f*

gib·lets ['dʒɪblɪts] *npl* frattaglie *fpl* (di volatili)

gid·di·ness ['gɪdɪnɪs] giramenti *mpl* di testa

gid·dy ['gɪdɪ] *adj*: **I feel ~** mi gira la testa

gift [gɪft] regalo *m*

gift·ed ['gɪftɪd] *adj* dotato

'**gift to·ken**, '**gift voucher** buono *m* d'aquisto

'**gift-wrap 1** *n* carta *f* da regalo **2** *v/t* (*pret & pp* **-ped**) impacchettare; **would you like it ~ped?** le faccio un pacco regalo?

gig [gɪg] F concerto *m*

gi·ga·byte ['gɪgəbaɪt] COMPUT gigabyte *m inv*

gi·gan·tic [dʒaɪ'gæntɪk] *adj* gigante

gig·gle ['gɪgl] **1** *v/i* ridacchiare **2** *n* risatina *f*

gig·gly ['gɪglɪ] *adj* ridacchiante

gill [gɪl] *of fish* branchia *f*

gilt [gɪlt] *n* doratura *f*; **~s** FIN titoli *mpl* obbligazionari

gim·mick ['gɪmɪk] trovata *f*

gim·mick·y ['gɪmɪkɪ] *adj* appariscente

gin [dʒɪn] gin *m inv*; **~ and tonic** gin and tonic *m inv*

gin·ger ['dʒɪndʒə(r)] **1** *n spice* zenzero *m* **2** *adj hair* rosso carota; *cat* rosso

gin·ger 'beer bibita *f* allo zenzero

'**gin·ger·bread** pan *m* di zenzero

gin·ger·ly ['dʒɪndʒəlɪ] *adv* con cautela

gip·sy ['dʒɪpsɪ] zingaro *m*, -a *f*

gi·raffe [dʒɪ'rɑːf] giraffa *f*

gir·der ['gɜːdə(r)] *n* trave *f*

girl [gɜːl] ragazza *f*

'**girl·friend** *of boy* ragazza *f*; *of girl* amica *f*

girl 'guide giovane esploratrice *f*

girl·ie ['gɜːlɪ] *adj* F da femminuccia F

'**girl·ie mag·a·zine** *pornographic* rivista *f* per soli uomini

girl·ish ['gɜːlɪʃ] *adj* tipicamente femminile

gi·ro ['dʒaɪərəʊ] bonifico *m*

gist [dʒɪst] sostanza *f*

give [gɪv] *v/t* (*pret* **gave**, *pp* **given**) dare; *present* fare; (*supply: electricity etc*) fornire; *talk, groan* fare; *party* dare; *pain, appetite* far venire; **~ her my love** salutala da parte mia

♦ **give away** *v/t as present* regalare; (*betray*) tradire; **give o.s. away** tradirsi

♦ **give back** *v/t* restituire

♦ **give in 1** *v/i surrender* arrendersi **2** *v/t* (*hand in*) consegnare

♦ **give off** *v/t smell, fumes* emettere

♦ **give onto** *v/t* (*open onto*) dare su

♦ **give out 1** *v/t leaflets etc* distribuire **2** *v/i of supplies, strength* esaurirsi

♦ **give up 1** *v/t smoking etc* rinunciare a; **he gave up smoking** ha smesso di fumare; **give o.s. up to the police** consegnarsi alla polizia **2** *v/i* (*cease habit*) smettere; (*stop making effort*) lasciar perdere

♦ **give way** *v/i of bridge etc* cedere; MOT dare la precedenza

give-and-'take concessioni *fpl* reciproche

giv·en ['gɪvn] *pp* → **give**

'**giv·en name** nome *m* di battesimo

gla·ci·er ['glæsɪə(r)] ghiacciaio *m*

glad [glæd] *adj* contento

glad·ly ['glædlɪ] *adv* volentieri

glam·or *Am* → **glamour**

glam·or·ize ['glæməraɪz] *v/t* esaltare

glam·or·ous ['glæmərəs] *adj* affascinante

glam·our ['glæmə(r)] fascino *m*

glance [glɑːns] **1** *n* sguardo *m*; **at first ~** a prima vista **2** *v/i* dare un'occhiata *o* uno sguardo

♦ **glance at** *v/t* dare un'occhiata *o* uno sguardo a

gland [glænd] ghiandola *f*

glan·du·lar fe·ver ['glændjʊlə(r)] mononucleosi *f*

glare [gleə(r)] **1** *n of sun, headlights* luce *f* abbagliante **2** *v/i of sun, headlights* splendere di luce abbagliante

♦ **glare at** *v/t* guardare di storto

G

glar·ing ['gleərɪŋ] *adj mistake* lampante

glar·ing·ly ['gleərɪŋlɪ] *adv:* **be ~ obvious** essere più che ovvio

glass [glɑ:s] *material* vetro *m*; *for drink* bicchiere *m*

glass 'case teca *f*

glasses *npl* occhiali *mpl*

'glass·house serra *f*

glaze [gleɪz] *n* smalto *m* trasparente

♦ **glaze over** *v/i of eyes* appannarsi

glazed [gleɪzd] *adj expression* assente

gla·zi·er ['gleɪzɪə(r)] *n* vetraio *m*

glaz·ing ['gleɪzɪŋ] vetri *mpl*

gleam [gli:m] **1** *n* luccichio *m* **2** *v/i* luccicare

glee [gli:] allegria *f*

glee·ful ['gli:fʊl] *adj* allegro

glib [glɪb] *adj* poco convincente

glib·ly ['glɪblɪ] *adv* in modo poco convincente

glide [glaɪd] *v/i of skier, boat* scivolare; *of bird, plane* planare

glid·er ['glaɪdə(r)] *n* aliante *m*

glid·ing ['glaɪdɪŋ] *n* SP volo *m* planato

glim·mer ['glɪmə(r)] **1** *n of light* barlume *m*; **~ of hope** barlume *m* di speranza **2** *v/i* emettere un barlume

glimpse [glɪmps] **1** *n* occhiata *f*; **catch a ~ of** intravedere **2** *v/t* intravedere

glint [glɪnt] **1** *n* luccichio *m* **2** *v/i of light, eyes* luccicare

glis·ten ['glɪsn] *v/i* scintillare

glit·ter ['glɪtə(r)] *v/i* brillare

glit·ter·ati *npl:* **the ~** il bel mondo

gloat [gləʊt] *v/i* gongolare

♦ **gloat over** *v/t* compiacersi di

glo·bal ['gləʊbl] *adj* (*worldwide*) mondiale; *without exceptions* globale

glo·bal e'con·o·my economia *f* mondiale

glo·bal 'mar·ket mercato *m* mondiale

glo·bal 'war·ming effetto *m* serra

globe [gləʊb] globo *m*; *model of earth* mappamondo *m*

gloom [glu:m] (*darkness*) penombra

f; *mood* tristezza *f*

gloom·i·ly ['glu:mɪlɪ] *adv* tristemente

gloom·y ['glu:mɪ] *adj room* buio; *mood, person* triste; *day* grigio

glo·ri·ous ['glɔːrɪəs] *adj weather, day* splendido; *victory* glorioso

glo·ry ['glɔːrɪ] *n* gloria *f*; (*beauty*) splendore *m*

gloss [glɒs] *n* (*shine*) lucido *m*; (*general explanation*) glossa *f*

♦ **gloss over** *v/t* sorvolare su

glos·sa·ry ['glɒsərɪ] glossario *f*

'gloss paint vernice *f* lucida

gloss·y ['glɒsɪ] **1** *adj paper* patinato **2** *n magazine* rivista *f* femminile

glove [glʌv] guanto *m*

'glove com·part·ment *in car* cruscotto *m*

'glove pup·pet burattino *m*

glow [gləʊ] **1** *n of light, fire* bagliore *m*; *in cheeks* colorito *m* vivo; *of candle* luce *f* fioca **2** *v/i of light* brillare; *her cheeks ~ed* è diventata rossa

glow·er ['glaʊə(r)] *v/i:* **~ at s.o.** guardare qu in cagnesco

glow·ing ['gləʊɪŋ] *adj description* entusiastico

glu·cose ['glu:kəʊs] glucosio *m*

glue [glu:] **1** *n* colla *f* **2** *v/t:* **~ sth to sth** incollare qc a qc; **be ~d to the TV** F essere incollato alla TV F

glum [glʌm] *adj* triste

glum·ly ['glʌmlɪ] *adv* tristemente

glut [glʌt] *n* eccesso *m*

glut·ton ['glʌtən] ghiottone *m*, -a *f*

glut·ton·y ['glʌtənɪ] ghiottoneria *f*

GMT [dʒi:em'ti:] *abbr* (= **Greenwich Mean Time**) ora *f* di Greenwich

gnarled [nɑ:ld] *adj branch, hands* nodoso

gnat [næt] moscerino *m*

gnaw [nɔ:] *v/t bone* rosicchiare

GNP [dʒi:en'pi:] *abbr* (= **gross national product**) PNL *m* (= prodotto *m* nazionale lordo)

go [gəʊ] **1** *n* (*try*) tentativo *m*; **it's my ~** tocca a me, è il mio turno; **have a ~ at sth** (*try*) fare un tentativo in qc; (*complain about*) lamentarsi di qc;

be on the ~ essere indaffarato; *in one ~* drink, write etc tutto in una volta **2** *v/i* ◊ (*pret* **went**, *pp* **gone**) andare; (*leave: of train, plane*) partire; (*leave: of people*) andare via; (*work, function*) funzionare; (*become*) diventare; (*come out: of stain etc*) andare via; (*cease: of pain etc*) sparire; (*match: of colours etc*) stare bene insieme; *~ shopping* / *~ jogging* andare a fare spese / andare a correre; *I must be ~ing* devo andare; *let's ~!* andiamo!; *~ for a walk* andare a fare una passeggiata; *~ to bed* andare a letto; *~ to school* andare a scuola; *how's the work ~ing?* come va il lavoro?; *they're ~ing for £50* (*being sold at*) li vendono a £50; *be all gone* (*finished*) essere finito; *I've gone 15 miles* ho fatto 15 miglia; *there are two days to ~ before ...* mancano due giorni a ...; *the story ~es that ...* la storia dice che ...; *to ~* Am food da asporto ◊ *future I'm ~ing to meet him tomorrow* lo incontrerò domani; *it's ~ing to snow* sta per nevicare

♦ *go ahead* *v/i and do sth* andare avanti; *go ahead!* (*on you go*) fai pure!

♦ *go ahead with* *v/t plans etc* andare avanti con

♦ *go along with* *v/t suggestion* concordare con

♦ *go at* *v/t* (*attack*) scagliarsi contro

♦ *go away* *v/i of person, pain* andare via; *of rain* smettere

♦ *go back* *v/i* (*return*) ritornare; (*date back*) rimontare; *we go back a long way* ci conosciamo da una vita; *go back to sleep* tornare a dormire

♦ *go by* *v/i of car, people, time* passare

♦ *go down* *v/i* scendere; *of sun, ship* tramontare; *of ship* affondare; *of swelling* diminuire; *will it go down well with them?* la prenderanno bene?

♦ *go for* *v/t* (*attack*) attaccare; *I don't much go for gin* non vado matto per il gin; *she really goes for him* le

piace davvero

♦ *go in* *v/i to room, house* entrare; *of sun* andare via; (*fit: of part etc*) andare

♦ *go in for* *v/t competition, race* iscriversi a; (*like, take part in*) dedicarsi a

♦ *go off* **1** *v/i* (*leave*) andarsene; *of bomb* esplodere; *of gun* sparare; *of alarm* scattare; *of light* spegnersi; *of milk etc* andare a male **2** *v/t* (*stop liking*) stufarsi di

♦ *go on* *v/i* (*continue*) andare avanti; (*happen*) succedere; *go on, do it!* encouraging dai, fallo!; *what's going on?* cosa sta succedendo?

♦ *go on at* *v/t* (*nag*) sgridare

♦ *go out* *v/i of person* uscire; *of light, fire* spegnersi

♦ *go out with* *v/t romantically* uscire con

♦ *go over* *v/t* (*check*) esaminare; (*do again*) rifare

♦ *go through* *v/t illness, hard times* passare; (*check*) controllare; (*read through*) leggere

♦ *go under* *v/i* (*sink*) affondare; *of company* fallire

♦ *go up* *v/i* salire

♦ *go without* **1** *v/t food etc* fare a meno di **2** *v/i* farne a meno

goad [gəʊd] *v/t* spronare

'**go-a·head 1** *n* via libera *m*; *get the ~* avere il via libera **2** *adj* (*enterprising, dynamic*) intraprendente

goal [gəʊl] (*sport: target*) rete *f*; (*sport: points*) gol *m inv*; (*objective*) obiettivo *m*

goal·ie ['gəʊlɪ] F portiere *m*

'**goal·keep·er** portiere *m*; '**goal kick** rimessa *f*; '**goal·mouth** area *f* di porta; '**goal·post** palo *m*

goat [gəʊt] capra *f*

gob·ble ['gɒbl] *v/t* tranguiare

♦ *gobble up* *v/t* tranguiare

gob·ble·dy·gook ['gɒbldɪguːk] F linguaggio *m* incomprensibile

'**go-be·tween** mediatore *m*, -trice *f*

gob-smacked ['gɒbsmækt] *adj* P sbigottito

god [gɒd] dio *m*; *thank God!* grazie a Dio!; *oh God!* Dio mio!

'**god·child** figlioccio *m*, -a *f*
'**god·daugh·ter** figliaccia *f*
god·dess ['gɒdɪs] dea *f*
'**god·fa·ther** also in mafia padrino *m*;
'**god·for·sak·en** ['gɒdfəseɪkən] adj
place, town dimenticato da Dio;
'**god·moth·er** madrina *f*; '**god·**
pa·rent man padrino *m*; woman
madrina *f*; '**god·send** benedizione
f; '**god·son** figlioccio *m*
go·fer ['gəʊfə(r)] F galoppino *m*, -a *f*
F
gog·gles ['gɒglz] *npl* occhialini *mpl*
go·ing ['gəʊɪŋ] *adj* price etc corrente;
~ **concern** azienda *f* florida
go·ings-on [gəʊɪŋz'ɒn] *npl* vicende
fpl
gold [gəʊld] **1** *n* oro *m* **2** *adj* d'oro
gold·en ['gəʊldn] *adj* sky, hair dorato
gold·en '**hand·shake** buonuscita *f*
gold·en '**wed·ding** (an·ni·ver·sa·ry) nozze *fpl* d'oro
'**gold·fish** pesce *m* rosso; '**gold mine**
fig miniera *f* d'oro; '**gold·smith**
orefice *m/f*
golf [gɒlf] golf *m*
'**golf ball** palla *f* da golf; '**golf club**
organization club *m inv* di golf; stick
mazza *f* da golf; '**golf course** campo *m* di golf
golf·er ['gɒlfə(r)] giocatore *m*, -trice
di golf
gon·do·la ['gɒndələ] gondola *f*
gon·do·lier [gɒndə'lɪə(r)] gondoliere *m*
gone [gɒn] *pp* → **go**
gong [gɒŋ] gong *m inv*
good [gʊd] **1** *adj* buono; weather, film
bello; actor, child bravo; **a ~ many**
un bel po' (di); **be ~ at** essere bravo
in; **be ~ for s.o.** fare bene a qu; **be ~**
for sth andare bene per qc; **~!**
bene!; **it's ~ to see you** è bello vederti **2** *n* bene *m*; **it did him no ~**
non gli ha fatto bene; **it did him a**
lot of ~ gli ha fatto molto bene;
what ~ is that to me? a che cosa mi
serve?; **the ~** il buono; people i buoni
good·bye [gʊd'baɪ] arrivederci; **say**

~ **to s.o., wish s.o.** ~ salutare qu
'**good-for-nothing** *n* buono *m*, -a *f*
nulla; **Good** '**Fri·day** venerdì *m inv*
santo; **good-hu·mored** Am, **good-**
hu·moured [gʊd'hju:məd] *adj* di
buon umore; **good-'look·ing**
[gʊd'lʊkɪŋ] *adj* attraente; **good-**
na·tured [gʊd'neɪtʃəd] di buon cuore
good·ness ['gʊdnɪs] bontà *f*; *thank*
~! grazie al cielo
goods [gʊdz] *npl* COM merce *fsg*
good'will buona volontà *f*
good·y-good·y ['gʊdigʊdi] *n* F san-
tarellino *m*, -a *f* F
goo·ey ['gu:i] *adj* appiccicoso
goof [gu:f] *v/i* F fare una gaffe
goose [gu:s] (*pl* **geese** [gi:s]) oca *f*
goose·ber·ry ['gʊzbərɪ] uva *f* spina
'**goose pim·ples** *npl* pelle *f* d'oca
gorge [gɔ:dʒ] **1** *n* gola *f* **2** *v/t*: ~ **o.s.**
on sth strafogarsi di qc
gor·geous ['gɔ:dʒəs] *adj* stupendo;
smell ottimo
go·ril·la [gə'rɪlə] gorilla *m*
gosh [gɒʃ] *int* caspita
go-'slow sciopero *m* bianco
Gos·pel ['gɒspl] in Bible vangelo *m*
'**gos·pel truth** sacrosanta verità *f inv*
gos·sip ['gɒsɪp] **1** *n* pettegolezzo *m*;
person pettegolo *m*, -a *f* **2** *v/i* spette-
golare
'**gos·sip col·umn** cronaca *f* rosa
'**gos·sip col·um·nist** giornalista *m/f*
di cronaca rosa
gossipy ['gɒsɪpɪ] *adj* letter pieno di
chiacchiere
got [gɒt] *pret & pp* → **get**
gour·met ['gʊəmeɪ] *n* buongustaio
m, -a *f*
gov·ern ['gʌvn] *v/t* country governare
gov·ern·ment ['gʌvnmənt] governo
m
gov·er·nor ['gʌvənə(r)] governatore
m
gown [gaʊn] (long dress) abito *m* lungo; (wedding dress) abito *m* da sposa; of academic, judge toga *f*; of
surgeon camice *m*

GP [dʒiː'piː] *abbr* (= *General Practitioner*) medico *m* generico

grab [græb] *v/t* (*pret & pp* **-bed**) afferrare; ~ *a bite to eat* fare uno spuntino rapido; ~ *some sleep* farsi una dormita

grace [greɪs] *of dancer etc* grazia *f*; *before meals* preghiera *f* (prima di un pasto)

grace·ful ['greɪsfʊl] *adj* aggraziato

grace·ful·ly ['greɪsfʊlɪ] *adv move* con grazia

gra·cious ['greɪʃəs] *adj person* cortese; *style* elegante; *living* agiato; *good ~!* santo cielo!

grade [greɪd] **1** *n* (*quality*) qualità *f inv*; EDU voto *m* **2** *v/t* classificare

'grade school *Am* scuola *f* elementare

gra·di·ent ['greɪdɪənt] pendenza *f*

grad·u·al ['grædʒʊəl] *adj* graduale

grad·u·al·ly ['grædʒʊəlɪ] *adv* gradualmente

grad·u·ate ['grædʒʊət] **1** *n* laureato *m*, -a *f* **2** *v/i from university* laurearsi

grad·u·a·tion [grædʒʊ'eɪʃn] laurea *f*; *ceremony* cerimonia *f* di laurea

graf·fi·ti [grəˈfiːtiː] graffiti *mpl*

graft [grɑːft] **1** *n* BOT innesto *m*; MED trapianto *m*; F (*hard work*) duro lavoro *m* **2** *v/t* BOT innestare; MED trapiantare

grain [greɪn] cereali *mpl*; *seed* granello *m*; *of rice, wheat* chicco *m*; *in wood* venatura *f*; **go against the ~** essere contro natura

gram [græm] grammo *m*

gram·mar ['græmə(r)] grammatica *f*

'gram·mar school liceo *m*

gram·mat·i·cal [grəˈmætɪkl] *adj* grammaticale

gram·mat·i·cal·ly *adv* grammaticalmente

grand [grænd] **1** *adj* grandioso; F (*very good*) eccezionale **2** *n* F (*£1000*) mille sterline *fpl*

'grand·dad ['grændæd] nonno *m*

'grand·child nipote *m/f*

'grand·daugh·ter nipote *f*

gran·deur ['grændʒə(r)] grandiosità *f*

'grand·fa·ther nonno *m*

grand·fa·ther clock pendolo *m*

gran·di·ose ['grændɪəʊs] *adj* grandioso

'grand·ma F nonna *f*; **'grandmoth·er** nonna *f*; **'grand·pa** F nonno *m*; **'grand·par·ents** *npl* nonni *mpl*; **grand pi'an·o** pianoforte *m* a coda; **grand 'slam** grande slam *m inv*; **'grand·son** nipote *m*; **'grandstand** tribuna *f*

gran·ite ['grænɪt] granito *m*

gran·ny ['grænɪ] F nonna *f*

'gran·ny flat appartamento *m* annesso

grant [grɑːnt] **1** *n money* sussidio *m*; *for university* borsa *f* di studio **2** *v/t visa* assegnare; *permission* concedere; *request, wish* esaudire; **take sth for ~ed** dare qc per scontato; **he takes his wife for ~ed** considera quello che fa sua moglie come dovuto

gran·ule ['grænjuːl] granello *m*

grape [greɪp] acino *m* d'uva; **~s** uva *fsg*

'grape·fruit pompelmo *m*; **'grapefruit juice** succo *m* di pompelmo; **'grape·vine**: *I heard on the ~ that ...* ho sentito dire che ...

graph [grɑːf] grafico *m*

graph·ic ['græfɪk] **1** *adj* grafico; (*vivid*) vivido **2** *n* COMPUT grafico *m*; **~s** grafica *f*

graph·ic·al·ly ['græfɪklɪ] *adv describe* in modo vivido

graph·ic de'sign·er grafico *m*, -a *f*

♦ **grap·ple with** ['græpl] *v/t attacker* lottare con; *problem etc* essere alle prese con

grasp [grɑːsp] **1** *n physical* presa *f*; *mental* comprensione *f* **2** *v/t physically, mentally* afferrare

grass [grɑːs] *n* erba *f*

'grass·hop·per cavalletta *f*; **grass roots** *npl people* massa *f* popolare; **grass 'wid·ow** donna *f* il cui marito è spesso assente; **grass 'wid·ow·er** uomo *m* la cui moglie è spesso assente

gras·sy ['grɑːsɪ] *adj* erboso

grate¹ [greɪt] *n metal* grata *f*

grate² [greɪt] **1** v/t in cooking grattugiare **2** v/i of sounds stridere

grate·ful ['greɪtful] adj grato; **be ~ to s.o.** essere grato a qu

grate·ful·ly ['greɪtfulɪ] adv con gratitudine

grat·er ['greɪtə(r)] grattugia f

grat·i·fy ['grætɪfaɪ] v/t (pret & pp **-ied**) soddisfare

grat·ing ['greɪtɪŋ] **1** n grata f **2** adj sound, voice stridente

grat·i·tude ['grætɪtjuːd] gratitudine f

gra·tu·i·tous [grə'tjuːɪtəs] adj gratuito

gra·tu·i·ty [grə'tjuːətɪ] (tip) mancia f

grave¹ [greɪv] n tomba f

grave² [greɪv] adj (serious) grave

grav·el ['grævl] n ghiaia f

'grave·stone lapide f

'grave·yard cimitero m

♦ **grav·i·tate towards** ['grævɪteɪt] v/t gravitare intorno a

grav·i·ty ['grævətɪ] PHYS forza f di gravità

gra·vy ['greɪvɪ] sugo m della carne

gray Am → **grey**

graze¹ [greɪz] v/i of cow, horse brucare

graze² [greɪz] **1** v/t arm etc graffiare **2** n graffio m

grease [griːs] n grasso m

grease-proof 'pa·per carta f oleata

greas·y ['griːsɪ] adj food, hair, skin grasso; hands, plate unto

great [greɪt] adj grande; F (very good) fantastico; **~ to see you!** sono contento di vederti!

Great 'Brit·ain Gran Bretagna f; **great-'grand·child** pronipote m/f; **great-'grand·daugh·ter** pronipote f; **great-'grand·fa·ther** bisnonno m; **great-'grand·moth·er** bisnonna f; **great-'grand·par·ents** npl bisnonni mpl; **great-'grand·son** pronipote m

great·ly ['greɪtlɪ] adv molto

great·ness ['greɪtnɪs] grandezza f

Greece [griːs] Grecia f

greed [griːd] avidità f; for food ingordigia f

greed·i·ly ['griːdɪlɪ] adv con avidità; eat con ingordigia

greed·y ['griːdɪ] adj avido; for food ingordo

Greek [griːk] **1** n greco m, -a f; language greco m **2** adj greco

green [griːn] adj verde; environmentally ecologico; **the Greens** POL i verdi

green 'beans npl fagiolini mpl; **'green belt** zona f verde tutt'intorno ad una città; **'green card** driving insurance carta f verde; **green 'fin·gers**: **have ~** avere il pollice verde; **'green·gro·cer** fruttivendolo m, -a f; **'green·horn** F pivello m, -a f F; **'green·house** serra f; **'green·house ef·fect** effetto m serra; **'green·house gas** gas m inv inquinante; **green 'pep·per** vegetable peperone m

greens [griːnz] npl verdura f

greet [griːt] v/t salutare

greet·ing ['griːtɪŋ] saluto m

'greet·ings card biglietto m d'auguri

gre·gar·i·ous [grɪ'geərɪəs] adj person socievole

gre·nade [grɪ'neɪd] granata f

grew [gruː] pret → **grow**

grey [greɪ] adj grigio; hair bianco; **be going ~** cominciare ad avere i capelli bianchi

grey-haired [greɪ'heəd] adj con i capelli bianchi

'grey·hound levriero m

grid [grɪd] grata f; on map reticolato m

'grid·lock in traffic ingorgo m

grief [griːf] dolore m

grief-strick·en ['griːfstrɪkn] adj addolorato

griev·ance ['griːvəns] rimostranza f

grieve [griːv] v/i essere addolorato; **~ for s.o.** essere addolorato per qu

grill [grɪl] **1** n for cooking grill m inv; metal frame griglia f; dish grigliata f; on window grata f **2** v/t food fare alla griglia; (interrogate) mettere sotto torchio

grille [grɪl] grata f

grim [grɪm] *adj* cupo; *determination* accanito

gri·mace ['grɪməs] *n* smorfia *f*

grime [graɪm] sporcizia *f*

grim·ly ['grɪmlɪ] *adv* con aria grave

grim·y ['graɪmɪ] *adj* sudicio

grin [grɪn] **1** *n* sorriso *m* **2** *v/i* (*pret & pp -ned*) sorridere

grind [graɪnd] *v/t* (*pret & pp* **ground**) *coffee, meat* macinare; **~ one's teeth** digrignare i denti

grip [grɪp] **1** *n on rope etc* presa *f*; *he's losing his ~ losing skills* sta perdendo dei colpi; *get to ~s with sth* affrontare qc **2** *v/t* (*pret & pp -ped*) afferrare; *of brakes* fare presa su; *be ~ped by sth by panic* essere preso da qc

gripe [graɪp] **1** *n on rope etc* presa *f* lamentarsi

grip·ping ['grɪpɪŋ] *adj* avvincente

gris·tle ['grɪsl] cartilagine *f*

grit [grɪt] **1** *n* (*dirt*) granelli *mpl; for roads* sabbia *f* **2** *v/t* (*pret & pp -ted*): **~ one's teeth** stringere i denti

grit·ty ['grɪtɪ] *adj* F *book, film etc* realistico

groan [grəʊn] **1** *n* gemito *m* **2** *v/i* gemere

gro·cer ['grəʊsə(r)] droghiere *m; at the ~'s* (*shop*) dal droghiere

gro·cer·ies ['grəʊsərɪz] *npl* generi *mpl* alimentari

gro·cer·y store ['grəʊsərɪ] drogheria *f*

grog·gy ['grɒgɪ] *adj* F intontito

groin [grɔɪn] ANAT inguine *m*

groom [gruːm] **1** *n for bride* sposo *m; for horse* stalliere *m* **2** *v/t horse* strigliare; (*train, prepare*) preparare; *well ~ed in appearance* ben curato

groove [gruːv] scanalatura *f*

grope [grəʊp] **1** *v/i in the dark* brancolare **2** *v/t sexually* palpeggiare
   ♦ **grope for** *v/t door handle* cercare a tastoni; *the right word* cercare di trovare

gross [grəʊs] *adj* (*coarse, vulgar*) volgare; *exaggeration* madornale; FIN lordo

gross do·mes·tic 'prod·uct pro-

dotto *m* interno lordo

gross na·tion·al 'prod·uct prodotto *m* nazionale lordo

grot·ty ['grɒtɪ] *adj* F *street, flat* squallido; *I feel ~* sto da schifo F

ground[1] [graʊnd] **1** *n* suolo *m; (area, for sport*) terreno *m; (reason*) motivo *m*, ragione *f*; ELEC terra *f*; *on the ~* per terra; *on the ~s of* a causa di **2** *v/t* ELEC mettere a terra

ground[2] [graʊnd] *pret & pp → grind

'ground con·trol controllo *m* da terra; **'ground crew** personale *m* di terra; **'ground floor** pianoterra *m* inv

ground·ing ['graʊndɪŋ] *in subject* basi *fpl; have a good ~ in* avere delle buone basi di

ground·less ['graʊndlɪs] *adj* infondato; **'ground plan** pianta *f* del piano terra; **'ground staff** SP personale *m* addetto alla manutenzione dei campi sportivi; *at airport* personale *m* di terra; **'ground·work** lavoro *m* di preparazione

group [gruːp] **1** *n* gruppo *m* **2** *v/t* raggruppare

group·ie ['gruːpɪ] F *ragazza f che segue un gruppo o cantante rock in tutti i concerti*

group 'ther·a·py terapia *f* di gruppo

grouse[1] [graʊs] (*pl* **grouse**) *bird* gallo *m* cedrone

grouse[2] [graʊs] **1** *n* F lamentela *f* **2** *v/i* F brontolare

grov·el ['grɒvl] *v/i fig* umiliarsi

grow [grəʊ] (*pret* **grew**, *pp* **grown**) **1** *v/i of child, animal, plant* crescere; *of number, amount* aumentare; *of business* svilupparsi; *let one's hair ~* farsi crescere i capelli; **~ old / tired** invecchiare / stancarsi; **~ into sth** diventare qc **2** *v/t flowers* coltivare
   ♦ **grow up** *of person* crescere; *of city* svilupparsi; *grow up!* comportati da adulto!

growl [graʊl] **1** *n* grugnito *m* **2** *v/i* ringhiare

grown [grəʊn] *pp → grow

grown-up ['grəʊnʌp] **1** *n* adulto *m*, -a *f* **2** *adj* adulto

growth [grəʊθ] *of person* crescita *f*; *of company* sviluppo *m*; (*increase*) aumento *m*; MED tumore *m*

grub[1] [grʌb] *of insect* larva *f*

grub[2] [grʌb] F (*food*) mangiare *m*

grub·by ['grʌbɪ] *adj* sporco

grudge [grʌdʒ] **1** *n* rancore *m*; *bear s.o. a ~* portare rancore a qu **2** *v/t* dare a malincuore; *~ s.o. sth* invidiare qc a qu

grudg·ing ['grʌdʒɪŋ] *adj* riluttante

grudg·ing·ly ['grʌdʒɪŋlɪ] *adv* a malincuore

gru·el·ing *Am*, **gru·el·ling** ['gruːəlɪŋ] *adj climb, task* estenuante

gruff [grʌf] *adj* burbero

grum·ble ['grʌmbl] *v/i* brontolare

grum·bler ['grʌmblə(r)] brontolone *m*, *-a f*

grump·y ['grʌmpɪ] *adj* scontroso

grunt [grʌnt] **1** *n* grugnito *m* **2** *v/i* grugnire

guar·an·tee [gærən'tiː] **1** *n* garanzia *f*; *~ period* periodo *m* di garanzia **2** *v/t* garantire

guar·an·tor [gærən'tɔː(r)] garante *m*

guard [gɑːd] **1** *n* guardia *m*; *be on one's ~ against* stare in guardia contro **2** *v/t* fare la guardia a
♦ **guard against** *v/t* guardarsi da

'guard dog cane *m* da guardia

guard·ed ['gɑːdɪd] *adj reply* cauto

guard·i·an ['gɑːdɪən] LAW tutore *m*, *-trice f*

guard·i·an 'an·gel angelo *m* custode

guer·ril·la [gə'rɪlə] guerrigliero *m*, *-a f*

guer·ril·la 'war·fare guerriglia *f*

guess [ges] **1** *n* supposizione *f*; *I give you three ~es* ti do tre possibilità di indovinare **2** *v/t the answer* indovinare; *I ~ so* suppongo di sì; *I ~ not* suppongo di no **3** *v/i* indovinare; *I guessed correctly* ho indovinato; *I was just ~ing* ho tirato a indovinare

'guess·work congettura *f*

guest [gest] *n* ospite *m/f*

'guest·house pensione *f*

'guest·room camera *f* degli ospiti

guf·faw [gʌ'fɔː] **1** *n* sghignazzata *f* **2** *v/i* sghignazzare

guid·ance ['gaɪdəns] consigli *mpl*

guide [gaɪd] **1** *n person, book* guida *f* **2** *v/t* guidare

'guide·book guida *f* turistica

guid·ed mis·sile ['gaɪdɪd] missile *m* guidato

'guide dog cane *m* per ciechi

guid·ed 'tour visita *f* guidata

guide·lines ['gaɪdlaɪnz] *npl* direttive *fpl*

guilt [gɪlt] colpa *f*; LAW colpevolezza *f*

guilt·y ['gɪltɪ] *adj also* LAW colpevole; *have a ~ conscience* avere la coscienza sporca

guin·ea pig ['gɪnɪpɪg] porcellino *m* d'india; *for experiments, fig* cavia *f*

guise [gaɪz]: *under the ~ of* dietro la maschera di

gui·tar [gɪ'tɑː(r)] chitarra *f*

gui'tar case custodia *f* della chitarra

gui·tar·ist [gɪ'tɑːrɪst] chitarrista *m/f*

gui·tar play·er chitarrista *m/f*

gulf [gʌlf] golfo *m*; *fig* divario *m*; *the Gulf* il Golfo

gull [gʌl] *n bird* gabbiano *m*

gul·let [gʌlɪt] ANAT esofago *m*

gul·li·ble ['gʌlɪbl] *adj* credulone

gulp [gʌlp] **1** *n of water* sorso *m*; *of air* boccata *f* **2** *v/i in surprise* deglutire
♦ **gulp down** *v/t drink* ingoiare; *food* tranguggiare

gum[1] [gʌm] *in mouth* gengiva *f*

gum[2] [gʌm] *n* (*glue*) colla *f*; (*chewing gum*) gomma *f*

gump·tion ['gʌmpʃn] F sale *m* in zucca F

gun [gʌn] *pistol, revolver, rifle* arma *f* da fuoco; (*cannon*) cannone *m*
♦ **gun down** *v/t* (*pret & pp -ned*) sparare a morte a

'gun·fire spari *mpl*; **'gun·man** uomo *m* armato; *robber* rapinatore *m*; **'gun·point**: *at ~* con un'arma puntata addosso; **'gun·shot** sparo *m*; **'gun·shot wound** ferita *f* da arma da fuoco

gur·gle ['gɜːgl] *v/i of baby, drain* gorgogliare

gu·ru ['guru] *fig* guru *m inv*

gush [gʌʃ] *v/i of liquid* sgorgare

gush·y ['gʌʃɪ] *adj* F (*enthusiastic*)

iper-entusiastico
gust [gʌst] raffica f
gus·to ['gʌstəʊ]: **with ~** con slancio
gust·y ['gʌstɪ] of weather ventoso; **~ wind** vento a raffiche
gut [gʌt] **1** n intestino m; F (stomach) pancia f **2** v/t (pret & pp **-ted**) (destroy) sventrare
guts [gʌts] npl F (courage) fegato m F
guts·y ['gʌtsɪ] adj F person che ha fegato; F thing to do che richiede fegato
gut·ter ['gʌtə(r)] on pavement canaletto m di scolo; on roof grondaia f
'gutter·press pej stampa f scandalistica
guv [gʌv] F capo m, -a f F
guy [gaɪ] F tipo m F; **hey, you ~s** ei, gente

guz·zle ['gʌzl] v/t ingozzarsi di
gym [dʒɪm] palestra f; (activity) ginnastica f
'gym class educazione f fisica
gym·na·si·um [dʒɪm'neɪzɪəm] palestra f
gym·nast ['dʒɪmnæst] ginnasta m/f
gym·nas·tics [dʒɪm'næstɪks] nsg ginnastica f
'gym shoes npl scarpe fpl da ginnastica
'gym teacher insegnante m/f di educazione fisica
gy·ne·col·o·gy etc Am → **gynaecology** etc
gy·nae·col·o·gy [gaɪnɪ'kɒlədʒɪ] ginecologia f
gy·nae·col·o·gist [gaɪnɪ'kɒlədʒɪst] ginecologo m, -a f
gyp·sy ['dʒɪpsɪ] zingaro m, -a f

H

hab·it ['hæbɪt] abitudine f; **get into the ~ of doing sth** prendere l'abitudine di fare qc
hab·it·a·ble ['hæbɪtəbl] adj abitabile
hab·i·tat ['hæbɪtæt] habitat m inv
ha·bit·u·al [hə'bɪtjʊəl] adj solito; smoker, drinker incallito
hack [hæk] n (poor writer) scribacchino m
hack·er ['hækə(r)] COMPUT hacker m/f inv
hack·neyed ['hæknɪd] adj trito
had [hæd] pret & pp → **have**
had·dock ['hædək] haddock m inv
haem·or·rhage ['hemərɪdʒ] **1** n emorragia f **2** v/i avere un'emorragia
hag·gard ['hægəd] adj tirato
hag·gle ['hægl] v/i contrattare
hail [heɪl] n grandine f
'hail·stone chicco m di grandine
'hail·storm grandinata f

hair [heə(r)] capelli mpl; single capello m; on body, of animal pelo m
'hair·brush spazzola f per capelli;
'hair·cut taglio m di capelli; **'hair·do** F pettinatura f; **'hair·dress·er** parrucchiere m, -a f; **at the ~'s** dal parrucchiere; **'hair·dri·er**, **'hair·dry·er** fon m inv
hair·less ['heəlɪs] adj glabro
'hair·pin forcina f; **hair·pin 'bend** tornante m; **hair·rais·ing** ['heəreɪzɪŋ] adj terrificante; **hair re·mov·er** [heərɪ'muːvə(r)] crema f depilatoria
'hair's breadth fig: **by a ~** per un pelo
hair·split·ting ['heəsplɪtɪŋ] n pedanteria f; **'hair spray** lacca f per capelli; **'hair·style** acconciatura f; **'hair·styl·ist** parrucchiere m, -a f
hair·y ['heərɪ] adj arm, animal peloso; F (frightening) preoccupante
half [hɑːf] **1** n (pl **halves** [hɑːvz])

metà *f inv*, mezzo *m*; **~ past ten** le dieci e mezza; **~ an hour** mezz'ora; **~ a pound** mezza libbra; **go halves with s.o. on sth** fare a metà di qc con qu **2** *adj* mezzo **3** *adv* a metà

half-heart-ed [hɑːf'hɑːtɪd] *adj* poco convinto; **half 'term** *vacanza f a metà trimestre*; **half 'time 1** *n* SP intervallo *m* **2** *adj*: **~ job** lavoro a mezza giornata; **~ score** risultato alla fine del primo tempo; **half'way 1** *adj stage, point* intermedio **2** *adv also fig* a metà strada; **~ finished** fatto a metà

hall [hɔːl] *large room* sala *f*; *hallway in house* ingresso *m*

Hal-low-e'en [hæləʊ'iːn] vigilia *f* d'Ognissanti

halo ['heɪləʊ] aureola *f*

halt [hɔːlt] **1** *v/i* fermarsi **2** *v/t* fermare **3** *n*: **come to a ~** arrestarsi

halve [hɑːv] *v/t* dimezzare

ham [hæm] prosciutto *m*

ham-burg-er ['hæmbɜːgə(r)] hamburger *m inv*

ham-mer ['hæmə(r)] **1** *n* martello *m* **2** *v/i* martellare; **~ at the door** picchiare alla porta

ham-mock ['hæmək] amaca *f*

ham-per¹ ['hæmpə(r)] *n for food* cestino *m*

ham-per² ['hæmpə(r)] *v/t (obstruct)* ostacolare

ham-ster ['hæmstə(r)] criceto *m*

hand [hænd] *n* mano *m*; *of clock* lancetta *f*; *(worker)* operaio *m*; **at ~, by ~** a portata di mano; **at first ~** di prima mano; **by ~** a mano; **on the one ~ ..., on the other ~ ...** da un lato ..., dall'altro ...; **in ~** *(being done)* in corso; **on your right ~** sulla tua destra; **~s off!** giù le mani!; **~s up!** mani in alto!; **change ~s** cambiare di mano; **give s.o. a ~** dare una mano a qu

♦ **hand down** *v/t* passare
♦ **hand in** *v/t* consegnare
♦ **hand on** *v/t* passare
♦ **hand out** *v/t* distribuire
♦ **hand over** *v/t* consegnare; *child to parent etc* dare

'hand-bag borsetta *f*; **'hand-book** manuale *m*; **'hand-brake** freno *m* a mano; **'hand-cuff** *v/t* ammanettare; **hand-cuffs** ['hæn(d)kʌfs] *npl* manette *fpl*

hand-i-cap ['hændɪkæp] handicap *m inv*

hand-i-capped ['hændɪkæpt] *adj also fig* handicappato

hand-i-craft ['hændɪkrɑːft] artigianato *m*

hand-i-work ['hændɪwɜːk] opera *f*

hand-ker-chief ['hæŋkəʃɪf] fazzoletto *m*

han-dle ['hændl] **1** *n* maniglia *f* **2** *v/t goods* maneggiare; *case, deal* trattare; *difficult person* prendere; **let me ~ this** lascia fare a me; **be able to ~ s.o.** saperci fare con qu

han-dle-bars ['hændlbɑːz] *npl* manubrio *msg*

'hand lug-gage bagaglio *m* a mano; **hand-made** [hæn(d)'meɪd] *adj* fatto a mano; **'hand-rail** corrimano *m inv*; **'hand-shake** stretta *f* di mano

hands-off [hændz'ɒf] *adj approach* teorico; **he has a ~ style of management** non partecipa direttamente agli aspetti pratici della gestione

hand-some ['hænsəm] *adj* bello

hands-on [hændz'ɒn] *adj experience* pratico; **he has a ~ style of management** partecipa direttamente agli aspetti pratici della gestione

'hand-writ-ing calligrafia *f*

hand-writ-ten ['hændrɪtn] *adj* scritto a mano

hand-y ['hændɪ] *adj tool, device* pratico; **it's ~ for the shops** è comodo per i negozi; **it might come in ~** potrebbe tornare utile

hang [hæŋ] **1** *v/t (pret & pp hung) picture* appendere; *person (pret & pp hanged)* impiccare **2** *v/i (pret & pp hung) of dress, hair* cadere; **his coat was ~ing behind the door** il suo cappotto era appeso dietro la porta **3** *n*: **get the ~ of** F capire

♦ **hang about** *v/i on streets* gironzolare; **hang about a minute!** F un attimo!

♦ hang on v/i (wait) aspettare
♦ hang on to v/t (keep) tenere
♦ hang up v/i TELEC riattaccare
han·gar ['hæŋə(r)] hangar m inv
hang·er ['hæŋə(r)] for clothes gruccia f
hang glid·er ['hæŋglaɪdə(r)] deltaplano m
hang glid·ing ['hæŋglaɪdɪŋ] deltaplano m
'hang·o·ver postumi mpl della sbornia
♦ hanker after ['hæŋkə(r)] v/t desiderare
han·kie, han·ky ['hæŋkɪ] F fazzoletto m
hap·haz·ard [hæp'hæzəd] adj a casaccio
hap·pen ['hæpn] v/i succedere; if you ~ to see him se ti capita di vederlo; what has ~ed to you? cosa ti è successo?
♦ happen across v/t trovare per caso
hap·pen·ing ['hæpnɪŋ] avvenimento m
hap·pi·ly ['hæpɪlɪ] adv allegramente; (gladly) volentieri; (luckily) per fortuna
hap·pi·ness ['hæpɪnɪs] felicità f inv
hap·py ['hæpɪ] adj felice
hap·py-go-'luck·y adj spensierato
'hap·py hour orario m in cui le consumazioni costano meno
har·ass [hə'ræs] v/t tormentare; sexually molestare
har·assed [hər'æst] adj stressato
har·ass·ment [hə'ræsmənt] persecuzione f; sexual ~ molestie fpl sessuali
har·bor Am, har·bour ['hɑːbə(r)] 1 n porto m 2 v/t criminal dar rifugio a; grudge covare
hard [hɑːd] adj duro; (difficult) difficile; facts, evidence concreto; drug pesante; ~ of hearing duro d'orecchio
'hard·back n libro m con copertina rigida; hard-boiled [hɑːd'bɔɪld] adj egg sodo; 'hard cop·y copia f stampata; 'hard core n (pornography)

pornografia f hard-core; hard 'cur·ren·cy valuta f forte; hard 'disk hard disk m inv
hard·en ['hɑːdn] 1 v/t indurire 2 v/i of glue indurirsi; of attitude irrigidirsi
'hard hat casco m; (construction worker) muratore m; hard·head·ed [hɑː'hedɪd] adj pratico; hard·heart·ed [hɑːd'hɑːtɪd] adj dal cuore duro; hard 'line linea f dura; hard·lin·er sostenitore m, -trice f della linea dura
hard·ly ['hɑːdlɪ] adv a malapena; ~ ever quasi mai; you can ~ expect him to ... non puoi certo aspettarti che lui ...; ~! ci mancherebbe!
hard·ness ['hɑːdnɪs] durezza f, (difficulty) difficoltà f inv
hard·'sell tecnica f aggressiva di vendita
hard·ship ['hɑːdʃɪp] difficoltà fpl economiche
hard 'shoul·der corsia f di emergenza; hard 'up adj al verde; 'hard·ware ferramenta fpl; COMPUT hardware m inv; 'hard·ware store negozio m di ferramenta; hard·work·ing [hɑːd'wɜːkɪŋ] adj che lavora duro
har·dy ['hɑːdɪ] adj resistente
hare [heə(r)] lepre f
hare·brained ['heəbreɪnd] adj pazzo
harm [hɑːm] 1 n danno m; it wouldn't do any ~ to ... non sarebbe una cattiva idea ... 2 v/t danneggiare
harm·ful ['hɑːmfʊl] adj dannoso
harm·less ['hɑːmlɪs] adj innocuo
har·mo·ni·ous [hɑː'məʊnɪəs] adj armonioso
har·mo·nize ['hɑːmənaɪz] v/i armonizzare
har·mo·ny ['hɑːmənɪ] armonia f
harp [hɑːp] n arpa f
♦ harp on about v/t F menarsela su F
har·poon [hɑː'puːn] arpione m
harsh [hɑːʃ] adj criticism, words duro; colour, light troppo forte
harsh·ly ['hɑːʃlɪ] adv duramente
har·vest ['hɑːvɪst] n raccolto m

H

hash [hæʃ] n F: **make a ~ of** fare un pasticcio di

hash·ish ['hæʃiːʃ] hashish m inv

'hash mark cancelletto m

haste [heɪst] n fretta f

has·ten ['heɪsn] v/i: **~ to do sth** affrettarsi a fare qc

hast·i·ly ['heɪstɪlɪ] adv in fretta

hast·y ['heɪstɪ] adj frettoloso

hat [hæt] cappello m

hatch [hætʃ] n for serving food passavivande m inv; on ship boccaporto m

♦ hatch out v/i of eggs schiudersi

hatch·et ['hætʃɪt] ascia f; **bury the ~** seppellire l'ascia di guerra

hate [heɪt] 1 n odio m 2 v/t odiare

ha·tred ['heɪtrɪd] odio m

haugh·ty ['hɔːtɪ] adj altezzoso

haul [hɔːl] 1 n of fish pescata f 2 v/t (pull) trascinare

haul·age ['hɔːlɪdʒ] autotrasporto m

'haul·age com·pa·ny impresa f di autotrasporto

haul·i·er ['hɔːlɪə(r)] autotrasportatore m

haunch [hɔːntʃ] anca f

haunt [hɔːnt] 1 v/t: **this place is ~ed** questo posto è infestato dai fantasmi 2 n ritrovo m

haunt·ing ['hɔːntɪŋ] adj tune indimenticabile

have [hæv] (pret & pp had) 1 v/t ◊ avere; breakfast, shower avere; **can I ~ ...?** posso avere ...?; **I'll ~ a coffee** prendo un caffè; **~ lunch/dinner** pranzare/cenare; **do you ~ ...?** ha ...? ◊ must: **~ (got) to** dovere; **I ~ (got) to go** devo andare ◊ causative: **~ sth done** far fare qc; **I had the printer fixed** ho fatto riparare la stampante; **I had my hair cut** mi sono tagliata i capelli 2 v/aux avere; with verbs of motion essere; **~ you seen her?** l'hai vista?; **I ~ come** sono venuto

♦ have back v/t: **when can I have it back?** quando posso riaverlo?

♦ have on v/t (wear) portare, indossare; **do you have anything on tonight?** (have planned) hai programmi per stasera?

ha·ven ['heɪvn] fig oasi f inv

hav·oc ['hævək] caos m inv; **play ~ with** scombussolare

hawk [hɔːk] also fig falco m

hay [heɪ] fieno m

'hay fe·ver raffreddore m da fieno

'hay stack pagliaio m

haz·ard ['hæzəd] n rischio m

'haz·ard lights npl MOT luci fpl di emergenza

haz·ard·ous ['hæzədəs] adj rischioso

haze [heɪz] foschia f

ha·zel ['heɪzl] n (tree) nocciolo m

'ha·zel·nut nocciola f

haz·y ['heɪzɪ] adj view, image indistinto; memories vago; **I'm a bit ~ about it** non ne sono certo

he [hiː] pron lui; **~'s French** è francese; **you're funny, ~'s not** tu sei spiritoso, lui no; **there ~ is** eccolo

head [hed] 1 n testa f; (boss, leader) capo m; of primary school direttore m, -trice f; of secondary school preside m/f; on beer schiuma f; of nail capocchia f; of queue, line inizio m; of tape recorder testina f; **£15 a ~** 15 sterline a testa; **~s or tails?** testa o croce?; **at the ~ of the list** in cima alla lista; **~ over heels** fall a capofitto; **~ over heels in love** pazzamente innamorato; **lose one's ~** (go crazy) perdere la testa 2 v/t (lead) essere a capo di; ball colpire di testa

'head·ache mal m di testa

'head·band fascia f per i capelli

head·er ['hedə(r)] in soccer colpo m di testa; in document intestazione f

'head·hunt v/t COM: **be ~ed** essere selezionato da un cacciatore di teste

'head·hunt·er COM cacciatore m di teste

head·ing ['hedɪŋ] in list titolo m

'head·lamp fanale m; 'head·land promontorio m; 'head·light fanale m; 'head·line n in newspaper titolo; **make the ~s** fare titolo; 'head·long adv fall a testa in giù; 'head·mas·ter in primary school direttore m; in secondary school preside m; 'head·mis·tress in primary *school* direttrice *f*; *in secondary school* preside *f*; **head 'of·fice** *of company* sede *f* centrale; **head·'on 1** *adv* crash frontalmente **2** *adj* crash frontale; **'head·phones** *npl* cuffie *fpl*; **'head·quar·ters** *npl* sede *fsg*; MIL quartier *msg* generale; **'head·rest** poggiatesta *m inv*; **'head·room** *for vehicle under bridge* altezza *f* utile; *in car* altezza *f* dell'abitacolo; **'head·scarf** foulard *m inv*; **'head·strong** *adj* testardo; **head 'teach·er** *in primary school* direttore *m*, -trice *f*; *in secondary school* preside *m/f*; **head 'wait·er** capocameriere *m*; **'head·wind** vento *m* di prua

head·y ['hedɪ] *adj drink, wine etc* inebriante

heal [hiːl] *v/t v/i* guarire

♦ **heal up** *v/i* cicatrizzarsi

health [helθ] salute *f*; (*public* ~) sanità *f inv*; **your** ~! (alla) salute!

'health care assistenza *f* sanitaria

'health farm beauty farm *f inv*; **'health food** alimenti *mpl* macrobiotici; **'health food store** negozio *m* di macrobiotica; **'health in·su·rance** assicurazione *f* contro le malattie; **'health re·sort** stazione *f* termale

health·y ['helθɪ] *adj also fig* sano

heap [hiːp] *n* mucchio *m*

♦ **heap up** *v/t* ammucchiare

hear [hɪə(r)] *v/t & v/i* (*pret & pp* **heard**) sentire

♦ **hear about** *v/t* sapere di

♦ **hear from** *v/t* (*have news from*) avere notizie di

heard [hɜːd] *pret & pp* → **hear**

hear·ing ['hɪərɪŋ] udito *m*; LAW udienza *f*; **be within / out of** ~ essere / non essere a portata di voce

'hear·ing aid apparecchio *m* acustico

'hear·say diceria *f*; **by** ~ per sentito dire

hearse [hɜːs] carro *m* funebre

heart [hɑːt] cuore *m*; *of problem etc* nocciolo *m*; **know sth by** ~ sapere qc a memoria

'heart at·tack infarto *m*; **'heart·beat** battito *m* cardiaco; **'heart·break·ing** ['hɑːtbreɪkɪŋ] *adj* straziante; **'heart·brok·en** *adj* affranto; **'heart·burn** bruciore *m* di stomaco; **'heart fail·ure** infarto *m*; **heart·felt** ['hɑːtfelt] *adj sympathy* sentito

hearth [hɑːθ] focolare *m*

heart·less ['hɑːtlɪs] *adj* spietato

heart·rend·ing ['hɑːtrendɪŋ] *adj plea, sight* straziante

hearts [hɑːts] *npl in cards* cuori *mpl*

'heart throb F idolo *m*

'heart trans·plant trapianto *m* cardiaco

heart·y ['hɑːtɪ] *adj appetite* robusto; *meal* sostanzioso; *person* gioviale

heat [hiːt] calore *m*; (*hot weather*) caldo *m*

♦ **heat up** *v/t* riscaldare

heat·ed ['hiːtɪd] *adj swimming pool* riscaldato; *discussion* animato

heat·er ['hiːtə(r)] *radiator* termosifone *m*; *electric, gas* stufa *f*; *in car* riscaldamento *m*

heath [hiːθ] brughiera *f*

hea·then ['hiːðn] *n* pagano *m*, -a *f*

heath·er ['heðə(r)] erica *f*

heat·ing ['hiːtɪŋ] riscaldamento *m*

'heat·proof, 'heat-re·sis·tant *adj* termoresistente; **'heat·stroke** colpo *m* di calore; **'heat·wave** ondata *f* di caldo

heave [hiːv] *v/t* (*lift*) sollevare

heav·en ['hevn] paradiso *m*; **good ~s!** santo cielo!

heav·en·ly ['hevnlɪ] *adj* F divino

heav·y ['hevɪ] *adj* pesante; *cold, rain, accent* forte; *traffic* intenso; *food* pesante; *smoker* accanito; *drinker* forte; *financial loss, casualties* ingente; **be a ~ sleeper** avere il sonno pesante

heav·y·-'du·ty *adj* resistente

heav·y·weight *adj* SP di pesi massimi

heck·le ['hekl] *v/t* interrompere di continuo

hec·tic ['hektɪk] *adj* frenetico

hedge [hedʒ] *n* siepe *f*

H

hedge·hog ['hedʒhɒg] riccio *m*

hedge·row ['hedʒrəʊ] siepe *f*

heed [hiːd] *v/t:* **pay ~ to ...** ascoltare ...

heel [hiːl] *of foot* tallone *m*, calcagno *m*; *of shoe* tacco *m*

'**heel bar** calzoleria *f* istantanea

hef·ty ['heftɪ] *adj* massiccio

height [haɪt] altezza *f*; *of aeroplane* altitudine *f*; **at the ~ of summer** nel pieno dell'estate

height·en ['haɪtn] *v/t effect, tension* aumentare

heir [eə(r)] erede *m*

heir·ess ['eərɪs] ereditiera *f*

held [held] *pret & pp →* **hold**

hel·i·cop·ter ['helɪkɒptə(r)] elicottero *m*

hell [hel] inferno *m*; **what the ~ are you doing / do you want?** F che diavolo fai / vuoi? F; **go to ~!** F va' all'inferno! F; **a ~ of a lot** F un casino F; **one ~ of a nice guy** F un tipo in gambissima

hel·lo [hə'ləʊ] *int informal* ciao; *more formal* buongiorno; buona sera; TELEC pronto; **say ~ to s.o.** salutare qu

helm [helm] NAUT timone *m*

hel·met ['helmɪt] *of motorcyclist* casco *m*; *of soldier* elmetto *m*

help [help] **1** *n* aiuto *m* **2** *v/t* aiutare; **~ o.s.** servirsi; **I can't ~ it** non ci posso far niente; **I couldn't ~ laughing** non ho potuto fare a meno di ridere

help·er ['helpə(r)] aiutante *m/f*

help·ful ['helpfʊl] *adj person* di aiuto; *advice* utile; **he was very ~** mi è stato di grande aiuto

help·ing ['helpɪŋ] *of food* porzione *f*

help·less ['helplɪs] *adj* (*unable to cope*) indifeso; (*powerless*) impotente

help·less·ly ['helplɪslɪ] *adv:* **we watched ~** guardavamo impotenti

help·less·ness ['helplɪsnɪs] impotenza *f*

'**help me·nu** COMPUT menu *m inv* della guida in linea

hem [hem] *n of dress etc* orlo *m*

hem·i·sphere ['hemɪsfɪə(r)] emisfero *m*

'**hem·line** orlo *m*

hen [hen] gallina *f*

hench·man ['hentʃmən] *pej* scagnozzo *m*

'**hen par·ty** equivalente *m* al femminile della festa d'addio al celibato

hen-pecked ['henpekt] *adj:* **~ husband** marito *m* succube della moglie

hep·a·ti·tis [hepə'taɪtɪs] epatite *f*

her [hɜː(r)] **1** *adj* il suo *m*, la sua *f*, i suoi *mpl*, le sue *fpl*; **~ ticket** il suo biglietto; **~ brother / sister** suo fratello / sua sorella **2** *pron direct object* la; *indirect object* le; *after prep* lei; **I know ~** la conosco; **I gave ~ the keys** le ho dato le chiavi; **this is for ~** questo è per lei; **who? ~ ~** chi? – lei

herb [hɜːb] *for medicines* erba *f* medicinale; *for flavouring* erba *f* aromatica

herb(al) '**tea** ['hɜːb(əl)] tisana *f*

herd [hɜːd] *n* mandria *f*

here [hɪə(r)] *adv* qui, qua; **~'s to you!** *as toast* salute!; **~ you are** *giving sth* ecco qui; **~!** *in roll-call* presente!

he·red·i·ta·ry [hə'redɪtərɪ] *adj disease* ereditario

he·red·i·ty [hə'redɪtɪ] ereditarietà *f inv*

her·i·tage ['herɪtɪdʒ] patrimonio *m*

her·mit ['hɜːmɪt] eremita *m/f*

her·ni·a ['hɜːnɪə] MED ernia *f*

he·ro ['hɪərəʊ] eroe *m*

he·ro·ic [hɪ'rəʊɪk] *adj* eroico

he·ro·i·cal·ly [hɪ'rəʊɪklɪ] *adv* eroicamente

her·o·in ['herəʊɪn] eroina *f*

'**her·o·in ad·dict** eroinomane *m/f*

her·o·ine ['herəʊɪn] eroina *f*

her·o·ism ['herəʊɪzm] eroismo *m*

her·on ['herən] airone *m*

her·pes ['hɜːpiːz] MED herpes *m*

her·ring ['herɪŋ] aringa *f*

hers [hɜːz] *pron* il suo *m*, la sua *f*, i suoi *mpl*, le sue *fpl*; **a friend of ~** un suo amico

her·self [hɜː'self] *pron reflexive* si;

emphatic se stessa; *after prep* sé, se stessa; *she must be proud of ~* deve'essere fiera di sé *o* se stessa; *she hurt ~* si è fatta male; *she told me so* ~ me l'ha detto lei stessa; *by ~* da sola

hes·i·tant ['hezɪtənt] *adj* esitante

hes·i·tant·ly ['hezɪtəntlɪ] *adv* con esitazione

hes·i·tate ['hezɪteɪt] *v/i* esitare

hes·i·ta·tion [hezɪ'teɪʃn] esitazione *f*

het·er·o·sex·u·al [hetərəʊ'seksjʊəl] *adj* eterosessuale

hey·day ['heɪdeɪ] tempi *mpl* d'oro

hi [haɪ] *int* ciao

hi·ber·nate ['haɪbəneɪt] *v/i* andare in letargo

hic·cup ['hɪkʌp] *n* singhiozzo *m*; (*minor problem*) intoppo *m*; *have the ~s* avere il singhiozzo

hid [hɪd] *pret* → **hide**

hid·den ['hɪdn] **1** *adj* nascosto **2** *pp* → **hide**

hid·den a'gen·da *fig* secondo fine *m*

hide¹ [haɪd] (*pret* **hid**, *pp* **hidden**) **1** *v/t* nascondere **2** *v/i* nascondersi

hide² [haɪd] *n of animal* pelle *f*

hide-and-'seek nascondino *m*

'hide·a·way rifugio *m*

hid·e·ous ['hɪdɪəs] *adj face, weather* orrendo; *crime* atroce

hid·ing¹ ['haɪdɪŋ] (*beating*) batosta *f*

hid·ing² ['haɪdɪŋ] *n*: *be in ~* tenersi nascosto; *go into ~* darsi alla macchia

'hid·ing place nascondiglio *m*

hi·er·ar·chy ['haɪərɑːkɪ] gerarchia *f*

hi-fi ['haɪfaɪ] hi-fi *m inv*

high [haɪ] **1** *adj building, price, mountain, note, temperature, salary* alto; *wind, speed* forte; *quality, hopes* buono; (*on drugs*) fatto F; *~ in the sky* in alto nel cielo; *have a very ~ opinion of …* stimare molto …; *it is ~ time he left* sarebbe ora che se ne andasse **2** *n in statistics* livello *m* record **3** *adv* in alto

'high·brow *adj* intellettuale; **'high·chair** seggiolone *m*; **high·'class** *adj* di (prima) classe; **High 'Court** Corte *f* Suprema; **high 'div·ing** tuffo *m*;

high·'fre·quen·cy *adj* ad alta frequenza; **high·'grade** *adj* di buona qualità; **high·hand·ed** [haɪ'hænd-ɪd] *adj* autoritario; **high-heeled** [haɪ'hiːld] *adj* col tacco alto; **'high jump** salto *m* in alto; **high·'lev·el** *adj* ad alto livello; **'high life** bella vita *f*; **'high·light 1** *n* (*main event*) clou *m inv*; *in hair* colpo *m* di sole **2** *v/t with pen* evidenziare; COMPUT selezionare; **'high·light·er** *pen* evidenziatore *m*

high·ly ['haɪlɪ] *adv desirable, likely* molto; *be ~ paid* essere pagato profumatamente; *think ~ of s.o.* stimare molto qu

high·ly 'strung *adj* nervoso

high per'form·ance *adj drill, battery* ad alto rendimento; **high-pitched** [haɪ'pɪtʃt] *adj* acuto; **'high point** clou *m inv*; **high-pow·ered** [haɪ'paʊəd] *adj engine* potente; *intellectual* di prestigio; **high 'pres·sure 1** *n weather* alta pressione *f* **2** *adj* TECH ad alta pressione; *salesman* aggressivo; **high 'priest** gran sacerdote *m*; **'high·rise** palazzone *m*; **'high school** scuola *f* superiore; **high so'ci·e·ty** alta società *f inv*; **high-speed 'train** treno *m* ad alta velocità; **'high street** via *f* principale; **high 'tech 1** *n* high-tech *m inv* **2** *adj* high tech; **high 'tide** marea *f*; **high-'volt·age** alta tensione *f*; **high 'wa·ter** alta marea *f*; **High·way 'Code** Codice *m* stradale

hi·jack ['haɪdʒæk] **1** *v/t* dirottare **2** *n* dirottamento *m*

hi·jack·er ['haɪdʒækə(r)] dirottatore *m*, -trice *f*

hike¹ [haɪk] **1** *n* camminata *f* **2** *v/i* fare camminate

hike² [haɪk] *n in prices* aumento *m*

hik·er ['haɪkə(r)] escursionista *m/f*

hik·ing ['haɪkɪŋ] escursionismo *m*

'hik·ing boots *npl* scarponcini *mpl* da camminata

hi·lar·i·ous [hɪ'leərɪəs] *adj* divertentissimo

hill [hɪl] collina *f*; (*slope*) altura *f*

hill·side ['hɪlsaɪd] pendio *m*

hill·top ['hɪltɒp] cima *f* della collina

hill·y ['hɪlɪ] *adj* collinoso

hilt [hɪlt] impugnatura *f*

him [hɪm] *pron direct object* lo; *indirect object* gli; *after prep* lui; *I know* ~ lo conosco; *I gave* ~ *the keys* gli ho dato le chiavi; *this is for* ~ questo è per lui; *who?* – ~ chi? – lui

him·self [hɪm'self] *pron* se stesso; *after prep* sé, se stesso; *he must be proud of* ~ dev'essere fiero di sé *o* se stesso; *he hurt* ~ si è fatto male; *he told me so* ~ me l'ha detto lui stesso; *by* ~ da solo

hind [haɪnd] *adj* posteriore

hin·der ['hɪndə(r)] *v/t* intralciare

hin·drance ['hɪndrəns] intralcio *m*

hind·sight ['haɪndsaɪt] *with* ~ con il senno di poi

hinge [hɪndʒ] cardine *m*

♦ **hinge on** *v/t* dipendere da

hint [hɪnt] *n* (*clue*) accenno *m*; (*piece of advice*) consiglio *m*; (*implied suggestion*) allusione *f*; *of red, sadness etc* punta *f*

hip [hɪp] *n* fianco *m*

hip 'pock·et tasca *f* posteriore

hip·po·pot·a·mus [hɪpə'pɒtəməs] ippopotamo *m*

hire ['haɪə(r)] *v/t room, hall* affittare; *workers, staff* assumere; *conjuror etc* ingaggiare

hire 'pur·chase acquisto *m* rateale

his [hɪz] **1** *adj* il suo *m*, la sua *f*, i suoi *mpl*, le sue *fpl*; ~ *bag* la sua valigia; ~ *brother* / *sister* suo fratello / sua sorella **2** *pron* il suo *m*, la sua *f*, i suoi *mpl*, le sue *fpl*; *a friend of* ~ un suo amico

hiss [hɪs] *v/i* sibilare

his·to·ri·an [hɪ'stɔːrɪən] storico *m*, -a *f*

his·tor·ic [hɪ'stɒrɪk] *adj* storico

his·tor·i·cal [hɪ'stɒrɪkl] *adj* storico

his·to·ry ['hɪstərɪ] storia *f*

hit [hɪt] **1** *v/t* (*pret & pp hit*) colpire; (*collide with*) sbattere contro; *I* ~ *my knee* ho battuto il ginocchio; *he was* ~ *by a bullet* è stato colpito da un proiettile; *it suddenly* ~ *me* (*I realized*) improvvisamente ho realizzato; ~ *town* (*arrive*) arrivare (in città) **2** *n* (*blow*) colpo *m*; (*success*) successo *m*

♦ **hit back** *v/i* reagire

♦ **hit on** *v/t idea* trovare

♦ **hit out at** *v/t* (*criticize*) attaccare

hit-and-run *adj:* ~ *accident* incidente *m* con omissione di soccorso

hitch [hɪtʃ] **1** *n* (*problem*) contrattempo *m*; *without a* ~ senza contrattempi **2** *v/t:* ~ *sth to sth* legare qc a qc; *with hook* agganciare qc a qc; ~ *a lift* chiedere un passaggio **3** *v/i* (*hitchhike*) fare l'autostop

♦ **hitch up** *v/t wagon, trailer* attaccare

hitch·hike *v/i* fare l'autostop

hitch·hik·er autostoppista *m/f*

hitch·hik·ing autostop *m inv*

hi-'tech 1 *n* high-tech *m inv* **2** *adj* high tech

hit·list libro *m* nero; **hit·man** sicario *m*; **hit-or-'miss** *adj:* *on a* ~ *basis* affidandosi al caso; **hit squad** commando *m*

HIV [eɪtʃaɪ'viː] *abbr* (= *human immunodeficiency virus*) HIV *m*

hive [haɪv] *for bees* alveare *m*

♦ **hive off** *v/t* (COM: *separate off*) separare

HIV-'pos·i·tive sieropositivo

hoard [hɔːd] **1** *n* provvista *f*; ~ *of money* gruzzolo *m* **2** *v/t* accumulare

hoard·er ['hɔːdə(r)] *persona f che non butta mai niente*

hoarse [hɔːs] *adj* rauco

hoax [həʊks] *n* scherzo *m*; *malicious* falso allarme *m*

hob [hɒb] *on cooker* piano *m* di cottura

hob·ble ['hɒbl] *v/i* zoppicare

hob·by ['hɒbɪ] hobby *m inv*

hock·ey ['hɒkɪ] hockey *m* (su prato)

hoist [hɔɪst] **1** *n* montacarichi *m inv* **2** *v/t* (*lift*) sollevare; *flag* issare

hold [həʊld] **1** *v/t* (*pret & pp held*) *in hand* tenere; (*support, keep in place*) reggere; *passport, licence* avere; *prisoner, suspect* trattenere; (*contain*) contenere; *job*, *post* occupare; *course* tenere; **~ hands** tenersi per mano; **~ one's breath** trattenere il fiato; **he can ~ his drink** regge bene l'alcol; **~ s.o. responsible** ritenere qu responsabile; **~ that ...** (*believe*, *maintain*) sostenere che ...; **~ the line** TELEC resti in linea **2** *n in ship*, *plane* stiva *f*; **catch ~ of sth** afferrare qc; **lose one's ~ on sth** *on rope etc* perdere la presa su qc

◆ **hold against** *v/t*: **hold sth against s.o.** volerne a qu per qc

◆ **hold back 1** *v/t crowds* contenere; *facts* nascondere **2** *v/i* (*hesitate*) esitare; **he's holding back** *not telling all* non sta dicendo tutta la verità

◆ **hold on** *v/i* (*wait*) attendere; TELEC restare in linea; **now hold on a minute!** aspetta un attimo!

◆ **hold on to** *v/t* (*keep*) tenere; *belief* aggrapparsi a

◆ **hold out 1** *v/t hand* tendere; *prospect* offrire **2** *v/i of supplies* durare; *of trapped miners etc* resistere

◆ **hold up 1** *v/t hand* alzare; *bank etc* rapinare; (*make late*) trattenere; **hold sth up as an example** portare qc ad esempio

◆ **hold with** *v/t* (*approve of*) essere d'accordo con

'**hold·all** borsone *m*

hold·er ['həʊldə(r)] (*container*) contenitore *m*; *of passport* titolare *m*; *of ticket* possessore *m*; *of record* detentore *m*, -trice *f*

'**hold·ing com·pa·ny** holding *f inv*

'**hold·up** (*robbery*) rapina *f*; (*delay*) ritardo *m*

hole [həʊl] buco *m*

hol·i·day ['hɒlədeɪ] vacanza *f*; *public giorno m festivo*; (*day off*) giorno *m* di ferie; **go on ~** andare in vacanza

hol·i·day·mak·er ['hɒlədeɪmeɪkə(r)] vacanziere *m*, -a *f*

Hol·land ['hɒlənd] Olanda *f*

hol·low ['hɒləʊ] *adj object* cavo, vuoto; *cheeks* infossato

hol·ly ['hɒlɪ] agrifoglio *m*

hol·o·caust ['hɒləkɔːst] olocausto *m*

hol·o·gram ['hɒləgræm] ologramma *m*

hol·ster ['həʊlstə(r)] fondina *f*

ho·ly ['həʊlɪ] *adj* santo

Ho·ly 'Spir·it Spirito *m* Santo

'**Ho·ly Week** settimana *f* santa

home [həʊm] **1** *n* casa *f*; (*native country*) patria *f*; *for old people* casa *f* di riposo; *for children* istituto *m*; **at ~** a casa; **make yourself at ~** fai come a casa tua; **at ~** SP in casa; **work from ~** lavorare da casa **2** *adv* a casa; **go ~** andare a casa; **is she ~ yet?** è tornata?

'**home ad·dress** indirizzo *m* di casa; **home 'bank·ing** home-banking *m inv*; '**home·com·ing** ritorno *m*; **home com'put·er** computer *m inv* (per casa)

home·less ['həʊmlɪs] *adj* senza tetto; **the ~** i senzacasa

'**home·lov·ing** *adj* casalingo

home·ly ['həʊmlɪ] *adj* semplice; (*welcoming*) accogliente

home'made *adj* fatto in casa, casalingo; '**home match** incontro *m* casalingo; **home 'mov·ie** filmino *m* (casalingo); '**Home Of·fice** Ministero *m* degli Interni

'**home page** home page *f*; **Home 'Sec·ret·ar·y** Ministro *m* degli Interni; '**home·sick** *adj*: **be ~** avere nostalgia di casa; '**home town** città *f inv* natale

home·ward ['həʊmwəd] *adv* verso casa

'**home·work** EDU compiti *mpl* a casa

'**home·work·ing** COM telelavoro *m inv*

hom·i·cide ['hɒmɪsaɪd] *crime* omicidio *m*; *Am*: *police department* (squadra *f*) omicidi *f*

hom·o·graph ['hɒməgræf] omografo *m*

ho·mo·pho·bi·a [həʊmə'fəʊbɪə] omofobia *f*

ho·mo·sex·u·al [həʊmə'seksjʊəl] **1** *adj* omosessuale **2** *n* omosessuale *m/f*

H

hon·est ['ɒnɪst] *adj* onesto

hon·est·ly ['ɒnɪstlɪ] *adv* onestamente; **~!** ma insomma!

hon·es·ty ['ɒnɪstɪ] onestà *f inv*

hon·ey ['hʌnɪ] miele *m*; F *(darling)* tesoro *m*

'hon·ey·comb favo *m*

'hon·ey·moon *n* luna *f* di miele

honk [hɒŋk] *v/t horn* suonare

hon·or *etc Am* → **honour** *etc*

hon·our ['ɒnə(r)] **1** *n* onore *m* **2** *v/t* onorare

hon·our·a·ble ['ɒnrəbl] *adj* onorevole

hood [hʊd] *over head* cappuccio *m*; *over cooker* cappa *f*; MOT: *on convertible* capote *f inv*

hood·lum ['huːdləm] gangster *m inv*

hoof [huːf] zoccolo *m*

hook [hʊk] gancio *m*; *for fishing* amo *m*; **off the ~** TELEC staccato

hooked [hʊkt] *adj*: **be ~ on s.o. / sth** essere fanatico di qu / qc; **be ~ on sth** *on drugs* essere assuefatto a qc

hook·er ['hʊkə(r)] F prostituta *f*; *in rugby* tallonatore *m*

hoo·li·gan ['huːlɪgən] teppista *m/f*

hoo·li·gan·is·m ['huːlɪgənɪzm] teppismo *m*

hoop [huːp] cerchio *m*

hoot [huːt] **1** *v/t horn* suonare **2** *v/i of car* suonare il clacson; *of owl* gufare

hoo·ver® ['huːvə(r)] **1** *n* aspirapolvere *m* **2** *v/t carpets, room* pulire con l'aspirapolvere

hop¹ [hɒp] *n plant* luppolo *m*

hop² [hɒp] *v/i (pret & pp -ped)* saltare

hope [həʊp] **1** *n* speranza *f*; **there's no ~ of that** non farci conto **2** *v/i* sperare; **~ for sth** augurarsi qc; **I – so** spero di sì; **I – not** spero di no **3** *v/t*: **I – you like it** spero che ti piaccia

hope·ful ['həʊpfʊl] *adj person* ottimista; *(promising)* promettente

hope·ful·ly ['həʊpflɪ] *adv say, wait* con ottimismo; *(I/we hope)* si spera

hope·less ['həʊplɪs] *adj position, prospect* senza speranza; *(useless: person)* negato F

ho·ri·zon [hə'raɪzn] orizzonte *m*

hor·i·zon·tal [hɒrɪ'zɒntl] *adj* orizzontale

hor·mone ['hɔːməʊn] ormone *m*

horn [hɔːn] *of animal* corno *m*; MOT clacson *m inv*

hor·net ['hɔːnɪt] calabrone *m*

horn-rimmed 'spec·ta·cles [hɔːnrɪmd] *npl* occhiali *mpl* con montatura di tartaruga

horn·y ['hɔːnɪ] *adj* F *sexually* arrapato P

hor·o·scope ['hɒrəskəʊp] oroscopo *m*

hor·ri·ble ['hɒrɪbl] *adj* orribile

hor·ri·fy ['hɒrɪfaɪ] *v/t (pret & pp -ied)* inorridire; **I was horrified** ero scioccato

hor·ri·fy·ing ['hɒrɪfaɪɪŋ] *adj experience* terrificante; *idea, prices* allucinante

hor·ror ['hɒrə(r)] orrore *m*; **the ~s of war** le atrocità della guerra

'hor·ror mov·ie film *m* dell'orrore

hors d'oeu·vre [ɔː'dɜːvr] antipasto *m*

horse [hɔːs] cavallo *m*

'horse·back *n*: **on ~** a cavallo; **horse 'chest·nut** ippocastano *m*; **'horse·pow·er** cavallo-vapore *m*; **'horse·shoe** ferro *m* di cavallo

hor·ti·cul·ture ['hɔːtɪkʌltʃə(r)] orticoltura *f*

hose [həʊz] *n* tubo *m* di gomma

hos·pice ['hɒspɪs] ospedale *m* per i malati terminali

hos·pi·ta·ble [hɒ'spɪtəbl] *adj* ospitale

hos·pi·tal ['hɒspɪtl] ospedale *m*; **go into ~** essere ricoverato (in ospedale)

hos·pi·tal·i·ty [hɒspɪ'tælətɪ] ospitalità *f inv*

host [həʊst] *n at party, reception* padrone *m* di casa; *of TV programme* presentatore *m*, -trice *f*

hos·tage ['hɒstɪdʒ] ostaggio *m*; **be taken ~** essere preso in ostaggio

hos·tel ['hɒstl] *for students* pensionato *m*; *(youth ~)* ostello *m* (della gioventù)

hos·tess ['həʊstɪs] *at party, reception*

padrona *f* di casa; *on aeroplane* hostess *f inv*

hos·tile ['hɒstaɪl] *adj* ostile

hos·til·i·ty [hɒ'stɪlətɪ] ostilità *f inv*

hot [hɒt] *adj weather, water* caldo; *(spicy)* piccante; F *(good)* bravo *(at sth* in qc); *it's* ~ fa caldo; *I'm* ~ ho caldo

'hot dog hot dog *m inv*

ho·tel [hǝʊ'tel] albergo *m*

'hot·plate piastra *f* riscaldante

'hot spot *military, political* zona *f* calda

hour ['aʊǝ(r)] ora *f*

hour·ly ['aʊǝlɪ] *adj pay, rate* a ora; *at* ~ *intervals* ad ogni ora

house [haʊs] 1 *n* casa *f*; POL camera *f*; THEA sala *f*; *at your* ~ a casa tua, da te 2 *v/t* [haʊz] alloggiare

'house·boat house boat *f inv*; 'house·break·ing furto *m* con scasso; 'house·hold famiglia *f*; 'house·hold 'name nome *m* conosciuto; 'house hus·band casalingo *m*; 'house·keep·er governante *f*; 'house·keep·ing *activity* governo *m* della casa; *money* soldi *mpl* per le spese di casa; house·warm·ing (par·ty) ['haʊswɔːmɪŋ] festa *f* per inaugurare la nuova casa; 'house·wife casalinga *f*; 'house·work lavori *mpl* domestici

hous·ing ['haʊzɪŋ] alloggi *mpl*; TECH alloggiamento *m*

hov·el ['hɒvl] tugurio *m*

hov·er ['hɒvǝ(r)] *v/i* librarsi

'hov·er·craft hovercraft *m inv*

how [haʊ] *adv* come; ~ *are you?* come stai?; ~ *about …?* che ne dici di …?; ~ *much?* quanto?; ~ *much is it? of cost* quant'è?; ~ *many?* quanti?; ~ *often?* ogni quanto?; ~ *odd / lovely!* che strano / bello!

how·ev·er *adv* comunque; ~ *big / rich they are* per quanto grandi / ricchi siano

howl [haʊl] *v/i of dog* ululare; *of person in pain* urlare; ~ *with laughter* sbellicarsi dalle risate

howl·er ['haʊlǝ(r)] *mistake* strafalcione *m*

hub [hʌb] *of wheel* mozzo *m*

'hub·cap coprimozzo *m*

♦ hud·dle to·geth·er ['hʌdl] *v/i* stringersi l'un l'altro

hue [hjuː] tinta *f*

huff [hʌf]: *be in a* ~ essere imbronciato

hug [hʌg] 1 *v/t (pret & pp* -ged *)* abbracciare 2 *n* abbraccio *m*

huge [hjuːdʒ] *adj* enorme

hull [hʌl] scafo *m*

hul·la·ba·loo [hʌlǝbǝ'luː] baccano *m*

hum [hʌm] *(pret & pp* -med *)* 1 *v/t song, tune* canticchiare 2 *v/i of person* canticchiare; *of machine* ronzare

hu·man ['hjuːmǝn] 1 *n* essere *m* umano 2 *adj* umano; ~ *error* errore *m* umano

hu·man 'be·ing essere *m* umano

hu·mane [hjuː'meɪn] *adj* umano

hu·man·i·tar·i·an [hjuːmænɪ'teǝrɪǝn] *adj* umanitario

hu·man·i·ty [hjuː'mænǝtɪ] umanità *f inv*

hu·man 'race genere *m* umano

hu·man re'sources *npl* risorse *fpl* umane

hum·ble ['hʌmbl] *adj origins, person* umile; *house* modesto

hum·drum ['hʌmdrʌm] *adj* monotono

hu·mid ['hjuːmɪd] *adj* umido

hu·mid·i·fi·er [hjuː'mɪdɪfaɪǝ(r)] umidificatore *m*

hu·mid·i·ty [hjuː'mɪdǝtɪ] umidità *f inv*

hu·mil·i·ate [hjuː'mɪlɪeɪt] *v/t* umiliare

hu·mil·i·at·ing [hjuː'mɪlɪeɪtɪŋ] *adj* umiliante

hu·mil·i·a·tion [hjuːmɪlɪ'eɪʃn] umiliazione *f*

hu·mil·i·ty [hjuː'mɪlǝtɪ] umiltà *f inv*

hu·mor *Am* → *humour*

hu·mor·ous ['hjuːmǝrǝs] *adj person* spiritoso; *story* umoristico

hu·mour ['hjuːmǝ(r)] umorismo *m*; *(mood)* umore *m*; *sense of* ~ senso dell'umorismo

hump [hʌmp] 1 *n of camel, person* gobba *f*; *on road* dosso *m* 2 *v/t* F (carry) portare

hunch [hʌntʃ] (idea) impressione f, of detective intuizione f

hun·dred ['hʌndrəd] cento m; **a ~ ...** cento ...

hun·dredth ['hʌndrəθ] n & adj centesimo, -a

'hun·dred·weight cinquanta chili (circa)

hung [hʌŋ] pret & pp → **hang**

Hun·gar·i·an [hʌŋ'geəriən] 1 adj ungherese 2 n person ungherese m/f; language ungherese m

Hun·ga·ry ['hʌŋgəri] Ungheria f

hun·ger ['hʌŋgə(r)] fame f

hung·o·ver [hʌŋ'əuvə(r)] adj: **feel ~** avere i postumi della sbornia

hun·gry ['hʌŋgri] adj affamato; **I'm ~** ho fame

hunk [hʌŋk] n tocco m; F (man) fusto m F

hun·ky-do·ry [hʌŋkɪ'dɔːri] adj F: **everything's ~** tutto va a meraviglia

hunt [hʌnt] 1 n for animals caccia f; for job, house, missing child ricerca f 2 v/t animal cacciare

♦ hunt for v/t cercare

hunt·er ['hʌntə(r)] cacciatore m, -trice f

hunt·ing ['hʌntɪŋ] caccia f

hur·dle ['hɜːdl] also fig ostacolo m

hur·dler ['hɜːdlə(r)] SP ostacolista m/f

hur·dles npl SP: **100 metres** i cento metri a ostacoli

hurl [hɜːl] v/t scagliare

hur·ray [hʊ'reɪ] int urrà!

hur·ri·cane ['hʌrɪkən] uragano m

hur·ried ['hʌrɪd] adj frettoloso

hur·ry ['hʌrɪ] 1 n fretta f; **be in a ~** avere fretta 2 v/i (pret & pp **-ied**) sbrigarsi

♦ hurry up 1 v/i sbrigarsi; **hurry up!** sbrigati! 2 v/t fare fretta a

hurt [hɜːt] 1 v/i (pret & pp **hurt**) v/i far male; **does it ~?** ti fa male? 2 v/t physically far male a; emotionally ferire

hus·band ['hʌzbənd] marito m

hush [hʌʃ] n silenzio m; **~!** silenzio!

♦ hush up v/t scandal etc mettere a tacere

husk [hʌsk] pula m

hus·ky ['hʌski] adj voice roco

hus·tle ['hʌsl] 1 n: **~ and bustle** trambusto m 2 v/t person spingere

hut [hʌt] capanno m

hy·a·cinth ['haɪəsɪnθ] giacinto m

hy·brid ['haɪbrɪd] n plant, animal ibrido m

hy·drant ['haɪdrənt] idrante m

hy·draul·ic [haɪ'drɔːlɪk] adj idraulico

hy·dro·e·lec·tric [haɪdrəʊɪ'lektrɪk] adj idroelettrico

'hy·dro·foil ['haɪdrəfɔɪl] boat aliscafo m

hy·dro·gen ['haɪdrədʒən] idrogeno m

'hy·dro·gen bomb bomba f H

hy·giene ['haɪdʒiːn] igiene f

hy·gien·ic [haɪ'dʒiːnɪk] adj igienico

hymn [hɪm] inno m (sacro)

hype [haɪp] n pubblicità f inv

hy·per·ac·tive [haɪpər'æktɪv] adj iperattivo

hy·per·mar·ket ['haɪpəmɑːkɪt] ipermercato m

hy·per·sen·si·tive [haɪpə'sensɪtɪv] adj ipersensibile

hy·per·ten·sion [haɪpə'tenʃn] ipertensione f

hy·per·text ['haɪpətekst] COMPUT ipertesto m

hy·phen ['haɪfn] trattino m

hyp·no·sis [hɪp'nəʊsɪs] ipnosi f

hyp·no·ther·a·py [hɪpnəʊ'θerəpi] ipnoterapia f

hyp·no·tize ['hɪpnətaɪz] v/t ipnotizzare

hy·po·chon·dri·ac [haɪpə'kɒndrɪæk] n ipocondriaco m, -a f

hy·poc·ri·sy [hɪ'pɒkrəsi] ipocrisia f

hyp·o·crite ['hɪpəkrɪt] ipocrita m/f

hyp·o·crit·i·cal [hɪpə'krɪtɪkl] adj ipocrita

hy·po·ther·mi·a [haɪpə'θɜːmɪə] ipotermia f

hy·poth·e·sis [haɪ'pɒθəsɪs] (pl **hypotheses** [haɪ'pɒθəsiːz]) ipotesi f inv

hy·po·thet·i·cal [haɪpə'θetɪkl] *adj*
ipotetico
hys·ter·ec·to·my [hɪstə'rektəmɪ]
isterectomia *f*
hys·te·ri·a [hɪ'stɪərɪə] isteria *f*
hys·ter·i·cal [hɪ'sterɪkl] *adj person,*
laugh isterico; F *(very funny)* buf-
fissimo; **become ~** avere una crisi
isterica
hys·ter·ics [hɪ'sterɪks] *npl laughter*
attacco *m* di risa; MED crisi *f*
isterica

I

I [aɪ] *pron* io; **~ am English** sono inglese; **you're crazy, ~'m not** tu sei
pazzo, io no
ice [aɪs] ghiaccio *m*; **break the ~** *fig*
rompere il ghiaccio
♦ **ice up** *v/i of engine, wings* ghiacciar-
si
ice·berg ['aɪsbɜːg] iceberg *m inv*;
'ice·box *Am* frigo *m*; **'ice·break·er**
ship rompighiaccio *m inv*; **'ice**
cream gelato *m*; **'ice cream par-**
lor *Am,* **'ice cream par·lour** gelateria *f*; **'ice cube** cubetto *m* di
ghiaccio
iced [aɪst] *adj drink* ghiacciato; *cake*
glassato
iced 'cof·fee caffè *m inv* freddo
'ice hock·ey hockey *m inv* sul ghiaccio; **'ice lol·ly** ghiacciolo *m*; **'ice**
rink pista *f* di pattinaggio; **'ice**
skate pattinare (sul ghiaccio); **'ice**
skat·ing pattinaggio *m* (sul ghiaccio)
i·ci·cle ['aɪsɪkl] ghiacciolo *m*
i·cing ['aɪsɪŋ] glassa *f*
i·con ['aɪkɒn] *cultural* mito *m*;
COMPUT icona *f*
icy ['aɪsɪ] *adj road, surface* ghiacciato;
welcome glaciale
ID [aɪ'diː] *abbr (= identity)*: **have you**
got any ~ on you? ha un documen-
to d'identità?
idea [aɪ'dɪə] idea *f*; **good ~!** ottima
idea!; **I have no ~** non ne ho la minima idea; **it's not a good ~ to …** non
è una buona idea …
i·deal [aɪ'dɪəl] *adj (perfect)* ideale;
it's not ~ but we'll take it non è
l'ideale ma lo prendiamo lo stesso
i·deal·is·tic [aɪdɪə'lɪstɪk] *adj person*
idealista; *views* idealistico
i·deal·ly [aɪ'dɪəlɪ] *adv*: **the hotel is ~**
situated l'albergo si trova in una
posizione ideale; **~, we would do it**
like this l'ideale sarebbe farlo così
i·den·ti·cal [aɪ'dentɪkl] *adj* identico;
~ twins gemelli *mpl* monozigotici
i·den·ti·fi·ca·tion [aɪdentɪfɪ'keɪʃn]
identificazione *f*, riconoscimento *m*;
papers etc documento *m* di riconoscimento o d'identità
i·den·ti·fy [aɪ'dentɪfaɪ] *v/t (pret & pp*
-ied) (recognize) identificare, riconoscere; *(point out)* individuare
i·den·ti·ty [aɪ'dentətɪ] identità *f inv*; **~**
card carta *f* d'identità; **a case of**
mistaken ~ uno scambio di persona
i·de·o·log·i·cal [aɪdɪə'lɒdʒɪkl] *adj*
ideologico
i·de·ol·o·gy [aɪdɪ'ɒlədʒɪ] ideologia *f*
id·i·om ['ɪdɪəm] *(saying)* locuzione *f*
idiomatica
id·i·o·mat·ic [ɪdɪə'mætɪk] *adj* naturale
id·i·o·syn·cra·sy [ɪdɪə'sɪŋkrəsɪ] piccola mania *f*
id·i·ot ['ɪdɪət] idiota *m/f*
id·i·ot·ic [ɪdɪ'ɒtɪk] *adj* idiota
i·dle ['aɪdl] **1** *adj person* disoccupato;
threat vuoto; *machinery* inattivo;
in an ~ moment in un momento

libero 2 *v/i of engine* girare al minimo

♦ **idle away** *v/t the time etc* trascorrere oziando

i·dol ['aɪdl] idolo *m*

i·dol·ize ['aɪdəlaɪz] *v/t* idolatrare

i·dyl·lic [ɪ'dɪlɪk] *adj* idilli(a)co

if [ɪf] *conj* se; **~ only you had told me** se (solo) me l'avessi detto

ig·nite [ɪg'naɪt] *v/t* dar fuoco a

ig·ni·tion [ɪg'nɪʃn] *in car* accensione *f*; **~ key** chiave *f* dell'accensione

ig·no·rance ['ɪgnərəns] ignoranza *f*

ig·no·rant ['ɪgnərənt] *adj* (*rude*) cafone; **be ~ of sth** ignorare qc

ig·nore [ɪg'nɔː(r)] *v/t* ignorare

ill [ɪl] *adj* ammalato; **fall ~, be taken ~** ammalarsi; **feel ~** sentirsi male; **look ~** avere una brutta cera; **feel ~ at ease** sentirsi a disagio

il·le·gal [ɪ'liːgl] *adj* illegale

il·le·gi·ble [ɪ'ledʒəbl] *adj* illeggibile

il·le·git·i·mate [ɪlɪ'dʒɪtɪmət] *adj child* illegittimo

ill-fat·ed [ɪl'feɪtɪd] *adj* sfortunato

il·li·cit [ɪ'lɪsɪt] *adj copy, imports* illegale; *pleasure, relationship* illecito

il·lit·e·rate [ɪ'lɪtərət] *adj* analfabeta

ill-man·nered [ɪl'mænəd] *adj* maleducato

ill-na·tured [ɪl'neɪtʃəd] *adj* d'indole cattiva

ill·ness ['ɪlnɪs] malattia *f*

il·log·i·cal [ɪ'lɒdʒɪkl] *adj* illogico

ill-tem·pered [ɪl'tempəd] *adj* irascibile

ill 'treat *v/t* maltrattare

il·lu·mi·nate [ɪ'luːmɪneɪt] *v/t building etc* illuminare

il·lu·mi·nat·ing [ɪ'luːmɪneɪtɪŋ] *adj remarks etc* chiarificatore

il·lu·sion [ɪ'luːʒn] illusione *f*

il·lus·trate ['ɪləstreɪt] *v/t* illustrare

il·lus·tra·tion [ɪlə'streɪʃn] (*picture*) illustrazione *f*; *with examples* esemplificazione *f*

il·lus·tra·tor   [ɪlə'streɪtə(r)] illustratore *m*, -trice *f*

ill 'will rancore *m*

im·age ['ɪmɪdʒ] immagine *f*; (*exact likeness*) ritratto *m*

'im·age-con·scious *adj* attento all'immagine

i·ma·gi·na·ble [ɪ'mædʒɪnəbl] *adj* immaginabile; **the biggest / smallest size ~** la misura più grande / piccola che si possa immaginare

i·ma·gi·na·ry [ɪ'mædʒɪnərɪ] *adj* immaginario

i·ma·gi·na·tion [ɪmædʒɪ'neɪʃn] immaginazione *f*, fantasia *f*; **it's all in your ~** è tutto frutto della tua immaginazione

i·ma·gi·na·tive [ɪ'mædʒɪnətɪv] *adj* fantasioso

i·ma·gine [ɪ'mædʒɪn] *v/t* immaginare; **I can just ~ it** me lo immagino; **you're imagining things** è frutto della tua immaginazione

im·be·cile ['ɪmbəsiːl] ebete *m/f*

IMF [aɪem'ef] *abbr* (= **International Monetary Fund**) FMI *m* (= **Fondo** *m* **Monetario Internazionale**)

im·i·tate ['ɪmɪteɪt] *v/t* imitare

im·i·ta·tion [ɪmɪ'teɪʃn] imitazione *f*; **learn by ~** imparare copiando

im·mac·u·late [ɪ'mækjʊlət] *adj* immacolato

im·ma·te·ri·al [ɪmə'tɪərɪəl] *adj* (*not relevant*) irrilevante

im·ma·ture [ɪmə'tʃʊə(r)] *adj* immaturo

im·me·di·ate [ɪ'miːdɪət] *adj* immediato; **the ~ family** i familiari più stretti; **the ~ problem** il problema più immediato; **in the ~ neighbourhood** nelle immediate vicinanze

im·me·di·ate·ly [ɪ'miːdɪətlɪ] *adv* immediatamente; **~ after the bank / church** subito dopo la banca / chiesa

im·mense [ɪ'mens] *adj* immenso

im·merse [ɪ'mɜːs] *v/t* immergere; **~ o.s. in** immergersi in

im·mer·sion heat·er [ɪ'mɜːʃn] scaldabagno *m* elettrico

im·mi·grant ['ɪmɪgrənt] *n* immigrato *m*, -a *f*

im·mi·grate ['ɪmɪgreɪt] *v/i* immigrare

im·mi·gra·tion [ɪmɪ'greɪʃn] *act* immigrazione f; **Immigration** government ment department ufficio m stranieri

im·mi·nent['ɪmɪnənt] adj imminente

im·mo·bi·lize [ɪ'məʊbɪlaɪz] v/t factory, person, car immobilizzare

im·mo·bi·liz·er [ɪ'məʊbɪlaɪzə(r)] on car immobilizzatore m

im·mod·e·rate [ɪ'mɒdərət] adj smodato

im·mor·al [ɪ'mɒrəl] adj immorale

im·mor·al·i·ty [ɪmɒ'rælɪtɪ] immoralità f inv

im·mor·tal [ɪ'mɔːtl] adj immortale

im·mor·tal·i·ty [ɪmɔː'tælɪtɪ] immortalità f inv

im·mune [ɪ'mjuːn] adj to illness, infection immune; from ruling, requirement esente

im'mune sys·tem MED sistema m immunitario

im·mu·ni·ty [ɪ'mjuːnɪtɪ] to infection immunità f inv; from ruling esenzione f; **diplomatic ~** immunità f inv diplomatica

im·pact ['ɪmpækt] n of meteorite, vehicle urto m; of new manager etc impatto m; (effect) effetto m

im·pair [ɪm'peə(r)] v/t danneggiare

im·paired [ɪm'peəd] adj danneggiato

im·par·tial [ɪm'pɑːʃl] adj imparziale

im·pass·a·ble [ɪm'pɑːsəbl] adj road impraticabile

im·passe ['æmpɑːs] in negotiations etc impasse m inv

im·pas·sioned [ɪm'pæʃnd] adj speech, plea appassionato

im·pas·sive [ɪm'pæsɪv] adj impassibile

im·pa·tience [ɪm'peɪʃəns] impazienza f

im·pa·tient [ɪm'peɪʃənt] adj impaziente

im·pa·tient·ly [ɪm'peɪʃəntlɪ] adv con impazienza

im·peach [ɪm'piːtʃ] v/t President mettere in stato d'accusa

im·pec·ca·ble [ɪm'pekəbl] adj impeccabile

im·pec·ca·bly [ɪm'pekəblɪ] adv impeccabilmente

im·pede [ɪm'piːd] v/t ostacolare

im·ped·i·ment [ɪm'pedɪmənt] in speech difetto m

im·pend·ing [ɪm'pendɪŋ] adj imminente

im·pen·e·tra·ble [ɪm'penɪtrəbl] adj impenetrabile

im·per·a·tive [ɪm'perətɪv] 1 adj essenziale 2 n GRAM imperativo m

im·per·cep·ti·ble [ɪmpɜ'septɪbl] adj impercettibile

im·per·fect [ɪm'pɜːfekt] 1 adj imperfetto 2 n GRAM imperfetto m

im·pe·ri·al [ɪm'pɪərɪəl] adj imperiale

im·per·son·al [ɪm'pɜːsənl] adj impersonale

im·per·so·nate [ɪm'pɜːsəneɪt] v/t as a joke imitare; illegally fingersi

im·per·ti·nence [ɪm'pɜːtɪnəns] impertinenza f

im·per·ti·nent [ɪm'pɜːtɪnənt] adj impertinente

im·per·tur·ba·ble [ɪmpə'tɜːbəbl] adj imperturbabile

im·per·vi·ous [ɪm'pɜːvɪəs] adj: ~ to indifferente a

im·pe·tu·ous [ɪm'petjʊəs] adj impetuoso

im·pe·tus ['ɪmpɪtəs] of campaign etc impeto m

im·ple·ment ['ɪmplɪmənt] 1 n utensile m 2 v/t implementare; measures attuare, implementare

im·pli·cate ['ɪmplɪkeɪt] v/t implicare; ~ s.o. in sth implicare qu in qc

im·pli·ca·tion [ɪmplɪ'keɪʃn] conseguenza f possibile; by ~ implicitamente

im·pli·cit [ɪm'plɪsɪt] adj implicito; trust assoluto

im·plore [ɪm'plɔː(r)] v/t implorare

im·ply [ɪm'plaɪ] v/t (pret & pp -ied) implicare; are you ~ing I was lying? stai insinuando che ho mentito?

im·po·lite [ɪmpə'laɪt] adj maleducato

im·port ['ɪmpɔːt] 1 n importazione f; item articolo m d'importazione 2 v/t importare

im·por·tance [ɪm'pɔːtəns] importanza f

im·por·tant [ɪmˈpɔːtənt] *adj* importante

im·por·ter [ɪmˈpɔːtə(r)] importatore *m*, -trice *f*

im·pose [ɪmˈpəʊz] *v/t tax* imporre; ~ **o.s. on s.o.** disturbare qu

im·pos·ing [ɪmˈpəʊzɪŋ] *adj* imponente

im·pos·si·bil·i·ty [ɪmpɒsɪˈbɪlɪtɪ] impossibilità *f inv*

im·pos·si·ble [ɪmˈpɒsɪbəl] *adj* impossibile

im·pos·tor [ɪmˈpɒstə(r)] impostore *m*, -a *f*

im·po·tence [ˈɪmpətəns] impotenza *f*

im·po·tent [ˈɪmpətənt] *adj* impotente

im·pov·e·rished [ɪmˈpɒvərɪʃt] *adj* impoverito

im·prac·ti·cal [ɪmˈpræktɪkəl] *adj person* senza senso pratico; *suggestion* poco pratico

im·press [ɪmˈpres] *v/t* fare colpo su; *be ~ed by s.o. / sth* essere colpito da qu / qc; *$500 an hour? – I'm ~ed* 500 dollari all'ora? – però; *terrible work, I'm not ~ed* pessimo lavoro, vergogna

im·pres·sion [ɪmˈpreʃn] impressione *f*; (*impersonation*) imitazione *f*; *make a good / bad ~ on s.o.* fare buona / cattiva impressione su qu; *I get the ~ that …* ho l'impressione che …

im·pres·sion·a·ble [ɪmˈpreʃənəbl] *adj* impressionabile

im·pres·sive [ɪmˈpresɪv] *adj* notevole

im·print [ˈɪmprɪnt] *n of credit card* impressione *f*

im·pris·on [ɪmˈprɪzn] *v/t* incarcerare

im·pris·on·ment [ɪmˈprɪznmənt] carcerazione *f*; *15 years' ~* 15 anni di carcere *o* reclusione

im·prob·a·ble [ɪmˈprɒbəbl] *adj* improbabile

im·prop·er [ɪmˈprɒpə(r)] *adj behaviour* sconveniente; *use* improprio

im·prove [ɪmˈpruːv] *v/t & v/i* migliorare

im·prove·ment [ɪmˈpruːvmənt] miglioramento *m*

im·pro·vise [ˈɪmprəvaɪz] *v/i* improvvisare

im·pu·dent [ˈɪmpjʊdənt] *adj* impudente

im·pulse [ˈɪmpʌls] impulso *m*; *do sth on an ~* fare qc d'impulso

ˈim·pulse buy acquisto *m* d'impulso

im·pul·sive [ɪmˈpʌlsɪv] *adj* impulsivo

im·pu·ni·ty [ɪmˈpjuːnətɪ]: *with ~* impunemente

im·pure [ɪmˈpjʊə(r)] *adj* impuro

in [ɪn] **1** *prep* ◊ *~ Birmingham / Milan* a Birmingham / Milano; *~ the street* per strada; *~ the box* nella scatola; *put it ~ your pocket* mettitelo in tasca; *wounded ~ the leg / arm* ferito alla gamba / al braccio ◊ *~ 1999* nel 1999; *~ two hours from now* tra due ore; *over period of* in due ore; *~ the morning* la mattina; *~ the summer* d'estate; *~ September* a *o* in settembre ◊ *~ English / Italian* in inglese / italiano; *~ a loud voice* a voce alta; *~ his style* nel suo stile; *~ yellow* di giallo ◊ *~ crossing the road* (*while*) mentre attraversava la strada; *~ agreeing to this* (*by virtue of*) accettando questo ◊ *~ his first novel* nel suo primo romanzo; *~ Dante* in Dante ◊ *three ~ all* tre in tutto; *one ~ ten* uno su dieci **2** *adv*: *be ~ at home* essere a casa; *in the building etc* esserci; *arrived: of train* essere arrivato; *in its position* essere dentro; *is she ~?* c'è?; *~ here / there* qui / lì (dentro) **3** *adj* (*fashionable, popular*) in, di moda

in·a·bil·i·ty [ɪnəˈbɪlɪtɪ] incapacità *f inv*

in·ac·ces·si·ble [ɪnəkˈsesɪbl] *adj* inaccessibile

in·ac·cu·rate [ɪnˈækjʊrət] *adj* inaccurato

in·ac·tive [ɪnˈæktɪv] *adj* inattivo

in·ad·e·quate [ɪnˈædɪkwət] *adj* inadeguato

in·ad·vis·a·ble [ɪnədˈvaɪzəbl] *adj* sconsigliabile

in·an·i·mate [ɪn'ænɪmət] *adj* inanimato

in·ap·pro·pri·ate [ɪnə'prəuprɪət] *adj* inappropriato

in·ar·tic·u·late [ɪnɑː'tɪkjʊlət] *adj* che si esprime male

in·at·ten·tive [ɪnə'tentɪv] *adj* disattento

in·au·di·ble [ɪn'ɔːdɪbl] *adj* impercettibile

in·au·gu·ral [ɪ'nɔːgjʊrəl] *adj speech* inaugurale

in·au·gu·rate [ɪ'nɔːgjʊreɪt] *v/t* inaugurare

in·born ['ɪnbɔːn] *adj* innato

in·breed·ing ['ɪnbriːdɪŋ] unioni *fpl* tra consanguinei

in·cal·cu·la·ble [ɪn'kælkjʊləbl] *adj damage* incalcolabile

in·ca·pa·ble [ɪn'keɪpəbl]] *adj* incapace; *be ~ of doing sth* essere incapace di fare qc

in·cen·di·a·ry de·vice [ɪn'sendɪərɪ] ordigno *m* incendiario

in·cense[1] ['ɪnsens] *n* incenso *m*

in·cense[2] [ɪn'sens] *v/t* fare infuriare

in·cen·tive [ɪn'sentɪv] incentivo *m*

in·ces·sant [ɪn'sesnt] *adj* incessante

in·ces·sant·ly [ɪn'sesntlɪ] *adv* incessantemente

in·cest ['ɪnsest] incesto *m*

inch [ɪntʃ] pollice *m*

in·ci·dent ['ɪnsɪdənt] incidente *m*

in·ci·den·tal [ɪnsɪ'dentl] *adj* casuale; *~ expenses* spese accessorie

in·ci·den·tal·ly [ɪnsɪ'dentlɪ] *adv (by the way)* a proposito

in·cin·e·ra·tor [ɪn'sɪnəreɪtə(r)] inceneritore *m*

in·ci·sion [ɪn'sɪʒn] incisione *f*

in·ci·sive [ɪn'saɪsɪv] *adj mind, analysis* acuto

in·cite [ɪn'saɪt] *v/t* incitare; *~ s.o. to do sth* istigare qu a fare qc

in·clem·ent [ɪn'klemənt] *adj weather* inclemente

in·cli·na·tion [ɪnklɪ'neɪʃn] *tendency, liking* inclinazione *f*

in·cline [ɪn'klaɪn] *v/t: be ~d to believe sth* essere propenso a cre-

dere qc; *be ~d to do sth* avere la tendenza di fare qc

in·close, in·clos·ure → *enclose, enclosure*

in·clude [ɪn'kluːd] *v/t* includere, comprendere

in·clud·ing [ɪn'kluːdɪŋ] *prep* compreso, incluso

in·clu·sive [ɪn'kluːsɪv] **1** *adj* price tutto compreso **2** *prep*: *~ of VAT* IVA compresa **3** *adv*: *from Monday to Thursday ~* dal lunedì al giovedì compreso

in·co·her·ent *adj* incoerente

in·come ['ɪnkʌm] reddito *m*

'in·come tax imposta *f* sul reddito

in·com·ing ['ɪnkʌmɪŋ] *adj flight, phonecall, mail* in arrivo; *tide* montante; *president* entrante

in·com·pa·ra·ble [ɪn'kɒmprəbl] *adj* incomparabile

in·com·pat·i·bil·i·ty [ɪnkəmpætɪ'bɪlɪtɪ] incompatibilità *f inv*

in·com·pat·i·ble [ɪnkəm'pætɪbl] *adj* incompatibile

in·com·pe·tence [ɪn'kɒmpɪtəns] incompetenza *f*

in·com·pe·tent [ɪn'kɒmpɪtənt] *adj* incompetente

in·com·plete [ɪnkəm'pliːt] *adj* incompleto

in·com·pre·hen·si·ble [ɪnkɒmprɪ'hensɪbl] *adj* incomprensibile

in·con·ceiv·a·ble [ɪnkən'siːvəbl] *adj* inconcepibile

in·con·clu·sive [ɪnkən'kluːsɪv] *adj* inconcludente

in·con·gru·ous [ɪn'kɒŋgrʊəs] *adj* fuori luogo

in·con·sid·er·ate [ɪnkən'sɪdərət] *adj* poco gentile

in·con·sis·tent [ɪnkən'sɪstənt] *adj* incoerente

in·con·so·la·ble [ɪnkən'səʊləbl] *adj* inconsolabile

in·con·spic·u·ous [ɪnkən'spɪkjʊəs] *adj* poco visibile; *make o.s. ~* passare inosservato

in·con·ve·ni·ence [ɪnkən'viːnɪəns] *n* inconveniente *m*

in·con·ve·ni·ent [ɪnkən'viːnɪənt] *adj*

scomodo; *time* poco opportuno

in·cor·po·rate [ɪn'kɔːpəreɪt] *v/t* includere

in·cor·rect [ɪnkə'rekt] *adj* answer errato; *behaviour* scorretto; **am I ~ in thinking ...?** sbaglio a pensare che ...?

in·cor·rect·ly [ɪnkə'rektlɪ] *adv* in modo errato

in·cor·ri·gi·ble [ɪn'kɒrɪdʒəbl] *adj* correggibile

in·crease [ɪn'kriːs] **1** *v/t & v/i* aumentare **2** *n* ['ɪnkriːs] aumento *m*; **on the ~** in aumento

in·creas·ing [ɪn'kriːsɪŋ] *adj* crescente

in·creas·ing·ly [ɪn'kriːsɪŋlɪ] *adv* sempre più

in·cred·i·ble [ɪn'kredɪbl] *adj* (*amazing, very good*) incredibile

in·crim·i·nate [ɪn'krɪmɪneɪt] *v/t* compromettere; **~ o.s.** compromettersi

in·cu·ba·tor ['ɪŋkjubeɪtə(r)] incubatrice *f*

in·cur [ɪn'kɜː(r)] *v/t* (*pret & pp* **-red**) *costs* affrontare; *debts* contrarre; *s.o.'s anger* esporsi a

in·cu·ra·ble [ɪn'kjʊərəbl] *adj* incurabile

in·debt·ed [ɪn'detɪd] *adj*: **be ~ to s.o.** essere (molto) obbligato a qu

in·de·cent [ɪn'diːsnt] *adj* indecente

in·de·ci·sive [ɪndɪ'saɪsɪv] *adj* indeciso

in·de·ci·sive·ness [ɪndɪ'saɪsɪvnɪs] indecisione *f*

in·deed [ɪn'diːd] *adv* (*in fact*) in effetti; (*yes, agreeing*) esatto; **very much ~** moltissimo; **thank you very much ~** grazie mille

in·de·fi·na·ble [ɪndɪ'faɪnəbl] *adj* indefinibile

in·def·i·nite [ɪn'defɪnɪt] *adj* indeterminato; **~ article** GRAM articolo *m* indeterminativo

in·def·i·nite·ly [ɪn'defɪnɪtlɪ] *adv* a tempo indeterminato

in·del·i·cate [ɪn'delɪkət] *adj* indelicato

in·dent ['ɪndent] **1** *n* in text rientro *m* a margine **2** *v/t* [ɪn'dent] *line*

rientrare il margine di

in·de·pen·dence [ɪndɪ'pendəns] indipendenza *f*

in·de·pen·dent [ɪndɪ'pendənt] *adj* indipendente

in·de·pen·dent·ly [ɪndɪ'pendəntlɪ] *adv* indipendentemente; **~ of** indipendentemente da

in·de·scri·ba·ble [ɪndɪ'skraɪbəbl] *adj* indescrivibile

in·de·scrib·a·bly [ɪndɪ'skraɪbəblɪ] *adv*: **~ beautiful** di una bellezza indescrivibile; **~ bad** pessimo

in·de·struc·ti·ble [ɪndɪ'strʌktəbl] *adj* indistruttibile

in·de·ter·mi·nate [ɪndɪ'tɜːmɪnət] *adj* indeterminato

in·dex ['ɪndeks] indice *m*

'in·dex card scheda *f*; 'in·dex finger indice *m*; in·dex-'linked *adj* indicizzato

In·di·a ['ɪndɪə] India *f*

In·di·an ['ɪndɪən] **1** *adj* indiano **2** *n* *person* indiano *m*, -a *f*; *American* indiano *m*, -a *f* d'America

In·di·an 'sum·mer estate *f* di San Martino

in·di·cate ['ɪndɪkeɪt] **1** *v/t* indicare **2** *v/i when driving* segnalare (il cambiamento di direzione)

in·di·ca·tion [ɪndɪ'keɪʃn] indicazione *f*

in·di·ca·tor ['ɪndɪkeɪtə(r)] *on car* indicatore *m* di direzione, freccia *f* F

in·dict [ɪn'daɪt] *v/t* incriminare

in·dif·fer·ence [ɪn'dɪfrəns] indifferenza *f*

in·dif·fer·ent [ɪn'dɪfrənt] *adj* indifferente; (*mediocre*) mediocre

in·di·ges·ti·ble [ɪndɪ'dʒestɪbl] *adj* indigesto

in·di·ges·tion [ɪndɪ'dʒestʃn] indigestione *f*

in·dig·nant [ɪn'dɪgnənt] *adj* indignato

in·dig·na·tion [ɪndɪg'neɪʃn] indignazione *f*

in·di·rect [ɪndɪ'rekt] *adj* indiretto

in·di·rect·ly [ɪndɪ'rektlɪ] *adv* indirettamente

in·dis·creet [ɪndɪ'skriːt] *adj* indiscreto

in·dis·cre·tion [ɪndɪ'skreʃn] indiscrezione *f*; *sexual* scappatella *f*

in·dis·crim·i·nate [ɪndɪ'skrɪmɪnət] *adj* indiscriminato

in·dis·pen·sa·ble [ɪndɪ'spensəbl] *adj* indispensabile

in·dis·posed [ɪndɪ'spəʊzd] *adj* (*not well*) indisposto

in·dis·pu·ta·ble [ɪndɪ'spjuːtəbl] *adj* indiscutibile

in·dis·pu·ta·bly [ɪndɪ'spjuːtəblɪ] *adv* indiscutibilmente

in·dis·tinct [ɪndɪ'stɪŋkt] *adj* indistinto

in·dis·tin·guish·a·ble [ɪndɪ'stɪŋgwɪʃəbl] *adj* indistinguibile

in·di·vid·u·al [ɪndɪ'vɪdjʊəl] **1** *n* individuo *m* **2** *adj* (*separate*) singolo; (*personal*) individuale

in·di·vid·u·a·list [ɪndɪ'vɪdjʊəlɪst] *adj* individualista

in·di·vid·u·al·ly [ɪndɪ'vɪdjʊəlɪ] *adv* individualmente

in·di·vis·i·ble [ɪndɪ'vɪzɪbl] *adj* indivisibile

in·doc·tri·nate [ɪn'dɒktrɪneɪt] *v/t* indottrinare

in·do·lence ['ɪndələns] indolenza *f*

in·do·lent ['ɪndələnt] *adj* indolente

In·do·ne·sia [ɪndə'niːʒə] Indonesia *f*

In·do·ne·sian [ɪndə'niːʒən] **1** *adj* indonesiano **2** *n person* indonesiano *m*, -a *f*

in·door ['ɪndɔː(r)] *adj activities, games* al coperto; *arena, swimming pool* coperto

in·doors [ɪn'dɔːz] *adv in building* all'interno; *at home* in casa

in·duc·tion course [ɪn'dʌkʃn] corso *m* d'avviamento

in·dulge [ɪn'dʌldʒ] **1** *v/t o.s., one's tastes* soddisfare **2** *v/i:* ~ *in sth* lasciarsi andare a qc; *in joke* permettersi qc

in·dul·gence [ɪn'dʌldʒəns] *of tastes, appetite etc* soddisfazione *f*; (*laxity*) indulgenza *f*

in·dul·gent [ɪn'dʌldʒənt] *adj* (*not strict enough*) indulgente

in·dus·tri·al [ɪn'dʌstrɪəl] *adj* industriale

in·dus·tri·al 'ac·tion agitazione *f* sindacale

in·dus·tri·al dis'pute vertenza *f* sindacale

in·dus·tri·al es'tate zona *f* industriale

in·dus·tri·al·ist [ɪn'dʌstrɪəlɪst] industriale *m*

in·dus·tri·al·ize [ɪn'dʌstrɪəlaɪz] **1** *v/t* industrializzare **2** *v/i* industrializzarsi

in·dus·tri·al 'waste scorie *fpl* industriali

in·dus·tri·ous [ɪn'dʌstrɪəs] *adj* diligente

in·dus·try ['ɪndəstrɪ] industria *f*

in·ef·fec·tive [ɪnɪ'fektɪv] *adj* inefficace

in·ef·fec·tu·al [ɪnɪ'fektʃʊəl] *adj person* inetto

in·ef·fi·cient [ɪnɪ'fɪʃənt] *adj* inefficiente

in·el·i·gi·ble [ɪn'elɪdʒɪbl] *adj:* **be ~ for sth** non avere diritto a qc

in·ept [ɪ'nept] *adj* inetto

in·e·qual·i·ty [ɪnɪ'kwɒlɪtɪ] disuguaglianza *f*

in·es·ca·pa·ble [ɪnɪ'skeɪpəbl] *adj* inevitabile

in·es·ti·ma·ble [ɪn'estɪməbl] *adj* inestimabile

in·ev·i·ta·ble [ɪn'evɪtəbl] *adj* inevitabile; **the ~ bottle of ...** l'immancabile bottiglia di ...

in·ev·i·ta·bly [ɪn'evɪtəblɪ] *adv* inevitabilmente

in·ex·cu·sa·ble [ɪnɪk'skjuːzəbl] *adj* imperdonabile

in·ex·haus·ti·ble [ɪnɪg'zɔːstəbl] *adj supply* inesauribile

in·ex·pen·sive [ɪnɪk'spensɪv] *adj* poco costoso, economico

in·ex·pe·ri·enced [ɪnɪk'spɪərɪənst] *adj* inesperto

in·ex·plic·a·ble [ɪnɪk'splɪkəbl] *adj* inspiegabile

in·ex·pres·si·ble [ɪnɪk'spresɪbl] *adj* inesprimibile

in·fal·li·ble [ɪn'fælɪbl] *adj* infallibile

in·fa·mous ['ɪnfəməs] adj famigerato

in·fan·cy ['ɪnfənsɪ] of person infanzia f; of state, institution stadio m iniziale

in·fant ['ɪnfənt] bambino m piccolo, bambina f piccola

in·fan·tile ['ɪnfəntaɪl] adj pej infantile

in·fan·try ['ɪnfəntrɪ] fanteria f

in·fan·try 'sol·dier fante m

'in·fant school scuola f elementare

in·fat·u·at·ed [ɪn'fætʃueɪtɪd] adj: be ~ with s.o. essere infatuato di qu

in·fect [ɪn'fekt] v/t of person contagiare; food, water contaminare; become ~ed of wound infettarsi; of person contagiarsi

in·fec·tion [ɪn'fekʃn] infezione f

in·fec·tious [ɪn'fekʃəs] adj disease infettivo, contagioso; fig: laughter contagioso

in·fer [ɪn'fɜː(r)] v/t (pret & pp -red): ~ sth from sth dedurre qc da qc

in·fe·ri·or [ɪn'fɪərɪə(r)] adj quality, workmanship inferiore; in rank subalterno

in·fe·ri·or·i·ty [ɪnfɪərɪ'ɒrətɪ] in quality inferiorità f inv

in·fe·ri·or·i·ty com·plex complesso m d'inferiorità

in·fer·tile [ɪn'fɜːtaɪl] adj sterile

in·fer·til·i·ty [ɪnfə'tɪlɪtɪ] sterilità f inv

in·fi·del·i·ty [ɪnfɪ'delɪtɪ] infedeltà f inv

in·fil·trate ['ɪnfɪltreɪt] v/t infiltrare

in·fi·nite ['ɪnfɪnɪt] adj infinito

in·fin·i·tive [ɪn'fɪnətɪv] GRAM infinito m

in·fin·i·ty [ɪn'fɪnətɪ] infinito m

in·firm [ɪn'fɜːm] adj infermo

in·fir·ma·ry [ɪn'fɜːmərɪ] infermeria f

in·fir·mi·ty [ɪn'fɜːmətɪ] infermità f inv

in·flame [ɪn'fleɪm] v/t passions accendere

in·flam·ma·ble [ɪn'flæməbl] adj infiammabile

in·flam·ma·tion [ɪnflə'meɪʃn] MED infiammazione f

in·flat·a·ble [ɪn'fleɪtəbl] adj dinghy gonfiabile

inflate [ɪn'fleɪt] v/t tyre, dinghy gonfiare; economy inflazionare

in·fla·tion [ɪn'fleɪʃən] inflazione f

in·fla·tion·a·ry [ɪn'fleɪʃənərɪ] adj inflazionistico

in·flec·tion [ɪn'flekʃn] of voice intonazione f

in·flex·i·ble [ɪn'fleksɪbl] adj attitude, person inflessibile

in·flict [ɪn'flɪkt] v/t: ~ sth on s.o. punishment infliggere qc a qu; wound, suffering procurare qc a qu

'in-flight adj: ~ entertainment intrattenimento a bordo

in·flu·ence ['ɪnfluəns] 1 n influenza f; be a good / bad ~ on s.o. avere una buona / cattiva influenza su qu; people who have ~ persone influenti; who were your main ~s? chi si è ispirato principalmente? 2 v/t s.o.'s thinking esercitare un'influenza su; decision influenzare

in·flu·en·tial [ɪnflu'enʃl] adj writer, philosopher, film-maker autorevole; she knows ~ people conosce gente influente

in·flu·en·za [ɪnflu'enzə] influenza f

in·form [ɪn'fɔːm] 1 v/t informare; ~ s.o. about sth informare qu di qc; please keep me ~ed tienimi informato 2 v/i denunciare; ~ on s.o. denunciare qu

in·for·mal [ɪn'fɔːml] adj informale

in·for·mal·i·ty [ɪnfɔː'mælɪtɪ] informalità f inv

in·form·ant [ɪn'fɔːmənt] informatore m, -trice f

in·for·ma·tion [ɪnfə'meɪʃn] informazione f; a bit of ~ un'informazione

in·for·ma·tion 'sci·ence informatica f

in·for·ma·tion 'sci·en·tist informatico m, -a f

in·for·ma·tion tech'nol·o·gy informatica f

in·form·a·tive [ɪn'fɔːmətɪv] adj article etc istruttivo; he wasn't very ~ non è stato di grande aiuto

in·form·er [ɪn'fɔːmə(r)] informatore m, -trice f

in·fra·red [ɪnfrə'red] adj infrarosso

in·fra·struc·ture [ˈɪnfrəstrʌktʃə(r)] infrastruttura f

in·fre·quent [ɪnˈfriːkwənt] adj raro

in·fu·ri·ate [ɪnˈfjʊərɪeɪt] v/t far infuriare

in·fu·ri·at·ing [ɪnˈfjʊərɪeɪtɪŋ] adj esasperante

in·fuse [ɪnˈfjuːz] v/i: *let the tea ~* lasciare in infusione il tè

in·fu·sion [ɪnˈfjuːʒn] (*herb tea*) infuso m

in·ge·ni·ous [ɪnˈdʒiːnɪəs] adj ingegnoso

in·ge·nu·i·ty [ɪndʒɪˈnjuːətɪ] ingegnosità f inv

in·got [ˈɪŋgət] lingotto m

in·gra·ti·ate [ɪnˈgreɪʃɪeɪt] v/t: *~ o.s. with s.o.* ingraziarsi qu

in·grat·i·tude [ɪnˈgrætɪtjuːd] ingratitudine f

in·gre·di·ent [ɪnˈgriːdɪənt] *for cooking* ingrediente m; *fig: for success* elemento m

in·hab·it [ɪnˈhæbɪt] v/t abitare

in·hab·it·a·ble [ɪnˈhæbɪtəbl] adj abitabile

in·hab·i·tant [ɪnˈhæbɪtənt] abitante m/f

in·hale [ɪnˈheɪl] **1** v/t inalare **2** v/i *when smoking* aspirare

in·ha·ler [ɪnˈheɪlə(r)] inalatore m

in·her·it [ɪnˈherɪt] v/t ereditare

in·her·i·tance [ɪnˈherɪtəns] eredità f inv

in·hib·it [ɪnˈhɪbɪt] v/t *growth, conversation etc* inibire

in·hib·it·ed [ɪnˈhɪbɪtɪd] adj inibito

in·hi·bi·tion [ɪnhɪˈbɪʃn] inibizione f

in·hos·pi·ta·ble [ɪnhɒˈspɪtəbl] adj inospitale

ˈin-house 1 adj aziendale **2** adv *work* all'interno dell'azienda

in·hu·man [ɪnˈhjuːmən] adj disumano

i·ni·tial [ɪˈnɪʃl] **1** adj iniziale **2** n iniziale f **3** v/t (*write initials on*) siglare (con le iniziali)

i·ni·tial·ly [ɪˈnɪʃlɪ] adv inizialmente

i·ni·ti·ate [ɪˈnɪʃɪeɪt] v/t avviare

i·ni·ti·a·tion [ɪnɪʃɪˈeɪʃn] avviamento m

i·ni·tia·tive [ɪˈnɪʃətɪv] iniziativa f; *do sth on one's own ~* fare qc di propria iniziativa; *take the ~* prendere l'iniziativa

in·ject [ɪnˈdʒekt] v/t *medicine, drug, fuel* iniettare; *capital* investire

in·jec·tion [ɪnˈdʒekʃn] MED, *of fuel* iniezione f; *of capital* investimento m

ˈin-joke: *it's an ~* è una battuta tra di noi / loro

in·jure [ˈɪndʒə(r)] v/t ferire; *~ o.s.* ferirsi

in·jured [ˈɪndʒəd] **1** adj *leg* ferito; *feelings* offeso **2** npl feriti mpl

ˈin·jury time SP minuti mpl di recupero

in·jus·tice [ɪnˈdʒʌstɪs] ingiustizia f

ink [ɪŋk] inchiostro m

ˈink-jet (**ˈprin·ter**) stampante f a getto d'inchiostro

in·land [ˈɪnlənd] adj *areas* dell'interno; *mail* nazionale; *sea* interno

In·land ˈRev·e·nue fisco m

in-laws [ˈɪnlɔːz] npl famiglia fsg della moglie / del marito; (*wife's / husband's parents*) suoceri mpl

in·lay [ˈɪnleɪ] n intarsio m

in·let [ˈɪnlet] *of sea* insenatura f; *in machine* presa f

in·mate [ˈɪnmeɪt] *of prison* detenuto m, -a f; *of mental hospital* ricoverato m, -a f

inn [ɪn] locanda f

in·nate [ɪˈneɪt] adj innato

in·ner [ˈɪnə(r)] adj interno

in·ner ˈcit·y centro m in degrado di una zona urbana; *~ decay* degrado del centro urbano

ˈin·ner·most adj *thoughts etc* più intimo

in·ner ˈtube camera f d'aria

in·nings [ˈɪnɪŋz] nsg *in cricket* turno m di battuta

in·no·cence [ˈɪnəsəns] innocenza f

in·no·cent [ˈɪnəsənt] adj innocente

in·noc·u·ous [ɪˈnɒkjʊəs] adj innocuo

in·no·va·tion [ɪnəˈveɪʃn] innovazione f

in·no·va·tive ['ɪnəvətɪv] adj innovativo

in·no·va·tor ['ɪnəveɪtə(r)] innovatore m, -trice f

in·nu·me·ra·ble [ɪ'njuːmərəbl] adj innumerevole

i·noc·u·late [ɪ'nɒkjʊleɪt] v/t vaccinare

i·noc·u·la·tion [ɪ'nɒkjʊ'leɪʃn] vaccinazione f

in·of·fen·sive [ɪnə'fensɪv] adj inoffensivo

in·or·gan·ic [ɪnɔː'gænɪk] adj inorganico

'in·pa·tient degente m/f

in·put ['ɪnpʊt] 1 n contributo m; COMPUT input m inv 2 v/t (pret & pp -ted or input) into project contribuire con; COMPUT inserire

in·quest ['ɪnkwest] inchiesta f giudiziaria

in·quire [ɪn'kwaɪə(r)] v/i domandare; ~ into sth svolgere indagini su qc

in·quir·y [ɪn'kwaɪərɪ] richiesta f di informazioni; (public ~) indagine f

in·quis·i·tive [ɪn'kwɪzətɪv] adj curioso

in·sane [ɪn'seɪn] adj pazzo

in·san·i·ta·ry [ɪn'sænɪtrɪ] adj antigienico

in·san·i·ty [ɪn'sænɪtɪ] infermità f mentale

in·sa·tia·ble [ɪn'seɪʃəbl] adj insaziabile

in·scrip·tion [ɪn'skrɪpʃn] iscrizione f

in·scru·ta·ble [ɪn'skruːtəbl] adj imperscrutabile

in·sect ['ɪnsekt] insetto m

in·sec·ti·cide [ɪn'sektɪsaɪd] insetticida m

'in·sect re·pel·lent insettifugo m

in·se·cure [ɪnsɪ'kjʊə(r)] adj insicuro

in·se·cu·ri·ty [ɪnsɪ'kjʊərɪtɪ] insicurezza f

in·sen·si·tive [ɪn'sensɪtɪv] adj insensibile

in·sen·si·tiv·i·ty [ɪnsensɪ'tɪvɪtɪ] insensibilità f inv

in·sep·a·ra·ble [ɪn'seprəbl] adj two issues inscindibile; two people inseparabile

in·sert ['ɪnsɜːt] 1 n in magazine etc inserto m 2 v/t [ɪn'sɜːt] inserire; ~ sth into sth inserire qc in qc

in·ser·tion [ɪn'sɜːʃn] (act) inserimento m

in·side [ɪn'saɪd] 1 n of house, box interno m; of road destra f, sinistra f; someone on the ~ at Lloyds qualcuno che lavora ai Lloyds; ~ out a rovescio; turn sth ~ out rivoltare qc; know sth ~ out sapere qc a menadito 2 prep dentro; ~ of 2 hours in meno di due ore 3 adv stay, remain, go, carry dentro; I've never been ~ non sono mai entrato 4 adj interno; ~ information informazioni riservate; ~ lane SP corsia f interna; on road corsia f di marcia; ~ pocket tasca f interna

in·sid·er [ɪn'saɪdə(r)]: an ~ from the Department ... un impiegato del Ministero ...

in·sid·er 'deal·ing FIN insider trading m inv

in·sides [ɪn'saɪdz] npl pancia fsg; intestines budella fpl

in·sid·i·ous [ɪn'sɪdɪəs] adj insidioso

in·sight ['ɪnsaɪt]: it offers an ~ into ... permette di capire ...; full of ~ molto intuitivo

in·sig·nif·i·cant [ɪnsɪg'nɪfɪkənt] adj insignificante

in·sin·cere [ɪnsɪn'sɪə(r)] adj falso

in·sin·cer·i·ty [ɪnsɪn'serɪtɪ] falsità f inv

in·sin·u·ate [ɪn'sɪnjʊeɪt] v/t (imply) insinuare

in·sist [ɪn'sɪst] v/i insistere; please keep it, I ~ tienilo, ci tengo!

♦ insist on v/t esigere; insist on doing sth insistere per fare qc

in·sis·tent [ɪn'sɪstənt] adj insistente

in·so·lent ['ɪnsələnt] adj insolente

in·sol·u·ble [ɪn'sɒljʊbl] adj problem insolubile; substance insolubile

in·sol·vent [ɪn'sɒlvənt] adj insolvente

in·som·ni·a [ɪn'sɒmnɪə] insonnia f

in·som·ni·ac [ɪn'sɒmnɪæk] persona f che soffre di insonnia

in·spect [ɪn'spekt] v/t work, tickets,

baggage controllare; *building, factory, school* ispezionare

in·spec·tion [ɪnˈspekʃn] *of work, tickets, baggage* controllo *m; of building, factory, school* ispezione *f*

in·spec·tor [ɪnˈspektə(r)] *in factory* ispettore *m, -trice f; on buses* controllore *m; of police* ispettore *m*

in·spi·ra·tion [ɪnspəˈreɪʃn] ispirazione *f; (very good idea)* lampo *m* di genio

in·spire [ɪnˈspaɪə(r)] *v/t respect etc* suscitare; **be ~d by s.o./sth** essere ispirato da qu/qc

in·sta·bil·i·ty [ɪnstəˈbɪlɪtɪ] *of character, economy* instabilità *f inv*

in·stall [ɪnˈstɔːl] *v/t computer, telephones, software* installare

in·stal·la·tion [ɪnstəˈleɪʃn] *of new equipment, software* installazione *f;* **military ~** struttura *f* militare

in·stall·ment, in·stall·ment *Am* [ɪnˈstɔːlmənt] *of story, TV drama etc* puntata *f; (payment)* rata *f*

in·stance [ˈɪnstəns] *(example)* esempio *m;* **for ~** per esempio

in·stant [ˈɪnstənt] **1** *adj* immediato **2** *n* istante *m;* **in an ~** in un attimo

in·stan·ta·ne·ous [ɪnstənˈteɪnɪəs] *adj* immediato

in·stant 'cof·fee caffè *m inv* istantaneo *o* solubile

in·stant·ly [ˈɪnstəntlɪ] *adv* istantaneamente

in·stead [ɪnˈsted] *adv* invece; **~ of** invece di

in·step [ˈɪnstep] collo *m* del piede

in·stinct [ˈɪnstɪŋkt] istinto *m*

in·stinc·tive [ɪnˈstɪŋktɪv] *adj* istintivo

in·sti·tute [ˈɪnstɪtjuːt] **1** *n* istituto *m* **2** *v/t new law* introdurre; *enquiry* avviare

in·sti·tu·tion [ɪnstɪˈtjuːʃn] *governmental* istituto *m; sth traditional* istituzione *f; (setting up)* avviamento *m*

in·struct [ɪnˈstrʌkt] *v/t (order)* dare istruzioni a; *(teach)* istruire; **~ s.o. to do sth** *(order)* dare istruzioni a qu di fare qc

in·struc·tion [ɪnˈstrʌkʃn] istruzione

f; **~s for use** istruzioni per l'uso

in·struc·tion man·u·al libretto *m* d'istruzioni

in·struc·tive [ɪnˈstrʌktɪv] *adj* istruttivo

in·struc·tor [ɪnˈstrʌktə(r)] istruttore *m, -trice f*

in·stru·ment [ˈɪnstrʊmənt] strumento *m*

in·sub·or·di·nate [ɪnsəˈbɔːdɪnət] *adj* insubordinato

in·suf·fi·cient [ɪnsəˈfɪʃnt] *adj* insufficiente

in·su·late [ˈɪnsjʊleɪt] *v/t* ELEC isolare; *against cold* isolare termicamente

in·su·lat·ing tape nastro *m* isolante

in·su·la·tion [ɪnsjʊˈleɪʃn] ELEC isolamento *m; against cold* isolamento *m* termico

in·su·lin [ˈɪnsjʊlɪn] insulina *f*

in·sult [ˈɪnsʌlt] **1** *n* insulto *m* **2** *v/t* [ɪnˈsʌlt] insultare

in·sur·ance [ɪnˈʃʊərəns] assicurazione *f*

in·sur·ance com·pa·ny compagnia *f* di assicurazioni; **in·sur·ance pol·i·cy** polizza *f* di assicurazione; **in·sur·ance pre·mi·um** premio *m* assicurativo

in·sure [ɪnˈʃʊə(r)] *v/t* assicurare

in·sured [ɪnˈʃʊəd] **1** *adj* assicurato; **be ~ed** essere assicurato **2** *n:* **the ~** l'assicurato

in·sur·moun·ta·ble [ɪnsəˈmaʊntəbl] *adj* insormontabile

in·tact [ɪnˈtækt] *adj (not damaged)* intatto

in·take [ˈɪnteɪk] *of college etc* (numero *m* di) iscrizioni *fpl*

in·te·grate [ˈɪntɪgreɪt] *v/t* integrare

in·te·grat·ed 'cir·cuit [ˈɪntɪgreɪtɪd] *adj* circuito *m* integrato

in·teg·ri·ty [ɪnˈtegrətɪ] integrità *f inv*

in·tel·lect [ˈɪntəlekt] intelletto *m*

in·tel·lec·tual [ɪntəˈlektjʊəl] **1** *adj* intellettuale **2** *n* intellettuale *m/f*

in·tel·li·gence [ɪnˈtelɪdʒəns] intelligenza *f; (information)* informazioni *fpl*

in·tel·li·gence of·fi·cer agente *m/f*

dei servizi segreti

in·tel·li·gence ser·vice servizi *mpl* segreti

in·tel·li·gent [ɪn'telɪdʒənt] *adj* intelligente

in·tel·li·gi·ble [ɪn'telɪdʒəbl] *adj* intelligibile

in·tend [ɪn'tend] *v/i:* **~ to do sth** (*do on purpose*) volere fare qc; (*plan to do*) avere intenzione di fare qc; *that's not what I ~ed* non è quello che intendevo

in·tense [ɪn'tens] *adj pleasure, heat, pressure* intenso; *concentration* profondo; *he's too ~* è troppo serio

in·ten·si·fy [ɪn'tensɪfaɪ] (*pret & pp -ied*) **1** *v/t effect, pressure* intensificare **2** *v/i of pain* acuirsi; *of fighting* intensificarsi

in·ten·si·ty [ɪn'tensətɪ] intensità *f inv*

in·ten·sive [ɪn'tensɪv] *adj* intensivo

in·ten·sive 'care (u·nit) MED (reparto *m* di) terapia *f* intensiva

in·ten·sive 'course corso *m* intensivo

in·tent [ɪn'tent] *adj* **be ~ on doing sth** (*determined to do*) essere deciso a fare qc; (*concentrating on*) essere intento a fare qc

in·ten·tion [ɪn'tenʃn] intenzione *f; I have no ~ of ...* (*refuse to*) non ho intenzione di ...

in·ten·tion·al [ɪn'tenʃənl] *adj* intenzionale

in·ten·tion·al·ly [ɪn'tenʃnlɪ] *adv* intenzionalmente

in·ter·ac·tion [ɪntər'ækʃn] interazione *f*

in·ter·ac·tive [ɪntər'æktɪv] *adj* interattivo

in·ter·cede [ɪntə'siːd] *v/i* intercedere

in·ter·cept [ɪntə'sept] *v/t* intercettare

in·ter·change ['ɪntətʃeɪndʒ] *Am* MOT interscambio *m*

in·ter·change·a·ble [ɪntə'tʃeɪndʒəbl] *adj* interscambiabile

in·ter·com ['ɪntəkɒm] citofono *m*

in·ter·course ['ɪntəkɔːs] *sexual* rapporto *m* sessuale

in·ter·de·pend·ent [ɪntədɪ'pendənt] *adj* interdipendente

in·ter·est ['ɪntrəst] **1** *n* interesse *m;* FIN: *rate* interesse *m; money paid / received* interessi *mpl;* **take an ~ in sth** interessarsi di qc **2** *v/t* interessare; *does that offer ~ you?* t'interessa l'offerta?

in·ter·est·ed ['ɪntrəstɪd] *adj* interessato; *be ~ in sth* interessarsi di qc; *thanks, but I'm not ~* grazie, non mi interessa

in·ter·est-free 'loan prestito *m* senza interessi

in·ter·est·ing ['ɪntrəstɪŋ] *adj* interessante

'in·ter·est rate FIN tasso *m* d'interesse

in·ter·face ['ɪntəfeɪs] **1** *n* interfaccia *f* **2** *v/i* interfacciarsi

in·ter·fere [ɪntə'fɪə(r)] *v/i* interferire
♦ **interfere with** *v/t* manomettere; *plans* intralciare

in·ter·fer·ence [ɪntə'fɪərəns] interferenza *f; on radio* interferenze *fpl*

in·te·ri·or [ɪn'tɪərɪə(r)] **1** *adj* interno **2** *n of house* interno *m; of country* entroterra *m*

in·te·ri·or dec·o·ra·tor arredatore *m,* -trice *f;* **in·te·ri·or de·sign** architettura *f* d'interni; **in·te·ri·or de·sign·er** architetto *m* d'interni

in·ter·lude ['ɪntəluːd] *at theatre, concert* intervallo *m;* (*period*) parentesi *f*

in·ter·mar·ry [ɪntə'mærɪ] *v/i* (*pret & pp -ied*) fare matrimoni misti

in·ter·me·di·a·ry [ɪntə'miːdɪərɪ] *n* intermediario *m,* -a *f*

in·ter·me·di·ate [ɪntə'miːdɪət] *adj* intermedio

in·ter·mis·sion [ɪntə'mɪʃn] *in theatre, cinema* intervallo *m*

in·tern [ɪn'tɜːn] *v/t* internare

in·ter·nal [ɪn'tɜːnl] *adj* interno

in·ter·nal com'bus·tion en·gine motore *m* a scoppio

in·ter·nal·ly [ɪn'tɜːnəlɪ] *adv:* **he's bleeding ~** ha un'emorragia interna; *not to be taken ~* per uso esterno

in·ter·na·tion·al [ɪntə'næʃnl] **1** *adj*

internazionale **2** *n match* partita *f* internazionale; *player* giocatore *m*, -trice *f* della nazionale

In·ter·na·tion·al Court of 'Jus·tice Corte *f* Internazionale di Giustizia

in·ter·na·tion·al·ly [ɪntə'næʃnəlɪ] *adv* a livello internazionale

In·ter·na·tion·al 'Mon·e·tar·y Fund Fondo *m* Monetario Internazionale

In·ter·net ['ɪntənet] Internet *m inv*; **on the ~** su Internet; **~ service provider** provider *m inv* di servizi Internet

in·ter·pret [ɪn'tɜ:prɪt] **1** *v/t linguistically* tradurre; *piece of music, comment etc* interpretare **2** *v/i* fare da interprete

in·ter·pre·ta·tion [ɪntɜ:prɪ'teɪʃn] *linguistic* traduzione *f; of piece of music, meaning* interpretazione *f*

in·ter·pret·er [ɪn'tɜ:prɪtə(r)] interprete *m/f*

in·ter·re·lat·ed [ɪntərɪ'leɪtɪd] *adj* correlato

in·ter·ro·gate [ɪn'terəgeɪt] *v/t* interrogare

in·ter·ro·ga·tion [ɪntərə'geɪʃn] interrogatorio *m*

in·ter·rog·a·tive [ɪntə'rɒgətɪv] *n* GRAM forma *f* interrogativa

in·ter·ro·ga·tor [ɪntərə'geɪtə(r)] interrogante *m/f*

in·ter·rupt [ɪntə'rʌpt] *v/t & v/i* interrompere

in·ter·rup·tion [ɪntə'rʌpʃn] interruzione *f*

in·ter·sect [ɪntə'sekt] **1** *v/t* intersecare **2** *v/i* intersecarsi

in·ter·sec·tion ['ɪntəsekʃn] (*crossroads*) incrocio *m*

in·ter·val ['ɪntəvl] intervallo *m*; **sunny ~s** schiarite

in·ter·vene [ɪntə'vi:n] *v/i of person, police etc* intervenire; *of time* trascorrere

in·ter·ven·tion [ɪntə'venʃn] intervento *m*

in·ter·view ['ɪntəvju:] **1** *n on TV, in paper* intervista *f; for job* intervista *f* d'assunzione, colloquio *m* di lavoro **2** *v/t on TV, for paper* intervistare; *for*

job sottoporre a intervista

in·ter·view·ee [ɪntəvju:'i:] *on TV* intervistato *m*, -a *f; for job* candidato *m*, -a *f*

in·ter·view·er ['ɪntəvju:ə(r)] *on TV, for paper* intervistatore *m*, -trice *f*; (*for job*) *persona f che conduce un'intervista d'assunzione*

in·tes·tine [ɪn'testɪn] intestino *m*

in·ti·ma·cy ['ɪntɪməsɪ] intimità *f inv*

in·ti·mate ['ɪntɪmət] *adj friend, thoughts* intimo; **be ~ with s.o.** *sexually* avere rapporti intimi con qu

in·tim·i·date [ɪn'tɪmɪdeɪt] *v/t* intimidire

in·tim·i·da·tion [ɪntɪmɪ'deɪʃn] intimidazione *f*

in·to ['ɪntʊ] *prep* in; **he put it ~ his suitcase** l'ha messo in valigia; **translate ~ English** tradurre in inglese; **be ~ sth** F (*like*) amare qc; (*be involved with*) interessarsi di qc; **be ~ drugs** fare uso di droga; **when you're ~ the job** quando sei pratico del lavoro

in·tol·e·ra·ble [ɪn'tɒlərəbl] *adj* intollerabile

in·tol·e·rant [ɪn'tɒlərənt] *adj* intollerante

in·tox·i·cat·ed [ɪn'tɒksɪkeɪtɪd] *adj* ubriaco

in·tran·si·tive [ɪn'trænsɪtɪv] *adj* intransitivo

in·tra·ve·nous [ɪntrə'vi:nəs] *adj* endovenoso

in·trep·id [ɪn'trepɪd] *adj* intrepido

in·tri·cate ['ɪntrɪkət] *adj* complicato

in·trigue ['ɪntri:g] **1** *n* intrigo *m* **2** *v/t* [ɪn'tri:g] intrigare; **I would be ~d to know ...** m'interesserebbe molto sapere ...

in·trigu·ing [ɪn'tri:gɪŋ] *adj* intrigante

in·tro·duce [ɪntrə'dju:s] *v/t person* presentare; *new technique etc* introdurre; **may I ~ ...?** permette che le presenti ...?

in·tro·duc·tion [ɪntrə'dʌkʃn] *to person* presentazione *f; to a new food, sport etc* approccio *m; in book, of new technique* introduzione *f*

in·tro·vert ['ɪntrəvɜːt] introverso *m*, -a *f*

in·trude [ɪn'truːd] *v/i* importunare

in·trud·er [ɪn'truːdə(r)] intruso *m*, -a *f*

in·tru·sion [ɪn'truːʒn] intrusione *f*

in·tu·i·tion [ɪntjuː'ɪʃn] intuito *m*

in·vade [ɪn'veɪd] *v/t* invadere

in·val·id¹ [ɪn'vælɪd] *adj* non valido

in·va·lid² ['ɪnvəlɪd] *n* MED invalido *m*, -a *f*

in·val·i·date [ɪn'vælɪdeɪt] *v/t* claim, theory invalidare

in·val·u·a·ble [ɪn'væljubl] *adj* help, contributor prezioso

in·var·i·a·bly [ɪn'veɪrɪəblɪ] *adv* (always) invariabilmente

in·va·sion [ɪn'veɪʒn] invasione *f*

in·vent [ɪn'vent] *v/t* inventare

in·ven·tion [ɪn'venʃn] invenzione *f*

in·ven·tive [ɪn'ventɪv] *adj* fantasioso

in·ven·tor [ɪn'ventə(r)] inventore *m*, -trice *f*

in·ven·to·ry ['ɪnvəntrɪ] inventario *m*

in·verse [ɪn'vɜːs] *adj* order inverso

in·vert [ɪn'vɜːt] *v/t* invertire

in·vert·ed 'com·mas [ɪn'vɜːtɪd] *npl* virgolette *fpl*

in·ver·te·brate [ɪn'vɜːtɪbrət] *n* invertebrato *m*

in·vest [ɪn'vest] *v/t & v/i* investire

in·ves·ti·gate [ɪn'vestɪgeɪt] *v/t* indagare su

in·ves·ti·ga·tion [ɪnvestɪ'geɪʃn] indagine *f*

in·ves·ti·ga·tive 'jour·nal·ism [ɪn'vestɪgətɪv] giornalismo *m* investigativo

in·vest·ment [ɪn'vestmənt] investimento *m*

in·ves·tor [ɪn'vestə(r)] investitore *m*, -trice

in·vig·or·at·ing [ɪn'vɪgəreɪtɪŋ] *adj* climate tonificante

in·vin·ci·ble [ɪn'vɪnsəbl] *adj* invincibile

in·vis·i·ble [ɪn'vɪzɪbl] *adj* invisibile

in·vi·ta·tion [ɪnvɪ'teɪʃn] invito *m*

in·vite [ɪn'vaɪt] *v/t* invitare; **can I ~ you for a meal?** posso invitarti a pranzo?

♦ **invite in** *v/t* invitare a entrare

in·voice ['ɪnvɔɪs] **1** *n* fattura *f* **2** *v/t customer* fatturare

in·vol·un·ta·ry [ɪn'vɒləntrɪ] *adj* involontario

in·volve [ɪn'vɒlv] *v/t* hard work, expense comportare; (concern) riguardare; **what does it ~?** che cosa comporta?; **get ~d with sth** entrare a far parte di qc; **get ~d with s.o.** emotionally, romantically legarsi a qu

in·volved [ɪn'vɒlvd] *adj* (complex) complesso

in·volve·ment [ɪn'vɒlvmənt] in a project etc partecipazione *f*; in a crime, accident coinvolgimento *m*

in·vul·ne·ra·ble [ɪn'vʌlnərəbl] *adj* invulnerabile

in·ward ['ɪnwəd] **1** *adj* direction verso l'interno; feeling, thoughts intimo **2** *adv* verso l'interno

in·ward·ly ['ɪnwədlɪ] *adv* dentro di sé

i·o·dine ['aɪədiːn] iodio *m*

IOU [aɪəʊ'juː] *abbr* (= **I owe you**) pagherò *m*

IQ [aɪ'kjuː] *abbr* (= **intelligence quotient**) quoziente *m* d'intelligenza

I·ran [ɪ'rɑːn] Iran *m*

I·ra·ni·an [ɪ'reɪnɪən] **1** *adj* iraniano **2** *n* person iraniano *m*, -a *f*

I·raq [ɪ'rɑːk] Iraq *m*

I·ra·qi [ɪ'rækɪ] **1** *adj* iracheno **2** *n* person iracheno *m*, -a *f*

Ire·land ['aɪələnd] Irlanda *f*

i·ris ['aɪərɪs] of eye iride *f*; flower iris *m* inv

I·rish ['aɪərɪʃ] *adj* irlandese

'I·rish·man irlandese *m*

'I·rish·wom·an irlandese *f*

i·ron ['aɪən] **1** *n* substance ferro *m*; for clothes ferro *m* da stiro **2** *v/t* shirts etc stirare

i·ron·ic(al) [aɪ'rɒnɪk(l)] *adj* ironico

i·ron·ing ['aɪənɪŋ]: **do the ~** stirare

'i·ron·ing board asse *m* da stiro

'i·ron·works stabilimento *m* siderurgico

i·ron·y ['aɪərənɪ] ironia *f*

ir·ra·tion·al [ɪ'ræʃənl] *adj* irrazionale

ir·rec·on·ci·la·ble [ɪrekən'saɪləbl] *adj* inconciliabile

ir·re·cov·er·a·ble [ɪrɪ'kʌvərəbl] *adj* irrecuperabile

ir·reg·u·lar [ɪ'regjʊlə(r)] *adj* irregolare

ir·rel·e·vant [ɪ'reləvənt] *adj* non pertinente

ir·rep·a·ra·ble [ɪ'repərəbl] *adj* irreparabile

ir·re·place·a·ble [ɪrɪ'pleɪsəbl] *adj object, person* insostituibile

ir·re·pres·si·ble [ɪrɪ'presəbl] *adj sense of humour* incontenibile; *person* che non si lascia abbattere

ir·re·proa·cha·ble [ɪrɪ'prəʊtʃəbl] *adj* irreprensibile

ir·re·sis·ti·ble [ɪrɪ'zɪstəbl] *adj* irresistibile

ir·re·spec·tive [ɪrɪ'spektɪv] *adj*: **~ of** a prescindere da

ir·re·spon·si·ble [ɪrɪ'spɒnsəbl] *adj* irresponsabile

ir·re·trie·va·ble [ɪrɪ'triːvəbl] *adj* irrecuperabile

ir·rev·e·rent [ɪ'revərənt] *adj* irriverente

ir·rev·o·ca·ble [ɪ'revəkəbl] *adj* irrevocabile

ir·ri·gate ['ɪrɪgeɪt] *v/t* irrigare

ir·ri·ga·tion [ɪrɪ'geɪʃn] irrigazione *f*

ir·ri·ga·tion ca·nal canale *m* d'irrigazione

ir·ri·ta·ble ['ɪrɪtəbl] *adj* irritabile

ir·ri·tate ['ɪrɪteɪt] *v/t* irritare

ir·ri·tat·ing ['ɪrɪteɪtɪŋ] *adj* irritante

ir·ri·ta·tion [ɪrɪ'teɪʃn] irritazione *f*

Is·lam ['ɪzlɑːm] Islam *m*

Is·lam·ic [ɪz'læmɪk] *adj* islamico

is·land ['aɪlənd] isola *f*; **(traffic) ~** isola *f* spartitraffico

is·land·er ['aɪləndə(r)] isolano *m*, -a *f*

i·so·late ['aɪsəleɪt] *v/t* isolare

i·so·lat·ed ['aɪsəleɪtɪd] *adj house, occurrence* isolato

i·so·la·tion [aɪsə'leɪʃn] *of a region* isolamento *m*; **in ~** *taken etc* da solo

i·so·la·tion ward reparto *m* d'isolamento

ISP [aɪes'piː] *abbr* (= **Internet service provider**) provider *m inv* di servizi Internet

Is·rael ['ɪzreɪl] Israele *m*

Is·rae·li [ɪz'reɪli] **1** *adj* israeliano **2** *n person* israeliano *m*, -a *f*

is·sue ['ɪʃuː] **1** *n* (*matter*) questione *f*; (*result*) risultato *m*; *of magazine* numero *m*; **the point at ~** il punto in discussione; **take ~ with s.o. / sth** prendere posizione contro qu / qc **2** *v/t passports, visa* rilasciare; *supplies* distribuire; *coins* emettere; *warning* dare

IT [aɪ'tiː] *abbr* (= **information technology**) IT *f*

it [ɪt] *pron* ◊ *as subject*: **what colour is ~? – ~ is red** di che colore è? – è rosso; **~'s raining** piove; **~'s me / him** sono io / è lui; **~'s Charlie here** TELEC sono Charlie; **that's ~!** (*that's right*) proprio così!; (*finished*) finito! ◊ *as object* lo *m*, la *f*; **I broke ~** l'ho rotto, -a; **I can't eat ~ all** non posso mangiarla tutta

I·tal·i·an [ɪ'tæljən] **1** *adj* italiano **2** *n person* italiano *m*, -a *f*; *language* italiano *m*

i·tal·ic [ɪ'tælɪk] *adj* in corsivo

I·ta·ly ['ɪtəlɪ] Italia *f*

itch [ɪtʃ] **1** *n* prurito *m* **2** *v/i* prudere

i·tem ['aɪtəm] *on agenda* punto *m* (all'ordine del giorno); *on shopping list* articolo *m*; *in accounts* voce *f*; **news ~** notizia *f*; **~ of clothing** capo *m* di vestiario

i·tem·ize ['aɪtəmaɪz] *v/t invoice* dettagliare

i·tin·e·ra·ry [aɪ'tɪnərərɪ] itinerario *m*

its [ɪts] *adj* il suo *m*, la sua *f*, i suoi *mpl*, le sue *fpl*

it's [ɪts] → **it is**; **it has**

it·self [ɪt'self] *pron reflexive* si; *emphatic* di per sé; **by ~** (*alone*) da solo; (*automatically*) da sé

i·vo·ry ['aɪvərɪ] avorio *m*

i·vy ['aɪvɪ] edera *f*

J

jab [dʒæb] v/t (pret & pp **-bed**) conficcare

jab·ber ['dʒæbə(r)] v/i parlare fitto fitto

jack [dʒæk] n MOT cric m inv; in cards fante m
♦ **jack up** v/t MOT sollevare con il cric

jack·et ['dʒækɪt] n giacca f; of book copertina f

jack·et po'ta·to patata f al forno con la buccia

'**jack·knife 1** n coltello m a serramanico **2** v/i: **the lorry ~d** il rimorchio dell'articolato si è messo di traverso

'**jack·pot** primo premio m; **hit the ~** vincere il primo premio; fig fare un terno al lotto

jade [dʒeɪd] giada f

jad·ed ['dʒeɪdɪd] adj spossato

jag·ged ['dʒægɪd] adj frastagliato

jail [dʒeɪl] n prigione f

jam¹ [dʒæm] for bread marmellata f

jam² [dʒæm] **1** n MOT ingorgo m; **be in a ~** F (difficulty) essere in difficoltà **2** v/t (pret & pp **-med**) (ram) ficcare; (cause to stick) bloccare; broadcast disturbare; **be ~med** of roads essere congestionato; of door, window essere bloccato **3** v/i (pret & pp **-med**) (stick) bloccarsi; (squeeze) stiparsi
♦ **jam on** v/t: **jam on the brakes** inchiodare

jam-'packed adj F pieno zeppo

jan·i·tor ['dʒænɪtə(r)] custode m

Jan·u·a·ry ['dʒænjʊərɪ] gennaio m

Ja·pan [dʒə'pæn] Giappone m

Jap·a·nese [dʒæpə'niːz] **1** adj giapponese **2** n person giapponese m/f; language giapponese m

jar¹ [dʒɑː(r)] n container barattolo m

jar² [dʒɑː(r)] v/i (pret & pp **-red**) of noise stridere; **~ on** dar fastidio a

jar·gon ['dʒɑːgən] gergo m

jaun·dice ['dʒɔːndɪs] itterizia f

jaun·diced ['dʒɔːndɪst] adj fig cinico

jaunt [dʒɔːnt] gita f

jaunt·y ['dʒɔːntɪ] adj sbarazzino

jav·e·lin ['dʒævlɪn] (spear) giavellotto m; event lancio m del giavellotto

jaw [dʒɔː] n mascella m

jay·walk·er ['dʒeɪwɔːkə(r)] pedone m indisciplinato

jazz [dʒæz] jazz m inv
♦ **jazz up** v/t F ravvivare

jeal·ous ['dʒeləs] adj geloso; **be ~ of ...** essere geloso di ...

jeal·ous·ly ['dʒeləslɪ] adv gelosamente

jeal·ous·y ['dʒeləsɪ] gelosia f

jeans [dʒiːnz] npl jeans mpl

jeep [dʒiːp] jeep f inv

jeer [dʒɪə(r)] **1** n scherno m **2** v/i schernire; **~ at** schernire

jel·ly ['dʒelɪ] gelatina f

'**jel·ly ba·by** bonbon m inv di gelatina; '**jel·ly bean** bonbon m inv di gelatina; '**jel·ly·fish** medusa f

jeop·ar·dize ['dʒepədaɪz] v/t mettere in pericolo

jeop·ar·dy ['dʒepədɪ]: **be in ~** essere in pericolo

jerk¹ [dʒɜːk] **1** n scossone m **2** v/t dare uno strattone

jerk² [dʒɜːk] F idiota m/f

jerk·y ['dʒɜːkɪ] adj movement a scatti

jer·sey ['dʒɜːzɪ] (sweater) maglia f; fabric jersey m inv

jest [dʒest] **1** n scherzo m; **in ~** per scherzo **2** v/i scherzare

Je·sus ['dʒiːzəs] Gesù m

jet [dʒet] **1** n of water zampillo m; (nozzle) becco m; airplane jet m inv **2** v/i (pret & pp **-ted**) travel volare

jet-'black adj (nero) corvino; '**jet en·gine** motore m a reazione; '**jet-lag** jet-lag m inv

jet·ti·son ['dʒetɪsn] *v/t* gettare; *fig* abbandonare

jet·ty ['dʒetɪ] molo *m*

Jew [dʒuː] ebreo *m*, -a *f*

jew·el ['dʒuːəl] gioiello *m*; *fig: person* perla *f*

jew·el·er *Am*, **jew·el·ler** ['dʒuːlə(r)] gioielliere *m*

jew·el·lery, **jew·el·ry** *Am* ['dʒuːlrɪ] gioielli *mpl*

Jew·ish ['dʒuːɪʃ] *adj* ebraico; *people* ebreo

jif·fy [dʒɪfɪ] F: **in a ~** in un batter d'occhio, in un attimo

jig·saw (puzzle) ['dʒɪgsɔː] puzzle *m inv*

jilt [dʒɪlt] *v/t* piantare F

jin·gle ['dʒɪŋgl] **1** *n song* jingle *m inv* **2** *v/i of keys, coins* tintinnare

jinx [dʒɪŋks] *n person* iettatore *m*, -trice *f*; *(bad luck)* **there's a ~ on this project** questo progetto è iellato

jit·ters ['dʒɪtəz] *npl* F: **get the ~** avere fifa F

jit·ter·y ['dʒɪtərɪ] *adj* F nervoso

job [dʒɒb] *(employment)* lavoro *m*; *(task)* compito *m*; **out of a ~** senza lavoro; **it's a good ~ you ...** meno male che tu ...; **you'll have a ~** *(it'll be difficult)* sarà un'impresa

'job cen·tre *Br* ufficio *m* di collocamento; **'job de·scrip·tion** elenco *m* delle mansioni; **'job hunt: be ~ing** cercare lavoro

job·less ['dʒɒblɪs] *adj* disoccupato

job sat·is'fac·tion soddisfazione *f* nel lavoro

jock·ey ['dʒɒkɪ] *n* fantino *m*

jog [dʒɒg] **1** *n* corsa *f*; **go for a ~** andare a fare footing **2** *v/i (pret & pp -ged) as exercise* fare footing **3** *v/t (pret & pp -ged) elbow etc* urtare; **~ s.o.'s memory** rinfrescare la memoria a qu

♦ **jog along** *v/i* F procedere

jog·ger ['dʒɒgə(r)] *person* persona *f* che fa footing; *Am shoe* scarpa *f* da ginnastica

jog·ging ['dʒɒgɪŋ] footing *m inv*; **go ~** fare footing

'**jog·ging suit** tuta *f* da ginnastica

join [dʒɔɪn] **1** *n* giuntura *f* **2** *v/i of roads, rivers* unirsi; *(become a member)* iscriversi **3** *v/t (connect)* unire; *person* unirsi a; *club* iscriversi a; *(go to work for)* entrare in; *of road* congiungersi a

♦ **join in** *v/i* partecipare

♦ **join up** *v/i* MIL arruolarsi

join·er ['dʒɔɪnə(r)] *n* falegname *m*

joint [dʒɔɪnt] **1** *n* ANAT articolazione *f*; *in woodwork* giunto *m*; *of meat* arrosto *m*; F *place* locale *m*; *of cannabis* spinello *m* **2** *adj (shared)* comune

joint ac'count conto *m* comune

joint 'ven·ture joint venture *f inv*

joke [dʒəʊk] **1** *n story* barzelletta *f*; *(practical ~)* scherzo *m*; **play a ~ on** fare uno scherzo a; **it's no ~** non è uno scherzo **2** *v/i (pretend)* scherzare

jok·er ['dʒəʊkə(r)] *in cards* jolly *m inv*; F burlone *m*, -a *f*

jok·ing ['dʒəʊkɪŋ]: **~ apart** scherzi a parte

jok·ing·ly ['dʒəʊkɪŋlɪ] *adv* scherzosamente

jol·ly ['dʒɒlɪ] *adj* allegro; **~ good** benissimo

jolt [dʒɒlt] **1** *n (jerk)* scossone *m* **2** *v/t (push)* urtare

jos·tle ['dʒɒsl] *v/t* spintonare

♦ **jot down** [dʒɒt] *v/t (pret & pp -ted)* annotare

jour·nal ['dʒɜːnl] *magazine* rivista *f*; *diary* diario *m*

jour·nal·is·m ['dʒɜːnəlɪzm] giornalismo *m*

jour·nal·ist ['dʒɜːnəlɪst] giornalista *m/f*

jour·ney ['dʒɜːnɪ] *n* viaggio *m*

jo·vi·al ['dʒəʊvɪəl] *adj* gioviale

joy [dʒɔɪ] gioia *f*

'**joy·stick** COMPUT joystick *m inv*

ju·bi·lant ['dʒuːbɪlənt] *adj* esultante

ju·bi·la·tion [dʒuːbɪ'leɪʃn] giubilo *m*

judge [dʒʌdʒ] **1** *n* giudice *m* **2** *v/t* giudicare; *competition* fare da giudice a **3** *v/i* giudicare

judg(e)·ment ['dʒʌdʒmənt] *n*

giudizio m; *I agreed, against my better* ~ ho accettato, pur pensando che fosse sbagliato; *an error of* ~ un errore di valutazione

'**Judg(e)·ment Day** il giorno m del giudizio

ju·di·cial [dʒuːˈdɪʃl] adj giudiziario

ju·di·cious [dʒuːˈdɪʃəs] adj giudizioso

ju·do [ˈdʒuːdəʊ] judo m inv

jug [dʒʌg] brocca f

jug·ger·naut [ˈdʒʌgənɔːt] bisonte m della strada F

jug·gle [ˈdʒʌgl] v/t fare giochi di destrezza con; *fig: conflicting demands* destreggiarsi fra; *figures* manipolare

jug·gler [ˈdʒʌglə(r)] giocoliere m

juice [dʒuːs] succo m

juic·y [ˈdʒuːsɪ] adj succoso; *news, gossip* piccante

juke·box [ˈdʒuːkbɒks] juke-box m inv

Ju·ly [dʒuˈlaɪ] luglio m

jum·ble [ˈdʒʌmbl] mucchio m

♦ **jumble up** v/t mescolare

'**jum·ble sale** vendita f di beneficenza

jum·bo (jet) [ˈdʒʌmbəʊ] jumbo m (jet)

'**jum·bo-sized** adj gigante

jump [dʒʌmp] **1** n salto m; (*increase*) impennata f; *give a* ~ *of surprise* sobbalzare **2** v/i saltare; (*increase*) aumentare rapidamente, avere un'impennata; *in surprise* sobbalzare; ~ *to one's feet* balzare in piedi; ~ *to conclusions* arrivare a conclusioni affrettate **3** v/t *fence etc* saltare; F (*attack*) aggredire; ~ *the queue* non rispettare la fila; ~ *the lights* passare col rosso

♦ **jump at** v/t *opportunity* prendere al balzo, cogliere al volo

jump·er[1] [ˈdʒʌmpə(r)] golf m inv

jump·er[2] [ˈdʒʌmpə(r)] SP saltatore m, -trice f

jump·y [ˈdʒʌmpɪ] adj nervoso

junc·tion [ˈdʒʌŋkʃn] *of roads* incrocio m

junc·ture [ˈdʒʌŋktʃə(r)] *fml: at this* ~ in questo frangente

June [dʒuːn] giugno m

jun·gle [ˈdʒʌŋgl] giungla f

jun·ior [ˈdʒuːnɪə(r)] **1** adj (*subordinate*) subalterno; (*younger*) giovane **2** n *in rank* subalterno m, -a f; *she is ten years my* ~ ha dieci anni meno di me

'**ju·nior school** scuola f elementare

junk [dʒʌŋk] (*rubbish*) robaccia f

'**junk food** alimenti mpl poco sani

junk·ie [ˈdʒʌŋkɪ] n F tossico m, -a f F

'**junk mail** posta f spazzatura; '**junk shop** negozio m di chincaglierie; '**junk·yard** deposito m di robivecchi

jur·is·dic·tion [dʒuərɪsˈdɪkʃn] LAW giurisdizione f

ju·ror [ˈdʒuərə(r)] n giurato m, -a f

ju·ry [ˈdʒuərɪ] n giuria f

just [dʒʌst] **1** adj giusto **2** adv (*barely*) appena; (*exactly*) proprio; (*only*) solo; *I've* ~ *seen her* l'ho appena vista; ~ *about* (*almost*) quasi; *I was* ~ *about to leave when ...* stavo proprio per andarmene quando ...; *a house* ~ *like that* una casa proprio così; *he left her* ~ *like that* l'ha lasciata così, senza spiegazioni; *he agreed* ~ *like that* ha accettato così, senza pensarci due volte; ~ *now* (*a few moments ago*) proprio ora; (*at the moment*) al momento; ~ *you wait!* aspetta un po'!; ~ *be quiet!* fai silenzio!; ~ *as rich* altrettanto ricco

jus·tice [ˈdʒʌstɪs] giustizia f

jus·ti·fi·a·ble [dʒʌstɪˈfaɪəbl] adj giustificabile

jus·ti·fi·a·bly [dʒʌstɪˈfaɪəblɪ] adv a ragione

jus·ti·fi·ca·tion [dʒʌstɪfɪˈkeɪʃn] giustificazione f

jus·ti·fy [ˈdʒʌstɪfaɪ] v/t (*pret & pp -ied*) *also text* giustificare

just·ly [ˈdʒʌstlɪ] adv giustamente

♦ **jut out** [dʒʌt] v/i (*pret & pp -ted*) sporgere

ju·ve·nile [ˈdʒuːvənaɪl] **1** adj minorile; *pej* puerile **2** n *fml* minore m/f

ju·ve·nile de·lin·quen·cy delinquenza *f* minorile

ju·ve·nile de·lin·quent delinquente
m/f minorile

K

k [keɪ] *abbr* (= **kilobyte**) k (=kilobyte
m inv); (= **thousand**) mille; **earn
25K** guadagnare 25 mila sterline

kan·ga·roo [kæŋgə'ruː] canguro *m*

ka·ra·te [kə'rɑːtɪ] karate *m inv*

ka·ra·te chop colpo *m* di karate

ke·bab [kɪ'bæb] spiedino *m* di carne

keel [kiːl] NAUT chiglia *f*

♦ **keel over** *v/i* of boat capovolgersi;
of structure crollare; *of person* cascare per terra; *faint* svenire

keen [kiːn] *adj person* entusiasta;
interest, competition vivo; **be ~ on
sth** essere appassionato di qc; **I'm
not ~ on the idea** l'idea non mi va
tanto; **he's ~ on her** lei gli piace
molto; **be ~ to do sth** aver molta
voglia di fare qc

keep [kiːp] **1** *n* (*maintenance*) vitto e
alloggio *m*; **for ~s** F per sempre **2** *v/t*
(*pret & pp* **kept**) tenere; (*not lose*)
mantenere; (*detain*) trattenere;
family mantenere; *animals* allevare;
~ a promise mantenere una promessa; **~ s.o. company** tenere compagnia a qu; **~ s.o. waiting** far
aspettare qu; **~ sth to o.s.** (*not tell*)
tenere qc per sé; **~ sth from s.o.** nascondere qc a qu; **~ s.o. from doing
sth** impedire a qu di fare qc; **~
trying!** continua a provare!; **don't ~
interrupting!** non interrompere in
continuazione! **3** *v/i* (*pret & pp*
kept) (*remain*) rimanere; *of food,
milk* conservarsi; **~ left** tenere la sinistra; **~ straight on** vai sempre
dritto; **~ still** stare fermo

♦ **keep away 1** *v/i* stare alla larga;
keep away from ... stai alla larga
da ... **2** *v/t* tenere lontano; **keep s.o.**

away from sth tenere qu lontano
da qc

♦ **keep back** *v/t* (*hold in check*) trattenere; *information* nascondere

♦ **keep down** *v/t voice* abbassare;
costs, inflation etc contenere; *food*
trattenere; **keep the noise down,
will you?** fate meno rumore!

♦ **keep in** *v/t in hospital* trattenere;
keep a pupil in punire uno studente
trattenendolo oltre l'orario scolastico

♦ **keep off 1** *v/t* (*avoid*) evitare; **keep
off the grass** non calpestare l'erba
2 *v/i*: **if the rain keeps off** se non
piove

♦ **keep on 1** *v/i* continuare; **keep on
doing sth** continuare a fare qc **2** *v/t
employee, coat* tenere

♦ **keep on at** *v/t* (*nag*) assillare

♦ **keep out 1** *v/t the cold* proteggere
da; *person* escludere **2** *v/i of room*
non entrare (**of** in); *of argument etc*
non immischiarsi (**of** in); **keep out
as sign** vietato l'ingresso; **you keep
out of this!** non immischiarti!

♦ **keep to** *v/t path, rules* seguire; **keep
to the point** non divagare

♦ **keep up 1** *v/i when walking, running etc* tener dietro **2** *v/t pace, payments* stare dietro a; *bridge, pants*
reggere

♦ **keep up with** *v/t* stare al passo con;
(*stay in touch with*) mantenere i rapporti con

keep·ing ['kiːpɪŋ]: **be in ~ with** essere in armonia con

'keep·sake ricordo *m*

keg [keg] barilotto *m*

ken·nel ['kenl] canile *m*

ken·nels ['kenlz] *npl* canile *m*

kept [kept] *pret & pp* → **keep**

kerb [kɜːb] orlo *m* del marciapiede

ker·nel ['kɜːnl] nocciolo *m*

ketch·up ['ketʃʌp] ketchup *m inv*

ket·tle ['ketl] bollitore *m*

key [kiː] **1** *n to door, drawer,* MUS chiave *f*; *on keyboard* tasto *m* **2** *adj (vital)* chiave **3** *v/t* COMPUT battere

♦ **key in** *v/t data* immettere

'key·board COMPUT, MUS tastiera *f*; **'key·board·er** COMPUT, MUS tastierista *m/f*; **'key·card** tessera *f* magnetica

keyed-up [kiːd'ʌp] *adj* agitato

'key·hole buco *m* della serratura; **'key·note 'speech** discorso *m* programmatico; **'key·ring** portachiavi *m inv*

kha·ki ['kɑːkɪ] *adj colour* cachi *inv*

kick [kɪk] **1** *n* calcio *m*; F *(thrill)* gusto *m*; *(just) for ~s* F (solo) per il gusto di farlo *v/t* dare un calcio a; F *habit* liberarsi da **3** *v/i* dare calci; SP calciare; *of horse* scalciare

♦ **kick around** *v/t (treat harshly)* maltrattare; F *(discuss)* discutere di; *kick a ball around* giocare a pallone

♦ **kick in** *v/i* P *(start to operate)* entrare in funzione

♦ **kick off** *v/i* F *(start)* iniziare; *of player* dare il calcio d'inizio

♦ **kick out** *v/t* buttar fuori; *be kicked out of the company/army* essere buttato fuori dalla ditta/dall'esercito

♦ **kick up** *v/t*: *kick up a fuss* fare una scenata

'kick·back F *(bribe)* tangente *f*

'kick·off SP calcio *m* d'inizio

kid [kɪd] **1** *n* F *(child)* bambino *m*, -a *f*; F *(young person)* ragazzo *m*, -a *f*; F **brother/sister** fratello/sorella minore **2** *v/t (pret & pp* **-ded)** F prendere in giro **3** *v/i (pret & pp* **-ded)** F scherzare; *I was only ~ding* stavo solo scherzando

kid·der ['kɪdə(r)] F burlone *m*, -a *f*

kid 'gloves: *handle s.o. with ~* trattare qu coi guanti

kid·nap ['kɪdnæp] *v/t (pret & pp* **-ped)** rapire, sequestrare

kid·nap·per ['kɪdnæpə(r)] rapitore *m*,-trice *f*, sequestratore *m*, -trice *f*

'kid·nap·ping ['kɪdnæpɪŋ] rapimento *m*, sequestro *m* (di persona)

kid·ney ['kɪdnɪ] ANAT rene *m*; *in cooking* rognone *m*

'kid·ney bean fagiolo *m* comune

'kid·ney ma·chine MED rene *m* artificiale

kill [kɪl] *v/t* uccidere; *plant, time* ammazzare; *be ~ed in an accident* morire in un incidente; *~ o.s.* suicidarsi; *~ o.s. laughing* F morire dalle risate

kil·ler ['kɪlə(r)] *(murderer)* assassino *m*, -a *f*; *(hired ~)* killer *m/f inv*; *flu can be a ~* si può morire d'influenza

kil·ling ['kɪlɪŋ] omicidio *m*; *make a ~* F *(lots of money)* fare un pacco di soldi F

kil·ling·ly ['kɪlɪŋlɪ] *adv*: *~ funny* divertentissimo

kiln [kɪln] fornace *f*

ki·lo ['kiːləʊ] chilo *m*

ki·lo·byte ['kɪləʊbaɪt] COMPUT kilobyte *m inv*

ki·lo·gram ['kɪləʊgræm] chilogrammo *m*

ki·lo·me·ter *Am*, **ki·lo·me·tre** [kɪ'lɒmɪtə(r)] chilometro *m*

kilt [kɪlt] kilt *m inv*

kind¹ [kaɪnd] *adj* gentile

kind² [kaɪnd] *n (sort)* tipo *m*; *(make, brand)* marca *f*; *all ~s of people* gente di tutti i tipi; *nothing of the ~!* niente affatto!; *~ of sad/strange* F un po' triste/strano

kin·der·gar·ten ['kɪndəgɑːtn] asilo *m*

kind-heart·ed [kaɪnd'hɑːtɪd] *adj* di buon cuore

kind·ly ['kaɪndlɪ] **1** *adj* gentile **2** *adv* gentilmente; *(please)* per cortesia

kind·ness ['kaɪndnɪs] *n* gentilezza *f*

king [kɪŋ] re *m inv*

king·dom ['kɪŋdəm] regno *m*

'king-size(d) *adj bed* matrimoniale grande; *cigarettes* lungo

kink [kɪŋk] *in hose etc* attorcigliamento *m*

kink·y ['kɪŋkɪ] *adj* F particolare F

kiosk ['kiːɒsk] edicola *f*

kip [kɪp] P pisolino *m*

kip·per ['kɪpə(r)] aringa *f* affumicata

kiss [kɪs] **1** *n* bacio *m* **2** *v/t* baciare **3** *v/i* baciarsi

kiss of 'life respirazione *f* bocca a bocca

kit [kɪt] kit *m inv*; (*equipment*) attrezzatura *f*; *for assembly* kit *m inv* di montaggio

kitch·en ['kɪtʃɪn] cucina *f*

kitch·en·ette [kɪtʃɪ'net] cucinino *m*

kitch·en 'sink: she packs everything but the ~ F si porta dietro tutta la casa

kite [kaɪt] aquilone *m*

kit·ten ['kɪtn] gattino *m*

kit·ty ['kɪtɪ] *money* cassa *f* comune

knack [næk] capacità *f inv*; **there's a ~ to it** bisogna saperlo fare

knead [niːd] *v/t dough* lavorare

knee [niː] *n* ginocchio *m*

'knee·cap *n* rotula *f*

kneel [niːl] *v/i* (*pret & pp* **knelt**) inginocchiarsi

'knee-length *adj* al ginocchio

knelt [nelt] *pret & pp* → **kneel**

knew [njuː] *pret* → **know**

knick·ers ['nɪkəz] *npl* mutandine *fpl*; **get one's ~ in a twist** P agitarsi

knick-knacks ['nɪknæks] *npl* F ninnoli *mpl*

knife [naɪf] **1** *n* (*pl* **knives** [naɪvz]) coltello *m* **2** *v/t* accoltellare

knight [naɪt] *n* cavaliere *m*

knit [nɪt] (*pret & pp* **-ted**) **1** *v/t* fare a maglia **2** *v/i* lavorare a maglia

♦ **knit together** *v/i of broken bone* saldarsi

knit·ting ['nɪtɪŋ] *sth being knitted* lavoro *m* a maglia; *activity* il lavorare *m* a maglia

'knit·ting nee·dle ferro *m* (da calza)

'knit·wear maglieria *f*

knob [nɒb] *on door* pomello *m*; *of butter* noce *f*

knock [nɒk] **1** *n on door* colpo *m*;

(*blow*) botta *f* **2** *v/t* (*hit*) colpire; *head, knee* battere; F (*criticize*) criticare **3** *v/i at the door* bussare (*at* a); **I ~ed my head** ho battuto la testa

♦ **knock around 1** *v/t* F (*beat*) picchiare **2** *v/i* F (*travel*) vagabondare

♦ **knock down** *v/t of car* investire; *object, building etc* buttar giù; F (*reduce the price of*) scontare

♦ **knock off 1** *v/t* P (*steal*) fregare P **2** *v/i* F (*stop work for the day*) smontare F

♦ **knock out** *v/t* (*make unconscious*) mettere K.O. F; *power lines etc* mettere fuori uso; (*eliminate*) eliminare

♦ **knock over** *v/t* far cadere; *of car* investire

'knock·down *adj*: **a ~ price** un prezzo stracciato

knock·er ['nɒkə(r)] *on door* battente *m*

knock-kneed [nɒk'niːd] *adj* con le gambe storte

'knock·out *in boxing* K.O. *m inv*

knot [nɒt] **1** *n* nodo *m* **2** *v/t* (*pret & pp* **-ted**) annodare

'knot·ty ['nɒtɪ] *adj problem* spinoso

know [nəʊ] **1** *v/t* (*pret* **knew**, *pp* **known**) *subject; person, place* conoscere; (*recognize*) riconoscere; **~ how to waltz** saper ballare il valzer **2** *v/i* (*pret* **knew**, *pp* **known**) sapere; **I don't ~** non so; **yes, I ~** sì, lo so **3** *n*: **be in the ~** F essere beninformato

'know-all F sapientone *m*, -a *f*

'know-how F know-how *m inv*

know·ing ['nəʊɪŋ] *adj* d'intesa

know·ing·ly ['nəʊɪŋlɪ] *adv* (*wittingly*) deliberatamente; *smile etc* con aria d'intesa

knowl·edge ['nɒlɪdʒ] conoscenza *f*; **to the best of my ~** per quanto ne sappia; **have a good ~ of ...** avere una buona conoscenza di ...

knowl·edge·a·ble ['nɒlɪdʒəbl] *adj* ferrato

known [nəʊn] *pp* → **know**

knuck·le ['nʌkl] nocca *f*

♦ **knuckle down** *v/i* F impegnarsi

♦ **knuckle under** *v/i* F cedere

KO [keɪ'əʊ] (*knockout*) K.O. *m inv*

K

Ko·ran [kə'rɑːn] Corano *m*
Ko·re·a [kə'riːə] Corea *f*
Ko·re·an [kə'riːən] **1** *adj* coreano **2** *n* coreano *m*, -a *f*; *language* coreano *m*

ko·sher ['kəʊʃə(r)] *adj* REL kasher; F a posto
kow·tow ['kaʊtaʊ] *v/i* F prostrarsi
ku·dos ['kjuːdɒs] gloria *f*

L

lab [læb] laboratorio *m*
la·bel ['leɪbl] **1** *n* etichetta *f* **2** *v/t baggage* mettere l'etichetta su
la·bor·a·to·ry [lə'bɒrətrɪ] laboratorio *m*
la·bor·a·to·ry tech·ni·cian tecnico *m* di laboratorio
la·bor *etc Am* → **labour** *etc*
la·bo·ri·ous [lə'bɔːrɪəs] *adj* laborioso
'la·bor u·ni·on *Am* sindacato *m*
la·bour ['leɪbə(r)] *n* (*work*) lavoro *m*; *in pregnancy* travaglio *m*; **be in ~** avere le doglie *fpl*
la·boured ['leɪbəd] *adj style, speech* pesante
la·bour·er ['leɪbərə(r)] manovale *m*
'La·bour Par·ty partito *m* laburista
'la·bour ward MED sala *f* travaglio
lace [leɪs] *n material* pizzo *m*; *for shoe* laccio *m*
♦ **lace up** *v/t shoes* allacciare
lack [læk] **1** *n* mancanza *f* **2** *v/t* mancare di **3** *v/i*: **be ~ing** mancare
lac·quer ['lækə(r)] *n for hair* lacca *f*
lad [læd] ragazzo *m*
lad·der ['lædə(r)] scala *f* (a pioli); Br: *in tights* sfilatura *f*
'lad·der·proof *adj Br* indemagliabile
la·den ['leɪdn] *adj* carico
la·dies (room) ['leɪdiːz] bagno *m* per donne
la·dle ['leɪdl] *n* mestolo *m*
la·dy ['leɪdɪ] signora *f*
'la·dy·bird coccinella *f*
'la·dy·like da signora; **she's not very ~** non è certo una signora
lag [læg] *v/t* (*pret & pp* **-ged**) *pipes* isolare

♦ **lag behind** *v/i* essere indietro
la·ger ['lɑːgə(r)] birra *f* (bionda)
la·goon [lə'guːn] laguna *f*
laid [leɪd] *pret & pp* → **lay**
laid-back [leɪd'bæk] *adj* rilassato
lain [leɪn] *pp* → **lie**
lake [leɪk] lago *m*
lamb [læm] *animal, meat* agnello *m*
lame [leɪm] *adj person* zoppo; *excuse* zoppicante
la·ment [lə'ment] **1** *n* lamento *m* **2** *v/t* piangere
lam·en·ta·ble ['læməntəbl] *adj* deplorevole
lam·i·nat·ed ['læmɪneɪtɪd] *adj surface* laminato; *paper* plastificato
lam·i·nat·ed 'glass vetro *m* laminato
lamp [læmp] lampada *f*
'lamp·post lampione *m*
'lamp·shade paralume *m*
land [lænd] **1** *n* terreno *m* (*shore*) terra *f* (*country*) paese *m*; **by ~** per via di terra; **on ~** sulla terraferma; **work on the ~** *as farmer* lavorare la terra **2** *v/t aeroplane* far atterrare; *job* accaparrarsi **3** *v/i of aeroplane* atterrare; *of ball, sth thrown* cadere, finire
land·ing ['lændɪŋ] *n of aeroplane* atterraggio *m*; *top of staircase* pianerottolo *m*
'land·ing field terreno *m* d'atterraggio; **'land·ing gear** carrello *m* d'atterraggio; **'land·ing strip** pista *f* d'atterraggio
'land·la·dy *of bar* proprietaria *f*; *of rented room* padrona *f* di casa; **'land·lord** *of bar* proprietario *m*; *of*

rented room padrone *m* di casa;
'land·mark punto *m* di riferimento; *fig* pietra *f* miliare; **'land own·er** proprietario *m*, -a *f* terriero, -a;
land·scape ['lændskeɪp] **1** *n* paesaggio *m* **2** *adv print* landscape, orizzontale

'land·slide frana *f*

land·slide 'vic·to·ry vittoria *f* schiacciante

lane [leɪn] *in country* viottolo *m*; (*alley*) vicolo *m*; MOT corsia *f*

lan·guage ['læŋgwɪdʒ] lingua *f*; (*speech, style*) linguaggio *m*

'lan·guage lab laboratorio *m* linguistico

lank [læŋk] *adj pej: hair* diritto

lank·y ['læŋkɪ] *adj person* allampanato

lan·tern ['læntən] lanterna *f*

lap¹ [læp] *n of track* giro *m* (di pista)

lap² [læp] *n of water* sciabordio *m*

♦ **lap up** *v/t* (*pret & pp* **-ped**) *drink, milk* leccare; *flattery* compiacersi di

lap³ [læp] *n of person* grembo *m*

la·pel [lə'pel] bavero *m*

lapse [læps] **1** *n* (*mistake, slip*) mancanza *f*; *of time* intervallo *m*; **~ of memory** vuoto *m* di memoria; **~ of taste** caduta *f* di tono **2** *v/i* scadere; **~ into** cadere in

'lap·top COMPUT laptop *m inv*

lar·ce·ny ['lɑːsənɪ] furto *m*

lard [lɑːd] lardo *m*

lar·der ['lɑːdə(r)] dispensa *f*

large [lɑːdʒ] *adj* grande; **at ~** in libertà

large·ly ['lɑːdʒlɪ] *adv* (*mainly*) in gran parte

lark [lɑːk] *bird* allodola *f*

lar·va ['lɑːvə] larva *f*

lar·yn·gi·tis [lærɪn'dʒaɪtɪs] laringite *f*

lar·ynx ['lærɪŋks] laringe *f*

la·ser ['leɪzə(r)] laser *m inv*

'la·ser beam raggio *m* laser

'la·ser print·er stampante *f* laser

lash¹ [læʃ] *v/t with whip* frustare

lash² [læʃ] *n* (*eyelash*) ciglio *m*

♦ **lash down** *v/t with rope* assicurare

♦ **lash out** *v/i with fists, words* menare colpi

lass [læs] ragazza *f*

last¹ [lɑːst] **1** *adj in series* ultimo; (*preceding*) precedente; **~ but one** penultimo; **~ night** ieri sera; **~ year** l'anno scorso **2** *adv* **he finished ~** ha finito per ultimo; *in race* è arrivato ultimo; **when I ~ saw him** l'ultima volta che l'ho visto; **~ but not least** per finire; **at ~** finalmente

last² [lɑːst] *v/i* durare

last·ing ['lɑːstɪŋ] *adj* duraturo

last·ly ['lɑːstlɪ] *adv* per finire

latch [lætʃ] chiavistello *m*

late [leɪt] **1** *adj* (*behind time*) in ritardo; *in day* tardi; **it's getting ~** si sta facendo tardi; *of* ~ recentemente; **the ~ 19th century** il tardo XIX secolo **2** *adv* tardi

late·ly ['leɪtlɪ] *adv* recentemente

lat·er ['leɪtə(r)] *adv* più tardi; **see you ~!** a più tardi; **~ on** più tardi

lat·est ['leɪtɪst] **1** *adj* ultimo, più recente **2** *n*: **at the ~** al più tardi

lathe [leɪð] *n* tornio *m*

la·ther ['lɑːðə(r)] *from soap* schiuma *f*; **the horse is in a ~** il cavallo è sudato

Lat·in ['lætɪn] **1** *adj* latino **2** *n* latino *m*

Lat·in A'mer·i·ca America *f* Latina

La·tin A'mer·i·can 1 *n* latino-americano *m*, -a *f* **2** *adj* latino-americano

lat·i·tude ['lætɪtjuːd] *geographical* latitudine *f*; (*freedom to act*) libertà *f inv* d'azione

lat·ter ['lætə(r)] *adj*: **the ~** quest'ultimo

laugh [lɑːf] **1** *n* risata *f*; **it was a ~** F ci siamo divertiti **2** *v/i* ridere

♦ **laugh at** *v/t* ridere di

'laugh·ing stock zimbello *m*; **become a ~** rendersi ridicolo

laugh·ter ['lɑːftə(r)] risata *f*; **sounds of ~** delle risate

launch [lɔːntʃ] **1** *n boat* lancia *f*; *of rocket, product* lancio *m*; *of ship* varo *m* **2** *v/t rocket, product* lanciare; *ship* varare

'launch cer·e·mo·ny cerimonia *f* di lancio

launch·(ing) pad rampa *f* di lancio

L

laun·der ['lɔ:ndə(r)] v/t clothes lavare e stirare; ~ **money** riciclare denaro sporco

laun·derette [lɔ:n'dret] lavanderia f automatica

laun·dry ['lɔ:ndrɪ] place lavanderia f; clothes bucato m

lau·rel ['lɒrəl] alloro m

lav·a·to·ry ['lævətrɪ] gabinetto m

lav·en·der ['lævəndə(r)] lavanda f

lav·ish ['lævɪʃ] adj meal lauto; reception, lifestyle sontuoso

law [lɔ:] legge f; **criminal / civil** ~ diritto m penale / civile; **against the** ~ contro la legge; **forbidden by** ~ vietato dalla legge

law-a·bid·ing ['lɔ:əbaɪdɪŋ] adj che rispetta la legge

'law court tribunale m

law·ful ['lɔ:fʊl] adj legale

law·less ['lɔ:lɪs] adj senza legge

lawn [lɔ:n] prato m all'inglese; **play on the** ~ giocare sul prato

'lawn mow·er tagliaerba m inv

'law·suit azione f legale

law·yer ['lɔ:jə(r)] avvocato m

lax [læks] adj permissivo

lax·a·tive ['læksətɪv] n lassativo m

lay[1] [leɪ] pret → **lie**

lay[2] [leɪ] v/t (pret & pp laid) (put down) posare; eggs deporre; V (sexually) scopare V

♦ **lay into** v/t (attack) aggredire

♦ **lay off** v/t workers licenziare; temporarily mettere in cassa integrazione

♦ **lay on** v/t (provide) offrire

♦ **lay out** v/t objects disporre; page impaginare

'lay·a·bout F scansafatiche m/f inv

'lay-by on road piazzola f di sosta

lay·er ['leɪə(r)] strato m

'lay·man laico m

'lay-off licenziamento m; **there have been 50** ~**s** temporary 50 operai sono stati messi in cassa integrazione

♦ **laze around** [leɪz] v/i oziare

la·zy ['leɪzɪ] adj person pigro; day passato a oziare

lb abbr (= **pound**) libbra f

LCD [elsi:'di:] abbr (= **liquid crystal**

display) display m inv a cristalli liquidi

lead[1] [li:d] **1** v/t (pret & pp led) procession, race essere in testa a; company, team essere a capo di; (guide, take) condurre **2** v/i (pret & pp led) in race, competition essere in testa; (provide leadership) dirigere; **a street ~ing off the square** una strada che parte dalla piazza; **a street ~ing into the square** una strada che sbocca sulla piazza; **where is this ~ing?** dove vuoi andare a parare? **3** n in race posizione f di testa; **be in the** ~ essere in testa; **take the** ~ passare in testa

♦ **lead on** v/i (go in front) guidare

♦ **lead up to** v/t preludere

lead[2] [li:d] for dog guinzaglio m

lead[3] [led] substance piombo m

lead·ed ['ledɪd] adj petrol con piombo

lead·er ['li:də(r)] person capo m; in race, on market leader m/f inv; in newspaper editoriale m

lead·er·ship ['li:dəʃɪp] of party etc direzione f, leadership f inv; **under his** ~ sotto la sua direzione; ~ **skills** capacità f di comando; ~ **contest** lotta f per la direzione

lead-free ['ledfri:] adj petrol senza piombo

lead·ing ['li:dɪŋ] adj runner in testa; company, product leader inv

'lead·ing-edge adj company, technology all'avanguardia

leaf [li:f] (pl **leaves** [li:vz]) foglia f

♦ **leaf through** v/t sfogliare

leaf·let ['li:flət] dépliant m inv

league [li:g] lega f; SP campionato m

leak [li:k] **1** n of water perdita f; of gas fuga f; **there's been a** ~ of information c'è stata una fuga di notizie **2** v/i of pipe perdere; of boat far acqua

♦ **leak out** v/i of air, gas fuoriuscire; of news trapelare

leak·y ['li:kɪ] adj pipe che perde; boat che fa acqua

lean[1] [li:n] **1** v/i be at an angle pendere; ~ **against sth** appoggiarsi a qc

2 v/t appoggiare; **~ sth against sth** appoggiare a qc a qc

lean² [li:n] adj meat magro; style, prose asciutto

leap [li:p] **1** n salto m; **a great ~ forward** un grande balzo in avanti **2** v/i saltare

'**leap year** anno m bisestile

learn [lɜ:n] **1** v/t imparare; (hear) apprendere; **~ how to do sth** imparare a fare qc **2** v/i imparare

learn·er ['lɜ:nə(r)] principiante m/f

'**learn·er driv·er** principiante m/f (alla guida)

learn·ing ['lɜ:nɪŋ] n (knowledge) sapere m; (act) apprendimento m

'**learn·ing curve** processo m di apprendimento; **be constantly on the ~** non finire mai di imparare

lease [li:s] **1** n (contratto m di) affitto m **2** v/t flat, equipment affittare

♦ **lease out** v/t flat, equipment dare in affitto

lease 'pur·chase acquisto m in leasing

leash [li:ʃ] for dog guinzaglio m

least [li:st] **1** adj (slightest) minimo; **I've the ~ debt** io ho il debito minore **2** adv meno **3** n minimo m; **not in the ~ suprised / disappointed** per niente sorpreso / deluso; **at ~** almeno

leath·er ['leðə(r)] **1** n pelle f, cuoio m **2** adj di pelle, di cuoio

leave [li:v] **1** n (holiday) congedo m; MIL licenza f; **on ~** in congedo, in licenza **2** v/t (pret & pp **left**) lasciare; room, house, office uscire da; station, airport partire da; (forget) dimenticare; **~ school** finire gli studi; **let's ~ things as they are** lasciamo le cose come stanno; **how did you ~ things with him?** come sei rimasto d'accordo con lui?; **~ s.o. / sth alone** lasciare stare qu / qc; **be left** rimanere; **there is nothing left** non è rimasto niente **3** v/i (pret & pp **left**) of person, plane, bus partire; **he's just left** è appena uscito

♦ **leave behind** v/t intentionally lasciare; (forget) dimenticare

♦ **leave on** v/t hat, coat non togliersi; TV, computer lasciare acceso

♦ **leave out** v/t word, figure omettere; (not put away) lasciare in giro; **leave me out of this** non mi immischiare in questa faccenda

'**leav·ing par·ty** festa f d'addio

lec·ture ['lektʃə(r)] **1** n lezione f **2** v/i at university insegnare

'**lec·ture hall** aula f magna

lec·tur·er ['lektʃərə(r)] professore m, -essa universitario, -a

LED [eli:'di:] abbr (= **light-emitting diode**) LED m inv

led [led] pret & pp → **lead¹**

ledge [ledʒ] of window davanzale m; on rock face sporgenza f

ledg·er ['ledʒə(r)] COM libro m mastro

leek [li:k] porro m

leer [lɪə(r)] n sexual sguardo m libidinoso; evil sguardo m malvagio

left¹ [left] **1** adj sinistro; POL di sinistra **2** n sinistra f; **on the ~** a sinistra; **on the ~ of sth** a sinistra di qc; **to the ~ turn**, look a sinistra **3** adv turn, look a sinistra

left² [left] pret & pp → **leave**

'**left-hand** adj sinistro; **left-hand 'drive** guida f a sinistra; **left-'handed** adj mancino; **left 'lug·gage (office)** deposito m bagagli; '**left-overs** npl food avanzi mpl; '**left-wing** adj POL di sinistra

leg [leg] of person gamba f; of animal zampa f; of turkey, chicken coscia f; of lamb cosciotto m; of journey tappa f; of competition girone m; **pull s.o.'s ~** prendere in giro qu

leg·a·cy ['legəsɪ] eredità f inv

le·gal ['li:gl] adj legale

le·gal ad'vis·er consulente m/f legale

le·gal·i·ty [lɪ'gælətɪ] legalità f inv

le·gal·ize ['li:gəlaɪz] v/t legalizzare

le·gend ['ledʒənd] leggenda f

le·gen·da·ry ['ledʒəndrɪ] adj leggendario

le·gi·ble ['ledʒəbl] adj leggibile

le·gis·late ['ledʒɪsleɪt] v/i legiferare

le·gis·la·tion [ledʒɪs'leɪʃn] legislazione f

le·gis·la·tive ['ledʒɪslətɪv] adj legislativo

le·gis·la·ture ['ledʒɪsləʧə(r)] POL legislatura f

le·git·i·mate [lɪ'dʒɪtɪmət] adj legittimo

'leg room spazio m per le gambe

lei·sure ['leʒə(r)] svago m; at your ~
con comodo

'lei·sure cen·ter Am, 'lei·sure centre centro m sportivo e ricreativo

lei·sure·ly ['leʒəlɪ] adj pace, lifestyle
tranquillo

'lei·sure time tempo m libero

le·mon ['lemən] limone m

le·mon·ade [lemə'neɪd] fizzy gazzosa f; made from lemon juice limonata
f

'le·mon juice succo m di limone

le·mon 'tea tè m inv al limone

lend [lend] v/t (pret & pp lent) prestare; ~ s.o. sth prestare qc a qu

length [leŋθ] lunghezza f; piece: of
material taglio m; at ~ describe,
explain a lungo; (eventually) alla fine

length·en ['leŋθən] v/t allungare

length·y ['leŋθɪ] adj speech, stay lungo

le·ni·ent ['liːnɪənt] adj indulgente

lens [lenz] of camera obiettivo m; of
spectacles lente f; of eye cristallino
m

'lens cov·er of camera copriobiet-
tivo m

Lent [lent] REL Quaresima f

lent [lent] pret & pp → lend

len·til ['lentl] lenticchia f

len·til 'soup minestra f di lenticchie

Leo ['liːəʊ] ASTR Leone m

leop·ard ['lepəd] leopardo m

le·o·tard ['liːətɑːd] body m inv

les·bi·an ['lezbɪən] 1 n lesbica f 2 adj
di/per lesbiche

less [les] adv (di) meno; eat/talk ~
parlare/mangiare (di) meno; ~ in-
teresting/serious meno interes-
sante/serio; it costs ~ costa (di)
meno; ~ than £200 meno di £200

less·en ['lesn] v/t & v/i diminuire

les·son ['lesn] lezione f

let [let] v/t (pret & pp let) (allow) lasciare; (rent) affittare; ~ s.o. do sth
lasciar fare qc a qu; ~ me go! lascia-
mi andare!; ~ him come in! fallo
entrare!; ~'s go stiamo/restiamo;
~'s not argue non litighia-
mo; ~ alone tanto meno; ~ go of sth
of rope, handle mollare qc

♦let down v/t hair sciogliersi; blinds
abbassare; (disappoint) deludere;
dress, trousers allungare

♦let in v/t to house far entrare

♦let off v/t not punish perdonare;
from car far scendere

♦let out v/t of room, building far uscire; jacket etc allargare; groan, yell
emettere

♦let up v/i (stop) smettere

le·thal ['liːθl] mortale

leth·ar·gic [lɪ'θɑːdʒɪk] adj fiacco

leth·ar·gy ['leθədʒɪ] fiacchezza f

let·ter ['letə(r)] lettera f

'let·ter·box on street buca f delle lettere; in door cassetta f della posta;
'let·ter·head heading intestazione
f; (headed paper) carta f intestata;
let·ter of 'cred·it COM lettera f di
credito

let·tuce ['letɪs] lattuga f

'let·up: without a ~ senza sosta

leu·ke·mia [luː'kiːmɪə] leucemia f

lev·el ['levl] 1 adj field, surface piano;
in competition, scores pari; draw ~
with s.o. in match pareggiare; he
drew ~ with the leading car ha
raggiunto l'auto in testa 2 n livello
m; on the ~ F (honest) onesto

lev·el 'cross·ing Br passaggio m a
livello

lev·el-head·ed [levl'hedɪd] adj posato

le·ver ['liːvə(r)] 1 n leva f 2 v/t: ~ sth
up/off sollevare/togliere qc con
una leva; ~ sth open aprire qc facendo leva

lev·er·age ['liːvrɪdʒ] forza f; (influence) influenza f

lev·y ['levɪ] v/t (pret & pp -ied) taxes
imporre

lewd [luːd] adj osceno

li·a·bil·i·ty [laɪə'bɪlətɪ] (*responsibility*) responsabilità *f inv*; F *person* morto; F *thing* peso *m*

li·a·ble ['laɪəbl] *adj* (*answerable*) responsabile; *it's ~ to break* (*likely*) è probabile che si rompa
♦ **liaise with** [lɪ'eɪz] *v/t* tenere i contatti con

li·ai·son [lɪ'eɪzɒn] (*contacts*) contatti *mpl*

li·ar ['laɪə(r)] bugiardo *m*, -a *f*

li·bel ['laɪbl] **1** *n* diffamazione *f* **2** *v/t* diffamare

lib·er·al ['lɪbrəl] *adj* (*broad-minded*), POL liberale; *portion etc* abbondante

lib·er·ate ['lɪbəreɪt] *v/t* liberare

lib·er·at·ed ['lɪbəreɪtɪd] *adj woman* emancipato

lib·er·a·tion [lɪbə'reɪʃn] liberazione *f*

lib·er·ty ['lɪbətɪ] libertà *f inv*; *at ~ of prisoner etc* in libertà; *be at ~ to do sth* poter fare qc

Li·bra ['liːbrə] ASTR Bilancia *f*

li·brar·i·an [laɪ'breərɪən] bibliotecario *m*, -a *f*

li·bra·ry ['laɪbrərɪ] biblioteca *f*

Lib·y·a ['lɪbɪə] Libia *f*

Lib·yan ['lɪbɪən] **1** *adj* libico **2** *n person* libico *m*, -a *f*

lice [laɪs] *pl* → **louse**

li·cence ['laɪsns] (*driving ~*) patente *f*; (*road tax ~*) bollo *m* (auto); *for TV* canone *m* (televisivo); *for gun* porto *m* d'armi; *for imports / exports* licenza *f*; *for dog* tassa *f*

li·cense ['laɪsns] *v/t issue ~* rilasciare la licenza a; *be ~d to sell alcohol* essere autorizzato alla vendita di alcolici; *the car isn't ~d* la macchina non ha il bollo **2** *n Am* → **licence**

'li·cense plate *Am* targa *f*

lick [lɪk] **1** *n* leccata *f*; *a ~ of paint* una passata di vernice **2** *v/t* leccare; *~ one's lips* leccarsi i baffi

lick·ing ['lɪkɪŋ] F (*defeat*): *get a ~* prendere una batosta

lid [lɪd] coperchio *m*

lie¹ [laɪ] **1** *n* bugia *f*; *tell ~s* dire bugie **2** *v/i* mentire

lie² [laɪ] *v/i* (*pret* **lay**, *pp* **lain**) *of person* sdraiarsi; *of object* stare; (*be situated*) trovarsi
♦ **lie down** *v/i* sdraiarsi

'lie-in: *have a ~* restare a letto fino a tardi

lieu [ljuː] *n*: *in ~ of* invece di

lieu·ten·ant [lef'tenənt] tenente *m*

life [laɪf] (*pl* **lives** [laɪvz]) vita *f*; *of machine* durata *f*; *of battery* autonomia *f*; *all her ~* tutta la vita; *that's ~!* così è la vita!

'life as·sur·ance *Br* assicurazione *f* sulla vita; 'life belt salvagente *m inv*; 'life·boat lancia *f* di salvataggio; 'life ex·pect·an·cy aspettativa *f* di vita; 'life·guard bagnino *m*, -a *f*; 'life his·to·ry ciclo *m* vitale; life im·pris·on·ment ergastolo *m*; 'life in·sur·ance assicurazione *f* sulla vita; 'life jack·et giubbotto *m* di salvataggio

life·less ['laɪflɪs] *adj* senza vita

life·like ['laɪflaɪk] *adj* fedele

'life·long *adj* di vecchia data; 'life-sav·ing *adj drug* salvavita; 'life-sized *adj* a grandezza naturale; 'life-threat·en·ing *adj* mortale; 'life·time *n*: *in my ~* in vita mia

lift [lɪft] **1** *v/t* sollevare **2** *v/i of fog* diradarsi **3** *n Br*: *in building* ascensore *m*; *in car* passaggio *m*; *give s.o. a ~* dare un passaggio a qu
♦ **lift off** *v/i of rocket* decollare

'lift-off *of rocket* decollo *m*

lig·a·ment ['lɪgəmənt] legamento *m*

light¹ [laɪt] **1** *n* luce *f*; *in the ~ of* alla luce di; *have you got a ~?* hai da accendere? **2** *v/t* (*pret & pp* **lit**) *fire, cigarette* accendere; (*illuminate*) illuminare **3** *adj not dark* chiaro

light² [laɪt] **1** *adj not heavy* leggero **2** *adv*: *travel ~* viaggiare leggero
♦ **light up 1** *v/t* (*illuminate*) illuminare **2** *v/i* (*start to smoke*) accendersi una sigaretta

'light bulb lampadina *f*

light·en¹ ['laɪtn] *v/t colour* schiarire

light·en² ['laɪtn] *v/t load* alleggerire
♦ **lighten up** *v/i of person* rilassarsi

light·er ['laɪtə(r)] *for cigarettes* accendino *m*

light-head·ed [laɪtˈhedɪd] *adj* (*dizzy*) stordito; **light-ˈheart·ed** [laɪtˈhɑːtɪd] *adj film* leggero; **ˈlight-house** faro *m*

light·ing [ˈlaɪtɪŋ] illuminazione *f*

light·ly [ˈlaɪtlɪ] *adv touch* leggermente; **get off ~** cavarsela con poco

light·ness [ˈlaɪtnɪs] leggerezza *f*

light·ning [ˈlaɪtnɪŋ] fulmine *m*

ˈlight·ning con·duc·tor parafulmine *m*

ˈlight pen penna *f* luminosa

ˈlight·weight *in boxing* peso *m* leggero

ˈlight year anno *m* luce

like¹ [laɪk] **1** *prep* come; **~ this / that** così; **what is she ~?** *in looks, character* com'è?; **it's not ~ him** *not his character* non è da lui; **look ~ s.o.** assomigliare a qu **2** *conj* F (*as*) come; **~ I said** come ho già detto

like² [laɪk] *v/t*: **I ~ it / her** mi piace; **I would ~ ...** vorrei ...; **I would ~ to ...** vorrei ...; **would you ~ ...?** ti va ...?; **would you ~ to ...?** ti va di ...?; **he ~s swimming** gli piace nuotare; **if you ~** se vuoi

like·a·ble [ˈlaɪkəbl] *adj* simpatico

like·li·hood [ˈlaɪklɪhʊd] probabilità *f inv*; **in all ~** molto probabilmente

like·ly [ˈlaɪklɪ] *adj* (*probable*) probabile; **not ~!** difficile!

like·ness [ˈlaɪknɪs] (*resemblance*) somiglianza *f*

ˈlike·wise [ˈlaɪkwaɪz] *adv* altrettanto

lik·ing [ˈlaɪkɪŋ] predilizione *f*; **is it to your ~?** *fml* è di tuo gradimento?; **take a ~ to s.o.** prendere qu in simpatia

li·lac [ˈlaɪlək] *flower* lillà *m inv*; *colour* lilla *m inv*

li·ly [ˈlɪlɪ] giglio *m*

li·ly of the ˈval·ley mughetto *m*

limb [lɪm] arto *m*

lime¹ [laɪm] *fruit* limetta *f*

lime² [laɪm] *substance* calce *f*

ˈlime·green *adj* verde *m* acido

ˈlime·light *n*: **be in the ~** essere in vista

lim·it [ˈlɪmɪt] **1** *n* limite *m*; **within ~s** entro certi limiti; **off ~s** off-limits;

that's the ~! F è il colmo! **2** *v/t* limitare

lim·i·ta·tion [lɪmɪˈteɪʃn] limite *m*

lim·it·ed ˈcom·pa·ny società *f inv* a responsabilità limitata

li·mo [ˈlɪməʊ] F limousine *f inv*

lim·ou·sine [ˈlɪməziːn] limousine *f inv*

limp¹ [lɪmp] *adj* floscio

limp² [lɪmp] *n*: **he has a ~** zoppica

line¹ [laɪn] *n on paper, road* linea *f*; *of people, trees* fila *f*; *of text* riga *f*; (*cord*) filo *m*; *of business* settore *m*; TELEC linea *f*; **the ~ is busy** è occupato; **hold the ~** rimanga in linea; **draw the ~ at sth** non tollerare qc; **~ of inquiry** pista *f*; **~ of reasoning** filo *m* del ragionamento; **stand in ~** *esp Am* fare la fila; **in ~ with ...** (*conforming with*) in linea con ...

line² [laɪn] *v/t* foderare

♦ **line up** *v/i* mettersi in fila

lin·e·ar [ˈlɪnɪə(r)] *adj* lineare

lin·en [ˈlɪnɪn] *material* lino *m*; *sheets etc* biancheria *f*

lin·er [ˈlaɪnə(r)] *ship* transatlantico *m*

lines·man [ˈlaɪnzmən] SP guardalinee *m inv*

lin·ger [ˈlɪŋgə(r)] *v/i of person* attardarsi; *of smell, pain* persistere

lin·ge·rie [ˈlænʒərɪ] lingerie *f inv*

lin·guist [ˈlɪŋgwɪst] *professional* linguista *m/f*; *person good at languages* poliglotta *m/f*

lin·guis·tic [lɪŋˈgwɪstɪk] *adj* linguistico

lin·ing [ˈlaɪnɪŋ] *of clothes* fodera *f*; *of brakes* guarnizione *f*

link [lɪŋk] **1** *n* (*connection*) legame *m*; *in chain* anello *m* **2** *v/t* collegare

♦ **link up** *v/i* riunirsi; TV collegarsi

li·on [ˈlaɪən] leone *m*

li·on·ess [ˈlaɪənes] leonessa *f*

lip [lɪp] labbro *m*; **~s** labbra

ˈlip-read *v/i* (*pret & pp* **-read** [red]) leggere le labbra

ˈlip·stick rossetto *m*

li·queur [lɪˈkjʊə(r)] liquore *m*

liq·uid [ˈlɪkwɪd] **1** *n* liquido *m* **2** *adj* liquido

liq·ui·date [ˈlɪkwɪdeɪt] *v/t* liquidare

liq·ui·da·tion [lɪkwɪˈdeɪʃn] liquidazione *f*; **go into** ~ andare in liquidazione

liq·ui·di·ty [lɪˈkwɪdɪtɪ] FIN liquidità *f inv*

liq·uid·ize [ˈlɪkwɪdaɪz] *v/t* frullare

liq·uid·iz·er [ˈlɪkwɪdaɪzə(r)] frullatore *m*

liq·uor [ˈlɪkə(r)] superalcolici *mpl*

liq·uo·rice [ˈlɪkərɪs] liquirizia *f*

lisp [lɪsp] **1** *n* lisca *f* **2** *v/i* parlare con la lisca

list [lɪst] **1** *n* elenco *m*, lista *f* **2** *v/t* elencare

lis·ten [ˈlɪsn] *v/i* ascoltare
♦ **listen in** *v/i* ascoltare (di nascosto)
♦ **listen to** *v/t radio, person* ascoltare

lis·ten·er [ˈlɪsnə(r)] *to radio* ascoltatore *m*, -trice *f*; **he's a good** ~ sa ascoltare

list·ings mag·a·zine [ˈlɪstɪŋz] guida *f* dei programmi radio / TV

list·less [ˈlɪstlɪs] *adj* apatico

lit [lɪt] *pret & pp* → **light**

li·ter *Am* → **litre**

lit·e·ral [ˈlɪtərəl] *adj* letterale

lit·e·ral·ly [ˈlɪtərəlɪ] *adv* letteralmente

lit·e·ra·ry [ˈlɪtərərɪ] *adj* letterario

lit·e·rate [ˈlɪtərət] *adj*: **be** ~ saper leggere e scrivere

lit·e·ra·ture [ˈlɪtrətʃə(r)] letteratura *f*; F (*leaflets*) opuscoli *mpl*

li·tre [ˈliːtə(r)] litro *m*

lit·ter [ˈlɪtə(r)] rifiuti *mpl*; *of animal* cucciolata *f*

'lit·ter bas·ket cestino *m* dei rifiuti

'lit·ter bin bidone *m* dei rifiuti

lit·tle [ˈlɪtl] **1** *adj* piccolo; **the ~ ones** i piccoli **2** *n*: **the ~ I know** il poco che so; **a ~** un po'; **a ~ bread / wine** un po' di pane / vino; **a ~ is better than nothing** meglio poco che niente **3** *adv*: **~ by ~** (a) poco a poco; **a ~ better / bigger** un po' meglio / più grande; **a ~ before 6** un po' prima delle 6

live¹ [lɪv] *v/i* (*reside*) abitare; (*be alive*) vivere
♦ **live on 1** *v/t rice, bread* vivere di **2** *v/i continue living* sopravvivere

♦ **live up**: **live it up** fare la bella vita
♦ **live up to** *v/t* essere all'altezza di
♦ **live with** *v/t* vivere con

live² [laɪv] **1** *adj broadcast* dal vivo **2** *adv broadcast* in diretta; *record* dal vivo; *ammunition* carico

live·li·hood [ˈlaɪvlɪhʊd] mezzi *mpl* di sostentamento; **earn one's ~** guadagnarsi da vivere

live·li·ness [ˈlaɪvlɪnɪs] vivacità *f inv*

live·ly [ˈlaɪvlɪ] *adj* vivace

liv·er [ˈlɪvə(r)] fegato *m*

live·stock [ˈlaɪvstɒk] bestiame *m*

liv·id [ˈlɪvɪd] *adj* (*angry*) furibondo

liv·ing [ˈlɪvɪŋ] **1** *adj* in vita **2** *n*: **earn one's** ~ guadagnarsi da vivere; **what do you do for a ~?** che lavoro fai?; **standard of ~** tenore *m* di vita

'liv·ing room salotto *m*, soggiorno *m*

liz·ard [ˈlɪzəd] lucertola *f*

load [ləʊd] **1** *n* carico *m*; **~s of** F un sacco di **2** *v/t* caricare; **~ sth onto sth** caricare qc su qc

load·ed [ˈləʊdɪd] *adj* F (*very rich*) ricco sfondato

loaf [ləʊf] *n* (*pl loaves* [ləʊvz]): **a ~ of bread** una pagnotta
♦ **loaf about** *v/i* F oziare

loaf·er [ˈləʊfə(r)] *shoe* mocassino *m*

loan [ləʊn] **1** *n* prestito *m*; **on** ~ in prestito **2** *v/t*: **~ s.o. sth** prestare qc a qu

loathe [ləʊð] *v/t* detestare

loath·ing [ˈləʊðɪŋ] disgusto *m*

lob·by [ˈlɒbɪ] *in hotel, theatre* atrio *m*; POL lobby *f inv*

lobe [ləʊb] *of ear* lobo *m*

lob·ster [ˈlɒbstə(r)] aragosta *f*

lo·cal [ˈləʊkl] **1** *adj people, bar* del posto; *produce* locale; **I'm not** ~ non sono del posto **2** *n* persona *f* del posto; **are you a ~?** sei del posto?

'lo·cal call TELEC telefonata *f* urbana; **lo·cal e'lec·tions** *npl* elezioni *fpl* amministrative; **lo·cal 'gov·ern·ment** amministrazione *f* locale

lo·cal·i·ty [ləʊˈkælətɪ] località *f inv*

lo·cal·ly [ˈləʊkəlɪ] *adv* live, *work* nella zona

lo·cal 'pro·duce prodotti *mpl* locali

'lo·cal time ora *f* locale

L

lo·cate [ləʊ'keɪt] v/t *new factory etc* situare; *identify position of* localizzare; **be ~d** essere situato

lo·ca·tion [ləʊ'keɪʃn] (*siting*) ubicazione f; *identifying position of* localizzazione f; **on ~** *film* in esterni; **the film was shot on ~ in …** gli esterni del film sono stati girati in …

loch lago m

lock¹ [lɒk] *of hair* ciocca f

lock² [lɒk] **1** n *on door* serratura f **2** v/t *door* chiudere a chiave; **~ sth in position** bloccare qc
♦ **lock away** v/t mettere sottochiave
♦ **lock in** v/t *person* chiudere dentro
♦ **lock out** v/t *of house* chiudere fuori
♦ **lock up** v/t *in prison* mettere dentro

lock·er ['lɒkə(r)] armadietto m

'**lock·er room** spogliatoio m

lock·et ['lɒkɪt] medaglione m

lock·smith ['lɒksmɪθ] fabbro m ferraio

lo·cust ['ləʊkəst] locusta f

lodge [lɒdʒ] **1** v/t *complaint* presentare **2** v/i *of bullet* conficcarsi

lodg·er ['lɒdʒə(r)] pensionante m/f

loft [lɒft] soffitta f

loft·y ['lɒftɪ] adj *peak* alto; *ideals* nobile

log [lɒg] *wood* ceppo m; *written record* giornale m
♦ **log off** v/i (*pret & pp* **-ged**) disconnettersi (*from* da)
♦ **log on** v/i connettersi
♦ **log on to** v/t connettersi a

'**log book** giornale m di bordo

log 'cab·in casetta f di legno

log·ger·heads ['lɒgəhedz]: **be at ~** essere ai ferri corti

lo·gic ['lɒdʒɪk] logica f

lo·gic·al ['lɒdʒɪkl] adj logico

lo·gic·al·ly ['lɒdʒɪklɪ] adv a rigor di logica; *arrange* in modo logico

lo·gis·tics [lə'dʒɪstɪks] npl logistica f

lo·go ['ləʊgəʊ] logo m inv

loi·ter ['lɔɪtə(r)] v/i gironzolare

lol·li·pop ['lɒlɪpɒp] lecca lecca m inv

'**lol·li·pop man/wo·man** Br uomo/donna che aiuta i bambini ad attraversare la strada

lol·ly ['lɒlɪ] (*ice lolly*) ghiacciolo m; F (*money*) grana f F

Lon·don ['lʌndən] Londra f

lone·li·ness ['ləʊnlɪnɪs] solitudine f

lone·ly ['ləʊnlɪ] adj *person* solo; *place* isolato

lon·er ['ləʊnə(r)] persona f solitaria

long¹ [lɒŋ] **1** adj lungo; **it's a ~ way** è lontano **2** adv: **don't be ~** torna presto **5 weeks is too ~** 5 settimane è troppo; **will it take ~?** ci vorrà tanto?; **that was ~ ago** è stato tanto tempo fa; **~ before then** molto prima di allora; **before ~** poco tempo dopo; **we can't wait any ~er** non possiamo attendere oltre; **he no ~er works here** non lavora più qui; **so ~ as** (*provided*) sempre che; **so ~!** arrivederci!

long² [lɒŋ] v/i: **~ for sth** desiderare ardentemente qc; **be ~ing to do sth** desiderare ardentemente fare qc

long-'dis·tance adj *phonecall* interurbano; *race* di fondo; *flight* intercontinentale

lon·gev·i·ty [lɒn'dʒevɪtɪ] longevità f inv

long·ing ['lɒŋɪŋ] n desiderio m

lon·gi·tude ['lɒŋgɪtjuːd] longitudine f

'**long jump** salto m in lungo; **long-'life milk** latte m a lunga conservazione; '**long-range** *missile* a lunga gittata; *forecast* a lungo termine; **long-sight·ed** [lɒŋ'saɪtɪd] adj presbite; **long-sleeved** [lɒŋ'sliːvd] adj a maniche lunghe; **long-'stand·ing** adj di vecchia data; '**long-term** adj *plans, investment* a lunga scadenza; *relationship* stabile; '**long wave** RAD onde fpl lunghe

long-wind·ed [lɒŋ'wɪndɪd] adj prolisso

loo [luː] F gabinetto m

look [lʊk] **1** n (*appearance*) aspetto m; (*glance*) sguardo m; **give s.o./ sth a ~** dare uno sguardo a qu/qc; **have a ~ at sth** examine dare un'occhiata a qc; **can I have a ~ around?** *in shop etc* posso dare un'occhiata?; **~s** (*beauty*) bellezza f **2** v/i guardare; (*search*) cercare;

(*seem*) sembrare; **you ~ tired /
different** sembri stanco / diverso
♦ **look after** *v/t* badare a
♦ **look ahead** *v/i fig* pensare al futuro
♦ **look around** *v/i in shop etc* dare
un'occhiata in giro; (~ *back*) guardarsi indietro
♦ **look at** *v/t* guardare; (*consider*)
considerare
♦ **look back** *v/i* guardare indietro
♦ **look down on** *v/t* disprezzare
♦ **look for** *v/t* cercare
♦ **look forward to** *v/t*: **look forward
to doing sth** non veder l'ora di fare
qc; **I'm looking forward to the
holidays** non vedo l'ora che arrivi-
no le vacanze; **I'm not looking
forward to it** non ne ho proprio voglia
♦ **look in on** *v/t* (*visit*) passare a trovare
♦ **look into** *v/t* (*investigate*) esaminare
♦ **look on 1** *v/i* (*watch*) rimanere a
guardare **2** *v/t*: **I look on you as a
friend** (*consider*) ti considero un
amico
♦ **look onto** *v/t garden, street* dare su
♦ **look out** *v/i of window etc* guardare
fuori; (*pay attention*) fare attenzione; **look out!** attento!
♦ **look out for** *v/t* cercare; (*be on
guard against*) fare attenzione a
♦ **look out of** *v/t window* guardare da
♦ **look over** *v/t house, translation* esaminare
♦ **look round** *v/t museum, city* visitare
♦ **look through** *v/t magazine, notes*
scorrere
♦ **look to** *v/t* (*rely on*) contare su
♦ **look up 1** *v/i from paper etc* sollevare lo sguardo; (*improve*) migliorare
2 *v/t word, phone number* cercare;
(*visit*) andare a trovare
♦ **look up to** *v/t* (*respect*) avere rispetto per
lookout *n person* sentinella *f; place*
posto *m* di guardia; **be on the ~** stare all'erta; **be on the ~ for**
accommodation etc cercare di trovare; *new staff etc* essere alla ricerca di

♦ **loom up** [luːm] *v/i* apparire
loon·y ['luːnɪ] **1** *n* F matto *m*, -a *f*
2 *adj* F matto
loop [luːp] *n* cappio *m*
'**loop·hole** *in law etc* scappatoia *f*
loose [luːs] *adj wire, button* allentato;
clothes ampio; *tooth* che tentenna;
morals dissoluto; *wording* vago; **~
change** spiccioli *mpl*; **~ ends of
problem, discussion** aspetti *mpl* da
esaminare
loose·ly ['luːslɪ] *adv tied* senza stringere; *worded* vagamente
loos·en ['luːsn] *v/t collar, knot* allentare
loot [luːt] **1** *n* bottino *m* **2** *v/t & v/i*
saccheggiare
loot·er ['luːtə(r)] saccheggiatore *m*,
-trice *f*
♦ **lop off** [lɒp] *v/t* (*pret & pp* **-ped**) tagliar via
lop-sid·ed [lɒp'saɪdɪd] *adj* sbilenco
Lord [lɔːd] (*God*) Signore *m*; **the
(House of) ~s** la camera dei Lord
Lord's 'Prayer il Padrenostro *m*
lor·ry ['lɒrɪ] *Br* camion *m inv*
lose [luːz] (*pret & pp* **lost**) **1** *v/t object*
perdere **2** *v/i* SP perdere; *of clock*
andare indietro; **I'm lost** mi sono
perso; **get lost!** F sparisci!
♦ **lose out** *v/i* rimetterci
los·er ['luːzə(r)] *in contest* perdente
m/f; F *in life* sfigato *m*, -a *f* F
loss [lɒs] perdita *f*; **make a ~** subire
una perdita; **be at a ~** essere perplesso
lost [lɒst] **1** *adj* perso **2** *pret & pp* →
lose
lost and 'found *Am*, **lost 'property of·fice** *Br* ufficio *m* oggetti smarriti
lot [lɒt] *n*: **the ~** tutto; **a ~, ~s** molto; **a
~ of ice cream, ~s of ice cream**
molto gelato; **a ~ of ice creams, ~s
of ice creams** molti gelati; **a ~
better / easier** molto meglio / più
facile
lo·tion ['ləʊʃn] lozione *f*
lot·te·ry ['lɒtərɪ] lotteria *f*
loud [laʊd] *adj music, voice, noise* forte; *colour* sgargiante

L

loud·speak·er altoparlante *m*; *for stereo* cassa *f* dello stereo

lounge [laʊndʒ] *in house* soggiorno *m*; *in hotel* salone *m*; *at airport* sala *f* partenze

♦ **lounge about** *v/i* poltrire

'**lounge suit** completo *m* da uomo

louse [laʊs] (*pl* **lice** [laɪs]) pidocchio *m*

lous·y ['laʊzɪ] *adj* F schifoso F; *I feel* ~ mi sento uno schifo

lout [laʊt] teppista *m/f*

lov·a·ble ['lʌvəbl] *adj* adorabile

love [lʌv] **1** *n* amore *m*; *in tennis* zero *m*; *be in* ~ essere innamorato; *fall in* ~ innamorarsi; *make* ~ fare l'amore; *make* ~ *to* fare l'amore con; *yes, my* ~ sì, tesoro **2** *v/t person, country, wine* amare; ~ *doing sth* amare fare qc

'**love af·fair** relazione *f*; '**love-life** vita *f* sentimentale; '**love let·ter** lettera *f* d'amore

love·ly ['lʌvlɪ] *adj face, colour, holiday* bello; *meal, smell* buono; *we had a* ~ *time* siamo stati benissimo

lov·er ['lʌvə(r)] amante *m/f*

lov·ing ['lʌvɪŋ] *adj* affettuoso

lov·ing·ly ['lʌvɪŋlɪ] *adv* amorosamente

low [ləʊ] **1** *adj bridge, price, voice* basso; *quality* scarso; *be feeling* ~ sentirsi giù; *be* ~ *on petrol* avere poca benzina **2** *n in weather* depressione *f*; *in sales, statistics* minimo *m*

'**low·brow** [ləʊbraʊ] *adj* di scarso spessore culturale; **low-'cal·o·rie** *adj* ipocalorico; '**low-cut** *adj dress* scollato

low·er ['ləʊə(r)] *v/t boat, sth to the ground* calare; *flag, hemline* ammainare; *pressure, price* abbassare

'**low-fat** *adj* magro

'**low-key** *adj* discreto; '**low·lands** *npl* bassopiano *m*; **low-'pres·sure ar·e·a** *f* di bassa pressione; '**low sea·son** bassa stagione *f*; '**low tide** bassa marea *f*

loy·al ['lɔɪəl] *adj* leale

loy·al·ly ['lɔɪəlɪ] *adv* lealmente

loy·al·ty ['lɔɪəltɪ] lealtà *f inv*

loz·enge ['lɒzɪndʒ] *shape* rombo *m*; *tablet* pastiglia *f*

LP [el'piː] *abbr* (= *long-playing re·cord*) LP *m inv* (= long-playing *m inv*)

Ltd *abbr* (= *limited*) s.r.l. (= società *f inv* a responsabilità limitata)

lu·bri·cant ['luːbrɪkənt] lubrificante *m*

lu·bri·cate ['luːbrɪkeɪt] *v/t* lubrificare

lu·bri·ca·tion [luːbrɪ'keɪʃn] lubrificazione *f*

lu·cid ['luːsɪd] *adj* (*clear*) chiaro; (*sane*) lucido

luck [lʌk] fortuna *f*; *bad* ~ sfortuna; *hard* ~! che sfortuna!; *good* ~ fortuna *f*; *good* ~! buona fortuna!

luck·i·ly ['lʌkɪlɪ] *adv* fortunatamente

luck·y ['lʌkɪ] *adj* fortunato; *you were* ~ hai avuto fortuna; *he's* ~ *to be alive* è vivo per miracolo; *that's* ~! che fortuna!

lu·cra·tive ['luːkrətɪv] *adj* redditizio

lu·di·crous ['luːdɪkrəs] *adj* ridicolo

lug [lʌg] *v/t* (*pret & pp* -**ged**) F trascinare

lug·gage ['lʌgɪdʒ] bagagli *mpl*

'**lug·gage rack** *in train* portabagagli *m inv*

luke·warm ['luːkwɔːm] *adj* tiepido

lull [lʌl] **1** *n in fighting* momento *m* di calma; *in conversation* pausa *f* **2** *v/t*: ~ *s.o. into a false sense of security* illudersi che tutto vada bene

lul·la·by ['lʌləbaɪ] ninnananna *f*

lum·ba·go [lʌm'beɪgəʊ] lombaggine *f*

lum·ber ['lʌmbə(r)] (*timber*) legname *m*

lu·mi·nous ['luːmɪnəs] *adj* luminoso

lump [lʌmp] *of sugar* zolletta *f*; (*swelling*) nodulo *m*

♦ **lump together** *v/t* mettere insieme

lump 'sum pagamento *m* unico

lump·y ['lʌmpɪ] *adj sauce* grumoso; *mattress* pieno di buchi

lu·na·cy ['luːnəsɪ] pazzia *f*

lu·nar ['luːnə(r)] *adj* lunare

lu·na·tic ['luːnətɪk] *n* pazzo *m*, -a *f*

lunch [lʌntʃ] pranzo *m*; *have* ~ pranzare

'lunch box cestino *m* del pranzo;
'lunch break pausa *f* pranzo;
'lunch hour pausa *f* pranzo;
'lunch•time ora *f* di pranzo

lung [lʌŋ] polmone *m*

'lung can•cer cancro *m* al polmone

♦ **lunge at** [lʌndʒ] *v/t* scagliarsi contro

lurch [lɜːtʃ] *v/i* barcollare

lure [luə(r)] **1** *n* attrattiva *f* **2** *v/t* attirare; **~ s.o. into a trap** far cadere qu in trappola

lu•rid [ˈluərɪd] *adj colour* sgargiante; *details* scandaloso

lurk [lɜːk] *v/i of person* appostarsi; *of doubt* persistere

lus•cious [ˈlʌʃəs] *adj* sensuale

lush [lʌʃ] *adj vegetation* lussureggiante

lust [lʌst] *n* libidine *f*

lux•u•ri•ous [lʌgˈʒuərɪəs] *adj* lussuoso

lux•u•ri•ous•ly [lʌgˈʒuərɪəslɪ] *adv* lussuosamente

lux•u•ry [ˈlʌkʃərɪ] **1** *n* lusso *m* **2** *adj* di lusso

LV *abbr* (= **luncheon voucher**) buono *m* pasto

lymph gland [ˈlɪmfglænd] ghiandola *f* linfatica

lynch [lɪntʃ] *v/t* linciare

lyr•i•cist [ˈlɪrɪsɪst] paroliere *m*

lyr•ics [ˈlɪrɪks] *npl* parole *fpl*, testi *mpl*

M

M [em] *abbr* (= **medium**) M (= medio)

MA [emˈeɪ] *abbr* (= **Master of Arts**) master *m inv*

ma'am [mæm] *Am* signora *f*

mac [mæk] F (*mackintosh*) impermeabile *m*

ma•chine [məˈʃiːn] **1** *n* macchina *f* **2** *v/t with sewing machine* cucire a macchina; TECH lavorare a macchina

ma'chine gun mitragliatrice *f*

ma•chine-'read•a•ble *adj* leggibile dalla macchina

ma•chin•e•ry [məˈʃiːnərɪ] (*machines*) macchinario *m*

ma•chine trans•la•tion traduzione *f* fatta dal computer

ma•chis•mo [məˈkɪzməʊ] machismo *m*

mach•o [ˈmætʃəʊ] *adj* macho *m*

mack•in•tosh [ˈmækɪntɒʃ] impermeabile *m*

mac•ro [ˈmækrəʊ] COMPUT macro *f*

mad [mæd] *adj* (*insane*) pazzo *m*; F (*angry*) furioso; **be ~ about** F andar matto per; **drive s.o. ~** far impazzire qu; **go ~** (*become insane*) impazzire; F *with enthusiasm* impazzire; **like ~** F *run, work* come un matto

mad•am [ˈmædəm] signora *f*

mad 'cow dis•ease F morbo *m* della mucca pazza

mad•den [ˈmædən] *v/t* (*infuriate*) esasperare

mad•den•ing [ˈmædnɪŋ] *adj* esasperante

made [meɪd] *pret & pp* → **make**

made-to-'meas•ure *adj* su misura

'mad•house *fig* manicomio *m*

mad•ly [ˈmædlɪ] *adv* come un matto; **~ in love** pazzamente innamorato

'mad•man pazzo *m*

mad•ness [ˈmædnɪs] pazzia *f*

Ma•don•na [məˈdɒnə] Madonna *f*

Ma•fi•a [ˈmæfɪə] Mafia *f*

mag•a•zine [mægəˈziːn] *printed* rivista *f*

mag•got [ˈmægət] verme *m*

Ma·gi ['meɪdʒaɪ] REL Re Magi *mpl*

ma·gic ['mædʒɪk] **1** *n* magia *f*; *tricks* giochi *mpl* di prestigio; *like ~* come per magia **2** *adj* magico

mag·i·cal ['mædʒɪkl] *adj powers, moment* magico

ma·gi·cian [mə'dʒɪʃn] *performer* mago *m*, -a *f*

ma·gic 'spell incantesimo *m*; **magic 'trick** gioco *m* di prestigio; **mag·ic 'wand** bacchetta *f* magica

magistrate ['mædʒɪstreɪt] magistrato *m*

mag·nan·i·mous [mæg'nænɪməs] *adj* magnanimo

mag·net ['mægnɪt] calamita *f*, magnete *m*

mag·net·ic [mæg'netɪk] *adj* calamitato; *also fig* magnetico

mag·net·ic 'stripe striscia *f* magnetizzata

mag·net·ism [mæg'netɪzm] *of person* magnetismo *m*

mag·nif·i·cence [mæg'nɪfɪsəns] magnificenza *f*

mag·nif·i·cent [mæg'nɪfɪsənt] *adj* magnifico

mag·ni·fy ['mægnɪfaɪ] *v/t* (*pret & pp* -*ied*) ingrandire; *difficulties* ingigantire

'mag·ni·fy·ing glass lente *f* d'ingrandimento

mag·ni·tude ['mægnɪtjuːd] *of problem* portata *f*, AST magnitudine *f*

ma·hog·a·ny [mə'hɒgənɪ] mogano *m*

maid [meɪd] *servant* domestica *f*; *in hotel* cameriera *f*

maid·en name ['meɪdn] nome *m* da ragazza; **maid·en 'speech** discorso *m* inaugurale; **maid·en 'voy·age** viaggio *m* inaugurale

mail [meɪl] **1** *n* posta *f*; *put sth in the ~* spedire qc **2** *v/t letter* spedire; *person* spedire a

'mail·box *Am* buca *f* delle lettere; *Am: of house* cassetta *f* delle lettere; COMPUT casella *f* postale

'mail·ing list mailing list *m inv*

'mail·man *Am* postino *m*; **mail·'or·der cat·a·log** *Am*, **mail·'or·der**

cat·a·logue catalogo *m* di vendita per corrispondenza; **mail·'or·der firm** ditta *f* di vendita per corrispondenza; **'mail·shot** mailing *m inv*

maim [meɪm] *v/t* mutilare

main [meɪn] *adj* principale

'main course piatto *m* principale; **main 'en·trance** entrata *f* principale; **'main·frame** mainframe *m inv*; **'main·land** terraferma *f*, continente *m*; *on the ~* sul continente

main·ly ['meɪnlɪ] *adv* principalmente

main 'road strada *f* principale

'main street corso *m*

main·tain [meɪn'teɪn] *v/t* mantenere; *pace, speed; relationship; machine, house; family; innocence, guilt* sostenere; *~ that* sostenere che

main·te·nance ['meɪntənəns] *of machine, house* manutenzione *f*; *money* alimenti *mpl*; *of law and order* mantenimento *m*

'main·te·nance costs *npl* spese *fpl* di manutenzione

'main·te·nance staff addetti *mpl* alla manutenzione

ma·jes·tic [mə'dʒestɪk] *adj* maestoso

maj·es·ty ['mædʒəstɪ] *(grandeur)* maestà *f inv*; *Her Majesty* Sua Maestà

ma·jor ['meɪdʒə(r)] **1** *adj (significant)* importante, principale; *in C ~* MUS in Do maggiore **2** *n* MIL maggiore *m*

ma·jor·i·ty [mə'dʒɒrətɪ] *also* POL maggioranza *f*; maggioranza *f*; *be in the ~* essere in maggioranza

make [meɪk] **1** *n brand* marca *f* **2** *v/t* (*pret & pp* made) fare; *decision* prendere; *(earn)* guadagnare; MATH fare; *~ s.o. do sth* (*force to*) far fare qc a qu; *(cause to)* spingere qu a fare qc; *you can't ~ me do it!* non puoi costringermi a farlo!; *~ s.o. happy / angry* far felice / arrabbiare qu; *~ s.o. happy / sad* rendere felice / triste qu; *~ a decision* prendere una decisione; *~ a telephone call* fare una telefonata; *made in Japan* made in Japan; *~ it catch bus, train,* *come, succeed, survive* farcela; ***what time do you ~ it?*** che ore fai?; **~ believe** far finta; **~ do with** arrangiarsi con; ***what do you ~ of it?*** cosa ne pensi?

♦ **make for** *v/t* (*go towards*) dirigersi verso

♦ **make off** *v/i* svignarsela

♦ **make off with** *v/t* (*steal*) svignarsela con

♦ **make out** *v/t list* fare; *cheque* compilare; (*see*) distinguere; (*imply*) far capire; *who shall I make the cheque out to?* a chi devo intestare l'assegno?

♦ **make over**. *make sth over to s.o.* cedere qc a qu

♦ **make up 1** *v/i of woman, actor* truccarsi; *after quarrel* fare la pace **2** *v/t story, excuse* inventare; *face* truccare; (*constitute*) costituire; *be made up of* essere composto da; *make up one's mind* decidersi; *make it up after quarrel* fare la pace

♦ **make up for** *v/t* compensare; *I'll make up for forgetting your birthday* mi farò perdonare di essermi scordato del tuo compleanno

make-be·lieve *n* finta *f*

mak·er['meɪkə(r)] *manufacturer* fabbricante *m/f*

make·shift ['meɪkʃɪft] *adj* improvvisato

make-up ['meɪkʌp] (*cosmetics*) trucco *m*

make-up bag trousse *f inv* da trucco

mal·ad·just·ed [mælə'dʒʌstɪd] *adj* disadattato

male[meɪl] **1** *adj* (*masculine*) maschile; *animal, bird, fish* maschio **2** *n man* uomo *m*; *animal, bird, fish* maschio *m*

male 'chau·vin·ism maschilismo *m*; **male chau·vin·ist 'pig** maschilista *m*; **male 'nurse** infermiere *m*

ma·lev·o·lent [mə'levələnt] *adj* malevolo

mal·func·tion [mæl'fʌŋkʃn] **1** *n* cattivo *m* funzionamento **2** *v/i* funzionare male

mal·ice['mælɪs] cattiveria *f*, malvagità *f*

ma·li·cious [mə'lɪʃəs] *adj* cattivo, malvagio

ma·lig·nant [mə'lɪɡnənt] *adj tumour* maligno

mall [mæl] (*shopping ~*) centro *m* commerciale

mal·nu·tri·tion [mælnjuː'trɪʃn] denutrizione *f*

mal·prac·tice [mæl'præktɪs] negligenza *f*

malt ('whis·ky) [mɔːlt] whisky *m inv* di malto

mal·treat[mæl'triːt] *v/t* maltrattare

mal·treat·ment [mæl'triːtmənt] maltrattamento *m*

mam·mal ['mæml] mammifero *m*

mam·moth ['mæməθ] *adj* (*enormous*) colossale

man [mæn] **1** *n* (*pl* **men** [men]) *person, human being* uomo *m*; (*human being*) uomo *m*; *humanity* umanità *f inv*; *in draughts* pedina *f* **2** *v/t* (*pret & pp* **-ned**) *telephones, front desk* essere di servizio a; *it was ~ned by a crew of three* aveva un equipaggio di tre uomini

man·age ['mænɪdʒ] **1** *v/t business, money* gestire; *money; suitcase*; *can you ~ the suitcase?* ce la fai a portare la valigia?; *~ to ...* riuscire a ... **2** *v/i cope, financially* tirare avanti; (*financially*); *can you ~?* ce la fai?

man·age·a·ble ['mænɪdʒəbl] *adj suitcase etc* maneggevole; *hair* docile; *able to be done* fattibile

man·age·ment ['mænɪdʒmənt] (*managing*) gestione *f*; (*managers*) direzione *f*; *under his ~* durante la sua gestione

man·age·ment 'buy·out acquisizione *f* di un'impresa da parte dei suoi dirigenti; **man·age·ment con'sult·ant** consulente *m/f* di gestione aziendale; **'man·age·ment stud·ies** corso *m* di formazione manageriale; **'man·age·ment team** team *m inv* manageriale

man·ag·er ['mænɪdʒə(r)] manager

M

m/f inv, direttore *m*, -trice *f*

man·a·ge·ri·al [mænɪˈdʒɪərɪəl] *adj* manageriale

man·ag·ing di'rec·tor direttore *m* generale

man·da·rin 'or·ange [mændərɪn] mandarino *m*

man·date ['mændeɪt] (*authority, task*) mandato *m*

man·da·to·ry ['mændətrɪ] *adj* obbligatorio

mane [meɪn] *of horse* criniera *f*

ma·neu·ver *Am* → **manoeuvre**

man·gle ['mæŋgl] *v/t* (*crush*) stritolare

man·han·dle ['mænhændl] *v/t person* malmenare; *object* caricare

man·hood ['mænhʊd] *maturity* età *f inv* adulta; (*virility*) virilità *f inv*

'man·hour ora *f* lavorativa

'man·hunt caccia *f* all'uomo

ma·ni·a ['meɪnɪə] (*craze*) mania *f*

ma·ni·ac ['meɪnɪæk] F pazzo *m*, -a *f*

man·i·cure ['mænɪkjʊə(r)] *n* manicure *f inv*

man·i·fest ['mænɪfest] **1** *adj* palese **2** *v/t* manifestare; **~ itself** manifestarsi

ma·nip·u·late [məˈnɪpjʊleɪt] *v/t person, bones* manipolare; *equipment* maneggiare

ma·nip·u·la·tion [mənɪpjʊˈleɪʃn] *of person, bones* manipolazione *f*; *of bones*

ma·nip·u·la·tive [məˈnɪpjʊlətɪv] *adj* manipolatore

man'kind umanità *f inv*

man·ly ['mænlɪ] *adj* virile

'man-made *adj* sintetico

man·ner ['mænə(r)] *of doing sth* maniera *f*, modo *m*; (*attitude*) modo *m* di fare

man·ners ['mænəz] *npl*: **good / bad ~** buone / cattive maniere *fpl*; **have no ~** essere maleducato

ma·noeu·vre [məˈnuːvə(r)] **1** *n* manovra *f* **2** *v/t* manovrare

man·or ['mænə(r)] maniero *m*

'man·pow·er manodopera *f*, personale *m*

man·sion ['mænʃn] villa *f*

'man·slaugh·ter omicidio *m* colposo

man·tel·piece ['mæntlpiːs] mensola *f* del caminetto

man·u·al ['mænjʊəl] **1** *adj* manuale **2** *n* manuale *m*

man·u·al·ly ['mænjʊəlɪ] *adv* manualmente

man·u·fac·ture [mænjʊˈfæktʃə(r)] **1** *n* manifattura *f* **2** *v/t equipment* fabbricare

man·u·fac·tur·er [mænjʊˈfæktʃər-ə(r)] fabbricante *m/f*

man·u·fac·tur·ing [mænjʊˈfæktʃər-ɪŋ] *adj industry* manifatturiero

ma·nure [məˈnjʊə(r)] letame *m*

man·u·script ['mænjʊskrɪpt] manoscritto *m*; *typed* dattiloscritto *m*

man·y ['menɪ] **1** *adj* molti; **~ times** molte volte; **not ~ people / taxis** poche persone / pochi taxi; **too ~ problems / beers** troppi problemi / troppe birre **2** *pron* molti *m*, molte *f*; **a great ~, a good ~** moltissimi; **how ~ do you need?** quanti te ne servono?; **as ~ as 200** ben 200

'man-year anno / uomo *m*

map [mæp] *n* cartina *f*; (*street ~*) pianta *f*, piantina *f*

♦ **map out** *v/t* (*pret & pp* **-ped**) pianificare

ma·ple ['meɪpl] acero *m*

mar [mɑː(r)] *v/t* (*pret & pp* **-red**) guastare

mar·a·thon ['mærəθən] *race* maratona *f*

mar·ble ['mɑːbl] *material* marmo *m*

March [mɑːtʃ] marzo *m*

march [mɑːtʃ] **1** *n* marcia *f*; (*demonstration*) dimostrazione *f*, manifestazione *f* **2** *v/i* marciare; *in protest* dimostrare, manifestare; **~ from A to B** *in protest* sfilare in corteo da A a B

march·er ['mɑːtʃə(r)] dimostrante *m/f*, manifestante *m/f*

mare [meə(r)] cavalla *f*, giumenta *f*

mar·ga·rine [mɑːdʒəˈriːn] margarina *f*

mar·gin ['mɑːdʒɪn] *of page* margine *m*; (COM: *profit margin*) margine *m* di guadagno; **by a narrow ~** di stretta misura

mar·gin·al ['mɑːdʒɪnl] *adj* (*slight*) leggero

mar·gin·al·ly ['mɑːdʒɪnlɪ] *adv* (*slightly*) leggermente

mar·i·hua·na, mar·i·jua·na [mærɪ'hwɑːnə] marijuana *f*

ma·ri·na [mə'riːnə] porticciolo *m*

mar·i·nade [mærɪ'neɪd] *n* marinata *f*

mar·i·nate ['mærɪneɪt] *v/t* marinare

ma·rine [mə'riːn] **1** *adj* marino **2** *n* MIL marina *f* militare

mar·i·tal ['mærɪtl] *adj* coniugale

mar·i·tal 'sta·tus stato *m* civile

mar·i·time ['mærɪtaɪm] *adj* marittimo

mar·jo·ram ['mɑːdʒərəm] maggiorana *f*

mark¹ [mɑːk] FIN marco *m*

mark² [mɑːk] **1** *n* (*stain*) macchia *f*; (*sign, token*) segno *m*; (*trace*) voto *m*; **leave one's ~** lasciare un segno **2** *v/t* (*stain*) macchiare; EDU correggere; (*indicate*) indicare; (*commemorate*) celebrare; **your essays will be ~ed out of ten** ai temi sarà assegnata una votazione da 1 a 10 **3** *v/i* of fabric macchiarsi

♦ **mark down** *v/t goods* ribassare

♦ **mark out** *v/t with a line etc* delimitare; (*fig: set apart*) distinguere

♦ **mark up** *v/t price* aumentare; *goods* aumentare il prezzo di

marked [mɑːkt] *adj* (*definite*) spiccato

mark·er ['mɑːkə(r)] (*highlighter*) evidenziatore *m*

mar·ket ['mɑːkɪt] **1** *n* mercato *m*; *for particular commodity*; (*stock ~*) mercato *m* azionario; **on the ~** sul mercato **2** *v/t* vendere

mar·ket·a·ble ['mɑːkɪtəbl] *adj* commercializzabile

mar·ket e'con·o·my economia *f* di mercato

'mar·ket for·ces *npl* forze *fpl* di mercato

mar·ket·ing ['mɑːkɪtɪŋ] marketing *m inv*

'mar·ket·ing cam·paign campagna

f di marketing; 'mar·ket·ing de·part·ment reparto *m* marketing; 'mar·ket·ing mix marketing mix *m inv*; 'mar·ket·ing strat·e·gy strategia *f* di marketing

mar·ket 'lead·er leader *m inv* del mercato; 'mar·ket·place *in town* piazza *f* del mercato; *for commodities* piazza *f*, mercato *m*; mar·ket re'search ricerca *f* di mercato; mar·ket 'share quota *f* di mercato

mark-up ['mɑːkʌp] ricarico *m*

mar·ma·lade ['mɑːməleɪd] marmellata *f* d'arance

mar·quee [mɑː'kiː] padiglione *f*

mar·riage ['mærɪdʒ] matrimonio *m*; *event* nozze *fpl*

'mar·riage cer·tif·i·cate certificato *m* di matrimonio

'mar·riage 'guid·ance coun·se·llor consulente *m/f* matrimoniale

mar·ried ['mærɪd] *adj* sposato; **be ~ to ...** essere sposato con ...

mar·ried 'life vita *f* coniugale

mar·ry ['mærɪ] *v/t* (*pret & pp* -ied) sposare; *of priest* unire in matrimonio; **get married** sposarsi

marsh [mɑːʃ] palude *f*

mar·shal ['mɑːʃl] *official* membro *m* del servizio d'ordine

marsh·mal·low [mɑːʃ'mæləʊ] caramella *f* soffice e gommosa

marsh·y ['mɑːʃɪ] *adj* paludoso

mar·tial arts [mɑːʃ'ɑːts] *npl* arti *fpl* marziali

mar·tial 'law legge *f* marziale

mar·tyr ['mɑːtə(r)] martire *m/f*

mar·tyred ['mɑːtəd] *adj fig* da martire

mar·vel ['mɑːvl] meraviglia *f*

♦ **marvel at** *v/t* meravigliarsi di

mar·vel·ous *Am*, mar·vel·lous ['mɑːvələs] *adj* meraviglioso

Marx·ism ['mɑːksɪzm] marxismo *m*

Marx·ist ['mɑːksɪst] **1** *adj* marxista **2** *n* marxista *m/f*

mar·zi·pan ['mɑːzɪpæn] marzapane *m*

mas·ca·ra [mæ'skɑːrə] mascara *m inv*

mas·cot ['mæskət] mascotte *f inv*

M

mas·cu·line ['mæskjʊlɪn] *adj* maschile

mas·cu·lin·i·ty [mæskjʊ'lɪnətɪ] (*virility*) virilità *f inv*

mash [mæʃ] *v/t* passare, schiacciare

mashed po·ta·toes [mæʃt] *npl* purè *m inv* di patate

mask [mɑːsk] **1** *n* maschera *f* **2** *v/t feelings* mascherare

'**mask·ing tape** nastro *m* adesivo di carta

mas·och·ism ['mæsəkɪzm] masochismo *m*

mas·och·ist ['mæsəkɪst] masochista *m/f*

ma·son ['meɪsn] scalpellino *m*

ma·son·ry ['meɪsnrɪ] muratura *f*

mas·que·rade [mæskə'reɪd] **1** *n fig* messinscena *f* **2** *v/i*: ~ **as** farsi passare per

mass¹ [mæs] **1** *n great amount* massa *f*; *the* ~**es** le masse; ~**es of** F un sacco di F **2** *v/i* radunarsi

mass² [mæs] REL messa *f*

mas·sa·cre ['mæsəkə(r)] **1** *n also fig* massacro *m* **2** *v/t also fig* massacrare

mas·sage ['mæsɑːʒ] **1** *n* massaggio *m* **2** *v/t* massaggiare; *figures* manipolare

'**mas·sage par·lor** *Am*, '**mas·sage par·lour** *euph* casa *f* d'appuntamenti

mas·seur [mæ'sɜː(r)] massaggiatore *m*

mas·seuse [mæ'sɜːz] massaggiatrice *f*

mas·sive ['mæsɪv] *adj* enorme; *heart attack* grave

mass 'me·di·a *npl* mass media *mpl*; **mass-pro'duce** *v/t* produrre in serie; **mass pro'duc·tion** produzione *f* in serie

mast [mɑːst] *of ship* albero *m*; *for radio signal* palo *m* dell'antenna

mas·ter ['mɑːstə(r)] **1** *n of dog* padrone *m*; *of ship* capitano *m*; *be a ~ of* essere un maestro di **2** *v/t skill, language* avere completa padronanza di; *situation* dominare

'**mas·ter bed·room** camera *f* da letto principale

'**mas·ter key** passe-partout *m inv*

mas·ter·ly ['mɑːstəlɪ] *adj* magistrale

'**mas·ter·mind 1** *n fig* cervello *m* **2** *v/t* ideare; **Mas·ter of 'Arts** master *m inv*; **mas·ter of 'cer·e·mo·nies** maestro *m* di cerimonie; '**mas·ter·piece** capolavoro *m*; '**mas·ter's (de·gree)** master *m inv*

mas·ter·y ['mɑːstərɪ] padronanza *f*

mas·tur·bate ['mæstəbeɪt] *v/i* masturbarsi

mat [mæt] *for floor* tappetino *m*; SP tappeto *m*; *for table* tovaglietta *f* all'americana

match¹ [mætʃ] *for cigarette* fiammifero *m*; *wax* cerino *m*

match² [mætʃ] **1** *n (competition)* partita *f*; *be no* ~ *for s.o.* non poter competere con su; *meet one's* ~ trovare pane per i propri denti **2** *v/t (be the same as)* abbinare; *(equal)* uguagliare **3** *v/i of colours, patterns* intonarsi

'**match·box** scatola *f* di fiammiferi

match·ing ['mætʃɪŋ] *adj* abbinato

'**match stick** fiammifero *m*

mate [meɪt] **1** *n of animal* compagno *m*, -a *f*; NAUT secondo *m*; F *friend* amico *m*, -a *f* **2** *v/i* accoppiarsi

ma·te·ri·al [mə'tɪərɪəl] **1** *n fabric* stoffa *f*, tessuto *m*; *substance* materia *f*; ~**s** occorrente *m* **2** *adj* materiale

ma·te·ri·al·ism [mə'tɪərɪəlɪzm] materialismo *m*

ma·te·ri·al·ist [mətɪərɪə'lɪst] materialista *m/f*

ma·te·ri·al·is·tic [mətɪərɪə'lɪstɪk] *adj* materialistico

ma·te·ri·al·ize [mə'tɪərɪəlaɪz] *v/i* materializzarsi

ma·ter·nal [mə'tɜːnl] *adj* materno

ma·ter·ni·ty [mə'tɜːnətɪ] maternità *f inv*

ma·ter·ni·ty dress vestito *m* prémaman; **ma·ter·ni·ty leave** congedo *m* per maternità; **ma·ter·ni·ty ward** reparto *m* maternità

math *Am* → **maths**

math·e·mat·i·cal [mæθə'mætɪkl] *adj* matematico

math·e·ma·ti·cian [mæθmə'tɪʃn]

matematico *m*, -a *f*

math·e·mat·ics [mæθ'mætɪks] matematica *f*

maths [mæθs] matematica *f*

mat·i·née ['mætɪneɪ] matinée *f inv*

ma·tri·arch ['meɪtrɪɑːk] matriarca *f*

ma·tri·arch·al [meɪtrɪ'ɑːkl] *adj* matriarcale

mat·ri·mo·ny ['mætrɪmənɪ] matrimonio *m*

matt [mæt] *adj* opaco

mat·ter ['mætə(r)] **1** *n* (*affair*) questione *f*, faccenda *f*; PHYS materia *f*; *as a ~ of course* per abitudine; *as a ~ of fact* a dir la verità; *what's the ~?* cosa c'è?; *no ~ what she says* qualsiasi cosa dica **2** *v/i* importare; *it doesn't ~* non importa

mat·ter-of-'fact *adj* distaccato

mat·tress ['mætrɪs] materasso *m*

ma·ture [mə'tjʊə(r)] **1** *adj* maturo **2** *v/i of person, insurance policy etc* maturare; *of wine* invecchiare

ma·tu·ri·ty [mə'tjʊərɪtɪ] maturità *f inv*

maul [mɔːl] *v/t also fig* sbranare

max·i·mize ['mæksɪmaɪz] *v/t* massimizzare

max·i·mum ['mæksɪməm] **1** *adj* massimo **2** *n* massimo *m*

May [meɪ] maggio *m*

may [meɪ] *v/aux* ◊ (*possibility*): *it ~ rain* potrebbe piovere, può darsi che piova; *you ~ be right* potresti aver ragione, può darsi che abbia ragione; *it ~ not happen* magari non succederà, può darsi che non succeda ◊ (*permission*): *~ I help / smoke?* posso aiutare / fumare?; *you ~ if you like* puoi farlo se vuoi

may·be ['meɪbiː] *adv* forse

'May Day il primo maggio

may·on·naise [meɪə'neɪz] maionese *f*

may·or ['meə(r)] sindaco *m*

maze [meɪz] *also fig* dedalo *m*, labirinto *m*

MB *abbr* (= *megabyte*) MB *m* (= megabyte *m inv*)

MBA [embiː'eɪ] *abbr* (= *master of business administration*) master

m inv in amministraztione aziendale

MBO [embiː'əʊ] *abbr* (= *management buyout*) acquisizione *f* di un'impresa da parte dei suoi dirigenti

MC [em'siː] *abbr* (= *master of ceremonies*) maestro *m* di cerimonie

MD [em'diː] *abbr* (= *Doctor of Medicine*) dottore *m* in medicina

me [miː] *pron direct & indirect object* mi; *after prep, stressed* me; *she knows ~* mi conosce; *she spoke to ~* mi ha parlato; *she spoke to ~ but not to him* ha parlato a me ma non a lui; *without ~* senza di me; *it's ~* sono io; *who? ~?* chi? io?

mead·ow ['medəʊ] prato *m*

mea·ger *Am*, **mea·gre** ['miːgə(r)] *adj* scarso

meal [miːl] pranzo *m*, pasto *m*; *enjoy your ~!* buon appetito!

'meal·time ora *f* di pranzo

mean¹ [miːn] *adj with money* avaro; (*nasty*) cattivo

mean² [miːn] (*pret & pp meant*) **1** *v/t* (*signify*) significare, voler dire; *do you ~ it?* (*intend*) dici sul serio?; *~ to do sth* avere l'intenzione di fare qc; *be ~t for* essere destinato a; *of remark* essere diretto a; *doesn't it ~ anything to you?* (*doesn't it matter?*) non conta niente per te? **2** *v/i*: *~ well* avere buone intenzioni

mean·ing ['miːnɪŋ] *of word* significato *m*

mean·ing·ful ['miːnɪŋfʊl] *adj* (*comprehensible*) comprensibile; (*constructive*) costruttivo; *glance* eloquente

mean·ing·less ['miːnɪŋlɪs] *adj sentence etc* senza senso; *gesture* vuoto

means [miːnz] *npl financial* mezzi *mpl*; (*nsg: way*) modo *m*; *~ of transport* mezzo *m* di trasporto; *by all ~* (*certainly*) certamente; *by no ~ rich / poor* lungi dall'essere ricco / povero; *by ~ of* per mezzo di

meant [ment] *pret & pp* → *mean²*

mean·time ['miːntaɪm] **1** *adv* intanto **2** *n*: *in the ~* nel frattempo

mean·while ['miːnwaɪl] **1** *adv* intan-

M

to **2** *n*: **in the ~** nel frattempo
mea·sles ['mi:zlz] *nsg* morbillo *m*
mea·sure ['meʒə(r)] **1** *n (step)* misura *f*, provvedimento *m*; **a ~ of success** *certain amount* un certo successo **2** *v/t* prendere le misure di **3** *v/i* misurare

♦ **measure out** *v/t amount* dosare; *area* misurare

♦ **measure up to** *v/t* dimostrarsi all'altezza di

mea·sure·ment ['meʒəmənt] *action* misurazione *f*; *(dimension)* misura *f*; **system of ~** sistema *m* di misura

meas·ur·ing jug ['meʒərɪŋ] misurino *m*

'**mea·sur·ing tape** metro *m* a nastro
meat [mi:t] carne *f*
'**meat·ball** polpetta *f*
'**meat·loaf** polpettone *m*
me·chan·ic [mɪ'kænɪk] meccanico *m*
me·chan·i·cal [mɪ'kænɪkl] *adj also fig* meccanico
me·chan·i·cal en·gi'neer ingegnere *m* meccanico
me·chan·i·cal en·gi'neer·ing ingegneria *f* meccanica
me·chan·i·cal·ly [mɪ'kænɪklɪ] *adv also fig* meccanicamente
mech·a·nism ['mekənɪzm] meccanismo *m*
mech·a·nize ['mekənaɪz] *v/t* meccanizzare
med·al ['medl] medaglia *f*
med·al·ist *Am*, **med·al·list** ['medəlɪst] vincitore *m*,-trice *f* di una medaglia
med·dle ['medl] *v/i (interfere)* immischiarsi; **~ with** *(tinker)* mettere le mani in
me·di·a ['mi:dɪə] *npl*: **the ~** i mass media *mpl*
'**me·di·a cov·er·age**: **it was given a lot of ~** gli è stato dato molto spazio in tv e sui giornali; **an event that got a lot of ~** un avvenimento di grande risonanza
med·i·ae·val [medɪ'i:vl] → **medieval**
'**me·di·a e·vent** spettacolo *m* sensazionale; **me·di·a 'hype** montatura *f*

della stampa; '**me·di·a stud·ies** scienze *fpl* delle comunicazioni
me·di·ate ['mi:dɪeɪt] *v/i* fare da mediatore *m*, -trice *f*
me·di·a·tion [mi:dɪ'eɪʃn] mediazione *f*
me·di·a·tor ['mi:dɪeɪtə(r)] mediatore *m*, -trice *f*
med·i·cal ['medɪkl] **1** *adj* medico **2** *n* visita *f* medica
'**med·i·cal cer·tif·i·cate** certificato *m* medico; '**med·i·cal ex·am·i·na·tion** visita *f* medica; '**med·i·cal his·to·ry** anamnesi *f inv*; '**med·i·cal pro·fes·sion** professione *f* medica; corpo *m* medico; '**med·i·cal re·cord** cartella *f* clinica
med·i·cat·ed ['medɪkeɪtɪd] *adj* medicato
med·i·ca·tion [medɪ'keɪʃn] medicina *f*
me·di·ci·nal [mɪ'dɪsɪnl] *adj* medicinale
medi·cine ['medsən] medicina *f*
'**medi·cine cab·i·net** armadietto *m* dei medicinali
medi·e·val [medɪ'i:vl] *adj* medievale
me·di·o·cre [mi:dɪ'əʊkə(r)] *adj* mediocre
me·di·oc·ri·ty [mi:dɪ'ɒkrətɪ] mediocrità *f inv*
medi·tate ['medɪteɪt] *v/i* meditare
medi·ta·tion [medɪ'teɪʃn] meditazione *f*
Med·i·ter·ra·ne·an [medɪtə'reɪnɪən] **1** *adj* mediterraneo **2** *n*: **the ~** il Mar Mediterraneo; *area* i paesi mediterranei
me·di·um ['mi:dɪəm] **1** *adj (average)* medio; *steak* cotto al punto giusto **2** *n in size* media *f*; *(vehicle)* strumento *m*; *(spiritualist)* medium *m/f inv*
me·di·um-sized ['mi:dɪəmsaɪzd] *adj* di grandezza media; **me·di·um 'term**: **in the ~** a medio termine; '**me·di·um wave** RAD onde *fpl* medie
med·ley ['medlɪ] *(assortment)* misto *m*

meek [miːk] *adj* mite

meet [miːt] **1** *v/t* (*pret & pp* **met**) incontrare; (*get to know*) conoscere; (*collect*) andare *o* venire a prendere; *in competition* affrontare; *of eyes* incrociare; (*satisfy*) soddisfare; **I'll ~ you there** ci vediamo lì **2** *v/i* (*pret & pp* **met**) incontrarsi; *in competition* affrontarsi; *of eyes* incrociarsi; *of committee etc* riunirsi; **have you two met?** (*do you know each other?*) vi conoscete? **3** *n Am* SP raduno *m* sportivo

♦ **meet with** *v/t person* avere un incontro con; *opposition, approval etc* incontrare; **it met with success/failure** ha avuto successo/è fallito

meet·ing [miːtɪŋ] incontro *m*; *of committee, in business* riunione *f*; appuntamento *m*; **he's in a ~** è in riunione

'meet·ing place luogo *m* d'incontro

meg·a·byte [meɡəbaɪt] COMPUT megabyte *m inv*

mel·an·chol·y [melənkəlɪ] *adj* malinconia *f*

mel·low [meləʊ] **1** *adj* maturo **2** *v/i of person* addolcirsi

me·lo·di·ous [mɪˈləʊdɪəs] *adj* melodioso

mel·o·dra·mat·ic [melədrəˈmætɪk] *adj* melodrammatico

mel·o·dy [melədɪ] melodia *f*

mel·on [melən] melone *m*

melt [melt] **1** *v/i* sciogliersi **2** *v/t* sciogliere

♦ **melt away** *v/i fig* svanire

♦ **melt down** *v/t metal* fondere

melt·ing pot [meltɪŋpɒt] *fig* crogiolo *m* di culture

mem·ber [membə(r)] *of family* componente *m/f*; *of club* socio *m*; *of organization* membro *m*

Mem·ber of 'Par·lia·ment deputato *m*

mem·ber·ship [membəʃɪp] iscrizione *f*; *number of members* numero *m* dei soci

'mem·ber·ship card tessera *f* d'iscrizione

mem·brane [membreɪn] membrana *f*

me·men·to [meˈmentəʊ] souvenir *m inv*

mem·o [meməʊ] circolare *f*

mem·oirs [memwɑːz] *npl* memorie *fpl*

'mem·o pad blocco *m* notes

mem·o·ra·ble [memərəbl] *adj* memorabile

me·mo·ri·al [mɪˈmɔːrɪəl] **1** *adj* commemorativo **2** *n also fig* memorial *m inv*

mem·o·rize [meməraɪz] *v/t* memorizzare

mem·o·ry [memərɪ] (*recollection*) ricordo *m*; *power of recollection* memoria *f*; COMPUT memoria *f*; **in ~ of** in memoria di

men [men] *pl* → **man**

men·ace [menɪs] **1** *n* (*threat*) minaccia *f*; *person* pericolo *m* pubblico; (*nuisance*) peste *f* **2** *v/t* minacciare

men·ac·ing [menɪsɪŋ] minaccioso

mend [mend] **1** *v/t* riparare **2** *n*: **be on the ~** *after illness* essere in via di guarigione

me·ni·al [miːnɪəl] *adj* umile

men·in·gi·tis [menɪnˈdʒaɪtɪs] meningite *f*

men·o·pause [menəpɔːz] menopausa *f*

'men's room *Am* bagno *m* (degli uomini)

men·stru·ate [menstrʊeɪt] *v/i* avere le mestruazioni

men·stru·a·tion [menstrʊˈeɪʃn] mestruazione *f*

men·tal [mentl] *adj* mentale; F (*crazy*) pazzo

men·tal a'rith·me·tic calcolo *m* mentale; **men·tal 'cru·el·ty** crudeltà *f inv* mentale; **'men·tal hos·pi·tal** ospedale *m* psichiatrico; **men·tal 'ill·ness** malattia *f* mentale

men·tal·i·ty [menˈtælətɪ] mentalità *f inv*

men·tal·ly [mentəlɪ] *adv inwardly* mentalmente; *calculate etc* a mente

M

men·tal·ly 'hand·i·capped adj handicappato mentale

men·tal·ly 'ill adj malato di mente

men·tion ['menʃn] **1** n cenno m; *he made no ~ of it* non ne ha fatto cenno **2** v/t accennare a; *she ~ed that ...* ha accennato al fatto che ...; *don't ~ it* (*you're welcome*) non c'è di che

men·tor ['mentɔ:(r)] guida f spirituale

men·u ['menjuː] *also* COMPUT menu *m inv*

MEP [emiː'piː] *abbr* (= *Member of the European Parliament*) eurodeputato *m*

mer·ce·na·ry ['mɜːsɪnərɪ] **1** adj mercenario **2** n MIL mercenario *m*

mer·chan·dise ['mɜːtʃəndaɪz] merce *f*

mer·chant ['mɜːtʃənt] commerciante *m/f*

mer·chant 'bank banca *f* d'affari

mer·chant 'bank·er banchiere *m* d'affari

mer·ci·ful ['mɜːsɪful] adj misericordioso

mer·ci·ful·ly ['mɜːsɪflɪ] adv (*thankfully*) per fortuna

mer·ci·less ['mɜːsɪlɪs] adj spietato

mer·cu·ry ['mɜːkjurɪ] mercurio *m*

mer·cy ['mɜːsɪ] misericordia *f*; *be at s.o.'s ~* essere alla mercé di qu

mere [mɪə(r)] adj semplice; *he's a ~ child* è solo un bambino

mere·ly ['mɪəlɪ] adv soltanto

merge [mɜːdʒ] v/i of two lines etc unirsi; of companies fondersi

merg·er ['mɜːdʒə(r)] COM fusione *f*

mer·it ['merɪt] **1** n (*worth*) merito *m*; (*advantage*) vantaggio *m* **2** v/t meritare

mer·ri·ment ['merɪmənt] ilarità *f inv*

mer·ry ['merɪ] adj allegro; *Merry Christmas!* Buon Natale!

'mer·ry-go-round giostra *f*

mesh [meʃ] in net maglia *f*

mess [mes] (*untidiness*) disordine *m*; (*trouble*) pasticcio *m*; *be a ~* of room, desk, hair essere in disordine; of situation, s.o.'s life essere un pasticcio

♦mess about, mess around 1 v/i (*waste time*) trastullarsi **2** v/t person menare per il naso

♦mess around with v/t (*play with*) giocare con; (*interfere with*) armeggiare con; *s.o.'s wife* avere una relazione con

♦mess up v/t room, papers mettere sottosopra; task, plans, marriage rovinare

mes·sage ['mesɪdʒ] also fig messaggio *m*

mes·sen·ger ['mesɪndʒə(r)] (*courier*) fattorino *m*, -a *f*

Mes·si·ah [me'saɪə] Messia *m*

mess·y ['mesɪ] adj room in disordine; person disordinato; job sporco; divorce, situation antipatico

met [met] pret & pp → **meet**

met·a·bol·ic [metə'bɒlɪk] adj metabolico

me·tab·o·lis·m [mətæ'bəlɪzm] metabolismo *m*

met·al ['metl] **1** adj in o di metallo **2** n metallo *m*

me·tal·lic [mɪ'tælɪk] adj metallico

met·a·phor ['metəfə(r)] metafora *f*

me·te·or ['miːtɪə(r)] meteora *f*

me·te·or·ic [miːtɪ'ɒrɪk] adj fig fulmineo

me·te·or·ite ['miːtɪəraɪt] meteorite *m* o *f*

me·te·o·ro·log·i·cal [miːtɪərə'lɒdʒɪkl] adj meteorologico

me·te·or·ol·o·gist [miːtɪə'rɒlədʒɪst] meteorologo *m*, -a *f*

me·te·o·rol·o·gy [miːtɪə'rɒlədʒɪ] meteorologia *f*

me·ter ['miːtə(r)] for gas etc contatore *m*; (*parking ~*) parchimetro *m*; Am: length metro *m*

'me·ter read·ing lettura *f* del contatore

meth·od ['meθəd] metodo *m*

me·thod·i·cal [mɪ'θɒdɪkl] adj metodico

me·thod·i·cal·ly [mɪ'θɒdɪklɪ] adv metodicamente

me·tic·u·lous [mɪ'tɪkjʊləs] adj meticoloso

me·tic·u·lous·ly [mɪˈtɪkjʊləslɪ] *adv* meticolosamente

me·tre [ˈmiːtə(r)] metro *m*

met·ric [ˈmetrɪk] *adj* metrico

me·trop·o·lis [mɪˈtrɒpəlɪs] metropoli *f inv*

met·ro·pol·i·tan [metrəˈpɒlɪtən] *adj* metropolitano

mew [mjuː] *n & v/i* → *miaow*

Mex·i·can [ˈmeksɪkən] **1** *adj* messicano **2** *n* messicano *m*, -a *f*

Mex·i·co [ˈmeksɪkəʊ] Messico *m*

mez·za·nine (**floor**) [ˈmezənɪn] mezzanino *m*

mi·aow [mɪaʊ] **1** *n* miao *m* **2** *v/i* miagolare

mice [maɪs] *pl* → *mouse*

mick·ey mouse [mɪkɪˈmaʊs] *adj* P *course, qualification* del piffero F

mi·cro·bi·ol·o·gy [ˈmaɪkrəʊ] microbiologia *f*; **ˈmi·cro·chip** microchip *m inv*; **ˈmi·cro·cli·mate** microclima *m*; **mi·cro·cosm** [ˈmaɪkrəʊkɒzm] microcosmo *m*; **ˈmi·cro·e·lec·tron·ics** microelettronica *f*; **ˈmi·cro·film** microfilm *m inv*; **ˈmi·cro·or·gan·ism** microrganismo *m*; **ˈmi·cro·phone** microfono *m*; **mi·cro·proces·sor** microprocessore *m*; **ˈmi·cro·scope** microscopio *m*; **mi·cro·scop·ic** [maɪkrəˈskɒpɪk] *adj* microscopico; **ˈmi·cro·wave** *oven* forno *m* a microonde

mid·air [mɪdˈeə(r)]: **in** ~ a mezz'aria

mid·day [mɪdˈdeɪ] mezzogiorno *m*

mid·dle [ˈmɪdl] **1** *adj* di mezzo **2** *n* mezzo *m*; **in the** ~ **of** *of floor, room* nel centro di, in mezzo a; *of period of time* a metà di; **be in the** ~ **of doing sth** stare facendo qc

ˈmid·dle-aged *adj* di mezz'età; **ˈMid·dle Ages** *npl* Medioevo *m*; **mid·dle ˈclass** *adj* borghese; **the** ~ **class(es)** *npl* la borghesia *f*; **Mid·dle ˈEast** Medio Oriente *m*; **ˈmid·dle-man** intermediario *m*; **mid·dle ˈman·age·ment** quadri *mpl* intermedi; **mid·dle ˈname** secondo nome *m*; **ˈmid·dle·weight** *boxer* peso *m* medio

mid·dling [ˈmɪdlɪŋ] *adj* medio

mid·field·er [mɪdˈfiːldə(r)] centrocampista *m*

midge [mɪdʒ] moscerino *m*

midg·et [ˈmɪdʒɪt] *adj* di dimensioni ridotte

ˈMid·lands *npl* regione *f* nell'Inghilterra centrale

ˈmid·night [ˈmɪdnaɪt] mezzanotte *f*; **at** ~ a mezzanotte; **ˈmid·sum·mer** piena estate *f*; **ˈmid·way** *adv* a metà strada; ~ **through** a metà di; **ˈmid·week** *adv* metà settimana; **ˈMid·west** *regione f medio-occidentale degli USA*; **ˈmid·wife** ostetrica *f*; **ˈmid·win·ter** pieno inverno *m*

might¹ [maɪt] *v/aux*: **I** ~ **be late** potrei far tardi; **it** ~ **rain** magari piove; **it** ~ **never happen** potrebbe non succedere mai; **I** ~ **have lost it** perhaps I did forse l'ho perso; **it would have been possible** avrei potuto perderlo; **he** ~ **have left** forse se n'è andato; **you** ~ **as well spend the night here** tanto vale che passi la notte qui; **you** ~ **have told me!** potevi dirmelo!

might² [maɪt] (*power*) forze *fpl*

might·y [ˈmaɪtɪ] **1** *adj* potente **2** *adv* F (*extremely*) molto

mi·graine [ˈmiːgreɪn] emicrania *f*

mi·grant work·er [ˈmaɪgrənt] emigrante *m/f*

mi·grate [maɪˈgreɪt] *v/i* emigrare; *of birds* migrare

mi·gra·tion [maɪˈgreɪʃn] emigrazione *f*; *of birds* migrazione *f*

mike [maɪk] F microfono *m*

Mi·lan [mɪˈlæn] Milano *f*

mild [maɪld] *adj* weather mite; *cheese, person* dolce; *curry* poco piccante; *punishment, sedative* leggero

mil·dew [ˈmɪldjuː] muffa *f*

mild·ly [ˈmaɪldlɪ] *adv* gentilmente; (*slightly*) moderatamente; **to put it** ~ a dir poco

mild·ness [ˈmaɪldnɪs] *of weather* mitezza *f*; *of person, voice* dolcezza *f*

mile [maɪl] miglio *m*; ~**s better**/ **easier** F molto meglio / più facile

mile·age [ˈmaɪlɪdʒ] chilometraggio *m*

M

'mile·stone *also fig* pietra *f* miliare

mil·i·tant ['mɪlɪtənt] **1** *adj* militante **2** *n* militante *m/f*

mil·i·ta·ry ['mɪlɪtrɪ] **1** *adj* militare **2** *n*: **the ~** l'esercito *m*, le forze *fpl* armate; **it's run by the ~** è in mano ai militari

mil·i·ta·ry a'cad·e·my accademia *f* militare; **mil·i·ta·ry po'lice** polizia *f* militare; **mil·i·tar·y 'serv·ice** servizio *m* militare

mi·li·tia [mɪ'lɪʃə] milizia *f*

milk [mɪlk] **1** *n* latte *m* **2** *v/t* mungere

'milk bot·tle bottiglia *f* del latte; **milk 'choc·o·late** cioccolato *m* al latte; **'milk float** furgone *m* del lattaio; **'milk jug** bricco *m* del latte; **'milk·man** lattaio *m*; **milk of mag'ne·sia** latte *m* di magnesia; **'milk·shake** frappé *m inv*

'milk·y ['mɪlkɪ] *adj* con tanto latte

Milk·y 'Way Via *f* Lattea

mill [mɪl] *for grain* mulino *m*; *for textiles* fabbrica *f*

♦ mill about, mill around *v/i* brulicare

mil·len·ni·um [mɪ'lenɪəm] millennio *m*

mil·li·gram ['mɪlɪgræm] milligrammo *m*

mil·li·me·ter *Am*, mil·li·me·tre ['mɪlɪmiːtə(r)] millimetro *m*

mil·lion ['mɪljən] milione *m*

mil·lion·aire [mɪljə'neə(r)] miliardario *m*, -a *f*

mime [maɪm] *v/t* mimare

mim·ic ['mɪmɪk] **1** *n* imitatore *m*, -trice *f* **2** *v/t* (*pret & pp* **-ked**) imitare

mince [mɪns] *v/t meat* carne *f* tritata

'mince·meat frutta *f* secca tritata

mince 'pie pasticcino *m* ripieno di frutta secca tritata

mind [maɪnd] **1** *n* mente *f*, cervello *m*; **it's all in your ~** è solo la tua immaginazione; **be out of one's ~** essere matto; **keep sth in ~** tenere presente qc; **I've a good ~ to ...** ho proprio voglia di ...; **change one's ~** cambiare idea; **it didn't enter my ~** non mi è passato per la testa; **give s.o. a piece of one's ~** cantarne quattro a qu; **make up one's ~** decidersi; **have sth on one's ~** essere preoccupato per qc; **keep one's ~ on sth** concentrarsi su qc **2** *v/t (look after)* tenere d'occhio; *children* badare a; *(heed)* fare attenzione a; **I don't ~ tea if that's all you've got** *(object to)* il tè va bene se non hai altro; **I don't ~ what we do** non importa cosa facciamo; **do you ~ if I smoke?, do you ~ my smoking?** le dispiace se fumo?; **would you ~ opening the window?** le dispiace aprire la finestra?; **~ the step!** attento al gradino!; **~ your own business!** fatti gli affari tuoi! **3** *v/i*: **~!** *(be careful)* attenzione!; **never ~!** non farci caso!; **I don't ~** è uguale o indifferente

mind-bog·gling ['maɪndbɒglɪŋ] *adj* incredibile

mind·less ['maɪndlɪs] *adj violence* insensato

mine[1] [maɪn] *pron* il mio *m*, la mia *f*, i miei *mpl*, le mie *fpl*; **a cousin of ~** un mio cugino

mine[2] [maɪn] **1** *n for coal etc* miniera *f* **2** *v/i*: **~ for** estrarre

mine[3] [maɪn] **1** *n explosive* mina *f* **2** *v/t* minare

'mine·field *also fig* campo *m* minato

min·er ['maɪnə(r)] minatore *m*

min·e·ral ['mɪnərəl] *n* minerale *m*

'min·e·ral wa·ter acqua *f* minerale

'mine·sweep·er NAUT dragamine *m inv*

min·gle ['mɪŋgl] *v/i of sounds, smells* mischiarsi; *at party* mescolarsi

min·i ['mɪnɪ] *skirt* mini *f inv*

min·i·a·ture ['mɪnɪtʃə(r)] *adj* in miniatura

'min·i·bus minibus *m inv*

'min·i·cab radiotaxi *m inv*

min·i·mal ['mɪnɪməl] *adj* minimo

min·i·mal·ism ['mɪnɪməlɪzm] minimalismo *m*

min·i·mize ['mɪnɪmaɪz] *v/t* minimizzare

min·i·mum ['mɪnɪməm] **1** adj minimo **2** n minimo m

min·i·mum 'wage salario m minimo garantito

min·ing ['maɪnɪŋ] industria f mineraria

'min·i·se·ries TV miniserie f inv

'min·i·skirt minigonna f

min·is·ter ['mɪnɪstə(r)] POL ministro m; REL pastore m

min·is·te·ri·al [mɪnɪ'stɪərɪəl] adj ministeriale

min·is·try ['mɪnɪstrɪ] POL ministero m

mink [mɪŋk] **1** adj fur di visone **2** n coat visone m

mi·nor ['maɪnə(r)] **1** adj piccolo; *in D ~* MUS in Re minore **2** n LAW minorenne m/f

mi·nor·i·ty [maɪ'nɒrətɪ] minoranza f; *be in the ~* essere in minoranza

mint [mɪnt] n herb menta f; chocolate cioccolato m alla menta; sweet mentina f

mi·nus ['maɪnəs] **1** n (~ sign) meno m **2** prep meno; *~ 10 degrees* 10 gradi sotto zero

mi·nus·cule ['mɪnəskjuːl] adj minuscolo

min·ute¹ ['mɪnɪt] of time minuto m; *in a ~* (soon) in un attimo; *just a ~* un attimo

mi·nute² [maɪ'njuːt] adj (tiny) piccolissimo; (detailed) minuzioso; *in ~ detail* minuziosamente

'mi·nute hand lancetta f dei minuti

mi·nute·ly [maɪ'njuːtlɪ] adv (in detail) minuziosamente; (very slightly) appena

min·utes ['mɪnɪts] npl of meeting verbale m

mir·a·cle ['mɪrəkl] miracolo m

mi·rac·u·lous [mɪ'rækjʊləs] adj miracoloso

mi·rac·u·lous·ly [mɪ'rækjʊləslɪ] adv miracolosamente

mi·rage ['mɪrɑːʒ] miraggio m

mir·ror ['mɪrə(r)] **1** n specchio m; MOT specchietto m **2** v/t riflettere; *be ~ed in sth* in water etc specchiarsi in qc; fig rispecchiarsi in qc

mirth [mɜːθ] ilarità f inv

mis·an·thro·pist [mɪ'zænθrəpɪst] misantropo m

mis·ap·pre·hen·sion [mɪsæprɪ'henʃn]: *be under a ~* sbagliarsi

mis·be·have [mɪsbə'heɪv] v/i comportarsi male

mis·be·hav·ior Am, mis·be·hav·iour [mɪsbə'heɪvjə(r)] comportamento m scorretto

mis·cal·cu·late [mɪs'kælkjʊleɪt] v/t & v/i calcolare male

mis·cal·cu·la·tion [mɪs'kælkjʊleɪʃn] errore m di calcolo

mis·car·riage ['mɪskærɪdʒ] MED aborto m spontaneo; *~ of justice* errore m giudiziario

mis·car·ry [mɪs'kærɪ] v/i (pret & pp -ied) of plan fallire

mis·cel·la·ne·ous [mɪsə'leɪnɪəs] adj eterogeneo

mis·chief ['mɪstʃɪf] (naughtiness) birichinate fpl

mis·chie·vous ['mɪstʃɪvəs] adj (naughty) birichino; (malicious) perfido

mis·con·cep·tion [mɪskən'sepʃn] idea f sbagliata

mis·con·duct [mɪs'kɒndʌkt] reato m professionale

mis·con·strue [mɪskən'struː] v/t interpretare male

mis·de·mea·nor Am, mis·de·mea·nour [mɪsdə'miːnə(r)] infrazione f

mi·ser ['maɪzə(r)] avaro m, -a f

mis·e·ra·ble ['mɪzrəbl] adj (unhappy) infelice; weather, performance deprimente

mi·ser·ly ['maɪzəlɪ] adj person avaro; amount misero

mis·e·ry ['mɪzərɪ] (unhappiness) tristezza f; (wretchedness) miseria f

mis·fire [mɪs'faɪə(r)] v/i of joke, scheme far cilecca; of engine perdere colpi

mis·fit ['mɪsfɪt] in society disadattato m, -a f

mis·for·tune [mɪs'fɔːtʃən] sfortuna f

mis·giv·ings [mɪs'gɪvɪŋz] npl dubbi mpl

mis·guid·ed [mɪs'gaɪdɪd] adj at-

M

tempts, theory sbagliato; **he was ~ in maintaining that ...** sbagliava a sostenere che ...

mis·han·dle [mɪs'hændl] *v/t situation* gestire male

mis·hap ['mɪshæp] incidente *m*

mis·in·form [mɪsɪn'fɔːm] *v/t* informare male

mis·in·ter·pret [mɪsɪn'tɜːprɪt] *v/t* interpretare male

mis·in·ter·pre·ta·tion [mɪsɪntɜːprɪ'teɪʃn] interpretazione *f* errata

mis·judge [mɪs'dʒʌdʒ] *v/t person, situation* giudicare male

mis·lay [mɪs'leɪ] *v/t* (*pret & pp* **-laid**) smarrire

mis·lead [mɪs'liːd] *v/t* (*pret & pp* **-led**) trarre in inganno

mis·lead·ing [mɪs'liːdɪŋ] *adj* fuorviante

mis·man·age [mɪs'mænɪdʒ] *v/t* gestire male

mis·man·age·ment [mɪs'mænɪdʒmənt] cattiva gestione *f*

mis·match ['mɪsmætʃ] discordanza *f*

mis·placed [mɪs'pleɪst] *adj loyalty, enthusiasm* malriposto

mis·print ['mɪsprɪnt] refuso *m*

mis·pro·nounce [mɪsprə'naʊns] *v/t* pronunciare male

mis·pro·nun·ci·a·tion [mɪsprənʌnsɪ'eɪʃn] errore *m* di pronuncia

mis·read [mɪs'riːd] *v/t* (*pret & pp* **-read** [red]) *word, figures* leggere male; *situation* interpretare male

mis·rep·re·sent [mɪsreprɪ'zent] *v/t facts, truth* travisare; **I've been ~ed** hanno travisato quello che ho detto

miss¹ [mɪs]: **Miss Smith** signorina Smith; **~!** signorina!

miss² [mɪs] **1** *n*: **give the meeting / party a ~** non andare alla riunione / festa **2** *v/t* (*not hit*) mancare; *emotionally* sentire la mancanza di; *bus, train, plane* perdere; (*not be present at*) mancare a; **I ~ you** mi manchi; **you've just ~ed him** he's *just gone* è appena uscito; **we must have ~ed the turnoff** ci dev'essere

sfuggito lo svincolo **3** *v/i* fallire

mis·shap·en [mɪs'ʃeɪpən] *adj* deforme

mis·sile ['mɪsaɪl] (*rocket*) missile *m*

miss·ing ['mɪsɪŋ] *adj* scomparso; **be ~** *of person, plane* essere disperso; **there's a piece ~** manca un pezzo

mis·sion ['mɪʃn] (*task, people*) missione *f*

mis·sion·a·ry ['mɪʃənrɪ] REL missionario *m*, -a *f*

mis·spell [mɪs'spel] *v/t* scrivere male

mist [mɪst] foschia *f*

♦ **mist over** *v/i of eyes* velarsi di lacrime

♦ **mist up** *v/i of mirror, window* appannarsi

mis·take [mɪ'steɪk] **1** *n* errore *m*, sbaglio *m*; **make a ~** fare un errore, sbagliarsi; **by ~** per errore **2** *v/t* (*pret* **mistook**, *pp* **mistaken**) sbagliare; **~ sth for sth** scambiare qc per qc

mis·tak·en [mɪ'steɪkən] **1** *adj* sbagliato; **be ~** sbagliarsi **2** *pp* → **mistake**

mis·ter ['mɪstə(r)] → **Mr**

mis·tress ['mɪstrɪs] *lover* amante *f*, *of servant, of dog* padrona *f*

mis·trust [mɪs'trʌst] **1** *n* diffidenza *f* **2** *v/t* diffidare di

mist·y ['mɪstɪ] *adj weather* nebbioso; *eyes* velato

mis·un·der·stand [mɪsʌndə'stænd] *v/t* (*pret & pp* **-stood**) fraintendere

mis·un·der·stand·ing [mɪsʌndə'stændɪŋ] *mistake* malinteso *m*, equivoco *m*; *argument* dissapore *m*

mis·use [mɪs'juːs] **1** *n* uso *m* improprio **2** *v/t* [mɪs'juːz] usare impropriamente

miti·ga·ting cir·cum·stances ['mɪtɪgeɪtɪŋ] *npl* circostanze *fpl* attenuanti

mit·ten ['mɪtn] muffola *f*

mix [mɪks] **1** *n* (*mixture*) mescolanza *f*, *in cooking* miscuglio *m*; *in cooking*: **ready to use** preparato *m* **2** *v/t* mescolare **3** *v/i socially* socializzare

♦ **mix up** *v/t* confondere; **mix sth up with sth** scambiare qc per qc; **be mixed up emotionally** avere disturbi emotivi; *of figures, papers* essere in disordine; *be mixed up in* essere coinvolto in; **get mixed up with** avere a che fare con

♦ **mix with** *v/t (associate with)* frequentare

mixed [mɪkst] *adj* misto; *reactions, reviews* contrastante; *I've got ~ feelings* sono combattuto

mixed 'mar·riage matrimonio *m* misto

mix·er ['mɪksə(r)] *for food* mixer *m inv*; *drink* bibita *f da mischiare a un superalcolico*; **she's a good ~** è molto socievole

mix·ture ['mɪkstʃə(r)] miscuglio *m*; *medicine* sciroppo *m*

mix-up ['mɪksʌp] confusione *f*

moan [məʊn] **1** *n of pain* lamento *m*, gemito *m*; *(complaint)* lamentela *f* **2** *v/i in pain* lamentarsi, gemere; *(complain)* lamentarsi

mob [mɒb] **1** *n* folla *f* **2** *v/t (pret & pp -bed)* prendere d'assalto

mo·bile ['məʊbaɪl] **1** *adj that can be moved* mobile; **she's less ~ now** non si può muovere tanto, ora **2** *n for decoration* mobile *m inv*; *phone* telefonino *m*

mo·bile 'home casamobile *f*

mo·bile 'phone telefono *m* cellulare

mo·bil·i·ty [mə'bɪlətɪ] mobilità *f inv*

mob·ster ['mɒbstə(r)] gangster *m inv*

mock [mɒk] **1** *adj* finto; *exam, election* simulato; *a ~Tudor house* una casa in stile Tudor **2** *v/t* deridere

mock·e·ry ['mɒkərɪ] *(derision)* scherno *m*; *(travesty)* farsa *f*

mock-up ['mɒkʌp] *(model)* modello *m*

mod cons [mɒd'kɒnz] *npl:* **with all ~** con tutti i comfort

mode [məʊd] *form* mezzo *m*; COMPUT modalità *f inv*

mod·el ['mɒdl] **1** *adj employee, husband* modello; *boat, plane in miniatura* **2** *n (miniature)* modellino *m*; *(pattern)* modello *m*; *(fashion ~)* indossatrice *f*; **male ~** indossatore *m* **3** *v/t* indossare **4** *v/i for designer* fare

l'indossatore/-trice; *for artist, photographer* posare

mo·dem ['məʊdem] modem *m inv*

mod·e·rate ['mɒdərət] **1** *adj* moderato **2** *n* POL moderato *m*, -a *f* **3** *v/t* ['mɒdəreɪt] moderare **4** *v/i* calmarsi

mod·e·rate·ly ['mɒdərətlɪ] *adv* abbastanza

mod·e·ra·tion [mɒdə'reɪʃn] *(restraint)* moderazione *f*; **in ~** con moderazione

mod·ern ['mɒdn] *adj* moderno

mod·ern·i·za·tion [mɒdənaɪ'zeɪʃn] modernizzazione *f*

mod·ern·ize ['mɒdənaɪz] **1** *v/t* modernizzare **2** *v/i of business, country* modernizzarsi

mod·ern 'lan·guages lingue *fpl* moderne

mod·est ['mɒdɪst] *adj* modesto

mod·es·ty ['mɒdɪstɪ] modestia *f*

mod·i·fi·ca·tion [mɒdɪfɪ'keɪʃn] modifica *f*

mod·i·fy ['mɒdɪfaɪ] *v/t (pret & pp -ied)* modificare

mod·u·lar ['mɒdjʊlə(r)] *adj furniture* modulare

mod·ule ['mɒdjuːl] modulo *m*; *(space ~)* modulo *m* spaziale

moist [mɔɪst] *adj* umido

moist·en ['mɔɪsn] *v/t* inumidire

mois·ture ['mɔɪstʃə(r)] umidità *f inv*

mois·tur·iz·er ['mɔɪstʃəraɪzə(r)] *for skin* idratante *m*

mo·lar ['məʊlə(r)] molare *m*

mold *etc Am* → **mould** *etc*

mole [məʊl] *on skin* neo *m*; *animal, spy* talpa *f*

mo·lec·u·lar [mə'lekjʊlə(r)] *adj* molecolare

mol·e·cule ['mɒlɪkjuːl] molecola *f*

mo·lest [mə'lest] *v/t child, woman* molestare

mol·ly·cod·dle ['mɒlɪkɒdl] *v/t* F coccolare

mol·ten ['məʊltən] *adj* fuso

mo·ment ['məʊmənt] attimo *m*, istante *m*; **at the ~** al momento; **for the ~** per il momento

mo·men·tar·i·ly [məʊmən'teərɪlɪ] *adv (for a moment)* per un momento; (*Am: in a moment*) da un momento all'altro

mo·men·ta·ry ['məʊməntrɪ] *adj* momentaneo

mo·men·tous [mə'mentəs] *adj* importante

mo·men·tum [mə'mentəm] impeto *m*

mon·arch ['mɒnək] monarca *m*

mon·ar·chy ['mɒnəkɪ] monarchia *f*

mon·as·tery ['mɒnəstrɪ] monastero *m*

mo·nas·tic [mə'næstɪk] *adj* monastico

Mon·day ['mʌndeɪ] lunedì *m inv*

mon·e·ta·ry ['mʌnɪtrɪ] *adj* monetario

mon·ey ['mʌnɪ] denaro *m*, soldi *mpl*

'**mon·ey belt** marsupio *m*; '**mon·ey mar·ket** mercato *m* monetario; '**mon·ey or·der** vaglia *m*

mon·grel ['mʌŋgrəl] cane *m* bastardo

mon·i·tor ['mɒnɪtə(r)] **1** *n* COMPUT monitor *m inv* **2** *v/t* osservare

monk [mʌŋk] frate *m*, monaco *m*

mon·key ['mʌŋkɪ] scimmia *f*; F (*child*) diavoletto *m*

♦**monkey about with** *v/t* F armeggiare con

'**mon·key wrench** chiave *f* a rullino

mon·o·gram ['mɒnəgræm] monogramma *m*

mon·o·grammed ['mɒnəgræmd] con il monogramma

mon·o·log *Am*, **mon·o·logue** ['mɒnəlɒg] monologo *m*

mo·nop·o·lize [mə'nɒpəlaɪz] *v/t also fig* monopolizzare

mo·nop·o·ly [mə'nɒpəlɪ] monopolio *m*

mo·not·o·nous [mə'nɒtənəs] *adj* monotono

mo·not·o·ny [mə'nɒtənɪ] monotonia *f*

mon·soon [mɒn'suːn] monsone *m*

mon·ster ['mɒnstə(r)] mostro *m*

mon·stros·i·ty [mɒn'strɒsɪtɪ] obbrobrio *m*

mon·strous ['mɒnstrəs] *adj* mostruoso

month [mʌnθ] mese *m*

month·ly ['mʌnθlɪ] **1** *adj* mensile **2** *adv* mensilmente **3** *n magazine* mensile *m*

mon·u·ment ['mɒnjʊmənt] monumento *m*

mon·u·ment·al [mɒnjʊ'mentl] *adj fig* monumentale

moo [muː] *v/i* muggire

mood [muːd] (*frame of mind*) umore *m*; (*bad* ~) malumore *m*; *of meeting, country* clima *m*; **be in a good / bad** ~ essere di cattivo / buon umore; **be in the ~ for** aver voglia di

mood·y ['muːdɪ] *adj* lunatico; (*bad-tempered*) di cattivo umore

moon [muːn] luna *f*

'**moon·light 1** *n* chiaro *m* di luna **2** *v/i* F lavorare in nero; '**moon·lit** *adj night* di luna piena

moor [mʊə(r)] *v/t boat* ormeggiare

moor·ings ['mʊərɪŋz] *npl* ormeggio *m*

moose [muːs] alce *m*

mop [mɒp] **1** *n for floor* mocio® *m*; *for dishes* spazzolino per i piatti **2** *v/t* (*pret & pp* **-ped**) *floor* lavare; *eyes, face* asciugare

♦**mop up** *v/t* raccogliere; MIL eliminare

mope [məʊp] *v/i* essere depresso

mo·ped ['məʊped] motorino *m*

mor·al ['mɒrəl] **1** *adj* morale; *person: of saldi principi morali* **2** *n of story* morale *f*; ~**s** principi *mpl* morali

mo·rale [mə'rɑːl] morale *m*

mo·ral·i·ty [mə'rælətɪ] moralità *f inv*

mor·bid ['mɔːbɪd] *adj* morboso

more [mɔː(r)] **1** *adj* più, altro; *some* ~ *tea?* dell'altro tè?; *a few* ~ *sandwiches* qualche altro tramezzino; *for* ~ *information* per maggiori informazioni; ~ *and* ~ *students / time* sempre più studenti / tempo; *there's no* ~ ... non c'è più ... **2** *adv* più; *with verbs di* più: ~ *important* più importante; ~ *often* più spesso; ~ *and* ~ sempre di più; ~ *or less* più o meno; *once* ~ ancora una volta; ~ *than 100* oltre 100; *I don't live* *there any* ~ non abito più lì **3** *pron*: *do you want some* ~? ne vuoi ancora?, ne vuoi dell'altro; *a little* ~ un altro po'

more·o·ver [mɔː'rəʊvə(r)] *adv* inoltre

morgue [mɔːg] obitorio *m*

morn·ing ['mɔːnɪŋ] mattino *m*, mattina *f*; *in the* ~ di mattina; (*tomorrow*) domattina; *this* ~ stamattina; *tomorrow* ~ domani mattina; *good* ~ buongiorno

morn·ing 'sick·ness nausee *fpl* mattutine

mo·ron ['mɔːrɒn] F idiota *m/f*

mo·rose [mə'rəʊs] *adj* imbronciato

mor·phine ['mɔːfiːn] morfina *f*

mor·sel ['mɔːsl] pezzetto *m*

mor·tal ['mɔːtl] **1** *adj* mortale **2** *n* mortale *m/f*

mor·tal·i·ty [mɔː'tælətɪ] mortalità *f inv*

mor·tar¹ ['mɔːtə(r)] MIL mortaio *m*

mor·tar² ['mɔːtə(r)] *cement* malta *f*

mort·gage ['mɔːgɪdʒ] **1** *n* mutuo *m* ipotecario *m* **2** *v/t* ipotecare

mor·tu·a·ry ['mɔːtjʊərɪ] camera *f* mortuaria

mo·sa·ic [məʊ'zeɪɪk] mosaico *m*

Mos·cow ['mɒskəʊ] Mosca *f*

Mos·lem ['mʊzlɪm] **1** *adj* islamico **2** *n* musulmano *m*, -a *f*

mosque [mɒsk] moschea *f*

mos·qui·to [mɒs'kiːtəʊ] zanzara *f*

moss [mɒs] muschio *m*

moss·y ['mɒsɪ] *adj* coperto di muschio

most [məʊst] **1** *adj* la maggior parte di; ~ *Saturdays* quasi tutti i sabati **2** *adv* (*very*) estremamente; ~ *beautiful / interesting* il più bello / interessante; *that's the one I like* ~ è quello che mi piace di più; ~ *of all* soprattutto **3** *pron* la maggior parte (*of* di); *at* (*the*) ~ al massimo; *make the* ~ *of* approfittare (al massimo) di

most·ly ['məʊstlɪ] *adv* per lo più

MOT [eməʊ'tiː] *Br* revisione *f* annuale obbligatoria dei veicoli

mo·tel [məʊ'tel] motel *m inv*

moth [mɒθ] falena *f*, (*clothes* ~) tarma *f*

'moth·ball naftalina *f*

moth·er ['mʌðə(r)] **1** *n* madre *f* **2** *v/t* fare da mamma a

'moth·er·board COMPUT scheda *f* madre

'moth·er·hood maternità *f inv*

Moth·er·ing 'Sun·day → *Mother's Day*

'moth·er-in-law (*pl mothers-in-law*) suocera *f*

moth·er·ly ['mʌðəlɪ] *adj* materno

moth·er-of-'pearl madreperla *f*; **'Moth·er's Day** Festa *f* della mamma; **'moth·er tongue** madrelingua *f*

mo·tif [məʊ'tiːf] motivo *m*

mo·tion ['məʊʃn] **1** *n* (*movement*) moto *m*; (*proposal*) mozione *f*; *set things in* ~ metter in moto le cose **2** *v/t*: *he ~ed me forward* mi ha fatto cenno di avvicinarmi

mo·tion·less ['məʊʃnlɪs] *adj* immobile

mo·ti·vate ['məʊtɪveɪt] *v/t person* motivare

mo·ti·va·tion [məʊtɪ'veɪʃn] motivazione *f*

mo·tive ['məʊtɪv] motivo *m*

mo·tor ['məʊtə(r)] motore *m*; *Br* F *car* macchina *f*

'mo·tor·bike moto *f*; **'mo·tor·boat** motoscafo *m*; **mo·tor·cade** ['məʊtəkeɪd] corteo *m* di auto; **'mo·tor·cy·cle** motocicletta *f*; **'mo·tor·cy·clist** motociclista *m/f*; **'mo·tor home** casamobile *f*

mo·tor·ist ['məʊtərɪst] automobilista *m/f*

'mo·tor me·chan·ic meccanico *m*; **'mo·tor rac·ing** automobilismo *m*; **'mo·tor·scoot·er** scooter *m inv*; **'mo·tor show** salone *m* dell'automobile; **'mo·tor ve·hi·cle** autoveicolo *m*; **'mo·tor·way** *Br* autostrada *f*

mot·to ['mɒtəʊ] motto *m*

mould¹ [məʊld] *on food* muffa *f*

mould² [məʊld] **1** *n* stampo *m* **2** *v/t also fig* plasmare

M

mould·y ['məʊldɪ] *adj* food ammuffi-to

mound [maʊnd] (*hillock*) collinetta *f*; *in baseball* pedana *f* del lanciatore; (*pile*) mucchio *m*

mount [maʊnt] **1** *n* (*horse*) cavalca-tura *f*; **Mount McKinlay** il Monte McKinlay **2** *v/t* steps salire; *horse* montare a; *bicycle* montare in; *campaign* organizzare; *jewel* monta-re; *photo*, *painting* incorniciare **3** *v/i* (*increase*) aumentare

♦ **mount up** *v/i* accumularsi

moun·tain ['maʊntɪn] montagna *f*

'**moun·tain bike** mountain bike *f inv*

moun·tain·eer [maʊntɪ'nɪə(r)] alpi-nista *m/f*

moun·tain·eer·ing [maʊntɪ'nɪərɪŋ] alpinismo *m*

moun·tain·ous ['maʊntɪnəs] *adj* montuoso

moun·tain 'res·cue serv·ice soc-corso *m* alpino

mount·ed po'lice ['maʊntɪd] polizia *f* a cavallo

mourn [mɔːn] **1** *v/t* piangere **2** *v/i*: ~ **for** piangere la morte di

mourn·er ['mɔːnə(r)] persona *f* che partecipa a un corteo funebre

mourn·ful ['mɔːnfʊl] *adj* triste

mourn·ing ['mɔːnɪŋ] lutto *m*; **be in** ~ essere in lutto; **wear** ~ portare il lut-to

mouse [maʊs] (*pl* **mice** [maɪs]) topo *m*; COMPUT mouse *m inv*

'**mouse mat** COMPUT tappetino *m* del mouse

mous·tache [mə'stɑːʃ] baffi *mpl*

mouth [maʊθ] *of person* bocca *f*; *of river* foce *f*

mouth·ful ['maʊθfʊl] *of food* bocco-ne *m*; *of drink* sorsata *f*

'**mouth·or·gan** armonica *f* a bocca; '**mouth·piece** *of instrument* bocchi-no *m*; (*spokesperson*) portavoce *m/f*; '**mouth·wash** collutorio *m*; '**mouth·wa·ter·ing** *adj* che fa veni-re l'acquolina

move [muːv] **1** *n* (*step*, *action*) mossa *f*; *change of house* trasloco *m*; **get a** ~ **on**! F spicciati!; **don't make a** ~! non

ti muovere! **2** *v/t* object spostare, muovere; (*transfer*) trasferire; *emo-tionally* commuovere; ~ **house** traslocare **3** *v/i* muoversi, spostarsi; (*transfer*) trasferirsi

♦ **move around** *v/i* in room muover-si; *from place to place* spostarsi

♦ **move away** *v/i* allontanarsi; *move house* traslocare

♦ **move in** *v/i* trasferirsi

♦ **move on** *v/i* ripartire; *in discussion* andare avanti; **move on to sth** pas-sare a qc

♦ **move out** *v/i* of house andare via; *of troops* ritirarsi

♦ **move up** *v/i* in league avanzare; (*make room*) spostarsi

move·ment ['muːvmənt] movimen-to *m*

mov·ie ['muːvɪ] film *m inv*; **go to a** ~ / **the ~s** andare al cinema

'**mov·ie thea·ter** *Am* cinema *m inv*

mov·ing ['muːvɪŋ] *adj* which can move mobile; *emotionally* commo-vente

mow [məʊ] *v/t* grass tagliare, falciare

♦ **mow down** *v/t* falciare

mow·er ['məʊə(r)] tosaerba *m inv*

MP [em'piː] *abbr* (= **Member of Par-liament**) deputato *m*; (= **Military Policeman**) polizia *f* militare

mph [empiː'eɪtʃ] *abbr* (= **miles per hour**) miglia *fpl* orarie

Mr ['mɪstə(r)] signor

Mrs ['mɪsɪz] signora

Ms [mɪz] signora *appellativo m usato sia per donne sposate che nubili*

Mt *abbr* (= **Mount**) M. (= monte *m*)

much [mʌtʃ] **1** *adj* molto; **so** ~ **money** tanti soldi; **how** ~ **sugar?** quanto zucchero?; **as** ~ **... as ...** tanto ... quanto ... **2** *adv* molto; **very** ~ moltissimo; **too** ~ troppo; **as** ~ **as ...** tanto quanto ...; **as** ~ **as a million dollars** addirittura un milio-ne di dollari; **I thought as** ~ me l'aspettavo **3** *pron* molto; **nothing** ~ niente di particolare; **there's not** ~ **left** non ne è rimasto, -a molto, -a

muck [mʌk] (*dirt*) sporco *m*

mu·cus ['mjuːkəs] muco *m*

mud [mʌd] fango *m*

mud·dle ['mʌdl] **1** *n* disordine *m*; *I'm in a ~* sono confuso **2** *v/t* confondere

♦ **muddle up** *v/t* (*mess up*) mettere in disordine; (*confuse*) confondere

mud·dy ['mʌdɪ] *adj* fangoso; *hands, boots* sporco di fango

mues·li ['muːzlɪ] müsli *m inv*

muf·fle ['mʌfl] *v/t* attutire; *voice* camuffare

muf·fler ['mʌflər] *Am* MOT marmitta *f*

♦ **muffle up** *v/i* coprirsi bene

mug[1] [mʌg] *for tea, coffee* tazzone *m*; F (*face*) faccia *f*

mug[2] [mʌg] *v/t* (*pret & pp* **-ged**) *attack* aggredire

mug·ger ['mʌgər] aggressore *m*

mug·ging ['mʌgɪŋ] aggressione *f*

mug·gy ['mʌgɪ] *adj* afoso

♦ **mull over** [mʌl] *v/t* riflettere su

mul·ti·lat·e·ral [mʌltɪ'lætərəl] *adj* POL multilaterale

mul·ti·lin·gual [mʌltɪ'lɪŋgwəl] *adj* multilingue *inv*

mul·ti·me·di·a [mʌltɪ'miːdɪə] **1** *adj* multimediale **2** *n* multimedialità *f inv*

mul·ti·na·tion·al [mʌltɪ'næʃnl] **1** *adj* multinazionale **2** *n* COM multinazionale *f*

mul·ti·ple ['mʌltɪpl] *adj* multiplo

mul·ti·ple 'choice ques·tion esercizio *m* a scelta multipla

mul·ti·ple scle·ro·sis sclerosi *f* multipla

'mul·ti·plex ('cin·e·ma) cinema *m inv* multisale

mul·ti·pli·ca·tion [mʌltɪplɪ'keɪʃn] moltiplicazione *f*

mul·ti·ply ['mʌltɪplaɪ] (*pret & pp* **-ied**) **1** *v/t* moltiplicare **2** *v/i* moltiplicarsi

multi-sto·rey (car park) [mʌltɪ'stɔːrɪ] parcheggio *m* a più piani

mum [mʌm] mamma *f*

mum·ble ['mʌmbl] **1** *n* borbottio *m* **2** *v/t & v/i* borbottare

mum·my ['mʌmɪ] mamma *f*

mumps [mʌmps] *nsg* orecchioni *mpl*

munch [mʌntʃ] *v/t & v/i* sgranocchiare

mu·ni·ci·pal [mjuː'nɪsɪpl] *adj* municipale

mu·ral ['mjʊərəl] murale *m*

mur·der ['mɜːdə(r)] **1** *n* omicidio *m* **2** *v/t person* uccidere; *song* rovinare

mur·der·er ['mɜːdərə(r)] omicida *m/f*

mur·der·ous ['mɜːdrəs] *adj rage, look* omicida

murk·y ['mɜːkɪ] *adj also fig* torbido

mur·mur ['mɜːmə(r)] **1** *n* mormorio *m* **2** *v/t* mormorare

mus·cle ['mʌsl] muscolo *m*

mus·cu·lar ['mʌskjʊlə(r)] *adj pain, strain* muscolare; *person* muscoloso

muse [mjuːz] *v/i* riflettere

mu·se·um [mjuː'zɪəm] museo *m*

mush·room ['mʌʃruːm] **1** *n* fungo *m* **2** *v/i* crescere rapidamente

mu·sic ['mjuːzɪk] musica *f*; *in written form* spartito *m*

mu·sic·al ['mjuːzɪkl] **1** *adj* musicale; *person* portato per la musica; *voice* melodioso **2** *n* musical *m inv*

'mu·sic(·al) box carillon *m inv*

mu·sic·al 'in·stru·ment strumento *m* musicale

mu·sic·ian [mjuː'zɪʃn] musicista *m/f*

mus·sel ['mʌsl] cozza *f*

must [mʌst] *v/aux* ◊ (*necessity*): *I ~ be on time* devo arrivare in orario; *I ~* devo; *I ~n't be late* non devo far tardi ◊ (*probability*): *it ~ be about 6 o'clock* devono essere circa le sei; *they ~ have arrived by now* ormai devono essere arrivati

mus·tache *Am →* **moustache**

mus·tard ['mʌstəd] senape *f*

must·y ['mʌstɪ] *adj smell* di stantio; *room* che sa di stantio

mute [mjuːt] *adj* muto

mut·ed ['mjuːtɪd] *adj* tenue

mu·ti·late ['mjuːtɪleɪt] *v/t* mutilare

mu·ti·ny ['mjuːtɪnɪ] **1** *n* ammutinamento *m* **2** *v/i* (*pret & pp* **-ied**) ammutinarsi

M

mut·ter ['mʌtə(r)] v/t & v/i farfugliare

mutton ['mʌtn] montone m

mu·tu·al ['mjuːtjʊəl] adj admiration reciproco; friend in comune

muz·zle ['mʌzl] **1** n of animal muso m; for dog museruola f **2** v/t: **~ the press** imbavagliare la stampa

my [maɪ] adj il mio m, la mia f, i miei mpl, le mie fpl; **~ bag** said by man/woman la mia valigia; **~ sister/brother** mia sorella/mio fratello

my·op·ic [maɪ'ɒpɪk] adj miope

my·self [maɪ'self] pron reflexive mi; emphatic io stesso; after prep me

stesso; **I've hurt ~** mi sono fatto male; **~, I'd prefer ...** quanto a me, preferirei ...; **by ~** da solo

mys·te·ri·ous [mɪ'stɪərɪəs] adj misterioso

mys·te·ri·ous·ly [mɪ'stɪərɪəslɪ] adv misteriosamente

mys·te·ry ['mɪstərɪ] mistero m

mys·tic ['mɪstɪk] adj mistico

mys·ti·fy ['mɪstɪfaɪ] v/t (pret & pp -ied) lasciare perplesso

myth [mɪθ] also fig mito m

myth·i·cal ['mɪθɪkl] adj mitico

my·thol·o·gy [mɪ'θɒlədʒɪ] mitologia f

N

nab [næb] v/t (pret & pp **-bed**) F take for o.s. prendere

nag [næg] (pret & pp **-ged**) **1** v/i of person brontolare di continuo **2** v/t assillare; **~ s.o. to do sth** assillare qu perché faccia qc

nag·ging ['nægɪŋ] adj person brontolone; doubt, pain assillante

nail [neɪl] for wood chiodo m; on finger, toe unghia f

'**nail clip·pers** npl tagliaunghie m inv; '**nail file** limetta f per unghie; '**nail pol·ish** smalto m per unghie; '**nail pol·ish re·mov·er** solvente m per unghie; '**nail scis·sors** npl forbicine fpl per unghie; '**nail var·nish** smalto m per unghie

na·ive [naɪ'iːv] adj ingenuo

naked ['neɪkɪd] adj nudo; **to the ~ eye** a occhio nudo

name [neɪm] **1** n nome m; **what's your ~?** come ti chiami?; **call s.o. ~s** insultare qu; **make a ~ for o.s.** farsi un nome **2** v/t chiamare

♦ **name after** v/t: **they named him after his grandfather** gli hanno messo il nome del nonno

♦ **name for** Am → **name after**

name·ly ['neɪmlɪ] adv cioè

'**name·sake** omonimo m, -a f

'**name·tag** on clothing etc targhetta f col nome

nan·ny ['nænɪ] bambinaia f

nap [næp] n sonnellino m; **have a ~** farsi un sonnellino

nape [neɪp] n: **~ of the neck** nuca f

nap·kin ['næpkɪn] (table ~) tovagliolo m; Am (sanitary ~) assorbente m

Na·ples ['neɪplz] Napoli f

nap·py ['næpɪ] pannolino m

nar·cot·ic [naː'kɒtɪk] n narcotico m

nar·rate [nə'reɪt] v/t raccontare, narrare

nar·ra·tion [nə'reɪʃn] narrazione f

nar·ra·tive ['nærətɪv] **1** n story racconto **2** adj poem, style narrativo

nar·ra·tor [nə'reɪtə(r)] narratore m, -trice f

nar·row ['nærəʊ] adj street, bed etc stretto; views, mind ristretto; victory di stretta misura

nar·row·ly ['nærəʊlɪ] adv win di stretta misura; **~ escape sth** scampare a qc per un pelo F

nar·row-mind·ed [nærəʊ'maɪndɪd] *adj* di idee ristrette

na·sal ['neɪzl] *adj voice* nasale

nas·ty ['nɑːstɪ] *adj person, thing to say, smell, weather* cattivo; *cut, wound, disease* brutto

na·tion ['neɪʃn] nazione *f*

na·tion·al ['næʃənl] **1** *adj* nazionale **2** *n* cittadino *m*, -a *f*

na·tion·al 'an·them inno *m* nazionale

na·tion·al 'debt debito *m* pubblico

na·tion·al·ism ['næʃənəlɪzm] nazionalismo *m*

na·tion·al·i·ty [næʃə'næləti] nazionalità *f inv*

na·tion·al·ize ['næʃənəlaɪz] *v/t industry etc* nazionalizzare

na·tion·al 'park parco *m* nazionale

na·tive ['neɪtɪv] **1** *adj* indigeno; **~ language** madrelingua *f* **2** *n (tribesman)* indigeno *m*, -a *f*; **she's a ~ of New York** è originaria di New York; **she speaks Chinese like a ~** parla cinese come una madrelingua

na·tive 'coun·try patria *f*

na·tive 'speak·er: English ~ persona *f* di madrelingua inglese

NATO ['neɪtəʊ] *abbr* (= **North Atlantic Treaty Organization**) NATO *f*

nat·u·ral ['nætʃrəl] *adj* naturale

nat·u·ral 'gas gas *m inv* naturale

nat·u·ral·ist ['nætʃrəlɪst] naturalista *m/f*

nat·u·ral·ize ['nætʃrəlaɪz] *v/t:* **become ~d** naturalizzarsi

nat·u·ral·ly ['nætʃərəlɪ] *adv (of course)* naturalmente; *behave, speak* con naturalezza; *(by nature)* per natura

nat·u·ral 'sci·ence scienze *fpl* naturali

nat·u·ral 'sci·en·tist studioso *m*, -a *f* di scienze naturali

na·ture ['neɪtʃə(r)] natura *f*

na·ture re'serve riserva *f* naturale

naugh·ty ['nɔːtɪ] *adj* cattivo; *photograph, word etc* spinto

nau·se·a ['nɔːzɪə] nausea *f*

nau·se·ate ['nɔːzɪeɪt] *v/t (fig: disgust)* disgustare

nau·se·at·ing ['nɔːzɪeɪtɪŋ] *adj smell, taste* nauseante; *person* disgustoso

nau·seous ['nɔːzɪəs] *adj:* **feel ~** avere la nausea

nau·ti·cal ['nɔːtɪkl] *adj* nautico

'nau·ti·cal mile miglio *m* nautico

na·val ['neɪvl] *adj* navale; *officer, uniform* della marina

'na·val base base *f* navale

na·vel ['neɪvl] ombelico *m*

nav·i·ga·ble ['nævɪgəbl] *adj river* navigabile

nav·i·gate ['nævɪgeɪt] *v/i in ship, in aeroplane* navigare; *in car* fare da navigatore / -trice; COMPUT navigare

nav·i·ga·tion [nævɪ'geɪʃn] navigazione *f*

nav·i·ga·tor ['nævɪgeɪtə(r)] *on ship, in aeroplane* ufficiale *m* di rotta; *in car* navigatore *m*, -trice *f*

na·vy ['neɪvɪ] marina *f* militare

na·vy 'blue 1 *n* blu *m inv* scuro **2** *adj* blu scuro

near [nɪə(r)] **1** *adv* vicino **2** *prep* vicino a; **~ the bank** vicino alla banca; **do you go ~ the bank?** va dalle parti della banca? **3** *adj* vicino; **the ~est stop** la fermata più vicina; **in the ~ future** nel prossimo futuro

near·by [nɪə'baɪ] *adv* live vicino

near·ly ['nɪəlɪ] *adv* quasi

near-sight·ed [nɪə'saɪtɪd] *adj* miope

neat [niːt] *adj room, desk, person* ordinato; *whisky* liscio; *solution* efficace; F *(terrific)* fantastico

ne·ces·sar·i·ly ['nesəserəlɪ] *adv* necessariamente

ne·ces·sa·ry ['nesəsərɪ] *adj* necessario; **it is ~ to ...** è necessario ..., bisogna ...

ne·ces·si·tate [nɪ'sesɪteɪt] *v/t* rende re necessario

ne·ces·si·ty [nɪ'sesɪtɪ] necessità *f inv*

neck [nek] collo *m*

neck·lace ['neklɪs] collana *f*

'neck·line *of dress* scollo *m*

née [neɪ] *adj:* **Lisa Higgins ~ Smart** Lisa Higgins nata Smart

need [niːd] **1** *n* bisogno *m*; **if ~ be** se necessario; **be in ~** *(be needy)* essere

bisognoso; **be in ~ of sth** aver bisogno di qc; **there's no ~ to be rude /
upset** non c'è bisogno di essere maleducato / triste **2** v/t avere bisogno di; **you'll ~ to buy one** dovrai comprarne uno; **you don't ~ to wait** non c'è bisogno che aspetti; **I ~ to talk to you** ti devo parlare; **~ I say more?** devo aggiungere altro?

nee·dle ['ni:dl] *for sewing, on dial* ago *m*; *on record player* puntina *f*

'nee·dle·work cucito *m*

need·y ['ni:dɪ] *adj* bisognoso

neg·a·tive ['negətɪv] **1** *adj* negativo **2** *n* ELEC polo *m* negativo; PHOT negativa *f*; **answer in the ~** rispondere negativamente

ne·glect [nɪ'glekt] **1** *n* trascuratezza *f* **2** v/t *garden, one's health* trascurare; **~ to do sth** trascurare di fare qc

ne·glect·ed [nɪ'glektɪd] *adj gardens, author* trascurato; **feel ~** sentirsi trascurato

neg·li·gence ['neglɪdʒəns] negligenza *f*

neg·li·gent ['neglɪdʒənt] *adj* negligente

neg·li·gi·ble ['neglɪdʒəbl] *adj quantity, amount* trascurabile

ne·go·ti·a·ble [nɪ'gəʊʃəbl] *adj salary, contract* negoziabile

ne·go·ti·ate [nɪ'gəʊʃɪeɪt] **1** v/i trattare **2** v/t *deal, settlement* negoziare; *obstacles* superare; *bend in road* affrontare

ne·go·ti·a·tion [nɪgəʊʃɪ'eɪʃn] negoziato *m*, trattativa *f*

ne·go·ti·a·tor [nɪ'gəʊʃɪeɪtə(r)] negoziatore *m*, -trice *f*

neigh [neɪ] v/i nitrire

neigh·bor *etc Am* → **neighbour** *etc*

neigh·bour ['neɪbə(r)] vicino *m*, -a *f*

neigh·bour·hood ['neɪbəhʊd] *in town* quartiere *m*; **in the ~ of** *fig* intorno a

neigh·bour·ing ['neɪbərɪŋ] *adj house, state* confinante

neigh·bour·ly ['neɪbəlɪ] *adj* amichevole

nei·ther ['naɪðə(r)] **1** *adj*: **~ player** nessuno dei due giocatori **2** *pron*

nessuno *m* dei due, nessuna *f* delle due, né l'uno né l'altro, né l'una né l'altra **3** *adv*: **~ ... nor ...** né ... né ... **4** *conj* neanche; **~ do I** neanch'io

ne·on light ['ni:ɒn] luce *f* al neon

neph·ew ['nevju:] nipote *m* (di zii)

nerd [nɜːd] P fesso *m*, -a *f* P; *in style* tamarro *m* P

nerve [nɜːv] nervo *m*; *(courage)* coraggio *m*; *(impudence)* faccia *f* tosta; **it's bad for my ~s** mi mette in agitazione; **get on s.o.'s ~s** dare sui nervi a qu

nerve-rack·ing ['nɜːvrækɪŋ] *adj* snervante

ner·vous ['nɜːvəs] *adj* nervoso; **be ~ about doing sth** essere ansioso all'idea di fare qc

ner·vous 'break·down esaurimento *m* nervoso

ner·vous 'en·er·gy: be full of ~ essere sovraeccitato

ner·vous·ness ['nɜːvəsnɪs] nervosismo *m*

ner·vous 'wreck: be a ~ avere i nervi a pezzi

nest [nest] *n* nido *m*

nes·tle ['nesl] v/i rannicchiarsi

net[1] [net] *for fishing* retino *m*; *for tennis* rete *f*

net[2] [net] *adj* COM netto

net 'cur·tain tenda *f* di tulle

net 'pro·fit guadagno *m* o utile *m* netto

net·tle ['netl] ortica *f*

'net·work *of contacts, cells* rete *f*; COMPUT network *m inv*

neu·rol·o·gist [njʊə'rɒlədʒɪst] neurologo *m*, -a *f*

neu·ro·sis [njʊə'rəʊsɪs] nevrosi *f inv*

neu·rot·ic [njʊ'rɒtɪk] *adj* nevrotico

neu·ter ['nju:tə(r)] v/t *animal* sterilizzare

neu·tral ['nju:trl] **1** *adj country* neutrale; *colour* neutro **2** *n gear* folle *m*; **in ~** in folle

neu·tral·i·ty [nju:'trælətɪ] neutralità *f inv*

neu·tral·ize ['nju:trəlaɪz] v/t neutralizzare

nev·er ['nevə(r)] *adv* mai; **~! in**

disbelief ma va'!; **you're ~ going to believe this** non ci crederesti mai; **you ~ promised, did you?** non l'avrai promesso, spero!

nev•er•'end•ing *adj* senza fine

nev•er•the•less [nevəðə'les] *adv* comunque, tuttavia

new [nju:] *adj* nuovo; **this system is still ~ to me** non sono ancora abituato al sistema; **I'm ~ to the job** sono nuovo del mestiere; **that's nothing ~** non è una novità

'new•born *adj* neonato

new•com•er ['nju:kʌmə(r)] nuovo arrivato *m*, nuova arrivata *f*

new•ly ['nju:lɪ] *adv* (*recently*) recentemente

'new•ly weds [wedz] *npl* sposini *mpl*

new 'moon luna *f* nuova

news [nju:z] *nsg* notizia *f*; *on TV, radio* notiziario *m*; novità *f inv*; **any ~?** ci sono novità?; **that's ~ to me** mi giunge nuovo

'news a•gen•cy agenzia *f* di stampa; **'news•a•gent** giornalaio *m*; **'news•cast** telegiornale *m*; **'news•cast•er** giornalista *m/f* televisivo, -a; **'news flash** notizia *f* flash; **'news•pa•per** giornale *m*; **'news•read•er** giornalista *m/f* radiotelevisivo, -a; **'news re•port** notiziario *m*; **'news•stand** edicola *f*; **'news•ven•dor** edicolante *m*

new 'year anno *m* nuovo; **Happy New Year!** buon anno!; **New Year's 'Day** capodanno *m*; **New Year's 'Eve** San Silvestro *m*; **New Zea•land** ['zi:lənd] Nuova Zelanda *f*; **New Zea•land•er** ['zi:ləndə(r)] neozelandese *m/f*

next [nekst] **1** *adj in time* prossimo; *in space* vicino; **the ~ week / month he came back again** la settimana / il mese dopo ritornò; **who's ~?** a chi tocca? **2** *adv* dopo; **~ to** (*beside*) accanto a; (*in comparison with*) a paragone di

next 'door 1 *adj*: **~ neighbour** vicino *m*, -a *f* di casa **2** *adv* live nella casa accanto

next of 'kin parente *m/f* prossimo

nib•ble ['nɪbl] *v/t* mordicchiare

nice [naɪs] *adj person* carino, gentile; *day, weather, party* bello; *meal, food* buono; **be ~ to your sister!** sii carino con tua sorella!; **that's very ~ of you** molto gentile da parte tua!

nice•ly ['naɪslɪ] *adv written, presented* bene

nice•ties ['naɪsətɪz] *npl*: **social ~** convenevoli *mpl*

niche [ni:ʃ] *in market* nicchia *f* (di mercato); *special position* nicchia *f*

nick [nɪk] *n cut* taglietto *m*; **in the ~ of time** appena in tempo

nick•el ['nɪkl] *material* nichel *m inv*; (*Am: coin*) moneta *f* da 5 centesimi di dollaro

'nick•name *n* soprannome *m*

niece [ni:s] nipote *f* (di zii)

nig•gard•ly ['nɪgədlɪ] *adj amount* misero; *person* tirchio

night [naɪt] notte *f*; (*evening*) sera *f*; **at ~** di notte / di sera; **last ~** ieri notte / ieri sera; **travel by ~** viaggiare di notte; **during the ~** durante la notte; **stay the ~** rimanere a dormire; **a room for 2 ~s** una stanza per due notti; **work ~s** fare il turno di notte; **good ~** buona notte; **in the middle of the ~** a notte fonda

'night•cap (*drink*) bicchierino *m* bevuto prima di andare a letto; **'night•club** night(-club) *m inv*; **'night•dress** camicia *f* da notte; **'night•fall: at ~** al calar della notte; **'night flight** volo *m* notturno; **'night•gown** camicia *f* da notte

night•ie ['naɪtɪ] F camicia *f* da notte

nigh•tin•gale ['naɪtɪŋgeɪl] usignolo *m*

'night•life vita *f* notturna

night•ly ['naɪtlɪ] *adj & adv* ogni sera; *late at night* ogni notte

'night•mare *also fig* incubo *m*; **'night por•ter** portiere *m* notturno; **'night school** scuola *f* serale; **'night shift** turno *m* di notte; **'night•shirt** camicia *f* da notte (*da uomo*); **'night•spot** locale *m* notturno; **'night•time: at ~, in the ~** di notte, la notte

nil [nɪl] SP zero *m*

nim·ble ['nɪmbl] *adj* agile

nine [naɪn] nove

nine·teen [naɪn'tiːn] diciannove

nine·teenth [naɪn'tiːnθ] *n & adj* diciannovesimo, -a

nine·ti·eth ['naɪntɪɪθ] *n & adj* novantesimo, -a

nine·ty ['naɪntɪ] novanta

ninth [naɪnθ] *n & adj* nono

nip [nɪp] (*pinch*) pizzico *m*; (*bite*) morso *m*

nip·ple ['nɪpl] capezzolo *m*

ni·tro·gen ['naɪtrədʒn] azoto *m*

no [nəʊ] **1** *adv* no **2** *adj* nessuno; *there's ~ coffee / tea left* non c'è più caffè / tè; *I have ~ family / money* non ho famiglia / soldi; *I'm ~ linguist / expert* non sono un linguista / esperto; *~ parking* sosta vietata; *~ smoking* vietato fumare

no·bil·i·ty [nəʊ'bɪlətɪ] nobiltà *f inv*

no·ble ['nəʊbl] *adj* nobile

no·bod·y ['nəʊbədɪ] *pron* nessuno; *~ knows* nessuno lo sa; *there was ~ at home* non c'era nessuno in casa

nod [nɒd] **1** *n* cenno *m* del capo **2** *v/i* (*pret & pp -ded*) fare un cenno col capo; *~ in agreement* annuire

♦ **nod off** *v/i* (*fall asleep*) appisolarsi

no-hop·er [nəʊ'həʊpə(r)] F buono *m*, -a *f* a nulla

noise [nɔɪz] (*sound*) rumore *m*; *loud, unpleasant* chiasso *m*

nois·y ['nɔɪzɪ] *adj* rumoroso; *children, party* chiassoso; *don't be so ~* non fate tanto rumore

nom·i·nal ['nɒmɪnl] *adj amount* simbolico

nom·i·nate ['nɒmɪneɪt] *v/t* (*appoint*) designare; *~ s.o. for a post* proporre qu come candidato per una posizione

nom·i·na·tion [nɒmɪ'neɪʃn] (*appointing*) nomina *f*; (*proposal*) candidatura *f*; *person proposed* candidato *m*, -a *f*

nom·i·nee [nɒmɪ'niː] candidato *m*, -a *f*

non ... [nɒn] non ...

non-al·co·hol·ic *adj* analcolico

non-a'ligned *adj* non allineato

non·cha·lant ['nɒnʃələnt] *adj* noncurante

non-com·mis·sioned 'of·fi·cer sottufficiale *m*

non-com'mit·tal *adj person, response* evasivo

non·de·script ['nɒndɪskrɪpt] *adj* ordinario

none [nʌn] *pron* nessuno *m*, -a *f*; *~ of the students* nessuno degli studenti; *~ of this money is mine* neanche una lira di questi soldi è mia; *there are ~ left* non ne sono rimasti; *there is ~ left* non ne è rimasto, non è rimasto niente

non'en·ti·ty nullità *f inv*

none·the·less [nʌnðə'les] *adv* nondimeno

non·ex'ist·ent *adj* inesistente

non'fic·tion opere *fpl* non di narrativa

non-(in)'flam·ma·ble *adj* non infiammabile

non·in·ter'fer·ence, non·in·ter'ven·tion non intervento *m*

non-'i·ron *adj shirt* che non si stira

'no-no: *that's a ~* F non si fa

no-'non·sense *adj approach* pragmatico

non'pay·ment mancato pagamento *m*

non·pol'lut·ing *adj* non inquinante

non·res·i·dent *n in country* non residente *m/f*; (*in hotel*) persona *f* chi non è cliente di un albergo

non-re·turn·a·ble [nɒnrɪ'tɜːnəbl] *adj* a fondo perduto

non·sense ['nɒnsəns] sciocchezze *fpl*; *don't talk ~* non dire sciocchezze; *~, it's easy!* sciocchezze, è facile!

non'skid *adj tyres* antidrucciolevole

non'slip *adj surface* antiscivolo *inv*

non'smok·er *person* non fumatore *m*, -trice *f*

non'stand·ard *adj* fuori standard, non di serie; *use of a word* che fa eccezione

non'stick *adj pans* antiaderente

non'stop 1 *adj flight, train* diretto; *chatter* continuo **2** *adv fly, travel* senza scalo; *chatter, argue* di continuo

non'swim·mer *persona f chi non sa nuotare*

non'u·nion *adj* non appartenente al sindacato

non'vi·o·lence non violenza *f*

non'vi·o·lent *adj* non violento

noo·dles ['nu:dlz] *npl* spaghetti *mpl* cinesi

nook [nʊk] angolino *m*

noon [nu:n] mezzogiorno *m*; **at ~** a mezzogiorno

noose [nu:s] cappio *m*

nor [nɔ:(r)] *adv conj* né; **~ do I** neanch'io, neanche a me

norm [nɔ:m] norma *f*

nor·mal ['nɔ:ml] *adj* normale

nor·mal·i·ty [nɔ:'mælətɪ] normalità *f inv*

nor·mal·ize ['nɔ:məlaɪz] *v/t relationships* normalizzare

nor·mal·ly ['nɔ:məlɪ] *adv* (*usually*) di solito; *in a normal way* normalmente

north [nɔ:θ] **1** *n* nord *m*; **to the ~ of** a nord di **2** *adj* settentrionale, nord *inv* **3** *adv travel* verso nord; **~ of** a nord di

North Am'er·i·ca America *f* del Nord; **North Am'er·i·can 1** *n* nordamericano *m*, -a *f* **2** *adj* nordamericano; **north'east** *n* nordest

nor·ther·ly ['nɔ:ðəlɪ] *adj wind* settentrionale; *direction* nord *inv*

nor·thern ['nɔ:ðən] *adj* settentrionale

nor·thern·er ['nɔ:ðənə(r)] settentrionale *m/f*

North Ko're·a Corea *f* del Nord; **North Ko're·an 1** *adj* nordcoreano **2** *n* nordcoreano *m*, -a *f*; **North 'Pole** polo *m* nord

north·wards ['nɔ:ðwədz] *adv travel* verso nord

north·west [nɔ:ð'west] *n* nordovest *m*

Nor·way ['nɔ:weɪ] Norvegia *f*

Nor·we·gian [nɔ:'wi:dʒn] **1** *adj* norvegese **2** *n person* norvegese *m/f*; *language* norvegese *m*

nose [nəʊz] naso *m*; **right under my**

~! proprio sotto il naso!

♦ **nose about** *v/i* F curiosare

'nose·bleed emorragia *f* nasale

nos·tal·gia [nɒ'stældʒɪə] nostalgia *f*

nos·tal·gic [nɒ'stældʒɪk] *adj* nostalgico

nos·tril ['nɒstrəl] narice *f*

nos·y ['nəʊzɪ] *adj* F curioso

not [nɒt] *adv* non; **~ this one, that one** non questo, quello; **~ a lot** non molto; *I hope ~* spero di no; *I don't know* non so; *I am ~ American* non sono americano; *he didn't help* non ha aiutato; **~ me** io no

no·ta·ble ['nəʊtəbl] *adj* notevole

no·ta·ry ['nəʊtərɪ] notaio *m*

notch [nɒtʃ] tacca *f*

note [nəʊt] *n short letter* biglietto *m*; MUS nota *f*; *memo to self* appunto *m*; *comment on text* nota *f*; *take ~s* prendere appunti; **take ~ of sth** prendere nota di qc

♦ **note down** *v/t* annotare

note·book taccuino *m*; COMPUT notebook *m inv*

not·ed ['nəʊtɪd] *adj* noto

'note·pad bloc-notes *m inv*

'note·pa·per carta *f* da lettere

noth·ing ['nʌθɪŋ] *pron* niente; **~ but** nient'altro che; **~ much** niente di speciale; **for ~** (*for free*) gratis; (*for no reason*) per un nonnulla; *I'd like* **~ better** non chiedo di meglio

no·tice ['nəʊtɪs] **1** *n on notice board, in street* avviso *m*; (*advance warning*) preavviso *m*; *in newspaper* annuncio *m*; *to leave job* preavviso *m*; *to leave house* disdetta *f*; **at short ~** con un breve preavviso; **until further ~** fino a nuovo avviso; **give s.o. his / her ~** *to quit job* dare il preavviso a qu; *to leave house* dare la disdetta a qu; *hand in one's* **~** *to employer* presentare le dimissioni; **four weeks'** **~** quattro settimane di preavviso; **take ~ of sth** fare caso a qc; **take no ~ of s.o. / sth** non fare caso a qu / qc **2** *v/t* notare

no·tice·a·ble ['nəʊtɪsəbl] *adj* sensibile

'notice board bacheca *f*

no·ti·fy ['nəʊtɪfaɪ] v/t (pret & pp **-ied**) informare

no·tion ['nəʊʃn] idea f

no·to·ri·ous [nəʊ'tɔːrɪəs] adj famigerato

nou·gat ['nuːgɑː] torrone m

nought [nɔːt] zero m

noun [naʊn] nome m, sostantivo m

nour·ish·ing ['nʌrɪʃɪŋ] adj nutriente

nour·ish·ment ['nʌrɪʃmənt] nutrimento m

nov·el ['nɒvl] n romanzo m

nov·el·ist ['nɒvlɪst] romanziere m, -a f

nov·el·ty ['nɒvltɪ] novità f inv

No·vem·ber [nəʊ'vembə(r)] novembre m

nov·ice ['nɒvɪs] principiante m/f

now [naʊ] adv ora, adesso; **~ and again**, **~ and then** ogni tanto; **by ~** ormai; **from ~ on** d'ora in poi; **right ~** subito; **just ~** (proprio) adesso; **~, ~!** su, su!; **~, where did I put it?** dunque, dove l'ho messo?

now·a·days ['naʊədeɪz] adv oggigiorno

no·where ['nəʊweə(r)] adv da nessuna parte; **there's ~ to sit** non c'è posto; **it's ~ near finished** è ben lontano dall'essere terminato

noz·zle ['nɒzl] bocchetta f

nu·cle·ar ['njuːklɪə(r)] adj nucleare; **nu·cle·ar 'en·er·gy** energia f nucleare; **nu·cle·ar 'fis·sion** fissione f nucleare; **'nu·cle·ar-free** adj denuclearizzato; **nu·cle·ar 'phys·ics** fisica f nucleare; **nu·cle·ar 'pow·er** energia f nucleare; **nu·cle·ar 'pow·er sta·tion** centrale f nucleare; **nu·cle·ar re'ac·tor** reattore m nucleare; **nu·cle·ar 'waste** scorie fpl radioattive; **nu·cle·ar 'weap·on** arma f nucleare

nude [njuːd] **1** adj nudo **2** n painting nudo m; **in the ~** nudo

nudge [nʌdʒ] v/t dare un colpetto di gomito a

nud·ist ['njuːdɪst] n nudista m/f

nui·sance ['njuːsns] seccatura f;

make a ~ of o.s. dare fastidio; **what a ~!** che seccatura!

nuke [njuːk] v/t F distruggere con armi atomiche

null and 'void [nʌl] adj nullo

numb [nʌm] adj intirizzito; emotionally impietrito

num·ber ['nʌmbə(r)] **1** n (figure) numero m, cifra f; (quantity) quantità f inv; of hotel room, house, phone number etc numero m **2** v/t put a number on contare

'number plate MOT targa f

nu·me·ral ['njuːmərəl] numero m

nu·me·rate ['njuːmərət] adj: **be ~** avere buone basi in matematica; of children saper contare

nu·me·rous ['njuːmərəs] adj numeroso

nun [nʌn] suora f

nurse [nɜːs] infermiere m, -a f

nur·se·ry ['nɜːsərɪ] school asilo m; in house stanza f dei bambini; for plants vivaio m

'nur·se·ry rhyme filastrocca f; **'nur·se·ry school** scuola f materna; **'nur·se·ry school teach·er** insegnante m/f di scuola materna

nurs·ing ['nɜːsɪŋ] professione f d'infermiere; **she went into ~** è diventata infermiera

'nurs·ing home for old people casa f di riposo

nut [nʌt] noce f; for bolt dado m; **~s** F (testicles) palle fpl

'nut·crack·ers npl schiaccianoci m inv

nu·tri·ent ['njuːtrɪənt] n sostanza f nutritiva

nu·tri·tion [njuː'trɪʃn] alimentazione f

nu·tri·tious [njuː'trɪʃəs] adj nutriente

nuts [nʌts] adj F (crazy) svitato; **be ~ about s.o.** essere pazzo di qu

'nut·shell: in a ~ in poche parole

nut·ty ['nʌtɪ] adj taste di noce; F (crazy) pazzo

ny·lon ['naɪlɒn] **1** n nylon m inv **2** adj di nylon

O

oak [əʊk] *tree* quercia *f*; *wood* rovere *m*

OAP [əʊeɪˈpiː] *abbr* (= **old age pensioner**) pensionato *m*, -a *f*

oar [ɔː(r)] remo *m*

o·a·sis [əʊˈeɪsɪs] (*pl* **oases** [əʊˈeɪsiːz]) *also fig* oasi *f inv*

oath [əʊθ] LAW giuramento *m*; (*swearword*) imprecazione *f*; **on ~** sotto giuramento

'oat·meal farina *f* d'avena

oats [əʊts] *npl* avena *f*

o·be·di·ence [əˈbiːdɪəns] ubbidienza *f*

o·be·di·ent [əˈbiːdɪənt] *adj* ubbidiente

o·be·di·ent·ly [əˈbiːdɪəntlɪ] *adv* docilmente

o·bese [əʊˈbiːs] *adj* obeso

o·bes·i·ty [əʊˈbiːsɪtɪ] obesità *f inv*

o·bey [əˈbeɪ] *v/t parents* ubbidire a; *law* osservare

o·bit·u·a·ry [əˈbɪtjʊərɪ] *n* necrologio *m*

ob·ject¹ [ˈɒbdʒɪkt] *n* (*thing*) oggetto *m*; (*aim*) scopo *m*; GRAM complemento *m*

ob·ject² [əbˈdʒekt] *v/i* avere da obiettare

♦ **object to** *v/t* essere contrario a

ob·jec·tion [əbˈdʒekʃn] obiezione *f*

ob·jec·tio·na·ble [əbˈdʒekʃnəbl] *adj* (*unpleasant*) antipatico

ob·jec·tive [əbˈdʒektɪv] **1** *adj* obiettivo **2** *n* obiettivo *m*

ob·jec·tive·ly [əbˈdʒektɪvlɪ] *adv* obiettivamente

ob·jec·tiv·i·ty [əbˈdʒektɪvətɪ] obiettività *f inv*

ob·li·ga·tion [ɒblɪˈgeɪʃn] obbligo *m*; **be under an ~ to s.o.** essere in debito con qu

ob·lig·a·to·ry [əˈblɪgətrɪ] *adj* obbligatorio

o·blige [əˈblaɪdʒ] *v/t*: **much ~d!** grazie mille!

o·blig·ing [əˈblaɪdʒɪŋ] *adj* servizievole

o·blique [əˈbliːk] **1** *adj reference* indiretto **2** *n in punctuation* barra *f*

o·blit·er·ate [əˈblɪtəreɪt] *v/t city* annientare; *memory* cancellare

o·bliv·i·on [əˈblɪvɪən] oblio *m*; **fall into ~** cadere in oblio

o·bliv·i·ous [əˈblɪvɪəs] *adj*: **be ~ of sth** essere ignaro di qc

ob·long [ˈɒblɒŋ] **1** *adj* rettangolare **2** *n* rettangolo *m*

ob·nox·ious [əbˈnɒkʃəs] *adj* offensivo; *smell* sgradevole

ob·scene [əbˈsiːn] *adj* osceno; *salary, poverty* vergognoso

ob·scen·i·ty [əbˈsenɪtɪ] oscenità *f inv*

ob·scure [əbˈskjʊə(r)] *adj* oscuro

ob·scu·ri·ty [əbˈskjʊərətɪ] oscurità *f inv*

ob·ser·vance [əbˈzɜːvns] osservanza *f*

ob·ser·vant [əbˈzɜːvnt] *adj* osservante

ob·ser·va·tion [ɒbzəˈveɪʃn] osservazione *f*

ob·ser·va·to·ry [əbˈzɜːvətrɪ] osservatorio *m*

ob·serve [əbˈzɜːv] *v/t* osservare

ob·serv·er [əbˈzɜːvə(r)] *n* osservatore *m*, -trice *f*

ob·sess [əbˈses] *v/t*: **be ~ed by / with** essere fissato con

ob·ses·sion [əbˈseʃn] fissazione *f*

ob·ses·sive [əbˈsesɪv] *adj person, behaviour* ossessivo

ob·so·lete [ˈɒbsəliːt] *adj model* obsoleto; *word* disusato, antiquato

ob·sta·cle [ˈɒbstəkl] *also fig* ostacolo

ob·ste·tri·cian [ɒbstəˈtrɪʃn] ostetrico *m*, -a *f*

ob·stet·rics [ɒbˈstetrɪks] ostetricia f

ob·sti·na·cy [ˈɒbstɪnəsɪ] ostinazione f

ob·sti·nate [ˈɒbstɪnət] adj ostinato

ob·sti·nate·ly [ˈɒbstɪnətlɪ] adv ostinatamente

ob·struct [əbˈstrʌkt] v/t road, passage ostruire; investigation, police ostacolare

ob·struc·tion [əbˈstrʌkʃn] on road etc ostruzione f

ob·struc·tive [əbˈstrʌktɪv] adj behaviour, tactics ostruzionista

ob·tru·sive [əbˈtruːsɪv] adj music invadente; colour stonato

ob·tain [əbˈteɪn] v/t ottenere

ob·tain·a·ble [əbˈteɪnəbl] adj products reperibile

ob·tuse [əbˈtjuːs] adj fig ottuso

ob·vi·ous [ˈɒbvɪəs] adj ovvio, evidente

ob·vi·ous·ly [ˈɒbvɪəslɪ] adv ovviamente, evidentemente; ~! ovviamente!

oc·ca·sion [əˈkeɪʒn] occasione f

oc·ca·sion·al [əˈkeɪʒənl] adj sporadico; I like the ~ whisky bevo un whisky ogni tanto

oc·ca·sion·al·ly [əˈkeɪʒnlɪ] adv ogni tanto

oc·cult [ɒˈkʌlt] 1 adj occulto 2 n: the ~ l'occulto m

oc·cu·pant [ˈɒkjʊpənt] of vehicle occupante m/f; of building, flat abitante m/f

oc·cu·pa·tion [ɒkjʊˈpeɪʃn] (job) professione f; of country occupazione f

oc·cu·pa·tion·al 'ther·a·pist [ɒkjʊˈpeɪʃnl] ergoterapeuta m/f

oc·cu·pa·tion·al 'ther·a·py ergoterapia f

oc·cu·py [ˈɒkjʊpaɪ] v/t (pret & pp -ied) occupare

oc·cur [əˈkɜː(r)] v/i (pret & pp -red) accadere; it ~red to me that ... mi è venuto in mente che ...

oc·cur·rence [əˈkʌrəns] evento m

o·cean [ˈəʊʃn] oceano m

o·ce·a·nog·ra·pher [əʊʃnˈɒgrəfə(r)] oceanografo m, -a f

o·ce·a·nog·ra·phy [əʊʃnˈɒgrəfɪ] oceanografia f

o'clock [əˈklɒk]: at five/six ~ alle cinque/sei; it's one ~ è l'una; it's three ~ sono le tre

Oc·to·ber [ɒkˈtəʊbə(r)] ottobre m

oc·to·pus [ˈɒktəpəs] polpo m

OD [əʊˈdiː] v/i: F ~ on drug fare un'overdose di

odd [ɒd] adj (strange) strano; (not even) dispari; the ~ one out l'eccezione f; 50 ~ 50 e rotti

'odd·ball F persona f stramba; he's an ~ è un tipo strambo

odds [ɒdz] npl: be at ~ with essere in disaccordo con; the ~ are 10 to one le probabilità sono 10 contro una; the ~ are that ... è probabile che ...; against all the ~ contro ogni aspettativa

odds and 'ends npl objects cianfrusaglie fpl; things to do cose fpl

'odds-on adj: the ~ favourite il favorito; it's ~ that ... è praticamente scontato che ...

o·di·ous [ˈəʊdɪəs] adj odioso

o·dor Am, **o·dour** [ˈəʊdə(r)] odore m

of [ɒv], [əv] prep di; the works ~ Dickens le opere di Dickens; it's made ~ steel è di acciaio; die ~ cancer morire di cancro; a friend ~ mine un mio amico; very nice ~ him molto gentile da parte sua; ~ the three this is ... dei tre questo è ...

off [ɒf] 1 prep: a lane ~ the main road not far from un sentiero poco lontano dalla strada principale; leading off un sentiero che parte dalla strada principale; £20 ~ the price 20 sterline di sconto; he's ~ his food ha perso l'appetito 2 adv: be ~ of light, TV etc essere spento; of gas, tap essere chiuso; (cancelled) essere annullato; of food essere finito; she was ~ today non era al lavoro oggi; you've left the lid ~ non hai messo il coperchio; we're ~ tomorrow leaving partiamo domani; I'm ~ to New York vado a New York; I must be ~ devo andare;

with his trousers / hat ~ senza pantaloni / cappello; **take a day** ~ prendere un giorno libero; **it's 3 miles** ~ dista 3 miglia; **it's a long way** ~ è molto lontano; **drive** ~ partire (in macchina); **walk** ~ allontanarsi; ~ **and on** ogni tanto **3** adj food andato a male; ~ **switch** interruttore m di spegnimento

of·fal ['ɒfl] frattaglie fpl

of·fence [ə'fens] LAW reato m; **take ~ at sth** offendersi per qc

of·fend [ə'fend] v/t (insult) offendere

of·fend·er [ə'fendə(r)] LAW delinquente m/f; **~s will be prosecuted** i trasgressori saranno perseguiti a norma di legge

of·fense Am → offence

of·fen·sive [ə'fensɪv] **1** adj behaviour, remark, offensivo; smell sgradevole **2** n (MIL: attack) offensiva f; **go onto the** ~ passare all'offensiva

of·fer ['ɒfə(r)] **1** n offerta f **2** v/t offrire; ~ **s.o. sth** offrire qc a qu

off'hand adj attitude disinvolto

of·fice ['ɒfɪs] ufficio m; (position) carica f

'**of·fice block** complesso m di uffici

'**of·fice hours** npl orario m d'ufficio

of·fi·cer ['ɒfɪsə(r)] MIL ufficiale m; in police agente m/f

of·fi·cial [ə'fɪʃl] **1** adj ufficiale **2** n funzionario m, -a f

of·fi·cial·ly [ə'fɪʃlɪ] adv ufficialmente

of·fi·ci·ate [ə'fɪʃɪeɪt] v/i officiare

of·fi·cious [ə'fɪʃəs] adj invadente

'**off-licence** Br negozio m di alcolici

'**off-line** adj & adv off-line

'**off-peak** adj rates ridotto; ~ **electricity** elettricità f a tariffa ridotta

'**off-sea·son 1** adj rates di bassa stagione **2** n bassa stagione f

'**off·set** v/t (pret & pp -set) losses, disadvantage compensare

'**off·shore** adj drilling rig, investment off-shore inv

'**off·side 1** adj wheel etc destro; on the left sinistro **2** adv SP in fuorigioco

'**off·spring** figli mpl; of animal piccoli mpl

off-the-'rec·ord adj ufficioso

'**off-white** adj bianco sporco

of·ten ['ɒfn] adv spesso

oil [ɔɪl] **1** n olio m; petroleum petrolio m; for central heating nafta f **2** v/t hinges, bearings oliare

'**oil change** cambio m dell'olio; '**oil·cloth** tela f cerata; '**oil com·pa·ny** compagnia f petrolifera; '**oil·field** giacimento m petrolifero; '**oil-fired** adj central heating a nafta; '**oil paint·ing** quadro m a olio; '**oil-pro·duc·ing coun·try** paese m produttore di petrolio; '**oil re·fin·e·ry** raffineria f di petrolio; '**oil rig** piattaforma f petrolifera; '**oil·skins** npl abiti mpl di tela cerata; '**oil slick** chiazza f di petrolio; '**oil tank·er** petroliera f; '**oil well** pozzo m petrolifero

oil·y ['ɔɪlɪ] adj unto

oint·ment ['ɔɪntmənt] pomata f

ok [əʊ'keɪ] adj, adv F: **is it ~ with you if ...?** ti va bene se ...?; **does that look ~?** ti sembra che vada bene?; **that's ~ by me** per me va bene; **are you ~?** well, not hurt stai bene?; **are you ~ for Friday?** ti va bene venerdì?; **he's ~** (is a good guy) è in gamba

old [əʊld] adj vecchio; (previous) precedente; **how ~ are you / is he?** quanti anni hai / ha?; **he's getting ~** sta invecchiando

old 'age vecchiaia f

old age 'pen·sion pensione f di anzianità

old-age 'pen·sion·er pensionato m, -a f

old 'peo·ple's home casa f di riposo (per anziani)

old-'fash·ioned adj antiquato

ol·ive ['ɒlɪv] oliva f

'**ol·ive oil** olio m d'oliva

O·lym·pic 'Games [ə'lɪmpɪk] npl Olimpiadi fpl, giochi mpl olimpici

om·e·let Am, **om·e·lette** ['ɒmlɪt] frittata f

om·i·nous ['ɒmɪnəs] adj sinistro

o·mis·sion [ə'mɪʃn] omissione f; on purpose esclusione f

o·mit [əˈmɪt] *v/t* (*pret & pp* **-ted**) omettere, escludere; *~ to do sth* tralasciare di fare qc

om·nip·o·tent [ɒmˈnɪpətənt] *adj* onnipotente

om·nis·ci·ent [ɒmˈnɪsɪənt] *adj* onnisciente

on [ɒn] **1** *prep* su; *~ the table / wall* sul tavolo/muro; *~ the bus / train* in autobus/treno; *get ~ the bus / train* salire sull'autobus/sul treno; *~ TV / the radio* alla tv/radio; *~ Sunday* domenica; *~ Sundays* di domenica; *~ the 1st of June* il primo di giugno; *be ~ holiday / sale / offer* essere in vacanza/vendita/offerta; *I'm ~ antibiotics* sto prendendo antibiotici; *this is ~ me* (*I'm paying*) offro io; *have you any money ~ you?* hai dei soldi con te?; *~ his arrival / departure* al suo arrivo/alla sua partenza; *~ hearing this* al sentire queste parole **2** *adv*: *be ~ of light, TV etc* essere acceso; *of gas, tap* essere aperto; *of machine* essere in funzione; *of handbrake* essere inserito; *it's ~ after the news of programme* è dopo il notiziario; *the meeting is ~ scheduled to happen* la riunione si fa; *put the lid ~* metti il coperchio; *with his jacket / hat ~* con la giacca/il cappello; *what's ~ tonight?* on TV cosa c'è stasera?; *I've got something ~ tonight planned* stasera ho un impegno; *you're ~ I accept your offer etc* d'accordo; *that's not ~* (*not allowed, not fair*) non è giusto; *~ you go* (*go ahead*) fai pure; *walk / talk ~* continuare a parlare/camminare; *and so ~* e così via; *~ and ~ talk etc* senza sosta **3** *adj*: *the ~ switch* l'interruttore m d'accensione

once [wʌns] **1** *adv* (*one time*) una volta; (*formerly*) un tempo; *~ again, ~ more* ancora una volta; *at ~* (*immediately*) subito; *all at ~* (*suddenly*) improvvisamente; (*all*) *at ~* (*together*) contemporaneamente; *~ upon a time there was ...* c'era una volta ...; *~ in a while* ogni tanto; *~*

and for all una volta per tutte; *for ~* per una volta **2** *conj* non appena; *~ you have finished* non appena hai finito

one [wʌn] **1** *n* (*number*) uno m **2** *adj* uno, -a; *~ day* un giorno **3** *pron* uno m, -a f; *which ~?* quale?; *that ~* quello m, -a f; *this ~* questo m, -a f; *by ~, enter, deal with* uno alla volta; *~ another* l'un l'altro, a vicenda; *what can ~ say / do?* cosa si può dire/fare?; *~ would have thought that ...* si sarebbe pensato che ...; *the more ~ thinks about it ...* più ci si pensa ...; *the little ~s* i piccoli; *I for ~* per quanto mi riguarda

one·off 1 *n* fatto m eccezionale; *person* persona f eccezionale **2** *adj* unico

one·par·ent 'fam·i·ly famiglia f monogenitore

one'self *pron reflexive* si; *after prep* se stesso m, -a f, sé; *cut ~* tagliarsi; *do sth ~* fare qc da sé; *do sth by ~* fare qc da solo

one·sid·ed [wʌnˈsaɪdɪd] *adj* unilaterale

one·track 'mind *hum*: *have a ~* essere fissato col sesso

'one·way street strada f a senso unico

'one·way tick·et biglietto m di sola andata

on·ion [ˈʌnjən] cipolla f

'on·line *adj & adv* on-line *inv*

'on·line serv·ice COMPUT servizio m on-line

on·look·er [ˈɒnlʊkə(r)] astante m

on·ly [ˈəʊnlɪ] **1** *adv* solo; *not ~ X but also Y* non solo X ma anche Y; *~ just* a malapena **2** *adj* unico; *~ son* unico figlio maschio

'on·set inizio m

'on·side *adv* SP non in fuorigioco

on·the·job 'train·ing training m *inv* sul lavoro

on·to [ˈɒntuː] *prep*: *put sth ~ sth* mettere qc sopra qc

on·wards [ˈɒnwədz] *adv* in avanti; *from ...* da ... in poi

ooze [uːz] **1** *v/i of liquid, mud* colare

2 *v/t: he ~s charm* è di una gentilezza esagerata

o·paque [əʊ'peɪk] *glass* opaco

OPEC ['əʊpek] *abbr* (= ***Organization of Petroleum Exporting Countries***) OPEC *f*

o·pen ['əʊpən] **1** *adj* aperto; *flower* sbocciato; (*honest, frank*) aperto, franco; ***in the ~ air*** all'aria aperta **2** *v/t* aprire **3** *v/i of door, shop* aprirsi; *of flower* sbocciare

♦ **open up** *v/i of person* aprirsi

o·pen-'air *adj meeting, concert* all'aperto; *pool* scoperto; **'o·pen day** giornata *f* di apertura al pubblico; **o·pen-'end·ed** *adj contract etc* aperto

o·pen·ing ['əʊpənɪŋ] *in wall etc* apertura *f*; *of film, novel etc* inizio *m*; (*job going*) posto *m* vacante

'o·pen·ing hours *npl* orario *m* d'apertura

o·pen·ly ['əʊpənlɪ] *adv* (*honestly, frankly*) apertamente

o·pen-mind·ed [əʊpən'maɪndɪd] *adj* aperto; **o·pen 'plan of·fice** open space *m inv*; **'o·pen tick·et** biglietto *m* aperto

op·e·ra ['ɒpərə] lirica *f*, opera *f*

'op·e·ra glass·es *npl* binocolo *m* da teatro; **'op·e·ra house** teatro *m* dell'opera; **'op·e·ra sing·er** cantante lirico *m*, -a *f*

op·e·rate ['ɒpəreɪt] **1** *v/i of company* operare; *of airline, bus service* essere in servizio; *of machine* funzionare; MED operare, intervenire **2** *v/t machine* far funzionare

♦ **operate on** *v/t* MED operare

'op·e·rat·ing in·struc·tions *npl* istruzioni *fpl* per l'uso

'op·e·rat·ing sys·tem COMPUT sistema *m* operativo

op·e·ra·tion [ɒpə'reɪʃn] operazione *f*; MED intervento *m* (chirurgico), operazione *f*; *of machine* funzionamento *m*; **~s** *of company* operazioni *fpl*; **have an ~** MED subire un intervento (chirurgico)

op·e·ra·tor ['ɒpəreɪtə(r)] TELEC centralinista *m/f*; *of machine* operatore

m, -trice *f*; (*tour ~*) operatore *m* turistico

o·pin·ion [ə'pɪnjən] opinione *f*, parere *m*; ***in my ~*** a mio parere

o'pin·ion poll sondaggio *m* d'opinione

op·po·nent [ə'pəʊnənt] avversario *m*, -a *f*

op·por·tune ['ɒpətjuːn] *adj fml* opportuno

op·por·tun·ist [ɒpə'tjuːnɪst] opportunista *m/f*

op·por·tu·ni·ty [ɒpə'tjuːnətɪ] opportunità *f inv*

op·pose [ə'pəʊz] *v/t* opporsi a; ***be ~d to ...*** essere contrario a ...; ***as ~d to ...*** piuttosto che ...

op·po·site ['ɒpəzɪt] **1** *adj direction* opposto; *meaning, views* contrario; *house* di fronte; ***the ~ side of the road*** l'altro lato della strada; ***the ~ sex*** l'altro sesso **2** *n* contrario *m*

op·po·site 'num·ber omologo *m*

op·po·si·tion [ɒpə'zɪʃn] opposizione *f*

op·press [ə'pres] *v/t the people* opprimere

op·pres·sive [ə'presɪv] *adj rule, dictator* oppressivo; *weather* opprimente

opt [ɒpt] *v/t:* ***~ to do sth*** optare per fare qc

op·ti·cal il·lu·sion ['ɒptɪkl] illusione *f* ottica

op·ti·cian [ɒp'tɪʃn] *dispensing* ottico *m*, -a *f*; *ophthalmic* optometrista *m/f*

op·ti·mism ['ɒptɪmɪzm] ottimismo *m*

op·ti·mist ['ɒptɪmɪst] ottimista *m/f*

op·ti·mist·ic [ɒptɪ'mɪstɪk] *adj attitude, view* ottimistico; *person* ottimista

op·timist·ic·ally [ɒptɪ'mɪstɪklɪ] *adv* ottimisticamente

optimum ['ɒptɪməm] **1** *adj* ottimale **2** *n* optimum *m inv*

op·tion ['ɒpʃn] possibilità *f inv*, opzione *f*; ***he had no other ~*** non ha avuto scelta

op·tion·al ['ɒpʃnl] *adj* facoltativo

op·tion·al 'ex·tras *npl* optional *m inv*

O

or [ɔː(r)] *conj* o; *he can't hear ~ see* non può né sentire né vedere; *~ else!* o guai a te!

o·ral ['ɔːrəl] *adj* orale

or·ange ['ɒrɪndʒ] **1** *adj colour* arancione **2** *n fruit* arancia *f*; *colour* arancione *m*

or·ange·ade ['ɒrɪndʒeɪd] aranciata *f*

'or·ange juice succo *m* d'arancia

or·ange 'squash aranciata *f* non gasata

o·ra·tor ['ɒrətə(r)] oratore *m*, -trice *f*

or·bit ['ɔːbɪt] **1** *n of earth* orbita *f*; *send sth into ~* lanciare in orbita qc **2** *v/t the earth* orbitare intorno a

or·chard ['ɔːtʃəd] frutteto *m*

or·ches·tra ['ɔːkɪstrə] orchestra *f*

or·chid ['ɔːkɪd] orchidea *f*

or·dain [ɔːˈdeɪn] *v/t priest* ordinare

or·deal [ɔːˈdiːl] esperienza *f* traumatizzante

or·der ['ɔːdə(r)] **1** *n* ordine *m*; *for goods, in restaurant* ordinazione *f*; *in ~ to do sth* così da fare qc; *he stood down in ~ that she could get the job* si è ritirato, così che lei potesse avere il lavoro; *out of ~* (*not functioning*) fuori servizio; (*not in sequence*) fuori posto; *he's out of ~* (*not doing the proper thing*) si sta comportando in modo scorretto **2** *v/t* ordinare; *~ s.o. to do sth* ordinare a qu di fare qc **3** *v/i* ordinare

or·der·ly ['ɔːdəlɪ] **1** *adj room, mind* ordinato; *crowd* disciplinato **2** *n in hospital* inserviente *m/f*

or·di·nal num·ber ['ɔːdɪnl] numero *m* ordinale

or·di·nar·i·ly [ɔːdɪˈneərɪlɪ] *adv* (*as a rule*) normalmente

or·di·nary ['ɔːdɪnərɪ] *adj* normale; *pej* ordinario; *nothing out of the ~* niente di straordinario

ore [ɔː(r)] minerale *m* grezzo

or·gan ['ɔːgən] ANAT, MUS organo *m*

or·gan·ic [ɔːˈgænɪk] *adj* *food, fertilizer* biologico

or·gan·i·cal·ly [ɔːˈgænɪklɪ] *adv* *grown* biologicamente

or·gan·is·m ['ɔːgənɪzm] organismo *m*

or·gan·i·za·tion [ɔːgənaɪˈzeɪʃn] organizzazione *f*

or·gan·ize ['ɔːgənaɪz] *v/t* organizzare

or·gan·ized 'crime criminalità *f inv* organizzata

or·gan·iz·er ['ɔːgənaɪzə(r)] *person* organizzatore *m*, -trice *f*

or·gas·m ['ɔːgæzm] orgasmo *m*

O·ri·ent ['ɔːrɪənt] Oriente *m*

O·ri·en·tal [ɔːrɪˈentl] **1** *adj* orientale **2** *n* orientale *m/f*

o·ri·en·tate ['ɔːrɪənteɪt] *v/t* (*direct*) orientare; *~ o.s.* (*get bearings*) orientarsi

or·i·gin ['ɒrɪdʒɪn] origine *f*; *of Chinese ~* di origine cinese

o·rig·i·nal [əˈrɪdʒənl] **1** *adj* originale **2** *n painting etc* originale *m*

o·rig·i·nal·i·ty [ərɪdʒɪˈælətɪ] originalità *f inv*

o·rig·i·nal·ly [əˈrɪdʒənəlɪ] *adv* (*at first*) in origine; *~ he comes from France* è di origini francesi

o·rig·i·nate [əˈrɪdʒɪneɪt] **1** *v/t scheme, idea* dare origine a **2** *v/i of idea, belief* avere origine

o·rig·i·na·tor [əˈrɪdʒɪneɪtə(r)] *of scheme etc* ideatore *m*, -trice *f*

or·na·ment ['ɔːnəmənt] soprammobile *m*

or·na·men·tal [ɔːnəˈmentl] *adj* ornamentale

or·nate [ɔːˈneɪt] *adj style, architecture* ornato

or·phan ['ɔːfn] *n* orfano *m*, -a *f*

or·phan·age ['ɔːfənɪdʒ] orfanotrofio *m*

or·tho·dox ['ɔːθədɒks] *adj also fig* ortodosso

or·tho·pe·dic [ɔːθəˈpiːdɪk] *adj* ortopedico

os·ten·si·bly [ɒˈstensəblɪ] *adv* apparentemente

os·ten·ta·tion [ɒstenˈteɪʃn] ostentazione *f*

os·ten·ta·tious [ɒstenˈteɪʃəs] *adj* ostentato

os·ten·ta·tious·ly [ɒstenˈteɪʃəslɪ]

adv con ostentazione

os·tra·cize ['ɒstrəsaɪz] *v/t* ostracizzare

oth·er ['ʌðə(r)] **1** *adj* altro; *the ~ day* l'altro giorno; *every ~ day* a giorni alterni; *every ~ person* una persona su due **2** *n* l'altro *m*, -a *f*; *the ~s* gli altri

oth·er·wise ['ʌðəwaɪz] *adv* altrimenti; *(differently)* diversamente

OTT [əʊtiː'tiː] *abbr* F (= *over the top*) esagerato

ot·ter ['ɒtə(r)] lontra *f*

ought [ɔːt] *v/aux*: *I/you ~ to know* dovrei/dovresti saperlo; *you ~ to have done it* avresti dovuto farlo

ounce [aʊns] oncia *f*

our ['aʊə(r)] *adj* il nostro *m*, la nostra *f*, i nostri *mpl*, le nostre *fpl*; *~ brother/sister* nostro fratello/nostra sorella

ours ['aʊəz] *pron* il nostro *m*, la nostra *f*, i nostri *mpl*, le nostre *fpl*

our·selves [aʊə'selvz] *pron reflexive* ci; *emphatic* noi stessi/nois stesse; *after prep* noi; *we did it ~* l'abbiamo fatto noi (stessi/stesse); *we talked about ~* abbiamo parlato di noi; *by ~* da soli

oust [aʊst] *v/t from office* esautorare

out [aʊt]: *be ~ of light, fire* essere spento; *of flower* essere sbocciato; *of sun* splendere; *not at home, not in building* essere fuori; *of calculations* essere sbagliato; *(be published)* essere uscito; *of secret* essere svelato; *no longer in competition* essere eliminato; *of workers* essere in sciopero; *(no longer in fashion)* essere out; *~ here in Dallas* qui a Dallas; *he's ~ in the garden* è in giardino; *(get) ~!* fuori!; *(get) ~ of my room!* fuori dalla mia stanza!; *that's ~!* (*out of the question*) è fuori discussione!; *he's ~ to win* fully intends to è deciso a vincere

out·board 'mo·tor motore *m* fuoribordo

'out·break *of war, disease* scoppio *m*

'out·build·ing annesso *m*

'out·burst *emotional* reazione *f* violenta; *~ of anger* esplosione *f* di

'out·cast *n* emarginato *m*, -a *f*

'out·come risultato *m*

'out·cry protesta *f*

'out·dat·ed *adj* sorpassato

out'do *v/t (pret -did, pp -done)* superare

'out·door *adj toilet, activities, life* all'aperto; *swimming pool* scoperto

out'doors *adv* all'aperto

out·er ['aʊtə(r)] *adj wall etc* esterno

out·er 'space spazio *m* intergalattico

'out·fit *(clothes)* completo *m*; *(company, organization)* organizzazione *f*

'out·go·ing *adj flight, mail* in partenza; *personality* estroverso

out'grow *v/t (pret -grew, pp -grown) bad habits, interests* perdere

out·ing ['aʊtɪŋ] *(trip)* gita *f*

out'last *v/t* durare più di

'out·let *of pipe* scarico *m*; *for sales* punto *m* di vendita

'out·line 1 *n of person, building etc* profilo *m*; *of plan, novel* abbozzo *m* **2** *v/t plans etc* abbozzare

out'live *v/t* sopravvivere a

'out·look *(prospects)* prospettiva *f*

'out·ly·ing *adj areas* periferico

out'num·ber *v/t* superare numericamente

out of *prep (motion)* fuori; *fall ~ the window* cadere fuori dalla finestra ◊ *(position)* da *20 miles ~ Newcastle* 20 miglia da Newcastle ◊ *(cause)* per; *~ jealousy/curiosity* per gelosia/curiosità ◊ *(without)* senza; *we're ~ petrol/beer* siamo senza benzina/birra ◊ *from a group* su *5 ~ 10* 5 su 10

out-of-'date *adj passport* scaduto; *values* superato

out-of-the-way *adj* fuori mano

'out·pa·tient paziente *m/f* esterno, -a

'out·pa·tients' (clin·ic) ambulatorio *m*

'out·per·form *v/t of machine, investment* rendere meglio di; *of company, economy* andare meglio di

'out·put 1 *n of factory* produzione *f*;

O

COMPUT output *m inv* **2** *v/t* (*pret &
pp* **-ted** *or* **output**) (*produce*) produrre; COMPUT: *signal* emettere

'out·rage 1 *n feeling* sdegno *m*; *act*
atrocità *f inv* **2** *v/t* indignare

out·ra·geous [aut'reɪdʒəs] *adj acts*
scioccante; *prices* scandaloso

'out·right 1 *adj winner* assoluto
2 *adv win* nettamente; *kill* sul colpo

out·run *v/t* (*pret* **-ran**, *pp* **-run**) *also
fig* superare; *run faster than* correre
più veloce di

'out·set *n*: **at / from the ~** all' / dal-
l'inizio

out·shine *v/t* (*pret & pp* **-shone**)
eclissare

'out·side 1 *adj surface, wall, lane*
esterno **2** *adv sit, go* fuori **3** *prep*
fuori da; (*apart from*) al di fuori di
4 *n of building, case etc* esterno *m*; **at
the ~** al massimo

out·side 'broad·cast trasmissione *f*
in esterna

out·sid·er [aut'saɪdə(r)] estraneo
m, -a *f*; *in election, race* outsider *m
inv*

'out·size *adj clothing* di taglia forte

'out·skirts *npl* periferia *f*

out·smart *v/t →* **outwit**

out·stand·ing *adj success, writer* eccezionale; FIN: *invoice, sums* da saldare

out·stretched ['autstretʃt] *adj hands*
teso

out·vote *v/t* mettere in minoranza

out·ward ['autwəd] *adj appearance*
esteriore; **~ journey** viaggio *m* d'andata

out·ward·ly ['autwədlɪ] *adv* esterior-
mente

out·weigh *v/t* contare più di

out·wit *v/t* (*pret & pp* **-ted**) riuscire a
gabbare

o·val ['əuvl] *adj* ovale

o·va·ry ['əuvərɪ] ovaia *f*

o·va·tion [əu'veɪʃn] ovazione *f*; **she
was given a standing ~** il pubblico
s'è alzato in piedi per applaudirla

ov·en ['ʌvn] *in kitchen* forno *m*; *in
factory* fornace *f*

'ov·en glove, 'ov·en mitt guanto *m*

da forno; **'ov·en·proof** *adj* pirofilo;
'ov·en·read·y *adj* pronto da mettere al forno

o·ver ['əuvə(r)] **1** *prep* (*above*) sopra,
su; (*across*) dall'altra parte; (*more
than*) oltre; (*during*) nel corso di; **~
the phone** al telefono; **travel all ~
Brazil** girare tutto il Brasile; **you
find them all ~ Brazil** si trovano
dappertutto in Brasile; **let's talk ~ a
meal** parliamone a pranzo; **we're ~
the worst** il peggio è passato; **~ and
above** oltre a **2** *adv* ~ (*finished*)
essere finito; (*left*) essere rimasto; **~
to you** (*your turn*) tocca a te; **~ in
Japan** in Giappone; **~here / there**
qui / lì; **it hurts all ~** mi fa male dappertutto; **painted white all ~** tutto
dipinto di bianco; **it's all ~** è finito;
I've told you ~ and ~ again te l'ho
detto mille volte; **do sth ~ again** rifare qc

o·ver·all ['əuvərɔːl] **1** *adj length* totale **2** *adv measure* complessivamente;
(*in general*) nell'insieme

o·ver·alls ['əuvərɔːlz] *npl* tuta *f* da
lavoro

o·ver·awe *v/t* intimidire; **be ~d by
s.o. / sth** essere intimidito da qu / qc

o·ver·bal·ance *v/i* perdere l'equilibrio

o·ver·bear·ing *adj* autoritario

'o·ver·board *adv*: **man ~!** uomo in
mare!; **go ~ for s.o. / sth** entusiasmarsi per qu / qc

'o·ver·cast *adj day, sky* nuvoloso

o·ver·charge *v/t customer* far pagare
più del dovuto a

'o·ver·coat cappotto *m*

o·ver·come *v/t* (*pret* **-came**, *pp*
-come) *difficulties, shyness* superare; **be ~ by emotion** essere sopraf-
fatto dall'emozione

o·ver·crowd·ed *adj* sovraffollato

o·ver·do *v/t* (*pret* **-did**, *pp* **-done**)
(*exaggerate*) esagerare; *in cooking*
stracuocere; **you're ~ing things**
taking on too much ti stai strapaz-
zando

o·ver·done *adj meat* stracotto

'o·ver·dose *n* overdose *f inv*

'o·ver·draft scoperto *m* (di conto); **have an ~** avere il conto scoperto

o·ver'draw *v/t* (*pret* **-drew**, *pp* **-drawn**): **~ one's account** andare allo scoperto; **be £800 ~n** essere (allo) scoperto di 800 sterline

o·ver'dressed *adj* troppo elegante

'o·ver·drive MOT overdrive *m inv*

o·ver'due *adj* bill, *rent* arretrato; *train*, *baby* in ritardo

o·ver'es·ti·mate *v/t* abilities, *value* sovrastimare

o·ver'ex·pose *v/t* photograph sovraesporre

'o·ver·flow[1] *n* pipe troppopieno *m*

o·ver'flow[2] *v/i* of water traboccare; *of river* strariparе

o·ver'grown *adj* garden coperto d'erbacce; **he's an ~ baby** è un bambinone

o·ver'haul *v/t* engine revisionare; *plans* rivedere

'o·ver·head[1] *adj* lights, *cables* in alto, aereo; *railway* soprelevato

'over·head[2] Am *nsg*, 'over·heads *npl* FIN costi *mpl* di gestione; **travel ~** spese *fpl* di viaggio

'o·ver·head pro·jec·tor lavagna *f* luminosa

o·ver'hear *v/t* (*pret* & *pp* **-heard**) sentire per caso

o·ver'heat·ed *adj* room, *engine* surriscaldato

o·ver'joyed [əʊvə'dʒɔɪd] *adj* felicissimo

'o·ver·kill: **that's ~** è un'esagerazione

'o·ver·land *adj* & *adv* via terra

o·ver'lap *v/i* (*pret* & *pp* **-ped**) (*partly cover*) sovrapporsi; (*partly coincide*) coincidere

'o·ver·leaf: **see ~** a tergo

o·ver'load *v/t* sovraccaricare

o·ver'look *v/t* of tall building etc dominare, dare su; *deliberately* chiudere un occhio su; *accidentally* non notare; **the room ~s the garden** la stanza dà sul giardino

o·ver'ly ['əʊvəlɪ] *adv* troppo; **not ~ ...** non particolarmente ...

'o·ver·night *adv* travel di notte; *stay* per la notte

o·ver'night 'bag piccola borsa *f* da viaggio

o·ver'paid *adj* strapagato

o·ver·pop·u·lat·ed [əʊvə'pɒpjuleɪtɪd] *adj* sovrappopolato

o·ver'pow·er *v/t* physically sopraffare

o·ver·pow·er·ing [əʊvə'paʊrɪŋ] *adj* smell asfissiante; *sense of guilt* opprimente

o·ver'priced [əʊvə'praɪst] *adj* troppo caro

o·ver·rat·ed [əʊvə'reɪtɪd] *adj* sopravvalutato

o·ver·re'act *v/i* reagire in modo eccessivo

o·ver'ride *v/t* (*pret* **-rode**, *pp* **-ridden**) annullare; *person* annullare la decisione di; (*be more important than*) prevalere su

o·ver'rid·ing *adj* concern principale

o·ver'rule *v/t* decision annullare

o·ver'run *v/t* (*pret* **-ran**, *pp* **-run**) *country* invadere; *time* sforare; **be ~ with** essere invaso da

o·ver'seas *adv* & *adj* all'estero

o·ver'see *v/t* (*pret* **-saw**, *pp* **-seen**) sorvegliare

o·ver'shad·ow *v/t* fig eclissare

'o·ver·sight svista *f*

o·ver·sim·pli·fi·ca·tion semplificazione *f* eccessiva

o·ver'sim·pli·fy *v/t* (*pret* & *pp* **-ied**) semplificare troppo

o·ver'sleep *v/i* (*pret* & *pp* **-slept**) non svegliarsi in tempo

o·ver'state *v/t* esagerare

o·ver'state·ment esagerazione *f*

o·ver'step *v/t* (*pret* & *pp* **-ped**): fig **~ the mark** passare il segno

o·ver'take *v/t* (*pret* **-took**, *pp* **-taken**) *in work*, *development* superare; MOT sorpassare

o·ver'throw[1] *v/t* (*pret* **-threw**, *pp* **-thrown**) *government* rovesciare

'o·ver·throw[2] *n* of government rovesciamento *m*

'o·ver·time Br **1** *n* straordinario *m* **2** *adv*: **work ~** fare lo straordinario

O

'o•ver•ture ['əʊvətjʊə(r)] MUS ouverture *f inv*; **make ~s to** fare approcci a

o•ver'turn 1 *v/t vehicle, object* ribaltare; *government* rovesciare **2** *v/i of vehicle* ribaltarsi

'o•ver•view visione *f* d'insieme

o•ver'weight *adj* sovrappeso

o•ver'whelm [əʊvə'welm] *v/t with work* oberare; *with emotion* sopraffare; **be ~ed by** *response* essere colpito da

o•ver•whelm•ing [əʊvə'welmɪŋ] *adj feeling* profondo; *majority* schiacciante

o•ver'work 1 *n* lavoro *m* eccessivo **2** *v/i* lavorare troppo **3** *v/t* far lavorare troppo

owe [əʊ] *v/t* dovere; **~ s.o. £500** dovere £500 a qu; **~ s.o. an apology** dovere delle scuse a qu; **how much**

do I ~ you? quanto le devo?

ow•ing to ['əʊɪŋ] *prep* a causa di

owl [aʊl] gufo *m*

own¹ [əʊn] *v/t* possedere

own² [əʊn] **1** *adj* proprio; **my ~ car** la mia macchina; **my ~ mother** proprio mia madre **2** *pron*: **a car of my ~** un'auto tutta mia; **on my / his ~** da solo

♦ **own up** *v/i* confessare

own•er ['əʊnə(r)] proprietario *m*, -a *f*

own•er•ship ['əʊnəʃɪp] proprietà *f inv*

ox [ɒks] bue *m*

ox•ide ['ɒksaɪd] ossido *m*

ox•y•gen ['ɒksɪdʒən] ossigeno *m*

oy•ster ['ɔɪstə(r)] ostrica *f*

oz *abbr* (= **ounce(s)**) oncia

o•zone ['əʊzəʊn] ozono *m*

'o•zone lay•er fascia *f* o strato *m* d'ozono

P

p [piː] *abbr* (= **penny**; **pence**) penny *m inv*

PA [piː'eɪ] *abbr* (= **personal assistant**) assistente *m/f* personale

pace [peɪs] **1** *n* (*step*) passo *m*; (*speed*) ritmo *m* **2** *v/i*: **~ up and down** camminare su e giù

'pace•mak•er MED pacemaker *m inv*; SP battistrada *m inv*

Pa•cif•ic [pə'sɪfɪk]: **the ~** (**Ocean**) il Pacifico

pac•i•fism ['pæsɪfɪzm] pacifismo *m*

pac•i•fist ['pæsɪfɪst] *n* pacifista *m/f*

pac•i•fy ['pæsɪfaɪ] *v/t* (*pret & pp* -**ied**) placare

pack [pæk] **1** *n* (*back~*) zaino *m*; *of cereal, food* confezione *f*; *of cigarettes* pacchetto *m*; *of peas etc* confezione *f*; *of cards* mazzo *m* **2** *v/t bag* fare; *item of clothing etc* mettere in valigia; *goods* imballare; *groceries* imbu-

stare **3** *v/i* fare la valigia / le valigie

pack•age ['pækɪdʒ] **1** *n* (*parcel*) pacco *m*; *of offers etc* pacchetto *m* **2** *v/t* confezionare

'pack•age deal *for holiday* offerta *f* tutto compreso

'pack•age tour viaggio *m* organizzato

pack•ag•ing ['pækɪdʒɪŋ] *also fig* confezione *f*

pack•ed [pækt] *adj* (*crowded*) affollato

pack•et ['pækɪt] confezione *f*; *of cigarettes, crisps* pacchetto *m*

pact [pækt] patto *m*

pad¹ [pæd] **1** *n piece of cloth etc* tampone *m*; *for writing* blocchetto *m* **2** *v/t* (*pret & pp* -**ded**) *with material* imbottire; *speech, report* farcire

pad² [pæd] *v/i* (*move quietly*) camminare a passi felpati

pad·ded ['pædɪd] *adj jacket, shoulders* imbottito

pad·ding ['pædɪŋ] *material* imbottitura *f; in speech etc* riempitivo *m*

pad·dle ['pædl] **1** *n for canoe* pagaia *f* **2** *v/i in canoe* pagaiare; *in water* sguazzare

pad·dling pool ['pædlɪŋpuːl] piscinetta *f* per bambini

pad·dock ['pædək] paddock *m inv*

pad·lock ['pædlɒk] **1** *n* lucchetto *m* **2** *v/t gate* chiudere col lucchetto; **~ X to Y** fissare col lucchetto X a Y

paed·i·at·ric *etc* → **pediatric** *etc*

page[1] [peɪdʒ] *n of book etc* pagina *f*

page[2] [peɪdʒ] *v/t (call)* chiamare con l'altoparlante; *with pager* chiamare col cercapersone

pag·er ['peɪdʒə(r)] cercapersone *m inv*

paid [peɪd] *pret & pp* → **pay**

paid em·ploy·ment occupazione *f* rimunerata

pail [peɪl] secchio *m*

pain [peɪn] *n* dolore *m*; **be in ~** soffrire; **take ~s to ...** fare il possibile per ...; **a ~ in the neck** F una rottura *f* di scatole F

pain·ful ['peɪnful] *adj (distressing)* doloroso; *(laborious)* difficile; **my leg is still ~** la gamba mi fa ancora male; **it is my ~ duty to inform you ...** siamo addolorati di comunicarle ...

pain·ful·ly ['peɪnflɪ] *adv (extremely, acutely)* estremamente

pain·kill·er ['peɪnkɪlə(r)] analgesico *m*

pain·less ['peɪnlɪs] *adj* indolore

pains·tak·ing ['peɪnzteɪkɪŋ] *adj* accurato

paint [peɪnt] **1** *n for wall, car* vernice *f; for artist* colore *m* **2** *v/t wall etc* pitturare; *picture* dipingere **3** *v/i as art form* dipingere

paint·brush ['peɪntbrʌʃ] pennello *m*

paint·er ['peɪntə(r)] *decorator* imbianchino *m; artist* pittore *m*, -trice *f*

paint·ing ['peɪntɪŋ] *activity* pittura *f;* *(picture)* quadro *m*

paint·work ['peɪntwɜːk] vernice *f*

pair [peə(r)] *of objects* paio *m; of animals, people* coppia *f*; **a ~ of shoes** un paio di scarpe

pa·ja·mas *Am* → **pyjamas**

Pa·ki·stan [pɑːkɪ'stɑːn] Pakistan *m*

Pa·ki·sta·ni [pɑːkɪ'stɑːnɪ] **1** *n* pakistano *m*, -a *f* **2** *adj* pakistano

pal [pæl] F *(friend)* amico *m*, -a *f*

pal·ace ['pælɪs] palazzo *m* signorile

pal·ate ['pælət] palato *m*

pa·la·tial [pə'leɪʃl] *adj* sfarzoso

pale [peɪl] *adj person* pallido; **~ pink / blue** rosa / celeste pallido

Pal·e·stine ['pæləstaɪn] Palestina *f*

Pal·e·stin·i·an [pælə'stɪnɪən] **1** *n* palestinese *m/f* **2** *adj* palestinese

pal·let ['pælɪt] pallet *m inv*

pal·lor ['pælə(r)] pallore *m*

palm[1] [pɑːm] *of hand* palma *f*

palm[2] [pɑːm] *tree* palma *f*

pal·pi·ta·tions [pælpɪ'teɪʃnz] *npl* MED palpitazioni *fpl*

pam·per ['pæmpə(r)] *v/t* viziare

pam·phlet ['pæmflɪt] volantino *m*

pan [pæn] **1** *n for cooking* pentola *f; for frying* padella *f* **2** *v/t (pret & pp -ned)* F *(criticize)* stroncare F

♦ **pan out** *v/i (develop)* sviluppare

pan·cake ['pænkeɪk] crêpe *f inv*

pan·da ['pændə] panda *m inv*

pan·de·mo·ni·um [pændɪ'məʊnɪəm] pandemonio *m*

♦ **pan·der to** ['pændə(r)] *v/t* assecondare

pane [peɪn]: **~ (of glass)** vetro *m*

pan·el ['pænl] pannello *m; of experts* gruppo *m; of judges* giuria *f*

pan·el·ling ['pænəlɪŋ] rivestimento *m* a pannelli

pang [pæŋ] *of remorse* fitta *f;* **~s of hunger** morsi *mpl* della fame

pan·ic ['pænɪk] **1** *n* panico *m* **2** *v/i (pret & pp -ked):* **don't ~** non farti prendere dal panico

'pan·ic buy·ing FIN acquisto *m* motivato dal panico; **'pan·ic sel·ling** FIN vendita *f* motivata dal panico; **'pan·ic-strick·en** *adj* in preda al panico

pan·o·ra·ma [pænə'rɑːmə] panorama *m*

P

pa·no·ra·mic [pænə'ræmɪk] *adj* view panoramico

pan·sy ['pænzɪ] *flower* viola *f* del pensiero

pant [pænt] *v/i* ansimare

pan·ties ['pæntɪz] *npl* mutandine *fpl*

pants [pænts] *npl* (*underpants*) mutande *fpl*; *esp Am* (*trousers*) pantaloni *mpl*

pan·ty·hose ['pæntɪhəʊz] *Am* collant *mpl*

pa·pal ['peɪpəl] *adj* pontificio

pa·per ['peɪpə(r)] 1 *n material* carta *f*; (*news~*) giornale *m*; (*wall~*) carta *f* da parati; *academic* relazione *f*; (*examination ~*) esame *m*; *~s* (*identity ~s, documents*) documenti *mpl*; *a piece of ~* un pezzo di carta 2 *adj* di carta 3 *v/t room, walls* tappezzare

'paperback tascabile *m*; paper 'bag sacchetto *m* di carta; 'paper boy ragazzo *m* che recapita i giornali a domicilio; 'paper clip graffetta *f*; 'paper cup bicchiere *m* di carta; 'paperwork disbrigo *m* delle pratiche

par [pɑː (r)] *in golf* par *m inv*; *be on a ~ with* essere allo stesso livello di; *feel below ~* non sentirsi bene

par·a·chute ['pærəʃuːt] 1 *n* paracadute *m inv* 2 *v/i* paracadutarsi 3 *v/t troops, supplies* paracadutare

par·a·chut·ist ['pærəʃuːtɪst] paracadutista *m/f*

pa·rade [pə'reɪd] 1 *n* (*procession*) sfilata *f* 2 *v/i* sfilare 3 *v/t knowledge, new car* fare sfoggio di

par·a·dise ['pærədaɪs] paradiso *m*

par·a·dox ['pærədɒks] paradosso *m*

par·a·dox·i·cal [pærə'dɒksɪkl] *adj* paradossale

par·a·dox·i·cal·ly [pærə'dɒksɪklɪ] *adv* paradossalmente

par·a·graph ['pærəgrɑːf] paragrafo *m*

par·al·lel ['pærəlel] 1 *n* (*in geometry*) parallela *f*; GEOG, *fig* parallelo *m*; *do two things in ~* fare due cose in parallelo 2 *adj also fig* parallelo 3 *v/t* (*match*) uguagliare

par·a·lyse ['pærəlaɪz] *v/t also fig* paralizzare

par·al·y·sis [pə'ræləsɪs] *also fig* paralisi *f inv*

par·a·med·ic [pærə'medɪk] *n* paramedico *m*, -a *f*

pa·ram·e·ter [pə'ræmɪtə(r)] parametro *m*

par·a·mil·i·tar·y [pærə'mɪlɪtrɪ] 1 *adj* paramilitare 2 *n* appartenente *m/f* ad un'organizzazione paramilitare

par·a·mount ['pærəmaʊnt] *adj* vitale; *be ~* essere di vitale importanza

par·a·noi·a [pærə'nɔɪə] paranoia *f*

par·a·noid ['pærənɔɪd] *adj* paranoico

par·a·pher·na·li·a [pærəfə'neɪlɪə] armamentario *m*

par·a·phrase ['pærəfreɪz] *v/t* parafrasare

par·a·pleg·ic [pærə'pliːdʒɪk] *n* paraplegico *m*, -a *f*

par·a·site ['pærəsaɪt] *also fig* parassita *m*

par·a·sol ['pærəsɒl] parasole *m*

par·a·troop·er ['pærətruːpə(r)] MIL paracadutista *m*

par·cel ['pɑːsl] *n* pacco *m*

♦ parcel up *v/t* impacchettare

parch [pɑːtʃ] *v/t* riardere; *be ~ed* F *of person* essere assetato

par·don ['pɑːdn] 1 *n* LAW grazia *f*; *I beg your ~?* (*what did you say*) prego?; *I beg your ~* (*I'm sorry*) scusi 2 *v/t* scusare; LAW graziare

pare [peə(r)] *v/t* (*peel*) pelare

par·ent ['peərənt] genitore *m*

pa·ren·tal [pə'rentl] *adj* dei genitori

'par·ent company società *f inv* madre

par·ent-'teach·er association organizzazione *f* composta da genitori e insegnanti

par·ish ['pærɪʃ] parrocchia *f*

park[1] [pɑːk] *n* parco *m*

park[2] [pɑːk] *v/t & v/i* MOT parcheggiare

par·ka ['pɑːkə] parka *m inv*

par·king ['pɑːkɪŋ] MOT parcheggio *m*; *no ~* sosta *f* vietata

'par·king brake *Am* freno *m* a mano;

'par·king disc disco *m* orario; 'par·king lot *Am* parcheggio *m*; 'par·king me·ter parchimetro *m*; 'par·king place parcheggio *m*; 'par·king tick·et multa *f* per sosta vietata

par·lia·ment ['pɑːləmənt] parlamento *m*

par·lia·men·ta·ry [pɑːljə'mentərɪ] *adj* parlamentare

pa·role [pə'rəʊl] 1 *n* libertà *f inv* vigilata; *be out on ~* essere rimesso in libertà vigilata 2 *v/t* concedere la libertà vigilata a

par·rot ['pærət] pappagallo *m*

pars·ley ['pɑːslɪ] prezzemolo *m*

part [pɑːt] 1 *n* parte *f*; *of machine* pezzo *m*; *Am: in hair* riga *f*; *take ~ in* prendere parte in 2 *adv* (*partly*) in parte 3 *v/i* separarsi 4 *v/t*: *~ one's hair* farsi la riga

♦ part with *v/t* separarsi da

'part ex·change permuta *f*; *take sth in ~ exchange* prendere qc in permuta

par·tial ['pɑːʃl] *adj* (*incomplete*) parziale; *be ~ to* avere un debole per

par·tial·ly ['pɑːʃəlɪ] *adv* parzialmente

par·ti·ci·pant [pɑː'tɪsɪpənt] partecipante *m/f*

par·ti·ci·pate [pɑː'tɪsɪpeɪt] *v/i* partecipare; *~ in sth* partecipare a qc

par·ti·ci·pa·tion [pɑːtɪsɪ'peɪʃn] partecipazione *f*

par·ti·cle ['pɑːtɪkl] PHYS particella *f*; *small amount* briciolo *m*

par·tic·u·lar [pə'tɪkjʊlə(r)] *adj* (*specific*) particolare; (*fussy*) pignolo; *in ~* in particolare

par·tic·u·lar·ly [pə'tɪkjʊləlɪ] *adv* particolarmente

part·ing ['pɑːtɪŋ] *of people* separazione *f*; *in hair* riga *f*

par·ti·tion [pɑː'tɪʃn] 1 *n* (*screen*) tramezzo *m*; (*of country*) suddivisione *f* 2 *v/t country* suddividere

♦ partition off *v/t* tramezzare

part·ly ['pɑːtlɪ] *adv* in parte

part·ner ['pɑːtnə(r)] COM socio *m*, -a *f*; *in relationship* partner *m/f inv*; *in particular activity* compagno *m*, -a *f*

part·ner·ship ['pɑːtnəʃɪp] COM società *f inv*; *in particular activity* sodalizio *m*

part of 'speech GRAM parte *f* del discorso; 'part own·er comproprietario *m*, -a *f*; 'part-time *adj & adv* part-time; part-'tim·er lavoratore *m*, -trice *f* part-time

par·ty ['pɑːtɪ] 1 *n* (*celebration*) festa *f*; POL partito *m*; (*group*) gruppo *m*; *be a ~ to* essere coinvolto in 2 *v/i* (*pret & pp -ied*) F far baldoria

pass [pɑːs] 1 *n* for getting into a place passi *m inv*; SP passaggio *m*; *in mountains* passo *m*; *make a ~ at* fare avances a 2 *v/t* (*hand*) passare; (*go past*) passare davanti a; (*overtake*) sorpassare; (*go beyond*) superare; (*approve*) approvare; SP passare; *~ an exam* superare un esame; *~ sentence* LAW emanare la sentenza; *~ the time* passare il tempo 3 *v/i* passare; *in exam* essere promosso

♦ pass around *v/t* far circolare

♦ pass away *v/i euph* spegnersi *euph*

♦ pass by 1 *v/t* (*go past*) passare davanti a 2 *v/i* (*go past*) passare

♦ pass on 1 *v/t* information, book, savings passare (*to* a) 2 *v/i* (*euph: die*) mancare euph

♦ pass out *v/i* (*faint*) svenire

♦ pass through *v/t town* passare per

♦ pass up *v/t opportunity* lasciarsi sfuggire

pass·a·ble ['pɑːsəbl] *adj road* transitabile; (*acceptable*) passabile

pas·sage ['pæsɪdʒ] (*corridor*) passaggio *m*; *from poem, book* passo *m*; *the ~ of time* il passare del tempo

pas·sage·way ['pæsɪdʒweɪ] corridoio *m*

pas·sen·ger ['pæsɪndʒə(r)] passeggero *m*, -a *f*

'pas·sen·ger seat sedile *m* del passeggero

pas·ser·by [pɑːsə'baɪ] (*pl passers-by*) passante *m/f*

pas·sion ['pæʃn] passione *f*

pas·sion·ate ['pæʃnət] adj appassionato

pas·sive ['pæsɪv] **1** adj passivo **2** n GRAM passivo m; **in the ~** al passivo

'pass mark EDU voto m sufficiente

Pass·o·ver ['pɑːsəʊvə(r)] REL Pasqua f ebraica

pass·port ['pɑːspɔːt] passaporto m

'pass·port control controllo m passaporti

pass·word ['pɑːswɜːd] parola f d'ordine; COMPUT password f inv

past [pɑːst] **1** adj (former) precedente; **in the ~ few days** nei giorni scorsi; **that's all ~ now** è acqua passata ormai **2** n passato m; **in the ~** nel passato **3** prep in position oltre; **it's half ~ two** sono le due e mezza; **it's ~ seven o'clock** sono le sette passate **4** adv: **run ~** passare di corsa

pas·ta ['pæstə] pasta f

paste [peɪst] **1** n (adhesive) colla f **2** v/t (stick) incollare

pas·tel ['pæstl] **1** n pastello m **2** adj pastello

pas·time ['pɑːstaɪm] passatempo m

past par·ti·ci·ple GRAM participio m passato

pas·tra·mi [pæ'strɑːmɪ] affettato m di carne di manzo speziata

pas·try ['peɪstrɪ] for pie pasta f (sfoglia); (small cake) pasticcino m

'past tense GRAM passato m

pas·ty ['peɪstɪ] adj complexion smorto

pat [pæt] **1** n colpetto m; affectionate buffetto m; **give s.o. a ~ on the back** fig dare una pacca sulla spalla a qu **2** v/t (pret & pp **-ted**) dare un colpetto a; affectionately dare un buffetto a

patch [pætʃ] **1** n on clothing pezza f; (period of time) periodo m; (area) zona f; **go through a bad ~** attraversare un brutto periodo; **~es of fog** banchi mpl di nebbia; **be not a ~ on** fig non essere niente a paragone di **2** v/t clothing rattoppare

♦ **patch up** v/t (repair temporarily) riparare alla meglio; quarrel risolvere

patch·work ['pætʃwɜːk] **1** n patch-

work m inv **2** adj quilt patchwork

patch·y ['pætʃɪ] adj quality irregolare; work, performance discontinuo, disuguale

pâ·té ['pæteɪ] pâté m inv

pa·tent ['peɪtnt] **1** adj palese **2** n for invention brevetto m **3** v/t invention brevettare

pa·tent 'leath·er vernice f

pa·tent·ly ['peɪtntlɪ] adv (clearly) palesemente

pa·ter·nal [pə'tɜːnl] adj paterno

pa·ter·nal·ism [pə'tɜːnlɪzm] paternalismo m

pa·ter·nal·is·tic [pətɜːnl'ɪstɪk] adj paternalistico

pa·ter·ni·ty [pə'tɜːnɪtɪ] paternità f inv

path [pɑːθ] sentiero m; fig strada f

pa·thet·ic [pə'θetɪk] adj invoking pity patetico; F (very bad) penoso

path·o·log·i·cal [pæθə'lɒdʒɪkl] adj patologico

pa·thol·o·gy [pə'θɒlədʒɪ] patologia f

pa·thol·o·gist [pə'θɒlədʒɪst] patologo m, -a f

pa·tience ['peɪʃns] pazienza f; Br: card game solitario m

pa·tient ['peɪʃnt] **1** n paziente m/f **2** adj paziente; **just be ~!** abbi pazienza!

pa·tient·ly ['peɪʃntlɪ] adv pazientemente

pat·i·o ['pætɪəʊ] terrazza f

pat·ri·ot ['peɪtrɪət] patriota m/f

pat·ri·ot·ic [peɪtrɪ'ɒtɪk] adj patriottico

pa·tri·ot·ism ['peɪtrɪətɪzm] patriottismo m

pa·trol [pə'trəʊl] **1** n pattuglia f; **be on ~** essere di pattuglia **2** v/t (pret & pp **-led**) streets, border pattugliare

pa'trol car autopattuglia f

pa'trol·man agente m/f di pattuglia

pa·tron ['peɪtrən] of artist patrocinatore m, -trice f; of charity patrono m, -essa f; of shop, cinema cliente m/f

pa·tron·age ['pætrənɪdʒ] of artist patronato m; of charity patrocinio m

pa·tron·ize ['pætrənaɪz] v/t shop essere cliente di; *person* trattare con condiscendenza

pa·tron·iz·ing ['pætrənaɪzɪŋ] *adj* condiscendente

pa·tron 'saint patrono *m*, -a *f*

pat·ter ['pætə(r)] **1** *n of rain etc* picchiettio *m*; F *of salesman* imbonimento *m* **2** *v/i* picchiettare

pat·tern ['pætn] *n on wallpaper, fabric* motivo *m*, disegno *m*; *for knitting, sewing* (carta) modello *m*; *in behaviour, events* schema *m*

pat·terned ['pætənd] *adj* fantasia *inv*

paunch [pɔ:nʧ] pancia *f*

pause [pɔ:z] **1** *n* pausa *f* **2** *v/i* fermarsi **3** *v/t tape* fermare

pave [peɪv] *v/t* pavimentare; **~ the way for** *fig* aprire la strada a

pave·ment ['peɪvmənt] *Br* marciapiede *m*

pav·ing stone ['peɪvɪŋ] lastra *f* di pavimentazione

paw [pɔ:] **1** *n of animal*, F (*hand*) zampa *f* **2** *v/t* F palpare

pawn¹ [pɔ:n] *n in chess* pedone *m*; *fig* pedina *f*

pawn² [pɔ:n] *v/t* impegnare

'pawn·bro·ker prestatore *m*, -trice *f* su pegno

'pawn·shop monte *m* di pietà

pay [peɪ] **1** *n* paga *f*; **in the ~ of** al soldo di **2** *v/t* (*pret & pp* **paid**) pagare; **~ attention** fare attenzione; **~ s.o. a compliment** fare un complimento a qu **3** *v/i* (*pret & pp* **paid**) pagare; (*be profitable*) rendere; **it doesn't ~ to ...** non conviene ...; **~ for purchase** pagare; **you'll ~ for this!** *fig* la pagherai!

◆ **pay back** *v/t person* restituire i soldi a; *loan* restituire; (*get revenge on*) farla pagare a

◆ **pay in** *v/t to bank* versare

◆ **pay off 1** *v/t debt* estinguere; *workers* liquidare; *corrupt official* comprare **2** *v/i* (*be profitable*) dare frutti

◆ **pay up** *v/i* pagare

pay·a·ble ['peɪəbl] *adj* pagabile

'pay·day giorno *m* di paga

pay·ee [peɪ'i:] beneficiario *m*, -a *f*

pay·er ['peɪə(r)] pagatore *m*, -trice *f*

pay·ment ['peɪmənt] pagamento *m*

'pay pack·et busta *f* paga; **'pay phone** telefono *m* pubblico; **'payroll** *money* stipendi *mpl*; *employees* personale *m*; **be on the ~** essere sul libro paga; **'pay·slip** busta *f* paga

PC [pi:'si:] *abbr* (= **personal computer**) PC *m inv*; (= **politically correct**) politicamente corretto; (= **police constable**) agente *m* di polizia

pea [pi:] pisello *m*

peace [pi:s] pace *f*

peace·a·ble ['pi:səbl] *adj person* pacifico

peace·ful ['pi:sful] *adj* tranquillo; *demonstration* pacifico

peace·ful·ly ['pi:sflɪ] *adv* tranquillamente; *demonstrate* pacificamente

peach [pi:ʧ] pesca *f*; *tree* pesco *m*

pea·cock ['pi:kɒk] pavone *m*

peak [pi:k] **1** *n* vetta *f*; *fig* apice *m* **2** *v/i* raggiungere il livello massimo

peak con·sump·tion periodo *m* di massimo consumo; **'peak hours** *npl* ore *fpl* di punta; **peak 'view·ing hours** *npl* prima serata *f*

pea·nut ['pi:nʌt] arachide *f*; **get paid ~s** F essere pagati una miseria F; **that's ~s to him** F sono briciole per lui

pea·nut 'but·ter burro *m* d'arachidi

pear [peə(r)] pera *f*; *tree* pero *m*

pearl [pɜ:l] perla *f*

peas·ant ['peznt] contadino *m*, -a *f*

peb·ble ['pebl] ciottolo *m*

peck [pek] **1** *n* (*bite*) beccata *f*; (*kiss*) bacetto *m* **2** *v/t* (*bite*) beccare; (*kiss*) dare un bacetto a

pe·cu·li·ar [pɪ'kju:lɪə(r)] *adj* (*strange*) strano; **~ to** (*special*) caratteristico di

pe·cu·li·ar·i·ty [pɪkju:lɪ'ærətɪ] (*strangeness*) stranezza *f*; (*special feature*) caratteristica *f*

ped·al ['pedl] **1** *n of bike* pedale *m* **2** *v/i turn ~s* pedalare; (*cycle*) andare in bicicletta

pe·dan·tic [pɪ'dæntɪk] *adj* pedante

ped·dle ['pedl] *v/t drugs* spacciare

ped·es·tal ['pedɪstl] *for statue* piedistallo *m*

pe·des·tri·an [pɪˈdestrɪən] *n* pedone *m*

pe·des·tri·an 'cros·sing passaggio *m* pedonale

pe·des·tri·an 'pre·cinct zona *f* pedonale

pe·di·at·ric [piːdɪˈætrɪk] *adj* pediatrico

pe·di·a·tri·cian [piːdɪəˈtrɪʃn] pediatra *m/f*

pe·di·at·rics [piːdɪˈætrɪks] pediatria *f*

ped·i·cure [ˈpedɪkjʊə(r)] pedicure *f inv*

ped·i·gree [ˈpedɪɡriː] **1** *n* pedigree *m inv* **2** *adj* di razza pura

pee [piː] *v/i* F fare pipì F

peek [piːk] **1** *n* sbirciata F **2** *v/i* sbirciare F

peel [piːl] **1** *n* buccia *f*; *of citrus fruit* scorza *f* **2** *v/t fruit, vegetables* sbucciare **3** *v/i of nose, shoulders* spellarsi; *of paint* scrostarsi

♦ **peel off 1** *v/t wrapper etc* togliere **2** *v/i of wrapper* venir via

peep [piːp] → **peek**

peep·hole [ˈpiːphəʊl] spioncino *m*

peer[1] [pɪə(r)] *n (equal)* pari *m/f inv*

peer[2] [pɪə(r)] *v/i* guardare; **~ through the mist** guardare attraverso la foschia; **~ at** scrutare

peeved [piːvd] *adj* F seccato

peg [peg] *n for coat* attaccapanni *m inv*; *for tent* picchetto *m*; **off the ~** prêt-à-porter

pe·jo·ra·tive [pɪˈdʒɒrətɪv] *adj* peggiorativo

pel·let [ˈpelɪt] pallina *f*; *(bullet)* pallino *m*

pelt [pelt] **1** *v/t*: **~ s.o with sth** tirare qc a qu **2** *v/i*: **they ~ed along the road** F sono sfrecciati per strada; **it's ~ing down** F piove a dirotto

pel·vis [ˈpelvɪs] pelvi *f inv*

pen[1] [pen] *n* penna *f*

pen[2] [pen] *(enclosure)* recinto *m*

pe·nal·ize [ˈpiːnəlaɪz] *v/t* penalizzare

pen·al·ty [ˈpenltɪ] ammenda *f*; *in soccer* rigore *m*; *in rugby* punizione *f*; **take the ~** battere il rigore / la punizione

'pen·al·ty ar·e·a SP area *f* di rigore; **'pen·al·ty clause** LAW penale *f*; **'pen·al·ty kick** *in soccer* calcio *m* di rigore; *in rugby* calcio *m* di punizione; **pen·al·ty 'shoot-out** rigori *mpl*; **'pen·al·ty spot** dischetto *m* di rigore

pence [pens] *npl* penny *m inv*

pen·cil [ˈpensɪl] matita *f*

pen·cil sharp·en·er temperamatite *m inv*

pen·dant [ˈpendənt] *necklace* pendaglio *m*

pend·ing [ˈpendɪŋ] **1** *prep* in attesa di **2** *adj*: **be ~** essere in sospeso

pen·e·trate [ˈpenɪtreɪt] *v/t* penetrare in

pen·e·trat·ing [ˈpenɪtreɪtɪŋ] *adj stare, scream* penetrante; *analysis* perspicace

pen·e·tra·tion [penɪˈtreɪʃn] penetrazione *f*

'pen friend amico *m*, -a *f* di penna

pen·guin [ˈpeŋɡwɪn] pinguino *m*

pen·i·cil·lin [penɪˈsɪlɪn] penicillina *f*

pe·nin·su·la [pəˈnɪnsjʊlə] penisola *f*

pe·nis [ˈpiːnɪs] pene *m*

pen·i·tence [ˈpenɪtəns] penitenza *f*

pen·i·tent [ˈpenɪtənt] *adj* pentito

pen·knife [ˈpennaɪf] temperino *m*

'pen name pseudonimo *m*

pen·nant [ˈpenənt] gagliardetto *m*

pen·ni·less [ˈpenɪləs] *adj* al verde

pen·ny [ˈpenɪ] penny *m inv*

'pen pal amico *m*, -a *f* di penna

pen·sion [ˈpenʃn] pensione *f*

♦ **pension off** *v/t* mandare in pensione

pen·sion·er [ˈpenʃnə(r)] pensionato *m*, -a *f*

'pen·sion fund fondo *m* pensioni

'pen·sion scheme schema *m* pensionistico

pen·sive [ˈpensɪv] *adj* pensieroso

Pen·ta·gon [ˈpentəɡɒn]: **the ~** il Pentagono

pen·tath·lon [penˈtæθlən] pentathlon *m inv*

Pen·te·cost [ˈpentɪkɒst] Pentecoste *f*

pent·house [ˈpenthaʊs] attico *m*

pent-up ['pentʌp] *adj* represso

pe·nul·ti·mate [pe'nʌltɪmət] *adj* penultimo

peo·ple ['piːpl] *npl* gente *f*, persone *fpl*; (*nsg: race, tribe*) popolazione *f*; **the ~** (*the citizens*) il popolo; **the American ~** gli americani; **~ say ...** si dice che ...

pep·per ['pepə(r)] *spice* pepe *m*; *vegetable* peperone *m*

pep·per·mint *sweet* mentina *f*; *flavouring* menta *f*

pep talk ['peptɔːk] discorso *m* d'incoraggiamento

per [pɜː(r)] *prep* a; **100 km ~ hour** 100 km all'ora; **£50 ~ night** 50 sterline a notte; **~ annum** all'anno

per·ceive [pə'siːv] *v/t with senses* percepire; (*view, interpret*) interpretare

per·cent [pə'sent] per cento

per·cen·tage [pə'sentɪdʒ] percentuale *f*

per·cep·ti·ble [pə'septəbl] *adj* percettibile

per·cep·ti·bly [pə'septəblɪ] *adv* percettibilmente

per·cep·tion [pə'sepʃn] *through senses* percezione *f*; (*insight*) sensibilità *f inv*

per·cep·tive [pə'septɪv] *adj person, remark* perspicace

perch [pɜːtʃ] **1** *n for bird* posatoio *m* **2** *v/i of bird* posarsi; *of person* appollaiarsi

per·co·late ['pɜːkəleɪt] *v/i of coffee* filtrare

per·co·la·tor ['pɜːkəleɪtə(r)] caffettiera *f* a filtro

per·cus·sion [pə'kʌʃn] percussioni *fpl*

per'cus·sion in·stru·ment strumento *m* a percussione

pe·ren·ni·al [pə'renɪəl] *n* BOT pianta *f* perenne

per·fect ['pɜːfɪkt] **1** *n* GRAM passato *m* prossimo **2** *adj* perfetto **3** *v/t* [pə'fekt] perfezionare

per·fec·tion [pə'fekʃn] perfezione *f*; **to ~** alla perfezione

per·fec·tion·ist [pə'fekʃnɪst] perfezionista *m/f*

per·fect·ly ['pɜːfɪktlɪ] *adv* perfettamente

per·fo·rat·ed ['pɜːfəreɪtɪd] *adj* line perforato

per·fo·ra·tions [pɜːfə'reɪʃnz] *npl* linea *fsg* perforata

per·form [pə'fɔːm] **1** *v/t* (*carry out*) eseguire; *of actors* rappresentare; *of musician* eseguire **2** *v/i of actor, musician, dancer* esibirsi; *of actor* recitare; **the car ~s well** la macchina dà ottime prestazioni

per·form·ance [pə'fɔːməns] *by actor* rappresentazione *f*; *by musician* esecuzione *f*; (*show*) spettacolo *m*; *of employee, company etc* rendimento *m*; *of machine* prestazioni *fpl*

per'form·ance car auto *f inv* di alte prestazioni

per·form·er [pə'fɔːmə(r)] artista *m/f*

per·fume ['pɜːfjuːm] profumo *m*

per·func·to·ry [pə'fʌŋktərɪ] *adj* superficiale

per·haps [pə'hæps] *adv* forse

per·il ['perəl] pericolo *m*

per·il·ous ['perələs] *adj* pericoloso

pe·rim·e·ter [pə'rɪmɪtə(r)] perimetro *m*

pe'rim·e·ter fence recinzione *f*

pe·ri·od ['pɪərɪəd] *time* periodo *m*; (*menstruation*) mestruazioni *fpl*; **I don't want to, ~!** *Am* non voglio, punto e basta!

pe·ri·od·ic [pɪərɪ'ɒdɪk] *adj* periodico

pe·ri·od·i·cal [pɪərɪ'ɒdɪkl] *n* periodico *m*

pe·ri·od·i·cal·ly [pɪərɪ'ɒdɪklɪ] *adv* periodicamente

pe·riph·e·ral [pə'rɪfərəl] **1** *adj not crucial* marginale **2** *n* COMPUT periferica *f*

pe·riph·e·ry [pə'rɪfərɪ] periferia *f*

per·ish ['perɪʃ] *v/i of rubber* deteriorarsi; *of person* perire

per·ish·a·ble ['perɪʃəbl] *adj food* deteriorabile

per·ish·ing ['perɪʃɪŋ] *adj* F: **it's ~** fa un freddo da cane F

per·jure ['pɜːdʒə(r)] *v/r*: **~ o.s.** spergiurare

per·ju·ry ['pɜːdʒərɪ] falso giuramento *m*

perk [pɜːk] *n of job* vantaggio *m*

♦ **perk up 1** *v/t* F tirare su di morale **2** *v/i* F animarsi

perk·y ['pɜːkɪ] *adj* F (*cheerful*) allegro

perm [pɜːm] **1** *n* permanente *f* **2** *v/t* fare la permanente a

per·ma·nent ['pɜːmənənt] *adj* permanente; *job, address* fisso

per·ma·nent·ly ['pɜːmənəntlɪ] *adv* permanentemente

per·me·a·ble ['pɜːmɪəbl] *adj* permeabile

per·me·ate ['pɜːmɪeɪt] *v/t* permeare

per·mis·si·ble [pə'mɪsəbl] *adj* permesso, ammissibile

per·mis·sion [pə'mɪʃn] permesso *m*

per·mis·sive [pə'mɪsɪv] *adj* permissivo

per·mis·sive so·ci·e·ty società *f inv* permissiva

per·mit ['pɜːmɪt] **1** *n* permesso *m* **2** *v/t* [pə'mɪt] (*pret & pp* **-ted**) permettere; ~ *s.o. to do sth* permettere a qu di fare qc

per·pen·dic·u·lar [pɜːpən'dɪkjʊlə(r)] *adj* perpendicolare

per·pet·u·al *adj* perenne

per·pet·u·al·ly [pə'petjʊəlɪ] *adv* perennemente

per·pet·u·ate [pə'petjʊeɪt] *v/t* perpetuare

per·plex [pə'pleks] *v/t* lasciare perplesso

per·plexed [pə'plekst] *adj* perplesso

per·plex·i·ty [pə'pleksɪtɪ] perplessità *f inv*

per·se·cute ['pɜːsɪkjuːt] *v/t* perseguitare

per·se·cu·tion [pɜːsɪ'kjuːʃn] persecuzione *f*

per·se·cu·tor [pɜːsɪ'kjuːtə(r)] persecutore *m*, -trice *f*

per·se·ver·ance [pɜːsɪ'vɪərəns] perseveranza *f*

per·se·vere [pɜːsɪ'vɪə(r)] *v/i* perseverare

per·sist [pə'sɪst] *v/i* persistere; ~ *in* persistere in

per·sis·tence [pə'sɪstəns] (*perseverance*) perseveranza *f*; (*continuation*) persistere *m*

per·sis·tent [pə'sɪstənt] *adj person, questions* insistente; *rain, unemployment etc* continuo

per·sis·tent·ly [pə'sɪstəntlɪ] *adv* (*continually*) continuamente

per·son ['pɜːsn] persona *f*; *in* ~ di persona

per·son·al ['pɜːsnl] *adj* personale; *don't make* ~ *remarks* non fare commenti personali

per·son·al as·sis·tant assistente *m/f* personale; '**per·son·al col·umn** annunci *mpl* personali; **per·son·al com·put·er** personal computer *m inv*; **per·son·al 'hy·giene** igiene *f* personale

per·son·al·i·ty [pɜːsə'nælətɪ] personalità *f inv*

per·son·al·ly ['pɜːsənəlɪ] *adv* personalmente; *don't take it* ~ non offenderti

per·son·al 'or·gan·iz·er agenda *f* elettronica; **per·son·al 'pro·noun** pronome *m* personale; **per·son·al 'ster·e·o** Walkman® *m inv*

per·son·i·fy [pə'sɒnɪfaɪ] *v/t* (*pret & pp* **-ied**) *of person* personificare

per·son·nel [pɜːsə'nel] *employees* personale *m*; *department* ufficio *m* del personale

per·son'nel man·a·ger direttore *m*, -trice *f* del personale

per·spec·tive [pə'spektɪv] PAINT prospettiva *f*; *get sth into* ~ vedere qc nella giusta prospettiva

per·spi·ra·tion [pɜːspɪ'reɪʃn] traspirazione *f*

per·spire [pə'spaɪə(r)] *v/i* sudare

per·suade [pə'sweɪd] *v/t* persuadere, convincere; ~ *s.o. to do sth* persuadere *o* convincere qu a fare qc

per·sua·sion [pə'sweɪʒn] persuasione *f*

per·sua·sive [pə'sweɪsɪv] *adj* persuasivo

per·ti·nent ['pɜːtɪnənt] *adj fml* pertinente

per·turb [pə'tɜːb] *v/t* inquietare

per·turb·ing [pə'tɜːbɪŋ] *adj* inquietante

pe·ruse [pə'ruːz] *v/t fml* leggere

per·va·sive [pə'veɪsɪv] *adj influence, ideas* diffuso

per·verse [pə'vɜːs] *adj* ostinato, irragionevole; *sexually* pervertito; **be ~** (*awkward*) essere un bastian contrario; **take a ~ delight in doing sth** provare un piacere perverso a fare qc

per·ver·sion [pə'vɜːʃn] *sexual* perversione *f*

per·vert ['pɜːvɜːt] *n sexual* pervertito *m*, -a *f*

pes·si·mism ['pesɪmɪzm] pessimismo *m*

pes·si·mist ['pesɪmɪst] pessimista *m/f*

pes·si·mist·ic [pesɪ'mɪstɪk] *adj attitude, view* pessimistico; *person* pessimista

pest [pest] animale / insetto *m* nocivo; F *person* peste *f*

pes·ter ['pestə(r)] *v/t* assillare; **~ s.o. to do sth** assillare qu perché faccia qc

pes·ti·cide ['pestɪsaɪd] pesticida *m*

pet [pet] **1** *n animal* animale *m* domestico; (*favourite*) favorito *m*, -a *f* **2** *adj* preferito **3** *v/t* (*pret & pp -ted*) *animal* accarezzare **4** *v/i* (*pret & pp -ted*) *of couple* pomiciare F

pet·al ['petl] petalo *m*

♦**pe·ter out** ['piːtə(r)] *v/i of rebellion, rain* cessare; *of path* finire

pe·tite [pə'tiːt] *adj* minuta

pe·ti·tion [pə'tɪʃn] *n* petizione *f*

'pet name nomignolo *m*

pet·ri·fied ['petrɪfaɪd] *adj* terrorizzato

pet·ri·fy ['petrɪfaɪ] *v/t* (*pret & pp -ied*) terrorizzare

pet·ro·chem·i·cal [petrəʊ'kemɪkl] *adj* petrolchimico

pet·rol ['petrl] benzina *f*

pe·tro·le·um [pɪ'trəʊlɪəm] petrolio *m*

'pet·rol gauge spia *f* della benzina,

'pet·rol pump pompa *f* della benzina; **'pet·rol sta·tion** stazione *f* di servizio

pet·ting ['petɪŋ] petting *m inv*

pet·ty ['petɪ] *adj person, behaviour* meschino; *details, problem* insignificante

pet·ty 'cash piccola cassa *f*

pet·u·lant ['petjʊlənt] *adj* petulante

pew [pjuː] banco *m* (di chiesa)

pew·ter ['pjuːtə(r)] peltro *m*

phar·ma·ceu·ti·cal [fɑːmə'sjuːtɪkl] *adj* farmaceutico

phar·ma·ceu·ti·cals [fɑːmə'sjuːtɪklz] *npl* farmaceutici *mpl*

phar·ma·cist ['fɑːməsɪst] farmacista *m/f*

phar·ma·cy ['fɑːməsɪ] farmacia *f*

phase [feɪz] fase *f*

♦**phase in** *v/t* introdurre gradualmente

♦**phase out** *v/t* eliminare gradualmente

PhD [piːeɪtʃ'diː] *abbr* (= *Doctor of Philosophy*) dottorato *m* di ricerca

phe·nom·e·nal [fɪ'nɒmɪnl] *adj* fenomenale

phe·nom·e·nal·ly [fɪ'nɒmɪnlɪ] *adv* straordinariamente

phe·nom·e·non [fɪ'nɒmɪnɒn] fenomeno *m*

phil·an·throp·ic [fɪlən'θrɒpɪk] *adj* filantropico

phi·lan·thro·pist [fɪ'lænθrəpɪst] filantropo *m*, -a *f*

phi·lan·thro·py [fɪ'lænθrəpɪ] filantropia *f*

Phil·ip·pines ['fɪlɪpiːnz] *npl*: **the ~** le Filippine *fpl*

phil·is·tine ['fɪlɪstaɪn] *n* ignorante *m/f*

phi·los·o·pher [fɪ'lɒsəfə(r)] filosofo *m*, -a *f*

phil·o·soph·i·cal [fɪlə'sɒfɪkl] *adj* filosofico

phi·los·o·phy [fɪ'lɒsəfɪ] filosofia *f*

pho·bi·a ['fəʊbɪə] fobia *f*

phone [fəʊn] **1** *n* telefono *m*; **be on the ~** *have one* avere il telefono; *be talking* essere al telefono **2** *v/t* telefonare a **3** *v/i* telefonare

'phone book guida *f* telefonica,

P

elenco telefonico *m*; 'phone booth cabina *f* telefonica; 'phone box cabina *f* telefonica; 'phone call telefonata *f*; 'phone card scheda *f* telefonica; 'phone num·ber numero *m* di telefono

pho·net·ics [fə'netɪks] fonetica *f*

pho·n(e)y ['fəʊnɪ] *adj* F falso

pho·to ['fəʊtəʊ] *n* foto *f*

'pho·to al·bum album *m* fotografico; 'pho·to·cop·i·er fotocopiatrice *f*; 'pho·to·cop·y 1 *n* fotocopia *f* 2 *v/t* (*pret & pp* -ied) fotocopiare

pho·to·gen·ic [fəʊtəʊ'dʒenɪk] *adj* fotogenico

pho·to·graph ['fəʊtəɡrɑːf] 1 *n* fotografia *f* 2 *v/t* fotografare

pho·tog·ra·pher [fə'tɒɡrəfə(r)] fotografo *m*, -a *f*

pho·tog·ra·phy [fə'tɒɡrəfɪ] fotografia *f*

phrase [freɪz] 1 *n* frase *f* 2 *v/t* esprimere

'phrase·book vocabolarietto *m* di frasi utili

phys·i·cal ['fɪzɪkl] 1 *adj* fisico 2 *n* MED visita *f* medica

phys·i·cal 'hand·i·cap *adj* handicap *m inv* fisico

phys·i·cal·ly ['fɪzɪklɪ] *adv* fisicamente

phys·i·cal·ly 'hand·i·cap·ped *adj*: be ~ essere portatore *m*, -trice *f* di handicap fisico

phy·si·cian [fɪ'zɪʃn] medico *m*

phys·i·cist ['fɪzɪsɪst] fisico *m*, -a *f*

phys·ics ['fɪzɪks] fisica *f*

phys·i·o·ther·a·pist [fɪzɪəʊ'θerəpɪst] fisioterapeuta *m/f*

phys·i·o·ther·a·py [fɪzɪəʊ'θerəpɪ] fisioterapia *f*

phy·sique [fɪ'ziːk] fisico *m*

pi·a·nist ['pɪənɪst] pianista *m/f*

pi·an·o [pɪ'ænəʊ] piano *m*

pick [pɪk] 1 *n*: take your ~ scegli quello che vuoi 2 *v/t* (*choose*) scegliere; *flowers, fruit* raccogliere; ~ one's nose mettersi le dita nel naso 3 *v/i*: ~ and choose fare il difficili

♦ pick at *v/t*: pick at one's food man-

giucchiare poco

♦ pick on *v/t treat unfairly* prendersela con; (*select*) scegliere

♦ pick out *v/t* (*identify*) riconoscere

♦ pick up 1 *v/t* prendere; *phone* sollevare; *baby* prendere in braccio; *from ground* raccogliere; (*collect*) andare / venire a prendere; *information* raccogliere; *in car* far salire; *man, woman* rimorchiare F; *language, skill* imparare; *habit, illness* prendere; (*buy*) trovare; *criminal* arrestare; pick up the tab F pagare (il conto) 2 *v/i* (*improve*) migliorare

pick·et ['pɪkɪt] 1 *n of strikers* picchetto *m* 2 *v/t* picchettare

'pick·et line cordone *m* degli scioperanti

pick·le ['pɪkl] *v/t* conservare sott'aceto

pick·les ['pɪklz] *npl* sottaceti *mpl*

'pick·pock·et borseggiatore *m*, -trice *f*

pick·y ['pɪkɪ] *adj* F difficile (da accontentare)

pic·nic ['pɪknɪk] 1 *n* picnic *m inv* 2 *v/i* (*pret & pp* -ked) fare un picnic

pic·ture ['pɪktʃə(r)] 1 *n photo* foto *f*; *painting* quadro *m*; *illustration* figura *f*; *film* film *m inv*; put / keep s.o. in the ~ mettere / tenere al corrente qu 2 *v/t* immaginare

'pic·ture book libro *m* illustrato

pic·ture 'post·card cartolina *f* illustrata

pic·tures ['pɪktʃəz] *npl* cinema *m*

pic·tur·esque [pɪktʃə'resk] *adj* pittoresco

pie [paɪ] *sweet* torta *f*; *savoury* pasticcio *m*

piece [piːs] pezzo *m*; a ~ of pie / bread una fetta di torta / pane; a ~ of advice un consiglio; go to ~s crollare; take to ~s smontare

♦ piece together *v/t broken plate* rimettere insieme; *facts, evidence* ricostruire

piece·meal ['piːsmiːl] *adv* poco alla volta

piece·work ['piːswɜːk] *n* lavoro *m* a cottimo

pier [pɪə(r)] *at seaside* pontile *m*

pierce [pɪəs] *v/t (penetrate)* trapassa-re; *ears* farsi i buchi in

pierc·ing ['pɪəsɪŋ] *noise* lacerante; *eyes* penetrante; *wind* pungente

pig [pɪg] *also fig* maiale *m*

pi·geon ['pɪdʒɪn] piccione *m*

'pi·geon·hole 1 *n* casella *f* **2** *v/t person* etichettare; *proposal* archiviare

pig·gy·bank ['pɪgɪbæŋk] salvada-naio *m*

pig·head·ed [pɪg'hedɪd] *adj* testardo

'pig·skin pelle *f* di cinghiale; **'pig·sty** *also fig* porcile *m*; **'pig·tail** *plaited* treccina *f*

pile [paɪl] mucchio *m*; **a ~ of work** un sacco di lavoro F

♦ **pile up 1** *v/i of work, bills* accumu-larsi **2** *v/t* ammucchiare

piles [paɪlz] *nsg* MED emorroidi *fpl*

pile-up ['paɪlʌp] MOT tampona-mento *m* a catena

pil·fer·ing ['pɪlfərɪŋ] piccoli furti *mpl*

pil·grim ['pɪlgrɪm] pellegrino *m*, -a *f*

pil·grim·age ['pɪlgrɪmɪdʒ] pellegri-naggio *m*

pill [pɪl] pastiglia *f*; **the ~** la pillola; **be on the ~** prendere la pillola

pil·lar ['pɪlə(r)] colonna *f*

'pil·lar box buca *f* delle lettere (a colonnina)

pil·lion ['pɪljən] *of motor bike* sellino *m* posteriore

pil·low ['pɪləʊ] *n* guanciale *m*

'pil·low·case, **'pil·low·slip** federa *f*

pi·lot ['paɪlət] **1** *n of aeroplane* pilota *m/f* **2** *v/t aeroplane* pilotare

'pi·lot plant stabilimento *m* pilota

'pi·lot scheme progetto *m* pilota

pimp [pɪmp] *n* ruffiano *m*

pim·ple ['pɪmpl] brufolo *m*

pin [pɪn] **1** *n for sewing* spillo *m*; *in bowling* birillo *m*; *(badge)* spilla *f*; ELEC spinotto *m* **2** *v/t (pret & pp -ned) (hold down)* immobilizzare; *(attach)* attaccare; *on lapel* appunta-re

♦ **pin down** *v/t:* **pin s.o. down to a date** far fissare una data a qu

♦ **pin up** *v/t notice* appuntare

PIN [pɪn] *abbr* (= **personal identification number**) numero *m* di codice segreto

pin·cers ['pɪnsəz] *npl tool* tenaglie *fpl*; *of crab* chele *fpl*

pinch [pɪntʃ] **1** *n* pizzico *m*; **at a ~** al massimo **2** *v/t* pizzicare **3** *v/i of shoes* stringere

pine[1] [paɪn] *n* pino *m*; **~ furniture** mobili *mpl* di pino

pine[2] [paɪn] *v/i:* **~ for** soffrire per la mancanza di

pine·ap·ple ['paɪnæpl] ananas *m inv*

ping [pɪŋ] **1** *n* suono *m* metallico **2** *v/i* fare un suono metallico

ping-pong ['pɪŋpɒŋ] ping-pong *m inv*

pink [pɪŋk] *adj* rosa *inv*

pin·na·cle ['pɪnəkl] *fig* apice *m*

pin·point *v/t* indicare con esattezza

pins and 'nee·dles *npl* formicolio *m*

'pin·stripe *adj* gessato

pint [paɪnt] pinta *f*

'pin-up (girl) pin-up *f inv*

pi·o·neer [paɪə'nɪə(r)] **1** *n fig* pionie-re *m*, -a *f* **2** *v/t* essere il/la pioniere di

pi·o·neer·ing [paɪə'nɪərɪŋ] *adj work* pionieristico

pi·ous ['paɪəs] *adj* pio

pip [pɪp] *n of fruit* seme *m*

pipe [paɪp] **1** *n for smoking* pipa *f*; *for water, gas, sewage* tubo *m* **2** *v/t* tra-sportare con condutture

♦ **pipe down** *v/i* F far silenzio

piped mu·sic [paɪpt'mjuːzɪk] musi-ca *f* di sottofondo

pipe·line conduttura *f*; **in the ~** *fig* in arrivo

pip·ing hot [paɪpɪŋ'hɒt] *adj* caldissi-mo

pi·rate [pɪʃ] *v/t software* piratare

Pis·ces ['paɪsiːz] ASTR Pesci *m/f inv*

piss [pɪs] **1** *v/i* P *(urinate)* pisciare P **2** *n (urine)* piscio *m* P; **take the ~out of s.o.** P prendere qu per il culo P

♦ **piss off** *v/i* P sparire; **piss off!** levati dalle palle! P

pissed [pɪst] *adj* P *(drunk)* sbronzo F; *Am (annoyed)* seccato

pis·tol ['pɪstl] pistola *f*

P

pis·ton ['pɪstən] pistone *m*

pit [pɪt] *n* (*hole*) buca *f*; (*coal mine*) miniera *f*

pitch[1] [pɪtʃ] *n* MUS intonazione *f*

pitch[2] [pɪtʃ] *v/t tent* piantare; *ball* lanciare

'**pitch black** *adj* buio pesto

pitch·er ['pɪtʃə(r)] *container* brocca *f*

pit·e·ous ['pɪtɪəs] *adj* pietoso

pit·fall ['pɪtfɔːl] *n* tranello *m*

pith [pɪθ] *of citrus fruit* parte *f* bianca della scorza

pit·i·ful ['pɪtɪfʊl] *adj sight* pietoso; *excuse, attempt* penoso

pit·i·less ['pɪtɪləs] *adj* spietato

pits [pɪts] *npl in motor racing* box *m inv*

'**pit stop** *in motor racing* sosta *f* ai box

pit·tance ['pɪtns] miseria *f*

pit·y ['pɪtɪ] **1** *n* pietà *f inv*; **it's a ~ that** è un peccato che; **what a ~!** che peccato!; **take ~ on** avere pietà di 2 *v/t* (*pret & pp -ied*) *person* avere pietà di

piv·ot ['pɪvət] *v/i* ruotare

piz·za ['piːtsə] pizza *f*

plac·ard ['plækɑːd] cartello *m*

place [pleɪs] **1** *n* posto *m*; *flat, house* casa *f*; **I've lost my ~** *in book* ho perso il segno; **at my/his ~** a casa mia/sua; **in ~ of** invece di; **feel out of ~** sentirsi fuori posto; **take ~** aver luogo; **in the first ~** (*firstly*) in primo luogo 2 *v/t* (*put*) piazzare; **I can't quite ~ you** non mi ricordo dove ci siamo conosciuti; **~ an order** fare un'ordinazione

'**place mat** tovaglietta *f* all'americana

plac·id ['plæsɪd] *adj* placido

pla·gia·rism ['pleɪdʒərɪzm] plagio *m*

pla·gia·rize ['pleɪdʒəraɪz] *v/t* plagiare

plague [pleɪg] **1** *n* peste *f* 2 *v/t* (*bother*) tormentare

plain[1] [pleɪn] *n* pianura *f*

plain[2] [pleɪn] **1** *adj* (*clear, obvious*) chiaro; *not fancy* semplice; *not pretty* scialbo; *not patterned* in tinta unita; (*blunt*) franco; **~ chocolate** cioccolato *m* fondente 2 *adv* semplicemente; **it's ~ crazy** è semplicemente matto

'**plain-clothes: in ~** in borghese

plain·ly ['pleɪnlɪ] *adv* (*clearly*) chiaramente; (*bluntly*) francamente; (*simply*) semplicemente

plain-'spo·ken *adj* franco

plain·tiff ['pleɪntɪf] LAW attore *m*, -trice *f*

plain·tive ['pleɪntɪv] *adj* lamentoso

plait [plæt] **1** *n in hair* treccia *f* 2 *v/t hair* intrecciare

plan [plæn] **1** *n* (*project, intention*) piano *m*; (*drawing*) progetto *m* 2 *v/t* (*pret & pp -ned*) (*prepare*) organizzare; (*design*) progettare; **~ to do, ~ on doing** avere in programma di 3 *v/i* (*pret & pp -ned*) pianificare

plane[1] [pleɪn] *n* (*aeroplane*) aereo *m*

plane[2] [pleɪn] *tool* pialla *f*

plan·et ['plænɪt] pianeta *m*

plank [plæŋk] *of wood* asse *f*; *fig: of policy* punto *m*

plan·ning ['plænɪŋ] pianificazione *f*; **at the ~ stage** allo stadio di progettazione

plant[1] [plɑːnt] **1** *n* pianta *f* 2 *v/t* piantare

plant[2] [plɑːnt] *n* (*factory*) stabilimento *m*; (*equipment*) impianto *m*

plan·ta·tion [plæn'teɪʃn] piantagione *f*

plaque [plæk] *on wall, teeth* placca *f*

plas·ter ['plɑːstə(r)] **1** *n on wall, ceiling* intonaco *m* 2 *v/t wall, ceiling* intonacare; **be ~ed with** essere ricoperto di

plas·ter cast ingessatura *f*

plas·tic ['plæstɪk] **1** *n* plastica *f*; F (*money*) carte *fpl* di credito 2 *adj made of ~* di plastica

plas·tic 'bag sacchetto *m* di plastica; **plas·tic 'mon·ey** carte *fpl* di credito; **plas·tic 'sur·geon** chirurgo *m* plastico; **plas·tic 'sur·ge·ry** chirurgia *f* plastica

plate [pleɪt] *n for food* piatto *m*; *sheet of metal* lastra *f*

pla·teau ['plætəʊ] altopiano *m*

plat·form ['plætfɔːm] (*stage*) palco

m; of railway station binario *m; fig: political* piattaforma *f*

plat·i·num ['plætinəm] **1** *n* platino *m* **2** *adj* di platino

plat·i·tude ['plætitju:d] banalità *f inv*

pla·ton·ic [plə'tɒnik] *adj relationship* platonico

pla·toon [plə'tu:n] *of soldiers* plotone *m*

plat·ter ['plætə(r)] *for meat, fish* vassoio *m*

plau·si·ble ['plɔ:zəbl] *adj* plausibile

play [pleɪ] **1** *n in theatre, on TV* commedia *f; of children,* TECH, SP gioco *m* **2** *v/i of children,* SP giocare; *of musician* suonare **3** *v/t* MUS suonare; *game* giocare a; *opponent* giocare contro; *(perform: Macbeth etc)* rappresentare; *particular role* interpretare; **~ a joke on** fare uno scherzo a

♦ **play around** *v/i* F *(be unfaithful):* **his wife's been playing around** sua moglie lo ha tradito; **her husband was playing around with his secretary** suo marito aveva una relazione con la segretaria

♦ **play down** *v/t* minimizzare

♦ **play up** *v/i of machine* dare noie; *of child* fare i capricci; *of tooth, bad back etc* fare male

play·act ['pleɪækt] *v/i (pretend)* fare la commedia

play·back ['pleɪbæk] playback *m inv*

play·boy ['pleɪbɔɪ] playboy *m inv*

play·er ['pleɪə(r)] SP giocatore *m,* -trice *f; musician* musicista *m/f; actor* attore *m,* -trice *f*

play·ful ['pleɪful] *adj punch, mood* scherzoso; *puppy* giocherellone

play·ground ['pleɪgraʊnd] *in school* cortile *m* per la ricreazione; *in park* parco *m* giochi

'**play·group** asilo *m*

play·ing card ['pleɪiŋkɑ:d] carta *f* da gioco

play·ing field ['pleɪiŋfi:ld] campo *m* sportivo

play·mate ['pleɪmeɪt] compagno *m,* -a *f* di gioco

play·wright ['pleɪraɪt] commediografo *m,* -a *f*

plc [pi:el'si:] *abbr (= public limited company)* società *f inv* a responsabilità limitata quotata in borsa

plea [pli:] **1** *n* appello *m*

plead [pli:d] *v/i:* **~ for** supplicare; **~ guilty / not guilty** dichiararsi colpevole / innocente; **~ with** supplicare

pleas·ant ['pleznt] *adj* piacevole

please [pli:z] **1** *adv* per favore; **more tea? – yes, ~** ancora tè? – sì, grazie; **~ do** fai pure, prego **2** *v/t* far piacere a; **~ yourself** fai come ti pare

pleased [pli:zd] *adj* contento; **~ to meet you** piacere!

pleas·ing ['pli:ziŋ] *adj* piacevole

pleas·ure ['pleʒə(r)] *(happiness, satisfaction)* contentezza *f; (as opposed to work)* piacere *m; (delight)* gioia *f;* **it's a ~** *(you're welcome)* è un piacere; **with ~** con vero piacere

pleat [pli:t] *n in skirt* piega *f*

pleat·ed skirt ['pli:tid] gonna *f* a pieghe

pledge [pledʒ] **1** *n (promise)* promessa *f* **2** *v/t (promise)* promettere

plen·ti·ful ['plentiful] *adj* abbondante

plen·ty ['plenti] *(abundance)* abbondanza *f;* **~ of** molto; **that's ~** basta così; **there's ~ for everyone** ce n'è per tutti

pli·a·ble *adj* flessibile

pli·ers *npl* pinze *fpl;* **a pair of ~** un paio di pinze

plight [plaɪt] situazione *f* critica

plod [plɒd] *v/i (pret & pp -ded) walk* trascinarsi

♦ **plod on** *v/i with a job* sgobbare

plod·der ['plɒdə(r)] *at work, school* sgobbone *m,* -a *f*

plot[1] [plɒt] *n land* appezzamento *m*

plot[2] [plɒt] **1** *n (conspiracy)* complotto *m; of novel* trama *f* **2** *v/t & v/i (pret & pp -ted)* complottare

plot·ter ['plɒtə(r)] cospiratore *m,* -trice *f;* COMPUT plotter *m inv*

plough, plow *Am* [plaʊ] **1** *n* aratro *m* **2** *v/t & v/i* arare

♦ **plough on** *v/i with profits* reinvestire

pluck [plʌk] *v/t eyebrows* pinzare; *chicken* spennare

P

♦ **pluck up** v/t: **pluck up courage** trovare il coraggio

plug [plʌg] **1** n for sink, bath tappo m; electrical spina f; (spark ~) candela f; for new book etc pubblicità f inv **2** v/t (pret & pp **-ged**) hole tappare; new book etc fare pubblicità a

♦ **plug away** v/i F sgobbare

♦ **plug in** v/t attaccare (alla presa)

plum [plʌm] **1** n susina f **2** adj: ~ **job** F un lavoro favoloso

plum·age ['pluːmɪdʒ] piumaggio m

plumb [plʌm] adj a piombo

♦ **plumb in** v/t washing machine collegare all'impianto idraulico

plumb·er ['plʌmə(r)] idraulico m

plumb·ing ['plʌmɪŋ] pipes impianto m idraulico

plume [pluːm] n piuma f

plum·met ['plʌmɪt] v/i of aeroplane precipitare; of share prices crollare

plump [plʌmp] adj person, chicken in carne; hands, feet, face paffuto

♦ **plump for** v/t scegliere

plunge [plʌndʒ] **1** n caduta f; in prices crollo m; **take the ~** fare il gran passo **2** v/i precipitare; of prices crollare **3** v/t knife conficcare; tomatoes immergere; **the city was ~d into darkness** la città fu immersa nel buio; **the news ~d him into despair** la notizia lo gettò nella disperazione

plung·ing ['plʌndʒɪŋ] adj neckline profonda

plu·per·fect ['pluː'pɜːfɪkt] n GRAM piuccheperfetto m

plu·ral ['plʊərəl] **1** n plurale m **2** adj plurale

plus [plʌs] **1** prep più **2** adj: **£500 ~** oltre 500 sterline **3** n symbol più m inv; (advantage) vantaggio m **4** conj (moreover, in addition) per di più

plush [plʌʃ] adj di lusso

'**plus sign** segno m più

ply·wood ['plaɪwʊd] compensato m

PM [piː'em] abbr (= **Prime Minister**) primo ministro m

p.m. [piː'em] abbr (= **post meri·diem**): **at 2** ~ alle 2 del pomeriggio; **at 10.30** ~ alle 10.30 di sera

pneu·mat·ic [njuː'mætɪk] adj pneumatico

pneu·mat·ic '**drill** martello m pneumatico

pneu·mo·ni·a [njuː'məʊnɪə] polmonite f

poach[1] [pəʊtʃ] v/t cook bollire; egg fare in camicia

poach[2] [pəʊtʃ] **1** v/i for game cacciare di frodo; for fish pescare di frodo **2** v/t cacciare / pescare di frodo

poached egg [pəʊtʃt'eg] uovo m in camicia

poach·er ['pəʊtʃə(r)] of salmon, game cacciatore / pescatore m di frodo

P.O. Box [piː'əʊbɒks] casella f postale

pock·et ['pɒkɪt] **1** n tasca f; **line one's ~s** arricchirsi; **be out of ~** rimetterci **2** adj (miniature) in miniatura **3** v/t intascare

pock·et '**cal·cu·la·tor** calcolatrice f tascabile

'**pocket book** Am (wallet) portafoglio m; (handbag) borsetta f

po·di·um ['pəʊdɪəm] podio m

po·em ['pəʊɪm] poesia f

po·et ['pəʊɪt] poeta m, -essa f

po·et·ic [pəʊ'etɪk] adj person, description poetico

po·et·ic '**jus·tice** giustizia f divina

po·et·ry ['pəʊɪtrɪ] poesia f

poig·nant ['pɔɪnjənt] adj commovente

point [pɔɪnt] **1** n of pencil, knife punta f; in competition, exam punto m; (purpose) senso m; (moment) punto m; in argument, discussion punto m; in decimals virgola f; **that's beside the** ~ non c'entra; **be on the** ~ **of** stare giusto per; **get to the** ~ venire al dunque; **that's a** ~ questo, in effetti, è vero; **the** ~ **is ...** il fatto è che ...; **you've got a** ~ **there** su questo, hai ragione; **I take your** ~ su questo, ti do ragione; **there's no** ~ **in waiting / trying** non ha senso aspettare / tentare **2** v/i indicare **3** v/t gun puntare (**at** contro)

♦ **point at** v/t with finger indicare col dito

◆ **point out** *v/t sights, advantages* indicare

◆ **point to** *v/t with finger* additare; *(fig: indicate)* far presupporre

'**point-blank 1** *adj refusal, denial* categorico; *at ~ range* a bruciapelo **2** *adv refuse, deny* categoricamente

point·ed ['pɔɪntɪd] *adj remark, question* significativo

point·er ['pɔɪntə(r)] *for teacher* bacchetta *f*; *(hint)* consiglio *m*; *(sign, indication)* indizio *m*

point·less ['pɔɪntləs] *adj* inutile; *it's ~ trying* è inutile tentare

'**point of sale** punto *m* vendita

'**point of view** punto *m* di vista

poise [pɔɪz] padronanza *f* di sé

poised [pɔɪzd] *adj person* posato

poi·son ['pɔɪzn] **1** *n* veleno *m* **2** *v/t* avvelenare

poi·son·ous ['pɔɪznəs] *adj* velenoso

poke [pəʊk] **1** *n* colpetto *m* **2** *v/t (prod)* dare un colpetto a; *(stick)* ficcare; *~ fun at* prendere in giro; *~ one's nose into* ficcare il naso in

◆ **poke around** *v/i* F curiosare

pok·er ['pəʊkə(r)] *card game* poker *m inv*

pok·y ['pəʊkɪ] *adj* F *(cramped)* angusto

Po·land ['pəʊlənd] Polonia *f*

po·lar ['pəʊlə(r)] *adj* polare

po·lar bear orso *m* polare

po·lar·ize ['pəʊləraɪz] *v/t* polarizzare

Pole [pəʊl] polacco *m*, -a *f*

pole[1] [pəʊl] *of wood, metal* paletto *m*

pole[2] [pəʊl] *of earth* polo *m*

'**pole star** stella *f* polare; '**pole-vault** salto *m* con l'asta; '**pole-vault·er** saltatore *m*, -trice *f* con l'asta

po·lice [pə'liːs] *n* polizia *f*

po·lice car auto *f* della polizia; **po·lice·man** poliziotto *m*; **po·lice state** stato *m* di polizia; **po·lice sta·tion** commissariato *m* di polizia; **po·lice·wo·man** donna *f* poliziotto

pol·i·cy[1] ['pɒlɪsɪ] politica *f*

pol·i·cy[2] ['pɒlɪsɪ] *(insurance ~)* polizza *f*

po·li·o ['pəʊlɪəʊ] polio *f*

Pol·ish ['pəʊlɪʃ] **1** *adj* polacco **2** *n* polacco *m*

pol·ish ['pɒlɪʃ] **1** *n product* lucido *m*; *(nail ~)* smalto *m* **2** *v/t* lucidare; *speech* rifinire

◆ **polish off** *v/t food* spazzolare F

◆ **polish up** *v/t skill* perfezionare

pol·ished ['pɒlɪʃt] *adj performance* impeccabile

po·lite [pə'laɪt] *adj* cortese

po·lite·ly [pə'laɪtlɪ] *adv* cortesemente

po·lite·ness [pə'laɪtnɪs] cortesia *f*

po·lit·i·cal [pə'lɪtɪkl] *adj* politico

po·lit·i·cal·ly cor·rect [pə'lɪtɪklɪ kə'rekt] *adj* politicamente corretto

pol·i·ti·cian [pɒlɪ'tɪʃn] uomo *m* politico, donna *f* politica

pol·i·tics ['pɒlətɪks] politica *f*; *what are his ~?* di che tendenze politiche è?

poll [pəʊl] **1** *n (survey)* sondaggio *m*; *the ~s (election)* le elezioni *fpl*; *go to the ~s (vote)* andare alle urne **2** *v/t people* fare un sondaggio tra; *votes* guadagnare

pol·len ['pɒlən] polline *m*

'**pol·len count** concentrazione *f* di polline

'**poll·ing booth** ['pəʊlɪŋ] cabina *f* elettorale; '**poll·ing day** giorno *m* delle elezioni; '**poll·ing sta·tion** seggio *m* elettorale

poll·ster ['pɒlstə(r)] esperto *m*, -a *f* di sondaggi

pol·lu·tant [pə'luːtənt] sostanza *f* inquinante

pol·lute [pə'luːt] *v/t* inquinare

pol·lu·tion [pə'luːʃn] inquinamento *m*

po·lo ['pəʊləʊ] SP polo *m*

'**po·lo neck** *adj sweater* a dolcevita

'**po·lo shirt** polo *f inv*

pol·y·es·ter [pɒlɪ'estə(r)] poliestere *m*

pol·y·sty·rene [pɒlɪ'staɪriːn] polistirolo *m*

pol·y·thene ['pɒlɪθiːn] polietilene *m*

pol·y·thene 'bag sacchetto *m* di plastica

P

pol·y·un·sat·u·rat·ed [pɒlɪʌnˈsætʃə-reɪtɪd] *adj* polinsaturo

pom·pous [ˈpɒmpəs] *adj* pomposo

pond [pɒnd] stagno *m*

pon·der [ˈpɒndə(r)] *v/i* riflettere

pon·tiff [ˈpɒntɪf] pontefice *m*

po·ny [ˈpəʊnɪ] pony *m inv*

'po·ny·tail coda *f* (di cavallo)

poo·dle [ˈpuːdl] barboncino *m*

pool¹ [puːl] (*swimming ~*) piscina *f*; *of water, blood* pozza *f*

pool² [puːl] *game* biliardo *m*

pool³ [puːl] **1** *n common fund* cassa *f* comune **2** *v/t resources* mettere insieme

'pool hall sala *f* da biliardo

pools [puːlz] *npl* totocalcio *m*; **do the ~** giocare al totocalcio

'pool table tavolo *m* da biliardo

poop·ed [puːpt] *adj* F stanco morto

poor [pʊə(r)] **1** *adj not wealthy, unfortunate* povero; *not good* misero; *be in ~ health* essere in cattiva salute; *~ old Tony!* povero Tony! **2** *n*: **the ~** i poveri

poor·ly [ˈpʊəlɪ] **1** *adv* male **2** *adj* (*unwell*) indisposto

pop¹ [pɒp] **1** *n noise* schiocco *m* **2** *v/i* (*pret & pp* **-ped**) *of balloon etc* scoppiare **3** *v/t* (*pret & pp* **-ped**) *cork* stappare; *balloon* far scoppiare

pop² [pɒp] **1** *n* MUS pop *m inv* **2** *adj* pop *inv*

pop³ [pɒp] *v/t* (*pret & pp* **-ped**) F (*put*) ficcare F; *~ one's head around the door* sbucare con la testa dalla porta

♦ **pop in** *v/i* F (*make a brief visit*) entrare un attimo

♦ **pop out** *v/i* F (*go out for a short time*) fare un salto fuori

♦ **pop up** *v/i* F (*appear suddenly*) saltare fuori

'pop con·cert concerto *m* pop

pop·corn [ˈpɒpkɔːn] popcorn *m inv*

pope [pəʊp] papa *m*

'pop group gruppo *m* pop

pop·py [ˈpɒpɪ] papavero *m*

'pop song canzone *m* pop

pop·u·lar [ˈpɒpjʊlə(r)] *adj* popolare; *belief, support* diffuso

pop·u·lar·i·ty [pɒpjʊˈlærətɪ] popolarità *f inv*

pop·u·late [ˈpɒpjʊleɪt] *v/t* popolare

pop·u·la·tion [pɒpjʊˈleɪʃn] popolazione *f*

porce·lain [ˈpɔːsəlɪn] **1** *n* porcellana *f* **2** *adj* di porcellana

porch [pɔːtʃ] porticato *m*; *Am* veranda *f*

por·cu·pine [ˈpɔːkjʊpaɪn] porcospino *m*

pore [pɔː(r)] *of skin* poro *m*

♦ **pore over** *v/t* studiare attentamente

pork [pɔːk] maiale *m*

porn [pɔːn] *n* F porno *m* F

porn(o) [pɔːn, ˈpɔːnəʊ] *adj* F porno *inv* F

por·no·graph·ic [pɔːnəˈgræfɪk] *adj* pornografico

porn·og·ra·phy [pɔːˈnɒgrəfɪ] pornografia *f*

po·rous [ˈpɔːrəs] *adj* poroso

port¹ [pɔːt] *n* (*harbour, drink*) porto *m*

port² [pɔːt] *adj* (*left-hand*) babordo; *on the ~ side* a babordo

por·ta·ble [ˈpɔːtəbl] **1** *adj* portatile **2** *n* portatile *m*

por·ter [ˈpɔːtə(r)] portiere *m*

port·hole [ˈpɔːthəʊl] NAUT oblò *m inv*

por·tion [ˈpɔːʃn] *n* parte *f*; *of food* porzione *f*

por·trait [ˈpɔːtreɪt] **1** *n* ritratto *m* **2** *adv print* verticale

por·tray [pɔːˈtreɪ] *v/t of artist, photographer* ritrarre; *of actor* interpretare; *of author* descrivere

por·tray·al [pɔːˈtreɪəl] *by actor* rappresentazione *f*; *by author* descrizione *f*

Por·tu·gal [ˈpɔːtjʊgl] Portogallo *m*

Por·tu·guese [pɔːtjʊˈgiːz] **1** *adj* portoghese **2** *n person* portoghese *m/f*; *language* portoghese *m*

pose [pəʊz] **1** *n* (*pretence*) posa *f* **2** *v/i for artist, photographer* posare; *~ as* farsi passare per **3** *v/t*: *~ a problem / a threat* creare un problema / una minaccia

P

posh [pɒʃ] *adj* F elegante; *pej* snob

po·si·tion [pəˈzɪʃn] **1** *n* posizione *f*; *what would you do in my ~?* cosa faresti al mio posto? **2** *v/t* sistemare, piazzare

pos·i·tive [ˈpɒzətɪv] *adj* positivo; *be ~ (sure)* essere certo

pos·i·tive·ly [ˈpɒzətɪvlɪ] *adv* (*downright*) decisamente; (*definitely*) assolutamente; *think* in modo positivo

pos·sess [pəˈzes] *v/t* possedere

pos·ses·sion [pəˈzeʃn] (*ownership*) possesso *m*; *thing owned* bene *m*; *~s* averi *mpl*

pos·ses·sive [pəˈzesɪv] *adj also* GRAM possessivo

pos·si·bil·i·ty [pɒsəˈbɪlətɪ] possibilità *f inv*

pos·si·ble [ˈpɒsəbl] *adj* possibile; *the shortest / quickest ~ ...* la ... più breve / veloce possibile; *the best ~ ...* la migliore ... possibile

pos·si·bly [ˈpɒsəblɪ] *adv* (*perhaps*) forse; *that can't ~ be right* non è possibile che sia giusto; *could you ~ tell me ...?* potrebbe per caso dirmi ...?

post¹ [pəʊst] **1** *n of wood, metal* palo *m* **2** *v/t notice* affiggere; *profits* annunciare; *keep s.o. ~ed* tenere informato qu

post² [pəʊst] **1** *n* (*place of duty*) posto *m* **2** *v/t soldier, employee* assegnare; *guards* piazzare

post³ [pəʊst] **1** *n* (*mail*) posta *f*; *by ~* per posta **2** *v/t letter* spedire (per posta); (*put in the mail*) imbucare

post·age [ˈpəʊstɪdʒ] affrancatura *f*

'post·age stamp *fml* francobollo *m*

post·al [ˈpəʊstl] *adj* postale

'post·al or·der vaglia *m* postale

'post·box buca *f* delle lettere; **'post·card** cartolina *f*; **'post·code** codice *m* di avviamento postale; **'post·date** *v/t* postdatare

post·er [ˈpəʊstə(r)] *n* manifesto *m*; *for decoration* poster *m inv*

pos·te·ri·or [pɒˈstɪərɪə(r)] *n* (*hum: buttocks*) posteriore *m*

pos·ter·i·ty [pɒˈsterətɪ] posteri *mpl*

post·grad·u·ate [ˈpəʊstgrædjʊɪt]

1 *n* studente *m* / studentessa *f* di un corso post-universitario **2** *adj* post-universitario

post·hu·mous [ˈpɒstjʊməs] *adj* postumo

post·hu·mous·ly [ˈpɒstjʊməslɪ] *adv* dopo la sua morte; *it was published ~* è stato pubblicato postumo

post·ing [ˈpəʊstɪŋ] (*assignment*) incarico *m*

post·man [ˈpəʊstmən] postino *m*

post·mark [ˈpəʊstmɑːk] timbro *m* postale

post·mor·tem [pəʊstˈmɔːtəm] autopsia *f*

'post of·fice ufficio *m* postale

post·pone [pəʊstˈpəʊn] *v/t* rinviare

post·pone·ment [pəʊstˈpəʊnmənt] rinvio *m*

pos·ture [ˈpɒstʃə(r)] posizione *f*

'post·war *adj* del dopoguerra

pot¹ [pɒt] *for cooking* pentola *f*; *for coffee* caffettiera *f*; *for tea* teiera *f*; *for plant* vaso *m*

pot² [pɒt] F (*marijuana*) erba *f* F

po·ta·to [pəˈteɪtəʊ] patata *f*

po·ta·to chips *Am*, **po·ta·to crisps** *Br npl* patatine *fpl*

'pot·bel·ly [ˈpɒtbelɪ] pancetta *f*

po·tent [ˈpəʊtənt] *adj* potente

po·ten·tial [pəˈtenʃl] **1** *adj* potenziale **2** *n* potenziale *m*

po·ten·tial·ly [pəˈtenʃəlɪ] *adv* potenzialmente

pot·hole [ˈpɒthəʊl] *in road* buca *f*

pot·ter [ˈpɒtə(r)] *n* vasaio *m*, -a *f*

pot·ter·y [ˈpɒtərɪ] *n activity* ceramica *f*; *items* vasellame *m*; *place* laboratorio *m* di ceramica

pot·ty [ˈpɒtɪ] *n for baby* vasino *m*

pouch [paʊtʃ] (*bag*) borsa *f*

poul·try [ˈpəʊltrɪ] *birds* volatili *mpl*; *meat* pollame *m*

pounce [paʊns] *v/i of animal* balzare; *fig* piombare

pound¹ [paʊnd] *n weight* libbra *f*; FIN sterlina *f*

pound² [paʊnd] *for strays* canile *m* municipale; *for cars* deposito *m* auto

pound³ [paʊnd] *v/i of heart* battere

P

forte; **~ on** (*hammer on*) picchiare su

pound 'ster·ling sterlina *f*

pour [pɔː(r)] **1** *v/t liquid* versare **2** *v/i*: **it's ~ing (with rain)** sta diluviando

♦ **pour out** *v/t liquid* versare; *troubles* sfogarsi raccontando

pout [paʊt] *v/i* fare il broncio

pov·er·ty ['pɒvətɪ] povertà *f inv*

pov·er·ty-strick·en ['pɒvətɪstrɪkn] *adj* poverissimo

pow·der ['paʊdə(r)] **1** *n* polvere *f*; *for face* cipria *f* **2** *v/t*: **~ one's face** mettersi la cipria

'**pow·der room** F toilette *f inv* per signore

pow·er ['paʊə(r)] **1** *n* (*strength*) forza *f*; *of engine* potenza *f*; (*authority*) potere *m*; (*energy*) energia *f*; (*electricity*) elettricità *f inv*; **in ~** POL al potere; **fall from ~** POL perdere il potere **2** *v/t*: **~ed by atomic energy** a propulsione atomica

'**pow·er-as·sist·ed steer·ing** servosterzo *m*; '**pow·er cut** interruzione *f* di corrente; '**pow·er fail·ure** guasto *m* alla linea elettrica

pow·er·ful ['paʊəfʊl] *adj* potente

pow·er·less ['paʊəlɪs] *adj* impotente; **be ~ to ...** non poter far niente per ...

'**pow·er line** linea *f* elettrica; '**pow·er sta·tion** centrale *f* elettrica; '**pow·er steer·ing** servosterzo *m*; '**pow·er u·nit** alimentatore *m*

PR [piː'ɑː(r)] *abbr* (= *public relations*) relazioni *fpl* pubbliche

prac·ti·cal ['præktɪkl] *adj* pratico

prac·ti·cal 'joke scherzo *m*

prac·tic·al·ly ['præktɪklɪ] *adv behave*, *think* in modo pratico; (*almost*) praticamente

prac·tice ['præktɪs] **1** *n* pratica *f*; (*training*) esercizio *m*; (*rehearsal*) prove *fpl*; (*custom*) consuetudine *f*; **in ~** (*in reality*) in pratica; **be out of ~** essere fuori allenamento **2** *v/t* & *v/i Am* → **practise**

prac·tise ['præktɪs] **1** *v/t* esercitarsi in; *law*, *medicine* esercitare **2** *v/i* esercitarsi

prag·mat·ic [præg'mætɪk] *adj* pragmatico

prag·ma·tism ['prægmətɪzm] pragmatismo *m*

prai·rie ['preərɪ] prateria *f*

praise [preɪz] **1** *n* lode *f* **2** *v/t* lodare

praise·wor·thy ['preɪzwɜːðɪ] *adj* lodevole

pram [præm] carrozzina *f*

prank [præŋk] *n* birichinata *f*

prat·tle ['prætl] *v/i* cianciare

prawn [prɔːn] gamberetto *m*

pray [preɪ] *v/i* pregare

prayer [preə(r)] preghiera *f*

preach [priːtʃ] **1** *v/i* predicare **2** *v/t* *sermon* predicare

preach·er ['priːtʃə(r)] predicatore *m*, -trice *f*

pre·am·ble [priː'æmbl] preambolo *m*

pre·car·i·ous [prɪ'keərɪəs] *adj* precario

pre·car·i·ous·ly [prɪ'keərɪəslɪ] *adv* precariamente

pre·cau·tion [prɪ'kɔːʃn] precauzione *f*

pre·cau·tion·a·ry [prɪ'kɔːʃnrɪ] *adj* *measure* di precauzione

pre·cede [prɪ'siːd] *v/t* precedere

pre·ce·dence ['presɪdəns] precedenza *f*; **take ~ over ...** avere la precedenza su ...

pre·ce·dent ['presɪdənt] *n* precedente *m*

pre·ce·ding [prɪ'siːdɪŋ] *adj* precedente

pre·cinct ['priːsɪŋkt] (*Am: district*) distretto *m*

pre·cious ['preʃəs] *adj* prezioso

pre·cip·i·tate [prɪ'sɪpɪteɪt] *v/t crisis* accelerare

pre·cip·i·ta·tion [prɪsɪpɪ'teɪʃn] *fml* precipitazione *f*

pré·cis ['preɪsiː] *n* riassunto *m*

pre·cise [prɪ'saɪs] *adj* preciso

pre·cise·ly [prɪ'saɪslɪ] *adv* precisamente

pre·ci·sion [prɪ'sɪʒn] precisione *f*

pre·co·cious [prɪ'kəʊʃəs] *adj child* precoce

pre·con·ceived [priːkən'siːvd] *adj*

idea preconcetto

pre·con·di·tion [prɪkən'dɪʃn] condizione *f* indispensabile

pred·a·tor ['predətə(r)] *animal* predatore *m*, -trice *f*

pred·a·to·ry ['predətrɪ] *adj* rapace

pre·de·ces·sor ['priːdɪsesə(r)] predecessore *m*

pre·des·ti·na·tion [priːdestɪ'neɪʃn] predestinazione *f*

pre·des·tined [priː'destɪnd] *adj*: **be ~ to** essere predestinato a

pre·dic·a·ment [prɪ'dɪkəmənt] situazione *f* difficile

pre·dict [prɪ'dɪkt] *v/t* predire

pre·dict·a·ble [prɪ'dɪktəbl] *adj* prevedibile

pre·dic·tion [prɪ'dɪkʃn] predizione *f*

pre·dom·i·nant [prɪ'dɒmɪnənt] *adj* predominante

pre·dom·i·nant·ly [prɪ'dɒmɪnəntlɪ] *adv* prevalentemente

pre·dom·i·nate [prɪ'dɒmɪneɪt] *v/i* predominare

preen [priːn] *v/t*: **~ o.s.** *fig* farsi bello

pre·fab·ri·cat·ed [priː'fæbrɪkeɪtɪd] *adj* prefabbricato

pref·ace ['prefɪs] *n* prefazione *f*

pre·fect ['priːfekt] EDU *studente m/ studentessa f* dell'ultimo anno di liceo *con responsabilità disciplinari*

pre·fer [prɪ'fɜː(r)] *v/t (pret & pp -red)* preferire; **~ X to Y** preferire X a Y; **~ to do** preferire fare

pref·er·a·ble ['prefərəbl] *adj* preferibile

pref·er·a·bly ['prefərəblɪ] *adv* preferibilmente

pref·er·ence ['prefərəns] preferenza *f*; **give ~ to** dare *o* accordare la preferenza a

pref·er·en·tial [prefə'renʃl] *adj* preferenziale

pre·fix ['priːfɪks] prefisso *m*

preg·nan·cy ['pregnənsɪ] gravidanza *f*

preg·nant ['pregnənt] *adj* incinta; **get ~** restare incinta

pre·heat ['priːhiːt] *v/t oven* far riscaldare

pre·his·tor·ic [priːhɪs'tɒrɪk] *adj* preistorico

pre·judge [priː'dʒʌdʒ] *v/t* giudicare a priori

prej·u·dice ['predʒudɪs] **1** *n* pregiudizio *m* **2** *v/t person* influenzare; *chances* pregiudicare

prej·u·diced ['predʒudɪst] *adj* prevenuto

prej·u·di·cial [predʒu'dɪʃl] *adj*: **be ~ to** essere pregiudizievole a

pre·lim·i·na·ry [prɪ'lɪmɪnərɪ] *adj* preliminare

prel·ude ['preljuːd] preludio *m*

pre·mar·i·tal [priː'mærɪtl] *adj* prematrimoniale

pre·ma·ture ['premətjuə(r)] *adj* prematuro

pre·med·i·tat·ed [priː'medɪteɪtɪd] *adj* premeditato

prem·i·er ['premɪə(r)] *n (Prime Minister)* premier *m inv*

prem·i·ère ['premɪeə(r)] *n* premiere *f inv*, prima *f*

prem·is·es ['premɪsɪz] *npl* locali *mpl*

pre·mi·um ['priːmɪəm] *n in insurance* premio *m*

pre·mo·ni·tion [premə'nɪʃn] premonizione *f*

pre·oc·cu·pied [prɪ'ɒkjupaɪd] *adj* preoccupato

pre·paid ['priːpeɪd] *adj* prepagato

prep·a·ra·tion [prepə'reɪʃn] preparazione *f*; **in ~ for** in vista di; **~s** preparativi *mpl*

pre·pare [prɪ'peə(r)] **1** *v/t* preparare; **be ~d to do sth** *(willing)* essere preparato a fare qc; **be ~d for sth** *(be expecting)* essere preparato per qc **2** *v/i* prepararsi

prep·o·si·tion [prepə'zɪʃn] preposizione *f*

pre·pos·sess·ing [priːpə'zesɪŋ] *adj* attraente

pre·pos·ter·ous [prɪ'pɒstərəs] *adj* ridicolo

prep school ['prepskuːl] *scuola f* privata di preparazione alla scuola superiore

pre·req·ui·site [priː'rekwɪzɪt] condizione *f* indispensabile

pre·rog·a·tive [prɪ'rɒgətɪv] prerogativa *f*

pre·scribe [prɪ'skraɪb] *v/t of doctor* prescrivere

pre·scrip·tion [prɪ'skrɪpʃn] MED ricetta *f* medica

pres·ence ['prezns] presenza *f*; **in the ~ of** in presenza di

pres·ence of 'mind presenza *f* di spirito

pres·ent¹ ['preznt] **1** *adj* (*current*) attuale; **be ~** essere presente **2** *n*: **the ~** *also* GRAM il presente; **at ~** al momento

pres·ent² ['preznt] *n* (*gift*) regalo *m*

pres·ent³ [prɪ'zent] *v/t award* consegnare; *bouquet* offrire; *programme* presentare; **~ s.o. with sth, ~ sth to s.o.** offrire qc a qu

pre·sen·ta·tion [preznˈteɪʃn] presentazione *f*

pres·ent-day [preznt'deɪ] *adj* di oggi

pres·ent·er [prɪ'zentə(r)] presentatore *m*, -trice *f*

pres·ent·ly ['prezntlɪ] *adv* (*at the moment*) attualmente; (*soon*) tra breve

'pres·ent tense presente *m*

pres·er·va·tion [prezə'veɪʃn] *of food* conservazione *f*; *of standards, peace etc* mantenimento *m*

pre·ser·va·tive [prɪ'zɜ:vətɪv] *n for wood*; *in food* conservante *m*

pre·serve [prɪ'zɜ:v] **1** *n* (*domain*) dominio *m* **2** *v/t standards, peace etc* mantenere; *wood etc* proteggere; *food* conservare

pre·serves [prɪ'zɜ:vz] *npl* conserve *fpl*

pre·side [prɪ'zaɪd] *v/i at meeting* presiedere; **~ over** *meeting* presiedere a

pres·i·den·cy ['prezɪdənsɪ] presidenza *f*

pres·i·dent ['prezɪdnt] presidente *m*

pres·i·den·tial [prezɪ'denʃl] *adj* presidenziale

press [pres] **1** *n*: **the ~** la stampa **2** *v/t button* premere; (*urge*) far pressione su; (*squeeze*) stringere; *clothes* stirare; *grapes, olives* spremere **3** *v/i*: **~ for** fare pressioni per ottenere

'press a·gen·cy agenzia *f* di stampa

'press con·fer·ence conferenza *f* stampa

press·ing ['presɪŋ] *adj* urgente

press-stud ['presstʌd] (bottone *m*) automatico

press-up ['presʌp] flessione *f* sulle braccia

pres·sure ['preʃə(r)] **1** *n* pressione *f*; **be under ~** (**to do**) essere sotto pressione (per fare) **2** *v/t* fare delle pressioni su

'pres·sure cook·er pentola *f* a pressione

'pres·sur·ize ['preʃəraɪz] *v/t person* fare delle pressioni su

pres·tige [pre'sti:ʒ] prestigio *m*

pres·ti·gious [pre'stɪdʒəs] *adj* prestigioso

pre·sum·a·ble [prɪ'zju:məbl] *adj* presumibile

pre·su·ma·bly [prɪ'zju:məblɪ] *adv* presumibilmente

pre·sume [prɪ'zju:m] *v/i* presumere; **~ to do** *fml* permettersi di fare

pre·sump·tion [prɪ'zʌmpʃn] *of innocence, guilt* presunzione *f*

pre·sump·tu·ous [prɪ'zʌmptjʊəs] *adj* impertinente

pre·sup·pose [pri:sə'pəʊz] *v/t* presupporre

pre-tax ['pri:tæks] *adj* al lordo d'imposta

pre·tence [prɪ'tens] finta *f*

pre·tend [prɪ'tend] **1** *v/t* fingere **2** *v/i* fare finta

pre·tense *Am* → **pretence**

pre·ten·tious [prɪ'tenʃəs] *adj* pretenzioso

pre·text ['pri:tekst] pretesto *m*

pret·ty ['prɪtɪ] **1** *adj* carino **2** *adv* (*quite*) piuttosto

pre·vail [prɪ'veɪl] *v/i* (*triumph*) prevalere

pre·vail·ing [prɪ'veɪlɪŋ] *adj* prevalente

pre·var·i·cate [prɪ'værɪkeɪt] *v/i* tergiversare

pre·vent [prɪ'vent] *v/t* prevenire; **~ s.o. (from) doing sth** impedire a qu di fare qc

pre·ven·tion [prɪ'venʃn] prevenzio-ne f

pre·ven·tive [prɪ'ventɪv] adj preventivo

pre·view ['priːvjuː] n of film, exhibition anteprima f

pre·vi·ous ['priːvɪəs] adj precedente; ~ **to** prima di

pre·vi·ous·ly ['priːvɪəslɪ] adv precedentemente

pre-war ['priːwɔː(r)] adj dell'ante-guerra

prey [preɪ] n preda f
♦ **prey on** v/t far preda di; fig: of conman etc approfittarsi di; **prey on s.o.'s mind** preoccupare qu

price [praɪs] 1 n prezzo m 2 v/t COM fissare il prezzo di

price·less ['praɪslɪs] adj (valuable) di valore inestimabile

'price tag cartellino m del prezzo

'price war guerra f dei prezzi

price·y ['praɪsɪ] adj F caro

prick[1] [prɪk] 1 n pain puntura f 2 v/t (jab) pungere

prick[2] [prɪk] n V (penis) cazzo m V; person testa f di cazzo V
♦ **prick up** v/t: **prick up one's ears** also fig drizzare le orecchie

prick·le ['prɪkl] on plant spina f

prick·ly ['prɪklɪ] adj plant spinoso; beard ispido; (irritable) permaloso

pride [praɪd] 1 n in person, achievement orgoglio m; (self-respect) amor m proprio 2 v/t: ~ **o.s. on** vantarsi di

priest [priːst] prete m

pri·ma·ri·ly [praɪ'meərɪlɪ] adv principalmente

pri·ma·ry ['praɪmərɪ] adj principale

'pri·ma·ry school scuola f elementare

prime [praɪm] 1 n: **be in one's** ~ essere nel fiore degli anni 2 adj example, reason principale; (very good) ottimo; **of** ~ **importance** della massima importanza

prime 'min·is·ter primo ministro m

'prime time TV programmi mpl tv di prima serata

prim·i·tive ['prɪmɪtɪv] adj also fig primitivo

prim·rose ['prɪmrəʊz] primula f

prince [prɪns] principe m

prin·cess [prɪn'ses] principessa f

prin·ci·pal ['prɪnsəpl] 1 adj principale 2 n of school preside m/f

prin·ci·pal·i·ty [prɪnsɪ'pælətɪ] principato m

prin·ci·pal·ly ['prɪnsəplɪ] adv principalmente

prin·ci·ple ['prɪnsəpl] principio m; **on** ~ per principio; **in** ~ in linea di principio

print [prɪnt] 1 n in book, newspaper etc caratteri mpl; photograph stampa f; mark impronta f; **out of** ~ esaurito 2 v/t stampare; (use block capitals) scrivere in stampatello
♦ **print out** v/t stampare

print·ed 'mat·ter ['prɪntɪdmætə(r)] stampe fpl

print·er ['prɪntə(r)] person tipografo m; machine stampante f

'print·ing press ['prɪntɪŋpres] pressa f tipografica

'print·out stampato m

pri·or ['praɪə(r)] 1 adj precedente 2 prep: ~ **to** prima di

pri·or·i·tize [praɪ'ɒrətaɪz] v/t (put in order of priority) classificare in ordine d'importanza; (give priority to) dare precedenza a

pri·or·i·ty [praɪ'ɒrətɪ] priorità f inv; **have** ~ avere la precedenza

pris·on ['prɪzn] prigione f

pris·on·er ['prɪznə(r)] prigioniero m, -a f; **take s.o.** ~ fare prigioniero qu

pris·on·er of 'war prigioniero m di guerra

pri·va·cy ['prɪvəsɪ] privacy f inv

pri·vate ['praɪvət] 1 adj privato 2 n MIL soldato m semplice; **in** ~ in privato

pri·vate 'en·ter·prise iniziativa f privata

pri·vate·ly ['praɪvətlɪ] adv (in private) in privato; (inwardly) dentro di sé; ~ **funded** finanziato da privati; ~ **owned** privato

'pri·vate sec·tor settore m privato

pri·va·ti·za·tion [praɪvətaɪ'zeɪʃn] privatizzazione f

P

pri·va·tize ['praɪvətaɪz] v/t privatizzare

priv·i·lege ['prɪvəlɪdʒ] special treatment privilegio m; (honour) onore m

priv·i·leged ['prɪvəlɪdʒd] adj privilegiato; (honoured) onorato

prize [praɪz] **1** n premio m **2** v/t dare molto valore a

prize·win·ner ['praɪzwɪnə(r)] vincitore m, -trice f

prize·win·ning ['praɪzwɪnɪŋ] adj vincente

pro¹ [prəʊ] n: **the ~s and cons** i pro e i contro

pro² [prəʊ] → **professional**

pro³ [prəʊ] prep: **be ~ ...** (in favour of) essere a favore di ...

prob·a·bil·i·ty [prɒbə'bɪlətɪ] probabilità f inv

prob·a·ble ['prɒbəbl] adj probabile

prob·a·bly ['prɒbəblɪ] adv probabilmente

pro·ba·tion [prə'beɪʃn] in job periodo m di prova; LAW libertà f inv vigilata; **on ~** in job in prova

pro·'ba·tion of·fi·cer funzionario m che sorveglia i vigilati

pro·'ba·tion pe·ri·od in job periodo m di prova

probe [prəʊb] **1** n (investigation) indagine f; scientific sonda f **2** v/t esplorare; (investigate) investigare

prob·lem ['prɒbləm] problema m; **no ~** non c'è problema

pro·ce·dure [prə'siːdʒə(r)] procedura f

pro·ceed [prə'siːd] **1** v/i of people proseguire; of work etc procedere **2** v/t: **~ to do sth** cominciare a fare qc

pro·ceed·ings [prə'siːdɪŋz] npl (events) avvenimenti mpl

pro·ceeds ['prəʊsiːdz] npl ricavato m

pro·cess ['prəʊses] **1** n processo m; **in the ~** while doing it nel far ciò **2** v/t food, raw materials trattare; data elaborare; application etc sbrigare; **~ed cheese** formaggio m fuso

pro·ces·sion [prə'seʃn] processione f

pro·claim [prə'kleɪm] v/t proclamare

proc·la·ma·tion [prɒklə'meɪʃn] proclamazione f

prod [prɒd] **1** n colpetto m **2** v/t (pret & pp **-ded**) dare un colpetto a

pro·di·gious [prə'dɪdʒəs] adj straordinario

prod·i·gy ['prɒdɪdʒɪ]: (**infant**) **~** bambino m, -a f prodigio

prod·uce¹ ['prɒdjuːs] n prodotti mpl

pro·duce² [prə'djuːs] v/t produrre; (bring about) dare origine a; (bring out) tirar fuori; play, play mettere in scena

pro·duc·er [prə'djuːsə(r)] produttore m, -trice f; of play regista m/f

prod·uct ['prɒdʌkt] prodotto m; (result) risultato m

pro·duc·tion [prə'dʌkʃn] produzione f; of play regia f; **a new ~ of ...** una nuova messa in scena di ...

pro·duc·tion ca·pac·i·ty capacità f inv produttiva

pro·duc·tion costs npl costi mpl di produzione

pro·duc·tive [prə'dʌktɪv] adj produttivo

pro·duc·tiv·i·ty [prɒdʌk'tɪvətɪ] produttività f inv

pro·fane [prə'feɪn] adj language sacrilego

pro·fan·i·ty [prə'fænətɪ] (swearword) imprecazione f

pro·fess [prə'fes] v/t dichiarare

pro·fes·sion [prə'feʃn] professione f

pro·fes·sion·al [prə'feʃnl] **1** adj not amateur professionale; advice, help di un esperto; piece of work da professionista; **turn ~** passare al professionismo **2** n professionista m/f

pro·fes·sion·al·ly [prə'feʃnlɪ] adv play sport a livello professionistico; (well, skilfully) in modo professionale

pro·fes·sor [prə'fesə(r)] professore m (universitario)

pro·fi·cien·cy [prə'fɪʃnsɪ] competenza f

pro·fi·cient [prə'fɪʃnt] adj competente

pro·file ['prəʊfaɪl] profilo *m*

prof·it ['prɒfɪt] **1** *n* profitto *m* **2** *v/i*: ~ **by**, ~ **from** trarre profitto da

prof·it·a·bil·i·ty [prɒfɪtə'bɪlətɪ] redditività *f inv*

prof·it·a·ble ['prɒfɪtəbl] *adj* redditizio

'prof·it cen·ter *Am*, 'prof·it cen·tre centro *m* di profitto

'prof·it mar·gin margine *m* di profitto

pro·found [prə'faʊnd] *adj* profondo

pro·found·ly [prə'faʊndlɪ] *adv* profondamente

pro·fuse [prə'fjuːs] *adj* abbondante

pro·fuse·ly [prə'fjuːslɪ] *adv* thank con grande effusione; bleed copiosamente

prog·no·sis [prɒg'nəʊsɪs] prognosi *f inv*

pro·gram ['prəʊgræm] **1** *n* COMPUT programma *m* **2** *v/t* (*pret & pp* -*med*) COMPUT programmare

pro·gram *Am*, pro·gramme ['prəʊgræm] **1** *n* programma *m* **2** *v/t* programmare

pro·gram·mer ['prəʊgræmə(r)] COMPUT programmatore *m*, -trice *f*

pro·gress ['prəʊgres] **1** *n* progresso *m*; make ~ fare progressi; in ~ in corso **2** *v/i* [prə'gres] (*advance in time*) procedere; (*move on*) avanzare; (*make progress*) fare progressi; how is the work ~ing? come procede il lavoro?

pro·gres·sive [prə'gresɪv] *adj* (*enlightened*) progressista; which progresses progressivo

pro·gres·sive·ly [prə'gresɪvlɪ] *adv* progressivamente

pro·hib·it [prə'hɪbɪt] *v/t* proibire

pro·hi·bi·tion [prəʊhɪ'bɪʃn] proibizione *f*; **Prohibition** il Proibizionismo

pro·hib·i·tive [prə'hɪbɪtɪv] *adj* prices proibitivo

proj·ect[1] ['prɒdʒekt] *n* (*plan*) piano *m*; (*undertaking*) progetto *m*; EDU ricerca *f*

pro·ject[2] [prə'dʒekt] **1** *v/t* figures, sales fare una previsione di; film

proiettare **2** *v/i* (*stick out*) sporgere in fuori

pro·jec·tion [prə'dʒekʃn] (*forecast*) proiezione *f*

pro·jec·tor [prə'dʒektə(r)] for slides proiettore *m*

pro·lif·ic [prə'lɪfɪk] *adj* writer, artist prolifico

pro·log *Am*, pro·logue ['prəʊlɒg] prologo *m*

pro·long [prə'lɒŋ] *v/t* prolungare

prom·i·nent ['prɒmɪnənt] *adj* nose, chin sporgente; (*significant*) prominente

prom·is·cu·i·ty [prɒmɪ'skjuːətɪ] promiscuità *f inv*

pro·mis·cu·ous [prə'mɪskjʊəs] *adj* promiscuo

prom·ise ['prɒmɪs] **1** *n* promessa *f* **2** *v/t* promettere; ~ **to** ... promettere di ...; ~ **sth to s.o.** promettere qc a qu **3** *v/i* promettere; **I** ~ lo prometto

prom·is·ing ['prɒmɪsɪŋ] *adj* promettente

pro·mote [prə'məʊt] *v/t* promuovere

pro·mot·er [prə'məʊtə(r)] of sports event promoter *m/f inv*

pro·mo·tion [prə'məʊʃn] promozione *f*; **get** ~ essere promosso

prompt [prɒmpt] **1** *adj* (*on time*) puntuale; (*speedy*) tempestivo **2** *adv*: **at two o'clock** ~ alle due in punto **3** *v/t* (*cause*) causare; actor dare l'imbeccata a **4** *n* COMPUT prompt *m inv*

prompt·ly ['prɒmptlɪ] *adv* (*on time*) puntualmente; (*immediately*) prontamente

prone [prəʊn] *adj*: **be** ~ **to** essere soggetto a

prong [prɒŋ] dente *m*

pro·noun ['prəʊnaʊn] pronome *m*

pro·nounce [prə'naʊns] *v/t* word pronunciare; (*declare*) dichiarare

pro·nounced [prə'naʊnst] *adj* accent spiccato; views preciso

pron·to ['prɒntəʊ] *adv* F immediatamente

pro·nun·ci·a·tion [prənʌnsɪ'eɪʃn] pronuncia *f*

proof [pruːf] *n* prova *f*; of book bozza *f*

prop [prɒp] **1** v/t (pret & pp **-ped**) appoggiare **2** n THEA materiale m di scena

♦ **prop up** v/t also fig sostenere

prop·a·gan·da [prɒpəˈgændə] propaganda f

pro·pel [prəˈpel] v/t (pret & pp **-led**) spingere; of engine, fuel azionare

pro·pel·lant [prəˈpelənt] in aerosol propellente m

pro·pel·ler [prəˈpelə(r)] elica f

prop·er [ˈprɒpə(r)] adj (real) vero e proprio; (correct) giusto; (fitting) appropriato

prop·er·ly [ˈprɒpəlɪ] adv (correctly) correttamente; (fittingly) in modo appropriato

'prop·er noun nome m proprio

prop·er·ty [ˈprɒpətɪ] proprietà f inv

prop·er·ty de'vel·op·er impresario m edile

proph·e·cy [ˈprɒfəsɪ] profezia f

proph·e·sy [ˈprɒfəsaɪ] v/t (pret & pp **-ied**) profetizzare

pro·por·tion [prəˈpɔːʃn] proporzione f

pro·por·tion·al [prəˈpɔːʃnl] adj proporzionale

pro·por·tion·al rep·re·sen'ta·tion POL rappresentanza f proporzionale

pro·pos·al [prəˈpəʊzl] proposta f

pro·pose [prəˈpəʊz] **1** v/t (suggest) proporre; ~ **to do sth** (plan) proporsi di fare qc **2** v/i make offer of marriage fare una proposta di matrimonio

prop·o·si·tion [prɒpəˈzɪʃn] **1** n proposta f **2** v/t woman fare proposte sessuali a

pro·pri·e·tor [prəˈpraɪətə(r)] proprietario m, -a f

pro·pri·e·tress [prəˈpraɪətrɪs] proprietaria f

prose [prəʊz] prosa f

pros·e·cute [ˈprɒsɪkjuːt] v/t LAW intentare azione legale contro; of lawyer sostenere l'accusa contro

pros·e·cu·tion [prɒsɪˈkjuːʃn] LAW azione f giudiziaria; (lawyers) accusa f

pros·pect [ˈprɒspekt] **1** n (chance, likelihood) probabilità f inv; thought of something in the future prospettiva f; **~s** for company, in job prospettive fpl **2** v/i: ~ **for** gold cercare

pro·spec·tive [prəˈspektɪv] adj potenziale; MP aspirante

pros·per [ˈprɒspə(r)] v/i prosperare

pros·per·i·ty [prɒˈsperətɪ] prosperità f inv

pros·per·ous [ˈprɒspərəs] adj prospero

pros·ti·tute [ˈprɒstɪtjuːt] n prostituta f; **male ~** prostituto m

pros·ti·tu·tion [prɒstɪˈtjuːʃn] prostituzione f

pros·trate [ˈprɒstreɪt] adj: **be ~ with grief** essere abbattuto dal dolore

pro·tect [prəˈtekt] v/t proteggere

pro·tec·tion [prəˈtekʃn] protezione f

pro'tec·tion mon·ey pizzo m F

pro·tec·tive [prəˈtektɪv] adj protettivo

pro·tec·tive 'cloth·ing indumenti mpl protettivi

pro·tec·tor [prəˈtektə(r)] protettore m, -trice f

pro·tein [ˈprəʊtiːn] proteina f

pro·test [ˈprəʊtest] **1** n protesta f **2** v/t [prəˈtest] protestare **3** v/i protestare; POL manifestare, protestare

Prot·es·tant [ˈprɒtɪstənt] **1** n protestante m/f **2** adj protestante

pro·test·er [prəˈtestə(r)] dimostrante m/f, manifestante m/f

pro·to·col [ˈprəʊtəkɒl] protocollo m

pro·to·type [ˈprəʊtətaɪp] prototipo m

pro·tract·ed [prəˈtræktɪd] adj prolungato

pro·trude [prəˈtruːd] v/i sporgere

pro·trud·ing [prəˈtruːdɪŋ] adj sporgente

proud [praʊd] adj orgoglioso, fiero; **be ~ of** essere fiero di

proud·ly [ˈpraʊdlɪ] adv con orgoglio

prove [pruːv] v/t dimostrare

prov·erb [ˈprɒvɜːb] proverbio m

pro·vide [prəˈvaɪd] v/t money, food fornire; opportunity offrire; ~ **s.o. with sth** fornire qu di qc

♦ **provide for** v/t *family* provvedere a; *of law etc* contemplare

pro·vid·ed [prə'vaɪdɪd] *conj*: ~ **(that)** *(on condition that)* a condizione che

prov·ince ['prɒvɪns] provincia f

pro·vin·cial [prə'vɪnʃl] *adj also pej* provinciale

pro·vi·sion [prə'vɪʒn] *(supply)* fornitura f; *of law, contract* disposizione f

pro·vi·sion·al [prə'vɪʒnl] *adj* provvisorio

pro·vi·so [prə'vaɪzəʊ] condizione f

prov·o·ca·tion [prɒvə'keɪʃn] provocazione f

pro·voc·a·tive [prə'vɒkətɪv] *adj* provocatorio; *sexually* provocante

pro·voke [prə'vəʊk] v/t *(cause)* causare; *(annoy)* provocare

prow [praʊ] NAUT prua f

prow·ess ['praʊɪs] abilità f inv

prowl [praʊl] v/i aggirarsi

prowl·er ['praʊlə(r)] tipo m sospetto

prox·im·i·ty [prɒk'sɪmətɪ] prossimità f inv

prox·y ['prɒksɪ] *(authority)* procura f; *person* procuratore m, -trice f, mandatario m, -a f

prude [pruːd]: **be a** ~ scandalizzarsi facilmente

pru·dence ['pruːdns] prudenza f

pru·dent ['pruːdnt] *adj* prudente

prud·ish ['pruːdɪʃ] *adj* che si scandalizza facilmente

prune¹ [pruːn] n prugna f

prune² [pruːn] v/t *plant* potare; *fig* ridurre

pry [praɪ] v/i *(pret & pp -ied)* essere indiscreto

♦ **pry into** v/t ficcare il naso in

PS ['piːes] abbr *(= postscript)* P.S. *(= post scriptum m inv)*

pseu·do·nym ['sjuːdənɪm] pseudonimo m

psy·chi·at·ric [saɪkɪ'ætrɪk] *adj* psichiatrico

psy·chi·a·trist [saɪ'kaɪətrɪst] psichiatra m/f

psy·chi·a·try [saɪ'kaɪətrɪ] psichiatria f

psy·chic ['saɪkɪk] *adj* psichico; *I'm not* ~! non sono un indovino!

psy·cho·an·a·lyse [saɪkəʊ'ænəlaɪz] v/t psicanalizzare

psy·cho·a·nal·y·sis [saɪkəʊən'æləsɪs] psicanalisi f

psy·cho·an·a·lyst [saɪkəʊ'ænəlɪst] psicanalista m/f

psy·cho·log·i·cal [saɪkə'lɒdʒɪkl] *adj* psicologico

psy·cho·log·i·cal·ly [saɪkə'lɒdʒɪklɪ] *adv* psicologicamente

psy·chol·o·gist [saɪ'kɒlədʒɪst] psicologo m, -a f

psy·chol·o·gy [saɪ'kɒlədʒɪ] psicologia f

psy·cho·path ['saɪkəpæθ] psicopatico m, -a f

psy·cho·so·mat·ic [saɪkəʊsə'mætɪk] *adj* psicosomatico

PT [piː'tiː] abbr *(= physical training)* educazione f fisica

PTO [piːtiː'əʊ] abbr *(= please turn over)* vedi retro

pub [pʌb] pub m inv

pu·ber·ty ['pjuːbətɪ] pubertà f inv

pu·bic hair [pjuː'bɪk'heə(r)] peli mpl del pube

pub·lic ['pʌblɪk] **1** *adj* pubblico **2** n: **the** ~ il pubblico; **in** ~ in pubblico

pub·li·ca·tion [pʌblɪ'keɪʃn] pubblicazione f

pub·lic 'hol·i·day giorno m festivo

pub·lic·i·ty [pʌb'lɪsətɪ] pubblicità f inv

pub·li·cize ['pʌblɪsaɪz] v/t *make known* far sapere in giro; COM reclamizzare

pub·lic 'li·bra·ry biblioteca f pubblica

pub·lic lim·it·ed 'com·pa·ny società f inv a responsabilità limitata quotata in borsa

pub·lic·ly ['pʌblɪklɪ] *adv* pubblicamente

pub·lic 'pros·e·cu·tor *pubblico ministero* m; **pub·lic re'la·tions** npl relazioni fpl pubbliche; **'pub·lic school** Br scuola f privata; **'pub·lic sec·tor** settore m pubblico; **pub·lic 'trans·port** mezzi mpl pubblici

pub·lish ['pʌblɪʃ] v/t pubblicare

pub·lish·er ['pʌblɪʃə(r)] editore m

pub·lish·ing ['pʌblɪʃɪŋ] editoria f

'pub·lish·ing com·pa·ny casa f editrice

pud·ding ['pʊdɪŋ] *dish* budino m; *part of meal* dolce m

pud·dle ['pʌdl] n pozzanghera f

puff [pʌf] **1** n *of wind, smoke* soffio m **2** v/i (*pant*) ansimare; **~ on a cigarette** tirare boccate da una sigaretta

puff·y ['pʌfɪ] adj *eyes, face* gonfio

puke [pjuːk] v/i F vomitare

pull [pʊl] **1** n *on rope* tirata f; F (*appeal*) attrattiva f; F (*influence*) influenza f **2** v/t (*drag*) tirare; (*tug*) dare uno strappo a; *tooth* togliere **3** v/i tirare; **~ a muscle** farsi uno strappo muscolare

♦ **pull ahead** v/i *in race, competition* portarsi in testa

♦ **pull apart** v/t (*separate*) separare

♦ **pull away** v/t spostare

♦ **pull down** v/t (*lower*) tirar giù; (*demolish*) demolire

♦ **pull in** v/i *of bus, train* arrivare

♦ **pull off** v/t togliere; F *deal etc* portare a termine

♦ **pull out 1** v/t tirar fuori; *troops* (far) ritirare **2** v/i *of agreement, competition*, MIL ritirarsi; *of ship* partire

♦ **pull over** v/i *of driver* accostarsi

♦ **pull through** v/i *from an illness* farcela F

♦ **pull together 1** v/i (*cooperate*) cooperare **2** v/t: **pull o.s. together** darsi una mossa F

♦ **pull up 1** v/t (*raise*) tirar su; *plant, weeds* strappare **2** v/i *of car etc* fermarsi

pul·ley ['pʊlɪ] puleggia f

pull·o·ver ['pʊləʊvə(r)] pullover m inv

pulp [pʌlp] *soft mass* poltiglia f; *of fruit* polpa f; *for paper-making* pasta f

pul·pit ['pʊlpɪt] pulpito m

pul·sate [pʌl'seɪt] v/i *of heart, blood* pulsare; *of rhythm* vibrare

pulse [pʌls] polso m

pul·ver·ize ['pʌlvəraɪz] v/t polverizzare

pump [pʌmp] **1** n pompa f **2** v/t pompare

♦ **pump up** v/t gonfiare

pump·kin ['pʌmpkɪn] zucca f

pun [pʌn] gioco m di parole

punch [pʌntʃ] **1** n *blow* pugno m; *implement* punzonatrice f **2** v/t *with fist* dare un pugno a; *hole* perforare; *ticket* forare

'punch line finale m

punc·tu·al ['pʌŋktjʊəl] adj puntuale

punc·tu·al·i·ty [pʌŋktjʊ'ælətɪ] puntualità f inv

punc·tu·al·ly ['pʌŋktjʊəlɪ] adv puntualmente

punc·tu·ate ['pʌŋktjʊeɪt] v/t mettere la punteggiatura in

punc·tu·a·tion ['pʌŋktjʊ'eɪʃn] punteggiatura f

punc·tu·a·tion mark segno m d'interpunzione

punc·ture ['pʌŋktʃə(r)] **1** n foratura f **2** v/t forare

pun·gent ['pʌndʒənt] adj acre; *taste* aspro

pun·ish ['pʌnɪʃ] v/t *person* punire

pun·ish·ing ['pʌnɪʃɪŋ] adj *pace, schedule* estenuante

pun·ish·ment ['pʌnɪʃmənt] punizione f

punk (rock) ['pʌŋkrɒk] MUS punk m inv

pu·ny ['pjuːnɪ] adj *person* gracile

pup [pʌp] cucciolo m

pu·pil[1] ['pjuːpl] *of eye* pupilla f

pu·pil[2] ['pjuːpl] (*student*) allievo m, -a f

pup·pet ['pʌpɪt] burattino m; *with strings* marionetta f

'pup·pet gov·ern·ment governo m fantoccio

pup·py ['pʌpɪ] cucciolo m

pur·chase[1] ['pɜːtʃəs] **1** n acquisto m **2** v/t acquistare

pur·chase[2] ['pɜːtʃəs] (*grip*) presa f

pur·chas·er ['pɜːtʃəsə(r)] acquirente m/f

pure [pjʊə(r)] adj puro; **~ new wool** pura lana f vergine

pure·ly ['pjʊəlɪ] adv puramente

pur·ga·to·ry ['pɜːgətrɪ] purgatorio *m*

purge [pɜːdʒ] **1** *n of political party* epurazione *f* **2** *v/t* epurare

pu·ri·fy ['pjʊərɪfaɪ] *v/t* (*pret & pp -ied*) water purificare

pu·ri·tan ['pjʊərɪtən] puritano *m*, -a *f*

pu·ri·tan·i·cal [pjʊərɪ'tænɪkl] *adj* puritano

pu·ri·ty ['pjʊərɪtɪ] purezza *f*

pur·ple ['pɜːpl] *adj* viola *inv*

pur·pose ['pɜːpəs] (*aim, object*) scopo *m*; **on** ~ di proposito

pur·pose·ful ['pɜːpəsfʊl] *adj* risoluto

pur·pose·ly ['pɜːpəslɪ] *adv* di proposito

purr [pɜː(r)] *v/i of cat* far le fusa

purse [pɜːs] *n for money* borsellino *m*; *Am* (*handbag*) borsetta *f*

pur·sue [pə'sjuː] *v/t person* inseguire; *career* intraprendere; *course of action* proseguire

pur·su·er [pə'sjuːə(r)] inseguitore *m*, -trice *f*

pur·suit [pə'sjuːt] (*chase*) inseguimento *m*; *of happiness etc* ricerca *f*; *activity* occupazione *f*; *those in* ~ gli inseguitori

pus [pʌs] pus *m inv*

push [pʊʃ] **1** *n* (*shove*) spinta *f*; *at the* ~ *of a button* premendo un pulsante **2** *v/t* (*shove*) spingere; *button* premere; (*pressurize*) fare pressioni su; F *drugs* spacciare; *be ~ed for* F essere a corto di; *be ~ing 40* F essere sulla quarantina **3** *v/i* spingere

♦ **push ahead** *v/i* andare avanti

♦ **push along** *v/t cart etc* spingere

♦ **push away** *v/t* respingere

♦ **push off 1** *v/t lid* spingere via **2** *v/i* F (*leave*) andarsene; **push off!** sparisci! F

♦ **push on** *v/i* (*continue*) continuare

♦ **push up** *v/t prices* far salire

push-but·ton ['pʊʃbʌtn] *adj* a tastiera

'**push·chair** passeggino *m*

push·er ['pʊʃə(r)] F *of drugs* spacciatore *m*, -trice *f*

push-up ['pʊʃʌp] flessione *f* sulle braccia

push·y ['pʊʃɪ] *adj* F troppo intraprendente

puss, pus·sy (**cat**) [pʊs, 'pʊsɪ (kæt)] F micio *m*, -a *f*

♦ **pus·sy·foot about** ['pʊsɪfʊt] *v/i* F tentennare

put [pʊt] *v/t* (*pret & pp put*) mettere; *question* porre; ~ *the cost at ...* stimare il costo intorno a ...

♦ **put across** *v/t ideas etc* trasmettere

♦ **put aside** *v/t* mettere da parte

♦ **put away** *v/t in cupboard etc* mettere via; *in institution* rinchiudere; (*consume*) far fuori; *money* mettere da parte

♦ **put back** *v/t* (*replace*) rimettere a posto

♦ **put by** *v/t money* mettere da parte

♦ **put down** *v/t* mettere giù; *deposit* versare; *rebellion* reprimere; *animal* abbattere; (*belittle*) sminuire; *in writing* scrivere; *put one's foot down in car* accelerare; (*be firm*) farsi valere; *put X down to Y* (*attribute*) attribuire X a Y

♦ **put forward** *v/t idea etc* avanzare

♦ **put in** *v/t* inserire; *overtime* fare; *time, effort* dedicare; *request, claim* presentare

♦ **put in for** *v/t* (*apply for*) fare domanda per

♦ **put off** *v/t light, radio, TV* spegnere; (*postpone*) rimandare; (*deter*) scoraggiare; (*repel*) disgustare; *the accident put me off driving* l'incidente mi ha fatto passare la voglia di guidare

♦ **put on** *v/t light, radio, TV* accendere; *tape, music* mettere su; *jacket, shoes, glasses* mettersi; *makeup* mettere; (*perform*) mettere in scena; (*assume*) affettare; *put on the brakes* frenare; *put on weight* ingrassare; *she's just putting it on* sta solo fingendo

♦ **put out** *v/t hand* allungare; *fire, light* spegnere

♦ **put through** *v/t*: *I'll put you through* (*to him*) glielo passo; *I'll put you through to sales* le passo l'ufficio vendite

P

♦ **put together** v/t (assemble) montare; (organize) organizzare

♦ **put up** v/t hand alzare; person ospitare; (erect) costruire; prices aumentare; poster, notice affiggere; money fornire; **put up for sale** mettere in vendita

♦ **put up with** v/t (tolerate) sopportare

putt [pʌt] v/t & v/i SP pattare

put·ty ['pʌtɪ] mastice m

puz·zle ['pʌzl] **1** n (mystery) mistero m; game rebus m inv; jigsaw puzzle m inv; crossword cruciverba m inv **2** v/t lasciar perplesso

puz·zling ['pʌzlɪŋ] adj inspiegabile

PVC [piːviːˈsiː] abbr (= **polyvinyl chloride**) PVC m inv (= polivinilcloruro m)

py·ja·mas [pəˈdʒɑːməz] npl pigiama m

py·lon ['paɪlən] pilone m

Q

quack¹ [kwæk] **1** n of duck qua qua m inv **2** v/i fare qua qua

quack² [kwæk] F (bad doctor) ciarlatano m, -a f; **I'm going to see the ~** vado dal dottore

quad·ran·gle ['kwɒdræŋgl] figure quadrilatero m; courtyard cortile m

quad·ru·ped ['kwɒdrʊped] quadrupede m

quad·ru·ple ['kwɒdrʊpl] v/i quadruplicare

quad·ru·plets ['kwɒdrʊplɪts] npl quattro gemelli mpl

quads [kwɒdz] npl F quattro gemelli mpl

quag·mire ['kwɒgmaɪə(r)] fig ginepraio m

quail [kweɪl] v/i perdersi d'animo

quaint [kweɪnt] adj pretty pittoresco; slightly eccentric: ideas etc curioso

quake [kweɪk] **1** n (earthquake) terremoto m **2** v/i also fig tremare

qual·i·fi·ca·tion [kwɒlɪfɪˈkeɪʃn] from university etc titolo m di studio; of remark etc riserva f; **have the right ~s for a job** skills avere tutti i requisiti per un lavoro

qual·i·fied ['kwɒlɪfaɪd] adj doctor, engineer etc abilitato; (restricted) con riserva; **I am not ~ to judge** non sono in grado di valutare

qual·i·fy ['kwɒlɪfaɪ] (pret & pp **-ied**) **1** v/t of degree, course etc abilitare; remark etc precisare **2** v/i (get certificate etc) ottenere la qualifica (**as** di); in competition qualificarsi; **our team has qualified for the semi-final** la nostra squadra è entrata in semifinale; **that doesn't ~ as ...** non può essere considerato ...

qual·i·ty ['kwɒlɪtɪ] qualità f inv

qual·i·ty con'trol controllo m (di) qualità

qualm [kwɑːm]: **have no ~s about ...** non aver scrupoli a ...

quan·da·ry ['kwɒndərɪ] n dilemma m; **be in a ~** avere un dilemma

quan·ti·fy ['kwɒntɪfaɪ] v/t (pret & pp **-ied**) quantificare

quan·ti·ty ['kwɒntətɪ] quantità f inv

quan·tum 'phys·ics ['kwɒntəm] teoria f fisica dei quanti

quar·an·tine ['kwɒrəntiːn] n quarantena f

quar·rel ['kwɒrəl] **1** n litigio m **2** v/i (pret & pp **-led**, Am **-ed**) litigare

quar·rel·some ['kwɒrəlsʌm] adj litigioso

quar·ry¹ ['kwɒrɪ] in hunt preda f

quar·ry² ['kwɒrɪ] for mining cava f

quart [kwɔːt] quarto m di gallone

quar·ter ['kwɔːtə(r)] **1** n quarto m;

part of town quartiere *m*; **a ~ of an hour** un quarto d'ora; (**a**) **~ to 5** le cinque meno un quarto; (**a**) **~ past 5** le cinque e un quarto **2** *v/t* dividere in quattro parti

quar·ter·'fi·nal partita *f* dei quarti *mpl* di finale

quar·ter·'fi·nal·ist concorrente *m/f* dei quarti di finale

quar·ter·ly ['kwɔ:təlɪ] **1** *adj* trimestrale **2** *adv* trimestralmente

quar·ters ['kwɔ:təz] *npl* MIL quartieri *mpl*

quar·tet [kwɔ:'tet] MUS quartetto *m*

quartz [kwɔ:ts] quarzo *m*

quash [kwɒʃ] *v/t rebellion* reprimere; *court decision* annullare

qua·ver ['kweɪvə(r)] **1** *n in voice* tremolio *m*; MUS croma *f* **2** *v/i of voice* tremolare

quay [ki:] banchina *f*

'quay·side banchina *f*

quea·sy ['kwi:zɪ] *adj* nauseato

queen [kwi:n] regina *f*

queen 'bee ape *f* regina

queer [kwɪə(r)] *adj* (*peculiar*) strano

queer·ly ['kwɪə(r)lɪ] *adv* stranamente

quell [kwel] *v/t* soffocare

quench [kwentʃ] *v/t also fig* spegnere

que·ry ['kwɪərɪ] **1** *n* interrogativo *m* **2** *v/t* (*pret & pp* **-ied**) *express doubt about* contestare; *check* controllare

quest [kwest] *n* ricerca *f*

ques·tion ['kwestʃn] **1** *n* domanda *f*; *matter* questione *f*; **in ~** (*being talked about*) in questione; (*in doubt*) in dubbio; **it's a ~ of money / time** è questione di soldi / tempo; **that's out of the ~** è fuori discussione **2** *v/t person* interrogare; (*doubt*) dubitare di; **that's not being ~ed** nessuno lo mette in dubbio

ques·tion·a·ble ['kwestʃnəbl] *adj* discutibile; (*dubious*) dubbio

ques·tion·er ['kwestʃnə(r)] *n* interrogatore *m*, -trice *f*

ques·tion·ing ['kwestʃnɪŋ] **1** *adj look, tone* interrogativo **2** *n* interrogatorio *m*

'ques·tion mark punto *m* interrogativo

'ques·tion mas·ter presentatore *m*, -trice *f* di quiz

ques·tion·naire [kwestʃə'neə(r)] *n* questionario *m*

queue [kju:] **1** *n* coda *f*, fila *f* **2** *v/i* fare la fila *o* la coda

queue-jump·er ['kju:dʒʌmpə(r)] persona *f* che non rispetta la coda

quib·ble ['kwɪbl] *v/i* cavillare

quick [kwɪk] *adj person* svelto; *reply, change* veloce; **be ~!** fai presto!, fai in fretta!; **let's have a ~ drink** beviamo qualcosa?; **can I have a ~ look?** posso dare un'occhiatina?; **that was ~!** già fatto?

quick·ie ['kwɪkɪ] F: **have a ~** *quick drink* bere qualcosa

quick·ly ['kwɪklɪ] *adv* rapidamente, in fretta

'quick·sand sabbie *fpl* mobili; **'quick·sil·ver** mercurio *m*; **quick·wit·ted** [kwɪk'wɪtɪd] *adj* sveglio

quid [kwɪd] F sterlina *f*; **50 ~** 50 sterline

qui·et ['kwaɪət] *adj voice, music* basso; *engine* silenzioso; *street, life, town* tranquillo; **keep ~ about sth** tenere segreto qc; **~!** silenzio!, stai zitto!

♦ **quieten down** ['kwaɪətn] **1** *v/t* calmare **2** *v/i* calmarsi

quiet·ly ['kwaɪətlɪ] *adv not loudly* silenziosamente, senza far rumore; (*without fuss*) semplicemente; (*peacefully*) tranquillamente

quiet·ness ['kwaɪətnɪs] *of night, street* tranquillità *f*, calma *f*; *of voice* dolcezza *f*

quilt [kwɪlt] *on bed* piumino *m*

quilt·ed ['kwɪltɪd] *adj* trapuntato

quin·ine ['kwɪni:n] chinino *m*

quin·tet [kwɪn'tet] MUS quintetto *m*

quip [kwɪp] **1** *n* battuta *f* (di spirito) **2** *v/i* (*pret & pp* **-ped**) scherzare

quirk [kwɜ:k] bizzarria *f*

quirk·y ['kwɜ:kɪ] *adj* bizzarro

quit [kwɪt] (*pret & pp* **quit**) **1** *v/t job* mollare F; **~ doing sth** smettere di fare qc **2** *v/i* (*leave job*) licenziarsi;

Q

COMPUT uscire; *get one's notice to ~ from landlord* ricevere la disdetta

quite [kwaɪt] *adv* (*fairly*) abbastanza; (*completely*) completamente; *not ~ ready* non ancora pronto; *I didn't ~ understand* non ho capito bene; *is that right? – not ~* giusto? – non esattamente; *~!* esatto!; *~ a lot drink, change* parecchio; *~ a lot better* molto meglio; *~ a few* un bel po'; *it was ~ a surprise / change* è stata una bella sorpresa / un bel cambiamento

quits [kwɪts] *adj*: *be ~ with s.o.* essere pari con qu

quit·ter ['kwɪtə(r)] F rinunciatario *m*, -a *f*

quiv·er ['kwɪvə(r)] *v/i* tremare

quiz [kwɪz] **1** *n* quiz *m inv* **2** *v/t* (*pret & pp -zed*) interrogare

'**quiz mas·ter** conduttore *m*, -trice *f* (di gioco a quiz)

'**quiz pro·gram** *Am*, '**quiz programme** gioco *m* a quiz

quo·ta ['kwəʊtə] quota *f*

quo·ta·tion [kwəʊ'teɪʃn] *from author* citazione *f*; *price* preventivo *m*; *give s.o. a ~ for sth* fare un preventivo a qu per qc

quo·ta·tion marks *npl* virgolette *fpl*

quote [kwəʊt] **1** *n from author* citazione *f*; *price* preventivo *m*; (*quotation mark*) virgoletta *f*; *in ~s* tra virgolette **2** *v/t* citare; *price* stimare; *~d on the Stock Exchange* quotato in Borsa **3** *v/i*: *~ from an author* citare un autore

R

rab·bi ['ræbaɪ] rabbino *m*

rab·bit ['ræbɪt] coniglio *m*

♦ **rab·bit on** *v/i* P blaterare

rab·ble ['ræbl] marmaglia *f*

rab·ble-rous·er ['ræblraʊzə(r)] agitatore *m*, -trice *f*

ra·bies ['reɪbiːz] *nsg* rabbia *f*, idrofobia *f*

race[1] [reɪs] *n of people* razza *f*

race[2] [reɪs] **1** *n* SP gara *f*; *the ~s* (*horse races*) le corse **2** *v/i* (*run fast*) correre; *he ~d against the world champion* ha gareggiato contro il campione del mondo **3** *v/t*: *I'll ~ you* facciamo una gara

'**race·course** ippodromo *m*; '**race·horse** cavallo *m* da corsa; '**race re·la·tions** *npl* rapporti *mpl* interrazziali; '**race riot** scontri *mpl* razziali; '**race·track** pista *f*; *for horses* ippodromo *m*

ra·cial ['reɪʃl] *adj* razziale; *~ equality* parità *f inv* razziale

rac·ing ['reɪsɪŋ] corse *fpl*

'**rac·ing car** auto *f inv* da corsa

'**rac·ing driv·er** pilota *m* automobilistico

ra·cis·m ['reɪsɪzm] razzismo *m*

ra·cist ['reɪsɪst] **1** *n* razzista *m/f* **2** *adj* razzista

rack [ræk] **1** *n for parking bikes* rastrelliera *f*; *for bags on train* portabagagli *m inv*; *for CDs* porta-CD *m inv* **2** *v/t*: *~ one's brains* scervellarsi

rack·et[1] ['rækɪt] SP racchetta *f*

rack·et[2] ['rækɪt] (*noise*) baccano *m*; *criminal activity* racket *m inv*

ra·dar ['reɪdɑː(r)] radar *m inv*

'**ra·dar screen** schermo *m* radar

'**ra·dar trap** autovelox® *m*

ra·di·al '*tire* *Am*, **ra·di·al** '*tyre* ['reɪdɪəl] pneumatico *m* radiale

ra·di·ance ['reɪdɪəns] splendore *m*

ra·di·ant ['reɪdɪənt] *adj smile* splendente; *appearance* raggiante

ra·di·ate ['reɪdɪeɪt] v/i *of heat, light* diffondersi

ra·di·a·tion [reɪdɪ'eɪʃn] PHYS radiazione *f*

ra·di·a·tor ['reɪdɪeɪtə(r)] *in room* termosifone *m*; *in car* radiatore *m*

rad·i·cal ['rædɪkl] **1** *adj* radicale **2** *n* radicale *m/f*

rad·i·cal·ism ['rædɪkəlɪzm] POL radicalismo *m*

rad·i·cal·ly ['rædɪklɪ] *adv* radicalmente

ra·di·o ['reɪdɪəʊ] radio *f inv*; **on the ~** alla radio; **by ~** via radio

ra·di·o·ac·tive [reɪdɪəʊ'æktɪv] *adj* radioattivo; **ra·di·o·ac·tive 'waste** scorie *fpl* radioattive; **ra·di·o·ac·tiv·i·ty** [reɪdɪəʊæk'tɪvətɪ] radioattività *f inv*; **ra·di·o a'larm** radiosveglia *f*

ra·di·og·ra·pher [reɪdɪ'ɒgrəfə(r)] radiologo *m*, -a *f*

ra·di·og·ra·phy [reɪdɪ'ɒgrəfɪ] radiografia *f*

'ra·di·o sta·tion stazione *f* radiofonica, radio *f inv*; **'ra·di·o tax·i** radiotaxi *m inv*; **ra·di·o'ther·a·py** radioterapia *f*

rad·ish ['rædɪʃ] *n* ravanello *m*

ra·di·us ['reɪdɪəs] *n* raggio *m*

raf·fle ['ræfl] *n* lotteria *f*

raft [rɑːft] *n* zattera *f*

raf·ter ['rɑːftə(r)] travicello *m*

rag [ræg] *n for cleaning etc* straccio *m*; **dressed in ~s** vestito di stracci

rage [reɪdʒ] **1** *n* rabbia *f*, collera *f*; **be in a ~** essere furioso; **be all the ~** F essere di moda **2** *v/i of person* infierire; *of storm* infuriare

rag·ged ['rægɪd] *adj* stracciato

raid [reɪd] **1** *n* raid *m inv* **2** *v/t of police, robbers* fare un raid in; *fridge, orchard* fare razzia in

raid·er ['reɪdə(r)] *on bank etc* rapinatore *m*, -trice *f*

rail [reɪl] *n on track* rotaia *f*; (*hand~*) corrimano *m*; (*barrier*) parapetto *m*; **curtain ~** bastone *m* per tende; **towel ~** portasciugamano *m inv*; **by ~** in treno

rail·ings ['reɪlɪŋz] *npl around park*

etc inferriata *f*

'rail·road railway → **railway** *etc*

rail·way ['reɪlweɪ] ferrovia *f*

'rail·way line linea *f* ferroviaria

'rail·way sta·tion stazione *f* ferroviaria

rain [reɪn] **1** *n* pioggia *f*; **in the ~** sotto la pioggia **2** *v/i* piovere; **it's ~ing** sta piovendo

'rain·bow arcobaleno *m*; **'rain·coat** impermeabile *m*; **'rain·drop** goccia *f* di pioggia; **'rain·fall** piovosità *f inv*; **'rain for·est** foresta *f* pluviale; **'rain·proof** *adj fabric* impermeabile; **'rain·storm** temporale *m*

rain·y ['reɪnɪ] *adj day* di pioggia; *weather* piovoso; **it's ~** piove molto

raise [reɪz] **1** *n esp Am: in salary* aumento *m* **2** *v/t shelf, question* sollevare; *offer* aumentare; *children* allevare; *money* raccogliere

rai·sin ['reɪzn] uva *f* passa

rake [reɪk] *n for garden* rastrello *m*

♦ **rake up** *v/t leaves* rastrellare; *fig* rivangare

ral·ly ['rælɪ] *n meeting* raduno *m*; MOT rally *m inv*; *in tennis* scambio *m*

♦ **rally round** (*pret & pp* **-ied**) *v/i* offrire aiuto **2** *v/t*: **rally round s.o.** aiutare qu

RAM [ræm] *abbr* COMPUT (= **random access memory**) RAM *f inv*

ram [ræm] **1** *n* montone *m* **2** *v/t* (*pret & pp* **-med**) *ship, car* sbattere contro

ram·ble ['ræmbl] **1** *n walk* escursione *f* **2** *v/i walk* fare passeggiate; *in speaking* divagare; *talk incoherently* vaneggiare

ram·bler ['ræmblə(r)] *walker* escursionista *m/f*

ram·bling ['ræmblɪŋ] *adj speech* sconnesso

ramp [ræmp] rampa *f*; *for raising vehicle* ponte *m* idraulico

ram·page ['ræmpeɪdʒ] **1** *v/i* scatenarsi **2** *n*: **go on the ~** scatenarsi

ram·pant ['ræmpənt] *adj inflation* dilagante

ram·part ['ræmpɑːt] bastione *m*

ram·shack·le [ˈræmʃækl] *adj* sgangherato

ran [ræn] *pret* → **run**

ranch [rɑ:nʃ] ranch *m inv*

ran·cid [ˈrænsɪd] *adj* rancido

ran·cour [ˈrænkə(r)] rancore *m*

R&D [ɑ:rənˈdi:] *abbr* (= **research and development**) ricerca *f* e sviluppo *m*

ran·dom [ˈrændəm] **1** *adj* casuale; ~ **sample** campione *m* casuale; **take a ~ sample** prendere un campione a caso **2** *n*: **at ~** a caso

ran·dy [ˈrændɪ] *adj* F arrapato

rang [ræŋ] *pret* → **ring**

range [reɪndʒ] **1** *n of products* gamma *f*; *of missile, gun* gittata *f*; *of salary* scala *f*; *of voice* estensione *f*; *of mountains* catena *f*; (*shooting ~*) poligono *m* (di tiro); **at close** ~ a distanza ravvicinata **2** *v/i*: ~ **from X to Y** variare da X a Y

rank [ræŋk] **1** *n* MIL grado *m*; *in society* rango *m*; **the ~s** MIL la truppa **2** *v/t* classificare

♦ **rank among** *v/t* classificarsi tra

ran·kle [ˈræŋkl] *v/i* bruciare

ran·sack [ˈrænsæk] *v/t* saccheggiare

ran·som [ˈrænsəm] *n* riscatto *m*; **hold s.o. to ~** tenere in ostaggio qu

ˈ**ran·som mon·ey** (soldi *mpl* del) riscatto *m*

rant [rænt] *v/i*: ~ **and rave** inveire

rap [ræp] **1** *n at door etc* colpo *m*; MUS rap *m inv* **2** *v/t* (*pret & pp* **-ped**) *table etc* battere

♦ **rap at** *v/t window etc* bussare a

rape[1] [reɪp] **1** *n* stupro *m* **2** *v/t* violentare

rape[2] [reɪp] *n* BOT colza *f*

ˈ**rape vic·tim** vittima *f* stupro

rap·id [ˈræpɪd] *adj* rapido

ra·pid·i·ty [rəˈpɪdətɪ] rapidità *f inv*

rap·id·ly [ˈræpɪdlɪ] *adv* rapidamente

rap·ids [ˈræpɪdz] *npl* rapide *fpl*

rap·ist [ˈreɪpɪst] violentatore *m*

rap·port [ræˈpɔ:(r)] rapporto *m*

rap·ture [ˈræpʃə(r)] *n*: **go into ~s over** andare in estasi per

rap·tur·ous [ˈræpʃərəs] *adj* entusiastico

rare [reə(r)] *adj* raro; *steak* al sangue

rare·ly [ˈreəlɪ] *adv* raramente

rar·i·ty [ˈreərətɪ] rarità *f inv*

ras·cal [ˈrɑ:skl] birbante *m/f*

rash[1] [ræʃ] *n* MED orticaria *f*

rash[2] [ræʃ] *adj action, behaviour* avventato

rash·er [ˈræʃə(r)] fettina *f*

rash·ly [ˈræʃlɪ] *adv* avventatamente

rasp·ber·ry [ˈrɑ:zbərɪ] lampone *m*

rat [ræt] *n* ratto *m*

rate [reɪt] **1** *n of exchange* tasso *m*; *of pay, pricing* tariffa *f*; (*speed*) ritmo *m*; ~ **of interest** FIN tasso *m* d'interesse; **at this ~** (*at this speed*) di questo passo; **at any ~** in ogni modo **2** *v/t* (*consider, rank*) reputare

rather [ˈrɑ:ðə(r)] *adv* piuttosto; **I would ~ stay here** preferirei stare qui; **or would you ~ ...?** o preferiresti ...?

rat·i·fi·ca·tion [rætɪfɪˈkeɪʃn] ratifica *f*

rat·i·fy [ˈrætɪfaɪ] *v/t* (*pret & pp* **-ied**) ratificare

rat·ings [ˈreɪtɪŋz] *npl* indice *m* d'ascolto

ra·ti·o [ˈreɪʃɪəʊ] proporzione *f*

ra·tion [ˈræʃn] **1** *n* razione *f* **2** *v/t supplies* razionare

ra·tion·al [ˈræʃənl] *adj* razionale

ra·tion·al·i·ty [ræʃəˈnælɪtɪ] razionalità *f inv*

ra·tion·al·i·za·tion [ræʃənəlaɪˈzeɪʃn] razionalizzazione *f*

ra·tion·al·ize [ˈræʃənəlaɪz] *v/t & v/i* razionalizzare

ra·tion·al·ly [ˈræʃənlɪ] *adv* razionalmente

ˈ**rat race** corsa *f* al successo

rat·tle [ˈrætl] **1** *n noise* rumore *m*; *toy* sonaglio *m* **2** *v/t* scuotere **3** *v/i* far rumore

♦ **rattle off** *v/t poem, list of names* snocciolare

♦ **rattle through** *v/t* fare di gran carriera

ˈ**rat·tle·snake** serpente *m* a sonagli

rau·cous [ˈrɔ:kəs] *adj* sguaiato

rav·age [ˈrævɪdʒ] **1** *n*: **the ~s of time** le ingiurie del tempo *v/t*: **~d by**

war devastato dalla guerra

rave [reɪv] **1** *v/i* delirare; **~ about sth** be very enthusiastic entusiasmarsi per qc **2** *n party* rave *m inv*

ra·ven ['reɪvn] corvo *m*

rav·e·nous ['rævənəs] *adj* famelico

rav·e·nous·ly ['rævənəslɪ] *adv* voracemente

rave re'view recensione *f* entusiastica

ra·vine [rə'viːn] burrone *m*

rav·ing ['reɪvɪŋ] *adv*: **~ mad** matto da legare

ra·vi·o·li ['rævɪəʊlɪ] *nsg* ravioli *mpl*

rav·ish·ing ['rævɪʃɪŋ] *adj* incantevole

raw [rɔː] *adj meat, vegetable* crudo; *sugar, iron* grezzo

raw ma'te·ri·al materia *f* prima

ray [reɪ] raggio *m*; **a ~ of hope** un raggio di speranza

raze [reɪz] *v/t*: **~ to the ground** radere al suolo

ra·zor ['reɪzə(r)] rasoio *m*

'**ra·zor blade** lametta *f* da barba

re [riː] *prep* COM con riferimento a

reach [riːtʃ] **1** *n*: *within* **~** vicino (*of* a); *within arm's reach* a portata (di mano); *out of* **~** non a portata (di di); *keep out of* **~** *of children* tenere lontano dalla portata dei bambini **2** *v/t city etc* arrivare a; *decision, agreement, conclusion* raggiungere; *can you* **~** *it?* ci arrivi?

♦ **reach out** *v/i* allungare la mano

re·act [rɪ'ækt] *v/i* reagire

re·ac·tion [rɪ'ækʃn] reazione *f*

re·ac·tion·a·ry [rɪ'ækʃnrɪ] **1** *n* POL reazionario *m*, -a *f* **2** *adj* POL reazionario

re·ac·tor [rɪ'æktə(r)] *nuclear* reattore *m*

read [riːd] (*pret & pp* **read** [red]) **1** *v/i* leggere; **~ to s.o.** leggere a qu **2** *v/t* leggere; (*study*) studiare

♦ **read out** *v/t aloud* leggere a voce alta

♦ **read up on** *v/t* documentarsi su

rea·da·ble ['riːdəbl] *adj handwriting* leggibile; *book* di piacevole lettura

read·er ['riːdə(r)] *person* lettore *m*, -trice *f*

read·i·ly ['redɪlɪ] *adv* (*willingly*) volentieri; (*easily*) facilmente

read·i·ness ['redɪnɪs] *for action* disponibilità *f inv*; *to agree* prontezza *f*

read·ing ['riːdɪŋ] *also from meter* lettura *f*

'**read·ing mat·ter** roba *f* da leggere

re·ad·just [riːə'dʒʌst] **1** *v/t equipment, controls* regolare **2** *v/i to conditions* riadattarsi

read-'on·ly file COMPUT file *m inv* di sola lettura

read-'on·ly mem·o·ry COMPUT memoria *f* di sola lettura

read·y ['redɪ] *adj* pronto; **get (o.s.)** **~** prepararsi; **get sth** **~** preparare qc

read·y 'cash contanti *mpl*; **read·y-made** *adj stew etc* precotto; *solution* bell'e pronto; **read·y-to-wear** *adj* confezionato

real [riːl] *adj* vero

'**real es·tate** proprietà *fpl* immobiliari

re·a·lis·m ['rɪəlɪzm] realismo *m*

re·a·list ['rɪəlɪst] realista *m/f*

re·a·lis·tic [rɪə'lɪstɪk] *adj* realistico

re·a·lis·tic·al·ly [rɪə'lɪstɪklɪ] *adv* realisticamente

re·al·i·ty [rɪ'ælətɪ] realtà *f inv*

re·a·li·za·tion [rɪəlaɪ'zeɪʃn] realizzazione *f*

re·a·lize ['rɪəlaɪz] *v/t* rendersi conto di, realizzare; FIN realizzare; *I – now that ...* ora capisco che ...

real·ly ['rɪəlɪ] *adv* veramente; **~?** davvero?; *not* **~** (*not much*) non proprio

real 'time *n* COMPUT tempo *m* reale

real-time *adj* COMPUT in tempo reale

reap [riːp] *v/t* mietere

re·ap·pear [riːə'pɪər] *v/i* riapparire

reappearance [riːə'pɪərəns] ricomparsa *f*

rear [rɪə(r)] **1** *n of building* retro *m*; *of train* parte *f* posteriore **2** *adj* posteriore

rear 'end F *of person* posteriore *m*

rear-'end *v/t*: **be ~ed** F essere tamponato

R

rear 'light *of car* fanalino *m* posteriore

re·arm [riː'ɑːm] **1** *v/t* riarmare **2** *v/i* riarmarsi

'rear·most *adj* ultimo

re·ar·range [riːə'reɪnʒ] *v/t furniture* spostare; *schedule* cambiare

rear-view 'mir·ror specchietto *m* retrovisore

rea·son ['riːzn] **1** *n faculty* ragione *f*; *(cause)* motivo *m*; *see / listen to ~* ascoltare ragione **2** *v/i*: *~ with s.o.* far ragionare con qu

rea·so·na·ble ['riːznəbl] *adj person, price* ragionevole; *weather, health* discreto; *a ~ number of people* un discreto numero di persone

rea·son·a·bly ['riːznəblɪ] *adv act, behave* ragionevolmente; *(quite)* abbastanza

rea·son·ing ['riːznɪŋ] ragionamento *m*

re·as·sure [riːə'ʃʊə(r)] *v/t* rassicurare

re·as·sur·ing [riːə'ʃʊərɪŋ] *adj* rassicurante

re·bate ['riːbeɪt] *money back* rimborso *m*

reb·el ['rebl] **1** *n* ribelle *m/f*; *~ forces* forze *fpl* ribelli **2** *v/i* [rɪ'bel] *(pret & pp -led)* ribellarsi

reb·el·lion [rɪ'belɪən] ribellione *f*

reb·el·lious [rɪ'belɪəs] *adj* ribelle

reb·el·lious·ly [rɪ'belɪəslɪ] *adv* con atteggiamento ribelle

reb·el·lious·ness [rɪ'belɪəsnɪs] spirito *m* di ribellione

re·boot [riː'buːt] *v/t & v/i* COMPUT riavviare

re·bound [rɪ'baʊnd] *v/i of ball etc* rimbalzare

re·buff [rɪ'bʌf] *n* secco rifiuto *m*

re·build ['riːbɪld] *v/t (pret & pp -built)* ricostruire

re·buke [rɪ'bjuːk] *v/t* rimproverare

re·call [rɪ'kɔːl] *v/t* richiamare; *(remember)* ricordare

re·cap ['riːkæp] *v/i (pret & pp -ped)* F ricapitolare

re·cap·ture [riː'kæptʃə(r)] *v/t criminal* ricatturare; *town* riconquistare

re·cede [rɪ'siːd] *v/i of flood waters* abbassarsi

re·ced·ing [rɪ'siːdɪŋ] *adj forehead, chin* sfuggente; *have a ~ hairline* essere stempiato

re·ceipt [rɪ'siːt] *for purchase* ricevuta *f*, scontrino *m*; *acknowledge ~ of sth* accusare ricevuta di qc; *~s* FIN introiti *mpl*

re·ceive [rɪ'siːv] *v/t* ricevere

re·ceiv·er [rɪ'siːvə(r)] *of letter* destinatario *m*, -a *f*; TELEC ricevitore *m*; *radio* apparecchio *m* ricevente

re·ceiv·er·ship [rɪ'siːvəʃɪp]: *be in ~* essere in amministrazione controllata

re·cent ['riːsnt] *adj* recente

re·cent·ly ['riːsntlɪ] *adv* recentemente

re·cep·tion [rɪ'sepʃn] *in hotel, company* reception *f inv*; *formal party* ricevimento *m*; *(welcome)* accoglienza *f*; *on radio, mobile phone* ricezione *f*

re·cep·tion desk banco *m* della reception

re·cep·tion·ist [rɪ'sepʃnɪst] receptionist *m/f inv*

re·cep·tive [rɪ'septɪv] *adj*: *be ~ to sth* essere ricettivo verso qc

re·cess ['riːses] *in wall etc* rientranza *f*; *of parliament* vacanza *f*

re·ces·sion [rɪ'seʃn] *economic* recessione *f*

re·charge [riː'tʃɑːdʒ] *v/t battery* ricaricare

re·ci·pe ['resəpɪ] ricetta *f*

're·ci·pe book ricettario *m*

re·cip·i·ent [rɪ'sɪpɪənt] destinatario *m*, -a *f*

re·cip·ro·cal [rɪ'sɪprəkl] *adj* reciproco

re·cit·al [rɪ'saɪtl] MUS recital *m inv*

re·cite [rɪ'saɪt] *v/t poem* recitare; *details, facts* enumerare

reck·less ['reklɪs] *adj* spericolato

reck·less·ly ['reklɪslɪ] *adv behave, drive* in modo spericolato; *spend* avventatamente

reck·on ['rekən] *v/i (think, consider)* pensare

♦ **reckon on** v/t contare su

♦ **reckon with** v/t: **have s.o./sth to reakon with** dover fare i conti con qu/qc

reck·on·ing ['rekəniŋ] calcoli mpl

re·claim [rɪ'kleɪm] v/t land bonificare

re·cline [rɪ'klaɪn] v/i sdraiarsi

re·clin·er [rɪ'klaɪnə(r)] chair poltrona f reclinabile

re·cluse [rɪ'kluːs] eremita m/f

rec·og·ni·tion [rekəg'nɪʃn] of state, s.o.'s achievements riconoscimento m; **have changed beyond ~** essere irriconoscibile

rec·og·niz·a·ble [rekəg'naɪzəbl] adj riconoscibile

rec·og·nize ['rekəgnaɪz] v/t riconoscere; **it can be ~d by ...** si riconosce da ...

re·coil [rɪ'kɔɪl] v/i indietreggiare

rec·ol·lect [rekə'lekt] v/t rammentare

rec·ol·lec·tion [rekə'lekʃn] ricordo m

rec·om·mend [rekə'mend] v/t consigliare

rec·om·men·da·tion [rekəmen'deɪʃn] consiglio m

rec·om·pense ['rekəmpens] n fml ricompensa f; LAW risarcimento m

rec·on·cile ['rekənsaɪl] v/t people, differences riconciliare; facts conciliare; **~ o.s. to ...** rassegnarsi a ...; **they are now ~d** si sono riconciliati

rec·on·cil·i·a·tion [rekənsɪlɪ'eɪʃn] of people, differences riconciliazione f; of facts conciliazione f

re·con·di·tion [riːkən'dɪʃn] v/t ricondizionare

re·con·nais·sance [rɪ'kɒnɪsns] MIL ricognizione f

re·con·sid·er [riːkən'sɪdə(r)] **1** v/t offer, one's position riconsiderare **2** v/i ripensare

re·con·struct [riːkən'strʌkt] v/t city, crime, life ricostruire

rec·ord¹ ['rekɔːd] n MUS disco m; SP etc record m inv, primato m; written document etc nota f; in database record m inv; **~s** archivio m; **say sth off the ~** dire qc ufficialmente;

have a criminal ~ avere precedenti penali; **he has a good ~ for punctuality/reliability** è sempre stato puntuale/affidabile

record² [rɪ'kɔːd] v/t electronically registrare; in writing annotare

'rec·ord-break·ing adj da record

re·cor·der [rɪ'kɔːdə(r)] MUS flauto m dolce

'rec·ord hold·er primatista m/f

re·cord·ing [rɪ'kɔːdɪŋ] registrazione f

re'cord·ing stu·di·o sala f di registrazione

rec·ord play·er ['rekɔːd] giradischi m inv

re·count [rɪ'kaʊnt] v/t (tell) raccontare

re-count ['riːkaʊnt] **1** n of votes nuovo conteggio m **2** v/t (count again) ricontare

re·coup [rɪ'kuːp] v/t financial losses rifarsi di

re·cov·er [rɪ'kʌvə(r)] **1** v/t stolen goods recuperare **2** v/i from illness rimettersi

re·cov·er·y [rɪ'kʌvərɪ] of stolen goods recupero m; from illness guarigione f; **he has made a speedy ~** è guarito in fretta

rec·re·a·tion [rekrɪ'eɪʃn] ricreazione f

rec·re·a·tion·al [rekrɪ'eɪʃnl] adj done for pleasure ricreativo

re·cruit [rɪ'kruːt] **1** n MIL recluta f; to company neoassunto m, -a f **2** v/t new staff assumere; members arruolare

re·cruit·ment [rɪ'kruːtmənt] assunzione f; MIL, POL reclutamento m

re'cruit·ment drive campagna f di arruolamento

rec·tan·gle ['rektæŋgl] rettangolo m

rec·tan·gu·lar [rek'tæŋgjʊlə(r)] adj rettangolare

rec·ti·fy ['rektɪfaɪ] v/t (pret & pp -ied) (put right) rettificare

re·cu·pe·rate [rɪ'kjuːpəreɪt] v/i recuperare

re·cur [rɪ'kɜː(r)] (pret & pp -red) v/i

R

of error, event ripetersi; *of symptoms* ripresentarsi

re·cur·rent [rɪ'kʌrənt] *adj* ricorrente

re·cy·cla·ble [riː'saɪkləbl] *adj* riciclabile

re·cy·cle [riː'saɪkl] *v/t* riciclare

re·cy·cling [riː'saɪklɪŋ] riciclo *m*

red [red] *adj* rosso; *in the ~* FIN in rosso

Red 'Cross Croce *f* Rossa

red·den ['redn] *v/i* (*blush*) arrossire

re·dec·o·rate [riː'dekəreɪt] *v/t* ritinteggiare; *change wallpaper* ritapezzare

re·deem [rɪ'diːm] *v/t debt* estinguere; *sinners* redimere

re·deem·ing [rɪ'diːmɪŋ]: *~ feature* aspetto *m* positivo

re·demp·tion [rɪ'dempʃn] REL redenzione *f*

re·de·vel·op [riːdɪ'veləp] *v/t part of town* risanare

red-'hand·ed [red'hændɪd] *adj*: *catch s.o. ~* cogliere qu in flagrante; **'red·head** rosso *m*, -a *f*; **red-'hot** *adj* rovente; **red-'let·ter day** giorno *m* memorabile; **red 'light** *at traffic lights* rosso *m*; **red 'light dis·trict** quartiere *m* a luci rosse; **red 'meat** carni *fpl* rosse

re·dou·ble [riː'dʌbl] *v/t*: *~ one's efforts* intensificare gli sforzi

red 'pep·per peperone *m* rosso

re·duce [rɪ'djuːs] *v/t* ridurre

re·duc·tion [rɪ'dʌkʃn] riduzione *f*

re·dun·dan·cy [rɪ'dʌndənsɪ] *Br at work* licenziamento *m*

re'dun·dan·cy no·tice *Br* avviso *m* di licenziamento

re'dun·dan·cy pay·ment *Br* indennità *f inv* di licenziamento

re·dun·dant [rɪ'dʌndənt] *adj* (*unnecessary*) superfluo; *Br be made ~ at work* essere licenziato; *Br make s.o. ~* licenziare qu

reed [riːd] BOT canna *f*

reef [riːf] *in sea* scogliera *f*

'reef knot nodo *m* piano

reek [riːk] *v/i* puzzare; *~ of ...* puzzare di ...

reel [riːl] *n of film* rullino *m*; *of thread* rocchetto *m*; *of tape* bobina *f*; *of fishing line* mulinello *m*

♦ **reel off** *v/t* snocciolare

re-e·lect *v/t* rieleggere

re-e·lec·tion rielezione *f*

re-'en·try *of spacecraft* rientro *m*

ref [ref] F arbitro *m*

re·fer [rɪ'fɜː(r)] (*pret & pp -red*): *~ a decision / problem to s.o.* rinviare una decisione / un problema a qu **2** *v/i*: *~ to ...* (*allude to*) riferirsi a ...; *dictionary etc* consultare ...

ref·er·ee [refə'riː] SP arbitro *m*; *for job* referenza *f*

ref·er·ence ['refərəns] (*allusion*) allusione *f*; *for job* referenza *f*; (*~ number*) (numero *m* di) riferimento *m*; *with ~ to* con riferimento a

'ref·er·ence book opera *f* di consultazione; **'ref·er·ence li·bra·ry** biblioteca *f* di consultazione; **'ref·er·ence num·ber** numero *m* di riferimento

ref·e·ren·dum [refə'rendəm] referendum *m inv*

re·fill ['riːfɪl] *v/t glass* riempire

re·fine [rɪ'faɪn] *v/t* raffinare

re·fined [rɪ'faɪnd] *adj manners, language* raffinato

re·fine·ment [rɪ'faɪnmənt] *to process, machine* miglioramento *m*

re·fin·e·ry [rɪ'faɪnərɪ] raffineria *f*

re·fla·tion ['riːfleɪʃn] reflazione *f*

reflect [rɪ'flekt] **1** *v/t light* riflettere; *be ~ed in ...* riflettersi in ... **2** *v/i* (*think*) riflettere

re·flec·tion [rɪ'flekʃn] *in water, glass etc* riflesso *m*; (*consideration*) riflessione *f*; *on ~* dopo aver riflettuto

re·flex ['riːfleks] *in body* riflesso *m*

re·flex re'ac·tion riflesso *m*

re·form [rɪ'fɔːm] **1** *n* riforma *f* **2** *v/t* riformare

re·form·er [rɪ'fɔːmə(r)] riformatore *m*, -trice *f*

re·frain¹ [rɪ'freɪn] *v/i fml*: *please ~ from smoking* si prega di non fumare

re·frain² [rɪ'freɪn] *n in song* ritornello *m*

re·fresh [rɪ'freʃ] *v/t person* ristorare; **feel ~ed** sentirsi ristorato

refresh·er course [rɪ'freʃə(r)] corso *m* di aggiornamento

re·fresh·ing [rɪ'freʃɪŋ] *adj drink* rinfrescante; *experience* piacevole

re·fresh·ments [rɪ'freʃmənts] *npl* rinfreschi *mpl*

re·fri·ge·rate [rɪ'frɪdʒəreɪt] *v/t:* **keep ~d** conservare in frigo

re·fri·ge·ra·tor [rɪ'frɪdʒəreɪtə(r)] frigorifero *m*

re·fu·el [riː'fjuːəl] **1** *v/t aeroplane* rifornire di carburante **2** *v/i of aeroplane, car* fare rifornimento

ref·uge ['refjuːdʒ] rifugio *m*; **take ~ from storm etc** ripararsi

ref·u·gee [refjuˈdʒiː] rifugiato *m*, -a *f*, profugo *m*, -a *f*

ref·u·gee camp campo *m* profughi

re·fund ['riːfʌnd] **1** *n* rimborso *m* **2** *v/t* [rɪ'fʌnd] rimborsare

re·fus·al [rɪ'fjuːzl] rifiuto *m*

re·fuse¹ [rɪ'fjuːz] *v/t & v/i* rifiutare; **~ to do sth** rifiutare di fare qc

ref·use² ['refjuːs] *(garbage)* rifiuti *mpl*

'ref·use col·lec·tion raccolta *f* dei rifiuti

'ref·use dump discarica *f* (dei rifiuti)

re·fute [rɪ'fjuːt] *v/t* confutare

re·gain [rɪ'geɪn] *v/t control, lost territory, the lead* riconquistare

re·gal ['riːgl] *adj* regale

re·gard [rɪ'gɑːd] **1** *n:* **have great ~ for s.o.** avere molta stima di qu; **in this ~** a questo riguardo; **with ~ to** riguardo a; *(kind)* **~s** cordiali saluti; **give my ~s to Paola** saluti a Paola; **with no ~ for ...** senza alcun riguardo per ... **2** *v/t:* **~ s.o. / sth as sth** considerare qu/qc come qc; **as ~s ...** riguardo a ...

re·gard·ing [rɪ'gɑːdɪŋ] *prep* riguardo a

re·gard·less [rɪ'gɑːdlɪs] *adv* lo stesso; **~ of** senza tener conto di

re·gime [reɪ'ʒiːm] *(government)* regime *m*

re·gi·ment ['redʒɪmənt] *n* reggimento *m*

re·gion ['riːdʒən] regione *f*; **in the ~ of** intorno a

re·gion·al ['riːdʒənl] *adj* regionale

re·gis·ter ['redʒɪstə(r)] **1** *n* registro *m* **2** *v/t birth, death: by individual* denunciare; *by authorities* registrare; *vehicle* iscrivere; *letter* assicurare; *emotion* mostrare; **send a letter ~ed** spedire una lettera assicurata **3** *v/i at university* iscriversi; **I'm ~ed with Dr Lee** il mio medico è il dottor Lee

re·gis·tered let·ter ['redʒɪstəd] (lettera *f*) assicurata *f*

re·gis·tra·tion [redʒɪ'streɪʃn] *Br (vehicle number)* numero *m* di targa; *at university* iscrizione *f*

re·gis·tra·tion num·ber *Br* MOT numero *m* di targa

re·gis·try of·fice ['redʒɪstrɪ] ufficio *m* di stato civile

re·gret [rɪ'gret] **1** *v/t (pret & pp* **-ted** *)* rammaricarsi di; *missed opportunity* rimpiangere; **we ~ to inform you that ...** siamo spiacenti di informarla che ... **2** *n* rammarico *m*

re·gret·ful [rɪ'gretfəl] *adj* di rammarico

re·gret·ful·ly [rɪ'gretfəlɪ] *adv* con rammarico

re·gret·ta·ble [rɪ'gretəbl] *adj* deplorevole

re·gret·ta·bly [rɪ'gretəblɪ] *adv* purtroppo

reg·u·lar ['regjʊlə(r)] **1** *adj* regolare; *(esp Am: ordinary)* normale **2** *n at bar etc* cliente *m/f* abituale

reg·u·lar·i·ty [regjʊ'lærətɪ] regolarità *f inv*

reg·u·lar·ly ['regjʊləlɪ] *adv* regolarmente

reg·u·late ['regʊleɪt] *v/t* regolare

reg·u·la·tion [regʊ'leɪʃn] *(rule)* regolamento *m*; *control* controllo *m*

re·hab ['riːhæb] F riabilitazione *f*

re·ha·bil·i·tate [riːhə'bɪlɪteɪt] *v/t ex-criminal* riabilitare

R

re·hears·al [rɪ'hɜːsl] prova *f*

re·hearse [rɪ'hɜːs] *v/t & v/i* provare

reign [reɪn] **1** *n* regno *m* **2** *v/i* regnare

re·im·burse [riːɪm'bɜːs] *v/t* rimborsare

rein [reɪn] redine *f*

re·in·car·na·tion [riːɪnkɑː'neɪʃn] reincarnazione *f*

re·in·force [riːɪn'fɔːs] *v/t* rinforzare

re·in·forced con·crete [riːɪn'fɔːst] cemento *m* armato

re·in·force·ments [riːɪn'fɔːsmənts] *npl* MIL rinforzi *mpl*

re·in·state [riːɪn'steɪt] *v/t* reintegrare

re·it·e·rate [riː'ɪtəreɪt] *v/t fml* ripetere

re·ject [rɪ'dʒekt] *v/t* respingere

re·jec·tion [rɪ'dʒekʃn] rifiuto *m*

re·lapse ['riːlæps] *n* MED ricaduta *f*; **have a ~** avere una ricaduta

re·late [rɪ'leɪt] **1** *v/t story* raccontare; **~ sth to sth** collegare qc a qc **2** *v/i*: **~ to ...** be connected with riferirsi a ...; **he doesn't ~ to people** non sa stabilire un rapporto con gli altri

re·lat·ed [rɪ'leɪtɪd] *adj by family* imparentato; *events, ideas etc* collegato

re·la·tion [rɪ'leɪʃn] *in family* parente *m/f*; (connection) rapporto *m*; **business / diplomatic ~s** rapporti d'affari / diplomatici

re·la·tion·ship [rɪ'leɪʃnʃɪp] rapporto *m*

rel·a·tive ['relətɪv] **1** *n* parente *m/f* **2** *adj* relativo; **X is ~ to Y** X è legato a Y

rel·a·tive·ly ['relətɪvlɪ] *adv* relativamente

re·lax [rɪ'læks] **1** *v/i* rilassarsi; **~!, don't get angry** rilassati! non te la prendere **2** *v/t* rilassare

re·lax·a·tion [riːlæk'seɪʃn] relax *m inv*; *of rules etc* rilassamento *m*

re·laxed [rɪ'lækst] *adj* rilassato

re·lax·ing [rɪ'læksɪŋ] *adj* rilassante

re·lay [riː'leɪ] **1** *v/t* trasmettere **2** *n*: **~ (race)** (corsa *f* a) staffetta *f*

re·lease [rɪ'liːs] **1** *n from prison* rilascio *m*; *of CD etc* uscita *f*; *of software* versione *f*; **this film is a new ~** è un film appena uscito **2** *v/t prisoner* rilasciare; *handbrake* togliere; *film, record* far uscire; *information* rendere noto

rel·e·gate ['relɪgeɪt] *v/t* relegare; **be ~d** SP essere retrocesso

rel·e·ga·tion [relɪ'geɪʃn] SP retrocessione *f*

re·lent [rɪ'lent] *v/i* cedere

re·lent·less [rɪ'lentlɪs] *adj* incessante, implacabile

re·lent·less·ly [rɪ'lentlɪslɪ] *adv* incessantemente

rel·e·vance ['reləvəns] pertinenza *f*

rel·e·vant ['reləvənt] *adj* pertinente

re·li·a·bil·i·ty [rɪlaɪə'bɪlətɪ] affidabilità *f inv*

re·li·a·ble [rɪ'laɪəbl] *adj* affidabile

re·li·a·bly [rɪ'laɪəblɪ] *adv*: **I am ~ informed that ...** so da fonte certa che ...

re·li·ance [rɪ'laɪəns] dipendenza *f*; **~ on s.o. / sth** dipendenza da qu / qc

re·li·ant [rɪ'laɪənt] *adj*: **be ~ on** dipendere da

rel·ic ['relɪk] reliquia *f*

re·lief [rɪ'liːf] sollievo *m*; **that's a ~** che sollievo; **in ~** in art in rilievo

re·lieve [rɪ'liːv] *v/t pressure, pain* alleviare; *(take over from)* dare il cambio a; **be ~d** *at news etc* essere sollevato

re·li·gion [rɪ'lɪdʒən] religione *f*

re·li·gious [rɪ'lɪdʒəs] *adj* religioso

re·li·gious·ly [rɪ'lɪdʒəslɪ] *adv* (conscientiously) religiosamente

re·lin·quish [rɪ'lɪŋkwɪʃ] *v/t* rinunciare a

rel·ish ['relɪʃ] **1** *n sauce* salsa *f*; (enjoyment) gusto *m* **2** *v/t idea, prospect* gradire

re·live [riː'lɪv] *v/t* rivivere

re·lo·cate [riːlə'keɪt] *v/i of business, employee* trasferirsi

re·lo·ca·tion [riːlə'keɪʃn] *of business, employee* trasferimento *m*

re·luc·tance [rɪ'lʌktəns] riluttanza *f*

re·luc·tant [rɪ'lʌktənt] *adj* riluttante; **be ~ to do sth** essere restio a fare qc

re·luc·tant·ly [rɪ'lʌktəntlɪ] *adv* a malincuore

♦ re·ly on [rɪ'laɪ] v/t (pret & pp -ied) contare su; rely on s.o. to do sth contare su qu perché faccia qc

re·main [rɪ'meɪn] v/i rimanere

re·main·der [rɪ'meɪndə(r)] 1 n also MATH resto m 2 v/t svendere

re·main·ing [rɪ'meɪnɪŋ] adj restante

re·mains [rɪ'meɪnz] npl of body resti mpl

re·make ['riːmeɪk] n of film remake m inv

re·mand [rɪ'mɑːnd] 1 v/t: ~ s.o. in custody ordinare la custodia cautelare di qu 2 n: be on ~ essere in attesa di giudizio

re·mark [rɪ'mɑːk] 1 n commento m 2 v/t osservare

re·mar·ka·ble [rɪ'mɑːkəbl] adj notevole

re·mark·a·bly [rɪ'mɑːkəblɪ] adv notevolmente

re·mar·ry [riː'mærɪ] v/i (pret & pp -ied) risposarsi

rem·e·dy ['remədɪ] n rimedio m

re·mem·ber [rɪ'membə(r)] 1 v/t ricordare; ~ to lock the door ricordati di chiudere la porta a chiave; ~ me to her dalle i miei saluti 2 v/i ricordare, ricordarsi

Re·mem·brance Day [rɪ'membrəns] 11 novembre, commemorazione f dei caduti in guerra

re·mind [rɪ'maɪnd] v/t: ~ s.o. of s.o. / sth ricordare qu / qc a qu

re·mind·er [rɪ'maɪndə(r)] promemoria m; COM: for payment sollecito m

rem·i·nisce [remɪ'nɪs] v/i rievocare il passato

rem·i·nis·cent [remɪ'nɪsənt] adj: be ~ of sth far venire in mente qc

re·miss [rɪ'mɪs] adj fml negligente

re·mis·sion [rɪ'mɪʃn] remissione f

rem·nant ['remnənt] resto m; of fabric scampolo m

re·morse [rɪ'mɔːs] rimorso m

re·morse·less [rɪ'mɔːslɪs] adj spietato

re·mote [rɪ'məʊt] adj village isolato; possibility, connection remoto; (aloof) distante; ancestor lontano

re·mote 'ac·cess COMPUT accesso m remoto

re·mote con'trol telecomando m

re·mote·ly [rɪ'məʊtlɪ] adv related, connected lontamente; just ~ possible vagamente possibile

re·mote·ness [rɪ'məʊtnəs] isolamento m

re·mov·a·ble [rɪ'muːvəbl] adj staccabile

re·mov·al [rɪ'muːvl] rimozione f; from home trasloco

re'mov·al firm ditta f di traslochi

re'mov·al van furgone m dei traslochi

re·move [rɪ'muːv] v/t top, lid togliere; MED asportare; doubt, suspicion eliminare

re·mu·ner·a·tion [rɪmjuːnə'reɪʃn] rimunerazione f

re·mu·ner·a·tive [rɪ'mjuːnərətɪv] adj rimunerativo

Re·nais·sance [rɪ'neɪsəns] Rinascimento m

re·name [riː'neɪm] v/t ribattezzare; file rinominare

ren·der ['rendə(r)] v/t service rendere; ~ s.o. helpless rendere infermo qu

ren·der·ing ['rendərɪŋ] of piece of music interpretazione f

ren·dez·vous ['rɒndeɪvuː] (meeting) incontro m

re·new [rɪ'njuː] v/t contract, licence rinnovare; feel ~ed sentirsi rinato

re·new·al [rɪ'njuːəl] of contract etc rinnovo m

re·nounce [rɪ'naʊns] v/t title, rights rinunciare a

ren·o·vate ['renəveɪt] v/t ristrutturare

ren·o·va·tion [renə'veɪʃn] ristrutturazione f

re·nown [rɪ'naʊn] fama f

re·nowned [rɪ'naʊnd] adj famoso

rent [rent] 1 n affitto m; for ~ affittasi 2 v/t flat affittare; car equipment, noleggiare; (~ out) affittare

rent·al ['rentl] for flat affitto m; for car noleggio m; for TV, phone canone m

R

'rent·al a·gree·ment contratto *m* di noleggio

rent-'free *adv* gratis

re·o·pen [riː'əʊpn] *v/t & v/i* riaprire

re·or·gan·i·za·tion [riːɔːgənaɪz'eɪʃn] riorganizzazione *f*

re·or·gan·ize [riː'ɔːgənaɪz] *v/t* riorganizzare

rep [rep] COM rappresentante *m/f*

re·paint [riː'peɪnt] *v/t* ridipingere

re·pair [rɪ'peə(r)] 1 *v/t* riparare 2 *n*: *in a good / bad state of ~* in buono / cattivo stato; *~s* riparazioni *fpl*

re'pair·man tecnico *m*

re·pa·tri·ate [riː'pætrɪeɪt] *v/t* rimpatriare

re·pa·tri·a·tion [riːpætrɪ'eɪʃn] rimpatrio *m*

re·pay [riː'peɪ] *v/t* (*pret & pp* -paid) *money* restituire; *person* ripagare

re·pay·ment [riː'peɪmənt] pagamento *m*

re·peal [rɪ'piːl] *v/t law* abrogare

re·peat [rɪ'piːt] 1 *v/t* ripetere; *am I ~ing myself?* l'ho già detto? 2 *n programme* replica *f*

re·peat 'busi·ness COM ulteriori ordini *mpl*

re·peat·ed [rɪ'piːtɪd] *adj* ripetuto

re·peat·ed·ly [rɪ'piːtɪdlɪ] *adv* ripetutamente

re·peat 'or·der COM ulteriore ordine *m*

re·pel [rɪ'pel] *v/t* (*pret & pp* -led) *invaders, attack* respingere; (*disgust*) ripugnare

re·pel·lent [rɪ'pelənt] 1 *n* (*insect ~*) insettifugo *m* 2 *adj* ripugnante

re·pent [rɪ'pent] *v/i* pentirsi

re·per·cus·sions [riːpə'kʌʃnz] *npl* ripercussioni *fpl*

rep·er·toire ['repətwɑː(r)] repertorio *m*

rep·e·ti·tion [repɪ'tɪʃn] ripetizione *f*

rep·e·ti·tive [rɪ'petɪtɪv] *adj* ripetitivo

re·place [rɪ'pleɪs] *v/t* (*put back*) mettere a posto *v/t* (*take the place of*) sostituire

re·place·ment [rɪ'pleɪsmənt] *person* sostituto *m*, -a *f; act* sostituzione *f; this is the ~ for the old model* que-

sto è il modello che sostituisce il vecchio

re·place·ment 'part pezzo *m* di ricambio

re·play ['riːpleɪ] 1 *n recording* replay *m inv; match* spareggio *m* 2 *v/t match* rigiocare

re·plen·ish [rɪ'plenɪʃ] *v/t container* riempire; *supplies* rifornire

rep·li·ca ['replɪkə] copia *f*

re·ply [rɪ'plaɪ] 1 *n* risposta *f* 2 *v/t & v/i* (*pret & pp* -ied) rispondere

re·port [rɪ'pɔːt] 1 *n* (*account*) resoconto *m; by journalist* servizio *m;* EDU pagella *f* 2 *v/t facts* fare un servizio su; *to authorities* denunciare; *~ one's findings to s.o.* riferire sulle proprie conclusioni a qu; *~ a person to the police* denunciare qualcuno alla polizia; *he is ~ed to be in London* si dice che sia a Londra 3 *v/i of journalist* fare un reportage; (*present o.s.*) presentarsi

♦report to *v/t in business* rendere conto a

re·port·er [rɪ'pɔːtə(r)] giornalista *m/f*

re·pos·sess [riːpə'zes] *v/t* COM riprenderci

rep·re·hen·si·ble [reprɪ'hensəbl] *adj* riprovevole

rep·re·sent [reprɪ'zent] *v/t* rappresentare

rep·re·sen·ta·tive [reprɪ'zentətɪv] 1 *n* rappresentante *m/f* 2 *adj* (*typical*) rappresentativo

re·press [rɪ'pres] *v/t* reprimere

re·pres·sion [rɪ'preʃn] POL repressione *f*

re·pres·sive [rɪ'presɪv] *adj* POL repressivo

re·prieve [rɪ'priːv] 1 *n* LAW sospensione *f* della pena capitale; *fig* proroga *f* 2 *v/t prisoner* sospendere l'esecuzione di

rep·ri·mand ['reprɪmɑːnd] *v/t* ammonire

re·print ['riːprɪnt] 1 *n* ristampa *f* 2 *v/t* ristampare

re·pri·sal [rɪ'praɪzl] rappresaglia *f; take ~s* fare delle rappresaglie; *in ~*

R

for per rappresaglia contro

re·proach [rɪˈprəʊtʃ] **1** *n* rimprovero *m*; **be beyond ~** essere irreprensibile **2** *v/t* rimproverare

re·proach·ful [rɪˈprəʊtʃfʊl] *adj* di rimprovero

re·proach·ful·ly [rɪˈprəʊtʃfʊlɪ] *adv* con aria di rimprovero

re·pro·duce [riːprəˈdjuːs] **1** *v/t* riprodurre **2** *v/i* riprodursi

re·pro·duc·tion [riːprəˈdʌkʃn] riproduzione *f*

re·pro·duc·tive [riːprəˈdʌktɪv] *adj* riproduttivo

rep·tile [ˈreptaɪl] rettile *m*

re·pub·lic [rɪˈpʌblɪk] repubblica *f*

re·pub·li·can [rɪˈpʌblɪkən] **1** *n* repubblicano *m*, -a *f* **2** *adj* repubblicano

re·pu·di·ate [rɪˈpjuːdɪeɪt] *v/t* (*deny*) respingere

re·pul·sive [rɪˈpʌlsɪv] *adj* ripugnante

rep·u·ta·ble [ˈrepjʊtəbl] *adj* rispettabile

rep·u·ta·tion [repjʊˈteɪʃn] reputazione *f*; **have a good / bad ~** avere una buona / cattiva reputazione

re·put·ed [repˈjʊtəd] *adj*: **be ~ to be** avere la fama di essere

re·put·ed·ly [repˈjʊtədlɪ] *adv* a quanto si dice

re·quest [rɪˈkwest] **1** *n* richiesta *f*; **on ~** su richiesta **2** *v/t* richiedere

re·quiem [ˈrekwɪəm] MUS requiem *m inv*

re·quire [rɪˈkwaɪə(r)] *v/t* (*need*) aver bisogno di; *it ~s great care* richiede molta cura; *as ~d by law* come prescritto dalla legge; *guests are ~d to ...* i signori clienti sono pregati di ...

re·quired [rɪˈkwaɪəd] *adj* (*necessary*) necessario

re·quire·ment [rɪˈkwaɪəmənt] (*need*) esigenza *f*; (*condition*) requisito *m*

req·ui·si·tion [rekwɪˈzɪʃn] *v/t* requisire

re·route [riːˈruːt] *v/t aeroplane etc* deviare

re·run [ˈriːrʌn] **1** *n of programme* replica *f* **2** *v/t* (*pret* *-ran*, *pp* *-run*) *programme* replicare

re·sched·ule [riːˈʃedjuːl] *v/t* stabilire di nuovo

res·cue [ˈreskjuː] **1** *n* salvataggio *m*; *come to s.o.'s ~* andare in aiuto a qu **2** *v/t* salvare

'res·cue par·ty squadra *f* di soccorso

re·search [rɪˈsɜːtʃ] *n* ricerca *f*
♦ **research into** *v/t* fare ricerca su

re·search and de'vel·op·ment ricerca *f* e sviluppo *m*

re'search as·sis·tant assistente ricercatore *m*, -trice *f*

re·search·er [rɪˈsɜːtʃə(r)] ricercatore *m*, -trice *f*

re'search proj·ect ricerca *f*

re·sem·blance [rɪˈzembləns] somiglianza *f*

re·sem·ble [rɪˈzembl] *v/t* (as)somigliare a

re·sent [rɪˈzent] *v/t* risentirsi per

re·sent·ful [rɪˈzentfʊl] *adj* pieno di risentimento

re·sent·ful·ly [rɪˈzentfʊlɪ] *adv* con risentimento

re·sent·ment [rɪˈzentmənt] risentimento *m*

res·er·va·tion [rezəˈveɪʃn] *of room, table* prenotazione *f*; *mental, special area* riserva *f*; *I have a ~* in hotel, restaurant ho prenotato

re·serve [rɪˈzɜːv] **1** *n* (*store*) riserva *f*; (*aloofness*) riserbo *m*; SP riserva *f*; *~s* FIN riserve *fpl*; *keep sth in ~* tenere qc di riserva **2** *v/t seat, table* prenotare; *judgment* riservarsi

re·served [rɪˈzɜːvd] *adj person, manner* riservato; *table, seat* prenotato

res·er·voir [ˈrezəvwɑː(r)] *for water* bacino *m* idrico

re·shuf·fle [ˈriːˌʃʌfl] **1** *n* POL rimpasto *m* **2** *v/t* POL rimpastare

re·side [rɪˈzaɪd] *v/i fml* risiedere

res·i·dence [ˈrezɪdəns] *fml*: *house etc* residenza *f*; (*stay*) permanenza *f*

'res·i·dence per·mit permesso *m* di residenza

'res·i·dent [ˈrezɪdənt] **1** *n* residente *m/f* **2** *adj living in a building* residente sul posto

res·i·den·tial [rezɪˈdenʃl] *adj district* residenziale

R

res·i·due ['rezɪdjuː] residuo *m*

re·sign [rɪ'zaɪn] **1** *v/t position* dimettersi da; **~ o.s. to** rassegnarsi a **2** *v/i from job* dimettersi

res·ig·na·tion [rezɪg'neɪʃn] *from job* dimissioni *fpl*; *mental* rassegnazione *f*

re·signed [re'zaɪnd] *adj* rassegnato; **we have become ~ to the fact that ...** ci siamo rassegnati al fatto che ...

re·sil·i·ent [rɪ'zɪlɪənt] *adj personality* che ha molte risorse; *material* resistente

res·in ['rezɪn] resina *f*

re·sist [rɪ'zɪst] **1** *v/t* resistere a **2** *v/i* resistere

re·sist·ance [rɪ'zɪstəns] resistenza *f*

re·sis·tant [rɪ'zɪstənt] *adj material* resistente; **~ to heat / rust** resistente al calore / alla ruggine

re·sit ['riːsɪt] *v/t exam* ridare

res·o·lute ['rezəluːt] *adj* risoluto

res·o·lu·tion [rezə'luːʃn] *(decision)* risoluzione *f*; *made at New Year etc* proposito *m*; *(determination)* risolutezza *f*; *of problem* soluzione *f*; *of image* risoluzione *f*

re·solve [rɪ'zɒlv] *v/t problem, mystery* risolvere; **~ to do sth** decidere di fare qc

re·sort [rɪ'zɔːt] *n place* località *f inv*; *holiday* ~ luogo *m* di villeggiatura; *ski* ~ stazione *f* sciistica; *as a last* ~ come ultima risorsa

♦ **resort to** *v/t violence, threats* far ricorso a

♦ **re·sound with** [rɪ'zaund] *v/t* risuonare di

re·sound·ing [rɪ'zaundɪŋ] *adj success, victory* clamoroso

re·source [rɪ'sɔːs] risorsa *f*; *financial* ~s *mpl* economici; *leave s.o. to his own* ~s lasciare qu in balia di se stesso

re·source·ful [rɪ'sɔːsful] *adj* pieno di risorse

re·spect [rɪ'spekt] **1** *n* rispetto *m*; *show* ~ avere rispetto per; *with* ~ *to* riguardo a; *in this / that* ~ quanto a questo; *in many* ~s sotto molti

aspetti; *pay one's last* ~s *to s.o.* rendere omaggio a qu **2** *v/t* rispettare

re·spect·a·bil·i·ty [rɪspektə'bɪlətɪ] rispettabilità *f inv*

re·spec·ta·ble [rɪ'spektəbl] *adj* rispettabile

re·spec·ta·bly [rɪ'spektəblɪ] *adv* rispettabilmente

re·spect·ful [rɪ'spektful] *adj* rispettoso

re·spect·ful·ly [rɪ'spektflɪ] *adv* con rispetto

re·spec·tive [rɪ'spektɪv] *adj* rispettivo

re·spec·tive·ly [rɪ'spektɪvlɪ] *adv* rispettivamente

res·pi·ra·tion [respɪ'reɪʃn] respirazione *f*

res·pi·ra·tor [respɪ'reɪtə(r)] MED respiratore *m*

re·spite ['respaɪt] tregua *f*; *without* ~ senza tregua

re·spond [rɪ'spɒnd] *v/i* rispondere

re·sponse [rɪ'spɒns] risposta *f*

re·spon·si·bil·i·ty [rɪspɒnsɪ'bɪlətɪ] responsabilità *f inv*; *accept* ~ *for* assumersi la responsabilità di; *a job with more* ~ un lavoro con più responsabilità

re·spon·si·ble [rɪ'spɒnsəbl] *adj* responsabile (*for* di); *job, position* di responsabilità

re·spon·sive [rɪ'spɒnsɪv] *adj audience* caloroso; *be* ~ *of brakes* rispondere bene

rest¹ [rest] **1** *n* riposo *m*; *set s.o.'s mind at* ~ tranquillizzare qu **2** *v/i* riposare; ~ *on ...* (*be based on*) basarsi su ...; (*lean against*) poggiare su ...; *it all* ~*s with him* dipende tutto da lui **3** *v/t* (*lean, balance*) appoggiare

rest² [rest] *n*: *the* ~ il resto *m*

res·tau·rant ['restrɒnt] ristorante *m*

'res·tau·rant car RAIL vagone *m* ristorante

'rest cure cura *f* del riposo

'rest·ful ['restful] *adj* riposante

'rest home casa *f* di riposo

rest·less ['restlɪs] *adj* irrequieto;

have a **~ night** passare una notte agitata

rest·less·ly ['restlɪslɪ] *adv* nervosamente

res·to·ra·tion [restə'reɪʃn] restauro *m*

re·store [rɪ'stɔː(r)] *v/t building etc* restaurare; *(bring back)* restituire

re·strain [rɪ'streɪn] *v/t dog, troops* frenare; *emotions* reprimere; **~ o.s.** trattenersi

re·straint [rɪ'streɪnt] *(self-control)* autocontrollo *m*

re·strict [rɪ'strɪkt] *v/t* limitare; *I'll* **~ myself to ...** mi limiterò a ...

re·strict·ed [rɪ'strɪktɪd] *adj view* limitato

re·strict·ed 'ar·e·a MIL zona *f* militare

re·stric·tion [rɪ'strɪkʃn] restrizione *f*

'rest room *Am* gabinetto *m*

re·sult [rɪ'zʌlt] *n* risultato *m*; *as a* **~ of this** in conseguenza a ciò

♦ **result from** *v/t* risultare da, derivare da

♦ **result in** *v/t* dare luogo a; **this resulted in him feeling even worse** questo ha fatto sì che stesse ancora peggio

re·sume [rɪ'zjuːm] *v/t & v/i* riprendere

ré·su·mé ['rezumeɪ] *Am* curriculum vitae *m inv*

re·sump·tion [rɪ'zʌmpʃn] ripresa *f*

re·sur·face [riː'sɜːfɪs] **1** *v/t roads* asfaltare **2** *v/i (reappear)* riaffiorare

Res·ur·rec·tion [rezə'rekʃn] REL resurrezione *f*

re·sus·ci·tate [rɪ'sʌsɪteɪt] *v/t* rianimare

re·sus·ci·ta·tion [rɪsʌsɪ'teɪʃn] rianimazione *f*

re·tail ['riːteɪl] **1** *adv* al dettaglio **2** *v/i:* **~ at ...** essere in vendita a ...

re·tail·er ['riːteɪlə(r)] dettagliante *m/f*

're·tail out·let punto *m* (di) vendita

're·tail price prezzo *m* al dettaglio

re·tain [rɪ'teɪn] *v/t* conservare

re·tain·er [rɪ'teɪnə(r)] FIN onorario *m*

re·tal·i·ate [rɪ'tælɪeɪt] *v/i* vendicarsi

re·tal·i·a·tion [rɪtælɪ'eɪʃn] rappresaglia *f*; *in* **~ for** per rappresaglia contro

re·tard·ed [rɪ'tɑːdɪd] *adj mentally* ritardato

re·think [riː'θɪŋk] *v/t (pret & pp* **-thought)** riconsiderare

re·ti·cence ['retɪsns] riservatezza *f*

re·ti·cent ['retɪsnt] *adj* riservato

re·tire [rɪ'taɪə(r)] *v/i from work* andare in pensione

re·tired [rɪ'taɪəd] *adj* in pensione

re·tire·ment [rɪ'taɪəmənt] pensione *f*; *act* pensionamento *m*

re·tire·ment age età *f inv* pensionabile

re·tir·ing [rɪ'taɪərɪŋ] *adj* riservato

re·tort [rɪ'tɔːt] **1** *n* replica *f* **2** *v/t* replicare

re·trace [rɪ'treɪs] *v/t:* **~ one's footsteps** ritornare sui propri passi

re·tract [rɪ'trækt] *v/t claws* ritrarre; *undercarriage* far rientrare; *statement* ritrattare

re·train [riː'treɪn] *v/i* riqualificarsi

re·treat [rɪ'triːt] **1** *v/i* ritirarsi **2** *n* MIL ritirata *f*; *place* rifugio *m*

re·trieve [rɪ'triːv] *v/t* recuperare

re·triev·er [rɪ'triːvə(r)] *dog* cane *m* da riporto

ret·ro·ac·tive [retrəʊ'æktɪv] *adj law etc* retroattivo

ret·ro·ac·tive·ly [retrəʊ'æktɪvlɪ] *adv* retroattivamente

ret·ro·grade ['retrəgreɪd] *adj move, decision* retrogrado

ret·ro·spect ['retrəspekt] *in* **~** ripensandoci

ret·ro·spec·tive [retrə'spekt ɪv] *n* retrospettiva *f*

re·turn [rɪ'tɜːn] **1** *n* ritorno *m*; *(giving back)* restituzione *f*; COMPUT *(tasto m)* invio *m*; *in tennis* risposta *f* al servizio; *tax* **~** dichiarazione *f* dei redditi; *by* **~ (of post)** a stretto giro di posta; **~s** *(profit)* rendimento *m*; *many happy* **~s (of the day)** cento di questi giorni; *in* **~ for** in cambio di **2** *v/t (give back)* restituire; *(put back)* rimettere; *favour, invitation* ri-

R

cambiare **3** v/i (*go back, come back*) ritornare; *of symptoms, doubts etc* ricomparire

re•turn 'flight volo *m* di ritorno; **re•turn 'jour•ney** viaggio *m* di ritorno; **re'turn match** partita *f* (del girone) di ritorno; **re'turn tick•et** biglietto *m* (di) andata e ritorno

re•u•ni•fi•ca•tion [riːjuːnɪfɪ'keɪʃn] riunificazione *f*

re•u•nion [riː'juːnɪən] riunione *f*

re•u•nite [riːjuː'naɪt] v/t riunire

re•us•a•ble [riː'juːzəbl] *adj* riutilizzabile

re•use [riː'juːz] v/t riutilizzare

rev [rev] *n*: **~s per minute** giri al minuto

♦ rev up v/t (*pret & pp* **-ved**) *engine* far andare su di giri

re•val•u•a•tion [riːvæljʊ'eɪʃn] rivalutazione *f*

re•veal [rɪ'viːl] v/t (*make visible*) mostrare; (*make known*) rivelare

re•veal•ing [rɪ'viːlɪŋ] *adj remark* rivelatore; *dress* scollato

♦ revel in ['revl] v/t (*pret & pp* **-led**, *Am* **-ed**) godere di

rev•e•la•tion [revə'leɪʃn] rivelazione *f*

re•venge [rɪ'vendʒ] *n* vendetta *f*; **take one's ~** vendicarsi; **in ~ for** per vendicarsi di

rev•e•nue ['revənjuː] reddito *m*

re•ver•be•rate [rɪ'vɜːbəreɪt] v/i *of sound* rimbombare

re•vere [rɪ'vɪə(r)] v/t riverire

rev•e•rence ['revərəns] rispetto *m*

Rev•e•rend ['revərənd] REL reverendo *m*

rev•e•rent ['revərənt] *adj* riverente

re•verse [rɪ'vɜːs] **1** *adj sequence* opposto; **in ~ order** in ordine inverso **2** *n* (*opposite*) contrario *m*; (*back*) rovescio *m*; MOT retromarcia *f* **3** v/t *sequence* invertire; **~ the car** fare marcia indietro; **~ the charges** TELEC telefonare a carico del destinatario **4** v/i MOT fare marcia indietro

revert [rɪ'vɜːt] v/i: **~ to** ritornare a

re•view [rɪ'vjuː] **1** *n of book, film* recensione *f*; *of troops* rivista *f*; *of situation etc* revisione *f* **2** v/t *book, film* recensire; *troops* passare in rivista; *situation etc* riesaminare

re•view•er [rɪ'vjuːə(r)] *of book, film* critico *m*, -a *f*

re•vise [rɪ'vaɪz] **1** v/t *opinion, text* rivedere; EDU ripassare **2** v/i EDU ripassare

re•vi•sion [rɪ'vɪʒn] *of opinion, text* revisione *f*; *for exam* ripasso *m*

re•viv•al [rɪ'vaɪvl] *of custom, old style etc* revival *m inv*; *of patient* ripresa *f*

re•vive [rɪ'vaɪv] **1** v/t *custom, old style etc* riportare alla moda; *patient* rianimare **2** v/i *of business etc* riprendersi

re•voke [rɪ'vəʊk] v/t *licence* revocare

re•volt [rɪ'vəʊlt] **1** *n* rivolta *f* **2** v/i ribellarsi

re•volt•ing [rɪ'vəʊltɪŋ] *adj* (*disgusting*) schifoso

rev•o•lu•tion [revə'luːʃn] rivoluzione *f*

rev•o•lu•tion•ar•y [revə'luːʃn ərɪ] **1** *n* POL rivoluzionario *m*, -a *f* **2** *adj* rivoluzionario

rev•o•lu•tion•ize [revə'luːʃnaɪz] v/t rivoluzionare

re•volve [rɪ'vɒlv] v/i ruotare

re•volv•er [rɪ'vɒlvə(r)] revolver *m inv*

re•volv•ing 'door [rɪ'vɒlvɪŋ] porta *f* girevole

re•vue [rɪ'vjuː] THEA rivista *f*

re•vul•sion [rɪ'vʌlʃn] ribrezzo *m*

re•ward [rɪ'wɔːd] **1** *n financial* ricompensa *f*; *benefit derived* vantaggio *m* **2** v/t *financially* ricompensare

re•ward•ing [rɪ'wɔːdɪŋ] *adj experience* gratificante

re•wind [riː'waɪnd] v/t (*pret & pp* **-wound**) *film, tape* riavvolgere

re•write [riː'raɪt] v/t (*pret* **-wrote**, *pp* **-written**) riscrivere

rhe•to•ric ['retərɪk] retorica *f*

rhe•to•ri•cal 'ques•tion [rɪ'tɒrɪkl] domanda *f* retorica

rheu•ma•tism ['ruːmətɪzm] reumatismo *m*

rhi·no·ce·ros [raɪ'nɒsərəs] rinoceronte *m*

rhu·barb ['ru:bɑ:b] rabarbaro *m*

rhyme [raɪm] **1** *n* rima *f* **2** *v/i* rimare; **~ with** fare rima con

rhythm ['rɪðm] ritmo *m*

rib [rɪb] ANAT costola *f*

rib·bon ['rɪbən] nastro *m*

rice [raɪs] riso *m*

rice 'pud·ding budino *m* di riso

rich [rɪtʃ] **1** *adj* (*wealthy*) ricco; *food* pesante **2** *n*: **the** ~ i ricchi *mpl*

rich·ly ['rɪtʃlɪ] *adv deserved* pienamente

rick·et·y ['rɪkətɪ] *adj* traballante

ric·o·chet ['rɪkəʃeɪ] *v/i* rimbalzare

rid [rɪd]: **get ~ of** sbarazzarsi di

rid·dance ['rɪdns] *n* F: **good ~!** che liberazione!

rid·den ['rɪdn] *pp* → **ride**

rid·dle ['rɪdl] **1** *n* indovinello *m* **2** *v/t*: **be ~d with** essere crivellato di

ride [raɪd] **1** *n on horse* cavalcata *f*; *in vehicle* giro *m*; (*journey*) viaggio *m*; **do you want a ~ into town?** *Am* vuoi uno strappo in città? **2** *v/t* (*pret* **rode**, *pp* **ridden**): **~ a horse** andare a cavallo; **~ a bike** andare in bicicletta **3** *v/i* (*pret* **rode**, *pp* **ridden**) *on horse* andare a cavallo; *on bike* andare; *in vehicle* viaggiare; **he rode home** è andato a casa in bicicletta

rid·er ['raɪdə(r)] *on horse* cavallerizzo *m*, -a *f*; *on bike* ciclista *m/f*

ridge [rɪdʒ] *raised strip* sporgenza *f*; *of mountain* cresta *f*; *of roof* punta *f*

rid·i·cule ['rɪdɪkjuːl] **1** *n* ridicolo *m* **2** *v/t* ridicolizzare

ri·dic·u·lous [rɪ'dɪkjuləs] *adj* ridicolo

ri·dic·u·lous·ly [rɪ'dɪkjuləslɪ] *adv* incredibilmente

rid·ing ['raɪdɪŋ] *on horseback* equitazione *f*

ri·fle ['raɪfl] *n* fucile *m*

rift [rɪft] *in earth* crepa *f*; *in party etc* spaccatura *f*

rig [rɪg] **1** *n* (*oil* ~) piattaforma *f* petrolifera **2** *v/t* (*pret & pp* **-ged**) *elections* manipolare

right [raɪt] **1** *adj* (*correct*) esatto; (*proper, just*) giusto; (*suitable*) adatto; *not left* destro; **be ~ of answer** essere esatto; *of person* avere ragione; *of clock* essere giusto; **put things ~** sistemare le cose;→ **alright 2** *adv* (*directly*) proprio; (*correctly*) bene; (*completely*) completamente; *not left* a destra; **~ now** (*immediately*) subito; (*at the moment*) adesso **3** *n civil, legal etc* diritto *m*; *not left* destra *f*; **the** ~ POL la destra; **on the** ~ a destra; **turn to the ~, take a ~** girare a destra; **be in the** ~ avere ragione; **know ~ from wrong** saper distinguere il bene dal male

right-'an·gle angolo *m* retto; **at ~s to ...** ad angolo retto con ...

right·ful ['raɪtful] *adj heir, owner etc* legittimo

'right·hand *adj* destro; **on the ~ side** a destra; **right·hand 'drive** MOT guida *f* a destra; *car* auto *f inv* con guida a destra; **right·hand·ed** [raɪt'hændɪd] *adj*: **be ~** usare la (mano) destra; **right·hand 'man** braccio *m* destro; **right of 'way** *in traffic* (diritto *m* di) precedenza *f*; *across land* diritto *m* di accesso; **right 'wing** *n* POL destra *f*; SP esterno *m* destro; **right-'wing** *adj* POL di destra; **right 'wing·er** POL persona *f* di destra; **right-wing ex'trem·ism** POL estremismo *m* di destra

rig·id ['rɪdʒɪd] *adj material, principles* rigido; *attitude* inflessibile

rig·or *Am* → **rigour**

rig·or·ous ['rɪgərəs] *adj* rigoroso

rig·or·ous·ly ['rɪgərəslɪ] *adv check, examine* rigorosamente

rig·our ['rɪgə(r)] *of discipline* rigore *m*; **the ~s of the winter** i rigori dell'inverno

rile [raɪl] *v/t* F irritare

rim [rɪm] *of wheel* cerchione *m*; *of cup* orlo *m*; *of spectacles* montatura *f*

ring¹ [rɪŋ] (*circle*) cerchio *m*; *on finger* anello *m*; *in boxing* ring *m inv*, quadrato *m*; *at circus* pista *f*

ring² [rɪŋ] **1** *n of bell* trillo *m*; *of voice* suono *m*; **give s.o. a ~** TELEC dare un colpo di telefono a qu **2** *v/t* (*pret* **rang**, *pp* **rung**) *bell* suonare; TELEC chiamare 3 *v/i* (*pret* **rang**, *pp* **rung**) *of bell* suonare; TELEC chiamare; *please ~ for attention* suonare il campanello

'ring·lead·er capobanda *m inv*; 'ring-pull linguetta *f*; 'ring road circonvallazione *f*

rink [rɪŋk] pista *f* di pattinaggio su ghiaccio

rinse [rɪns] 1 *n for hair colour* cachet *m inv* 2 *v/t* sciaquare

ri·ot ['raɪət] 1 *n* sommossa *f* 2 *v/i* causare disordini

ri·ot·er ['raɪətə(r)] dimostrante *m/f*

'riot police reparti *mpl* (di polizia) antisommossa

rip [rɪp] 1 *n in cloth etc* strappo *m* 2 *v/t* (*pret & pp* **-ped**) *cloth etc* strappare; *~ sth open* aprire qc strappandolo

♦ rip off *v/t* F *customers* fregare F

♦ rip up *v/t letter*, *sheet* strappare

ripe [raɪp] *adj fruit* maturo

rip·en ['raɪpn] *v/i of fruit* maturare

ripe·ness ['raɪpnɪs] *of fruit* maturazione *f*

'rip-off *n* F fregatura *f* F

rip·ple ['rɪpl] *on water* increspatura *f*

rise [raɪz] 1 *v/i* (*pret* **rose**, *pp* **risen**) *from chair etc* alzarsi; *of sun* sorgere; *of price*, *temperature* aumentare; *of water level* salire 2 *n* aumento *m*; *~ to power* salita *f* al potere; *give ~ to* dare origine a

ris·en ['rɪzn] *pp* → **rise**

ris·er ['raɪzə(r)] *n*: *be an early / be a late ~* essere mattiniero / alzarsi sempre tardi

risk [rɪsk] 1 *n* rischio *m*; *take a ~* correre un rischio 2 *v/t* rischiare; *let's ~ it* proviamo

risk·y ['rɪskɪ] *adj* rischioso

ri·sot·to [rɪs'ɒtəʊ] risotto *m*

ris·qué [rɪ'skeɪ] *adj* osé

rit·u·al ['rɪtjʊəl] 1 *n* rituale *m* 2 *adj* rituale

ri·val ['raɪvl] 1 *n in sport*, *love* rivale *m/f*; *in business* concorrente *m/f* 2 *v/t* competere con; *I can't ~ that* non posso competere con quello

ri·val·ry ['raɪvlrɪ] rivalità *f inv*

riv·er ['rɪvə(r)] fiume *m*

'riv·er·bank sponda *f* del fiume; 'riv·er·bed letto *m* del fiume; 'riv·er·side 1 *adj* sul fiume 2 *n* riva *f* del fiume

riv·et ['rɪvɪt] 1 *n* ribattino *m* 2 *v/t* rivettare

riv·et·ing ['rɪvɪtɪŋ] *adj* avvincente

Riv·i·e·ra [rɪvɪ'eərə] *n*: *the Italian ~* la riviera (ligure)

road [rəʊd] strada *f*; *it's just down the ~* è qui vicino

'road·block posto *m* di blocco; 'road hog pirata *m* della strada; 'road hold·ing *of vehicle* tenuta *f* di strada; 'road map carta *f* automobilistica; road 'safe·ty sicurezza *f* sulle strade; 'road·side: *at the ~* sul ciglio della strada; 'road-sign cartello *m* stradale; 'road·way carreggiata *f*; 'road works *npl* lavori *mpl* stradali; 'road·wor·thy *adj* in buono stato di marcia

roam [rəʊm] *v/i* vagabondare

roar [rɔ:(r)] 1 *n of engine* rombo *m*; *of lion* ruggito *m*; *of traffic* fragore *m* 2 *v/i of engine* rombare; *of lion* ruggire; *of person* gridare; *~ with laughter* ridere fragorosamente

roast [rəʊst] 1 *n beef etc* arrosto *m* 2 *v/t chicken*, *potatoes* arrostire; *coffee beans*, *peanuts* tostare 3 *v/i of food* arrostire; *in hot room*, *climate* scoppiare di caldo

roast 'beef arrosto *m* di manzo

'roast·ing tin [rəʊstɪŋ] teglia *f* per arrosti

roast 'pork arrosto *m* di maiale

rob [rɒb] *v/t* (*pret & pp* **-bed**) *person*, *bank* rapinare; *I've been ~bed* mi hanno rapinato

rob·ber ['rɒbə(r)] rapinatore *m*, -trice *f*

rob·ber·y ['rɒbərɪ] rapina *f*

robe [rəʊb] *of judge* toga *f*; *of priest* tonaca *f*; *Am* (*dressing gown*) vestaglia *f*

rob·in ['rɒbɪn] pettirosso *m*

ro·bot ['rəʊbɒt] robot *m inv*

ro·bust [rəʊ'bʌst] *adj* robusto

rock [rɒk] 1 *n* roccia *f*; MUS rock *m inv*; *on the ~s drink* con ghiaccio;

marriage in crisi **2** *v/t baby* cullare; *cradle* far dondolare; (*surprise*) sconvolgere **3** *v/i on chair* dondolarsi; *of boat* dondolare

'rock band gruppo *m* rock; **rock 'bot•tom: reach ~** toccare il fondo; 'rock-bot•tom *adj prices* bassissimo; 'rock climb•er rocciatore *m*, -trice *f*; 'rock climb•ing roccia *f*

rock•et ['rɒkɪt] **1** *n* razzo *m* **2** *v/i of prices etc* salire alle stelle

rock•ing chair ['rɒkɪŋ] sedia *f* a dondolo

'rock•ing horse cavallo *m* a dondolo

rock 'n' roll [rɒknˈrəʊl] rock and roll *m inv*

'rock star rockstar *f inv*

rock•y ['rɒkɪ] *adj shore* roccioso; (*shaky*) instabile

rod [rɒd] sbarra *f*; *for fishing* canna *f*

rode [rəʊd] *pret* → ride

ro•dent ['rəʊdnt] roditore *m*

rogue [rəʊg] briccone *m*, -a *f*

role [rəʊl] ruolo *m*

'role mod•el modello *m* di comportamento

roll [rəʊl] **1** *n of bread* panino *m*; *of film* rullino *m*; *of thunder* rombo *m*; (*list, register*) lista *f* **2** *v/i of ball etc* rotolare; *of boat* dondolare **3** *v/t: ~ sth into a ball* appallottolare qc; *~ sth along the ground* far rotolare qc

♦ roll over **1** *v/i* rigirarsi **2** *v/t person, object* girare; *loan, agreement* rinnovare

♦ roll up **1** *v/t sleeves* arrotolare **2** *v/i* F (*arrive*) arrivare

'roll call appello *m*

roll•er ['rəʊlə(r)] *for hair* bigodino *m*

'roll•er blade® *n* roller blade *m inv*; 'roll•er blind tenda *f* a rullo; roll•er coast•er ['rəʊləkəʊstə(r)] montagne *fpl* russe; 'roll•er skate *n* pattino *m* a rotelle

roll•ing pin ['rəʊlɪŋ] matterello *m*

ROM [rɒm] *abbr* COMPUT (= **read only memory**) ROM *f inv*

Ro•man ['rəʊmən] **1** *adj* romano **2** *n* Romano *m*, -a *f*

Ro•man 'Cath•o•lic **1** *n* REL cattoli-

co *m*, -a *f* **2** *adj* cattolico

ro•mance [rəˈmæns] (*affair*) storia *f* d'amore; *novel* romanzo *m* rosa; *film* film *m inv* d'amore

ro•man•tic [rəʊˈmæntɪk] *adj* romantico

ro•man•tic•al•ly [rəʊˈmæntɪklɪ] *adv* romanticamente; *~ involved with s.o.* legato sentimentalmente a qu

Rome [rəʊm] Roma *f*

roof [ru:f] tetto *m*; *have a ~ over one's head* avere un tetto sulla testa

'roof rack MOT portabagagli *m inv*

room [ru:m] stanza *f*; (*bedroom*) camera *f* (da letto); (*space*) posto *m*; *there's no ~ for ...* non c'è posto per ...

'room mate compagno *m*, -a *f* di stanza; 'room ser•vice servizio *m* in camera; room 'tem•per•a•ture temperatura *f* ambiente

room•y ['ru:mɪ] *adj house, car etc* spazioso; *clothes* ampio

root [ru:t] *n* radice *f*; *~s of person* radici *fpl*

♦ root for *v/t* F fare il tifo per

♦ root out *v/t* (*get rid of*) eradicare; (*find*) scovare

rope [rəʊp] corda *f*, fune *f*; *show s.o. the ~s* F insegnare il mestiere a qu

♦ rope off *v/t* transennare

ro•sa•ry ['rəʊzərɪ] REL rosario *m*

rose[1] [rəʊz] BOT rosa *f*

rose[2] [rəʊz] *pret* → rise

rose•ma•ry ['rəʊzmərɪ] rosmarino *m*

ros•trum ['rɒstrəm] podio *m*

ros•y ['rəʊzɪ] *adj* roseo

rot [rɒt] **1** *n* marciume *m* **2** *v/i* (*pret & pp -ted*) marcire

ro•ta ['rəʊtə] turni *mpl*; *actual document* tabella *f* dei turni; *on a ~ basis* a turno

ro•tate [rəʊˈteɪt] **1** *v/i of blades, earth* ruotare **2** *v/t* girare; *crops* avvicendare

ro•ta•tion [rəʊˈteɪʃn] *around the sun etc* rotazione *f*; *in ~* a turno

rot•ten ['rɒtn] *adj food, wood etc* marcio; F (*very bad*) schifoso F; *what ~ luck!* che scalogna!; *what a ~ thing*

R

to do! che carognata!

rough [rʌf] **1** *adj* hands, skin, surface ruvido; *ground* accidentato; (*coarse*) rozzo; (*violent*) violento; *crossing* movimentato; *seas* grosso; (*approximate*) approssimativo; **~ draft** abbozzo *m* **2** *adv*: **sleep ~** dormire all'addiaccio **3** *v/t*: ~ **it** F vivere senza confort **4** *n in golf* erba f alta

♦**rough up** *v/t* F malmenare

rough·age ['rʌfidʒ] *in food* fibre *fpl*

rough·ly ['rʌfli] *adv* (*approximately*) circa; (*harshly*) bruscamente; **~ speaking** grosso modo

rou·lette [ru:'let] roulette *f inv*

round [raʊnd] **1** *adj* rotondo; **in ~ figures** in cifra tonda **2** *n of postman, doctor* giro *m*; *of toast* fetta *f*; *of drinks* giro *m*; *of competition* girone *m*; *in boxing match* round *m inv* **3** *v/t the corner* girare **4** *adv & prep* → *around*

♦**round off** *v/t edges* smussare; *meeting, night out* chiudere

♦**round up** *v/t figure* arrotondare; *suspects, criminals* radunare

round·a·bout ['raʊndəbaʊt] **1** *adj route, way of saying sth* indiretto **2** *n on road* rotatoria *f*; **'round-the-world** *adj* intorno al mondo; **round trip 'tick·et** *Am* biglietto *m* (di) andata e ritorno; **'round-up** *of cattle* raduno *m*; *of suspects, criminals* retata *f*; *of news* riepilogo *m*

rouse [raʊz] *v/t from sleep* svegliare; *interest, emotions* risvegliare

rous·ing ['raʊzɪŋ] *adj speech, finale* entusiasmante

route [ru:t] *of car* itinerario *m*; *of plane, ship* rotta *f*; *of bus* percorso *m*

rou·tine [ru:'ti:n] **1** *adj* abituale **2** *n* routine *f*; **as a matter of ~** d'abitudine

row[1] [raʊ] *n* (*line*) fila *f*; **5 days in a ~** 5 giorni di fila

row[2] [raʊ] *v/t & v/i boat* remare

row[3] [raʊ] *n* (*quarrel*) litigio *m*; (*noise*) baccano *m*

row·dy ['raʊdɪ] *adj* turbolento

row·ing boat ['raʊɪŋ] barca *f* a remi

roy·al ['rɔɪəl] *adj* reale

roy·al·ty ['rɔɪəltɪ] (*royal persons*) reali *mpl*; *on book, recording* royalty *f inv*

rub [rʌb] *v/t* (*pret & pp -bed*) sfregare, strofinare

♦**rub down** *v/t to clean* levigare

♦**rub in** *v/t cream, ointment* far penetrare; **don't rub it in!** *fig* non rivoltare il coltello nella piaga!

♦**rub off 1** *v/t dirt* togliere (strofinando) **2** *v/i*: **it rubs off on you** ti si comunica

♦**rub out** *v/t with eraser* cancellare

rub·ber ['rʌbə(r)] **1** *n* gomma *f* **2** *adj* di gomma

rub·ber 'band elastico *m*

rub·ber 'gloves *npl* guanti *mpl* di gomma

rub·bish ['rʌbɪʃ] immondizia *f*; (*poor quality*) porcheria *f*; (*nonsense*) sciocchezza *f*; **don't talk ~!** non dire sciocchezze!

'rub·bish bin pattumiera *f*

rub·ble ['rʌbl] macerie *fpl*

ru·by ['ru:bɪ] *jewel* rubino *m*

ruck·sack ['rʌksæk] zaino *m*

rud·der ['rʌdə(r)] timone *m*

rud·dy ['rʌdɪ] *adj complexion* rubicondo

rude [ru:d] *adj person, behaviour* maleducato; *language* volgare; **a ~ word** una parolaccia; **it's ~ to ...** è cattiva educazione ...

rude·ly ['ru:dlɪ] *adv* (*impolitely*) scortesemente

rude·ness ['ru:dnɪs] maleducazione *f*

ru·di·men·ta·ry [ru:dɪ'mentərɪ] *adj* rudimentale

ru·di·ments ['ru:dɪmənts] *npl* rudimenti *mpl*

rue·ful ['ru:fʊl] *adj* rassegnato

rue·ful·ly ['ru:fəlɪ] *adv* con aria rassegnata

ruf·fi·an ['rʌfɪən] delinquente *m/f*

ruf·fle ['rʌfl] **1** *n* (*on dress*) gala *f* **2** *v/t hair* scompigliare; *person* turbare; **get ~d** agitarsi

rug [rʌg] tappeto *m*; (*blanket*) coperta *f* (da viaggio)

rug·by ['rʌgbɪ] SP rugby *m inv*

R

rug·by 'league rugby *m inv* a tredici; **'rug·by match** partita *f* di rugby; **'rug·by play·er** giocatore *m* di rugby; **rug·by 'un·ion** rugby *m inv* a quindici

rug·ged ['rʌgɪd] *adj coastline* frastagliato; *face, features* marcato

ru·in ['ruːɪn] **1** *n* rovina *f*; **~s** rovine; **in ~s** *city, building* in rovina; *plans, career* rovinato **2** *v/t* rovinare; **be ~ed** *financially* essere rovinato

rule [ruːl] **1** *n of club, game* regola *f*; (*authority*) dominio *m*; *for measuring* metro *m* (a stecche); **as a ~** generalmente **2** *v/t country* governare; **the judge ~d that ...** il giudice ha stabilito che ... **3** *v/i of monarch* regnare

♦ **rule out** *v/t* escludere

rul·er ['ruːlə(r)] *for measuring* righello *m*; *of state* capo *m*

rul·ing ['ruːlɪŋ] **1** *n* decisione *f* **2** *adj party* di governo

rum [rʌm] *drink* rum *m inv*

rum·ble ['rʌmbl] *v/i of stomach* brontolare; *of thunder* rimbombare

♦ **rum·mage around** ['rʌmɪdʒ] *v/i* frugare

ru·mour ['ruːmə(r)] **1** *n* voce *f* **2** *v/t: it is ~ed that ...* corre voce che ...

rump [rʌmp] *of animal* groppa *f*

rum·ple ['rʌmpl] *v/t clothes, paper* spiegazzare

rump·'steak bistecca *f* di girello

run [rʌn] **1** *n on foot* corsa *f*; *distance* tragitto *m*; *in tights* sfilatura *f*; **go for a ~** andare a correre; **go for a ~ in the car** andare a fare un giro in macchina; **make a ~ for it** scappare; **a criminal on the ~** un evaso, un'evasa; **in the short ~/in the long ~** sulle prime / alla lunga; **a ~ on the dollar** una forte richiesta di dollari; **it's had a three year ~** *of play* ha tenuto cartellone per tre anni **2** *v/i* (*pret ran, pp run*) *of person, animal* correre; *of river* scorrere; *of trains, buses* viaggiare; *of paint, makeup* sbavare; *of nose* colare; *of play* tenere il cartellone; *of software* girare; *of engine, machine*

funzionare; **don't leave the tap ~ning** non lasciare il rubinetto aperto; **~ for President** *in election* candidarsi alla presidenza **3** *v/t* (*pret ran, pp run*) correre; (*take part in: race*) partecipare a; *business, hotel, project etc* gestire; *software* lanciare; *car* usare; *risk* correre; **can I ~ you to the station?** ti porto alla stazione?; **he ran his eye down the page** diede uno sguardo alla pagina

♦ **run across** *v/t* imbattersi in

♦ **run away** *v/i* scappare

♦ **run down 1** *v/t* (*knock down*) investire; (*criticize*) parlare male di; *stocks* ridurre **2** *v/i of battery* scaricarsi

♦ **run into** *v/t* (*meet*) imbattersi in; *difficulties* trovare

♦ **run off 1** *v/i* scappare **2** *v/t* (*print off*) stampare

♦ **run out** *v/i of contract, time* scadere; *of supplies* esaurirsi

♦ **run out of** *v/t patience* perdere; *supplies* rimanere senza; **I ran out of petrol** ho finito la benzina; **we are running out of time** il tempo sta per scadere

♦ **run over 1** *v/t* (*knock down*) investire; **can we run over the details again?** possiamo rivedere i particolari? **2** *v/i of water etc* traboccare

♦ **run through** *v/t rehearse, go over* rivedere

♦ **run up** *v/t debts, large bill* accumulare; *clothes* mettere insieme

run·a·way ['rʌnəweɪ] *n* ragazzo *m*, -a *f* scappato di casa

run-'down *adj person* debilitato; *part of town, building* fatiscente

rung[1] [rʌŋ] *of ladder* piolo *m*

rung[2] [rʌŋ] *pp →* **ring**

run·ner ['rʌnə(r)] *athlete* velocista *m/f*

run·ner 'beans *npl* fagiolini *mpl*

run·ner-'up secondo *m*, -a *f* classificato (-a)

run·ning ['rʌnɪŋ] **1** *n* SP corsa *f*; *of business* gestione *f* **2** *adj:* **for two days ~** per due giorni di seguito

R

run·ning 'wa·ter acqua f corrente

run·ny ['rʌnɪ] adj substance liquido; nose che cola

'run-up SP rincorsa f; **in the ~ to** nel periodo che precede …

'run·way pista f

rup·ture ['rʌptʃə(r)] **1** n rottura f; MED lacerazione f; (hernia) ernia f **2** v/i of pipe etc scoppiare

ru·ral ['rʊərəl] adj rurale

ruse [ruːz] stratagemma m

rush [rʌʃ] **1** n corsa f; **do sth in a ~** fare qc di corsa; **be in a ~** andare di fretta; **what's the big ~?** che fretta c'è? **2** v/t person mettere fretta o premura a; meal mangiare in fretta; **~ s.o. to hospital / the airport** portare qu di corsa all'ospedale / aeroporto **3** v/i affrettarsi

'rush hour ora f di punta

Rus·sia ['rʌʃə] Russia f

Rus·sian ['rʌʃən] **1** adj russo **2** n russo m, -a f; language russo m

rust [rʌst] **1** n ruggine f **2** v/i arrugginirsi

rus·tle ['rʌsl] **1** n of silk, leaves fruscio m **2** v/i of silk, leaves frusciare

'rust-proof adj a prova di ruggine

rust re·mov·er ['rʌstrɪmuːvə(r)] smacchiatore m per la ruggine

rust·y ['rʌstɪ] adj also fig arrugginito; **I'm a little ~** sono un po' arrugginito

rut [rʌt] in road solco m; **be in a ~** fig essersi fossilizzato

ruth·less ['ruːθlɪs] adj spietato

ruth·less·ly adv spietatamente

ruth·less·ness ['ruːθlɪsnɪs] spietatezza f

rye [raɪ] segale f

'rye bread pane m di segale

S

sab·bat·i·cal [sə'bætɪkl] n of academic anno m sabbatico

sab·o·tage ['sæbətɑːʒ] **1** n sabotaggio m **2** v/t sabotare

sab·o·teur [sæbə'tɜː(r)] sabotatore m, -trice f

sac·cha·rin ['sækərɪn] n saccarina f

sa·chet ['sæʃeɪ] of shampoo, cream etc bustina f

sack [sæk] **1** n bag sacco m; **get the ~** F essere licenziato **2** v/t F licenziare

sa·cred ['seɪkrɪd] adj sacro

sac·ri·fice ['sækrɪfaɪs] **1** n sacrificio m; **make ~s** fig fare sacrifici **2** v/t sacrificare

sac·ri·lege ['sækrɪlɪdʒ] sacrilegio m

sad [sæd] adj triste; state of affairs deplorevole

sad·dle ['sædl] **1** n sella f **2** v/t horse sellare; **~ s.o. with sth** fig affibbiare qc a qu

sa·dism ['seɪdɪzm] sadismo m

sa·dist ['seɪdɪst] sadista m/f

sa·dis·tic [sə'dɪstɪk] adj sadistico

sad·ly ['sædlɪ] adv tristemente; (regrettably) purtroppo

sad·ness ['sædnɪs] tristezza f

safe [seɪf] **1** adj not dangerous sicuro; not in danger al sicuro; driver prudente; **is it ~ to walk here?** non è pericoloso camminare qui? **2** n cassaforte f

'safe·guard 1 n protezione f, salvaguardia f; **as a ~ against** per proteggersi contro **2** v/t proteggere

safe'keep·ing: give sth to s.o. for ~ dare qc in custodia a qu

safe·ly ['seɪflɪ] adv arrive, complete first test etc senza problemi; drive prudentemente; assume tranquillamente

safe·ty ['seɪftɪ] sicurezza f

'safe·ty belt cintura f di sicurezza; **'safe·ty-con·scious** adj attento ai problemi di sicurezza; **safe·ty 'first** prudenza *f*; **'safe·ty pin** spilla *f* di sicurezza

sag [sæg] **1** *n in ceiling* incurvatura *f* **2** *v/i* (*pret & pp* **-ged**) *of ceiling* incurvarsi; *of rope* allentarsi

sa·ga ['sɑ:gə] saga *f*

sage [seɪdʒ] *n herb* salvia *f*

Sa·git·tar·i·us [sædʒɪ'teərɪəs] ASTR Sagittario *m*

said [sed] *pret & pp* → **say**

sail [seɪl] **1** *n of boat* vela *f*; *trip* veleggiata *f*; **go for a ~** fare un giro in barca (a vela) **2** *v/t yacht* pilotare **3** *v/i* fare vela; (*depart*) salpare

'sail·board 1 *n* windsurf *m inv* **2** *v/i* fare windsurf

'sail·board·ing windsurf *m inv*

sail·ing ['seɪlɪŋ] SP vela *f*

'sail·ing boat barca *f* a vela

'sail·ing ship veliero *m*

sail·or ['seɪlə(r)] marinaio *m*; **be a bad/good ~** soffrire / non soffrire il mal di mare

saint [seɪnt] santo *m*, -a *f*

sake [seɪk] *n*: **for my/your ~** per il mio/il tuo bene; **for the ~ of** per; **for the ~ of peace** per amor di pace

sal·ad ['sæləd] insalata *f*

sal·ad 'dress·ing condimento *m* per l'insalata

sal·a·ry ['sælərɪ] stipendio *m*

'sal·a·ry scale scala *f* salariale

sale [seɪl] vendita *f*; **at reduced prices** svendita *f*, saldi *mpl*; **for ~ sign** in vendita; **be on ~** essere in vendita

sales [seɪlz] *npl department* reparto *m* vendite

'sales as·sist·ant, **'sales clerk** *Am in shop* commesso *m*, -a *f*; **'sales fig·ures** *npl* fatturato *m*; **'sales·man** venditore *m*; **sales 'man·ag·er** direttore *m*, -trice *f* delle vendite; **'sales meet·ing** riunione *f* marketing e vendite; **sales wom·an** venditrice *f*

sa·lient ['seɪlɪənt] *adj* saliente

sa·li·va [sə'laɪvə] saliva *f*

salm·on ['sæmən] (*pl salmon*) salmone *m*

sa·loon [sə'lu:n] MOT berlina *f*; *Am*: *bar* bar *m inv*

salt [sɒlt] **1** *n* sale *m* **2** *v/t food* salare

'salt·cel·lar saliera *f*; **salt 'wa·ter** acqua *f* salata; **'salt-wa·ter fish** pesce *m* di mare

salt·y ['sɒltɪ] *adj* salato

sal·u·tar·y ['sæljutərɪ] *adj experience* salutare

sa·lute [sə'lu:t] **1** *n* MIL saluto *m*; **take the ~** ricevere i saluti **2** *v/t & v/i* salutare

sal·vage ['sælvɪdʒ] *v/t from wreck* ricuperare

sal·va·tion [sæl'veɪʃn] salvezza *f*

Sal·va·tion 'Ar·my Esercito *m* della Salvezza

same [seɪm] **1** *adj* stesso **2** *pron* stesso; **the ~** lo stesso, la stessa; **Happy New Year – the ~ to you** Buon anno! – Grazie e altrettanto!; **he's not the ~ any more** non è più lo stesso; **all the ~** (*even so*) lo stesso; **men are all the ~** gli uomini sono tutti uguali; **it's all the ~ to me** per me è uguale **3** *adv*: **the ~** allo stesso modo; **I still feel the ~ about that** la penso sempre allo stesso modo

sam·ple ['sɑ:mpl] **1** *n* campione *m* **2** *v/t food, product* provare

san·a·to·ri·um [sænə'tɔ:rɪəm] casa *f* di cura

sanc·ti·mo·ni·ous [sæŋktɪ'məunɪəs] *adj* moraleggiante

sanc·tion ['sæŋkʃn] **1** *n* (*approval*) approvazione *f*; (*penalty*) sanzione *f* **2** *v/t* (*approve*) sancire

sanc·ti·ty ['sæŋktətɪ] santità *f*

sanc·tu·a·ry ['sæŋktjʊərɪ] REL santuario *m*; *for wild animals* riserva *f*

sand [sænd] **1** *n* sabbia *f* **2** *v/t with sandpaper* smerigliare

san·dal ['sændl] sandalo *m*

'sand·bag sacchetto *m* di sabbia; **'sand·blast** *v/t* sabbiare; **sand dune** duna *f*

sand·er ['sændə(r)] *tool* smerigliatrice *f*

'sand·pa·per 1 *n* carta *f* smerigliata **2** *v/t* smerigliare

'sand·stone arenaria *f*

sand·wich ['sænwɪdʒ] **1** n tramezzino **m 2** v/t: *be ~ed between two ...*
essere incastrato tra due ...

sand·y ['sændɪ] adj *beach* sabbioso;
full of sand pieno di sabbia; *hair*
rossiccio

sane [seɪn] adj sano di mente

sang [sæŋ] pret → **sing**

san·i·ta·ry ['sænɪtərɪ] adj *conditions*
igienico; *installations* sanitario

'san·i·ta·ry tow·el assorbente m
(igienico)

san·i·ta·tion [sænɪ'teɪʃn] (*sanitary
installations*) impianti mpl igienici;
(*removal of waste*) fognature fpl

san·i·ty ['sænətɪ] sanità f inv mentale

sank [sæŋk] pret → **sink**

San·ta Claus ['sæntəklɔːz] Babbo m
Natale

sap [sæp] **1** n *in tree* linfa f **2** v/t (*pret
& pp* **-ped**) *s.o.'s energy* indebolire

sap·phire ['sæfaɪə(r)] n *jewel* zaffiro
m

sar·casm ['sɑːkæzm] sarcasmo m

sar·cas·tic [sɑː'kæstɪk] adj sarcastico

sar·cas·tic·al·ly [sɑː'kæstɪklɪ] adv
sarcasticamente

sar·dine [sɑː'diːn] sardina f

Sar·din·i·a [sɑː'dɪnɪə] Sardegna f

Sar·din·i·an [sɑː'dɪnɪən] **1** adj sardo
2 n sardo m, -a f

sar·don·ic [sɑː'dɒnɪk] adj sardonico

sar·don·ic·al·ly [sɑː'dɒnɪklɪ] adv sar-
donicamente

sash [sæʃ] *on dress* fusciacca f; *on
uniform* fascia f; *on window* vetro m
scorrevole (di finestra a ghigliottina)

Sa·tan ['seɪtn] Satana m

satch·el ['sætʃl] *for schoolchild* cartella f

sat·el·lite ['sætəlaɪt] satellite m

'sat·el·lite dish antenna f parabolica

sat·el·lite T'V TV f inv satellitare

sat·in ['sætɪn] adj satin m inv

sat·ire ['sætaɪə(r)] satira f

sa·tir·i·cal [sə'tɪrɪkl] adj satirico

sat·i·rist ['sætərɪst] satirista m

sat·i·rize ['sætəraɪz] v/t satireggiare

sat·is·fac·tion [sætɪs'fækʃn] soddisfazione f; *is that to your ~?* è di suo
gradimento?

sat·is·fac·to·ry [sætɪs'fæktərɪ] adj
soddisfacente; *just good enough* sufficiente; *this is not ~* non è sufficiente

satisfy ['sætɪsfaɪ] v/t (*pret & pp* **-ied**)
customers, needs, curiosity soddisfare; *requirement* rispondere a; – *s.o.'s
hunger* sfamare qu; *I am satisfied
had enough to eat* sono sazio; *I am
satisfied that ...* (*convinced*) sono
convinto che ...; *I hope you're
satisfied!* sei contento?

Sat·ur·day ['sætədeɪ] sabato m

sauce [sɔːs] salsa f, sugo m

'sauce·pan pentola f

sau·cer ['sɔːsə(r)] piattino m

sauc·y ['sɔːsɪ] adj *person, dress* provocante

Sa·u·di A·ra·bi·a [saʊdɪə'reɪbɪə]
Arabia f Saudita

Sa·u·di A·ra·bi·an [saʊdɪə'reɪbɪən]
1 adj saudita **2** n *person* saudita m/f

sau·na ['sɔːnə] sauna f

saun·ter ['sɔːntə(r)] v/i passeggiare;
he ~ed in at 10.30 è arrivato tranquillamente alle 10.30

saus·age ['sɒsɪdʒ] salsiccia f

sav·age ['sævɪdʒ] **1** adj *animal* selvaggio; *attack, criticism* feroce **2** n
selvaggio m, -a f

sav·age·ry ['sævɪdʒrɪ] ferocia f

save [seɪv] **1** v/t (*rescue*) salvare;
money, time, effort risparmiare; (*collect*) raccogliere; COMPUT salvare;
goal parare; *you could ~ yourself a
lot of effort* potresti risparmiarti
parecchi sforzi **2** v/i (*put money
aside*) risparmiare; SP parare **3** n SP
parata f

♦ **save up for** v/t risparmiare per

sav·er ['seɪvə(r)] *person* risparmiatore m, -trice f

sav·ing ['seɪvɪŋ] risparmio m

sav·ings ['seɪvɪŋz] npl risparmi mpl

'sav·ings ac·count libretto m di risparmio; **savings and 'loan** Am →
building society; **'sav·ings bank**
cassa f di risparmio

sa·vior *Am*, **sa·viour** ['seɪvjə(r)] REL salvatore *m*

sa·vor *etc Am* → **savour** *etc*

sa·vour ['seɪvə(r)] **1** *n* sapore *m* **2** *v/t* assaporare

sa·voury ['seɪvərɪ] *adj not sweet* salato (*non dolce*)

saw[1] [sɔː] **1** *n tool* sega *f* **2** *v/t* segare

saw[2] [sɔː] *pret* → **see**

♦ **saw off** *v/t* segare via

'**saw·dust** segatura *f*

sax·o·phone ['sæksəfəʊn] sassofono *m*

say [seɪ] **1** *v/t* (*pret & pp* **said**) dire; ***can I ~ something?*** posso dire una cosa?; ***that is to ~*** sarebbe a dire; ***what do you ~ to that?*** cosa ne dici?; ***what does the note ~?*** cosa dice il biglietto? **2** *n:* ***have one's ~*** dire la propria; ***have a ~ in sth*** avere voce in capitolo in qc

say·ing ['seɪɪŋ] detto *m*

scab [skæb] *on skin* crosta *f*

scaf·fold·ing ['skæfəldɪŋ] *on building* impalcature *fpl*

scald [skɔːld] *v/t* scottare; ***~ o.s.*** scottarsi

scale[1] [skeɪl] *on fish* scaglia *f*

scale[2] [skeɪl] **1** *n of map*, MUS scala *f*; *on thermometer* scala *f* graduata; *of project* portata *f*; ***on a large ~*** su vasta scala; ***on a small ~*** su scala ridotta **2** *v/t cliffs etc* scalare

♦ **scale down** *v/t* ridurre

scale 'draw·ing disegno *m* in scala

scales [skeɪlz] *npl for weighing* bilancia *fsg*

scal·lop ['skɒləp] *n* capasanta *f*

scalp [skælp] *n* cuoio *m* capelluto

scal·pel ['skælpl] bisturi *m*

scam [skæm] F truffa *f*

scam·pi ['skæmpɪ] *gamberoni mpl in pastella fritti*

scan [skæn] **1** *v/t* (*pret & pp* **-ned**) *horizon* scrutare; *page* scorrere; *foetus* fare l'ecografia di; *brain* fare la TAC di; COMPUT scannerizzare **2** *n* (*brain ~*) TAC *f inv*; *of foetus* ecografia *f*

♦ **scan in** *v/t* COMPUT scannerizzare

scan·dal ['skændl] scandalo *m*

scan·dal·ize ['skændəlaɪz] *v/t* scandalizzare

scan·dal·ous ['skændələs] *adj* scandaloso

Scan·di·na·vi·a   [skændɪ'neɪvɪə] Scandinavia *f*

scan·ner ['skænə(r)] scanner *m inv*

scant [skænt] *adj* scarso

scant·i·ly ['skæntɪlɪ] *adv:* ***~ clad*** succintamente vestito

scant·y ['skæntɪ] *adj clothes* succinto

scape·goat ['skeɪpgəʊt] capro *m* espiatorio

scar [skɑː(r)] **1** *n* cicatrice *f* **2** *v/t* (*pret & pp* **-red**) *face* lasciare cicatrici su; *fig* segnare

scarce [skeəs] *adj in short supply* scarso; ***make o.s. ~*** squagliarsela F

scarce·ly ['skeəslɪ] *adv* appena; ***there was ~ anything left*** non rimaneva quasi più niente

scar·ci·ty ['skeəsɪtɪ] scarsità *f inv*

scare [skeə(r)] **1** *v/t* spaventare; ***be ~d of*** avere paura di **2** *n* (*panic, alarm*) panico *m*; ***give s.o. a ~*** mettere paura a qu

♦ **scare away** *v/t* far scappare

'**scare·crow** spaventapasseri *m inv*

scare·mon·ger ['skeəmʌngə(r)] allarmista *m/f*

scarf [skɑːf] *around neck* sciarpa *f*; *over head* foulard *m inv*

scar·let ['skɑːlət] *adj* scarlatto

scar·let 'fe·ver scarlattina *f*

scar·y ['skeərɪ] *adj* che fa paura

scath·ing ['skeɪðɪŋ] *adj* caustico

scat·ter ['skætə(r)] **1** *v/t leaflets, seeds* spargere; *crowd* disperdere **2** *v/i of people* disperdersi

scat·ter·brained ['skætəbreɪnd] *adj* sventato

scat·tered ['skætəd] *adj family, villages* sparpagliato; ***~ showers*** precipitazioni sparse

scat·ty ['skætɪ] *adj* sventato

scav·enge ['skævɪndʒ] *v/i* frugare tra i rifiuti

scav·eng·er ['skævɪndʒə(r)] *animal* animale *m* necrofago; (*person*) persona *f* che fruga tra i rifiuti

sce·na·ri·o [sɪ'nɑːrɪəʊ] scenario *m*

S

scene [si:n] scena *f*; (*argument*) scenata *f*; **make a ~** fare una scenata; **~s** THEA scenografia *f*; *jazz / rock* **~** il mondo del jazz / rock; **behind the ~s** dietro le quinte

sce·ne·ry ['si:nǝrɪ] paesaggio *m*; THEA scenario *m*

scent [sent] *n of roses* profumo *m*; *of animal* odore *m*

scep·tic ['skeptɪk] scettico *m*, -a *f*

scep·ti·cal ['skeptɪkl] *adj* scettico

scep·ti·cal·ly ['skeptɪklɪ] *adv* scetticamente

scep·ti·cism ['skeptɪsɪzm] scetticismo *m*

sched·ule ['ʃedjuːl] **1** *n of events, work* programma *m*; *for trains* orario *m*; **be on ~** *of work, of train etc* essere in orario; **be behind ~** *of work, of train etc* essere in ritardo **2** *v/t put on schedule* programmare; **it's ~d for completion next month** il completamento dei lavori è previsto per il mese prossimo

sched·uled 'flight ['ʃedju:ld] volo *m* di linea

scheme [ski:m] **1** *n* (*plan*) piano *m*; (*plot*) complotto *m* **2** *v/i* (*plot*) complottare, tramare

schem·ing ['ski:mɪŋ] *adj* intrigante

schiz·o·phre·ni·a [skɪtsǝ'fri:nɪǝ] schizofrenia *f*

schiz·o·phren·ic [skɪtsǝ'frenɪk] **1** *n* schizofrenico *m*, -a *f* **2** *adj* schizofrenico

schol·ar ['skɒlǝ(r)] studioso *m*, -a *f*

schol·ar·ly ['skɒlǝ(r)lɪ] *adj* dotto

schol·ar·ship ['skɒlǝʃɪp] (*scholarly work*) erudizione *f*; (*financial award*) borsa *f* di studio

school [sku:l] scuola *f*

'school bag (*satchel*) cartella *f*; **'school·boy** scolaro *m*; **'school·children** scolari *mpl*; **'school days** *npl* tempi *mpl* della scuola; **'school·girl** scolara *f*; **'school·mas·ter** maestro *m*; **'school·mate** compagno *m*, -a *f* di scuola; **'school·mis·tress** maestra *f*; **'school·teach·er** insegnante *m/f*

sci·at·i·ca [saɪ'ætɪkǝ] sciatica *f*

sci·ence ['saɪǝns] scienza *f*

sci·ence 'fic·tion fantascienza *f*

sci·en·tif·ic [saɪǝn'tɪfɪk] *adj* scientifico

sci·en·tist ['saɪǝntɪst] scienziato *m*, -a *f*

scis·sors ['sɪzǝz] *npl* forbici *fpl*

scoff[1] [skɒf] *v/t food* sbafare

scoff[2] [skɒf] *v/i* (*mock*) canzonare

♦ **scoff at** *v/t* deridere

scold [skǝʊld] *v/t* sgridare

scone [skɒn] focaccina *f* o dolcetto *m* da mangiare con il tè

scoop [sku:p] **1** *n for grain, flour* paletta *f*; *for ice cream* cucchiaio *m* dosatore; *of ice cream* pallina *f*; (*story*) scoop *m inv* **2** *v/t* (*pick up*) raccogliere

♦ **scoop up** *v/t* sollevare tra le braccia

scoot·er ['sku:tǝ(r)] *with motor* scooter *m inv*; *child's* monopattino *m*

scope [skǝʊp] portata *f*; (*opportunity*) possibilità *f inv*

scorch [skɔːtʃ] *v/t* bruciare

scorch·ing hot ['skɔːtʃɪŋ] *adj* torrido

score [skɔː(r)] **1** *n* SP punteggio *m*; (*written music*) spartito *m*; *of film etc* colonna *f* sonora; **what's the ~?** SP a quanto sono / siamo?; **have a ~ to settle with s.o.** avere un conto in sospeso con qu; **keep** (**the**) **~** tenere il punteggio **2** *v/t goal, point* segnare; (*cut*) incidere **3** *v/i* segnare; (*keep the score*) tenere il punteggio

'score·board segnapunti *m inv*

scor·er ['skɔːrǝ(r)] *of goal, point* marcatore *m*, -trice *f*; (*score-keeper*) segnapunti *m/f inv*

scorn [skɔːn] **1** *n* disprezzo *m*; **pour ~ on sth** deridere qc **2** *v/t idea, suggestion* disprezzare

scorn·ful ['skɔːnfʊl] *adj* sprezzante

scorn·ful·ly ['skɔːnfʊlɪ] *adv* sprezzantemente

Scor·pi·o ['skɔːpɪǝʊ] ASTR Scorpione *m*

Scot [skɒt] scozzese *m/f*

Scotch [skɒtʃ] (*whisky*) scotch *m inv*

Scotch 'tape® *Am* scotch® *m*

scot-'free *adv*: **get off ~** farla franca

Scot·land ['skɒtlənd] Scozia *f*

Scots·man ['skɒtsmən] scozzese *m*

Scots·wom·an ['skɒtswʊmən] scozzese *f*

Scot·tish ['skɒtɪʃ] *adj* scozzese

scoun·drel ['skaʊndrəl] birbante *m/f*

scour¹ ['skaʊə(r)] *v/t* (*search*) setacciare

scour² ['skaʊə(r)] *v/t pans* sfregare

scout [skaʊt] *n* (*boy ~*) boy-scout *m inv*

scowl [skaʊl] **1** *n* sguardo *m* torvo **2** *v/i* guardare storto

scram [skræm] *v/i* (*pret* & *pp* **-med**) F filare

scram·ble ['skræmbl] **1** *n* (*rush*) corsa *f* **2** *v/t message* rendere indecifrabile **3** *v/i climb* inerpicarsi; **he ~d to his feet** si rialzò in fretta

scram·bled 'eggs ['skræmbld] *npl* uova *fpl* strapazzate

scrap [skræp] **1** *n metal* rottame *m*; (*fight*) zuffa *f*; (*little bit*) briciolo *m* **2** *v/t* (*pret* & *pp* **-ped**) *plan, project* abbandonare

'scrap·book album *m inv*

scrape [skreɪp] **1** *n on paintwork* graffio *m* **2** *v/t paintwork, one's arm etc* graffiare; *vegetables* raschiare; **~ a living** sbarcare il lunario

♦ scrape through *v/i in exam* passare per il rotto della cuffia

'scrap heap cumulo *m* di rottami; **good for the ~** da buttare via; **scrap 'met·al** rottami *mpl*; **scrap 'pa·per** carta *f* già usata

scrap·py ['skræpɪ] *adj work, writing* senza capo né coda

scratch [skrætʃ] **1** *n mark* graffio *m*; **have a ~** *to stop itching* grattarsi; **start from ~** ricominciare da zero; **not up to ~** non all'altezza **2** *v/t* (*mark*) graffiare; *because of itch* grattare **3** *v/i of cat, nails* graffiare

scrawl [skrɔːl] **1** *n* scarabocchio *m* **2** *v/t* scarabocchiare

scraw·ny ['skrɔːnɪ] *adj* scheletrico

scream [skriːm] **1** *n* urlo *m*; **~s of laughter** risate *fpl* fragorose **2** *v/i* urlare

screech [skriːtʃ] **1** *n of tyres* stridio *m*; (*scream*) strillo *m* **2** *v/i of tyres* stridere; (*scream*) strillare

screen [skriːn] **1** *n in room, hospital* paravento *m*; *of smoke* cortina *f*; *cinema*, COMPUT, *of television* schermo *m*; **on the ~** *in film* sullo schermo; **on (the) ~** COMPUT su schermo **2** *v/t* (*protect, hide*) riparare; *film* proiettare; *for security reasons* vagliare

'screen·play sceneggiatura *f*; 'screen sav·er COMPUT salvaschermo *m inv*; 'screen test *for film* provino *m*

screw [skruː] **1** *n* vite *f* (metallica); V (*sex*) scopata *f* V **2** *v/t* V scopare V; (*cheat*) fregare F; **~ sth to sth** avvitare qc a qc

♦ screw up **1** *v/t eyes* strizzare; *piece of paper* appallottolare; F (*make a mess of*) mandare all'aria **2** *v/i* F (*make a bad mistake*) fare un casino F

'screw·driv·er cacciavite *m*

screwed 'up [skruːd'ʌp] *adj* F *psychologically* complessato

'screw top *on bottle* tappo *m* a vite

screw·y ['skruːɪ] *adj* F svitato

scrib·ble ['skrɪbl] **1** *n* scarabocchio *m* **2** *v/t* & *v/i* (*write quickly*) scarabocchiare

scrimp [skrɪmp] *v/i*: **~ and scrape** risparmiare fino all'ultimo soldo

script [skrɪpt] *for film, play* copione *m*; (*form of writing*) scrittura *f*

scrip·ture ['skrɪptʃə(r)]: **the (Holy) Scriptures** le Sacre Scritture *fpl*

'script·writ·er sceneggiatore *m*, -trice *f*

scroll [skrəʊl] *n* rotolo *m* di pergamena

♦ scroll down *v/i* COMPUT far scorrere il testo in avanti

♦ scroll up *v/i* COMPUT far scorrere il testo indietro

scrounge [skraʊndʒ] *v/t* scroccare

scroung·er ['skraʊndʒə(r)] scroccone *m*, -a *f*

scrub [skrʌb] *v/t* (*pret* & *pp* **-bed**) *floors, hands* sfregare (con spazzola)

scrub·bing brush ['skrʌbɪŋ] *for floor* spazzolone *m*

scruff·y ['skrʌfɪ] *adj* trasandato

scrum [skrʌm] *in rugby* mischia *f*

♦ **scrunch up** [skrʌntʃ] *v/t plastic cup etc* accartocciare

scru·ples ['skru:plz] *npl* scrupoli *mpl*; **have no ~ about doing sth** non avere scrupoli a fare qc

scru·pu·lous ['skru:pjʊləs] *adj* scrupoloso

scru·pu·lous·ly ['skru:pjʊləslɪ] *adv* (*meticulously*) scrupolosamente

scru·ti·nize ['skru:tɪnaɪz] *v/t text* esaminare attentamente; *face* scrutare

scru·ti·ny ['skru:tɪnɪ] attento esame *m*; **come under ~** essere sottoposto ad attento esame

scu·ba div·ing ['sku:bə] immersione *f* subacquea

scuf·fle ['skʌfl] *n* tafferuglio *m*

sculp·tor ['skʌlptə(r)] scultore *m*, -trice *f*

sculp·ture ['skʌlptʃə(r)] scultura *f*

scum [skʌm] *on liquid* schiuma *f*; (*pej: people*) feccia *f*

sea [si:] mare *m*; **by the ~** al mare

'sea·bed fondale *m* marino; **'sea·bird** uccello *m* marino; **'sea·far·ing** ['si:feərɪŋ] *adj nation* marinaro; **'sea·food** frutti *mpl* di mare; **'sea·front** lungomare *m inv*; **'sea·go·ing** *adj vessel* d'alto mare; **'sea·gull** gabbiano *m*

seal¹ [si:l] *n animal* foca *f*

seal² [si:l] **1** *n on document* sigillo *m*; TECH chiusura *f* ermetica **2** *v/t container* chiudere ermeticamente

♦ **seal off** *v/t area* bloccare l'accesso a

'sea lev·el: above / below ~ sopra / sotto il livello del mare

seam [si:m] *n on garment* cucitura *f*; *of ore* filone *m*

'sea·man marinaio *m*

seam·stress ['si:mstrɪs] sarta *f*

'sea·port porto *m* marittimo

'sea pow·er *nation* potenza *f* marittima

search [sɜ:tʃ] **1** *n for s.o. / sth* ricerca *f*; *of person, building* perquisizione *f*; **in ~ of** alla ricerca di **2** *v/t person,*

building, baggage perquisire; *area* perlustrare

♦ **search for** *v/t* cercare

search·ing ['sɜ:tʃɪŋ] *adj look* penetrante

'search·light riflettore *m*; **'search par·ty** squadra *f* di ricerca; **'search war·rant** mandato *m* di perquisizione

'sea·shore riva *f* (del mare)

'sea·sick *adj* con il mal di mare; **be ~** avere il mal di mare; **get ~** soffrire il mal di mare; **'sea·side** *n: at the ~** al mare; **go to the ~** andare al mare; **~ resort** località *f* balneare

sea·son ['si:zn] *n* stagione *f*; **in / out of ~** in / fuori stagione

sea·son·al ['si:znl] *adj* stagionale

sea·soned ['si:znd] *adj wood* stagionato; *traveller, campaigner etc* esperto

sea·son·ing ['si:znɪŋ] condimento *m*

'sea·son tick·et abbonamento *m*

seat [si:t] **1** *n* posto *m*; *of trousers* fondo *m*; POL seggio *m*; **please take a ~** si accomodi **2** *v/t* (*have seating for*) avere posti a sedere per; **please remain ~ed** state seduti, per favore

'seat belt cintura *f* di sicurezza

'sea ur·chin riccio *m* di mare

'sea·weed alga *f*

se·clud·ed [sɪ'klu:dɪd] *adj* appartato

se·clu·sion [sɪ'klu:ʒn] isolamento *m*

sec·ond¹ ['sekənd] **1** *n of time* secondo *m*; **just a ~** un attimo **2** *adj* secondo **3** *adv come in* secondo **4** *v/t motion* appoggiare

se·cond² [sɪ'kɒnd] *v/t: be ~ed to* essere assegnato a

sec·on·da·ry ['sekəndrɪ] *adj* secondario

sec·on·da·ry ed·u·ca·tion istruzione *f* secondaria

sec·ond 'best *adj* secondo (dopo il migliore); **sec·ond 'big·gest** *adj* secondo in ordine di grandezza; **sec·ond 'class** *adj ticket* di seconda classe; **sec·ond 'floor** secondo piano *m*; *Am* terzo piano; **sec·ond 'gear** MOT seconda *f* (marcia); **'sec·ond·hand** *n on clock* lancetta *f* dei secondi; **'sec·ond-hand** *adj & adv* di seconda mano

sec·ond·ly ['sekəndlɪ] *adv* in secondo luogo

sec·ond-'rate *adj* di second'ordine

sec·ond 'thoughts: *I've had ~ thoughts* ci ho ripensato

se·cre·cy ['si:krəsɪ] segretezza *f*

se·cret ['si:krət] **1** *n* segreto *m*; *do sth in ~* fare qc in segreto **2** *adj* segreto

se·cret 'a·gent agente *m* segreto

sec·re·tar·i·al [sekrə'teərɪəl] *adj tasks, job* di segretaria

sec·re·tar·y ['sekrətərɪ] segretario *m*, -a *f*; POL ministro *m*

Sec·re·tar·y of 'State *in USA* Segretario *m* di Stato

se·crete [sɪ'kri:t] *v/t (give off)* secernere; *(hide away)* nascondere

se·cre·tion [sɪ'kri:ʃn] secrezione *f*

se·cre·tive ['si:krətɪv] *adj* riservato

se·cret·ly ['si:krətlɪ] *adv* segretamente

se·cret po'lice polizia *f* segreta

se·cret 'ser·vice servizio *m* segreto

sect [sekt] setta *f*

sec·tion ['sekʃn] sezione *f*

sec·tor ['sektə(r)] settore *m*

sec·u·lar ['sekjʊlə(r)] *adj* laico

se·cure [sɪ'kjʊə(r)] **1** *adj shelf etc* saldo *feeling* sicuro; *job* stabile **2** *v/t shelf etc* assicurare; *s.o.'s help, finances* assicurarsi

se·cu·ri·ty [sɪ'kjʊərətɪ] *in job* sicurezza *f*; *in relationship* stabilità *f inv*; *for investment* garanzia *f*; *at airport etc* sicurezza *f*

se'cu·ri·ties mar·ket FIN mercato *m* dei titoli

se'cu·ri·ty a·lert stato *m* di allarme; **se'cu·ri·ty check** controllo *m* di sicurezza; **se'cu·ri·ty-con·scious** *adj* attento alla sicurezza; **se'cu·ri·ty forces** *npl police* forze *fpl* dell'ordine; **se'cu·ri·ty forces** *npl* forze *fpl* di sicurezza; **se'cu·ri·ty guard** guardia *f* giurata; **se'cu·ri·ty risk** minaccia *f* per la sicurezza

se·date [sɪ'deɪt] *v/t* somministrare sedativi a

se·da·tion [sɪ'deɪʃn]: *be under ~* essere sotto l'effetto di sedativi

sed·a·tive ['sedətɪv] *n* sedativo *m*

sed·en·ta·ry ['sedəntərɪ] *adj job* sedentario

sed·i·ment ['sedɪmənt] sedimento *m*

se·duce [sɪ'dju:s] *v/t* sedurre

se·duc·tion [sɪ'dʌkʃn] seduzione *f*

se·duc·tive [sɪ'dʌktɪv] *adj smile, look* seducente; *offer* allettante

see [si:] *v/t (pret saw, pp seen)* vedere; *(understand)* capire; *romantically* uscire con; *I ~ capisco; can I ~ the manager?* vorrei vedere il direttore; *you should ~ a doctor* dovresti andare dal medico; *~ s.o. home* accompagnare a casa qu; *I'll ~ you to the door* t'accompagno alla porta; *~ you!* F ciao! F

♦ **see about** *v/t (look into)* provvedere a; *I'll see about it* ci penso io

♦ **see off** *v/t at airport etc* salutare; *(chase away)* scacciare

♦ **see out** *v/t*: **see s.o. out** accompagnare qu alla porta

♦ **see to** *v/t*: **see to sth** occuparsi di qc; **see to it that sth gets done** assicurarsi che qc venga fatto

seed [si:d] *single* seme *m*; *collective* semi *mpl*; *in tennis* testa *f* di serie; *go to ~ of person, district* ridursi male

seed·ling ['si:dlɪŋ] semenzale *m*

seed·y ['si:dɪ] *adj bar, district* squallido

see·ing (that) ['si:ɪŋ] *conj* visto che

seek [si:k] *v/t & v/i (pret & pp sought)* cercare

seem [si:m] *v/i* sembrare; *it seems that ...* sembra che ...

seem·ing·ly ['si:mɪŋlɪ] *adv* apparentemente

seen [si:n] *pp* → **see**

seep [si:p] *v/i of liquid* filtrare

♦ **seep out** *v/i of liquid* filtrare

see·saw ['si:sɔ:] *n* altalena *f* (a bilico)

seethe [si:ð] *v/i fig* fremere di rabbia

'see-through *adj dress, material* trasparente

seg·ment ['segmənt] segmento *m*; *of orange* spicchio *m*

S

seg·ment·ed [seg'mentɪd] *adj* frazionato

seg·re·gate ['segrɪgeɪt] *v/t* separare

seg·re·ga·tion [segrɪ'geɪʃn] segregazione *f*

seis·mol·o·gy [saɪz'mɒlədʒɪ] sismologia *f*

seize [siːz] *v/t s.o., s.o.'s arm* afferrare; *power* prendere; *opportunity* cogliere; *of Customs, police etc* sequestrare

♦ **seize up** *v/i of engine* grippare

sei·zure ['siːʒə(r)] MED attacco *m; of drugs etc* sequestro *m*

sel·dom ['seldəm] *adv* raramente

se·lect [sɪ'lekt] **1** *v/t* selezionare **2** *adj* (*exclusive*) scelto

se·lec·tion [sɪ'lekʃn] scelta *f; that/ those chosen* selezione *f*

se·lec·tion pro·cess procedimento *m* di selezione

se·lec·tive [sɪ'lektɪv] *adj* selettivo

self [self] (*pl* **selves** [selvz]) io *m*

self-ad·dressed 'en·ve·lope [selfə'drest] busta *f* col proprio nome e indirizzo *m;* **self-as'sur·ance** sicurezza *f* di sé; **self-as'sured** [selfə'ʃʊəd] *adj* sicuro di sé; **self-ca·ter·ing a'part·ment** appartamento *m* indipendente con cucina; **self-'cen·tered** *Am*, **self-'cen·tred** [self'sentəd] *adj* egocentrico; **self-'clean·ing** *adj oven* autopulente; **self-con'fessed** [selfkən'fest] *adj* dichiarato; **self-'con·fi·dence** fiducia *f* in se stessi; **self-'con·fi·dent** *adj* sicuro di sé; **self-'con·scious** *adj* insicuro; *smile* imbarazzato; *feel ~* sentirsi a disagio; **self-'con·scious·ness** disagio *m;* **self-con'tained** [selfkən'teɪnd] *adj flat* indipendente; **self con'trol** autocontrollo *m;* **self-de'fence**, **self-de'fense** *Am personal* legittima difesa *f; of state* autodifesa *f;* **self-'dis·ci·pline** autodisciplina *f;* **self-'doubt** dubbi *mpl* personali; **self-em·ployed** [selfɪm'plɔɪd] *adj* autonomo; **self-e'steem** autostima *f;* **self-'ev·i·dent** *adj* evidente; **self-ex'pres·sion** espressione *f* di sé;

self-'gov·ern·ment autogoverno *m;* **self-'in·ter·est** interesse *m* personale

self·ish ['selfɪʃ] *adj* egoista

self·less ['selflɪs] *adj person* altruista; *attitude, dedication* altruistico

self-made 'man [self'meɪd] self-made man *m inv;* **self-'pit·y** autocommiserazione *f;* **self-'por·trait** autoritratto *m;* **self-pos'sessed** *adj* padrone di sé; **self-re'li·ant** *adj* indipendente; **self-re'spect** dignità *f inv;* **self-'right·eous** *adj pej* presuntuoso; **self-'sat·is·fied** *adj pej* soddisfatto di sé; **self-'ser·vice** *adj* self-service; **self-ser·vice 'res·tau·rant** self-service *m inv;* **self-taught** [self'tɔːt] *adj* autodidatta

sell [sel] (*pret & pp* **sold**) **1** *v/t* vendere; *you have to ~ yourself* devi saperti vendere **2** *v/i of products* vendere

♦ **sell out of** *v/t* esaurire; *we are sold out of candles* abbiamo esaurito le candele

♦ **sell up** *v/i* vendere

'sell-by date data *f* di scadenza; *be past its ~* essere scaduto

sell·er ['selə(r)] venditore *m*, -trice *f*

sell·ing ['selɪŋ] *n* COM vendita *f*

'sell·ing point COM punto *m* forte (che fa vendere il prodotto)

Sel·lo·tape® ['seləteɪp] scotch® *m*

se·men ['siːmən] sperma *m*

se·mes·ter [sɪ'mestər] *Am* semestre *m*

sem·i ['semɪ] *n* → **semidetached 'house**

'sem·i·cir·cle semicerchio *m*

sem·i'cir·cu·lar *adj* semicircolare

sem·i·'co·lon punto e virgola *m*

sem·i·con'duc·tor ELEC semiconduttore *m*

sem·i·de·tached ('house) [semɪdɪ'tætʃt] villa *f* bifamiliare

semi·fi·nal semifinale *f*

sem·i·nar ['semɪnɑː(r)] seminario *m*

sem·i'skilled *adj* parzialmente qualificato

sen·ate ['senət] senato *m*

sen·a·tor ['senətə(r)] senatore *m*, -trice *f*

send [send] *v/t* (*pret & pp* **sent**) mandare; **~ sth to s.o.** mandare qc a qu; **~ s.o. to s.o.** mandare qu da qu; **~ her my best wishes** mandale i miei saluti

♦ **send back** *v/t* mandare indietro

♦ **send for** *v/t doctor, help* (mandare a) chiamare

♦ **send in** *v/t troops* inviare; *next interviewee* far entrare; *application form* spedire

♦ **send off** *v/t letter, fax etc* spedire; *footballer* espellere

♦ **send up** *v/t* (*mock*) prendere in giro

send·er ['sendə(r)] *of letter* mittente *m/f*

se·nile ['si:naɪl] *adj pej* rimbambito

se·nil·i·ty [sɪ'nɪlətɪ] *pej* rimbambimento *m*

se·ni·or ['si:nɪə(r)] *adj* (*older*) più anziano; *in rank* di grado superiore; **be ~ to s.o.** *in rank* essere di grado superiore rispetto a qu

se·ni·or 'cit·i·zen anziano *m*, -a *f*

se·ni·or·i·ty [si:nɪ'ɒrətɪ] *in job* anzianità *f inv*

sen·sa·tion [sen'seɪʃn] (*feeling*) sensazione *f*; (*surprise event*) scalpore *m*; **be a ~** essere sensazionale

sen·sa·tion·al [sen'seɪʃnl] *adj* sensazionale

sense [sens] **1** *n* (*meaning*) significato *m*; (*purpose, point*) senso *m*; (*common sense*) buonsenso *m*; (*sight, smell etc*) senso *m*; (*feeling*) sensazione; **in a ~** = in un certo senso; **talk ~, man!** ragiona!; **come to one's ~s** tornare in sé; **it doesn't make ~** non ha senso; **there's no ~ in trying / waiting** non ha senso provare / aspettare **2** *v/t* sentire

sense·less ['senslɪs] *adj* (*pointless*) assurdo

sen·si·ble ['sensəbl] *adj person, decision* assennato; *advice* sensato; *clothes, shoes* pratico

sen·si·bly ['sensəblɪ] *adv* assennatamente

sen·si·tive ['sensətɪv] *adj* sensibile

sen·si·tiv·i·ty [sensə'tɪvətɪ] sensibilità *f inv*

sen·sor ['sensə(r)] sensore *m*

sen·su·al ['sensjʊəl] *adj* sensuale

sen·su·al·i·ty [sensjʊ'ælətɪ] sensualità *f inv*

sen·su·ous ['sensjʊəs] *adj* sensuale

sent [sent] *pret & pp →* **send**

sen·tence ['sentəns] **1** *n* GRAM frase *m*; LAW condanna *f* **2** *v/t* LAW condannare

sen·ti·ment ['sentɪmənt] (*sentimentality*) sentimentalismo *m*; (*opinion*) opinione *f*

sen·ti·men·tal [sentɪ'mentl] *adj* sentimentale

sen·ti·men·tal·i·ty [sentɪmen'tælətɪ] sentimentalismo *m*

sen·try ['sentrɪ] sentinella *f*

sep·a·rate ['sepərət] **1** *adj* separato **2** *v/t* ['sepəreɪt] separare; **~ sth from sth** separare qc da qc **3** *v/i* *of couple* separarsi

sep·a·rat·ed ['sepəreɪtɪd] *adj couple* separato

sep·a·rate·ly ['sepərətlɪ] *adv* separatamente

sep·a·ra·tion [sepə'reɪʃn] separazione *f*

Sep·tem·ber [sep'tembə(r)] settembre *m*

sep·tic ['septɪk] *adj* infetto; **go ~** *of wound* infettarsi

se·quel ['si:kwəl] seguito *m*

se·quence ['si:kwəns] sequenza *f*; **in ~** di seguito; **out of ~** fuori tempo; **the ~ of events** l'ordine dei fatti

se·rene [sɪ'ri:n] *adj* sereno

ser·geant ['sɑ:dʒənt] sergente *m*

se·ri·al ['sɪərɪəl] *n* serial *m inv*

se·ri·al·ize ['sɪərɪəlaɪz] *v/t novel on TV* trasmettere a puntate

'se·ri·al kill·er serial killer *m/f inv*; **'se·ri·al num·ber** *of product* numero *m* di serie; **'se·ri·al port** COMPUT porta *f* seriale

se·ries ['sɪəri:z] *nsg* serie *f inv*

se·ri·ous ['sɪərɪəs] *adj illness, situation, damage* grave; *person, company* serio; **I'm ~** dico sul serio; **listen,**

this is ~ ascolta, è una cosa seria; **we'd better take a ~ look at it** dovremo considerarlo seriamente

se·ri·ous·ly ['sɪərɪəslɪ] *adv injured* gravemente; *(extremely)* estremamente; **~ though, ...** scherzi a parte, ...; **~?** davvero?; **take s.o. ~** prendere sul serio qu

se·ri·ous·ness ['sɪərɪəsnɪs] *of person* serietà *f inv; of situation, illness etc* gravità *f inv*

ser·mon ['sɜːmən] predica *f*

ser·vant ['sɜːvənt] domestico *m*, -a *f*

serve [sɜːv] **1** *n in tennis* servizio *m* **2** *v/t food, customer, one's country,* servire; **it ~s you/him right** ti/gli sta bene **3** *v/i give out food, in tennis* servire; *as politician etc* prestare servizio

♦ **serve up** *v/t meal* servire

serv·er ['sɜːvə(r)] COMPUT server *m inv*

serv·ice ['sɜːvɪs] **1** *n to customers, community* servizio *m; for vehicle, machine* manutenzione *f; for vehicle* revisione *f; in tennis* servizio *m;* **~s** servizi; **the ~s** MIL le forze armate **2** *v/t vehicle* revisionare; *machine* fare la manutenzione di

'serv·ice ar·e·a area *f* di servizio; 'serv·ice charge *in restaurant, club* servizio *m;* 'serv·ice in·dus·try settore *m* terziario; 'serv·ice·man MIL militare *m;* 'serv·ice pro·vid·er COMPUT fornitore *m* di servizi; 'serv·ice sec·tor settore *m* terziario; 'serv·ice sta·tion stazione *f* di servizio

serv·i·ette [sɜːvɪ'et] tovagliolino *m*

ser·vile ['sɜːvaɪl] *adj pej* servile

serv·ing ['sɜːvɪŋ] *n of food* porzione *f*

ses·sion ['seʃn] *of parliament* sessione *f; with psychiatrist, consultant etc* seduta *f*

set [set] **1** *n of tools* set *m inv; of dishes, knives* servizio *m; of books* raccolta *f; group of people* cerchia *f;* MATH insieme *m;* (THEA: *scenery)* scenografia *f; where a film is made* set *m inv; in tennis* set *m inv;* **television ~** televisore *m* **2** *v/t (pret & pp set) (place)* mettere; *film, novel etc* ambientare; *date, time, limit* fissare; *mechanism* regolare; *alarm clock* mettere; *broken limb* ingessare; *jewel* montare; *(typeset)* comporre; **~ the table** apparecchiare (la tavola); **~ a task for s.o.** assegnare un compito a qu **3** *v/i (pret & pp set) of sun* tramontare; *of glue* indurirsi **4** *adj views, ideas* rigido; *(ready)* pronto; **be dead ~ on (doing) sth** essere deciso a fare qc; **be very ~ in one's ways** essere abitudinario; **~ book/reading** *in course* libro/lettura in programma; **~ meal** menù *m inv* fisso

♦ **set apart** *v/t:* **set sth apart from sth** distinguere qc da qc

♦ **set aside** *v/t for future use* mettere da parte

♦ **set back** *v/t in plans etc* ritardare; **it set me back £400** F mi è costato 400 sterline

♦ **set off 1** *v/i on journey* partire **2** *v/t explosion* causare; *chain reaction, alarm* far scattare

♦ **set out 1** *v/i on journey* partire **2** *v/t ideas, proposal, goods* esporre; **set out to do sth** *(intend)* proporsi di fare qc

♦ **set to** *v/i start on a task* mettersi all'opera

♦ **set up 1** *v/t new company* fondare; *system* mettere in opera; *equipment, machine* piazzare; F *(frame)* incastrare F **2** *v/i in business* mettersi in affari

'set·back contrattempo *m*

set·tee [se'tiː] *(couch, sofa)* divano *m*

set·ting ['setɪŋ] *n of novel etc* ambientazione *f; of house* posizione *f*

set·tle ['setl] **1** *v/i of bird, dust, beer* posarsi; *of building* assestarsi; *to live* stabilirsi **2** *v/t dispute* comporre; *issue, uncertainty* risolvere; *s.o.'s debts, the bill* saldare; *nerves, stomach* calmare; **that ~s it!** è deciso!

♦ **settle down** *v/i (stop being noisy)* calmarsi; *(stop wild living)* mettere la testa a posto; *in an area* stabilirsi

◆**settle for** v/t (*take, accept*) accontentarsi di

◆**settle up** v/i (*pay*) regolare i conti; *in hotel etc* pagare il conto

set·tled ['setld] *adj weather* stabile

set·tle·ment ['setlmənt] *of dispute* composizione f; (*payment*) pagamento m

set·tler ['setlə(r)] *in new country* colonizzatore m, -trice f

'**set·up** n (*structure*) organizzazione f; (*relationship*) relazione f; F (*frameup*) montatura f

sev·en ['sevn] sette

sev·en·teen [sevn'tiːn] diciassette

sev·en·teenth [sevn'tiːnθ] diciassettesimo, -a

sev·enth ['sevnθ] n & adj settimo, -a

sev·en·ti·eth ['sevntɪɪθ] n & adj settantesimo, -a

sev·en·ty ['sevntɪ] settanta

sev·er ['sevə(r)] v/t *arm, cable etc* recidere; *relations* troncare

sev·e·ral ['sevrl] **1** *adj* parecchi **2** *pron* parecchi m, -ie f

se·vere [sɪ'vɪə(r)] *adj illness* grave; *penalty, teacher, face* severo; *winter, weather* rigido

se·vere·ly [sɪ'vɪəlɪ] *adv punish* severamente; *speak, stare* duramente; *injured, disrupted* gravemente

se·ver·i·ty [sɪ'verətɪ] *of illness* gravità f inv; *of look etc* durezza f; *of penalty* severità f inv; *of winter* rigidità f inv

sew [səʊ] v/t & v/i (*pret* -ed, pp **sewn**) cucire

◆**sew on** v/t *button* attaccare

sew·age ['suːɪdʒ] acque fpl di scolo

'**sew·age plant** impianto m per il riciclaggio delle acque di scolo

sew·er ['suːə(r)] fogna f

sew·ing ['səʊɪŋ] n cucito m

'**sew·ing ma·chine** macchina f da cucire

sex [seks] sesso m; **have ~ with** avere rapporti sessuali con

sex·ist ['seksɪst] **1** *adj* sessista **2** n sessista m/f

sex·u·al ['seksjʊəl] *adj* sessuale

sex·u·al as·sault violenza f sessuale;

sex·u·al ha·rass·ment molestie fpl sessuali; **sex·u·al 'in·ter·course** rapporti mpl sessuali

sex·u·al·i·ty [seksjʊ'ælətɪ] sessualità f inv

sex·u·al·ly ['seksjʊlɪ] *adv* sessualmente

sex·u·al·ly trans·mit·ted dis'ease [seksjʊltrænz'mɪtɪd] malattia f venerea

'**sex·y** ['seksɪ] *adj* sexy inv

shab·bi·ly ['ʃæbɪlɪ] *adv dressed* in modo trasandato; *treat* in modo meschino

shab·bi·ness ['ʃæbɪnɪs] *of coat etc* trasandatezza f

shab·by ['ʃæbɪ] *adj coat etc* trasandato; *treatment* meschino

shack [ʃæk] baracca f

shade [ʃeɪd] **1** n *for lamp* paralume m; *of colour* tonalità f inv; **in the ~** all'ombra **2** v/t *from sun, light* riparare

shad·ow ['ʃædəʊ] n ombra f

shad·y ['ʃeɪdɪ] *adj spot* all'ombra; *character, dealings* losco

shaft [ʃaːft] *of axle* albero m; *of mine* pozzo m

shag·gy ['ʃægɪ] *adj hair* arruffato; *dog* dal pelo arruffato

shake [ʃeɪk] **1** n: **give sth a good ~** dare una scrollata a qc **2** v/t (*pret* **shook**, pp **shaken**) scuotere; *emotionally* sconvolgere; **~ hands** stringersi la mano; **~ hands with s.o.** stringere la mano a qu **3** v/i *of hands, voice, building* tremare

shak·en ['ʃeɪkən] **1** *adj emotionally* scosso **2** pp → **shake**

'**shake-up** rimpasto m

'**shak·y** ['ʃeɪkɪ] *adj table etc* traballante; *after illness, shock* debole; *grasp of sth, grammar etc* incerto; *voice, hand* tremante

shall [ʃæl] v/aux ◊ *future*: **I ~ do my best** farò del mio meglio; **I shan't see them** non li vedrò ◊ *suggesting*: **~ we go now?** andiamo?

shal·low ['ʃæləʊ] *adj water* poco profondo; *person* superficiale

sham·bles ['ʃæmblz] nsg casino m F

shame [ʃeɪm] **1** *n* vergogna *f*; **bring ~ on ...** disonorare ...; **what a ~!** che peccato!; **~ on you!** vergognati! **2** *v/t*: **~ s.o. into doing sth** indurre qu a fare qc per vergogna

shame·ful [ˈʃeɪmful] *adj* vergognoso

shame·ful·ly [ˈʃeɪmfulɪ] *adv* vergognosamente

shame·less [ˈʃeɪmlɪs] *adj* svergognato

sham·poo [ʃæmˈpuː] **1** *n* shampoo *m inv*; **a ~ and set** shampoo e messa in piega **2** *v/t* fare lo shampoo a

shape [ʃeɪp] **1** *n* forma *f* **2** *v/t clay* dar forma a; *person's life, character* forgiare; *the future* determinare

shape·less [ˈʃeɪplɪs] *adj dress etc* informe

shape·ly [ˈʃeɪplɪ] *adv figure* ben fatto

share [ʃeə(r)] **1** *n* parte *f*, FIN azione *f*; **do one's ~ of the work** fare la propria parte del lavoro **2** *v/t* dividere; *s.o.'s feelings, opinions* condividere **3** *v/i* dividere; **do you mind sharing with Patrick?** ti dispiace dividere con Patrick?

♦ **share out** *v/t* spartire

ˈ**share·hold·er** azionista *m/f*

shark [ʃɑːk] *fish* squalo *m*

sharp [ʃɑːp] **1** *adj knife* affilato; *mind, pain* acuto; *taste* aspro **2** *adv* MUS in dieisis; **at 3 o'clock** ~ alle 3 precise

sharp·en [ˈʃɑːpn] *v/t knife* affilare; *skills* raffinare

sharp ˈprac·tice pratiche *fpl* poco oneste

shat [ʃæt] *pret & pp → shit*

shat·ter [ˈʃætə(r)] **1** *v/t glass* frantumare; *illusions* distruggere **2** *v/i of glass* frantumarsi

shat·tered [ˈʃætəd] *adj* F (*exhausted*) esausto; (*very upset*) sconvolto

shat·ter·ing [ˈʃætərɪŋ] *adj news, experience* sconvolgente; *effect* tremendo

shave [ʃeɪv] **1** *v/t* radere **2** *v/i* farsi la barba **3** *n*: **have a ~** farsi la barba; **that was a close ~** ce l'abbiamo fatta per un pelo

♦ **shave off** *v/t beard* tagliarsi; *from piece of wood* piallare

shav·en [ˈʃeɪvn] *adj head* rasato

shav·er [ˈʃeɪvə(r)] *electric* rasoio *m*

shav·ing brush [ˈʃeɪvɪŋ] pennello *m* da barba

ˈ**shav·ing soap** sapone *m* da barba

shawl [ʃɔːl] scialle *m*

she [ʃiː] *pron* lei; **~ has three children** ha tre figli; **you're funny, ~'s not** tu sei spiritoso, lei no; **there ~ is** eccola

shears [ʃɪəz] *npl for gardening* cesoie *fpl*; *for sewing* forbici *fpl*

sheath [ʃiːθ] *n for knife* guaina *f*, *contraceptive* preservativo *m*

shed[1] [ʃed] *v/t* (*pret & pp shed*) *blood* spargere; *tears* versare; *leaves* perdere; **~ light on** *fig* fare luce su

shed[2] [ʃed] *n* baracca *f*

sheep [ʃiːp] (*pl sheep*) pecora *f*

ˈ**sheep·dog** cane *m* pastore

sheep·ish [ˈʃiːpɪʃ] *adj* imbarazzato

ˈ**sheep·skin** *adj lining* di montone

sheer [ʃɪə(r)] *adj madness, luxury* puro; *drop, cliffs* ripido

sheet [ʃiːt] *for bed* lenzuolo *m*; *of paper* foglio *m*; *of metal, glass* lastra *f*

shelf [ʃelf] (*pl shelves* [ʃelvz]) mensola *f*; **shelves** scaffale *msg*, ripiani *mpl*

ˈ**shelf-life** *of product* durata *f* di conservazione

shell [ʃel] **1** *n of mussel etc* conchiglia *f*; *of egg* guscio *m*; *of tortoise* corazza *f*; MIL granata *f*; **come out of one's ~** *fig* uscire dal guscio **2** *v/t peas* sbucciare; MIL bombardare

ˈ**shell·fire** bombardamento *m*; **come under ~** essere bombardato

ˈ**shell·fish** crostacei *mpl*

shel·ter [ˈʃeltə(r)] **1** *n* (*refuge*) riparo *m*; *construction* rifugio *m* **2** *v/i from rain, bombing etc* ripararsi **3** *v/t* (*protect*) proteggere

shel·tered [ˈʃeltəd] *adj place* riparato; **lead a ~ life** vivere nella bambagia

shelve [ʃelv] *v/t fig* accantonare

shep·herd [ˈʃepəd] *n* pastore *m*

sher·ry [ˈʃerɪ] sherry *m inv*

shield [ʃiːld] **1** *n* scudo *m*; *sports trophy* scudetto *m*; TECH schermo *m* di protezione *f* **2** *v/t* (*protect*) proteggere

shift [ʃɪft] **1** *n* (*change*) cambiamento *m*; *period of work* turno *m* **2** *v/t* (*move*) spostare; *stains etc* togliere **3** *v/i* (*move*) spostarsi; *of wind* cambiare direzione; *that's ~ing!* F è un bolide!

'**shift key** COMPUT tasto *m* shift; '**shift work** turni *mpl*; '**shift work-er** turnista *m/f*

'**shift·y** ['ʃɪftɪ] *adj pej* losco

'**shift·y-look·ing** *adj pej* dall'aria losca

shil·ly-shal·ly ['ʃɪlɪʃælɪ] *v/i* (*pret & pp -ied*) F tentennare

shim·mer ['ʃɪmə(r)] *v/i* luccicare

shin [ʃɪn] *n* stinco *m*

shine [ʃaɪn] **1** *v/i* (*pret & pp* **shone**) *of sun, shoes, metal* splendere; *fig: of student etc* brillare **2** *v/t* (*pret & pp* **shone**) *torch etc* puntare **3** *n* *on shoes etc* lucentezza *f*

shin·gle ['ʃɪŋgl] *on beach* ciottoli *mpl*

shin·gles ['ʃɪŋglz] *nsg* MED fuoco *m* di Sant'Antonio

shin·y ['ʃaɪnɪ] *adj surface* lucido

ship [ʃɪp] **1** *n* nave *f* **2** *v/t* (*pret & pp -ped*) (*send*) spedire; (*send by sea*) spedire via mare

ship·ment ['ʃɪpmənt] (*consignment*) carico *m*

'**ship·own·er** armatore *m*

ship·ping ['ʃɪpɪŋ] *n* (*sea traffic*) navigazione *f*; (*sending*) trasporto *m* (via mare)

'**ship·ping com·pa·ny** compagnia *f* di navigazione

'**ship·shape** *adj* in perfetto ordine; '**ship·wreck 1** *n* naufragio *m* **2** *v/t*: *be ~ed* naufragare; '**ship·yard** cantiere *m* navale

shirk [ʃɜːk] *v/t* scansare

shirk·er ['ʃɜːkə(r)] scansafatiche *m/f inv*

shirt [ʃɜːt] camicia *f*; *in his ~ sleeves* in maniche di camicia

shit [ʃɪt] **1** *n* F merda *f* P; *bad quality goods, work* stronzata *f* P **2** *v/i* (*pret & pp* **shat**) cagare P **3** *int* merda P

shit·ty ['ʃɪtɪ] *adj* F di merda P

shiv·er ['ʃɪvə(r)] **1** *v/i* rabbrividire **2** *n* brivido *m*

shock [ʃɒk] **1** *n* shock *m inv*; ELEC scossa *f*; *be in ~* MED essere in stato di shock **2** *v/t* scioccare; *be ~ed by* essere scioccato da

'**shock ab·sorb·er** MOT ammortizzatore *m*

shock·ing ['ʃɒkɪŋ] *adj behaviour, poverty* scandaloso; F *very bad* allucinante F

shock·ing·ly ['ʃɒkɪŋlɪ] *adv behave* scandalosamente; *bad, late, expensive* terribilmente

shod·dy ['ʃɒdɪ] *adj goods* scadente; *behaviour* meschino

shoe [ʃuː] scarpa *f*

'**shoe·horn** calzascarpe *m inv*; '**shoe·lace** laccio *m* di scarpa; '**shoe·mak·er**, '**shoe mend·er** calzolaio *m*; '**shoe-shop** negozio *m* di scarpe; '**shoe·string** *n*: *do sth on a ~* fare qc con pochi soldi

shone [ʃɒn] *pret & pp* → **shine**

♦ **shoo away** [ʃuː] *v/t children, chicken* scacciare

shook [ʃʊk] *pret* → **shake**

shoot [ʃuːt] **1** *n* BOT germoglio *m* **2** *v/t v/t* (*pret & pp* **shot**) sparare; *film* girare; *~ s.o. in the leg* colpire qu alla gamba; *~ s.o. for desertion* fucilare qu per diserzione

♦ **shoot down** *v/t aeroplane* abbattere

♦ **shoot off** *v/i* (*rush off*) precipitarsi

♦ **shoot up** *v/i of prices* salire alle stelle; *of children* crescere molto; *of new suburbs, buildings etc* spuntare; F *of drug addict* farsi F

shoot·ing star ['ʃuːtɪŋ] stella *f* cadente

shop [ʃɒp] **1** *n* negozio *m*; *talk ~* parlare di lavoro **2** *v/i* (*pret & pp -ped*) fare acquisti; *go ~ping* andare a fare spese

'**shop as·sis·tant** commesso *m*, -a *f*; '**shop·keep·er** negoziante *m/f*; **shop·lift·er** ['ʃɒplɪftə(r)] taccheggiatore *m*, -trice *f*; **shop·lift·ing** ['ʃɒplɪftɪŋ] *n* taccheggio *m*

S

shop·per ['ʃɒpə(r)] *person* acquirente *m/f*

shop·ping ['ʃɒpɪŋ] *activity* fare spese; *items* spesa *f*; ***do one's ~*** fare la spesa

'**shop·ping bag** borsa *f* per la spesa; '**shop·ping cen·ter** *Am*, '**shop·ping cen·tre** centro *m* commerciale; '**shop·ping list** lista *f* della spesa; '**shop·ping mall** centro *m* commerciale

shop 'stew·ard rappresentante *m/f* sindacale

shop 'win·dow vetrina *f*

shore [ʃɔː(r)] riva *f*; ***on ~*** not at sea a terra

short [ʃɔːt] **1** *adj* in *length*, *distance* corto; in *height* basso; in *time* breve; ***be ~ of*** essere a corto di **2** *adv*: ***cut a vacation / meeting ~*** interrompere una vacanza / riunione; ***stop a person ~*** interrompere una persona; ***go ~ of*** fare a meno di; ***in ~*** in breve

short·age ['ʃɔːtɪdʒ] mancanza *f*

short 'cir·cuit *n* corto *m* circuito; **short·com·ing** ['ʃɔːtkʌmɪŋ] difetto *m*; '**short cut** scorciatoia *f*

short·en ['ʃɔːtn] **1** *v/t* accorciare **2** *v/i* accorciarsi

'**short·fall** deficit *m inv*; in *hours etc* mancanza *f*; '**short·hand** *n* stenografia *f*; **short·'hand·ed** *adj*: ***be ~*** essere a corto di personale; '**short·list** *n of candidates* rosa *f* dei candidati

short-lived ['ʃɔːtlɪvd] *adj* di breve durata

'**short·ly** ['ʃɔːtlɪ] *adv* (*soon*) tra breve; ***~ before / after*** poco prima / dopo

short·ness ['ʃɔːtnɪs] *of visit* brevità *f inv*; in *height* bassa statura *f*

shorts [ʃɔːts] *npl* calzoncini *mpl*

short·sight·ed [ʃɔːt'saɪtɪd] *adj also fig* miope; **short-sleeved** ['ʃɔːtsliːvd] *adj* a maniche corte; **short-staffed** [ʃɔːt'stɑːft] *adj* a corto di personale; **short 'sto·ry** racconto *m*; **short-tem·pered** [ʃɔːt'tempəd] *adj* irascibile; '**short-term** *adj* a bre-

ve termine; '**short time** *n*: ***be on ~*** *of workers* lavorare a orario ridotto; '**short wave** RAD onde *fpl* corte

shot [ʃɒt] **1** *n from gun* sparo *m*; (*photograph*) foto *f*; (*injection*) puntura *f*; ***be a good / poor ~*** essere un buon / pessimo tiratore; ***like a ~*** *accept, run off* come un razzo **2** *pret & pp* → **shoot**

'**shot·gun** fucile *m* da caccia

should [ʃʊd] *v/aux*: ***what ~ I do?*** cosa devo fare?; ***you ~n't do that*** non dovresti farlo; ***that ~ be long enough*** dovrebbe essere lungo abbastanza; ***you ~ have heard him!*** avresti dovuto sentirlo!

shoul·der ['ʃəʊldə(r)] *n* ANAT spalla *f*

'**shoul·der bag** borsa *f* a tracolla; '**shoul·der blade** scapola *f*; '**shoulder strap** spallina *f*

shout [ʃaʊt] **1** *n* grido *m*, urlo *m* **2** *v/t & v/i* gridare, urlare

♦ **shout at** *v/i* urlare a

shout·ing ['ʃaʊtɪŋ] *n* urla *fpl*

shove [ʃʌv] **1** *n* spinta *f* **2** *v/t & v/i* spingere

♦ **shove in** *v/i* passare davanti; ***he shoved in in front of me*** mi è passato davanti

♦ **shove off** *v/i* F (*go away*) levarsi di torno

shov·el ['ʃʌvl] **1** *n* pala *f* **2** *v/t* spalare

show [ʃəʊ] **1** *n* THEA, TV spettacolo *m*; (*display*) manifestazione *f*; ***on ~*** *at exhibition* esposto; ***it's all done for ~*** *pej* è tutta una scena **2** *v/t* (*pret -ed*, *pp shown*) *passport, ticket* mostrare; *interest, emotion* dimostrare; *at exhibition* esporre; *film* proiettare; ***~ s.o. sth***, ***~ sth to s.o.*** mostrare qc a qu **3** *v/i* (*pret -ed*, *pp shown*) (*be visible*) vedersi; ***does it ~?*** si vede?; ***what's ~ing at the cinema?*** cosa danno al cinema?

♦ **show around** *v/t* far visitare

♦ **show in** *v/t* far entrare

♦ **show off 1** *v/t* skills mettere in risalto **2** *v/i pej* mettersi in mostra

♦ **show up 1** *v/t s.o.'s shortcomings etc* far risaltare; ***don't show me up in public*** non farmi fare brutta figura

2 v/i F (*arrive, turn up*) farsi vedere F; (*be visible*) notarsi

'show busi·ness il mondo dello spettacolo

'show·case *n* vetrinetta *f*; *fig* vetrina *f*

'show·down regolamento *m* di conti

show·er ['ʃaʊə(r)] **1** *n* of rain acquazzone *m*; *to wash* doccia *f*; *take a* ~ fare una doccia **2** v/i fare la doccia **3** v/t: ~ *s.o. with praise* coprire qu di lodi

'show·er cap cuffia *f* da doccia; 'show·er cur·tain tenda *f* della doccia; 'show·er·proof *adj* impermeabile

show-jump·er ['ʃəʊdʒʌmpə(r)] cavaliere *m*, cavallerizza *f* di concorso ippico

'show·jump·ing concorso *m* ippico

'show-off *pej* esibizionista *m/f*

'show·room show-room *m inv*; *in ~ condition* mai usato

show·y ['ʃəʊɪ] *adj* appariscente

shrank [ʃræŋk] *pret →* **shrink**

shred [ʃred] **1** *n* of paper strisciolina *f*, of cloth brandello *m*; of evidence, etc briciolo *m* **2** v/t (*pret & pp -ded*) *paper* stracciare; *in cooking* sminuzzare

shred·der ['ʃredə(r)] *for documents* distruttore *m* di documenti

shrewd [ʃruːd] *adj person, businessman* scaltro; *investment* oculato

shrewd·ly ['ʃruːdlɪ] *adv* oculatamente

shrewd·ness ['ʃruːdnɪs] oculatezza *f*

shriek [ʃriːk] **1** *n* strillo *m* **2** v/i strillare

shrill [ʃrɪl] *adj* stridulo

shrimp [ʃrɪmp] gamberetto *m*

shrine [ʃraɪn] santuario *m*

shrink¹ [ʃrɪŋk] v/i (*pret* **shrank**, *pp* **shrunk**) of material restringersi; *level of support etc* diminuire

shrink² [ʃrɪŋk] *n* F (*psychiatrist*) strizzacervelli *m/f inv*

'shrink-wrap v/t cellofanare

'shrink-wrap·ping *process* cellofanatura *f*; *material* cellophane® *m inv*

shriv·el ['ʃrɪvl] v/i avvizzire

Shrove 'Tues·day [ʃrəʊv] martedì *m* grasso

shrub [ʃrʌb] arbusto *m*

shrub·be·ry ['ʃrʌbərɪ] arboreto *m*

shrug [ʃrʌg] **1** *n* alzata *f* di spalle **2** v/i (*pret & pp -ged*) alzare le spalle **3** v/t (*pret & pp -ged*): ~ *one's shoulders* alzare le spalle

shrunk [ʃrʌŋk] *pp →* **shrink**

shud·der ['ʃʌdə(r)] **1** *n* of fear, disgust brivido *m*; of earth etc tremore *m* **2** v/i with fear, disgust rabbrividire; of earth, building tremare; *I ~ to think* non oso immaginare

shuf·fle ['ʃʌfl] **1** v/t cards mescolare **2** v/i in walking strascicare i piedi; *he ~d into the bathroom* è andato in bagno strascicando i piedi

shun [ʃʌn] v/t (*pret & pp -ned*) evitare

shut [ʃʌt] (*pret & pp* **shut**) **1** v/t chiudere **2** v/i of door, box chiudersi; of shop, bank chiudere; *they were ~* era chiuso

♦ shut down **1** v/t business chiudere; computer spegnere **2** v/i of business chiudere i battenti; of computer spegnersi

♦ shut off v/t chiudere

♦ shut up v/i F (be quiet) star zitto; *shut up!* zitto!

shut·ter ['ʃʌtə(r)] on window battente *m*; PHOT otturatore *m*

'shut·ter speed PHOT tempo *m* di apertura

shut·tle ['ʃʌtl] v/i fare la spola

'shut·tle·bus *at airport* bus *m inv* navetta; 'shut·tle·cock SP volano *m*; 'shut·tle ser·vice servizio *m* navetta

shy [ʃaɪ] *adj* timido

shy·ness ['ʃaɪnɪs] timidezza *f*

Si·a·mese 'twins [saɪə'miːz] *npl* fratelli *mpl* / sorelle *fpl* siamesi

Si·cil·i·an [sɪ'sɪlɪən] **1** *adj* siciliano **2** *n* siciliano *m*, -a *f*

Sic·i·ly ['sɪsɪlɪ] Sicilia *f*

sick [sɪk] *adj* malato; *sense of humour* crudele; *I feel ~ about to vomit* ho la nausea; *I'm going to be ~ vomit* ho voglia di vomitare; *be ~ of* (*fed up*

S

with) essere stufo di

sick·en ['sıkn] **1** *v/t* (*disgust*) disgustare **2** *v/i*: **be ~ing for sth** covare qc

sick·en·ing ['sıknıŋ] *adj* disgustoso

'sick leave *n*: **be on ~** essere in (congedo per) malattia

sick·ly ['sıklı] *adj person* delicato; *smell* stomachevole

sick·ness ['sıknıs] malattia *f*; (*vomiting*) nausea *f*

'sick·ness ben·e·fit *Br* indennità *f inv* di malattia

side [saıd] *n of box, house* lato *m*; *of person, mountain* fianco *m*; *of page, record* facciata *f*; SP squadra *f*; **take ~s** (*favour one side*) prendere posizione; **take ~s with** partegiare per; **I'm on your ~** sono dalla tua (parte); **~ by ~** fianco a fianco; **at the ~ of the road** sul ciglio della strada; **on the big / small ~** piuttosto grande / piccolo

◆ **side with** *v/t* prendere le parti di

'side·board credenza *f*; **'sideburns** *npl* basette *fpl*; **'side dish** contorno *m*; **'side ef·fect** effetto *m* collaterale; **'side·light** MOT luce *f* di posizione; **'side·line 1** *n* attività *f inv* collaterale **2** *v/t* sentirsi sminuito; **'side·step** *v/t* (*pret & pp -ped*) scansare; *fig* schivare; **'side street** via *f* laterale; **'side·track** *v/t* distrarre; **get ~ed by** essere distratto da; **'side·walk** *Am* marciapiede *m*; **side·ways** ['saıdweız] *adv* di lato

siege [si:dʒ] assedio *m*; **lay ~ to** assediare

sieve [sıv] *n* setaccio *m*

sift [sıft] *v/t* setacciare

◆ **sift through** *v/t details, data* passare al vaglio

sigh [saı] **1** *n* sospiro *m*; **heave a ~ of relief** tirare un respiro di sollievo **2** *v/i* sospirare

sight [saıt] *n* vista *f*; **~s of city** luoghi *mpl* da visitare; **catch ~ of** intravedere; **know by ~** conoscere di vista; **be within ~ of** essere visibile da; **out of ~ of** non visibile da; **out of ~** fuori dalla vista di; **what a ~ you are!**

come sei conciato!; **lose ~ of** *main objective etc* perdere di vista

sight·see·ing ['saıtsi:ıŋ] *n* visita *f* turistica; **I enjoy ~** mi piace visitare i posti; **go ~** fare un giro turistico

'sight·see·ing tour giro *m* turistico

'sight·seer ['saıtsi:ə(r)] turista *m/f*

sign [saın] **1** *n* (*indication*) segno *m*; (*road ~*) segnale *m*; *outside shop* insegna *f*; **it's a ~ of the times** è tipico dei nostri giorni **2** *v/t & v/i document* firmare

◆ **sign in** *v/i* firmare il registro (all'arrivo)

◆ **sign up** *v/i* (*join the army*) arruolarsi

sig·nal ['sıgnl] **1** *n* segnale *m*; **be sending out the right / wrong ~s** *fig* lanciare il messaggio giusto / sbagliato **2** *v/i of driver* segnalare

sig·na·to·ry ['sıgnətrı] *n* firmatario *m*, -a *f*

sig·na·ture ['sıgnətʃə(r)] firma *f*

sig·na·ture 'tune sigla *f* musicale

sig·net ring ['sıgnıtrıŋ] anello *m* con sigillo

sig·nif·i·cance [sıg'nıfıkəns] importanza *f*; (*meaning*) significato *m*

sig·nif·i·cant [sıg'nıfıkənt] *adj event etc* significativo; (*quite notable*) notevole

sig·nif·i·cant·ly [sıg'nıfıkəntlı] *adv larger, more expensive* notevolmente

sig·ni·fy ['sıgnıfaı] *v/t* (*pret & pp -ied*) significare

'sign lan·guage linguaggio *m* dei segni

'sign·post cartello *m* stradale

si·lence ['saıləns] **1** *n* silenzio *m*; **in ~ work, march** in silenzio; **~!** silenzio! **2** *v/t* mettere a tacere

si·lenc·er ['saılənsə(r)] *on gun* silenziatore *m*; *on car* marmitta *f*

si·lent ['saılənt] *adj* silenzioso; *film* muto; **stay ~** *not comment* tacere

sil·hou·ette [sılu:'et] *n* sagoma *f*

sil·i·con ['sılıkən] silicio *m*

sil·i·con 'chip chip *m inv* al silicio

sil·i·cone ['sılıkəʊn] silicone *m*

silk [sılk] **1** *n* seta *f* **2** *adj shirt etc* di seta

silk·y ['sɪlkɪ] *adj hair, texture* setoso

sil·li·ness ['sɪlɪnɪs] stupidità *f inv*

sil·ly ['sɪlɪ] *adj* stupido

si·lo ['saɪləʊ] silo *m*

sil·ver ['sɪlvə(r)] **1** *n metal* argento *m*; **~ objects** argenteria *f* **2** *adj ring* d'argento; *colour* argentato

sil·ver-plat·ed [sɪlvə'pleɪtɪd] *adj* placcato d'argento; **'sil·ver·ware** argenteria *f*; **sil·ver 'wed·ding** nozze *fpl* d'argento

sim·i·lar ['sɪmɪlə(r)] *adj* simile

sim·i·lar·i·ty [sɪmɪ'lærətɪ] rassomiglianza *f*

sim·i·lar·ly ['sɪmɪləlɪ] *adv* allo stesso modo

sim·mer ['sɪmə(r)] *v/i in cooking* sobbollire; *with rage* ribollire

♦ **simmer down** *v/i* calmarsi

sim·ple ['sɪmpl] *adj method, life, dress* semplice; *person* semplciotto

sim·ple-mind·ed [sɪmpl'maɪndɪd] *adj pej* semplciotto

sim·pli·ci·ty [sɪm'plɪsətɪ] semplicità *f inv*

sim·pli·fy ['sɪmplɪfaɪ] *v/t (pret & pp -ied)* semplificare

sim·plis·tic [sɪm'plɪstɪk] *adj* semplicistico

sim·ply ['sɪmplɪ] *adv (absolutely)* assolutamente; *in a simple way* semplicemente; *it is ~ the best* è assolutamente il migliore

sim·u·late ['sɪmjʊleɪt] *v/t* simulare

sim·ul·ta·ne·ous [sɪml'teɪnɪəs] *adj* simultaneo

sim·ul·ta·ne·ous·ly [sɪml'teɪnɪəslɪ] *adv* simultaneamente

sin [sɪn] **1** *n* peccato *m* **2** *v/i (pret & pp -ned)* peccare

since [sɪns] **1** *prep* da; **~ last week** dalla scorsa settimana **2** *adv* da allora; *I haven't seen him* ~ non lo vedo da allora **3** *conj in expressions of time* da quando; *(seeing that)* visto che; *~ you left* da quando sei andato via; *ever ~ I have known her* da quando la conosco; *~ you don't like it* visto che non ti piace

sin·cere [sɪn'sɪə(r)] *adj* sincero

sin·cere·ly [sɪn'sɪəlɪ] *adv* con sinceri-

tà; *hope* sinceramente; *Yours ~* Distinti saluti

sin·cer·i·ty [sɪn'serətɪ] sincerità *f inv*

sin·ful ['sɪnfʊl] *adj* peccaminoso

sing [sɪŋ] *v/t & v/i (pret* **sang***, pp* **sung***)* cantare

singe [sɪndʒ] *v/t* bruciacchiare

sing·er ['sɪŋə(r)] cantante *m/f*

sin·gle ['sɪŋgl] **1** *adj (sole)* solo; *(not double)* singolo; *bed, sheet* a una piazza; *(not married)* single; *with reference to Europe* single; *there wasn't a ~ ...* non c'era nemmeno un ...; *in ~ file* in fila indiana **2** *n* MUS singolo *m*; *(~ room)* (camera *f*) singola *f*; *ticket* biglietto *m* di sola andata; *person* single *m/f inv*; *~s in tennis* singolo

♦ **single out** *v/t (choose)* prescegliere; *(distinguish)* distinguere

sin·gle-breast·ed [sɪŋgl'brestɪd] *adj* a un petto; **sin·gle-'hand·ed** [sɪŋgl'hændɪd] *adj & adv* da solo; **sin·gle-mind·ed** [sɪŋgl'maɪndɪd] *adj* determinato; **Sin·gle 'Mar·ket** mercato *m* unico; **sin·gle 'moth·er** ragazza *f* madre; **sin·gle 'pa·rent** genitore *m* single; **sin·gle pa·rent 'fam·i·ly** famiglia *f* monoparentale; **sin·gle 'room** (camera *f*) singola *f*

sin·gu·lar ['sɪŋgjʊlə(r)] **1** *adj* GRAM singolare **2** *n* GRAM singolare *m*; *in the ~* al singolare

sin·is·ter ['sɪnɪstə(r)] *adj* sinistro

sink [sɪŋk] **1** *n* lavandino *m* **2** *v/i (pret* **sank***, pp* **sunk***) of ship* affondare; *of object* andare a fondo; *of sun* calare; *of interest rates, pressure etc* scendere; *he sank onto the bed* crollò sul letto **3** *v/t (pret* **sank***, pp* **sunk***) ship* (far) affondare; *funds* investire

♦ **sink in** *v/i of liquid* penetrare; *it still hasn't really sunk in* of realization ancora non mi rendo conto

sin·ner ['sɪnə(r)] peccatore *m*, -trice *f*

si·nus ['saɪnəs] seno *m* paranasale; *my ~es are blocked* ho il naso bloccato

si·nus·i·tis [saɪnə'saɪtɪs] MED sinusite *f*

S

sip [sɪp] **1** *n* sorso *m* **2** *v/t* (*pret & pp* **-ped**) sorseggiare

sir [sɜː(r)] signore *m*; **Sir Charles** Sir Charles

si·ren ['saɪrən] sirena *f*

sir·loin ['sɜːlɔɪn] controfiletto *m*

sis·ter ['sɪstə(r)] sorella *f*; *in hospital* (infermiera *f*) caposala *f*

'sis·ter-in-law (*pl* **sisters-in-law**) cognata *f*

sit [sɪt] (*pret & pp* **sat**) **1** *v/i* sedere; (*sit down*) sedersi; *for a portrait* posare; *of objects* stare; *of committee, assembly etc* riunirsi **2** *v/t* exam dare

♦ **sit down** *v/i* sedersi

♦ **sit up** *v/i in bed* mettersi a sedere; *straighten back* star seduto bene; *wait up at night* rimanere alzato

sit·com ['sɪtkɒm] sitcom *f inv*

site [saɪt] **1** *n* luogo *m* **2** *v/t new offices etc* situare

sit·ting ['sɪtɪŋ] *n of committee, court* sessione *f*; *for artist* seduta *f*; *for meals* turno *m*

'sit·ting room salotto *m*

sit·u·at·ed ['sɪtjʊeɪtɪd] *adj* situato; **be ~** trovarsi

sit·u·a·tion [sɪtjʊ'eɪʃn] situazione *f*; *of building etc* posizione *f*

six [sɪks] sei

six·teen [sɪks'tiːn] sedici

six·teenth [sɪks'tiːnθ] *n & adj* sedicesimo, -a

sixth [sɪksθ] *adj* sesto

six·ti·eth ['sɪkstɪɪθ] *n & adj* sessantesimo, -a

six·ty ['sɪkstɪ] sessanta

size [saɪz] dimensioni *fpl*; *of clothes* taglia *f*, misura *f*; *of shoes* numero *m*

♦ **size up** *v/t* valutare

size·a·ble ['saɪzəbl] *adj* considerevole

siz·zle ['sɪzl] *v/i* sfrigolare

skate [skeɪt] **1** *n* pattino *m* **2** *v/i* pattinare

skate·board ['skeɪtbɔːd] *n* skateboard *m inv*

skate·board·er ['skeɪtbɔːdə(r)] skateboarder *m/f inv*

skate·board·ing ['skeɪtbɔːdɪŋ] skateboard *m inv*

skat·er ['skeɪtə(r)] pattinatore *m*, -trice *f*

skat·ing ['skeɪtɪŋ] *n* pattinaggio *m*

'skat·ing rink pista *f* di pattinaggio

skel·e·ton ['skelɪtn] scheletro *m*

'skel·e·ton key passe-partout *m inv*

'skep·tic *etc Am* → **sceptic** *etc*

sketch [sketʃ] **1** *n* abbozzo *m*; THEA sketch *m inv* **2** *v/t* abbozzare

'sketch·book album *m* da disegno

sketch·y ['sketʃɪ] *adj knowledge etc* lacunoso

skew·er ['skjʊə(r)] *n* spiedino *m*

ski [skiː] **1** *n* sci *m inv* **2** *v/i* sciare

'ski boots *npl* scarponi *mpl* da sci

skid [skɪd] **1** *n* sbandata *f* **2** *v/i* (*pret & pp* **-ded**) sbandare

ski·er ['skiːə(r)] sciatore *m*, -trice *f*

ski·ing ['skiːɪŋ] sci *m inv*; **go ~** andare a sciare

'ski in·struc·tor maestro *m*, -a *f* di sci

skil·ful ['skɪlfʊl] *adj* abile

skil·ful·ly ['skɪlflɪ] *adv* abilmente

'ski lift impianto *m* di risalita

skill [skɪl] (*ability*) abilità *f inv*; **what ~s do you have?** quali capacità possiede?

skilled [skɪld] *adj* abile

skilled 'work·er operaio *m*, -a *f* specializzato, -a

skill·ful *etc Am* → **skilful** *etc*

skim [skɪm] *v/t* (*pret & pp* **-med**) *surface* sfiorare; *milk* scremare

♦ **skim off** *v/t the best* selezionare

♦ **skim through** *v/t text* scorrere

skimmed 'milk [skɪmd] latte *m* scremato

skimp·y ['skɪmpɪ] *adj account etc* scarso; *dress* succinto

skin [skɪn] **1** *n of person, animal* pelle *f*; *of fruit* buccia *f* **2** *v/t* (*pret & pp* **-ned**) scoiare

'skin div·ing immersioni *fpl* subacquee

skin·flint ['skɪnflɪnt] F spilorcio *m* F

'skin graft innesto *m* epidermico

skin·ny ['skɪnɪ] *adj* magro

'skin-tight *adj* aderente

skip [skɪp] **1** *n little jump* salto *m* **2** *v/i* (*pret & pp* **-ped**) saltellare; *with skipping rope* saltare **3** *v/t* (*pret & pp*

-ped) (*omit*) saltare

'ski pole racchetta *f* da sci

skip·per ['skɪpə(r)] NAUT skipper *m inv*; *of team* capitano *m*

skip·ping rope ['skɪpɪŋ] corda *f* (per saltare)

'ski re·sort stazione *f* sciistica

skirt [skɜːt] *n* gonna *f*

'ski run pista *f* da sci

skit·tle ['skɪtl] birillo *m*

skit·tles ['skɪtlz] *nsg* (*game*) birilli *mpl*

skive [skaɪv] *v/i* F fare lo scansafatiche F

skull [skʌl] cranio *m*

sky [skaɪ] cielo *m*

'sky·light lucernario *m*; **'sky·line** profilo *m* (contro il cielo); **'sky-scrap·er** ['skaɪskreɪpə(r)] grattacielo *m*

slab [slæb] *of stone* lastra *f*; *of cake etc* fetta *f*

slack [slæk] *adj rope* allentato; *person, work* negligente; *period* lento

slack·en ['slækn] *v/t rope* allentare; *pace* rallentare

♦ **slacken off** *v/i* rallentare

slacks [slæks] *npl* pantaloni *mpl* casual

♦ **slag off** [slæg] *v/t* P parlare male di

slain [sleɪn] *pp* → **slay**

slam [slæm] *v/t & v/i* (*pret & pp* **-med**) *door* sbattere

♦ **slam down** *v/t* sbattere

slan·der ['slɑːndə(r)] **1** *n* diffamazione *f* **2** *v/t* diffamare

slan·der·ous ['slɑːndərəs] *adj* diffamatorio

slang [slæŋ] slang *m inv*; *of a specific group* gergo *m*

slant [slɑːnt] **1** *v/i* pendere **2** *n* pendenza *f*; *given to a story* angolazione *f*

slant·ing ['slɑːntɪŋ] *adj roof* spiovente

slap [slæp] **1** *n blow* schiaffo *m* **2** *v/t* (*pret & pp* **-ped**) schiaffeggiare

'slap·dash *adj work* frettoloso; *person* pressapochista

slap-up 'meal F pranzo *m* coi fiocchi

slash [slæʃ] **1** *n cut* taglio *m*; *in punctuation* barra *f* **2** *v/t skin, painting* squarciare; *prices, costs* abbattere; **~ one's wrists** tagliarsi le vene

slate [sleɪt] *n* ardesia *f*

slaugh·ter ['slɔːtə(r)] **1** *n of animals* macellazione *f*; *of people, troops* massacro *m* **2** *v/t animals* macellare; *people, troops* massacrare

'slaugh·ter·house *for animals* macello *m*

Slav [slɑːv] *adj* slavo

slave [sleɪv] *n* schiavo *m*, -a *f*

'slave-driv·er F negriero, -a *f* F

sla·ve·ry schiavitù *f inv*

slay [sleɪ] *v/t* (*pret* **slew**, *pp* **slain**) ammazzare

sleaze [sliːz] POL corruzione *f*

slea·zy ['sliːzɪ] *adj bar, characters* sordido

sled(ge) [sled, sledʒ] *n* slitta *f*

'sledge ham·mer mazza *f*

sleep [sliːp] **1** *n* sonno *m*; **go to ~** addormentarsi; **I need a good ~** ho bisogno di una bella dormita; **I couldn't get to ~** non sono riuscito a dormire **2** *v/i* (*pret & pp* **slept**) dormire

♦ **sleep in** *v/i* (*have a long lie*) dormire fino a tardi

♦ **sleep on** *v/t proposal, decision* dormire su; **sleep on it** dormirci su

♦ **sleep with** *v/t* (*have sex with*) andare a letto con

sleep·er ['sliːpə(r)] RAIL: *on track* traversina *f*; (*sleeping car*) vagone *m* letto; *train* treno *m* notturno; **be a light / heavy ~** avere il sonno leggero / pesante

sleep·i·ly ['sliːpɪlɪ] *adv* con aria assonnata

'sleep·ing bag ['sliːpɪŋ] sacco *m* a pelo; **'sleep·ing car** RAIL vagone *m* letto; **'sleep·ing part·ner** *Br* COM socio *m* inattivo; **'sleep·ing pill** sonnifero *m*

sleep·less ['sliːplɪs] *adj night* in bianco

'sleep walk·er sonnambulo *m*, -a *f*

S

'sleep walk·ing sonnambulismo *m*

sleep·y ['sliːpɪ] *adj child* assonnato; *town* addormentato; **I'm ~** ho sonno

sleet [sliːt] *n* nevischio *m*

sleeve [sliːv] *of jacket etc* manica *f*

sleeve·less ['sliːvlɪs] *adj* senza maniche

sleigh [sleɪ] *n* slitta *f*

sleight of 'hand [slaɪt] gioco *m* di prestigio

slen·der ['slendə(r)] *adj figure, arms* snello; *chance, income, margin* piccolo

slept [slept] *pret & pp* → **sleep**

slew [sluː] *pret* → **slay**

slice [slaɪs] **1** *n also fig* fetta *f* **2** *v/t loaf etc* affettare

sliced 'bread [slaɪst] pane *m* a cassetta; **the greatest thing since ~** F il non plus ultra

slick [slɪk] **1** *adj performance* brillante; *(pej: cunning)* scaltro **2** *n of oil* chiazza *f* di petrolio

slid [slɪd] *pret & pp* → **slide**

slide [slaɪd] **1** *n for kids* scivolo *m*; PHOT diapositiva *f*; *in hair* fermacapelli *m inv* **2** *v/i (pret & pp slid)* scivolare; *of exchange rate etc* calare **3** *v/t (pret & pp slid)* far scivolare

slid·ing door [slaɪdɪŋ'dɔː(r)] porta *f* scorrevole

slight [slaɪt] **1** *adj person, figure* gracile; *(small)* leggero; **no, not in the ~est** no, per nulla **2** *n (insult)* offesa *f*

slight·ly ['slaɪtlɪ] *adv* leggermente

slim [slɪm] **1** *adj* slanciato; *chance* scarso **2** *v/i (pret & pp -med)* dimagrire; **I'm ~ming** sono a dieta

slime [slaɪm] melma *f*

slim·y ['slaɪmɪ] *adj liquid* melmoso; *person* viscido

sling [slɪŋ] **1** *n for arm* fascia *f* a tracolla **2** *v/t (pret & pp slung) (throw)* lanciare

slip [slɪp] **1** *n on ice etc* scivolata *f*; *(mistake)* errore *m*; **a ~ of paper** un foglietto; **a ~ of the tongue** un lapsus; **give s.o. the ~** seminare qu **2** *v/i (pret & pp -ped) on ice etc* scivolare; *of quality etc* peggiorare; **he ~ped out of the room** è sgattaiolato fuori dalla stanza **3** *v/t (pret & pp -ped) (put)* far scivolare; **he ~ped it into his briefcase** l'ha fatto scivolare nella valigetta; **it ~ped my mind** mi è passato di mente

♦ **slip away** *v/i of time* passare; *of opportunity* andare sprecato; *(die quietly)* spirare

♦ **slip off** *v/t jacket etc* togliersi

♦ **slip on** *v/t jacket etc* infilarsi

♦ **slip out** *v/i (go out)* sgattaiolare

♦ **slip up** *v/i make mistake* sbagliarsi

slipped 'disc [slɪpt] ernia *f* del disco

slip·per ['slɪpə(r)] pantofola *f*

slip·pery ['slɪpərɪ] *adj* scivoloso

'slip road rampa *f* di accesso

slip·shod ['slɪpʃɒd] *adj* trascurato

'slip-up *(mistake)* errore *m*

slit [slɪt] **1** *n (tear)* strappo *m*; *(hole)* fessura *f*; *in skirt* spacco *m* **2** *v/t (pret & pp slit)* envelope, packet aprire (tagliando); *throat* tagliare

slith·er ['slɪðə(r)] *v/i* strisciare

sliv·er ['slɪvə(r)] scheggia *f*

slob [slɒb] *pej* sudicione *m*, -a *f*

slob·ber ['slɒbə(r)] *v/i* sbavare

slog [slɒg] *n* faticata *f*

slo·gan ['sləʊgən] slogan *m inv*

slop [slɒp] *v/t (pret & pp -ped)* rovesciare, versare

slope [sləʊp] **1** *n* pendenza *f*; *of mountain* pendio *m*; **built on a ~** costruito in pendio **2** *v/i* essere inclinato; **the road ~s down to the sea** la strada scende fino al mare

slop·py ['slɒpɪ] *adj work, editing* trascurato; *in dressing* sciatto; *(too sentimental)* sdolcinato

sloshed [slɒʃt] *adj* F *(drunk)* sbronzo F

slot [slɒt] **1** *n* fessura *f*; *in schedule* spazio *m*

♦ **slot in** *(pret & pp -ted)* **1** *v/t* infilare **2** *v/i* infilarsi

'slot ma·chine *for vending* distributore *m* automatico; *for gambling* slot-machine *f inv*

slouch [slaʊtʃ] *v/i*: **don't ~!** su con la schiena!

slov·en·ly ['slʌvnlɪ] *adj* sciatto

slow [sləʊ] *adj* lento; *be ~ of clock* essere indietro

♦ **slow down** *v/t & v/i* rallentare

'**slow·coach** *Br* F lumaca f F

'**slow·down** *in production* rallentamento *m*

slow·ly ['sləʊlɪ] *adv* lentamente

slow 'mo·tion *n*: *in ~* al rallentatore

slow·ness ['sləʊnɪs] lentezza f

'**slow·poke** *Am* F lumaca f F

slug [slʌg] *n animal* lumaca f

slug·gish ['slʌgɪʃ] *adj* lento

slum [slʌm] *n* slum *m inv*

slump [slʌmp] **1** *n in trade* crollo *m* **2** *v/i economically* crollare; *(collapse: of person)* accasciarsi

slung [slʌŋ] *pret & pp* → **sling**

slur [slɜː(r)] **1** *n* calunnia f **2** *v/t* (*pret & pp* **-red**) *words* biascicare

slurp [slɜːp] *v/t* bere rumorosamente

slurred [slɜːd] *adj speech* impappinato

slush [slʌʃ] fanghiglia f; *(pej: sentimental stuff)* smancerie fpl

'**slush fund** fondi *mpl* neri

slush·y ['slʌʃɪ] *adj snow* ridotto in fanghiglia; *film, novel* sdolcinato

slut [slʌt] *pej* sgualdrina f

sly [slaɪ] *adj* scaltro; *on the ~* di nascosto

smack [smæk] **1** *n on the bottom* sculacciata f; *in the face* schiaffo *m* **2** *v/t child* picchiare; *bottom* sculacciare

small [smɔːl] **1** *adj* piccolo **2** *n*: *the ~ of the back* le reni

small 'change spiccioli *mpl*; **small hours** *npl*: *the ~* le ore *fpl* piccole; **small·pox** ['smɔːlpɒks] vaiolo *m*; '**small print** parte f scritta in caratteri minuti; '**small talk** conversazione f di circostanza

smarm·y ['smɑːmɪ] *adj* F untuoso

smart [smɑːt] **1** *adj* (*elegant*) elegante; (*intelligent*) intelligente; *pace* svelto; *get ~ with* F fare il furbo con F **2** *v/i* (*hurt*) bruciare

smart al·ec(k) ['smɑːtælɪk] F sapientone *m* F; '**smart ass** P sapientone *m*; '**smart card** smart card f *inv*

♦ **smarten up** ['smɑːtn] *v/t* sistemare; **smarten o.s. up** mettersi in ghingheri

smart·ly ['smɑːtlɪ] *adv dressed* elegantemente

smash [smæʃ] **1** *n noise* fracasso *m*; (*car crash*) scontro *m*; *in tennis* schiacciata f **2** *v/t break* spaccare; *hit hard* sbattere; *~ sth to pieces* mandare in frantumi qc **3** *v/i break* frantumarsi; *the driver ~ed into ...* l'automobilista si è schiantato contro ...

♦ **smash up** *v/t place* distruggere

smash 'hit F successone *m*

smash·ing ['smæʃɪŋ] *adj* F fantastico

smat·ter·ing ['smætərɪŋ] *of a language* infarinatura f

smear [smɪə(r)] **1** *n of ink etc* macchia f; MED striscio *m*; *on character* calunnia f **2** *v/t*; *character* calunniare; *~ mud over the wall* imbrattare il muro di fango

'**smear cam·paign** campagna f diffamatoria

smell [smel] **1** *n* odore *m*; *it has no ~* non ha odore; *sense of ~* olfatto *m*, odorato *m* **2** *v/t* sentire odore di; *test by smelling* sentire **3** *v/i unpleasantly* puzzare; (*sniff*) odorare; *what does it ~ of?* che odore ha?; *you ~ of beer* puzzi di birra; *it ~s good* ha un buon profumino

smell·y ['smelɪ] *adj* puzzolente; *it's so ~ in here* qui dentro c'è puzza

smile [smaɪl] **1** *n* sorriso *m* **2** *v/i* sorridere

♦ **smile at** *v/t* sorridere a

smirk [smɜːk] **1** *n* sorriso *m* compiaciuto **2** *v/i* sorridere con compiacimento

smog [smɒg] smog *m inv*

smoke [sməʊk] **1** *n* fumo *m*; *have a ~* fumare **2** *v/t cigarettes etc* fumare; *bacon* affumicare **3** *v/i* fumare; *I don't ~* non fumo

smok·er ['sməʊkə(r)] *person* fumatore *m*, -trice f

smok·ing ['sməʊkɪŋ] fumo *m*; *no ~* vietato fumare

'**smok·ing com·part·ment** RAIL

carrozza *m* fumatori

smok·y ['sməʊkɪ] *adj room, air* pieno di fumo

smol·der *Am* → **smoulder**

smooth [smuːð] **1** *adj surface, skin, sea* liscio; *sea* liscio; *transition* senza problemi; *pej: person* melliflui **2** *v/t hair* lisciare

♦ **smooth down** *v/t with sandpaper etc* levigare

♦ **smooth out** *v/t paper, cloth* lisciare

♦ **smooth over** *v/t:* **smooth things over** appianare le cose

smooth·ly ['smuːðlɪ] *adv without any problems* senza problemi

smoth·er ['smʌðə(r)] *v/t flames, person* soffocare; **~ s.o. with kisses** coprire qu di baci

smoul·der ['sməʊldə(r)] *v/i of fire* covare sotto la cenere; *fig: with anger, desire* consumarsi (**with** di)

smudge [smʌdʒ] **1** *n* sbavatura *f* **2** *v/t* sbavare

smug [smʌg] *adj* compiaciuto

smug·gle ['smʌgl] *v/t* contrabbandare

smug·gler ['smʌglə(r)] contrabbandiere *m*, -a *f*

smug·gling ['smʌglɪŋ] contrabbando *m*

smug·ly ['smʌglɪ] *adv* con compiacimento

smut·ty ['smʌtɪ] *adj joke, sense of humour* sconcio

snack [snæk] *n* spuntino *m*

'snack bar snack bar *m inv*

snag [snæg] *n (problem)* problema *m*

snail [sneɪl] *n* chiocciola *f*, *in cooking* lumaca *f*

snake [sneɪk] *n* serpente *m*

snap [snæp] **1** *n sound* botto *m*; PHOT foto *f* **2** *v/t (pret & pp -ped) break* spezzare; *(say sharply)* dire bruscamente **3** *v/i (pret & pp -ped) break* spezzarsi **4** *adj decision, judgement* immediato

♦ **snap up** *v/t bargains* accaparrarsi

snap·py ['snæpɪ] *adj person, mood* irritabile; F *(quick)* rapido; *(elegant)* elegante

'snap·shot istantanea *f*

snarl [snɑːl] **1** *n of dog* ringhio *m* **2** *v/i* ringhiare

snatch [snætʃ] **1** *v/t* afferrare; *(steal)* scippare; *(kidnap)* rapire **2** *v/i* strappare di mano

snaz·zy ['snæzɪ] *adj* F chic

sneak [sniːk] **1** *n (telltale)* spione *m*, -a *f* **2** *v/t (remove, steal)* rubare; **~ a glance at** dare una sbirciatina a **3** *v/i (tell tales)* fare la spia; **~ out of ...** sgattaiolare furti da ...

sneak·ing ['sniːkɪŋ] *adj:* **have a ~ suspicion that ...** avere il vago sospetto che ...

sneak·y ['sniːkɪ] *adj* F *(crafty)* scaltro

sneer [snɪə(r)] **1** *n* sogghigno *m* **2** *v/i* sogghignare

sneeze [sniːz] **1** *n* starnuto *m* **2** *v/i* starnutire

sniff [snɪf] **1** *v/i to clear nose* tirare su col naso; *of dog* fiutare **2** *v/t smell* annusare

snig·ger ['snɪgə(r)] **1** *n* risolino *m* **2** *v/i* ridacchiare

snip [snɪp] *n* F *(bargain)* affare *m*

snip·er ['snaɪpə(r)] cecchino *m*

sniv·el ['snɪvl] *v/i pej* frignare

snob [snɒb] snob *m/f inv*

snob·ber·y ['snɒbərɪ] snobismo *m*

snob·bish ['snɒbɪʃ] *adj* snob *inv*

snook·er ['snuːkə(r)] biliardo *m*

snoop [snuːp] *n* ficcanaso *m/f inv*

♦ **snoop around** *v/i* ficcanasare

snoot·y ['snuːtɪ] *adj* snob *inv*

snooze [snuːz] **1** *n* sonnellino *m*; **have a ~** fare un sonnellino **2** *v/i* sonnecchiare

snore [snɔː(r)] *v/i* russare

snor·ing ['snɔːrɪŋ] *n* russare *m*

snor·kel ['snɔːkl] *n* boccaglio *m*

snort [snɔːt] *v/i* sbuffare

snout [snaʊt] *of pig* grugno *m*; *of dog* muso *m*

snow [snəʊ] **1** *n* neve *f* **2** *v/i* nevicare

♦ **snow under** *v/t:* **be snowed under with ...** essere sommerso di ...

'snow·ball palla *f* di neve; **'snow·bound** *adj* isolato dalla neve; **'snow chains** *npl* MOT catene *fpl* da neve; **'snow·drift** cumulo *m* di

neve; **'snow·drop** bucaneve *m inv*;
'snow·flake fiocco *m* di neve;
'snow·man pupazzo *m* di neve;
'snow·storm tormenta *f*

snow·y ['snəʊɪ] *adj weather* nevoso; *roofs, hills* innevato

snub [snʌb] **1** *n* affronto *m* **2** *v/t* (*pret & pp* **-bed**) snobbare

snub-nosed ['snʌbnəʊzd] *adj* col naso all'insù

snug [snʌg] *adj* al calduccio; (*tight-fitting*) attillato

♦ **snuggle down** ['snʌgl] *v/i* accoccolarsi

♦ **snuggle up to** *v/t* rannicchiarsi accanto a

so [səʊ] **1** *adv* così; **~ hot / cold** così caldo / freddo; **not ~ much** non così tanto; **~ much better / easier** molto meglio / più facile; **you shouldn't eat / drink ~ much** non dovresti mangiare / bere così tanto; **I miss you ~** mi manchi tanto; **~ am / do I** anch'io; **~ is she / does she** anche lei; **and ~ on** e così via **2** *pron*: **I hope / think ~** spero / penso di sì; **I don't think ~** non credo, credo di no; **you didn't tell me – I did ~** non me l'hai detto – e invece sì; **50 or ~** circa 50 **3** *conj* (*for that reason*) così; (*in order that*) così che; **and ~ I missed the train** e così ho perso il treno; **~ (that) I could come too** così che potessi venire anch'io; **~ what?** E allora?

soak [səʊk] *v/t* (*steep*) mettere a bagno; *of water, rain* inzuppare

♦ **soak up** *v/t liquid* assorbire; **soak up the sun** crogiolarsi al sole

soaked [səʊkt] *adj* fradicio; **be ~ to the skin** essere bagnato fradicio

soak·ing (**wet**) ['səʊkɪŋ] *adj* bagnato fradicio

so-and-so ['səʊənsəʊ] F *unknown person* tal dei tali *m/f inv*; (*euph: annoying person*) impiastro *m*

soap [səʊp] *n for washing* sapone *m*

'soap (**op·e·ra**) soap (opera) *f inv*, telenovela *f*

soap·y ['səʊpɪ] *adj water* saponato

soar [sɔ:(r)] *v/i of rocket etc* innalzar-

si; *of prices* aumentare vertiginosamente

sob [sɒb] **1** *n* singhiozzo *m* **2** *v/i* (*pret & pp* **-bed**) singhiozzare

so·ber ['səʊbə(r)] *adj* (*not drunk*) sobrio; (*serious*) serio

♦ **sober up** *v/i* smaltire la sbornia

so-'called *adj* cosiddetto

soc·cer ['sɒkə(r)] calcio *m*

'soc·cer hoo·li·gan hooligan *m/f inv*

so·cia·ble ['səʊʃəbl] *adj* socievole

so·cial ['səʊʃl] *adj* sociale

so·cial 'dem·o·crat socialdemocratico *m*, -a *f*

so·cial·is·m ['səʊʃəlɪzm] socialismo *m*

so·cial·ist ['səʊʃəlɪst] **1** *adj* socialista **2** *n* socialista *m/f*

so·cial·ize ['səʊʃəlaɪz] *v/i* socializzare

'soc·ial life vita *f* sociale; **so·cial 'sci·ence** scienza *f* sociale; **so·cial se·cu·ri·ty** *Br* sussidio *m* della previdenza sociale; **so·cial 'serv·i·ces** *Br npl* servizi *mpl* sociali; **'so·cial work** assistenza *f* sociale; **'so·cial work·er** assistente *m/f* sociale

so·ci·e·ty [sə'saɪətɪ] società *f inv*; (*organization*) associazione *f*

so·ci·ol·o·gist [səʊsɪ'ɒlədʒɪst] sociologo *m*, -a *f*

so·ci·ol·o·gy [səʊsɪ'ɒlədʒɪ] sociologia *f*

sock¹ [sɒk] calzino *m*

sock² [sɒk] **1** *n* F (*punch*) pugno *m* **2** *v/t* F (*punch*) dare un pugno a

sock·et ['sɒkɪt] *for light bulb* portalampada *m inv*; *in wall* presa *f* (di corrente); *of eye* orbita *f*

so·da ['səʊdə] (*~ water*) seltz *m inv*

sod·den ['sɒdn] *adj* zuppo

so·fa ['səʊfə] divano *m*

'so·fa-bed divano *m* letto

soft [sɒft] *adj pillow* soffice; *chair, skin* morbido; *light, colour* tenue; *music* soft; *voice* sommesso; (*lenient*) indulgente; **have a ~ spot for** avere un debole per

soft 'drink bibita *f* analcolica

'soft drug droga *f* leggera

soft·en ['sɒfn] **1** *v/t butter etc* ammor-

S

bidire; *position* attenuare; *impact, blow* attutire **2** *v/i of butter, ice-cream* ammorbidirsi

soft·ly ['sɒftlɪ] *adv speak* sommessamente

soft 'toy giocattolo *m* di pezza

soft·ware ['sɒftweə(r)] software *m inv*

sog·gy ['sɒgɪ] *adj* molle e pesante

soil [sɔɪl] **1** *n* (*earth*) terra *f* **2** *v/t* sporcare

so·lar 'en·er·gy ['səʊlə(r)] energia *f* solare; 'so·lar pan·el pannello *m* solare; 'solar system sistema *m* solare

sold [səʊld] *pret* & *pp* → sell

sol·dier ['səʊldʒə(r)] soldato *m*
♦ soldier on *v/i* perseverare

sole¹ [səʊl] *n of foot* pianta *f* (del piede); *of shoe* suola *f*

sole² [səʊl] *adj* unico; (*exclusive*) esclusivo

sole³ [səʊl] (*fish*) sogliola *f*

sole·ly ['səʊlɪ] *adv* solamente; *be ~ responsible* essere il solo/la sola responsabile

sol·emn ['sɒləm] *adj* solenne

so·lem·ni·ty [sə'lemnɪtɪ] solennità *f inv*

sol·emn·ly ['sɒləmlɪ] *adv* solennemente

so·li·cit [sə'lɪsɪt] *v/i of prostitute* adescare

so·lic·i·tor [sə'lɪsɪtə(r)] avvocato *m*

sol·id ['sɒlɪd] *adj* (*hard*) solido; (*without holes*) compatto; *gold, silver* massiccio; (*sturdy*) robusto; *evidence* concreto; *support* forte; *a ~ hour* un'ora intera

sol·i·dar·i·ty [sɒlɪ'dærɪtɪ] solidarietà *f inv*

sol·id·i·fy [sə'lɪdɪfaɪ] *v/i* (*pret* & *pp -ied*) solidificarsi

sol·id·ly ['sɒlɪdlɪ] *adv* built solidamente; *in favour of sth* all'unanimità

so·lil·o·quy [sə'lɪləkwɪ] *on stage* monologo *m*

sol·i·taire ['sɒlɪteər] *Am: card game* solitario *m*

sol·i·ta·ry ['sɒlɪtərɪ] *adj life, activity* solitario; (*single*) solo

sol·i·ta·ry con'fine·ment isolamento *m*

sol·i·tude ['sɒlɪtjuːd] solitudine *f*

so·lo ['səʊləʊ] **1** *n* MUS assolo *m* **2** *adj performance* solista; *flight* in solitario

so·lo·ist ['səʊləʊɪst] solista *m/f*

sol·u·ble ['sɒljʊbl] *adj substance* solubile; *problem* risolvibile

so·lu·tion [sə'luːʃn] soluzione *f*

solve [sɒlv] *v/t* risolvere

sol·vent ['sɒlvənt] **1** *adj financially* solvibile **2** *n* solvente *m*

som·ber *Am*, som·bre ['sɒmbə(r)] *adj* (*dark*) scuro; (*serious*) tetro

some [sʌm] **1** *adj* (*unspecified amount*) un po' di, del; (*unspecified number*) qualche, dei *m*, delle *f*; *would you like ~ water?* vuoi un po' d'acqua *o* dell'acqua?; *would you like ~ biscuits?* vuoi dei biscotti *o* qualche biscotto?; *~ people say that ...* alcuni dicono che ... **2** *pron* (*unspecified amount*) un po'; (*unspecified number*) alcuni *m*, -e *f*; *would you like ~?* ne vuoi un po'?; *give me ~* dammene un po'; *~ of the students* alcuni studenti

some·bod·y ['sʌmbədɪ] *pron* qualcuno; 'some·day *adv* un giorno; 'some·how *adv* (*by one means or another*) in qualche modo; (*for some unknown reason*) per qualche motivo; 'some·one *pron* → somebod·y

som·er·sault ['sʌməsɔːlt] **1** *n* capriola *f* **2** *v/i* fare una capriola

'some·thing *pron* qualcosa; *would you like ~ to drink/eat?* vuoi (qualcosa) da mangiare/bere?; *is ~ wrong?* c'è qualcosa che non va?; 'some·time *adv* (*one of these days*) uno di questi giorni; *~ last year* l'anno scorso; 'some·times ['sʌmtaɪmz] *adv* a volte; 'some·what *adv* piuttosto; 'some·where **1** *adv* da qualche parte **2** *pron* un posto; *let's go ~ quiet* andiamo in un posto tranquillo

son [sʌn] figlio *m*

so·na·ta [sə'nɑːtə] MUS sonata *f*

song [sɒŋ] canzone *f*; *of birds* canto *m*

'song·bird uccello *m* canoro

'song·writ·er compositore *m*, -trice *f*

'son-in-law (*pl* **sons-in-law**) genero *m*

son·net ['sɒnɪt] sonetto *m*

soon [suːn] *adv* presto; **as ~ as** non appena; **as ~ as possible** prima possibile; **~er or later** presto o tardi; **the ~er the better** prima è, meglio è; **how ~ can you be ready?** fra quanto sei pronto?

soot [sʊt] fuliggine *f*

soothe [suːð] *v/t* calmare

so·phis·ti·cat·ed [sə'fɪstɪkeɪtɪd] *adj* sofisticato

so·phis·ti·ca·tion [sə'fɪstɪkeɪʃn] *of person* raffinatezza *f*; *of machine* complessità *f inv*

sop·py ['sɒpɪ] *adj* F sdolcinato

so·pra·no [sə'prɑːnəʊ] *n* soprano *m/f*

sor·did ['sɔːdɪd] *adj affair, business* sordido

sore [sɔː(r)] **1** *adj* (*painful*) dolorante; **is it ~?** fa male? **2** *n* piaga *f*

sore 'throat mal *m* di gola

sor·row ['sɒrəʊ] *n* dispiacere *m*, dolore *m*

sor·ry ['sɒrɪ] *adj day, sight* triste; (**I'm**) **~!** *apologizing* scusa!; *polite form* scusi!; **I'm ~** *regretting* mi dispiace; **I won't be ~ to leave here** non vedo l'ora di andarmene da qui; **I feel ~ for her** mi dispiace per lei

sort [sɔːt] **1** *n* tipo *m*; **~ of ...** F un po' ...; **is it finished? – ~ of** F è terminato? – quasi **2** *v/t* separare; COMPUT ordinare

♦ **sort out** *v/t papers* mettere in ordine; *problem* risolvere; **sort things out** sistemare le cose

SOS [esəʊ'es] SOS *m inv*

so-'so *adv* F così così

sought [sɔːt] *pret & pp* → **seek**

soul [səʊl] anima *f*; **the poor ~** il poverino, la poverina

sound[1] [saʊnd] **1** *adj* (*sensible*) valido; (*healthy*) sano; *sleep* profondo; *structure, walls* solido **2** *adv*: **be ~ asleep** dormire profondamente

sound[2] [saʊnd] **1** *n* suono *m*; (*noise*) rumore *m* **2** *v/t* (*pronounce*) pronunciare; MED auscultare; **~ one's horn** suonare il clacson **3** *v/i*: **that ~s interesting** sembra interessante; **that ~s like a good idea** mi sembra un'ottima idea; **she ~ed unhappy** dalla voce sembrava infelice

♦ **sound out** *v/t* sondare l'opinione di

'sound bar·ri·er muro *m* del suono

'sound·bite slogan *m inv*

'sound ef·fects *npl* effetti *mpl* sonori

sound·ly ['saʊndlɪ] *adv sleep* profondamente; *beaten* duramente

'sound·proof *adj* insonorizzato

'sound·track colonna *f* sonora

soup [suːp] minestra *f*

'soup bowl scodella *f*

souped-up [suːpt'ʌp] *adj* F truccato F

'soup plate piatto *m* fondo

'soup spoon cucchiaio *m* da minestra

sour ['saʊə(r)] *adj apple, orange* aspro; *milk, expression, comment* acido

source [sɔːs] *n* fonte *f*; *of river* sorgente *f*

sour 'cream panna *f* acida

south [saʊθ] **1** *adj* meridionale, del sud **2** *n* sud *m*; **to the ~ of** a sud di **3** *adv* verso sud

South 'Af·ric·a Repubblica *f* Sudafricana

South 'Af·ri·can 1 *adj* sudafricano **2** *n* sudafricano *m*, -a *f*

South A'mer·i·ca Sudamerica *m*

South A'mer·i·can 1 *adj* sudamericano **2** *n* sudamericano *m*, -a *f*

south'east 1 *n* sud-est *m* **2** *adj* sud-orientale **3** *adv* verso sud-est; **it's ~ of ...** è a sud-est di ...

south'east·ern *adj* sud-orientale

south·er·ly ['sʌðəlɪ] *adj* meridionale

south·ern ['sʌðən] *adj* del sud

south·ern·er ['sʌðənə(r)] abitante *m/f* del sud

south·ern·most ['sʌðənməʊst] *adj* più a sud

South 'Pole polo *m* sud

south·wards ['saʊθwədz] *adv* verso sud

south·'west 1 *n* sud-ovest *m* 2 *adj* sud-occidentale 3 *adv* verso sud-ovest; *it's ~ of ...* è a sud-ovest di ...

south'west·ern *adj* sud-occidentale

sou·ve·nir [suːvə'nɪə(r)] souvenir *m inv*

sove·reign ['sɒvrɪn] *adj state* sovrano

sove·reign·ty ['sɒvrɪntɪ] *of state* sovranità *f inv*

So·vi·et ['səʊvɪət] *adj* sovietico

So·vi·et 'U·nion Unione *f* Sovietica

sow¹ [saʊ] *n* (*female pig*) scrofa *f*

sow² [səʊ] *v/t seeds* seminare

sown [səʊn] *pp* → **sow²**

soy·a bean ['sɔɪə] seme *m* di soia

soy(a) 'sauce salsa *f* di soia

spa [spaː] località *f inv* termale

space [speɪs] *n* spazio *m*; *in car park* posto *m*

♦ space out *v/t* distanziare

'space·bar COMPUT barra *f* spaziatrice; **'space·craft** veicolo *m* spaziale; **'space·ship** astronave *f*; **'space shut·tle** shuttle *m inv*; **'space sta·tion** stazione *f* spaziale; **'space·suit** tuta *f* spaziale

spa·cious ['speɪʃəs] *adj* spazioso

spade [speɪd] *for digging* vanga *f*, *~s in card game* picche

'spade·work *fig* preparativi *mpl*

spa·ghet·ti [spə'getɪ] *nsg* spaghetti *mpl*

Spain [speɪn] Spagna *f*

span [spæn] *v/t* (*pret & pp* -ned) coprire; *of bridge* attraversare

Span·iard ['spænjəd] spagnolo *m*, -a *f*

Span·ish ['spænɪʃ] 1 *adj* spagnolo 2 *n language* spagnolo *m*

spank [spæŋk] *v/t* sculacciare

spank·ing ['spæŋkɪŋ] sculaccione *m*

span·ner ['spænə(r)] *Br* chiave *f* inglese

spare [speə(r)] 1 *v/t* (*do without*) fare a meno di; *can you ~ £50?* mi puoi prestare 50 sterline?; *can you ~ the time?* hai tempo?; *have money/*

time to ~ avere soldi / tempo d'avanzo; *there were 5 to ~* (*left over, in excess*) ce n'erano 5 d'avanzo 2 *adj* in più 3 *n* ricambio *m*

spare 'part pezzo *m* di ricambio; **spare 'ribs** *npl* costine *fpl* di maiale; **spare 'room** stanza *f* degli ospiti; **spare 'time** tempo *m* libero; **spare 'tire** *Am*, **spare 'tyre** MOT ruota *f* di scorta

spar·ing ['speə(r)ɪŋ] *adj*: *be ~ with* andarci piano con F

spa·ring·ly ['speə(r)ɪŋlɪ] *adv* con moderazione

spark [spaːk] *n* scintilla *f*

spark·ing plug ['spaːkɪŋ] candela *f*

sparkle ['spaːkl] *v/i* brillare

spark·ling 'wine ['spaːklɪŋ] vino *m* frizzante

'spark plug candela *f*

spar·row ['spærəʊ] passero *m*

sparse [spaːs] *adj vegetation* rado

sparse·ly ['spaːslɪ] *adv*: *~ populated* scarsamente popolato

spar·tan ['spaːtn] *adj* spartano

spas·mod·ic [spæz'mɒdɪk] *adj* irregolare

spat [spæt] *pret & pp* → **spit**

spate [speɪt] *fig* ondata *f*

spa·tial ['speɪʃl] *adj* spaziale

spat·ter ['spætə(r)] *v/t mud, paint* schizzare

speak [spiːk] (*pret* **spoke**, *pp* **spoken**) 1 *v/i* parlare; *we're not ~ing* (*to each other*) (*we've quarrelled*) non ci rivolgiamo la parola; *~ing* TELEC sono io 2 *v/t foreign language* parlare; *the truth* dire; *~ one's mind* dire quello che si pensa

♦ speak for *v/t* parlare a nome di

♦ speak out *v/i* prendere posizione; *say what you think* farsi sentire

♦ speak up *v/i* (*speak louder*) parlare ad alta voce

speak·er ['spiːkə(r)] oratore *m*, -trice *f*; *of sound system* cassa *f*

spear [spɪə(r)] lancia *f*

spear·mint ['spɪəmɪnt] menta *f*

spe·cial ['speʃl] *adj* speciale; (*particular*) particolare

spe·cial ef·fects *npl* effetti *mpl* speciali

spe·cial·ist ['speʃlɪst] specialista *m/f*

spe·cial·i·ty [speʃɪ'ælətɪ] specialità *f inv*

spe·cial·ize ['speʃəlaɪz] *v/i* specializzarsi; **~ in ...** specializzarsi in; **we ~ in ...** siamo specializzati in …

spe·cial·ly ['speʃlɪ] *adv* → **especially**

spe·cial·ty ['speʃəltɪ] *Am* specialità *f inv*

spe·cies ['spiːʃiːz] *nsg* specie *f inv*

spe·cif·ic [spə'sɪfɪk] *adj* specifico

spe·cif·i·cal·ly [spə'sɪfɪklɪ] *adv* specificamente

spec·i·fi·ca·tions [spesɪfɪ'keɪʃnz] *npl of machine etc* caratteristiche *fpl* tecniche, specifiche *fpl*

spec·i·fy ['spesɪfaɪ] *v/t* (*pret & pp* **-ied**) specificare

spe·ci·men ['spesɪmən] campione *m*

speck [spek] *of dust, soot* granello *m*

specs [speks] *npl* F (*spectacles*) occhiali *mpl*

spec·ta·cle ['spektəkl] (*impressive sight*) spettacolo *m*; (**a pair of**) **~s** (un paio di) occhiali *mpl*

spec·tac·u·lar [spek'tækjʊlə(r)] *adj* spettacolare

spec·ta·tor [spek'teɪtə(r)] spettatore *m*, -trice *f*

spec'ta·tor sport sport *m inv* spettacolo

spec·trum ['spektrəm] *fig* gamma *f*

spec·u·late ['spekjʊleɪt] *v/i* fare congetture (**on** su); FIN speculare

spec·u·la·tion [spekjʊ'leɪʃn] congetture *fpl*; FIN speculazione *f*

spec·u·la·tor ['spekjʊleɪtə(r)] FIN speculatore *m*, -trice *f*

sped [sped] *pret & pp* → **speed**

speech [spiːtʃ] (*address*) discorso *m*; *in play* monologo *m*; (*ability to speak*) parola *f*; (*way of speaking*) linguaggio *m*; **faculty / power of ~** facoltà / uso della parola; **her ~ was slurred** biascicava le parole

speech de·fect difetto *m* del linguaggio

speech·less ['spiːtʃlɪs] *adj* with

shock, surprise senza parole

'speech ther·a·pist logopedista *m/f*; **speech 'ther·a·py** logopedia *f*; **'speech writ·er** ghost writer *m inv*

speed [spiːd] **1** *n* velocità *f inv*; (*quickness*) rapidità *f inv*; **at a ~ of 150 mph** a una velocità di 150 miglia orarie; **reduce your ~** rallentare **2** *v/i* (*pret & pp* **sped**) (*go quickly*) andare a tutta velocità; (*drive too quickly*) superare il limite di velocità

♦ **speed by** *v/i* sfrecciare; *of days* volare

♦ **speed up 1** *v/i* andare più veloce **2** *v/t* accelerare

'speed·boat motoscafo *m*

'speed bump dosso *m* di rallentamento

speed·i·ly ['spiːdɪlɪ] *adv* rapidamente

speed·ing ['spiːdɪŋ] *n when driving* eccesso *m* di velocità

'speed·ing fine multa *f* per eccesso di velocità

'speed lim·it *on roads* limite *m* di velocità

speed·om·e·ter [spiː'dɒmɪtə(r)] tachimetro *m*

'speed trap *sistema m con cui la polizia individua chi supera il limite di velocità*

speed·y ['spiːdɪ] *adj* rapido

spell[1] [spel] **1** *v/t*: **how do you ~ ...?** come si scrive …?; **could you ~ that please?** me lo può dettare lettera per lettera? **2** *v/i* sapere come si scrivono le parole

spell[2] [spel] *n* (*period of time*) periodo *m*; (*turn*) turno *m*

'spell·bound *adj* incantato; **'spell·check** COMPUT controllo *m* ortografico; **do a ~ on ...** fare il controllo ortografico di …; **'spell·check·er** COMPUT correttore *m* ortografico

spell·ing ['spelɪŋ] ortografia *f*

spend [spend] *v/t* (*pret & pp* **spent**) *money* spendere; *time* passare

'spend·thrift *n pej* spendaccione *m*, -a *f*

spent [spent] *pret & pp* → **spend**

sperm [spɜːm] spermatozoo *m*; *(semen)* sperma *m*

'sperm bank banca *f* dello sperma

'sperm count numero *m* degli spermatozoi

sphere [sfɪə(r)] *also fig* sfera *f*; **~ of influence** sfera d'influenza

spice [spaɪs] *n (seasoning)* spezia *f*

spic·y ['spaɪsɪ] *adj food* piccante

spi·der ['spaɪdə(r)] ragno *m*

'spi·der's web ragnatela *f*

spike [spaɪk] *n on railings* spunzone *m*; *on plant* spina *f*; *on animal* aculeo *m*; *on running shoes* chiodo *m*

spill [spɪl] **1** *v/t* versare **2** *v/i* versarsi **3** *n of oil etc* fuoriuscita *f*

spin[1] [spɪn] **1** *n* giro *m*; *on ball* effetto *m* **2** *v/t (pret & pp* **spun***)* far girare; *ball* imprimere l'effetto a **3** *v/i (pret & pp* **spun***) of wheel* girare; **my head is ~ning** mi gira la testa

spin[2] [spɪn] *v/t (pret & pp* **spun***) wool, cotton* filare; *web* tessere

♦ **spin around** *v/i of person, car* girarsi

♦ **spin out** *v/t* F far durare

spin·ach ['spɪnɪdʒ] spinaci *mpl*

spin·al ['spaɪnl] *adj* spinale

spin·al 'col·umn colonna *f* vertebrale, spina *f* dorsale

spin·al 'cord midollo *m* spinale

'spin doc·tor F persona *f* incaricata di far apparire un personaggio politico nella luce migliore; **'spin-dry** *v/t* centrifugare; **'spin-dry·er** centrifuga *f*

spine [spaɪn] *of person, animal* spina *f* dorsale; *of book* dorso *m*; *on plant, hedgehog* spina *f*

spine·less ['spaɪnlɪs] *adj (cowardly)* smidollato

'spin-off applicazione *f* secondaria

spin·ster ['spɪnstə(r)] zitella *f*

spin·y ['spaɪnɪ] *adj* spinoso

spi·ral ['spaɪrəl] **1** *n* spirale *f* **2** *v/i (rise quickly)* salire vertiginosamente

spi·ral 'stair·case scala *f* a chiocciola

spire ['spaɪə(r)] spira *f*, guglia *f*

spir·it ['spɪrɪt] *n* spirito *m*; **we did it in a ~ of cooperation** abbiamo agito per spirito di collaborazione

spir·it·ed ['spɪrɪtɪd] *adj debate* animato; *defence* energico; *performance* brioso

'spir·it lev·el livella *f* a bolla d'aria

spir·its[1] ['spɪrɪts] *npl (alcohol)* superalcolici *mpl*

spir·its[2] ['spɪrɪts] *npl (morale)* morale *msg*; **be in good / poor ~** essere su / giù di morale

spir·i·tu·al ['spɪrɪtjʊəl] *adj* spirituale

spir·it·u·al·ism ['spɪrɪtjʊəlɪzm] spiritismo *m*

spir·it·u·al·ist ['spɪrɪtjʊəlɪst] *n* spiritista *m/f*

spit [spɪt] *v/i (pret & pp* **spat***) of person* sputare; **it's ~ting with rain** pioviggina

♦ **spit out** *v/t food, liquid* sputare

spite [spaɪt] *n* dispetto *m*; **in ~ of** malgrado

spite·ful ['spaɪtfʊl] *adj* dispettoso

spite·ful·ly ['spaɪtfəlɪ] *adv* dispettosamente

spit·ting 'im·age ['spɪtɪŋ]: **be the ~ of s.o.** essere il ritratto sputato di qu

splash [splæʃ] **1** *n (noise)* tonfo *m*; *(small amount of liquid)* schizzo *m*; *of colour* macchia *f* **2** *v/t person* schizzare; *water, mud* spruzzare **3** *v/i of waves* infrangersi

♦ **splash down** *v/i of spacecraft* ammarare

♦ **splash out** *v/i in spending* spendere un sacco di soldi **(on** per)

'splash-down ammaraggio *m*

splen·did ['splendɪd] *adj* magnifico

splen·dor *Am*, **splen·dour** ['splendə(r)] magnificenza *f*

splint [splɪnt] *n* MED stecca *f*

splin·ter ['splɪntə(r)] **1** *n* scheggia *f* **2** *v/i* scheggiarsi

'splin·ter group gruppo *m* scissionista

split [splɪt] **1** *n in leather* strappo *m*; *in wood* crepa *f*; *(disagreement)* spaccatura *f*; *(division, share)* divisione *f* **2** *v/t (pret & pp* **split***) leather* strappare; *wood, logs* spaccare; *(cause disagreement in)* spaccare; *(divide)*

dividere **3** v/i (*pret & pp* **split**) *of leather* strapparsi; *of wood* spaccarsi; (*disagree*) spaccarsi
♦ **split up** v/i *of couple* separarsi
split per·son·al·i·ty PSYCH sdoppiamento *m* della personalità
split·ting ['splɪtɪŋ] *adj:* **~ headache** feroce mal *m inv* di testa
splut·ter ['splʌtə(r)] v/i farfugliare
spoil [spɔɪl] v/t *child* viziare; *surprise, party* rovinare
'spoil·sport F guastafeste *m/f*
spoilt [spɔɪlt] *adj child* viziato; **be ~ for choice** avere (solo) l'imbarazzo della scelta
spoke[1] [spəʊk] *of wheel* raggio *m*
spoke[2] [spəʊk] *pret →* **speak**
spo·ken ['spəʊkən] *pp →* **speak**
spokes·man ['spəʊksmən] portavoce *m*
spokes·per·son ['spəʊkspɜːsən] portavoce *m/f*
spokes·wom·an ['spəʊkswʊmən] portavoce *f*
sponge [spʌndʒ] *n* spugna *f*
♦ **sponge off / on** v/t F vivere alle spalle di
'sponge cake pan *m inv* di Spagna
spong·er ['spʌndʒə(r)] F scroccone *m*, -a *f*
spon·sor ['spɒnsə(r)] **1** *n for immigration* garante *m/f inv*; *for membership* socio *m*, -a *f* garante; *of TV programme, sports event, for fundraising* sponsor *m inv* **2** v/t *for immigration, membership* garantire per; *TV programme, sports event* sponsorizzare
spon·sor·ship ['spɒnsəʃɪp] sponsorizzazione *f*
spon·ta·ne·ous [spɒn'teɪnɪəs] *adj* spontaneo
spon·ta·ne·ous·ly [spɒn'teɪnɪəslɪ] *adv* spontaneamente
spook·y ['spuːkɪ] *adj* F sinistro
spool [spuːl] *n* bobina *f*
spoon [spuːn] *n* cucchiaio *m*
'spoon·feed v/t (*pret & pp* **-fed**) *fig* scodellare la pappa a
spoon·ful ['spuːnfʊl] cucchiaio *f*
spo·rad·ic [spə'rædɪk] *adj* sporadico

sport [spɔːt] *n* sport *m inv*
sport·ing ['spɔːtɪŋ] *adj* sportivo; **a ~ gesture** un gesto sportivo
'sports car [spɔːts] auto *f inv* sportiva; **'sports cen·ter** *Am*, **'sports cen·tre** *indoor* palazzetto *m* dello sport; **'sports jack·et** giacca *f* sportiva; **'sports·man** sportivo *m*; **'sports med·i·cine** medicina *f* dello sport; **'sports news** *nsg* notizie *fpl* sportive; **'sports page** pagina *f* dello sport; **'sports·wear** abbigliamento *m* sportivo; **'sports·wom·an** sportiva *f*
sport·y ['spɔːtɪ] *adj* sportivo
spot[1] [spɒt] (*pimple*) brufolo *m*; *caused by measles* puntino *m*; *part of pattern* pois *m inv*; **a ~ of ...** (*a little*) un po' di ...
spot[2] [spɒt] (*place*) posticino *m*; **on the ~** (*in the place in question*) sul posto; (*immediately*) immediatamente; **put s.o. on the ~** mettere in difficoltà qu
spot[3] [spɒt] v/t (*pret & pp* **-ted**) (*notice*) notare; (*identify*) trovare
spot 'check *n* controllo *m* casuale
spot·less ['spɒtlɪs] *adj* pulitissimo
'spot·light *n* faretto *m*
spot·ted ['spɒtɪd] *adj fabric* a pois
spot·ty ['spɒtɪ] *adj with pimples* brufoloso
spouse [spaʊs] *fml* coniuge *m/f*
spout [spaʊt] **1** *n* beccuccio *m* **2** v/i *of liquid* sgorgare **3** v/t F: **~ nonsense** ciarlare
sprain [spreɪn] **1** *n* slogatura *f* **2** v/t slogarsi
sprang [spræŋ] *pret →* **spring**
sprawl [sprɔːl] v/i stravaccarsi; *of city* estendersi; **send s.o. ~ing** *of punch* mandare qu a gambe all'aria
sprawl·ing ['sprɔːlɪŋ] *adj city, suburbs* tentacolare
spray [spreɪ] **1** *n of sea water, from fountain* spruzzi *mpl*; *for hair* lacca *f*; (*container*) spray *m inv* **2** v/t spruzzare; **~ s.o. / sth with sth** spruzzare qu / qc di qc
'spray·gun pistola *f* a spruzzo
spread [spred] **1** *n of disease, religion*

etc diffusione *f*; F *big meal* banchetto *m*; **2** *v/t* (*pret & pp* **spread**) (*lay*) stendere; *butter, jam* spalmare; *news, rumour, disease* diffondere; *arms, legs* allargare **3** *v/i* (*pret & pp* **spread**) diffondersi; *of butter* spalmarsi

'**spread·sheet** COMPUT spreadsheet *m inv*

spree [spriː] F: *go* (*out*) *on a* ~ *having fun* andare a far baldoria; *go on a shopping* ~ andare a fare spese folli

sprig [sprɪɡ] *n* rametto *m*

spright·ly ['spraɪtlɪ] *adj* arzillo

spring[1] [sprɪŋ] *n season* primavera *f*

spring[2] [sprɪŋ] *n device* molla *f*

spring[3] [sprɪŋ] **1** *n* (*jump*) balzo *m*; (*stream*) sorgente *f* **2** *v/i* (*pret* **sprang**, *pp* **sprung**) scattare; ~ *from* derivare da

'**spring·board** trampolino *m*; **spring 'chick·en** *hum*: *she's no* ~ non è più una ragazzina; **spring-'clean·ing** pulizie *fpl* di primavera; **spring 'on·ion** cipollotto *m*; '**spring·time** primavera *f*

spring·y ['sprɪŋɪ] *adj mattress, walk* molleggiato; *ground* morbido; *material* elastico

sprin·kle ['sprɪŋkl] *v/t* spruzzare; ~ *sth with* cospargere qc di

sprin·kler ['sprɪŋklə(r)] *for garden* irrigatore *m*; *in ceiling* sprinkler *m inv*

sprint [sprɪnt] **1** *n*: scatto *m*; *the 100 metres* ~ i cento metri piani **2** *v/i* fare uno scatto

sprint·er ['sprɪntə(r)] SP velocista *m/f*

sprout [spraʊt] **1** *v/i of seed* spuntare **2** *n* germoglio *m*; (*Brussels*) ~*s* cavolini *mpl* di Bruxelles

spruce [spruːs] *adj* curato

sprung [sprʌŋ] *pp* → **spring**

spun [spʌn] *pret & pp* → **spin**

spry [spraɪ] *adj* arzillo

spud [spʌd] F patata *f*

spur [spɜː(r)] *n* sperone *m*; *fig* sprone *m*; *on the* ~ *of the moment* su due piedi

♦ **spur on** *v/t* (*pret & pp* **-red**) (*encourage*) spronare

spurt [spɜːt] **1** *n*: *put on a* ~ *in race* fare uno scatto; *in work* accelerare il ritmo **2** *v/i of liquid* sprizzare

sput·ter ['spʌtə(r)] *v/i of engine* scoppiettare

spy [spaɪ] **1** *n* spia *f* **2** *v/i* (*pret & pp* **-ied**) fare la spia **3** *v/t* (*pret & pp* **-ied**) F scorgere

♦ **spy on** *v/t* spiare

squab·ble ['skwɒbl] **1** *n* bisticcio *m* **2** *v/i* bisticciare

squal·id ['skwɒlɪd] *adj* squallido

squal·or ['skwɒlə(r)] squallore *m*

squan·der ['skwɒndə(r)] *v/t money* dilapidare

square [skweə(r)] **1** *adj in shape* quadrato; ~ *mile* miglio quadrato **2** *n in shape* quadrato *m*; *in town* piazza *f*; *in board game* casella *f*; MATH quadrato *m*; *we're back to* ~ *one* siamo punto e a capo

♦ **square up** *v/i* (*settle up*) fare i conti

square 'root radice *f* quadrata

squash[1] [skwɒʃ] *n vegetable* zucca *f*

squash[2] [skwɒʃ] *n game* squash *m inv*

squash[3] [skwɒʃ] **1** *v/t* (*crush*) schiacciare **2** *n*: *orange / lemon* ~ sciroppo *m* d'arancia / limone

squat [skwɒt] **1** *adj in shape* tozzo **2** *v/i* (*pret & pp* **-ted**) (*sit*) accovacciarsi; *illegally* occupare abusivamente

squat·ter ['skwɒtə(r)] squatter *m inv*, occupante *m/f* abusivo, -a

squeak [skwiːk] **1** *n of mouse* squittio *m*; *of hinge* cigolio *m* **2** *v/i of mouse* squittire; *of hinge* cigolare; *of shoes* scricchiolare

squeak·y ['skwiːkɪ] *adj hinge* cigolante; *shoes* scricchiolante; *voice* stridulo

squeak·y 'clean *adj* F pulito

squeal [skwiːl] **1** *n of pain, laughter* strillo *m*; *of brakes* stridore *m* **2** *v/i* strillare; *of brakes* stridere

squeam·ish ['skwiːmɪʃ] *adj*: *be* ~ avere lo stomaco delicato

squeeze [skwiːz] **1** *n of hand,*

shoulder stretta *f*; *a ~ of lemon* una spruzzata di limone **2** *v/t hand* stringere; *orange, lemon* spremere; *sponge* strizzare

♦ **squeeze in 1** *v/i to a car etc* infilarsi **2** *v/t* infilare

♦ **squeeze up** *v/i to make space* stringersi

squid [skwɪd] calamaro *m*

squint [skwɪnt] *n* strabismo *m*

squirm [skwɜːm] *v/i* (*wriggle*) contorcersi; *~* (*with embarrassment*) morire di vergogna

squir·rel ['skwɪrəl] scoiattolo *m*

squirt [skwɜːt] **1** *v/t* spruzzare **2** *n* F *pej* microbo *m* F

St *abbr* (= *saint*) S. (= santo *m*, santa *f*); (= *street*) v. (= via *f*)

stab [stæb] **1** *n* F: *have a ~ at doing sth* provare a fare qc **2** *v/t* (*pret & pp -bed*) *person* accoltellare

sta·bil·i·ty [stə'bɪlətɪ] stabilità *f inv*

sta·bil·ize ['steɪbɪlaɪz] **1** *v/t prices, boat* stabilizzare **2** *v/i of prices etc* stabilizzarsi

sta·ble¹ ['steɪbl] *n building* stalla *f*; *establishment* scuderia *f*

sta·ble² ['steɪbl] *adj* stabile

stack [stæk] **1** *n* (*pile*) pila *f*; (*smokestack*) ciminiera *f*; *~s of* F un sacco di F **2** *v/t* mettere in pila

sta·di·um ['steɪdɪəm] stadio *m*

staff [stɑːf] *npl* (*employees*) personale *msg*; (*teachers*) corpo *m* insegnante

'**staff·room** *in school* sala *f* professori

stag [stæg] cervo *m*

stage¹ [steɪdʒ] *in life, project etc* fase *f*; *of journey* tappa *f*

stage² [steɪdʒ] **1** *n* THEA palcoscenico *m*; *go on the ~ become actor* fare teatro **2** *v/t play* mettere in scena; *demonstration* organizzare

stage 'door ingresso *m* degli artisti;

'**stage fright** attacco *m* di panico;

'**stage hand** macchinista *m/f*

stag·ger ['stægə(r)] **1** *v/i* barcollare **2** *v/t* (*amaze*) sbalordire; *holidays, breaks etc* scaglionare

stag·ger·ing ['stægərɪŋ] *adj* sbalorditivo

stag·nant ['stægnənt] *adj also fig* stagnante

stag·nate [stæg'neɪt] *v/i of person, mind* vegetare

stag·na·tion [stæg'neɪʃn] ristagno *m*

'**stag par·ty** (*festa f di*) addio *m* al celibato

stain [steɪn] **1** *n* (*dirty mark*) macchia *f*; *for wood* mordente *m* **2** *v/t* (*dirty*) macchiare; *wood* dare il mordente a **3** *v/i of wine etc* macchiare; *of fabric* macchiarsi

stained-glass 'win·dow [steɪnd] vetrata *f* colorata

stain·less 'steel ['steɪnlɪs] **1** *n* acciaio *m* inossidabile **2** *adj* d'acciaio inossidabile

'**stain re·mov·er** smacchiatore *m*

stair [steə(r)] scalino *m*; *the ~s* le scale

'**stair·case** scala *f*

stake [steɪk] **1** *n of wood* paletto *m*; *when gambling* puntata *f*; (*investment*) partecipazione *f*; *be at ~* essere in gioco **2** *v/t tree* puntellare; *money* puntare

stale [steɪl] *adj bread* raffermo; *air* viziato; *fig: news* vecchio

'**stale·mate** *in chess* stallo *m*; *fig* punto *m* morto

stalk¹ [stɔːk] *n of fruit* picciolo *m*; *of plant* gambo *m*

stalk² [stɔːk] *v/t animal* seguire; *person* perseguitare (con telefonate, lettere ecc)

stalk·er ['stɔːkə(r)] *persona f che perseguita qualcun altro con telefonate, lettere ecc*

stall¹ [stɔːl] *n at market* bancarella *f*; *for cow, horse* box *m inv*

stall² [stɔːl] **1** *v/i of engine* spegnersi; *of vehicle* fermarsi; (*play for time*) temporeggiare **2** *v/t engine* far spegnere; *people* trattenere

stal·li·on ['stæljən] stallone *m*

stalls [stɔːlz] *npl* platea *f*

stal·wart ['stɔːlwət] *adj support, supporter* fedele

stam·i·na ['stæmɪnə] resistenza *f*

stam·mer ['stæmə(r)] **1** *n* balbuzie *f* **2** *v/i* balbettare

stamp¹ [stæmp] **1** *n for letter* francobollo *m*; (*date ~ etc*) timbro *m* **2** *v/t letter* affrancare; *document, passport* timbrare; **~ed addressed envelope** busta *f* affrancata per la risposta

stamp² [stæmp] *v/t*: **~ one's feet** pestare i piedi

'**stamp col·lec·ting** filatelia *f*; '**stamp col·lec·tion** collezione *f* di francobolli; '**stamp col·lec·tor** collezionista *m/f* di francobolli

♦ **stamp out** *v/t* (*eradicate*) eliminare

stam·pede [stæm'piːd] **1** *n of cattle etc* fuga *f* precipitosa; *of people* fuggi-fuggi *m inv* **2** *v/i of cattle etc* fuggire precipitosamente; *of people* precipitarsi

stance [stɑːns] (*position*) presa *f* di posizione

stand [stænd] **1** *n at exhibition* stand *m inv*; (*witness ~*) banco *m* dei testimoni; (*support, base*) base *f*; **take the ~** LAW testimoniare **2** *v/i* (*pret & pp* **stood**) (*be situated: of person*) stare; *of object, building* trovarsi; *as opposed to sit* stare in piedi; (*rise*) alzarsi in piedi; **~ still** stare fermo; **where do you ~ on the issue?** qual è la tua posizione sulla questione? **3** *v/t* (*pret & pp* **stood**) (*tolerate*) sopportare; (*put*) mettere; **you don't ~ a chance** non hai alcuna probabilità; **~ s.o. a drink** offrire da bere a qu; **~ one's ground** non mollare, tenere duro

♦ **stand back** *v/i* farsi indietro

♦ **stand by 1** *v/i* (*not take action*) stare a guardare; (*be ready*) tenersi pronto **2** *v/t person* stare al fianco di; *decision* mantenere

♦ **stand down** *v/i* (*withdraw*) ritirarsi

♦ **stand for** *v/t* (*tolerate*) tollerare; (*mean*) significare; *freedom etc* rappresentare

♦ **stand in for** *v/t* sostituire

♦ **stand out** *v/i* spiccare; *of person, building* distinguersi

♦ **stand up 1** *v/i* alzarsi in piedi **2** *v/t* F *on date* dare buca a F

♦ **stand up for** *v/t* difendere

♦ **stand up to** *v/t* far fronte a

stan·dard ['stændəd] **1** *adj* (*usual*) comune; *model, size* standard *inv* **2** *n* (*level*) livello *m*; (*expectation*) aspettativa *f*; TECH standard *m inv*; **moral ~s** principi *mpl*; **be / not be up to ~** essere / non essere di buona qualità

stan·dard·ize ['stændədaɪz] *v/t* standardizzare

'**stan·dard lamp** *Br* lampada *f* a stelo

stan·dard of 'li·ving tenore *m* di vita

'**stand·by 1** *n ticket* biglietto *m* stand-by; **on ~** *at airport* in lista d'attesa; **on ~** *of troops etc* pronto

'**stand·by pas·sen·ger** passeggero *m*, -a *f* in lista d'attesa

stand·ing ['stændɪŋ] *n in society etc* posizione *f*; (*repute*) reputazione *f*; **a musician of some ~** un musicista di una certa importanza; **a friendship of long ~** un'amicizia di lunga durata

stand·ing 'or·der FIN ordine *m* permanente

'**stand·ing room** posto *m* in piedi

stand·off·ish [stænd'ɒfɪʃ] *adj* scostante; '**stand·point** punto *m* di vista; '**stand·still**; **be at a ~** essere fermo; **bring to a ~** fermare

stank [stæŋk] *pret* → **stink**

stan·za ['stænzə] *of poem* stanza *f*

sta·ple¹ ['steɪpl] *n* (*foodstuff*) alimento *m* base

sta·ple² ['steɪpl] **1** *n* (*fastener*) graffa *f* **2** *v/t* pinzare

sta·ple 'di·et alimentazione *f* base

'**sta·ple gun** pistola *f* sparachiodi

sta·pler ['steɪplə(r)] pinzatrice *f*

star [stɑː(r)] **1** *n in sky* stella *f*; *fig* star *f inv* **2** *v/t* (*pret & pp* **-red**) *a film ~ring Julia Roberts* un film interpretato da Julia Roberts **3** *v/i* (*pret & pp* **-red**): *he ~ed in Psycho* è il protagonista di Psycho

'**star·board** *adj* a tribordo

starch [stɑːtʃ] *in foodstuff* amido *m*

stare [steə(r)] **1** *n* sguardo *m* fisso **2** *v/i* fissare; **~ at** fissare

'**star·fish** stella *f* di mare

stark [stɑːk] **1** *adj landscape* desolato; *colour scheme* austero; *reminder, contrast etc* brusco **2** *adv*: **~ naked** completamente nudo

star·ling ['stɑːlɪŋ] storno *m*

star·ry ['stɑːrɪ] *adj night* stellato

star·ry-eyed [stɑːrɪ'aɪd]] *adj person* idealista

start [stɑːt] **1** *n (beginning)* inizio *m*; **make a ~ on sth** iniziare qc; **get off to a good / bad ~** *in marriage, career* cominciare bene / male; *from the ~* dall'inizio; *well, it's a ~!* è pur sempre un inizio! **2** *v/i* iniziare, cominciare; *of engine, car* partire; **~ing from tomorrow** a partire da domani **3** *v/t* cominciare; *engine, car* mettere in moto; *business* mettere su; **~ to do sth, ~ doing sth** cominciare a fare qc

start·er ['stɑːtə(r)] *part of meal* antipasto *m*; *of car* motorino *m* d'avviamento; *in race* starter *m inv*

'start·ing point punto *m* di partenza

'start·ing sal·a·ry stipendio *m* iniziale

star·tle ['stɑːtl] *v/t* far trasalire

star·tling ['stɑːtlɪŋ] *adj* sorprendente

starv·a·tion [stɑː'veɪʃn] fame *f*

starve [stɑːv] *v/i* soffrire la fame; **~ to death** morire di fame; **I'm starving** F sto morendo di fame

state[1] [steɪt] **1** *n of car, house etc* stato *m*, condizione *f*; *(country)* stato *m*; **the States** gli Stati Uniti; **be in a ~** essere agitato **2** *adj* di stato; *school* statale; *banquet etc* ufficiale

state[2] [steɪt] *v/t* dichiarare

'State De·part·ment *in USA* Ministero *m* degli Esteri

state·ment ['steɪtmənt] *to police* deposizione *f*; *(announcement)* dichiarazione *f*; *(bank ~)* estratto *m* conto

state of e·mer·gen·cy stato *m* d'emergenza

state-of-the-'art *adj* allo stato dell'arte

states·man ['steɪtsmən] statista *m*

state 'vis·it visita *f* ufficiale

stat·ic (e·lec·tric·i·ty) ['stætɪk] elettricità *f inv* statica

sta·tion ['steɪʃn] **1** *n* stazione *f* **2** *v/t guard etc* disporre; **be ~ed at** *of soldier* essere di stanza in / a

sta·tion·a·ry ['steɪʃnərɪ] *adj* fermo

sta·tion·er's ['steɪʃənərz] cartoleria *f*

sta·tion·er·y ['steɪʃənərɪ] articoli *mpl* di cancelleria

sta·tion 'man·ag·er dirigente *m* della stazione ferroviaria

'sta·tion wag·on *Am* giardiniera *f*

sta·tis·ti·cal [stə'tɪstɪkl] *adj* statistico

sta·tis·ti·cal·ly [stə'tɪstɪklɪ] *adv* statisticamente

sta·tis·ti·cian [stætɪs'tɪʃn] esperto *m*, -a *f* di statistica

sta·tis·tics [stə'tɪstɪks] *nsg science* statistica *f*; *npl figures* statistiche *fpl*

stat·ue ['stætjuː] statua *f*

sta·tus ['steɪtəs] posizione *f*

'sta·tus bar COMPUT barra *f* di stato

'sta·tus sym·bol status symbol *m inv*

stat·ute ['stætjuːt] statuto *m*

staunch [stɔːntʃ] *adj* leale

stay [steɪ] **1** *n* soggiorno *m* **2** *v/i in a place* stare; *in a condition* restare; **~ in a hotel** stare in albergo; **~ right there!** non ti muovere!; **~ put** non muoversi

♦ **stay away** *v/i* stare alla larga

♦ **stay away from** *v/t* stare alla larga da

♦ **stay behind** *v/i* rimanere

♦ **stay up** *v/i (not go to bed)* rimanere alzato

stead·i·ly ['stedɪlɪ] *adv improve etc* costantemente; *look* fisso

stead·y ['stedɪ] **1** *adj voice, hands* fermo; *job, boyfriend* fisso; *beat* regolare; *improvement, decline, progress* costante **2** *adv*: **be going ~** fare coppia fissa; **~ on!** calma! **3** *v/t (pret & pp -ied) bookcase etc* rendere saldo; **~ o.s.** ritrovare l'equilibrio

steak [steɪk] bistecca *f*, carne *f* (di manzo)

steal [stiːl] *(pret stole, pp stolen)* **1** *v/t money etc* rubare **2** *v/i (be a thief)* rubare; **~ in / out** *(move quietly)* entrare / uscire furtivamente

S

stealth·y ['stelθι] *adj* furtivo

steam [stiːm] **1** *n* vapore *m* **2** *v/t food* cuocere al vapore

♦ **steam up 1** *v/i of window* appannarsi **2** *v/t*: **be steamed up** F *angry* essere furibondo

steam·er ['stiːmə(r)] *for cooking* vaporiera *f*

'steam i·ron ferro *m* a vapore

steel [stiːl] **1** *n* acciaio *m* **2** *adj* d'acciaio

'steel·work·er operaio *m* di acciaieria

'steel·works acciaieria *f*

steep[1] [stiːp] *adj hill etc* ripido; F *prices* alto; **that's a bit ~ expensive** è un po' caro

steep[2] [stiːp] *v/t (soak)* lasciare a bagno

stee·ple ['stiːpl] campanile *m*

'stee·ple·chase *in athletics* corsa *f* ad ostacoli

steep·ly ['stiːplɪ] *adv*: **climb ~** *of path* salire ripidamente; *of prices* salire vertiginosamente

steer[1] [stɪə(r)] *n animal* manzo *m*

steer[2] [stɪə(r)] *v/t car, boat* manovrare; *person* guidare; *conversation* spostare

steer·ing ['stɪərɪŋ] *of motor vehicle* sterzo *m*

'steer·ing wheel volante *m*

stem[1] [stem] *n of plant, glass* stelo *m*; *of word* radice *f*

♦ **stem from** *v/t* derivare da

stem[2] [stem] *v/t (pret & pp -med) (block)* arginare

stench [stentʃ] puzzo *m*

sten·cil ['stensɪl] **1** *n* stencil *m inv* **2** *v/t (pret & pp -led, Am -ed) pattern* disegnare con lo stencil

step [step] **1** *n (pace)* passo *m*; *(stair)* gradino *m*; *(measure)* provvedimento *m*; **~ by ~** poco a poco **2** *v/i (pret & pp -ped)* mettere il piede; **~ into / out of** salire in / scendere da

♦ **step down** *v/i from post etc* dimettersi

♦ **step forward** *v/i also fig* farsi avanti

♦ **step up** *v/t* F *(increase)* aumentare

'step·broth·er fratellastro *m*; **'step·daugh·ter** figliastra *f*; **'step·fa·ther** patrigno *m*; **'step·lad·der** scala *f* a libretto; **'step·moth·er** matrigna *f*

step·ping stone ['stepɪŋ] pietra *f* di un guado; *fig* trampolino *m* di lancio

'step·sis·ter sorellastra *f*

'step·son figliastro *m*

ster·e·o ['sterɪəʊ] *n (sound system)* stereo *m inv*

ster·e·o·type ['sterɪəʊtaɪp] *n* stereotipo *m*

ster·ile ['steraɪl] *adj* sterile

ster·il·ize ['sterəlaɪz] *v/t* sterilizzare

ster·ling ['stɜːlɪŋ] *n* FIN sterlina *f*

stern[1] [stɜːn] *adj* severo

stern[2] [stɜːn] *n* NAUT poppa *f*

stern·ly ['stɜːnlɪ] *adv* severamente

ster·oids ['sterɔɪdz] *npl* anabolizzanti *mpl*

steth·o·scope ['steθəskəʊp] fonendoscopio *m*

stew [stjuː] *n* spezzatino *m*

stew·ard ['stjuːəd] *n on plane, ship* steward *m inv*; *at demonstration, meeting* membro *m* del servizio d'ordine

stew·ard·ess [stjuːə'des] *on plane, ship* hostess *f inv*

stewed [stjuːd] *adj apples, plums* cotto

stick[1] [stɪk] *n wood* rametto *m*; *(walking ~)* bastone *m*; **out in the ~s** F a casa del diavolo F

stick[2] [stɪk] *(pret & pp stuck)* **1** *v/t with adhesive* attaccare; *needle, knife* conficcare; F *(put)* mettere **2** *v/i (jam)* bloccarsi; *(adhere)* attaccarsi

♦ **stick around** *v/i* F restare

♦ **stick by** *v/t* F: **stick by s.o.** rimanere al fianco di qu

♦ **stick out** *v/i (protrude)* sporgere; *(be noticeable)* spiccare

♦ **stick to** *v/t* F *(keep to)* attenersi a; *(follow)* seguire

♦ **stick together** *v/i* F restare uniti

♦ **stick up** *v/t poster, leaflet* affiggere

♦ **stick up for** *v/t* F difendere

stick·er ['stɪkə(r)] adesivo *m*

'stick·ing plas·ter cerotto *m*

'stick-in-the-mud F abitudinario *m*,
-a *f*

stick·y ['stɪkɪ] *adj hands, surface* appiccicoso; *label* adesivo

stiff [stɪf] **1** *adj brush, cardboard,
leather* rigido; *muscle, body* anchilosato; *mixture, paste* sodo; *in manner*
freddo; *drink, competition* forte; *fine*
salato **2** *adv*: **be scared ~** F essere
spaventato a morte F; **be bored ~** F
essere annoiato a morte F

stiff·en ['stɪfn] *v/i* irrigidirsi

♦ **stiffen up** *v/i of muscle* anchilosarsi

stiff·ly ['stɪflɪ] *adv* rigidamente; *fig*
freddamente

stiff·ness ['stɪfnəs] *of muscles* indolenzimento *m*; *of material* rigidità *f*;
fig: of manner freddezza *f*

sti·fle ['staɪfl] *v/t also fig* soffocare

sti·fling ['staɪflɪŋ] *adj* soffocante

stig·ma ['stɪgmə] vergogna *f*

sti·let·tos [stɪ'letəʊz] *npl (shoes)*
scarpe *fpl* col tacco a spillo

still¹ [stɪl] **1** *adj (motionless)* immobile; *without wind* senza vento; *drink*
non gas(s)ato; *it was very ~ outside* tutto era calmo fuori **2** *adv*:
keep / stand ~! stai fermo!

still² [stɪl] *adv (yet)* ancora; *(nevertheless)* comunque; **she ~ hasn't finished** non ha ancora finito; **they
are ~ my parents** sono pur sempre
i miei genitori; **~ more** *(even more)*
ancora più

'still·born *adj* nato morto

still *'life* natura *f* morta

stilt·ed ['stɪltɪd] *adj* poco naturale

stilts [stɪlts] *npl* trampoli *mpl*

stim·u·lant ['stɪmjʊlənt] stimolante
m

stim·u·late ['stɪmjʊleɪt] *v/t* stimolare

stim·u·lat·ing ['stɪmjʊleɪtɪŋ] *adj* stimolante

stim·u·la·tion [stɪmjʊ'leɪʃn] stimolazione *f*

stim·u·lus ['stɪmjʊləs] *(incentive)* stimolo *m*

sting [stɪŋ] **1** *n from bee* puntura *f*;
actual organ pungiglione *m*; *from
jellyfish* pizzico *m* **2** *v/t (pret & pp
stung)* *of bee* pungere; *of jellyfish*

pizzicare **3** *v/i (pret & pp stung)* *of
eyes, scratch* bruciare

sting·ing ['stɪŋɪŋ] *adj remark, criticism* pungente

sting·y ['stɪndʒɪ] *adj* F tirchio F

stink [stɪŋk] **1** *n (bad smell)* puzza *f*; F
(fuss) putiferio *m* F; **kick up a ~**
fare un casino F **2** *v/i (pret stank, pp
stunk)* *(smell bad)* puzzare; F *(be
very bad)* fare schifo F

stint [stɪnt] *n* periodo *m*; **do a ~ in
the army** arruolarsi nell'esercito
per un periodo; **do you want to do
a ~ now?** vuoi darmi il cambio?

♦ **stint on** *v/t* F lesinare su

stip·u·late ['stɪpjʊleɪt] *v/t & v/i* stabilire

stip·u·la·tion [stɪpjʊ'leɪʃn] condizione *f*

stir [stɜː(r)] **1** *n*: **give the soup a ~**
mescolare la minestra; **cause a ~**
fare scalpore **2** *v/t (pret & pp -red)*
mescolare **3** *v/i (pret & pp -red)* *of
sleeping person* muoversi

♦ **stir up** *v/t* fomentare

'stir-fry *v/t (pret & pp -ied)* saltare
(in padella)

stir·ring ['stɜːrɪŋ] *adj music, speech*
commovente

stitch [stɪtʃ] **1** *n in sewing* punto *m*; *in
knitting* maglia *f*; **-es** MED punti *mpl*
(di sutura); **be in -es** *laughing* ridere a crepapelle; **have a ~** avere una
fitta al fianco **2** *v/t sew* cucire

♦ **stitch up** *v/t wound* suturare

stitch·ing ['stɪtʃɪŋ] *(stitches)* cucitura
f

stock [stɒk] **1** *n (reserves)* provvista
f; COM: *of store* stock *m inv*; *animals*
bestiame *m*; FIN titoli *mpl*; *for soup
etc* brodo *m*; **in ~ / out of ~** disponibile / esaurito; **take ~** fare il punto
2 *v/t* COM vendere

♦ **stock up on** *v/t* fare provvista di

'stock·brok·er agente *m/f* di cambio; **'stock cube** dado *m (da brodo)*; **'stock ex·change** borsa *f* valori

stock·ing ['stɒkɪŋ] calza *f (da donna)*

stock·ist ['stɒkɪst] rivenditore *m*

S

'stock mar·ket mercato *m* azionario; **stock·mar·ket 'crash** crollo *m* del mercato azionario; **'stock·pile 1** *n of food, weapons* scorta *f* **2** *v/t* fare scorta di; **'stock·room** magazzino *m*; **stock-'still** *adv*: **stand ~** stare immobile; **'stock·tak·ing** inventario *m*

stock·y ['stɒkɪ] *adj* tarchiato

stodg·y ['stɒdʒɪ] *adj food* pesante

sto·i·cal ['stəʊɪkl] *adj* stoico

sto·i·cism ['stəʊɪsɪzm] stoicismo *m*

stole [stəʊl] *pret* → **steal**

stol·en ['stəʊlən] *pp* → **steal**

stom·ach ['stʌmək] **1** *n* stomaco *m*; *(abdomen)* pancia *f* **2** *v/t (tolerate)* sopportare

'stom·ach·ache mal *m* di stomaco

stone [stəʊn] *n material* pietra *f*; *(pebble)* sasso *m*; *(precious ~)* pietra *f* preziosa; *in fruit* nocciolo *m*

stoned [stəʊnd] *adj* F *on drugs* fatto F

stone-'deaf *adj* sordo (come una campana)

'stone·wall *v/i* F menare il can per l'aia

ston·y ['stəʊnɪ] *adj ground, path* sassoso

stood [stʊd] *pret & pp* → **stand**

stool [stuːl] *seat* sgabello *m*

stoop [stuːp] **1** *n*: **walk with a ~** camminare con la schiena curva **2** *v/i (bend down)* chinarsi; *(have bent back)* essere curvo

stop [stɒp] **1** *n for train, bus* fermata *f*; **come to a ~** fermarsi; **put a ~ to** mettere fine a **2** *v/t (pret & pp -ped)* *(put an end to)* mettere fine a; *(prevent)* fermare; *(cease)* smettere; *person, car, bus* fermare; **it has ~ped raining** ha smesso di piovere; **I ~ped her from leaving** le ho impedito di andar via; **~ a cheque** bloccare un assegno **3** *v/i (pret & pp -ped)* *(come to a halt)* fermarsi; *of rain, noise* smettere

♦ **stop by** *v/i (visit)* passare

♦ **stop off** *v/i* fermarsi, fare sosta; *at post office* passare a

♦ **stop over** *v/i* fare sosta

♦ **stop up** *v/t sink* intasare

'stop·gap *person* tappabuchi *m/f inv*; *thing* soluzione *f* temporanea

'stop·o·ver *n* sosta *f*; *in air travel* scalo *m* intermedio

'stop·per ['stɒpə(r)] tappo *m*

stop sign (segnale *m* di) stop *m inv*

'stop·watch cronometro *m*

stor·age ['stɔːrɪdʒ]: **put sth in ~** mettere qc in magazzino; **not much space for ~** poco spazio per riporre la roba

'stor·age ca·pac·i·ty COMPUT capacità *f* di memoria

'stor·age space spazio *m* per riporre la roba

store [stɔː(r)] **1** *n large shop* negozio *m*; *(stock)* riserva *f*; *(storehouse)* deposito *m* **2** *v/t* tenere; COMPUT memorizzare

'store·room magazzino *m*

sto·rey ['stɔːrɪ] piano *m*

stork [stɔːk] *n* cicogna *f*

storm [stɔːm] *n* tempesta *f*

'storm warn·ing avviso *m* di tempesta

storm·y ['stɔːmɪ] *adj also fig* tempestoso

sto·ry¹ ['stɔːrɪ] *(tale)* racconto *m*; *(account)* storia *f*; *(newspaper article)* articolo *m*; F *(lie)* bugia *f*

sto·ry² ['stɔːrɪ] *Am* → **storey**

stout [staut] *adj person* robusto; *defender* tenace

stove [stəʊv] *for cooking* cucina *f*; *for heating* stufa *f*

stow [stəʊ] *v/t* riporre

♦ **stow away** *v/i* imbarcarsi clandestinamente

'stow·a·way *n* passeggero *m*, -a *f* clandestino, -a

strag·gler ['stræglə(r)] persona *f* che rimane indietro

straight [streɪt] **1** *adj line* retto; *hair, whisky* liscio; *back, knees* dritto; *(honest, direct)* onesto; *(tidy)* in ordine; *(conservative)* convenzionale; *(not homosexual)* etero; **keep a ~ face** non ridere **2** *adv (in a straight line)* dritto; *(directly, immediately)* dritto, direttamente; *(clearly: think)* con chiarezza; **stand up ~!** stai dritto!; **look s.o. ~ in the eye** guardare qu dritto negli occhi; **go ~** F *of criminal* rigare dritto; **give it to me ~** F dimmi francamente; **~ ahead** avanti dritto; **carry ~ on** proseguire dritto; **~away, ~ off** immediatamente; **~ out** say sth chiaro e tondo

straight·en ['streɪtn] v/t raddrizzare

♦ **straighten out 1** v/t situation sistemare; F person mettere in riga F **2** v/i of road tornare diritto

♦ **straighten up** v/i raddrizzarsi

straight'for·ward adj (honest, direct) franco; (simple) semplice

strain¹ [streɪn] **1** n physical sforzo m; mental tensione f **2** v/t (injure) affaticare; fig: finances, budget gravare su

strain² [streɪn] v/t vegetables scolare; oil, fat etc filtrare

strain³ [streɪn] n of virus ceppo m

strained [streɪnd] adj teso

strain·er ['streɪnə(r)] for vegetables etc colino m

strait [streɪt] GEOG stretto m

strait·laced [streɪt'leɪst] adj puritano

strand¹ [strænd] n of wool, thread filo m; of hair ciocca f

strand² [strænd] v/t piantare in asso F; **be ~ed** essere bloccato

strange [streɪndʒ] adj (odd, curious) strano; (unknown, foreign) sconosciuto

strange·ly ['streɪndʒlɪ] adv (oddly) stranamente; **~ enough** strano ma vero

strang·er ['streɪndʒə(r)] person you don't know sconosciuto m, -a f; **I'm a ~ here myself** non sono di queste parti

stran·gle ['stræŋgl] v/t person strangolare

strap [stræp] n of bag tracolla f; of bra, dress bretellina f, spallina f; of watch cinturino m; of shoe listino m

♦ **strap in** v/t (pret & pp **-ped**) with seatbelt allacciare la cintura di sicurezza a

♦ **strap on** v/t allacciare

strap·less ['stræplɪs] adj senza spalline

stra·te·gic [strəˈtiːdʒɪk] adj strategico

strat·e·gy ['strætədʒɪ] strategia f

straw¹ [strɔː] paglia f; **that's the last ~!** questa è la goccia che fa traboccare il vaso!

straw² [strɔː] for drink cannuccia f

straw·ber·ry ['strɔːbərɪ] fragola f

stray [streɪ] **1** adj animal randagio; bullet vagante **2** n dog, cat randagio m **3** v/i of animal smarrirsi; of child allontanarsi; fig: of eyes, thoughts vagare

streak [striːk] **1** n of dirt, paint stria f, fig: of nastiness etc vena f **2** v/i move quickly sfrecciare **3** v/t: **be ~ed with** essere striato di

streak·y ['striːkɪ] adj striato

stream [striːm] **1** n ruscello m; fig: of people, complaints fiume m; **come on ~** of plant entrare in attività; of oil arrivare **2** v/i riversarsi

stream·er ['striːmə(r)] stella f filante

'stream·line v/t fig snellire

'stream·lined adj car, plane aerodinamico; fig: organization snellito

street [striːt] strada f; in address via f

'street·car Am tram m inv; **'street·light** lampione m; **'street·light·ing** illuminazione f stradale; **'street value** of drugs valore m di mercato; **'street·walk·er** F passeggiatrice f; **'street·wise** adj scafato F

strength [streŋθ] of person, wind, emotion, currency forza f; (strong point) punto m forte

strength·en ['streŋθn] **1** v/t rinforzare **2** v/i consolidarsi

stren·u·ous ['strenjʊəs] adj faticoso

stren·u·ous·ly ['strenjʊəslɪ] adv deny recisamente

stress [stres] **1** n (emphasis) accento m; (tension) stress m inv; **be under ~** essere sotto pressione **2** v/t syllable accentare; importance etc sottolineare

stressed 'out [strest] adj stressato

stress·ful ['stresful] adj stressante

S

stretch [stretʃ] **1** *n of land, water* tratto *m*; **at a ~** *(non-stop)* di fila **2** *adj fabric* elasticizzato **3** *v/t material* tendere; *small income* far bastare; **~ the rules** F fare uno strappo (alla regola); **he ~ed out his hand** allungò la mano; **a job that ~es me** un lavoro che mi impegna **4** *v/i to relax muscles* stirarsi; *to reach sth* allungarsi; *(spread)* estendersi; *of fabric*: *give* cedere; *of fabric*: *sag* allargarsi; **~ from X to Y** *(extend)* estendersi da X a Y

stretch·er ['stretʃə(r)] barella *f*

strict [strɪkt] *adj person* severo; *instructions, rules* tassativo

strict·ly ['strɪktlɪ] *adv*: **be brought up ~** ricevere un'educazione rigida; **it is ~ forbidden** è severamente proibito

strictness ['strɪktnəs] severità *f inv*

strid·den ['strɪdn] *pp* → **stride**

stride [straɪd] **1** *n* falcata *f*; **take sth in one's ~** affrontare qc senza drammi; **make great ~s** *fig* far passi da gigante **2** *v/i* (*pret* **strode**, *pp* **stridden**) procedere a grandi passi; **he strode up to me** avanzò verso di me

stri·dent ['straɪdnt] *adj* stridulo; *fig*: *demands* veemente

strike [straɪk] **1** *n of workers* sciopero *m*; *of oil* scoperta *f*; **be on ~** essere in sciopero; **go on ~** entrare in sciopero **2** *v/i* (*pret & pp* **struck**) *of workers* scioperare; *(attack)* aggredire; *of disaster* colpire; *of clock* suonare **3** *v/t* (*pret & pp* **struck**) *(hit)* colpire; *match* accendere (sfregando); *of idea, thought* venire in mente a; *oil* trovare; **~ one's head against sth** battere la testa contro qc; **she struck me as being ...** mi ha dato l'impressione di essere ...

♦ **strike out** *v/t* depennare

'strike·break·er crumiro *m*, -a *f*

strik·er ['straɪkə(r)] *person on strike* scioperante *m/f*; *in football* bomber *m inv*, cannoniere *m*, punta *f*

strik·ing ['straɪkɪŋ] *adj (marked)* marcato; *(eye-catching)* impressio-

nante; *(attractive)* attraente; *colour* forte

string [strɪŋ] *n (cord)* spago *m*; *of violin, tennis racket* corda *f*; **the ~s** MUS gli archi; **pull ~s** esercitare la propria influenza; **a ~ of** *(series)* una serie di

♦ **string along 1** *v/i* (*pret & pp* **strung**) F: **do you mind if I string along?** posso venire anch'io? **2** *v/t* (*pret & pp* **strung**) F: **string s.o. along** menare qu per il naso

♦ **string up** *v/t* F impiccare

stringed 'in·stru·ment [strɪŋd] strumento *m* ad arco

strin·gent ['strɪndʒənt] *adj* rigoroso

'string play·er suonatore *m*, -trice *f* di strumento ad arco

strip [strɪp] **1** *n* striscia *f*; *(comic ~)* fumetto *m*; *of soccer player* divisa *f* **2** *v/t* (*pret & pp* **-ped**) *(remove)* staccare; *bed* disfare; *(undress)* spogliare; **~ s.o. of sth** spogliare qu di qc **3** *v/i* (*pret & pp* **-ped**) *(undress)* spogliarsi; *of stripper* fare lo spogliarello

'strip club locale *m* di spogliarelli

stripe [straɪp] striscia *f*; *indicating rank* gallone *m*

striped [straɪpt] *adj* a strisce

'strip joint F → **strip club**

strip·per ['strɪpə(r)] spogliarellista *f*; **male ~** spogliarellista *m*

'strip show spogliarello *m*

strip'tease spogliarello *m*

strive [straɪv] *v/i* (*pret* **strove**, *pp* **striven**): **~ to do sth** sforzarsi di fare qc; **~ for sth** lottare per (ottenere) qc

striv·en ['strɪvn] *pp* → **strive**

strobe (light) [strəʊb] luce *f* stroboscopica

strode [strəʊd] *pret* → **stride**

stroke [strəʊk] **1** *n* MED ictus *m inv*; *when painting* pennellata *f*; *in swimming* bracciata *f*; *style of swimming* stile *m* di nuoto; **~ of luck** colpo di fortuna; **she never does a ~** *(of work)* non fa mai un bel niente **2** *v/t* accarezzare

stroll [strəʊl] **1** *n* passeggiata *f*; **go for**

a ~ fare una passeggiata **2** *v/i* fare due passi; **she ~ed back to the office** tornò in ufficio in tutta calma

strong [strɒŋ] *adj person, wind, drink, currency* forte; *structure* resistente; *candidate* valido; *taste, smell* intenso; *views, beliefs* fermo; *arguments* convincente; *objections* energico; **~ support** largo consenso

'**strong·hold** *fig* roccaforte *f*

strong·ly ['strɒŋlɪ] *adv believe, object* fermamente; *built* solidamente; **feel ~ about sth** avere molto a cuore qc

strong-mind·ed [strɒŋ'maɪndɪd] *adj* risoluto; '**strong point** (punto *m*) forte *m*; '**strong·room** camera *f* blindata; **strong-'willed** [strɒŋ-'wɪld] *adj* deciso

strove [strəʊv] *pret* → **strive**

struck [strʌk] *pret & pp* → **strike**

struc·tur·al ['strʌktʃərl] *adj* strutturale

struc·ture ['strʌktʃə(r)] **1** *n something built* costruzione *f*; *of novel, society etc* struttura *f* **2** *v/t* strutturare

strug·gle ['strʌgl] **1** *n* (*fight*) colluttazione *f*; *fig* lotta *f*; (*hard time*) fatica *f* **2** *v/i with a person* lottare; (*have a hard time*) faticare; **~ to do sth** faticare a fare qc

strum [strʌm] *v/t* (*pret & pp* **-med**) strimpellare

strung [strʌŋ] *pret & pp* → **string**

strut [strʌt] *v/i* (*pret & pp* **-ted**) camminare impettito

stub [stʌb] **1** *n of cigarette* mozzicone *m*; *of cheque, ticket* matrice *f* **2** *v/t* (*pret & pp* **-bed**): **~ one's toe** urtare il dito del piede

♦ **stub out** *v/t* spegnere

stub·ble ['stʌbl] *on man's face* barba *f* ispida

stub·born ['stʌbən] *adj person* testardo; *defence, refusal, denial* ostinato

stub·by ['stʌbɪ] *adj* tozzo

stuck [stʌk] **1** *pret & pp* → **stick** **2** *adj* F: **be ~ on s.o.** essere cotto di qu F

stuck-'up *adj* F presuntuoso

stu·dent ['stjuːdnt] studente *m*, -essa *f*

stu·dent 'nurse infermiere *m*, -a *f* tirocinante

stu·dent 'teach·er insegnante *m/f* tirocinante

stu·di·o ['stjuːdɪəʊ] studio *m*; (*recording ~*) sala *f* di registrazione

stu·di·ous ['stjuːdɪəs] *adj* studioso

stud·y ['stʌdɪ] **1** *n* studio *m* **2** *v/t & v/i* (*pret & pp* **-ied**) studiare

stuff [stʌf] **1** *n* roba *f* **2** *v/t turkey* farcire; **~ sth into sth** ficcare qc in qc

stuff·ing ['stʌfɪŋ] *for turkey* farcia *f*; *in chair, teddy bear* imbottitura *f*

stuff·y ['stʌfɪ] *adj room* mal ventilato; *person* inquadrato

stum·ble ['stʌmbl] *v/i* inciampare

♦ **stumble across** *v/t* trovare per caso

♦ **stumble over** *v/t* inciampare in; *words* incespicare in

stum·bling-block ['stʌmblɪŋ] *fig* scoglio *m*

stump [stʌmp] **1** *n of tree* ceppo *m* **2** *v/t of question, questioner* sconcertare

♦ **stump up** *v/t* F sganciare F

stun [stʌn] *v/t* (*pret & pp* **-ned**) *of blow* stordire; *of news* sbalordire

stung [stʌŋ] *pret & pp* → **sting**

stunk [stʌŋk] *pp* → **stink**

stun·ning ['stʌnɪŋ] *adj* (*amazing*) sbalorditivo; (*very beautiful*) splendido

stunt [stʌnt] *n for publicity* trovata *f* pubblicitaria; *in film* acrobazia *f*

'**stunt·man** *in film* cascatore *m*

stu·pe·fy ['stjuːpɪfaɪ] *v/t* (*pret & pp* **-ied**) sbalordire

stu·pen·dous [stjuː'pendəs] *adj* (*marvellous*) fantastico; *mistake* enorme

stu·pid ['stjuːpɪd] *adj* stupido

stu·pid·i·ty [stjuː'pɪdətɪ] stupidità *f inv*

stu·por ['stjuːpə(r)] stordimento *m*; **in a drunken ~** stordito dall'alcool

stur·dy ['stɜːdɪ] *adj* robusto

stut·ter ['stʌtə(r)] *v/i* balbettare

sty [staɪ] *for pig* porcile *m*

style [staɪl] *n* stile *m*; (*fashion*) moda *f*; (*fashionable elegance*) classe *f*; (*hair~*) pettinatura *f*; **go out of ~** passare di moda

styl·ish ['staɪlɪʃ] *adj* elegante

styl·ist ['staɪlɪst] (*hair ~*) parrucchiere *m*, -a *f*

sub·com·mit·tee ['sʌbkəmɪtɪ] sottocommissione *f*

sub·con·scious [sʌb'kɒnʃəs] *adj* subconscio; **the ~** (**mind**) il subconscio

sub·con·scious·ly [sʌb'kɒnʃəslɪ] *adv* inconsciamente

sub·con·tract [sʌbkən'trakt] *v/t* subappaltare

sub·con·trac·tor [sʌbkən'traktə(r)] subappaltatore *m*, -trice *f*

sub·di·vide [sʌbdɪ'vaɪd] *v/t* suddividere

sub·due [səb'djuː] *v/t* sottomettere

sub·dued [səb'djuːd] *adj* person, voice pacato; *light, colour* soffuso

sub·head·ing ['sʌbhedɪŋ] sottotitolo *m*

sub·hu·man [sʌb'hjuːmən] *adj* subumano

sub·ject ['sʌbdʒɪkt] **1** *n* of monarch suddito *m*, -a *f*; (*topic*) argomento *m*; EDU materia *f*; GRAM soggetto *m*; **change the ~** cambiare argomento **2** *adj*: **be ~ to** essere soggetto a; **~ to availability** nei limiti della disponibilità **3** *v/t* [səb'dʒekt] sottoporre; **be ~ed to criticism** essere criticato

sub·jec·tive [səb'dʒektɪv] *adj* soggettivo

sub·junc·tive [səb'dʒʌŋktɪv] GRAM congiuntivo *m*

sub·let ['sʌblet] *v/t* (*pret & pp* **-let**) subaffittare

sub·ma·chine gun mitra *m*

sub·ma·rine ['sʌbməriːn] sottomarino *m*, sommergibile *m*

sub·merge [səb'mɜːdʒ] **1** *v/t* sommergere **2** *v/i* of submarine immergersi

sub·mis·sion [səb'mɪʃn] (*surrender*) sottomissione *f*; request to committee etc richiesta *f*

sub·mis·sive [səb'mɪsɪv] *adj* sottomesso

sub·mit [səb'mɪt] (*pret & pp* **-ted**) **1** *v/t* plan, proposal presentare **2** *v/i* sottomettersi

sub·or·di·nate [sə'bɔːdɪnət] **1** *adj* employee, position subalterno **2** *n* subalterno *m*, -a *f*

sub·poe·na [sə'piːnə] **1** *n* citazione *f* **2** *v/t* person citare in giudizio

♦ **subscribe to** [səb'skraɪb] *v/t* magazine etc abbonarsi a; *theory* condividere

sub·scrib·er [səb'skraɪbə(r)] *to magazine* abbonato *m*, -a *f*

sub·scrip·tion [səb'skrɪpʃn] abbonamento *m*

sub·se·quent ['sʌbsɪkwənt] *adj* successivo

sub·se·quent·ly ['sʌbsɪkwəntlɪ] *adv* successivamente

sub·side [səb'saɪd] *v/i* of waters, winds calare; *of building* sprofondare; *of fears, panic* calmarsi

sub·sid·i·a·ry [səb'sɪdɪərɪ] *n* filiale *f*

sub·si·dize ['sʌbsɪdaɪz] *v/t* sovvenzionare

sub·si·dy ['sʌbsɪdɪ] sovvenzione *f*

♦ **subsist on** *v/t* vivere di

sub·sis·tence farm·ing [səb'sɪstəns] agricoltura *f* di sussistenza

sub·sis·tence lev·el livello *m* minimo di vita

sub·stance ['sʌbstəns] (*matter*) sostanza *f*

sub·stan·dard [sʌb'stændəd] *adj* scadente

sub·stan·tial [səb'stænʃl] *adj* considerevole; *meal* sostanzioso

sub·stan·tial·ly [səb'stænʃlɪ] *adv* (*considerably*) considerevolmente; (*in essence*) sostanzialmente

sub·stan·ti·ate [səb'stænʃɪeɪt] *v/t* comprovare

sub·stan·tive [səb'stæntɪv] *adj* sostanziale

sub·sti·tute ['sʌbstɪtjuːt] **1** *n* for person sostituto *m*, -a *f*; for commodity alternativa *f*; SP riserva *f* **2** *v/t*: **~ X for Y** sostituire Y con X **3** *v/i*: **~ for s.o.** sostituire qu

sub·sti·tu·tion [sʌbstɪˈtjuːʃn] (*act*) sostituzione *f*; *make a ~* SP fare una sostituzione

sub·ti·tle [ˈsʌbtaɪtl] *n* sottotitolo *m*

sub·tle [ˈsʌtl] *adj* hint, difference sottile; *flavour* delicato

sub·tract [səbˈtrækt] *v/t* number sottrarre

sub·urb [ˈsʌbɜːb] sobborgo *m*; *the ~s* la periferia

sub·ur·ban [səˈbɜːbən] *adj* di periferia

sub·ur·bi·a [səˈbɜːbɪə] periferia *f*

sub·ver·sive [səbˈvɜːsɪv] **1** *adj* sovversivo **2** *n* sovversivo *m*, -a *f*

sub·way [ˈsʌbweɪ] *Br* (*passageway*) sottopassaggio *m*; *Am* metropolitana *f*

sub'ze·ro *adj*: *~ temperatures* temperature sottozero

suc·ceed [səkˈsiːd] **1** *v/i* (*be successful*) avere successo; *to throne* succedere; *~ in doing sth* riuscire a fare qc **2** *v/t* (*come after*) succedere a

suc·ceed·ing [səkˈsiːdɪŋ] *adj* successivo

suc·cess [səkˈses] successo *m*; *be a ~* avere successo

suc·cess·ful [səkˈsesful] *adj* person affermato; *marriage, party* riuscito; *be ~* riuscire; *he's very ~* è arrivato

suc·cess·ful·ly [səkˈsesflɪ] *adv* con successo; *we ~ completed ...* siamo riusciti a portare a termine ...

suc·ces·sion [səkˈseʃn] (*sequence*) sfilza *f*; *to the throne* successione *f*; *in ~* di seguito

suc·ces·sive [səkˈsesɪv] *adj* successivo; *three ~ days* tre giorni di seguito

suc·ces·sor [səkˈsesə(r)] successore *m*

suc·cinct [səkˈsɪŋkt] *adj* succinto

suc·cu·lent [ˈsʌkjʊlənt] *adj* succulento

suc·cumb [səˈkʌm] *v/i* (*give in*) cedere; *~ to temptation* cedere alla tentazione

such [sʌtʃ] **1** *adj* (*of that kind*) del genere; *~ a* (*so much of a*) un / una tale; *~ as* come; *~ people* gente del ge-

nere; *he made ~ a fuss* ha fatto una tale scenata; *there is no ~ word as ...* la parola ... non esiste **2** *adv* così; *~ nice people* gente così simpatica; *as ~* (*in that capacity*) in quanto tale; *as ~* (*in itself*) di per sé

suck [sʌk] **1** *v/t* lollipop etc succhiare; *~ one's thumb* succhiarsi il dito **2** *v/i*: *it ~s* P (*is awful*) fa schifo P
♦ **suck up** *v/t* assorbire; *dust* aspirare
♦ **suck up to** *v/t* F leccare i piedi a F

suck·er [ˈsʌkə(r)] F person pollo F

suc·tion [ˈsʌkʃn] aspirazione *f*

sud·den [ˈsʌdn] *adj* improvviso; *all of a ~* all'improvviso

sud·den·ly [ˈsʌdnlɪ] *adv* improvvisamente

suds [sʌdz] *npl* (*soap ~*) schiuma *fsg*

sue [suː] **1** *v/t* fare causa a **2** *v/i* fare causa

suede [sweɪd] *n* pelle *f* scamosciata

suf·fer [ˈsʌfə(r)] **1** *v/i* (*be in great pain*) soffrire; (*deteriorate*) risentirne; *be ~ing from* soffrire di **2** *v/t* loss, setback subire

suf·fer·ing [ˈsʌfərɪŋ] *n* sofferenza *f*

suf·fi·cient [səˈfɪʃnt] *adj* sufficiente

suf·fi·cient·ly [səˈfɪʃntlɪ] *adv* abbastanza

suf·fo·cate [ˈsʌfəkeɪt] *v/t & v/i* soffocare

suf·fo·ca·tion [sʌfəˈkeɪʃn] soffocamento *m*

sug·ar [ˈʃʊgə(r)] **1** *n* zucchero *m* **2** *v/t* zuccherare

'sug·ar bowl zuccheriera *f*

sug·gest [səˈdʒest] *v/t* proporre, suggerire; *I ~ that we stop now* propongo di fermarci ora

sug·ges·tion [səˈdʒestʃən] *n* proposta *f*, suggerimento *m*

su·i·cide [ˈsuːɪsaɪd] *n* suicidio *m*; *commit ~* suicidarsi

'su·i·cide pact *n* patto *m* suicida

suit [suːt] **1** *n* for man vestito *m*, completo *m*; *for woman* tailleur *m inv*; *in cards* seme *m* **2** *v/t* of clothes, colour stare bene a; *~ yourself!* F fai come ti pare!; *be ~ed for sth* essere fatto per qc

sui·ta·ble [ˈsuːtəbl] *adj* adatto

S

sui·ta·bly ['suːtəblɪ] *adv* adeguatamente

'suit·case valigia *f*

suite [swiːt] *of rooms* suite *f inv*; *of furniture* divano *m* e poltrone *fpl* coordinati; MUS suite *f inv*

sul·fur *etc Am* → **sulphur** *etc*

sulk [sʌlk] *v/i* fare il broncio

sulk·y ['sʌlkɪ] *adj* imbronciato

sul·len ['sʌlən] *adj* crucciato

sul·phur ['sʌlfə(r)] zolfo *m*

sul·phur·ic acid [sʌl'fjuːrɪk] acido *m* solforico

sul·try ['sʌltrɪ] *adj climate* afoso; *sexually* sensuale

sum [sʌm] somma *f*; *in arithmetic* addizione *f*; *a large ~ of money* una forte somma di denaro; *that's the ~ total of his efforts* quello è tutto quello che ha fatto

♦ **sum up** (*pret & pp* **-med**) **1** *v/t* (*summarize*) riassumere; (*assess*) valutare **2** *v/i* LAW riepilogare

sum·ma·rize ['sʌməraɪz] *v/t* riassumere

sum·ma·ry ['sʌmərɪ] *n* riassunto *m*

sum·mer ['sʌmə(r)] estate *f*

sum·mit ['sʌmɪt] *of mountain* vetta *f*; POL summit *m inv*

'sum·mit meet·ing → **summit**

sum·mon ['sʌmən] *v/t* convocare

♦ **summon up** *v/t strength* raccogliere

sum·mons ['sʌmənz] *nsg* LAW citazione *f*

sump [sʌmp] *for oil* coppa *f* dell'olio

sun [sʌn] sole *m*; *in the ~* al sole; *out of the ~* all'ombra; *he has had too much ~* ha preso troppo sole

'sun·bathe *v/i* prendere il sole; **'sun·bed** lettino *m* solare; **'sun·block** protezione *f* solare totale; **'sun·burn** scottatura *f*; **'sun·burnt** *adj* scottato

Sun·day ['sʌndeɪ] domenica *f*

'sun·dial meridiana *f*

sun·dries ['sʌndrɪz] *npl* varie *fpl*

sung [sʌŋ] *pp* → **sing**

'sun·glass·es *npl* occhiali *mpl* da sole

sunk [sʌŋk] *pp* → **sink**

sunk·en ['sʌŋkn] *adj cheeks* incavato

sun·ny ['sʌnɪ] *adj day* di sole; *spot* soleggiato; *disposition* allegro; *it's ~* c'è il sole

'sun·rise alba *f*; **'sun·set** tramonto *m*; **'sun·shade** ombrellone *m*; **'sun·shine** (luce *f* del) sole *m*; **'sun·stroke** colpo *m* di sole; **'sun·tan** abbronzatura *f*; *get a ~* abbronzarsi

su·per ['suːpə(r)] *adj* F fantastico

su·perb [suː'pɜːb] *adj* magnifico

su·per·fi·cial [suːpə'fɪʃl] *adj* superficiale

su·per·flu·ous [suː'pɜːfluəs] *adj* superfluo

su·per'hu·man *adj efforts* sovrumano

su·per·in·tend·ent [suːpərɪn'tendənt] *of police* commissario *m*

su·pe·ri·or [suː'pɪərɪə(r)] **1** *adj* (*better*) superiore **2** *n in organization, society* superiore *m*

su·per·la·tive [suː'pɜːlətɪv] **1** *adj* (*superb*) eccellente **2** *n* GRAM superlativo *m*

'su·per·mar·ket supermarket *m inv*, supermercato *m*

su·per·nat·u·ral 1 *adj powers* soprannaturale **2** *n*: *the ~* il soprannaturale

'su·per·pow·er POL superpotenza *f*

su·per·son·ic [suːpə'sɒnɪk] *adj flight, aircraft* supersonico

su·per·sti·tion [suːpə'stɪʃn] *n* superstizione *f*

su·per·sti·tious [suːpə'stɪʃəs] *adj person* superstizioso

su·per·vise ['suːpəvaɪz] *v/t* supervisionare

su·per·vi·sor ['suːpəvaɪzə(r)] *at work* supervisore *m*

sup·per ['sʌpə(r)] cena *f*

sup·ple ['sʌpl] *adj person, limbs* snodato; *material* flessibile

sup·ple·ment ['sʌplɪmənt] supplemento *m*

sup·pli·er [sə'plaɪə(r)] *n* COM fornitore *m*

sup·ply [sə'plaɪ] **1** *n* fornitura *f*; *~ and demand* domanda e offerta; *supplies* rifornimenti **2** *v/t* (*pret &*

pp **-ied**) *goods* fornire; **~ s.o. with sth** fornire qc a qu; **be supplied with** *fitted with etc* essere dotato di

sup·port [sə'pɔːt] **1** *n for structure* supporto *m*; (*backing*) sostegno *m* **2** *v/t building, structure* sostenere; *financially* mantenere; (*back*) sostenere; *football team* fare il tifo per

sup·port·er [sə'pɔːtə(r)] sostenitore *m*, -trice *f*; *of football team etc* tifoso *m*, -a *f*

sup·port·ive [sə'pɔːtɪv] *adj*: **be ~ towards s.o.** dare il proprio appoggio a qu

sup·pose [sə'pəʊz] *v/t* (*imagine*) supporre; **I ~ so** suppongo di sì; **it is ~d to** ... (*is meant to*) dovrebbe ...; (*is said to*) dicono che ...; **you are not ~d to** ... (*not allowed to*) non dovresti ...

sup·pos·ed·ly [sə'pəʊzɪdlɪ] *adv* presumibilmente

sup·pos·i·to·ry [sə'pɒzɪtrɪ] MED supposta *f*

sup·press [sə'pres] *v/t rebellion etc* reprimere

sup·pres·sion [sə'preʃn] repressione *f*

su·prem·a·cy [suː'preməsɪ] supremazia *f*

su·preme [suː'priːm] *adj* supremo

sur·charge ['sɜːtʃɑːdʒ] *for travel* sovrapprezzo *m*; *for mail* soprattassa *f*

sure [ʃʊə(r)] **1** *adj* sicuro; **I'm ~** sono sicuro; **be ~ about sth** essere sicuro di qc; **make ~ that** ... assicurarsi che ... **2** *adv* certamente; **~ enough** infatti; **~!** F certo!

sure·ly ['ʃʊəlɪ] *adv* certamente; (*gladly*) volentieri; **~ that's not right!** non può essere!; **oh, ~ you've heard of him** non puoi non conoscerlo

sur·e·ty ['ʃʊərətɪ] *for loan* cauzione *f*

surf [sɜːf] **1** *n on sea* spuma *f* **2** *v/t the Net* navigare

sur·face ['sɜːfɪs] **1** *n of table, object, water* superficie *f*; **on the ~** *fig* superficialmente, in apparenza **2** *v/i of swimmer, submarine* risalire in su-

perficie, riemergere; (*appear*) farsi vivo

'sur·face mail posta *f* ordinaria

'surf·board tavola *f* da surf

surf·er ['sɜːfə(r)] *on sea* surfista *m/f*

surf·ing ['sɜːfɪŋ] surf *m inv*; **go ~** fare surf

surge [sɜːdʒ] *n in electric current* sovratensione *f* transitoria; *in demand* impennata *f*; *of interest, financial growth etc* aumento *m*

♦ **surge forward** *v/i of crowd* buttarsi avanti

sur·geon ['sɜːdʒən] chirurgo *m*

sur·ge·ry ['sɜːdʒərɪ] intervento *m* chirurgico; *Br: place of work* ambulatorio *m*; **undergo ~** sottoporsi a un intervento chirurgico; **~ hours** orario *m* d'ambulatorio

sur·gi·cal ['sɜːdʒɪkl] *adj* chirurgico

sur·gi·cal·ly ['sɜːdʒɪklɪ] *adv* chirurgicamente

sur·ly ['sɜːlɪ] *adj* scontroso

sur·mount [sə'maʊnt] *v/t difficulties* sormontare

sur·name ['sɜːneɪm] cognome *m*

sur·pass [sə'pɑːs] *v/t* superare

sur·plus ['sɜːpləs] **1** *n* surplus *m inv* **2** *adj* eccedente

sur·prise [sə'praɪz] **1** *n* sorpresa *f*; **it'll come as no ~ to hear that** ... non ti sorprenderà sapere che ... **2** *v/t* sorprendere; **be ~d** essere sorpreso; **look ~d** avere l'aria sorpresa

sur·pris·ing [sə'praɪzɪŋ] *adj* sorprendente

sur·pris·ing·ly [sə'praɪzɪŋlɪ] *adv* sorprendentemente

sur·ren·der [sə'rendə(r)] **1** *v/i of army* arrendersi **2** *v/t weapons etc* consegnare **3** *n* resa *f*

sur·ro·gate 'moth·er ['sʌrəgət] madre *f* biologica

sur·round [sə'raʊnd] **1** *v/t* circondare; **be ~ed by** ... essere circondato da ... **2** *n of picture etc* bordo *m*

sur·round·ing [sə'raʊndɪŋ] *adj* circostante

sur·round·ings [sə'raʊndɪŋz] *npl of village etc* dintorni *mpl*; *fig* ambiente *m*

sur·vey ['sɜːveɪ] **1** *n of modern literature etc* quadro *m* generale; *of building* perizia *f*; *poll* indagine *f* **2** *v/t* [sə'veɪ] (*look at*) osservare; *building* periziare

sur·vey·or [sə'veɪə(r)] perito *m*

sur·viv·al [sə'vaɪvl] sopravvivenza *f*

sur·vive [sə'vaɪv] **1** *v/i* sopravvivere; *how are you? – I'm surviving* come stai? – si tira avanti; *his two surviving daughters* le due figlie ancora in vita **2** *v/t* sopravvivere a

sur·vi·vor [sə'vaɪvə(r)] superstite *m/f*; *he's a ~ fig* se la cava sempre

sus·cep·ti·ble [sə'septəbl] *adj emotionally* impressionabile; *be ~ to the cold / heat* soffrire il freddo / caldo

sus·pect ['sʌspekt] **1** *n* indiziato *m*, -a *f* **2** *v/t* [sə'spekt] *person* sospettare; (*suppose*) supporre

sus·pect·ed [sə'spektɪd] *adj murderer* presunto; *cause, heart attack etc* sospetto

sus·pend [sə'spend] *v/t* (*hang*) sospendere; *from office, duties* sospendere

sus·pend·ers [sə'spendəz] *npl* giarrettiere *fpl*; *Am* (*braces*) bretelle *fpl*

sus·pense [sə'spens] suspense *f inv*

sus·pen·sion [sə'spenʃn] sospensione *f*

sus'pen·sion bridge ponte *m* sospeso

sus·pi·cion [sə'spɪʃn] sospetto *m*

sus·pi·cious [sə'spɪʃəs] *adj causing suspicion* sospetto; *feeling suspicion* sospettoso; *be ~ of* sospettare di

sus·tain [sə'steɪn] *v/t* sostenere

sus·tain·a·ble [sə'steɪnəbl] *adj* sostenibile

swab [swɒb] tampone *m*

swag·ger ['swægə(r)] *n* andatura *f* spavalda

swal·low¹ ['swɒləʊ] **1** *v/t liquid, food* inghiottire **2** *v/i* inghiottire

swal·low² ['swɒləʊ] *n bird* rondine *f*

swam [swæm] *pret* → **swim**

swamp [swɒmp] **1** *n* palude *f* **2** *v/t*: *be ~ped with* essere sommerso da

swamp·y ['swɒmpɪ] *adj ground* paludoso

swan [swɒn] cigno *m*

swap [swɒp] (*pret & pp -ped*) **1** *v/t*: *~ sth for sth* scambiare qc con qc **2** *v/i* fare scambio

swarm [swɔːm] **1** *n of bees* sciame *m* **2** *v/i*: *the town was ~ing with ...* la città brulicava di ...

swar·thy ['swɔːðɪ] *adj face, complexion* scuro

swat [swɒt] *v/t* (*pret & pp -ted*) *insect, fly* schiacciare

sway [sweɪ] **1** *n* (*influence, power*) influenza *f* **2** *v/i* barcollare

swear [sweə(r)] (*pret swore, pp sworn*) **1** *v/i* (*use swearword*) imprecare; *~ at s.o.* dire parolacce a qu **2** *v/t* (*promise*) giurare; LAW, *on oath* giurare

♦ **swear in** *v/t*: *the witness was sworn in* il testimone ha prestato giuramento

'swear·word parolaccia *f*

sweat [swet] **1** *n* sudore *m*; *covered in ~* tutto sudato **2** *v/i* sudare

'sweat band fascia *f* asciugasudore

sweat·er ['swetə(r)] maglione *m*

'sweat·shirt felpa *f*

sweat·y ['swetɪ] *adj hands* sudato; *smell* di sudore

Swede [swiːd] svedese *m/f*

Swe·den ['swiːdn] Svezia *f*

Swe·dish ['swiːdɪʃ] **1** *adj* svedese **2** *n* svedese *m*

sweep [swiːp] **1** *v/t* (*pret & pp swept*) *floor, leaves* spazzare **2** *n* (*long curve*) curva *f*

♦ **sweep up** *v/t mess* spazzare via

sweep·ing ['swiːpɪŋ] *adj changes* radicale; *a ~ statement* una generalizzazione

sweet [swiːt] **1** *adj taste, tea* dolce; F (*kind*) gentile; F (*cute*) carino **2** *n* caramella *f*; (*dessert*) dolce *m*

sweet and 'sour *adj* agrodolce

'sweet·corn mais *m inv*

sweet·en ['swiːtn] *v/t drink, food* zuccherare

sweet·en·er ['swiːtnə(r)] *for drink* dolcificante *m*

'**sweet·heart** innamorato *m*, -a *f*

swell [swel] **1** *v/i* of wound, limb gonfiarsi **2** *n* of the sea mare *m* lungo

swell·ing ['swelɪŋ] *n* MED gonfiore *m*

swel·ter·ing ['sweltərɪŋ] *adj* heat, day afoso, soffocante

swept [swept] *pret & pp* → **sweep**

swerve [swɜːv] *v/i* of driver, car sterzare (bruscamente)

swift [swɪft] *adj* rapido

swim [swɪm] **1** *v/i* (*pret* **swam**, *pp* **swum**) nuotare; *go ~ming* andare a nuotare; *my head is ~ming* mi gira la testa **2** *n* nuotata *f*; *go for a ~* andare a nuotare

swim·mer ['swɪmə(r)] nuotatore *m*, -trice *f*

swim·ming ['swɪmɪŋ] nuoto *m*

'**swim·ming baths** *npl* piscina *f* pubblica; '**swim·ming cos·tume** costume *m* da bagno; '**swim·ming pool** piscina *f*

swin·dle ['swɪndl] **1** *n* truffa *f* **2** *v/t* truffare; *~ s.o. out of sth* estorcere qc a qu (con l'inganno)

swine [swaɪn] F person mascalzone *m*

swing [swɪŋ] **1** *n* of pendulum etc oscillazione *f*; for child altalena *f*; *a ~ to the left* una svolta verso la sinistra **2** *v/t* (*pret & pp* **swung**) far dondolare; *~ one's hips* ancheggiare **3** *v/i* (*pret & pp* **swung**) dondolare; (*turn*) girare; of public opinion etc indirizzarsi

swing-'door porta *f* a vento

Swiss [swɪs] **1** *adj* svizzero **2** *n* person svizzero *m*, -a *f*; *the ~* gli svizzeri

switch [swɪtʃ] **1** *n* for light interruttore *m*; (*change*) cambiamento *m* **2** *v/t* (*change*) cambiare **3** *v/i* (*change*) cambiare; *~ to* passare a

♦ **switch off** *v/t* spegnere

♦ **switch on** *v/t* accendere

'**switch·board** centralino *m*

'**switch·o·ver** to new system passaggio *m*

Swit·zer·land ['swɪtsələnd] Svizzera *f*

swiv·el ['swɪvl] *v/i* (*pret & pp* **-led**,

Am **-ed**) of chair, monitor girarsi

swol·len ['swəʊlən] *adj* gonfio

swoop [swuːp] *v/i* of bird scendere in picchiata

♦ **swoop down on** *v/t* prey scendere in picchiata su

♦ **swoop on** *v/t* of police etc piombare su

sword [sɔːd] spada *f*

swore [swɔː(r)] *pret* → **swear**

sworn [swɔːn] *pp* → **swear**

swum [swʌm] *pp* → **swim**

swung [swʌŋ] *pret & pp* → **swing**

syc·a·more ['sɪkəmɔː] sicomoro *m*

syl·la·ble ['sɪləbl] sillaba *f*

syl·la·bus ['sɪləbəs] programma *m*

sym·bol ['sɪmbəl] simbolo *m*

sym·bol·ic [sɪmˈbɒlɪk] *adj* simbolico

sym·bol·ism ['sɪmbəlɪzm] simbolismo *m*

sym·bol·ist ['sɪmbəlɪst] simbolista *m/f*

sym·bol·ize ['sɪmbəlaɪz] *v/t* simboleggiare

sym·met·ri·c(al) [sɪˈmetrɪkl] *adj* simmetrico

sym·me·try ['sɪmətrɪ] simmetria *f*

sym·pa·thet·ic [sɪmpəˈθetɪk] *adj* (*showing pity*) compassionevole; (*understanding*) comprensivo; *be ~ towards an idea* simpatizzare per un'idea

♦ **sympathize with** ['sɪmpəθaɪz] *v/t* person, views capire

sym·pa·thiz·er ['sɪmpəθaɪzə(r)] *n* POL simpatizzante *m/f*

sym·pa·thy ['sɪmpəθɪ] *n* (*pity*) compassione *f*; (*understanding*) comprensione *f*; *don't expect any ~ from me!* non venire a lamentarti da me!

sym·pho·ny ['sɪmfənɪ] sinfonia *f*

'**sym·pho·ny or·ches·tra** orchestra *f* sinfonica

symp·tom ['sɪmptəm] also fig sintomo *m*

symp·to·mat·ic [sɪmptəˈmætɪk] *adj*: *be ~ of* fig essere sintomatico di

syn·chro·nize ['sɪŋkrənaɪz] *v/t* sincronizzare

syn·o·nym ['sɪnənɪm] sinonimo *m*

S

sy·non·y·mous [sɪˈnɒnɪməs] *adj* sinonimo; *be ~ with fig* essere sinonimo di

syn·tax [ˈsɪntæks] sintassi *f inv*

syn·the·siz·er [ˈsɪnθəsaɪzə(r)] MUS sintetizzatore *m*

syn·thet·ic [sɪnˈθetɪk] *adj* sintetico

syph·i·lis [ˈsɪfɪlɪs] sifilide *f*

Syr·i·a [ˈsɪrɪə] Siria *f*

Syr·i·an [ˈsɪrɪən] **1** *adj* siriano **2** *n* siriano *m*, -a *f*

sy·ringe [sɪˈrɪndʒ] *n* siringa *f*

syr·up [ˈsɪrəp] sciroppo *m*

sys·tem [ˈsɪstəm] (*method*) metodo *m*, sistema *m*; (*orderliness*) ordine *m*; (*computer*) sistema *m*; *the braking ~* il sistema di frenata; *the digestive ~* l'apparato digerente

sys·te·mat·ic [sɪstəˈmætɪk] *adj* approach, person sistematico

sys·tem·at·i·cal·ly [sɪstəˈmætɪklɪ] *adv* sistematicamente

sys·tems **'an·a·lyst** [ˈsɪstəmz] COMPUT analista *m/f* di sistemi

T

tab [tæb] *n for pulling* linguetta *f*; *in text* tabulazione *f*

ta·ble [ˈteɪbl] *n* tavolo *m*; *of figures* tabella *f*, tavola *f*; *sit at the ~* sedersi a tavola

'ta·ble·cloth tovaglia *f*; **'ta·ble lamp** lampada *f* da tavolo; **ta·ble of 'con·tents** indice *m*; **'ta·ble·spoon** cucchiaio *m* da tavola

ta·blet [ˈtæblɪt] MED compressa *f*

'ta·ble ten·nis ping pong *m*

tab·loid [ˈtæblɔɪd] *n newspaper* quotidiano *m* formato tabloid; *pej* quotidiano *m* scandalistico

ta·boo [təˈbuː] *adj* tabù *m inv*

ta·cit [ˈtæsɪt] *adj* tacito

ta·ci·turn [ˈtæsɪtɜːn] *adj* taciturno

tack [tæk] **1** *n* (*nail*) chiodino *m* **2** *v/t* (*sew*) imbastire **3** *v/i of yacht* virare di bordo

tack·le [ˈtækl] **1** *n* (*equipment*) attrezzatura *f*; SP: *in rugby* placcaggio *m*; *in football, hockey* contrasto *m* **2** *v/t in rugby* placcare; *in football, hockey* contrastare; *problem, intruder* affrontare

tack·y [ˈtækɪ] *adj paint* fresco; *glue* appiccicoso; F (*cheap, poor quality*) di cattivo gusto

tact [tækt] tatto *m*

tact·ful [ˈtæktfʊl] *adj* pieno di tatto

tact·ful·ly [ˈtæktflɪ] *adv* con grande tatto

tac·ti·cal [ˈtæktɪkl] *adj* tattico

tac·tics [ˈtæktɪks] *npl* tattica *f*

tact·less [ˈtæktlɪs] *adj* privo di tatto

tad·pole [ˈtædpəʊl] girino *m*

tag [tæg] (*label*) etichetta *f*

♦**tag along** *v/i* (*pret & pp -ged*) accodarsi

tail [teɪl] *n* coda *f*

'tail·back coda *f*; **'tail coat** frac *m inv*; **'tail light** luce *f* posteriore

tai·lor [ˈteɪlə(r)] sarto *m*, -a *f*

tai·lor-made [teɪləˈmeɪd] *adj suit, solution* (*fatto*) su misura

'tail·wind vento *m* in coda

taint·ed [ˈteɪntɪd] *adj* contaminato

Tai·wan [taɪˈwɑːn] Taiwan *f*

Tai·wan·ese [taɪwəˈniːz] **1** *adj* taiwanese **2** *n* taiwanese *m/f*; *dialect* taiwanese *m*

take [teɪk] *v/t* (*pret* **took**, *pp* **taken**) prendere; (*transport*) portare; (*accompany*) accompagnare; (*accept: money, gift*) accettare; *maths, French, photograph, exam, shower, stroll* fare; (*endure*) sopportare; (*require*) richiedere; *how long does it ~?*

quanto ci vuole?; *I'll ~ it when shopping* lo prendo

♦ **take after** v/t aver preso da

♦ **take apart** v/t (*dismantle*) smontare; F (*criticize, beat*) fare a pezzi F

♦ **take away** v/t (*pain*) far sparire; (*remove: object*) togliere; MATH sottrarre; *take sth away from s.o.* togliere qc a qu; *to take away food* da asporto

♦ **take back** v/t (*return: object*) riportare; (*receive back*) riprendere; *person* riaccompagnare; (*accept back: husband etc*) rimettersi insieme a; *I take back what I said* ritiro quello che ho detto; *that takes me back of music, thought etc* mi riporta al passato

♦ **take down** v/t *from shelf* tirare giù; *scaffolding* smontare; *trousers* allungare; (*write down*) annotare

♦ **take in** v/t (*take indoors*) portare dentro; (*give accommodation*) ospitare; (*make narrower*) stringere; (*deceive*) imbrogliare; (*include*) includere

♦ **take off 1** v/t *clothes, 10%* togliere; (*mimic*) imitare; *can you take a bit off here?* to barber può spuntare un po' qui?; *take a day / week off* prendere un giorno / una settimana di ferie **2** v/i *of aeroplane* decollare; (*become popular*) far presa

♦ **take on** v/t *job* intraprendere; *staff* assumere

♦ **take out** v/t *from bag, pocket* tirare fuori; *stain, appendix, tooth, word* togliere; *money from bank* prelevare; *to dinner etc* portar fuori; *insurance policy* stipulare, fare; *take it out on s.o.* prendersela con qu

♦ **take over 1** v/t *company etc* assumere il controllo di; *tourists take over the town* i turisti invadono la città **2** v/i *of new management etc* assumere il controllo; (*do sth in s.o.'s place*) dare il cambio

♦ **take to** v/t (*like*) prendere in simpatia; (*form habit of*) prendere l'abitudine di; *take to drink* darsi all'alcol; *he immediately took to*

the idea la nuova idea gli è piaciuto subito

♦ **take up** v/t *carpet etc* togliere; (*carry up*) portare sopra; (*shorten*) accorciare; *judo, Spanish, new job* incominciare; *offer* accettare; *space, time* occupare; *I'll take you up on your offer* accetto la tua offerta

'**take-away** *meal* piatto *m* da asporto; (*restaurant*) ristorante *m* che prepara piatti da asporto

'**take-home pay** stipendio *m* in busta

tak-en ['teɪkən] pp → **take**

'**take-off** decollo *m*; (*impersonation*) imitazione *f*; '**take-o-ver** COM rilevamento *m*; '**take-o-ver bid** offerta *f* pubblica di acquisto, OPA *f*

ta-kings ['teɪkɪnz] npl incassi mpl

tal-cum pow-der ['tælkəmpaudə(r)] talco *m*

tale [teɪl] storia *f*

tal-ent ['tælənt] talento *m*

tal-ent-ed ['tæləntɪd] adj pieno di talento; *he's not very ~* non ha molto talento

'**tal-ent scout** talent scout *m/f inv*

talk [tɔːk] **1** v/i parlare; *can I talk to ...?* posso parlare con ...?; *I'll ~ to him about it* gliene parlo **2** v/t *English etc* parlare; *business, politics* parlare di; *~ s.o. into doing sth* convincere qu a fare qc; *~ s.o. out of doing sth* dissuadere qu dal fare qc **3** n (*conversation*) conversazione *f*; (*lecture*) conferenza *f*; *~s* (*negotiations*) trattative fpl, negoziati mpl; *he's all ~* pej è tutto chiacchiere

♦ **talk back** v/i ribattere

♦ **talk down to** v/t trattare dall'alto in basso

♦ **talk over** v/t discutere di

talk-a-tive ['tɔːkətɪv] adj loquace

talk-ing-to ['tɔːkɪŋtuː] sgridata *f*

'**talk show** talk show *m inv*

tall [tɔːl] adj alto

tall 'or-der bella impresa *f*

tall 'sto-ry baggianata *f*

tal-ly ['tælɪ] **1** n conto *m* **2** v/i (pret & pp **-ied**) quadrare

♦ **tally with** v/t quadrare con

tame [teɪm] *adj animal* addomestica-
to; *joke etc* blando

♦ **tamper with** ['tæmpə(r)] *v/t* manomettere

tam·pon ['tæmpɒn] tampone *m*

tan [tæn] **1** *n from sun* abbronzatura
f; *colour* marrone *m* rossiccio **2** *v/i*
(*pret & pp* **-ned**) *in sun* abbronzarsi
3 *v/t* (*pret & pp* **-ned**) *leather* conciare

tan·dem ['tændəm] *bike* tandem *m
inv*

tan·gent ['tændʒənt] MATH tangente
f

tan·ge·rine [tændʒə'riːn] tangerino
m

tan·gi·ble ['tændʒɪbl] *adj* tangibile

tan·gle ['tæŋgl] *n* nodo *m*

♦ **tangle up**: *get tangled up of string
etc* aggrovigliarsi

tan·go ['tæŋgəʊ] *n* tango *m*

tank [tæŋk] recipiente *m*; MOT serbatoio *m*; MIL carro *m* armato; *for skin
diver* bombola *f* (d'ossigeno)

tank·er ['tæŋkə(r)] *ship* nave *f* cisterna; *truck* autocisterna *f*

tanned [tænd] *adj* abbronzato

Tan·noy® ['tænɔɪ] altoparlante *m*

tan·ta·liz·ing ['tæntəlaɪzɪŋ] *adj* allettante; *smell* stuzzicante

tan·ta·mount ['tæntəmaʊnt] *adj*: *be
~ to* essere equivalente a

tan·trum ['tæntrəm] capricci *mpl*;
throw a ~ fare (i) capricci

tap [tæp] **1** *n* rubinetto *m* **2** *v/t* (*pret
& pp* **-ped**) (*hit*) dare un colpetto a;
phone mettere sotto controllo; *he
was ~ping his fingers on the table*
tamburellava con le dita sul tavolo

♦ **tap into** *v/t resources* attingere a

tap dance *n* tip tap *m*

tape [teɪp] **1** *n magnetic* nastro *m* magnetico; *recorded* cassetta *f*; (*sticky*)
nastro *m* adesivo; *on ~* registrato
2 *v/t conversation etc* registrare; *~
sth to sth* attaccare qc a qc col nastro adesivo

tape deck registratore *m*; **tape
drive** COMPUT unità *f inv* di backup
a nastro; **tape meas·ure** metro *m* a
nastro

tap·er ['teɪpə(r)] *v/i* assottigliarsi

♦ **taper off** *v/i of production* calare
gradualmente; *of figures* decrescere

tape re·cord·er registratore *m* a
cassette

tape re·cord·ing registrazione *f* su
cassetta

ta·pes·try ['tæpɪstrɪ] arazzo *m*

tape·worm ['teɪpwɜːm] verme *m* solitario

tar [tɑː(r)] *n* catrame *m*

tar·get ['tɑːgɪt] **1** *n in shooting* bersaglio *m*; *for sales, production* obiettivo
m **2** *v/t market* rivolgersi a

tar·get 'au·di·ence target *m inv* di
pubblico; **tar·get date** data *f* fissa-
ta; **tar·get 'fig·ure** target *m inv*;
tar·get group COM gruppo *m*
target; **tar·get language** lingua *f*
d'arrivo; **tar·get mar·ket** mercato
m target

tar·iff ['tærɪf] (*price*) tariffa *f*; (*tax*)
tassa *f*

tar·mac ['tɑːmæk] *at airport* pista *f*

tar·nish ['tɑːnɪʃ] *v/t metal* ossidare;
reputation macchiare

tar·pau·lin [tɑː'pɔːlɪn] tela *f* cerata

tart¹ [tɑːt] *n* torta *f*

tart² [tɑːt] *n* F (*prostitute*) sgualdrina
f; *pej: woman* stronza *f*

tar·tan ['tɑːtn] tartan *m*

task [tɑːsk] compito *m*

task force task force *f inv*

tas·sel ['tæsl] nappa *f*

taste [teɪst] **1** *n* gusto *m*; *he has no ~*
non ha nessun gusto **2** *v/t food* assaggiare; (*experience: freedom etc*)
provare; *I can't ~ anything* non
sento nessun sapore **3** *v/i*: *it ~s
like ...* ha sapore di ...; *it ~s very
nice* è molto buono

taste buds *npl* papille *fpl* gustative

taste·ful ['teɪstfʊl] *adj* di gusto

taste·ful·ly ['teɪstfəlɪ] *adv* con gusto

taste·less ['teɪstlɪs] *adj food* insapore; *remark, person* privo di gusto

tast·ing ['teɪstɪŋ] *of wine* degustazione *f*

tast·y ['teɪstɪ] *adj* gustoso

tat·tered ['tætəd] *adj clothes, book*
malridotto

tat·ters ['tætəz]: *in ~ of clothes* a brandelli; *of reputation, career* a pezzi

tat·too [tə'tuː] *n* tatuaggio *m*

tat·ty ['tætɪ] *adj* F malandato

taught [tɔːt] *pret & pp* → **teach**

taunt [tɔːnt] **1** *n* scherno *m* **2** *v/t* schernire

Tau·rus ['tɔːrəs] ASTR Toro *m*

taut [tɔːt] *adj* teso

taw·dry ['tɔːdrɪ] *adj* pacchiano

tax [tæks] **1** *n* tassa *f*; *before / after ~* al lordo/al netto di imposte **2** *v/t* tassare

tax·a·ble 'in·come reddito *m* imponibile

tax·a·tion [tæk'seɪʃn] tassazione *f*

'tax avoid·ance elusione *f* fiscale; **'tax brack·et** fascia *f* di reddito; **'tax code** codice *m* fiscale; **'tax-de·duct·i·ble** *adj* deducibile dalle imposte; **'tax disc** *for car* bollo *m* (di circolazione); **'tax eva·sion** evasione *f* fiscale; **'tax-free** *adj* esentasse *inv*

tax·i ['tæksɪ] taxi *m inv*

'tax·i dri·ver tassista *m/f*

tax·ing ['tæksɪŋ] *adj* estenuante

'tax in·spect·or ispettore *m*, -trice *f* fiscale

'tax·i rank, tax·i stand stazione *f* dei taxi

'tax·man fisco *m*; **'tax ·pay·er** contribuente *m/f*; **'tax re·turn** *form* dichiarazione *f* dei redditi; **'tax year** anno *m* fiscale

TB [tiː'biː] *abbr* (= *tuberculosis*) tbc *f* (= tubercolosi *f*)

tea [tiː] *drink* tè *m inv*; *meal* cena *f*

tea·bag ['tiːbæg] bustina *f* di tè

teach [tiːtʃ] (*pret & pp* **taught**) **1** *v/t subject* insegnare; *person* insegnare a; *~ s.o. to do sth* insegnare a qu a fare qc **2** *v/i* insegnare

tea·cher ['tiːtʃə(r)] insegnante *m/f*

tea·cher 'train·ing tirocinio *m* per insegnanti

tea·ching ['tiːtʃɪŋ] *profession* insegnamento *m*

'tea·ching aid sussidio *m* didattico

'tea cloth strofinaccio *m* da cucina;

'tea·cup tazza *f* da tè; **'tea drink·er** bevitore *m*, -trice *f* di tè

teak [tiːk] tek *m*

'tea leaf foglia *f* di tè

team [tiːm] *in sport* squadra *f*; *at work* équipe *f inv*

'team mate compagno *m*, -a *f* di squadra; **team 'spirit** spirito *m* d'équipe; **'team·work** lavoro *m* d'équipe

tea·pot ['tiːpɒt] teiera *f*

tear¹ [teə(r)] **1** *n in cloth etc* strappo *m* **2** *v/t* (*pret* **tore**, *pp* **torn**) *paper, cloth* strappare; *be torn between two alternatives* essere combattuto tra due alternative **3** *v/i* (*pret* **tore**, *pp* **torn**) (*run fast, drive fast*) sfrecciare

♦ **tear down** *v/t poster* strappare; *building* buttar giù

♦ **tear out** *v/t* strappare

♦ **tear up** *v/t paper* distruggere; *agreement* rompere

tear² [tɪə(r)] *n in eye* lacrima *f*; *burst into ~s* scoppiare a piangere; *be in ~s* essere in lacrime

tear·drop ['tɪədrɒp] lacrima *f*

tear·ful ['tɪəful] *adj person* in lacrime; *look, voice* piangente

'tear gas gas *m inv* lacrimogeno

tea·room sala *f* da tè

tease [tiːz] *v/t person* prendere in giro; *animal* stuzzicare

'tea serv·ice, 'tea set servizio *m* da tè; **'tea·spoon** cucchiaino *m* da caffè; **'tea strain·er** colino *m* da tè

teat [tiːt] capezzolo *m*; *made of rubber* tettarella *f*

'tea to·wel strofinaccio *m* da cucina

tech·ni·cal ['teknɪkl] *adj* tecnico

tech·ni·cal·i·ty [teknɪ'kælətɪ] (*technical nature*) tecnicismo *m*; LAW vizio *m* di procedura; *that's just a ~* è solo un dettaglio

tech·ni·cal·ly ['teknɪklɪ] *adv* tecnicamente

tech·ni·cian [tek'nɪʃn] tecnico *m*

tech·nique [tek'niːk] tecnica *f*

tech·no·log·i·cal [teknə'lɒdʒɪkl] *adj* tecnologico

tech·no·lo·gy [tek'nɒlədʒɪ] tecnologia *f*

tech·no·phob·i·a [teknə'fəʊbɪə] tecnofobia *f*

ted·dy bear ['tedɪbeə(r)] orsacchiotto *m*

te·di·ous ['tiːdɪəs] *adj* noioso

tee [tiː] *n in golf* tee *m inv*

teem [tiːm] *v/i* pullulare; *be ~ing with rain* piovere a dirotto; *be ~ing with tourists/ants* pullulare di turisti/formiche

teen·age ['tiːneɪdʒ] *adj problems* degli adolescenti; *gangs* di ragazzi; *~ boy/girl* ragazzo *m*/ragazza *f* adolescente; *~ fashions* moda giovane

teen·ag·er ['tiːneɪdʒə(r)] adolescente *m/f*

teens [tiːnz] *npl* adolescenza *f*; *be in one's ~* essere adolescente; *reach one's ~* entrare nell'adolescenza

tee·ny ['tiːnɪ] *adj* F piccolissimo

teeth [tiːθ] *pl* → **tooth**

teethe [tiːð] *v/i* mettere i denti

teething problems *npl* difficoltà *fpl* iniziali

tee·to·tal [tiː'təʊtl] *adj person* astemio; *party* senza alcolici

tee·to·tal·ler [tiː'təʊtlə(r)] astemio *m*, -a *f*

tel·e·com·mu·ni·ca·tions [telɪkəmjuːnɪ'keɪʃnz] telecomunicazioni *fpl*

tel·e·gram ['telɪgræm] telegramma *m*

tel·e·graph pole ['telɪgrɑːfpəʊl] palo *m* del telegrafo

tel·e·path·ic [telɪ'pæθɪk] *adj* telepatico; *you must be ~!* devi avere poteri telepatici!

te·lep·a·thy [tɪ'lepəθɪ] telepatia *f*

tel·e·phone ['telɪfəʊn] **1** *n* telefono *m*; *be on the ~* *be speaking* essere al telefono; *possess a phone* avere il telefono **2** *v/t person* telefonare a **3** *v/i* telefonare

'tel·e·phone bill bolletta *f* del telefono; **'tel·e·phone book** guida *f* telefonica; **'tel·e·phone booth** cabina *f* telefonica; **'tel·e·phone box** cabina *f* telefonica; **'tel·e·phone call** telefonata *f*; **'tel·e·phone con·ver-**

sa·tion conversazione *f* telefonica; **'tel·e·phone di·rec·to·ry** elenco *m* telefonico; **'tel·e·phone ex·change** centralino *m* telefonico; **'tel·e·phone mes·sage** messaggio *m* telefonico; **'tel·e·phone num·ber** numero *m* telefonico

tel·e·pho·to lens [telɪfəʊtəʊ'lenz] teleobiettivo *m*

tel·e·sales ['telɪseɪlz] vendita *f* telefonica

tel·e·scope ['telɪskəʊp] telescopio *m*

tel·e·scop·ic lens [telɪskɒpɪk'lenz] lente *f* telescopica

tel·e·thon ['telɪθɒn] telethon *m inv*

tel·e·vise ['telɪvaɪz] *v/t* trasmettere in televisione

tel·e·vi·sion ['telɪvɪʒn] televisione *f*; *set* televisione *f*, televisore *m*; *on ~* alla televisione; *watch ~* guardare la televisione

'tel·e·vi·sion au·di·ence pubblico *m* televisivo; **'tel·e·vi·sion li·cence** canone *m* (televisivo); **'tel·e·vi·sion pro·gramme** programma *m* televisivo; **'tel·e·vi·sion set** televisore *m*; **'tel·e·vi·sion stu·di·o** studio *m* televisivo

tell [tel] (*pret & pp told*) **1** *v/t* dire; *story* raccontare; *~ s.o. sth* dire qc a qu; *don't ~ Mum* non dirlo alla mamma; *~ s.o. to do sth* dire a qu di fare qc; *I've been told that ...* mi hanno detto che ...; *it's hard to ~* è difficile a dirsi; *you never can ~* non si può mai dire; *~ X from Y* distinguere X da Y; *I can't ~ the difference between ...* non vedo nessuna differenza tra ...; *you're ~ing me!* F a chi lo dici! F **2** *v/i (have effect)* farsi sentire; *the heat is ~ing on him* il caldo si fa sentire su di lui; *time will ~* il tempo lo dirà

◆ **tell off** *v/t* rimproverare

tell·er ['telə(r)] *in bank* cassiere *m*, -a *f*

tell·ing ['telɪŋ] *adj argument* efficace; *a ~ sign* un segnale chiaro

tell·ing 'off rimprovero *m*; *give s.o. a ~* rimproverare qu

tell·tale ['telteɪl] **1** *adj* signs rivelatore **2** *n* spione *m*, spiona *f*

tel·ly ['telɪ] F tele *f*

temp [temp] **1** *n* employee impiegato *m*, -a interinale **2** *v/i* fare lavori interinali

tem·per ['tempə(r)] (*bad ~*): **have a terrible ~** essere irascibile; **be in a ~** essere arrabbiato; **keep one's ~** mantenere la calma; **lose one's ~** perdere le staffe

tem·pe·ra·ment ['tempərəmənt] temperamento *m*

tem·pe·ra·men·tal [temprə'mentl] *adj* (*moody*) lunatico; *machine* imprevedibile

tem·pe·rate ['tempərət] *adj* temperato

tem·pe·ra·ture ['temprətʃə(r)] temperatura *f*; (*fever*) febbre *f*; **have a ~** avere la febbre; **take s.o.'s ~** prendere la temperatura a qu

tem·ple¹ ['templ] REL tempio *m*

tem·ple² ['templ] ANAT tempia *f*

tem·po ['tempəu] ritmo *m*; MUS tempo *m*

tem·po·rar·i·ly [tempə'reərɪlɪ] *adv* temporaneamente

tem·po·ra·ry ['tempərərɪ] *adj* temporaneo, provvisorio

tempt [tempt] *v/t* tentare

temp·ta·tion [temp'teɪʃn] tentazione *f*

tempt·ing ['temptɪŋ] *adj* allettante; *meal* appetitoso

ten [ten] dieci

te·na·cious [tɪ'neɪʃəs] *adj* tenace

te·nac·i·ty [tɪ'næsɪtɪ] tenacità *f*

ten·ant ['tenənt] inquilino *m*, -a *f*, locatario *m*, -a *f fml*; *in office* affittuario *m*, -a *f*

tend¹ [tend] *v/t* (*look after*) prendersi cura di

tend² [tend] *v/i*: **~ to do sth** tendere a fare qc, avere la tendenza a fare qc; **~ towards sth** avere una tendenza verso qc

ten·den·cy ['tendənsɪ] tendenza *f*

ten·der¹ ['tendə(r)] *adj* (*sore*) sensibile; (*affectionate*) tenero; *steak* tenero

ten·der² ['tendə(r)] *n* COM offerta *f* ufficiale

ten·der·ness ['tendənɪs] (*soreness*) sensibilità *f*; *of kiss, steak* tenerezza *f*

ten·don ['tendən] tendine *m*

ten·nis ['tenɪs] tennis *m*

'ten·nis ball palla *f* da tennis; **'tennis court** campo *m* da tennis; **'tennis pla·yer** tennista *m/f*; **'ten·nis rack·et** racchetta *f* da tennis

ten·or ['tenə(r)] MUS tenore *m*

tense¹ [tens] *n* GRAM tempo *m*

tense² [tens] *adj* voice, person teso; moment, atmosphere carico di tensione

♦ **tense up** *v/i of muscles* contrarre; *of person* irrigidirsi

ten·sion ['tenʃn] tensione *f*

tent [tent] tenda *f*

ten·ta·cle ['tentəkl] tentacolo *m*

ten·ta·tive ['tentətɪv] *adj* esitante

ten·ter·hooks ['tentəhuks]: **be on ~** essere sulle spine

tenth [tenθ] *n & adj* decimo, -a

tep·id ['tepɪd] *adj* water, reaction tiepido

term [tɜːm] periodo *m*; of office durata *f* in carica; EDU: of three months trimestre *m*; of two months bimestre *m*; (condition, period) termine *m*; **be on good / bad ~s with s.o.** essere in buoni / cattivi rapporti con qu; **in the long / short ~** a lungo / breve termine; **come to ~s with sth** venire a patti con qc

ter·mi·nal ['tɜːmɪnl] **1** *n at airport, for containers*, COMPUT terminale *m*; *for buses* capolinea *m inv*; ELEC morsetto *m* **2** *adj illness* in fase terminale

ter·mi·nal·ly ['tɜːmɪnəlɪ] *adv*: **~ ill** malato (in fase) terminale

ter·mi·nate ['tɜːmɪneɪt] **1** *v/t contract, pregnancy* interrompere **2** *v/i* terminare

ter·mi·na·tion [tɜːmɪ'neɪʃn] of contract, pregnancy interruzione *f*

ter·mi·nol·o·gy [tɜːmɪ'nɒlədʒɪ] terminologia *f*

ter·mi·nus ['tɜːmɪnəs] for buses capolinea *m inv*; *for trains* stazione *f* di testa

ter·race ['terəs] *of houses* fila *f* di case a schiera; *on hillside, at hotel* terrazza *f*

ter·raced house [terəst'haʊs] casa *f* a schiera

ter·ra cot·ta [terə'kɒtə] *adj* di terracotta

ter·rain [tə'reɪn] terreno *m*

ter·res·tri·al [tə'restrɪəl] **1** *n* terrestre *m/f* **2** *adj television* di terra

ter·ri·ble ['terəbl] *adj* terribile

ter·ri·bly ['terəblɪ] *adv play* malissimo; *(very)* molto

ter·rif·ic [tə'rɪfɪk] *adj* eccezionale; *~!* bene!

ter·rif·i·cal·ly [tə'rɪfɪklɪ] *adv (very)* eccezionalmente

ter·ri·fy ['terɪfaɪ] *v/t* (*pret & pp* **-ied**) terrificare; *be terrified* essere terrificato

ter·ri·fy·ing ['terɪfaɪɪŋ] *adj* terrificante

ter·ri·to·ri·al [terɪ'tɔːrɪəl] *adj* territoriale

ter·ri·to·ri·al 'wa·ters *npl* acque *fpl* territoriali

ter·ri·to·ry ['terɪtərɪ] *also fig* territorio *m*

ter·ror ['terə(r)] terrore *m*

ter·ror·is·m ['terərɪzm] terrorismo *m*

ter·ror·ist ['terərɪst] terrorista *m/f*

'ter·ror·ist at·tack attentato *m* terroristico

'ter·ror·ist or·gan·i·za·tion organizzazione *f* terroristica

ter·ror·ize ['terəraɪz] *v/t* terrorizzare

terse [tɜːs] *adj* brusco

test [test] **1** *n* prova *f*, test *m inv*; *for driving, medical* esame *m*; *blood ~* analisi *f inv* del sangue **2** *v/t soup, bathwater* provare; *machine, theory* testare; *person, friendship* mettere alla prova; *~ the water fig* tastare il terreno

tes·ta·ment ['testəmənt] testimonianza *f* (**to** di); *Old / New Testament* REL Vecchio / Nuovo Testamento

'test-drive: go for a ~ fare un giro di prova

tes·ti·cle ['testɪkl] testicolo *m*

tes·ti·fy ['testɪfaɪ] *v/i* (*pret & pp* **-ied**) LAW testimoniare

tes·ti·mo·ni·al [testɪ'məʊnɪəl] referenze *fpl* scritte

tes·ti·mo·ny ['testɪmənɪ] LAW testimonianza *f*

'test tube provetta *f*

'test tube ba·by bambino *m*, -a *f* (concepito, -a) in provetta

tes·ty ['testɪ] *adj* suscettibile

te·ta·nus ['tetənəs] tetano *m*

teth·er ['teðə(r)] **1** *v/t horse* legare **2** *n*: *be at the end of one's ~* essere allo stremo

text [tekst] testo *m*

'text·book libro *m* di testo

tex·tile ['tekstaɪl] tessuto *m*

tex·ture ['tekstʃə(r)] consistenza *f*

Thai [taɪ] **1** *adj* tailandese **2** *n person* tailandese *m/f*; *language* tailandese *m*

Thai·land ['taɪlænd] Tailandia *f*

than [ðæn] *adv*: *older / faster ~* più vecchio / veloce di me; *she's more French ~ Italian* è più francese che italiana

thank [θæŋk] *v/t* ringraziare; *~ you* grazie; *no ~ you* no, grazie

thank·ful ['θæŋkfʊl] *adj* riconoscente

thank·ful·ly ['θæŋkfʊlɪ] *adv* con riconoscenza; *(luckily)* fortunatamente

thank·less ['θæŋklɪs] *adj* ingrato

thanks [θæŋks] *npl* ringraziamenti *mpl*; *~!* grazie!; *~ to* grazie a

that [ðæt] **1** *adj* quel; *with masculine nouns before s+consonant, gn, ps and z* quello; *~ one* quello **2** *pron* quello *m*, -a *f*; *what is ~?* cos'è?; *who is ~?* chi è?; *~'s mine* è mio; *~'s tea* quello è tè; *~'s very kind* è molto gentile **3** *relative pron* che; *the person / car ~ you saw* la persona / macchina che hai visto; *the day ~ he was born* il giorno in cui è nato **4** *adv (so)* così; *~ big / expensive* così grande / caro **5** *conj* che; *I think ~ ...* credo che ...

thaw [θɔː] *v/i of snow* sciogliersi; *of*

frozen food scongelare

the [ðə] *il m, la f; i mpl, le fpl; with masculine nouns before s+consonant, gn, ps and z* lo *m,* gli *mpl; before vowel* l' *m/f,* gli *mpl;* **to ~ bathroom** al bagno; **~ sooner ~ better** prima è, meglio è

the·a·ter *Am* → theatre

the·a·tre ['θɪətə(r)] teatro *m*

'**the·a·tre crit·ic** critico *m* teatrale

the·a·tre·go·er ['θɪətəgəʊə(r)] frequentatore *m,* -trice *f* di teatro

the·at·ri·cal [θɪ'ætrɪkl] *also fig* teatrale

theft [θeft] furto *m*

their [ðeə(r)] *adj* il loro *m,* la loro *f;* i loro *mpl,* le loro *fpl;* (*his or her*) il suo *m,* la sua *f,* i suoi *mpl,* le sue *fpl;* **~ daughter/son** la loro figlia/il loro figlio

theirs [ðeəz] *pron* il loro *m,* la loro *f;* i loro *mpl,* le loro *fpl;* **it was an idea of ~** è stata una loro idea

them [ðem] *pron direct object* li *m,* le *f; referring to things* essi *m,* esse *f; indirect object* loro, gli; *after preposition* loro; *referring to things* essi *m,* esse *f;* (*him or her*) lo *m,* la *f;* **I know ~** li/le conosco; **I sold it to ~** gliel'ho venduto, l'ho venduto a loro

theme [θiːm] tema *m*

'**theme park** parco *m* a tema

'**theme song** canzone *f* principale

them·selves [ðem'selvz] *pron reflexive* si; *emphatic* loro stessi *mpl,* loro stesse *fpl; after prep* se stessi/stesse; **they ~** loro stessi/stesse; **they enjoyed ~** si sono divertiti; **they only think about ~** pensano solo a se stessi/stesse; **by ~** (*alone*) da soli *mpl,* da sole *fpl*

then [ðen] *adv* (*at that time*) allora; (*after that*) poi; (*deducing*) allora; **by ~** allora

the·o·lo·gian [θɪə'ləʊdʒɪən] teologo *m,* -a *f*

the·ol·o·gy [θɪ'ɒlədʒɪ] teologia *f*

the·o·ret·i·cal [θɪə'retɪkl] *adj* teorico

the·o·ret·i·cal·ly [θɪə'retɪklɪ] *adv* teoricamente

the·o·ry ['θɪərɪ] teoria *f;* **in ~** in teoria

ther·a·peu·tic [θerə'pjuːtɪk] *adj* terapeutico

ther·a·pist ['θerəpɪst] terapista *m/f,* terapeuta *m/f*

ther·a·py ['θerəpɪ] terapia *f*

there [ðeə(r)] *adv* lì, là; **over ~** là; **down ~** laggiù; **~ is ...** c'è; **~ are ...** ci sono; **is ~ ...?** c'è ...?; **are ~ ...?** ci sono ...?; **isn't ~?** non c'è ...?; **aren't ~?** non ci sono ...?; **~ you are** *giving sth* ecco qui; *finding sth* ecco; *completing sth* ecco fatto; **~ and back** andata e ritorno; **~ he is!** eccolo!; **~, ~!** *comforting* su, dai!

there·a·bouts [ðeərə'baʊts] *adv* giù di lì

there·fore [ðeəfɔː(r)] *adv* quindi, pertanto

ther·mom·e·ter [θə'mɒmɪtə(r)] termometro *m*

ther·mos flask ['θɜːməsflɑːsk] termos *m inv*

ther·mo·stat ['θɜːməstæt] termostato *m*

these [ðiːz] **1** *adj* questi **2** *pron* questi *m,* -e *f*

the·sis ['θiːsɪs] (*pl* theses ['θiːsiːz]) tesi *f inv*

they [ðeɪ] *pron* ◊ **~'re going to the theatre** vanno a teatro; **~'re going to the theatre, we're not** loro vanno a teatro, noi no; **there ~ are** eccoli *mpl,* eccole *fpl* ◊ **if anyone looks at this, ~ will see that ...** se qualcuno lo guarda, vedrà che ...; **~ say that ...** si dice che ...; **~ are going to change the law** cambieranno la legge

thick [θɪk] *adj* spesso; *hair* folto; *fog, forest* fitto; *liquid* denso; F (*stupid*) ottuso

thick·en ['θɪkən] *v/t sauce* inspessire

thick·set ['θɪkset] *adj* tarchiato

thick·skinned ['θɪkskɪnd] *adj fig* insensibile

thief [θiːf] (*pl* thieves [θiːvz]) ladro *m,* -a *f*

thigh [θaɪ] coscia *f*

thim·ble ['θɪmbl] ditale *m*

thin [θɪn] *adj* sottile; *person* magro;

T

hair rado; *liquid* fluido

thing [θɪŋ] cosa *f*; **~s** (*belongings*) cose *fpl*; **how are ~s?** come vanno le cose?; **it's a good ~ you told me** è un bene che tu me l'abbia detto; **what a ~ to do/say!** che razza di cosa da fare/dire!

thing·um·a·jig ['θɪŋʌmədʒɪg] F coso *m*, cosa *f* F

think [θɪŋk] *v/i* (*pret & pp* **thought**) pensare; **I ~ so** penso o credo di sì; **I don't ~ so** non credo; **I ~ so too** lo penso anch'io; **what do you ~?** cosa ne pensi?; **what do you ~ of it?** cosa ne pensi?; **I can't ~ of anything more** non mi viene in mente niente'altro; **~ hard!** pensaci bene!; **I'm ~ing about emigrating** sto pensando di emigrare

♦ **think over** *v/t* riflettere su

♦ **think through** *v/t* analizzare a fondo

♦ **think up** *v/t plan* escogitare

'**think tank** comitato *m* di esperti

thin-skinned [θɪn'skɪnd] *adj fig* sensibile

third [θɜːd] *n & adj* terzo, -a

third·ly ['θɜːdlɪ] *adv* in terzo luogo

'**third-par·ty** terzi *mpl*; **third-par·ty in'sur·ance** assicurazione *f* sulla responsabilità civile; **third 'per·son** GRAM terza persona *f*; '**third-rate** *adj* scadente; **Third 'World** Terzo Mondo *m*

thirst [θɜːst] sete *f*

thirsty ['θɜːstɪ] *adj* assetato; **be ~** avere sete

thir·teen [θɜː'tiːn] tredici

thir·teenth [θɜː'tiːnθ] *n & adj* tredicesimo, -a

thir·ti·eth ['θɜːtɪɪθ] *n & adj* trentesimo, -a

thir·ty ['θɜːtɪ] trenta

this [ðɪs] **1** *adj* questo; **~ one** questo (qui) **2** *pron* questo *m*, -a *f*; **~ is easy** è facile; **~ is ...** *introducing s.o.* questo/questa è ...; TELEC sono ...; **3** *adv*: **~ big/high** grande/alto così

thorn [θɔːn] spina *f*

thorn·y ['θɔːnɪ] *adj also fig* spinoso

thor·ough ['θʌrə] *adj search, know-*

ledge approfondito; *person* scrupoloso

thor·ough·bred ['θʌrəbred] *horse* purosangue *inv*

thor·ough·ly ['θʌrəlɪ] *adv clean, search for* accuratamente; *know, understand* perfettamente; *agree, spoil* completamente; **~ stupid** stupidissimo

those [ðəʊz] **1** *adj* quelli; *with masculine nouns before s+consonant, gn, ps and z* quegli **2** *pron* quelli *m*, -e *f*; *with masculine nouns before s+consonant, gn, ps and z* quegli

though [ðəʊ] **1** *conj* (*although*) benché; **~ it might fail** benché possa non riuscire; **say it as ~ you meant it** dillo come se lo sentissi davvero; **it looks as ~ ...** sembra che ... **2** *adv* però; **it's not finished** ~ non è finito, però

thought [θɔːt] **1** *n* pensiero *m* **2** *pret & pp* → **think**

thought·ful ['θɔːtfʊl] *adj* pensieroso; *reply* meditato; (*considerate*) gentile

thought·ful·ly [əθɔːtflɪ] *adv* (*pensively*) con aria pensierosa; (*considerately*) gentilmente

thought·less ['θɔːtlɪs] *adj* sconsiderato

thought·less·ly ['θɔːtlɪslɪ] *adv* in modo sconsiderato

thou·sand ['θaʊznd] mille; **a ~ pounds** mille sterline; **~s of** migliaia di

thou·sandth ['θaʊzndθ] *n & adj* millesimo, -a

thrash [θræʃ] *v/t* picchiare; SP battere

♦ **thrash about** *v/i with arms etc* sferrare colpi in aria

♦ **thrash out** *v/t solution* mettere a punto

thrash·ing ['θræʃɪŋ] botte *fpl*; SP batosta *f*

thread [θred] **1** *n* filo *m*; *of screw* filettatura *f* **2** *v/t needle* infilare il filo in; *beads* infilare

thread·bare ['θredbeə(r)] *adj* liso

threat [θret] minaccia *f*

threat·en ['θretn] *v/t* minacciare

threat·en·ing ['θretnɪŋ] *adj* minaccioso; **~ letter** lettera *f* minatoria

three [θriː] tre

three 'quart·ers tre quarti *mpl*

thresh [θreʃ] *v/t corn* trebbiare

thresh·old ['θreʃhəʊld] *of house, new era* soglia *f*; **on the ~ of** sulla soglia di

threw [θruː] *pret → **throw***

thrift [θrɪft] parsimonia *f*

thrift·y ['θrɪftɪ] *adj* parsimonioso

thrill [θrɪl] **1** *n* emozione *f*; *physical feeling* brivido *m* **2** *v/t*: **be ~ed** essere emozionato

thrill·er ['θrɪlə(r)] giallo *m*

thrill·ing ['θrɪlɪŋ] *adj* emozionante

thrive [θraɪv] *v/i of plant* crescere rigoglioso; *of business, economy* prosperare

throat [θrəʊt] gola *f*; **have a sore ~** avere mal di gola

throat loz·enge pastiglia *f* per la gola

throb [θrɒb] *v/i (pret & pp -**bed**)* pulsare; *of heart* battere; *of music* rimbombare

throb·bing ['θrɒbɪŋ] pulsazione *f*; *of heart* battito *m*; *of music* rimbombo *m*

throne [θrəʊn] trono *m*

throng [θrɒŋ] *n* calca *f*

throt·tle ['θrɒtl] **1** *n on motorbike* manetta *f* di accelerazione; *on boat* leva *f* di accelerazione **2** *v/t (strangle)* strozzare

♦ **throttle back** *v/i* decelerare

through [θruː] **1** *prep (across)* attraverso; *(during)* durante; *(by means of)* tramite; **go ~ the city** attraversare la città; **~ the winter / summer** per tutto l'inverno / tutta l'estate; **arranged ~ him** organizzato tramite lui **2** *adv*: **wet ~** completamente bagnato; **watch a film ~** guardare un film fino alla fine **3** *adj*: **be ~** *of couple* essersi lasciati; **have arrived**: *of news etc* essere arrivato; **you're ~** TELEC è in linea; **I'm ~ with ...** *(finished with)* ho finito con ...; **I'm ~ with him** ho chiuso con lui

'through flight volo *m* diretto

through·out [θruː'aʊt] **1** *prep*: **~ the**

night per tutta la notte **2** *adv (in all parts)* completamente

'through train treno *m* diretto

throw [θrəʊ] **1** *v/t (pret **threw**, pp **thrown**)* lanciare; *into bin etc* gettare; *of horse* disarcionare; *(disconcert)* sconcertare; *party* dare **2** *n* lancio *m*

♦ **throw away** *v/t* buttare via, gettare

♦ **throw off** *v/t jacket etc* togliersi in fretta; *cold etc* liberarsi di

♦ **throw on** *v/t clothes* mettersi in fretta

♦ **throw out** *v/t old things* buttare via; *from bar, house etc* buttare fuori; *plan* scartare

♦ **throw up** **1** *v/t ball* lanciare; **throw up one's hands** alzare le mani al cielo **2** *v/i (vomit)* vomitare

'throw-a·way *adj remark* buttato lì; *(disposable)* usa e getta *inv*

'throw-in SP rimessa *f*

thrown [θrəʊn] *pp → **throw***

thrush [θrʌʃ] *bird* tordo *m*

thrust [θrʌst] *v/t (pret & pp **thrust**) (push hard)* spingere; *knife* conficcare; **~ sth into s.o.'s hands** ficcare qc in mano a qu; **~ one's way through the crowd** farsi largo tra la folla

thud [θʌd] *n* tonfo *m*

thug [θʌg] *hooligan* teppista *m*; *tough guy* bullo *m*

thumb [θʌm] **1** *n* pollice *m* **2** *v/t*: **~ a lift** fare l'autostop

thump [θʌmp] **1** *n blow* pugno *m*; *noise* colpo *m* **2** *v/t person* dare un pugno a; **~ one's fist on the table** dare un pugno sul tavolo **3** *v/i of heart* palpitare; **~ on the door** battere alla porta

thun·der ['θʌndə(r)] *n* tuono *m*

thun·der·ous ['θʌndərəs] *adj applause* fragoroso

thun·der·storm ['θʌndəstɔːm] temporale *m*

'thun·der·struck *adj* allibito

thun·der·y ['θʌndərɪ] *adj weather* temporalesco

Thurs·day ['θɜːzdeɪ] giovedì *m inv*

T

thus [ðʌs] *adv* (*in this way*) così

thwart [θwɔːt] *v/t person, plans* ostacolare

thyme [taɪm] timo *m*

thy·roid gland ['θaɪrɔɪdglænd] tiroide *f*

Ti·ber ['taɪbə(r)] Tevere *m*

tick [tɪk] **1** *n of clock* ticchettio *m*; *in text* segno *m* **2** *v/i of clock* ticchettare **3** *v/t with a ~* segnare
♦ **tick off** *v/t* rimproverare; *item in a list* segnare

tick·et ['tɪkɪt] biglietto *m*; *in cloakroom* scontrino *m*

'**ti·cket col·lec·tor** bigliettaio *m*, *-a f*;
'**ti·cket in·spec·tor** controllore *m*;
'**ti·cket ma·chine** distributore *m* di biglietti; '**ti·cket of·fice** biglietteria *f*

tick·ing ['tɪkɪŋ] *noise* ticchettio *m*

tick·le ['tɪkl] **1** *v/t person* fare il solletico a **2** *v/i of material* dare prurito; *of person* fare il solletico

tick·lish ['tɪklɪʃ] *adj*: **be ~** soffrire il solletico

ti·dal wave ['taɪdlweɪv] onda *f* di marea

tide [taɪd] marea *f*; **high ~** alta marea; **low ~** bassa marea; **the ~ is in / out** c'è l'alta / la bassa marea
♦ **tide over** *v/t* togliere d'impiccio

ti·di·ness ['taɪdɪnɪs] ordine *m*

ti·dy ['taɪdɪ] *adj* ordinato
♦ **tidy away** *v/t* (*pret & pp -ied*) mettere a posto
♦ **tidy up 1** *v/t room, shelves* mettere in ordine; **tidy o.s. up** darsi una sistemata **2** *v/i* mettere in ordine

tie [taɪ] **1** *n* (*necktie*) cravatta *f*, (SP: *even result*) pareggio *m*; **he doesn't have any ~s** non ha legami **2** *v/t knot, hands* legare; **~ a knot** fare un nodo; **~ two ropes together** annodare due corde **3** *v/i* SP pareggiare
♦ **tie down** *v/t with rope* legare; (*restrict*) vincolare
♦ **tie up** *v/t person, laces, hair* legare; *boat* ormeggiare; **I'm tied up tomorrow** sono impegnato domani

tier [tɪə(r)] *of hierarchy* livello *m*; *in stadium* anello *m*

ti·ger ['taɪgə(r)] tigre *f*

tight [taɪt] **1** *adj clothes* stretto; *security* rigido; *rope* teso; *hard to move* bloccato; *not leaving much time* giusto; *schedule* serrato; F (*drunk*) sbronzo F **2** *adv*: **hold s.o. / sth ~** tenere qu / qc stretto; **shut sth ~** chiudere bene qc

tight·en ['taɪtn] *v/t screw* serrare; *belt* stringere; *rope* tendere; *control, security* intensificare
♦ **tighten up** *v/i in discipline, security* intensificare il controllo

tight-fist·ed [taɪt'fɪstɪd] *adj* taccagno

tight·ly ['taɪtlɪ] *adv* → **tight** *adv*

tight·rope ['taɪtrəʊp] fune *f* (per funamboli)

tights [taɪts] *npl* collant *mpl*

tile [taɪl] *on floor* mattonella *f*; *on wall* piastrella *f*; *on roof* tegola *f*

till[1] [tɪl] *prep & conj* → **until**

till[2] [tɪl] *n* (*cash register*) cassa *f*

till[3] [tɪl] *v/t soil* arare

tilt [tɪlt] **1** *v/t* inclinare **2** *v/i* inclinarsi

tim·ber ['tɪmbə(r)] legname *m*

time [taɪm] tempo *m*; *by the clock* ora *f*, (*occasion*) volta *f*; **~ is up** il tempo è scaduto; **for the ~ being** al momento; **have a good ~** divertirsi; **have a good ~!** divertiti!; **what's the ~?, what ~ is it?** che ora è?, che ore sono?; **by the ~ you finish** quando avrai finito; **the first ~** la prima volta; **four ~s** quattro volte; **~ and again** ripetutamente; **all the ~** per tutto il tempo; **I've been here for some ~** sono qui da un po'; **take your ~** fai con calma; **for a ~** per un po' (di tempo); **at any ~** in qualsiasi momento; (**and**) **about ~!** era ora!; **two / three at a ~** due / tre alla volta; **at the same ~** *speak, reply etc* contemporaneamente; (*however*) nel contempo; **in ~** in tempo; (*eventually*) col tempo; **on ~** in orario; **in no ~** in un attimo

'**time bomb** bomba *f* a orologeria;
'**time clock** *in factory* bollatrice *f*;

'time-con·sum·ing *adj* lungo; **'time dif·fer·ence** fuso *m* orario; **'time-lag** scarto *m* di tempo; **'time lim·it** limite *m* temporale

time·ly ['taɪmlɪ] *adj* tempestivo

tim·er ['taɪmə(r)] cronometro *m*; *person* cronometrista *m/f*; *on oven* timer *m inv*

'time-sav·ing *adj* risparmio *m* di tempo; **'time·scale** *of project* cronologia *f*; **'time share** *Br* (*house, apartment*) multiproprietà *f inv*; **'time switch** interruttore *m* a tempo; **'time·ta·ble** orario *m*; **'time·warp** trasposizione *f* temporale; **'time zone** zona *f* di fuso orario

tim·id ['tɪmɪd] *adj* timido

tim·id·ly ['tɪmɪdlɪ] *adv* timidamente

tim·ing ['taɪmɪŋ] (*choosing a time*) tempismo *m*; *that's good ~!* che tempismo!

tin [tɪn] *metal* stagno *m*; *container* barattolo *m*

tin·foil ['tɪnfɔɪl] carta *f* stagnola

tinge [tɪndʒ] *n of colour, sadness* sfumatura *f*

tin·gle ['tɪŋgl] *v/i* pizzicare

♦ **tinker with** ['tɪŋkə(r)] *v/t* armeggiare con

tin·kle ['tɪŋkl] *n of bell* tintinnio *m*

tinned [tɪnd] *adj* in scatola

'tin o·pen·er apriscatole *m inv*

tin·sel ['tɪnsl] fili *mpl* d'argento

tint [tɪnt] **1** *n of colour* sfumatura *f*; *in hair* riflessant *m* **2** *v/t hair* fare dei riflessi a

tint·ed ['tɪntɪd] *glasses* fumé *inv*

ti·ny ['taɪnɪ] *adj* piccolissimo

tip[1] [tɪp] *n of stick, finger* punta *f*; *of cigarette* filtro *m*

tip[2] [tɪp] **1** *n* (*piece of advice*) consiglio *m*; *money* mancia *f* **2** *v/t* (*pret & pp -ped*) *waiter etc* dare la mancia a

♦ **tip off** *v/t* fare una soffiata a

♦ **tip over** *v/t jug, liquid* rovesciare; *he tipped water all over me* mi ha rovesciato dell'acqua addosso

'tip-off soffiata *f*

tipped [tɪpt] *adj cigarettes* col filtro

Tipp-Ex® *n* bianchetto *m*

tip·sy ['tɪpsɪ] *adj* alticcio

tip·toe ['tɪptəʊ]: *on ~* sulla punta dei piedi

tire[1] ['taɪə(r)] **1** *v/t* stancare **2** *v/i* stancarsi; *he never ~s of it* non se ne stanca mai

tire[2] ['taɪə(r)] *Am n* → **tyre**

tired ['taɪəd] *adj* stanco; *be ~ of s.o. / sth* essere stanco di qu / qc

tired·ness ['taɪədnɪs] stanchezza *f*

tire·less ['taɪəlɪs] *adj* instancabile

tire·some ['taɪəsəm] *adj* (*annoying*) fastidioso

tir·ing ['taɪrɪŋ] *adj* stancante

Ti·rol → **Tyrol**

tis·sue ['tɪʃuː] ANAT tessuto *m*; (*handkerchief*) fazzolettino *m* (di carta)

'tis·sue pa·per carta *f* velina

tit[1] [tɪt] *bird* cincia *f*

tit[2] [tɪt]: *~ for tat* pan per focaccia

tit[3] [tɪt] V (*breast*) tetta *f* V

ti·tle ['taɪtl] titolo *m*; LAW diritto *m*

'ti·tle-hold·er SP detentore *m*, -trice *f* del titolo

'ti·tle role *in play, film* ruolo *m* principale

tit·ter ['tɪtə(r)] *v/i* ridacchiare

to [tuː], *unstressed* [tə] **1** *prep* a; *~ Italy* in Italia; *~ Rome* a Roma; *let's go ~ my place* andiamo a casa mia; *walk ~ the station* andare a piedi alla stazione; *~ the north / south of ...* a nord / sud di ...; *give sth ~ s.o.* dare qc a qu; *from Monday ~ Wednesday* da lunedì a mercoledì; *from 10 ~ 15 people* tra 10 e 15 persone; *count ~ 20* contare fino a venti; *it's 5 ~ 11* sono le undici meno cinque **2** *with verbs*: *~ speak, ~ see* parlare, vedere; *learn ~ drive* imparare a guidare; *nice ~ eat* buono da mangiare; *too heavy ~ carry* troppo pesante da trasportare; *~ be honest ...* per essere franco ...; *~ learn Italian in order to* per imparare l'italiano **3** *adv*: *~ and fro* avanti e indietro

toad [təʊd] rospo *m*

toad·stool ['təʊdstuːl] fungo *m* velenoso

toast [təʊst] **1** n pane m tostato; (drinking) brindisi m inv; **propose a ~ to s.o.** fare un brindisi in onore di qu **2** v/t bread tostare; drinking fare un brindisi a

to·bac·co [təˈbækəʊ] tabacco m

to·bac·co·nist [təˈbækənɪst] tabaccaio m

to·bog·gan [təˈbɒgən] n toboga m inv

to·day [təˈdeɪ] oggi

tod·dle [ˈtɒdl] v/i of child gattonare

tod·dler [ˈtɒdlə(r)] bambino m, -a f ai primi passi

to-do [təˈduː] F casino m F

toe [təʊ] **1** n dito m del piede; of shoes, socks punta f; **big ~** alluce m **2** v/t: **~ the line** attenersi alle direttive

toe·nail [ˈtəʊneɪl] unghia f del piede

tof·fee [ˈtɒfɪ] caramella f al mou

to·geth·er [təˈgeðə(r)] adv insieme

toil [tɔɪl] n duro lavoro m

toi·let [ˈtɔɪlɪt] gabinetto m; place bagno m, gabinetto m; **go to the ~** andare in bagno

'toi·let pa·per carta f igienica

toil·et·ries [ˈtɔɪlɪtrɪz] npl prodotti mpl da toilette

'toi·let roll rotolo m di carta igienica

to·ken [ˈtəʊkən] (sign) pegno m; for gambling gettone m; (gift ~) buono m

told [təʊld] pret & pp → **tell**

tol·e·ra·ble [ˈtɒlərəbl] adj pain etc tollerabile; (quite good) accettabile

tol·e·rance [ˈtɒlərəns] tolleranza f

tol·e·rant [ˈtɒlərənt] adj tollerante

tol·e·rate [ˈtɒləreɪt] v/t noise, person tollerare; **I won't ~ it!** non intendo tollerarlo!

toll[1] [təʊl] v/i of bell suonare

toll[2] [təʊl] n (deaths) bilancio m delle vittime

toll[3] [təʊl] n for bridge, road pedaggio m

'toll booth casello m

'toll road strada f a pedaggio

to·ma·to [təˈmɑːtəʊ] pomodoro m

to·ma·to 'ketch·up ketchup m inv

to·ma·to 'sauce for pasta etc salsa f o

sugo m di pomodoro; (ketchup) ketchup m

tomb [tuːm] tomba f

tom·boy [ˈtɒmbɔɪ] maschiaccio m

tomb·stone [ˈtuːmstəʊn] lapide f

tom·cat [ˈtɒmkæt] gatto m (maschio)

to·mor·row [təˈmɒrəʊ] domani; **the day after ~** dopodomani; **~ morning** domattina, domani mattina

ton [tʌn] tonnellata f

tone [təʊn] of colour, musical instrument tonalità f inv; of conversation etc tono m; of neighbourhood livello m sociale; **~ of voice** tono di voce

♦tone down v/t demands, criticism moderare il tono di

ton·er [ˈtəʊnə(r)] toner m inv

tongs [tɒŋz] npl pinze fpl; for hair ferro m arricciacapelli

tongue [tʌŋ] n lingua f

ton·ic [ˈtɒnɪk] MED ricostituente m

'ton·ic (wa·ter) acqua f tonica

to·night [təˈnaɪt] stanotte; (this evening) stasera

ton·sil [ˈtɒnsl] tonsilla f

ton·sil·li·tis [tɒnsɪˈlaɪtɪs] tonsillite f

too [tuː] adv (also) anche; (excessively) troppo; **me ~** anch'io; **~ big / hot** troppo grande / caldo; **~ much rice** troppo riso; **~ many mistakes** troppi errori; **eat ~ much** mangiare troppo

took [tʊk] pret → **take**

tool [tuːl] attrezzo m; fig strumento m

toot [tuːt] v/t F suonare

tooth [tuːθ] (pl teeth [tiːθ]) dente m

'tooth·ache mal m di denti

'tooth·brush spazzolino m da denti

tooth·less [ˈtuːθlɪs] sdentato

'tooth·paste dentifricio m

'tooth·pick stuzzicadenti m inv

top [tɒp] **1** n of mountain, tree cima f; of wall, screen parte f alta; of page, list, street inizio m; (lid: of bottle etc, pen) tappo m; of the class, league testa f; (clothing) maglia f; (MOT: gear) marcia f più alta; **on ~ of** in cima a; **at the ~ of** list, tree, mountain in cima a; league in testa a; page, street all'inizio di; **get to the ~** of company etc arrivare in cima; **get to the ~** of *mountain* arrivare alla vetta; **be over the ~** (*exaggerated*) essere esagerato **2** *adj branches* più alto; *floor* ultimo; *management* di alto livello; *official* di alto rango; *player* migliore; *speed, note* massimo **3** *v/t* (*pret & pp* **-ped**): **~ped with cream** ricoperto di crema

♦ **top up** *v/t glass* riempire; **top up the tank** fare il pieno

top ʼhat tuba *f*

top·ic [ˈtɒpɪk] argomento *m*

top·ic·al [ˈtɒpɪkl] *adj* attuale

top·less [ˈtɒplɪs] *adj* topless *inv*

top·most [ˈtɒpməʊst] *adj branches, floor* più alto

top·ping [ˈtɒpɪŋ] *on pizza* guarnizione *f*

top·ple [ˈtɒpl] **1** *v/i* crollare **2** *v/t government* far cadere

top ʼse·cret *adj* top secret *inv*

top·sy-tur·vy [tɒpsɪˈtɜːvɪ] *adj* sottosopra *inv*

torch [tɔːtʃ] *Br* pila *f*; *with flame* torcia *f*

tore [tɔː(r)] *pret* → **tear**

tor·ment [ˈtɔːment] **1** *n* tormento *m* **2** *v/t* [tɔːˈment] *person, animal* tormentare; **~ed by doubt** tormentato dal dubbio

torn [tɔːn] *pp* → **tear**

tor·na·do [tɔːˈneɪdəʊ] tornado *m*

tor·pe·do [tɔːˈpiːdəʊ] **1** *n* siluro *m* **2** *v/t* silurare; *fig* far saltare

tor·rent [ˈtɒrənt] torrente *m*; *of lava* fiume *m*; *of abuse, words* valanga *f*

tor·ren·tial [təˈrenʃl] *adj rain* torrenziale

tor·toise [ˈtɔːtəs] tartaruga *f*

tor·ture [ˈtɔːtʃə(r)] **1** *n* tortura *f* **2** *v/t* torturare

toss [tɒs] **1** *v/t ball* lanciare; *rider* disarcionare; *salad* mescolare; **~ a coin** fare testa o croce **2** *v/i*: **~ and turn** rigirarsi

to·tal [ˈtəʊtl] **1** *n* totale *m* **2** *adj amount, disaster* totale; *stranger* perfetto

to·tal·i·tar·i·an [təʊtælɪˈteərɪən] *adj* totalitario

to·tal·ly [ˈtəʊtəlɪ] *adv* totalmente, completamente

tot·ter [ˈtɒtə(r)] *v/i of person* barcollare

touch [tʌtʃ] **1** *n* tocco *m*; *sense* tatto *m*; *small detail* tocco *m*; *in rugby* touche *f*; **he felt a ~ on his shoulder** si è sentito toccare sulla spalla; **lose one's ~** perdere la mano; **kick the ball into ~** calciare la palla fuoricampo; **lose ~ with s.o.** perdere i contatti con qu; **keep in ~ with s.o.** rimanere in contatto con qu; **we kept in ~** siamo rimasti in contatto; **be out of ~** with *news* non essere al corrente; *with people* non avere contatti; **a ~ of** *little bit* un po' di ... **2** *v/t* toccare; *emotionally* commuovere **3** *v/i* toccare; *of two lines etc* toccarsi

♦ **touch down** *v/i of aeroplane* atterrare; SP fare meta

♦ **touch on** *v/t* (*mention*) accennare a

♦ **touch up** *v/t photo* ritoccare; *sexually* palpeggiare

touch-and-ʼgo: **it was ~** la situazione era critica

touch·down [ˈtʌtʃdaʊn] *of aeroplane* atterraggio *m*

touch·ing [ˈtʌtʃɪŋ] *adj* commovente

touch·line [ˈtʌtʃlaɪn] SP linea *f* laterale

ʼ**touch screen** schermo *m* tattile

touch·y [ˈtʌtʃɪ] *adj person* suscettibile

tough [tʌf] *adj person* forte; *question, exam, meat, punishment* duro; *material* resistente

♦ **toughen up** [ˈtʌfn] *v/t person* rendere più forte

ʼ**tough guy** F duro *m* F

tour [tʊə(r)] **1** *n* visita *f* **2** *v/t area* fare il giro di

ʼ**tour guide** guida *f* turistica

tour·ism [ˈtʊərɪzm] turismo *m*

tour·ist [ˈtʊərɪst] turista *m/f*

ʼ**tour·ist at·trac·tion** attrazione *f* turistica; ʼ**tour·ist in·dus·try** industria *f* del turismo; ʼ**tour·ist (in·for·ˈma·tion) of·fice** azienda *f* (autonoma) di soggiorno; ʼ**tour·ist sea·son** stagione *f* turistica

T

tour·na·ment ['tʊənəmənt] torneo *m*

'tour op·er·a·tor operatore *m* turistico

tous·led ['taʊzld] *adj hair* scompigliato

tout [taʊt] *n* bagarino *m*

tow [təʊ] **1** *v/t car, boat* rimorchiare **2** *n:* **give s.o. a ~** rimorchiare qu

♦ **tow away** *v/t car* portare via col carro attrezzi

to·wards [tə'wɔːdz] *prep* verso; *rude ~* maleducato nei confronti di; *work ~ (achieving) sth* lavorare per (raggiungere) qc

tow·el ['taʊəl] asciugamano *m*

tow·er ['taʊə(r)] torre *f*

♦ **tower over** *v/t* sovrastare

'tow·er block condominio *m* a torre

town [taʊn] città *f inv; opposed to city* cittadina *f*

town 'cen·tre centro *m*; **town 'coun·cil** consiglio *m* comunale; **town 'coun·cil·lor** consigliere *m*, -a *f* comunale; **town 'hall** municipio *m*

'tow·rope cavo *m* da rimorchio

tox·ic ['tɒksɪk] *adj* tossico

tox·ic 'waste scorie *fpl* tossiche

tox·in ['tɒksɪn] BIO tossina *f*

toy [tɔɪ] giocattolo *m*

♦ **toy with** *v/t object* giocherellare con; *idea* accarezzare

'toy shop negozio *m* di giocattoli

trace [treɪs] **1** *n of substance* traccia *f* **2** *v/t (find)* rintracciare; *(follow: footsteps)* seguire; *(draw)* tracciare

track [træk] *n (path)* sentiero *m; on race course* pista *f; (race course)* circuito *m;* RAIL binario *m; on record, CD* brano *m;* **keep ~ of sth** tenersi al passo con qc; *keep record of* registrare

♦ **track down** *v/t* rintracciare

'track·suit tuta *f* (da ginnastica)

trac·tor ['træktə(r)] trattore *m*

trade [treɪd] **1** *n (commerce)* commercio *m; (profession, craft)* mestiere *m* **2** *v/i (do business)* essere in attività; *~ in sth* commerciare in qc **3** *v/t (exchange)* scambiare; *~ sth for sth* scambiare qc con qc

♦ **trade in** *v/t when buying* dare in permuta

'trade fair fiera *f* campionaria

'trade·mark marchio *m* registrato

trad·er ['treɪdə(r)] commerciante *m/f*

trade 'se·cret segreto *m* industriale

trades·man ['treɪdzmən] *plumber etc* operaio *m; milkman etc* fornitore *m*

trade(s) 'u·nion sindacato *m*

tra·di·tion [trə'dɪʃn] tradizione *f*

tra·di·tion·al [trə'dɪʃnl] *adj* tradizionale

tra·di·tion·al·ly [trə'dɪʃnlɪ] *adv* tradizionalmente

traf·fic ['træfɪk] *n on roads, in drugs* traffico *m; at airport* traffico *m* aereo

♦ **traffic** *v/i (pret & pp* **-ked**) *drugs* trafficare

'traf·fic cop F vigile *m* (urbano); **'traf·fic is·land** isola *f* salvagente; **'traf·fic jam** ingorgo *m*; **'traf·fic lights** *npl* semaforo *m*; **'traf·fic po·lice** polizia *f* stradale; **'traf·fic sign** segnale *m* stradale; **'traf·fic war·den** ausiliario *m* (del traffico)

tra·ge·dy ['trædʒədɪ] tragedia *f*

tra·gic ['trædʒɪk] *adj* tragico

trail [treɪl] **1** *n (path)* sentiero *m; of person, animal* tracce *fpl; of blood* scia *f* **2** *v/t (follow)* seguire; *(drag)* trascinare; *caravan etc* trainare **3** *v/i (lag behind)* trascinarsi; **they're ~ing 3-1** stanno perdendo 3 a 1

trail·er ['treɪlə(r)] *pulled by vehicle* rimorchio *m; of film* trailer *m inv;* Am *(caravan)* roulotte *f inv*

train[1] [treɪn] *n* treno *m;* **go by ~** andare in treno

train[2] [treɪn] **1** *v/t team, athlete* allenare; *employee* formare; *dog* addestrare **2** *v/i of team, athlete* allenarsi; *of teacher etc* fare il tirocinio

train·ee [treɪ'niː] apprendista *m/f*

train·er ['treɪnə(r)] SP allenatore *m*, -trice *f; of dog* addestratore *m*, -trice *f*

train·ers ['treɪnəz] *npl shoes* scarpe *fpl* da ginnastica

train·ing [treɪnɪŋ] *of new staff*

formazione *f*; SP allenamento *m*; **be in** ~ SP allenarsi; **be out of** ~ SP essere fuori allenamento

'train·ing course corso *m* di formazione

'train·ing scheme programma *m* di formazione

'train sta·tion stazione *f* ferroviaria

trait [treɪt] tratto *m*

trai·tor ['treɪtə(r)] traditore *m*, -trice *f*

tram [træm] tram *m inv*

tramp [træmp] **1** *n* (*vagabond*) barbone *m*, -a *f* **2** *v/i* camminare con passo pesante

tram·ple ['træmpl] *v/t*: **be ~d to death** morire travolto; **be ~d underfoot** essere calpestato

◆ trample on *v/t person, object* calpestare

tram·po·line ['træmpəlin] trampolino *m*

trance [trɑːns] trance *f inv*; **go into a** ~ cadere in trance

tran·quil ['træŋkwɪl] *adj* tranquillo

tran·quil·li·ty [træŋ'kwɪlətɪ] tranquillità *f*

tran·quil·liz·er ['træŋkwɪlaɪzə(r)] tranquillante *m*

trans·act [træn'zækt] *v/t deal, business* trattare

trans·ac·tion [træn'zækʃn] transazione *f*

trans·at·lan·tic [trænzət'læntɪk] *adj* transatlantico

tran·scen·den·tal [trænsen'dentl] *adj* trascendentale

tran·script ['trænskrɪpt] trascrizione *f*

trans·fer [træns'fɜː(r)] **1** *v/t* (*pret & pp* -**red**) trasferire; LAW cedere **2** *v/i* (*pret & pp* -**red**) cambiare **3** *n* ['trænsfɜː(r)] trasferimento *m*; LAW cessione *f*; *of money* bonifico *m* bancario

trans·fer·a·ble [træns'fɜːrəbl] *adj* ticket trasferibile

'trans·fer fee *for football player* prezzo *m* d'acquisto

trans·form [træns'fɔːm] *v/t* trasformare

trans·form·a·tion [trænsfə'meɪʃn] trasformazione *f*

trans·form·er [træns'fɔːmə(r)] ELEC trasformatore *m*

trans·fu·sion [træns'fjuːʒn] trasfusione *f*

tran·sis·tor [træn'zɪstə(r)] transistor *m inv*; *radio* radiolina *f*

tran·sit ['trænsɪt]: **in** ~ *of goods, passengers* in transito

tran·si·tion [træn'sɪʒn] transizione *f*

tran·si·tion·al [træn'sɪʒnl] *adj* di transizione

'tran·sit lounge *at airport* sala *f* passeggeri in transito

'tran·sit pas·sen·ger passeggero *m*, -a *f* in transito

trans·late [træns'leɪt] *v/t* tradurre

trans·la·tion [træns'leɪʃn] traduzione *f*

trans·la·tor [træns'leɪtə(r)] traduttore *m*, -trice *f*

trans·mis·sion [trænz'mɪʃn] trasmissione *f*

trans·mit [trænz'mɪt] *v/t* (*pret & pp* -**ted**) news, programme, disease trasmettere

trans·mit·ter [trænz'mɪtə(r)] for radio, TV trasmettitore *m*

trans·par·en·cy [træns'pærənsɪ] PHOT diapositiva *f*

trans·par·ent [træns'pærənt] *adj* trasparente

trans·plant [træns'plɑːnt] **1** *v/t* MED trapiantare **2** *n* ['trænsplɑːnt] MED trapianto *m*

trans·port [træn'spɔːt] **1** *v/t* goods, people trasportare **2** *n* ['trænspɔːt] of goods, people trasporto *m*; **means of transport** mezzo *m* di trasporto; **public** ~ i trasporti pubblici

trans·por·ta·tion [trænspɔː'teɪʃn] of goods, people trasporto *m*; **means of** ~ mezzo *m* di trasporto

trans·ves·tite [træns'vestaɪt] travestito *m*

trap [træp] **1** *n* trappola *f*; question tranello *m*; **set a** ~ **for s.o.** tendere una trappola a qu **2** *v/t* (*pret & pp* -**ped**) animal intrappolare; person incastrare; **be** ~**ped** by enemy, *flames, landslide etc* essere intrappolato

trap·door ['træpdɔː(r)] botola *f*

tra·peze [trə'piːz] trapezio *m*

trap·pings ['træpɪŋz] *npl of power* segni *mpl* esteriori

trash [træʃ] (*garbage*) spazzatura *f*; *poor product* robaccia *f*; *despicable person* fetente *m/f*

trash·y ['træʃi] *adj goods, novel* scadente

trau·mat·ic [trɔː'mætɪk] *adj* traumatico

trau·ma·tize ['trɔːmətaɪz] *v/t* traumatizzare

trav·el ['trævl] **1** *n* viaggiare *m*; **~s** viaggi *mpl* **2** *v/i* (*pret & pp* **-led**, *Am* **-ed**) viaggiare; *I ~ to work by train* vado a lavorare in treno **3** *v/t* (*pret & pp* **-led**, *Am* **-ed**) *miles* percorrere

'**trav·el a·gen·cy** agenzia *f* di viaggio; '**trav·el a·gent** agente *m/f* di viaggio; '**trav·el bag** borsa *f* da viaggio; '**trav·el ex·pens·es** *npl* spese *fpl* di viaggio; '**trav·el in·sur·ance** assicurazione *f* di viaggio

trav·el·er *Am*, **trav·el·ler** ['trævələ(r)] viaggiatore *m*, -trice *f*

'**trav·el·er's check** *Am*, '**trav·el·ler's cheque** traveller's cheque *m inv*

'**trav·el pro·gram** *Am*, '**trav·el pro·gramme** *on TV etc* programma *m* di viaggi

trawl·er ['trɔːlə(r)] peschereccio *m*

tray [treɪ] *for food, photocopier* vassoio *m*; *to go in oven* teglia *f*

treach·er·ous ['tretʃərəs] *adj* traditore, infido

treach·er·y ['tretʃəri] tradimento *m*

tread [tred] **1** *n* passo *m*; *of staircase* gradino *m*; *of tyre* battistrada *m inv* **2** *v/i* (*pret* **trod**, *pp* **trodden**) camminare

♦ **tread on** *v/t s.o.'s foot* pestare

trea·son ['triːzn] tradimento *m*

trea·sure ['treʒə(r)] **1** *n also person* tesoro *m* **2** *v/t gift etc* custodire gelosamente

trea·sur·er ['treʒərə(r)] tesoriere *m*, -a *f*

treat [triːt] **1** *n* trattamento *m* speciale; *it was a real ~* è stato magnifico; *I have a ~ for you* ho una sorpresa per te; *it's my ~* (*I'm paying*) offro io **2** *v/t* trattare; *illness* curare; *~ s.o. to sth* offrire qc a qu

treat·ment ['triːtmənt] trattamento *m*; *of illness* cura *f*

treat·y ['triːti] trattato *m*

tre·ble¹ ['trebl] *n* MUS: *boy's voice* voce *f* bianca; *register* alti *mpl*

tre·ble² ['trebl] **1** *adv*: *~ the price* il triplo del prezzo **2** *v/i* triplicarsi

tree [triː] albero *m*

trem·ble ['trembl] *v/i* tremare

tre·men·dous [trɪ'mendəs] *adj* (*very good*) fantastico; (*enormous*) enorme

tre·men·dous·ly [trɪ'mendəslɪ] *adv* (*very*) incredibilmente; (*a lot*) moltissimo

trem·or ['tremə(r)] *of earth* scossa *f*

trench [trentʃ] trincea *f*

trend [trend] tendenza *f*

trend·y ['trendɪ] *adj* alla moda

tres·pass ['trespəs] *v/i* invadere una proprietà privata; *no ~ing* divieto d'accesso

♦ **trespass on** *v/t s.o.'s land, privacy* invadere; *s.o.'s rights, time* abusare di

tres·pass·er ['trespəsə(r)] intruso *m*, -a *f*

tri·al ['traɪəl] LAW processo *m*; *of equipment* prova *f*; *on ~* LAW sotto processo; *stand ~ for sth* essere processato per qc; *have sth on ~ equipment* avere qc in prova

tri·al pe·ri·od periodo *m* di prova

tri·an·gle ['traɪæŋgl] triangolo *m*

tri·an·gu·lar [traɪ'æŋgjʊlə(r)] *adj* triangolare

tribe [traɪb] tribù *f inv*

tri·bu·nal [traɪ'bjuːnl] tribunale *m*

tri·bu·ta·ry ['trɪbjʊtəri] *of river* affluente *m*

trick [trɪk] **1** *n to deceive* stratagemma *m*; (*knack*) trucco *m*; *a ~ of the light* un effetto di luce; *play a ~ on s.o.* fare uno scherzo a qu **2** *v/t* ingannare; **~ s.o. into doing sth** convincere qu con l'inganno a fare qc

trick·e·ry ['trɪkərɪ] truffa *f*

trick·le ['trɪkl] **1** *n* filo *m*; **a ~ of replies** poche risposte sporadiche **2** *v/i* gocciolare

trick·ster ['trɪkstə(r)] truffatore *m*, -trice *f*

trick·y ['trɪkɪ] *adj (difficult)* complicato

tri·cy·cle ['traɪsɪkl] triciclo *m*

tri·fle ['traɪfl] *n (triviality)* inezia *f*; *pudding* zuppa *f* inglese

tri·fling ['traɪflɪŋ] *adj* insignificante

trig·ger ['trɪgə(r)] *n on gun* grilletto *m*; *on camcorder* pulsante *m* (di accensione)

♦ **trigger off** *v/t* scatenare

trim [trɪm] **1** *adj (neat)* ordinato; *figure* snello **2** *v/t (pret & pp* **-med**) *hair, hedge* spuntare; *budget, costs* tagliare; *(decorate): dress* ornare **3** *n (light cut)* spuntata *f*; *in good ~* in buone condizioni

trim·ming ['trɪmɪŋ] *on clothes* ornamento *m*; **with all the ~s** con tutti gli annessi e connessi

trin·ket ['trɪŋkɪt] ninnolo *m*

tri·o ['triːəʊ] MUS trio *m*

trip [trɪp] **1** *n (journey)* viaggio *m*, gita *f* **2** *v/i (pret & pp* **-ped**) *(stumble)* inciampare *(over* in) **3** *v/t (pret & pp* **-ped**) *(make fall)* fare inciampare

♦ **trip up 1** *v/t (make fall)* fare inciampare; *cause to make a mistake* confondere **2** *v/i (stumble)* inciampare; *(make a mistake)* sbagliarsi

tripe [traɪp] trippa *f*

trip·le ['trɪpl] → **treble²**

trip·lets ['trɪplɪts] *npl* tre gemelli *mpl*

tri·pod ['traɪpɒd] PHOT treppiedi *m inv*

trite [traɪt] *adj* trito

tri·umph ['traɪʌmf] *n* trionfo *m*

triv·i·al ['trɪvɪəl] *adj* banale

triv·i·al·i·ty [trɪvɪ'ælətɪ] banalità *f inv*

trod [trɒd] *pret* → **tread**

trod·den ['trɒdn] *pp* → **tread**

trol·ley ['trɒlɪ] *in supermarket, at*

airport carrello *m*

trom·bone [trɒm'bəʊn] trombone *m*

troops [truːps] *npl* truppe *fpl*

tro·phy ['trəʊfɪ] trofeo *m*

tro·pic ['trɒpɪk] tropico *m*

trop·i·cal ['trɒpɪkl] *adj* tropicale

trop·ics ['trɒpɪks] *npl* tropici *mpl*

trot [trɒt] *v/i (pret & pp* **-ted**) trottare

trou·ble ['trʌbl] **1** *n (difficulties)* problemi *mpl*; *(inconvenience)* fastidio *m*; *(disturbance)* disordini *mpl*; **go to a lot of ~ to do sth** darsi molto da fare per fare qc; **no ~!** nessun problema!; **the ~ with you is ...** il tuo problema è ...; **get into ~** mettersi nei guai **2** *v/t (worry)* preoccupare; *(bother, disturb)* disturbare; *of back, liver etc* dare dei fastidi a

'**trou·ble-free** senza problemi

'**trou·ble·mak·er** attaccabrighe *m/f inv*

'**trou·ble·shoot·er** *(mediator)* mediatore *m*, trice *f*

'**trou·ble·shoot·ing** mediazione *f*; *in software manual* ricerca *f* problemi e soluzioni

trou·ble·some ['trʌblsəm] *adj* fastidioso

trou·sers ['traʊzəz] *npl* pantaloni *mpl*; **a pair of ~** un paio di pantaloni

'**trou·ser suit** tailleur *m inv* pantaloni

trout [traʊt] *(pl* **trout**) trota *f*

tru·ant ['truːənt]: **play ~** marinare la scuola

truce [truːs] tregua *f*

truck [trʌk] *(lorry)* camion *m inv*

trudge [trʌdʒ] **1** *v/i* arrancare; **~ around the shops** trascinarsi per i negozi **2** *n* camminata *f* stancante

true [truː] *adj* vero; **come ~** *of hopes, dream* realizzarsi

trul·y ['truːlɪ] *adv* davvero; **Yours ~** distinti saluti

trum·pet ['trʌmpɪt] tromba *f*

trum·pet·er ['trʌmpɪtə(r)] trombettiere *f*

trun·cheon ['trʌntʃn] manganello *m*

trunk [trʌŋk] *of tree, body* tronco *m*; *of elephant* proboscide *f*; *(large case)*

baule *m*; *Am* MOT bagagliaio *m inv*
trunks [trʌŋks] *npl for swimming* calzoncini *mpl* da bagno
trust [trʌst] **1** *n* fiducia *f*; FIN fondo *m* fiduciario; COM trust *m inv* **2** *v/t* fidarsi di; *I ~ you* mi fido di te
trusted ['trʌstɪd] *adj* fidato
trust·ee [trʌs'tiː] amministratore *m*, -trice *f* fiduciario, -a
trust·ful, trust·ing ['trʌstful, 'trʌstɪŋ] *adj* fiducioso
trust·wor·thy ['trʌstwɜːðɪ] *adj* affidabile
truth [truːθ] verità *f inv*
truth·ful ['truːθful] *adj account* veritiero; *person* sincero
try [traɪ] **1** *v/t* (*pret & pp* -**ied**) provare; LAW processare; *~ to do sth* provare a fare qc, cercare di fare qc **2** *v/i* (*pret & pp* -**ied**) provare, tentare; *you must ~ harder* devi provare con più impegno **3** *n* tentativo *m*; *in rugby* meta *f*; *can I have a ~?* *of food* posso assaggiare?; *at doing sth* posso fare un tentativo?
♦ **try on** *v/t clothes* provare
♦ **try out** *v/t new machine, method* provare
try·ing ['traɪɪŋ] *adj* (*annoying*) difficile
T-shirt ['tiːʃɜːt] maglietta *f*
tub [tʌb] (*bath*) vasca *f* da bagno; *of liquid* tinozza *f*; *for yoghurt, icecream* barattolo *m*
tub·by ['tʌbɪ] *adj* tozzo
tube [tjuːb] (*pipe*) tubo *m*; (*underground railway*) metropolitana *f*; *of toothpaste, ointment* tubetto *m*
tube·less ['tjuːblɪs] *adj tyre* senza camera d'aria
tu·ber·cu·lo·sis [tjuːbɜːkjʊ'ləʊsɪs] tubercolosi *f*
tuck [tʌk] **1** *n in dress* pince *f inv* **2** *v/t*: *~ sth into sth* infilare qc in qc
♦ **tuck away** *v/t* (*put away*) mettere via; (*eat quickly*) sbafare; *be tucked away of house, village* essere nascosto
♦ **tuck in 1** *v/t children* rimboccare le coperte a; *sheets* rimboccare **2** *v/i* (*eat*) mangiare; (*start eating*) incominciare a mangiare
♦ **tuck up** *v/t sleeves etc* rimboccarsi; *tuck s.o. up in bed* rimboccare le coperte a qu
Tues·day ['tjuːzdeɪ] martedì *m inv*
tuft [tʌft] ciuffo *m*
tug [tʌg] **1** *n* (*pull*) tirata *f*; NAUT rimorchiatore *m*; *I felt a ~ at my sleeve* mi sono sentito tirare la manica **2** *v/t* (*pret & pp* -**ged**) (*pull*) tirare
tu·i·tion [tjuː'ɪʃn] lezioni *fpl*
tu·lip ['tjuːlɪp] tulipano *m*
tum·ble ['tʌmbl] *v/i* ruzzolare; *of wall, prices* crollare
tum·ble·down ['tʌmbldaʊn] *adj* in rovina, fatiscente
tum·ble-dry·er ['tʌmbldraɪə(r)] asciugatrice *f*
tum·bler ['tʌmblə(r)] *for drinker* bicchiere *m* (senza stelo); *in circus* acrobata *m/f*
tum·my ['tʌmɪ] F pancia *f*
'tum·my ache mal *m* di pancia
tu·mour ['tjuːmə(r)] tumore *m*
tu·mult ['tjuːmʌlt] tumulto *m*
tu·mul·tu·ous [tjuː'mʌltjʊəs] *adj* tumultuoso
tu·na ['tjuːnə] tonno *m*; *~ salad* insalata *f* di tonno
tune [tjuːn] **1** *n* motivo *m*; *in ~ instrument* accordato; *person* intonato; *out of ~ instrument* scordato; *person* stonato **2** *v/t instrument* accordare; *engine* mettere a punto
♦ **tune in** *v/i of radio, TV* sintonizzarsi
♦ **tune in to** *v/t radio, TV* sintonizzarsi su
♦ **tune up 1** *v/i of orchestra, players* accordare gli strumenti **2** *v/t engine* mettere a punto
tune·ful ['tjuːnful] *adj* melodioso
tun·er ['tjuːnə(r)] (*hi-fi*) sintonizzatore *m*, tuner *m inv*
tune-up ['tjuːnʌp] *of engine* messa *f* a punto
tu·nic ['tjuːnɪk] tunica *f*; *protective* grembiule *m*; *of uniform* giacca *f*
tun·nel ['tʌnl] *n* galleria *f*, tunnel *m inv*
tur·bine ['tɜːbaɪn] turbina *f*

tur·bu·lence ['tɜːbjʊləns] *in air travel* turbolenza *f*

tur·bu·lent ['tɜːbjʊlənt] *adj* turbolento

turf [tɜːf] tappeto *m* erboso; (*piece*) zolla *f*

Tu·rin [tjʊ'rɪn] Torino *f*

Turk [tɜːk] turco *m*, -a *f*

Tur·key ['tɜːkɪ] Turchia *f*

tur·key ['tɜːkɪ] tacchino *m*

Turk·ish ['tɜːkɪʃ] **1** *adj* turco **2** *n language* turco *m*

tur·moil ['tɜːmɔɪl] agitazione *f*

turn [tɜːn] **1** *n* (*rotation*) giro *m*; *in road* curva *f*; *in variety show* numero *m*; **take ~s in doing sth** fare a turno a fare qc; **it's my ~** è il mio turno, tocca a me; **it's not your ~ yet** non è ancora il tuo turno; **take a ~ at the wheel** prendere il volante per un po'; **do s.o. a good ~** fare un favore a qu **2** *v/t wheel, corner* girare; **~ one's back on s.o.** girare le spalle a qu **3** *v/i of driver, car, wheel* girare; (*become*) diventare; **~ right / left here** gira a destra / sinistra qui; **it has ~ed sour / cold** è diventato acido / freddo; **he has ~ed 40** ha compiuto 40 anni

♦ **turn around 1** *v/t object* girare; *company* dare una svolta positiva a; (COM: *deal with*) eseguire; *order* evadere **2** *v/i of person* girarsi; *of driver* girare

♦ **turn away 1** *v/t* (*send away*) mandare via **2** *v/i* (*walk away*) andare via; (*look away*) girarsi dall'altra parte

♦ **turn back 1** *v/t edges, sheets* ripiegare **2** *v/i of walkers etc* tornare indietro; *in course of action* tirarsi indietro

♦ **turn down** *v/t offer, invitation* rifiutare; *volume, TV, heating* abbassare; *edge, collar* ripiegare

♦ **turn in 1** *v/i* (*go to bed*) andare a letto **2** *v/t to police* denunciare

♦ **turn off 1** *v/t TV, engine* spegnere; *tap* chiudere; F (*sexually*) far passare la voglia a **2** *v/i of driver* svoltare

♦ **turn on 1** *v/t TV, engine* accendere;

tap aprire; F (*sexually*) eccitare **2** *v/i of machine* accendersi

♦ **turn out 1** *v/t lights* spegnere **2** *v/i: as it turned out* come è emerso; **it turned out well** è andata bene

♦ **turn over 1** *v/i in bed* girarsi; *of vehicle* capottare **2** *v/t object, page* girare; FIN fatturare

♦ **turn up 1** *v/t collar, volume, heating* alzare **2** *v/i* (*arrive*) arrivare

turn·ing ['tɜːnɪŋ] svolta *f*

'turn·ing point svolta *f* decisiva

tur·nip ['tɜːnɪp] rapa *f*

'turn·out *of people* affluenza *f*; **'turn-o·ver** FIN fatturato *m*; *of staff* ricambio *m*; **'turn·stile** cancelletto *m* girevole; **'turn·ta·ble** piatto *m*; **'turn-up** *on trousers* risvolto *m*

tur·quoise ['tɜːkwɔɪz] *adj* turchese

tur·ret ['tʌrɪt] *of castle, tank* torretta *f*

tur·tle ['tɜːtl] tartaruga *f* marina

tur·tle·neck 'sweat·er maglia *f* a lupetto

Tus·ca·ny ['tʌskənɪ] Toscana *f*

tusk [tʌsk] zanna *f*

tu·tor ['tjuːtə(r)] EDU *insegnante universitario che segue un piccolo gruppo di studenti*; (*private*) ~ insegnante *m/f* privato, -a

tu·to·ri·al [tjuː'tɔːrɪəl] *n at university* incontro *m* con il tutor

tu·xe·do [tʌk'siːdəʊ] *Am* smoking *m inv*

TV [tiː'viː] tv *f inv*; **on ~** alla tv

T'V din·ner piatto *m* pronto; **T'V gui·de** guida *f* dei programmi tv; **T'V pro·gramme** programma *m* televisivo

twang [twæŋ] **1** *n in voice* suono *m* nasale **2** *v/t guitar string* vibrare

tweez·ers ['twiːzəz] *npl* pinzette *fpl*

twelfth [twelfθ] *n & adj* dodicesimo, -a

twelve [twelv] dodici

twen·ti·eth ['twentɪɪθ] *n & adj* ventesimo, -a

twen·ty ['twentɪ] venti

twice [twaɪs] *adv* due volte; **~ as much** il doppio; **~ as fast** veloce due volte tanto

twid·dle ['twɪdl] *v/t* girare; **~ one's**

thumbs girarsi i pollici
twig [twɪg] *n* ramoscello *m*
twi·light ['twaɪlaɪt] crepuscolo *m*
twin [twɪn] gemello *m*
'twin beds *npl* due lettini *mpl*
twinge [twɪndʒ] *of pain* fitta *f*
twin·kle ['twɪŋkl] *v/i of stars, eyes*
scintillare
twin 'room camera *f* a due letti
'twin town città *f inv* gemellata
twirl [twɜːl] **1** *v/t* fare roteare **2** *n of*
cream etc ricciolo *m*
twist [twɪst] **1** *v/t* attorcigliare; **~**
one's ankle prendere una storta
2 *v/i of road* snodarsi; *of river* serpeggiare **3** *n in rope* attorcigliata *f*;
in road curva *f*; *in plot, story* svolta *f*
twist·y ['twɪstɪ] *adj road* contorto
twit [twɪt] F scemo *m*, -a *f*
twitch [twɪtʃ] **1** *n nervous* spasmo *m*
2 *v/i (jerk)* contrarsi
twit·ter ['twɪtə(r)] *v/i* cinguettare
two [tuː] due; *the ~ of them* loro due
'two-faced *adj* falso; 'two-piece
(*woman's suit*) tailleur *m inv*;
'two-stroke *adj engine* a due tempi;
two-way 'traf·fic traffico *m* nei

due sensi di marcia
ty·coon [taɪ'kuːn] magnate *m*
type [taɪp] **1** *n (sort)* tipo *m*; *what ~*
of ...? che tipo di ...? **2** *v/t & v/i* (*use*
a keyboard) battere (a macchina)
type·writ·er ['taɪpraɪtə(r)] macchina
f da scrivere
ty·phoid ['taɪfɔɪd] febbre *f* tifoide
ty·phoon [taɪ'fuːn] tifone *m*
ty·phus ['taɪfəs] tifo *m*
typ·i·cal ['tɪpɪkl] *adj* tipico; *that's ~*
of you / him! tipico!
typ·i·cal·ly ['tɪpɪklɪ] *adv*: *~ American*
tipicamente americano; *he would ~*
arrive late arriva sempre tardi
typ·ist ['taɪpɪst] dattilografo *m*, -a *f*
ty·ran·ni·cal [tɪ'rænɪkl] *adj* tirannico
ty·ran·nize [tɪ'rænaɪz] *v/t* tiranneggiare
ty·ran·ny ['tɪrənɪ] tirannia *f*
ty·rant ['taɪrənt] tiranno *m*, -a *f*
tyre ['taɪə(r)] gomma *f*, pneumatico
m
Ty·rol [tɪ'rɒl] Tirolo *m*
Ty·ro·le·an [tɪrə'liːən] *adj* tirolese
Tyr·rhe·ni·an Sea [taɪ'riːnɪən] mar
m Tirreno

U

ug·ly ['ʌglɪ] *adj* brutto
UK [juː'keɪ] *abbr* (= *United King-*
dom) Regno *m* Unito
ul·cer ['ʌlsə(r)] ulcera *f*
ul·ti·mate ['ʌltɪmət] *adj* (*best, defini-*
tive) definitivo; (*final*) ultimo;
(*basic*) fondamentale
ul·ti·mate·ly ['ʌltɪmətlɪ] *adv* (*in the*
end) in definitiva
ul·ti·ma·tum [ʌltɪ'meɪtəm] ultimatum *m inv*
ul·tra·sound ['ʌltrəsaʊnd] MED ecografia *f*
ul·tra·vi·o·let [ʌltrə'vaɪələt] *adj* ultravioletto

um·bil·i·cal cord [ʌm'bɪlɪkl] cordone *m* ombelicale
um·brel·la [ʌm'brelə] ombrello *m*
um·pire ['ʌmpaɪə(r)] *n* arbitro *m*
ump·teen [ʌmp'tiːn] *adj* F ennesimo
UN [juː'en] *abbr* (= *United Nations*)
ONU *f inv* (= Organizzazione *f* delle Nazioni Unite)
un·a·ble [ʌn'eɪbl] *adj*: *be ~ to do sth*
not know how to non saper fare qc;
not be in a position to non poter fare
qc
un·ac·cept·a·ble [ʌnək'septəbl] *adj*
inaccettabile; *it is ~ that ...* è inac-

cettabile che …

un·ac·count·a·ble [ʌnəˈkaʊntəbl] *adj* inspiegabile

un·ac·cus·tomed [ʌnəˈkʌstəmd] *adj*: **be ~ to sth** non essere abituato a qc

un·a·dul·ter·at·ed [ʌnəˈdʌltəreɪtɪd] *adj* (*fig: absolute*) puro; *activities* anti-americano

u·nan·i·mous [juːˈnænɪməs] *adj verdict* unanime; **be ~ on** essere unanimi su

u·nan·i·mous·ly [juːˈnænɪməslɪ] *adv vote, decide* all'unanimità

un·ap·proach·a·ble [ʌnəˈprəʊtʃəbl] *adj person* inavvicinabile

un·armed [ʌnˈɑːmd] *adj person* disarmato; **~ combat** combattimento senz'armi

un·as·sum·ing [ʌnəˈsjuːmɪŋ] *adj* senza pretese

un·at·tached [ʌnəˈtætʃt] *adj without a partner* libero

un·at·tend·ed [ʌnəˈtendɪd] *adj* incustodito; **leave sth ~** lasciare qc incustodito

un·au·thor·ized [ʌnˈɔːθəraɪzd] *adj* non autorizzato

un·a·void·a·ble [ʌnəˈvɔɪdəbl] *adj* inevitabile

un·a·void·a·bly [ʌnəˈvɔɪdəblɪ] *adv* inevitabilmente; **be ~ detained** essere trattenuto per cause di forza maggiore

un·a·ware [ʌnəˈweə(r)] *adj*: **be ~ of** non rendersi conto di

un·a·wares [ʌnəˈweəz] *adv*: **catch s.o. ~** prendere qu alla sprovvista

un·bal·anced [ʌnˈbælənst] *adj* non equilibrato; PSYCH squilibrato

un·bear·a·ble [ʌnˈbeərəbl] *adj* insopportabile

un·beat·a·ble [ʌnˈbiːtəbl] *adj team, quality* imbattibile

un·beat·en [ʌnˈbiːtn] *adj team* imbattuto

un·be·liev·a·ble [ʌnbɪˈliːvəbl] *adj* incredibile

un·bi·as(s)ed [ʌnˈbaɪəst] *adj* imparziale

un·block [ʌnˈblɒk] *v/t pipe* sbloccare

un·born [ʌnˈbɔːn] *adj* non ancora nato

un·break·a·ble [ʌnˈbreɪkəbl] *adj plates* infrangibile; *world record* imbattibile

un·but·ton [ʌnˈbʌtn] *v/t* sbottonare

un·called-for [ʌnˈkɔːldfɔː(r)] *adj* ingiustificato

un·can·ny [ʌnˈkænɪ] *adj resemblance, skill* sorprendente; (*worrying: feeling*) inquietante

un·ceas·ing [ʌnˈsiːsɪŋ] *adj* incessante

un·cer·tain [ʌnˈsɜːtn] *adj future, weather* incerto; *origins* dubbio; **what will happen? - it's ~** cosa succederà? – non si sa; **be ~ about sth** non essere certo su qc

un·cer·tain·ty [ʌnˈsɜːtntɪ] *of the future* incertezza *f*; **there is still ~ about …** ci sono ancora dubbi su …

un·checked [ʌnˈtʃekt] *adj*: **let sth go ~** non controllare qc

un·cle [ˈʌŋkl] zio *m*

un·com·for·ta·ble [ʌnˈkʌmftəbl] *adj* scomodo; **feel ~ about sth** sentirsi a disagio per qc; **I feel ~ with him** mi sento a disagio con lui

un·com·mon [ʌnˈkɒmən] *adj* raro; **it's not ~** non è raro

un·com·pro·mis·ing [ʌnˈkɒmprəmaɪzɪŋ] *adj* fermo; *in a negative way* intransigente

un·con·cerned [ʌnkənˈsɜːnd] *adj* indifferente; **be ~ about s.o. / sth** non darsi pensiero di qu / qc

un·con·di·tion·al [ʌnkənˈdɪʃnl] *adj* incondizionato

un·con·scious [ʌnˈkɒnʃəs] *adj* MED svenuto; PSYCH inconscio; **knock s.o. ~** stordire qu con un colpo; **be ~ of sth** (*not aware*) non rendersi conto di qc

un·con·trol·la·ble [ʌnkənˈtrəʊləbl] *adj anger, desire, children* incontrollabile

un·con·ven·tion·al [ʌnkənˈvenʃnl] *adj* poco convenzionale

un·co·op·er·a·tive [ʌnkəʊˈɒprətɪv] *adj* poco cooperativo

un·cork [ʌnˈkɔːk] *v/t bottle* stappare

U

un·cov·er [ʌnˈkʌvə(r)] v/t scoprire

un·dam·aged [ʌnˈdæmɪdʒd] adj intatto

un·daunt·ed [ʌnˈdɔːntɪd] adj: **carry on ~** continuare imperterrito

un·de·cid·ed [ʌndɪˈsaɪdɪd] adj question irrisolto; **be ~ about sth** essere indeciso su qc

un·de·ni·a·ble [ʌndɪˈnaɪəbl] adj innegabile

un·de·ni·a·bly [ʌndɪˈnaɪəblɪ] adv innegabilmente

un·der [ˈʌndə(r)] **1** prep (beneath) sotto; (less than) meno di; **it is ~ review / investigation** viene rivisto / indagato; **it is ~ construction** è in costruzione **2** adv (anaesthetized) sotto anestesia

un·der·age adj: **~ drinking** alcolismo m minorile

ˈun·der·arm adv throw sottinsù

ˈun·der·car·riage carrello m d'atterraggio

ˈun·der·cov·er adj agent segreto

un·der·cut v/t (pret & pp **-cut**) COM vendere a minor prezzo di

ˈun·der·dog: **they were the ~s** dovevano perdere

un·der·done adj meat al sangue; not cooked enough non cotto abbastanza

un·der·es·ti·mate v/t person, skills, task sottovalutare

un·der·ex·posed adj PHOT sottoesposto

un·der·fed adj malnutrito

un·der·go v/t (pret **-went**, pp **-gone**) surgery, treatment sottoporsi a; experiences vivere; **~ refurbishment** venire ristrutturato

un·der·grad·u·ate studente m, -essa f universitario, -a

ˈun·der·ground **1** adj passages etc sotterraneo; POL: resistance, newspaper etc clandestino **2** adv work sottoterra; **go ~** POL entrare in clandestinità **3** n RAIL metropolitana f

ˈun·der·growth sottobosco m

un·der·hand adj (devious) subdolo

un·der·lie v/t (pret **-lay**, pp **-lain**) (form basis of) essere alla base di

un·der·line v/t text sottolineare

un·der·ly·ing adj causes, problems di fondo

un·der·mine v/t s.o.'s position minare

un·der·neath [ʌndəˈniːθ] prep adv sotto **2** adv sotto

ˈun·der·pants npl mutande fpl da uomo

ˈun·der·pass for pedestrians sottopassaggio m

un·der·priv·i·leged [ʌndəˈprɪvɪlɪdʒd] adj svantaggiato

un·der·rate v/t sottovalutare

ˈun·der·shirt Am canottiera f

un·der·sized [ʌndəˈsaɪzd] adj troppo piccolo

ˈun·der·skirt sottogonna f

un·der·staffed [ʌndəˈstɑːft] adj a corto di personale

un·der·stand [ʌndəˈstænd] (pret & pp **-stood**) **1** v/t capire; **I ~ that you ...** mi risulta che tu ...; **they are understood to be in Canada** pare che siano in Canada **2** v/i capire

un·der·stand·able [ʌndəˈstændəbl] adj comprensibile

un·der·stand·a·bly [ʌndəˈstændəblɪ] adv comprensibilmente

un·der·stand·ing [ʌndəˈstændɪŋ] **1** adj person comprensivo **2** n of problem, situation comprensione f; (agreement) intesa f; **on the ~ that we agree a price** a patto che ci troviamo d'accordo sul prezzo

ˈun·der·state·ment understatement m inv

un·der·take v/t (pret **-took**, pp **-taken**) task intraprendere; **~ to do sth** impegnarsi a fare qc

ˈun·der·tak·er impresario m di pompe funebri

ˈun·der·tak·ing (enterprise) impresa f; (promise) promessa f

un·der·val·ue v/t sottovalutare

ˈun·der·wear biancheria f intima

ˈun·der·weight adj sottopeso

ˈun·der·world criminal malavita f inv; in mythology inferi mpl

un·der·write v/t (pret **-wrote**, pp **-written**) FIN sottoscrivere

un·de·served [ʌndɪ'zɜːvd] *adj* immeritato

un·de·sir·a·ble [ʌndɪ'zaɪərəbl] *adj features, changes* indesiderato; *person* poco raccomandabile; **~ el·e·ment** *person* persona indesiderabile

un·dis·put·ed [ʌndɪ'spjuːtɪd] *adj champion, leader* indiscusso

un·do [ʌn'duː] *v/t* (*pret* **-did,** *pp* **-done**) *parcel, wrapping* disfare; *shirt* sbottonare; *shoes, shoelaces* slacciare; *s.o. else's work* annullare, sciupare

un·doubt·ed·ly [ʌn'daʊtɪdlɪ] *adv* indubbiamente

un·dreamt-of [ʌn'dremtɒv] *adj riches* impensato

un·dress [ʌn'dres] **1** *v/t* spogliare; **get ~ed** spogliarsi **2** *v/i* spogliarsi

un·due [ʌn'djuː] *adj* (*excessive*) eccessivo

un·du·ly [ʌn'djuːlɪ] *adv punished, blamed* ingiustamente; (*excessively*) eccessivamente

un·earth [ʌn'ɜːθ] *v/t ancient remains* portare alla luce; (*fig: find*) scovare

un·earth·ly [ʌn'ɜːθlɪ] *adv:* **at this ~ hour** a quest'ora (impossibile)

un·eas·y [ʌn'iːzɪ] *adj relationship, peace* precario; **feel ~ about** non sentirsela di

un·eat·a·ble [ʌn'iːtəbl] *adj* immangiabile

un·e·co·nom·ic [ʌniːkə'nɒmɪk] *adj* poco redditizio

un·ed·u·cat·ed [ʌn'edjʊkeɪtɪd] *adj* senza istruzione

un·em·ployed [ʌnɪm'plɔɪd] *adj* disoccupato; **the ~** i disoccupati

un·em·ploy·ment [ʌnɪm'plɔɪmənt] disoccupazione *f;* **~ benefit** sussidio *m* di disoccupazione

un·end·ing [ʌn'endɪŋ] *adj* interminabile

un·e·qual [ʌn'iːkwəl] *adj* disuguale; **be ~ to the task** non essere all'altezza del compito

un·er·ring [ʌn'erɪŋ] *adj judgement, instinct* infallibile

un·e·ven [ʌn'iːvn] *adj quality* irregolare; *ground* accidentato

un·e·ven·ly [ʌn'iːvnlɪ] *adv distributed, applied* in modo irregolare; **~ matched** *of two contestants* mal assortiti

un·e·vent·ful [ʌnɪ'ventful] *adj day, journey* tranquillo

un·ex·pec·ted [ʌnɪk'spektɪd] *adj* inatteso

un·ex·pec·ted·ly [ʌnɪk'spektɪdlɪ] *adv* inaspettatamente

un·fair [ʌn'feə(r)] *adj* ingiusto

un·faith·ful [ʌn'feɪθful] *adj husband, wife* infedele; **be ~ to s.o.** essere infedele a qu

un·fa·mil·i·ar [ʌnfə'mɪljə(r)] *adj* sconosciuto; **be ~ with sth** non conoscere qc

un·fas·ten [ʌn'fɑːsn] *v/t belt* slacciare

un·fa·vo·ra·ble *Am,* **un·fa·vou·ra·ble** [ʌn'feɪvərəbl] *adj report, review* negativo; *weather conditions* sfavorevole

un·feel·ing [ʌn'fiːlɪŋ] *adj person* insensibile

un·fin·ished [ʌn'fɪnɪʃt] *adj job, letter, building* non terminato; *business* in sospeso; **leave sth ~** non terminare qc

un·fit [ʌn'fɪt] *adj physically* fuori forma; **be ~ to ...** *morally* non essere degno di ...; **~ to eat/drink** non commestibile/non potabile

un·flap·pa·ble [ʌn'flæpəbl] *adj* F calmo, imperturbabile

un·fold [ʌn'fəʊld] **1** *v/t sheets, letter* spiegare; *one's arms* aprire **2** *v/i of story etc* svolgersi; *of view* spiegarsi

un·fore·seen [ʌnfɔː'siːn] *adj* imprevisto

un·for·get·ta·ble [ʌnfə'getəbl] *adj* indimenticabile

un·for·giv·a·ble [ʌnfə'gɪvəbl] *adj* imperdonabile; **that was ~ (of you)** è una mancanza imperdonabile

un·for·tu·nate [ʌn'fɔːtʃənət] *adj people* sfortunato; *event, choice of words* infelice; **that's ~ for you** è spiacevole per lei

un·for·tu·nate·ly [ʌn'fɔːtʃənətlɪ] *adv* sfortunatamente

U

un·found·ed [ʌnˈfaʊndɪd] *adj* infondato

un·friend·ly [ʌnˈfrendlɪ] *adj* poco amichevole; *software* di non facile uso

un·fur·nished [ʌnˈfɜːnɪʃt] *adj* non ammobiliato

un·god·ly [ʌnˈgɒdlɪ] *adj*: **at this ~ hour** ad un'ora impossibile

un·grate·ful [ʌnˈgreɪtfʊl] *adj* ingrato

un·hap·pi·ness [ʌnˈhæpɪnɪs] infelicità *f inv*

un·hap·py [ʌnˈhæpɪ] *adj* infelice; *customers etc* non soddisfatto; **be ~ with the service / an explanation** non essere soddisfatto del servizio / della giustificazione

un·harmed [ʌnˈhɑːmd] *adj* illeso

un·health·y [ʌnˈhelθɪ] *adj person* malaticcio; *conditions* malsano; *food, atmosphere* poco sano; *economy* traballante; *balance sheet* in passivo

un·heard-of [ʌnˈhɜːdɒv] *adj* inaudito

un·hoped-for *adj* insperato

un·hurt [ʌnˈhɜːt] *adj* illeso

un·hy·gi·en·ic [ʌnhaɪˈdʒiːnɪk] *adj* non igienico

u·ni·fi·ca·tion [juːnɪfɪˈkeɪʃn] unificazione *f*

u·ni·form [ˈjuːnɪfɔːm] **1** *n of school pupil, air hostess* divisa *f*; *of soldier* divisa *f*, uniforme *f* **2** *adj* uniforme

u·ni·fy [ˈjuːnɪfaɪ] *v/t (pret & pp -ied)* unificare

u·ni·lat·e·ral [juːnɪˈlætrəl] *adj* unilaterale

un·i·ma·gi·na·ble [ʌnɪˈmædʒɪnəbl] *adj* inimmaginabile

un·i·ma·gi·na·tive [ʌnɪˈmædʒɪnətɪv] *adj* senza fantasia

un·im·por·tant [ʌnɪmˈpɔːtənt] *adj* senza importanza

un·in·hab·i·ta·ble [ʌnɪnˈhæbɪtəbl] *adj* inabitabile

un·in·hab·it·ed [ʌnɪnˈhæbɪtɪd] *adj building* disabitato; *region* deserto

un·in·jured [ʌnˈɪndʒəd] *adj* incolume

un·in·tel·li·gi·ble [ʌnɪnˈtelɪdʒəbl] *adj* incomprensibile

un·in·ten·tion·al [ʌnɪnˈtenʃnl] *adj* involontario

un·in·ten·tion·al·ly [ʌnɪnˈtenʃnlɪ] *adv* involontariamente

un·in·te·rest·ing [ʌnˈɪntrəstɪŋ] *adj* poco interessante

un·in·ter·rupt·ed [ʌnɪntəˈrʌptɪd] *adj sleep, work* ininterrotto

u·nion [ˈjuːnɪən] POL unione *f*; *(trade ~)* sindacato *m*

u·nique [juːˈniːk] *adj (also very good)* unico; **with his own ~ humour / style** con quel senso dell'umorismo / quello stile tutto suo

u·nit [ˈjuːnɪt] *of measurement* unità *f inv*; *(section: of machine, structure)* elemento *m*; *(part with separate function)* unità *f inv*; *(department)* reparto *m*; MIL unità *f inv*; **we must work together as a ~** dobbiamo lavorare insieme come squadra

u·nit 'cost COM costo *m* unitario

u·nite [juːˈnaɪt] **1** *v/t* unire **2** *v/i* unirsi

u·nit·ed [juːˈnaɪtɪd] *adj* unito

U·nit·ed 'King·dom Regno *m* Unito

U·nit·ed 'Na·tions Nazioni *fpl* Unite

U·nit·ed 'States (of A'mer·i·ca) Stati *mpl* Uniti (d'America)

u·ni·ty [ˈjuːnətɪ] unità *f inv*

u·ni·ver·sal [juːnɪˈvɜːsl] *adj* universale

u·ni·ver·sal·ly [juːnɪˈvɜːsəlɪ] *adv* universalmente

u·ni·verse [ˈjuːnɪvɜːs] universo *m*

u·ni·ver·si·ty [juːnɪˈvɜːsətɪ] **1** *n* università *f inv*; **he is at a ~** fa l'università **2** *adj* universitario

un·just [ʌnˈdʒʌst] *adj* ingiusto

un·kempt [ʌnˈkempt] *adj hair* scarmigliato; *appearance* trasandato

un·kind [ʌnˈkaɪnd] *adj* cattivo

un·known [ʌnˈnəʊn] **1** *adj* sconosciuto **2** *n*: **a journey into the ~** un viaggio nell'ignoto

un·lead·ed [ʌnˈledɪd] *adj* senza piombo

un·less [ənˈles] *conj* a meno che; **~ he pays us tomorrow** a meno che non ci paghi domani; **~ I am mistaken** se non mi sbaglio

un·like [ʌn'laɪk] *prep* diverso da; *it's ~ him to drink so much* non è da lui bere così tanto; *the photograph was completely ~ her* la foto non le somigliava per niente; *~ Tom, I ...* a differenza di Tom, io ...

un·like·ly [ʌn'laɪklɪ] *adj* improbabile; *he is ~ to win* è improbabile che vinca; *it is ~ that ...* è improbabile che ...

un·lim·it·ed [ʌn'lɪmɪtɪd] *adj* illimitato

un·load [ʌn'ləʊd] *v/t lorry, goods* scaricare

un·lock [ʌn'lɒk] *v/t* aprire (con la chiave)

un·luck·i·ly [ʌn'lʌkɪlɪ] *adv* sfortunatamente

un·luck·y [ʌn'lʌkɪ] *adj day, choice, person* sfortunato; *that was so ~ for you!* che sfortuna hai avuto!

un·made-up [ʌnmeɪd'ʌp] *adj face* acqua e sapone

un·manned [ʌn'mænd] *adj spacecraft* senza equipaggio

un·mar·ried [ʌn'mærɪd] *adj* non sposato

un·mis·ta·ka·ble [ʌnmɪ'steɪkəbl] *adj* inconfondibile

un·moved [ʌn'muːvd] *adj: be ~ emotionally* non essere commosso

un·mu·si·cal [ʌn'mjuːzɪkl] *adj person* non portato per la musica; *sounds* disarmonico

un·nat·u·ral [ʌn'næt̬ərl] *adj* non normale; *it's not ~ to be annoyed* è naturale non essere seccati

un·ne·ces·sa·ry [ʌn'nesəsrɪ] *adj* non necessario; *comment, violence* gratuito

un·nerv·ing [ʌn'nɜːvɪŋ] *adj* inquietante

un·no·ticed [ʌn'nəʊtɪst] *adj* inosservato; *it went ~* passare inosservato

un·ob·tain·a·ble [ʌnəb'teɪnəbl] *adj goods* introvabile; TELEC non ottenibile

un·ob·tru·sive [ʌnəb'truːsɪv] *adj* discreto

un·oc·cu·pied [ʌn'ɒkjʊpaɪd] *adj building, house* vuoto; *post* vacante;

room libero; *he doesn't like being ~ person* non gli piace stare senza far niente

un·of·fi·cial [ʌnə'fɪʃl] *adj world record, leader* non ufficiale; *announcement* ufficioso

un·of·fi·cial·ly [ʌnə'fɪʃlɪ] *adv* non ufficialmente

un·pack [ʌn'pæk] **1** *v/t* disfare **2** *v/i* disfare le valige

un·paid [ʌn'peɪd] *adj work* non retribuito

un·pleas·ant [ʌn'pleznt] *adj person, thing to say* antipatico; *smell, taste* sgradevole; *he was very ~ to her* si è comportato malissimo con lei

un·plug [ʌn'plʌg] *v/t* (*pret & pp -ged*) TV, *computer* staccare (la spina di)

un·pop·u·lar [ʌn'pɒpjʊlə(r)] *adj person* mal visto; *decision* impopolare; *an ~ teacher with the students* un insegnante che non ha la simpatia degli studenti

un·pre·ce·den·ted [ʌn'presɪdentɪd] *adj* senza precedenti; *it was ~ for a woman to be ...* è senza precedenti che una donna sia ...

un·pre·dict·a·ble [ʌnprɪ'dɪktəbl] *adj person, weather* imprevedibile

un·pre·ten·tious [ʌnprɪ'tenʃəs] *adj person, style, hotel* senza pretese

un·prin·ci·pled [ʌn'prɪnsɪpld] *adj* senza scrupoli

un·pro·duc·tive [ʌnprə'dʌktɪv] *adj meeting, discussion* sterile; *soil* improduttivo

un·pro·fes·sion·al [ʌnprə'feʃnl] *adj person, workmanship* poco professionale; *it is ~ not to ...* è mancanza di professionalità non ...; *~ behaviour of doctor etc* scorrettezza *f* professionale

un·prof·it·a·ble [ʌn'prɒfɪtəbl] *adj* non redditizio

un·pro·nounce·a·ble [ʌnprə'naʊnsəbl] *adj* impronunciabile

un·pro·tect·ed [ʌnprə'tektɪd] *adj borders* indifeso; *machine* non riparato; *~ sex* sesso non protetto

U

un·pro·voked [ʌnprə'vəʊkt] *adj*
attack non provocato

un·qual·i·fied [ʌn'kwɒlɪfaɪd] *adj*
worker, instructor non qualificato;
doctor, teacher non abilitato

un·ques·tio·na·bly [ʌn'kwestʃnəblɪ]
adv (*without doubt*) indiscutibilmente

un·ques·tio·ning [ʌn'kwestʃnɪŋ] *adj*
attitude, loyalty assoluto

un·rav·el [ʌn'rævl] *v/t* (*pret & pp*
-led, *Am* **-ed**) *string* dipanare; *knitting* disfare; *mystery, complexities*
risolvere

un·rea·da·ble [ʌn'riːdəbl] *adj book*
illeggibile

un·re·al [ʌn'rɪəl] *adj creature* irreale;
impression inverosimile; **this is ~!** F
incredibile!

un·rea·lis·tic [ʌnrɪə'lɪstɪk] *adj person* poco realista; *expectations* poco
realistico

un·rea·so·na·ble [ʌn'riːznəbl] *adj
person* irragionevole; *demand, expectation* eccessivo

un·re·lat·ed [ʌnrɪ'leɪtɪd] *adj issues*
senza (alcuna) attinenza; *people*
non imparentato

un·re·lent·ing [ʌnrɪ'lentɪŋ] *adj* incessante

un·rel·i·a·ble [ʌnrɪ'laɪəbl] *adj* poco
affidabile

un·rest [ʌn'rest] agitazione *f*

un·re·strained [ʌnrɪ'streɪnd] *adj
emotions* incontrollato, sfrenato

un·road·wor·thy [ʌn'rəʊdwɜːðɪ] *adj*
non sicuro

un·roll [ʌn'rəʊl] *v/t carpet, scroll*
srotolare

un·ru·ly [ʌn'ruːlɪ] *adj* indisciplinato

un·safe [ʌn'seɪf] *adj bridge, vehicle,
wiring, district* pericoloso; **~ to
drink / eat** non potabile / non commestibile; **it is ~ to ...** è rischioso ...

un·san·i·tary [ʌn'sænɪtrɪ] *adj
conditions, drains* antigienico

un·sat·is·fac·to·ry [ʌnsætɪs'fæktrɪ]
adj poco soddisfacente

un·sa·vou·ry [ʌn'seɪvrɪ] *adj person,
reputation*, poco raccomandabile;
district brutto

un·scathed [ʌn'skeɪðd] *adj* (*not injured*) incolume; (*not damaged*)
intatto

un·screw [ʌn'skruː] *v/t* svitare

un·scru·pu·lous [ʌn'skruːpjələs] *adj*
senza scrupoli

un·self·ish [ʌn'selfɪʃ] *adj person* altruista; *act, gesture, behaviour* altruistico

un·set·tled [ʌn'setld] *adj issue* irrisolto; *weather, stock market* instabile; *lifestyle* irrequieto; *bills* non pagato

un·shav·en [ʌn'ʃeɪvn] *adj* non rasato

un·sight·ly [ʌn'saɪtlɪ] *adj* brutto

un·skilled [ʌn'skɪld] *adj* non specializzato

un·so·cia·ble [ʌn'səʊʃəbl] *adj* poco
socievole

un·so·phis·ti·cat·ed [ʌnsə'fɪstɪkeɪ-
tɪd] *adj person, beliefs* semplice;
equipment rudimentale

un·sta·ble [ʌn'steɪbl] *adj person*
squilibrato; *structure, area, economy*
instabile

un·stead·y [ʌn'stedɪ] *adj ladder* malsicuro; **be ~ on one's feet** non reggersi bene sulle gambe

un·stint·ing [ʌn'stɪntɪŋ] *adj support*
incondizionato; *generosity* illimitato; *praise* senza riserve; **be ~ in
one's efforts** prodigarsi negli sforzi

un·stuck [ʌn'stʌk] *adj*: **come ~** *of
notice etc* staccarsi; F *of plan etc* fallire

un·suc·cess·ful [ʌnsək'sesful] *adj
writer etc* di scarso successo; *candidate, party* sconfitto; *attempt* fallito;
he tried but was ~ ha provato ma
non ha avuto fortuna

un·suc·cess·ful·ly [ʌnsək'sesflɪ]
adv try, apply senza successo

un·suit·a·ble [ʌn'suːtəbl] *adj partner,
clothing* inadatto; *thing to say,
language* inappropriato; **be ~ for**
non essere adatto per; **they're ~ for
each other** non sono fatti l'uno per
l'altra

un·sus·pect·ing [ʌnsəs'pektɪŋ] *adj*
ignaro

un·swerv·ing [ʌnˈswɜːvɪŋ] *adj* loyalty, devotion incrollabile

un·think·a·ble [ʌnˈθɪŋkəbl] *adj* impensabile

un·ti·dy [ʌnˈtaɪdɪ] *adj* room, desk, hair in disordine

un·tie [ʌnˈtaɪ] *v/t* knot disfare; *laces* slacciare; *prisoner* slegare

un·til [ənˈtɪl] **1** *prep* fino a; *I can wait ~ tomorrow* posso aspettare fino a domani; *from Monday ~ Friday* da lunedì a venerdì; *not ~ Friday* non prima di venerdì; *it won't be finished ~ July* non sarà finito prima di luglio **2** *conj* finché (non); *can you wait ~ I'm ready?* puoi aspettare che sia pronta?; *they won't do anything ~ you say so* non faranno niente finché non glielo dici tu

un·time·ly [ʌnˈtaɪmlɪ] *adj* death prematuro

un·tir·ing [ʌnˈtaɪrɪŋ] *adj* efforts instancabile

un·told [ʌnˈtəʊld] *adj* riches incalcolabile; *suffering* indescrivibile; *story* inedito

un·trans·lat·a·ble [ʌntrænsˈleɪtəbl] *adj* intraducibile

un·true [ʌnˈtruː] *adj* falso

un·used¹ [ʌnˈjuːzd] *adj* goods mai usato

un·used² [ʌnˈjuːst] *adj*: *be ~ to sth* non essere abituato a qc; *be ~ to doing sth* non essere abituato a fare qc

un·u·su·al [ʌnˈjuːʒʊəl] *adj* insolito; *it's ~ for them not to write* non è da loro non scrivere

un·u·su·al·ly [ʌnˈjuːʒʊəlɪ] *adv* insolitamente

un·veil [ʌnˈveɪl] *v/t* memorial, statue etc scoprire

un·well [ʌnˈwel] *adj*: *be / feel ~* stare / sentirsi male

un·will·ing [ʌnˈwɪlɪŋ] *adj*: *be ~ to do sth* non essere disposto a fare qc

un·will·ing·ly [ʌnˈwɪlɪŋlɪ] *adv* malvolentieri

un·wind [ʌnˈwaɪnd] (*pret & pp -wound*) **1** *v/t* tape svolgere **2** *v/i* of

tape svolgersi; *of story* dipanarsi; F (*relax*) rilassarsi

un·wise [ʌnˈwaɪz] *adj* avventato, imprudente

un·wrap [ʌnˈræp] *v/t* (*pret & pp -ped*) gift aprire, scartare

un·writ·ten [ʌnˈrɪtn] *adj* law, rule tacito

un·zip [ʌnˈzɪp] *v/t* (*pret & pp -ped*) dress etc aprire (la chiusura lampo di); COMPUT espandere

up [ʌp] **1** *adv*: ~ *in the sky / ~ on the roof* in alto nel cielo / sul tetto; ~ *here / there* quassù / lassù; *be ~* (*out of bed*) essere in piedi; *of sun* essere sorto; (*be built*) essere costruito; *of shelves* essere montato; *of prices, temperature* essere aumentato; (*have expired*) essere scaduto; *the road is ~* ci sono lavori in corso; *what's ~?* F che c'è?; ~ *to the year 1989* fino al 1989; *he came ~ to me* mi si è avvicinato; *what are you ~ to these days?* cosa fai di bello?; *what are those kids ~ to?* cosa stanno combinando i bambini?; *be ~ to something* (*bad*) stare architettando qualcosa; *I don't feel ~ to it* non me la sento; *it's ~ to you* dipende da te; *it is ~ to them to solve it* their duty sta a loro risolverlo; *be ~ and about* after illness essersi ristabilito **2** *prep*: *further ~ the mountain* più in alto sulla montagna; *he climbed ~ the tree* si è arrampicato sull'albero; *they ran ~ the street* corsero per strada; *the water goes ~ this pipe* l'acqua sale su per questo tubo; *we travelled ~ to Milan* siamo arrivati fino a Milano **3** *n*: ~*s and downs* alti e bassi *mpl*

'up·bring·ing educazione *f*

'up·com·ing *adj* (*forthcoming*) prossimo

up·date 1 *v/t* file, records aggiornare; ~ *s.o. on sth* mettere qu al corrente di qc **2** *n* (*'update*) of files, records aggiornamento *m*; software version upgrade *m inv*; *can you give me an ~ on the situation?* può darmi gli ultimi aggiornamenti sulla situazione?

up·grade *v/t computers, equipment etc* aggiornare; *memory* potenziare, aumentare; *(replace with new versions)*; *passenger* promuovere a una classe superiore; *product* migliorare; **I ~d the monitor** ho comprato un monitor migliore; **we could ~ you to a bigger room** possiamo offrirle una camera più grande

up·heav·al [ʌp'hiːvl] *emotional* sconvolgimento *m*; *physical* scombussolamento *m*; *political, social* sconvolgimento *m*

up·hill [ʌp'hɪl] **1** *adv*: *go / walk ~* salire **2** *adj* ['ʌphɪl] *climb* in salita; *struggle* arduo

up·hold *v/t (pret & pp -held) traditions, rights* sostenere; *(vindicate)* confermare

up·hol·ster·y [ʌp'həʊlstərɪ] *coverings of chairs* tappezzeria *f*; *padding of chairs* imbottitura *f*

'up·keep *of old buildings, parks etc* manutenzione *f*

'up·load *v/t* COMPUT caricare

up·mar·ket *adj restaurant, hotel* elegante; *product* di qualità

upon [ə'pɒn] *prep* → **on**

up·per ['ʌpə(r)] *adj part of sth* superiore; *deck, rooms* di sopra; *the earth's ~ atmosphere* la parte più alta dell'atmosfera terrestre; *the ~ Thames* l'alto Tamigi

up·per 'class *adj accent* aristocratico; *family* dell'alta borghesia

up·per 'clas·ses *npl* alta borghesia *f*

'up·right 1 *adj citizen* onesto **2** *adv sit* (ben) dritto

'up·right (pi·an·o) pianoforte *m* verticale

'up·ris·ing insurrezione *f*

'up·roar *loud noise* trambusto *m*; *(protest)* protesta *f*

up·set 1 *v/t (pret & pp -set) drink, glass* rovesciare; *(make sad)* fare stare male; *(distress)* sconvolgere; *(annoy)* seccare **2** *adj (sad)* triste; *(distressed)* sconvolto; *(annoyed)* seccato; *be / get ~* prendersela

(about per*); get ~ about sth* prendersela per qc; *have an ~ stomach* avere l'intestino in disordine

up·set·ting *adj*: *it's so ~ (for me)* mi fa stare male, mi turba

'up·shot *(result, outcome)* risultato *m*

'up·side vantaggio *m*

up·side 'down *adv* capovolto; *turn sth ~* capovolgere qc

up·stairs 1 *adv* di sopra **2** *adj room* al piano di sopra

'up·start novellino *m* che si comporta in modo arrogante

up·stream *adv* a monte; *follow the river ~* risalire la corrente

'up·take: *be quick on the ~* capire le cose al volo; *be slow on the ~* essere lento nel capire

up·tight *adj F (nervous)* nervoso; *(inhibited)* inibito

up-to-'date *adj information* aggiornato; *fashions* più attuale

'up turn *in economy* ripresa *f*

up·wards ['ʌpwədz] *adv fly, move* in su; *~ of 10,000* oltre 10.000

u·ra·ni·um [jʊ'reɪnɪəm] uranio *m*

ur·ban ['ɜːbən] *adj areas, population* urbano; *redevelopment* urbanistico

ur·ban·i·za·tion [ɜːbənər'zeɪʃn] urbanizzazione *f*

ur·chin ['ɜːtʃɪn] monello *m*, -a *f*

urge [ɜːdʒ] **1** *n (forte)* desiderio *m* **2** *v/t*: *~ s.o. to do sth* raccomandare (caldamente) a qu di fare qc

♦ **urge on** *v/t (encourage)* incitare

ur·gen·cy ['ɜːdʒənsɪ] urgenza *f*; *the ~ of the situation* la gravità della situazione

ur·gent ['ɜːdʒənt] *adj job, letter* urgente; *be in ~ need of sth* avere bisogno urgente di qc; *is it ~?* è urgente?

u·ri·nate ['jʊərɪneɪt] *v/i* orinare

u·rine ['jʊərɪn] urina *f*

urn [ɜːn] urna *f*

us [ʌs] *pron direct & indirect object* ci; *when two pronouns are used* ce; *after prep* noi; *they know ~* ci conoscono; *don't leave ~* non ci lasciare, non lasciarci; *she gave ~ the keys* ci ha dato le chiavi; *she gave them to ~*

ce le ha date; *that's for ~* quello è per noi; *who's that? – it's ~* chi è? – siamo noi

US [juːˈes] *abbr* (= *United States*) USA *mpl*

USA [juːesˈeɪ] *abbr* (= *United States of America*) USA *mpl*

us·a·ble [ˈjuːzəbl] *adj* utilizzabile

us·age [ˈjuːzɪdʒ] *linguistic* uso *m*

use [juːz] **1** *v/t* tool, skills, knowledge usare, utilizzare; word, s.o.'s car usare; *a lot of petrol* consumare; *pej: person* usare; *I could ~ a drink* F berrei volentieri qualcosa **2** *n* [juːs] uso *m*; *be of great ~* essere di grande aiuto a qu; *be of no ~ to s.o.* non essere d'aiuto a qu; *is that of any ~?* ti è d'aiuto?; *it's no ~* non c'è verso; *it's no ~ trying / waiting* non serve a niente provare / aspettare

♦ **use up** *v/t* finire

used¹ [juːzd] *adj* car etc usato

used² [juːst] *adj*: *be ~ to s.o. / sth* essere abituato a qu / qc; *get ~ to s.o. / sth* abituarsi a qu / qc; *be ~ to doing sth* essere abituato a fare qc; *get ~ to doing sth* abituarsi a fare qc

used³ [juːst]: *I ~ to know him* lo conoscevo; *I ~ to like him* un tempo mi piaceva; *I don't work there now, but I ~ to* ora non più, ma una volta lavoravo lì

use·ful [ˈjuːsful] *adj* information, gadget utile; person di grande aiuto

use·ful·ness [ˈjuːsfulnɪs] utilità *f inv*

use·less [ˈjuːslɪs] *adj* information, advice inutile; F person incapace; machine, computer inservibile; *feel ~* sentirsi inutile; *it's ~ trying there isn't any point* non serve a niente provare

us·er [ˈjuːzə(r)] *of product* utente *m/f*

us·er'friend·ly *adj* software, device di facile uso

ush·er [ˈʌʃə(r)] *n* (at wedding) persona *f* che accompagna gli invitati ai loro posti; in a cinema maschera *f*

♦ **usher in** *v/t* new era inaugurare

ush·er·ette [ʌʃəˈret] maschera *f*

u·su·al [ˈjuːʒʊəl] *adj* solito; *it's not ~ for this to happen* non succede quasi mai; *as ~* come al solito; *the ~, please* il solito, per favore

u·su·al·ly [ˈjuːʒʊəlɪ] *adv* di solito

u·ten·sil [juːˈtensl] utensile *m*

u·te·rus [ˈjuːtərəs] utero *m*

u·til·i·ty [juːˈtɪlətɪ] (usefulness) utilità *f inv*; *public utilities* servizi pubblici

u·til·ize [ˈjuːtɪlaɪz] *v/t* utilizzare

ut·most [ˈʌtməʊst] **1** *adj* massimo **2** *n*: *do one's ~* fare (tutto) il possibile

ut·ter [ˈʌtə(r)] **1** *adj* totale **2** *v/t* sound emettere; word proferire

ut·ter·ly [ˈʌtəlɪ] *adv* totalmente

U-turn [ˈjuːtɜːn] inversione *f* a U; *fig: in policy* dietro-front *m inv*

V

va·can·cy [ˈveɪkənsɪ] at work posto *m* vacante; in hotel camera *f* libera; *~ for a driver* as advert autista cercasi; *do you have any vacancies?* avete bisogno di personale?; *"no vacancies"* "completo"

va·cant [ˈveɪkənt] *adj* building vuoto; room libero; position vacante; look, expression assente

va·cant·ly [ˈveɪkəntlɪ] *adv* con sguardo assente

va·cate [veɪˈkeɪt] *v/t* room lasciar libero

va·ca·tion [veɪˈkeɪʃn] *Am* vacanza *f*;

be on ~ essere in vacanza

vac·cin·ate ['væksɪneɪt] *v/t* vaccinare; *be ~d against ...* essere vaccinato contro ...

vac·cin·a·tion [væksɪ'neɪʃn] vaccinazione *f*

vac·cine ['væksiːn] vaccino *m*

vac·u·um ['vækjʊəm] **1** *n also fig* vuoto *m* **2** *v/t floors* passare l'aspirapolvere su

'**vac·u·um clean·er** aspirapolvere *m inv*; '**vac·u·um flask** termos *m inv*; **vac·u·um-'packed** *adj* sottovuoto

vag·a·bond ['vægəbɒnd] *n* vagabondo *m*, -a *f*

va·gi·na [və'dʒaɪnə] vagina *f*

va·gi·nal ['vædʒɪnl] *adj* vaginale

va·grant ['veɪgrənt] *n* vagabondo *m*, -a *f*

vague [veɪg] *adj* vago; *I'm still ~ about it* non ho ancora le idee chiare al riguardo

vague·ly ['veɪglɪ] *adv* vagamente

vain [veɪn] **1** *adj person* vanitoso; *hope* vano **2** *n: in ~* invano; *their efforts were in ~* i loro sforzi sono stati inutili

val·en·tine ['væləntaɪn] (*card*) biglietto *m* per San Valentino; *Valentine's Day* San Valentino

val·et ['væleɪ] **1** *n person* cameriere *m* personale **2** *v/t* ['vælət]: *have one's car ~ed* far lavare la macchina dentro e fuori

'**val·et ser·vice** *for clothes* servizio *m* di lavanderia; *for cars* servizio *m* completo di lavaggio

val·iant ['væliənt] *adj* valoroso

val·iant·ly ['væliəntlɪ] *adv* valorosamente

val·id ['vælɪd] *adj* valido

val·i·date ['vælɪdeɪt] *v/t with official stamp* convalidare; *s.o.'s alibi* confermare

va·lid·i·ty [və'lɪdətɪ] *of reason, argument* validità *f inv*

val·ley ['vælɪ] valle *f*

val·u·a·ble ['væljʊəbl] **1** *adj* prezioso **2** *n: ~s* oggetti *mpl* di valore

val·u·a·tion [væljʊ'eɪʃn] valutazione

f; *at his ~* secondo la sua valutazione

val·ue ['væljuː] **1** *n* valore *m*; *be good ~* essere conveniente; *get ~ for money* fare un affare; *rise/fall in ~* aumentare/perdere di valore **2** *v/t s.o.'s friendship, one's freedom* tenere a; *I ~ your advice* ci tengo alla tua opinione; *have an object ~d* far valutare un oggetto

'**val·ue-ad·ded tax** imposta *f* sul valore aggiunto

valve [vælv] valvola *f*

van [væn] furgone *m*

van·dal ['vændl] vandalo *m*

van·dal·is·m ['vændəlɪzm] vandalismo *m*

van·dal·ize ['vændəlaɪz] *v/t* vandalizzare

van·guard ['vængɑːd] *n* avanguardia *f*; *be in the ~ of* essere all'avanguardia di

va·nil·la [və'nɪlə] **1** *n* vaniglia *f* **2** *adj ice cream* alla vaniglia; *flavour* di vaniglia

van·ish ['vænɪʃ] *v/i* sparire

van·i·ty ['vænətɪ] *of person* vanità *f inv*

'**van·i·ty case** beauty-case *m inv*

van·tage point ['vɑːntɪdʒ] *on hill etc* punto *m* d'osservazione

va·por *Am* → **vapour**

va·por·ize ['veɪpəraɪz] *v/t* vaporizzare

va·pour ['veɪpə(r)] vapore *m*

'**va·pour trail** *of aeroplane* scia *f*

var·i·a·ble ['veərɪəbl] **1** *adj* variabile **2** *n* MATH, COMPUT variabile *f*

var·i·ant ['veərɪənt] *n* variante *f*

var·i·a·tion [veərɪ'eɪʃn] variazione *f*

var·i·cose 'vein ['værɪkəʊs] vena *f* varicosa

var·ied ['veərɪd] *adj range, diet* vario; *life* movimentato

va·ri·e·ty [və'raɪətɪ] varietà *f inv*; (*type*) tipo *m*; THEA varietà *f inv*; *a ~ of things to do* varie cose da fare

var·i·ous ['veərɪəs] *adj* (*several*) vario; (*different*) diverso

var·nish ['vɑːnɪʃ] **1** *n for wood* vernice *f*; (*nail ~*) smalto *m* **2** *v/t wood*

V

var·nish verniciare; *nails* smaltare

var·y ['veərɪ] *v/t & v/i* (*pret & pp* **-ied**) variare **2** *v/t* variare

vase [vɑːz] vaso *m*

vas·ec·to·my [və'sektəmɪ] vasectomia *f*

vast [vɑːst] *adj desert, knowledge* vasto; *improvement* immenso

vast·ly [vɑːstlɪ] *adv* immensamente

VAT [viːeɪ'tiː, væt] *abbr* (= **value added tax**) IVA *f* (= imposta *f* sul valore aggiunto)

Vat·i·can ['vætɪkən]: **the ~** il Vaticano

vau·de·ville ['vɔːdvɪl] *Am* varietà *f inv*

vault¹ [vɒlt] *n in roof* volta *f; cellar* cantina *f; ~s of bank* caveau *m inv*

vault² [vɒlt] **1** *n* SP volteggio *m* **2** *v/t* saltare

VCR [viːsiːˈɑː(r)] *abbr* (= **video cassette recorder**) videoregistratore *m*

veal [viːl] (carne *f* di) vitello *m*

veer [vɪə(r)] *v/i of car* sterzare; *of wind, party* cambiare direzione

veg [vedʒ] F verdure *fpl*

ve·gan ['viːgn] **1** *n* vegetaliano *m*, -a *f* **2** *adj* vegetaliano

vege·ta·ble ['vedʒtəbl] verdura *f*

ve·ge·tar·i·an [vedʒɪˈteərɪən] **1** *n* vegetariano *m*, -a *f* **2** *adj* vegetariano

ve·ge·tar·i·an·ism [vedʒɪˈteərɪənɪzm] vegetarianismo *m*

veg·e·ta·tion [vedʒɪˈteɪʃn] vegetazione *f*

ve·he·mence ['viːəməns] veemenza *f*

ve·he·ment ['viːəmənt] *adj* veemente

ve·he·ment·ly ['viːəməntlɪ] *adv* veementemente

ve·hi·cle ['viːɪkl] veicolo *m; for information etc* mezzo *m*

veil [veɪl] **1** *n* velo *m* **2** *v/t* velare

vein [veɪn] ANAT vena *f; in this ~* *fig* su questo tono

Vel·cro® ['velkrəʊ] velcro *m*

ve·loc·i·ty [vɪˈlɒsətɪ] velocità *f inv*

vel·vet ['velvɪt] *n* velluto *m*

vel·vet·y ['velvɪtɪ] *adj* vellutato

ven·det·ta [venˈdetə] vendetta *f*

vend·ing ma·chine ['vendɪŋ] distributore *m* automatico

vend·or ['vendə(r)] LAW venditore *m*, -trice *f*

ve·neer [vəˈnɪə(r)] *on wood* impiallacciatura *f; of politeness etc* parvenza *f*

ven·e·ra·ble ['venərəbl] *adj* venerabile

ven·e·rate ['venəreɪt] *v/t* venerare

ven·e·ra·tion [venəˈreɪʃn] venerazione *f*

ve·ne·re·al dis·ease [vɪˈnɪərɪəl] malattia *f* venerea

Ve·ne·tian [vəˈniːʃn] **1** *adj* veneziano **2** *n* veneziano *m*, -a *f*

ve·ne·tian 'blind veneziana *f*

ven·geance ['vendʒəns] vendetta *f; with a ~* a più non posso

Ven·ice ['venɪs] Venezia *f*

ven·i·son ['venɪsn] (carne *f* di) cervo *m*

ven·om ['venəm] *also fig* veleno *m*

ven·om·ous ['venəməs] *also fig* velenoso

vent [vent] *n for air* presa *f* d'aria; *give ~ to feelings, emotions* dare sfogo a

ven·ti·late ['ventɪleɪt] *v/t room, building* ventilare

ven·ti·la·tion [ventɪˈleɪʃn] ventilazione *f*

ven·ti·la·tion shaft condotto *m* di aerazione

ven·ti·la·tor ['ventɪleɪtə(r)] ventilatore *m;* MED respiratore *m*

ven·tril·o·quist [venˈtrɪləkwɪst] ventriloquo *m*, -a *f*

ven·ture ['ventʃə(r)] **1** *n* impresa *f* **2** *v/i* avventurarsi

ven·ue ['venjuː] *for meeting, concert etc* luogo *m*

ve·ran·da [vəˈrændə] veranda *f*

verb [vɜːb] verbo *m*

verb·al ['vɜːbl] verbale

verb·al·ly ['vɜːbəlɪ] verbalmente

ver·ba·tim [vɜːˈbeɪtɪm] *adv* parola per parola

ver·dict ['vɜːdɪkt] LAW verdetto *m;* (*opinion, judgment*) giudizio *m; a ~*

of guilty / not guilty un verdetto di colpevolezza / non colpevolezza

verge [vɜːdʒ] *n of road* bordo *m*; **be on the ~ of ...** *ruin, collapse* essere sull'orlo di ...; **on the ~ of tears** sul punto di piangere

♦ **verge on** *v/t* rasentare

ver·i·fi·ca·tion [verɪfɪˈkeɪʃn] verifica *f*

ver·i·fy [ˈverɪfaɪ] *v/t (pret & pp -ied)* verificare

ver·mi·cel·li [vɜːmɪˈtʃelɪ] *nsg* vermicelli *mpl*

ver·min [ˈvɜːmɪn] *npl* animali *mpl* nocivi

ver·mouth [ˈvɜːməθ] vermut *m inv*

ver·nac·u·lar [vəˈnækjʊlə(r)] *n* vernacolo *m*

ver·sa·tile [ˈvɜːsətaɪl] *adj* versatile

ver·sa·til·i·ty [vɜːsəˈtɪlətɪ] versatilità *f inv*

verse [vɜːs] *poetry* poesia *f*; *part of poem, song* strofa *f*

versed [vɜːst] *adj:* **be well ~ in a subject** essere versato in una materia

ver·sion [ˈvɜːʃn] versione *f*

ver·sus [ˈvɜːsəs] *prep* SP, LAW contro

ver·te·bra [ˈvɜːtɪbrə] vertebra *f*

ver·te·brate [ˈvɜːtɪbreɪt] *n* vertebrato *m*

ver·ti·cal [ˈvɜːtɪkl] *adj* verticale

ver·ti·go [ˈvɜːtɪɡəʊ] vertigini *fpl*

ver·y [ˈverɪ] **1** *adv* molto; **was it cold? – not ~** faceva freddo? – non molto; **~ fast / easy** molto veloce / semplice, velocissimo / semplicissimo; **the ~ best** il meglio **2** *adj:* **at that ~ moment** in quel preciso momento; **that's the ~ thing I need** è proprio quello che mi serve; **the ~ thought** il solo pensiero; **right at the ~ top / bottom** proprio in cima / in fondo

ves·sel [ˈvesl] NAUT natante *m*

vest [vest] canottiera *f*; *Am (waistcoat)* gilè *m inv*

ves·tige [ˈvestɪdʒ] vestigio *m* (*pl* vestigia *f*); **not a ~ of truth** neanche un'ombra di verità

vet[1] [vet] *n (veterinary surgeon)* veterinario *m*, -a *f*

vet[2] [vet] *v/t (pret & pp -ted)* *applicants etc* passare al vaglio

vet·e·ran [ˈvetərən] **1** *n* veterano *m*, -a *f*; MIL reduce *m/f* **2** *adj* veterano

vet·e·ri·na·ry 'sur·geon [ˈvetərɪnərɪ] veterinario *m*, -a *f*

ve·to [ˈviːtəʊ] **1** *n* veto *m* **2** *v/t* mettere il veto a

vex [veks] *v/t (concern, worry)* preoccupare

vexed [vekst] *adj (worried)* preoccupato; **the ~ question of ...** la questione controversa di ...

vi·a [ˈvaɪə] *prep* attraverso

vi·a·ble [ˈvaɪəbl] *adj life form, company* in grado di sopravvivere; *alternative, plan* fattibile

vi·brate [vaɪˈbreɪt] *v/i* vibrare

vi·bra·tion [vaɪˈbreɪʃn] vibrazione *f*

vic·ar [ˈvɪkə(r)] parroco *m* anglicano

vic·ar·age [ˈvɪkərɪdʒ] casa *f* del parroco

vice[1] [vaɪs] *for holding* morsa *f*

vice[2] [vaɪs] vizio *m*

vice 'pres·i·dent vice-presidente *m*

'vice squad buoncostume *f*

vi·ce ver·sa [vaɪsˈvɜːsə] *adv* viceversa

vi·cin·i·ty [vɪˈsɪnətɪ] *n:* **in the ~ of ...** *the church etc* nelle vicinanze di ...; *£500 etc* approssimativamente ...

vi·cious [ˈvɪʃəs] *adj dog* feroce; *attack, criticism* brutale

vi·cious 'cir·cle circolo *m* vizioso

vi·cious·ly [ˈvɪʃəslɪ] *adv* brutalmente

vic·tim [ˈvɪktɪm] vittima *f*

vic·tim·ize [ˈvɪktɪmaɪz] *v/t* perseguitare

vic·tor [ˈvɪktə(r)] vincitore *m*, -trice *f*

vic·to·ri·ous [vɪkˈtɔːrɪəs] *adj army* vittorioso; *team* vincente

vic·to·ry [ˈvɪktərɪ] vittoria *f*; **win a ~ over ...** riportare una vittoria su ...

vid·e·o [ˈvɪdɪəʊ] **1** *n video m inv*; *tape* videocassetta *f*; *(VCR)* videoregistratore *m* **2** *v/t* registrare

'vid·e·o cam·e·ra videocamera *f*;
'vid·e·o cas·sette videocassetta *f*;
'vid·e·o con·fer·ence TELEC

videoconferenza *f*; **'vid·e·o game** videogame *m inv*; **'vid·e·o·phone** videotelefono *m*; **'vid·e·o re·cord·er** videoregistratore *m*; **'vid·e·o re·cord·ing** videoregistrazione *f*; **'vid·e·o·tape** videocassetta *f*; **'vid·e·o·tape li·bra·ry** videoteca *f*

vie [vaɪ] *v/i* competere

Vi·et·nam [vɪet'næm] Vietnam *m*

Vi·et·nam·ese [vɪetnə'miːz] **1** *adj* vietnamita *m/f* **2** *n* vietnamita *m/f*; *language* vietnamita *m*

view [vjuː] **1** *n* veduta *f*; *of situation* parere *m*; **in ~ of** considerato; **be on ~ of paintings** essere esposto; **with a ~ to** con l'intenzione di **2** *v/t events, situation* vedere; *TV programme* guardare; *house for sale* vedere **3** *v/i* (*watch TV*) guardare la TV

view·er ['vjuːə(r)] *TV* telespettatore *m*, -trice *f*

'view·find·er PHOT mirino *m*

'view·point punto *m* di vista

vig·or *Am* → **vigour**

vig·or·ous ['vɪɡərəs] *adj* vigoroso

vig·or·ous·ly ['vɪɡərəslɪ] *adv* vigorosamente

vig·our ['vɪɡə(r)] vigore *m*

vile [vaɪl] *adj* disgustoso

vil·la ['vɪlə] villa *f*

vil·lage ['vɪlɪdʒ] paese *m*

vil·lag·er ['vɪlɪdʒə(r)] abitante *m/f* (del paese)

vil·lain ['vɪlən] cattivo *m*, -a *f*; F *criminal* delinquente *m/f*

vin·di·cate ['vɪndɪkeɪt] *v/t show to be correct* confermare; *show to be innocent* scagionare; **I feel ~d by the report** il resoconto mi dà ragione

vin·dic·tive [vɪn'dɪktɪv] *adj* vendicativo

vin·dic·tive·ly [vɪn'dɪktɪvlɪ] *adv* vendicativamente

vine [vaɪn] (*grape~*) vite *f*; *climber* rampicante *m*

vin·e·gar ['vɪnɪɡə(r)] aceto *m*

'vine·yard ['vɪnjɑːd] vigneto *m*

vin·tage ['vɪntɪdʒ] **1** *n of wine* annata *f* **2** *adj* (*classic*) d'annata

vi·o·la [vɪ'əʊlə] MUS viola *f*

vi·o·late ['vaɪəleɪt] *v/t* violare

vi·o·la·tion [vaɪə'leɪʃn] violazione *f*

vi·o·lence ['vaɪələns] violenza *f*; **outbreaks of ~** episodi di violenza

vi·o·lent ['vaɪələnt] *adj* violento; **have a ~ temper** avere un carattere violento

vi·o·lent·ly ['vaɪələntlɪ] *adv* violentemente; **fall ~ in love** innamorarsi follemente

vi·o·let ['vaɪələt] *n colour* viola *m*; *plant* viola *f*

vi·o·lin [vaɪə'lɪn] violino *m*

vi·o·lin·ist [vaɪə'lɪnɪst] violinista *m/f*

VIP [viːaɪ'piː] *abbr* (= **very important person**) VIP *m/f*

vi·per ['vaɪpə(r)] *snake* vipera *f*

vi·ral ['vaɪrəl] *adj infection* virale

vir·gin ['vɜːdʒɪn] vergine *m/f*

vir·gin·i·ty [vɜː'dʒɪnətɪ] verginità *f inv*; **lose one's ~** perdere la verginità

Vir·go ['vɜːɡəʊ] ASTR Vergine *f*

vir·ile ['vɪraɪl] *adj* virile

vi·ril·i·ty [vɪ'rɪlətɪ] virilità *f inv*

vir·tu·al ['vɜːtjʊəl] *adj* effettivo; COMPUT virtuale

vir·tu·al·ly ['vɜːtjʊəlɪ] *adv* (*almost*) praticamente

vir·tu·al re·al·i·ty ['vɜːtjʊ] realtà *f* virtuale

vir·tue ['vɜːtjuː] virtù *f inv*; **in ~ of** in virtù di

vir·tu·o·so [vɜːtʊ'əʊzəʊ] MUS virtuoso *m*, -a *f*

vir·tu·ous ['vɜːtjʊəs] *adj* virtuoso

vir·u·lent ['vɪrʊlənt] *adj disease* virulento; *fig: attack, hatred* feroce

vi·rus ['vaɪərəs] MED, COMPUT virus *m inv*

vi·sa ['viːzə] visto *m*

vise [vaɪz] *Am* → **vice¹**

vis·i·bil·i·ty [vɪzə'bɪlətɪ] visibilità *f inv*

vis·i·ble ['vɪzəbl] *adj object, difference* visibile; *anger* evidente; **not ~ to the naked eye** invisibile ad occhio nudo

vis·i·bly ['vɪzəblɪ] *adv different* visibilmente; **he was ~ moved** era visibilmente emozionato

vi·sion ['vɪʒn] (*eyesight*) vista *f*; REL *etc* visione *f*

vis·it ['vɪzɪt] **1** *n* visita *f*; **pay a ~ to**

V

the doctor / dentist andare dal medico / dentista; *pay s.o. a ~* fare una visita a qu **2** *v/t person* andare a trovare; *place, country, city* visitare; *doctor, dentist* andare da

vis·it·ing card ['vɪzɪtɪŋ] biglietto *m* da visita

'vis·it·ing hours *npl at hospital* orario *m* delle visite

vis·it·or ['vɪzɪtə(r)] *(guest)* ospite *m*; *to museum etc* visitatore *m*, -trice *f*; *(tourist)* turista *m/f*

vi·sor ['vaɪzə(r)] visiera *f*

vis·u·al ['vɪzjʊəl] *adj organs, memory* visivo; *arts* figurativo

vis·u·al 'aid sussidio *m* visivo

vis·u·al dis'play u·nit videoterminale *m*

vis·u·al·ize ['vɪzjʊəlaɪz] *v/t* immaginare; *(foresee)* prevedere

vis·u·al·ly im'paired ['vɪzjʊəlɪ] *adj* videoleso

vi·tal ['vaɪtl] *adj (essential)* essenziale; *it is ~ that ...* è essenziale che ...

vi·tal·i·ty [vaɪ'tælətɪ] *of person, city etc* vitalità *f inv*

vi·tal·ly ['vaɪtəlɪ] *adv*: *~ important* di vitale importanza

vi·tal 'or·gans *npl* organi *mpl* vitali

vi·tal sta·tis·tics *npl of woman* misure *fpl*

vit·a·min ['vɪtəmɪn] vitamina *f*

'vit·a·min pill (confetto *m* di) vitamina *f*

vit·ri·ol·ic [vɪtrɪ'ɒlɪk] *adj* caustico

vi·va·cious [vɪ'veɪʃəs] *adj* vivace

vi·vac·i·ty [vɪ'væsətɪ] vivacità *f inv*

viv·id ['vɪvɪd] *adj* vivido

viv·id·ly ['vɪvɪdlɪ] in modo vivido

V-neck ['viːnek] maglione *m* con scollo a V

vo·cab·u·la·ry [və'kæbjʊlərɪ] vocabolario *m*; *list of words* glossario *m*

vo·cal ['vəʊkl] *adj to do with the voice* vocale; *expressing opinions* eloquente; *become ~* cominciare a farsi sentire

'vo·cal cords *npl* corde *fpl* vocali

'vo·cal group MUS gruppo *m* vocale

vo·cal·ist ['vəʊkəlɪst] MUS cantante *m/f*

vo·ca·tion [və'keɪʃn] *(calling)* vocazione *f* (*for* a); *(profession)* professione *f*

vo·ca·tion·al [və'keɪʃnl] *adj guidance* professionale

vod·ka ['vɒdkə] vodka *f inv*

vogue [vəʊg] *n* moda *f*; *be in ~* essere in voga

voice [vɔɪs] **1** *n* voce *f* **2** *v/t opinions* esprimere

'voice mail segreteria *f* telefonica

void [vɔɪd] **1** *n* vuoto *m* **2** *adj*: *~ of* privo di

vol·a·tile ['vɒlətaɪl] *adj personality, moods* volubile

vol·ca·no [vɒl'keɪnəʊ] vulcano *m*

vol·ley ['vɒlɪ] *n of shots* raffica *f*; *in tennis* volée *f inv*

'vol·ley·ball pallavolo *f*

volt [vəʊlt] volt *m inv*

volt·age ['vəʊltɪdʒ] voltaggio *m*; *high ~* alta tensione *f*

vol·ume ['vɒljuːm] volume *m*

vol·ume con'trol volume *m*

vol·un·tar·i·ly [vɒlən'teərɪlɪ] *adv* spontaneamente

vol·un·ta·ry ['vɒləntərɪ] *adj helper* volontario; *~ work* volontariato

vol·un·teer [vɒlən'tɪə(r)] **1** *n* volontario *m*, -a *f* **2** *v/i* offrirsi volontario

vo·lup·tu·ous [və'lʌptjʊəs] *adj woman, figure* giunonico

vom·it ['vɒmɪt] **1** *n* vomito *m* **2** *v/i* vomitare

♦ vomit up *v/t* vomitare

vo·ra·cious [və'reɪʃəs] *adj appetite* vorace

vo·ra·cious·ly [və'reɪʃəslɪ] *eat* voracemente; *fig: read* avidamente

vote [vəʊt] **1** *n* voto *m*; *right to vote* diritto *m* di voto **2** *v/i* POL votare; *~ for / against s.o. / sth* votare a favore di / contro qu / qc **3** *v/t*: *they ~d him President* l'hanno eletto presidente; *I ~ we stay behind* propongo di rimanere

♦ vote in *v/t new member* eleggere

♦ vote on *v/t issue* mettere ai voti

♦ vote out *v/t of office* respingere

vot·er ['vəʊtə(r)] POL elettore *m*, -trice *f*

vot·ing ['vəʊtɪŋ] POL votazione f

'vot·ing booth cabina f elettorale

♦ **vouch for** [vaʊtʃ] v/t truth of sth garantire; person garantire per

vouch·er ['vaʊtʃə(r)] buono m

vow [vaʊ] **1** n voto m **2** v/t: ~ **to do sth** giurare di fare qc

vow·el [vaʊl] vocale f

voy·age ['vɔɪɪdʒ] n by sea, in space viaggio m

V-sign ['viːsaɪn] for victory segno m di vittoria; **give s.o. the ~** mandare qu a quel paese

vul·gar ['vʌlgə(r)] adj person, language volgare

vul·ne·ra·ble ['vʌlnərəbl] adj vulnerabile

vul·ture ['vʌltʃə(r)] avvoltoio m

W

wad [wɒd] n of cotton wool batuffolo m; of paper fascio m; of banknotes mazzetta f

wad·dle ['wɒdl] v/i camminare ondeggiando

wade [weɪd] v/i guadare

♦ **wade through** v/t: **I've still got this lot to wade through** devo ancora leggermi tutto questo

wa·fer ['weɪfə(r)] biscuit cialda f; REL ostia f

'wa·fer-thin adj sottilissimo

waf·fle¹ ['wɒfl] n (to eat) tipo m di cialda

waf·fle² ['wɒfl] v/i parlare a vuoto

wag [wæg] (pret & pp **-ged**) **1** v/t finger scuotere; **the dog ~ged its tail** il cane scodinzolò **2** v/i: **the dog's tail was ~ging** il cane scodinzolava

wage¹ [weɪdʒ] v/t: ~ **war against** also fig fare la guerra a

wage² [weɪdʒ] n paga f; ~**s** paga f

'wage earn·er salariato m, -a f;
'wage freeze blocco m dei salari;
'wage ne·go·ti·a·tions npl rivendicazioni fpl salariali; **'wage pack·et** fig busta f paga

wag·gle ['wægl] v/t ears, loose screw, tooth etc far muovere; ~ **one's hips** ancheggiare

wag·gon Am, **wag·on** ['wægən] RAIL carro m merci; **be on the ~** F non bere alcolici

wail [weɪl] **1** n of person gemito m; of baby vagito m; of siren ululato m **2** v/i of person gemere; of baby vagire; of siren ululare

waist [weɪst] vita f

'waist·coat gilè m inv

'waist·line vita f

wait [weɪt] **1** n attesa f **2** v/i aspettare; **we'll ~ until he's ready** aspetteremo che sia pronto; **I can't ~ to ...** non vedo l'ora di ... **2** v/t meal ritardare

♦ **wait for** v/t aspettare; **wait for me!** aspettami!

♦ **wait on** v/t (serve) servire

♦ **wait up** v/i restare alzato ad aspettare

wait·er ['weɪtə(r)] cameriere m; ~**!** cameriere!

wait·ing ['weɪtɪŋ] n attesa f; **no ~ sign** divieto m di sosta

'wait·ing list lista f d'attesa

'wait·ing room sala f d'attesa

wait·ress ['weɪtrɪs] cameriera f

waive [weɪv] v/t (renounce) rinunciare a; (dispense with) fare al meno di, lasciar perdere

wake¹ [weɪk] (pret **woke**, pp **woken**) **1** v/i: ~ (**up**) svegliarsi **2** v/t svegliare

wake² [weɪk] n of ship scia f; **in the ~ of** fig a seguito di; **follow in the ~ of** seguire le tracce di

'wake-up call sveglia f (telefonica)

Wales [weɪlz] Galles *m*

walk [wɔːk] **1** *n* camminata *f*; *it's a long ~ to the office* è una bella camminata fino all'ufficio; *it's a short ~ to the office* l'ufficio è a due passi; *go for a ~* fare due passi **2** *v/i* camminare; *as opposed to taking the car, bus etc* andare a piedi; (*hike*) passeggiare; *learn to ~* imparare a camminare; *we ~ed for hours* abbiamo camminato per ore; *she ~ed over to the window* andò alla finestra **3** *v/t dog* portare fuori; *I'll ~ you home* ti accompagno a casa; *~ the streets* (*walk around*) girare in lungo e in largo

♦ **walk out** *v/i of husband etc, from theatre* andarsene; (*go on strike*) scendere in sciopero

♦ **walk out on** *v/t spouse, family* abbandonare

'**walk·a·bout** bagno *m* di folla; *go ~ F of monarch, politician* fare un bagno di folla

walk·er ['wɔːkə(r)] (*hiker*) escursionista *m/f*; *for baby* girello *m*; *for old person* deambulatore *m*; *be a slow/fast ~* avere il passo lento/spedito

walk·ie-'talk·ie [wɔːkɪ'tɔːkɪ] walkie-talkie *m inv*

walk·ing ['wɔːkɪŋ] *n as opposed to driving* camminare *m*; (*hiking*) escursionismo *m*; *it's within ~ distance* ci si arriva a piedi

'**walk·ing stick** bastone *m* da passeggio

'**walk·ing tour** escursionismo *m*

'**Walk·man**® walkman *m inv*; '**walk·out** *strike* sciopero *m* selvaggio; '**walk·over** (*easy win*) vittoria *f* facile

wall [wɔːl] *external* muro *m*; *internal* parete *f*; *fig: of silence etc* muro *m*; *go to the ~ of company* andare in rovina; *~s of a city* mura *fpl*; *drive s.o. up the ~* F far diventare matto qu

wal·let ['wɒlɪt] portafoglio *m*

wal·lop ['wɒləp] **1** *n* F *blow* colpo *m* **2** *v/t* F colpire; *opponent* stracciare F

'**wall·pa·per 1** *n* tappezzeria *f*, carta *f* da parati **2** *v/t* tappezzare

wall-to-'wall *adj*: *~ carpet* moquette *f*

wal·nut ['wɔːlnʌt] noce *f*

waltz [wɔːlts] *n* valzer *m inv*

wan [wɒn] *adj face* pallido

wan·der ['wɒndə(r)] *v/i* (*roam*) gironzolare; (*stray*) allontanarsi; *my attention began to ~* mi sono distratto

♦ **wander around** *v/i* girare

wane [weɪn] *v/i of interest, enthusiasm* calare

wan·gle ['wæŋgl] *v/t* F rimediare F

want [wɒnt] **1** *n: for ~ of* per mancanza di **2** *v/t* volere; (*need*) avere bisogno di; *~ to do sth* volere fare qc; *I ~ to stay here* voglio stare qui; *do you ~ to come too? – no, I don't ~ to* vuoi venire anche tu? – no, grazie; *you can have whatever you ~* puoi avere tutto ciò che vuoi; *it's not what I ~ed* non è quello che volevo; *she ~s you to go back* vuole che torni indietro; *he ~s a haircut* dovrebbe tagliarsi i capelli **3** *v/i: ~ for nothing* non mancare di niente

'**want ad** annuncio *m* economico

want·ed ['wɒntɪd] *adj by police* ricercato

want·ing ['wɒntɪŋ] *adj: be ~ in* mancare di

wan·ton ['wɒntən] *adj cruelty, neglect* gratuito

war [wɔː(r)] *n* guerra *f*; *fig* lotta *f*; *be at ~* essere in guerra

war·ble ['wɔːbl] *v/i of bird* gorgheggiare

ward [wɔːd] *n in hospital* corsia *f*; *child* minore *m* sotto tutela

♦ **ward off** *v/t blow* parare; *attacker* respingere; *cold* combattere

war·den ['wɔːdn] (*traffic ~*) vigile *m* urbano; *of hostel* direttore *m*, -trice *f*; *of nature reserve* guardiano *m*, -a *f*; *Am: of prison* agente *m/f* di custodia

ward·er ['wɔːdə(r)] agente *m/f* di custodia

'**ward·robe** *for clothes* armadio *m*; *clothes* guardaroba *m*

ware·house ['weəhaʊs] magazzino *m*

'war·fare guerra *f*

'war·head testata *f*

war·i·ly ['weərɪlɪ] *adv* con aria guardinga

warm [wɔ:m] **1** *adj* caldo; *welcome, smile* caloroso; *it's ~ of weather* fa caldo; *it's ~ in here* qui c'è caldo; *are you ~ enough?* ti fa freddo? **2** *v/t:* → **warm up**

♦ **warm up 1** *v/t* scaldare **2** *v/i* scaldarsi; *of athlete etc* fare riscaldamento

warm·heart·ed ['wɔ:mhɑ:tɪd] *adj* cordiale

warm·ly ['wɔ:mlɪ] *adv dressed* con abiti pesanti; *welcome, smile* calorosamente

warmth [wɔ:mθ] calore *m*; *of welcome, smile* calorosità *f inv*

'warm-up SP riscaldamento *m*

warn [wɔ:n] *v/t* avvertire

warn·ing ['wɔ:nɪŋ] *n* avvertimento *m*; *without ~* senza preavviso

warp [wɔ:p] **1** *v/t wood* deformare; *character* segnare **2** *v/i of wood* deformarsi

warped [wɔ:pt] *adj fig* contorto

'war·plane aereo *m* militare

war·rant ['wɒrənt] **1** *n* mandato *m* **2** *v/t (deserve, call for)* giustificare

war·ran·ty ['wɒrəntɪ] *(guarantee)* garanzia *f*; *be under ~* essere in garanzia

war·ri·or ['wɒrɪə(r)] guerriero *m*, -a *f*

'war·ship nave *f* da guerra

wart [wɔ:t] verruca *f*

'war·time tempo *m* di guerra

war·y ['weərɪ] *adj* guardingo; *be ~ of* diffidare di

was [wɒz] *pret* → **be**

wash [wɒʃ] **1** *n:* **have a ~** darsi una lavata; *that skirt needs a ~* quella gonna va lavata **2** *v/t* lavare; *~ one's hands / hair* lavarsi le mani / i capelli **3** *v/i* lavarsi

♦ **wash up** *v/i Br (wash the dishes)* lavare i piatti

wash·a·ble ['wɒʃəbl] *adj* lavabile

'wash·ba·sin, 'wash·bowl lavandino *m*

washed out [wɒʃt'aʊt] *adj* sfinito

wash·er ['wɒʃə(r)] *for tap etc* guarnizione *f*; → **washing machine**

wash·ing ['wɒʃɪŋ] *washed clothes* bucato *m*; *clothes to be washed* biancheria *f* da lavare; *do the ~* fare il bucato

wash·ing ma·chine lavatrice *f*

'wash·ing pow·der detersivo *m* per bucato

wash·ing-'up: *do the ~* lavare i piatti

wash·ing-'up liq·uid detersivo *m* per i piatti

wasp [wɒsp] vespa *f*

waste [weɪst] **1** *n* spreco *m*; *from industrial process* rifiuti *mpl*; *it's a ~ of time / money* è tempo sprecato / sono soldi sprecati **2** *adj material* di scarto **3** *v/t* sprecare

♦ **waste away** *v/i* deperire

'waste dis·pos·al (unit) tritarifiuti *m inv*

waste·ful ['weɪstfʊl] *adj person* sprecone; *methods, processes* dispendioso

'waste·land distesa *f* desolata; **waste·'pa·per** cartaccia *f*; **waste·pa·per 'bas·ket** cestino *m* della cartaccia; **'waste prod·uct** scorie *fpl* industriali

watch [wɒtʃ] **1** *n timepiece* orologio *m*; MIL guardia *f*; *keep ~* stare all'erta **2** *v/t film, TV* guardare; *(spy on)* sorvegliare; *(look after)* tenere d'occhio **3** *v/i* guardare

♦ **watch for** *v/t* aspettare

♦ **watch out** *v/i* fare attenzione; *watch out!* attento!

♦ **watch out for** *v/t* fare attenzione a

'watch·dog *fig* comitato *m* di controllo

watch·ful ['wɒtʃfʊl] *adj* vigile

'watch·mak·er orologiaio *m*, -a *f*

wa·ter ['wɔ:tə(r)] **1** *n* acqua *f*; *~s* NAUT acque (territoriali) **2** *v/t plant* annaffiare **3** *v/i of eyes* lacrimare; *my mouth is ~ing* ho l'acquolina in bocca

W

♦ **water down** v/t drink diluire

wa·ter can·non idrante m; **'wa·ter·col·or** Am, **'wa·ter·col·our** n acquerello m; **'wa·ter·cress** crescione m

wa·tered 'down ['wɔːtəd] adj fig edulcorato

'wa·ter·fall cascata f

wa·ter·ing can ['wɔːtərɪŋ] annaffiatoio m

'wa·ter·ing hole hum bar m inv

'wa·ter lev·el livello m delle acque; **'wa·ter lil·y** ninfea f; **wa·ter·logged** ['wɔːtəlɒgd] adj allagato; **'wa·ter main** conduttura f dell'acqua; **'wa·ter mark** filigrana f; **'wa·ter mel·on** anguria f, cocomero m; **'wa·ter pol·lu·tion** inquinamento m dell'acqua; **'wa·ter·proof** adj impermeabile

'wa·ter·shed fig svolta f; TV ora f dopo la quale sono ammessi programmi per un pubblico adulto; **'wa·ter·side** n: **at the** ~ sulla riva; **'wa·ter·ski·ing** sci m inv nautico; **'wa·ter·tight** adj compartment stagno; fig inattaccabile; **'wa·ter·way** corso m d'acqua navigabile; **'wa·ter·wings** npl braccioli mpl; **'wa·ter·works**: **turn on the** ~ F piangere

wa·ter·y ['wɔːtəri] adj acquoso

watt [wɒt] watt m inv

wave[1] [weɪv] n in sea onda f

wave[2] [weɪv] **1** n of hand saluto m (con la mano) **2** v/i with hand salutare (con la mano); ~ **to s.o.** salutare qu (con la mano) **3** v/t flag etc sventolare

'wave·length RAD lunghezza f d'onda; **be on the same** ~ fig essere sulla stessa lunghezza d'onda

wa·ver ['weɪvə(r)] v/i vacillare

wav·y ['weɪvi] adj hair, line ondulato

wax [wæks] n for floor, furniture cera f; in ear cerume m

way [weɪ] **1** n (method, manner) modo m; (manner) maniera f; (route) strada f; **this** ~ (like this) così; (in this direction) da questa parte; **by the** ~ (incidentally) a proposito; **by** ~ **of** (via) passando per; (in the form

of) come; **in a** ~ (in certain respects) in un certo senso; **be under** ~ essere in corso; **give** ~ MOT dare la precedenza; (collapse) crollare; **X has given** ~ **to Y** (been replaced by) Y ha preso il posto di X; **have one's (own)** ~ averla vinta; **OK, we'll do it your** ~ OK, faremo come dici tu; **lead the** ~ also fig fare strada; **lose one's** ~ smarrirsi; **be in the** ~ (be an obstruction) essere d'intralcio; **it's on the** ~ **to the station** è sulla strada della stazione; **I was on my** ~ **to the station** stavo andando alla stazione; **no** ~! neanche per sogno!; **there's no** ~ **he can do it** è impossibile che ce la faccia **2** adv F (much); **it's** ~ **too soon to decide** è veramente troppo presto per decidere; **they are** ~ **behind with their work** sono molto indietro con il lavoro

way 'in entrata f; **way of 'life** stile m di vita; **way 'out** n uscita f; fig: from situation via f d'uscita

we [wiː] pron noi; ~'**re the best** siamo i migliori; **they're going, but** ~'**re not** loro vanno, noi no

weak [wiːk] adj physically, morally debole; tea, coffee leggero

weak·en ['wiːkn] **1** v/t indebolire **2** v/i indebolirsi

weak·ling ['wiːklɪŋ] morally smidollato m, -a f; physically mingherlino m, -a f

weak·ness ['wiːknɪs] debolezza f; **have a** ~ **for sth** (liking) avere un debole per qc

wealth [welθ] ricchezza f; **a** ~ **of** una grande abbondanza di

wealth·y ['welθi] adj ricco

weap·on ['wepən] arma f

wear [weə(r)] **1** n: ~ **(and tear)** usura f; **clothes for everyday** ~ vestiti per tutti i giorni; **clothes for evening** ~ abiti da sera **2** v/t (pret **wore**, pp **worn**) (have on) indossare; (damage) logorare **3** v/i (pret **wore**, pp **worn**) (wear out) logorarsi; (last) durare

♦ **wear away 1** v/i consumarsi **2** v/t consumare

♦ **wear down** v/t resistance fiaccare

♦ **wear off** v/i of effect, feeling svanire

♦ **wear out 1** v/t (tire) estenuare; shoes consumare **2** v/i of shoes, carpet consumarsi

wea·ri·ly ['wɪərɪlɪ] adv stancamente

wear·ing ['weərɪŋ] adj (tiring) stancante

wear·y ['wɪərɪ] adj stanco

weath·er ['weðə(r)] **1** n tempo m; **be feeling under the ~** sentirsi poco bene **2** v/t crisis superare

'**weath·er-beat·en** adj segnato; '**weath·er fore·cast** previsioni fpl del tempo; '**weath·er·man** meteorologo m

weave [wiːv] **1** v/t (pret **wove**, pp **woven**) cloth tessere; basket intrecciare **2** v/i (move) zigzagare

web [web] of spider ragnatela f; **the Web** COMPUT il web m inv, la Rete f inv

webbed 'feet piedi mpl palmati

'**web page** pagina f web

'**web site** sito m web

wed·ding ['wedɪŋ] matrimonio m

'**wed·ding an·ni·ver·sa·ry** anniversario m di matrimonio; '**wed·ding cake** torta f nuziale; '**wed·ding day** giorno m del matrimonio; '**wed·ding dress** abito m or vestito m da sposa; '**wed·ding ring** fede f

wedge [wedʒ] **1** n to hold sth in place zeppa f; of cheese etc fetta f **2** v/t: ~ **open** tenere aperto

Wed·nes·day ['wenzdeɪ] mercoledì m inv

wee [wiː] adj F piccolo; **a ~ bit** un pochino

weed [wiːd] **1** n erbaccia f **2** v/t diserbare

♦ **weed out** v/t (remove) eliminare

'**weed-kill·er** diserbante m

weed·y ['wiːdɪ] adj F mingherlino

week [wiːk] settimana f; **a ~ tomorrow** una settimana a domani

'**week·day** giorno m feriale

week'end fine m settimana, weekend m inv; **at or Am on the ~** durante il fine settimana

week·ly ['wiːklɪ] **1** adj settimanale

2 n magazine settimanale m **3** adv settimanalmente

weep [wiːp] v/i (pret & pp **wept**) piangere

weep·y ['wiːpɪ] adj: **be ~** essere piagnucoloso

wee-wee 1 n F pipì f inv **2**; **do a ~** fare la pipì **2** v/i F fare la pipì

weigh [weɪ] v/t & v/i pesare

♦ **weigh down** v/t: **be weighed down with** with bags curvarsi sotto il peso di; with worries essere oppresso da

♦ **weigh on** v/t preoccupare

♦ **weigh up** v/t (assess) valutare

weight [weɪt] of person, object peso m; **put on / lose ~** ingrassare / dimagrire

♦ **weight down** v/t fermare con pesi

weight·less·ness ['weɪtləsnəs] assenza f di peso

'**weight·lift·er** pesista m/f

'**weight·lift·ing** sollevamento m pesi

weight·y ['weɪtɪ] adj fig: important importante

weir [wɪə(r)] chiusa f

weird [wɪəd] adj strano

weird·ly ['wɪədlɪ] adv stranamente

weird·o ['wɪədəʊ] n F pazzoide m/f

wel·come ['welkəm] **1** adj benvenuto; **make s.o. ~** accogliere bene qu; **it makes a ~ change** è un gradito cambiamento; **you're ~!** prego!; **you're ~ to try some** serviti pure **2** n also fig accoglienza f; fig: to news, proposal accoglienza f **3** v/t guests etc accogliere; fig: decision etc rallegrarsi di; **she ~s a challenge** apprezza le sfide

weld [weld] v/t saldare

weld·er ['weldə(r)] saldatore m, -trice f

wel·fare ['welfeə(r)] bene m inv

wel·fare 'state stato m sociale; '**wel·fare work** assistenza f sociale; '**wel·fare work·er** assistente m/f sociale

well¹ [wel] n for water, oil pozzo m

well² [wel] **1** adv bene; **~ done!** bravo!; **as ~** (too) anche; **as ~ as** in addition to oltre a; **it's just as ~ you**

told me hai fatto bene a dirmelo; *very ~ acknowledging an order* benissimo; *when you don't agree with sth but are doing it anyway* va bene; *~, ~! surprise* bene, bene!; *~ ... uncertainty, thinking* beh ... **2** *adj:* *be ~* stare bene; *feel ~* sentirsi bene; *get ~ soon!* guarisci presto!

well-'bal·anced *adj* person, meal equilibrato; *meal, diet* equilibrato; **well-be'haved** *adj* educato; **well-'be·ing** benessere *m*; **well-'built** *adj* ben fatto; *euph (fat)* robusto; **well-'done** *adj* meat ben cotto; **well-'dressed** *adj* ben vestito; **well-'earned** *adj* meritato; **well-'heeled** *adj* F danaroso

wel·lies ['weliz] *npl* F → **wellingtons**

well-in'formed *adj* ben informato

wel·ling·tons ['weliŋtənz] *npl* stivali *mpl* di gomma

well-'known *adj* famoso; **well-'made** *adj* ben fatto; **well-'man·nered** *adj* ben educato; **well-'mean·ing** *adj* spinto da buone intenzioni; **well-'off** *adj* benestante; **well-'paid** *adj* ben pagato; **well-'read** *adj* colto; **well-'timed** *adj* tempestivo; **well-to-'do** *adj* abbiente; **well-'worn** *adj* liso

Welsh [welʃ] **1** *adj* gallese **2** *n* language gallese *m*; *the ~* i gallesi

went [went] *pret* → **go**

wept [wept] *pret & pp* → **weep**

were [wɜː(r)] *pret pl* → **be**

west [west] **1** *n* ovest *m*, occidente *m*; *the West* POL l'Occidente; *western part of a country* parte *f* occidentale del paese **2** *adj* occidentale **3** *adv* verso ovest; *~ of* a ovest di

west·er·ly ['westəlɪ] *adj* occidentale; *in a ~ direction* verso ovest

west·ern ['westən] **1** *adj* occidentale; *Western* occidentale **2** *n* (*film*) western *m inv*

West·ern·er ['westənə(r)] *n* occidentale *m/f*

west·ern·ized ['westənaɪzd] *adj* occidentalizzato

west·ward ['westwəd] *adv* verso ovest

wet [wet] *adj* bagnato; (*rainy*) piovoso; *~ paint as sign* vernice fresca; *be ~ through* essere fradicio

wet 'blan·ket F guastafeste *m/f inv*

'wet suit *for diving* muta f

whack [wæk] **1** *n* F (*blow*) colpo *m*; F (*share*) parte *f* **2** *v/t* F colpire

whacked [wækt] *adj* F stanco morto

whack·ing ['wækɪŋ] *adj* F enorme

whale [weɪl] balena *f*

whal·ing ['weɪlɪŋ] caccia *f* alla balena

wharf [wɔːf] *n* banchina *f*

what [wɒt] **1** *pron* (che) cosa; *~ is that?* (che) cos'è?; *~ is it?* (*what do you want*) (che) cosa c'è?; *~?* cosa?; *astonishment* (che) cosa?; *it's not ~ I meant* non è ciò che volevo dire; *~ about some dinner?* e se mangiassimo qualcosa?; *~ about heading home?* e se ce ne andassimo a casa?; *~ is the date today?* quanti ne abbiamo oggi?; *~ for?* (*why*) perché?; *so ~?* e allora? **2** *adj* che *inv*, quale; *~ colour is the car?* di che colore è la macchina?; *~ university are you at?* in quale università studi? **3** *adv:* *~ a brilliant idea!* che bella idea!

what·ev·er [wɒt'evə(r)] **1** *pron*; *I'll do ~ you want* farò (tutto) quello che vuoi; *~ I do, it'll be a probem* qualsiasi cosa faccia, ci saranno problemi; *~ the season regardless of* in qualunque stagione; *~ people say* qualunque cosa dica la gente; *~ gave you that idea?* cosa mai te lo ha fatto pensare? **2** *adj* qualunque; *you have no reason ~ to worry* non hai nessun motivo di preoccuparti

wheat [wiːt] grano *m*, frumento *m*

whee·dle ['wiːdl] *v/t* F: *~ sth out of s.o.* ottenere qc da qu con lusinghe

wheel [wiːl] **1** *n* ruota *f*; (*steering ~*) volante *m* **2** *v/t* bicycle spingere **3** *v/i* *of birds* roteare

♦ **wheel around** *v/i* voltarsi

'wheel·bar·row carriola *f*; **'wheel·chair** sedia *f* a rotelle; **'wheel**

W

clamp ceppo *m* bloccaruote

wheeze [wiːz] *v/i* ansimare

when [wen] *adv conj* quando **2** *conj* quando; *~ I was a child* quand'ero bambino

when·ev·er [wen'evə(r)] *adv* (*each time*) ogni volta che; *regardless of when* in qualunque momento

where [weə(r)] **1** *adv* dove **2** *conj* dove; *this is ~ I used to live* io abitavo qui

where·a·bouts [weərə'baʊts] **1** *adv* dove **2** *npl*: *know s.o.'s ~* sapere dove si trova qu

where·as [weər'æz] mentre

wher·ev·er [weər'evə(r)] **1** *conj* dovunque; *~ you go* dovunque tu vada **2** *adv* dove; *~ can he be?* dove sarà mai?

whet [wet] *v/t v/t* (*pret & pp -ted*) *appetite* stuzzicare

wheth·er [ˈweðə(r)] *pron* se

which [wɪtʃ] **1** *adj* quale; *~ one is yours?* qual è il tuo? **2** *pron interrogative* quale; *relative che*; *on / in* ~ su / in cui; *take one, it doesn't matter ~* prendine uno, non importa quale

which·ev·er [wɪtʃ'evə(r)] **1** *adj* qualunque **2** *pron* quello che *m*, quella che *f*; *~ of the methods* qualunque metodo

whiff [wɪf] *unpleasant* zaffata *f*; *catch a ~ of* sentire

while [waɪl] **1** *conj* mentre; (*although*) benché **2** *n*: *a long ~ ago* molto tempo fa; *wait a long ~* aspettare molto *o* lungo; *for a ~* per un po'; *in a ~* fra poco; *I'll wait a ~ longer* aspetto un altro po'

♦ **while away** *v/t* passare

whim [wɪm] capriccio *m*

whim·per [ˈwɪmpə(r)] **1** *n of person, baby* gemito *m*; *of animal* mugolio *m* **2** *v/i of person, baby* gemere; *of animal* mugolare

whine [waɪn] *v/i of dog* guaire; F (*complain*) piagnucolare

whip [wɪp] **1** *n* frusta *f* **2** *v/t* (*pret & pp -ped*) (*beat*) sbattere; *cream* montare; F (*defeat*) stracciare F

♦ **whip out** *v/t* F tirar fuori (fulmineamente)

♦ **whip up** *v/t* (*arouse*) sobillare; F *meal* improvvisare

whipped cream [wɪpt] panna *f* montata

whip·ping [ˈwɪpɪŋ] (*beating*) bastonata *f*; F (*defeat*) batosta *f*

'whip·ping cream panna *f* da montare

'whip·round F colletta *f*; *have a ~* fare una colletta

whirl [wɜːl] **1** *n*: *my mind is in a ~* mi gira la testa **2** *v/i of blades etc* roteare; *of leaves* volteggiare; *of person* girarsi

'whirl·pool *in river* mulinello *m*; *for relaxation* vasca *f* per idromassaggio

whirr [wɜː(r)] *v/i* ronzare

whisk [wɪsk] **1** *n* frusta *f*; *mechanical* frullino *m* **2** *v/t eggs* frullare

♦ **whisk away** *v/t* togliere in fretta

whis·kers [ˈwɪskəz] *npl of man* basette *fpl*; *of animal* baffi *mpl*

whis·ky whisky *m inv*

whis·per [ˈwɪspə(r)] **1** *n* bisbiglio *m*; (*rumour*) voce *f* **2** *v/t & v/i* bisbigliare

whis·tle [ˈwɪsl] **1** *n sound* fischio *m*; *device* fischietto *m* **2** *v/i* fischiare **3** *v/t* fischiettare

whis·tle-blow·er [ˈwɪslbləʊə(r)] F *persona f che denuncia irregolarità all'interno della propria azienda*

white [waɪt] **1** *n colour* bianco *m*; *of egg* albume *m*, bianco *m* F; *person* bianco *m*, -a *f* **2** *adj* bianco; *person* bianco; *go ~* sbiancare (in viso)

white 'Christ·mas natale *m* con la neve; **white 'cof·fee** Br caffè *m inv* con latte *o* panna; **white-col·lar 'work·er** impiegato *m*, -a *f*; **'White House** Casa *f* Bianca; **white 'lie** bugia *f* innocente; **white 'meat** carne *f* bianca; **'white-wash 1** *n* calce *f*; *fig* copertura *f* **2** *v/t* imbiancare (con calce); **white 'wine** vino *m* bianco

Whit·sun [ˈwɪtsn] Pentecoste *f*

whit·tle [ˈwɪtl] *v/t wood* intagliare

♦ **whittle down** *v/t* ridurre

whiz(z) [wɪz] *n*: **be a ~ at** F essere un genio in
♦ **whizz by, whizz past** *v/i of time, car* sfrecciare

'whizz-kid F mago *m*, -a f F

who [huː] *pron interrogative* chi; *relative* che; **the man ~ I was talking to** l'uomo con cui parlavo; **I don't know ~ to believe** non so a chi credere

who·dun(n)·it [huːˈdʌnɪt] giallo *m*

who·ev·er [huːˈevə(r)] *pron* chiunque; *(interrogative)* chi mai; **~ can that be?** chi sarà mai?

whole [həʊl] **1** *adj*: **the ~ town** tutta la città; **two ~ hours / days** ben due ore / giorni; **a ~ chicken** un pollo intero; **he drank / ate the ~ lot** ha bevuto / mangiato tutto; **it's a ~ lot easier / better** è molto più facile / meglio **2** *n* tutto *m*; **the ~ of the United States** tutti gli Stati Uniti; **on the ~** nel complesso

whole-heart·ed [həʊlˈhɑːtɪd] *adj* senza riserve; **whole-heart·ed·ly** [həʊlˈhɑːtɪdlɪ] *adv* senza riserve; **whole-meal 'bread** pane *m* integrale; **'whole·sale 1** *adj* all'ingrosso; *fig* in massa **2** *adv* all'ingrosso; **whole·sal·er** [ˈhəʊlseɪlə(r)] grossista *m/f*; **whole·some** [ˈhəʊlsəm] *adj* sano

whol·ly [ˈhəʊlɪ] *adv* completamente

whol·ly owned 'sub·sid·i·ar·y consociata *f* interamente controllata

whom [huːm] *pron fml* chi; **to / for ~** a cui

whoop·ing cough [ˈhuːpɪŋ] pertosse *f*

whop·ping [ˈwɒpɪŋ] *adj* F enorme

whore [hɔː(r)] *n* puttana *f*

whose [huːz] **1** *pron interrogative* di chi; *relative* il / la cui; **~ is this?** di chi è questo?; **a man ~ wife ...** un uomo la cui moglie ...; **a country ~ economy is booming** un paese dall'economia fiorente **2** *adj* di chi; **~ bike is that?** di chi è quella bici?; **~ car are we taking?** che macchina prendiamo?

why [waɪ] *adv* perché; **that's ~** ecco perché; **~ not?** perché no?; **the reason ~ he left** il motivo per cui se ne è andato

wick·ed [ˈwɪkɪd] *adj* (*evil*) malvagio; (*mischievous*) malizioso

wick·er [ˈwɪkə(r)] *adj* di vimini

wick·er 'chair poltrona *f* di vimini

wick·et [ˈwɪkɪt] porta *f*

wide [waɪd] *adj* largo; *experience* vasto; *range* ampio; **be 12 metres ~** essere largo 12 metri

wide-a'wake *adj* sveglio

wide·ly [ˈwaɪdlɪ] *adv used, known* largamente; **it is ~ believed that ...** è una credenza diffusa che ...

wid·en [ˈwaɪdn] **1** *v/t* allargare **2** *v/i* allargarsi

wide-'o·pen *adj* spalancato; **wide-'rang·ing** *adj* di largo respiro; **'wide·spread** *adj* diffuso

wid·ow [ˈwɪdəʊ] *n* vedova *f*

wid·ow·er [ˈwɪdəʊə(r)] vedovo *m*

width [wɪdθ] larghezza *f*; *of fabric* altezza *f*

wield [wiːld] *v/t weapon* brandire; *power* esercitare

wife [waɪf] (*pl* **wives** [waɪvz]) moglie *f*

wig [wɪg] parrucca *f*

wig·gle [ˈwɪgl] *v/t*: **~ one's hips** ancheggiare; *loose screw etc* muovere

wild [waɪld] **1** *adj animal, flowers* selvatico; *teenager, party* scatenato; (*crazy: scheme*) folle; *applause* fragoroso; **be ~ about ...** (*keen on*) andare pazzo per ...; **go ~** impazzire; (*become angry*) andare su tutte le furie; **run ~** *of children* scatenarsi; *of plants* crescere senza controllo **2** *n*: **the ~s** le zone sperdute

wil·der·ness [ˈwɪldənɪs] *empty place* deserto *m*; *fig*: *garden etc* giungla *f*

'wild·fire: **spread like ~** allargarsi a macchia d'olio; **'wild·goose chase** ricerca *f* inutile; **'wild·life** fauna *f*; **~ programme** programma *m* sulla natura

wild·ly [ˈwaɪldlɪ] *adv* F terribilmente

wil·ful [ˈwɪlfʊl] *adj person* ostinato; *action* intenzionale; *action*

will¹ [wɪl] *n* LAW testamento *m*

will² [wɪl] *n* (*willpower*) volontà *f inv*

will³ [wɪl] *v/aux*: **I ~ let you know tomorrow** ti farò sapere entro domani; **~ you be there?** ci sarai?; **I won't be back** non tornerò; **you ~ call me, won't you?** mi chiamerai, vero?; **I'll pay for this ~ no you won't** questo lo pago io – no, lascia stare; **the car won't start** la macchina non parte; **~ you tell her that …?** dille che …; **~ you have some more tea?** vuoi dell'altro tè?; **~ you stop that!** smettila!

will-ful *Am* → **wilful**

will-ing [wɪl] *adj* disponibile; **are you ~ to pay more?** sei disposto a pagare di più?; **he was not ~ to accept** non ha voluto accettare

will-ing-ly [wɪlɪŋlɪ] *adv* volentieri

will-ing-ness [wɪlɪŋnɪs] disponibilità *f inv*

wil-low [wɪləʊ] salice *m*

will-pow-er [wɪl] F forza *f* di volontà

wil-ly-nil-ly [wɪlɪnɪlɪ] *adv* (*at random*) a casaccio

wilt [wɪlt] *v/i of plant* appassire

wi-ly [waɪlɪ] *adj* astuto

wimp [wɪmp] F pappamolle *m/f*

win [wɪn] **1** *n* vittoria *f* **2** *v/t & v/i* (*pret & pp* **won**) vincere

♦ **win back** *v/t* riconquistare

wince [wɪns] *v/i* fare una smorfia

wind¹ [wɪnd] **1** *n* vento *m*; (*flatulence*) aria *f*; **get ~ of …** venire a sapere … **2** *v/t* **~ s.o.** togliere il fiato a qu

wind² [waɪnd] (*pret & pp* **wound**) **1** *v/i of path* snodarsi; *of plant* avvolgersi **2** *v/t* avvolgere

♦ **wind down 1** *v/i*: **the party began to wind down** la gente cominciò ad andar via dalla festa **2** *v/t car window* abbassare; *business* chiudere gradualmente

♦ **wind up 1** *v/t clock* caricare; *car window* tirar su; *speech, presentation* concludere; *business, affairs, company* chiudere **2** *v/i*: **wind up in hospital** finire in ospedale

wind-bag [wɪnd] F trombone *m*

wind-fall *fig* colpo *m* di fortuna

wind-ing [waɪndɪŋ] *adj* tortuoso

wind in-stru-ment strumento *m* a fiato

wind-mill mulino *m*

win-dow [wɪndəʊ] *of house* finestra *f*; *of shop* vetrina *f*; *of car, train* finestrino *m*; COMPUT finestra *f*; **in the ~** *of shop* in vetrina

win-dow box fioriera *f*; **win-dow clean-er** lavavetri *m/f inv*; **win-dow-pane** vetro *m* (della finestra); **win-dow seat** *on plane, train* posto *m* di finestrino; **window-shop** *v/i* (*pret & pp* **-ped**): **go ~ping** guardare le vetrine; **win-dow-sill** [wɪndəʊsɪl]

wind-screen parabrezza *m inv*; **wind-screen wip-er** tergicristallo *m*; **wind-shield** *Am* parabrezza *m inv* **wind-surf-er** *person* windsurfista *m/f*; *board* windsurf *m inv*; **wind-surf-ing** windsurf *m inv*

wind-y [wɪndɪ] *adj weather, day* ventoso; **it's getting ~** si sta alzando il vento

wine [waɪn] vino *m*

wine bar enoteca *f*, bar *m inv*; **wine cel-lar** cantina *f*; **wine glass** bicchiere *m* da vino; **wine list** lista *f* dei vini; **wine mak-er** viticoltore *m*, -trice *f*; **wine mer-chant** *company* azienda *f* vinicola; *individual* vinaio *m*, -a *f*

wing [wɪŋ] *n also* SP ala *f*

wing-span apertura *f* alare

wink [wɪŋk] **1** *n* occhiolino *m*; **I didn't sleep a ~** F non ho chiuso occhio **2** *v/i of person* strizzare gli occhi; **~ at s.o.** fare l'occhiolino a qu

win-ner [wɪnə(r)] vincitore *m*, -trice *f*

win-ning [wɪnɪŋ] *adj* vincente

win-ning post traguardo *m*

win-nings [wɪnɪŋz] *npl* vincita *fsg*

win-ter [wɪntə(r)] *n* inverno *m*

win-ter sports *npl* sport *m inv* invernali

win-try [wɪntrɪ] *adj* invernale

wipe [waɪp] *v/t* (*dry*) asciugare; (*clean*) pulire; *tape* cancellare

♦ **wipe out** v/t (*kill, destroy*) distruggere; *debt* estinguere

wip·er ['waɪpə(r)] → **windscreen wiper**

wire ['waɪə(r)] **1** adj metallico **2** n fil m di ferro; ELEC filo m elettrico

wire·less ['waɪələs] radio f inv

wire 'net·ting rete f metallica

wir·ing ['waɪərɪŋ] n ELEC impianto m elettrico

wir·y ['waɪərɪ] adj person dal fisico asciutto

wis·dom ['wɪzdəm] saggezza f

'wis·dom tooth dente m del giudizio

wise [waɪz] adj saggio

'wise·crack n F spiritosaggine f

'wise guy pej spiritoso m

wise·ly ['waɪzlɪ] adv act saggiamente

wish [wɪʃ] **1** n desiderio m; **make a ~** esprimere un desiderio; *against his family's ~es* contro il volere della famiglia; *best ~es for birthday etc* tanti auguri; *as greetings* cordiali saluti **2** v/t volere; *I ~ that he'd stop* vorrei che la smettesse; *~ s.o. well* fare tanti auguri a qu; *I ~ed him good luck* gli ho augurato buona fortuna **3** v/i: *wish for* desiderare

'wish·bone forcella f (di pollo)

wish·ful 'think·ing ['wɪʃful] illusione f

wish·y-wash·y ['wɪʃɪwɒʃɪ] adj person insulso; colour slavato

wisp [wɪsp] of hair ciocca f; of smoke filo m

wist·ful ['wɪstful] adj malinconico

wist·ful·ly ['wɪstfəlɪ] adv malinconicamente

wit [wɪt] (*humour*) spirito m; person persona f di spirito; *be at one's ~s' end* non sapere più che fare; *keep one's ~s about one* non perdere la testa; *be scared out of one's ~s* essere spaventato a morte

witch [wɪtʃ] strega f

'witch-hunt fig caccia f alle streghe

with [wɪð] prep con; (*proximity*) con; (*agency*) con; (*cause*) di; (*possession*) con; *shiver ~ fear* tremare di paura; *a girl ~ blue eyes* una ragazza dagli o con gli occhi azzurri; *~ a*

smile / a wave con un sorriso / un gesto della mano; *are you ~ me?* (*do you understand*) mi segui?; *~ no money* senza soldi

withdraw [wɪð'drɔː] (*pret -drew, pp -drawn*) **1** v/t complaint, application, troops ritirare; *money from bank* prelevare; *troops ritirare* **2** v/i ritirarsi; ritirarsi

with·draw·al [wɪð'drɔːəl] of complaint, application, troops ritiro m; of money prelievo m; of troops ritiro m; from drugs crisi f inv di astinenza

with'draw·al symp·toms npl sindrome f da astinenza

with·drawn [wɪð'drɔːn] adj person chiuso

with·er ['wɪðə(r)] v/i seccare

with·hold v/t (pret & pp -held) information nascondere; consent rifiutare; payment trattenere

with·in prep (inside) dentro; in expressions of time nel giro di, entro; in expressions of distance a meno di; *is it ~ walking distance?* ci si arriva a piedi?; *we kept ~ the budget* abbiamo rispettato il budget; *it is not ~ my power* non rientra nelle mie competenze; *~ reach* a portata di mano

with·out prep senza; *~ you / him* senza (di) te / lui; *~ looking / asking* senza guardare / chiedere; *~ his seeing* senza che lo vedesse

with·stand v/t (pret & pp -stood) resistere a

wit·ness ['wɪtnɪs] **1** n testimone m/f; testimone m/f **2** v/t accident, crime essere testimone di; signature attestare l'autenticità di

'wit·ness box banco m dei testimoni

wit·ti·cis·m ['wɪtɪsɪzm] arguzia f

wit·ty ['wɪtɪ] adj arguto

wob·ble ['wɒbl] v/i of person vacillare; of object traballare

wob·bly ['wɒblɪ] adj person vacillante; object traballante; voice, hand tremante

wok [wɒk] wok m inv

woke [wəʊk] pret → **wake**

wok·en ['wəʊkn] *pp* → **wake**

wolf [wʊlf] **1** *n* (*pl* **wolves** [wʊlvz]) *animal* lupo *m*; (*fig: womanizer*) donnaiolo *m* **2** *v/t*: ~ (**down**) divorare

'**wolf whis·tle** *n* fischio *m*

'**wolf-whis·tle** *v/i*: ~ **at s.o.** fischiare dietro a qu

wom·an ['wʊmən] (*pl* **women** ['wɪmɪn]) donna *f*

wom·an 'doc·tor dottoressa *f*

wom·an 'driv·er autista *f*

wom·an·iz·er ['wʊmənaɪzə(r)] donnaiolo *m*

wom·an 'priest donna *f* sacerdote

womb [wuːm] utero *m*

wom·en [wɪmɪn] *pl* → **woman**

women's lib [wɪmɪnz'lɪb] movimento *m* di liberazione della donna

women's lib·ber [wɪmɪnz'lɪbə(r)] femminista *f*

won [wʌn] *pret & pp* → **win**

won·der ['wʌndə(r)] **1** *n* (*amazement*) stupore *m*, meraviglia *f*; *of science etc* meraviglia *f*; *no* ~*!* non mi stupisce!; *it's a* ~ *that* ... è incredibile che ... **2** *v/i* pensare **3** *v/t* domandarsi; *I* ~ *if you could help* mi chiedevo se potessi aiutarmi

won·der·ful ['wʌndəful] *adj* stupendo

won·der·ful·ly ['wʌndəflɪ] *adv* (*extremely*) estremamente

won't [wəʊnt] → **will not**

wood [wʊd] legno *m*; *for fire* legna *f*; (*forest*) bosco *m*

wood·ed ['wʊdɪd] *adj* boscoso

wood·en ['wʊdn] *adj* made of wood di legno

wood·peck·er ['wʊdpekə(r)] picchio *m*; '**wood·wind** MUS fiati *mpl*; '**wood·work** *parts made of wood* strutture *fpl* in legno; *activity* lavorazione *f* del legno

wool [wʊl] lana *f*

wool·en *Am*, **wool·len** ['wʊlən] **1** *adj* di lana **2** *n* indumento *m* di lana

word [wɜːd] **1** *n* parola *f*; (*news*) notizie *fpl*; (*promise*) parola *f*; *is there any* ~ *from* ...? ci sono notizie da ...?; *you have my* ~ hai la mia

parola; *have* ~*s* (*argue*) litigare; *have a* ~ *with s.o.* parlare con qu **2** *v/t article, letter* formulare

word·ing ['wɜːdɪŋ] formulazione *f*

word 'pro·cess·ing trattamento *m* testi

word 'pro·ces·sor *software* word processor *m inv*

wore [wɔː(r)] *pret* → **wear**

work [wɜːk] **1** *n* lavoro *m*; *out of* ~ disoccupato; *be at* ~ essere al lavoro; *I go to* ~ *by bus* vado a lavorare in autobus **2** *v/i of person* lavorare; *study* studiare; *of machine*, (*succeed*) funzionare; (*succeed*) funzionare; *I used to* ~ *with him* lavoravamo insieme; *how does it* ~*? of device* come funziona? **3** *v/t employee* far lavorare; *machine* far funzionare

♦ **work off** *v/t bad mood, anger* sfogare; *flab* smaltire

♦ **work out** *v/t problem* capire; *solution* trovare **2** *v/i at gym* fare ginnastica; *of relationship etc* funzionare

♦ **work out to** *v/t* (*add up to*) ammontare a

♦ **work up** *v/t*: **work up enthusiasm** entusiasmarsi; *I worked up an appetite* mi è venuto appetito; *get worked up* (*get angry*) infuriarsi; (*get nervous*) agitarsi

work·a·ble ['wɜːkəbl] *adj solution* realizzabile

work·a·hol·ic [wɜːkə'hɒlɪk] *n* F stacanovista *m/f*

'**work·day** *hours of work* giornata *f* lavorativa; *not a holiday* giorno *m* feriale

work·er ['wɜːkə(r)] lavoratore *m*, -trice *f*; *she's a good* ~ lavora bene

'**work·force** forza *f* lavoro

work·ing ['wɜːkɪŋ] *adj day, week* lavorativo; *clothes* da lavoro; *lunch* di lavoro; *in* ~ *order* funzionante; '**work·ing class** classe *f* operaia; '**work·ing-class** *adj* operaio; '**work·ing con·di·tions** *npl* condizioni *fpl* di lavoro; **work·ing 'day** → **workday**; '**work·ing hours** *npl* orario *m* di lavoro; **work·ing**

'knowledge conoscenza *f* di base; work·ing 'moth·er madre *f* che lavora

'work·load carico *m* di lavoro; 'work·man operaio *m*; 'work·man·like *adj* professionale; 'work·man·ship fattura *f*; work of 'art opera *f* d'arte; 'work·out allenamento *m*; 'work per·mit permesso *m* di lavoro; 'work·shop laboratorio *m*; *for mechanic* officina *f*; *(seminar)* workshop *m inv*; 'work sta·tion work station *f inv*; 'work·top piano *m* di lavoro; work-to-'rule sciopero *m* bianco

world [wɜːld] mondo *m*; the ~ of computers / the theatre il mondo dei computer / del teatro; out of this ~ F fantastico

World 'Cup mondiali *mpl* (di calcio); world-'class *adj* di livello internazionale; world-'fa·mous *adj* di fama mondiale

world·ly ['wɜːldlɪ] *adj goods* materiale; *not spiritual* terreno; *power* temporale; *person* mondano

world 'pow·er potenza *f* mondiale; world 'rec·ord record *m inv* mondiale; world 'war guerra *f* mondiale; 'world·wide 1 *adj* mondiale 2 *adv* a livello mondiale

worm [wɜːm] *n* verme *m*

worn [wɔːn] *pp* → wear

worn-'out *adj shoes, carpet, part* logoro; *person* esausto, sfinito

wor·ried ['wʌrɪd] *adj* preoccupato

wor·ried·ly ['wʌrɪdlɪ] *adv* con aria preoccupata

wor·ry ['wʌrɪ] 1 *n* preoccupazione *f* 2 *v/t (pret & pp -ied)* preoccupare; *(upset)* turbare 3 *v/i (pret & pp -ied)* proccuparsi; it will be alright, don't ~! andrà tutto bene, non preoccuparti!

wor·ry·ing ['wʌrɪɪŋ] *adj* preoccupante

worse [wɜːs] 1 *adj* peggiore; things will get ~ le cose peggioreranno 2 *adv* peggio

wors·en ['wɜːsn] *v/i* peggiorare

wor·ship ['wɜːʃɪp] 1 *n* culto *m* 2 *v/t*

(pret & pp -ped) venerare; *fig* adorare

worst [wɜːst] 1 *adj* peggiore 2 *adv* peggio 3 *n*: the ~ il peggio; if the ~ comes to the ~ nel peggiore dei casi

worst-case scen·a·ri·o: the ~ la peggiore delle ipotesi

worth [wɜːθ] 1 *adj*: be ~ valere; it's ~ reading / seeing vale la pena leggerlo / vederlo; be ~ it valerne la pena 2 *n* valore *m*; £20 ~ of petrol 20 sterline di benzina

worth·less ['wɜːθlɪs] *adj object* senza valore; *person* inetto

worth'while *adj cause* lodevole; be ~ *(beneficial, useful)* essere utile; *(worth the effort, worth doing)* valere la pena

worth·y ['wɜːðɪ] *adj* degno; *cause* lodevole; be ~ of *(deserve)* meritare

would [wʊd] *v/aux*: I ~ help if I could ti aiuterei se potessi; I said that I ~ go ho detto che sarei andato; I told him I ~ not leave unless ... gli ho detto che non me ne sarei andato se non ...; ~ you like to go to the cinema? vuoi andare al cinema?; ~ you mind if I smoked? la disturba se fumo?; ~ you tell her that ...? le dica che ...; ~ you close the door? le dispiace chiudere la porta?; I ~ have told you but ... te l'avrei detto ma ...; I ~ not have been so angry if ... non mi sarei arrabbiato tanto se ...

wound¹ [wuːnd] 1 *n* ferita *f* 2 *v/t also with remark* ferire; *with remark* ferire

wound² [waʊnd] *pret & pp* → wind²

wove [wəʊv] *pret* → weave

wov·en ['wəʊvn] *pp* → weave

wow [waʊ] *int* wow

wrap [ræp] *v/t (pret & pp -ped) parcel, gift* incartare; *(wind, cover)* avvolgere

♦ wrap up *v/i against the cold* coprirsi bene

wrap·per ['ræpə(r)] incarto *m*

wrap·ping ['ræpɪŋ] involucro *m*

'wrap·ping pa·per carta *f* da regalo

wreath [riːθ] corona *f; for funeral* corona *f* funebre

wreck [rek] **1** *n of ship* relitto *m; of car* carcassa *f;* **be a nervous ~** sentirsi un rottame **2** *v/t ship* far naufragare; *car* demolire; *plans, career, marriage* distruggere

wreck·age ['rekɪdʒ] *of car, plane* rottami *mpl; of marriage, career* brandelli *mpl*

wrench [rentʃ] **1** *n tool* chiave *f* inglese; *injury* slogatura *f* **2** *v/t injure* slogarsi; *(pull)* strappare

wres·tle ['resl] *v/i* fare la lotta

♦ **wrestle with** *v/t problems* lottare con

wres·tler ['reslə(r)] lottatore *m,* -trice *f*

wrest·ling ['reslɪŋ] lotta *f* libera

'wres·tling match incontro *m* di lotta libera

wrig·gle ['rɪgl] *v/i (squirm)* dimenarsi; *along the ground* strisciare

♦ **wriggle out of** *v/t* sottrarsi a

♦ **wring out** *v/t (pret & pp* **wrung**) *cloth* strizzare

wrin·kle ['rɪŋkl] **1** *n in skin* ruga *f; in clothes* grinza *f* **2** *v/t clothes* stropicciare **3** *v/i of clothes* stropicciarsi

wrist [rɪst] polso *m*

'wrist·watch orologio *m* da polso

write [raɪt] *(pret* **wrote,** *pp* **written**) **1** *v/t* scrivere; *cheque* fare **2** *v/i* scrivere; *of author* scrivere; *(send a letter)* scrivere

♦ **write down** *v/t* annotare, scrivere

♦ **write off** *v/t debt* cancellare; *car* distruggere

writ·er ['raɪtə(r)] autore *m,* -trice *f; professional* scrittore *m,* -trice *f*

'write-up F recensione *f*

writhe [raɪð] *v/i* contorcersi

writ·ing ['raɪtɪŋ] *as career* scrivere *m; (hand-writing)* scrittura *f; (words)* scritta *f; (script)* scritto *m;* **in ~** per iscritto

'writ·ing pa·per carta *f* da lettere

writ·ten ['rɪtn] *pp* → **write**

wrong [rɒŋ] **1** *adj* sbagliato; **be ~ of person** sbagliare; *of answer* essere errato; *morally* essere ingiusto; **it's ~ to steal** non si deve rubare; **what's ~?** cosa c'è?; **there is something ~ with the car** la macchina ha qualcosa che non va **2** *adv* in modo sbagliato; **go ~** *of person* sbagliare; *of marriage, plan etc* andar male **3** *n immoral action* torto *m; immorality* male *m;* **be in the ~** avere torto

wrong·ful ['rɒŋfʊl] *adj* illegale

wrong·ly ['rɒŋlɪ] *adv* erroneamente

wrong 'num·ber numero *m* sbagliato

wrote [rəʊt] *pret* → **write**

wrought 'i·ron [rɔːt] ferro *m* battuto

wrung [rʌŋ] *pret & pp* → **wring**

wry [raɪ] *adj* beffardo

X

xen·o·pho·bi·a [zenəʊ'fəʊbɪə] xenofobia *f*

X-ray ['eksreɪ] **1** *n* raggio *m* X; *picture* radiografia *f;* **have an ~** farsi fare una radiografia **2** *v/t* radiografare

xy·lo·phone [zaɪlə'fəʊn] xilofono *m*

Y

yacht [jɒt] *for pleasure* yacht *m inv*; *for racing* imbarcazione *f* da diporto

yacht·ing ['jɒtɪŋ] navigazione *f* da diporto

yachts·man ['jɒtsmən] diportista *m*

Yank [jæŋk] *n* F yankee *m inv*

yank [jæŋk] *v/t* dare uno strattone a

yap [jæp] *v/i* (*pret & pp* **-ped**) *of small dog* abbaiare; F *talk a lot* chiacchierare

yard¹ [jɑːd] *of prison, institution etc* cortile *m*; *for storage* deposito *m* all'aperto

yard² [jɑːd] *measurement* iarda *f*

'yard·stick *fig* metro *m*

yarn [jɑːn] *n* (*thread*) filato *m*; F *story* racconto *m*

yawn [jɔːn] **1** *n* sbadiglio *m* **2** *v/i* sbadigliare

year [jɪə(r)] anno *m*; *I've known here for ~s* la conosco da (tanti) anni; *it will last for ~s* durerà anni; *we were in the same ~ at school* frequentavamo lo stesso anno; *be six ~s old* avere sei anni

year·ly ['jɪəlɪ] **1** *adj* annuale **2** *adv* annualmente; *twice ~* due volte (al)l'anno

yearn [jɜːn] *v/i*: *~ to do sth* struggersi dal desiderio di fare qc

♦ **yearn for** *v/t* desiderare ardentemente

yearn·ing ['jɜːnɪŋ] *n* desiderio *m* struggente

yeast [jiːst] lievito *m*

yell [jel] **1** *n* urlo *m* **2** *v/t & v/i* urlare

yel·low ['jeləʊ] **1** *n* giallo *m* **2** *adj* giallo

yel·low 'pag·es® *npl* pagine *fpl* gialle

yelp [jelp] **1** *n* guaito *m* **2** *v/i* guaire

yen [jen] FIN yen *m inv*

yes [jes] *int* sì; *say ~* dire di sì

'yes·man *pej* yes man *m inv*

yes·ter·day ['jestədeɪ] **1** *adv* ieri; *the day before ~* l'altro ieri **2** *n* ieri *m inv*

yet [jet] **1** *adv* finora; *the fastest ~* il più veloce finora; *as ~ up to now* per ora; *it is as ~ undecided* rimane ancora da decidere; *have you finished ~?* (non) hai (ancora) finito?; *he hasn't arrived ~* non è ancora arrivato; *is he here ~? – not ~* è arrivato? – non ancora; *~ bigger/longer* ancora più grande/lungo **2** *conj* eppure; *~ I'm not sure* eppure non sono sicuro

yield [jiːld] **1** *n from fields etc* raccolto *m*; *from investment* rendita *f* **2** *v/t fruit, harvest* dare, produrre; *interest* fruttare **3** *v/i* (*give way*) cedere

yob [jɒb] P teppista *m/f*

yo·ga ['jəʊgə] yoga *m*

yog·hurt ['jɒgət] yogurt *m inv*

yolk [jəʊk] tuorlo *m*

you [juː] *pron* ◊ *subject: familiar singular* tu; *familiar polite plural* voi; *polite singular* lei; *do ~ know him?* lo conosci/conosce/conoscete?; *~ go, I'll stay* tu vai/lei vada/voi andate, io resto ◊ *direct object: familiar singular* ti; *familiar polite plural* vi; *polite singular* la; *he knows ~* ti/vi/la conosce ◊ *indirect object: familiar singular* ti; *when two pronouns are used* te; *familiar polite plural* vi; *when two pronouns are used* ve; *polite singular* le; *did he talk to ~?* ti/vi/le ha parlato?; *I need to talk to ~* devo parlarti/parlarvi/parlarle; *I told ~* te/ve l'ho detto, glielo ho detto ◊ *after prep familiar singular* te; *familiar polite plural* voi; *polite singular* lei; *this is for ~* questo è per te/voi/lei ◊ *impersonal: ~ never know* non si sa mai; *~ have to pay* si deve pagare; *fruit is good for ~* la frutta fa bene

young [jʌŋ] *adj* giovane

young·ster ['jʌŋstə(r)] ragazzo *m*, -a *f*

your [jɔː(r)] *adj familiar singular* il tuo *m*, la tua *f*, i tuoi *mpl*, le tue *fpl; polite singular* il suo *m*, la sua *f*, i suoi *mpl*, le sue *fpl; familiar & polite plural* il vostro *m*, la vostra *f*, i vostri *mpl*, le vostre *fpl; ~ **brother** tuo / suo / vostro fratello

yours [jɔːz] *pron familiar singular* il tuo *m*, la tua *f*, i tuoi *mpl*, le tue *fpl; polite singular* il suo *m*, la sua *f*, i suoi *mpl*, le sue *fpl; familiar & polite plural* il vostro *m*, la vostra *f*, i vostri *mpl*, le vostre *fpl; **a friend of ~** un tuo / suo / vostro amico; ... *at end of letter* saluti ...; **~ sincerely** distinti saluti

your'self *pron reflexive* ti; *reflexive polite* si; *emphatic* tu stesso *m*, tu stessa *f, emphatic polite* lei stesso *m*,

lei stessa *f; did you hurt ~?* ti sei / si è fatto male?; *you said so* — l'hai detto tu stesso / l'ha detto lei stesso; *keep it for ~* tienilo per te / lo tenga per sé; *by ~* da solo

your'selves *pron reflexive* vi; *emphatic* voi stessi *mpl*, voi stesse *fpl; did you hurt ~?* vi siete fatti male?; *can you do it ~?* potete farlo da voi?; *by ~* da soli *mpl*, da sole *fpl*

youth [juːθ] *n age* gioventù *f;* (*young man*) ragazzo *m;* (*young people*) giovani *mpl*

'youth club circolo *m* giovanile

youth·ful ['juːθfʊl] *adj* giovanile; *ideas* giovane; *idealism* di gioventù

'youth hos·tel ostello *m* della gioventù

Yu·go·sla·vi·a [juːgəˈslɑːvɪə] Jugoslavia *f*

Yu·go·sla·vi·an [juːgəˈslɑːvɪən] **1** *adj* jugoslavo **2** *n* jugoslavo *m*, -a *f*

yup·pie ['jʌpɪ] F yuppie *m/f inv*

Z

zap [zæp] *v/t* (*pret & pp* **-ped**) F COMPUT (*delete*) cancellare; (*kill*) annientare; (*hit*) colpire; (*send*) mandare

◆ **zap along** *v/i* F *move fast* sfrecciare

zapped [zæpt] *adj* F (*exhausted*) stanchissimo

zap·per ['zæpə(r)] *for changing TV channels* telecomando *m*

zap·py ['zæpɪ] *adj* F *car, pace* veloce; (*lively, energetic*) brioso

zeal [ziːl] zelo *m*

ze·bra ['zebrə] zebra *f*

ze·bra 'cross·ing *Br* strisce *fpl* pedonali

ze·ro ['zɪərəʊ] zero *m; 10 below ~* 10 (gradi) sotto zero

◆ **zero in on** *v/t* (*identify*) identificare

ze·ro 'growth crescita *f* zero

zest [zest] (*enthusiasm*) gusto *m;* (*peel*) scorza *f*

zig-zag ['zɪgzæg] **1** *n* zigzag *m inv* **2** *v/i* (*pret & pp* **-ged**) zigzagare

zilch [zɪltʃ] F un bel niente

zinc [zɪŋk] zinco *m*

zip [zɪp] (*cerniera f*) lampo *f*

◆ **zip up** *v/t* (*pret & pp* **-ped**) *dress, jacket* allacciare; COMPUT zippare, comprimere

'zip code *Am* codice *m* di avviamento postale

zo·di·ac ['zəʊdɪæk] ASTR zodiaco *m; signs of the ~* segni *mpl* zodiacali

zom·bie ['zɒmbɪ] F (*idiot*) cretino *m*, -a *f; feel like a ~ exhausted*

Z

sentirsi uno zombie
zone [zəʊn] zona f
zonked [zɒŋkt] *adj* P (*exhausted*)
stanco morto
zoo [zuː] zoo *m inv*
zo·o·log·i·cal [zuːə'lɒdʒɪkl] *adj* zoo-
logico

zo·ol·o·gist [zuː'ɒlədʒɪst] zoologo
m, -a *f*
zo·ol·o·gy [zuː'ɒlədʒɪ] zoologia *f*
zoom [zuːm] *v/i* F *move fast* sfrecciare
◆ **zoom in on** *v/t* PHOT zumare su
zoom 'lens zoom *m inv*
zuc·chi·ni [zuː'kiːnɪ] *Am* zucchino *m*

Z

Italian Verb Conjugations

You can find the conjugation pattern of an Italian verb by looking up the infinitive form in the dictionary. The numbers and letters given there after the infinitive refer to the conjugation patterns listed below.

The tables (**1a**, **2a**, **3a**, **4a**) show the full conjugations. The verb stem is given in ordinary type and the endings in *italics*. Compound tenses are given at **1a**. The three main conjugations (-are, -ere, -ire) are divided into four sets so as to illustrate the two different stress patterns of the second conjugation. Variations in form, stress pattern and vowel length are then shown for each of these four sets.

An underscore shows the stressed vowel in each conjugated form.

First Conjugation

1a mandare. The stem remains the same with regard to both spelling and pronunciation.

I. Simple Tenses

	indicativo			condizionale
pr	*imperf*	*p.r.*	*fut*	
mando	mandavo	mandai	manderò	manderei
mandi	mandavi	mandasti	manderai	manderesti
manda	mandava	mandò	manderà	manderebbe
mandiamo	mandavamo	mandammo	manderemo	manderemmo
mandate	mandavate	mandaste	manderete	mandereste
mandano	mandavano	mandarono	manderanno	manderebbero

congiuntivo		imperativo
pr	*imperf*	
mandi	mandassi	—
mandi	mandassi	manda
mandi	mandasse	mandi
mandiamo	mandassimo	mandiamo
mandiate	mandaste	mandate
mandino	mandassero	mandino

Participio presente: mandante   *Participio passato*: mandato
Gerundio presente: mandando

II. Compound Tenses

1. Active voice
(Formed by placing *avere* before the verb form *participio passato*)

Infinito
passato: aver mand*ato*

Gerundio
passato: avendo mand*ato*

Indicativo
passato pross: ho mand*ato*
trapassato prossimo: avevo mand*ato*

futuro anteriore: avrò mand*ato*

Condizionale
passato: avrei mand*ato*

Congiuntivo
passato: abbia mand*ato*
trapassato: avessi mand*ato*

2. Passive voice
(formed by placing *essere* before the verb form *participio passato*)

Infinito
presente: essere mand*ato, -a, -i, -e*
passato: essere stato (stata, stati, state) mand*ato, -a, -i, -e*

Gerundio
presente: essendo mand*ato, -a, -i, -e*
passato: essendo stato (stata, stati, state) mand*ato, -a, -i, -e*

Indicativo
presente: sono mand*ato, -a*
imperf: ero mand*ato, -a*
passato remoto: fui mand*ato, -a*
passato prossimo: sono stato (stata) mand*ato, -a*
trap. prossimo: ero stato (stata)

mand*ato, -a*
fut semplice: sarò mand*ato, -a*
fut anteriore: sarò stato (stata) mand*ato, -a*

Condizionale
presente: sarei mand*ato, -a*
passato: sarei stato (stata) mand*ato, -a*

Congiuntivo
presente: sia mand*ato, -a*
imperf: fossi mand*ato, -a*
passato: sia stato (stata) mand*ato, -a*
trapassato: fossi stato (stata) mand*ato, -a*

Imperativo
sii mand*ato, -a*

This pattern applies to the compound tenses of all verbs

pr ind	p.r.	fut	pr congiunt	imper

1b celare. The stressed, closed *-e* in the stem becomes an open *e*.

celo	celai	celerò	celi	—
celiamo	celammo	celeremo	celiamo	celiamo
celano	celarono	celeranno	celino	celino
		pp: celato		

1c lodare. The stressed, closed *-o* in the stem becomes an open *o*.

lodo	lodai	loderò	lodi	—
lodiamo	lodammo	loderemo	lodiamo	lodiamo
lodano	lodarono	loderanno	lodino	lodino
		pp: lodato		

1d cercare. The final consonant in the verb stem, *-c*, becomes *ch* before *i* and *e*.

cerco	cercai	cercherò	cerchi	—
cerchiamo	cercammo	cercheremo	cerchiamo	cerchiamo
cercano	cercarono	cercheranno	cerchino	cerchino
		pp: cercato		

pr ind	p.r.	fut	pr congiunt	imper

1e pagare. The final consonant in the verb stem, -g, becomes gh before i and e.

pago	pagai	pagherò	paghi	—
paghiamo	pagammo	pagheremo	paghiamo	paghiamo
pagano	pagarono	pagheranno	paghino	paghino
	pp: pagato			

1f baciare. The i is dropped if it is followed immediately by a second i or an e.

bacio	baciai	bacerò	baci	—
baciamo	baciammo	baceremo	baciamo	baciamo
baciano	baciarono	baceranno	bacino	bacino
	pp: baciato			

1g pigliare. The i is dropped if it is followed immediately by a second i.

piglio	pigliai	piglierò	pigli	—
pigliamo	piagliammo	piglieremo	pigliamo	pigliamo
pigliano	pigliarono	piglieranno	piglino	piglino
	pp: pigliato			

1h inviare. Verb forms in which the i is stressed retain the i even if it is followed by another i.

invio	inviai	invierò	invii	—
inviamo	inviammo	invieremo	inviamo	inviamo
inviano	inviarono	invieranno	inviino	inviino
	pp: inviato			

1i annoiare. Verbs ending in –iare with an unstressed i and a preceding vowel, drop the i which would be added.

annoio	annoiai	annoierò	annoi	—
annoiamo	annoiammo	annoieremo	annoiamo	annoiamo
annoiano	annoiarono	annoieranno	annoino	annoino
	pp: annoiato			

1k studiare. Verbs ending in –iare with an unstressed i and a preceding consonant, usually drop the i which would be added, even when the i in the verb stem is stressed: i.e. tu studi. Verbs ending in –liare always have -lii, eg esiliare, esilii.

studio	studiai	studierò	studi	—
studiamo	studiammo	studieremo	studiamo	studiamo
studiano	studiarono	studieranno	studino	studino
	pp: studiato			

1l abitare. In the verb forms in which the stem is stressed, the stress comes on the first syllable.

abito	abitai	abiterò	abiti	—
abitiamo	abitammo	abiteremo	abitiamo	abitiamo
abitano	abitarono	abiteranno	abitino	abitino
	pp: abitato			

pr ind	p.r.	fut	pr congiunt	imper

1m collaborare. In the verb forms in which the stem is stressed, the stress comes on the second syllable.

collaboro	collaborai	collaborerò	collabori	—
collaboriamo	collaborammo	collaboreremo	collaboriamo	collaboriamo
collaborano	collaborarono	collaboreranno	collaborino	collaborino

pp: collaborato

1n aggomitolare. In the verb forms in which the stem is stressed, the stress comes on the third or fourth syllable.

aggomitolo	~mitolai	~mitolerò	~mitoli	—
~mitoliamo	~mitolammo	~mitoleremo	~mitoliamo	~mitoliamo
~mitolano	~mitolarono	~mitoleranno	~mitolino	~mitolino

pp: aggomitolato

1o giocare. The stressed –o in the stem can be extended to –uo, but this is rarer.

gi(u)oco	giocai	giocherò	gi(u)ochi	—
giochiamo	giocammo	giocheremo	giochiamo	giochiamo
gi(u)ocano	giocarono	giocheranno	gi(u)ochino	gi(u)ochino

pp: giocato

1p andare. Two stems: and- and vad-. In fut and cond the e at the start of the ending is dropped.

vado	andai	andrò	vada	—
vai	andasti	andrai	vada	va, va', vai,
va	andò	andrà	vada	vada
andiamo	andammo	andremo	andiamo	andiamo
andate	andaste	andrete	andiate	andate
vanno	andarono	andranno	vadano	vadano

pp: andato

1q stare. Verb stem sta; p.r. (stetti etc); imperf del congiunt (stessi etc) as in the 2nd Conjugation; in fut and cond e becomes a.

sto	stetti	starò	stia	—
stai	stesti	starai	stia	sta', stai
sta	stette	starà	stia	stia
stiamo	stemmo	staremo	stiamo	stiamo
state	steste	starete	stiate	state
stanno	stettero	staranno	stiano	stiano

pp: stato

1r dare. Verb stem da; imperf del congiunt dessi etc; in the p.r. alternative forms detti, dette, dettero.

do	diedi, detti	darò	dia	—
dai	desti	darai	dia	da', dai
dà	diede, dette	darà	dia	dia
diamo	demmo	daremo	diamo	diamo
date	deste	darete	diate	date
danno	diedero, dettero	daranno	diano	diano

pp: dato

Second Conjugation – First Pattern

2a temere. The stem remains the same with regard to both spelling and pronunciation.

I. Simple Tenses

	indicativo			condizionale
pr	*imperf*	*p.r.*	*fut*	
temo	temevo	temei, temetti	temerò	temerei
temo	temevo	temei, temetti	temerò	temerei
temi	temevi	temesti	temerai	temeresti
teme	temeva	temette	temerà	temerebbe
temiamo	temevamo	tememmo	temeremo	temeremmo
temete	temevate	temeste	temerete	temereste
temono	temevano	temettero, temerono	temeranno	temerebbero

	congiuntivo		imperativo
pr	*imperf*		
tema	temessi	—	
tema	temessi	temi	
tema	temesse	tema	
temiamo	temessimo	temiamo	
temiate	temeste	temete	
temano	temessero	temano	

Participio presente: temente   *Participio passato*: temuto

Gerundio presente: temendo

II. Compound Tenses

Auxiliary verb *essere* or *avere*, followed by *participio passato* (see 1a).

pr ind	*p.r.*	*fut*	*pr congiunt*	*imper*

2b avere. In *fut* and *cond* the final *e* in the ending is omitted.

ho	ebbi	avrò	abbia	—
hai	avesti	avrai	abbia	abbi
ha	ebbe	avrà	abbia	abbia
abbiamo	avemmo	avremo	abbiamo	abbiamo
avete	aveste	avrete	abbiate	abbiate
hanno	ebbero	avranno	abbiano	abbiano
		pp: avuto		

2c cadere. In *fut* and *cond* the final *e* in the ending is omitted.

cado	caddi	cadrò	cada	—
cadiamo	cademmo	cadremo	cadiamo	cadiamo
cadono	caddero	cadranno	cadano	cadano
		pp: caduto		

2d calere. Used almost exclusively in 3rd person singular; now obsolete.

cale	calse	—	caglia	—
		pp: caluto		

pr ind	*p.r.*	*fut*	*pr congiunt*	*imper*

2e dolere. In *pr*, *g* is added between the verb stem and the ending *o* or *a*. In *fut* and *cond* *l* becomes *r* and the final *e* of the ending is dropped.

dolgo	dolsi	dorrò	dolga	—
duole	dolse	dorrà	dolga	dolga
dogliamo	dolemmo	dorremo	dogliamo	dogliamo
dolgono	dolsero	dorranno	dolgano	dolgano
		pp: doluto		

2f dovere. In the forms with the emphasis on the stem vowel, *o* becomes *e*. Omission of *e* in *fut* and *cond*.

devo	dovetti	dovrò	debba, deva	—
devi	dovesti	dovrai	debba, deva	devi
deve	dovette	dovrà	debba, deva	debba, deva
dobbiamo	dovemmo	dovremo	dobbiamo	dobbiamo
dovete	doveste	dovrete	dobbiate	dovete
devono	dovettero	dovranno	debbano, devano	debbano, devano
		pp: dovuto		

2g lucere. Used only in 3rd person singular and plural of *pr dell'ind* (luce, lucono), *imperf* (luceva, lucevano), *fut* (lucerà, luceranno), *pr del congiunt* (luca, lucano), and *imperf del congiunt* (lucesse, lucessero). Also *p pr* lucente, *ger* lucendo.

2h parere. In *fut* and *cond* the final *e* in the ending is omitted.

paio	parvi	parrò	paia	—
pa(r)iamo	paremmo	parremo	pa(r)iamo	—
paiono	parvero	parranno	paiano	—
		pp: parso		

2i persuadere.

persuado	persuasi	persuaderò	persuada	—
persuadiamo	persuademmo	persuaderemo	persuadiamo	persuadiamo
persuadono	persuasero	persuaderanno	persuadano	persuadano
		pp: persuaso		

2k piacere.

piaccio	piacqui	piacerò	piaccia	—
piacciamo	piacemmo	piaceremo	piacciamo	piacciamo
piacciono	piacquero	piaceranno	piacciano	piacciano
		pp: piaciuto		

2l potere. In *fut* and *cond* the final *e* in the ending is omitted.

posso	potei	potrò	possa	—
puoi	potesti	potrai	possa	—
può	poté	potrà	possa	—
possiamo	potemmo	potremo	possiamo	—
potete	poteste	potrete	possiate	—
possono	poterono	potranno	possano	—
		pp: potuto		

pr ind	*p.r.*	*fut*	*pr congiunt*	*imper*

2m rimanere. In *pr* g is added between stem and ending *o* or *a*; *p.r.* ending in *–si* and *pp* ending in *–sto* drop the *–n* from the stem; in *fut* and *cond* n becomes r.

rimango	rimasi	rimarrò	rimanga	—
rimaniamo	rimanemmo	rimarremo	rimaniamo	rimaniamo
rimangono	rimasero	rimarranno	rimangano	rimangano
	pp: rimasto			

2n sapere. In *fut* and *cond* the *e* is dropped; 2nd person plural of *imperf* formed from *congiunt*.

so	seppi	saprò	sappia	—
sai	sapesti	saprai	sappia	sappi
sa	seppe	saprà	sappia	sappia
sappiamo	sapemmo	sapremo	sappiamo	sappiamo
sapete	sapeste	saprete	sappiate	sappiate
sanno	seppero	sapranno	sappiano	sappiano
	p pr: sapiente		*pp:* saputo	

2o sedere. The *e* in the stem becomes *ie* in forms with the emphasis on the stem vowel; in *pr* alternative forms with *segg…*

siedo, seggo	sedei	sederò	sieda, segga	—
sediamo	sedemmo	sederemo	sediamo	sediamo
siedono, seggono	sederono	sederanno	siedano, seggano	siedano, seggano
	pp: seduto			

2p solere. Only used in *pr*, *p.r.*, *ger* and *pp*. In *pr dell'ind* (except 2nd person singular: *suoli*) and *congiunt* it follows the pattern of *volgere*.

soglio	solei	—	soglia	—
sogliamo	—	—	sogliamo	—
sogliono	—	—	sogliano	—
	ger: solendo		*pp:* solito	

2q tenere. Addition of *g* between stem and ending *o* or *a*. In *fut* and *cond* n becomes r.

tengo	tenni	terrò	tenga	—
tieni	tenesti	terrai	tenga	tieni
teniamo	tenemmo	terremo	teniamo	teniamo
tengono	tennero	terranno	tengano	tengano
	pp: tenuto			

2r valere. Addition of *g* between stem and ending *o* or *a*. In *fut* and *cond* n becomes r.

valgo	valsi	varrò	valga	—
valiamo	valemmo	varremo	valiamo	valiamo
valgono	valsero	varranno	valgano	valgano
	pp: valso			

pr ind	p.r.	fut	pr congiunt	imper

2s vedere. In *fut* and *cond* the final *e* in the ending is omitted.

vedo	vidi	vedrò	veda	—
vediamo	vedemmo	vedremo	vediamo	vediamo
vedono	videro	vedranno	vedano	vedano

pp: visto

2t volere. In *fut* and *cond l* becomes *r* and the final *e* of the ending is omitted; 2nd person plural of *imper* from the *congiunt*.

voglio	volli	vorrò	voglia	—
vuoi	volesti	vorrai	voglia	vogli
vuole	volle	vorrà	voglia	voglia
vogliamo	volemmo	vorremo	vogliamo	vogliamo
volete	voleste	vorrete	vogliate	vogliate
vogliono	vollero	vorranno	vogliano	vogliano

pp: voluto

Second Conjugation – Second Pattern

3a vendere. The stem remains the same with regard to both spelling and pronunciation.

I. Simple Tenses

	indicativo			condizionale
pr	imperf	p.r.	fut	
vendo	vendevo	vendetti, vendei	venderò	venderei
vendi	vendevi	vendesti	venderai	venderesti
vende	vendeva	vendette	venderà	venderebbe
vendiamo	vendevamo	vendemmo	venderemo	venderemmo
vendete	vendevate	vendeste	venderete	vendereste
vendono	vendevano	vendettero, venderono	venderanno	venderebbero

congiuntivo		imperativo
pr	imperf	
venda	vendessi	—
venda	vendessi	vendi
venda	vendesse	venda
vendiamo	vendessimo	vendiamo
vendiate	vendeste	vendete
vendano	vendessero	vendano

Participio presente: vendente   *Participio passato*: venduto*
        Gerundio presente: vendendo

Participio passato of *spandere* is *spanto*.

II. Compound Tenses

Auxiliary verb *essere* or *avere*, followed by *participio passato* (see 1a).

pr ind	p.r.	fut	pr congiunt	imper

3b chiudere.

chiudo	chiusi	chiuderò	chiuda	—
chiudiamo	chiudemmo	chiuderemo	chiudiamo	chiudiamo
chiudono	chiusero	chiuderanno	chiudano	chiudano
		pp: chiuso		

3c prendere.

prendo	presi	prenderò	prenda	—
prendiamo	prendemmo	prenderemo	prendiamo	prendiamo
prendono	presero	prenderanno	prendano	prendano
		pp: preso		

3d fingere. The *pp* of *stringere* is *stretto*.

fingo	finsi	fingerò	finga	—
fingiamo	fingemmo	fingeremo	fingiamo	fingiamo
fingono	finsero	fingeranno	fingano	fingano
		pp: finto		

3e addurre. Shorter form of *adducere*.

adduco	addussi	addurrò	adduca	—
adduci	adducesti	addurrai	adduca	adduci
adduce	addusse	addurrà	adduca	adduca
adduciamo	adducemmo	addurremo	adduciamo	adduciamo
adducete	adduceste	addurrete	adduciate	adduciate
adducono	addussero	addurranno	adducano	adducano
		pp: addotto		

3f assistere. In *p.r.* alternative forms end in *–etti*.

assisto	assistei	assisterò	assista	—
assistiamo	assistemmo	assisteremo	assistiamo	assistiamo
assistono	assisterono	assisteranno	assistano	assistano
		pp: assistito		

3g assolvere.

assolvo	assolsi, ~vetti	assolverò	assolva	—
assolviamo	assolvemmo	assolveremo	assolviamo	assolviamo
assolvono	assolsero, assolvettero	assolveranno	assolvano	assolvano
		pp: assolto		

3h assumere.

assumo	assunsi	assumerò	assuma	—
assumiamo	assumemmo	assumeremo	assumiamo	assumiamo
assumono	assunsero	assumeranno	assumano	assumano
		pp: assunto		

pr ind	p.r.	fut	pr congiunt	imper

3i bere. Conjugated according to the pattern of *bevere*. In *fut* and *cond* v becomes *r* and the *e* of the ending is dropped.

bevo	bevvi, bevetti	berrò	beva	—
bevi	bevesti	berrai	beva	bevi
beve	bevve, bevette	berrà	beva	beva
beviamo	bevemmo	berremo	beviamo	beviamo
bevete	beveste	berrete	beviate	bevete
bevono	bevvero, bevettero	berranno	bevano	bevano

pp: bevuto

3k chiedere.

chiedo	chiesi	chiederò	chieda	—
chiediamo	chiedemmo	chiederemo	chiediamo	chiediamo
chiedono	chiesero	chiederanno	chiedano	chiedano

pp: chiesto

3l concedere.

concedo	concessi, concedetti	concederò	conceda	—
concediamo	concedemmo	concederemo	concediamo	concediamo
concedono	concessero, concedettero	concederanno	concedano	concedano

pp: concesso

3m connettere.

connetto	connessi, connettei	connetterò	connetta	—
connettiamo	connettemmo	connetteremo	connettiamo	connettiamo
connettono	connessero, connetterono	connetteranno	connettano	connettano

pp: connesso

3n conoscere.

conosco	conobbi	conoscerò	conosca	—
conosciamo	conoscemmo	conosceremo	conosciamo	conosciamo
conoscono	conobbero	conosceranno	conoscano	conoscano

pp: conosciuto

3o correre.

corro	corsi	correrò	corra	—
corriamo	corremmo	correremo	corriamo	corriamo
corrono	corsero	correranno	corrano	corrano

pp: corso

pr ind	*p.r.*	*fut*	*pr congiunt*	*imper*

3p cuocere. In unstressed syllables *uo* becomes *o*. *Imperf* cocevo or cocessi.

cuocio	cossi	cuocerò	cuocia	—
cociamo	cocemmo	cuoceremo	cociamo	cociamo
cuociono	cossero	cuoceranno	cuociano	cuociano
		pp: cotto		

3q decidere.

decido	decisi	deciderò	decida	—
decidiamo	decidemmo	decideremo	decidiamo	decidiamo
decidono	decisero	decideranno	decidano	decidano
		pp: deciso		

3r deprimere.

deprimo	depressi	deprimerò	deprima	—
deprimiamo	deprimemmo	deprimeremo	deprimiamo	deprimiamo
deprimono	depressero	deprimeranno	deprimano	deprimano
		pp: depresso		

3s devolvere.

devolvo	devolvei, devolvetti	devolverò	devolva	—
devolviamo	devolvemmo	devolveremo	devolviamo	devolviamo
devolvono	devolverono, devolvettero	devolveranno	devolvano	devolvano
		pp: devoluto, devolto		

3t dire.

dico	dissi	dirò	dica	—
dici	dicesti	dirai	dica	
dice	disse	dirà	dica	
diciamo	dicemmo	diremo	diciamo	diciamo
dite	diceste	direte	diciate	dite
dicono	dissero	diranno	dicano	dicano
		pp: detto		

3u dirigere.

dirigo	diressi	dirigerò	diriga	—
dirigiamo	dirigemmo	dirigeremo	dirigiamo	dirigiamo
dirigono	diressero	dirigeranno	dirigano	dirigano
		pp: diretto		

3v discutere.

discuto	discussi	discuterò	discuta	—
discutiamo	discutemmo	discuteremo	discutiamo	discutiamo
discutono	discussero	discuteranno	discutano	discutano
		pp: discusso		

pr ind	p.r.	fut	pr congiunt	imper

3w esigere.

esigo	esigei, esigetti	esigerò	esiga	—
esigiamo	esigemmo	esigeremo	esigiamo	esigiamo
esigono	esigerono, esigettero	esigeranno	esigano	esigano

pp: esatto

3x esimere. Has no *pp*, and the *p.r. esimei* is rarely used. Instead the corresponding forms of *esentare* are used. Otherwise regular, following the pattern of *vendere* 3a.

3y espellere.

espello	espulsi	espellerò	espella	—
espelliamo	espellemmo	espelleremo	espelliamo	espelliamo
espellono	espulsero	espelleranno	espellano	espellano

pp: espulso

3z essere. Completely irregular. *Imperf dell'ind*: ero, eri, era, eravamo, eravate, erano; *imperf del congiunt*: fossi, fossi, fosse, fossimo, foste, fossero.

sono	fui	sarò	sia	—
sei	fosti	sarai	sia	sii
è	fu	sarà	sia	sia
siamo	fummo	saremo	siamo	siamo
siete	foste	sarete	siate	siate
sono	furono	saranno	siano	siano

pp: stato

3aa fare. Shorter form of *facere*. *Imperf* regular, following the pattern of *facere*: *facevo* etc

faccio	feci	farò	faccia	—
fai	facesti	farai	faccia	fa', fai
fa	fece	farà	faccia	faccia
facciamo	facemmo	faremo	facciamo	facciamo
fate	faceste	farete	facciate	fate
fanno	fecero	faranno	facciano	facciano

pp: fatto

3bb fondere.

fondo	fusi	fonderò	fonda	—
fondiamo	fondemmo	fonderemo	fondiamo	fondiamo
fondono	fusero	fonderanno	fondano	fondano

pp: fuso

3cc leggere.

leggo	lessi	leggerò	legga	—
leggiamo	leggemmo	leggeremo	leggiamo	leggiamo
leggono	lessero	leggeranno	leggano	leggano

pp: letto

pr ind	p.r.	fut	pr congiunt	imper

3dd mescere.

mesco	mescei	mescerò	mesca	—
mesciamo	mescemmo	mesceremo	mesciamo	mesciamo
mescono	mescerono	mesceranno	mescano	mescano
		pp: mesciuto		

3ee mettere.

metto	misi	metterò	metta	—
mettiamo	mettemmo	metteremo	mettiamo	mettiamo
mettono	misero	metteranno	mettano	mettano
		pp: messo		

3ff muovere. In unstressed syllables *uo* becomes *o*.

muovo	mossi	muoverò	muova	—
muoviamo	movemmo	muoveremo	muoviamo	muoviamo
muovono	mossero	muoveranno	muovano	muovano
		pp: mosso		

3gg nascere.

nasco	nacqui	nascerò	nasca	—
nasciamo	nascemmo	nasceremo	nasciamo	nasciamo
nascono	nacquero	nasceranno	nascano	nascano
		pp: nato		

3hh nascondere.

nascondo	nascosi	nasconderò	nasca	—
nascondiamo	nascondemmo	nasconderemo	nascondiamo	nascondiamo
nascondono	nascosero	nasconderanno	nascondano	nascondano
		pp: nascosto		

3ii nuocere. In unstressed syllables *uo* becomes *o*.

nuoccio	nocqui	nuocerò	nuoccia	—
nociamo	nocemmo	nuoceremo	nociamo	nuociamo
nuocciono	nocquero	nuoceranno	nuocciano	nuocciano
		pp: nociuto		

3kk piovere. Used only in the 3rd person singular and plural, in the two participial forms and in the *ger*; *pr ind* piove, piovono; *p.r.* piovve, piovvero; *fut* pioverà, pioveranno; *pr congiunt* piova, piovano; *pp* piovuto.

3ll porre. When followed by an *r* in *fut* and *cond* n becomes *r*.

pongo	posi	porrò	ponga	—
poni	ponesti	porrai	ponga	poni
pone	pose	porrà	ponga	ponga
poniamo	ponemmo	porremo	poniamo	poniamo
ponete	poneste	porrete	poniate	ponete
pongono	posero	porranno	pongano	pongano
		pp: posto		

pr ind	p.r.	fut	pr congiunt	imper

3mm prefiggere.

prefiggo	prefissi	prefiggerò	prefigga	—
prefiggiamo	prefiggemmo	prefiggeremo	prefiggiamo	prefiggiamo
prefiggono	prefissero	prefiggeranno	prefiggano	prefiggano
		pp: prefisso		

3nn recere. Addition of *i* between stem and endings *o, a, u*.

recio	recetti	recerò	recia	—
reciamo	recemmo	receremo	reciamo	reciamo
reciono	recettero	receranno	reciano	reciano
		pp: reciuto		

3oo redigere.

redigo	redassi	redigerò	rediga	—
redigiamo	redigemmo	redigeremo	redigiamo	redigiamo
redigono	redassero	redigeranno	redigano	redigano
		pp: redatto		

3pp redimere.

redimo	redensi	redimerò	redima	—
redimiamo	redimemmo	redimeremo	redimiamo	redimiamo
redimono	redensero	redimeranno	redimano	redimano
		pp: redento		

3qq riflettere. In *p.r.* and in *pp* in the sense of "think about" forms usually end in –*ei* and –*uto*; in the sense of "reflect back" usually –*ssi*, -*sso*.

rifletto	riflettei, riflessi	rifletterò	rifletta	—
riflettiamo	riflettemmo	rifletteremo	riflettiamo	riflettiamo
riflettono	rifletterono, riflesse	rifletteranno	riflettano	riflettano
	pp: riflettuto, riflesso			

3rr rompere.

rompo	ruppi	romperò	rompa	—
rompiamo	rompemmo	romperemo	rompiamo	rompiamo
rompono	ruppero	romperanno	rompano	rompano
		pp: rotto		

3ss scegliere. The stem ending *gli* becomes *lg* before endings *o* and *a*.

scelgo	scelsi	sceglierò	scelga	—
scegli	scegliesti	sceglierai	scelga	scegli
sceglie	scelse	sceglierà	scelga	scelga
scegliamo	scegliemmo	sceglieremo	scegliamo	scegliamo
scegliete	sceglieste	sceglierete	scegliate	scegliete
scelgono	scelsero	sceglieranno	scelgano	scelgano
		pp: scelto		

pr ind	p.r.	fut	pr congiunt	imper

3tt scrivere.

scrivo	scrissi	scriverò	scriva	—
scriviamo	scrivemmo	scriveremo	scriviamo	scriviamo
scrivono	scrissero	scriveranno	scrivano	scrivano
		pp: scritto		

3uu spargere.

spargo	sparsi	spargerò	sparga	—
spargiamo	spargemmo	spargeremo	spargiamo	spargiamo
spargono	sparsero	spargeranno	spargano	spargano
		pp: sparso		

3vv spegnere. The stem sound *gn* becomes *ng* before the endings *o* and *a*.

spengo	spensi	spegnerò	spenga	—
spegni	spegnesti	spegnerai	spenga	spegni
spegne	spense	spegnerà	spenga	spenga
spegniamo	spegnemmo	spegneremo	spegniamo	spegniamo
spegnete	spegneste	spegnerete	spegniate	spegnete
spengono	spensero	spegneranno	spengano	spengano
		pp: spento		

3ww svellere.

svello	svelsi	svellerò	svella	—
svelliamo	svellemmo	svelleremo	svelliamo	svelliamo
svellono	svelsero	svelleranno	svellano	svellano
		pp: svelto		

3xx trarre.

traggo	trassi	trarrò	tragga	—
trai	traesti	trarrai	tragga	trai
trae	trasse	trarrà	tragga	tragga
traiamo	traemmo	trarremo	traiamo	traiamo
traete	traeste	trarrete	traiate	traete
traggono	trassero	trarranno	traggano	traggano
		pp: tratto		

3yy vigere. Common only in the following forms: 3rd person singular and plural of *ind pr*, *imperf* and *fut*; *cond*; *congiunt imperf* and *p pr*. *Ind pr*: vige, vigono; *imperf*: vigeva, vigevano; *fut*: vigerà, vigeranno. *Congiunt imperf*: vigesse, vigessero. *Cond*: vigerebbe, vigerebbero. *P pr*: vigente.

3zz vivere.

vivo	vissi	vivrò	viva	—
viviamo	vivemmo	vivremo	viviamo	viviamo
vivono	vissero	vivranno	vivano	vivano
		pp: vissuto		

Third Conjugation

4a partire. The stem remains the same with regard to both spelling and pronunciation.

I. Simple Tenses

	indicativo			condizionale
pr	*imperf*	*p.r.*	*fut*	
parto*	partivo	partii	partirò	partirei
parti	partivi	partisti	partirai	partiresti
parte	partiva	partì	partirà	partirebbe
partiamo	partivamo	partimmo	partiremo	partiremmo
partite	partivate	partiste	partirete	partireste
partono*	partivano	partirono	partiranno	partirebbero

	congiuntivo	imperativo
pr	*imperf*	
parta*	partissi	—
parta*	partissi	parti
parta*	partisse	parta*
partiamo	partissimo	partiamo
partiate	partiste	partite
partano*	partissero	partano*

Participio presente: partente *Participio passato*: partito
Gerundio presente: partendo

* In *cucire* and *sdrucire* an *i* is added before *a* and *o*: *cucio, sdrucio* etc.

II. Compound Tenses

Auxiliary verb *essere* or *avere*, followed by *participio passato* (see 1a).

pr ind	*p.r.*	*fut*	*pr congiunt*	*imper*

4b sentire. The stressed, closed *-e* of stem ending becomes an open *-e*.

sento	sentii	sentirò	senta	—
sentiamo	sentimmo	sentiremo	sentiamo	sentiamo
sentono	sentirono	sentiranno	sentano	sentano
		pp: sentito		

4c dormire. The stressed, closed *-o* of stem ending becomes an open *-o*.

dormo	dormii	dormirò	dorma	—
dormiamo	dormimmo	dormiremo	dormiamo	dormiamo
dormono	dormirono	dormiranno	dormano	dormano
		pp: dormito		

pr ind	p.r.	fut	pr congiunt	imper

4d finire. In the 1st, 2nd and 3rd person singular and 3rd person plural of *pr* (*ind* and *congiunt*) and *imper*, *isc* is added between stem and ending.

finisco	finii	finirò	finisca	—
finisci	finisti	finirai	finisca	finisci
finisce	finì	finirà	finisca	finisca
finiamo	finimmo	finiremo	finiamo	finiamo
finite	finiste	finirete	finiate	finite
finiscono	finirono	finiranno	finiscano	finiscano
		pp: finito		

4e apparire.

appaio, apparisco	apparvi, apparsi, apparii	apparirò	appaia apparisca	—
appariamo	apparimmo	appariremo	appariamo	appariamo
appaiono, appariscono	apparvero, apparsero, apparirono	appariranno	appaiano, appariscano	appaiano, appariscano
		pp: apparso		

4f aprire.

apro	apersi, aprii	aprirò	apra	—
apriamo	aprimmo	apriremo	apriamo	apriamo
aprono	apersero, aprirono	apriranno	aprano	aprano
		pp: aperto		

4g compire. In most forms of the *pr ind*, *pr congiunt* and *imperf*, *compire* is conjugated according to the pattern of *compiere*. An *i* is therefore added between the stem and the ending except in forms whose ending begins with an *i*.

compio	compii	compirò	compia	—
compiamo	compimmo	compiremo	compiamo	compiamo
compiono	compirono	compiranno	compiano	compiano
	pp: compito, compiuto; *p pr*: compiente; *ger*: compiendo			

4h gire. Defective verb. Apart from the forms listed below, is used only in the *imperf* (*ind* and *congiunt*) and in the *cond*. This verb is now obsolete.

—	—	girò	—	—
—	gisti	girai	—	—
—	gì	girà	—	—
—	gimmo	giremo	—	—
gite	giste	girete	—	gite
—	girono	giranno	—	—
		pp: gito		

pr ind	p.r.	fut	pr congiunt	imper

4i ire. Defective verb. This verb is now obsolete. It was used only in *imperf dell'ind* (*ivo* etc) and in the following forms and persons:

	2nd pers sg isti			
—		1st pers pl iremo	—	—
2nd pers pl ite	—	2nd pers pl irete	—	2nd pers pl ite
—	3rd pers sg irono	3rd pers pl iranno	—	—
		pp: ito		

4k morire.

muoio	morii	mor(i)rò	muoia	—
moriamo	morimmo	mor(i)remo	moriamo	moriamo
muoiono	morirono	mor(i)ranno	muoiano	muoiano
		pp: morto		

4l olire. Defective verb. Used only in *imperf dell'ind* 3rd person singular (*oliva*) and 3rd person plural (*olivano*) and in *p pr* (*olente*). This verb is now obsolete.

4m salire. *Pr* as 4a, adding a *g* before *o* and *a*.

salgo	salii	salirò	salga	—
saliamo	salimmo	saliremo	saliamo	saliamo
salgono	salirono	saliranno	salgano	salgano
		pp: salito		

4n udire. *Pr* as 4a, with *u* becoming *o* in the forms in which the stem is stressed.

odo	udii	ud(i)rò	oda	—
udiamo	udimmo	ud(i)remo	udiamo	udiamo
odono	udirono	ud(i)ranno	odano	odano
		pp: udito		

4o uscire.

esco	uscii	uscirò	esca	—
esci	uscisti	uscirai	esca	esci
esce	uscì	uscirà	esca	esca
usciamo	uscimmo	usciremo	usciamo	usciamo
uscite	usciste	uscirete	usciate	uscite
escono	uscirono	usciranno	escano	escano
		pp: uscito		

4p venire.

vengo	venni	verrò	venga	—
vieni	venisti	verrai	venga	vieni
viene	venne	verrà	venga	venga
veniamo	venimmo	verremo	veniamo	veniamo
venite	veniste	verrete	veniate	venite
vengono	vennero	verranno	vengano	vengano
		pp: venuto		

Note sul verbo inglese

a) Coniugazione

Modo indicativo

1. Il tempo presente mantiene la stessa forma dell'infinito in tutte le persone, ad eccezione della 3ª singolare, a cui si aggiunge una -s all'infinito; ad es. *he brings*. Se l'infinito termina con una sibilante (ch, sh, ss, zz) si aggiunge -es, ad esempio *he passes*. Questa *s* ha due diverse pronunce: dopo una consonante sorda, si pronuncia sorda, ad es. *he paints* [peɪnts]; dopo una consonante sonora, si pronuncia sonora, ad es. *he sends* [sendz]; la pronuncia di -es è sonora, inoltre, quando la *e* fa parte della desinenza oppure della lettera finale dell'infinito, ad es. *he washes* ['wɒʃɪz], *he urges* ['ɜːdʒɪz]. Nei verbi che terminano per -y, la terza persona si forma sostituendo alla y -ies, ad es. *he worries, he tries*; sono tuttavia regolari i verbi che all'infinito hanno una vocale davanti alla -y, ad es. *he plays*. Il verbo *to be* è irregolare in tutte le persone: *I am, you are, he is, we are, you are, they are*. Altri tre verbi fanno eccezione alla terza persona singolare: *do - he does, go - he goes, have - he has*.

   Negli altri tempi, tutte le persone restano invariate. Il **passato** ed il **participio passato** si formano aggiungendo -ed all'infinito, ad es. *I passed, passed*, oppure aggiungendo soltanto -d nei verbi che all'infinito terminano in -e, ad es. *I faced, faced*. (Sono molti i verbi irregolari; cfr. sotto). Questa desinenza -(e)d si pronuncia generalmente [t]: *passed* [pɑːst], *faced* [feɪst]; tuttavia, quando compare negli infiniti che terminano con una consonante sonora, con un suono consonantico sonoro o con una *r*, si pronuncia [d]: *warmed* [wɔːmd], *moved* [muːvd], *feared* [fɪəd]. Quando l'infinito termina con -d o -t, la desinenza -ed si pronuncia [ɪd]. Quando l'infinito termina in -y, quest'ultima si trasforma in -ie, e quindi si aggiunge la -d: *try - tried* [traɪd], *pity - pitied* ['pɪtiːd]. I **tempi passati composti** si formano con l'ausiliare *to have* ed il participio passato: **passato prossimo** *I have faced*, **trapassato prossimo** *I had faced*. Con l'ausiliare *will* (*shall*) e l'infinito si forma il **futuro**, ad es. *I shall face;* con l'ausiliare *would* (*should*) si forma il **condizionale**, ad es. *I should face*.

   Per ciascun tempo esiste inoltre la forma continuata, che si costruisce con il verbo *to be* (= essere) e il participio presente (cfr. sotto): *I am going, I was writing, I had been staying, I shall be waiting*, ecc.

2. In inglese, il **congiuntivo** non esiste quasi più, ad eccezione di alcuni casi particolari (*if I were you, so be it, it is proposed that a vote be taken*, ecc.). Al presente, mantiene la stessa forma dell'infinito per tutte le persone, *that I go, that he go*, ecc.

3. In inglese, il **participio presente** ed il **gerundio** hanno la stessa forma e si costruiscono aggiungendo all'infinito la desinenza -ing: *painting, sending*. Tuttavia: 1) nei verbi che all'infinito terminano in -e muta, la desinenza fa cadere questa vocale, ad es. *love - loving, write - writing* (fanno eccezione *dye - dyeing, singe - singeing*, che conservano la -e:); 2) il participio presente dei verbi *die, lie, vie*, ecc. si scrive *dying, lying, vying*, ecc.

4. Esiste una classe di verbi in parte irregolari, che terminano con una sola consonante preceduta da vocale semplice accentata. In questi verbi, prima di aggiungere la desinenza -ing o -ed si raddoppia la consonante:

lob	lob**bed**	lob**bing**	compel	compel**led**	compel**ling**
wed	wed**ded**	wed**ding**	control	control**led**	control**ling**
beg	beg**ged**	beg**ging**	bar	bar**red**	bar**ring**
step	step**ped**	step**ping**	stir	stir**red**	stir**ring**

I verbi che terminano per -l, quando preceduta da vocale atona, raddoppiano la consonante dei due participi nell'ortografia inglese della Gran Bretagna, ma non in quella americana:

travel travel**led**, *Am* travel**ed**   travel**ling**, *Am* traveling

Nei verbi che terminano in -c, si sostituisce -ck alla c, prima di aggiungere le desinenze -ed e -ing:

traffic traffi**cked** traffi**cking**

5. La **forma passiva** si forma esattamente come in italiano, con il verbo *to be* ed il participio passato: *I am obliged, he was fined, they will be moved*, ecc.

b) Verbi irregolari inglesi

Si riportano le tre forme principali di ciascun verbo: infinito, passato, participio passato.

alight	alighted, alit	alighted, alit	**cling**	clung	clung
arise	arose	arisen	**come**	came	come
awake	awoke	awoken, awaked	**cost**	cost	cost
be (am, is, are)	was (were)	been	**creep**	crept	crept
bear	bore	borne	**crow**	crowed, crew	crowed
beat	beat	beaten	**cut**	cut	cut
become	became	become	**deal**	dealt	dealt
begin	began	begun	**dig**	dug	dug
behold	beheld	beheld	**do**	did	done
bend	bent	bent	**draw**	drew	drawn
beseech	besought,	besought,	**dream**	dreamt,	dreamt,
	beseeched	beseeched		dreamed	dreamed
bet	bet, betted	bet, betted	**drink**	drank	drunk
bid	bade, bid	bidden, bid	**drive**	drove	driven
bind	bound	bound	**dwell**	dwelt,	dwelt,
bite	bit	bitten		dwelled	dwelled
bleed	bled	bled	**eat**	ate	eaten
blow	blew	blown	**fall**	fell	fallen
break	broke	broken	**feed**	fed	fed
breed	bred	bred	**feel**	felt	felt
bring	brought	brought	**fight**	fought	fought
broadcast	broadcast	broadcast	**find**	found	found
build	built	built	**flee**	fled	fled
burn	burnt, burned	burnt, burned	**fling**	flung	flung
burst	burst	burst	**fly**	flew	flown
bust	bust(ed)	bust(ed)	**forbear**	forbore	forborne
buy	bought	bought	**forbid**	forbad(e)	forbidden
cast	cast	cast	**forecast**	forecast(ed)	forecast(ed)
catch	caught	caught	**forget**	forgot	forgotten
choose	chose	chosen	**forgive**	forgave	forgiven
cleave (*cut*)	clove, cleft	cloven, cleft	**forsake**	forsook	forsaken

freeze	froze	frozen	**shrink**	shrank	shrunk
get	got	got, *Am* gotten	**shut**	shut	shut
give	gave	given	**sing**	sang	sung
go	went	gone	**sink**	sank	sunk
grind	ground	ground	**sit**	sat	sat
grow	grew	grown	**slay**	slew	slain
hang	hung.	hung,	**sleep**	slept	slept
	(*v/t*) hanged	(*v/t*) hanged	**slide**	slid	slid
have	had	had	**sling**	slung	slung
hear	heard	heard	**slink**	slunk	slunk
heave	heaved,	heaved,	**slit**	slit	slit
	NAUT hove	NAUT hove	**smell**	smelt, smelled	smelt, smelled
hew	hewed	hewed, hewn	**smite**	smote	smitten
hide	hid	hidden	**sow**	sowed	sown, sowed
hit	hit	hit	**speak**	spoke	spoken
hold	held	held	**speed**	sped, speeded	sped, speeded
hurt	hurt	hurt	**spell**	spelt, spelled	spelt, spelled
keep	kept	kept	**spend**	spent	spent
kneel	knelt, kneeled	knelt, kneeled	**spill**	spilt, spilled	spilt, spilled
know	knew	known	**spin**	spun, span	spun
lay	laid	laid	**spit**	spat	spat
lead	led	led	**split**	split	split
lean	leaned, leant	leaned, leant	**spoil**	spoiled, spoilt	spoiled, spoilt
leap	leaped, leapt	leaped, leapt	**spread**	spread	spread
learn	learned, learnt	learned, learnt	**spring**	sprang,	sprung
leave	left	left		*Am* sprung	
lend	lent	lent	**stand**	stood	stood
let	let	let	**stave**	staved, stove	staved, stove
lie	lay	lain	**steal**	stole	stolen
light	lighted, lit	lighted, lit	**stick**	stuck	stuck
lose	lost	lost	**sting**	stung	stung
make	made	made	**stink**	stunk, stank	stunk
mean	meant	meant	**strew**	strewed	strewed, strewn
meet	met	met	**stride**	strode	stridden
mow	mowed	mowed, mown	**strike**	struck	struck
pay	paid	paid	**string**	strung	strung
plead	pleaded, pled	pleaded, pled	**strive**	strove	striven
prove	proved	proved, proven	**swear**	swore	sworn
put	put	put	**sweep**	swept	swept
quit	quit(ted)	quit(ted)	**swell**	swelled	swollen
read [ri:d]	read [red]	read [red]	**swim**	swam	swum
rend	rent	rent	**swing**	swung	swung
rid	rid	rid	**take**	took	taken
ride	rode	ridden	**teach**	taught	taught
ring	rang	rung	**tear**	tore	torn
rise	rose	risen	**tell**	told	told
run	ran	run	**think**	thought	thought
saw	sawed	sawn, sawed	**thrive**	throve	thriven
say	said	said	**throw**	threw	thrown
see	saw	seen	**thrust**	thrust	thrust
seek	sought	sought	**tread**	trod	trodden
sell	sold	sold	**understand**	understood	understood
send	sent	sent	**wake**	woke, waked	woken, waked
set	set	set	**wear**	wore	worn
sew	sewed	sewed, sewn	**weave**	wove	woven
shake	shook	shaken	**wed**	wed(ded)	wed(ded)
shear	sheared	sheared, shorn	**weep**	wept	wept
shed	shed	shed	**wet**	wet(ted)	wet(ted)
shine	shone	shone	**win**	won	won
shit	shit(ted). shat	shit(ted), shat	**wind**	wound	wound
shoe	shod	shod	**wring**	wrung	wrung
shoot	shot	shot	**write**	wrote	written
show	showed	shown			

Numbers – Numerali

Cardinal numbers – I numeri cardinali

0	*zero* zero	80	*eighty* ottanta
1	*one* uno	90	*ninety* novanta
2	*two* due	100	*one/a hundred* cento
3	*three* tre	101	*one/a hundred* centouno *and one*
4	*four* quattro	102	*one/a hundred* centodue *and two*
5	*five* cinque		
6	*six* sei	200	*two hundred* duecento
7	*seven* sette	201	*two hundred and one* duecento uno
8	*eight* otto		
9	*nine* nove	300	*three hundred* trecento
10	*ten* dieci	400	*four hundred* quattrocento
11	*eleven* undici	500	*five hundred* cinquecento
12	*twelve* dodici	600	*six hundred* seicento
13	*thirteen* tredici	700	*seven hundred* settecento
14	*fourteen* quattordici	800	*eight hundred* ottocento
15	*fifteen* quindici	900	*nine hundred* novecento
16	*sixteen* sedici	1,000	*one/a thousand* mille
17	*seventeen* diciassette	1,001	*one/a thousand* milleuno/ *and one* mille e uno
18	*eighteen* diciotto		
19	*nineteen* diciannove	2,000	*two thousand* duemila
20	*twenty* venti	3,000	*three thousand* tremila
21	*twenty-one* ventuno	4,000	*four thousand* quattromila
22	*twenty-two* ventidue	5,000	*five thousand* cinquemila
23	*twenty-three* ventitrè		
28	*twenty-eight* ventotto	10,000	*ten thousand* diecimila
29	*twenty-nine* ventinove	100,000	*one/a hundred* centomila *thousand*
30	*thirty* trenta		
40	*forty* quaranta	1,000,000	*one/a million* un milione
50	*fifty* cinquanta	2,000,000	*two million* due milioni
60	*sixty* sessanta	1,000,000,000	*one/a billion* un miliardo
70	*seventy* settanta		

Notes:

i) In Italian numbers a comma is used for decimals:

   1,25   **one point two five**   uno virgola venticinque

ii) A full stop is used where, in English, we would use a comma:

   1.000.000 = 1,000,000

Italian can also write numbers like this using a space instead of a comma:

   1 000 000 = 1,000,000

Ordinal numbers – I numeri ordinali

1st	*first*	1°	il primo, la prima
2nd	*second*	2°	secondo
3rd	*third*	3°	terzo
4th	*fourth*	4°	quarto
5th	*fifth*	5°	quinto
6th	*sixth*	6°	sesto
7th	*seventh*	7°	settimo
8th	*eighth*	8°	ottavo
9th	*ninth*	9°	nono
10th	*tenth*	10°	decimo
11th	*eleventh*	11°	undicesimo
12th	*twelfth*	12°	dodicesimo
13th	*thirteenth*	13°	tredicesimo
14th	*fourteenth*	14°	quattordicesimo
15th	*fifteenth*	15°	quindicesimo
16th	*sixteenth*	16°	sedicesimo
17th	*seventeenth*	17°	diciassettesimo
18th	*eighteenth*	18°	diciottesimo
19th	*nineteenth*	19°	diciannovesimo
20th	*twentieth*	20°	ventesimo
21st	*twenty-first*	21°	ventunesimo
22nd	*twenty-second*	22°	ventiduesimo
30th	*thirtieth*	30°	trentesimo
40th	*fortieth*	40°	quarantesimo
50th	*fiftieth*	50°	cinquantesimo
60th	*sixtieth*	60°	sessantesimo
70th	*seventieth*	70°	settantesimo
80th	*eightieth*	80°	ottantesimo
90th	*ninetieth*	90°	novantesimo
100th	*hundredth*	100°	centesimo
101st	*hundred and first*	101°	centunesimo
103rd	*hundred and third*	103°	centotreesimo
200th	*two hundredth*	200°	duecentesimo
1000th	*thousandth*	1000°	millesimo
1001st	*thousand and first*	1001°	millesimo primo
2000th	*two thousandth*	2000°	duemillesimo
1000000th	*millionth*	1000000°	milionesimo

Note:

Italian ordinal numbers are ordinary adjectives and consequently must agree:

her 13th granddaughter   la sua tredicesima nipote

Fractions – Frazioni

½	*one half, a half*	un mezzo
⅓	*one third, a third*	un terzo
⅔	*two thirds*	due terzi
¼	*one quarter, a quarter*	un quarto
¾	*three quarters*	tre quarti
⅕	*one fifth, a fifth*	un quinto
⅒	*one tenth, a tenth*	un decimo
1½	*one and a half*	uno e mezzo
2¾	*two and three quarters*	due e tre quarti
¹⁄₁₀₀	*one hundredth, a hundredth*	un centesimo
¹⁄₁₀₀₀	*one thousandth, a thousandth*	un millesimo

Approximate numbers – Valori approssimativi

a couple	un paio
about ten	una decina
about twenty	una ventina
about eighty	un'ottantina
about a hundred	un centinaio
hundreds (of people)	centinaia (di persone)
about a thousand	un migliaio
thousands	migliaia

Headword in **bold** Lemma in **grassetto**	**im•pact** ['ɪmpækt] *n of meteorite, vehicle* urto *m*; *of new manager etc* impatto *m*; *(effect)* effetto *m*
International Phonetic Alphabet Trascrizione fonetica internazionale	**in•sult** ['ɪnsʌlt] **1** *n* insulto *m* **2** *v/t* [ɪn'sʌlt] insultare
Translation in normal characters with gender shown in *italics* Traduzione in carattere normale, genere dei sostantivi in *corsivo*	**cou•ri•er** ['kʊrɪə(r)] *(messenger)* corriere *m*; *with tourist party* accompagnatore *m* turistico, accompagnatrice *f* turistica
Hyphenation points Dei punti dividono il lemma in sillabe	**con•sum•er con•fi•dence** fiducia *f* dei consumatori; **con•sum•er goods** *npl* beni *mpl* di consumo
Stress shown in headwords ' indica la sillaba accentata	**mouth•wa•ter•ing** *adj* che fa venire l'acquolina
Examples and phrases in **bold italics** Esempi e locuzioni in **grassetto corsivo**	**i•deal•ly** [aɪ'dɪəlɪ] *adv*: **the hotel is ~ situated** l'albergo si trova in una posizione ideale; **~, we would do it like this** l'ideale sarebbe farlo così
Indicating words in *italics* Discriminazioni di significato in *corsivo*	**montaggio** *m* (*pl* -ggi) TECH assembly; *di film* editing **definire** <4d> define; *(risolvere)* settle **imbalsamare** <1a> embalm; *animale* stuff **land•ing** ['lændɪŋ] *n of aeroplane* atterraggio *m*; *top of staircase* pianerottolo *m*